# An Index
# to Book Reviews
# in the Humanities

## Volume 27
## 1986

Phillip Thomson
Williamston, Michigan

This volume of the Index contains data collected up to 31 December 1986.

This is an index to book reviews in humanities periodicals. Beginning with volume 12 of this Index (dated 1971), the former policy of selectively indexing reviews of books in certain subject categories only was dropped in favor of a policy of indexing all reviews in the periodicals indexed, with the one exception of children's books — the reviews of which will not be indexed.

The form of the entries used is as follows:

Author. Title.
    Reviewer. Identifying Legend.

The author's name used is the name that appears on the title-page of the book being reviewed, as well as we are able to determine, even though this name is known to be a pseudonym. The title only is shown; subtitles are included only where they are necessary to identify a book in a series. The identifying legend consists of the periodical, each of which has a code number, and the date and page number of the periodical where the review is to be found. PMLA abbreviations are also shown (when a periodical has such an abbreviation, but such abbreviations are limited to four letters) immediately following the code number of the periodical. To learn the name of the periodical in which the review appears, it is necessary to refer the code number to the numerically-arranged list of periodicals beginning on page iii. This list also shows the volume and number of the periodical issues indexed in this volume.

Reviews are indexed as they appear and no attempt is made to hold the title until all the reviews are published. For this reason it is necessary to refer to previous and subsequent volumes of this Index to be sure that the complete roster of reviews of any title is seen. As an aid to the user, an asterisk (*) has been added immediately following any title that was also indexed in Volume 26 (1985) of this Index.

Authors with hyphenated surnames are indexed under the name before the hyphen, and the name following the hyphen is not cross-indexed. Authors with more than one surname, but where the names are not hyphenated, are indexed under the first of the names and the last name is cross-indexed. When alphabetizing surnames containing umlauts, the umlauts are ignored. Editors are always shown in the author-title entry, and they are cross-indexed (except where the editor's surname is the same as that of the author). Translators are shown only when they are necessary to identify the book being reviewed (as in the classics), and they are not cross-indexed unless the book being reviewed has no author or editor. Certain reference works and anonymous works that are known primarily by their title are indexed under

that title and their editors are cross-indexed.

A list of abbreviations used is shown on page ii.

## ABBREVIATIONS

```
Anon.........Anonymous
Apr..........April
Aug..........August
Bk...........Book
Comp(s)......Compiler(s)
Cont.........Continued
Dec..........December
Ed(s)........Editor(s) [or] Edition(s)
Fasc.........Fascicule
Feb..........February
Jan..........January
Jul..........July
Jun..........June
Mar..........March
No...........Number
Nov..........November
Oct..........October
Prev.........Previous volume of this Index
Pt...........Part
Rev..........Revised
Sep..........September
Ser..........Series
Supp.........Supplement
Trans........Translator(s)
Vol..........Volume
* (asterisk)....This title was also shown
                in the volume of this Index
                immediately preceding this
                one
```

The periodicals in which the reviews appear are identified in this Index by a number. To supplement this number, and to promote ready identification, PMLA abbreviations are also given following this number. Every attempt will be made to index those issues shown here as "missing" in a later volume of this Index.

The following is a list of the periodicals indexed in volume 27:

2(AfrA) - African Arts. Los Angeles.
    Nov84 thru Aug85 (vol 18 complete)
4 - Agenda. London.
    Spring-Summer85 and Autumn-Winter 85/86 (vol 23 complete)
9(AlaR) - Alabama Review. University.
    Jan85 thru Oct85 (vol 38 complete)
16 - American Art Journal. New York.
    Winter85 thru Autumn85 (vol 17 complete)
18 - American Film. Washington.
    Oct85 thru Sep86 (vol 11 complete)
24 - American Journal of Philology. Baltimore.
    Spring85 thru Winter85 (vol 106 complete)
26(ALR) - American Literary Realism, 1870-1910. Arlington.
    Spring/Autumn85 (vol 18 complete)
27(AL) - American Literature. Durham.
    Mar85 thru Dec85 (vol 57 complete)
29(APR) - The American Poetry Review. Philadelphia.
    Jan-Feb86 thru Nov-Dec86 (vol 15 complete)
30 - American Poetry. Jefferson.
    Fall85 thru Spring86 (vol 3 complete)
31(ASch) - American Scholar. Washington.
    Winter84/85 thru Autumn85 (vol 54 complete)
35(AS) - American Speech. University.
    Spring85 thru Winter85 (vol 60 complete)
37 - The Américas. Washington.
    Jan-Feb85 thru Nov-Dec85 (vol 37 complete)
38 - Anglia. Tübingen.
    Band 103 complete
39 - Apollo. London.
    Jan85 thru Dec85 (vols 121 and 122 complete)
40 - AEB: Analytical and Enumerative Bibliography. De Kalb.
    Vol8No2 and Vol8No3
42(AR) - Antioch Review. Yellow Springs.
    Winter85 thru Fall85 (vol 43 complete)
43 - Architectura. München.
    Band 15 complete
44 - Architectural History. London.
    Vol 28 [no reviews indexed]
45 - Architectural Record. New York.
    Jan85 thru Dec85 (vol 173 complete)
46 - Architectural Review. London.
    Jan85 thru Dec85 (vols 177 and 178 complete)
48 - Archivo Español de Arte. Madrid.
    Jan-Mar85 thru Oct-Dec85 (vol 58 complete)

49 - Ariel. Calgary.
    Jan85 thru Oct85 (vol 16 complete)
50(ArQ) - Arizona Quarterly. Tucson.
    Spring85 thru Winter85 (vol 41 complete)
52 - Arcadia. Berlin.
    Band 20 complete
53(AGP) - Archiv für Geschichte der Philosophie. Berlin.
    Band 67 complete
54 - Art Bulletin. New York.
    Mar85 thru Dec85 (vol 67 complete)
55 - Art News. New York.
    Jan85 thru Dec85 (vol 84 complete)
57 - Artibus Asiae. Ascona.
    Vol 46 complete [no reviews indexed]
59 - Art History. London.
    Mar85 thru Dec85 (vol 8 complete)
60 - Arts of Asia. Hong Kong.
    Jan-Feb85 thru Nov-Dec85 (vol 15 complete)
61 - Atlantic Monthly. Boston.
    Jan86 thru Dec86 (vols 257 and 258 complete)
62 - Artforum. New York.
    Sep85 thru Summer86 (vol 24 complete)
63 - Australasian Journal of Philosophy. Bundoora.
    Mar85 thru Dec85 (vol 63 complete)
64(Arv) - ARV: Scandinavian Yearbook of Folklore. Stockholm.
    Vol 39 and Vol 40
67 - AUMLA [Journal of the Australasian Universities Language and Literature Assn.] Epping.
    May85 and Nov85 (no 63 and no 64)
70 - American Notes and Queries. Owingsville.
    Sep/Oct84 thru May/Jun86 (vols 23 and 24 complete)
71(ALS) - Australian Literary Studies. St. Lucia.
    May85 and Oct85 (vol 12 no 1 and 2)
72 - Archiv für das Studium der neueren Sprachen und Literaturen. Berlin.
    Band 222 complete
77 - Biography. Honolulu.
    Winter85 thru Fall85 (vol 8 complete)
78(BC) - Book Collector. London.
    Spring85 thru Winter85 (vol 34 complete)
81 - Boundary 2. Binghamton.
    Spring/Fall84 and Winter/Spring85 (vol 12 no 3, vol 13 complete)
83 - The British Journal for Eighteenth-Century Studies. Oxford.
    Spring85 and Autumn85 (vol 8 complete)
84 - The British Journal for the Philosophy of Science. Oxford.
    Mar85 thru Dec85 (vol 36 complete)
85(SBHC) - Studies in Browning and His Circle. Waco.
    Vol 13
86(BHS) - Bulletin of Hispanic Studies. Liverpool.
    Jan85 thru Oct85 (vol 62 complete)
87(BB) - Bulletin of Bibliography. Westport.
    Mar85 thru Dec85 (vol 42 complete)

88 - Blake, An Illustrated Quarterly.
Albuquerque.
Summer85 thru Spring86 (vol 19
complete)
89(BJA) - The British Journal of Aesthetics. Oxford.
Winter85 thru Autumn85 (vol 25
complete)
90 - Burlington Magazine. London.
Jan85 thru Dec85 (vol 127 complete)
91 - The Black Perspective in Music.
Cambria Heights.
Spring85 and Fall85 (vol 13 complete)
92(BH) - Bulletin Hispanique. Bordeaux.
Jan-Jun84 and Jul-Dec84 (vol 86
complete)
95(CLAJ) - CLA Journal. Atlanta.
Sep85 thru Jun86 (vol 29 complete)
97(CQ) - The Cambridge Quarterly. Cambridge.
Vol 14 complete
98 - Critique. Paris.
Jan-Feb85 thru Dec85 (vol 41 complete)
99 - Canadian Forum. Toronto.
Apr85 thru Mar86 (vol 65 complete)
102(CanL) - Canadian Literature. Vancouver.
Winter84 thru Fall85 (no 103 thru
no 106)
104(CASS) - Canadian-American Slavic
Studies/Revue canadienne-américaine
d'études slaves. Irvine.
Spring85 thru Winter85 (vol 19 complete)
105 - Canadian Poetry. London, Ontario.
Spring/Summer85 and Fall/Winter85
(no 16 and no 17)
106 - The Canadian Review of American
Studies. Winnipeg.
Spring85 thru Winter85 (vol 16 complete)
107(CRCL) - Canadian Review of Comparative
Literature/Revue Canadienne de Littérature Comparée. South Edmonton.
Mar85 thru Sep85 (vol 12 no 1-3)
108 - Canadian Theatre Review. Toronto.
Spring85 thru Winter85 (no 42 thru
no 45)
110 - Carolina Quarterly. Chapel Hill.
Fall85 thru Spring86 (vol 38 complete)
111 - Cauda Pavonis. Pullman.
Spring86 and Fall86 (vol 5 complete)
112 - Celtica. Dublin.
Vol 16 and Vol 17
114(ChiR) - Chicago Review. Chicago.
Winter85 and Spring86 (vol 35 no 2
and 3) [no reviews indexed]
115 - The Centennial Review. East Lansing.
Winter84 thru Fall85 (vols 28 and
29 complete)
116 - Chinese Literature: Essays, Articles,
Reviews. Madison.
Jul84 (vol 6 no 1/2)
121(CJ) - Classical Journal. Greenville.
Oct/Nov85 thru Apr/May86 (vol 81
complete)
122 - Classical Philology. Chicago.
Jan85 thru Oct85 (vol 80 complete)

123 - Classical Review. Oxford.
Vol 35 complete
124 - Classical World. Pittsburgh.
Sep/Oct85 thru Jul/Aug86 (vol 79
complete)
125 - Clio. Ft. Wayne.
Fall84 thru Summer85 (vol 14 complete)
126(CCC) - College Composition and Communication. Urbana.
Feb85 thru Dec85 (vol 36 complete)
127 - Art Journal. New York.
Winter84 and Spring85 thru Win-
ter85 (vol 44 no 4, vol 45 complete)
128(CE) - College English. Urbana.
Jan85 thru Dec85 (vol 47 complete)
129 - Commentary. New York.
Jan86 thru Dec86 (vols 81 and 82
complete)
130 - Comparative Drama. Kalamazoo.
Spring85 thru Winter85/86 (vol 19
complete)
131(CL) - Comparative Literature. Eugene.
Winter85 thru Fall85 (vol 37 complete)
133 - Colloquia Germanica. Bern.
Band17Heft3/4, Band18Heft1 thru
Band18Heft3
134(CP) - Concerning Poetry. Bellingham.
Vol 18No1/2
136 - Conradiana. Lubbock.
Vol 18 complete
138 - Conjunctions. Boston.
No7 and No8
139 - American Craft. New York.
Feb/Mar85 thru Dec85/Jan86 (vol 45
complete)
140(CH) - Crítica Hispánica. Johnson
City.
Vol 7 complete
141 - Criticism. Detroit.
Winter85 thru Fall85 (vol 27 complete)
142 - Philosophy and Social Criticism.
Chestnut Hill.
Summer85 thru Summer86 (vol 11
no 1-3)
143 - Current Musicology. New York.
Issue 37/38
145(Crit) - Critique. Washington.
Fall85 thru Summer86 (vol 27 complete)
148 - Critical Quarterly. Manchester.
Spring85 thru Winter85 (vol 27
complete)
149(CLS) - Comparative Literature Studies.
Urbana.
Spring85 thru Winter85 (vol 22
complete)
150(DR) - Dalhousie Review. Halifax.
Winter85/85 thru Summer85 (vol 64
no 4, vol 65 no 1 and 2)
151 - Dancemagazine. New York.
Jan85 thru Dec85 (vol 59 complete)
152(UDQ) - The Denver Quarterly. Denver.
Summer85 thru Spring/Summer86
(vol 20 no 1 thru vol 20 no 4/vol
21 no 1)
153 - Diacritics. Baltimore.
Spring85 thru Winter85 (vol 15 complete)

154 - Dialogue. Waterloo.
Spring85 thru Winter85 (vol 24 complete)

155 - The Dickensian. London.
Spring85 thru Autumn85 (vol 81 complete)

156(ShJW) - Deutsche Shakespeare-Gesellschaft West Jahrbuch. Bochum.
Jahrbuch1985

157 - Drama/The Quarterly Theatre Review. London.
No 155 thru no 158

158 - Dickens Quarterly. Amherst.
Mar85 thru Dec85 (vol 2 complete)

159 - Diachronica. Hildesheim.
Spring85 and Fall85 (vol 2 complete)

160 - Diálogos. Río Piedras.
Apr85 and Nov85 (vol 20 complete)

161(DUJ) - Durham University Journal. Durham.
Jun84 thru Jun85 (vol 76 no 2, vol 77 complete)

165(EAL) - Early American Literature. Chapel Hill.
Winter85/86 thru Winter86/87 (vol 20 no 3, vol 21 complete)

167 - Erkenntnis. Dordrecht.
Jan85 thru Nov85 (vols 22 and 23 complete)

168(ECW) - Essays on Canadian Writing. Toronto.
Summer85 (no 31) [no reviews indexed]

172(Edda) - Edda. Oslo.
1985/1 thru 1985/6 (vol 85 complete)

173(ECS) - Eighteenth-Century Studies. Northfield.
Fall85 thru Summer86 (vol 19 complete)

174(Éire) - Éire-Ireland. St. Paul.
Spring85 thru Winter85 (vol 20 complete)

175 - English. Oxford.
Spring85 thru Autumn85 (vol 34 complete)

176 - Encounter. London.
Jun85 and Jan86 thru Nov86 (vol 65 no 1, vol 66 complete, vol 76 no 1-4)

177(ELT) - English Literature in Transition. Greensboro.
Vol 28 complete

178 - English Studies in Canada. Edmonton.
Mar85 thru Dec85 (vol 11 complete)

179(ES) - English Studies. Lisse.
Feb85 thru Dec85 (vol 66 complete)

181 - Epoch. Ithaca.
Vol 35 no 1 [no reviews indexed]

183(ESQ) - ESQ: A Journal of the American Renaissance. Pullman.
Vol 31 complete

184(EIC) - Essays in Criticism. Oxford.
Jan85 thru Oct85 (vol 35 complete)

185 - Ethics. Chicago.
Oct85 thru Jul86 (vol 96 complete)

186(ETC.) - Etc. San Francisco.
Spring85 thru Winter85 (vol 42 complete)

187 - Ethnomusicology. Ann Arbor.
Winter86 thru Fall86 (vol 30 complete)

188(ECr) - L'Esprit Créateur. Baton Rouge.
Spring85 thru Winter85 (vol 25 complete)

189(EA) - Etudes Anglaises. Paris.
Jan-Mar86, Apr-Jun86 and Oct-Dec86 (vol 39 no 1, 2 and 4) [issue dated Jul-Sep86 missing]

191(ELN) - English Language Notes. Boulder.
Sep85 thru Jun86 (vol 23 complete)

192(EP) - Les Études Philosophiques. Paris.
Jan-Mar85 thru Oct-Dec85

193(ELit) - Études Littéraires. Québec.
Spring-Summer85 thru Winter85 (vol 18 complete)

196 - Fabula. Berlin.
Band 26 complete

198 - The Fiddlehead. Fredericton.
Spring85 thru Winter85 (no 143-146)

199 - Field. Oberlin.
Fall85 and Spring86 (no 33 and 34)

203 - Folklore. London.
Vol 96 complete

204(FdL) - Forum der Letteren. Den Haag.
Mar85 thru Dec85 (vol 26 complete)

205(ForL) - Forum Linguisticum. Lake Bluff.
Aug84 and Dec84 (vol 8 no 2 and 3) [Apr84 issue missing]

206(FoLi) - Folia Linguistica. The Hague.
Vol 19 complete

207(FR) - French Review. Champaign.
Oct85 thru May86 (vol 59 complete)

208(FS) - French Studies. London.
Jan85 thru Oct85 (vol 39 complete)

209(FM) - Le Français Moderne. Paris.
Apr85 and Oct85 (vol 53 complete)

210(FrF) - French Forum. Lexington.
Jan85 thru Sep85 (vol 10 complete)

214 - Gambit. London.
Vol 11 no 42/43 [no reviews indexed]

215(GL) - General Linguistics. University Park.
Vol 25 complete

219(GaR) - Georgia Review. Athens.
Spring85 thru Winter85 (vol 39 complete)

220(GL&L) - German Life and Letters. Oxford.
Oct85 thru Jul86 (vol 39 complete) [no reviews indexed]

221(GQ) - German Quarterly. Cherry Hill.
Winter85 thru Fall85 (vol 58 complete)

222(GR) - Germanic Review. Washington.
Winter85 thru Fall85 (vol 60 complete)

223 - Genre. Norman.
Spring85 thru Winter85 (vol 18 complete)

224(GRM) - Germanisch-Romanische Monatsschrift. Heidelberg.
Band 35 complete

228(GSLI) - Giornale storico della letteratura italiana. Torino.
Vol 162 complete

234 - The Hemingway Review. Ada.
Fall85 and Spring86 (vol 5 complete)

236 - The Hiram Poetry Review. Hiram.
Spring-Summer85 and Fall-Winter85 (no 38 and 39)

238 - Hispania. University.
    Mar85 thru Dec85 (vol 68 complete)
239 - Hispanic Linguistics. Pittsburgh.
    Vol 1 no 1 and vol 2 no 1 [vol 1
    no 2 missing]
240(HR) - Hispanic Review. Philadelphia.
    Winter85 thru Autumn85 (vol 53 com-
    plete)
241 - Hispanófila. Chapel Hill.
    Jan85 thru Sep85 (no 83-85)
244(HJAS) - Harvard Journal of Asiatic
    Studies. Cambridge.
    Jun85 and Dec85 (vol 45 complete)
249(HudR) - Hudson Review. New York.
    Spring85 thru Winter86 (vol 38
    complete)
250(HLQ) - The Huntington Library Quarter-
    ly. San Marino.
    Winter85 thru Autumn85 (vol 48
    complete)
257(IRAL) - IRAL: International Review
    of Applied Linguistics in Language
    Teaching. Heidelberg.
    Feb85 thru Nov85 (vol 23 complete)
258 - International Philosophical Quar-
    terly. New York and Namur.
    Mar85 thru Dec85 (vol 25 complete)
259(IIJ) - Indo-Iranian Journal. Dor-
    drecht.
    Jan85 thru Oct85 (vol 28 complete)
260(IF) - Indogermanische Forschungen.
    Berlin.
    Band 90
262 - Inquiry. Oslo.
    Mar85 thru Dec85 (vol 28 complete)
263(RIB) - Revista Interamericana de Bib-
    liografía/Inter-American Review of
    Bibliography. Washington.
    Vol 35 complete
264(I&L) - Ideologies and Literature.
    Minneapolis/Valencia.
    Vol 1 complete
268(IFR) - The International Fiction
    Review. Fredericton.
    Winter86 and Summer86 (vol 13 com-
    plete)
269(IJAL) - International Journal of
    American Linguistics. Chicago.
    Jan85 thru Oct85 (vol 51 complete)
271 - The Iowa Review. Iowa City.
    Winter85 thru Fall85 (vol 15 com-
    plete)
272(IUR) - Irish University Review. Dublin.
    Spring85 and Autumn85 (vol 15 com-
    plete)
275(IQ) - Italian Quarterly. New Bruns-
    wick.
    Summer/Fall84 and Winter/Spring/
    Summer85 (vol 25 no 97/98, vol 26
    no 99/100/101)
276 - Italica. Madison.
    Spring85 thru Winter85 (vol 62
    complete)
278(IS) - Italian Studies. Hull.
    Vol 40
279 - International Journal of Slavic
    Linguistics and Poetics. Columbus.
    Vol 29 and vol 30
283 - Jabberwocky - The Journal of the
    Lewis Carroll Society. Burton-on-
    Trent.
    Winter83/84 thru Summer84, Winter
        [continued]

84/85 (vol 13 no 1-3, vol 14 no 1)
    [Autumn84 issue missing]
284 - The Henry James Review. Baton
    Rouge.
    Spring85 (vol 6 no 3) [Winter85
    issue missing]
285(JapQ) - Japan Quarterly. Tokyo.
    Jan-Mar85 thru Oct-Dec85 (vol 32
    complete)
287 - Jewish Frontier. New York.
    Jan85 thru Nov-Dec85 (vol 52 com-
    plete)
289 - The Journal of Aesthetic Education.
    Urbana.
    Spring85 thru Winter85 (vol 19
    complete)
290(JAAC) - Journal of Aesthetics and Art
    Criticism. Greenvale.
    Fall85 thru Summer86 (vol 44 com-
    plete)
292(JAF) - Journal of American Folklore.
    Washington.
    Jan/Mar85 thru Oct/Dec85 (vol 98
    complete)
293(JASt) - Journal of Asian Studies. Ann
    Arbor.
    Nov84 thru Aug85 (vol 44 complete)
294 - Journal of Arabic Literature. Leiden.
    Vol 16
295(JML) - Journal of Modern Literature.
    Philadelphia.
    Mar85 thru Nov85 (vol 12 complete)
296(JCF) - Journal of Canadian Fiction.
    Montreal.
    No 34 [no reviews indexed]
297(JL) - Journal of Linguistics. Cam-
    bridge.
    Mar85 and Sep85 (vol 21 complete)
298 - Journal of Canadian Studies/Revue
    d'études canadiennes. Peterborough.
    Spring85 thru Winter85/86 (vol
    20 complete)
300 - Journal of English Linguistics.
    Whitewater.
    Apr85 and Oct85 (vol 18 complete)
301(JEGP) - Journal of English and Ger-
    manic Philology. Champaign.
    Jan85 thru Oct85 (vol 84 complete)
302 - Journal of Oriental Studies. Hong
    Kong.
    Vol 21 no 1 [entries wholly in
    Chinese are not indexed]
303(JoHS) - Journal of Hellenic Studies.
    London.
    Vol 105
304(JHP) - Journal of Hispanic Philology.
    Tallahassee.
    Winter85 thru Fall85 (vol 9 no 2
    and 3, vol 10 no 1)
305(JIL) - The Journal of Irish Literature.
    Newark.
    Jan85 thru Sep85 (vol 14 complete)
307 - Journal of Literary Semantics. Hei-
    delberg.
    May85 thru Dec85 (vol 14 complete)
308 - Journal of Music Theory. New Haven.
    Spring85 and Fall85 (vol 29 com-
    plete)
309 - Journal of Musicological Research.
    London.
    Vol 6 complete

311(JP) - Journal of Philosophy. New York.
Jan85 thru Dec85 (vol 82 complete)
313 - Journal of Roman Studies. London.
Vol 75
314 - Journal of South Asian Literature.
East Lansing.
Winter-Spring85 and Summer-Fall85
(vol 20 complete)
316 - Journal of Symbolic Logic. Pasadena.
Mar85 thru Dec85 (vol 50 complete)
317 - Journal of the American Musicological Society. Philadelphia.
Spring85 thru Fall85 (vol 38 complete)
318(JAOS) - Journal of the American Oriental Society. New Haven.
Jan-Mar84 thru Oct-Dec84 (vol 104
complete)
319 - Journal of the History of Philosophy.
St. Louis.
Jan86 thru Oct86 (vol 24 complete)
320(CJL) - Canadian Journal of Linguistics.
Ottawa.
Spring85 thru Winter85 (vol 30
complete)
321 - The Journal of Value Inquiry. Dordrecht.
Vol 19 complete
322(JHI) - Journal of the History of Ideas.
Philadelphia.
Jan-Mar85 thru Oct-Dec85 (vol 46
complete)
323 - JBSP: Journal of the British Society
for Phenomenology. Manchester.
Jan85 thru Oct85 (vol 16 complete)
324 - Journal of the Royal Society of Arts.
London.
Dec85 thru Nov86 (vol 134 complete)
326 - Journal of the William Morris Society. London.
Summer85 and Winter85/86 (vol 6
no 3 and 4)
329(JJQ) - James Joyce Quarterly. Tulsa.
Fall85 thru Summer86 (vol 23 complete)
339(KSMB) - The Keats-Shelley Memorial
Assn. Bulletin. Heslington.
No 36 [no reviews indexed]
340(KSJ) - Keats-Shelley Journal. New
York.
Vol 34
341 - Konsthistorisk Tidskrift. Stockholm.
Vol 54 complete
342 - Kant-Studien. Berlin.
Band 76 complete
343 - Komparatistische Hefte. Bayreuth.
Heft 11 and Heft 12
344 - The Kenyon Review. Gambier.
Winter86 thru Fall86 (vol 8 complete)
345(KRQ) - Kentucky Romance Quarterly.
Lexington.
Vol 32 complete
349 - Language and Style. Flushing.
Winter85 thru Fall85 (vol 18 com-
plete)
350 - Language. Baltimore.
Mar86 thru Dec86 (vol 62 complete)
351(LL) - Language Learning. Ann Arbor.
Mar85 thru Dec85 (vol 35 complete)

352(LATR) - Latin American Theatre Review.
Lawrence.
Fall85 and Spring86 (vol 19 complete)
353 - Linguistics. Amsterdam.
Vol 23 complete
354 - The Library. London.
Mar85 thru Dec85 (vol 7 complete)
355(LSoc) - Language in Society. New York.
Mar85 thru Dec85 (vol 14 complete)
356(LR) - Les Lettres Romanes. Louvain.
Feb/May85 thru Nov85 (vol 39 complete)
357 - Legacy. Amherst.
Spring86 (vol 3 no 1)
361 - Lingua. Amsterdam.
Jan85 thru Dec85 (vols 65-67 complete)
362 - The Listener. London.
2Jan86 thru 19&25Dec86 (vols 115
and 116 complete)
363(LitR) - The Literary Review. Madison.
Fall85 thru Summer86 (vol 29 complete)
364 - London Magazine. London.
Apr/May85 thru Mar86 (vol 25 complete)
365 - Literary Research Newsletter. Brock-
port.
Winter-Spring85 thru Fall85 (vol
10 complete)
366 - Literature and History. London.
Spring85 and Autumn85 (vol 11 complete)
367(L&P) - Literature and Psychology.
Normal.
Vol 31 no 4, vol 32 complete
376 - Malahat Review. Victoria.
Mar85 thru Dec85 (no 70-73) [the
actual Dec85 issue is cover-dated
Jan86]
377 - Manuscripta. St. Louis.
Jul84 thru Nov85 (vol 28 no 2 and
3, vol 29 complete)
379(MedR) - Medioevo romanzo. Bologna.
Apr85 thru Dec85 (vol 10 complete)
380 - Master Drawings. New York.
Winter84 (vol 22 no 4)
381 - Meanjin Quarterly. Parkville.
Mar85 thru Dec85 (vol 44 complete)
382(MAE) - Medium Aevum. Oxford.
1985/1 and 1985/2 (vol 54 complete)
384 - Merkur. Stuttgart.
Jan85 thru Dec85 (Band 39 complete)
385(MQR) - Michigan Quarterly Review. Ann
Arbor.
Winter86 thru Fall86 (vol 25 complete)
389(MQ) - The Midwest Quarterly. Pitts-
burg.
Autumn85 thru Summer86 (vol 27
complete)
390 - Midstream. New York.
Jan85 thru Dec85 (vol 31 complete)
391 - Milton Quarterly. Athens.
Mar85 thru Dec85 (vol 19 complete)
392 - The Mississippi Quarterly.
Mississippi State.
Winter84/85 thru Fall85 (vol 38
complete)
393(Mind) - Mind. Oxford.
Jan85 thru Oct85 (vol 94 complete)

394 – Mnemosyne. Leiden.
Vol 38 complete
395(MFS) – Modern Fiction Studies. West
Lafayette.
Spring85 thru Winter85 (vol 31 complete)
396(ModA) – Modern Age. Bryn Mawr.
Winter85 thru Fall85 (vol 29 complete)
397(MD) – Modern Drama. Toronto.
Mar85 thru Dec85 (vol 28 complete)
399(MLJ) – Modern Language Journal. Madison.
Spring85 thru Winter85 (vol 69
complete)
400(MLN) – MLN [Modern Language Notes].
Baltimore.
Jan85 thru Dec85 (vol 100 complete)
401(MLQ) – Modern Language Quarterly.
Seattle.
Jun84 thru Dec84 (vol 45 no 2-4)
402(MLR) – Modern Language Review. London.
Jan85 thru Oct85 (vol 80 complete)
403(MLS) – Modern Language Studies. Par-
amus.
Winter85 thru Fall85 (vol 15 complete)
404 – Modern Haiku. Madison.
Winter-Spring85 thru Autumn85 (vol
16 complete)
405(MP) – Modern Philology. Chicago.
Aug85 thru May86 (vol 83 complete)
406 – Monatshefte. Madison.
Spring85 thru Winter85 (vol 77
complete)
407(MN) – Monumenta Nipponica. Tokyo.
Spring85 thru Winter85 (vol 40 complete)
410(M&L) – Music and Letters. London.
Jan85 thru Oct85 (vol 66 complete)
412 – Music Review. Cambridge.
Feb83 thru Aug/Nov84 (vols 44 and
45 complete)
414(MusQ) – Musical Quarterly. New York.
Vol 71 complete
415 – The Musical Times. London.
Jan85 thru Dec85 (vol 126 complete)
418(MR) – Massachusetts Review. Amherst.
Spring85 thru Winter85 (vol 26
complete)
424 – Names. New York.
Mar-Jun85 thru Dec85 (vol 33 complete)
432(NEQ) – New England Quarterly. Boston.
Mar85 thru Dec85 (vol 58 complete)
434 – New England Review and Bread Loaf
Quarterly. Lyme.
Autumn84 thru Summer86 (vols 7 and
8 complete)
435 – New Orleans Review. New Orleans.
Spring85 thru Winter85 (vol 12 complete)
436(NewL) – New Letters. Kansas City.
Fall85 thru Summer85 (vol 52 complete) [no reviews indexed]
438 – The New Scholasticism. Washington.
Winter85 thru Autumn85 (vol 59
complete)
439(NM) – Neuphilologische Mitteilungen.
Helsinki.
1985/1 thru 1985/4 (vol 86 complete)

440 – New York Folklore. Saranac Lake.
Vol 11 no 1-4 [no reviews indexed]
441 – New York Times Book Review. New
York.
5Jan86 thru 28Dec86 (vol 91 complete)
442(NY) – New Yorker. New York.
6Jan86 thru 29Dec86 (vol 61 no 46-
52, vol 62 no 1-45) [vol 62 begins
with the 24Feb86 issue]
445(NCF) – Nineteenth-Century Fiction.
Berkeley.
Jun85 thru Mar86 (vol 40 complete)
446(NCFS) – Nineteenth-Century French
Studies. Fredonia.
Fall-Winter85/86 and Spring-Summer
86 (vol 14 complete)
447(N&Q) – Notes and Queries. Oxford.
Mar84 thru Dec84 (vol 31 complete)
448 – Northwest Review. Eugene.
Vol 23 complete
449 – Noûs. Bloomington.
Mar85 thru Dec85 (vol 19 complete)
450(NRF) – La Nouvelle Revue Française.
Paris.
Jan85 thru Dec85 (vols 65 and 66
complete)
451 – 19th Century Music. Berkeley.
Summer85 thru Spring86 (vol 9
complete)
452(NJL) – Nordic Journal of Linguistics.
Oslo.
Vol 8 complete
453(NYRB) – The New York Review of Books.
New York.
16Jan86 thru 18Dec86 (vol 32 no
21/22, vol 33 no 1-20)
454 – Novel. Providence.
Fall85 thru Spring86 (vol 19 complete)
455 – The North American Review. Cedar
Falls.
Mar85 thru Dec85 (vol 270 complete)
460(OhR) – The Ohio Review. Athens.
No 36 and no 37
461 – The Ontario Review. Princeton.
Spring-Summer85 and Fall-Winter
85/86 (no 22 and 23) [no reviews
indexed]
462(OL) – Orbis Litterarum. Copenhagen.
Vol 40 complete
463 – Oriental Art. Richmond.
Spring85 thru Winter85/86 (vol 31
complete)
464 – Orbis. Louvain.
Vol 31 fasc 1/2
466 – Oxford Studies in Ancient Philosophy.
Oxford.
Vols 1, 2 and 3
468 – Paideuma. Orono.
Fall84 thru Fall/Winter85 (vol 13
no 2 and 3, vol 14 complete)
469 – Parabola. New York.
Vol 11 complete
470 – Papers of the Bibliographical Society of Canada/Cahiers de la Société
bibliographique du Canada. Toronto.
Vol 23
471 – Pantheon. München.
Vol 43 [no reviews indexed]

472 - Parnassus: Poetry in Review. New
York.
Spring/Summer/Fall/Winter85 and
Spring/Summer86 (vol 12 no 2/vol
13 no 1, vol 13 no 2)
473(PR) - Partisan Review. Boston.
Vol 52 no 2-4
475 - Papers on French Seventeenth Century
Literature. Seattle and Tübingen.
Vol 12 complete
476 - Journal of Arts Management and Law
[ex-Performing Arts Review]. Washington.
Spring82 thru Winter86 (vols 12-15
complete)
477(PLL) - Papers on Language and Literature. Edwardsville.
Winter85 thru Fall85 (vol 21 complete)
478 - Philosophy and Literature. Baltimore.
Apr85 and Oct85 (vol 9 complete)
479(PhQ) - Philosophical Quarterly. Oxford.
Jan85 thru Oct85 (vol 35 complete)
480(P&R) - Philosophy and Rhetoric. University Park.
Vol 18 complete
481(PQ) - Philological Quarterly. Iowa
City.
Winter85 thru Fall85 (vol 64 complete)
482(PhR) - Philosophical Review. Ithaca.
Jan85 thru Oct85 (vol 94 complete)
483 - Philosophy. Cambridge.
Jan85 thru Oct85 (vol 60 complete)
484(PPR) - Philosophy and Phenomenological Research. Providence.
Sep85 thru Jun86 (vol 46 complete)
485(PE&W) - Philosophy East and West.
Honolulu.
Jan85 thru Oct85 (vol 35 complete)
486 - Philosophy of Science. East Lansing.
Sep84 thru Dec85 (vol 51 no 3 and
4, vol 52 complete)
487 - Phoenix. Toronto.
Spring85 thru Winter85 (vol 39
complete)
488 - Philosophy of the Social Sciences.
Waterloo.
Mar85 thru Dec85 (vol 15 complete)
489(PJGG) - Philosophisches Jahrbuch.
Freiburg.
Band 92 complete
490 - Poetica. Amsterdam.
Band 17 complete
491 - Poetry. Chicago.
Apr85 thru Mar86 (vols 146 and 147
complete)
493 - Poetry Review. London.
Jan85 thru Feb86 (vol 74 no 4, vol
75 complete)
495(PoeS) - Poe Studies. Pullman.
Jun85 and Dec85 (vol 18 complete)
496 - Poet Lore. Washington.
Spring85 thru Winter86 (vol 80
complete)
497(PolR) - Polish Review. New York.
Vol 30 complete
498 - Popular Music and Society. Bowling
Green.
Vol 9 no 3 and 4, vol 10 no 1 and
2

500 - Post Script. Jacksonville.
Fall85 thru Spring/Summer86 (vol 5
complete)
502(PrS) - Prairie Schooner. Lincoln.
Spring85 thru Winter85 (vol 59
complete)
503 - The Private Library. Pinner.
Winter83 thru Winter85 (vol 6 no
4, vols 7 and 8 complete)
505 - Progressive Architecture. Cleveland.
Jan85 thru Dec85 (vol 66 complete)
506(PSt) - Prose Studies. London.
May85 thru Dec85 (vol 8 complete)
507 - Print. New York.
Jan/Feb85 thru Nov/Dec85 (vol 39
complete)
510 - The Piano Quarterly. Wilmington.
Winter85/86 thru Fall86 (vol 34
complete)
513 - Perspectives of New Music. Seattle.
Fall-Winter84 and Spring-Summer85
(vol 23 complete)
517(PBSA) - Papers of the Bibliographical
Society of America. New York.
Vol 79 complete
518 - Philosophical Books. Oxford.
Jan85 thru Oct85 (vol 26 complete)
519(PhS) - Philosophical Studies. Dordrecht.
Jan85 thru Nov85 (vols 47 and 48
complete)
520 - Phronesis. Assen.
Vol 30 complete
526 - Quarry. Kingston.
Winter85 thru Autumn85 (vol 34
complete)
529(QQ) - Queen's Quarterly. Kingston.
Spring85 thru Winter85 (vol 92
complete)
532(RCF) - The Review of Contemporary
Fiction. Elmwood Park.
Spring85 thru Fall85 (vol 5 complete)
533 - Raritan. New Brunswick.
Summer85 thru Spring86 (vol 5 complete)
534(RALS) - Resources for American Literary Study. College Park.
Spring83 and Autumn83 (vol 13 complete)
535(RHL) - Revue d'Histoire Littéraire de
la France. Paris.
Jan-Feb85 thru Nov-Dec85 (vol 85
complete)
536(Rev) - Review. Charlottesville.
Vol 7
537 - Revue de Musicologie. Paris.
Vol 71 no 1/2 [vol 70 no 2 is
missing]
538(RAL) - Research in African Literatures.
Austin.
Spring85 thru Winter85 (vol 16
complete)
539 - Renaissance and Reformation/Renais-
sance et Réforme. Toronto.
Nov85 thru Aug86 (vol 9 no 4, vol
10 no 1-3)
540(RIPh) - Revue Internationale de Philosophie. Wetteren.
Vol 39 complete
541(RES) - Review of English Studies.
Oxford.
Feb85 thru Nov85 (vol 36 complete)

542 – Revue Philosophique de la France et de l'Étranger. Paris.
Jan–Mar85 thru Oct–Dec85 (vol 175 complete)
543 – Review of Metaphysics. Washington.
Sep84 thru Jun86 (vols 38 and 39 complete)
545(RPh) – Romance Philology. Berkeley.
Aug84 thru May86 (vols 38 and 39 complete)
546(RR) – Romanic Review. New York.
Jan85 thru Nov85 (vol 76 complete)
547(RF) – Romanische Forschungen. Frankfurt am Main.
Band 97 complete
548 – Revista Española de Lingüística. Madrid.
Jan–Jun85 and Jul–Dec85 (vol 15 complete)
549(RLC) – Revue de Littérature Comparée. Paris.
Jan–Mar85 thru Oct–Dec85 (vol 59 complete)
550(RusR) – Russian Review. Cambridge.
Jan85 thru Oct85 (vol 44 complete)
551(RenQ) – Renaissance Quarterly. New York.
Spring85 thru Winter85 (vol 38 complete)
552(REH) – Revista de estudios hispánicos. Poughkeepsie.
Jan85 thru Oct85 (vol 19 complete)
553(RLiR) – Revue de Linguistique Romane. Strasbourg.
Jan–Jun85 and Jul–Dec85 (vol 49 complete)
554 – Romania. Paris.
Vol 105 no 1 and 2/3
555 – Revue de Philologie. Paris.
Vol 59 fasc 1
556 – Russell. Hamilton.
Summer85 and Winter85/86 (vol 5 complete)
558(RLJ) – Russian Language Journal. East Lansing.
Fall84 (vol 38 no 131) and Vol 139 no 132/134
559 – Russian Linguistics. Dordrecht.
Vol 9 complete
560 – Salmagundi. Saratoga Springs.
Winter–Spring85 thru Fall85/Winter86 (no 66 thru 68/69)
561(SFS) – Science-Fiction Studies. Montréal.
Mar85 thru Nov85 (vol 12 complete)
562(Scan) – Scandinavica. Norwich.
May85 and Nov85 (vol 24 complete)
563(SS) – Scandinavian Studies. Lawrence.
Winter85 thru Autumn85 (vol 57 complete)
564 – Seminar. Toronto.
Feb85 thru Nov85 (vol 21 complete)
565 – Stand Magazine. Newcastle upon Tyne.
Winter84/85 thru Autumn85 (vol 26 complete)
566 – The Scriblerian. Philadelphia.
Autumn85 and Spring86 (vol 18 complete)
567 – Semiotica. Amsterdam.
Vol 53 complete thru vol 58 complete

568(SCN) – Seventeenth-Century News. University Park.
Spring–Summer85 thru Winter85 (vol 43 complete)
569(SR) – Sewanee Review. Sewanee.
Winter85 thru Fall85 (vol 93 complete)
570(SQ) – Shakespeare Quarterly. Washington.
Spring85 thru Winter85 (vol 36 complete)
571(ScLJ) – Scottish Literary Journal. Aberdeen.
May85 thru Winter85 (vol 12 complete plus supp 22 and supp 23)
572 – Shaw: The Annual of Bernard Shaw Studies. University Park.
Vol 6
573(SSF) – Studies in Short Fiction. Newberry.
Winter85 thru Fall85 (vol 22 complete)
574(SEEJ) – Slavic and East European Journal. Tucson.
Spring85 thru Winter85 (vol 29 complete)
575(SEER) – Slavonic and East European Review. London.
Jan85 thru Oct85 (vol 63 complete)
576 – Journal of the Society of Architectural Historians. Philadelphia.
Mar85 thru Dec85 (vol 44 complete)
577(SHR) – Southern Humanities Review. Auburn.
Winter85 thru Fall85 (vol 19 complete)
578 – Southern Literary Journal. Chapel Hill.
Spring86 and Fall86 (vol 18 no 2, vol 19 no 1)
579(SAQ) – South Atlantic Quarterly. Durham.
Winter85 thru Autumn85 (vol 84 complete)
580(SCR) – The South Carolina Review. Clemson.
Fall85 and Spring86 (vol 18 complete)
581 – Southerly. Sydney.
Mar85 thru Dec85 (vol 45 complete)
583 – Southern Speech Communication Journal. Tampa.
Fall85 thru Summer86 (vol 51 complete)
584(SWR) – Southwest Review. Dallas.
Winter85 thru Autumn85 (vol 70 complete)
585(SoQ) – The Southern Quarterly. Hattiesburg.
Fall–Winter85 thru Summer86 (vol 24 complete)
587(SAF) – Studies in American Fiction. Boston.
Spring85 and Autumn85 (vol 13 complete)
588(SSL) – Studies in Scottish Literature. Columbia.
Vol 20
589 – Speculum. Cambridge.
Jan85 thru Oct85 (vol 60 complete)
590 – Studies in the Humanities. Indiana.
Dec85 and Jun86 (vol 12 no 2, vol 13 no 1)

591(SIR) - Studies in Romanticism. Boston.
Spring85 thru Winter85 (vol 24 complete)
592 - Studio International. London.
Vol 198 complete
593 - Symposium. Washington.
Spring85 thru Winter85/86 (vol 39 complete)
594 - Studies in the Novel. Denton.
Spring85 thru Winter85 (vol 17 complete)
596(SL) - Studia Linguistica. Malmö.
Vol 39 complete
597(SN) - Studia Neophilologica. Stockholm.
Vol 57 complete
598(SoR) - The Southern Review. Baton Rouge.
Winter86 thru Autumn86 (vol 22 complete)
599 - Style. De Kalb.
Spring85 thru Winter85 (vol 19 complete)
600 - Simiolus. Utrecht.
Vol 15 complete
601(SuF) - Sinn und Form. Berlin.
Jan-Feb85 thru May-Jun85 (Band 37 Heft 1-3)
602 - Sprachkunst. Vienna.
Band 16 complete
603 - Studies in Language. Amsterdam.
Vol 9 complete
604 - Spenser Newsletter. Chapel Hill.
Winter85 thru Fall85 (vol 16 complete)
605(SC) - Stendhal Club. Grenoble.
15Oct85 thru 15Jul86 (vol 28 complete)
606 - Synthese. Dordrecht.
Jan85 thru Dec85 (vols 62-65 complete [no reviews indexed]
607 - Tempo. London.
Mar85 thru Dec85 (no 152-155)
608 - TESOL Quarterly. Washington.
Mar86 thru Dec86 (vol 20 complete)
609 - Theater. New Haven.
Winter85 thru Summer/Fall86 (vol 17 complete)
610 - Theatre Research International. Oxford.
Spring85 thru Autumn85 (vol 10 complete)
611(TN) - Theatre Notebook. London.
Vol 39 complete
612(ThS) - Theatre Survey. Albany.
May85 and Nov85 (vol 26 complete)
615(TJ) - Theatre Journal. Baltimore.
Mar85 thru Dec85 (vol 37 complete)
616 - Thalia. Ottawa.
Spring/Summer85 and Fall/Winter85 (vol 8 complete)
617(TLS) - Times Literary Supplement. London.
3Jan86 thru 26Dec86 (no 4318-4369)
618 - Trivia. North Amherst.
Winter85 and Summer85 (no 6 and 7)
619 - Transactions of the Charles S. Peirce Society. Buffalo.
Winter85 thru Fall85 (vol 21 complete)
627(UTQ) - University of Toronto Quarterly. Toronto.
Fall84 thru Summer86 (vols 54 and
[continued]

55 complete) [in Summer85 issue, only the "Humanities" section is indexed]
628(UWR) - University of Windsor Review. Windsor.
Fall-Winter85 (vol 19 no 1)
635(VPR) - Victorian Periodicals Review. Edwardsville.
Spring85 thru Winter85 (vol 18 complete)
636(VP) - Victorian Poetry. Morgantown.
Spring85 thru Winter85 (vol 23 complete)
637(VS) - Victorian Studies. Bloomington.
Autumn84 thru Summer86 (vols 28 and 29 complete)
639(VQR) - Virginia Quarterly Review. Charlottesville.
Winter85 thru Autumn85 (vol 61 complete)
646(WWR) - Walt Whitman Quarterly Review. Iowa City.
Summer85 thru Spring86 (vol 3 complete)
647 - Wascana Review. Regina.
Winter85 and Fall85 (vol 20 complete)
648(WCR) - West Coast Review. Burnaby.
Jun85 thru Apr86 (vol 20 complete)
649(WAL) - Western American Literature. Logan.
May85 thru Feb86 (vol 20 complete)
650(WF) - Western Folklore. Glendale.
Jan85 thru Oct85 (vol 44 complete)
651(WHR) - Western Humanities Review. Salt Lake City.
Spring85 thru Winter85 (vol 39 complete)
654(WB) - Weimarer Beiträge. Berlin.
1/1985 thru 12/1985 (vol 31 complete)
656(WMQ) - William and Mary Quarterly. Williamsburg.
Jan85 thru Oct85 (vol 42 complete)
658 - Winterthur Portfolio. Chicago.
Spring85 thru Winter85 (vol 20 complete)
659(ConL) - Contemporary Literature. Madison.
Spring86 thru Winter86 (vol 27 complete)
660(Word) - Word. Elmont.
Apr85 thru Dec85 (vol 36 complete)
661(WC) - The Wordsworth Circle. Philadelphia.
Winter85 thru Fall85 (vol 16 complete)
676(YR) - Yale Review. New Haven.
Summer85 thru Summer86 (vol 74 no 4, vol 75 complete)
677(YES) - The Yearbook of English Studies. London.
Vol 15
678(YCGL) - Yearbook of Comparative and General Literature. Bloomington.
No 34
679 - Zeitschrift für allgemeine Wissenschaftstheorie. Stuttgart.
Band 16 complete
680(ZDP) - Zeitschrift für deutsche Philologie. Berlin.
Band 104 complete

682(ZPSK) - Zeitschrift für Phonetik,
Sprachwissenschaft und Kommunikations-
forschung. Berlin.
Band 38 complete
683 - Zeitschrift für Kunstgeschichte.
München.
Band 48 complete
684(ZDA) - Zeitschrift für deutsches Altertum und deutsche Literatur [Anzeiger
section]. Stuttgart.
Band 114 complete
685(ZDL) - Zeitschrift für Dialektologie
und Linguistik. Wiesbaden.
1/1985 thru 3/1985 (vol 52 complete)
687 - Zeitschrift für Philosophische Forschung. Meisenheim/Glan.
Jan-Mar85 thru Oct-Dec85 (Band 39
complete)
688(ZSP) - Zeitschrift für slavische Philologie. Heidelberg.
Band 45 Heft 1
700 - Shenandoah. Lexington.
Vol 36 no 1-3 [no reviews indexed]
702 - Shakespeare Studies. New York.
Vol 17
703 - Sulfur. Ypsilanti.
No 13 thru no 15 (vol 5 complete)
704(SFR) - Stanford French Review. Saratoga.
Spring85 thru Winter85 (vol 9 complete)
705 - The Wallace Stevens Journal. Potsdam.
Spring85 and Fall85 (vol 9 complete)
706 - Studia Leibnitiana. Stuttgart.
Band 17 complete
707 - Sight and Sound. London.
Winter84/85 thru Autumn85 (vol 54
complete)
708 - Studi Linguistici Italiani. Rome.
Vol 11 complete

Each year we are unable (for one reason
or another) to index the reviews appearing
in all of the periodicals scanned. The
following is a list of the periodicals
whose reviews were not included in this
volume of the Index. Every attempt will
be made to index these reviews in the next
volume of the Index:

137 - CV/II: Contemporary Verse Two.
Winnipeg.
202(FMod) - Filología Moderna. Madrid.
261 - Indian Linguistics. Pune.
273(IC) - Islamic Culture. Hyderabad.
299 - Journal of Beckett Studies. London.
398(MPS) - Modern Poetry Studies. Buffalo.
411 - Music Analysis. Oxford.
457(NRFH) - Nueva Revista de Filología
Hispánica. Mexico City.
459 - Obsidian. Detroit.
465 - The Opera Quarterly. Chapel Hill.
494 - Poetics Today. Jerusalem.
521 - Philosophical Investigations. Oxford.
544 - Rhetorica. Berkeley.
582(SFQ) - Southern Folklore Quarterly.
Gainesville.
595(ScS) - Scottish Studies. Edinburgh.
613 - Thought. Bronx.
701(SinN) - Sin Nombre. San Juan.

Aaron, D. - see Inman, A.C.
Aaron, S. Stage Fright.
  D. Cavett, 61:Jun86-80
Aarsleff, H. From Locke to Saussure.*
  W. Keach, 591(SIR):Summer85-271
  T.J. Taylor, 541(RES):May85-245
Aarts, F. and J. English Syntactic Struc-
  tures.
  F.W. Gester, 72:Band222Heft2-373
  G. Leitner, 38:Band103Heft1/2-115
Aarts, J. and W. Meijs, eds. Corpus Lin-
  guistics.
  R.L. Brandson, 320(CJL):Winter85-482
Abbey, E. Beyond the Wall.
  J.A. Herndon, 649(WAL):May85-71
Abbey, L. The Antlered Boy.
  A.L. Amprimoz, 526:Spring85-80
  S. Hutchison, 102(CanL):Spring85-164
Abbott, D., ed. Mississippi Writers.
  (Vol 1)
  639(VQR):Autumn85-120
Abbott, H.P. Diary Fiction.*
  L.L. Doan, 395(MFS):Winter85-866
  B. Duyfhuizen, 454:Winter86-171
Abbott, J.E. The Life of Eknath. Life of
  Tukaram.
  F.M. Smith, 318(JAOS):Oct-Dec84-785
Abbott, L.K. Love is the Crooked Thing.
  A. Hempel, 441:16Mar86-10
  442(NY):23Jun86-98
Abbott, R.H. That Day in Gordon.
  D. Unger, 441:28Sep86-34
Abdala, B., Jr. and M. Aparecida Pascho-
  alin. História Social da literatura
  Portuguesa.
  R. Sousa, 264(I&L):[N.S.]Vol 1No1/2-
  281
Abdulaziz, M., W. Smalzer and H. Abdulazia.
  The Computer Book.
  J. Kimball, 608:Jun86-327
  W. Poole, 399(MLJ):Winter85-447
Abel, E. and E.K., eds. The "Signs"
  Reader.
  V. Middleton, 577(SHR):Summer85-258
Abel, E., M. Hirsch and E. Langland, eds.
  The Voyage In.*
  P.A. Vernon, 577(SHR):Summer85-260
Abel, E.K. Terminal Degrees.
  A. Hacker, 453(NYRB):13Feb86-35
Abel, L. The Intellectual Follies.
  B.P. Solomon, 473(PR):Vol152No3-282
Abel, R. The French Cinema: The First
  Wave, 1915-1929.*
  P. Baxter, 529(QQ):Autumn85-616
  B. Salt, 707:Spring85-147
  42(AR):Spring85-253
  295(JML):Nov85-438
Abel, R. The Progress of a Fire.
  M. Gorra, 441:19Jan86-12
Abellán, M.L. Censura y creación liter-
  aria en España (1939-1976).
  J-L. Marfany, 86(BHS):Apr85-212
Aberbach, D. At the Handles of the Lock.
  S. Pinsker, 395(MFS):Winter85-863
Abercrombie, S. Architecture as Art.
  R. Kimball, 45:Feb85-83
Abish, W. How German Is It.
  D. Saalmann, 145(Crit):Spring85-105
  [inadvertently deleted from prev vol]
Abodaher, D. Iacocca.
  J.K. Galbraith, 453(NYRB):10Apr86-11

Abou-Assaf, A., P. Bordreuil and A. Mil-
  lard. La Statue de Tell Fekherye et son
  inscription bilingue assyroaraméenne.
  S.A. Kaufman, 318(JAOS):Jul-Sep84-571
Abou Saif, L. A Bridge Through Time.
  A. Soueif, 617(TLS):15Aug86-886
Abraham, C. Norman Satirists in the Age
  of Louis XIII.
  T. Allott, 208(FS):Jul85-331
Abraham, C. On the Structure of Molière's
  "Comédies-Ballets."*
  J.L. Pallister, 568(SCN):Spring-
  Summer85-21
Abraham, G., ed. The New Oxford History
  of Music. (Vol 6)
  P. Williams, 617(TLS):13Jun86-638
Abraham, W., ed. Satzglieder im Deutschen.
  L.A. Connolly, 603:Vol9No1-123
Abrahams, E. The Lyrical Left.
  K.S. Lynn, 129:Oct86-83
Abrahams, R.D., ed. African Folktales.*
  R. Finnegan, 538(RAL):Fall85-384
  H. Scheub, 2(AfrA):Feb85-23
Abrahams, R.D. The Man-of-Words in the
  West Indies.*
  W. Harris, 538(RAL):Fall85-431
  T. Kochman, 355(LSoc):Sep85-390
Abrahams, R.D. and J.F. Szwed, eds. After
  Africa.
  B. Brown, 355(LSoc):Mar85-130
  S.D. Glazier, 538(RAL):Spring85-93
Abrahams, W., ed. Prize Stories 1986: The
  O. Henry Awards.
  C. Benfey, 441:27Apr86-22
Abramovič, S.L. Puškin v 1836 godu (pred-
  ystorija poslednej duèli).
  W.N. Vickery, 279:Vol130-181
Abrams, M., D. Gerard and N. Timms, eds.
  Values and Social Change in Britain.
  P. Addison, 617(TLS):14Mar86-284
Abramson, J. and B. Franklin. Where They
  Are Now.
  L. Greenhouse, 441:23Feb86-12
Abravanel, Y. Siḥot ʿal ha-Ahavah. (M.
  Dorman, trans)
  A.M. Lesley, 551(RenQ):Spring85-145
Abrioux, Y. Ian Hamilton Finlay.
  M. Francis, 62:Jan86-15
  D. Thomas, 362:9Jan86-30
  A. Young, 617(TLS):16May86-543
Abse, D. One-Legged on Ice.*
  T. Tierney, 502(PrS):Spring85-106
Abse, D. A Poet in the Family. A Strong
  Dose of Myself.
  P. Lewis, 565:Spring85-43
Absire, A. 118, rue Terminale.
  M.G. Rose, 207(FR):Dec85-329
Abû-l-'Alâ al-Ma'arrî. L'Épître du pardon.
  (V-M. Monteil, ed and trans)
  F. Trémolières, 450(NRF):Jun85-83
Abusch, A. Der Deckname.
  I. Hiebel, 601(SuF):Mar-Apr85-386
Accad, E. L'Excisée.
  C. Zimra, 207(FR):May86-990
Accarie, M. and A. Queffelec, eds.
  Mélanges de langue et de littérature
  médiévales offerts à Alice Planche.
  G. Eckard, 553(RLiR):Jul-Dec85-440
Acharhian, H. Hayots Andsnanunneri Bar-
  haran.
  A.M. Avakian, 424:Dec85-283
Achenbaum, W.A. Social Security.
  R. Pear, 441:15Jun86-21

Achinstein, P., ed. The Concept of Evidence.
  A. Boyer, 542:Jul-Sep85-358
Achinstein, P. The Nature of Explanation.*
  J.H. Fetzer, 486:Sep84-516
  R. Harré, 543:Sep85-137
  P. Horwich, 482(PhR):Oct85-583
  C.B. McCullagh, 63:Dec85-549
"800 Jahre Franz von Assisi."
  P. Dinzelbacher, 684(ZDA):Band114Heft1-29
Acker, K. Don Quixote.
  A. Haverty, 617(TLS):23May86-554
  T. Le Clair, 441:30Nov86-10
Ackerley, C. and L.J. Clipper. A Companion to "Under the Volcano."*
  R. Binns, 102(CanL):Summer85-157
  R.T. Chapman, 268(IFR):Winter86-54
  G.P. Jones, 627(UTQ):Summer85-447
  M.B. Pringle, 395(MFS):Summer85-370
  295(JML):Nov85-523
Ackerman, B. Reconstructing American Law.
  J.M. O'Fallon, 185:Oct85-201
Ackerman, D. Lady Faustus.
  L. Goldstein, 472:Spring/Summer/Fall/Winter85-446
Ackerman, D. On Extended Wings.*
  L. Goldstein, 385(MQR):Fall86-736
Ackerman, G.M. The Life and Work of Jean-Léon Gérôme.
  M. Warner, 617(TLS):5Sep86-956
Ackland, V. For Sylvia.*
  J. Johnston, 441:13Jul86-24
Ackroyd, P. T.S. Eliot.*
  A. Brink, 556:Summer85-77
  E.K. Hay, 432(NEQ):Sep85-485
  J. MacVean, 4:Autumn-Winter85/86-210
  R.B. Martin, 77:Fall85-365
  W. Phillips, 473(PR):Vol52No4-444
  C. Rawson, 493:Jan85-51
  295(JML):Nov85-472
  639(VQR):Spring85-48
Ackroyd, P. Hawksmoor.*
  J. Mellors, 364:Oct85-86
  J.C. Oates, 441:19Jan86-3
  442(NY):3Mar86-104
Ackroyd, P. The Last Testament of Oscar Wilde.*
  G. Davenport, 569(SR):Spring85-321
"Actes du Colloque Louise Michel."
  S. Michaud, 535(RHL):Nov/Dec85-1076
Acton, E. The Best of Eliza Acton. (E. Ray, ed)
  617(TLS):21Nov86-1327
Acton, H. Three Extraordinary Ambassadors.
  U.L., 278(IS):Vol40-136
"Actualité de Bonstetten."
  N. King, 208(FS):Jan85-81
"Actualité de l'histoire de la langue française."
  R. Martin, 553(RLiR):Jul-Dec85-419
Adair, G. Alice Through the Needle's Eye.*
  639(VQR):Autumn85-128
Adair, G. Myths and Memories.
  S. French, 617(TLS):17Oct86-1174
  C. McCabe, 362:2Oct86-24
Adair, G. and N. Roddick. A Night at the Pictures.
  D. Robinson, 617(TLS):17Jan86-69
Adam, H. and K. Moodley. South Africa without Apartheid.
  J.E. Spence, 617(TLS):15Aug86-882
  L. Thompson, 453(NYRB):23Oct86-3

Adam, J. Employment and Wage Policies in Poland, Czechoslovakia and Hungary since 1950.
  A. Nove, 617(TLS):10Jan86-31
Adam, R. - see Livy
Adams, A. Return Trips.*
  A. Boston, 617(TLS):31Jan86-112
Adams, A. Rich Rewards.
  L.T. Blades, 145(Crit):Summer86-187
Adams, A., ed and trans. The Romance of Yder.*
  T. Hunt, 402(MLR):Oct85-932
  E. Kennedy, 447(N&Q):Dec84-529
  D.D.R. Owen, 382(MAE):1985/2-324
Adams, A. Superior Women.*
  W.H. Pritchard, 249(HudR):Spring85-124
  639(VQR):Spring85-61
Adams, A., with M.S. Alinder. Ansel Adams.* (British title: An Autobiography.)
  R. Adams, 617(TLS):16May86-528
Adams, B. London Illustrated, 1604-1851.*
  P. Stockham, 503:Summer85-92
Adams, C. - see Henning, R.
Adams, D.J. - see de La Chesnaye des Bois, A.
Adams, H. Joyce Cary's Trilogies.*
  R. Bloom, 174(Éire):Winter85-149
  E.E. Christian, 594:Fall85-311
  E.D. Ermarth, 301(JEGP):Oct85-576
  D.E. Latané, Jr., 577(SHR):Fall85-382
Adams, H. The Fourth Widow.
  P-L. Adams, 61:Aug86-91
Adams, H. History of the United States of America During the Administrations of Thomas Jefferson. History of the United States of American During the Administrations of James Madison. (E.N. Harbert, ed of both)
  C.V. Woodward, 441:6Jul86-3
Adams, H. Mont Saint Michel and Chartres. (R. Carney, ed)
  617(TLS):21Nov86-1327
Adams, H. Philosophy of the Literary Symbolic.*
  D.E. Latané, Jr., 577(SHR):Fall85-382
  D.T. O'Hara, 401(MLQ):Sep84-311
Adams, J. The Financing of Terror.
  M. Clark, 362:21Aug86-22
  C. Townshend, 617(TLS):29Aug86-928
Adams, J. and S. Iqbal. Exports, Politics, and Economic Development.
  I-D. Pal, 293(JASt):May85-626
Adams, J.N. The Latin Sexual Vocabulary.*
  F.R.D. Goodyear, 123:Vol35No2-316
  D.R. Shackleton Bailey, 122:Jan85-83
Adams, M. Designs for Living.
  D. Duerden, 538(RAL):Fall85-452
Adams, P.G. Travel Literature and the Evolution of the Novel.*
  H. Anderson, 594:Winter85-420
  M. Golden, 579(SAQ):Autumn85-442
  E-M. Kroller, 102(CanL):Winter84-64
  I.S. Maclaren, 627(UTQ):Winter85/86-204
  P. Parrinder, 366:Autumn85-308
  S. Pickering, 569(SR):Winter85-xii
  P. Rogers, 506(PSt):May85-80
  P. Sabor, 529(QQ):Spring85-199
  M. Seidel, 301(JEGP):Jan85-133
Adams, R. Los Angeles Spring.
  A. Grundberg, 441:7Dec86-20

Adams, R.  Summer Nights.
  C. Reid, 617(TLS):6Jun86-611
Adams, R.M.  Heartland of Cities.
  T.C. Young, Jr., 318(JAOS):Apr-Jun84-369
Adams, R.N.  Paradoxical Harvest.
  D. Greenberg, 637(VS):Winter85-357
Adams, V.  The Media and the Falklands Campaign.
  R. Fox, 362:20Nov86-26
Adamson, D.  Balzac: "Illusions perdues."*
  L. Kamm, 207(FR):Apr86-790
Adamson, G.  Le Procédé de Raymond Roussel.*
  J.H. Matthews, 593:Fall85-227
Adamson, I.  The Identity of Ulster.
  R. Fréchet, 189(EA):Apr-Jun86-237
Adamson, W.L.  Hegemony and Revolution.
  W. Hartley, 275(IQ):Summer/Fall84-171
Adamson, W.L.  Marx and the Disillusionment of Marxism.
  T.B., 185:Jul86-905
Adcock, B.  Nettles.
  J. Saunders, 565:Autumn85-73
Adcock, F.  Selected Poems.*
  P. Bland, 364:Oct85-82
Addiss, S.  The World of Kameda Bōsai.
  B. Klein, 407(MN):Winter85-462
Adelard of Bath.  The First Latin Translation of Euclid's "Elements" Commonly Ascribed to Adelard of Bath, Books I-VIII and Books X.36-XV.2.  (H.L.L. Busard, ed)
  M. Masi, 589:Oct85-931
Aden, J.M.  Pope's Once and Future Kings.
  H-J. Müllenbrock, 38:Band103Heft1/2-217
Adeney, M. and J. Lloyd.  The Miners' Strike 1984-5.
  M. Crick, 617(TLS):24Oct86-1184
  N. Jones, 362:2Oct86-22
Adhyatman, S. and A. Ridho.  Martavans in Indonesia.  (2nd ed)
  J. Shaw, 60:May-Jun85-133
Adisa, O.P.  Bake-Face and Other Guava Stories.
  J. Olshan, 441:2Nov86-26
Adler, C.  Selected Letters of Cyrus Adler.  (I. Robinson, ed)
  J.D. Sarna, 129:Feb86-68
Adler, H. and H.J. Schrimpf, eds.  Karin Struck — Materialien.
  H.W. Panthel, 72:Band222Heft2-362
Adler, I. and B. Bayer, with I. Shalem, eds.  Yuval.
  D. Wulstan, 410(M&L):Oct85-378
Adler, M.J.  Six Great Ideas.
  S.J. Seleman, 438:Autumn85-493
Adler, M.J.  Ten Philosophical Mistakes.*
  639(VQR):Autumn85-135
Adler, R.  Reckless Disregard.
  M.E. Frankel, 441:9Nov86-1
Adler, S., ed.  Cultural Language Differences.
  C.T. Adger, 350:Mar86-230
Adler, W.  Jan Wildens.
  C.B., 90:Feb85-109
Adonis.  Transformations of the Lover.
  D. McDuff, 565:Summer85-72
Adorno, T.W.  Aesthetic Theory.*  (G. Adorno and R. Tiedemann, eds)
  L. Zuidervaart, 290(JAAC):Winter85-195

Adorno, T.W.  Notes sur la littérature.
  R. Rochlitz, 98:Jun-Jul85-607
Adriaansens, H.P.M.  Talcott Parsons and the Conceptual Dilemma.
  B. Green, 488:Mar85-93
Adrian, A.A.  Dickens and the Parent-Child Relationship.*
  J. Vogel, 158:Jun85-69
Adrian-Adrianowska, K.  Wspomnienia.
  S.L. Cuba, 497(PolR):Vol30No1-105
Adriani, G.  Degas: Pastels, Oil Sketches, Drawings.*
  J. Hayes, 324:May86-413
Aebischer, P.  Etudes de stratigraphie linguistique.
  H. Meier, 72:Band222Heft1-208
Aepinus, F.U.T.  Aepinus's Essay on the Theory of Electricity and Magnetism.  (R.W. Home, ed)
  W.F. Ryan, 575(SEER):Jan85-122
Aeschylus.  Choephori.  (A.F. Garvie, ed)
  J.H.C. Leach, 617(TLS):29Aug86-943
Aeschylus.  Prometheus Bound.  (M. Griffith, ed)
  D. Bain, 303(JoHS):Vol 105-180
Afshar, H.  Iran.
  F. Halliday, 617(TLS):20Jun86-667
"After the War Was Over."
  J. Manning, 441:26Jan86-21
Agard, F.B.  A Course in Romance Linguistics.  (Vol 1)
  J.A. Creore, 320(CJL):Fall85-349
  J.N. Green, 353:Vol23No1-163
  J. Klausenburger, 207(FR):Apr86-835
Agard, F.B.  A Course in Romance Linguistics.  (Vol 2)
  J.A. Creore, 320(CJL):Fall85-349
  R.P. de Gorog, 159:Fall85-231
  J.N. Green, 353:Vol23No1-163
  J. Klausenburger, 207(FR):Apr86-835
Agassi, J., ed.  Psychiatric Diagnosis.
  N. Laor, 488:Sep85-333
Agassi, J.  Science and Society.
  B. Baigrie, 488:Jun85-228
Agassi, J.  Towards a Rational Philosophical Anthropology.
  J.R. Wettersten, 679:Band16Heft1-167
"The Age of Vermeer and De Hooch."
  C. Ford, 59:Jun85-234
Ageyev, M.  Novel with Cocaine.*
  J. Updike, 442(NY):28Apr86-117
Aggarwal, P.C.  Halfway to Equality.
  B.R. Joshi, 293(JASt):May85-628
Agheana, I.T.  The Prose of Jorge Luis Borges.
  G.R. McMurray, 238:Dec85-785
  T. Running, 263(RIB):Vol35No2-207
Agnon, S.Y.  A Simple Story.*
  442(NY):3Mar86-104
Agrawal, D.P.  The Archaeology of India.
  G.F. Dales, 293(JASt):Nov84-220
Agresto, J.  The Supreme Court and Constitutional Democracy.
  A.S., 185:Oct85-211
Agthe, J.  Luba Hemba.
  E.N. Quarcoopome, 2(AfrA):Nov84-21
Aguilar, R.A.  Armengol and O.U. Somoza, eds.  Palabra nueva.
  F. De León, 238:Sep85-533
Aharoni, Y.  The Archaeology of the Land of Israel.  (M. Aharoni, ed)
  E.S. Meltzer, 318(JAOS):Jul-Sep84-579

3

Ahearn, B. Zukofsky's "A."*
  M. Davidson, 405(MP):Aug85-95
Ahearn, C. Luna-Verse.
  L. Boone, 102(CanL):Winter84-136
Ahearn, E.J. Rimbaud.*
  P. Newman-Gordon, 704(SFR):Spring85-
  110.
Ahern, E.M. and H. Gates, eds. The Anthro-
pology of Taiwanese Society.
  C.F. Blake, 302:Vol21No1-80
Ahlqvist, A., ed. Papers from the 5th
International Conference on Historical
Linguistics.
  B. Ó Cuív, 112:Vol 16-212
Ahlström, G.W. Royal Administration and
National Religion in Ancient Palestine.
  P.E. Dion, 318(JAOS):Oct-Dec84-763
Ahmad, J.A. Lost in the Crowd.
  D. Raffat, 441:13Apr86-29
Ahrens, R., ed. Shakespeare im Unterricht.
Shakespeare: Didaktisches Handbuch.
  J.L. Gunther, 570(SQ):Summer85-240
Ai. Sin.
  D. Wojahn, 441:8Jun86-38
Aichholzer, P. Darstellungen römischer
Sagen.
  M. Loudon, 313:Vol75-279
Aikin, J.P. German Baroque Drama.
  P. Skrine, 402(MLR):Jan85-210
  M.R. Sperberg-McQueen, 400(MLN):Apr85-
  665
Ailes, A. The Origins of the Royal Arms
of England.
  B.B. Rezak, 589:Apr85-373
Ainsley, J. Archibald Campbell Jordan.
  H. Scheub, 538(RAL):Fall85-465
Aird, C. A Dead Liberty.
  T.J. Binyon, 617(TLS):19Sep86-1029
Aithal, P.K.P. - see Devasvāmin
Aitken, W.R. Scottish Literature in
English and Scots.*
  D.S. Mack, 447(N&Q):Jun84-268
Ajami, F. The Arab Predicament.*
  A.T. Sullivan, 396(ModA):Fall85-365
Ajami, F. The Vanished Imam.
  M.C. Bateson, 441:25May86-5
  D. Ignatius, 61:Jun86-77
  E. Mortimer, 453(NYRB):9Oct86-17
Akenson, D.H. The Irish in Ontario.
Being Had.
  C. Byrne, 150(DR):Spring85-146
Akhmatova, A. Poems.* (L. Coffin, ed and
trans)
  J. Aleshire, 434:Winter84-272
Akhmatova, A. Sochineniia. (Vol 3) (G.P.
Struve and others, eds)
  S. Ketchian, 550(RusR):Jan85-78
Akindynos, G. Letters of Gregory Akindy-
nos. (A.C. Hero, ed and trans)
  A. Papadakis, 589:Oct85-932
Akiner, S. - see Janovič, S.
Akivaga, S.K. and A.B. Odaga. Oral Litera-
ture.
  P. Amuka, 538(RAL):Fall85-430
Akkerman, E., P. Masereeuw and W. Meijs.
Designing a Computerized Lexicon for
Linguistic Purposes.
  S. Cumming, 350:Sep86-728
Akmajian, A., R.A. Demers and R.M. Harnish.
Linguistics. (2nd ed)
  S.M. Embleton, 320(CJL):Spring85-84

Akrasanee, N. and H.C. Reiger, eds. ASEAN-
EEC Economic Relations.
  L. Lim, 293(JASt):May85-689
Akrigg, G.P.V. - see King James VI & I
Aksyonov, V. The Burn.*
  R.E. Peterson, 574(SEEJ):Winter85-488
  639(VQR):Spring85-62
"Akten zur deutschen auswärtigen Politik,
1918-1945." (Ser A, Vol 2)
  F.L. Carsten, 575(SEER):Jul85-465
"Akten zur deutschen auswärtigen Politik,
1918-1945." (Ser B, Vol 20)
  F.L. Carsten, 575(SEER):Jan85-139
"Akten zur deutschen auswärtigen Politik
1918-1945." (Ser B, Vol 21)
  F.L. Carsten, 575(SEER):Jan85-141
Alabaster, O. What You Can Do to Prevent
Cancer.
  639(VQR):Autumn85-135
Alain-Fournier. The Lost Domain (Le Grand
Meaulnes).
  R. Clarke, 362:27Nov86-26
Alain-Fournier, H. Towards the Lost
Domain.
  R. Clarke, 362:27Nov86-26
de Alarcón, P.A. Obras olvidadas. (C. De
Coster, ed)
  D. Quinn, 238:Sep85-517
Alas, L. La Regenta.* (J. Rutherford,
trans)
  A.M. Gullón, 240(HR):Spring85-250
  R.B. Klein, 552(REH):Jan85-139
Alatis, J.E. and J.C. Staczek, eds. Per-
spectives on Bilingualism and Bilingual
Education.
  R.B. Le Page, 353:Vol23No4-638
Alatri, P. D'Annunzio.
  J.R. Woodhouse, 402(MLR):Jan85-189
Alazraki, J. En busca del unicorno.*
  S. Boldy, 86(BHS):Oct85-403
Alba, R.D., ed. Ethnicity and Race in the
U.S.A.
  N. Glazer, 617(TLS):13Jun86-655
Alberigo, G. and others. La chrétienté en
débat, histoire, formes et problèmes
actuels.
  M. Adam, 542:Jul-Sep85-366
Alberoni, F. Movement and Institution.*
  L.G., 185:Jan86-449
Albert, K. Das gemeinsame Sein.
  R. Margreiter, 489(PJGG):Band92Heft1-
  212
Albertsen, L.L. Neuere deutsche Metrik.
  N. Gabriel, 680(ZDP):Band104Heft4-635
Albery, N. The House of Kanzē.*
  A. Becker, 441:7Sep86-22
  442(NY):13Oct86-156
Albisetti, J.C. Secondary School Reform
in Imperial Germany.
  G.R. Batho, 161(DUJ):Jun84-288
Albrecht, D. Designing Dreams.
  P. Goldberger, 441:7Dec86-17
Albrecht, E. and others, eds. Wörterbuch
Logik, Semiotik, Methodologie: Russische-
Deutsche/Deutsch-Russisch.
  J. Dölling, 682(ZPSK):Band38Heft4-449
  W. Kasack, 688(ZSP):Band45Heft1-222
Albrecht, G., comp. Internationale Bibli-
ographie zur Geschichte der deutschen
Literatur von den Anfängen bis zur Gegen-
wart.
  G. Wenzel, 654(WB):9/1985-1580

Albright, D. Lyricality in English Litera-
ture.
  A.T. McKenzie, 566:Spring86-225
  A. Williams, 88:Spring86-144
Albright, D. Tennyson.
  A.S. Byatt, 617(TLS):14Nov86-1274
Albright, T. Art in the San Francisco Bay
Area, 1945-1980.
  S. Boettger, 62:Dec85-14
  P. Failing, 55:Nov85-29
  P. Selz, 127:Spring85-75
Albury, R. The Politics of Objectivity.
  G. Sargeant, 63:Mar85-107
Alcalá, Á. - see Servet, M.
Alcock, J. Sonoran Desert Spring.
  T. Halliday, 617(TLS):4Jul86-745
Alcosser, S. A Fish to Feed All Hunger.
  H. Raz, 152(UDQ):Spring/Summer86-180
Alcover, M. Poullain de la Barre.*
  I. Maclean, 208(FS):Jan85-74
Alcuin. The Bishops, Kings, and Saints of
York. (P. Godman, ed)
  D. Ganz, 589:Jan85-115
  H. Sauer, 447(N&Q):Dec84-523
Aldcroft, D.H. The British Economy.
(Vol 1)
  R. Floud, 617(TLS):1Aug86-834
Aldea Vaquero, Q., T. Marín Martínez and J.
Vives Gatell, eds. Diccionario de his-
toria eclesiástica de España.
  A.E. Foley, 240(HR):Spring85-231
Alden, J. and D.C. Landis, eds. European
Americana.* (Vols 1 and 2)
  J.A.L. Lemay, 534(RALS):Spring83-26
  D.W. McLeod, 470:Vol23-109
Alden, J.R. Stephen Sayre.
  P. Marshall, 83:Autumn85-221
Alden, M.J. Bronze Age Population Fluctua-
tions in the Argolid from the Evidence
of Mycenaean Tombs.
  W.G. Cavanagh, 303(JoHS):Vol 105-220
Alderink, L.J. Creation and Salvation in
Ancient Orphism.*
  J. Mansfield, 394:Vol38fasc3/4-436
Alderson, J.C. and A.H. Urquhart, eds.
Reading in a Foreign Language.
  A.D. Cohen, 608:Dec86-747
Aldiss, B.W. Helliconia Winter.*
  639(VQR):Autumn85-125
Aldiss, B.W., with D. Wingrove. Trillion
Year Spree.
  J. Clute, 617(TLS):31Oct86-1223
Aldridge, A.O. Early American Literature.*
  C. Kretzoi, 107(CRCL):Sep85-525
Aldridge, A.O. Tom Paine's American Ideol-
ogy.
  R.A. Ferguson, 27(AL):Oct85-490
  W.B. Peach, 656(WMQ):Oct85-545
  S. Rosswurm, 173(ECS):Summer86-549
Aldridge, J.W. The American Novel and the
Way We Live Now.*
  C. Werner, 301(JEGP):Jul85-461
Alegría, C. Flowers from the Volcano.
  H.J.F. De Aguilar, 472:Spring/Summer/
    Fall/Winter85-369
Aleichem, S. The Nightingale.*
  R. Bar, 441:26Jan86-20
Alekseev, A.A. - see Sobolevskij, A.I.
Aler, J., ed. Gestalten um Stefan George.
  W.H. McClain, 221(GQ):Fall85-620
  M. Winkler, 133:Band18Heft2-183

Aleshkovsky, Y. Kangaroo.
  W. Herrick, 441:27Apr86-9
  J. Updike, 442(NY):28Apr86-120
Alessio, G.C. - see "Cronaca di Novalesa"
Alessio, G.C. - see Florentini, B.
Alexander, B. Korea.
  R. Halloran, 441:3Aug86-19
Alexander, C. The Early Writings of
Charlotte Brontë.*
  P. Thomson, 541(RES):Nov85-587
Alexander, C. - see Brontë, C.
Alexander, C., with others. The Produc-
tion of Houses.
  R. Banham, 617(TLS):3Jan86-15
Alexander, C.C. Here the Country Lies.
  D. Anfam, 59:Jun85-261
Alexander, G.I. Fortis and Lenis in Ger-
manic.
  G.S. Nathan, 350:Mar86-210
Alexander, H. Fans.*
  B. Scott, 39:Mar85-209
Alexander, J.C. Theoretical Logic in
Sociology.* (Vol 1)
  S.P. Turner, 488:Mar85-77
Alexander, J.C. Theoretical Logic in
Sociology.* (Vol 2)
  S.P. Turner, 488:Jun85-211
Alexander, J.C. Theoretical Logic in
Sociology.* (Vol 3)
  S.P. Turner, 488:Sep85-365
Alexander, J.C. Theoretical Logic in
Sociology.* (Vol 4)
  S.P. Turner, 488:Dec85-513
Alexander, J.J.G., T.J. Brown and J. Gibbs -
see Wormald, F.
Alexander, L. The Big Stick.
  R. Cohen, 441:16Mar86-20
Alexander, M. Old English Literature.*
  G. Bourquin, 189(EA):Jan-Mar86-115
  S.A.J. Bradley, 382(MAE):1985/2-284
  M. Dodsworth, 175:Spring85-93
  E.G. Stanley, 447(N&Q):Mar84-99
Alexander, P. Navigable Waterways.*
  M. Boruch, 460(OhR):No36-123
  G. Schulman, 491:Nov85-106
  W. Zander, 363(LitR):Spring86-379
  639(VQR):Autumn85-131
Alexander, W. Films on the Left.
  B. Nichols, 106:Summer85-231
Alexander of Aphrodisias. On Fate. (R.W.
Sharples, ed and trans)
  J. Dillon, 303(JoHS):Vol 105-195
  D. Frede, 466:Vol2-279
  N. White, 482(PhR):Jan85-127
Alexandre-Garner, C. "Le Quatuor d'Alex-
andrie."
  R. Silhol, 189(EA):Apr-Jun86-233
"Alfar (Revista de Casa América-Galicia)
1922-1929."
  L. Litvak, 240(HR):Summer85-380
Alföldi-Rosenbaum, E. and J. Ward-Perkins.
Justinianic Mosaic Pavements in Cyrena-
ican Churches.
  S. Campbell, 487:Spring85-96
Alfonsi, F. Alberto Moravia in America.
  L. Kibler, 276:Autumn85-264
Alfonso X. Alfonso el Sabio: Lapidario
[and] Libro de las formas & ymagenes.
(R.C. Diman and L.W. Winget, eds)
  J. Snow, 86(BHS):Jan85-130
Alfonso X. Calila e Dimna. (J.M. Cacho
Blecua and M.J. Lacarra, eds)
  F. López Estrada, 240(HR):Summer85-351

Alfonso X. Cantigas de Santa María. (J.
Filgueira Valverde, trans)
A.J. Cárdenas, 304(JHP):Spring85-247
Alfonso X. "Lapidario" (Según el manu-
scrito escurialense h.I.15). (S. Rodrí-
guez M. Montalvo, ed)
J. Snow, 86(BHS):Jan85-130
Alfonso XI. Libro de la Montería - Based
on Escorial MS Y-II-19.* (D.P. Seniff,
ed)
S.N. Dworkin, 545(RPh):Nov85-271
J. Snow, 86(BHS):Jan85-132
Alford, J.A. and D.P. Seniff. Literature
and Law in the Middle Ages.
K.H. Van D'Elden, 589:Oct85-935
Alford, S.E. Irony and the Logic of the
Romantic Imagination.
D. Simpson, 88:Winter85/86-106
Alfroy, J-M. La Fugue du père.
C-M. Senninger, 207(FR):Apr86-809
Algar, H. - see Imam Khomeini
Alger, H., Jr. Mabel Parker, or, The Hid-
den Treasure.
N. Baym, 441:20Jul86-10
Alhaique Pettinelli, R. L'immaginario
cavalleresco nel Rinascimento ferrarese.
M. Pieri, 400(MLN):Jan85-181
Ali, S.H. The Malays.
D.K. Mauzy, 293(JASt):Nov84-241
Ali, T. Can Pakistan Survive?
A.S. Ahmed, 293(JASt):Nov84-239
Ali, T. An Indian Dynasty.* (British
title: The Nehrus and the Gandhis.)
N. Mansergh, 617(TLS):10Jan86-30
Alic, M. Hypatia's Heritage.
P. Phillips, 617(TLS):16May86-524
Alighieri, D. - see under Dante Alighieri
Alinei, M. and others - see "Atlas Lin-
guarum Europae (ALE)"
Alkire, L.G., Jr., ed. New Periodical
Title Abbreviations.
K.B. Harder, 424:Sep85-204
Alkire, L.G., Jr. Periodical Title Abbre-
viations. (4th ed)
K.B. Harder, 424:Dec85-281
Alkon, P. and R. Folkenflik. Samuel
Johnson.
J. Abbott, 324:Nov86-843
S. Soupel, 189(EA):Apr-Jun86-218
D. Womersley, 617(TLS):24Jan86-84
"All About Shanghai."
R. Harris, 617(TLS):6Jun86-617
Allaby, M. - see "The Oxford Dictionary of
Natural History"
Allaigre, C. Sémantique et littérature.
N. Salvador Miguel, 86(BHS):Apr85-196
Allain, L. Dostoëvski et l'autre.
L.M. Porter, 395(MFS):Winter85-824
Allain, M. and P. Souvestre. Fantômas.
Delacorta, 441:20Jul86-6
442(NY):8Sep86-136
Allaire, S. Le modèle syntaxique des sys-
tèmes corrélatifs.
B. Damamme-Gilbert, 209(FM):Apr85-98
Allan, M. William Robinson, 1838-1935.
M.L. Simo, 637(VS):Winter85-334
Allanbrook, W.J. Rhythmic Gesture in
Mozart.*
J.R. Stevens, 317:Summer85-393
Allard, G.H., comp. Johannis Scoti Eriu-
genae Periphyseon: Indices generales.
S. Gersh, 589:Apr85-376

Allardt, E. and others, eds. Nordic
Democracy. (E.J. Friis, ed and trans)
E.S. Einhorn, 563(SS):Summer85-350
Allbeury, T. Mission Berlin.
N. Callendar, 441:5Oct86-28
Allchin, B., ed. South Asian Archaeology,
1981.
P. Rissman, 293(JASt):May85-629
Allchin, B. and R. The Rise of Civiliza-
tion in India and Pakistan.
R. Thapar, 318(JAOS):Apr-Jun84-336
Allegra, G. Il regno interiore.
L. Litvak, 240(HR):Winter85-109
Allegra, G. - see de Torquemada, A.
Allemann, B. and S. Reichert - see Celan,
P.
Allen, C.V. Time/Steps.
W.J. Harding, 441:27Jul186-18
Allen, D. Finally Truffaut.
D. Coward, 617(TLS):21Feb86-200
617(TLS):19Dec86-1434
Allen, D. Overnight in the Guest House of
the Mystic.*
M. Jarman, 249(HudR):Summer85-332
639(VQR):Winter85-27
Allen, D.G. and D.D. Hall, eds. Seven-
teenth-Century New England.
E. Emerson, 165(EAL):Spring86-78
Allen, E. A Woman's Place in the Novels
of Henry James.*
P.J. Eakin, 445(NCF):Sep85-240
E. Prioleau, 27(AL):May85-335
C. Wegelin, 395(MFS):Summer85-391
295(JML):Nov85-499
Allen, G.C. Appointment in Japan.
G. Akita, 293(JASt):May85-610
Allen, G.W. Waldo Emerson.*
J.S. Martin, 106:Summer85-205
Allen, I.L. The Language of Ethnic Con-
flict.
J. Algeo, 424:Sep85-190
B. Allen, 650(WF):Apr85-152
A.R. Bower, 355(LSoc):Dec85-533
Allen, J.B. and T.A. Moritz. A Distinc-
tion of Stories.*
D.J. McMillan, 38:Band103Heft1/2-194
Allen, J.J. The Reconstruction of a
Spanish Golden Age Playhouse.*
M-A. Börger-Reese, 240(HR):Autumn85-
493
J. Dowling, 612(ThS):Nov85-191
Allen, J.S. The Romance of Commerce and
Culture.
O.B. Hardison, Jr., 569(SR):Spring85-
xxvi
Allen, L. Burma.*
R. Nalley, 441:23Feb86-23
Allen, M. Animals in American Literature.
D. Seed, 447(N&Q):Dec84-573
Allen, M. La passion de Juliette.
R. Benson, 102(CanL):Spring85-171
Allen, M. Red Saturday.
D. Devlin, 157:No157-50
Allen, M.J.B. The Platonism of Marsilio
Ficino.*
L.G. Westerink, 551(RenQ):Winter85-722
Allen, M.J.B. and K. Muir - see Shake-
speare, W.
Allen, M.S. We Are Called Human.*
P.J. Lindholdt, 577(SHR):Winter85-81
Allen, P.G. The Sacred Hoop.
E. Jahner, 469:Vol 11No4-102

Allen, R., ed. "King Horn."
  R. Hanna 3d, 589:Oct85-936
Allen, R. The Traveling Woman.
  J. Shaw, 441:8Jun86-36
Allen, R.E. The Attalid Kingdom.*
  S.R.F. Price, 303(JoHS):Vol 105-217
Allen, R.E. The Oxford Minidictionary of
Spelling.
  J. Pauchard, 189(EA):Oct-Dec86-493
Allen, R.E. Plato's "Parmenides."*
  O. Delgado de Torres, 543:Dec84-375
  R. Heinaman, 303(JoHS):Vol 105-186
  S. Peterson, 482(PhR):Jul85-399
Allen, R.R. - see "The Eighteenth Century:
A Current Bibliography"
Allen, R.S. Loyalist Literature.
  K.L. Morrison, 102(CanL):Winter84-73
Allen, V.F. Inside English.
  D.L. Hammond, 399(MLJ):Autumn85-328
Allen, W. All in a Lifetime.
  P. Craig, 617(TLS):19Dec86-1428
Allen, W. Get Out Early.
  C. Hawtree, 617(TLS):12Dec86-1408
Allen, W. Tradition and Dream.
  617(TLS):15Aug86-899
Allen, W.B. - see Ames, F.
Allende, I. De amor y de sombra.
  C. Delacre Capestany, 37:Sep-Oct85-58
Allende, I. The House of the Spirits.*
  M. Gorra, 249(HudR):Winter86-666
  J. Mellors, 364:Jul85-97
  C. Rooke, 376:Sep85-140
  362:7Aug86-26
Allett, J. New Liberalism.
  J.L. Herkless, 637(VS):Winter85-349
Allilueva, S. The Faraway Music.
  A.S. Grossman, 129:Feb86-72
Allingham, M. The Fashion in Shrouds.
  P. Craig, 617(TLS):18Jul86-792
Allison, G.T., A. Carnesale and J.S. Nye,
eds. Hawks, Doves and Owls.*
  M. MccGwire, 617(TLS):31Oct86-1214
Allison, H.E. Kant's Transcendental Ideal-
ism.*
  E. Förster, 311(JP):Dec85-734
  T. Humphrey, 543:Dec85-345
  A. Melnick, 482(PhR):Jan85-134
Allison, L. Right Principles.
  R.E. Goodin, 185:Apr86-635
Allman, E.J. Player-King and Adversary.*
  R.P. Merrix, 702:Vol 17-240
Allmand, C.T. Lancastrian Normandy, 1415-
1450.
  A.J. Elder, 589:Oct85-939
  A.R. Smith, 382(MAE):1985/2-310
Allott, M., ed. Essays on Shelley.*
  P.M.S. Dawson, 677(YES):Vol 15-310
Allouch, J. Lettre pour lettre.
  A. Reix, 542:Jul-Sep85-352
Alloway, L. Network.
  D. Carrier, 55:Jan85-38
Almansi, G. and C. Béguin, eds. Theatre
of Sleep.
  B. Tonkin, 362:10Jul86-27
Almeder, R. The Philosophy of Charles S.
Peirce.
  J. Boler, 486:Dec85-648
Almeida, O.T., ed. The Sea Within.
  L.R. Guyer, 238:Dec85-781
Almendros, N. A Man With a Camera.*
  W. Lassally, 707:Autumn85-304

Almon, B. Deep North.
  J. Ditsky, 649(WAL):Nov85-256
  S. Scobie, 376:Mar85-160
Aloni, A. Le Muse di Archiloco.*
  J. Russo, 24:Spring85-128
Alonso, S. Tensión semántica (lenguaje y
estilo).
  J.B. Hall, 86(BHS):Jul85-308
Alp, S. Beiträge zur Erforschung des
hethitischen Tempels.
  G. Beckman, 318(JAOS):Jul-Sep84-583
Alpers, P.J. The Poetry of the "Faerie
Queene."
  J. van Dorsten, 179(ES):Oct85-467
Alpers, S. The Art of Describing.*
  J. Białostocki, 54:Sep85-520
  G. Martin, 39:Jan85-66
Alpert, M. La reforma militar de Azaña
(1931-1933).
  P. Preston, 86(BHS):Jul85-317
Alphand, A. Les Promenades de Paris.
  C. Matheu, 45:Oct85-109
Alphéus, K. Kant und Scheler.*  (B.
Wolandt, ed)
  G. Geismann, 489(PJGG):Band92Heft1-197
  R. Zimmer, 53(AGP):Band67Heft3-342
Alsberg, J. Modern Art and its Enigma.*
  B. Kennedy, 89(BJA):Winter85-77
Alsen, E. Salinger's Glass Stories as a
Composite Novel.
  A. Nadel, 395(MFS):Summer85-417
Alster, B., ed. Death in Mesopotamia.
  P. Machinist, 318(JAOS):Jul-Sep84-568
Alston, R.C. A Bibliography of the En-
glish Language from the Invention of
Printing to the Year 1800.  (Vol 12, Pt
1)
  D. Shaw, 617(TLS):24Oct86-1203
Altenberg, P. Télégrammes de l'âme.
  J-M. le Sidaner, 450(NRF):Oct85-108
Alter, I. The Good Man's Dilemma.
  P. Freese, 72:Band222Heft1-203
  J.L. Halio, 677(YES):Vol 15-359
Alter, R. Motives for Fiction.*
  W.B. Bache, 395(MFS):Winter85-846
Alther, L. Other Women.*
  639(VQR):Spring85-61
Althoff, G. and J. Wollasch. Die Toten-
bücher von Merseburg, Magdeburg und
Lüneburg.
  P.J. Geary, 589:Jul85-675
Altick, R.D. Paintings from Books.
  G. Cavaliero, 324:Aug86-628
Altieri, C. Act and Quality.*
  R.W. Dasenbrock, 435:Spring85-92
Altieri, C. Self and Sensibility in Con-
temporary American Poetry.*
  A. Golding, 30:Spring86-92
Altman, D. AIDS and the New Puritanism.
  R. Davenport-Hines, 617(TLS):18Jul86-
780
Altman, D. AIDS in the Mind of America.
  J. Lieberson, 453(NYRB):16Jan86-43
Altmann, A., E.J. Engel and F. Bamberger
- see Mendelssohn, M.
Alvar, M. Estudios Léxicos.
  D.A. Pharies, 238:May85-329
Alvar, M. and others. El comentario de
textos, 4.
  M.A. Diz, 238:Mar85-63
Alvarez, A. Offshore.
  J. Hunter, 617(TLS):10Oct86-1129
  A. Schmitz, 441:18May86-25

Álvarez, M.S. - see under Sánchez Álvarez, M.

Álvarez, N.E. Análisis arquetípico, mítico y simbológico de Pedro Páramo.
    M.J. Doudoroff, 238:Sep85-529
    E.P. Mocega-González, 140(CH):Vol7No1-87

Álvarez Barrientos, J. - see de Cañizares, J.

Alvarez-Detrell, T. and M.G. Paulson. The Gambling Mania On and Off the Stage in Pre-Revolutionary France.*
    B.G. Mittman, 207(FR):Dec85-321

Alvarez Gardeazábal, G. Pepe Botellas.
    A.F. Bolaños, 238:May85-323

Alvarez-Pereyre, J. The Poetry of Commitment in South Africa.
    C. Hope, 364:Jul85-78

Alvey, R.G. Dulcimer Maker.
    J.A. Burrison, 292(JAF):Oct/Dec85-489

Alvis, J. and T.G. West, eds. Shakespeare as Political Thinker.
    A.B. Kernan, 677(YES):Vol 15-279

Amado, J. Sea of Death.
    S. White, 448:Vol23No2-106

Amadou, R. - see de Saint-Martin, L-C.

Amann, E. Cicada Voices.* (G. Swede, ed)
    R. Stevenson, 102(CanL):Spring85-148

Amastae, J. and L. Elías-Olivares, eds. Spanish in the United States.*
    J.R. Gutiérrez, 355(LSoc):Sep85-395

Ambert, A.N. and S.E. Melendez. Bilingual Education.
    E. Gonzales-Berry, 399(MLJ):Autumn85-299

Ambler, E. Here Lies.*
    P-L. Adams, 61:Nov86-139
    R. Lourie, 441:17Aug86-14
    442(NY):29Sep86-135

Ambrière, M. - see de Balzac, H.

Ambrose, A. and M. Lazerowitz. Essays in the Unknown Wittgenstein.
    A. Janik, 319:Oct86-573

Amelang, J.S. Honored Citizens of Barcelona.
    I.A.A. Thompson, 617(TLS):3Oct86-1094

"American Literary Scholarship, 1980." (J.A. Robbins, ed)
    A. Hook, 447(N&Q):Dec84-564

Amerine, M.A. and E. Roessler. Wines. (2nd ed)
    J. Ronsheim, 42(AR):Spring85-248

Ames, F. Works of Fisher Ames.* (S. Ames, ed; rev by W.B. Allen)
    J.M. Banner, Jr., 396(ModA):Fall85-378

Ames, R.T. The Art of Rulership.*
    A.S. Cus, 543:Jun85-881

"Ami and Amile."* (S. Danon and S.N. Rosenberg, trans)
    T.D. Hemming, 208(FS):Jan85-61

Amichai, Y. The Selected Poetry of Yehuda Amichai. (C. Bloch and S. Mitchell, eds and trans) Travels.
    E. Hirsch, 441:3Aug86-14
    G. Josipovici, 617(TLS):17Oct86-1158

Amiot, A-M. Baudelaire de l'illuminisme.
    I. Faller, 208(FS):Apr85-223
    E.K. Kaplan, 207(FR):Dec85-300

Amis, K. The Old Devils.
    B. Morrison, 617(TLS):12Sep86-994
    B. Morton, 362:16Oct86-22

Amis, K. and J. Cochrane, eds. The Great British Songbook.
    G. Ewart, 617(TLS):26Dec86-1453

Amis, M. Money.*
    P. Lewis, 565:Spring85-43

Amis, M. The Moronic Inferno.
    S. Fender, 362:14Aug86-23
    R. Poirier, 617(TLS):18Jul86-785

Amjad-Ali, C. and W.A. Pitcher, eds. Liberation and Ethics.
    H.L.H., 185:Jul86-891

"Among the Flowers: The Hua-chien chi." (L. Fusek, trans)
    J.T. Wixted, 293(JASt):Nov84-163

Amoore, S. and others. Poetry Introduction 6.
    J. Mole, 176:Jan86-61
    C. Rawson, 617(TLS):7Feb86-137

Amor y Vázquez, J. and A.D. Kossoff, eds. Homenaje a Juan López-Morillas.
    D. Gies, 403(MLS):Fall85-361

Amorós, A. Introducción a la literatura.
    B. McGuirk, 86(BHS):Apr85-189

Amory, M. - see Fleming, A.

Amos, A.C. Linguistic Means of Determining the Dates of Old English Literary Texts.*
    J. Roberts, 677(YES):Vol 15-268

Amos, W. The Originals.*
    C. Hawtree, 364:Feb86-103

Amossy, R. Les Jeux de l'allusion littéraire dans "Un Beau Ténébreux" de Julien Gracq.*
    M. Moser-Verrey, 107(CRCL):Mar85-170

Ampalavanar, R. The Indian Minority and Political Change in Malaya, 1945-1957.
    J.N. Parmer, 293(JASt):Feb85-452

Amprimoz, A. Sur le Damier des tombes.
    N. Bishop, 102(CanL):Spring85-132

Amprimoz, A.L. Germain Nouveau dit Humilis.* La Poésie érotique de Germain Nouveau.*
    R. Little, 402(MLR):Jul85-723
    F.R. Smith, 208(FS):Jan85-96

Amsenga, B.J. and others, eds. Miscellanea Slavica.
    E.R. Sicher, 402(MLR):Apr85-507

"Amsterdam 1920-1960."
    R. Padovan, 46:Jan85-4

Anand, R.P. and P.V. Quisumbing, eds. ASEAN.
    C.D. Neher, 293(JASt):May85-661

Anania, M. The Sky at Ashland.
    T. Swiss, 441:30Nov86-17

Anastaplo, G. The Artist as Thinker.*
    D. St. John, 577(SHR):Fall85-369

Anaxagoras. The Fragments of Anaxagoras.* (D. Sider, ed)
    W.J. Verdenius, 394:Vol38fasc3/4-403

Ancelet, B.J. and E. Morgan, Jr. The Makers of Cajun Music/Musiciens cadiens et créoles.*
    A. Prévos, 207(FR):Mar86-629

Anctil, P. and G. Caldwell, eds. Juifs et réalités juives au Québec.
    B. Godard, 627(UTQ):Summer85-489

Andaya, B.W. and L.Y. A History of Malaysia.
    C.A. Trocki, 293(JASt):Feb85-453

Anderegg, M.A. David Lean.
    S. Kauffmann, 385(MQR):Winter86-136

Anderer, P. Other Worlds.
    V.C. Gessel, 407(MN):Winter85-431
    S. Goldstein, 395(MFS):Winter85-861
Anderman, J. Poland Under Black Light.
    N. Berry, 176:May86-57
    M. Simpson, 441:16Mar86-14
Andersen, D.S. Den humanistiske skole-
    komedie i Danmark.
    N.L. Jensen, 562(Scan):May85-71
Andersen, F.G., O. Holzapfel and T. Pettit.
    The Ballad as Narrative.*
    G. Boyes, 203:Vol96No1-125
    R. Wehse, 196:Band26Heft3/4-346
Andersen, L.P. - see "Partalopa saga"
Andersen, M. L'autrement pareille.
    B. Godard, 102(CanL):Fall85-101
Andersen, P.T. Stein Mehren — en logos-
    dikter.
    S. Lyngstad, 563(SS):Summer85-347
    A.G. Michaelsen, 562(Scan):May85-96
Andersen, R. Robert Coover.
    K. Hume, 402(MLR):Jan85-150
Andersen, R., ed. Pidginization and Creol-
    ization as Language Acquisition.*
    S. Jones and T. Pica, 355(LSoc):Mar85-
    90
Anderson, B. Imagined Communities.
    J. Breuilly, 488:Mar85-65
Anderson, C. In the Mother Tongue.
    M. Kumin, 219(GaR):Spring85-169
Anderson, D. - see Cavalcanti, G.
Anderson, D. - see Smith, R.
Anderson, D.K. The Works of Charles T.
    Griffes.*
    P. Dickinson, 415:Jun85-349
    C. MacDonald, 607:Sep85-43
Anderson, E.R. Cynewulf.
    J.P. Hermann, 301(JEGP):Apr85-249
    E.G. Stanley, 447(N&Q):Dec84-524
Anderson, F. A People's Army.*
    L.D. Cress, 432(NEQ):Jun85-302
Anderson, G. Eros sophistes.*
    G.N. Sandy, 303(JoHS):Vol 105-202
Anderson, J. Ballet and Modern Dance.
    B. Zuck, 441:21Sep86-20
Anderson, J. The Food of Portugal.
    F. Fabricant, 441:7Dec86-17
Anderson, J., ed. Language Form and Lin-
    guistic Variation.*
    C.D. Grijns, 361:May85-105
Anderson, J. The Only Daughter.*
    C. Rooke, 376:Sep85-140
Anderson, J. Sir Walter Scott and History,
    with Other Papers.*
    P. Garside, 677(YES):Vol 15-307
Anderson, J. - see Wind, E.
Anderson, J.C., Jr. The Historical Topog-
    raphy of the Imperial Fora.
    T.P. Wiseman, 313:Vol75-229
Anderson, J.H. Biographical Truth.*
    G.M. MacLean, 141:Spring85-215
    J.M. Steadman, 301(JEGP):Apr85-257
Anderson, J.K. Hunting in the Ancient
    World.
    P. Green, 617(TLS):25Apr86-456
Anderson, J.Q., E.W. Gaston, Jr. and J.W.
    Lee, eds. Southwestern American Litera-
    ture.
    L. Rodenberger, 649(WAL):Feb86-365
Anderson, L. We Can't All Be Heroes, You
    Know.*
    D. Flower, 249(HudR):Summer85-306

Anderson, M.R. Art in a Desacralized
    World.
    J.G. Nelson, 637(VS):Spring86-466
Anderson, P. In the Tracks of Historical
    Materialism.*
    T. Eagleton, 153:Winter85-2
    J.A. Winders, 659(ConL):Spring86-73
Anderson, P. Sinister Forces.
    D. Cole, 441:3Aug86-18
Anderson, P.V., R.J. Brockmann and C.R.
    Miller, eds. New Essays in Technical
    and Scientific Communication.
    F.J. D'Angelo, 126(CCC):Dec85-493
Anderson, R. Federico García Lorca.
    D. Harris, 402(MLR):Oct85-965
    F.H. Londré, 610:Spring85-85
Anderson, R. Night Calls.
    N. Callendar, 441:20Apr86-32
Anderson, R.A. Service for the Dead.
    K. Kalfus, 441:30Nov86-22
Anderson, R.D. Education and Opportunity
    in Victorian Scotland.
    J.S. Hurt, 637(VS):Spring85-544
Anderson, R.N., with R. Coller and R.F.
    Pestano. Filipinos in Rural Hawaii.
    A.B. Chen, 293(JASt):May85-660
Anderson, R.O. Fundamentals of the Petro-
    leum Industry.
    L. Milazzo, 584(SWR):Winter85-130
Anderson, S. Sherwood Anderson: Selected
    Letters.* (C.E. Modlin, ed)
    D.D. Anderson, 534(RALS):Autumn83-241
    W.B. Rideout, 27(AL):Mar85-182
Anderson, S. Letters to Bab.* (W.A.
    Sutton, ed) Kit Brandon.
    C. Benfey, 453(NYRB):30Jan86-16
Anderson, V.P. Robert Browning as a Reli-
    gious Poet.
    M.G. McBride, 85(SBHC):Vol 13-113
Anderson, W. Dante the Maker.
    J.S. Russell, 545(RPh):May85-552
Anderson, W.C. Between the Library and
    the Laboratory.
    J. Altena, 111:Fall86-9
    T.E.D. Braun, 207(FR):May86-976
    J. Undank, 210(FrF):May85-242
    A.C. Vila, 400(MLN):Dec85-1168
    639(VQR):Spring85-43
Anderson, W.L. and J.A. Lewis. A Guide
    to Cherokee Documents in Foreign
    Archives.
    P.H. Wood, 579(SAQ):Spring85-230
Anderson, W.S. Essays on Roman Satire.
    A.M. Bowie, 161(DUJ):Jun84-280
Anderson, W.S. and D.R. Cox, eds. The
    Technical Reader. (2nd ed)
    C. Waddell, 126(CCC):Dec85-495
Anderson, W.W. Children's Play and Games
    in Rural Thailand.
    J.R. Hanks, 293(JASt):Aug85-881
Andors, P. The Unfinished Liberation of
    Chinese Women, 1949-1980.
    E. Honig, 293(JASt):Feb85-329
de Andrade, C.D. - see under Drummond de
    Andrade, C.
Andreas-Salomé, L. Lettre ouverte à Freud.
    (D. Miermont, trans) Carnets intimes
    des dernières années. (E. Pfeiffer, ed)
    A. Reix, 542:Jan-Mar85-44
Andrew, C. Her Majesty's Secret Service.*
    (British title: Secret Service.)
    D. Cannadine, 453(NYRB):27Mar86-43
                                    [continued]

9

Andrew, C. Her Majesty's Secret Service.
[continuing]
  M. Howard, 441:16Feb86-6
  Z. Steiner, 617(TLS):4Jul86-727
Andrew, J.D. Concepts in Film Theory.
  A. Casebier, 290(JAAC):Fall85-83
Andrews, H.K. The Oxford Harmony. (Vol 2)
  P. Standford, 415:Aug85-464
Andrews, W. Voltaire.
  U. van Runset, 535(RHL):Mar/Apr85-300
Andrews, W.L., ed. Critical Essays on
W.E.B. Du Bois.
  J. Weixlmann, 659(ConL):Spring86-48
Andrews, W.L., ed. Sisters of the Spirit.
  F.S. Foster, 441:24Aug86-10
Andrews, W.L. To Tell a Free Story.
  I. Duffield, 617(TLS):17Oct86-1170
  F.S. Foster, 441:24Aug86-10
Andrianne, R. Literatur und Gesellschaft
im französischsprachigen Belgien.
  J.M. Klinkenberg, 553(RLiR):Jan-Jun85-
  227
  H-J. Lope, 547(RF):Band97Heft1-486
Andrianov, B. Na Velikoj Russkoj Ravnine.
  G.F. Holliday, 558(RLJ):Fall84-290
Andrieux, F. - see Charpentier, G.
Andrieux, N. and E. Baumgartner. Systèmes
morphologiques de l'ancien français.
(Vol A)
  R. de Gorog, 589:Jul85-633
  J. Picoche, 209(FM):Oct85-276
  D.H. Robinson, 402(MLR):Oct85-925
Anesko, M. "Friction with the Market."
  A. Bendixen, 441:30Nov86-23
Ang, I. Watching Dallas.
  N. Shulman, 617(TLS):2May86-471
Ang, L. - see under Li Ang
Angadi, P. The Done Thing.
  A. Robinson, 617(TLS):6Jun86-623
Angadi, P. The Governess.*
  D. Gess, 441:30Mar86-18
Angel, L. The Silence of the Mystic.
  J.R. Horne, 154:Summer85-291
Angelet, C. Symbolisme et invention for-
melle dans les premiers écrits d'André
Gide (Le Traité du Narcisse, Le Voyage
d'Urien, Paludes).*
  P. Pollard, 208(FS):Apr85-228
Angelou, M. All God's Children Need
Traveling Shoes.
  H.A. Baker, Jr., 441:11May86-14
  442(NY):14Apr86-110
Angelou, M. Singin' and Swingin' and
Gettin' Merry Like Christmas.
  J. Neville, 617(TLS):24Jan86-98
Angenot, M. La Parole pamphlétaire.*
  P. Bleton, 193(ELit):Autumn85-443
Anglemyer, M. and E.R. Seagreaves, eds.
The Natural Environment.
  S.N., 185:Jan86-465
Anglès, A. André Gide et le premier
groupe de "La Nouvelle Revue Française."
(Vol 2)
  P. Fawcett, 617(TLS):30Oct86-1110
  J-F. Revel, 176:Nov86-34
"The Anglo-Saxon Chronicle: A Collabora-
tive Edition; MS B." (Vol 4) (S. Taylor,
ed)
  J.J. Campbell, 301(JEGP):Oct85-543
  T.A. Shippey, 179(ES):Jun85-272
  E.G. Stanley, 541(RES):Nov85-546

Angulo, D. and A.E. Pérez Sánchez. A
Corpus of Spanish Drawings. (Vol 3)
  E. Harris, 617(TLS)7Mar86-245
Anhalt, I. Alternative Voices.*
  R. Falck, 627(UTQ):Summer85-513
  A.M. Gillmor, 529(QQ):Spring85-218
Aniel, J-P. Les maisons de Chartreux.
  C. Bruzelius, 589:Apr85-377
Anker, Ø. and E. Beyer, eds. "Og nu vil
jeg tale ut" — "men nu vil jeg også
tale ud."
  Ø. Rottem, 562(Scan):May85-59
Ankersmit, F.R. Narrative Logic.
  L.B. Cebik, 125:Spring85-338
Annan, N. Leslie Stephen.*
  S. Pickering, 569(SR):Fall85-lxxxiii
  E.F. Shields, 529(QQ):Winter85-828
Annas, J., ed. Oxford Studies in Ancient
Philosophy.* (Vol 1)
  J.K., 185:Oct85-220
Annas, J. and J. Barnes. The Modes of
Scepticism.*
  S. Everson, 520:Vol30No3-305
Annibaldi, C. and M. Monna, eds. Bibliog-
rafia e catalogo delle opere di Goffredo
Petrassi.
  J.C.G. Waterhouse, 410(M&L):Oct85-383
Annichiarico, A.M. and others, eds.
Tirante il Bianco.
  L. Mendia, 379(MedR):Apr85-146
"Annual Review of Applied Linguistics
1983." (R.B. Kaplan, ed)
  J. Walz, 399(MLJ):Autumn85-313
Anonimo romano. Cronica.* (G. Porta, ed)
[shown in prev under Romano, A.]
  G. Lepschy, 402(MLR):Jan85-181
Anscombe, I. Omega and After.
  M. Goldstein, 569(SR):Fall85-624
Anscombe, I. A Woman's Touch.*
  L. Dyett, 139:Feb/Mar85-52
Anscombre, J-C. and O. Ducrot. L'argumen-
tation dans la langue.*
  M. Dominicy, 540(RIPh):Vol39fasc4-450
  H. Nølke, 209(FM):Oct85-269
  F. Recanati, 192(EP):Oct-Dec85-549
Ansoff, H.I. Corporate Strategy.
  J. Turner, 617(TLS):11Jul86-751
Anstey, S. - see Thomas, R.S.
Anstruther, I. Oscar Browning.
  J. Marcus, 637(VS):Spring85-556
Antébi, E. and D. Fishlock. Biotechnology.
  R. Wright, 441:5Oct86-54
"Anthologie de la Poésie chinoise clas-
sique."
  J. Shapiro, 549(RLC):Jan-Mar85-87
Anthony, G. Gwen Pharis Ringwood.
  D. Staines, 402(MLR):Apr85-449
Anthony, P. Shade of the Tree.
  G. Jonas, 441:20Apr86-27
Anthony, P.D. John Ruskin's Labour.*
  J. Loesberg, 506(PSt):May85-91
  F.G. Townsend, 637(VS):Winter86-342
Antoine, G. Vis-à-vis ou le double regard
critique.*
  R. Ricatte, 535(RHL):Jan/Feb85-135
Antoine, R. La tragédie du roi Christophe.
  R. Spötter, 343:Heft12-113
Antokoletz, E. The Music of Béla Bartók.*
  A. Cross, 415:Nov85-671
  J. Samson, 607:Dec85-54
Anton, J.P., ed. Science and the Sciences
in Plato.
  J. Moline, 53(AGP):Band67Heft1-92

Antonielli, S. Letteratura del disagio.
E. Esposito, 228(GSLI):Vol 162fasc519-463
de Antonio, E. and M. Tuchman. Painters Painting.*
G. van Hensbergen, 90:Dec85-912
Antonius, S. The Lord.
S. Altinel, 617(TLS):13Jun86-646
Anyidoho, K. and others, eds. Cross Rhythms.
D.J. Crowley, 650(WF):Jan85-74
P.M. Peek, 538(RAL):Fall85-425
Anz, H., P. Kemp and F. Schmöe, eds. Kierkegaard und die deutsche Philosophie seiner Zeit.
L.R. Wilkinson, 563(SS):Summer85-333
Anz, H., P. Lübke and F. Schmöe, eds. Die Rezeption Søren Kierkegaards in der deutschen und dänischen Philosophie und Theologie.
L.R. Wilkinson, 563(SS):Summer85-333
Anz, T. and M. Stark, eds. Expressionismus.*
V. Žmegač, 224(GRM):Band35Heft1-105
Anzieu, D. Freud's Self-Analysis.
P. Gay, 617(TLS):30ct86-1085
Aparici Llanas, M.P. Las novelas de tesis de Benito Pérez Galdós.
A.G. Andreu, 240(HR):Spring85-248
B.J. Dendle, 86(BHS):Apr85-205
Apel, F. Literarische Übersetzung.
C. Grawe, 67:May85-79
Apel, K-O. Charles S. Peirce.*
R. Tursman, 488:Mar85-85
Apel, W. Die italienische Violinmusik im 17. Jahrhundert.
M. Talbot, 410(M&L):Apr85-139
Apollinaire, G. Le Poète assassiné. (M. Décaudin, ed)
G. Rees, 208(FS):Apr85-229
Apollinaire, G. Le Poète Assassiné.*
(British title: The Poet Assassinated and Other Stories.) (R. Padgett, trans)
R. Stella, 703:No13-136
D.J. Taylor, 176:Jun86-55
Apostel, L. and E. Story. African Philosophy.
B. Hallen, 488:Mar85-109
Apostolidès, J-M. Les métamorphoses de Tintin.
J. Baetens, 567:Vol55No3/4-313
Appel, A. Time After Time.
P. Glasser, 441:26Jan86-12
Appel, R. Immigrant Children Learning Dutch.
J.W. de Vries, 204(FdL):Mar85-66
Appelfeld, A. The Retreat.*
D.J. Enright, 364:Mar86-104
Appelfeld, A. To the Land of the Cattails.
R. Alter, 441:2Nov86-1
Appignanesi, R. Italia Perversa.* (Pt 1)
S. MacDonald, 441:23Nov86-24
Apple, M. Free Agents.
N. Shack, 617(TLS):10Oct86-1130
639(VQR):Winter85-24
Apple, M. The Oranging of America.
N. Shack, 617(TLS):10Oct86-1130
Appleby, D.P. The Music of Brazil.*
D.J. Crowley, 292(JAF):Jan/Mar85-110
Appleby, J. Capitalism and a New Social Order.*
R. Ketcham, 656(WMQ):Jul85-399

Appleman, P. Darwin's Ark.
639(VQR):Spring85-56
Appleyard, B. Richard Rogers.
J.M. Richards, 617(TLS):2May86-464
Apreszjan, J.D. and E. Páll. Orosz ige — magyar ige.
I.A. Mel'čuk, 206(FoLi):Vol 19No1/2-253
Apte, M.L. Humor and Laughter.*
J. Porteous, 529(QQ):Winter85-818
Apter, D.E. and N. Sawa. Against the State.*
C. Johnson, 293(JASt):May85-612
J.V. Koschmann, 407(MN):Autumn85-365
Apter, E. Pas de Vacances pour le Commissaire.
P.A. Berger, 399(MLJ):Spring85-87
Apter, T.E. Fantasy Literature.
R. Cardinal, 529(QQ):Autumn85-549
Apuleius. Platon und seine Lehre. (P. Siniscalco, ed)
J. den Boeft, 394:Vol38fasc3/4-462
A. Meredith, 161(DUJ):Jun84-282
Aquila, R. The Iroquois Restoration.
R.L. Haan, 656(WMQ):Jan85-134
Aquila, R.E. Representational Mind.*
J.V. Buroker, 518:Apr85-87
R. Meerbote, 342:Band76Heft4-464
E. Schaper, 323:May85-202
V.S. Wike, 543:Sep85-139
Aquinas, T. Questions on the Soul. (J.H. Robb, trans)
B.C. Bazan, 543:Jun85-910
Aquinas, T. Saint Thomas d'Aquin, "Questions disputées sur la vérité": Question XI. (B. Jollès, ed and trans)
J. Jolivet, 542:Apr-Jun85-249
Aquinas, T. Sancti Thomae de Aquino: "Questiones disputatae de malo." (Vol 23) (P-M. Gils, with others, eds)
B.C. Bazán, 154:Spring85-172
Arabi, O. Wittgenstein, langage et ontologie.
M. Malherbe, 192(EP):Apr-Jun85-257
Arac, J., W. Godzich and W. Martin, eds. The Yale Critics.*
N. Cotton, 435:Spring85-101
M.W. Jennings, 221(GQ):Winter85-97
de Aragon, A.C. - see under Cubillo de Aragon, A.
Arakin, V.D. Sopostavitel'naja tipologija skandinavskix jazykov.
Y. Tambovtsev, 350:Jun86-459
Arana Cañedo-Argüelles, J. Ciencia y Metafísica en el Kant precrítico (1746-1764).
M.P.M. Caimi, 342:Band76Heft2-219
Aranza, J. Backward Masking Unmasked.
R.S. Denisoff, 498:Vol9No4-72
Araya, G., H. Haverkate and K. van Leuven, eds. Homenaje a Andrés Bello en el bicentenario de su nacimiento (1781-1981).
R. Wright, 545(RPh):Aug85-142
Arblaster, A. The Rise and Decline of Western Liberalism.
639(VQR):Summer85-94
Arbuckle, E.S. - see Martineau, H.
Arbur, R. Leigh Brackett, Marion Zimmer Bradley, Anne McCaffrey.
L. Leith, 561(SFS):Mar85-103
Arce, J. Caesaraugusta, ciudad romana.
N. Mackie, 313:Vol75-288

Archambault, G. The Man With a Flower In His Mouth.
  R.A. Cavell, 102(CanL):Fall85-108
Archambault, G. Le Regard oblique.
  N.B. Bishop, 627(UTQ):Summer85-482
Archer, J. The Literature of British Domestic Architecture 1715-1842.
  H. Colvin, 617(TLS):17Jan86-54
  J.S. Curl, 505:Oct85-147
Archer, J. A Matter of Honor.
  V. Glendinning, 617(TLS):5Dec86-1368
  W. Hood, 441:27Jul86-18
  G. Kaufman, 362:3Jul86-30
Archer, J.H.G., ed. Art and Architecture in Victorian Manchester.*
  S. Pepper, 46:Oct85-77
Archer, L. Raymond Erith.
  C. Aslet, 617(TLS):28Feb86-221
Archer, R. and D. Simmonds. A Star is Torn.
  B. Case, 617(TLS):7Nov86-1245
  R. Christiansen, 362:30Oct86-27
Archer, S. Richard Hooker.
  R.W. Dyson, 161(DUJ):Jun84-315
Archer, W. William Archer on Ibsen. (T. Postlewait, ed)
  M. Quinn, 572:Vol6-165
  T.F. Van Laan, 130:Winter85/86-368
Archibald, D. Yeats.*
  W.E. Hall, 637(VS):Autumn84-191
"The Architecture of Frank Gehry."
  P. Goldberger, 441:7Dec86-16
"Archives de philosophie du droit." (Vol 28)
  J-L. Gardies, 542:Jan-Mar85-65
Arciniegas, G. America in Europe.
  P-L. Adams, 61:Mar86-111
  N. Bliven, 442(NY):5May86-129
Ardao, A. and others. Francisco Romero, maestro del la filosofía latinoamericana.
  A. Reix, 542:Jan-Mar85-75
Ardeleanu, I., V. Arimia and M. Muşat, eds. 23 August 1944.
  D. Deletant, 617(TLS):7Mar86-240
Arditti, R., R.D. Klein and S. Minden, eds. Test-Tube Women.
  C. Overall, 154:Winter85-728
Ardizzone, T. Heart of the Order.
  R. Ward, 441:19Oct86-38
Ardouin, P. Maurice Scève, Pernette du Guillet, Louise Labé.
  D.G. Coleman, 535(RHL):Jul/Aug85-678
de Arellano y Lynch, R.W.R. - see under Ramírez de Arellano y Lynch, R.W.
Arenas, R. El Central.
  S. White, 448:Vol23No2-106
Arenas, R. Farewell to the Sea.*
  J. Butt, 617(TLS):30May86-587
  M. Wood, 453(NYRB):27Mar86-34
Arenas, R. Lecturas fáciles: Lazarillo de Tormes. (J. Olivio Jiménez, ed)
  L.S. Glaze, 399(MLJ):Spring85-108
Arenas, R. El palacio de las blanquísimas mofetas.
  J. Olivares, 240(HR):Autumn85-467
Arendt, H. Between Past and Future.
  W. Heuer, 384:Dec85-1096
Arendt, H. La vie de l'esprit.* (Vol 2)
  A. Enegrén, 192(EP):Oct-Dec85-551
Arendt, H. Vom Leben des Geistes. Das Urteilen.
  W. Heuer, 384:Dec85-1099

Arendt, H. and K. Jaspers. Hannah Arendt, Karl Jaspers: Briefwechsel 1926-1969. (L. Köhler and H. Saner, eds)
  M. Davies, 617(TLS):13Jun86-642
  W. Heuer, 384:Dec85-1096
Arens, H. Kommentar zu Goethes Faust I.
  H. Eichner, 406:Winter85-469
Arens, W. The Original Sin.
  R. Dinnage, 453(NYRB):4Dec86-39
Arensberg, A. Group Sex.
  T. Janowitz, 441:5Oct86-22
Argetsinger, G.S. Ludvig Holberg's Comedies.*
  F. Brun, 615(TJ):Mar85-134
Arguedas, J.M. Deep Rivers.
  S. White, 448:Vol23No3-150
Arian, A. Politics in Israel.
  B. Wasserstein, 617(TLS):10Oct86-1123
Arias, R. The Spanish Sacramental Plays.
  D. Rogers, 86(BHS):Jul85-307
Aricò, A.C. - see under Caracciolo Aricò, A.
Ariès, P. Images of Man and Death.
  D.J. Enright, 362:9Jan86-28
  442(NY):6Jan86-86
Ariès, P. Le Temps de l'histoire.
  B. Stock, 617(TLS):5Sep86-983
Ariès, P. and G. Duby, eds. Histoire de la vie privèe. (Vols 1 and 2)
  B. Stock, 617(TLS):5Sep86-983
Ariosti, O. Alfeo. (G. Venturini, ed)
  M. Pieri, 400(MLN):Jan85-181
Ariosto, L. Satire. (C. Segre, ed) Erbolato. (G. Ronchi, ed) Lettere. (A. Stella, ed)
  E. Bigi, 228(GSLI):Vol 162fasc517-133
Aris, M. View of Medieval Bhutan.*
  R. Hillenbrand, 59:Jun85-265
Aristides, P.A. Elio Aristide, "Discorsi sacri." (S. Nicosia, ed and trans)
  D.A. Russell, 123:Vol35No1-183
Aristides Quintilianus. On Music.* (T.J. Mathiesen, ed and trans)
  E.K. Borthwick, 123:Vol35No2-258
Aristophanes. Knights. (A.H. Sommerstein, ed and trans)
  L. Edmunds, 24:Fall85-381
Aristotle. Aristote, "La Poétique." (R. Dupont-Roc and J. Lallot, eds and trans)
  W.J. Verdenius, 394:Vol38fasc1/2-201
Aristotle. Aristoteles, "Kategorien." (K. Oehler, trans)
  M. Kerkhoff, 160:Apr85-191
Aristotle. Aristotle's "De generatione et corruptione."* (C.J.F. Williams, ed and trans)
  J. Longrigg, 123:Vol35No2-386
Aristotle. Aristotle's "Eudemian Ethics."* (Bks 1, 2 and 8) (M.J. Woods, ed and trans)
  S.R.L. Clark, 393(Mind):Jul85-487
  D.T. Devereux, 482(PhR):Jul85-401
  D.C. Lindenmuth, 543:Sep85-174
Aristotle. Aristotle's "Physics" Books III and IV.* (E. Hussey, ed and trans)
  M.L. Gill, 482(PhR):Apr85-270
  L. Judson, 123:Vol35No1-74
  G.A. Press, 518:Jan85-14
Aristotle. Les attributions (Catégories).* (Y. Pelletier, with others, eds and trans)
  M.B. Ewbank, 543:Mar86-577

12

Aristotle. Nicomachean Ethics. (T. Irwin, trans)
R.K., 185:Jul86-911
Aristotle. The Politics. (C. Lord, ed and trans)
R.G.M., 185:Apr86-684
Arkell, D. Alain-Fournier.
R. Clarke, 362:27Nov86-26
Arksey, L., N. Pries and M. Reed, eds. American Diaries.* (Vol 1)
J.S. Batts, 470:Vol123-100
C.R. Davis, 568(SCN):Winter85-64
Arlacchi, P. Mafia Business.
E.J. Dionne, Jr., 441:3Aug86-22
E.J. Hobsbawm, 617(TLS):27Jun86-701
I. Thomson, 362:14Aug86-23
Armand, M. and M. Aymard - see "European Bibliography of Soviet, East European and Slavonic Studies"
Armengaud, F. La pragmatique.
C. Plantin, 540(RIPh):Vol139fasc4-470
Armengol, P.O. - see under Ortiz Armengol, P.
Armi, C.E. Masons and Sculptors in Roman-esque Burgundy.
T.A. Heslop, 39:Jan85-71
Armistead, S.G. and J.H. Silverman. En torno al romancero sefardí (Hispanismo y balcanismo de la tradición judeo-española).*
O. Anahory-Librowicz, 545(RPh):Feb86-379
Armitage, G.E. Across the Autumn Grass.
C. Hawtree, 617(TLS):25Jul86-818
Armitage, G.E. A Season of Peace.*
P. Glasser, 441:15Jun86-21
Armogathe, D. and M. Piper - see Michel, L.
Armour, P. The Door of Purgatory.
S. Bemrose, 278(IS):Vol40-111
S. Botterill, 402(MLR):Jan85-182
L. Pertile, 382(MAE):1985/2-343
Arms, G. and others - see Howells, W.D.
Arms, G. and C.K. Lohmann - see Howells, W.D.
Armstrong, D.M. What Is a Law of Nature?*
J. Butterfield, 393(Mind):Jan85-164
F.I. Dretske, 84:Mar85-79
J.H. Fetzer, 518:Apr85-120
L.J. O'Neill, 63:Jun85-233
M. Tiles, 483:Oct85-557
Armstrong, D.M. and N. Malcolm. Conscious-ness and Causality.
M. Adam, 542:Oct-Dec85-567
F.J., 185:Jan86-445
D. Locke, 393(Mind):Apr85-302
A. Morton, 84:Sep85-341
Armstrong, G. - see Vidal, G.
Armstrong, G., Jr. The Soviet Law of Property.
E. Huskey, 550(RusR):Oct85-403
Armstrong, J.A. Nations Before National-ism.*
D.E. Pienkos, 497(PolR):Vol30No4-458
Armstrong, P. and S. Feldman. A Midwife's Story.
R.M. Brown, 441:23Nov86-37
Armstrong, P.B. The Phenomenology of Henry James.*
J.F. Desmond, 478:Apr85-110
E.S. Fussell, 27(AL):Mar85-139
R.P. Hoople, 106:Spring85-57
D. Kirby, 639(VQR):Winter85-175
R.B. Yeazell, 536(Rev):Vol7-43

Armstrong, T., ed. Amerikanische Malerei 1930-1980.
C. Scherrmann, 384:Sep/Oct85-939
Arnáez, E. Orfebrería religiosa en la provincia de Segovia hasta 1700.*
A.G.S.C., 90:May85-312
Arnaud, N. - see Mirbeau, O.
Arnaut Daniel. The Poetry of Arnaut Daniel.* (J.J. Wilhelm, ed and trans)
L.M. Paterson, 208(FS):Jul85-320
A.E. Van Vleck, 545(RPh):Nov85-279
Arnell, P. and T. Bickford, eds. James Stirling.
P. Buchanan, 46:Aug85-66
J. Jacobus, 505:Jul85-133
Arnell, P. and T. Bickford, with I. Zaknic, eds. Charles Gwathmey and Robert Siegel.*
S. Lavin, 505:Dec85-99
Arney, W.R. and B.J. Bergen. Medicine and the Management of Living.
D.E.S., 185:Jan86-466
Arnhart, L. Aristotle on Political Reason-ing.*
J.V. Wagner, 543:Mar85-617
Arnheim, R. New Essays on the Psychology of Art.
C. McGee, 441:4May86-41
Arnold, A., ed. Sherlock Holmes auf der Hintertreppe.
R.J. Rundell, 406:Fall85-383
Arnold, A.J. Modernism and Negritude.*
H. Cohen, 131(CL):Winter85-95
Arnold, B. Back Road Caller.
T. Enslin, 138:No8-252
Arnold, B. German Knighthood 1050-1300.
S. Airlie, 617(TLS):4Apr86-354
Arnold, C. Lost Time.
V. MacKay, 617(TLS):30May86-588
Arnold, E. Life Drawing.
W. Blythe, 441:30Mar86-18
Arnold, H.L., ed. Karl Krolow.
R.E. Schade, 221(GQ):Summer85-480
Arnold, H.L. and T. Buck, eds. Positionen des Dramas.
T. Reber, 193(ELit):Spring-Summer85-199
Arnold, M. Willa Cather's Short Fiction.*
J.W. Gargano, 573(SSF):Spring85-249
M.A. O'Connor, 27(AL):Mar85-151
A.H. Petry, 50(ArQ):Summer85-187
S.J. Rosowski, 649(WAL):May85-68
295(JML):Nov85-456
Arnott, W.G. - see Menander
Arntzen, H. Musil-Kommentar zu dem Roman "Der Mann ohne Eigenschaften."
W. Hoffmeister, 406:Fall85-371
Aron, J-P. Les Modernes.*
C.J. Stivale, 207(FR):Oct85-163
Aron, J-P. The Office.
S. Dieckman, 615(TJ):Mar85-123
Aronis, C. An Annotated Bibliography of ESL Materials.*
K.A. Mullen, 399(MLJ):Spring85-117
T. Pica, 355(LSoc):Sep85-425
Aronowitz, S. The Crisis in Historical Materialism.
R.S. Gottlieb, 142:Winter86-87
Aronson, A. American Set Design.*
A. Feinsod, 615(TJ):Dec85-518
Aronson, J.L. A Realist Philosophy of Science.
R. Harré, 486:Sep85-483

13

Arqués Jover, A. Colección de pintores, escultores desconocidos. (I.V. Bernabé and L. Hernández Guardiola, eds)
M. Estella, 48:Jul-Sep85-315
Arquillo Torres, F. and others. El Retablo Mayor de la Catedral de Seville. (M. Ferrand and M. González, eds)
F-A. de Montêquin, 576:Dec85-396
Arrabal, F. The Burial of the Sardine.
J. Byrne, 532(RCF):Spring85-142
Arrabal, F. ... y pondrán esposas a las flores. (P.L. Podol, ed)
M.T. Halsey, 238:Dec85-777
Arrian. Flavius Arrien: "Histoire d'Alexandre."* (P. Savinel, trans)
M. Canto, 98:Jun-Jul85-618
Arrian. History of Alexander and Indica.* (Vol 2: Anabasis Alexandri, Bks 5-8, Indica.) (P.A. Brunt, ed)
P.A. Stadter, 123:Vol35No1-26
Arrington, L.J. Brigham Young.*
639(VQR):Autumn85-118
Arrow, K.J. Collected Papers. (Vol 1)
R.H., 185:Apr86-660
F. Hahn, 617(TLS):1Aug86-833
Arrow, K.J. Collected Papers. (Vols 2-6)
F. Hahn, 617(TLS):1Aug86-833
"Art of Our Time: The Saatchi Collection."
G. van Hensbergen, 90:Nov85-817
Arthur, E. Bad Guys.
S. Birkerts, 441:7Dec86-34
"Arthurian Literature, I."* (R. Barber, ed)
M. Lambert, 402(MLR):Oct85-893
"Arthurian Literature, II."* (R. Barber, ed)
P.J.C. Field, 447(N&Q):Jun84-254
"Arthurian Literature III." (R. Barber, ed)
C. Clark, 179(ES):Aug85-359
M. Lambert, 402(MLR):Oct85-893
"Arthurian Literature IV." (R. Barber, ed)
M-M. Dubois, 189(EA):Jan-Mar86-89
Arthurs, H.W. Without the Law.
P. McAuslan, 617(TLS):31Jan86-120
D. Philips, 637(VS):Summer86-629
Artinian, R.W. Maupassant Criticism.
H. Redman, Jr., 546(RR):Mar85-220
"Artists Against War and Fascism."
H. Kramer, 441:27Apr86-19
Artmann, H.C. Under the Cover of a Hat.
R.A. Berman, 441:2Nov86-26
"Arts du Spectacle et histoire des idées."
C. Meyer, 537:Vol71No1/2-195
"Aruṇantis Śivajñānasiddhiyār." (H.W. Schomerus, trans) (H. Berger, A. Dhamotharan and D.B. Kapp, eds)
J.W. de Jong, 259(IIJ):Jul85-227
Arvey, V. In One Lifetime.
E. Southern, 91:Spring85-122
Asaf'yev, B.V. A Book about Stravinsky.*
S. Karlinsky, 550(RusR):Jul85-281
Asals, F. Flannery O'Connor.*
J. Cunningham, 577(SHR):Winter85-72
Asche, U. Roms Weltherrschaftsidee und Aussenpolitik in der Spätantike im Spiegel der Panegyrici Latini.
C.E.V. Nixon, 313:Vol75-254
Aschenbrenner, K. Analysis of Appraisive Characterization.*
D.W. Crawford, 543:Jun86-755

Aschenbrenner, K. A Companion to Kant's "Critique of Pure Reason."
R. Meerbote, 319:Oct86-564
Asenbaum, P. and others. Otto Wagner — Möbel und Innenräume.
V.J. Behal, 683:Band48Heft2-271
Asencio, J.J.G. - see under Gómez Asencio, J.J.
Asensio, G.R. - see under Ramallo Asensio, G.
Ash, J. The Branching Stairs.*
M. Hulse, 493:Jan85-65
G. Szirtes, 148:Summer85-51
Ash, T.G. "Und Willst Du Nicht Mein Bruder Sein ... " Die DDR Heute.
G.A. Craig, 453(NYRB):25Sep86-62
Ashbery, J. Selected Poems.*
C. Rawson, 617(TLS):4Jul86-723
D. Revell, 152(UDQ):Spring/Summer86-185
Ashbery, J. A Wave.*
G. Ward, 97(CQ):Vol 14No2-163
455:Mar85-65
639(VQR):Winter85-27
Ashbrook, W. Donizetti and his Operas.*
J.B., 412:Feb83-59
W. Dean, 410(M&L):Jul85-272
Ashihara, Y. The Aesthetic Townscape.
D.W. Crawford, 318(JAOS):Summer86-416
Ashley, M. Dancing for Balanchine.*
R. Bailey, 151:Jan85-44
M. Mudrick, 249(HudR):Autumn85-520
S.L. Odom, 529(QQ):Winter85-824
Ashley, M. and T. Jeeves. The Complete Index to Astounding/Analog.
R.M.P., 561(SFS):Jul85-225
Ashmun, L.F., comp. Resettlement of Indochinese Refugees in the United States.
D.W. Haines, 293(JASt):Feb85-455
Ashton, D. About Rothko.*
D. Upright, 90:Apr85-240
M. Welish, 473(PR):Vol52No3-299
Ashton, R. Little Germany.
P. Gay, 617(TLS):5Sep86-961
D. Widgery, 362:17Jul86-29
Ashton, R. Reformation and Revolution, 1558-1660.
S.E. Lehmberg, 551(RenQ):Summer85-333
R. Smolinski, 568(SCN):Winter85-58
Ashton, S. and P. Tuson. India Office Library and Records.
J. Katz, 617(TLS):29Aug86-951
Ashton-Warner, S. I Passed This Way.
L. Jones, 49:Oct85-127
Ashworth, W. The Late, Great Lakes.
J. Koslow, 441:22Jun86-27
Asimov, I., M.H. Greenberg and C.G. Waugh, eds. Sherlock Holmes through Time and Space.
E.S. Lauterbach, 395(MFS):Summer85-382
Asimov, L. Foundation and Earth.
G. Jonas, 441:23Nov86-30
Aspiz, H. Walt Whitman and the Body Beautiful.
J. Gatta, 183(ESQ):Vol31No4-272
Asquith, H.H. Letters to Venetia Stanley. (M. and E. Brock, eds)
J.L. Godfrey, 377:Jul84-116
Assad, T.J. Tennysonian Lyric.
D.W. Tyree, 637(VS):Summer86-643

"Assays."* (Vol 1) (P.A. Knapp and M.A.
Stugrin, eds)
   G. Bourquin, 189(EA):Jan-Mar86-90
   A.A. MacDonald, 179(ES):Aug85-363
"Assays." (Vol 2) (P.A. Knapp, ed)
   G. Bourquin, 189(EA):Jan-Mar86-90
   V. Edden, 541(RES):Nov85-621
   A.A. MacDonald, 179(ES):Aug85-363
Asselain, J-C. Histoire économique de la
France du XVIIIème siècle à nos jours.
   J.S. Dugan, 207(FR):May86-1006
"Assessment of Best Practical Environment-
al Options for Management of Low and
Intermediate-level Solid Radioactive
Waste."
   M. Warnock, 617(TLS):17Oct86-1155
Assiniwi, B. Il n'y a plus d'Indiens.
   J. Moss, 102(CanL):Fall85-145
de Assis, J.M.M. - see under Machado de
Assis, J.M.
Assouline, P. L'Epuration des intel-
lectuels.
   P. McCarthy, 617(TLS):6Jun86-625
Astarita, M.L. Avidio Cassio.
   F. Millar, 123:Vol35No2-412
Astley, T. Beachmasters.*
   V. Young, 441:22Jun86-12
Astor, B. The Last Blossom on the Plum
Tree.
   C. Gaiser, 441:29Jun86-8
Astorquiza Pizarro, F., ed. Bio-biblio-
grafía de la filosofía en Chile, desde
el siglo XVI hasta 1980.
   J.C. Torchia Estrada, 263(RIB):
      Vol35No4-459
Astrachan, A. How Men Feel.
   R. Hansen, 441:10Aug86-6
Athanasopulos, C. Contemporary Theater.
   E.A. Langhans, 612(ThS):Nov85-187
Athanassiadi-Fowden, P. Julian and Hellen-
ism.*
   P.W. van der Horst, 394:Vol38fasc1/2-
      218
Athill, D. After a Funeral.
   R. Dinnage, 617(TLS):28Feb86-212
   M. Jones, 362:6Mar86-26
Atikian, M.B. and H. Armenians' Names.
   A.M. Avakian, 424:Sep85-181
Atil, E., ed. Suleymanname.
   E. Kolb, 441:16Nov86-25
Atkins, E.W. The Elgar-Atkins Friendship.
   P.M. Young, 410(M&L):Jan85-55
Atkins, G.D. Reading Deconstruction/Decon-
structive Reading.*
   R. Salvaggio, 173(ECS):Fall85-127
   R. Wolfs, 204(FdL):Mar85-59
Atkinson, B. Sean O'Casey. (R.G. Lowery,
ed)
   H. Pyle, 541(RES):Feb85-123
Atkinson, C.W. Mystic and Pilgrim.
   C.K. Zacher, 589:Apr85-469
Atkinson, J. Martin Luther.
   D.W.H. Arnold, 161(DUJ):Dec84-136
Atkinson, M. Plotinus, "Ennead" v.i.*
   A.H. Armstrong, 123:Vol35No1-201
   D.J. O'Meara, 543:Dec85-346
   J. Whittaker, 303(JoHS):Vol 105-196
Atkinson, P. Language, Structure and
Reproduction.
   R.K.S. Macaulay, 350:Dec86-956
"The Atlanta Exposition Cookbook."
   W. and C. Cowen, 639(VQR):Spring85-64

"Atlante Lessicale Toscano." (Vols 1-4)
   R.A. Hall, Jr., 545(RPh):May85-510
Atlas, A.W. Music at the Aragonese Court
of Naples.
   D. Fallows, 617(TLS):14Mar86-273
Atlas, J. The Great Pretender.
   L. Fiedler, 441:18May86-13
"Atlas Linguarum Europae (ALE)." (Vol 1,
fasc 1) (M. Alinei and others, eds)
   G. Cubbin, 297(JL):Sep85-524
   Z. Topolińska, 685(ZDL):3/1985-373
Atleson, J.B. Values and Assumptions in
American Labor Law.
   D.C., 185:Oct85-224
Attali, J. Un Homme d'influence.
   A.J. Sherman, 617(TLS):23May86-550
Attfield, R. The Ethics of Environmental
Concern.
   M. Adam, 542:Jan-Mar85-90
   J. Bordo, 529(QQ):Spring85-205
   S.R.L. Clark, 518:Jul85-184
   R. Elliot, 63:Dec85-499
   S.N., 185:Jan86-464
Attius, H. Estetik och moral.
   S.P. Sondrup, 563(SS):Summer85-357
Attridge, D. The Rhythms of English
Poetry.*
   B. Bjorklund, 301(JEGP):Jan85-113
   R.D. Cureton, 35(AS):Summer85-157
   A. Elliott, 541(RES):May85-244
Attridge, D. and D. Ferrer, eds. Post-
Structuralist Joyce.
   J. Kidd, 617(TLS):5Sep86-980
   P. McGee, 223:Summer85-193
   M. Norris, 329(JJQ):Spring86-365
Atwood, M. Bluebeard's Egg.*
   E. Brady, 198:Summer85-88
   R. Towers, 441:23Nov86-11
Atwood, M. Bodily Harm.
   R. Rubenstein, 298:Spring85-120
Atwood, M. The Handmaid's Tale.
   J. Fitzgerald, 99:Oct85-30
   M. McCarthy, 441:9Feb86-1
   K.C. O'Brien, 362:1May86-30
   C. Rooke, 376:Jan86-120
   L. Sage, 617(TLS):21Mar86-307
   J.L. Slonczewski, 344:Fall86-120
   J. Updike, 442(NY):12May86-118
Atwood, M. Interlunar.*
   A. Blott, 198:Winter85-90
   J.F. Hulcoop, 102(CanL):Winter84-88
   S. Scobie, 376:Mar85-160
Atwood, M. Murder in the Dark.*
   L. Weir, 102(CanL):Winter84-86
Atwood, M., ed. The New Oxford Book of
Canadian Verse in English.
   G. Woodcock, 677(YES):Vol 15-239
Atwood, M. Second Words.*
   R. Gibbs, 178:Mar85-113
   E. Jewinski, 628(UWR):Fall-Winter85-78
Aubailly, J-C. Le monologue, le dialogue
et la sottie.
   B.C. Bowen, 551(RenQ):Autumn85-544
Aubert de Gaspé fils, P. L'Influence d'un
livre. (A. Sénécal, ed)
   E.J. Talbot, 207(FR):Apr86-777
Aubineau, M. Un traité inédit de christol-
ogie de Sévérien de Gabala.
   R. Goulet, 192(EP):Apr-Jun85-251
Aubrac, L. Ils partiront dans l'ivresse.
   R.M. Webster, 207(FR):Apr86-834
Aubrey, J. Brief Lives. (R. Barber, ed)
   S. Archer, 568(SCN):Spring-Summer85-17

15

Auchincloss, L. Diary of a Yuppie.
J.J. Osborn, Jr., 441:31Aug86-6
R. Towers, 453(NYRB):18Dec86-29
Auchincloss, L. Honourable Men.*
V. Bogdanor, 362:17Apr86-28
B. Morton, 617(TLS):25Apr86-453
Aucouturier, M. - see "Cahiers Léon Tol-
stoÏ"
Auden, W.H. and C. Isherwood. Journey to
a War.
617(TLS):6Jun86-631
Audouin, R. - see "Politique économique"
Audouze, J. and G. Israël, eds. The Cam-
bridge Atlas of Astronomy.
E.J. Chaisson, 441:9Mar86-25
Auer, J.C.P. Bilingual Conversation.
N.R. Mahecha, 350:Dec86-953
Auerbach, N. Romantic Imprisonment.
M. Gordon, 454:Spring86-278
A. Goreau, 441:5Jan86-5
Auerbach, N. Woman and the Demon.*
K. Kroeber, 403(MLS):Fall85-358
Augustijn, C., P. Fraenkel and M. Lein-
hard - see Bucer, M.
Augustine, N.R. Augustine's Laws.
A. Feinberg, 441:16Mar86-21
Auletta, K. Greed and Glory on Wall
Street.
J.K. Galbraith, 453(NYRB):10Apr86-11
L. Minard, 441:19Jan86-6
Aumont, J. and others. L'Esthétique du
film.
T. Conley, 207(FR):Feb86-501
Aune, B. Metaphysics.
M. McGinn, 617(TLS):28Nov86-1338
Auring, S. and others. Dansk litteratur-
historie, 5.
A. Aarseth, 172(Edda):1985/4-255
Aurobindo, S. - see under Sri Aurobindo
Auroux, S. L'Illuminismo francese e la
tradizione logica di Port-Royal.
W. Büttemeyer, 53(AGP):Band67Heft2-218
Aury, D., J-C. Zylberstein and B. Leuil-
liot - see Paulhan, J.
Ausband, S.C. Myth and Meaning, Myth and
Order.*
J.B. Vickery, 577(SHR):Fall85-368
Ausfeld, M.L. and V.M. Mechlenburg. Ad-
vancing American Art.
F.V. O'Connor, 127:Winter84-393
Ausländer, R. Ich höre das Herz des
Oleanders.
J. Osborne, 617(TLS):31Jan86-104
Austen, C. Reminiscences. (D. Le Faye,
ed)
B. Brophy, 617(TLS):14Nov86-1284
Austen, J. Volume the First.
42(AR):Summer85-368
Austen, J. and C. Brontë. The Juvenilia
of Jane Austen and Charlotte Brontë.
(F. Beer, ed)
617(TLS):15Aug86-899
Auster, P. Ghosts.
R. Goldstein, 441:29Jun86-13
442(NY):18Aug86-73
Austerman, W.R. Sharps Rifles and Spanish
Mules.
L. Milazzo, 584(SWR):Autumn85-547
Austin, G. Phänomenologie der Gebärde
bei Hugo von Hofmannsthal.
J. Koppensteiner, 406:Summer85-236

Austin, N. Archery at the Dark of the
Moon.
R.B. Rutherford, 447(N&Q):Sep84-409
Austin, S. Parmenides.
J. Barnes, 617(TLS):28Nov86-1338
Austin, T.R. Language Crafted.
J.V. Catano, 599:Fall85-403
C. Ruhl, 350:Dec86-932
"Autour de David."
R. Wrigley, 90:Jun85-393
Auty, M. and N. Roddick, eds. British
Cinema Now.
D. Robinson, 617(TLS):17Jan86-69
"Aux origines de 'Pandora' et d''Aurelia.'"
G. Malandain, 535(RHL):Sep/Oct85-888
Avalle-Arce, J.B. - see de Cervantes
Saavedra, M.
Avalle-Arce, J.B. and G. Cervantes Martín
- see de Vega Carpio, L.
Avanesova, R.I. - see Borunova, S.N., V.L.
Voroncova and N.A. Es'kova
Avedon, R. In the American West: 1979-
1984.*
I. Jeffrey, 364:Feb86-80
Avella-Wildhalm, G., L. Lutz and U. and R.
Mattejiet - see "Lexikon des Mittelal-
ters"
"Les Aventures de Sindbad le marin." (R.R.
Khawam, trans)
J-L. Gautier, 450(NRF):Sep85-104
Averroes. Averroes' Middle Commentaries
on Aristotle's "Categories" and "De
Interpretatione." (C.E. Butterworth,
trans)
P.V. Spade, 319:Jan86-117
Averroes. Middle Commentary on Aris-
totle's "Topics." Middle Commentary on
Aristotle's "Categories." Middle Com-
mentary on Aristotle's "De Interpreta-
tione." (C.E. Butterworth and A.A.
al-Magid Haridi, eds of all)
S. Harvey, 543:Dec84-376
Avigdor, E. Coquettes et Précieuses.
Z. Youssef, 535(RHL):Jan/Feb85-93
Avins, C. Border Crossings.*
O. Markof-Belaeff, 550(RusR):Jul85-318
S.F. Orth, 574(SEEJ):Spring85-113
Avis, N. — abandoned outport —.
L.A. Davidson, 404:Summer85-54
Avishai, B. The Tragedy of Zionism.*
E. Alexander, 129:Feb86-28
J.S. Auerbach, 390:Nov85-55
A. Margalit, 453(NYRB):23Oct86-52
Avni, O. Tics, Tics et Tics.
L. Edson, 446(NCFS):Spring-Summer86-
374
Avril, F. and M-T. Gousset, with C. Rabel.
Manuscrits enluminés de la Bibliothèque
Nationale: Manuscrits enluminés
d'origine italienne. (Vol 2)
R. Gibbs, 90:Dec85-905
Avril, F. and Y. Zaluska. Manuscrits
enluminés de la Bibliothèque Nationale:
Manuscrits enluminés d'origine italienne.
(Vol 1)
R. Gibbs, 90:Dec85-905
Avtorkhanov, A. Memuary.
Y. Felshtinsky, 550(RusR):Jan85-114
Awoonor, K. The Breast of the Earth.
E. Palmer, 538(RAL):Winter85-619
Awouma, J-M. Contes et fables.
S. Domowitz, 538(RAL):Fall85-400

Awouma, J-M. and J-I. Noah. Contes et
fables du Cameroun.
    S. Domowitz, 538(RAL):Fall85-400
Axelos, K. Systématique ouverte.
    M. Adam, 542:Jan-Mar85-76
    T. Cordellier, 450(NRF):May85-88
    C. Roëls, 192(EP):Jul-Sep85-417
Axelrod, A. Charles Brockden Brown.*
    B. Christophersen, 651(WHR):Spring85-
    77
Axer, J. The Style and the Composition of
Cicero's Speech "Pro Q. Roscio Comoedo."
    J.G.F. Powell, 123:Vol35No2-391
Axionov, V. Paysages de papier.
    J. Blot, 450(NRF):Sep85-109
Axtell, J. The Invasion Within.*
    M. Abley, 617(TLS):13Jun86-652
Axton, M., ed. Three Tudor Classical
Interludes.
    D. Kay, 447(N&Q):Sep84-426
    A.A. MacDonald, 179(ES):Apr85-162
Ayala, F. La estructura narrativa y otras
experiencias literarias.
    E. Irizarry, 238:May85-304
de Ayala, P.L. - see under López de Ayala,
P.
Ayala Mallory, N. Bartolomé Esteban
Murillo.
    D. Angulo Íñiguez, 48:Jan-Mar85-93
Aycock, W.M. and S.P. Cravens, eds. Calde-
rón de la Barca at the Tercentenary.
    G. Edwards, 402(MLR):Jan85-197
    P.S. Finch, 345(KRQ):Vol132No3-335
Ayer, A.J. Freedom and Morality and Other
Essays.*
    O.J., 185:Jan86-433
Ayer, A.J. Voltaire.
    M. Cranston, 617(TLS):5Dec86-1384
    G. May, 441:2Nov86-32
    A. Ryan, 362:20ct86-26
    442(NY):8Dec86-154
Ayer, A.J. Wittgenstein.*
    483:Jul85-416
Ayers, E.L. Vengeance and Justice.
    D.A. Pyron, 639(VQR):Autumn85-741
Ayling, S. A Portrait of Sheridan.*
    M. Meyer, 364:Jun85-96
Aylmer, G.E. Rebellion or Revolution?
    B. Worden, 617(TLS):1Aug86-846
Aymes, J-R. La déportation sous le Pre-
mier Empire.
    G. Dufour, 92(BH):Jul-Dec84-546
Aziz, M. - see James, H.
al-Azmeh, A. Ibn Khaldun.
    F. Shehadi, 318(JAOS):Jul-Sep84-593


van Baak, J.J. The Place of Space in Nar-
ration.
    E.R. Sicher, 402(MLR):Jan85-253
    E.R. Sicher, 575(SEER):Jan85-99
Baasner, R. - see von Ebner-Eschenbach, M.
Babington Smith, C. Champion of Homoeop-
athy.
    N. Roberts, 617(TLS):13Jun86-642
Babson, S., with others. Working Detroit.
    N. Faires, 385(MQR):Spring86-468
"Babylon on the Rhone." (R. Coogan, trans)
    B.G. Kohl, 589:Apr85-476
Bacchi, C.L. Liberation Deferred?*
    H.J. Maroney, 529(QQ):Summer85-431

Baccouche, B. and S. Azmi. Conversations
in Modern Standard Arabic.
    D.R. Magrath, 399(MLJ):Summer85-168
Bach, H.I. The German Jew.*
    R.S. Levy, 129:Jan86-72
Bach, S. Final Cut.*
    F. Raphael, 617(TLS):21Feb86-200
    362:4Dec86-32
Bache, C. Verbal Aspect.
    S. Midgette, 350:Dec86-940
Bache-Wiig, H., ed. Sinn og samfunn.
    S. Lyngstad, 562(Scan):May85-82
Bachelard, G. Water and Dreams.
    D.P. Slattery, 435:Fall85-81
Bachmaier, P. and others - see Jacobi, F.H.
Bachmann, C., J. Lindenfeld and J. Simonin.
Langage et communications sociales.*
    Y. Winkin, 209(FM):Apr85-127
Bachmann, I. Franza.
    F. de Martinoir, 450(NRF):Dec85-93
Bachofer, W., W. von Hahn and D. Möhn, eds.
Rückläufiges Wörterbuch der Mittelhoch-
deutschen Sprache.
    H. Kolb, 72:Band222Heft1-155
Bächtold, J.M., J.J. Sturzenegger and R.
Trüb - see Weber, A. and J.M. Bächtold
Backhouse, J., D.H. Turner and L. Webster,
eds. The Golden Age of Anglo-Saxon Art.
    I. Wood, 59:Jun85-228
Bäcklund, U. "Realize" and "Recognize."
    A. Tellier, 189(EA):Apr-Jun86-239
Backscheider, P.R. A Being More Intense.
    R.A. Erickson, 173(ECS):Spring86-410
    F.M. Keener, 566:Autumn85-75
Bacon, R. Roger Bacon's Philosophy of
Nature.* (D.C. Lindberg, ed and trans)
    W.A. Wallace, 543:Jun85-892
Baconnet, M. Midi, la nuit.
    G.R. Montbertrand, 207(FR):Dec85-330
Bacou, R. La donnation Arï et Suzanne
Redon, Musée du Louvre.
    H. Dorra, 90:Aug85-541
Badash, L. Kapitza, Rutherford, and the
Kremlin.*
    639(VQR):Summer85-81
Badawi, M.M. Modern Arabic Literature and
the West.
    R. Ostle, 617(TLS):21Nov86-1326
Badolato, F., ed. George Gissing.
    R.L. Selig, 637(VS):Summer86-623
Badsha, O., ed. South Africa.
    J. Haskins, 441:24Aug86-18
Baer, E. Metalwork in Medieval Islamic
Art.
    R. Katzenstein, 589:Oct85-941
de Baere, G. - see van Ruusbroec, J.
von Baeyer, H. Rainbows, Snowflakes, and
Quarks.
    42(AR):Spring85-254
Bagehot, W. The Collected Works. (Vols
12-15) (N. St. John-Stevas, ed)
    J. Critchley, 362:22May86-29
    R.T. Shannon, 617(TLS):29Aug86-927
Bagge, S. and A. Nedkvitne - see "Regesta
Norvegica III, 1301-1319"
Bagley, F.R.C., ed and trans. The Muslim
World. (Pt 4, fasc 1)
    J.O. Voll, 318(JAOS):Apr-Jun84-391
Bagni, P. Guercino a Cento.
    N.W. Neilson, 90:May85-309
Bahr, E., E.P. Harris and L.G. Lyon, eds.
Humanität und Dialog.*
    H.B. Nisbet, 402(MLR):Jul85-754

17

Bail, M. Ian Fairweather.*
  E. Cross, 592:Vol 198No1011-52
Bailbé, J-M. - see Janin, J.
Bailet, D.S. Die Frau als Verführte und
  als Verführerin in der deutschen und
  französischen Literatur des 18. Jahr-
  hunderts.
  A. Scott-Prelorentzos, 107(CRCL):Sep85-
  540
Bailey, A.C. England, First and Last.*
  J. Morgan, 617(TLS):25Apr86-445
Bailey, C. The Sociology of Production in
  Rural Malay Society.
  M. Nash, 293(JASt):Nov84-254
Bailey, C-J.N. and R. Harris, eds. Devel-
  opmental Mechanisms of Language.
  L.M. Stanford, 320(CJL):Winter85-495
Bailey, D. Swim For Your Life.
  A.S. Brennan, 198:Winter85-114
  T. Middlebro', 102(CanL):Summer85-173
Bailey, D.R.S. - see under Shackleton
  Bailey, D.R.
Bailey, H. Hannie Richards.*
  C.L. Mithers, 441:16Mar86-20
Bailey, K., M. Long and S. Peck, eds.
  Second Language Acquisition Studies.
  J. La Motte, 355(LSoc):Jun85-265
Bailey, P. Gabriel's Lament.
  G. Strawson, 617(TLS):26Sep86-1058
  B. Tonkin, 362:20ct86-23
Bailey, P.J. Reading Stanley Elkin.
  S. Moore, 70:May/Jun86-156
Bailey, R.W. and M. Görlach, eds. English
  as a World Language.*
  F.W. Gester, 72:Band222Heft1-169
  A.M. Kinloch, 320(CJL):Spring85-97
  J. Pride, 355(LSoc):Sep85-379
Bailey, T. The Ambrosian Alleluias.
  D. Fallows, 415:Apr85-241
Baillie, W., ed. "Gratiae Theatrales," or
  A Choice Ternary of English Plays (1662).
  A.H. Andreadis, 568(SCN):Fall85-33
Bailly-Herzberg, J. Dictionnaire de
  l'Estampe en France 1830-1950.
  A.G., 90:Dec85-918
Bailyn, B. The Peopling of British North
  America.
  E. Wright, 441:17Aug86-6
Bain, D.H. Sitting in Darkness.
  I. Buruma, 453(NYRB):16Jan86-27
Bain, D.M. - see Menander
Bainbridge, B. English Journey.
  W.S. Peterson, 396(ModA):Summer85-261
Bainbridge, B. Filthy Lucre, or The Trag-
  edy of Andrew Ledwhistle and Richard
  Soleway.
  L. Duguid, 617(TLS):17Oct86-1168
Bainbridge, B. Mum and Mr. Armitage.*
  N. Berry, 176:May86-55
Baines, D. Migration in a Mature Economy.
  J.M. Winter, 617(TLS):25Jul86-822
Baines, E. The Birth Machine.*
  P. Lewis, 565:Winter84/85-42
Baines, J. Fecundity Figures.
  K. Kitchen, 617(TLS):27Jun86-712
Baines, J. Mandelstam: The Later Poetry.
  E. Sampson, 558(RLJ):Fall84-297
Baioni, G. Kafka.
  M.M. Anderson, 221(GQ):Fall85-626
Baird, I.F., ed. Scottish Feilde and
  Flodden Feilde.
  N.H. Keeble, 382(MAE):1985/2-322
Baird-Smith, R. - see "Winter's Tales"

Bairoch, P. De Jéricho à Mexico, Villes
  et Économie dans l'Histoire.
  H. Cronel, 450(NRF):Nov85-107
Bak, J.M. and G. Benecke, eds. Religion
  and Rural Revolt.
  M. Raeff, 104(CASS):Summer85-239
Bakalla, M.H. Arabic Linguistics.*
  M.R. Zughoul, 257(IRAL):Aug85-259
Baker, C. The Echoing Green.*
  G. Bornstein, 661(WC):Fall85-180
  R. Gleckner, 27(AL):Mar85-158
  S.M. Sperry, 191(ELN):Sep85-79
  295(JML):Nov85-432
Baker, D.C. - see Chaucer, G.
Baker, D.C., J.L. Murphy and L.B. Hall,
  Jr., eds. The Late Medieval Religious
  Plays of Bodleian MSS Digby 133 and e
  Museo 160.*
  R. Beadle, 382(MAE):1985/2-319
Baker, D.V. Cornish Prelude.
  C. Causley, 617(TLS):11Apr86-383
Baker, G.P. and P.M.S. Hacker. Frege.*
  D. Bell, 393(Mind):Jan85-160
  G. Currie, 518:Jan85-18
  J.N. Mohanty, 319:Oct86-568
  G.E. Rosado Haddock, 160:Apr85-171
Baker, G.P. and P.M.S. Hacker. Language,
  Sense and Nonsense.*
  J. Bogen, 262:Dec85-467
  P. Engel, 542:Jan-Mar85-46
  J.T. Jensen, 350:Mar86-205
  J. Heal, 393(Mind):Apr85-307
  L. Stevenson, 483:Apr85-270
  J.E. Tiles, 518:Apr85-98
Baker, G.P. and P.M.S. Hacker. Scepticism,
  Rules and Language.*
  E. Craig, 479(PhQ):Apr85-212
  C. Diamond, 518:Jan85-26
  P. Engel, 542:Jan-Mar85-45
  J. Heal, 393(Mind):Apr85-307
  D.M.S., 185:Apr86-671
  483:Jan85-147
Baker, G.P. and P.M.S. Hacker. Wittgen-
  stein. (Vol 2)
  J.F.M. Hunter, 617(TLS):19Sep86-1037
Baker, H.A., Jr. Blues, Ideology, and
  Afro-American Literature.*
  K. Byerman, 395(MFS):Winter85-730
  J. Weixlmann, 659(ConL):Spring86-48
  295(JML):Nov85-392
Baker, J.M. The Music of Alexander
  Scriabin.
  A. Pople, 617(TLS):4Jul86-739
Baker, J.R. Fuel-Injected Dreams.
  M. Bell, 441:4May86-38
Baker, L. The Percys of Mississippi.*
  E. Current-Garcia, 577(SHR):Spring85-
  190
  R.D. Launius, 392:Winter84/85-94
  V.A. Makowsky, 536(Rev):Vol7-305
Baker, L.F. and others. Collage. (2nd ed)
  G.R. Montbertrand, 207(FR):May86-1018
Baker, M. Our Three Selves.*
  S. Pickering, 569(SR):Fall85-lxxxiii
Baker, P. and C. Corne. Isle de France
  Creole.*
  H. Wise, 208(FS):Jul85-376
Baker, R.S. The Dark Historic Page.*
  D. Bradshaw, 447(N&Q):Dec84-544
Baker, W. The Libraries of George Eliot
  and George Henry Lewes.*
  W. Myers, 677(YES):Vol 15-320

Baker, W.J. Jesse Owens.
C. Mead, 441:3Aug86-17
Bakerman, J.S. and M.J. De Marr, eds.
Adolescent Female Portraits in the
American Novel: 1961-1981.
L. Pannill, 70:Jan/Feb85-95
"Baker's Dozen."
J.K. Keefer, 198:Winter85-95
Bakhash, S. The Reign of the Ayatollahs.*
C. Heywood, 617(TLS):21Mar86-293
Bakhtin, M. Problems of Dostoevsky's
Poetics. (C. Emerson, ed and trans)
M. Dodsworth, 175:Summer85-185
J. Frank, 453(NYRB):23Oct86-56
S. Monas, 473(PR):Vol52No4-452
C.V. Ponomareff, 627(UTQ):Spring86-310
W.G. Regier, 223:Spring85-74
Bakhtine, M. Esthétique de la création
verbale.
L. Arénilla, 450(NRF):Mar85-101
Bakker, B.H. - see Zola, É.
Bakker, R.T. The Dinosaur Heresies.
J.N. Wilford, 441:26Oct86-14
Bal, M., F. van Dijk Hemmes and G. van
Ginneken. En Sara in haar tent lachte ...
J.P. Fokkelman, 204(FdL):Mar85-79
Balakian, A., ed. The Symbolist Movement
in the Literature of European Languages.*
D.M. Kosinski, 127:Summer85-163
H-J. Lope, 52:Band20Heft2-216
Balakian, P. Sad Days of Light.*
P. Filkins, 363(LitR):Spring86-362
Balan, J., ed. Identifications.*
A. van Herk, 49:Jul85-112
Balas, R. and D. Rice. Qu'est-ce qui se
passe? (2nd ed)
B. Ebling 2d, 207(FR):Feb86-493
L.R. Polly, 399(MLJ):Winter85-408
Balbert, P. and P.L. Marcus, eds. D.H.
Lawrence.*
J.M. Coetzee, 453(NYRB):16Jan86-33
Balbus, I.D. Marxism and Domination.
R.S. Gottlieb, 142:Winter86-87
Balcer, J.M. and others. Studien zum
attischen Seebund.
C. Steppler, 123:Vol135No2-407
Bald, S.R. Novelists and Political Con-
sciousness.
R.J. Lewis, 293(JASt):Feb85-415
Baldassarri, G. Il sonno di Zeus.
M. Pieri, 400(MLN):Jan85-181
Baldi, P., ed. Papers from the XIIth Lin-
guistic Symposium on Romance Languages.*
F. Nuessel, 361:Jan85-166
B. Peeters, 547(RF):Band97Heft4-431
Baldick, C. The Social Mission of English
Criticism, 1848-1932.*
C. Dawson, 541(RES):Nov85-588
J. Fekete, 141:Winter85-97
B. Knights, 637(VS):Spring85-560
R.N. MacKenzie, 635(VPR):Summer85-80
W. Ruddick, 366:Autumn85-296
Baldinger, K. Dictionnaire onomasiolo-
gique de l'ancien gascon.* (fasc 1, 4
and 5) (rev by I. Popelar)
K. Klingebiel, 545(RPh):May86-448
Baldinger, K. Dictionnaire onomasiolo-
gique de l'ancien gascon.* (fasc 2 and
3) (rev by I. Popelar)
K. Klingebiel, 545(RPh):May86-448
G.F. Meier, 682(ZPSK):Band38Heft6-782

Baldinger, K. Dictionnaire onomasiolo-
gique de l'ancien occitan.* (fasc 1-3
plus supp) (rev by I. Popelar)
K. Klingebiel, 545(RPh):May86-448
Baldinger, K. Vers une sémantique moderne.
G. Kleiber, 553(RLiR):Jan-Jun85-195
Baldwin, B. Suetonius.*
K.R. Bradley, 122:Jul85-254
Baldwin, B. - see "Timarion"
Baldwin, J. Evidence of Things Not Seen.*
I. Bamforth, 617(TLS):19Sep86-1025
Baldwin, J. The Price of the Ticket.*
T. Tanner, 617(TLS):24Jan86-75
Baldwin, J. - see "The Essential Whole
Earth Catalog"
Baldwin, M. King Horn.*
J. Saunders, 565:Spring85-72
Baldwin, N. To All Gentleness.
C. Clausen, 27(AL):Mar85-140
Baldwin, S., ed. The Medieval Castilian
Bestiary.
G.A. Shipley, 86(BHS):Apr85-195
Balestrazzi, A.M. Jules Renard.
M. Autrand, 535(RHL):Sep/Oct85-894
Balfour, M. Britain and Joseph Chamber-
lain.
J. Turner, 617(TLS):31Jan86-106
Balibar, F. Galilée, Newton lus par Ein-
stein.
A. Boyer, 542:Jul-Sep85-360
Balić, S. Die Kultur der Bosniaken.
(Supp 1)
U. Schamiloglu, 318(JAOS):Oct-Dec84-
779
Balk, C. Bindweed.
A. Brumer, 441:6Jul86-23
Ball, J. Paul and Thomas Sandby, Royal
Academicians.*
C. Fox, 324:Jan86-130
L. Herrmann, 90:Jun85-392
Ball, M.J. and G.E. Jones, eds. Welsh
Phonology.
M.O. Tallerman, 297(JL):Sep85-523
T.A. Watkins, 112:Vol 17-173
Ball, W. A Sense of Direction.
J.C. Palmer, 615(TJ):Oct85-396
Ballantine, C. Music and its Social Mean-
ings.
L. Pike, 410(M&L):Oct85-381
Ballard, G. Memoirs of Several Ladies of
Great Britain. (R. Perry, ed)
M.W. Brownley, 566:Spring86-204
Ballard, J.G. Empire of the Sun.*
M. Hollington, 381:Jun85-269
Ballesta, J.C. - see under Cano Ballesta,
J.
Ballestero, J.B. - see under Bernales
Ballestero, J.
Ballestero, M. Poesía y reflexión.
R. Warner, 86(BHS):Apr85-190
Ballesteros, O.A. Bilingual-Bicultural
Education.
G. González, 399(MLJ):Autumn85-299
Balliett, W. American Musicians.
J. Litweiler, 441:21Dec86-11
Balliett, W. Jelly Roll, Jabbo, and Fats.
M.L. Stewart, 187:Fall86-572
"Ballistic Missile Defense Technologies."
Lord Zuckerman, 453(NYRB):30Jan86-32
Ballmer, T. and W. Brennenstuhl. Speech
Act Classification.*
E.W. Schneider, 685(ZDL):2/1985-242

Ballmer, T.T. and M. Pinkal, eds.
Approaching Vagueness.
  B. Hlebec, 361:Jul85-261
Balmas, N.C. - see under Clerici Balmas, N.
Balmori, D., S.F. Voss and M. Wortman.
Notable Family Networks in Latin America.*
  R.E. McCaa, 263(RIB):Vol35No2-208
Balmuth, M.S. and R.J. Rowland, Jr., eds.
Studies in Sardinian Archaeology.
  T.W. Potter, 123:Vol35No2-413
Balsamo, L. La bibliografia.
  C. Fahy, 354:Dec85-359
Baltz, L. San Quentin Point.
  A. Grundberg, 441:7Dec86-20
de Balzac, H. Annette et le criminel. (A. Lorant, ed)
  C. Massol-Bedoin, 535(RHL):Mar/Apr85-307
de Balzac, H. La Peau de chagrin.* (M. Ambrière, ed)
  M. Tilby, 208(FS):Jan85-87
de Balzac, J-L.G. Épîtres latines.* (J. Jehasse and B. Yon, eds and trans)
  R. Tebib, 535(RHL):Sep/Oct85-863
Bamber, L. Comic Women, Tragic Men.*
  P. Bement, 541(RES):Feb85-82
  C. Kahn, 403(MLS):Fall85-329
  S. Snyder, 702:Vol 17-244
Bamborschke, U. Der altčechische Tandariuš nach den 3 überlieferten Handschriften mit Einleitung und Wortregister.
  F. Otten, 688(ZSP):Band45Heft1-210
Bamford, C. - see Milosz, O.V.D.
Bammesberger, A. English Etymology.
  R.W. Wescott, 350:Sep86-713
Bammesberger, A., ed. Das etymologischen Wörterbuch, Fragen der Konzeption und Gestaltung.*
  C.F. Justus, 159:Spring85-89
  F.B.J. Kuiper, 259(IIJ):Jul85-207
Bammesberger, A. A Handbook of Irish: Essentials of Modern Irish.*
  H.L.C. Tristram, 464:Vol32fasc1/2-289
Bammesberger, A. A Handbook of Irish. (Vols 2 and 3)
  R.A. Fowkes, 660(Word):Apr85-91
Bammesberger, A. Lateinische Sprachwissenschaft.
  P. Baldi, 215(GL):Vol25No2-128
  P. Flobert, 555:Vol59fasc1-133
  J.T. Jensen, 350:Mar86-208
  D.G. Miller, 159:Spring85-83
Bammesberger, A., ed. Problems of Old English Lexicography.
  M. Cummings, 350:Dec86-942
Bammesberger, A. A Sketch of Diachronic English Morphology.
  C.R. Barrett, 159:Fall85-239
  S.M. Embleton, 350:Mar86-212
  R.L. Thomson, 215(GL):Vol25No2-133
Banac, I. The National Question in Yugoslavia.*
  T. Stoianovich, 104(CASS):Spring85-109
  M. Wheeler, 575(SEER):Oct85-613
  639(VQR):Winter85-8
Bance, A. Theodor Fontane: The Major Novels.*
  C.D. Cossar, 402(MLR):Jan85-220
  H.H.H. Remak, 222(GR):Fall85-151
Bance, A.F., ed. Weimar Germany.*
  P. Milbouer, 221(GQ):Winter85-147

Bancquart, M-C. Anatole France.
  J. Aeply, 450(NRF):Mar85-97
Bancquart, M-C. Les Tarots d'Ulysse.
  T.H. Brown, 207(FR):Feb86-479
Bandarage, A. Colonialism in Sri Lanka.
  L.A. Wickremeratne, 293(JASt):Feb85-417
Bandelier, A. and others, eds. Table de concordances rythmique et syntaxique des "Poésies" d'Arthur Rimbaud.* (Vol 2)
  C. Chadwick, 208(FS):Jul85-356
Bandelier, A.F. The Southwestern Journals of Adolph F. Bandelier 1889-1892. (C.H. Lange, C.L. Riley and E.M. Lange, eds)
  L. Milazzo, 584(SWR):Autumn85-547
Bandem, I.M. and F.E. de Boer. Kaja and Kelod.*
  H. Chung, 187:Spring/Summer86-365
Bandy, A.C. - see Lydus, J.
Banerjee, H. Agrarian Society of the Punjab, 1849-1901.
  I.J. Kerr, 293(JASt):Nov84-222
Banerjee, S. India's Simmering Revolution.
  B.P. Lamb, 293(JASt):Aug85-854
Banerji, A.K. Aspects of Indo-British Economic Relations, 1858-1898.
  A.W. Heston, 293(JASt):Feb85-418
Banes, S. Democracy's Body.
  G. Jackson, 151:Apr85-84
Banfield, A. Unspeakable Sentences.*
  L. Haegman, 349:Fall85-393
Banfield, E.C. The Democratic Muse.*
  D.M., 185:Oct85-210
  C. Mitze, 476:Fall84-97
  F.V. O'Connor, 127:Winter84-393
Banfield, S. Sensibility and English Song.
  W. Mellers, 415:Sep85-537
  M. Smith, 607:Sep85-37
Bang, H. Reportager. (C.K. Hansen, ed)
  G.C. Schoolfield, 563(SS):Autumn85-466
Bang, H. Tina.
  A. Born, 562(Scan):Nov85-231
Bange, E. An den Grenzen der Sprache.
  G. Ernst, 535(RHL):Sep/Oct85-900
Bango Torviso, I. and F. Marías. Bosch.
  90:Aug85-547
Banham, J. and J. Harris, eds. William Morris and the Middle Ages.*
  R. Dellamora, 637(VS):Spring86-471
Banham, R. A Concrete Atlantis.
  N. Adams, 617(TLS):10Oct86-1133
  J. Coolidge, 441:4May86-13
Banks, I. Walking on Glass.*
  S.R. Delany, 441:2Mar86-37
Banks, K. The Tyrian Veil.
  S. Kamboureli, 102(CanL):Winter84-138
Banks, L.R. Casualties.
  J-A. Goodwin, 617(TLS):3Oct86-1114
Banks, R. Continental Drift.*
  W. Lesser, 467:Autumn85-467
  42(AR):Fall85-503
Banks, R. Success Stories.
  J.W. Aldridge, 441:22Jun86-22
  I. Fonseca, 617(TLS):22Aug86-920
Bann, S. The Clothing of Clio.
  D. Bellos, 208(FS):Jan85-101
  R. Dellamora, 637(VS):Spring86-471
  C. Parker, 366:Autumn85-292
  639(VQR):Spring85-52
Banner, L.W. American Beauty.
  K. Walden, 529(QQ):Summer85-425

21

Barrell, J. The Dark Side of the Land-
scape.
   D.H. Solkin, 54:Sep85-507
Barrell, J. English Literature in History
1730-1780.*
   J. Black, 161(DUJ):Jun84-297
   J. Black, 566:Spring86-207
Barrell, J. The Political Theory of Paint-
ing from Reynolds to Hazlitt.
   A. Graham-Dixon, 362:23Oct86-23
Barrenechea, A.M. - see Cortázar, J.
Barrère, J-B. Victor Hugo.
   L. Bishop, 546(RR):Mar85-217
   M-F. Guyard, 535(RHL):Nov/Dec85-1075
Barret, P. Vie et mort d'un bureaucrate
ordinaire.
   R.C. Lamont, 207(FR):Mar86-639
Barreto-Rivera, R. Nimrod's Tongue.
   S. Scobie, 376:Jan86-123
Barrett, A.A. and R.W. Liscombe. Francis
Rattenbury and British Columbia.*
   M.L. Clausen, 576:May85-191
Barrett, T. Japanese Papermaking.*
   S. Hughes, 407(MN):Spring85-120
Barrett, W. Death of the Soul.
   J. Teichman, 441:7Sep86-24
Barrett, W., A. MacKay and D. Griffin.
Atlantic Wildflowers.
   M.J. Harvey, 150(DR):Summer85-322
Barri, N. Clause-Models in Antiphontean
Greek.
   A. Sideras, 260(IF):Band90-313
Barrie, P. Devotions.
   N. Shulman, 617(TLS):4Jul86-732
Barrientos, J.Á. - see under Álvarez
Barrientos, J.
Barrier, M. Carl Barks and the Art of the
Comic Book.
   R. Johnson, 453(NYRB):26Jun86-22
Barringer, C., ed. Norwich in the Nine-
teenth Century.
   R. Lawton, 637(VS):Spring86-491
Barrio Loza, J.Á. Los Beaugrant en el con-
texto de la escultura manierista vasca.
   M. Estella, 48:Apr-Jun85-169
Barrios, L.E. Hierba, montañas, y el
árbol de la vida en San Pedro Sacatepé-
quez, Guatemala.
   M. Schevill, 37:Nov-Dec85-59
Barroll, J.L., ed. Medieval and Renais-
sance Drama in England. (Ser 3, Vol 1)
   S. Billington, 610:Summer85-161
Barron, H.S. Those Who Stayed Behind.
   B. Pruitt, 432(NEQ):Jun85-315
Barron, S. German Expressionist Sculpture.
   J. Lloyd, 59:Mar85-128
Barrow, J.D. and F.J. Tipler. The Anthro-
pic Cosmological Principle.
   T. Ferris, 441:16Feb86-20
   M. Gardner, 453(NYRB):8May86-22
Barrow, R. Injustice, Inequality and
Ethics.
   R.H. Kane, 543:Jun86-756
Barrow, T.F., S. Armitage and W.E. Tydeman,
eds. Reading into Photography.
   Y. Michaud, 98:Aug-Sep85-761
Barrows, S., with W. Novak. Mayflower
Madam.
   F. King, 441:5Oct86-15
Barry, A. - see Barnes, D.
Barry, B. and R. Hardin, eds. Rational
Man and Irrational Society?
   J.L. McGregor, 529(QQ):Spring85-210

Barry, S. The Rhetorical Town.
   T. Eagleton, 493:Aug85-64
Barry, S. The Water-Colourist.
   T. Eagleton, 565:Winter84/85-68
Barry, T., B. Wood and D. Preusch. The
Other Side of Paradise.
   639(VQR):Spring85-59
Barstow, S. Just You Wait and See.
   V. Cunningham, 617(TLS):23May86-552
Bartles, H. Epos — die Gattung in der
Geschichte.
   D.H. Green, 402(MLR):Jan85-207
Barth, J. The Friday Book.
   B.H., 395(MFS):Winter85-763
Barth, R. The Co-op Kill.
   T.J. Binyon, 617(TLS):31Oct86-1224
Barth, R.L. Forced-Marching to the Styx.
   J. Mole, 176:Nov86-63
Barthel, M. The Jesuits. (M. Howson, ed
and trans)
   J. Hitchcock, 31(ASch):Autumn85-555
Barthelme, D. Paradise.
   E. Jolley, 441:26Oct86-7
   442(NY):17Nov86-151
Barthelme, F. Second Marriage.*
   42(AR):Winter85-123
   639(VQR):Winter85-25
Barthelme, F. Tracer.*
   R. Kaveney, 617(TLS):21Mar86-307
Barthes, R. La chambre claire.
   C. Assouly-Piquet, 98:Aug-Sep85-812
Barthes, R. L'Aventure sémiologique.
   T. Eagleton, 617(TLS):2May86-477
Barthes, R. The Responsibility of Forms.
   T. Eagleton, 617(TLS):2May86-477
   H. Vendler, 453(NYRB):8May86-44
Barthes, R. The Rustle of Language.*
(French title: Le Bruissement de la
langue.)
   H. Brodkey, 441:20Apr86-13
   H. Vendler, 453(NYRB):8May86-44
Bärthlein, K., ed. Zur Geschichte der
Philosophie. (Vol 2)
   W. Steinbeck, 342:Band76Heft3-351
Bartholomeusz, D. "The Winter's Tale" in
Performance in England and America,
1611-1976.*
   C.J. Carlisle, 570(SQ):Autumn85-364
   T. Haring-Smith, 615(TJ):May85-256
   M. Hattaway, 541(RES):Feb85-85
Bartholomew, D.A. and L.C. Schoenhals.
Bilingual Dictionaries for Indigenous
Languages.
   Y. Lastra de Suárez, 355(LSoc):Dec85-
569
Bartled, F. Albert Camus ou le mythe et
le mime.
   G. Cesbron, 535(RHL):Jan/Feb85-132
Bartlett, D.B. and J.B. Steele. Forever
More.
   M. Warnock, 617(TLS):17Oct86-1155
Bartlett, E. Strange Territory.*
   R. Pybus, 565:Summer85-62
Bartlett, J. History of the Universe.*
   F. Tuten, 62:Jan86-12
Bartlett, R. Gerald of Wales, 1146-1223.
   R.W. Pfaff, 589:Jan85-117
Bartley, J. Invocations.*
   T. Goldie, 102(CanL):Winter84-146
Bartley, W.W. 3d - see Popper, K.R.

Bartning, I. Remarques sur la syntaxe et
la sémantique des pseudo-adjectifs
dénominaux en français.
H.B-Z. Shyldkrot, 545(RPh):May86-488
Bartolus. Politica e diritto nel trecento
italiano. (D. Quaglioni, ed)
K.H. Van D'Elden, 589:Jul85-751
Barton, A. Ben Jonson, Dramatist.
R. Gill, 175:Autumn85-256
W.D. Kay, 615(TJ):Oct85-385
T. Minter, 157:No157-51
C.G. Thayer, 191(ELN):Jun86-68
Barton, J. Playing Shakespeare.
H. Hunt, 610:Summer85-173
Barton, M. - see "British Music Yearbook,
1985"
Bartrip, P.W.J. and S.B. Burman. The
Wounded Soldiers of Industry.
R. Glen, 637(VS):Summer85-706
Bartsch, R. and T. Vennemann. Grundzüge
der Sprachtheorie.*
B. Peeters, 257(IRAL):May85-168
Bartusiak, M. Thursday's Universe.
L.A. Marschall, 441:21Dec86-9
Baruchello, G. and H. Martin. Why
Duchamp.*
J. Yau, 703:No15-174
Barwise, J. and J. Perry. Situations and
Attitudes.
M.U. Coyne, 543:Sep84-107
M.J. Cresswell, 482(PhR):Apr85-293
S. McConnell-Ginet, 350:Jun86-433
de Bary, W.T. Neo-Confucian Orthodoxy and
the Learning of the Mind and Heart.
J. Ching, 302:Vol21No1-63
de Bary, W.T. The Quest for Liberalism in
the Chinese Past.
P. Cohen, 485(PE&W):Jul85-305
Barzun, J. Critical Questions on Music
and Letters, Culture and Biography,
1940-1980. (B. Friedland, ed)
B.H.B., 412:May83-145
Barzun, J. A Stroll with William James.*
J.R. Vile, 396(ModA):Spring85-183
L. Willson, 569(SR):Spring85-279
Bascapè, G.C. and M. del Piazzo, with L.
Borgia. Insegne e simboli.
B.B. Rezak, 589:Jul85-634
Bascetta, C. Scritti sulla lingua ital-
iana. (E. Cardone, ed)
P. Trifone, 708:Vol 11fasc2-287
Bascom, H. Apata.
R. Deveson, 617(TLS):24Oct86-1187
Bashkina, N.N. and others, eds. The
United States and Russia.
J.M. Hartley, 575(SEER):Oct85-595
Bashkirtseff, M. The Journal of Marie
Bashkirtseff.
P. Spender, 362:8May86-26
Basho and others. One Man's Moon. (C.
Corman, trans)
R. Spiess, 404:Summer85-56
Basie, C., with A. Murray. Good Morning
Blues.
M.S. Harper, 441:2Feb86-6
E.J. Hobsbawn, 453(NYRB):16Jan86-3
R.G. O'Meally, 617(TLS):11Jul86-764
Basinger, J. The "It's a Wonderful Life"
Book.
N. Gabler, 441:7Dec86-68
Basinger, J. The World War II Combat Film.
W. Paul, 18:Sep86-69

Baskin, J.R. Pharaoh's Counsellors.
S.D. Benin, 589:Apr85-380
Baskir, L.M. and W.A. Strauss. Chance and
Circumstance.
J.G. Dunne, 453(NYRB):25Sep86-25
Bass, D. and F. Wells, with R. Ridgeway.
Seven Summits.
J. Howe, 441:27Jul86-19
Bassan, F. Alfred de Vigny et la Comédie-
Française.
B.T. Cooper, 446(NCFS):Fall-
Winter85/86-167
Bassan, F. - see de Chateaubriand, F.R.
Bassein, B.A. Women and Death.*
J. Eis, 219(GaR):Summer85-459
Basset, L. Les emplois périphrastiques du
verbe grec mellein.
C.J. Ruijgh, 361:Apr85-323
Bassett, J.E. Faulkner.
P.R. Broughton, 534(RALS):Spring83-41
Bassi, E. and others - see Cataneo, P. and
others
Bassnett-McGuire, S. Luigi Pirandello.*
R. Andrews, 278(IS):Vol40-151
S.V. Longman, 615(TJ):Oct85-392
Basso, B. Frau Musika. (Vol 2)
E. Selfridge-Field, 410(M&L):Apr85-129
Basso, E.B. A Musical View of the
Universe.
P. Henley, 617(TLS):28Feb86-224
Bassy, A-M. - see de La Fontaine, J.
Bastian, H. Mummenschanz.
H. Kokott, 680(ZDP):Band104Heft3-458
Bastos, A.R. - see under Roa Bastos, A.
Bataille, G. Visions of Excess.
D. Kuspit, 62:Oct85-13
Bataille, G.M. and K.M. Sands. American
Indian Women.*
A. Krupat, 27(AL):Mar85-164
Batchelor, J. The Edwardian Novelists.*
P. Miles, 447(N&Q):Jun84-274
Batchelor, R.E. and M.H. Offord. A Guide
to Contemporary French Usage.
M. Renouard, 208(FS):Apr85-246
Bates, B. The Way of Wyrd.
639(VQR):Winter85-24
Bates, D. The Fashoda Incident of 1898.
D. Killingray, 637(VS):Summer85-703
Bates, D. Normandy before 1066.*
J. Johns, 382(MAE):1985/1-141
Bates, M.J. Wallace Stevens.*
P. Brazeau, 705:Fall85-121
H. Vendler, 453(NYRB):20Nov86-42
Bateson, M.C. With a Daughter's Eye.
A.S. Grossman, 77:Summer85-265
D. Tannen, 350:Mar86-198
Bator, P.M. The International Trade in
Art.
J.H. Merryman, 476:Fall83-84
Batsleer, J. and others. Rewriting
English.
C. Baldick, 617(TLS):16May86-539
Battaglia, S. Grande dizionario della
lingua italiana. (Vol 12)
A. Castelvecchi, 708:Vol 11fasc1-119
Battestin, M.C. - see Fielding, H.
Battin, M.P. Ethical Issues in Suicide.
M. Wreen, 321:Vol 19No3-245
Battin, W. In the Solar Wind.
F. Allen, 496:Fall85-179
E. Butscher, 496:Spring85-47
J.D. McClatchy, 249(HudR):Spring85-161
639(VQR):Winter85-28

"The Battle of Maldon." (D.G. Scragg, ed)
H. Gneuss, 38:Band103Heft3/4-452
Battye, C. The Brewhouse Private Press,
1963-1983.
D. Chambers, 503:Spring84-45
Batz, M. and H. Schroth. Theater zwischen
Tür und Angel.
H-J. Greif, 193(ELit):Spring-Summer85-
200
Baudelaire, C. Baudelaire Revisited.
(rev) (K.E. Lappin, trans)
L.B. Hyslop, 399(MLJ):Spring85-86
Baudelaire, C. My Heart Laid Bare and
Other Prose Writings. (N. Cameron,
trans)
V. Brombert, 617(TLS):26Sep86-1051
Baudelaire, C. Selected Letters. (R.
Lloyd, ed and trans)
J. Barnes, 453(NYRB):20Nov86-18
V. Brombert, 617(TLS):26Sep86-1051
Baudelaire, C. 66 Translations from
Charles Baudelaire's "Les Fleurs du Mal."
(J. McGowan, trans)
G. Gauthier, 236:Fall-Winter85-32
Baudot, G. and T. Todorov, eds. Récits
aztèques de la conquête.
M. Olender, 98:Nov85-1132
Baudrillard, J. The Mirror of Production.
Towards a Political Economy of the Sign.
J. Valente, 153:Summer85-54
Bauer, C., ed and trans. Cries from a
Wounded Madrid.
639(VQR):Winter85-27
Bauer, E., ed. Heinrich Hallers Überset-
zung der "Imitatio Christi."
H. Tiefenbach, 685(ZDL):2/1985-273
Bauer, H. and B. Rupprecht. Corpus der
barocken Deckenmalerei in Deutschland.
(Vols 1 and 2)
B.W. Lindemann, 683:Band48Heft3-399
Bauer, L. English Word-Formation.*
I. Kenesei, 603:Vol9No3-429
H. Sauer, 38:Band103Heft1/2-137
T.J. Taylor, 541(RES):Aug85-389
Bauer, M. Oskar Panizza.
P.D.G. Brown, 222(GR):Summer85-119
Bauer, O.G. Richard Wagner.
D. Unruh, 615(TJ):May85-259
Bauer, R. and J. Wertheimer, eds. Das
Ende des Stegreifspiels — Die Geburt des
Nationaltheaters.*
J. Voisine, 549(RLC):Jan-Mar85-98
Bauer, Y. American Jewry and the Holo-
caust.
B. Wasserstein, 390:Feb85-56
Bauer-Eberhardt, U. Die Italienischen
Miniaturen des 13.-16. Jahrhunderts.
K. Sutton, 90:Jul85-462
Baugh, G.C., ed. A History of Shropshire.
(Vol 11)
A. Gomme, 617(TLS):29Aug86-944
Baugh, J. Black Street Speech.*
S.S. Mufwene, 35(AS):Summer85-161
A.K. Spears, 355(LSoc):Mar85-101
Baum, J. The Calculating Passion of Ada
Byron.
B. Maddox, 441:50ct86-44
Bauman, J. Winter in the Morning.
R.K. Angress, 441:6Apr86-23
Bauman, R. Let Your Words Be Few.*
B. Nelson, 568(SCN):Spring-Summer85-11
Baumann, C.C. Wilhelm Müller.
J.F. Fetzer, 406:Summer85-228

Baumann, G. Sprache und Selbstbegegnung.
H. Ammerlahn and J. Rieckmann,
107(CRCL):Sep85-544
Baumann, U. Rom und die Juden.
M.D. Goodman, 123:Vol35No1-138
T. Rajak, 313:Vol75-305
Baumann, W. Der Widerspenstigen Zähmung.
W.F. Schwarz, 196:Band26Heft3/4-347
Baumer, R.V. and J.R. Brandon, eds. San-
skrit Drama in Performance.
S. Oleksiw, 318(JAOS):Jul-Sep84-601
Baumgarten, A.G. Texte zur Grundlegung
der Ästhetik.* (H.R. Schweizer, ed and
trans) Philosophische Betrachtungen
über einige Bedingungen des Gedichtes.*
(H. Paetzold, ed and trans)
D. Dahlstrom, 543:Mar86-553
E. Schaper, 89(BJA):Summer85-278
Baumgarten, A.G. Theoretische Aesthetik.
(H.R. Schweizer, ed and trans)
D. Dahlstrom, 543:Mar86-553
Baumgarten, A.I. The Phoenician History
of Philo of Byblos.
R.A. Oden, Jr., 318(JAOS):Jul-Sep84-
581
Baurmeister, U. and others - see Renouard,
P.
von Bawey, P. Rhetorik der Utopie.
R.C. Reimer, 406:Fall185-378
Baxter, C. Harmony of the World.*
R.M. Davis, 573(SSF):Summer85-358
G. Johnson, 385(MQR):Summer86-616
Baxter, C. Through the Safety Net.*
G. Johnson, 385(MQR):Summer86-616
J. Saari, 42(AR):Fall185-498
Baxter, G. Jodhpurs in the Quantocks.
B. Bainbridge, 617(TLS):26Dec86-1453
Baxter, J. and L. Koffman. Police.
M.B. Carter, 617(TLS):10Jan86-29
Baxter, M.G. One and Inseparable.
P.D. Erickson, 432(NEQ):Jun85-304
639(VQR):Winter85-12
Baxter, S.B., ed. England's Rise to Great-
ness, 1660-1763.*
J. Black, 161(DUJ):Dec84-103
M. Fitzpatrick, 83:Autumn85-225
Bayard, S.P., ed. Dance to the Fiddle,
March to the Fife.*
C. Goertzen, 187:Winter86-180
Bayer, H. Gral.
D.H. Green, 402(MLR):Oct85-971
Bayer, K. Sämtliche Werke.
K. Ramm, 384:Nov85-1011
Bayer, K. Sprechen und Situation. (2nd
ed)
I. Bax, 350:Jun86-475
Bayle, E. and others - see Jubert, P.
Bayles, M.D. Reproductive Ethics.*
H. Kuhse, 63:Jun85-249
A. Schafer, 154:Winter85-731
Bayley, E.R. Joe McCarthy and the Press.
J. Braeman, 106:Fall185-353
Bayley, P. and D. Coleman, eds. The
Equilibrium of Wit.*
A. Blanc, 535(RHL):Jan/Feb85-83
Bayley, S. Sex, Drink and Fast Cars.
S. Hey, 362:27Nov86-28
Bayley, S., P. Garner and D. Sudjic.
Twentieth-Century Style and Design.
J. Woudhuysen, 362:11Dec86-22
Baylon, C. and P. Fabre. Les noms de
lieux et de personnes.*
K.E.M. George, 208(FS):Jul85-373

25

Bayly, C.A. - see Stokes, E.
Baym, N. Novels, Readers, and Reviewers.*
  M.D. Bell, 534(RALS):Spring83-73
  W.L. Hedges, 445(NCF):Jun85-105
  R.W.B. Lewis, 432(NEQ):Jun85-282
  T. Martin, 27(AL):May85-324
Bayne-Powell, R. Catalogue of Portrait
  Miniatures in the Fitzwilliam Museum,
  Cambridge.
  G. Reynolds, 39:Nov85-402
Baynes-Cope, A.D. The Study and Conserva-
  tion of Globes.
  N. Barker, 617(TLS):20Jun86-686
Bazin, A. French Cinema of the Occupation
  and Resistance.
  A.G. Robson, 399(MLJ):Winter85-409
Bazire, J. and J.E. Cross, eds. Eleven
  Old English Rogationtide Homilies.*
  M. Clayton, 382(MAE):1985/2-289
  T.H. Leinbaugh, 541(RES):Aug85-395
Beacco, J-C. and M. Darot. Analyses de
  discours — lecture et expression.
  C. Kramsch, 399(MLJ):Summer85-170
Beach, D., ed. Aspects of Schenkerian
  Theory.*
  P. McCreless, 308:Spring85-169
Beach, E.L. The United States Navy: 200
  Years.
  R.F. Weigley, 441:31Aug86-11
Beadle, R., ed. The York Plays.*
  S. Carpenter, 541(RES):May85-253
  C.W. Marx, 382(MAE):1985/2-316
  A.H. Nelson, 402(MLR):Jan85-115
  O.S. Pickering, 72:Band222Heft2-391
Beadle, R. and P.M. King, eds. York
  Mystery Plays.
  C. Davidson, 589:Oct85-1042
Beal, B. and R. MacLeod. Prairie Fire.
  J.R. Miller, 298:Fall85-156
  G.W., 102(CanL):Summer85-195
Bealer, G. Quality and Concept.*
  J. Buhl, 167:Aug85-203
  N.B. Cocchiarella, 316:Jun85-554
  H. Hochberg, 486:Sep84-514
  E. Sosa, 311(JP):Jul85-382
Bean, H. False Match.
  C.L. Crow, 649(WAL):May85-90
Bean, M.C. The Development of Word Order
  Paterrns in Old English.
  G. Russom, 301(JEGP):Jan85-117
Bear, G. Blood Music.*
  J. Clute, 617(TLS):11Jul86-767
Beard, J. Hors d'Oeuvres and Canapes.
  W. and C. Cowen, 639(VQR):Autumn85-140
Beare, M. - see Sachs, H.
Beato, F. and R. von Stillfried, with P.
  Loti. Once Upon a Time.
  442(NY):17Nov86-155
Beattie, A. Love Always.*
  M. Gorra, 249(HudR):Winter86-660
Beattie, A. Where You'll Find Me.
  T.R. Edwards, 441:12Oct86-10
Beattie, G. Survivors of Steel City.
  N. Fountain, 362:4Sep86-30
Beattie, J.M. Crime and the Courts in
  England 1660-1880.
  J.A. Sharpe, 617(TLS):8Aug86-869
Beattie, S. The New Sculpture.*
  M. Stocker, 637(VS):Winter85-347
Beatus Liebanensis and Eterius Oxomensis.
  Adversus Elipandum, libri duo. (B.
  Löfstedt, ed)
  P. Meyvaert, 589:Oct85-1043

Beauchamp, G. Jack London.
  E. Labor, 26(ALR):Spring/Autumn85-265
Beauchamp, H. Les Enfants et le jeu drama-
  tique.
  L. Robert, 193(ELit):Winter85-233
Beauchamp, T.L. and A. Rosenberg. Hume
  and the Problem of Causation.
  T. Horgan, 482(PhR):Apr85-278
Beaufret, J. Notes sur la philosophie en
  France au XIXe siècle.
  M. Adam, 542:Jul-Sep85-331
de Beaugrande, R. Text Production.
  A.A. Glatthorn, 355(LSoc):Dec85-537
de Beaugrande, R-A. and W.U. Dressler.
  Introduction to Text Linguistics.*
  (German title: Einführung in die Text-
  linguistik.)
  K-E. Sommerfeldt, 682(ZPSK):
    Band38Heft6-753
de Beaujoyeulx, B. Le Balet comique,
  1581.*
  J.C. Nash, 207(FR):Dec85-289
Beauman, S. The Royal Shakespeare Com-
  pany.*
  W.A. Armstrong, 611(TN):Vol39No2-93
de Beaumarchais, P.A.C. Le Mariage de
  Figaro. (P. Larthomas, ed)
  G. von Proschwitz, 209(FM):Oct85-251
Beaumont, A. Busoni the Composer.*
  C. MacDonald, 607:Dec85-47
Beaumont, B. - see Flaubert, G. and I.S.
  Turgenev
Beausoleil, C. Une certaine fin de siècle.
  R. Giroux, 102(CanL):Spring85-124
de Beauvoir, S. Adieux.
  42(AR):Spring85-250
Bebbington, D.W. The Nonconformist Con-
  science.
  J.H.Y. Briggs, 637(VS):Spring85-546
Bec, P. Manuel pratique d'occitan moderne.
  V. Mark, 545(RPh):Aug84-93
Beccaria, C. Complete Works. (Vols 1 and
  2) (L. Firpo, F. Francioni and G. Gas-
  pari, eds)
  F. Venturi, 617(TLS):3Oct86-1096
Bech, G. Studien über das deutsche Verbum
  infinitum.* (2nd ed)
  A.L. Lloyd, 133:Band18Heft2-189
Bech, S.C. Storhandelens by.
  G.S. Argetsinger, 563(SS):Spring85-217
Béchade, H.D. Les romans comiques de
  Charles Sorel.
  G. Berger, 475:Vol 12No22-282
Bechler, Z., ed. Contemporary Newtonian
  Research.
  B.S. Eastwood, 173(ECS):Fall85-103
Bechtel, G. and J-C. Carrière. Diction-
  naire de la bêtise.
  W.D. Redfern, 149(CLS):Summer85-277
Beck, B. L'Enfant chat.
  R. Linkhorn, 207(FR):Oct85-146
Beck, C.L. and A.W. Burks, eds. Aspects
  of Meiji Modernization.
  R.F. Hackett, 293(JASt):Feb85-392
Beck, J.M. Joseph Howe.* (Vols 1 and 2)
  K.G. Pryke, 529(QQ):Summer85-385
Beck, K. Cultivating the Wasteland.
  M. Mayer, 476:Summer84-88
Beck, L.W. - see Kant, I.
Becker, A. Claudel et saint Augustin, une
  parenté spirituelle.
  M. Adam, 542:Jul-Sep85-311

26

Becker, C. Émile Zola, "Germinal."
Y. Chevrel, 535(RHL):May/Jun85-510
Becker, C.J., ed. Studies in Northern Coinages of the Eleventh Century.
J-P. Callu, 555:Vol59fasc1-171
Becker, E. When the War was Over.
E. MacFarquhar, 441:26Oct86-22
Becker, H-J. Die frühe Nietzsche-Rezeption in Japan (1893-1903).
J.C. Maraldo, 407(MN):Autumn85-369
Becker, J. Traditional Music in Modern Java.
W. Howard, 318(JAOS):Apr-Jun84-346
Becker, J-J. The Great War and the French People.
G. Best, 617(TLS):3Oct86-1109
Becker, L.C. and K. Kipnis, eds. Property.
H.K., 185:Jan86-437
von Becker, P. Der überraschte Voyeur.
D. Bentz, 193(ELit):Spring-Summer85-214
Becker, R.H. - see Wagner, H.R. and C.L. Camp
Becker, T. Die Bürgschaft.
P. Graves, 617(TLS):16May86-537
Beckett, D. Stephenson's Britain.
A.J. Peacock, 637(VS):Spring86-495
Beckett, J.V. The Aristocracy in England 1660-1914.
D. Cannadine, 617(TLS):19Dec86-1431
Beckett, L. Richard Wagner: "Parsifal."
J.B., 412:May84-146
Beckett, S. Collected Poems 1930-1978.
P. Collier, 402(MLR):Apr85-478
Beckett, S. The Complete Dramatic Works.
A. Jenkins, 617(TLS):14Nov86-1281
Beckett, S. Disjecta.* (R. Cohn, ed)
M.G. Rose, 130:Winter85/86-380
W.B. Worthen, 615(TJ):Dec85-514
Bečková, M. Jan Amos Komenský a Polsko.
A. Měšťan, 688(ZSP):Band45Heft1-221
Bédard, E. and J. Maurais, eds. La Norme linguistique.*
C.A. Demharter, 207(FR):Dec85-326
M. Heller, 355(LSoc):Jun85-266
T.R. Wooldridge, 627(UTQ):Summer85-487
Bédard, E. and D. Monnier. Conscience linguistique des jeunes Québécois.
M. Heller, 355(LSoc):Jun85-267
Bedient, C. In the Heart's Last Kingdom.
L. Casper, 651(WHR):Winter85-366
G. Cologne-Brookes, 617(TLS):5Sep86-960
Bedini, S.A. Thomas Jefferson and His Copying Machines.
G. James, 324:Oct86-766
R.M. Jellison, 656(WMQ):Jul85-423
Bedriomo, É. Proust, Wagner et la coïncidence des arts.
G. Jacques, 356(LR):Aug85-234
Bedser, A., with A. Bannister. Twin Ambitions.
A. Ross, 617(TLS):11Jul86-770
Beechcroft, W. Chain of Vengeance.
N. Callendar, 441:22Jun86-25
Beehler, B.M., T.K. Pratt and D.A. Zimmerman. Birds of New Guinea.
R.W. Ashford, 617(TLS):5Dec86-1385
Beeman, R.B. The Evolution of the Southern Backcountry.
M.L. Nicholls, 656(WMQ):Jul85-424
Beer, F. - see Austen, J. and C. Brontë

Beer, G. Darwin's Plots.*
R. Ashton, 541(RES):Aug85-442
P. Conradi, 148:Spring85-25
R.G. Hampson, 175:Autumn85-259
R. Keefe, 158:Sep85-106
J.S., 636(VP):Summer85-220
A. Welsh, 637(VS):Summer85-677
Beer, G. and M. Harris - see Meredith, G.
Beer, J., ed. "A Passage to India."
L. Mackinnon, 617(TLS):7Mar86-258
Beer, J. Summer Tales.
H. Wagener, 133:Band18Heft1-85
Beer, L.W. Freedom of Expression in Japan.*
Haruhara Akihiko, 285(JapQ):Apr-Jun85-209
Beer, P. and F. Godwin. Wessex.
D.A.N. Jones, 362:6Mar86-25
Beer, R. The Blind Corral.
C. Salzberg, 441:22Jun86-26
442(NY):7Jul86-82
Beer, T. Tarka Country.
J.W. Blench, 161(DUJ):Jun84-312
Beeston, A.F.L., ed and trans. The Espistle on Singing Girls of Jāḥiẓ.
I.J. Boullata, 318(JAOS):Apr-Jun84-382
Beeston, A.F.L. Sabaic Grammar.
P. Swiggers, 350:Jun86-469
Beeston, A.F.L. and others, eds. Arabic Literature to the End of the Umayyad Period.
J. Mattock, 294:Vol 16-150
Beetham, D. Marxists in Face of Fascism.
T. Deutscher, 208(FS):Jul85-367
"Beethoven-Jahrbuch." (Vol 10) (M. Staehelin, ed)
R. Bockholdt, 537:Vol71No1/2-204
Beetles, C. S.R. Badmin and the English Landscape.
A. Whittick, 324:May86-419
Beffroy de Reigny, L-A. Nicodème dans la lune ou La Révolution pacifique, folie en prose en trois actes. (M. Sajous, ed)
M. Cook, 402(MLR):Apr85-467
W. Wrage, 207(FR):Dec85-298
Bégin, L. and others. Pragmatisme et pensée contemporaine.
Y. Gauthier, 154:Summer85-357
Béhague, G., ed. Performance Practice.
H. Burnett, 414:Vol71No3-381
M. Herndon, 187:Spring/Summer86-346
Behar, R. Santa Maria del Monte.
J.S. Amelang, 441:28Sep86-27
Behler, E. Die Zeitschriften der Brüder Schlegel.
F. Jolles, 83:Spring85-117
Behlmer, G. Child Abuse and Moral Reform in England, 1870-1908.
J.A. Banks, 637(VS):Winter85-310
Behlmer, R., ed. Inside Warner Bros. (1935-1951).*
K. Brownlow, 617(TLS):23May86-551
P. Craig, 18:Oct85-79
Behnke, D.A. Religious Issues in Nineteenth Century Feminism.
B. Todd, 106:Fall85-329
Behr, C. T.S. Eliot.
R.Z. Temple, 536(Rev):Vol7-329
Behrendt, S.C. The Moment of Explosion.*
K. Kroeber, 88:Fall85-75
D.M. Welch, 481(PQ):Summer85-424

Bei Dao. Notes from the City of the Sun.
(B.S. McDougall, ed and trans)
J.C. Kinkley, 293(JASt):May85-596
Beichman, A. Herman Wouk.
J. Braham, 395(MFS):Winter85-740
Beicken, P., ed. Franz Kafka: Die Verwand-
lung.
H. Reiss, 133:Band18Heft1-94
Beidler, P.D. American Literature and the
Experience of Vietnam.*
G.F. Manning, 106:Summer85-237
G.O. Taylor, 27(AL):Dec85-695
Beier, A.L. Masterless Men.
R. Mayne, 176:Jul/Aug86-50
K. Wrightson, 617(TLS):11Apr86-380
Beier, A.L. and R. Finlay, eds. London
1500-1700.
R. Mayne, 176:Jul/Aug86-49
Beierwaltes, W. - see Schelling, F.W.J.
Beiner, R. Political Judgment.*
R. Marlin, 529(QQ):Autumn85-634
Beinhart, L. No One Rides For Free.
N. Callendar, 441:18May86-38
Beissel, H. Season of Blood.
A. Morton, 526:Autumn85-94
"Beiträge zur Geschichte der Ölskizze vom
16. bis zum 18. Jahrhundert.
E. Young, 39:Jul85-79
Beja, M., S.E. Gontarski and P. Astier,
eds. Samuel Beckett.*
K. Worth, 541(RES):Nov85-599
Bekes, P. and M. Bielefeld. Peter Rühm-
korf.
A. Phelan, 402(MLR):Oct85-1002
Bekkering, H. Orpheus en Euridice in
Vlaanderen.
P.F. Schmitz, 204(FdL):Mar85-77
Belaief, L. Toward a Whiteheadian Ethics.
J.W.D., 185:Apr86-685
G.W. Stroh, 619:Summer85-442
Beland, M. Chansons de voyageurs, cour-
eurs de bois et forestiers.
B. Cavanagh, 627(UTQ):Summer85-515
Béland, P. and I. Cronin. Money.
P. O'Toole, 441:26Oct86-39
Belchem, J. "Orator" Hunt.
W. Thomas, 617(TLS):7Mar86-238
de' Beldomandi, P. Contrapunctus. (J.
Herlinger, ed)
E.A. Lippman, 143:Issue37/38-205
de' Beldomandi, P. Prosdocimo de' Beldo-
mandi Contrapunctus/Counterpoint. (J.
Herlinger, ed and trans)
M. Huglo, 537:Vol171No1/2-198
Belenky, M.F. and others. Women's Ways of
Knowing.
S. Neustadtl, 441:5Oct86-38
Belgrave, R. and M. Cornell, eds. Energy
Self-Sufficiency for the UK?
P. McDonald, 617(TLS):25Jul86-820
Běličová, H. Modální báze jednoduché
věty a souvětí (K porovnávací syntaxi
češtiny a ruštiny).
D. Short, 575(SEER):Oct85-576
Lady Bell. At the Works.*
S.G. Bell, 637(VS):Summer86-627
Bell, A.O., with A. McNeillie - see Woolf,
V.
Bell, C.H. Olivier Messiaen.
A.W., 412:Aug/Nov84-299
Bell, D. Frege's Theory of Judgement.*
H. Jackson, 316:Mar85-254
J.M. Jiménez, 160:Apr85-181

Bell, D. Spinoza in Germany from 1670 to
the Age of Goethe.
W. Bartuschat, 687:Jul-Sep85-473
K.F. Hilliard, 83:Spring85-118
H.B. Nisbet, 402(MLR):Apr85-496
W. Schröder, 319:Jul86-410
Bell, D. and L. Thurow. The Deficits.
C. Johnson, 617(TLS):16May86-523
J.H. Makin, 441:17Aug86-15
J. Tobin, 453(NYRB):25Sep86-43
Bell, D.G. Early Loyalist Saint John.
E. Jones, 298:Fall85-149
Bell, I.A. Defoe's Fiction.
J. Richetti, 617(TLS):18Apr86-428
Bell, I.F.A. Critic as a Scientist.*
P. Makin, 677(YES):Vol 15-347
Bell, I.F.A., ed. Henry James.*
J.A. Ward, 395(MFS):Winter85-723
Bell, I.F.A., ed. Ezra Pound.
W. Harmon, 577(SHR):Spring85-181
S. Moore, 70:Mar/Apr85-122
D. Seed, 447(N&Q):Jun84-286
A. Woodward, 541(RES):May85-297
Bell, J. Policy Arguments in Judicial
Decisions.
A.S., 185:Oct85-224
Bell, J. and L. Choyce, eds. Visions from
the Edge.
D. Ketterer, 561(SFS):Mar85-91
Bell, M. Drawn by Stones, by Earth, by
Things that Have Been in the Fire.*
A. Dillon, 50(ArQ):Winter85-377
R. Jackson, 502(PrS):Winter85-109
P. Stitt, 219(GaR):Spring85-188
Bell, M. Old Snow Just Melting.
W.S. Di Piero, 569(SR):Winter85-140
R. McDowell, 249(HudR):Autumn85-511
Bell, M. The Sentiment of Reality.*
W.J. Palmer, 395(MFS):Summer85-333
M. Price, 402(MLR):Apr85-403
Bell, M. The Turkey Shoot.
D. Cooper, 441:6Apr86-23
Bell, M. - see Hawthorne, N.
Bell, M.D. The Development of American
Romance.*
H-W. Schaller, 38:Band103Heft1/2-251
E. Wagenknecht, 677(YES):Vol 15-315
Bell, M.S. Straight Cut.
E. Sirkin, 441:12Oct86-13
442(NY):22Sep86-117
Bell, R.M. Holy Anorexia.
N. Cohn, 453(NYRB):30Jan86-3
M. Lefkowitz, 617(TLS):25Apr86-438
Bell, S.H. A Man Flourishing.
S. Altinel, 617(TLS):26Dec86-1456
Bell, S.M. Nathalie Sarraute.*
E. Smyth, 535(RHL):May/Jun85-520
Bell, V.M. Robert Lowell.
R. Pooley, 677(YES):Vol 15-364
R. Tillinghast, 569(SR):Winter85-viii
Bellah, R.N. and others. Habits of the
Heart.*
N. Bliven, 442(NY):21Apr86-119
R.E. Goodin, 185:Jan86-431
Bellamy, E. Looking Backward.
K.M. Roemer, 26(ALR):Spring/Autumn85-
258
Bellamy, G. The Nudists.
C. Hawtree, 617(TLS):14Feb86-162
Bellamy, J.D., ed. American Poetry
Observed.
M. Cornis-Pop, 455:Mar85-68

Benito Doménech, F. Pinturas y pintores
en el Real Colegio de Corpus Christi.
E.H., 90:Apr85-244
F. Marías, 48:Apr-Jun85-164
Benjamin, A. - see Mandela, W.
Benjamin, R. and S.L. Elkin, eds. The
Democratic State.
J.K., 185:Jul86-896
Benjamin, W. Origine du drame baroque
allemand.
T. Cordellier, 450(NRF):Dec85-88
R. Rochlitz, 98:Dec85-1190
Benko, S. Pagan Rome and the Early Chris-
tians.*
G.P. Corrington, 124:May-Jun86-348
Benn, G. Briefe. (Vols 1 and 2 ed by H.
Steinhagen and J. Schröder, Vol 3 ed by
A.C. Fehn)
J.D. Barlow, 406:Winter85-500
Benn, G. Sämtliche Werke. (Gedichte 1
and 2) (G. Schuster, ed)
M. Hofmann, 617(TLS):26Sep86-1055
Benn, S.I. and G.F. Gaus, eds. Public and
Private in Social Life.
L.B. Green, 185:Apr86-647
Bennassar, B. La España del Siglo de Oro.
B.M. Damiani, 240(HR):Winter85-97
Bennett, B.A. and D.G. Wilkins. Donatello.
B. Boucher, 39:Jan85-67
D.F. Zervas, 90:Dec85-904
Bennett, B.T. - see Shelley, M.W.
Bennett, J. A Study of Spinoza's Ethics.*
A. Collier, 518:Oct85-212
Bennett, J.R. Bibliography of Stylistics
and Related Criticism, 1967-1983.
K. Hodges, 349:Fall85-399
Bennett, P.R. - see "A Kikuyu Market
Literature"
Bennett, W.J. To Reclaim a Legacy.
A. Hacker, 453(NYRB):13Feb86-35
Benni, S. Terra!
E. Korn, 617(TLS):26Sep86-1057
Bennigsen, A. and S.E. Wimbush. Mystics
and Commissars.
J. Baldick, 617(TLS):26Sep86-1073
Bennington, G. Sententiousness and the
Novel.
P. France, 617(TLS):4Apr86-366
Bennion, E. Antique Dental Instruments.
C. Lawrence, 617(TLS):26Dec86-1445
Bennis, H. and F. Beukema, eds. Lin-
guistics in the Netherlands 1985.
J. Hoeksema, 350:Sep86-705
Bennis, H. and T. Hoekstra. De Syntaxis
Van Het Nederlands.
A. Evers, 204(FdL):Mar85-72
Bennis, H. and W.U.S. Lessen Kloeke, eds.
Linguistics in the Netherlands.
J. van Voorst, 320(CJL):Spring85-113
de Benoist, A. - see Renan, E.
Benrekassa, G. Le Concentrique et l'excen-
trique.*
D. Brewer, 188(ECr):Fall85-97
Benrekassa, G. La Politique et sa mém-
oire.*
D. Brewer, 188(ECr):Fall85-97
M. Waddicor, 535(RHL):Mar/Apr85-300
Benser, C.C. Egon Wellesz (1885-1974).
W. Mellers, 617(TLS):7Mar86-244
Benson, E. J.M. Synge.*
A.P. Hinchliffe, 148:Spring85-87
D. Krause, 397(MD):Mar85-182

Benson, J.J. The True Adventures of John
Steinbeck, Writer.*
J.R. Bryer, 27(AL):Oct85-513
T. Hayashi, 577(SHR):Fall85-380
T. Ludington, 534(RALS):Spring83-105
J.J. Waldmeir, 115:Summer84-252
Benson, M. Nelson Mandela.
J.M. Coetzee, 453(NYRB):8May86-3
S.J. Ungar, 441:27Apr86-17
Benson, M. - see Mandela, W.
Benson, R. German Expressionist Drama.*
D. Fogg, 610:Spring85-82
Benson, R.L., G. Constable and C.D. Lanham,
eds. Renaissance and Renewal in the
Twelfth Century.
D.H. Green, 402(MLR):Jul85-678
Benson, R.M. Once Upon a Death.
C. Hardesty, 455:Sep85-70
Benstock, B., ed. Critical Essays on
James Joyce.
R. Battaglia, 329(JJQ):Spring86-376
Benstock, B. James Joyce.
M. Mortimer, 617(TLS):5Sep86-980
L. Orr, 329(JJQ):Summer86-507
van Benthem, J.F.A.K. The Logic of Time.
D. Christie, 543:Jun85-882
Bentley, G.E. The Profession of Player in
Shakespeare's Time 1590-1642.
R.A. Foakes, 551(RenQ):Autumn85-579
A. Gurr, 405(MP):May86-428
T. Helton, 568(SCN):Fall85-30
E.J. Jensen, 130:Winter85/86-363
639(VQR):Winter85-20
Bentley, G.E., Jr. and others. Essays on
the Blake Followers.
R. Lister, 88:Fall85-80
Bentley, I. and D. Gržan-Butina, eds.
Jože Plečnik.
R.G. Dyck, 505:Oct85-147
Bentley, J. Restless Bones.
J. McManners, 617(TLS):3Jan86-8
Bentley, J.H. Humanists and Holy Writ.*
A. Grafton, 589:Apr85-383
R.F. O'Toole, 377:Nov84-175
R.D. Sider, 551(RenQ):Spring85-142
Bentley, M. Politics Without Democracy.
A. Hawkins, 637(VS):Summer86-654
Bentley, U. Private Accounts.
J. Stephen, 617(TLS):100ct86-1131
Benton, T. The Rise and Fall of Struc-
tural Marxism.
T. Eagleton, 208(FS):Apr85-239
Benveniste, M. Conflicts and Contradic-
tions.
F. Ajami, 441:2Mar86-1
A. Margalit, 453(NYRB):23Oct86-52
Benvenuti, A.T. and M.P. Mussini Sacchi -
see under Tissoni Benvenuti, A. and M.P.
Mussini Sacchi
Benvenuto, B. and R. Kennedy. The Works
of Jacques Lacan.
E. Wright, 617(TLS):15Aug86-880
Benvenuto, R. Emily Brontë.
B.T. Gates, 637(VS):Autumn84-194
Benzie, W. Dr. F.J. Furnivall.*
H. Aarsleff, 637(VS):Autumn85-175
C.D. Benson, 589:Oct85-1043
G. Wing, 178:Jun85-256
Benziman, U. Sharon.
D.K. Shipler, 441:5Jan86-11
"Beowulf." (M. Osborn, trans)
N. Jacobs, 184(EIC):Jul85-260
639(VQR):Winter85-18

"Beowulf." (M.J. Swanton, ed and trans)
  H. Peters, 72:Band222Heft2-384
Berad, C. and others, eds. Goethe Proceedings.
  H. Reiss, 133:Band18Heft3-272
de Berceo, G. Milagros de Nuestra Señora. (M. Gerli, ed)
  J.E. Ackerman, 304(JHP):Fall85-71
de Berceo, G. Obras completas. (Vol 5) (B. Dutton, ed)
  I. Macpherson, 86(BHS):Apr85-194
Bercovitch, S., ed. Reconstructing American Literary History.
  A. Wald, 441:28Sep86-35
Bercovitch, S. and M. Jehlen, eds. Ideology and Classic American Literature.
  C. Baldick, 617(TLS):14Nov86-1273
Bercuson, D.J., R. Bothwell and J.L. Granatstein. The Great Brain Robbery.*
  B. Neatby, 298:Spring85-153
  R.R. Pierson, 298:Spring85-154
Berend, I.T. and G. Ranki. The Hungarian Economy in the Twentieth Century.
  A. Nove, 617(TLS):10Jan86-31
Berenson, M. Mary Berenson, A Self-Portrait from Her Diaries and Letters.* (B. Strachey and J. Samuels, eds)
  V.H. Winner, 639(VQR):Summer85-559
Beres, L.R. Mimicking Sisyphus.
  S.L., 185:Jan86-460
Beres, L.R. Reason and Realpolitik.
  M.T., 185:Jan86-460
Beres, L.R., ed. Security or Armageddon.
  A.J. Pierre, 441:24Aug86-10
Beresford, M.W. Time and Place.
  D.M. Palliser, 617(TLS):1Aug86-846
Berg, B.J. The Crisis of the Working Mother.
  A.R. Hochschild, 441:11May86-15
Berg, J. and others. Sozialgeschichte der deutschen Literatur von 1918 bis zur Gegenwart.*
  J. Rosellini, 406:Fall85-369
van den Berg, K. Playhouse and Cosmos.
  K. Brown, 617(TLS):22Aug86-917
Berg, K.W. and G. Åhmansson, eds. Mothers — Saviours — Peacemakers.
  R.S. ten Cate, 562(Scan):Nov85-235
  B. Lide, 563(SS):Spring85-213
Berg, M. The Age of Manufactures 1700-1820.*
  R. Mayne, 176:Jul/Aug86-50
Berg, W.J., M. Grimaud and G. Moskos. Saint/Oedipus.*
  L. Hill, 402(MLR):Jan85-172
Bergala, A. Initiation à la sémiologie du récit en images.
  S. Fischer, 207(FR):Oct85-180
Berger, A. Das Bad in der byzantinischen Zeit.
  D.D. Abrahamse, 589:Jan85-119
Berger, B. and P.L. The War Over the Family.
  J. Patrick, 396(ModA):Winter85-84
Berger, C. Der Autor und sein Held.
  W. Jehser, 654(WB):1/1985-156
Berger, C. Forms of Farewell.
  A. Filreis, 432(NEQ):Dec85-631
  J.G. Kronick, 705:Fall85-124
  295(JML):Nov85-557
Berger, C. Science, God, and Nature in Victorian Canada.*
  P.B. Waite, 529(QQ):Spring85-183

Berger, F.R. Happiness, Justice and Freedom.*
  J. Skorupski, 518:Oct85-193
Berger, H., A. Dhamotharan and D.B. Kapp – see "Aruṇantis Śivajñānasiddhiyār"
Berger, J. And Our Faces, My Heart, Brief as Photos.*
  R. Buckeye, 532(RCF):Fall85-196
  J. Coleman, 592:Vol 198No1009-53
Berger, J. The Dialect of Holy Island.
  W. Viereck, 685(ZDL):2/1985-248
Berger, J. The Sense of Sight. (L. Spencer, ed)
  D. Kuspit, 62:Jan86-12
  V. Young, 441:23Feb86-23
Berger, P.L. The Capitalist Revolution.
  L.C. Thurow, 441:7Sep86-9
Berger, T. Nowhere.*
  J. Clute, 617(TLS):21Feb86-198
Berger, U. Das Verhängnis oder Die Liebe des Paul Fleming.
  K. Kiesant, 654(WB):1/1985-113
Bergeron, D.M., ed. Pageantry in the Shakespearean Theater.
  I-S. Ewbank, 617(TLS):25Apr86-451
  639(VQR):Autumn85-122
Bergeron, D.H. and S. Lindenbaum, eds. Research Opportunities in Renaissance Drama, XXVI (1983).
  S.J. Steen, 568(SCN):Fall85-37
Berges, W. and H.J. Rieckenberg. Die älteren Hildesheimer Inschriften bis zum Tode Bischof Hezilos (†1079).
  M.E. Stoller, 589:Apr85-470
Bergez, D. Éluard ou le rayonnement de l'être.
  M-C. Dumas, 535(RHL):Jul/Aug85-697
Berginz-Plank, G. Literaturrezeption in einer Kleinstadt.*
  H.L. Cafferty, 221(GQ):Winter85-150
Bergland, R. The Fabric of Mind.
  S.A. Green, 441:23Nov86-19
Bergmann, B.R. The Economic Emergence of Women.
  W. Kaminer, 441:26Oct86-43
Bergmann, R., P. Pauly and M. Schlaefer. Einführung in die deutsche Sprachwissenschaft.*
  W. Sanders, 685(ZDL):3/1985-359
Bergner, H., ed. Lyrik des Mittelalters. (Pts 1 and 2)
  H. Kratz, 133:Band18Heft2-163
  H. Sievert, 654(WB):12/1985-2102
  K. Trimborn, 52:Band20Heft2-203
Bergner, H. – see Chaucer, G.
Bergner, J.T. The Rise of Formalism in Social Science.
  D. Jonsson, 488:Mar85-116
Bergquist, M.F. Ibero-Romance Philology.
  E. Blasco Ferrer, 379(MedR):Apr85-151
Bergr Sokkason. Helgastaðabók: Nikulás saga. (S. Jónsdóttir, S. Karlsson and S. Tómasson, eds)
  M.E. Kalinke, 301(JEGP):Oct85-587
Bergreen, L. James Agee.*
  B. Maine, 27(AL):May85-348
  R. Weber, 639(VQR):Spring85-360
  295(JML):Nov85-441
Bergson, A. and H.S. Levine, eds. The Soviet Economy.
  G. Grossman, 550(RusR):Jan85-81
  C.W. Lawson, 575(SEER):Jan85-150

31

Beringer, R.E. and others. Why the South
Lost the Civil War.
  C.V. Woodward, 453(NYRB):17Jul86-3
Berio, L., with R. Delmonte and B. András
Varga. Luciano Berio: Two Interviews.*
(D. Osmond-Smith, ed and trans)
  M. Smith, 607:Jun85-42
Berka, K. and L. Kreiser. Logik-Texte.
  J. Dölling, 682(ZPSK):Band38Heft4-443
Berkeley, G. Critical and Interpretive
Essays. (C. Turbayne, ed)
  D. Berlioz-Letellier, 540(RIPh):Vol39
  fasc3-270
  L. Déchery, 192(EP):Oct-Dec85-551
Berkhout, C.T. and M.M. Gatch, eds.
Anglo-Saxon Scholarship: the First Three
Centuries.*
  C. Sisam, 541(RES):May85-247
Berkoff, S. West, Lunch, Harry's Christ-
mas.
  D. Devlin, 157:No157-50
Berkow, I. Red.
  W. Sheed, 441:8Jun86-1
Berkowitz, D.S. - see Morison, R.
Berkowitz, G.M. Sir John Vanbrugh and the
End of Restoration Comedy.*
  P. Holland, 402(MLR):Apr85-422
Berkson, C. Elephanta: The Cave of Shiva.*
(Text by W.D. O'Flaherty, G. Michell and
C. Berkson)
  F.M. Asher, 293(JASt):Nov84-233
Berkvam, D.D. Enfance et maternité dans
la littérature française des XIIe et
XIIIe siècles.*
  T.D. Hemming, 208(FS):Apr85-182
Berkvam, M.L., with P.L. Smith - see
Hennin, P.M.
Berlanstein, L.R. The Working People of
Paris, 1871-1914.*
  639(VQR):Autumn85-115
Berlász, J., ed. Die Bibliothek Dern-
schwam.
  H.D. Gebauer, 354:Dec85-371
Berle, W. Heinrich Mann und die Weimarer
Republik.*
  M.S. Fries, 221(GQ):Spring85-298
Berlin, I. and others, eds. Freedom.
(Ser 1, Vol 1)
  L.F. Litwack, 441:14Sep86-34
  442(NY):10Feb86-113
Berlin, I. and R. Hoffman, eds. Slavery
and Freedom in the Age of the American
Revolution.*
  M. Drimmer, 656(WMQ):Jan85-144
Berlin, N. Eugene O'Neill.*
  A.P. Hinchliffe, 148:Spring85-87
Berlinger, J. Das zeitgenössische
deutsche Dialektgedicht.
  C.J. Wickham, 221(GQ):Fall85-642
Berlinger, R. - see Seidl, H.
Berlinger, R. and W. Schräder - see Seidl,
H.
Berlinski, D. Black Mischief.
  J. Schmidt, 441:27Apr86-23
Berman, A.J. - see Cook, J.
Berman, E. In Africa With Schweitzer.
  S.J. Kra, 441:14Dec86-31
Berman, J. The Talking Cure.
  D. Gunn, 617(TLS):30May86-595
Berman, R. Culture and Politics.
  C. Mitze, 476:Fall84-97

Bermejo Martínez, E. La pintura de los
primitivos flamencos en España.* (Vol
2)
  L.C., 90:Apr85-244
Bernabé, I.V. and L. Hernández Guardiola -
see Arqués Jover, A.
Bernal Leongómez, J. Elementos de gramá-
tica generativa.
  M.M. Azevedo, 545(RPh):Nov84-237
Bernales Ballestero, J. - see Sánchez
Gordillo, A.A.
Bernanos, G. Nouvelle Histoire de Mou-
chette. (B. Stefanson, ed)
  J.C. Whitehouse, 208(FS):Apr85-230
Bernard, I. - see de La Chaussée, P.C.N.
Bernard, J. Low Life.
  B. Bainbridge, 617(TLS):26Dec86-1453
Bernard, M. La Mort de la bien-aimée.
  F. Trémolières, 450(NRF):Feb85-82
Bernardi, J. - see St. Gregory of Nazian-
zus
Bernardin de Saint-Pierre, J.H. Paul et
Virginie. (E. Guitton, ed)
  D.G. Charlton, 208(FS):Oct85-479
  J. Proust, 547(RF):Band97Heft4-476
  P. Stewart, 207(FR):Apr86-785
Bernardini, P.A. Mito e attualità nelle
odi di Pindaro.
  C. Carey, 123:Vol35No2-381
  M.M. Willcock, 303(JoHS):Vol 105-182
Bernardo, A.S. and A.L. Pellegrini, eds.
Dante, Petrarch, Boccaccio.
  C.G., 278(IS):Vol40-109
Bernd, C.A. and others, eds. Goethe Pro-
ceedings.
  A. Hoelzel, 400(MLN):Apr85-667
  H.B. Nisbet, 402(MLR):Jul85-756
Berndt, R. A History of the English Lan-
guage.
  H. Penzl, 300:Apr85-71
Berner, R.C. Archival Theory and Practice
in the United States.
  S.C. Morton, 87(BB):Mar85-44
Bernet, C. Le Vocabulaire des tragédies
de Jean Racine.*
  H.T. Barnwell, 402(MLR):Apr85-715
  D. Fourny, 546(RR):Mar85-216
  R. Jolivet, 209(FM):Oct85-250
  N. Musso, 553(RLiR):Jul-Dec85-490
Bernhard, T. Auslöschung.
  S. Plaice, 617(TLS):30ct86-1088
Bernhard, T. Gathering Evidence.
  W. Abish, 441:16Feb86-12
  G. Steiner, 442(NY):21Jul86-92
Bernhard, T. Le Neveu de Wittgenstein.
  L. Kovacs, 450(NRF):May85-106
Bernheimer, C. Flaubert and Kafka.*
  D. Aynesworth, 345(KRQ):Vol32No1-109
  D. Barnouw, 221(GQ):Spring85-257
  J. Bem, 535(RHL):Sep/Oct85-893
  D. Faber, 549(RLC):Jul-Sep85-360
  A. Green, 208(FS):Apr85-222
  N. Schor, 546(RR):Mar85-218
  R. Sieburth, 131(CL):Summer85-283
Bernheimer, C. and C. Kahane, eds. In
Dora's Case.
  K. Mele, 367(L&P):Vol32No4-64
Bernier, O. Secrets of Marie Antoinette.
  F. Simon, 441:26Jan86-24
Bernikow, L. Alone in America.
  B. Pace, 441:20Jul86-19
Bernstein, B. Plane Crazy.
  T. Ferrell, 441:9Mar86-25

Bernstein, E.  German Humanism.
  F.L. Borchardt, 221(GQ):Spring85-274
Bernstein, G.L.  Haruko's World.*
  L.L. Cornell, 293(JASt):Nov84-200
Bernstein, J.M.  The Philosophy of the
  Novel.
  A. Easthope, 366:Spring85-130
  J.A. Varsava, 395(MFS):Summer85-454
Bernstein, R.J.  Beyond Objectivism and
  Relativism.*
  M. Adam, 542:Oct-Dec85-567
  C.W. Gowans, 258:Jun85-207
  J. Habermas, 384:Sep/Oct85-904
  R. Hanna, 543:Sep84-109
  C. Larmore, 482(PhR):Oct85-577
  J. Llewelyn, 518:Apr85-113
  B. Sullivan, 142:Summer85-85
Béroalde de Verville.  Le Moyen de par-
  venir.  (H. Moreau and A. Tournon, eds)
  N. Kenny, 208(FS):Apr85-196
  J.L. Pallister, 475:Vol 12No23-726
Berquet, G. and J-P. Collinet - see Con-
  rart, V.
Berrêdo Carneiro, P.E. and P. Arbousse-
  Bastide - see Comte, A.
Berrêdo Carneiro, P.E. and P. Arnaud - see
  Comte, A.
Berreman, G.D.  The Politics of Truth.
  W.L. Rowe, 293(JASt):Nov84-222
Berrendonner, A.  L'Eternel Grammairien.
  N. Gueunier, 209(FM):Apr85-128
  F. Kerleroux, 355(LSoc):Jun85-242
Berres, T.  Die Entstehung der Aeneis.
  W. Moskalew, 24:Winter85-527
Berriot, F. - see Bodin, J.
Berruer, P.  Georges Brassens: "La Marguer-
  ite et le chrysanthème."
  J. Abrate, 207(FR):Mar86-631
Berruer, P.  Jacques Brel va bien.
  J. Abrate, 207(FR):Mar86-633
Berry, C.J.  Hume, Hegel and Human Nature.
  R.H. Popkin, 543:Mar85-619
Berry, D.  The Creative Vision of Guil-
  laume Apollinaire.*
  M. Cranston, 345(KRQ):Vol32No1-104
  H. Merkl, 72:Band222Heft2-480
Berry, E.  Shakespeare's Comic Rites.*
  D. Birch, 610:Autumn85-235
Berry, J.  Chain of Days.
  S. O'Brien, 493:Aug85-66
  S. Rae, 364:Aug-Sep85-129
  S. Romer, 617(TLS):20Jun86-677
Berry, J., ed.  News from Babylon.*
  M. Horovitz, 565:Autumn85-59
Berry, J., J. Foose and T. Jones.  Up From
  the Cradle of Jazz.
  H. Mandel, 441:14Dec86-24
Berry, J.M.  The Interest Group Society.
  R.E.G., 185:Apr86-667
Berry, M.E.  Hideyoshi.*
  H. Ooms, 318(JAOS):Apr-Jun84-351
Berry, M.F.  Why ERA Failed.
  K. Luker, 441:19Oct86-7
Berry, P. and A. Bishop - see Brittain, V.
  and W. Holtby
Berry, R.  Shakespeare and the Awareness
  of the Audience.*
  R. Kift, 157:No157-51
Berry, R.J.  The Natural History of Orkney.
  J. Buxton, 617(TLS):21Mar86-314

Berry, W.  Collected Poems: 1957-1982.*
  R. McDowell, 249(HudR):Winter86-681
  D. Smith, 491:Oct85-40
  P. Stitt, 219(GaR):Fall85-635
Berry, W.  Structural Functions in Music.
  J.R., 412:May83-147
Berry, W.  The Wild Birds.
  H.F. Mosher, 441:13Apr86-22
Bers, V.  Greek Poetic Syntax in the Clas-
  sical Age.*
  A.C. Moorhouse, 123:Vol35No1-94
Bersani, L.  The Death of Stéphane Mal-
  larmé.
  J.E. Jackson, 535(RHL):Jan/Feb85-121
Berschin, W.  Grieschisch-lateinisches Mit-
  telalter von Hieronymus zu Nikolaus von
  Kues.*
  P. Dronke, 545(RPh):May85-531
Berschin, W., ed and trans.  Vitae Sanctae
  Wiboradae.
  K. Kunze, 684(ZDA):Band114Heft4-108
Bersier, G.  Wunschbild und Wirklichkeit.
  H. Rowland, 406:Fall85-358
Bertau, K.  Über Literaturgeschichte.
  W.H. Jackson, 402(MLR):Oct85-975
Bertau, K.  Wolfram von Eschenbach.
  W.H. Jackson, 402(MLR):Oct85-975
  W. McConnell, 221(GQ):Summer85-448
Berthiaume, G.  Les rôles du "mâgeiros."*
  F.I. Zeitlin, 487:Autumn85-284
Berthier, P.  Stendhal et la Sainte
  Famille.*
  G. May, 207(FR):Dec85-299
  G. Strickland, 208(FS):Jan85-84
Berthoff, A.E.  Reclaiming the Imagination.
  J.F. Slevin, 128(CE):Fall85-514
Berthoff, W.  The Ferment of Realism.*
  A.W. Bellringer, 402(MLR):Oct85-918
Berthold, R.M.  Rhodes in the Hellenistic
  Age.*
  L. Migeotte, 487:Winter85-400
  E.E. Rice, 123:Vol35No2-320
Berthold von Moosburg.  Expositio super
  Elementationem theologicam Procli.  (M.R.
  Pagnoni-Sturlese and L. Sturlese, eds)
  H. Boese, 684(ZDA):Band114Heft4-133
Bertholf, R.J. - see Niedecker, L.
Bertholf, R.J. and A.S. Levitt, eds.  Wil-
  liam Blake and the Moderns.
  J. Williams, 366:Spring85-142
Bertier, J. and others - see Plotinus
Bertier, P., ed.  Stendhal: l'écrivain, la
  société et le pouvoir.
  L. Le Guillou, 535(RHL):Sep/Oct85-883
Bertolucci, A.  La camera da letto.
  F. Donini, 617(TLS):15Aug86-893
Berton, P.  The Promised Land.
  J.R. Miller, 298:Fall85-156
  G.W., 102(CanL):Spring85-175
Bertram, P.  White Spaces in Shakespeare.*
  E.A.J. Honigmann, 677(YES):Vol 15-280
Bertran de Born.  The Poems of the Trouba-
  dour Bertran de Born.  (W.D. Paden, T.
  Sankovitch and P.H. Stäblein, eds)
  D.D.R. Owen, 617(TLS):29Aug86-950
Bertrand de Muñoz, M.  La Guerra Civil
  española en la novela.
  M. Lentzen, 547(RF):Band97Heft2/3-332
  J-L. Marfany, 86(BHS):Oct85-401
Bertsch, K.A. and L.S. Shaw.  The Nuclear
  Weapons Industry.
  A.C., 185:Jan86-462

Besch, W., O. Reichmann and S. Sonderegger, eds. Sprachgeschichte. (Vol 1)
M. Görlach, 660(Word):Dec85-266
Beschloss, M.R. Mayday.
N. Bliven, 442(NY):23Jun86-96
A. Dallin, 441:4May86-7
J. Ranelagh, 617(TLS):5Dec86-1367
Besly, E. and R. Bland. The Cunetio Treasure.
C.E. King, 123:Vol35No2-423
Besmer, F.E. Horses, Musicians, and Gods.
C.A. Waterman, 538(RAL):Fall85-457
Besnier, P. - see Rostand, E.
Bessai, D. and D. Kerr, eds. Showing West.*
R. Skene, 108:Fall85-140
Bessière, J., ed. Figures féminines et Roman.
L. Czyba, 535(RHL):Sep/Oct85-906
Bessiere, J. and J. Darras - see Larbaud, V.
Bessis, M. Corpuscules.
C. Debru, 98:Jun-Jul85-731
Best, D. Feeling and Reason in the Arts.
R.A. Smith, 290(JAAC):Spring86-302
Best, G. Humanity in Warfare.
C. Debenedetti, 529(QQ):Spring85-162
Best, N. Tennis and the Masai.
J. Melmoth, 617(TLS):16May86-536
Best, T.W. Reynard the Fox.*
D. Blamires, 402(MLR):Jan85-113
Besterman, T. - see de Voltaire, F.M.A.
Bethea, D.M. Khodasevich.*
L. Nelson, Jr., 569(SR):Spring85-309
G.S. Smith, 575(SEER):Jul85-445
Bethell, L., ed. The Cambridge History of Latin America.* (Vols 1 and 2)
M.H. Sable, 263(RIB):Vol35No4-460
Bethell, N. The Great Betrayal.
M.R.D. Foot, 176:Jun85-63
Betken, W.T., ed. "Romeo and Juliet."
I-S. Ewbank, 617(TLS):25Apr86-451
Bettelheim, B. Freud and Man's Soul.*
(French title: Freud et l'âme humaine.)
A. Reix, 542:Jul-Sep85-353
Bettelheim, B. Surviving the Holocaust.
617(TLS):15Aug86-899
Bettey, J.H. Wessex from AD 1000.
M. Havinden, 617(TLS):4Jul86-741
Bettoni, C. Italian in North Queensland.
E. Radtke, 72:Band222Heft2-440
Betts, W.W. - see Schultz, J.W.
Betz, H.D., ed. The Greek Magical Papyri in Translation. (Vol 1)
P. Parsons, 617(TLS):21Nov86-1316
Betz, P.F. - see Wordsworth, W.
Beugnot, B., ed. Voyages.
T.J. Reiss, 188(ECr):Fall85-99
Bevan, J. - see Walton, I.
Bever, T.G., J.M. Carroll and L.A. Miller, eds. Talking Minds.
R. Whitney, 350:Mar86-226
Beversluis, J. C.S. Lewis and the Search for Rational Religion.
B. Murray, 395(MFS):Winter85-806
295(JML):Nov85-521
Bevington, D. Action is Eloquence.*
J. Farness, 191(ELN):Dec85-72
J.E. Howard, 551(RenQ):Autumn85-576
P.C. McGuire, 615(TJ):Dec85-511
I. Pálffy, 610:Autumn85-237
639(VQR):Winter85-18

Beye, C.R. Epic and Romance in the "Argonautica" of Apollonius.*
J.E.G. Zetzel, 24:Fall85-383
Beyer, C.J. Nature et valeur dans la philosophie de Montesquieu.*
G. Barthel, 547(RF):Band97Heft2/3-318
S. Mason, 83:Spring85-113
M.H. Waddicor, 208(FS):Oct85-472
Beyrau, D. Militär und Gesellschaft im vorrevolutionären Russland.
M. Raeff, 104(CASS):Spring85-65
Beyrie, J. Galdós et son mythe.
N. Clémessy, 92(BH):Jul-Dec84-549
van Beysterveldt, A. Amadís-Esplandián-Calisto.*
J.R. Maier, 238:Dec85-768
Béziau, R. Les Débuts littéraires de Gobineau à Paris.
J. Boissel, 535(RHL):Mar/Apr85-315
Bhabra, H.S. Gestures.
C. Goodrich, 441:29Jun86-24
J. Mellors, 362:12Jun86-29
A. Sattin, 617(TLS):28Mar86-342
Bhakari, S.K. Indian Warfare.
J.W. Spellman, 318(JAOS):Apr-Jun84-345
Bhargava, M.L. Netaji Subhas Bose in South-East Asia.
L.A. Gordon, 293(JASt):May85-630
Bhargava, P.L. Fundamentals of Hinduism.
R.W. Larivière, 318(JAOS):Apr-Jun84-338
Bhaskar, R. Philosophy and the Human Sciences. (Vol 2)
S. Richmond, 488:Jun85-235.
Bhatt, N.R., ed. Mataṅgapārames̄varāgama (Kriyāpāda, Yogapāda et Caryāpāda), avec le commentaire de Bhaṭṭa Rāmakaṇṭha.
J.P. Olivelle, 318(JAOS):Apr-Jun84-338
Bhuiyan, M.A.W. Emergence of Bangladesh and Role of Awami League.
D.C. Makeig, 293(JASt):Feb85-418
Biagini, H.E., E. Ardissone and R. Sassi. La "Revista de Filosofía."
J.C. Torchia Estrada, 263(RIB): Vol35No2-214
Bialer, S. The Soviet Paradox.
D. Holloway, 453(NYRB):12Jun86-18
P. Reddaway, 441:27Jul86-1
Bialostosky, D.H. Making Tales.*
G.W. Ruoff, 661(WC):Fall85-155
C. Salvesen, 301(JEGP):Jul85-448
Bianchi, L. L'errore di Aristotele.
J. Jolivet, 542:Apr-Jun85-243
Bianchi, S. La Révolution culturelle de l'An II.
B. Valdman, 704(SFR):Winter85-439
Bianchi, S.M. and D. Spain. American Women in Transition.
B. Farah, 441:28Sep86-27
Bianciotto, G., ed and trans. Bestiaires du Moyen Age.
S. Kay, 545(RPh):Aug85-128
Bianciotto, G. and M. Salvat, eds. Epopée animale, Fable, Fabliau.
G. Roques, 553(RLiR):Jul-Dec85-423
Bianconi, P. and others. Il Sacro Monte sopra Varese.
W. Hood, 54:Jun85-333
Biard, J.D. Lexique pour l'explication de texte.
R. Gibson, 208(FS):Jan85-119

Birdsell, S. Night Travellers.
F.W. Kaye, 502(PrS):Spring85-103
L. Spalding, 99:Aug/Sep85-28
Bireley, R. Religion and Politics in the
Age of the Counterreformation.
L.W. Spitz, 377:Mar85-51
Birke, L. Women, Feminism and Biology.
J. Gelb, 441:21Sep86-28
Birkett, M.E. Lamartine and the Poetics
of Landscape.*
R. Lloyd, 208(FS):Jul85-352
C. Ménage, 535(RHL):Jul/Aug85-686
Birmingham, S. The Le Baron Secret.
D. Cole, 441:12Jan86-9
Birn, R. Aksel Sandemose.
M.C. Hunt, 395(MFS):Summer85-444
S. Lyngstad, 563(SS):Winter85-104
Birnbaum, H. and M.S. Flier, eds. Medie-
val Russian Culture.
W.K. Hanak, 589:Oct85-944
J.L. Perkowski, 574(SEEJ):Fall85-339
W.F. Ryan, 575(SEER):Oct85-577
Birnbaum, L. Red Dawn at Lexington.
P-L. Adams, 61:May86-99
C.R. Herron, 441:27Jul86-19
Birnbaum, P. Dimensions du pouvoir.
R. Gervais, 154:Spring85-170
Birney, E. Words on Waves.
M. Page, 648(WCR):Apr86-72
Birringer, J.H. Marlowe's "Dr. Faustus"
and "Tamburlaine."*
C.W. Cary, 130:Spring85-95
M. Charney, 551(RenQ):Spring85-165
K. Tetzeli von Rosador, 72:Band222
Heft2-399
"The Birth of Solidarity." (A. Kemp-Welch,
trans)
J. Woodall, 575(SEER):Jan85-153
Birx, H.J. Theories of Evolution.
C.G. Holland, 529(QQ):Summer85-423
"La Bisaccia dello Sheikh."
A. Schimmel, 318(JAOS):Oct-Dec84-777
Bischof, W. and others. After the War Was
Over.
M. Ignatieff, 617(TLS):3Jan86-5
Bischoff, P., ed. America, the Melting
Pot.
M. Diedrich, 72:Band222Heft2-427
Bishop, A. - see Brittain, V.
Bishop, C. The Devil's Diamond.
M. Rubio, 102(CanL):Fall85-115
Bishop, D.H., ed. Thinkers of the Indian
Renaissance.
H.W. French, 258:Sep85-335
Bishop, E. The Collected Prose.* (R.
Giroux, ed)
B. Costello, 473(PR):Vol52No2-153
J. Mazzaro, 569(SR):Winter85-iv
Bishop, E. The Complete Poems 1927-1979.*
P. Storace, 472:Spring/Summer/Fall/
Winter85-163
Bishop, I. Chaucer's "Troilus and Cris-
eyde."*
G. Morgan, 677(YES):Vol 15-272
Bishop, L. The Romantic Hero and His
Heirs in French Literature.
A. Gruzinska, 446(NCFS):Spring-
Summer86-352
B.L. Knapp, 207(FR):Apr86-787
Bishton, D. Black Heart Man.
362:6Nov86-36

Bissell, R.W. Orazio Gentileschi and the
Poetic Tradition in Caravaggesque Paint-
ing.*
J. Gash, 59:Jun85-249
Bissett, B. Seagull on Yonge Street.*
L. York, 102(CanL):Spring85-145
Bisson, T.N., ed. Fiscal Accounts of Cata-
lonia under the Early Count-Kings (1151-
1213).
P. Linehan, 617(TLS):7Nov86-1259
Bissoondath, N. Digging Up the Mountains.
H. Kureishi, 441:17Aug86-10
A. Maja-Pearce, 617(TLS):6Jun86-623
Bitov, A. Life in Windy Weather. (P.
Meyer, ed)
R.A. Maguire, 441:14Sep86-33
Bitsilli, P.M. Chekhov's Art.
S. Golub, 615(TJ):Mar85-128
Bittinger, M.L. Logic, Proof, and Sets.
(2nd ed)
A. Leggett, 316:Sep85-860
Bittner, R. Moralisches Gebot oder Auto-
nomie.*
M. Forschner, 687:Oct-Dec85-600
Bixler, P. Frances Hodgson Burnett.
M.G. Sprengnether, 26(ALR):Spring/
Autumn85-294
Bjerregaard, R., ed. Heltinde Historier.
F. Ingwersen, 563(SS):Autumn85-455
Björk, L.A. - see Hardy, T.
Björkman, S. "L'incroyable, romanesque,
picaresque épisode barbaresque."
G. Merk, 553(RLiR):Jul-Dec85-462
Björkvall, G., G. Iversen and R. Jonsson,
eds. Corpus troporum, III.*
P. Jeffery, 589:Apr85-471
Bjørnson, B. Jeg velger mig april. De
gode gjerninger redder verden.
Ø. Rottem, 562(Scan):May85-59
Bjørnvig, T. The Pact.
M.C. Hunt, 395(MFS):Summer85-444
Bjørnvig, T. Pagten.
E. Cederborg, 172(Edda):1985/5-319
Blachman, M.J., W.M. Leo Grande and K.E.
Sharpe, eds. Confronting Revolution.
A. Husarska, 441:23Nov86-25
Black, D. Peep Show.
M. Bloom, 441:8Jun86-36
Black, D. The Plague Years.
R. Davenport-Hines, 617(TLS):18Jul86-
780
K. Leishman, 441:27Jul86-12
Black, H.L. and E. Mr. Justice and Mrs.
Black.
J.P. MacKenzie, 441:20Apr86-23
Black, I. A Gambling Style of Government.
K.G. Tregonning, 293(JASt):May85-662
Black, J. The British and the Grand Tour.*
S. Soupel, 189(EA):Oct-Dec86-458
Black, J. The Italian Romantic Libretto.
J. Rosselli, 617(TLS):3Jan86-17
Black, M.H. Cambridge University Press:
1584-1984.*
J.R., 185:Jan86-456
Black, P.R. Ernst Kaltenbrunner.*
F.L. Carsten, 575(SEER):Jan85-142
Black Elk. The Sixth Grandfather. (R.J.
De Mallie, ed)
W.T. Hagan, 649(WAL):Nov85-261
Blackall, E.A. The Novels of the German
Romantics.*
J.K. Brown, 591(SIR):Fall85-436
[continued]

Blackall, E.A. The Novels of the German Romantics. [continuing]
R.D. Fulton, 594:Spring85-108
G. Hoffmeister, 400(MLN):Apr85-668
R. Hunter-Lougheed, 627(UTQ):Summer85-501
D.F. Mahoney, 221(GQ):Winter85-120
R. Paulin, 402(MLR):Jul85-758
Blackbourn, D. and G. Eley. The Peculiarities of German History.*
G.A. Craig, 453(NYRB):30Jan86-20
Blackburn, G.W. Education in the Third Reich.
W.J. Miller, 377:Nov85-209
Blackburn, S. Spreading the Word.*
P. Lamarque, 478:Oct85-212
R.M. Sainsbury, 84:Jun85-211
M. Smith, 63:Dec85-543
N. Tennant, 518:Apr85-65
C. Wright, 393(Mind):Apr85-310
Blackmore, R. - see Powys, J.C.
Blackmur, R.P. Selected Essays of R.P. Blackmur. (D. Donoghue, ed)
H. Marten, 441:8Jun86-29
Blackwell, K. The Spinozistic Ethics of Bertrand Russell.
S. Brown, 617(TLS):31Jan86-119
Blackwell, K. and others - see Russell, B.
Blackwell, M.J. C.J.L. Almqvist and Romantic Irony.*
S.P. Sondrup, 301(JEGP):Oct85-590
L. Vinge, 562(Scan):May85-74
Blades, J. Percussion Instruments and their History.
A.F.L.T., 412:Aug/Nov84-304
Blaicher, G. Die Erhaltung des Lebens.
P. Wenzel, 156(ShJW):Jahrbuch1985-255
Blaicher, G. Freie Zeit — Langeweile — Literatur.
D. Rolle, 38:Band103Heft3/4-497
Blainey, A. Immortal Boy.
J.M.B., 179(ES):Aug85-373
W. St. Clair, 617(TLS):18Apr86-428
Blair, F. Isadora.
A. Kisselgoff, 441:16Mar86-21
Blair, R. Robert Blair's "The Grave," Illustrated by William Blake.* (R.N. Essick and M.D. Paley, eds)
D. Fuller, 161(DUJ):Dec84-119
Blair, W. and V. Fischer - see Twain, M.
Blair, W. and R.I. McDavid, Jr., eds. The Mirth of a Nation.*
E.L. Galligan, 569(SR):Spring85-283
D.L.F. Nilsen, 424:Sep85-177
Blais, M-C. Anna's World.
J. Fitzgerald, 99:May85-31
Blais, M-C. Veiled Countries/Lives.
M.T. Lane, 198:Summer85-100
K.W. Meadwell, 526:Spring85-78
Blais, S. Apport de la toponymie ancienne aux études sur le français québécois et nordaméricain.
N. O'Nan, 424:Sep85-181
Blaise, C. Resident Alien.
P. West, 441:120ct86-44
Lord Blake and C.S. Nicholls - see "The Dictionary of National Biography 1971-1980"
Blake, K. Love and the Woman Question in Victorian Literature.*
R. Gagnier, 637(VS):Autumn85-159

Blake, N. and K. Pole, eds. Dangers of Deterrence.
S.C. Patten, 154:Winter85-713
Blake, N. and K. Pole, eds. Objections to Nuclear Defence.
D.L., 185:Oct85-223
B. Paskins, 518:Oct85-227
Blake, N.F. Shakespeare's Language.*
M. de Grazia, 570(SQ):Winter85-507
J. Schäfer, 72:Band222Heft2-400
A. Ward, 447(N&Q):Jun84-264
Blake, N.F. The Textual Tradition of the "Canterbury Tales."
A. Wawn, 617(TLS):28Nov86-1356
Blake, P. - see Hayward, M.
Blake, R. The Conservative Party from Peel to Thatcher.*
A. Hartley, 176:Apr86-43
Blake, R. The Decline of Power 1915-1964.*
S.R. Slaymaker 2d, 441:25May86-15
Blake, W. America: A Prophecy [and] Europe: A Prophecy. Songs of Experience.
J. La Belle, 88:Fall85-83
Blake, W. Annotations to Richard Watson. (8th ed) (G.I. James, ed)
N.O. Warner, 88:Winter85/86-116
Blake, W. Oeuvres de William Blake.* (Vol 4) (J. Blondel, ed and trans)
D. Fuller, 161(DUJ):Dec84-118
Blake, W. Songs of Innocence and Songs of Experience. [facsimile]
R.N. Essick, 88:Summer85-39
Blakeley, P.R. and J.N. Grant, eds. Eleven Exiles.
K.L. Morrison, 102(CanL):Winter84-73
Blalock, H. Basic Dilemmas in the Social Sciences.
K.S., 185:Jul86-899
Blamires, H. Twentieth-Century English Literature.
F. McCombie, 447(N&Q):Dec84-541
Blanc, C. and P. de Haller - see Euler, L.
Blanc, J., J.M. Cartier and P. Lederlin. En avant la musique, 1.
J.J. Smith, 207(FR):Mar86-659
Blanc, J., P. Lederlin and J.M. Cartier. En avant la musique, 2.
J.J. Smith, 207(FR):May86-1020
Blanc, O. La Dernière Lettre.*
J. Aeply, 450(NRF):Feb85-105
Blanch, R.J. "Sir Gawain and the Green Knight."
C. Clark, 179(ES):Aug85-360
D. Mehl, 72:Band222Heft2-475
382(MAE):1985/2-346
Blanchard, A. Essai sur la composition des comédies de Ménandre.
S.M. Goldberg, 303(JoHS):Vol 105-191
Blanchard, J. La pastorale en France aux XIVe et XVe siècles.
J.M. Ferrier, 208(FS):Oct85-452
M. Zink, 545(RPh):May86-517
Blanchard, J., ed. Le Pastoralet.*
A.T. Harrison, 589:Apr85-385
M. Zink, 545(RPh):May86-517
Blanchard, M.E. In Search of the City.
R. Terdiman, 446(NCFS):Spring-Summer86-366
Blanchard, W.H. Revolutionary Morality.
M.A. Miller, 550(RusR):Jan85-71

Blanche, J-É. Nouvelles lettres à André
Gide (1891-1925). (G-P. Collet, ed)
   C. Angelet, 535(RHL):Jul/Aug85-697
   D.H. Walker, 208(FS):Oct85-492
Blanchet, P. Le Français régional de
Provence.
   S. Thiolier-Méjean, 209(FM):Oct85-253
Blanchot, M. The Gaze of Orpheus. (P.A.
Sitney, ed) Death Sentence. When the
Time Comes. The Madness of the Day.
Vicious Circles.
   G. Sorrentino, 441:25May86-23
Bland, P. The Crusoe Factor.*
   H. Lomas, 364:Apr/May85-117
Blank, D.L. Ancient Philosophy and Gram-
mar.*
   D.M. Schenkeveld, 394:Vol38fasc3/4-424
Blanning, T.C.W. The French Revolution in
Germany.
   M. Hughes, 83:Spring85-97
Blanpied, J.W. Time and the Artist in
Shakespeare's English Histories.*
   R.C. Hassel, Jr., 702:Vol 17-247
Blanquat, J. and J-F. Botrel, eds. Clarín
y sus editores (1884-1893).
   F. García Sarriá, 86(BHS):Apr85-207
Blanshard, B. Four Reasonable Men.*
   W.W., 185:Jan86-452
   639(VQR):Spring85-50
Blaser, R. Syntax.
   R.B. Hatch, 648(WCR):Apr86-3
   J. Owens, 102(CanL):Winter84-93
Blasier, C. The Giant's Rival.*
   S.N. MacFarlane, 104(CASS):Spring85-98
Blass, F. and A. Debrunner. Grammatik des
neutestamentlichen Griechisch. (15th ed
rev by F. Rehkopf)
   A. Sideras, 260(IF):Band90-305
Blau, E. Ruskinian Gothic.
   S. Muthesius, 54:Mar85-167
Blaug, M. Great Economists before Keynes.
   D.J. O'Keeffe, 617(TLS):19Dec86-1420
Blaukopf, H. - see Mahler, G. and R.
Strauss
Blaukopf, K. Musik im Wandel der Gesell-
schaft.
   E.A. Lippman, 143:Issue37/38-206
Blayney, P.W.M. The Texts of "King Lear"
and their Origins.* (Vol 1)
   W.C. Ferguson, 40(AEB):Vol8No2-138
   P. Werstine, 570(SQ):Spring85-120
Blázquez, J.M. Mosaicos romanos de la
Real Academia de la Historia, Ciudad
Real, Toledo, Madrid y Cuenca. Mosaicos
romanos de Sevilla, Granada, Cádiz y
Murcia.
   A.A. Barrett, 124:Mar-Apr86-282
   N. Mackie, 123:Vol35No2-349
Blázquez, J.M. Primitivas religiones
ibéricas. (Vol 2)
   J. Elay, 318(JAOS):Oct-Dec84-774
Blázquez, J.M. and T. Ortego. Mosaicos
romanos de Soria.
   A.A. Barrett, 124:Mar-Apr86-282
   N. Mackie, 123:Vol35No2-349
Blecua, A. Manual de crítica textual.*
   L. Kasten, 238:May85-298
Blecua, J.M.C. and M.J. Lacarra - see
Cacho Blecua, J.M. and M.J. Lacarra
Blei, N. The Ghost of Sandburg's Phizzog.
   R. Ratner, 441:12Oct86-28
Bleikasten, A. Arp.
   R. Cardinal, 208(FS):Oct85-497

Bleikasten, A. Parcours de Faulkner.*
   M. Millgate, 189(EA):Oct-Dec86-485
Bleiler, E.F., ed. Science Fiction Writ-
ers. The Guide to Supernatural Fiction.
   L. Hatfield, 128(CE):Mar85-275
Blejwas, S.A. Realism in Polish Politics.
   S.R. Burant, 497(PolR):Vol30No3-306
Blessing, R. Poems and Stories.*
   F. Muratori, 448:Vol23No3-142
   V. Trueblood, 271:Winter85-136
Bleznick, D.W., ed. Studies on "Don
Quijote" and Other Cervantine Works.
   N.L. Hutman, 238:Sep85-515
Bliss, M. Banting.
   G.W., 102(CanL):Spring85-175
Blissett, W. The Long Conversation.*
   K.H. Staudt, 659(ConL):Fall86-409
Blitzer, W. Between Washington and Jerusa-
lem.
   P. Grose, 441:9Mar86-26
   B. Wasserstein, 617(TLS):10Oct86-1123
Blixen, K. Vinter – Eventyr. Kongesøn-
nerne og andre efterladte fortaellinger.
Samlede Essays.
   E. Cederborg, 172(Edda):1985/5-319
"Blixeniana 1985."
   E. Cederborg, 172(Edda):1985/5-319
Bloch, C. Spelling the Word.
   J. Drury, 617(TLS):28Feb86-228
Bloch, C. and S. Mitchell - see Amichai, Y.
Bloch, E. Briefe 1903-1975.* (U. Opolka
and others, eds)
   H-M. Lohmann, 384:Dec85-1089
Bloch, E. The Principle of Hope.
   M. Tanner, 617(TLS):22Aug86-923
   L. Wieseltier, 441:23Nov86-44
Bloch, M. - see Simpson, W. and Edward
VIII
Bloch, R. La divination dans l'Antiquité.
   A. Reix, 542:Apr-Jun85-231
Bloch, R.H. Etymologies and Genealogies.*
   J. Beck, 545(RPh):Aug85-92
   L.J. Friedman, 589:Jan85-121
   S. Huot, 405(MP):May86-414
   N.J. Lacy, 207(FR):Oct85-123
   J. Leeker, 547(RF):Band97Heft2/3-290
   P. Zumthor, 131(CL):Spring85-180
Bloch-Michel, J. L'Evanouie.
   R. Buss, 617(TLS):21Mar86-306
Block, H-U. Maschinelle Übersetzung kom-
plexer französischer Nominalsyntagmen
ins Deutsche.
   G. Kleiber, 553(RLiR):Jul-Dec85-500
Block, L. When the Sacred Ginmill Closes.
   N. Callendar, 441:20Jul86-20
Blodgett, E.D. Configuration.*
   B. Godard, 49:Jul85-108
   C.R. La Bossière, 268(IFR):Winter86-36
   C.R. La Bossière, 403(MLS):Fall85-378
   W. Pache, 52:Band20Heft1-80
Blofeld, J. Les mantras, ou la puissance
des mots sacrés.
   A. Reix, 542:Oct-Dec85-541
Blom, M.H. and T.E. - see Ewing, J.H.
Blomberg, M. Observations on the Dodwell
Painter.*
   D.C. Kurtz, 123:Vol35No1-156
Blomberg, M. and others. Corpus Vasorum
Antiquorum. (Sweden, Vol 2)
   T. Rasmussen, 303(JoHS):Vol 105-237

Blome, P. Die figürliche Bildwelt Kretas in der geometrischen und früharchaischen Periode.
E.A. Moignard, 303(JoHS):Vol 105-242
Blomeyer, G. and B. Tietze. Die Andere Bauarbeit.
W. Segal, 46:May85-80
Blonde, F. Greek Lamps from Thorikos.
D.M. Bailey, 303(JoHS):Vol 105-240
Blondel, J. - see Blake, W.
Blondel, M. Action (1893).
J.M. Somerville, 258:Sep85-336
Bloom, A. Prodigal Sons.
F. Kermode, 441:27Apr86-12
Bloom, E.A., L.D. Bloom and E. Leites. Educating the Audience.
A. Bony, 189(EA):Apr-Jun86-215
Bloom, H. Agon.*
A. Wordsworth, 541(RES):Aug85-458
Bloom, K. American Song.
E. Southern, 91:Spring85-124
Bloomfield, M.W., ed. Allegory, Myth, and Symbol.*
J. Kleinstück, 38:Band103Heft3/4-522
Bloor, D. Wittgenstein.
J. Burnheim, 63:Jun85-241
V.M. Cooke, 258:Sep85-329
H.O. Mounce, 84:Sep85-344
D.S., 185:Oct85-216
B-M. Schiller, 319:Jan86-137
Blot, J. Tout l'été.
A. Clerval, 450(NRF):Nov85-98
Blotner, J. Faulkner.*
S.S. Baskett, 115:Summer85-383
P.R. Broughton, 27(AL):Mar85-160
P.R. Broughton, 534(RALS):Spring83-41
A.F. Kinney, 395(MFS):Summer85-411
Blotner, J. - see Faulkner, W.
Bloxom, M.D. Pickaxe and Pencil.
F.V. O'Connor, 127:Winter84-393
Bluche, F. and J-F. Solnon. La véritable hiérarchie sociale de l'ancienne France.*
M. Bannister, 208(FS):Jul85-340
Bluger, M. On Nights Like This.
B. Pirie, 102(CanL):Summer85-181
Blüher, K.A. Die französische Novelle.
W. Krömer, 547(RF):Band97Heft4-459
Blüher, K.A., ed. Paul Valéry.
N. Suckling, 208(FS):Oct85-493
Bluhm, W.T. Force or Freedom?*
T.S.S., 185:Apr86-683
Blum, D. Bad Karma.
M. Gallagher, 441:7Sep86-23
Blum, D.S. Walter Lippmann.
639(VQR):Spring85-59
Blum, R. Kallimachos und die Literatur-verzeichnung bei den Griechen.
K.J. McKay, 394:Vol138fasc3/4-413
Blume, D. Wandmalerei als Ordenspropaganda.
J. Cannon, 90:Apr85-234
Blume, J. Letters to Judy.
C. Rumens, 617(TLS):28Nov86-1342
E. Winship, 441:8Jun86-12
Blümel, W. Die aiolischen Dialekte.
K. Mickey, 303(JoHS):Vol 105-203
Blumenberg, H. Arbeit am Mythos.*
U. Breth, 224(GRM):Band35Heft1-96
Blumenthal, E. Joseph Chaikin.*
G.L. Ratliff, 615(TJ):Dec85-525
Blumenthal, M. Days We Would Rather Know.*
D. Wojahn, 491:Jun85-174
639(VQR):Winter85-27

Blumenthal, M. Laps.*
D. Wojahn, 491:Jun85-174
Blumenthal, P. Semantische Dichte.*
W. Brandt, 685(ZDL):2/1985-270
Blumenthal, P. La Syntaxe du message.*
N.C.W. Spence, 208(FS):Apr85-247
Blumenthal, S. The Rise of the Counter-Establishment.
G. Hodgson, 441:5Oct86-7
J. Muravchik, 129:Oct86-84
Blumenthal, U-R., ed. Carolingian Essays.
P. Meyvaert, 589:Oct85-1044
Blunden, A. - see Mann, T.
Blunden, E. Cricket Country.
G. Moorhouse, 364:Aug-Sep85-154
Blunt, A. Guide to Baroque Rome.*
H. Hibbard, 576:May85-183
Blunt, A. - see "Paul Fréart de Chantelou"
Blunt, W. Slow on the Feather.
C. Brown, 617(TLS):14Nov86-1266
Blustein, J. Parents and Children.
G.B. Matthews, 311(JP):Jun85-330
Bly, C. Backbone.*
W.D. Everman, 455:Jun85-62
Bly, P. Pérez Galdós: "La de Bringas."
K. Kohut, 72:Band222Heft2-465
Bly, P.A. Galdós's Novel of the Historical Imagination.*
M. Gordon, 402(MLR):Jul85-739
Bly, R. The Man in the Black Coat Turns.
D. Lehman, 473(PR):Vol52No3-302
Bly, R. Selected Poems.
J. Peseroff, 441:25May86-2
Bly, R. Talking All Morning.
R. McDowell, 249(HudR):Autumn85-510
Bly, R. - see Rilke, R.M.
Blyth, A., ed. Opera on Record, 3.
E. Forbes, 415:May85-286
Blythe, R. Divine Landscapes.
M. Drabble, 362:27Mar86-28
V. Glendinning, 441:30Nov86-32
442(NY):24Nov86-150
Blythe, R. The Stories of Ronald Blythe.*
P. Lewis, 364:Aug-Sep85-147
J. Mellors, 362:9Jan86-29
Boakes, R. From Darwin to Behaviourism.
M. Midgley, 84:Dec85-459
Boardman, J. Greek Sculpture: The Classical Period.
B.F. Cook, 617(TLS):30May86-593
E. Esdaile, 324:Jun86-468
Boardman, J. The Parthenon and its Sculptures.
E. Esdaile, 324:Jun86-468
Boardman, J., J. Griffin and O. Murray, eds. The Oxford History of the Classical World.
D.J.R. Bruckner, 441:5Oct86-12
P. Levi, 176:Jul/Aug86-45
R. Seager, 617(TLS):3Oct86-1108
Boardman, M.E. Defoe and the Uses of Narrative.*
L.A. Curtis, 403(MLS):Fall85-350
Boaretto, C. - see Paulhan, J. and F. Ponge
Boatwright, J., ed. Shenandoah.
D. Stern, 441:19Jan86-16
Bobrowski, J. Shadow Lands.
T. Eagleton, 565:Spring85-66
Boccaccio, G. Decameron. (J. Payne, trans; rev by C.S. Singleton)
A.K. Cassell, 400(MLN):Jan85-178
J.L. Smarr, 149(CLS):Summer85-265

39

Boccaccio, G. The Decameron. (K. Speight, ed)
J. Usher, 278(IS):Vol40-119
Bock, A. Japanese Film Directors.
D. Bordwell, 18:Jun86-63
Bock, C. The Head-Hunters of Borneo.
617(TLS):25Apr86-459
Bock, H.M., ed. Cinegraph. (Installments 2-4)
S. Johnston, 707:Spring85-149
S.S. Prawer, 617(TLS):17Jan86-69
Bock, P. - see Ragaz, L.
Bockelkamp, M. Analytische Forschungen zu Handschriften des 19. Jahrhunderts.
J. Voisine, 549(RLC):Jan-Mar85-106
Bockstoce, J.R. Whales, Ice, and Men.
P-L. Adams, 61:Dec86-104
Bodde, D. Essays on Chinese Civilization. (C. Le Blanc and D. Borei, eds)
C. Mackerras, 302:Vol21No1-50
J.S. Major, 485(PE&W):Apr85-217
Boddy, M., J. Lovering and K. Bassett. Sunbelt City?
N. Deakin, 617(TLS):7Nov86-1239
Bode, C. - see Barnum, P.T.
Bödefeld, H. Untersuchungen zur Datierung der Alexandergeschichte des Q. Curtius Rufus.*
E.E. Rice, 123:Vol35No1-192
Bodel, J. Le Jeu de saint Nicolas. (A. Henry, ed)
K. Schoell, 547(RF):Band97Heft2/3-296
Bodin, J. Colloque entre sept scavans qui sont de differens sentimens des secrets cachez des choses relevees. (F. Berriot, ed)
P. Burke, 208(FS):Oct85-460
"Karl Bodmer's America." (D.C. Hunt and M.V. Gallagher, eds)
S.T. Swank, 658:Winter85-301
Body, J. and others - see Giraudoux, J.
Boedeker, D. Descent from Heaven.
C.A. Rubino, 124:Jul-Aug86-415
Boehm, C. Blood Revenge.
C.W. Bracewell, 575(SEER):Oct85-634
Boehm, T. On the Construction of Flutes/ Über der Flötenbau.
N. O'Loughlin, 415:May85-287
de Boer, T. Foundations of a Critical Psychology.
N.E. Wetherick, 323:Jan85-102
Boës, A. La Lanterne magique de l'histoire.
G. Bremner, 402(MLR):Apr85-465
W.F. Edmiston, 207(FR):Mar86-618
W.D. Howarth, 208(FS):Oct85-480
R. Niklaus, 535(RHL):Jan/Feb85-99
Boesak, A. and C. Villa-Vicencio, eds. A Call for an End to Unjust Rule.
J.E. Spence, 617(TLS):15Aug86-882
Boesche, R. - see de Tocqueville, A.
von Boeselager, D. Antike Mosaiken in Sizilien.
G.W.M. Harrison, 124:May-Jun86-347
R.J.A. Wilson, 313:Vol75-299
Boethius. Boethian Number Theory. (M. Masi, trans)
W. Knorr, 589:Oct85-946
Bogan, L. The Blue Estuaries.
D. Dorian, 472:Spring/Summer/Fall/ Winter85-144
Bogarde, D. Backcloth.
A. Walker, 617(TLS):19Sep86-1027

Bogdanos, T. Pearl.
E. Vasta, 589:Jul85-641
Bogel, F.V. Acts of Knowledge.
R.D. Lund, 403(MLS):Fall85-342
Bogel, F.V. Literature and Insubstantiality in Later Eighteenth-Century England.*
L. Damrosch, Jr., 536(Rev):Vol7-57
R. Markley, 141:Spring85-211
B. Redford, 173(ECS):Spring86-414
Bogen, J. and J.E. McGuire, eds. How Things Are.
D.C. Lindenmuth, 543:Jun86-757
Bogin, R. Abraham Clark and the Quest for Equality in the Revolutionary Era, 1774-1794.*
C. Bonwick, 83:Autumn85-222
Bohlmann, O. Yeats and Nietzsche.*
G.K. Blank, 149(CLS):Winter85-549
Böhme, G. Anthropologie in pragmatischer Hinsicht.
F. Vollhardt, 384:Dec85-1100
Böhme, H. and G. Das Andere der Vernunft.
W. Steinbeck, 342:Band76Heft4-471
Bohn, W. Apollinaire et l'homme sans visage.
J. Schultz, 343:Heft11-128
Bohnen, K., S-A. Jørgensen and F. Schmöe, eds. Dänische "Guldader"-Literatur und Goethezeit.
H. Eichner, 406:Winter85-469
P.M. Mitchell, 563(SS):Spring85-222
Bohórquez C., J.G. - see under Gútemberg Bohórquez C., J.
des Bois, A.D.L. - see under de La Chesnaye des Bois, A.
du Bois, P. History, Rhetorical Description and the Epic: From Homer to Spenser.*
K.M. Lea, 541(RES):May85-254
Boissard, J. A Time to Choose.
442(NY):6Jan86-85
Boisvert, L., M. Juneau and C. Poirier, eds. Travaux de Linguistique Québécoise 3.
H.J. Wolf, 547(RF):Band97Heft4-442
Boitani, P. Chaucer and Boccaccio.
H.H. Schless, 589:Jul85-644
Boitani, P., ed. Chaucer and the Italian Trecento.
I. Bishop, 541(RES):Nov85-557
J. Simpson, 382(MAE):1985/2-306
Boitani, P. English Medieval Narrative in the Thirteenth and Fourteenth Centuries.*
G. Bourquin, 189(EA):Jan-Mar86-115
P. Gradon, 541(RES):Feb85-69
Boixo, J.C.G. - see under González Boixo, J.C.
Bojič, V. and W. Oschlies. Lehrbuch der mazedonischen Sprache.
P. Hill, 575(SEER):Oct85-574
Bok, D. Higher Learning.
F.M. Hechinger, 441:12Oct86-28
Bok, S. Secrets.
P. Gilbert, 483:Jan85-143
Boklund-Lagopoulou, K., ed. Sēmeiotikē kai Koinōnia.
M. Herzfeld, 567:Vol56No1/2-153
Boland, L.A. The Foundations of Economic Method.
J. Birner, 84:Jun85-215
Bolcomb, W. - see Rochberg, G.
Bold, A., ed. W.H. Auden.
N. Jenkins, 617(TLS):13Jun86-643

41

Bonnaud, P. Terres et langages/Peuples et régions.
   H. Goebl, 547(RF):Band97Heft2/3-271
Bonnefis, P. Comme Maupassant.
   G. Woollen, 402(MLR):Jan85-173
Bonnefis, P. L'Innommable.
   D.F. Bell, 400(MLN):Sep85-884
   J. Best, 446(NCFS):Spring-Summer86-377
   B. Nelson, 208(FS):Jul85-358
Bonnefis, P. Jules Vallès.
   W.D. Redfern, 208(FS):Jan85-93
Bonnefoy, Y. Things Dying Things Newborn.
   S. Romer, 617(TLS):26Sep86-1050
Bonnell, F.W. and F.C. Conrad Aiken.
   W. McPheron, 87(BB):Mar85-42
Bonnell, P. and F. Sedwick. Conversation in French.
   Y. de la Quérière, 207(FR):Feb86-494
Bonnell, V.E. Roots of Rebellion.*
   H. Hogan, 550(RusR):Apr85-206
Bonnell, V.E., ed. The Russian Worker.*
   O. Crisp, 575(SEER):Apr85-303
Bonner, E. Alone Together.
   E.D. Dahrendorf, 617(TLS):24Oct86-1182
   S.F. Starr, 441:2Nov86-11
Bonner, W.H. Harp on the Shore. (G. Levine, ed)
   R. Sattelmeyer, 183(ESQ):Vol31No3-190
Bonnerot, J. and A. - see Sainte-Beuve, C.A.
Bonnet, H., with B. Brun. Matinée chez la princesse de Guermantes.
   E. Dezon-Jones, 535(RHL):Jan/Feb85-127
le Bonniec, H. Arnobe, "Contre Les Gentils," Tome 1, Livre i.
   J. Harries, 123:Vol35No1-192
Bono, B.J. Literary Transvaluation.*
   N. Gross, 124:Mar-Apr86-285
   R.S. Miola, 570(SQ):Winter85-502
   A. Patterson, 551(RenQ):Autumn85-570
Bonsack, E. Dvalinn.
   J. Hunter, 402(MLR):Jul85-741
   L. Motz, 563(SS):Winter85-77
Bonsiepen, W. and R. Heede - see Hegel, G.W.F.
"The Book Beautiful and the Binding as Art."
   P. Morgan, 40(AEB):Vol8No2-126
"Bookman's Price Index." (Vol 22) (D.F. McGrath, ed)
   R.A. Gekoski, 677(YES):Vol 15-255
"Bookman's Price Index." (Vol 26) (D.F. McGrath, ed)
   H. Schnelling, 568(SCN):Fall85-47
Boomer, B.P. - see under Pastor Boomer, B.
Boon, J.A. Other Tribes, Other Scribes.*
   J. Benthall, 567:Vol57No3/4-381
Boonham, N., ed. Royal Society of British Sculptors: Anniversary Journal 1904-1984.
   R.S., 90:Nov85-821
Boorstin, D.J. The Discoverers.*
   B.C. Shafer, 529(QQ):Spring85-187
Booth, A. The Roads to Sata.
   M. Howard, 441:7Dec86-14
   A. Thwaite, 176:Apr86-65
   F. Tuohy, 617(TLS):6Jun86-617
Booth, M. British Poetry 1964 to 1984.
   C. Rawson, 617(TLS):7Feb86-137
Booth, M. Carpet Sahib.
   A. Robinson, 362:20Nov86-27
Booth, M. Hiroshima Joe.
   S. Lardner, 442(NY):25Aug86-93
   M.J. Salter, 441:4May86-15

Booth, M. Looking for the Rainbow Sign.*
   J. Saunders, 565:Autumn85-73
Booth, M., ed. Tenfold.
   D. McDuff, 565:Winter84/85-73
Booth, M.R., ed. Victorian Theatrical Trades.*
   P. Mudford, 447(N&Q):Dec84-535
Booth, M.W. The Experience of Songs.*
   J.A. Winn, 402(MLR):Apr85-409
Booth, P. Relations.
   M. Rudman, 441:14Dec86-32
Booth, S. Dance with the Devil.
   B. Allan, 529(QQ):Summer85-265
   F. Wood, 364:Apr/May85-156
Booth, S. "King Lear," "Macbeth," Indefinition, and Tragedy.*
   R. Fraser, 405(MP):May86-423
   M.B. Rose, 536(Rev):Vol7-19
   J.R. Siemon, 301(JEGP):Apr85-266
   K. Tetzeli von Rosador, 156(ShJW): Jahrbuch1985-229
Booth, W.C. The Rhetoric of Fiction. (2nd ed)
   D.R. Schwarz, 569(SR):Summer85-480
Booth, W.C. and M.W. Gregory. The Harper and Row Reader.
   L.H. Peterson, 126(CCC):Dec85-499
Boralevi, L.C. - see under Campos Boralevi, L.
Borchmeyer, D. Das Theater Richard Wagners.
   G. Jordan, 221(GQ):Winter85-133
Borck, J.S. - see "The Eighteenth Century: A Current Bibliography"
Bord, J. and C. Ancient Mysteries of Britain.
   T.A. Shippey, 617(TLS):30May86-583
Bordeaux, J-L. François Le Moyne and his Generation, 1688-1737.
   P. Conisbee, 90:Dec85-908
Bordes, P. Le Serment du Jeu de Paume de Jacques-Louis David.
   D.M. Hunter, 90:Feb85-101
Bordin, R. Frances Willard.
   E. Griffith, 441:14Dec86-33
Bordinat, P. and S.B. Blaydes. Sir William Davenant.*
   M. De Porte, 402(MLR):Jan85-123
Bordman, G. American Operetta.
   G. Maschio, 615(TJ):May85-237
Bordman, G. The Oxford Companion to American Theatre.*
   M.A. Reilingh, 615(TJ):Dec85-516
   O. Trilling, 157:No157-52
Bordwell, D. Narration in the Fiction Film.
   R. Maltby, 617(TLS):24Oct86-1202
Bordwell, D., J. Staiger and K. Thompson. The Classical Hollywood Cinema.*
   B. Allan, 529(QQ):Winter85-821
   R.B. Palmer, 500:Spring/Summer86-88
Borel, P. Champavert. (J-L. Steinmetz, ed)
   R. Chambers, 446(NCFS):Spring-Summer86-355
Borer, A. Rimbaud en Abyssinie. Un Sieur Rimbaud se disant négociant.
   J.A. Ferguson, 208(FS):Oct85-490
Boretzky, N. Kreolsprachen, Substrate und Sprachwandel.
   J. Holm, 350:Mar86-225
Borges, J.L. Conférences.
   A. Calame, 450(NRF):Jul-Aug85-176

Borges, J.L.  Other Inquisitions.
  S. White, 448:Vol23No2-106
Borges, J.L.  Seven Nights.*
  A. Schelling, 703:No14-155
Borges, J.L. and A.B. Casares.  Nouveaux
  Contes de Bustos Domecq.
  A. Calame, 450(NRF):May85-104
Borges, J.L., with M. Kodama.  Atlas.
  N. Rankin, 617(TLS):20Jun86-674
  442(NY):10Nov86-148
Borgeson, P.W., Jr.  Hacia el hombre nuevo.
  J. Roy, 263(RIB):Vol35No4-461
Borgheggiani, P.A. and G.T. Brunelli.
  France et étranger dans la "Revue de
  littérature comparée," 1921-1980.
  O. Novel, 549(RLC):Oct-Dec85-445
Borgmann, A.  Technology and the Character
  of Contemporary Life.
  L.G., 185:Jan86-444
Borkenau, F.  End and Beginning.* (German
  title: Ende und Anfang.) (R. Lowenthal,
  ed)
  H. Pross, 384:Aug85-696
Borkenau, F.  Spanish Cockpit.
  H. Francis, 362:17Jul86-25
Borkin, A.  Problems in Form and Function.*
  R.A. Hudson, 297(JL):Mar85-262
Bormann, E.G.  The Force of Fantasy.
  C.L. Waagen, 583:Summer86-385
de Born, B. - see under Bertran de Born
Borne, E.  Les nouveaux inquisiteurs.
  M. Adam, 542:Jan-Mar85-76
Bornemark, K-O.  The Messenger Must Die.
  N. Callendar, 441:28Dec86-15
  442(NY):8Dec86-156
Bornet, V.D.  The Presidency of Lyndon B.
  Johnson.
  J.O. Robertson, 106:Winter85-465
Bornstein, D.  The Lady in the Tower.
  V.M. Lagorio, 377:Jul84-110
  J.W. Nicholls, 402(MLR):Jan85-111
Borochov, B.  Class Struggle and the Jew-
  ish Nation. (M. Cohen, ed)
  J.J. Goldberg, 287:Jan85-24
de Boron, R. - see under Robert de Boron
Borowski, I.E., R.B. Jachmann and R.B.
  Wasianski.  Kant intime.
  J. Stéfan, 450(NRF):Jun85-72
Borrás, A.A., ed.  The Theatre and His-
  panic Life.
  M.G. Paulson, 238:Mar85-72
Borràs, M.L.  Picabia.*
  S. Whitfield, 617(TLS):18Apr86-423
Borson, R.  The Whole Night, Coming Home.
  D. Livesay, 102(CanL):Fall85-141
  S. Scobie, 376:Mar85-161
  P.K. Smith, 99:Oct85-32
Borthwick, J.S.  The Student Body.
  N. Callendar, 441:16Nov86-38
Boruch, M.  View from the Gazebo.
  A. Turner, 199:Spring86-85
Borunova, S.N., V.L. Voroncova and N.A.
  Es'kova.  Orfozpičeskij slovar' russkogo
  jazyka. (R.I. Avanesova, ed)
  W. Lehfeldt, 559:Vol9No1-22
Borutti, S.  Significato, Saggio sulla
  semantica filosofica del '900.
  P. Engel, 542:Jan-Mar85-68
Bosco, F.C. - see under Cortesi Bosco, F.
Bose, M.  A Maidan View.
  A.L. Le Quesne, 617(TLS):5Sep86-987
Bosha, F.J.  Faulkner's "Soldiers' Pay."*
  J.J. Tucker, 106:Spring85-83

Bošković-Stulli, M., ed.  Šingala-mingala.*
  B. Schultze, 196:Band26Heft3/4-350
Bosl, K.  Gesellschaftsgeschichte Italiens
  im Mittelalter.
  D.J. Osheim, 589:Oct85-948
Bosley, E.C.  Techniques for Articulatory
  Disorders.
  A.S. Kaye, 361:Jan85-164
Bosley, K. - see de La Ceppède, J.
Boslough, J.  Stephen Hawking's Universe.*
  C. Small, 529(QQ):Winter85-880
Bosse, M.  Fire in Heaven.
  J. Bass, 441:9Feb86-25
Bossy, J.  Christianity in the West 1400-
  1700.*
  B. Bradshaw, 617(TLS):2May86-480
Bostock, W.W.  The Organization and Co-
  Ordination of "La Francophonie."
  H.F. Bostick, 399(MLJ):Winter85-410
Boström, H-O.  Thor Fagerkvist 1884-1960.
  T. Grünberger, 341:Vol54No1-41
Boswell, J.  Christianisme, tolérance
  sociale et homosexualité.
  H. Cronel, 450(NRF):Oct85-102
Boswell, J.  The Heart of Boswell. (M.
  Harris, ed)
  F.H. Ellis, 403(MLS):Winter85-80
Boswell, T.D. and J.R. Curtis.  The Cuban-
  American Experience.
  M. Glazer, 292(JAF):Jul/Sep85-360
Bosworth, A.B.  A Historical Commentary on
  Arrian's History of Alexander. (Vol 1)
  G. Schepens, 394:Vol138fasc3/4-417
Bosworth, D.  From My Father, Singing.
  N. Perrin, 441:23Mar86-18
Bosworth, P.  Diane Arbus.*
  S. Mernit, 219(GaR):Spring85-209
Bosworth, R.  Italy and the Approach of
  the First World War.
  J. Pollard, 278(IS):Vol40-151
Botha, R.P.  The Conduct of Linguistic
  Inquiry.
  A.M. Zwicky, 297(JL):Mar85-258
Botha, R.P.  A Galilean Analysis of Afri-
  kaans Reduplication.
  R. Beard, 350:Dec86-949
von Bothmer, D.  The Amasis Painter and
  His World.
  A.W. Johnston, 617(TLS):27Jun86-712
Böttcher, H-E., ed.  Recht Justiz Kritik.
  H. Pross, 384:Sep/Oct85-918
Bottomore, T., ed.  A Dictionary of Marx-
  ist Thought.*
  S. Hook, 176:Jan86-71
Boucé, P-G., ed.  Sexuality in Eighteenth-
  Century Britain.*
  T. Eagleton, 447(N&Q):Mar84-129
  G. Midgley, 541(RES):Aug85-465
  G.R.R., 588(SSL):Vol20-323
  P. Wagner, 72:Band222Heft2-476
Bouchard, G.  Le procès de la métaphore.
  A. Leclerc, 154:Winter85-655
Bouchelle, J.H., ed.  With Tennyson at the
  Keyboard.*
  B.N., 636(VP):Summer85-225
Bouchier, D.  The Feminist Challenge.
  C.C., 185:Apr86-678
Bouillon, J-P.  Art Nouveau.
  P-L. Adams, 61:Feb86-87
Boulanger, D.  Les Noces du merle.*
  F. de Martinoir, 450(NRF):Oct85-94

du Boulay, A.  Christie's Pictorial History of Chinese Ceramics.*
  39:Sep85-238
Boulding, K.E.  Human Betterment.  The World as a Total System.
  W. Leontief, 441:12Jan86-7
Boulding, K.E. and L. Senesh.  The Optimum Utilization of Knowledge.
  J.G., 185:Oct85-221
Boulez, P.  Orientations.  (J-J. Nattiez, ed)
  H. Cole, 362:21Aug86-25
  P. Griffiths, 617(TLS):29Aug86-941
Bouloiseau, M.  The Jacobin Republic, 1792-1794.
  P.M. Jones, 83:Autumn85-230
Boulton, J. - see Whiteley, O.
Boulton, J.T. and A. Robertson - see Lawrence, D.H.
Boulton, M., ed.  The Old French "Evangile de l'Enfance."
  G. Roques, 552(RLiR):Jan-Jun85-241
Bouma, H. and D.G. Bouwhuis, eds.  Attention and Performance, X.
  W. Grabe, 350:Jun86-477
Boumelha, P.  Thomas Hardy and Women.*
  H.L. Weatherby, 569(SR):Winter85-162
Bouraoui, H.  The Critical Strategy.
  P. McCallum, 178:Mar85-135
Bourassa, A.G.  Surrealism and Quebec Literature.
  N.B. Bishop, 376:Mar85-164
  J. Warwick, 102(CanL):Summer85-146
Bourdieu, P.  Distinction.
  S. Hoffmann, 453(NYRB):10Apr86-45
  M. Warner, 400(MLN):Dec85-1133
Bourdieu, P.  Homo academicus.*
  P. Desan, 207(FR):Oct85-159
Bourgeacq, J.  "L'enfant noir" de Camara Laye.
  C.L. Dehon, 207(FR):Feb86-454
  A. King, 538(RAL):Winter85-589
Bourgeois, A.P.  Art of the Yaka and Suku.
  J.M. Janzen, 2(AfrA):Aug85-14
Bourgeois, J-L.  Spectacular Vernacular.
  S. Ehrlich, 2(AfrA):Aug85-12
Bourget, J-L.  Le Mélodrame hollywoodien.
  M. Le Fanu, 189(EA):Oct-Dec86-489
Bourgoin, E.  Foreign Languages and Your Career.  (3rd ed)
  C.K. Knop, 207(FR):Mar86-660
Bourhis, R.Y., ed.  Conflict and Language Planning in Quebec.*
  M. Canale, 399(MLJ):Autumn85-292
Bourmeyster, A., ed.  Le 14 décembre 1825.
  P.J. O'Meara, 575(SEER):Jan85-126
Bourne, J. and others.  Lacquer.
  U. Roberts, 60:Jan-Feb85-128
Bourne, J.M.  Patronage and Society in Nineteenth-Century England.
  D. Cannadine, 617(TLS):27Jun86-715
Bourne, K.  Palmerston: The Early Years 1784-1841.*
  A.J. Heesom, 161(DUJ):Jun84-286
Bourne, P.G.  Fidel.
  S.K. Purcell, 441:19Oct86-24
Bourne, R.  The Letters of Randolph Bourne.  (E.J. Sandeen, ed)
  C.L.P. Silet, 534(RALS):Autumn83-235
Bournoutian, G.A.  Eastern Armenia in the Last Decades of Persian Rule 1807-1828.
  D.S.M. Williams, 575(SEER):Jan85-124

Bourquin, G.  "Piers Plowman."
  J. Simpson, 382(MAE):1985/2-302
Bourquin, J.  La dérivation suffixale (théorisation et enseignement) au XIXe siècle.
  H. Bonnard, 209(FM):Oct85-265
Boursier, N.  Le Centre et la Circonférence.
  D. Jourlait, 627(UTQ):Summer85-452
  D. Kuizenga, 207(FR):Feb86-464
  A.K. Mortimer, 210(FrF):Sep85-365
de Bouscal, D.G. - see under Guérin de Bouscal, D.
Bouton, M.M.  Agrarian Radicalism in South India.
  J. Brow, 617(TLS):19Sep86-1040
Bouveresse, J.  Le philosophe chez les autophages.*
  R. Schmit, 542:Oct-Dec85-542
Bouveresse, J.  Rationalité et cynisme.
  M. Jarrety, 450(NRF):May85-91
Bouvier, J-C., ed.  Tradition orale et identité culturelle.
  H. Goldberg, 545(RPh):Aug84-41
Bouwsma, O.K.  Without Proof or Evidence.*  (J.L. Craft and R.E. Hustwit, eds)
  E. Sprague, 518:Jul85-151
Bove, E.  My Friends.*  (German title: Meine Freunde.)
  M. Ward, 441:20Apr86-22
  442(NY):16Jun86-121
de Bovelles, C.  Le livre du néant.  (P. Magnard, ed and trans)
  J. Jolivet, 542:Apr-Jun85-254
de Bovelles, C.  Le Livre du Sage.  (P. Magnard, trans)
  J. Chomarat, 535(RHL):Nov/Dec85-1057
Bovykin, V.I.  Formirovanie finansovogo kapitala v Rossii (konets XIX v.-1908 g.).
  A.J. Rieber, 550(RusR):Oct85-423
Bowen, B.C.  Words and the Man in French Renaissance Literature.*
  J. Sproxton, 402(MLR):Jan85-162
Bowen, D.  Paul Cardinal Cullen and the Shaping of Modern Irish Catholicism.*
  W. Schoenl, 637(VS):Autumn85-171
Bowen, E.  The Mulberry Tree.  (H. Lee, ed)
  P. Craig, 617(TLS):17Oct86-1152
Bowen, E.G.  Dewi Sant/Saint David.
  D. Johnston, 112:Vol 16-206
Bowen, H.R. and J.H. Schuster.  American Professors.
  J. Conarroe, 617(TLS):21Nov86-1301
  A. Hacker, 453(NYRB):13Feb86-35
Bowen, J.  The Girls.
  C. Hawtree, 617(TLS):25Apr86-453
Bowen, R.W., ed.  E.H. Norman.
  A.H. Ion, 529(QQ):Autumn85-620
Bowen, Z.R. and J.F. Carens, eds.  A Companion to Joyce Studies.*
  R.M. Kain, 395(MFS):Summer85-347
Bower, N.  The Animal Connection.
  D. Devlin, 157:No158-45
Bowering, G.  Craft Slices.
  S. Scobie, 376:Jan86-127
Bowering, M.  The Sunday Before Winter.
  M. Madoff, 102(CanL):Winter84-141
Bowers, F. - see Marlowe, C.
Bowers, F. - see Nabokov, V.

Bowers, J.S.  The Theory of Grammatical
Relations.
  W.M. Christie, 205(ForL):Aug84-183
  H. Czepluch, 260(IF):Band90-251
Bowers, N.  James Dickey.
  S.C., 219(GaR):Summer85-460
  295(JML):Nov85-466
Bowersock, G.W.  Roman Arabia.*
  M.D. Goodman, 313:Vol75-306
  D. Kennedy, 24:Fall85-385
  B.M. Levick, 123:Vol35No2-330
  R.J. Rowland, Jr., 124:Jan-Feb86-195
Bowie, N.E., ed.  Making Ethical Decisions.
  T.D., 185:Jul86-891
Bowie, R.  Hearing the Light.
  L. Forestier, 496:Winter86-245
Bowlby, R.  Just Looking.
  R.L. Selig, 637(VS):Summer86-623
Bowles, E.A.  La pratique musicale au
Moyen Age/Musical Performance in the
Late Middle Ages.*
  C. Meyer, 537:Vol71No1/2-199
Bowles, J.  Selected Letters of Jane
Bowles 1935-1970.  (M. Dillon, ed)
  P. Keegan, 617(TLS):21Nov86-1326
Bowles, P.  Midnight Mass.
  P. Keegan, 617(TLS):21Nov86-1236
  J. Mellors, 362:16Jan86-30
  P. Parker, 364:Jun85-107
Bowles, P.  Without Stopping.
  P. Keegan, 617(TLS):21Nov86-1326
Bowles, S. and H. Gintis.  Democracy and
Capitalism.
  S. Berger, 441:8Jun86-31
Bowman, A.K., H.M. Cockle and others.  The
Oxyrhynchus Papyri.  (Vol 50)
  W. Luppe, 123:Vol35No2-355
Bowman, A.K. and J.D. Thomas.  Vindolanda:
The Latin Writing Tablets.
  R. Coles, 123:Vol35No1-171
Bowring, R. - see "Murasaki Shikibu: Her
Diary and Poetic Memoirs"
Bowron, E.P. - see Clark, A.M.
Boxill, B.R.  Blacks and Social Justice.
  C.N.S., 185:Apr86-674
Boyd, M.  Gay Priest.
  A.N. Williams, 441:12Oct86-29
Boyd, M.  Half Laughing Half Crying.
  V. Young, 441:13Apr86-23
Boyd, M.  Kiowa Voices.  (Vol 1)
  D.N. Brown, 187:Spring/Summer86-362
Boyd, M.  Domenico Scarlatti.
  W. Dean, 617(TLS):26Dec86-1444
Boyd, R. and P.J. Richerson.  Culture and
the Evolutionary Process.
  J.M. Smith, 453(NYRB):6Nov86-11
Boyd, W.  School Ties.
  A. Buckeridge, 364:Nov85-106
Boyd, W.  Stars and Bars.*
  M. Gorra, 249(HudR):Winter86-659
Boyd-Bowman, P.  Léxico hispanoamericano
del siglo XVIII.
  R. de Gorog, 545(RPh):May85-475
  R. Wright, 86(BHS):Oct85-408
Boydell, B.  The Crumhorn and other Renais-
sance Windcap Instruments.
  A. Lumsden, 415:Nov85-673
Boyden, J., ed.  Stick to the Music.
  K. Spence, 415:Apr85-226
Boyer, J.W.  Breaking Camp.
  B. Brown, 95(CLAJ):Dec85-250
Boyer, M.C.  Dreaming the Rational City.*
  K. Crossman, 106:Winter85-443

Boyer, M.C.  Manhattan Manners.
  442(NY):14Apr86-111
Boyer, P.  By the Bomb's Early Light.*
  D.J. Kevles, 442(NY):17Feb86-100
  D. Seideman, 617(TLS):14Mar86-268
Boyer, R.  The Daisy Ducks.
  N. Callendar, 441:21Sep86-37
Boyers, R.  Atrocity and Amnesia.
  E. Goodheart, 344:Summer86-125
Boyes, R. and J. Moody.  The Priest Who
Had to Die.
  G. Theiner, 617(TLS):14Nov86-1269
Boylan, C.  Last Resorts.
  D. Kirk, 441:16Feb86-16
Boylan, M.  Method and Practice in Aris-
totle's Biology.*
  A. Gotthelf, 543:Sep84-112
Boyle, A.J., ed.  Seneca Tragicus.
  D. Little, 67:Nov85-250
Boyle, K. and T. Hadden.  Ireland.*
  R. Fréchet, 189(EA):Oct-Dec86-476
Boyle, T.  Only the Dead Know Brooklyn.
  N. Callendar, 441:23Feb86-32
Boyle, T.C.  Greasy Lake and Other
Stories.*
  N. Shack, 617(TLS):31Jan86-112
Boyman, A.  Fragments du Narcisse.
  K.D. Levy, 207(FR):Oct85-141
Boyne, W.J.  The Leading Edge.
  R. Witkin, 441:12Oct86-29
Boyne, W.J. and S.L. Thompson.  The Wild
Blue.
  M. Buck, 441:23Nov86-24
Bozolli, B., ed.  Town and Countryside in
the Transvaal.
  E.I. Steinhart, 538(RAL):Spring85-136
Bozzolo, C. and H. Loyau, eds.  La Cour
Amoureuse dite de Charles VI.  (Vol 1)
  G. Fässler-Caccia, 547(RF):Band97
  Heft2/3-306
de Brabant, S. - see under Siger de Bra-
bant
Bracciolini, G.F.P. - see under Poggio
Bracciolini, G.F.
Brachin, P.  The Dutch Language.
  T.F. Shannon, 350:Dec86-948
Bracken, H.M.  Mind and Language.
  K.M. Squadrito, 319:Oct86-559
Bracken, P.  The Command and Control of
Nuclear Forces.*
  R.H. Falls, 529(QQ):Winter85-886
Brackenbury, A.  Breaking Ground and Other
Poems.*
  T. Warr, 493:Apr85-60
Brackenbury, R.  Crossing the Water.
  L. Chamberlain, 617(TLS):18Apr86-416
  J. Mellors, 362:12Jun86-29
Brackertz, K.  Artemidor von Daldis, Das
Traumbuch.
  A.H.M. Kessels, 394:Vol38fasc3/4-421
Bradbrook, M.C.  Women and Literature 1779-
1982.
  P. Boumelha, 541(RES):May85-282
Bradbury, M.  Saul Bellow.
  K. Watson, 447(N&Q):Jun84-281
Bradbury, M.  The Modern American Novel.*
  G. Davenport, 569(SR):Summer85-499
  T. Docherty, 541(RES):Nov85-607
  J. Klinkowitz, 301(JEGP):Apr85-291
Bradbury, M.  Rates of Exchange.*
  J.R. Banks, 148:Spring85-79
Bradbury, M.  Why Come to Slaka?
  D.J. Enright, 617(TLS):24Oct86-1199

Bradbury, M. and H. Temperley, eds. Introduction to American Studies.
J. Osborne, 402(MLR):Apr85-412
Bradby, D. Modern French Drama, 1940-1980.
C. Campos, 208(FS):Oct85-502
D. Jeffery, 610:Summer85-190
J.A. Thompson, 615(TJ):Oct85-383
Braden, G. Renaissance Tragedy and the Senecan Tradition.
P. Conrad, 617(TLS):14Mar86-279
A.L. Motto and J.R. Clark, 121(CJ):Dec85/Jan86-176
639(VQR):Autumn85-120
Bradford, B.T. Act of Will.
A. Postman, 441:20Jul86-18
Bradford, M.E. Generations of the Faithful Heart.*
T.J. Fleming, 396(ModA):Summer85-265
Bradley, B.L. Zu Rilkes "Malte Laurids Brigge."*
R. Delphendahl, 406:Summer85-244
Bradley, I. - see Gilbert, W.S. and A.S. Sullivan
Bradley, J. Allied Intervention in Russia.
K. Neilson, 104(CASS):Spring85-78
Bradley, J.L., ed. Ruskin: The Critical Heritage.*
S. Emerson, 184(EIC):Apr85-173
J. Loesberg, 506(PSt):May85-91
F.G. Townsend, 637(VS):Winter86-342
G. Wihl, 405(MP):May86-438
Bradley, K. and A. Gelb. Worker Capitalism.
W.L.M., 185:Apr86-659
Bradley, S.A.J., ed and trans. Anglo-Saxon Poetry.
M.J. Alexander, 382(MAE):1985/2-287
Bradsher, H.S. Afghanistan and the Soviet Union.
C.R. Saivetz, 550(RusR):Apr85-217
Brady, F. James Boswell: The Later Years 1769-1795.*
D. Daiches, 173(ECS):Spring86-412
R.B. Schwartz, 569(SR):Spring85-xxii
P.M. Spacks, 219(GaR):Spring85-182
42(AR):Winter85-120
Brady, K. The Short Stories of Thomas Hardy.*
B.F. Fisher 4th, 573(SSF):Summer85-365
C.E. May, 637(VS):Winter85-325
N. Page, 178:Mar85-97
G.G. Wickens, 627(UTQ):Fall84-123
M. Williams, 447(N&Q):Jun84-273
Brady, P. Le Bouc émissaire chez Emile Zola.
L.K. Martin, 188(ECr):Winter85-116
D. Place, 208(FS):Jan85-94
Braekman, W.L., ed. The "Demaundes off Love."
G. Bourquin, 189(EA):Jan-Mar85-116
Bragger, J.D. and R.A. Ariew. Chère Fran-çoise.* (2nd ed)
R.J. Melpignano, 399(MLJ):Autumn85-305
Bragger, J.D. and R.A. Ariew. Le Monde français. (2nd ed)
R. Danner, 399(MLJ):Winter85-411
M-N. Little, 207(FR):Dec85-311
Bragger, J.D. and D.B. Rice. Allons-y!*
J.W. Zdenek, 399(MLJ):Summer85-172
Braham, J. A Sort of Columbus.*
A.S. Knowles, 594:Winter85-422

Brahms, C. and N. Sherrin. Too Dirty for the Windmill.
F. Raphael, 617(TLS):6Jun86-609
Brake, L. and others - see "The Year's Work in English Studies"
Brakel, L.F. - see "The Story of Muhammad Hanafiyyah"
Brall, H. Gralsuche und Adelsheil.
D.H. Green, 402(MLR):Oct85-971
Bramah, E. Kai Lung's Golden Hours.
D.J. Enright, 617(TLS):27Jun86-705
Bramble, F. Dead of Winter.
T.J.B., 617(TLS):28Feb86-216
Brams, S.J. Superior Beings.*
42(AR):Winter85-125
Brams, S.J. Superpower Games.
T.C. Holyoke, 42(AR):Fall85-497
Bramsbäck, B. Folklore and W.B. Yeats.
R. Frèchet, 189(EA):Oct-Dec86-473
Bramwell, A. Blood and Soil.
I. Kershaw, 617(TLS):19Dec86-1416
Branca, V. Poliziano e l'umanesimo della parola.*
M. Cocco, 589:Jul85-646
Branca, V. and C. Ossola, eds. Cultura e società nel Rinascimento tra Riforme e Manierismi.
A. Buck, 547(RF):Band97Heft2/3-337
M.R. Maniates, 551(RenQ):Autumn85-513
Brancaforte, B. "Guzmán de Alfarache."
P. Márquez Villanueva, 240(HR):Autumn85-491
Branch, E.M. and R.H. Hirst, with H.E. Smith - see Twain, M.
Brand, M. and G.D. Lowry. Akbar's India.
A. Topsfield, 617(TLS):1Aug86-832
Brandell, G. Strindberg — ett författerliv. (Vol 3)
M. Robinson, 562(Scan):May85-87
B. Steene, 563(SS):Winter85-97
Branden, B. The Passion of Ayn Rand.
P.L. Berger, 441:6Jul86-13
T. Teachout, 129:Jul86-68
Brandenburg, D. and K. Brüsehoff. Die Seldschuken.
R. Hillenbrand, 59:Jun85-265
Brandmeyer, R. Biedermeierroman und Krise der ständischen Ordnung.
A.T. Alt, 406:Summer85-231
O.F. Best, 221(GQ):Fall85-612
Brandon, R. Left, Right and Centre.
M. Laski, 362:17Apr86-29
Brandon, R. The Spiritualists.*
F.B. Smith, 637(VS):Summer86-613
Brands, H. "Cogito ergo sum."*
J. Lechner, 342:Band76Heft1-107
Brandt, A.M. No Magic Bullet.*
R. Davenport-Hines, 617(TLS):18Jul86-780
Brandt, B. London in the Thirties.*
J. Sturman, 55:Apr85-28
Brandt, G.W., ed. British Television Drama.*
P. Davison, 677(YES):Vol 15-362
Brandt, N. The Man Who Tried to Burn New York.
P. Clinton, 441:9Nov86-33
Brandt, R., ed. Rechtsphilosophie der Aufklärung.
W. Naucke, 687:Jan-Mar85-147
Brandt, U. and others - see von Meysenbug, M.

Brandt, W. Arms and Hunger.
T. Jacoby, 441:24Aug86-14
442(NY):18Aug86-75
Branner, H.C. The Poet and the Girl;
Anguish; The Mountains.
W.G. Jones, 562(Scan):Nov85-243
Branner, R. St. Louis and the Court Style
in Gothic Architecture. Burgundian
Gothic Architecture.
617(TLS):10Oct86-1147
Brannigan, A. The Social Bases of Scien-
tific Discoveries.
H.M. Collins, 488:Sep85-377
Brantley, R.E. Locke, Wesley, and the
Method of English Romanticism.
L. Damrosch, Jr., 173(ECS):Spring86-
438
P.M.S. Dawson, 148:Summer85-67
R.M. Ryan, 661(WC):Fall85-182
J.C. Villalobos, 250(HLQ):Summer85-313
Branzi, A. The Hot House.
K.D. Stein, 45:Jul85-79
Brasch, C. Indirections.
L. Jones, 49:Oct85-127
Brasch, J.D. and J. Sigman. Hemingway's
Library.
J. Meyers, 50(ArQ):Winter85-370
Brashers, K. Sing the Cows Home.
R. Bendix, 650(WF):Jan85-64
E. Dettmer, 292(JAF):Apr/Jun85-231
Brassell, T. Tom Stoppard.
M. Hinden, 659(ConL):Fall86-400
Braswell, M.F. The Medieval Sinner.*
J.V. Fleming, 589:Jul85-649
Brater, E., ed. Beckett at 80/Beckett in
Context.
A. Jenkins, 617(TLS):14Nov86-1281
442(NY):19May86-120
Bratton, J.S. The Impact of Victorian
Children's Fiction.
J. Sutherland, 447(N&Q):Jun84-272
Braude, S.E. The Limits of Influence.
P. Forbes, 362:24Jul86-23
Braudel, F. L'Identité de la France.
E. Weber, 617(TLS):22Aug86-906
Braudy, L. The Frenzy of Renown.
S. Jacoby, 441:7Sep86-12
Brault, J. Moments fragiles.
N. Bishop, 102(CanL):Spring85-132
Braun, A. Studien zu Syntax und Morphol-
ogie der Steigerungsformen im Englischen.
A. Fill, 38:Band103Heft1/2-128
Braun, C. Kritische Theorie versus Kritiz-
ismus.*
H. Hermann, 342:Band76Heft1-114
Braun, H. The Assassination of Gaitán.
C. Abel, 617(TLS):15Aug86-883
Braun, O. A Comintern Agent in China,
1932-1939.*
L.N. Shaffer, 293(JASt):Nov84-152
Braun, P., ed. Fremdwort-Diskussion.
A.W. Stanforth, 685(ZDL):1/1985-123
Braun, T. Disraeli the Novelist.*
M. Hardman, 677(YES):Vol 15-316
Braun, V. Hinze-Kunze-Roman.
M. Hofmann, 617(TLS):14Feb86-173
Braun, V. Stücke.
U. Heukenkamp, 601(SuF):Jan-Feb85-208
Braund, D.C. Rome and the Friendly King.
R.K. Sherk, 124:Sep-Oct85-52
Braunmuller, A.R., ed. The Captive Lady.
J.R. Elliott, Jr., 541(RES):May85-273

Braveboy-Wagner, J.A. The Venezuela-
Guyana Border Dispute.
L.B. Rout, Jr., 263(RIB):Vol35No1-63
Bravo, B. SULÁN.
É. Will, 555:Vol59fasc1-108
Bray, B. and I. Landy-Houillon, eds.
Lettres portugaises, Lettres d'une Péru-
vienne, et autres romans d'amour par
lettres.*
C. Habib, 535(RHL):Jan/Feb85-96
Braybrooke, D. Ethics in the World of
Business.*
R. Bronaugh, 154:Autumn85-545
Brazeau, P. Parts of a World.*
G.S. Lensing, 534(RALS):Spring83-70
A. Morris, 481(PQ):Spring85-290
Breakwell, G. The Quiet Rebel.
F. Cairncross, 617(TLS):4Apr86-349
"Ian Breakwell's Diary 1964-1985."
362:3Jul86-34
Brecher, C. and R.D. Horton. Setting
Municipal Priorities 1986.
J. Cohn, 129:May86-74
Brecht, B. Briefe 1913-1956.* (G.
Glaeser, ed)
J. Goldhahn, 654(WB):1/1985-163
Brecht, B. Fear and Misery of the Third
Reich [and] Señora Carrar's Rifles.
A. Vivis, 157:No155-53
Brecht, W. Unser Leben in Augsburg,
damals.
P. Brady, 617(TLS):14Mar86-281
Bredin, J-D. The Affair.* (French title:
L'Affaire.)
A. Horne, 61:Feb86-83
S. McConnell, 129:May86-68
R.O. Paxton, 453(NYRB):27Feb86-3
G. Wright, 441:26Jan86-11
442(NY):17Mar86-110
Breen, T.H. Tobacco Culture.
A. Boyer, 441:5Jan86-17
Breeze, D.J. The Northern Frontiers of
Roman Britain.
L. Keppie, 123:Vol35No2-421
de Breffny, B. Irish Family Names.
K.B. Harder, 424:Sep85-200
Bregman, J. Synesius of Cyrene.*
G. Fowden, 122:Jul85-281
Breisach, E. Historiography.
H.N. Tuttle, 125:Fall84-95
Breitner, K. and T. Leibnitz, eds. Kata-
log der Sammlung Anthony van Hoboken in
der Musiksammlung der Österreichischen
Nationalbibliothek. (Vol 2)
O. Neighbour, 410(M&L):Apr85-157
Breitweiser, M.R. Cotton Mather and
Benjamin Franklin.
A. Delbanco, 165(EAL):Winter85/86-278
P.F. Gura, 432(NEQ):Sep85-492
Breivik, L.E. Existential "There."*
J. Esser, 38:Band103Heft3/4-421
Breman, J. The Village on Java and the
Early-Colonial State.
R.R. Jay, 293(JASt):Aug85-883
Bremmer, J. The Early Greek Concept of
the Soul.*
C. Gill, 303(JoHS):Vol 105-205
M.L. West, 123:Vol35No1-56
Bremner, G. Order and Chance.*
J.R. Loy, 173(ECS):Fall85-123
Brémond, C., J. Le Goff and J-C. Schmitt.
L'"Exemplum."*
C. Daxelmüller, 196:Band26Heft1/2-139

Brenan, G. and R. Partridge. Best of
Friends. (X. Fielding, ed)
  R. Carr, 617(TLS):28Nov86-1333
Brendon, P. Ike.
  T. Hoopes, 441:30Nov86-29
Breneman, L.N. and B. Once Upon a Time.
  J. Creagh, 583:Fall85-83
Brenkert, G.G. Marx's Ethics of Freedom.*
  S.B. Smith, 543:Sep84-115
  B. Warren, 63:Dec85-564
Brennan, A. Shakespeare's Dramatic Struc-
tures.
  K. Brown, 617(TLS):22Aug86-917
"Christopher Brennan." (T. Sturm, ed)
  A. Clark, 71(ALS):May85-143
Brennan, J. The Cuisine of Asia.
  W. and C. Cowen, 639(VQR):Autumn85-138
Brenner, A. Colour Terms in the Old Test-
ament.
  D.R. Hillers, 318(JAOS):Oct-Dec84-767
Brenner, G. Concealments in Hemingway's
Works.*
  K.G. Johnston, 27(AL):Mar85-152
Brent, A. Philosophy and Educational
Foundations.
  D.W. Hamlyn, 518:Jul85-166
Brentano, C. Sämtliche Erzählungen.
  H.M.K. Riley, 133:Band17Heft3/4-346
Brentano, F. Sensory and Noetic Conscious-
ness. (O. Kraus and L.L. McAllister,
eds)
  J.J. Drummond, 543:Sep85-141
Brentano, F. The Theory of Categories.
  J.W. Koterski, 438:Summer85-362
Brenzel, B.M. Daughters of the State.*
  B. Todd, 106:Fall85-329
Brereton, G.E. and J.M. Ferrier - see "Le
Menagier de Paris"
Brereton, J.M. The British Soldier.
  H. Strachan, 617(TLS):4Jul86-742
Bresee, C. Sea Island Yankee.
  A. Harvey, 441:1Jun86-14
Breslin, J. Table Money.
  J. Carroll, 441:18May86-9
  442(NY):2Jun86-107
Breslin, J.E.B. From Modern to Contempor-
ary.*
  P. Balakian, 27(AL):Mar85-149
  M. Perloff, 191(ELN):Jun86-61
  295(JML):Nov85-433
Bresnan, J., ed. Crisis in the Philip-
pines.
  P.G. Hollie, 441:14Dec86-25
  D. Wilson, 617(TLS):5Dec86-1366
Bresnan, J., ed. The Mental Representa-
tion of Grammatical Relations.*
  I. Griffiths and R. Harris, 567:
Vol53No1/3-179
Bréton, G. Journal 1867-1871.
  A-C. Faitrop, 207(FR):May86-1010
Brett, C.E.B. Buildings of Belfast. (2nd
ed)
  A. Gomme, 617(TLS):27Jun86-713
Brett, G. Through Our Own Eyes.
  A. Barnett, 362:4Dec86-32
Brett, L. Our Selves Unknown.*
  S. Gardiner, 364:Apr/May85-141
Brett, P., comp. Benjamin Britten: "Peter
Grimes."*
  J.B., 412:Aug/Nov84-300

Brett, S. Dead Giveaway.
  P-L. Adams, 61:Jun86-83
  T.J. Binyon, 617(TLS):19Sep86-1029
  N. Callendar, 441:1Jun86-46
Brett, S. A Nice Class of Corpse.
  T.J. Binyon, 617(TLS):31Oct86-1224
Brett, S. A Shock to the System.*
  639(VQR):Autumn85-115
Brettell, R.R. and S.F. McCullagh. Degas
in The Art Institute of Chicago.
  A.A. McLees, 207(FR):Apr86-831
  C. Stuckey, 90:Jul85-466
Bretz, M.L. Concha Espina.
  B.J. Dendle, 552(REH):Oct85-139
Bretz, M.L., T. Dvorak and C. Kirschner.
Pasajes.
  M.S. Finch, 399(MLJ):Spring85-109
  W.T. Little, 238:May85-335
Breuer, H-P. - see Butler, S.
Brewer, A. A Guide to Marx's "Capital."
  T.M., 185:Apr86-668
Brewer, A.M. and M. Browne, eds. Diction-
aries, Encyclopedias, and Other Word-
Related Books. (3rd ed)
  P. Larkin, 677(YES):Vol 15-254
Brewer, D. English Gothic Literature.
  H. Cooper, 382(MAE):1985/2-295
  M. Dodsworth, 175:Spring85-93
  P. Gradon, 447(N&Q):Sep84-417
Brewer, D. An Introduction to Chaucer.*
  M. Dodsworth, 175:Summer85-184
  382(MAE):1985/2-346
Brewer, D. and E. Frankl. Arthur's Brit-
ain.
  T.A. Shippey, 617(TLS):30May86-583
Brewer, P.J. Shaker Communities, Shaker
Lives.
  A.A. Rhodes, 441:7Sep86-23
Brewster, E. A House Full of Women.*
  N. Besner, 102(CanL):Winter84-119
Breyer, B.J.S. - see Trollope, A.
Breytenbach, B. End Papers.
  J. Campbell, 617(TLS):19Sep86-1028
  D. Caute, 362:17Jul86-26
  B. Robbins, 441:30Nov86-21
Breytenbach, B. Mouroir.
  J. Campbell, 617(TLS):19Sep86-1028
Breytenbach, B. The True Confessions of
an Albino Terrorist.*
  J. Campbell, 617(TLS):19Sep86-1028
  J. Levine, 676(YR):Summer86-610
Brezzi, P. and M. Lorch, eds. Umanesimo a
Roma nel Quattrocento.
  K.R. Bartlett, 539:Nov85-283
Brial, J-M. Georges Brassens.
  J. Abrate, 207(FR):Mar86-631
Brick, H. Daniel Bell and the Decline of
Intellectual Radicalism.
  D.J. Singal, 617(TLS):21Nov86-1301
Bridel, P. Aventicum III.
  J.F. Drinkwater, 313:Vol75-292
Bridges, R. The Selected Letters of
Robert Bridges, With the Correspondence
of Robert Bridges and Lionel Muirhead.*
  (Vols 1 and 2) (D.E. Stanford, ed)
  J.F. Cotter, 249(HudR):Summer85-343
Bridgman, N. La musique à Venise.
  M-A. Lescourret, 98:Oct85-1037
Bridgman, R. Dark Thoreau.*
  R. Sattelmeyer, 183(ESQ):Vol31No3-190

Broda, R. and E. Jöst, eds. Wintermärchen in der Provinz.
  C.J. Wickham, 406:Fall85-384
Brode, P. Sir John Beverley Robinson.
  G.W., 102(CanL):Fall85-185
Brodeau, V. Poésies. (H.M. Tomlinson, ed)
  E. Balmas, 535(RHL):Mar/Apr85-289
  E. Guild, 208(FS):Jan85-65
Broder, P.J. The American West.
  R. Tyler, 584(SWR):Autumn85-559
Broderick, G. A Handbook of Late Spoken Manx.
  M. Ó Murchú, 112:Vol 17-164
  R.L. Thomson, 215(GL):Vol25No3-202
Brodersen, M. Walter Benjamin.
  R. Rochlitz, 98:Apr85-410
Brodeur, P. Outrageous Misconduct.*
  M. Kempton, 453(NYRB):30Jan86-31
Brodsky, G., J. Troyer and D. Vance, eds. Contemporary Readings in Social and Political Ethics.
  T.D., 185:Apr86-692
Brodsky, J. Less Than One.
  J. Bayley, 453(NYRB):12Jun86-3
  D. Bethea, 441:13Jul86-3
  F. Eberstadt, 129:Nov86-74
  H. Gifford, 617(TLS):19Sep86-1019
Brodsky, L.D. and R.W. Hamblin, eds. Faulkner.* (Vol 2)
  P.R. Broughton, 534(RALS):Spring83-41
Brodsky, L.D. and R.W. Hamblin, eds. Faulkner. (Vols 3 and 4)
  A. Ponder, 578:Fall86-96
Brodsky, M. Circuits and Wedding Feast.
  L. Gordon, 441:14Sep86-30
Brodsky, P.P. Russia in the Works of Rainer Maria Rilke.
  J. Simons, 104(CASS):Summer85-229
Brody, J. Lectures de Montaigne.*
  P. Henry, 131(CL):Spring85-187
  F. Lestringant, 535(RHL):Jan/Feb85-80
  I. Maclean, 208(FS):Apr85-193
  S. Rendall, 153:Summer85-44
Broich, U. and others - see Schirmer, W.F.
Broilo, F. Iscrizioni lapidarie latine del Museo Nazionale Concordiese di Portogruaro (I a.C.-III d.C.). (Vol 1)
  M.H. Crawford, 313:Vol75-319
Broilo, F. Iscrizioni lapidarie latine del Museo Nazionale Concordiese di Portogruaro (I a.C.-III d.C.). (Vol 2)
  T.R.S. Broughton, 124:Jul-Aug86-424
  M.H. Crawford, 313:Vol75-319
Brokken, H.M. Het ontstaan van de Hoekse en Kabeljauwse twisten.
  B. Lyon, 589:Jan85-101
Brolin, B.C. Flight of Fancy.
  J. Giovannini, 441:26Jan86-15
Broman, B.M. Old Homes of Bangkok.
  U. Roberts, 60:Jan-Feb85-134
Brombert, V. Victor Hugo and the Visionary Novel.*
  J.P. Houston, 207(FR):Mar86-621
  E. Weber, 31(ASch):Summer85-418
Brome, A. Poems. (R.R. Dubinski, ed)
  R.A. Anselment, 539:Nov85-275
  A. Rudrum, 178:Mar85-91
Brommer, F. Odysseus.
  J. Boardman, 123:Vol35No1-208
Brömser, B. Funktionale Satzperspektive im Englischen.
  J. Esser, 38:Band103Heft1/2-118

Bromwich, D. Hazlitt.*
  P.M.S. Dawson, 506(PSt):May85-84
  P. Faulkner, 161(DUJ):Jun85-277
  J.C. Robinson, 536(Rev):Vol7-65
Bromwich, R. Aspects of the Poetry of Dafydd ap Gwilym.
  G. Ruddock, 617(TLS):6Jun86-624
Bromwich, R. - see Dafydd ap Gwilym
Brøndsted, M., ed. Kortprosa i Norden.
  A. Bolckmans, 562(Scan):May85-104
Bronk, W. Vectors and Smoothable Curves.*
  K. Oderman, 271:Spring-Summer85-204
Bronner, S.E. and D. Kellner, eds. Passion and Rebellion.
  J. Lloyd, 59:Mar85-128
  J.M. Ritchie, 402(MLR):Jan85-227
Bronner, S.J. American Folk Art.
  M.J. Young, 292(JAF):Jul/Sep85-362
Brontë, C. The Poems of Charlotte Brontë.* (T. Winnifrith, ed)
  C. Alexander, 67:Nov85-263
  S. Davies, 148:Autumn85-35
  P. Morgan, 179(ES):Dec85-568
Brontë, C. Something about Arthur.* (C. Alexander, ed)
  T. Winnifrith, 677(YES):Vol 15-318
Brontë, P.B. The Poems of Patrick Branwell Brontë.* (T. Winnifrith, ed)
  R.G. Collins, 636(VP):Summer85-202
Bronzwaer, W., with K. Fens and J. Kuin, eds. T.S. Eliot, Gedichten.
  T.A. Westendorp, 204(FdL):Jun85-159
Brook, S. New York Days, New York Nights.
  639(VQR):Autumn85-136
Brook-Shepherd, G. November 1918.
  P. Brown, 106:Spring85-107
Brooke, C. A History of Gonville and Caius College.
  R. Shannon, 617(TLS):12Dec86-1395
Brooke, C.N.L. and R.A.B. Mynors - see Map, W.
Brooke, J. - see Walpole, H.
Brooke-Rose, C. A Rhetoric of the Unreal.*
  R. Cardinal, 529(QQ):Autumn85-549
Brooke-Rose, C. Xorandor.
  T.M. Disch, 441:3Aug86-10
  B. Morton, 617(TLS):11Jul86-767
  J. Turner, 362:7Aug86-25
Brookes, O. Forget Me Knots.
  S. Laschever, 441:24Aug86-19
Brookhiser, R. The Outside Story.
  G.A. Fossedal, 129:Jun86-78
  T. Noah, 441:1Jun86-29
Brookhiser, R. - see Buckley, W.F., Jr.
Brookner, A. Jacques-Louis David.
  617(TLS):19Dec86-1434
Brookner, A. Family and Friends.*
  S. Lardner, 442(NY):10Mar86-121
  J. Mellors, 364:Oct85-86
  D.J. Taylor, 176:Jun86-54
Brookner, A. Hotel du Lac.*
  D. Flower, 249(HudR):Summer85-309
  42(AR):Fall85-503
  639(VQR):Summer85-92
Brookner, A. A Misalliance.
  P. Craig, 617(TLS):29Aug86-932
  B. Tonkin, 362:4Sep86-22
Brooks, C. William Faulkner: First Encounters.*
  J.B. Wittenberg, 115:Spring84-147

[continued]

Brown, J. Velázquez. [continuing]
  A. Arikha, 453(NYRB):6Nov86-27
  L. Gowing, 441:10Aug86-1
  L. Gowing, 617(TLS):1Aug86-831
Brown, J. and J.H. Elliott. A Palace for
a King.
  L. Gowing, 617(TLS):1Aug86-831
Brown, J., with B. Tucker. James Brown.
  M. Watkins, 441:30Nov86-23
Brown, J.A.C. The Social Psychology of
Industry.
  J. Turner, 617(TLS):11Jul86-751
Brown, J.C. Immodest Acts.
  N. Cohn, 453(NYRB):30Jan86-3
  M. Lefkowitz, 617(TLS):25Apr86-438
  R. Mayne, 176:Jul/Aug86-49
  F. Randall, 441:19Jan86-27
Brown, J.L. Valéry Larbaud.
  A. Connell, 107(CRCL):Sep85-451
  S. Taylor-Horrex, 208(FS):Jan85-107
Brown, J.L. Shards.
  P. Mahillon, 450(NRF):Jul-Aug85-180
Brown, J.P. A Reader's Guide to the
Nineteenth-Century English Novel.
  A.L. Harris, 268(IFR):Winter86-50
  B.V. Qualls, 637(VS):Spring86-498
  G.B. Tennyson, 445(NCF):Sep85-248
Brown, J.R. Discovering Shakespeare.*
  K. Muir, 677(YES):Vol 15-278
Brown, J.R., ed. Focus on "Macbeth."*
  K. Tetzeli von Rosador, 156(ShJW):
  Jahrbuch1985-229
Brown, J.W. Fictional Meals and Their
Function in the French Novel 1789-1848.
  G. Gourdeau-Wilson, 627(UTQ):Summer85-
  454
Brown, J.W. Modos de ser/Modos de ver.
  L.S. Glaze, 399(MLJ):Autumn85-320
  B.C. Leetch, 238:Dec85-802
Brown, L. English Dramatic Form 1660-
1760.*
  D. Hughes, 402(MLR):Apr85-421
Brown, L. Alexander Pope.*
  P-G. Boucé, 189(EA):Jan-Mar86-78
  W. Hutchings, 148:Autumn85-73
  639(VQR):Autumn85-121
Brown, L. Victorian News and Newspapers.
  R. Altick, 617(TLS):21Feb86-185
Brown, M.E. Burns and Tradition.
  W.F.H. Nicolaisen, 588(SSL):Vol20-290
Brown, M.W. Tongues of Flame.
  K. Morton, 441:24Aug86-6
Brown, N.B. Hugo and Dostoevsky.
  M. Finlay, 107(CRCL):Mar85-163
Brown, P. Genèse de l'Antiquité tardive.*
Society and the Holy in Late Antiquity.*
(French title: La société et le sacré
dans l'Antiquité tardive.) Le culte des
saints, son essor et sa fonction dans la
chrétienté latine.
  B. Judic, 98:Oct85-1003
Brown, R., ed. The Architectural Out-
siders.
  J. Brandon-Jones, 324:Aug86-629
  E. Chaney, 617(TLS):3Jan86-16
Brown, R. Civil Wars.
  L. Simon, 502(PrS):Summer85-113
Brown, R. The Haunted House.
  J. Winterson, 617(TLS):1Aug86-844
Brown, R. James Joyce and Sexuality.
  J. Kidd, 617(TLS):5Sep86-980
  M. Shechner, 329(JJQ):Summer86-503

Brown, R. The Nature of Social Laws.
  O. Letwin, 483:Apr85-276
  M. Mandelbaum, 185:Jan86-427
Brown, R.E. and D.W. Macdonald, eds.
Social Odours in Mammals.
  M. Ridley, 617(TLS):5Sep86-986
Brown, R.J. Timber-Framed Buildings of
England.
  J. Munby, 617(TLS):31Oct86-1230
Brown, R.M. High Hearts.
  M. Childress, 441:20Apr86-22
Brown, S., ed. Caribbean Poetry Now.
  T. Eagleton, 565:Spring85-66
Brown, S. Leibniz.*
  S.E., 185:Apr86-670
  N. Jolley, 319:Jan86-129
Brown, S.C., ed. Objectivity and Cultural
Divergence.
  B. Mayo, 518:Jul85-178
Brown, S.J. Thomas Chalmers and the Godly
Commonwealth.
  H.D. Rack, 637(VS):Winter85-324
Brown, V. - see Loew, E.A.
Brown, V.P. and L. Owens. The World of
the Southern Indians.
  L.R. Atkins, 9(AlaR):Jan85-69
Brown, W. and H. Senior. Victorious in
Defeat.
  E. Jones, 298:Fall85-149
Browne, G.A. Stone 588.
  B. Tritel, 441:23Feb86-23
Browne, P.F. Sassenach.
  442(NY):27Oct86-144
Browne, R., ed. Music Theory.*
  S. Ehrenkreutz, 309:Vol6No3-260
Browne, T. Pseudodoxia Epidemica.* (R.
Robbins, ed)
  D. Novarr, 402(MLR):Jul85-694
Browning, C.R. Fateful Months.
  I. Kershaw, 617(TLS):7Nov86-1242
Browning, E.B. The Letters of Elizabeth
Barrett Browning to Mary Russell Mitford
1836-1854.* (M.B. Raymond and M.R.
Sullivan, eds)
  P. Drew, 402(MLR):Jan85-133
Browning, R. Robert Browning: The Poems.*
(J. Pettigrew, ed; completed by T.J.
Collins)
  P. Drew, 402(MLR):Apr85-445
Browning, R., ed. The Greek World.*
  C.M. Woodhouse, 617(TLS):3Jan86-18
Browning, R. Medieval and Modern Greek.
(2nd ed)
  D. Holton, 123:Vol35No1-97
Browning, R. More than Friend. (M. Mere-
dith, ed)
  R. Langbaum, 441:26Jan86-21
Browning, R. The Poetical Works of Robert
Browning.* (Vol 1) (I. Jack and M.
Smith, eds)
  P. Drew, 402(MLR):Jan85-134
  C.D. Ryals, 301(JEGP):Oct85-562
Browning, R. The Poetical Works of Robert
Browning.* (Vol 2) (I. Jack and M.
Smith, eds)
  M. Hicks, 148:Summer85-87
  C.D. Ryals, 301(JEGP):Oct85-562
Browning, R.M. Deutsche Lyrik des Barock.
  R. Ambacher, 406:Summer85-220
Browning, R.M., ed. Goethe, Hölderlin,
Nietzsche, and Others.
  R. Spuler, 399(MLJ):Autumn85-308

Brunvand, J.H.  The Choking Doberman and Other "New" Urban Legends.
  R.D. Bethke, 650(WF):Apr85-147
  J. Erickson, 196:Band26Heft1/2-142
Brunvand, J.H.  The Mexican Pet.
  P-L. Adams, 61:Oct86-103
  S. Simon, 441:6Jul86-8
Bruscagli, R.  Stagioni della civiltà estense.*
  M. Pieri, 400(MLN):Jan85-181
Brush, S.G., C.W.F. Everitt and E. Garber - see Maxwell, J.C.
Brushwood, J.S.  Genteel Barbarism.*
  C.J. Alonso, 403(MLS):Summer85-93
Brushwood, J.S.  La novela hispano-americana del siglo XX.
  C.M. del Río, 238:Dec85-783
Brüske, W.  Untersuchungen zur Geschichte des Lutizenbundes.  (2nd ed)
  H.P. King, 575(SEER):Apr85-294
Bruss, E.W.  Beautiful Theories.
  D.H. Hirsch, 569(SR):Summer85-465
  S.R. Suleiman, 141:Summer85-307
Bruyère, N.  Méthode et dialectique dans l'oeuvre de La Ramée — Renaissance et âge classique.
  K. Meerhoff, 204(FdL):Sep85-226
de Bruyn, L.  Mob-Rule and Riots.
  G. Bourquin, 189(EA):Apr-Jun86-240
Bryan, J. 3d.  Merry Gentlemen (and One Lady).*
  442(NY):17Mar86-111
Bryan, T.A.  Censorship and Social Conflict in the Spanish Theatre.*
  J. Lyon, 86(BHS):Jul85-321
Bryant, D.  Lyric Poets of the Southern T'ang.
  R.W. Bodman, 293(JASt):Feb85-360
  Wong Siu-Kit, 302:Vol21No1-66
Bryant, S.M. - see Pérez de Hita, G.
Bryant, W.C.  The Letters of William Cullen Bryant.  (Vol 4) (W.C. Bryant 2d and T.G. Voss, eds)
  D.A. Ringe, 27(AL):Dec85-660
Bryce, J.  Cosimo Bartoli (1503-1572).*
  J.R. Woodhouse, 278(IS):Vol40-130
Bryce, J.C. - see Smith, A.
Bryer, A. and D. Winfield.  The Byzantine Monuments and Topography of the Pontos.
  J. Howard-Johnston, 617(TLS):17Oct86-1172
Bryer, J.R., ed.  The Short Stories of F. Scott Fitzgerald.*
  A.H. Petry, 403(MLS):Fall85-368
Bryfonski, D., ed.  Contemporary Authors, Autobiography Series.  (Vol 1)
  J. Klinkowitz, 534(RALS):Spring83-62
  42(AR):Spring85-251
Brykman, G.  Berkeley.
  A.R., 540(RIPh):Vol39fasc3-280
Bryson, J.  Evil Angels.
  J. Neville, 617(TLS):14Feb86-157
Bryson, N.  Tradition and Desire.*
  B. Gosskurth, 90:Aug85-539
  R. Jay, 446(NCFS):Spring-Summer86-387
  R.A. Kingcaid, 207(FR):Dec85-322
  W. Leeks, 59:Sep85-366
Bryson, N.  Word and Image.*
  S.S. Bryson, 188(ECr):Spring85-91
  P. Joannides, 97(CQ):Vol 14No3-240
Brzezinski, J., ed.  Consciousness.
  J-M. Gabaude, 542:Jul-Sep85-354

Brzezinski, Z.  Game Plan.
  E.A. Cohen, 129:Sep86-61
  P. Johnson, 441:29Jun86-11
  442(NY):4Aug86-87
Buache, F.  Le Cinema Allemand (1918-1933).
  P. Warren, 193(ELit):Spring-Summer85-201
Bubner, R.  Geschichtsprozesse und Handlungsnormen.
  J. Habermas, 384:Sep/Oct85-900
Bucco, M.  René Wellek.
  C. Norris, 402(MLR):Jan85-138
Bucco, M.  Western American Literary Criticism.
  F. Erisman, 26(ALR):Spring/Autumn85-267
  S.E. Marovitz, 26(ALR):Spring/Autumn85-269
  D.E. Wylder, 649(WAL):Aug85-182
Bucer, M.  Martini Buceri opera omnia.  (Ser 2, Vol 1) (C. Augustijn, P. Fraenkel and M. Leinhard, eds)
  L.V.R., 568(SCN):Spring-Summer85-27
  R.J. Schoeck, 551(RenQ):Winter85-733
Buch, H.C.  The Wedding at Port-au-Prince.
  R. Guy, 441:2Nov86-20
Buchan, D.  Scottish Tradition.*
  D. McDuff, 565:Winter84/85-73
Buchan, J.  The Thirty-Nine Steps.
  K. Hillier, 364:Dec85/Jan86-153
Buchanan, G.  Tragedies.*  (P. Sharratt and P.G. Walsh, eds and trans)
  J.W. Binns, 123:Vol35No1-227
  P. Ford, 402(MLR):Jan85-161
  P. Godman, 541(RES):Nov85-563
  G. Schrenck, 535(RHL):Sep/Oct85-858
Buchanan, P.H.  Margaret Tudor, Queen of Scots.
  C. Bingham, 617(TLS):18Apr86-427
Buchanan, W.J.  Present Danger.
  J. Bass, 441:20Apr86-22
Buchloh, B.H.D., S. Guilbaut and D. Solkin, eds.  Modernism and Modernity.
  F. Frascina, 59:Dec85-515
Buchner, E.  Die Sonnenuhr des Augustus.
  P. Pattenden, 123:Vol35No1-217
  A. Wallace-Hadrill, 313:Vol75-245
Buchner, H., W.G. Jacobs and A. Pieper - see Schelling, F.W.J.
Buchner, H. and J. Jantzen - see Schelling, F.W.J.
Bucholz, A.  Hans Delbrück and the German Military Establishment.
  G. Best, 617(TLS):10Jan86-32
Buchthal, H.  Art of the Mediterranean World, A.D. 100 to 1400.
  W.B. Denny, 589:Jul85-653
Buck, M.  Politics, Finance and the Church in the Reign of Edward II.
  R.M. Haines, 589:Jan85-130
  G.L. Harriss, 382(MAE):1985/2-297
Buck, N. and others.  The London Employment Problem.
  N. Deakin, 617(TLS):7Nov86-1239
Buck, R.J.  Agriculture and Agricultural Practice in Roman Law.
  F.R. Bliss, 124:Sep-Oct85-59
Buck, W.  Mahabharata.  Ramayana.
  W.L. Smith, 318(JAOS):Jul-Sep84-607
Buckland, T., ed.  Traditional Dance.  (Vol 2)
  S. Billington, 203:Vol196No2-262

Buñuel, L. Obra literaria. (A. Sánchez
Vidal, ed)
   J. Cano Ballesta, 400(MLN):Mar85-452
Buñuel, L., with J-C. Carrière. My Last
Sigh.* (French title: Mon Dernier
Soupir; British title: My Last Breath.)
   42(AR):Spring85-253
Buonarroti il Giovane, M. La fiera.* (U.
Limentani, ed)
   G. Aquilecchia, 278(IS):Vol40-138
   J.R. Woodhouse, 402(MLR):Jan85-185
Burbank, R. Twentieth Century Music.
   M. Rochester, 415:Feb85-97
a Búrc, É. and L. MacCoisdeala. Eochair,
Mac Rí in Éirinn.
   B. Ó Cuív, 112:Vol 16-196
Burchfield, R. The English Language.*
   W.N. Francis, 350:Sep86-712
   H. Käsmann, 38:Band103Heft3/4-411
   J. Pauchard, 189(EA):Apr-Jun86-194
Burchfield, R.W. - see "A Supplement to
the Oxford English Dictionary"
Burck, E. Historische und epische Tradi-
tion bei Silius Italicus.
   D.C. Feeney, 123:Vol35No2-390
Burck, F.W. Mothers Talking.
   C. Klein, 441:10Aug86-19
Burdon, E. I Used To Be An Animal, But
I'm All Right Now.
   362:6Nov86-36
Burford, B. The Threshing Floor.
   J. Winterson, 617(TLS):22Aug86-921
Burford, E.J. Wits, Wenchers and Wantons.
   D. Sacks, 441:12Oct86-14
Bürger, P. Theory of the Avant-Garde.*
   M. Calinescu, 125:Winter85-205
   R. Shattuck, 453(NYRB):18Dec86-66
Burger, R. "The Phaedo."
   R.K., 185:Jul86-912
   J.P. Schiller, 319:Oct86-547
Burgess, A. But Do Blondes Prefer Gentle-
men?
   N. Ramsey, 441:30Mar86-19
Burgess, A. Flame Into Being.*
   J.M. Coetzee, 453(NYRB):16Jan86-33
   R. Lewis, 176:Jan86-42
   S. Silvers, 364:Oct85-102
Burgess, A. Ernest Hemingway and His
World.
   W. Sheed, 453(NYRB):12Jun86-5
Burgess, A. Homage to Qwert Yuiop.
   R. Craft, 617(TLS):6Jun86-608
Burgess, A. The Kingdom of the Wicked.*
   R. Lewis, 176:Jan86-41
   P. Vansittart, 364:Jun85-100
Burgess, A. Ninety-nine Novels.
   J. Breen, 381:Mar85-142
Burgess, A. The Pianoplayers.
   P-L. Adams, 61:Nov86-140
   W. Brandmark, 362:11Sep86-22
   V. Cunningham, 617(TLS):29Aug86-933
   G. Lyons, 441:2Nov86-7
   442(NY):3Nov86-166
Burgess, G.S. Chrétien de Troyes: "Erec
et Enide."
   A.H. Diverres, 208(FS):Jan85-60
   E.P. Wisotzka, 207(FR):Feb86-457
   382(MAE):1985/2-347
Burgess, G.S. Marie de France.
   A. Vanderheyden, 356(LR):Aug85-223
Burgess, M. A Guide to Science Fiction
and Fantasy in the Library of Congress
   [continued]

Classification Scheme.
   C.E., 561(SFS):Mar85-104
Burgess, T., ed. Education for Capability.
   K. Alexander, 324:Jul86-535
Burgess, T. and E. Adams. Records of
Achievement at 16.
   A. Jones, 324:Sep86-693
Bürgisser, M. Untersuchungen zur Wortbild-
ung im Althochdeutschen und Altnieder-
deutschen.
   J. Erben, 684(ZDA):Band114Heft1-1
Burgoon, J.K. and T. Saine. The Unspoken
Dialogue.
   G.W. Beattie, 567:Vol57No3/4-375
Burian, J. Svoboda: Wagner.*
   D. Unruh, 615(TJ):May85-259
Buridan, J. John Buridan on Self-
Reference.* (G.E. Hughes, ed)
   I. Angelelli, 316:Sep85-859
   C.J. Martin, 482(PhR):Jul85-406
Buridan, J. Iohannes Buridanus, "Quaes-
tiones in praedicamenta." (J. Schneider,
ed)
   P.O. Lewry, 589:Oct85-953
Burke, E. Selected Letters of Edmund
Burke. (H.C. Mansfield, Jr., ed)
   I.K., 185:Apr86-687
   R. Nisbet, 31(ASch):Winter84/85-121
   639(VQR):Winter85-9
Burke, J.J., Jr. and D. Kay, eds. The
Unknown Samuel Johnson.*
   J.D. Fleeman, 541(RES):Nov85-573
   R. Halsband, 301(JEGP):Jan85-129
   S.E. Longmire, 405(MP):Nov85-197
Burke, J.L. The Convict.
   A. Codrescu, 441:5Jan86-16
Burke, T.E. The Philosophy of Popper.*
   A. O'Hear, 393(Mind):Jan85-167
Burkert, W. Greek Religion.*
   J. Barnes, 520:Vol30No2-217
Burkert, W. Homo Necans.*
   J.N. Bremmer, 123:Vol35No2-312
Burkhardt, F. and F. Bowers - see James, W.
Burkhardt, F. and F. Bowers, with I.K.
Skrupskelis - see James, W.
Burkhardt, H. Logik und Semiotik in der
Philosophie von Leibniz.*
   K.E. Kaehler, 53(AGP):Band67Heft2-212
Burkholder, J.P. Charles Ives.
   W. Mellers, 617(TLS):7Feb86-143
Burl, A. Megalithic Brittany.
   C. Chippindale, 617(TLS):6Jun86-629
Burlakoff, N. and C. Lindahl, eds. Folk-
lore on Two Continents.
   R.D. Bethke, 650(WF):Jan85-68
Burland, B. Love is a Durable Fire.
   T. Cook, 441:22Jun86-27
"Burlesque et obscénité chez les trouba-
dours."
   F. Delay, 450(NRF):Feb85-106
Burley, W.J. Wycliffe and the Quiet
Virgin.
   T.J. Binyon, 617(TLS):27Jun86-711
Burling, R. Learning a Field Language.
   M.L. Bender, 350:Mar86-224
Burmeister, B. Streit um den Nouveau
Roman.
   A. Burkart, 654(WB):10/1985-1747
Burn, G. Pocket Money.
   S. Hey, 362:18/25Dec86-56
Burn, L. and R. Glynn. Beazley Addenda.
   B.B. Shefton, 123:Vol35No2-420

Burnett, A.P.  The Art of Bacchylides.
  P. Wilson, 617(TLS):30May86-593
Burnett, A.P.  Three Archaic Poets.*
  R. Jenkyns, 487:Summer85-165
Burnett, C.  One More Time.
  R. Plunkett, 441:19Oct86-31
Burnett, D. and M. Schiff.  Contemporary
  Canadian Art.*
  D. Farr, 529(QQ):Autumn85-604
  J.H. Kaplan, 102(CanL):Spring85-122
Burnett, J.  Destiny Obscure.
  N. Hackett, 77:Fall85-369
Burnett, P., ed.  The Penguin Book of
  Caribbean Verse in English.
  L. Mackinnon, 617(TLS):24Oct86-1185
Burnett, T.A.J.  The Rise and Fall of a
  Regency Dandy.
  A. Nicholson, 677(YES):Vol 15-309
Burnett, V.  A Comedy of Eros.
  E. McNamara, 102(CanL):Winter84-113
Burney, F.  Cecilia.
  J. Bayley, 617(TLS):27Jun86-695
Burney, F.  The Journals and Letters of
  Fanny Burney (Madame d'Arblay).*  (Vols
  11 and 12)  (J. Hemlow, with A. Douglas
  and P. Hawkins, eds)
  K.C. Phillipps, 506(PSt):Dec85-97
Burnheim, J.  Is Democracy Possible?
  V. Bogdanor, 617(TLS):7Mar86-241
Burnley, D.  A Guide to Chaucer's Lan-
  guage.*
  N. Davis, 541(RES):Nov85-554
  W.A. Quinn, 599:Summer85-287
  R.A. Waldron, 179(ES):Oct85-465
Burns, B.  The Novels of Thomas Love Pea-
  cock.
  B.R., 148:Autumn85-91
Burns, C.  Snakewrist.
  A. Sattin, 617(TLS):5Sep86-978
Burns, C.A.  Henry Céard et le Natural-
  isme.*
  P. Cogny, 535(RHL):Jan/Feb85-115
Burns, E. - see Stein, G. and C. Van Vech-
  ten
Burns, O.A.  Cold Sassy Tree.
  639(VQR):Summer85-91
Burns, R.  A Dance for the Moon.
  M. Stimpson, 617(TLS):27Jun86-710
Burns, R.  Ground Money.
  442(NY):16Jun86-123
Burns, R.  The Letters of Robert Burns.
  (2nd ed)  (G.R. Roy, ed)
  D. Dunn, 617(TLS):25Jul86-803
Burns, R. - see Sanesi, R.
Burns, R.I.  Muslims, Christians, and Jews
  in the Crusader Kingdom of Valencia.
  639(VQR):Winter85-9
Burns, R.I.  Society and Documentation in
  Crusader Valencia.
  P. Linehan, 617(TLS):4Apr86-354
Burns, R.I., ed.  The Worlds of Alfonso
  the Learned and James the Conqueror.
  R.A. Fletcher, 617(TLS):18Jul86-796
Burns, R.W.  British Television: The For-
  mative Years.
  N. Moss, 362:11Dec86-26
Burns, T.S.  A History of the Ostrogoths.
  N. Wagner, 684(ZDA):Band114Heft2-41
Burnshaw, S.  Robert Frost Himself.
  R.W. Flint, 441:30Nov86-24

Burnyeat, M., ed.  The Skeptical Tradi-
  tion.*
  L. Groarke, 154:Winter85-746
  E. de Olaso, 319:Jan86-118
Burr, D.  Eucharistic Presence and Conver-
  sion in Late Thirteenth-Century Francis-
  can Thought.
  G.J. Etzkorn, 589:Oct85-955
Burr, E.E.  The Journal of Esther Edwards
  Burr, 1754-1757.*  (C.F. Karlsen and L.
  Crumpacker, eds)
  C. Bushman, 658:Summer/Autumn85-201
Burra, E.  Well, Dearie!*  (W. Chappell,
  ed)
  A. Ross, 364:Dec85/Jan86-126
Burresi, M. and A. Caleca.  Andrea, Nino e
  Tommaso, scultori pisani.
  J. Gardner, 90:Aug85-535
Burridge, T.  Clement Attlee.
  H.G. Pitt, 364:Mar86-92
  M. Pugh, 617(TLS):21Mar86-296
  442(NY):10Nov86-145
Burrison, J.A.  Brothers in Clay.*
  C. Counts, 139:Jun/Jul85-52
  G.H. Greer, 650(WF):Jan85-54
  R.B. St. George, 292(JAF):Apr/Jun85-
  220
Burroughs, W.  The Adding Machine.
  J. Campbell, 617(TLS):24Jan86-76
  A. Schmitz, 441:17Aug86-23
Burroughs, W.  Queer.*
  A. Mars-Jones, 617(TLS):18Apr86-415
Burrow, J.A.  The Ages of Man.
  A. Murray, 617(TLS):10Oct86-1127
Burrow, J.A.  Essays on Medieval Litera-
  ture.*
  D. Pearsall, 179(ES):Feb85-80
  E. Wilson, 541(RES):Aug85-402
Burrow, J.A.  Medieval Writers and their
  Work.*
  N.F. Blake, 72:Band222Heft1-178
  P.M. Kean, 541(RES):Feb85-142
Burrow, T. and M.B. Emeneau.  A Dravidian
  Etymological Dictionary.*  (2nd ed)
  K.R. Norman, 361:Jul85-272
Burrs, M.  The Blue Pools of Paradise.
  J. Orange, 102(CanL):Winter84-103
Burssenbrugge, M-M.  The Heat Bird.
  C. Wright, 448:Vol23No1-118
Burstein, P.  Discrimination, Jobs, and
  Politics.
  N. Glazer, 617(TLS):13Jun86-655
Burstyn, V., ed.  Women Against Censor-
  ship.*
  M. Kadar, 99:Aug/Sep85-36
Burt, L.W.  Tribalism in Crisis.
  B.W. Dippie, 106:Spring85-31
Burt, R.  Rockerama.
  R.S. Denisoff, 498:Vol9No4-67
Burt, S.  Floral Street.
  D. Profumo, 617(TLS):17Jan86-57
  R. Seidman, 441:4May86-40
Burton, G.  Heartbreak Hotel.
  B. Harvey, 441:14Dec86-24
Burton, R.  Bird Behaviour.*
  E. Dunn, 617(TLS):30May86-602
Burton, R.  Classical Poets in the "Flor-
  ilegium Gallicum."
  R.C. Lounsbury, 124:Jul-Aug86-423
Bury, J.P.T.  France: 1814-1940.  (5th ed)
  R.A. Hartzell, 207(FR):May86-1009
Bury, J.P.T.  Gambetta's Final Years.
  D.H. Barry, 161(DUJ):Jun85-261

Bury, J.P.T. and R.P. Tombs. Thiers 1797-1877.
D.H. Pinkney, 617(TLS):19Dec86-1417
Busacker, K. Shakespeares "Julius Caesar."
J.L. Gunther, 570(SQ):Summer85-240
Busard, H.L.L. - see Adelard of Bath
Busby, K. Gauvain in Old French Literature.*
D. Kelly, 545(RPh):Feb85-386
Busby, K., ed and trans. Raoul de Houdenc, "Le Roman des Eles," the Anonymous "Ordene de Chevalierie."*
A.T. Harrison, 207(FR):Dec85-286
W.G. Van Emden, 402(MLR):Jan85-157
K. Varty, 382(MAE):1985/2-329
Busby, K., ed. Three Anglo-Norman Redactions of L'Ordene de Chevalerie.
G. Roques, 553(RLiR):Jan-Jun85-239
Busby, M. Preston Jones.
D.E. Wylder, 649(WAL):Aug85-187
Busch, B.C. The War Against the Seals.
S. Mills, 617(TLS):6Jun86-612
Busch, F. Sometimes I Live in the Country.
C. Baxter, 441:1Jun86-35
Busch, F. Too Late American Boyhood Blues.
W.H. Pritchard, 249(HudR):Spring85-128
639(VQR):Spring85-61
Busch, L. and W.B. Lacy. Science, Agriculture, and the Politics of Research.
F.A. Hilenski, 577(SHR):Summer85-277
Busch, W. Max und Moritz, polyglott.
J. Amsler, 549(RLC):Jul-Sep85-357
Buschinger, D. and A. Crépin, eds.
Comique, satire et parodie dans la tradition renardienne et les fabliaux.
D. Blamires, 402(MLR):Jul85-749
Bush, M.L. Noble Privilege.
J.B. Henneman, 589:Jul85-655
Bush, R. T.S. Eliot.*
M. Alexander, 4:Spring-Summer85-177
S.S. Baskett, 115:Fall84/Winter85-148
J.S. Brooker, 405(MP):Feb86-325
R.I. Scott, 648(WCR):Apr86-69
G. Smith, 27(AL):Mar85-143
R.Z. Temple, 536(Rev):Vol7-329
L. Thiesmeyer, 184(EIC):Oct85-350
295(JML):Nov85-472
Bush, S. and A. Booth. Life on the Line.
R.P. Knowles, 198:Spring85-84
Bushman, R.L. King and People in Provincial Massachusetts.
J. Butler, 432(NEQ):Dec85-614
Bushman, R.L. Joseph Smith and the Beginnings of Mormonism.*
L. Arrington, 432(NEQ):Sep85-469
D. Martin, 617(TLS):7Mar86-251
Bushnaq, I., ed and trans. Arab Folktales.
B. Harlow, 441:6Apr86-12
442(NY):26May86-106
Bushnell, J. Mutiny Amid Repression.
F. Kazemzadeh, 441:16Feb86-13
Busi, A. Seminario sulla gioventù. Vita standard di un venditore provvisorio di collant.
P. Hainsworth, 617(TLS):9May86-497
Buss, R. Vigny: "Chatterton."
W.D. Howarth, 208(FS):Jul85-353
Busse, T.V. The Professor's Book of First Names.
E.D. Lawson, 424:Dec85-279

Bussmann, H. Lexikon der Sprachwissenschaft.
H. Haider, 603:Vol9No3-463
J. Lüdtke, 547(RF):Band97Heft4-429
D. Nehls, 257(IRAL):May85-167
Bussy-Rabutin. Correspondance avec le Père René Rapin. (C. Rouben, ed)
D.C. Potts, 402(MLR):Apr85-463
P. Wolfe, 475:Vol 12No22-376
"Solomon D. Butcher: Photographing the American Dream." (J.E. Carter, ed)
442(NY):24Mar86-128
Buthlay, K. Hugh MacDiarmid.*
D.S. Robb, 447(N&Q):Dec84-532
Butler, A.J. The Arab Conquest of Egypt and the Last Thirty Years of the Roman Dominion. (2nd ed rev by P.M. Fraser)
W.J. Aerts, 394:Vol38fasc3/4-449
Butler, A.M. Daughters of Joy, Sisters of Mercy.
L. Milazzo, 584(SWR):Autumn85-547
Butler, C. Computers in Linguistics.
G. Sampson, 617(TLS):29Aug86-949
Butler, C. Statistics in Linguistics.
P. Dunkel, 608:Sep86-549
Butler, C. Interpretation, Deconstruction, and Ideology.*
P. Barry, 175:Summer85-169
Butler, D. The Men Who Mastered Time.
P. Reading, 617(TLS):31Oct86-1225
Butler, G. Coffin on the Water.
T.J. Binyon, 617(TLS):10Oct86-1131
M. Laski, 362:3Jul86-32
Butler, J. The Huguenots in America.
J.F. Bosher, 656(WMQ):Jan85-136
A. Friedlander, 173(ECS):Spring86-398
Butler, J. Jujitsu for Christ.
M. Kirby, 441:23Nov86-9
442(NY):17Nov86-151
Butler, L.S. Samuel Beckett and the Meaning of Being.*
S.E. Gontarski, 395(MFS):Summer85-372
W.B. Worthen, 615(TJ):Dec85-514
295(JML):Nov85-447
Butler, L.S. and A.D. Watson, eds. The North Carolina Experience.
R.F. Dolle, 568(SCN):Winter85-64
Butler, M., ed. Burke, Paine, Godwin, and the Revolution Controversy.
P.M.S. Dawson, 148:Summer85-67
C.B. Jones, 506(PSt):May85-82
I.K., 185:Apr86-687
A. Morvan, 189(EA):Apr-Jun86-224
Butler, M. Theatre and Crisis, 1632-1642.*
C. Hill, 366:Autumn85-301
Butler, R. Balzac and the French Revolution.*
I. Collins, 366:Spring85-146
Butler, R. Zola: "La Terre."
L. Kamm, 207(FR):Apr86-790
B. Nelson, 208(FS):Jan85-95
R. Stanley, 446(NCFS):Spring-Summer86-379
Butler, S., ed. Common Ground.
T. Curtis, 493:Feb86-62
Butler, S. The Note-Books of Samuel Butler. (Vol 1) (H-P. Breuer, ed)
T.L. Jeffers, 177(ELT):Vol28No4-422
H.H. Watts, 395(MFS):Summer85-341
Butler, W.E., ed. The Legal System of the Chinese Soviet Republic (1931-1934).
P. Potter, 293(JASt):May85-573

Butlin, M. and E. Joll. The Paintings of
J.M.W. Turner.* (rev)
  L. Herrmann, 90:Jan85-47
  A. Wilton, 39:Oct85-316
Butlin, R. Ragtime in Unfamiliar Bars.
  T. Dooley, 617(TLS):20Jun86-677
  W. Scammell, 148:Winter85-65
Bütner, T.T. Las lenguas de los Andes
Centrales.
  J. Bustamante García, 548:Jul-Dec85-
  471
Butor, M. The Spirit of Mediterranean
Places.
  E. Roditi, 441:31Aug86-10
Butrica, J.L. The Manuscript Tradition of
Propertius.
  K. Gries, 124:Jul-Aug86-412
  S. Schierling, 377:Nov84-181
Butson, T.G. The Tsar's Lieutenant.*
  G.C. Furr, 550(RusR):Oct85-427
Butt, J. Miguel de Unamuno: "San Manuel
Bueno, Mártir."*
  K. Kohut, 72:Band222Heft2-465
Butt, R. The Unfinished Task.
  J. Critchley, 362:17Jul86-27
Butterfield, R.W., ed. Modern American
Poetry.*
  L. Coupe, 148:Winter85-88
Butterick, G.F. - see Olson, C.
Butterworth, B., B. Comrie and Ö. Dahl,
eds. Explanations for Language Univer-
sals.
  P. Ramat, 361:Aug85-375
Butterworth, C.E., with A.A. al-Magid
Haridi - see Averroes
Butterworth, M. The Five Million Dollar
Prince.
  N. Callendar, 441:21Sep86-36
Butterworth, N. A Dictionary of American
Composers.
  P. Dickinson, 410(M&L):Jan85-58
Buttitta, A. Semiotica e antropologia.
  M. Herzfeld, 567:Vol56No1/2-153
Büttner, F.O. Imitatio pietatis.
  K.E. Haney, 589:Jul85-657
Büttner, G. Samuel Beckett's Novel
"Watt."*
  F.N. Smith, 395(MFS):Winter85-813
de Butts, M.C.L. - see Lee, A.
van Buuren, C., ed. "The Buke of the
Sevyne Sagis."*
  R.S. Allen, 382(MAE):1985/2-321
van Buuren, M. Ongebaande wegen.
  W. de Moor, 204(FdL):Dec85-317
Buxbaum, M.H. Benjamin Franklin, 1721-
1906.*
  O. Seavey, 405(MP):Nov85-200
Buxton, R.G.A. Persuasion in Greek
Tragedy.
  A.L. Brown, 303(JoHS):Vol 105-200
Buys, W., T. Sill and R. Beck. Speaking
by Doing.
  S. Irujo, 399(MLJ):Summer85-216
Buzzati, D. The Tartar Steppe.
  D.J. Taylor, 176:Jun86-55
Bykau, W. Zeichen des Unheils.
  A. Hiersche, 654(WB):5/1985-858
Bynum, D.E. The Daemon in the Wood.
  J.J. Duggan, 589:Jul85-659
Byock, J.L. Feud in the Icelandic Saga.*
  P. Hallberg, 562(Scan):May85-66
Byrd, D. Charles Olson's Maximus.
  H.M. Dennis, 677(YES):Vol 15-356

Bryd, M. "Tristram Shandy."*
  M. New, 173(ECS):Summer86-553
  S. Soupel, 189(EA):Apr-Jun86-222
Byrd, W.S. Letters from a Young Shaker.
(S.J. Stein, ed)
  R. Minkoff, 441:8Jun86-37
Byrne, J.A. The Headhunters.
  M. Bender, 441:17Aug86-23
Byrne, M.S., ed. The Lisle Letters: An
Abridgement.
  E.Z. Tabuteau, 115:Spring84-146
Byrne, R. Skyscraper.
  J.V. Iovine, 45:Mar85-77
Byron, C.M. The Fanciest Dive.
  R. Blount, Jr., 441:9Mar86-11

Cabezas, O. Fire from the Mountain.*
  S. White, 448:Vol23No3-150
Cabrera, V. Juan Benet.*
  D.K. Herzberger, 400(MLN):Mar85-441
Cabrera Infante, G. Holy Smoke.
  J. Butt, 617(TLS):29Aug86-946
  J. Rubins, 453(NYRB):8May86-35
  A. Schmitz, 441:2Mar86-25
Caccia, F. and A. D'Alfonso, eds. Quêtes.
  M. Mantovani, 102(CanL):Fall85-81
Cacho Blecua, J.M. and M.J. Lacarra - see
Alfonso X
Cadogan, M. Richmal Crompton.
  G. Avery, 617(TLS):5Dec86-1378
  N. Williams, 362:13Nov86-26
Cadogan, M. and P. Craig. You're a Brick,
Angela.
  617(TLS):25Apr86-459
Cadsby, H. and M. Jacobs, eds. The Third
Taboo.*
  B. Pell, 102(CanL):Spring85-136
Cadwallader, E.H. Searchlight on Values.
  J.N. Mohanty, 543:Mar86-559
  J.B.S., 185:Jul86-903
Cady, E.H. Young Howells and John Brown.
  B. Morton, 617(TLS):1Aug86-838
Caelius Rufus, M. Marco Celio Rufo,
"Lettere." (A. Cavarzere, ed)
  P. Flobert, 555:Vol59fasc1-134
Caesar, M. and P. Hainsworth, eds. Writ-
ers and Society in Contemporary Italy.*
  B.M., 278(IS):Vol40-160
Cagianelli, F. and D. Della Croce. Giulio
Briccialdi e il suo Tempo.
  M.S.K., 412:May83-149
Cagli, B., P. Gossett and A. Zedda - see
Rossini, G.
Cagni, L. Briefe aus dem Iraq Museum (TIM
II).
  W.L. Moran, 318(JAOS):Jul-Sep84-573
Cahalan, J.M. Great Hatred, Little Room.*
  W.A. Dumbleton, 637(VS):Spring85-548
Cahan, A. Grandma Never Lived in America.
(M. Rischin, ed)
  A. Knopf, 441:11May86-25
"Cahiers Léon Tolstoï." (Vol 1) (M.
Aucouturier, ed)
  R.F. Christian, 575(SEER):Apr85-289
  P. Carden, 104(CASS):Summer85-210
"Cahiers mennaisiens." (No 16-17)
  J. Gaulmier, 535(RHL):May/Jun85-494
"Cahiers Marcel Proust." (No 11)
  B. Brun, 549(RLC):Jul-Sep85-363
  E.D. Jones, 535(RHL):Jan/Feb85-124

59

"Cahiers Stendhal." (No 1) (J-J. Hamm, ed)
 E.J. Talbot, 446(NCFS):Spring-Summer86-
 400
Cahill, J. The Distant Mountains.*
 J. Silbergeld, 54:Mar85-168
Cahill, T., with R. Ewing. Buried Dreams.
 M. Gallagher, 441:30Mar86-19
Cahn, W. Romanesque Bible Illumination.
 J. Folda, 589:Jan85-133
 C.M. Kauffmann, 54:Mar85-155
Caiger-Smith, A. Lustre Pottery.
 B. Gray, 39:Dec85-500
Cain, W.E. The Crisis in Criticism.*
 D. Bialostosky, 454:Winter86-164
 M. Bucco, 649(WAL):Nov85-262
 P.H. Fry, 639(VQR):Autumn85-718
 F. Gado, 573(SSF):Spring85-254
 K. Johnston, 128(CE):Apr85-407
 D. Morton, 651(WHR):Summer85-178
Caird, J. A Distant Urn.
 C. Milton, 571(ScLJ):Winter85-59
Cairncross, A. The Price of War.
 R. Floud, 617(TLS):28Nov86-1337
Caistor, N., ed. Nunca Más.
 E. Crawley, 617(TLS):16May86-522
Caizzi, F.D. - see under Decleva Caizzi, F.
Calame, A. - see Regnard, J-F.
Calandra, D. New German Dramatists.*
 J. Schlueter, 397(MD):Mar85-184
Calder, A. Revolutionary Empire.
 J.P. Greene, 656(WMQ):Jan85-127
Calder, D.G. Cynewulf.*
 R.W.V. Elliott, 677(YES):Vol 15-269
 L.H. Malmberg, 161(DUJ):Dec84-110
Calder, D.G. and others - see "Sources and
 Analogues of Old English Poetry"
Calder, J. and others. As No Other Dare
 Fail.
 A. Jenkins, 617(TLS):14Nov86-1281
Calder, N. The English Channel.
 442(NY):14Jul86-84
Calder, W.M. 3d - see von Wilamowitz-
 Moellendorff, U.
Calderan, R. - see Plautus
Calderón de la Barca, P. La cisma de
 Inglaterra. (F. Ruiz Ramón, ed)
 J.A. Madrigal, 140(CH):Vol7No1-100
Calderón de la Barca, P. Entremeses,
 jácaras y mojigangas. (E. Rodríguez and
 A. Tordera, eds)
 H.W. Sullivan, 240(HR):Summer85-369
Calderón de la Barca, P. Fieras afemina
 amor. (E.M. Wilson, ed)
 J.A. Madrigal, 345(KRQ):Vol32No4-430
Calderón de la Barca, P. El gran teatro
 del mundo. (D. Ynduráin, ed)
 W. Hunter, 86(BHS):Oct85-407
Calderón de la Barca, P. Guárdate de la
 agua mansa (Beware of Still Waters).
 (D.M. Gitlitz, trans)
 M.D. McGaha, 238:May85-302
Calderwood, J.L. If It Were Done.
 C. Baldick, 617(TLS):14Nov86-1273
Calderwood, J.L. To Be and Not To Be.*
 H.R. Coursen, 702:Vol 17-260
 J.E. Hirsh, 401(MLQ):Jun84-193
 M. Mayer, 156(ShJW):Jahrbuch1985-238
 J. Orrell, 610:Spring85-73
 M.B. Rose, 536(Rev):Vol7-19
Caldicott, C.E.J. - see Guérin de Bouscal,
 D.

Caldwell, M. and W. Kendrick, eds. The
 Treasury of English Poetry.
 C. Clausen, 569(SR):Winter85-157
Caldwell, P. The Puritan Conversion Nar-
 rative.*
 L. Hönnighausen, 72:Band222Heft2-425
 D. Leverenz, 656(WMQ):Jan85-131
 S. Robbins, 568(SCN):Winter85-63
Calet, H. Rêver à la Suisse.
 C. Dis, 450(NRF):Jan85-93
Calic, E. Reinhard Heydrich.
 639(VQR):Spring85-48
Califano, J.A., Jr. America's Health Care
 Revolution.
 R.H. Ebert, 441:23Mar86-34
Calimani, R. Storia del Ghetto di Venezia.
 B. Pullan, 617(TLS):11Jul86-756
Calin, W. A Muse for Heroes.*
 P.E. Bennett, 402(MLR):Oct85-926
 R.F. Cook, 589:Jul85-662
 K.D. Uitti, 405(MP):May86-416
Calingaert, E.F. and J. Days. Pasta and
 Rice Italian Style.
 W. and C. Cowen, 639(VQR):Autumn85-141
Calisher, H. The Bobby-Soxer.
 M. Dickstein, 441:30Mar86-5
Calkins, R.G. Illustrated Books of the
 Middle Ages.*
 C. Nordenfalk, 589:Jan85-135
 P.E. Webber, 377:Jul84-104
Callaghan, M. A Time For Judas.*
 M. Abley, 102(CanL):Winter84-66
Callaghan, M.R. Confessions of a Prodigal
 Daughter.*
 C. Ames, 441:5Jan86-16
Callahan, H. Water's Edge.
 M. Nesbit, 59:Mar85-132
Callahan, S. Adrift.
 J. Koslow, 441:12Jan86-21
Callahan, W.J. Church, Politics and
 Society in Spain, 1750-1874.*
 639(VQR):Winter85-8
Callan, E. Auden.*
 M. Kirkham, 529(QQ):Summer85-405
Callard, D.A. "Pretty Good for a Woman."*
 M. Jefferson, 441:2Mar86-12
Callary, E. and L.E. Seits, eds. The How,
 Why, and Whence of Names.
 R.M. Rennick, 424:Sep85-196
Callebat, L. and others. Vitruve, "De
 Architectura."
 J.N. Adams, 123:Vol35No1-191
Callender, J.B. Studies in the Nominal
 Sentence in Egyptian and Coptic.
 M.L. Bender, 350:Mar86-221
Callimachus. Callimaco: Inni. (V.G. Lanz-
 ara, ed and trans)
 N. Hopkinson, 123:Vol35No2-384
Callinicos, A. Is There a Future for Marx-
 ism?
 A. Parker, 153:Winter85-57
Callison, C.S. Land-to-the-Tiller in the
 Mekong Delta.
 J.A. Dixon, 293(JASt):May85-663
Calloway, S. Designs for Interiors.
 D. Johnson, 453(NYRB):4Dec86-3
Calmann, J. The Letters of John Calmann.
 J. Grigg, 362:19Jun86-27
Calvesi, M. and E. Coen. Boccioni.
 S. Berresford, 90:Apr85-238
Calvin, J. Des Scandales. (O. Fatio,
 with C. Rapin, eds)
 F. Higman, 208(FS):Apr85-191

Calvin, W.H.  The River that Flows Uphill.
R. Lewis, 441:14Dec86-30
Calvino, I.  Difficult Loves.*
I. Malin, 532(RCF):Spring85-146
I. Thomson, 364:Dec85/Jan86-154
Calvino, I.  Sotto il sole giaguaro.
L. Sage, 617(TLS):26Sep86-1057
Calvocoressi, R., ed.  Oskar Kokoschka
1886-1980.
N. Lynton, 617(TLS):3Oct86-1086
Camacho Martínez, R.  Málaga barroca,
arquitectura religiosa de los siglos
XVII y XVIII.
J.R. Buendía, 48:Jul-Sep85-315
Camarena Laucirica, J.  Cuentos tradicion-
ales recopilados en la provincia de
Ciudad Real.
F. Delpech, 92(BH):Jul-Dec84-568
Camargo, A., E. Raposo and S. Flaksman.
O Nordeste e a Política.
D.J. Viera, 399(MLJ):Autumn85-315
Camden, A.  Blow by Blow.
H.B.R., 412:Aug/Nov84-302
Camden, W.  Remains concerning Britain.*
(R.D. Dunn, ed)
J.P. Carley, 539:Nov85-308
70:May/Jun85-165
Cameron, A.  The Journey.
D. Harrison, 649(WAL):May85-89
Cameron, A., A. Kingsmill and A.C. Amos.
Old English Word Studies.
R.H. Bremmer, Jr., 179(ES):Aug85-380
S. Cooper, 382(MAE):1985/2-290
C.B. Hieatt, 178:Jun85-231
T.H. Leinbaugh, 589:Jan85-214
I. Mönkkönen, 439(NM):1985/4-599
Cameron, A. and A. Kuhrt, eds.  Images of
Women in Antiquity.
S. Murnaghan, 124:Mar-Apr86-276
Cameron, C.  The Name Givers.
K.B. Harder, 424:Sep85-187
Cameron, E.  Irving Layton.
P.K. Smith, 99:Nov85-38
Cameron, E., ed.  Hugh MacLennan: 1982.*
J. Kertzer, 178:Mar85-117
Cameron, N.  The Complete Poems of Norman
Cameron. (W. Hope, ed)
R. Fuller, 364:Aug-Sep85-150
Cameron, P.  One Way or Another.
V.K. Burg, 441:22Jun86-11
A.H.G. Phillips, 617(TLS):5Sep86-978
Cameron, S.  Writing Nature.
D. Donoghue, 617(TLS):25Apr86-435
Camic, C.  Experience and Enlightenment.
A.T. McKenzie, 125:Fall84-109
Caminero, J.  Víctima o verdugo.
J. Iffland, 238:Dec85-772
Camoin, F.  Why Men Are Afraid of Women.
J. Voelker, 573(SSF):Summer85-361
639(VQR):Winter85-25
Camp, D. - see Lindsay, V.
Camp, J.M.  The Athenian Agora.
M. Vickers, 617(TLS):12Sep86-1007
Camp, J.M. 2d and W.B. Dinsmoor, Jr.
Ancient Athenian Building Methods.
J.J. Coulton, 123:Vol35No1-214
Camp, W.  Stroke Counterstroke.
R. Jones, 362:8May86-26
J.K.L. Walker, 617(TLS):14Feb86-162
de la Campa, A.R. and R. Chang-Rodriguez,
eds.  Poesía hispanoamericana colonial.
S. Siegelman, 263(RIB):Vol35No3-326

Campbell, A.  Island to Island.
L. Jones, 49:Oct85-127
Campbell, A.  No Memory of a Move.*
T. Whalen, 102(CanL):Winter84-75
Campbell, D. and S. Connor.  On the Record.
L. Burnard, 617(TLS):25Jul86-813
Campbell, D.A.  The Golden Lyre.*
M.R. Halleran, 134(CP):Vol 18No1/2-135
Campbell, D.A. - see "Greek Lyric"
Campbell, G.  A Dissertation on Miracles.
M. Wertheimer, 480(P&R):Vol 18No3-189
Campbell, I.  Lewis Grassic Gibbon.
A.T. McKenzie, 395(MFS):Winter85-816
Campbell, J.  Gate Fever.
L. Taylor, 617(TLS):2May86-470
Campbell, J.  Grammatical Man.
R.R. van Oirsouw, 307:Dec85-200
Campbell, J.  Invisible Country.
J. Steffen, 364:Jul85-111
Campbell, J.B.  The Emperor and the Roman
Army: 31 B.C. - A.D. 235.
J.J. Wilkes, 313:Vol75-239
Campbell, J.L., with F. Collinson, eds and
trans.  Hebridean Folksongs III.
B.D.H. Miller, 447(N&Q):Sep84-423
Campbell, M.  Studies in the Third Book of
Apollonius Rhodius' "Argonautica."*
R.L. Hunter, 303(JoHS):Vol 105-192
Campbell, M.W.  The Silent Song of Mary
Eleanor.
G. Noonan, 102(CanL):Winter84-116
Campbell, P.N.  Form and the Art of
Theatre.
A. Graham-White, 615(TJ):Dec85-520
Campbell, R.  In La-La Land We Trust.
N. Callendar, 441:28Dec86-15
Campbell, R.  The Junkyard Dog.
N. Callendar, 441:14Sep86-38
Campbell, T. and others, eds.  Human
Rights.
M. Levine, 617(TLS):22Aug86-905
Campbell, W.  Villi the Clown.
R.G. Suny, 550(RusR):Apr85-200
Campbell, W.D.  Forty Acres and a Goat.
A. Friesinger, 441:16Nov86-25
Campos Boralevi, L.  Bentham and the
Oppressed.
G.L., 185:Apr86-679
"The Canadian Encyclopedia."
J. Hutcheson, 99:Dec85-22
Canal, R.  La Malédiction de l'éphémère.
R. Buss, 617(TLS):3Oct86-1112
Canals Vidal, F.  Cuestiones de fundamenta-
ción.
A. Reix, 542:Oct-Dec85-551
Canary, R.H.  T.S. Eliot.*
L.S. Dembo, 405(MP):Aug85-85
R.Z. Temple, 536(Rev):Vol7-329
Cañas, D.  Lecturas fáciles: ¿Qué dice el
periódico?  (J. Olivio Jiménez, ed)
L.S. Glaze, 399(MLJ):Spring85-108
Cancogni, M.  A Friendship.
S. MacDonald, 441:27Apr86-22
Candau, F.J.C. - see under Cevallos Candau,
F.J.
Candaux, J-D. and others - see de
Charrière, I.
Candaux, J-D. and B. Lescaze, eds.  Cinq
siècles d'imprimerie genevoise.*
J-L. Gautier, 535(RHL):Mar/Apr85-333
D.J. Shaw, 354:Sep85-274

Candida, B. Bronzetti, terrecotte, placchette rinascimentali di ispirazione classica alla Ca' d'Oro e al Museo Correr di Venezia.
R. Adam, 555:Vol59fasc1-163
Cañedo-Argüelles, J.A. - see under Arana Cañedo-Argüelles, J.
Canetti, E. The Conscience of Words.*
(French title: La Conscience des mots.)
P. Brady, 617(TLS):3Oct86-1085
D.A.N. Jones, 362:8May86-23
Canetti, E. Earwitness.
D.J. Enright, 362:23Oct86-29
Canetti, E. The Human Province.*
I. Parry, 617(TLS):22Aug86-923
Canetti, E. The Numbered.*
D. Devlin, 157:No156-49
Canetti, E. The Play of the Eyes.
D.J. Enright, 453(NYRB):17Jul86-9
J.P. Stern, 441:10Aug86-12
Canfield, J.V. Wittgenstein.*
J.O. Nelson, 543:Dec84-380
Canfora, L. Studi sull'"Athenaion politeia" pseudosenofontea.*
B.M. Mitchell, 123:Vol35No1-118
Canh, N.V. Vietnam Under Communism, 1975-1982.
N.V. Long, 293(JASt):Feb85-337
de Cañizares, J. El anillo de Giges. (J. Álvarez Barrientos, ed)
A.V. Ebersole, 240(HR):Autumn85-499
Cannadine, D., ed. Patricians, Power and Politics in Nineteenth-Century Towns.
M.J. Winstanley, 637(VS):Spring85-561
Canny, N. The Upstart Earl.
J. McGuire, 272(IUR):Autumn85-258
Cano Ballesta, J. - see de Larra, M.J.
"Cantar de Mío Cid/Chanson de mon Cid."*
(J. Horrent, ed and trans)
M. Rössner, 72:Band222Heft2-461
Cantarella, G.M. Ecclesiologia e politica nel papato di Pasquale II.
U-R. Blumenthal, 589:Jan85-137
Cantini Guidotti, G. Tre inventari di bicchierai toscani fra Cinque e Seicento.
M. Pozzi, 228(GSLI):Vol 162fasc520-591
Cantor, G.N. and M.J.S. Hodge, eds. Conceptions of Ether.
J. Worrall, 84:Mar85-81
Cantor, J. The Death of Che Guevara.*
G. Davenport, 569(SR):Spring85-321
D.R. Murray, 529(QQ):Summer85-392
Cantor, P.A. Creature and Creator.
P.M. Dawson, 148:Summer85-67
A.K. Mellor, 191(ELN):Sep85-77
Cantrell, J.A. James Nasmyth and the Bridgewater Foundry.
T.C. Barker, 617(TLS):11Jul86-752
Cantwell, R. Bluegrass Breakdown.*
R.M. Marovich, Jr., 650(WF):Apr85-144
L. Martin, 187:Fall86-587
Canz, I.G. Grammaticae universalis tenuia rudimenta.
P. Swiggers, 350:Jun86-454
"Robert Capa Photographs."* (R. Whelan and C. Capa, eds)
M. Ignatieff, 617(TLS):3Jan86-5
442(NY):6Jan86-86
Capaldi, N. Out of Order.*
B.R.B., 185:Jul86-920
J.V. Wagner, 543:Dec85-347

Čapek, K. War with the Newts. (M. and R. Weatherall, trans) War with the Newts. (E. Osers, trans)
I. Hajek, 617(TLS):7Feb86-150
Capieu, H. La Source et l'estuaire.
C.A. Demharter, 207(FR):May86-995
Caplan, P.J. The Myth of Women's Masochism.*
M. Jay, 362:9Oct86-24
Caplat, M. Dinghies to Divas.
R. Anderson, 415:Oct85-604
Caplin, L.E., ed. The Business of Art.
J.S. Eagle, 476:Winter83-77
Caponigro, P. Megaliths.
A. Grundberg, 441:7Dec86-21
Capote, T. Answered Prayers.
A.R. Lee, 362:6Nov86-26
J. Melmoth, 617(TLS):5Dec86-1369
Capozzi, R. Carlo Bernari tra fantasia e realtà.
C. Klopp, 276:Spring85-75
Cappelli, A. The Elements of Abbreviation in Medieval Latin Paleography.
C.B. Faulhaber, 545(RPh):Nov85-237
Cappiello, R. Oh Lucky Country.
S. Gunew, 381:Dec85-517
Cappon, A.P. Aspects of Wordsworth and Whitehead.
J.A. Hodgson, 478:Apr85-116
Capriglione, J.C. Prassagora di Cos.
J. Longrigg, 303(JoHS):Vol 105-209
Caprile, J-P. and H. Jungraithmayr, eds. Préalables à la reconstruction du Proto-Tchadique.
G.F. Meier, 682(ZPSK):Band38Heft2-175
Caputo, J.D. Heidegger and Aquinas.
J.L. Marsh, 258:Jun85-201
Caputo-Mayr, M.L. and J.M. Herz. Franz Kafkas Werke.
R.R. Nicolai, 564:Nov85-312
J.J. White, 402(MLR):Jan85-225
Caracciolo Aricò, A. - see Manin, D. and G. Boerio
Caradec, F., ed. Dictionnaire du français argotique et populaire.
L. Vines, 399(MLJ):Spring85-92
Caradec, F. Feu Willy avec ou sans Colette.
J. Aeply, 450(NRF):Jul-Aug85-157
Caraman, P. The Lost Empire.
D. Bates, 617(TLS):18Apr86-426
Caramello, C. Silverless Mirrors.*
M. Dekoven, 395(MFS):Winter85-766
S.E. Grace, 106:Winter85-483
J. Mellard, 599:Fall85-400
K. Tölölyan, 454:Spring86-264
Carandini, A., A. Ricci and M. De Vos. Filosofiana, the Villa of Piazza Armerina.
R. Ling, 313:Vol75-294
Caravaggi, B.B. - see Hardy, A.
Cárcel Ortí, V., ed. Correspondencia Diplomática del Nuncio Amat (1833-1840).
P. Deacon, 86(BHS):Apr85-203
Card, J.V. An Anatomy of "Penelope."
B. Benstock, 395(MFS):Winter85-784
J. Kidd, 617(TLS):5Sep86-980
L. Tucker, 329(JJQ):Fall85-98
Cárdenas, H.U. and M. Álvarez Álvarez - see Urrutia Cárdenas, H. and M. Álvarez Álvarez

Cardinal, C. Les Montres du Louvre. (Vol 1)
  H.H., 90:Oct85-728
Cardone, E. - see Bascetta, C.
Cardonne-Arlyck, E. La métaphore raconte.
  R. Chambers, 210(FrF):Jan85-121
  C. Toloudis, 207(FR):May86-989
Cardoza, A.L. Agrarian Elites and Italian Fascism.
  A. Orde, 161(DUJ):Jun84-292
Cardozo-Freeman, I., with E.P. Delorme. The Joint.
  A.W. Futrell, 35(AS):Fall85-250
Cardwell, M. - see Dickens, C.
Cardwell, R.A. - see de Icaza, F.A.
Careless, J.M.S. Toronto to 1918.
  L.R., 102(CanL):Fall85-168
Carena, C., M. Manfredini and L. Piccirilli - see Plutarch
Caretta, V. The Snarling Muse.
  C.L. Caywood, 579(SAQ):Spring85-228
Carettoni, G. Das Haus des Augustus auf dem Palatin.
  R. Ling, 123:Vol35No1-218
  A. Wallace-Hadrill, 313:Vol75-245
Carey, F. and A. Griffiths. The Print in Germany, 1880-1933.
  I. Rogoff, 90:Apr85-241
Carey, G.W. and J.V. Schall, eds. Essays on Christianity and Political Philosophy.
  R. Williamson, 396(ModA):Spring85-179
Carey, H. Mansfield Forbes and his Cambridge.
  J. Holloway, 97(CQ):Vol 14No2-155
  A.W. Price, 161(DUJ):Jun85-288
Carey, J., ed. William Golding.
  P. Reading, 617(TLS):17Oct86-1153
Carey, P. Illywhacker.*
  P. Lewis, 364:Apr/May85-148
  P. Lewis, 565:Summer85-50
Cargile, J. Paradoxes.
  J. Hawthorn, 316:Mar85-250
Carillo, C. Shepherd Avenue.
  M. Bell, 441:6Apr86-22
Carkeet, D. I Been There Before.
  S. Kenney, 441:26Jan86-28
Carl, W. Sinn und Bedeutung.
  J.N. Mohanty, 543:Sep84-116
Carlen, A. Theatergeschichte des deutschen Wallis.*
  E. Harvolk, 684(ZDA):Band114Heft2-86
Carleton, D.E. Red Scare!*
  L. Milazzo, 584(SWR):Summer85-415
Carlisle, D. Ragged But Right.
  M.R. Winchell, 585(SoQ):Spring86-91
Carlisle, E.F. Loren Eiseley.*
  P. Klopfer, 579(SAQ):Winter85-105
  D. Seed, 447(N&Q):Dec84-573
Carlo, P. Stolen Flower.
  N. Callendar, 441:16Nov86-38
Carlson, L. Dialogue Games.
  D. Schiffrin, 355(LSoc):Mar85-98
Carlson, M. Theories of the Theatre.*
  G. Playfair, 157:No156-49
Carlson, S. Women of Grace.
  295(JML):Nov85-500
Carlton, B. The Return to the Forbidden Planet.
  D. Devlin, 157:No157-50
Carlyle, T. A Carlyle Reader.* (G.B. Tennyson, ed)
  P. Morgan, 635(VPR):Winter85-162

Carlyle, T. Carlyle's Latter-Day Pamphlets.* (M.K. Goldberg and J.P. Seigel, eds)
  R.L. Tarr, 536(Rev):Vol7-239
Carlyle, T. and J.W. The Collected Letters of Thomas and Jane Welsh Carlyle.* (Vols 8 and 9) (C.R. Sanders and K.J. Fielding, eds)
  S. Monod, 402(MLR):Apr85-440
Carlyle, T. and J.W. The Collected Letters of Thomas and Jane Welsh Carlyle. (Vols 10-12) (C.R. Sanders, general ed)
  A. Hayter, 617(TLS):5Dec86-1380
Carlyle, T. and J. Ruskin. The Correspondence of Thomas Carlyle and John Ruskin.* (G.A. Cate, ed)
  R.L. Tarr, 536(Rev):Vol7-239
Carman, W.Y. Richard Simkin's Uniforms of the British Army.
  N. Powell, 39:Jul85-78
Carmassi, C. La letteratura tedesca nei periodici italiani del primo ottocento (1800-1847).
  I. Solbrig, 133:Band18Heft2-178
Carmichael, A.G. Plague and the Poor in Renaissance Florence.
  F. Gilbert, 453(NYRB):9Oct86-43
Carmona, M. La France de Richelieu.
  J-C. Vuillemin, 207(FR):Feb86-505
Carne-Ross, D.S. Pindar.*
  R. Hamilton, 124:Jul-Aug86-414
  P. Wilson, 617(TLS):30May86-593
Carnegie, T. Indy 500.
  J. Radosta, 441:7Dec86-68
"Carnegie Treasures Cookbook."
  W. and C. Cowen, 639(VQR):Autumn85-140
Carneiro, P.E.B. - see under Berrêdo Carneiro, P.E.
Carney, R. American Dreaming.*
  C. Rickey, 62:Nov85-11
Carney, R. - see Adams, H.
Carnovsky, M., with P. Sander. The Actor's Eye.
  H.K. Chinoy, 615(TJ):Mar85-117
Carnoy, M. The State and Political Theory.
  T.M., 185:Jan86-439
Caro, M.A. Notas a la "Ortología y métrica" de don Andrés Bello.
  J.R. Craddock, 545(RPh):Aug85-144
Carozzi, M. Voltaire's Attitude toward Geology.*
  T.E.D. Braun, 207(FR):Feb86-467
Carp, E.W. To Starve the Army at Pleasure.*
  D.L. Ammerman, 656(WMQ):Oct85-541
  639(VQR):Winter85-9
Carpenter, B. The Poetic Avant-Garde in Poland, 1918-1939.*
  P. Coates, 575(SEER):Apr85-292
Carpenter, D. Jokes for the Apocalypse.
  B. Selinger, 647:Fall85-83
Carpenter, D.B. - see Emerson, E.T.
Carpenter, H. O.U.D.S.*
  O. Trilling, 157:No157-52
Carpenter, H. Secret Gardens.*
  M. Burgan, 637(VS):Summer86-640
  G.B. Tennyson, 445(NCF):Mar86-493
Carpenter, H. and M. Prichard. The Oxford Companion to Children's Literature.
  M-A. Thompson, 526:Winter85-79
Carpenter, K. and B. Steinbrink. Ausbruch und Abenteuer.
  W. Braungart, 196:Band26Heft3/4-351

Carpenter, K.E., ed. Books and Society in History.*
  T.R. Adams, 517(PBSA):Vol79No4-567
  P. Saenger, 173(ECS):Fall85-94
Carpenter, K.J. The History of Scurvy and Vitamin C.
  R. Porter, 617(TLS):7Nov86-1253
Carpentier, G. Les Manuscrits de la marmotte.
  L. di Benedetto, 207(FR):Feb86-482
Carpio, L.D. - see under de Vega Carpio, L.
Carr, A.D. Medieval Anglesey.
  J.A. Meisel, 589:Apr85-473
Carr, F. Mozart and Constanze.
  W.J. Allanbrook, 410(M&L):Apr85-159
Carr, G.J. and E. Sagarra, eds. Irish Studies in Modern Austrian Literature.
  W.G. Sebald, 402(MLR):Jan85-224
Carr, I. Miles Davis.
  D.M., 91:Fall85-229
Carr, J.L. The Battle of Pollock's Crossing.*
  J. Mellors, 364:Jun85-102
Carr, J.L. A Season in Sinji.
  M. Meyer, 364:Aug-Sep85-157
Carr, R. The Civil War in Spain.
  H. Francis, 362:17Jul86-25
Carr, R. Spain 1808-1975. (2nd ed)
  J-L. Marfany, 86(BHS):Jul85-310
Carr, V.S. Dos Passos.
  J. Rohrkemper, 395(MFS):Summer85-402
  295(JML):Nov85-469
Carrard, P. Malraux ou le récit hybride, essai sur les techniques narratives dans "L'Espoir."
  C. Moatti, 535(RHL):Mar/Apr85-326
Carrasco, D. Quetzalcoatl and the Irony of Empire.*
  W.R. Fowler, Jr., 529(QQ):Spring85-175
Carrasco García, A. Escultores, pintores y plateros del Bajo Renacimiento en Llerena.
  M. Estella, 48:Apr-Jun85-166
le Carré, J. A Perfect Spy.
  N. Annan, 453(NYRB):29May86-3
  F. Conroy, 441:13Apr86-1
  B. Morrison, 617(TLS):11Apr86-381
  L. Rose, 61:May86-94
  M. Warnock, 362:20Mar86-28
  442(NY):19May86-119
Carrell, S.L. Le Soliloque de la passion féminine ou le dialogue illusoire.*
  J. Bloch, 208(FS):Jul85-341
Carretta, V. The Snarling Muse.*
  O.W. Ferguson, 569(SR):Summer85-1vi
  T. Lockwood, 401(MLQ):Sep84-297
  A.H. de Quehen, 627(UTQ):Spring85-289
Carrick, P. Medical Ethics in Antiquity.
  T.F. Murphy, 258:Dec85-434
Carrier, L.S. Experience and the Objects of Perception.
  E. Sosa, 543:Sep85-142
Carrier, R. The Hockey Sweater.
  P. Miller, 526:Winter85-91
Carrier, R. Lady With Chains.
  J. Mills, 198:Autumn85-85
  D. Pope, 526:Spring85-93
  H.L. Thomas, 102(CanL):Fall85-128
Carrier, R. De l'amour dans la ferraille.
  R. Beaudoin, 102(CanL):Fall85-124
  E. Hamblet, 207(FR):Feb86-483
Carrière, J.M. It's Good to Tell You.
  L. Löfstedt, 439(NM):1985/2-285

Carrillo, F. Semiolingüística de la novela picaresca.
  G. Díaz-Migoyo, 86(BHS):Jul85-302
  H.H. Reed, 238:Dec85-769
Carringer, R.L. The Making of "Citizen Kane."*
  R. Davies, 617(TLS):28Nov86-1331
Carrington, C. Rudyard Kipling.
  617(TLS):19Dec86-1434
Carrithers, M., S. Collins and S. Lukes, eds. The Category of the Person.
  J. Dunn, 617(TLS):25Jul86-825
Carrive, P. La philosophie des passions chez Bernard Mandeville.
  M. Conche, 192(EP):Apr-Jun85-258
  M. Conche, 192(EP):Oct-Dec85-552
Carroll, D. Australian Contemporary Drama 1909-1982.
  G.A. Wilkes, 581:Jun85-243
Carroll, J. The Cultural Theory of Matthew Arnold.*
  C. Dawson, 541(RES):Nov85-588
  A.C. Dooley, 405(MP):Aug85-55
Carroll, J. Supply of Heroes.
  M. Binchy, 441:5Oct86-15
Carroll, J.M. What's In a Name?
  A. Lehrer, 350:Dec86-709
Carroll, L. Alice's Adventures in Wonderland. (S.H. Goodacre, ed)
  J. Bump, 637(VS):Winter85-316
  P. Heath, 40(AEB):Vol8No3-204
Carroll, L. Lewis Carroll's Alice: Through the Looking Glass, and What Alice Found There. (S.H. Goodacre, ed)
  J. Bump, 637(VS):Winter85-316
Carroll, L. Journaux. (P. Blanchard, trans)
  C. Jordis, 450(NRF):Jan85-106
Carroll, W.C. The Metamorphoses of Shakespearean Comedy.
  R. Berry, 529(QQ):Winter85-860
Carruth, H. Asphalt Georgics.*
  M. Oliver, 344:Summer86-129
Carruth, H. The Selected Poetry of Hayden Carruth.
  M.L. Rosenthal, 441:11May86-17
Carruth, H. Working Papers.* If You Call This Cry a Song. The Sleeping Beauty. Effluences from the Sacred Caves.
  T. Swiss, 569(SR):Winter85-149
Carson, J. Colonial Virginia Cookery.
  639(VQR):Autumn85-137
Carsten, F.L. Britain and the Weimar Republic.
  639(VQR):Spring85-54
Carsten, F.L. The First Austrian Republic 1918-1938.
  A. Glees, 617(TLS):30Oct86-1089
Carstensen, F.V. American Enterprise in Foreign Markets.
  639(VQR):Winter85-7
Carswell, C. The Savage Pilgrimage.
  J. Lane, 402(MLR):Jul85-706
Carswell, J. Government and the Universities in Britain.
  N. Annan, 617(TLS):11Apr86-375
  G. Warnock, 362:10Apr86-25
Carter, A. Saints and Strangers.
  C. Newman, 441:7Sep86-1
Carter, A., ed. Wayward Girls Wicked Women.
  J-A. Goodwin, 617(TLS):19Dec86-1428

Carter, B. The Moon in the Weir.
J.W. Blench, 161(DUJ):Jun85-292
Carter, D.T. When the War Was Over.
639(VQR):Autumn85-116
Carter, J. The Blood of Abraham.*
A. Watson, 617(TLS):14Feb86-160
Carter, J. and G. Pollard. An Enquiry
into the Nature of Certain Nineteenth
Century Pamphlets.* (2nd ed) (N. Barker
and J. Collins, eds)
D. Chambers, 503:Winter83-186
W.E. Fredeman, 536(Rev):Vol7-259
Carter, J.C. The Sculpture of the Sanctu-
ary of Athena Polias at Priene.*
R.R.R. Smith, 303(JoHS):Vol 105-233
Carter, J.E. - see "Solomon D. Butcher:
Photographing the American Dream"
Carter, M. George Orwell and the Problem
of Authentic Existence.
R.J. Voorhees, 395(MFS):Winter85-810
Carter, R., - ed. Thirties Poets.
A. Haberer, 189(EA):Apr-Jun86-230
Carter, R. and D. Burton, eds. Literary
Text and Language Study.*
R. Fowler, 677(YES):Vol 15-256
Carter, R., B. Day and P. Meggs. Typo-
graphic Design, Form and Communication.
507:Sep/Oct85-125
Carter, R.B. Descartes' Medical Philos-
ophy.
N.J. Wells, 438:Summer85-371
Carter, R.E. Dimensions of Moral Educa-
tion.*
B. Hendley, 154:Autumn85-548
Cartier-Bresson, H. Photoportraits.*
M. Ignatieff, 617(TLS):3Jan86-5
I. Jeffrey, 364:Feb86-81
Cartland, B. The Romance of Food.
W. and C. Cowen, 639(VQR):Autumn85-140
Cartledge, P.A. and F.D. Harvey, eds.
Crux.
S. Hornblower, 617(TLS):1Aug86-848
Carton, E. The Rhetoric of American
Romance.
E.A. Dryden, 445(NCF):Mar86-479
Cartwright, N. How the Laws of Physics
Lie.*
J.H. Fetzer, 518:Apr85-120
M.R. Forster, 486:Sep85-478
G. Joseph, 482(PhR):Oct85-580
M. Tiles, 483:Jan85-133
Carusi, A. and G.B. Valsecchi, eds.
Dynamics of Comets.
J. North, 617(TLS):7Feb86-131
de Carvalho, J. Obra completa. (Vols 1-4)
(J.V. de Pina Martins, ed)
C.B. Schmitt, 319:Jan86-134
Carver, M. Dilemmas of the Desert War.
D. Graham, 617(TLS):10Oct86-1125
Carver, R. Cathedral.*
P. Schnapp, 649(WAL):Aug85-168
Carver, R. Fires.*
J. Mellors, 364:Apr/May85-145
Carver, R. Where Water Comes Together
With Other Water.
C. Muske, 441:9Feb86-28
D. Smith, 491:Oct85-38
639(VQR):Autumn85-131
Carver, R. - see Kittredge, W.
Cary, M. Different Drummers.
C.H. Bruner, 538(RAL):Winter85-609
R.A. Paredes, 395(MFS):Winter85-858
Casagrande, G. - see Beni, P.

Casagrande, J. The Sound System of
French.*
A. Azoulay-Vicente, 215(GL):Vol25No4-
276
A. Brunelle, 320(CJL):Fall85-337
Casanova de Seingalt, J. Icosameron. (R.
Zurer, ed and trans)
D. Coward, 617(TLS):3Oct86-1097
Casares, A.B. - see under Bioy Casares, A.
Cascardi, A.J. The Limits of Illusion.*
C.C. Soufas, Jr., 304(JHP):Fall85-88
A. Vivis, 157:No155-53
Casebeer, E. Hermann Hesse, de Siddharta
au Jeu des perles de verre. (M. Meyer,
ed and trans)
A. Reix, 542:Jan-Mar85-52
Casella, M.T. Tra Boccaccio e Petrarca.
G. Velli, 400(MLN):Jan85-175
Casertano, G. Democrito: Dall'atomo alla
città.*
M.E. Reesor, 124:Jan-Feb86-204
Casertano, G. Il piacere, l'amore e la
morte nelle dottrine dei presocratici.
(Vol 1)
C.C.W. Taylor, 303(JoHS):Vol 105-207
Casey, P. After Thunder.
M. Harmon, 272(IUR):Autumn85-234
Cashman, S.D. America in the Gilded Age.
W. Nugent, 579(SAQ):Summer85-331
L. Shore, 529(QQ):Autumn85-601
Cason, C. 90° in the Shade.
F. Hobson, 9(AlaR):Jan85-67
Caspar, G. Im Umgang.
K. Walther, 601(SuF):May-Jun85-660
Caspar, G., ed. Über Bodo Uhse.
K. Walther, 601(SuF):May-Jun85-660
Cass, G. Stylistic Deficiency in the
English of German Advanced Learners in
Teacher Education.
T. Pica, 355(LSoc):Sep85-426
Cassar-Pullicino, J. Studies in Maltese
Folklore.
A. Smith, 203:Vol96No2-267
Cassedy, S. - see Bely, A.
Cassel, C., M. McCally and H. Abraham, eds.
Nuclear Weapons and Nuclear War.
J.M., 185:Jan86-461
Cassell, A.K. Dante's Fearful Art of
Justice.
T. Barolini, 551(RenQ):Winter85-705
P. Shaw, 617(TLS):31Jan86-122
Cassidy, F.G. - see "Dictionary of Amer-
ican Regional English"
Cassidy, F.G. and R.B. Le Page, eds. Dic-
tionary of Jamaican English. (2nd ed)
M. Görlach, 38:Band103Heft1/2-157
Cassin, B., ed and trans. Si Parménide.*
A. Villani, 192(EP):Apr-Jun85-260
Cassirer, E. Individu et cosmos dans la
philosophie de la Renaissance.*
J. Jolivet, 542:Apr-Jun85-252
Cassity, T. Hurricane Lamp.
J. Ash, 441:20Apr86-19
Casson, A.J. My Favourite Watercolours,
1919 to 1957.
W.N., 102(CanL):Winter84-190
Cassou, J. Les Inconnus dans la cave.
J. Bens, 450(NRF):Feb85-86
Cassutt, M. The Star Country.
G. Jonas, 441:21Sep86-31
Cast, D. The Calumny of Apelles.
R.W. Hanning, 54:Dec85-690

Casteneda, C. The Fire from Within.
  E. Covello, 649(WAL):Aug85-169
Castañeda, H-N. Sprache und Erfahrung.
  J. Habermas, 384:Sep/Oct85-899
Castañeda, H-N. Thinking and Doing.
  P. Gärdenfors, 316:Mar85-248
Castellaccio, A. Aspetti di storia italo-
catalana.
  J.L. Shneidman, 589:Jul85-736
Castellani, A., ed. La prosa italiana
delle origini.* (Pt 1)
  M. Pozzi, 228(GSLI):Vol 162fasc520-591
  H. Stammerjohann, 547(RF):Band97
    Heft2/3-282
Castellanos, J. Raimon Casellas i el
Modernisme.
  A. Yates, 402(MLR):Oct85-967
Castellanos, J. Plácido, poeta social y
político.
  A. Gutiérrez de la Solana, 238:May85-
    314
Castelletti, C. Stravaganze d'amore.
  V. Kapp, 72:Band222Heft2-479
Castellucci, J. The Big Dance.
  A. Gottlieb, 441:13Jul86-26
  H. Klehr, 129:Jul86-60
    442(NY):8Sep86-138
Castelvetro, L. Castelvetro on the Art of
Poetry. (A. Bongiorno, ed and trans)
  J.R. Clark, 377:Nov85-199
de Castera, B. Recueil de philosophie
comparée.
  M. Adam, 542:Jan-Mar85-78
Castex, P-G. Horizons romantiques.*
  A.A. McLees, 207(FR):Oct85-133
Castiglioni, L. Lezioni intorno alle
Georgiche di Virgilio e altri studi.
  P. Flobert, 555:Vol59fasc1-140
Castiglioni, L. Viaggio: Travels in the
United States of North America, 1785-87.
  M. Jehlen, 173(ECS):Fall85-143
Castillo, D.A. The Translated World.
  C. Baldick, 617(TLS):28Mar86-341
del Castillo, M. La Gloire de Dina.
  F-E. Dorenlot, 207(FR):Dec85-335
Castillo-Feliú, G.I. Lecturas básicas.
(3rd ed)
  R.B. Klein, 399(MLJ):Winter85-434
Castle, F.T. Gilbert Green.
  G. O'Brien, 441:13Jul86-18
Castle, T. Clarissa's Ciphers.*
  J.E. Aikins, 627(UTQ):Fall84-106
Castle, T., ed. Basil Hume.
  I. Ker, 617(TLS):7Nov86-1238
Castleman, R. American Impressions.
  C. McGee, 441:12Jan86-21
Castleman, R. and W. Wittrock, eds. Henri
de Toulouse-Lautrec.
  M.A. Stevens, 617(TLS):18Apr86-423
Castley, A. and T. Wight. Business Situa-
tions French.
  D.E. Rivas, 399(MLJ):Spring85-86
Castor, G. and T. Cave, eds. Neo-Latin
and the Vernacular in Renaissance
France.*
  J.W. Binns, 123:Vol35No1-228
  B.C. Bowen, 301(JEGP):Oct85-547
  J. Britnell, 161(DUJ):Jun85-265
  J. Supple, 402(MLR):Jul85-712
Castoriadis, C. Domaines de l'homme.
  S. Khilnani, 617(TLS):12Dec86-1404
Castronovo, D. Edmund Wilson.*
  N. Berry, 617(TLS):14Feb86-170

Castrop, H. Die varronische Satire in
England 1660-1690.
  B. Nugel, 566:Autumn85-14
Casway, J.I. Owen Roe O'Neill and the
Struggle for Catholic Ireland.*
  M.E. Daly, 272(IUR):Spring85-104
Catalano, F. Francesco Sforza.
  P. Clarke, 539:Nov85-291
"Catálogo de Monumentos y Conjuntos de la
Communidad Valencia/Cataleg de Monuments
i Conjunts de la Comunitat Valenciana."
  A.E. Pérez Sánchez, 48:Jan-Mar85-87
"Catalogue de l'exposition Christian Bol-
tanski."
  K. Kirishima, 98:Aug-Sep85-934
"Catalogue général des livres imprimés."
  [Bibliothèque Nationale] (Auteurs, col-
  lectivités-auteurs, anonymes, 1970-1979;
  Série en caractères non latins, Vol 1:
  Caractères cyrilliques; Russe.)
  J. Dietze, 559:Vol9No1-110
"Catalogue of Manuscripts in the Houghton
Library, Harvard University." (Vol 1)
  A. Bell, 617(TLS):29Aug86-951
Cataneo, P. and others. Scritti di archi-
tettura. (E. Bassi and others, eds)
  J.B. Bury, 617(TLS):15Aug86-892
Cate, C. The War of the Two Emperors.*
  D. Murray, 441:20Jul86-19
    442(NY):3Mar86-106
Cate, G.A. - see Carlyle, T. and J. Ruskin
Cátedra, P.M., ed. Alonso de Córdoba,
Conmemoración breve de los reyes de
Portugal [together with] Surtz, R.E.,
ed. Un sermón castellano del siglo XV
con motivo de la fiesta del Corpus
Christi.
  M.E. Ciavarelli, 240(HR):Winter85-95
Cathcart, A. The Comeback.
  I. Bamforth, 617(TLS):2May86-478
Cathcart, L.L. American Still Life 1948-
1983.
  J.L., 90:Jun85-397
Cattermole, P. and P. Moore. The Story of
the Earth.
  K.E. Jermy, 324:Dec85-66
Cattin, G. Music of the Middle Ages I.*
  J. Caldwell, 410(M&L):Oct85-403
Caudwell, C. Collected Poems.
  H. Francis, 362:17Jul86-25
Caudwell, S. The Shortest Way to Hades.*
  N. Callendar, 441:19Jan86-17
Caughey, J.L. Imaginary Social Worlds.
  H.F. Smith, 106:Winter85-451
Caunitz, W.J. Suspects.
  T.S. Purdum, 441:7Sep86-22
Causley, C. Secret Destinations.*
  H.S. Bhabra, 493:Apr85-59
Caute, D. The Espionage of the Saints.
  A. Kenny, 362:6Feb86-28
  O.R. McGregor, 617(TLS):4Apr86-348
Caute, D. News from Nowhere.
  D.A.N. Jones, 362:9Oct86-24
  D. Montrose, 617(TLS):26Sep86-1058
Cauthen, K. Process Ethics.
  E.H.C., 185:Jul86-889
Cavafy, C.P. Collected Poems.
  D. McDuff, 565:Summer85-72
Cavailles, J. Méthode axiomatique et
formalisme.
  H. Sinaceur, 98:Oct85-974

Cavaion, D. and P. Cazzola, eds. Leskovi-
ana.
  L. Pedrotti, 574(SEEJ):Summer85-208
Cavalcanti, G. Pound's Cavalcanti.* (D.
Anderson, ed)
  J.J. Wilhelm, 468:Fall84-299
Cavalcanti, P. and P. Piccone - see
Gramsci, A.
Cavarzere, A. - see Caelius Rufus, M.
Cave, K. - see Farington, J.
Cave, R. The Private Press. (2nd ed)
  D. McKitterick, 78(BC):Summer85-241
Cavell, E. Sometimes a Great Nation.
  W.N., 102(CanL):Fall85-199
Cavell, S. The Senses of Walden.
  J. Parini, 249(HudR):Spring85-117
Cavell, S. Themes Out of School.
  J. Parini, 249(HudR):Spring85-116
Cavell, S. The World Viewed.
  G. Mazzotta, 153:Summer85-2
Caviedes, C.N. The Southern Cone.
  P.W. Drake, 263(RIB):Vol35No2-209
Cavillac, M. Gueux et marchands dans le
"Guzmán de Alfarache" (1599-1604).
  J.A. Whitenack, 240(HR):Spring85-240
Cavitch, D. My Soul and I.
  D.S. Reynolds, 441:2Feb86-14
Cawley, A.C. and others. The Revels His-
tory of Drama in English.* (Vol 1)
  S. Carpenter, 541(RES):Nov85-552
  A.A. MacDonald, 179(ES):Aug85-365
  M. Rose, 366:Autumn85-299
  W. Tydeman, 610:Spring85-72
Caws, M.A. Yves Bonnefoy.
  M. Bishop, 207(FR):Apr86-797
  S. Lawall, 188(ECr):Summer85-101
Caws, M.A. The Eye in the Text.*
  R. Cardinal, 402(MLR):Apr85-471
Caws, M.A. A Metapoetics of the Passage.*
  R. Cardinal, 402(MLR):Apr85-471
  S. Lawall, 131(CL):Fall85-357
Caws, M.A. Reading Frames in Modern Fic-
tion.*
  C. Shloss, 454:Spring86-267
Caws, M.A., ed. Writing in a Modern
Temper.*
  J. Cruickshank, 208(FS):Jul85-370
Cazabon, M.J. Views of Trinidad from Draw-
ings by M.J. Cazabon.
  G.K. Lewis, 617(TLS):24Jan86-96
Cazden, N., H. Haufrecht and N. Studer,
eds. Folk Songs of the Catskills.*
  R.D. Bethke, 292(JAF):Jan/Mar85-114
Cazden, N., H. Haufrecht and N. Studer.
Notes and Sources for Folk Songs of the
Catskills.
  R.D. Bethke, 292(JAF):Jan/Mar85-114
Cazden, R.E. A Social History of the
German Book Trade in America to the
Civil War.
  W.R. Tannhof, 517(PBSA):Vol79No4-589
Cazeaux, J. La trame et la chaîne ou les
structures littéraires et l'exégèse dans
cinq des traités de Philon d'Alexandrie.
L'épée du Logos et le soleil de midi.
  É. des Places, 555:Vol59fasc1-129
Cazel, F.A., Jr., ed. Roll of Divers
Accounts for the Early Years of the
Reign of Henry III.
  589:Jan85-216
Cazelles, B. Le corps de sainteté d'après
Jehan Bouche d'Or, Jehan Paulus et
                                    [continued]

quelques vies des XIIe et XIIIe siècles.*
  J. Beck, 589:Jul85-664
  G. Eckard, 553(RLiR):Jan-Jun85-232
  U. Ernst, 547(RF):Band97Heft2/3-299
  P. Rickard, 208(FS):Apr85-183
Cazotte, J. Correspondance de Jacques
Cazotte. (G. Décote, ed)
  C. Todd, 208(FS):Jan85-80
Cea, J.C.M. - see under Martín Cea, J.C.
Cebik, L.B. Fictional Narrative and Truth.
  M. Benton, 89(BJA):Summer85-289
  D. Morton, 395(MFS):Winter85-842
de Ceccatty, R. L'Or et la poussière.
  J. Kirkup, 617(TLS):5Sep86-979
Cecchetti, D. Petrarca, Pietramala e
Clamanges.*
  A.S. Bernardo, 545(RPh):Aug84-111
  R. Jacoff, 589:Jan85-216
Cecchetti, G. - see Leopardi, G.
Cecchin, G., ed. Americani sul Grapps.
  V. Meyers, 234:Fall85-47
Cecil, D. - see MacCarthy, D.
Cederroth, S. The Spell of the Ancestors
and the Power of Mekkah.
  J.L. Ecklund, 293(JASt):Feb85-456
Cejtlin, S.N. Rečevye ošibki i ix predu-
preždenie.
  J.L. Conrad, 558(RLJ):Fall84-273
Celan, P. Gesammelte Werke. (B. Allemann
and S. Reichert, eds)
  O. Davies, 402(MLR):Oct85-1002
  J. Glenn, 221(GQ):Fall85-634
Celan, P. Last Poems. Collected Prose.
  R. Kelly, 441:9Nov86-21
Celant, G., ed. Coerenza in coerenza.
  C.J., 90:Nov85-820
Celeyrette-Pietri, N. "Agathe" ou "Le
Manuscrit trouvé dans une cervelle" de
Valéry.
  P. Gifford, 208(FS):Apr85-227
Céline, L-F. Conversations with Professor
Y.
  N. Ramsey, 441:31Aug86-13
Céline, L-F. Maudits soupirs pour une
autre fois.
  P. McCarthy, 617(TLS):6Jun86-625
Céline, L-F. Romans. (Vol 1) (H. Godard,
ed)
  L. Davis, 208(FS):Apr85-231
Cella, C.R. Mary Johnston.
  P. Drew, 402(MLR):Apr85-446
Celli, T. and G. Pugliese. Tullio Serafin.
  H. Sachs, 617(TLS):3Jan86-17
Cendrars, B. Gold.
  K. Davis, 649(WAL):Aug85-179
Cenerini, L. L'eclissi della fortuna.
  E.B. Quallio, 475:Vol12No22-288
Censorinus. Censorini "de die natali"
liber ad Q. Caerellium. (N. Sallmann,
ed)
  P. Flobert, 555:Vol59fasc1-143
  A. Grafton, 123:Vol35No1-46
Censorinus. Le jour natal. (G. Rocca-
Serra, trans)
  J. Mansfeld, 394:Vol38fasc1/2-234
Centeno, Y.K. 5 Aproximações. A Simbo-
logia Alquimica no Conto da Serpente
Verde de Goethe. Simbolos de Totalidade
na Obra de Hermann Hesse. Subsidios
para o Estudo de Thomas Vaughan. A
Alquimia do Amor. A Alquimia e o
"Fausto" de Goethe. Fernando Pessoa.
                                    [continued]

[continuing]
Fernando Pessoa e a Filosofia Hermética.
    S. Reckert, 111:Fall86-5
"A Century of Collecting 1882-1982, Man-
    chester City Art Galleries."
    90:May85-312
Cercignani, F. Shakespeare's Works and
    Elizabethan Pronunciation.*
    J. Schäfer, 402(MLR):Apr85-419
Cerdà i Surroca, M.A. Els pre-refaelites
    a Catalunya.
    J.L. Marfany, 86(BHS):Jul85-323
Cerezo Galán, P. La voluntad de aventura.
    N.R. Orringer, 238:Mar85-68
Čermák, F., J. Hromek and M.J. Machač,
    eds. Slovník české frazeologie a idio-
    matiky.
    R.B. Pynsent, 575(SEER):Apr85-282
Černjavskaja, T. and V. Rudenko. Sovet-
    skaja Kul'tura.
    G.F. Holliday, 558(RLJ):Fall84-290
Cernuda, L. La realidad y el deseo.*
    (M.J. Flys, ed)
    M.P. Predmore, 240(HR):Summer85-378
    R. Warner, 86(BHS):Oct85-401
Cerny, L. Beautie and the Use Thereof.
    A. van der Weel, 551(RenQ):Winter85-
    761
Ceronetti, G. Albergo Italia.
    J. Keates, 617(TLS):26Sep86-1061
Cerquiglini, B. La parole médiévale.
    G. Kleiber, 553(RLiR):Jan-Jun85-220
Cerquiglini, B. - see Robert de Boron
Cerquiglini, J. - see Christine de Pisan
Cersowksy, P. Phantastische Literatur im
    ersten Viertel des 20. Jahrhunderts.
    L. Weissberg, 400(MLN):Apr85-670
de Cervantes Saavedra, M. The Adventures
    of Don Quixote de la Mancha. (T.
    Smollett, trans)
    M. Amis, 61:Mar86-104
de Cervantes Saavedra, M. Novelas ejem-
    plares.* (J.B. Avalle-Arce, ed)
    F.P. Casa, 240(HR):Winter85-102
    F. Pierce, 86(BHS):Jul85-306
Césaire, A. Aimé Césaire: The Collected
    Poetry.* (C. Eshleman and A. Smith, eds
    and trans)
    R.D.E. Burton, 402(MLR):Apr85-474
    R. Jones, 208(FS):Apr85-232
    D. McDuff, 565:Summer85-72
Cesari, G. Critique de la raison délir-
    ante.
    M. Adam, 542:Jul-Sep85-354
Cevallos Candau, F.J. Juan Bautista de
    Aguirre y el barroco colonial.
    W.C. Bryant, 238:May85-312
    F. Dauster, 240(HR):Summer85-386
Cevasco, G.A. John Gray.
    D. Rutenberg, 637(VS):Winter85-336
Chabot, D. Moon Country.
    A.S. Brennan, 198:Winter85-114
    B. Kingstone, 99:Oct85-31
Chabot, J. L'Autre Moi.*
    R. Killick, 402(MLR):Jul85-718
Chadwick, H. Augustine.
    A. Kenny, 362:15May86-24
    R.A. Markus, 617(TLS):15Aug86-896
Chadwick, H. Boethius: The Consolations
    of Music, Logic, Theology, and Philos-
    ophy.*
    B. McGinn, 122:Jul85-285

Chadwick, O. Hensley Henson.
    J.R.D. Honey, 161(DUJ):Jun85-255
Chaeremon. Chaeremon, Egyptian Priest and
    Stoic Philosopher. (P.W. Van der Horst,
    ed and trans)
    J.G. Griffiths, 123:Vol35No2-310
Chafets, Z. Double Vision.
    A. Wohl, 390:Mar85-61
Chafets, Z. Heroes and Hustlers, Hard
    Hats and Holy Men.
    M. Morrison, 129:Jul86-62
    J.R. Moskin, 441:13Apr86-13
Chahine, S.A. Regards sur le théâtre
    d'Arthur Adamov.
    N. Lane, 207(FR):Feb86-473
Chaika, E. Language.*
    T.C. Frazer, 300:Apr85-79
Chailley, J., ed. Précis de musicologie.
    (2nd ed)
    D. Charlton, 415:Sep85-597
Chainey, G. A Literary History of
    Cambridge.*
    G. Cavaliero, 324:Mar86-271
Chalfont, A. Star Wars.
    F. Lewis, 441:25May86-21
    M. MccGwire, 617(TLS):31Oct86-1214
    S.P. Rosen, 129:Jul86-58
Challe, R. Difficultés sur la religion
    proposées au père Malebranche.* (F.
    Deloffre and M. Menemencioglu, eds)
    M. Cardy, 83:Autumn85-246
    S. O'Cathasaigh, 208(FS):Jul85-343
    R. Ouellet, 207(FR):Mar86-613
Challe, R. Journal d'un voyage fait aux
    Indes orientales (1690-1691). (2nd ed)
    (F. Deloffre and M. Menemencioglu, eds)
    R. Ouellet, 207(FR):Feb86-465
Challiand, G. L'Enjeu africain.
    H. Cronel, 450(NRF):Mar85-109
Chamberlain, B.J. and R.M. Harmon. A Dic-
    tionary of Informal Brazilian Portuguese
    (with English Index).
    M.J. Curran, 238:May85-334
    R.D. Dennis, 399(MLJ):Autumn85-316
    M. Silverman, 263(RIB):Vol35No2-210
Chamberlain, J.S. Ibsen.*
    J. Haugan, 562(Scan):May85-79
Chambers, I. Popular Culture.
    S. French, 617(TLS):17Oct86-1174
Chambers, J. Milestones 1.*
    I. Carr, 617(TLS):11Apr86-402
    B.L. Hampton, 187:Spring/Summer86-332
    D.M., 91:Fall85-229
    B. Morrow, 138:No8-248
Chambers, J. Milestones 2.*
    I. Carr, 617(TLS):11Apr86-402
    B. Morrow, 138:No8-248
Chambers, J., Jr., ed. Black English.
    M. Farr, 355(LSoc):Mar85-108
Chambers, R. Story and Situation.*
    S. Jeffords, 577(SHR):Fall85-365
    D. Kramer, 573(SSF):Spring85-252
    W. Ray, 210(FrF):May85-248
    W.B. Warner, 141:Spring85-207
Chambers-Schiller, L.V. Liberty, A Better
    Husband.
    L.W. Banner, 656(WMQ):Jul85-427
Champe, F.W. The Matachines Dance of the
    Upper Rio Grande.
    D.N. Brown, 187:Spring/Summer86-362
    G.R. Smith, 292(JAF):Jan/Mar85-118
    J.D. Sweet, 650(WF):Jan85-59

Champigny, R.  Sartre and Drama.*
  M. Autrand, 535(RHL):May/Jun85-520
Chan, A., R. Madsen and J. Unger.  Chen
  Village.
  N. Diamond, 293(JASt):Aug85-785
Chan, A.B.  Arming the Chinese.*
  O.Y.K. Wou (Wu), 302:Vol21No1-77
Chance, J.  Woman as Hero in Old English
  Literature.
  A.J. Frantzen, 70:Mar/Apr86-124
Chance, N.A.  China's Urban Villagers.
  G. Bennett, 293(JASt):Nov84-154
Chand, M.  The Painted Cage.
  S. Altinel, 617(TLS):21Nov86-1324
Chanda, N.  Brother Enemy.
  R. Manning, 441:28Dec86-5
Chandler, D.L.  Henry Flagler.
  R. Lenzner, 441:28Sep86-37
Chandler, D.P.  A History of Cambodia.
  M. Vickery, 293(JASt):Feb85-458
Chandler, J.K.  Wordsworth's Second Nature.
  K. Swann, 661(WC):Fall85-158
Chandler, R.  Selected Letters of a Ray-
  mond Chandler.  (F. MacShane, ed)
  J.S. Whitley, 402(MLR):Jan85-146
Chandonnet, A.F.  Auras, Tendrils.
  B. Pirie, 102(CanL):Summer85-181
Chandos, J.  Boys Together.*
  J. Halperin, 637(VS):Winter86-335
Chandra, G.S.S.  Heirloom.
  D. McDuff, 565:Winter84/85-73
Chandra, P.  On the Study of Indian Art.
  R. Lipsey, 293(JASt):May85-631
Chandra, P.  The Sculpture of India, 3000
  BC - 1300 AD.
  J.C. Harle, 617(TLS):4Apr86-369
Chanel, P. - see Cocteau, J.
Chaney, E. and N. Ritchie, eds.  Oxford,
  China and Italy.*
  D.E. Rhodes, 278(IS):Vol40-162
Chang, H.C.  Chinese Literature 3.*
  M.K. Hom, 293(JASt):Nov84-155
Chang, K.C.  Art, Myth, and Ritual.*
  L. Vandermeersch, 244(HJAS):Dec85-712
Chang, R.T.  The Justice of the Western
  Consular Courts in Nineteenth-Century
  Japan.*
  W. Gray, 293(JASt):Aug85-836
Chang-Rodríguez, R.  Violencia y subver-
  sión en la prosa colonial hispanoamer-
  icana, siglos XVI y XVII.*
  L.H. Dowling, 238:Mar85-72
Chanin, P.  The Natural History of Otters.
  J. Birdsall, 617(TLS):21Mar86-314
Channels, N.L.  Social Science Methods in
  the Legal Process.
  B.G.H., 185:Jul86-914
Channing, W.E.  Selected Writings.  (D.
  Robinson, ed)
  A. Delbanco, 165(EAL):Spring86-75
Chanoff, D. and D. Van Toai.  Portrait of
  the Enemy.
  A.R. Isaacs, 441:30Nov86-23
de Chantelou, P.F.  Paul Fréart de Chante-
  lou: Diary of the Cavaliere Bernini's
  Visit to France.  (A. Blunt, ed; M.
  Corbett, trans)
  R.M. Adams, 453(NYRB):8May86-9
  J. Montagu, 617(TLS):28Mar86-321
Chantraine, H.  Novaesium VIII.  (2nd ed)
  M.H. Crawford, 313:Vol75-321
Chaplin, P.  Albany Park.
  V. Glendinning, 617(TLS):6Jun86-609

Chapman, C.B.  Physicians, Law, and Ethics.
  I. McGilchrist, 617(TLS):7Nov86-1251
  D.E.S., 185:Jan86-466
Chapman, E.L.  The Magic Labyrinth of
  Philip José Farmer.
  G.K. Wolfe, 561(SFS):Nov85-345
Chapman, G.  A Passionate Prodigality.
  I. Jeffrey, 364:Jul85-105
Chapman, M.  South African English Poetry.
  C. Hope, 364:Jul85-78
Chapman, R.  The Language of English Lit-
  erature.
  A. Ward, 447(N&Q):Sep84-420
Chapman, R.  The Treatment of Sounds in
  Language and Literature.*
  A. Welsh, 191(ELN):Mar86-72
Chapman, T.  Time.*
  R.C. Hoy, 486:Dec84-694
Chapon, F.  Mystère et splendeurs de
  Jacques Doucet, 1853-1929.*
  L.J. Austin, 208(FS):Jan85-98
Chappell, F.  Castle Tzingal.
  M.J. Bugeja, 219(GaR):Winter85-896
  M. Jarman, 249(HudR):Summer85-331
  R.T. Smith, 577(SHR):Fall85-390
Chappell, F.  I Am One of You Forever.*
  G.C., 569(SR):Spring85-xxxix
  B. Cooley, 110:Winter86-87
Chappell, F.  Source.
  L. Erdrich, 441:1Jun86-36
Chappell, W. - see Burra, E.
Chappuzeau, S.  Le Cercle des femmes [et]
  L'Académie des femmes.*  (J. Crow, ed)
  R. Horville, 535(RHL):Sep/Oct85-868
Char, R.  Oeuvres complètes.*
  L. Herlin, 450(NRF):Jan85-87
  E. Marty, 98:Jun-Jul85-719
Charcot, J-M. and P. Richer.  Les Démon-
  iaques dans l'art [suivi de] Charcot,
  J-M.  La foi qui guérit.  (J. Fédida and
  G. Didi-Huberman, eds)
  P. Dubrunquez, 450(NRF):Jun85-73
  J-M. Gros, 98:Aug-Sep85-889
du Chardin, P.  Le Roman de la Conscience
  malheureuse.*
  C. Foucart, 72:Band222Heft1-153
  R. Galle, 547(RF):Band97Heft4-461
de la Charité, M. - see under Macé de la
  Charité
Charles, M.  L'Arbre et la source.
  T. Cave, 617(TLS):18Apr86-429
Charles, S.R.  Josquin des Prez.
  J. Milsom, 410(M&L):Jul85-276
Charleston, R.J.  English Glass and the
  Glass Used in England, circa 400-1940.*
  G. Wills, 39:Jan85-70
Charlesworth, J.H., ed.  The Old Testament
  Pseudepigrapha.  (Vol 2)
  G. Vermes, 617(TLS):27Jun86-718
Charlesworth, J.H.  The Old Testament
  Pseudepigrapha and the New Testament.
  G. Vermes, 617(TLS):27Jun86-718
Charlesworth, M.  The Glass House.
  S. Altinel, 617(TLS):1Aug86-844
"The Charlottesville Tapes."
  P.S. Kennedy-Grant, 45:Aug85-73
Charlton, D.  Grétry and the Growth of
  Opéra-comique.
  W. Dean, 617(TLS):10Oct86-1138
Charlton, D.G., ed.  France.  (2nd ed)
  C. Lloyd, 161(DUJ):Jun84-283

Charlton, D.G., ed. The French Romantics.*
 J-F. Brière, 207(FR):Feb86-510
 J. Cruickshank, 208(FS):Apr85-216
Charlton, D.G. New Images of the Natural
 in France.*
 P.V. Conroy, Jr., 207(FR):Feb86-509
 L.J. Jordanova, 208(FS):Oct85-480
Charlton, P. John Stainer and the Musical
 Life of Victorian Britain.*
 W.J. Gatens, 410(M&L):Apr85-153
Charlton, T. Guide to Courses and Careers
 in Art, Craft and Design.
 C. Pemberton, 324:Oct86-764
Charmé, S.L. Meaning and Myth in the
 Study of Lives.
 H.E. Barnes, 478:Oct85-227
Charmley, J. Duff Cooper.
 D. Pryce-Jones, 617(TLS):16May86-527
 A. Watkins, 362:17Apr86-26
Charmley, J. - see Shuckburgh, E.
Charney, M. Joe Orton.*
 A.P. Hinchliffe, 148:Summer85-91
Charpentier, G. Gustave inédites à ses
 parents. (F. Andrieux, ed)
 R. Orledge, 410(M&L):Apr85-141
Charpin, D. and J-M. Durand. Documents
 Cunéiformes de Strasbourg. (Vol 1)
 R.F.G. Sweet, 318(JAOS):Apr-Jun84-372
de Charrière, I. [Belle de Zuylen]
 Oeuvres complètes. (Vol 4) (J-D. Can-
 daux and others, eds)
 K. Kloocke, 547(RF):Band97Heft4-477
 M. Mat-Hasquin, 535(RHL):Mar/Apr85-306
de Charrière, I. [Belle de Zuylen]
 Oeuvres complètes.* (Vols 5 and 6)
 (J-D. Candaux and others, eds)
 K. Kloocke, 547(RF):Band97Heft4-477
Charrin, A-V. Le petit monde du grand
 Corbeau.
 J. Verrier, 549(RLC):Oct-Dec85-448
Charron, F. François.
 E. Dansereau, 102(CanL):Fall85-106
Charters, S. Louisiana Black.
 A.H.G. Phillips, 617(TLS):28Nov86-1358
Chartier, R., ed. Pratiques de la lecture.
 Q.M. Hope, 207(FR):Feb86-504
Charyn, J. Metropolis.
 D. Stern, 441:27Jul86-10
Charyn, J. War Cries Over Avenue C.*
 I. Malin, 532(RCF):Fall85-196
Chase, A. Playing God in Yellowstone.
 P. Shabecoff, 441:1Jun86-15
 442(NY):16Jun86-122
Chase, J. Exterior Decoration.
 K.J. Weitze, 576:May85-188
Chase, K. Eros and Psyche.
 A. Jumeau, 189(EA):Apr-Jun86-225
 S. Tick, 637(VS):Spring86-475
Chase-Riboud, B. Valide.
 W. Smith, 441:10Aug86-22
Chastain, T. and others. Murder in Manhat-
 tan.
 M. Stasio, 441:2Nov86-33
Chastel, A. The Sack of Rome, 1527.*
 (French title: Le Sac de Rome, 1527.)
 C.H. Clough, 324:Mar86-274
 E. Darragon, 98:Jun-Jul85-661
 W. Gundersheimer, 54:Mar85-156
 M. Jarrety, 450(NRF):Jan85-102
de Chateaubriand, F.R. Moïse. (F. Bassan,
 ed)
 J-C. Morisot, 446(NCFS):Fall-
 Winter85/86-166

Chatman, S. Antonioni, or, the Surface of
 the World.
 P. Brunette, 18:Jul/Aug86-75
Chatterjee, M. Gandhi's Religious Thought.
 D. Bishop, 258:Sep85-331
Chattopadhyaya, A. Atīśa and Tibet.
 K.G. Zysk, 318(JAOS):Oct-Dec84-783
Chattopadhyaya, D., ed. Studies in the
 History of Science in India.
 D. Riepe, 486:Dec84-698
Chattopadhyaya, S. Reflections on the
 Tantras.
 F.M. Smith, 318(JAOS):Oct-Dec84-786
Chaucer, G. The Canterbury Tales. (D.
 Wright, trans)
 P.N. Furbank, 362:1May86-26
 A. Wawn, 617(TLS):28Nov86-1356
Chaucer, G. The Canterbury Tales/Die
 Canterbury-Erzählungen. (H. Bergner, ed)
 K. Gamerschlag, 72:Band222Heft1-179
Chaucer, G. Chaucer: "The Book of the
 Duchess." (H. Phillips, ed)
 J.D. Burnley, 541(RES):Aug85-409
 J. Frankis, 161(DUJ):Jun85-264
 J. Lawlor, 382(MAE):1985/2-308
Chaucer, G. The Manciple's Tale. (D.C.
 Baker, ed)
 N.F. Blake, 40(AEB):Vol8No2-134
Chaucer, G. The Nun's Priest's Tale. (D.
 Pearsall, ed)
 R. Hanna 3d, 40(AEB):Vol8No3-184
Chaucer, G. Troilus and Criseyde.* (B.A.
 Windeatt, ed)
 D.C. Baker, 191(ELN):Mar86-65
 J.D. Burnley, 179(ES):Jun85-276
 J. Ferster, 184(EIC):Oct85-345
Chaudenson, R. Textes créoles anciens (La
 Réunion et Ile Maurice).*
 J. Verrier, 549(RLC):Jan-Mar85-110
Chaudhuri, K.N. Trade and Civilisation in
 the Indian Ocean.
 C. Wickham, 617(TLS):12Sep86-998
Chaudhuri, S. Infirm Glory.*
 M. Shapiro, 402(MLR):Apr85-417
Chaudhury, R.H. and N.R. Ahmed. Female
 Status in Bangladesh.
 H. Papanek, 293(JASt):Nov84-127
de la Chaussée, F. Initiation à la phoné-
 tique de l'ancien français. (3rd ed)
 J. Klare, 682(ZPSK):Band38Heft2-176
 J. Klausenburger, 545(RPh):Feb85-324
 J. Kramer, 547(RF):Band97Heft1-57
 M. Offord, 208(FS):Apr85-188
 C. Schmitt, 72:Band222Heft1-215
Chaussinand-Nogaret, G. Madame Roland.
 A. Forrest, 617(TLS):21Mar86-310
Chávez, D. The Last of the Menu Girls.
 B.L. Clark, 441:12Oct86-28
Chawaf, C. Les Surfaces de l'orage. La
 Vallée incarnate.
 R.D. Frye, 207(FR):Mar86-641
Cheatwood, K.T-H. Elegies for Patrice.
 B. Brown, 95(CLAJ):Dec85-250
Chedzoy, A. William Barnes.
 C.H. Sisson, 617(TLS):20Jun86-676
Cheetham, F. English Medieval Alabasters.
 N. Coldstream, 90:Feb85-95
 C.R. Dodwell, 39:May85-351
Cheever, S. Home Before Dark.*
 R.G. Collins, 534(RALS):Spring83-33
 F.R. Cunningham, 268(IFR):Winter86-38
 R. Merrill, 27(AL):Oct85-512
 [continued]

Cheever, S. Home Before Dark. [continuing]
  D. Revell, 395(MFS):Summer85-419
  V.C. Wang, 573(SSF):Summer85-362
  295(JML):Nov85-458
Chefdor, M., R. Quinones and A. Wachtel,
  eds. Modernism.
  A.W. Litz, 617(TLS):10Oct86-1142
Chekhov, A. Late-Blooming Flowers and
  Other Stories. (I.C. Chertok and J.
  Gardner, trans)
  V. Belenkaya, 573(SSF):Spring85-239
Chell, S. The Dynamic Self.
  R. Donahoo, 85(SBHC):Vol 13-115
Ch'en, C-Y. - see Hsün Yüeh
Chen, F.T-S. China Policy and National
  Security.
  M. Schaller, 293(JASt):Aug85-806
Ch'en Tsu-yu. Chin-tai Chung-kuo ch'a-yeh
  te fa-chan yü shih-chieh shih-ch'ang.
  R.P. Gardella, 293(JASt):May85-575
Cheney, R.C. Names on the Face of Montana.
  M.M. Bryant, 424:Mar-Jun85-96
Cheng, F. Chinese Poetic Writing.
  J.J.Y. Liu, 293(JASt):Nov84-157
Cheng, H-L., ed and trans. Nāgārjuna's
  "Twelve Gate Treatise."
  J.W. de Jong, 259(IIJ):Jul85-228
Cheng, N. Life and Death in Shanghai.
  D. Davin, 617(TLS):22Aug86-909
Cheng Te-k'un. Studies in Chinese Archae-
  ology.
  H.A. Peters, 293(JASt):Nov84-158
Cheng Te-k'un. Studies in Chinese Art.
  M. Cummings, 293(JASt):May85-577
Chénieux-Gendron, J. Le surréalisme.
  P. Somville, 542:Jul-Sep85-349
Chénieux-Gendron, J. Le Surréalisme et le
  roman 1922-1950.
  W. Bohn, 210(FrF):Jan85-119
  M-C. Dumas, 535(RHL):Nov/Dec85-1079
  J.H. Matthews, 210(FrF):Sep85-367
  H. Peyre, 207(FR):Dec85-305
Chenu, J. - see Peirce, C.S.
Cherchari, A. Réception de la littérature
  africaine d'expression française jus-
  qu'en 1970.*
  C. Dunton, 538(RAL):Spring85-108
  R. Jones, 208(FS):Apr85-243
Cherlin, A.J. and F.F. Furstenberg, Jr.
  The New American Grandparent.
  M. Scarf, 441:21Sep86-13
Chernin, K. The Flame Bearers.
  A. Roiphe, 441:9Nov86-12
Chernin, K. In My Mother's House.*
  R. Scherer, 287:May85-23
Chernoff, M. Bop.
  F. Prose, 441:21Sep86-11
Chernus, I. Mysticism in Rabbinic Judaism.
  P. Schäfer, 318(JAOS):Jul-Sep84-537
Cherpack, C. Logos in Mythos.
  H. Josephs, 210(FrF):Sep85-366
  V. Mylne, 402(MLR):Jan85-165
  J. Whatley, 207(FR):Feb86-461
Chertok, S. Posledniaia liubov' Maiakov-
  skogo.
  R. Tempest, 550(RusR):Apr85-191
Chéry-Aynesworth, J. Approche rhétorique
  de la dialectique des sens chez Bernanos.
  (Vol 2)
  J.C. Whitehouse, 402(MLR):Oct85-949

Cheshire, J. Variation in an English Dia-
  lect.*
  A. Brunelle, 320(CLJ):Fall85-339
  W.N. Francis, 660(Word):Dec85-243
Chesler, P. Mothers on Trial.
  W. Kaminer, 441:5Jan86-10
Chesney, E.A. The Countervoyage of Rabe-
  lais and Ariosto.*
  M. Smith, 447(N&Q):Jun84-259
Chesnut, M. The Private Mary Chesnut.*
  (C.V. Woodward and E. Muhlenfeld, eds)
  F.D. Williams, 115:Summer85-386
Chester, L. Tooth and Claw.
  S. Fry, 362:6Nov86-23
Cheuse, A. The Grandmothers' Club.
  P-L. Adams, 61:Nov86-139
  J. Charyn, 441:26Oct86-11
Chevalier, J-C. and P. Encrevé, eds. Vers
  une histoire sociale de la linguistique.
  P. Swiggers, 350:Mar86-206
Chevalier, M. Cuentos folklóricos espa-
  ñoles del Siglo de Oro.
  D. Devoto, 92(BH):Jan-Jun84-239
  A.L. Galanes, 240(HR):Summer85-365
Chevalier, M. Tipos cómicos y folklore
  (siglos XVI-XVII). Cuentos españoles de
  los siglos XVI y XVII.
  D. Devoto, 92(BH):Jan-Jun84-239
Chevallier, M. La Part du feu.
  T. Greene, 207(FR):Dec85-332
Chevrel, Y. Le Naturalisme.*
  E. Höfner, 72:Band222Heft2-351
  R. Ripoll, 535(RHL):Jan/Feb85-112
  F. Wolfzettel, 224(GRM):Band35Heft4-
  471
Chevrel, Y., ed. Le naturalisme dans les
  littératures de langues européennes.*
  C. Rodiek, 52:Band20Heft3-320
Ch'i, H-S. Nationalist China at War.
  D.R. Reynolds, 293(JASt):Nov84-160
Ch'i-fang, H. - see under Ho Ch'i-fang
dalla Chiara, M.L. Italian Studies in the
  Philosophy of Science.
  P. Engel, 98:Mar85-309
Chiarini, G. Lessing e Plauto.
  H. Zehnacker, 555:Vol59fasc1-137
Chibnall, M. Anglo-Norman England 1066-
  1166.
  W.L. Warren, 617(TLS):25Apr86-442
Child, J. Geopolitics and Conflict in
  South America.
  E. Duran, 263(RIB):Vol35No3-325
Childers, T. The Nazi Voter.
  J. Caplan, 529(QQ):Spring85-66
Childress, M. A World Made of Fire.
  639(VQR):Winter85-23
Chin Kin Wah. The Defense of Malaysia and
  Singapore.
  T.J. Bellows, 293(JASt):Aug85-885
Chingen. Miraculous Tales of the Lotus
  Sutra from Ancient Japan.
  M.H. Childs, 407(MN):Summer85-251
Chinol, E. Falsi nell'arte.
  G. Norman, 617(TLS):11Apr86-379
Chinoy, H.K. and L.W. Jenkins. Women in
  American Theatre.
  E. Hamilton, 476:Summer82-78
Chiodi-Tischer, U. Die Mundert von Sisco
  (Korsika).
  M. Pfister, 72:Band222Heft2-438
Chirat, R. Catalogue des films français
  de long métrage.
  R.M. Webster, 207(FR):Apr86-823

Chirat, R.  Le Cinéma des années 30.
  R.M. Webster, 207(FR):Apr86-822
Chirat, R.  Le Cinéma français des années
de guerre.
  N. Greene, 207(FR):Mar86-635
Chisholm, A.  Bernard van Dieren.
  L. East, 415:Sep85-537
Chisholm, A.  Faces of Hiroshima.*
  J. Haylock, 364:Oct85-99
Chisholm, J.E., ed.  The Pseudo-Augustin-
ian "Hypomnesticon" against the Pelag-
ians and the Celestians.  (Vol 2)
  W.S. Babcock, 589:Apr85-474
Chisholm, R.M.  The First Person.
  P. van Inwagen, 449:Mar85-122
  J. Kim, 484(PPR):Mar86-483
Chisholm, R.M.  The Foundations of Know-
ing.*
  P. Helm, 449:Mar85-111
Chislett, A.  Quiet is the Land.*
  N. Besner, 102(CanL):Spring85-128
Chitnis, A.C.  The Scottish Enlightenment
and Early Victorian English Society.
  P. Mandler, 617(TLS):2May86-467
Chittick, W.C., ed and trans.  A Shicite
Anthology.
  A. Schimmel, 318(JAOS):Oct-Dec84-778
Choate, P. and J.K. Linger.  The High-Flex
Society.
  H. Goodman, 441:26Oct86-28
Chodkiewicz, M.  Le Sceau des saints.
  J. Baldick, 617(TLS):26Sep86-1073
Chojnacki, S.  Major Themes in Ethiopian
Painting.
  B. Juel-Jensen, 354:Mar85-64
Chomarat, J.  Grammaire et rhetorique chez
Erasme.
  C.R. Thompson, 551(RenQ):Spring85-113
Chomarat, J. - see Valla, L.
Chomsky, N.  Turning the Tide.
  A. Tonelson, 441:13Apr86-28
  L. Whitehead, 362:30Oct86-28
"Choreography by George Balanchine."*
  M. Mudrick, 249(HudR):Autumn85-520
Chotiner, B.A.  Khrushchev's Party Reform.
  D. Schwartz, 550(RusR):Oct85-432
Chouillet, A-M. and S. Auroux - see de
Condillac, É.B.
Chowder, K.  Jadis.*
  42(AR):Fall85-502
Chowdhury, A.  Agrarian Social Relations
and Rural Development in Bangladesh.
  J.P. Thorp, 293(JASt):Nov84-223
Choyce, L., ed.  The Cape Breton Collec-
tion.
  E. Thompson, 198:Autumn85-72
Choyce, L.  Fast Living.*
  A. Munton, 198:Winter85-100
Chrétien, J-L.  Lueur du secret.
  M. Adam, 542:Oct-Dec85-548
  F. Wybrands, 450(NRF):Dec85-85
Chrétien de Troyes.  Lancelot, or, The
Knight of the Cart.*  (W.W. Kibler, ed
and trans)
  G.S. Burgess, 545(RPh):Nov85-266
Chrétien de Troyes.  Perceval, or, The
Story of the Grail.  (R.H. Cline, trans)
  A.J. Brumlik, 545(RPh):Nov85-261
  T. Hunt, 208(FS):Apr85-178
Chrisman, K.  Dreaming in the Dust.
  A. Barnet, 441:13Apr86-23

Chrisman, M.U.  Lay Culture, Learned
Culture.*  Bibliography of Strasbourg
Imprints, 1480-1599.*
  B.T. Chambers, 517(PBSA):Vol79No1-148
Christ, C.T.  Victorian and Modern
Poetics.*
  L.R. Pratt, 637(VS):Winter86-333
  J.S., 636(VP):Summer85-222
  H. Witemeyer, 141:Summer85-328
  295(JML):Nov85-433
Christ, K.  The Romans.
  G.P. Verbrugghe, 124:Jan-Feb86-194
Christensen, D.E., ed.  Contemporary Ger-
man Philosophy.  (Vol 1)
  L.S. Stepelevich, 543:Mar85-620
Christensen, E. and A.W. Ehlers, comps.
Dansk litteraturhistorisk bibliografi
1976-1977.
  K.H. Ober, 563(SS):Winter85-111
Christensen, J.  Coleridge's Blessed
Machine of Language.*
  R.L. Brett, 541(RES):Feb85-106
Christian, R.F. - see Tolstoy, L.N.
Christians, D.  Die Sprachrubrik der "Liter-
aturnaya Gazeta" von 1964 bis 1978.
  J.M. Kirkwood, 575(SEER):Apr85-283
Christiansen, R.  Prima Donna.*
  J. Steane, 415:Feb85-97
Christie, A.  An Honest Woman.
  L. Prinz, 441:6Apr86-22
Christie, I.  Arrows of Desire.
  L. Anderson, 617(TLS):16May86-529
Christie, I.R.  Stress and Stability in
Late Eighteenth-Century Britain.*
  I. Kramnick, 173(ECS):Summer86-534
Christin, A-M., ed.  Ecritures: Systèmes
idéographiques et pratiques expressives.
  M. David, 542:Jan-Mar85-85
Christine de Pisan.  The Book of the City
of Ladies.*
  P.F. Dembowski, 545(RPh):Aug85-125
Christine de Pisan.  Cent Ballades d'Amant
et de Dame.  (J. Cerquiglini, ed)
  G. Mombello, 545(RPh):Aug84-103
Christman, M.C.S.  Adventurous Pursuits.
  J.R. Biggs, 656(WMQ):Jan85-155
Christmann, H.H.  Romanistik und Anglistik
an der deutschen Universität im 19. Jahr-
hundert.
  P. Swiggers, 350:Sep86-703
Christmas, L.  The Ribbon and the Ragged
Square.
  R. Davidson, 617(TLS):9May86-515
Christopher, G.B.  Milton and the Science
of the Saints.*
  M. Evans, 541(RES):May85-270
  A. Low, 403(MLS):Fall85-332
Christopher, N.  A Short History of the
Island of Butterflies.
  D. Wojahn, 441:8Jun86-38
Christopher, N.  The Soloist.
  I. Kapp, 441:20Apr86-26
Christopher, R.C.  Second to None.
  S. Chira, 441:26Oct86-37
Christopher, W. and others.  American Hos-
tages in Iran.*
  T. Jacoby, 617(TLS):5Dec86-1367
Christy, J.  Travelin Light.
  S. Lehman, 102(CanL):Winter84-115
"Le Chrysanthème solitaire."  (J. Pigeot
and K. Kosugi, trans)
  J. Bésineau, 407(MN):Winter85-427

Chryssafis, G. A Textual and Stylistic Commentary on Theocritus' "Idyll" XXV.
W. Beck, 24:Summer85-250
Chu-Chang, M., with V. Rodriguez, eds. Asian and Pacific-American Perspectives in Bilingual Education.
V.O. Chattergy, 355(LSoc):Sep85-419
Chudakov, A.P. Chekhov's Poetics.*
S. Golub, 615(TJ):Mar85-128
Chukovsky, K.I. The Art of Translation.* (L.G. Leighton, ed and trans)
K. Kostsinsky, 550(RusR):Jan85-96
R.E. Peterson, 574(SEEJ):Summer85-221
Chung, P.C. Palace Women in the Northern Sung (960-1126).
S. Cahill, 318(JAOS):Jul-Sep84-562
"Church Organs."
A. Bond, 415:Dec85-756
Churchill, W.S. The Irrepressible Churchill. (K. Halle, comp)
P-L. Adams, 61:Mar86-111
Churchland, P.M. Matter and Consciousness.*
J.J.C. Smart, 393(Mind):Apr85-306
Chute, B.J. The Good Woman.
D. Cole, 441:21Dec86-14
Chute, C. The Beans of Egypt, Maine.* (British title: The Beans.)
D. Flower, 249(HudR):Summer85-304
Chvany, C.V. and R.D. Brecht, eds. Morphosyntax in Slavic.*
C. Rudin, 574(SEEJ):Fall85-353
"CIAM."
R. Padovan, 46:Jan85-4
Cianci, G., ed. Wyndham Lewis.
P.M.S. Dawson, 541(RES):Feb85-124
Ciardi, J. Selected Poems.
D. Wojahn, 491:Jun85-169
639(VQR):Spring85-55
Ciardi, R.P. and L. Tongiorgi Tomasi - see under Paolo Ciardi, R. and L. Tongiorgi Tomasi
Ciccone, S.D., I. Bonomi and A. Masini - see under De Stefanis Ciccone, S., I. Bonomi and A. Masini
Cicero. Philippics. (D.R. Shackleton Bailey, ed and trans)
T.P. Wiseman, 617(TLS):26Sep86-1072
Cienkowski, W. Język dla wszystkich.
Z. Weigt, 688(ZSP):Band45Heft1-203
de la Cierva, R. Francisco Franco.
P. Preston, 617(TLS):30ct86-1093
Cifuentes, L.F. - see under Fernández Cifuentes, L.
Cikovsky, N., Jr. - see Morse, S.F.B.
"Cimelia."
R.S. Wieck, 517(PBSA):Vol79No3-445
Ciment, J. Small Claims.
L. Zeidner, 441:19Oct86-30
Ciment, M. John Boorman.
J-L. Bourget, 189(EA):Oct-Dec86-490
D. Robinson, 617(TLS):24Oct86-1202
Ciment, M. Conversations with Losey.
D. Robinson, 617(TLS):24Oct86-1202
Cinotti, M. Michelangelo Merisi detto il Caravaggio.*
E. Cropper, 551(RenQ):Autumn85-532
Cioffi, F. Formula Fiction?
D.M. Hassler, 395(MFS):Summer85-465
D.J. Weinstock, 561(SFS):Mar85-97
Cioranescu, A. Le Masque et le visage.*
H.G. Hall, 402(MLR):Apr85-462
C.N. Smith, 208(FS):Jul85-332

Cipolla, G. - see Tasso, T.
"Circulating Film Library Catalog." [The Museum of Modern Art]
R. Anderson, 500:Fall85-67
Ciria, A. Política y cultura popular.
M. Navarro, 263(RIB):Vol35No4-464
Citino, D. The Appassionata Poems.
M.J. Bugeja, 577(SHR):Winter85-83
Ciucci, G. and others. The American City.*
T.J. McDonald, 385(MQR):Spring86-459
Čivikov, G. Interpretationsprobleme Moderner Lyrik am Beispiel Paul Celans.
B. Bjorklund, 222(GR):Spring85-79
"Civilisation et communication."
E.C. Knox, 207(FR):Oct85-157
Cixous, H. Angst.
N. Irving, 617(TLS):21Mar86-306
Cixous, H. Inside.
M. Hirsch, 441:7Dec86-70
Cixous, H. and C. Clément. The Newly Born Woman.
A. Barnet, 441:24Aug86-19
Clagett, M. Archimedes in the Middle Ages. (Vol 5, Pts 1-5)
J.F. Daly, 377:Nov85-192
Clampitt, A. The Kingfisher.*
D. Lehman, 473(PR):Vol52No3-302
Clampitt, A. What the Light Was Like.*
N. Corcoran, 617(TLS):14Mar86-267
S.M. Gilbert, 491:Dec85-156
W. Logan, 472:Spring/Summer/Fall/Winter85-463
R. McDowell, 249(HudR):Winter86-688
J. Mole, 176:Nov86-57
M. Oliver, 344:Summer86-129
639(VQR):Summer85-96
Clanchy, M.T. From Memory to Written Record.
A. Lutz, 38:Band103Heft1/2-179
Clancy, L. Xavier Herbert.
L.T. Hergenhan, 402(MLR):Apr85-448
Clancy, L. The Novels of Vladimir Nabokov.*
C.S. Ross, 268(IFR):Winter86-43
J.P. Shute, 395(MFS):Winter85-757
295(JML):Nov85-530
Clancy, T. Red Storm Rising.
R. Lekachman, 441:27Jul86-7
de Claramonte, A. Deste agua no beberé. (A. Rodríguez López-Vázquez, ed)
C. Ganelin, 238:Dec85-771
J.A. Madrigal, 345(KRQ):Vol32No4-430
Clare, J. John Clare: "The Parish." (E. Robinson and D. Powell, eds)
W.H., 148:Winter85-91
Clare, J. John Clare's Autobiographical Writings.* (E. Robinson, ed)
T.N.C., 506(PSt):Dec85-100
E. Strickland, 661(WC):Fall85-204
Clare, J. The Later Poems of John Clare, 1837-1864. (E. Robinson and D. Powell, eds)
E. Strickland, 661(WC):Fall85-204
Clare, J. The Letters of John Clare. (M. Storey, ed)
T. Paulin, 617(TLS):20Jun86-675
Clare, J. The Natural History Prose Writings of John Clare. (M. Grainger, ed)
T.N.C., 506(PSt):Dec85-100
P.M.S. Dawson, 148:Summer85-86
E. Strickland, 661(WC):Fall85-204
L.J. Swingle, 340(KSJ):Vol34-194

Clare, J. The Rural Muse.* (R.K.R. Thornton, ed)
J.R. Watson, 161(DUJ):Dec84-127
"John Clare." (E. Robinson and D. Powell, eds)
P.M.S. Dawson, 148:Summer85-86
R. Raimond, 189(EA):Jan-Mar86-99
E. Strickland, 661(WC):Fall85-204
Clareson, T.D. and T.L. Wymer, eds.
Voices for the Future. (Vol 3)
K.L. Spencer, 561(SFS):Mar85-98
Clark, A. The Comic Art of Reg Parlett.
B. Bainbridge, 617(TLS):26Dec86-1453
Clark, A. - see Giscard d'Estaing, V.
Clark, A.M. Pompeo Batoni. (E.P. Bowron, ed)
F. Haskell, 453(NYRB):27Mar86-7
L. Stainton, 617(TLS):10Jan86-40
Clark, A.M. Murder Under Trust.*
K. Muir, 402(MLR):Jul85-689
Clark, A.R. La France dans l'histoire selon Bernanos.
J.C. Whitehouse, 402(MLR):Oct85-949
S. Wilson, 208(FS):Jul85-366
Clark, D. Storm Centre.
T.J. Binyon, 617(TLS):27Jun86-711
Clark, D.R. Yeats at Songs and Choruses.
J.P. Frayne, 301(JEGP):Apr85-284
Clark, E. Camping Out.
C. Kizer, 441:4May86-11
Clark, I. Limited Nuclear War.*
E.P., 185:Jan86-458
Clark, J.C.D. English Society 1688-1832.
L. Colley, 617(TLS):14Mar86-271
J. Dunn, 362:17Jul86-28
Clark, K. and M. Holquist. Mikhail Bakhtin.*
M. Dodsworth, 175:Summer85-185
D. Donoghue, 533:Fall85-107
J. Frank, 453(NYRB):27Mar86-7
W.G. Regier, 223:Spring85-74
P.S. Yaeger, 659(ConL):Summer86-246
639(VQR):Autumn85-118
Clark, P. Marmaduke Pickthall.
M. Ruthven, 617(TLS):5Sep86-964
Clark, R., ed. James Fenimore Cooper.
B. Lee, 617(TLS):27Jun86-704
Clark, R. History and Myth in American Fiction, 1823-52.
D.E. Jones, 27(AL):Dec85-665
Clark, R. and J. McDonough. Imaginary Crimes.
H. Krasnick, 608:Sep86-545
Clark, R.J. and others. Design in America.
H.A. Harrison, 658:Summer/Autumn85-216
Clark, R.J. and T.S. Hines. Los Angeles Transfer.
K.J. Weitze, 576:May85-188
Clark, R.W. The Life of Ernst Chain.
A. Saunders, 617(TLS):14Mar86-283
Clark, R.W. Works of Man.*
442(NY):13Jan86-87
Clark, S. The Elizabethan Pamphleteers.*
J. van Dorsten, 179(ES):Oct85-467
D. Norbrook, 541(RES):Nov85-622
D. Traister, 517(PBSA):Vol79No4-581
Clark, S. and J.S. Donnelly, Jr., eds.
Irish Peasants.
D.H. Akenson, 637(VS):Winter85-317
M.E. Daly, 272(IUR):Spring85-104
A.J. Heesom, 161(DUJ):Jun85-263
D.A. Wilson, 529(QQ):Spring85-191

Clark, S.L. and J.N. Wasserman. Thomas Hardy and the Tristan Legend.
P. Coustillas, 189(EA):Jan-Mar86-106
K. Gamerschlag, 72:Band222Heft2-417
Clark, T. Jack Kerouac.
G.F. Butterick, 432(NEQ):Mar85-152
C.P. Wilson, 27(AL):May85-349
Clark, T.J. The Painting of Modern Life.*
D. Carrier, 290(JAAC):Winter85-203
E. Heartney, 55:Dec85-27
A. Rifkin, 59:Dec85-488
T. Shapiro, 207(FR):Apr86-825
D. Sutton, 39:Nov85-326
Clark, V.P., P.A. Eschholz and A.F. Rosa, eds. Language.
T.E. Murray, 660(Word):Dec85-247
Clark, W.B. Critical Essays on Robert Penn Warren.
R. Gray, 677(YES):Vol 15-355
Clarke, A. Proud Empires.
S. Rae, 617(TLS):24Oct86-1188
Clarke, A.C. The Songs of Distant Earth.
C. Greenland, 617(TLS):31Oct86-1224
G. Jonas, 441:11May86-23
Clarke, A.R. La France dans l'Histoire selon Bernanos - see under Clark, A.R.
Clarke, C. Narratives.
C. Hernton, 472:Spring/Summer/Fall/Winter85-518
Clarke, D.D. Language and Action.
R.T. Denny, 355(LSoc):Dec85-554
Clarke, D.P. Descartes' Philosophy of Science.
J.R. Milton, 208(FS):Apr85-198
Clarke, E. and C. Perry. English Cottage Gardens.
S. Brownmiller, 441:1Jun86-31
Clarke, F.G. Will-o'-the Wisp.
D. Saunders, 575(SEER):Apr85-306
Clarke, F.R.C. Healey Willan.*
A.M. Gillmor, 529(QQ):Spring85-221
W.R., 412:May83-139
Clarke, G. Selected Poems.
T. Curtis, 493:Feb86-62
S. Rae, 364:Aug-Sep85-129
Clarke, G.E. Saltwater Spirituals and Deeper Blues.
A. Munton, 198:Winter85-100
Clarke, G.W. - see Saint Cyprian
Clarke, J. and C. Critcher. The Devil Makes Work.
R.E. Pahl, 617(TLS):14Mar86-284
Clarke, M. The Cutting Season.
A. Cimon, 99:Jan86-37
Clarke, M. and N. Penny, eds. The Arrogant Connoisseur.
G.B. Tatum, 576:Dec85-398
Clarke, P. - see Paul of Venice
Clarke, P.B. Black Paradise.
A.D. Jones, 617(TLS):23May86-558
Clarke, S. Jah Music.
P. O'Gorman, 187:Winter86-159
Classen, C.J. Die Stadt im Spiegel der Descriptiones und Laudes urbium in der antiken und mittelalterlichen Literatur bis zum Ende des zwölften Jahrhunderts.
J-M. André, 555:Vol59fasc1-171
Claudian. Claudii Claudiani "De Bello Gildonico." (E.M. Olechowska, ed and trans)
W.E. Heus, 394:Vol38fasc1/2-238
Clausen, C. The Place of Poetry.
J.G. Vance, 577(SHR):Winter85-80
Clausen, C.A. - see Nilsson, S.

Cobarrubias, J. and J.A. Fishman, eds.
Progress in Language Planning.*
  M. Ó Siadhail, 112:Vol 16-189
Cobb, J.B., Jr. and F.I. Gamwell, eds.
Existence and Actuality.
  A.J.R., 185:Apr86-669
Cobb, J.C. Industrialization and Southern
Society, 1877-1984.
  639(VQR):Winter85-8
Cobb, R. A Classical Education.*
  R. Fuller, 364:Apr/May85-139
Cobb, R. People and Places.*
  S. Romer, 617(TLS):17Jan86-55
  A. Ross, 364:Oct85-98
Cobbold, D. Evening Faces.
  G. Davenport, 569(SR):Spring85-321
Coburn, B. Nepali Aama.
  B.N. Aziz, 293(JASt):Nov84-224
Cocco, M., ed. Roman de Cardenois.
  P. Ménard, 545(RPh):Aug85-121
Cockburn, C. Cockburn in Spain.
  H. Francis, 362:17Jul86-25
Cockburn, J.S., ed. Calendar of Assize
Records, Home Circuit Indictments,
Elizabeth I and James I: Introduction.
  J.A. Sharpe, 617(TLS):6Jun86-628
Cocke, R. Veronese's Drawings.*
  J.B. Shaw, 90:May85-308
  L. Vertova, 39:Jul85-75
Cockerham, H. - see Gautier, T.
Cocks, A.S. - see "The V&A Album 4"
Cocks, A.S. and C. Truman. The Thyssen-
Bornemisza Collection.*
  C. Gere, 90:Jan85-45
Cocks, G. Psychotherapy in the Third
Reich.*
  W. Kluback, 390:Oct85-60
  E. Kurzweil, 473(PR):Vol52No2-144
Cockshut, A.O.J. The Art of Autobiography
in 19th and 20th Century England.*
  M. Moran, 556:Summer85-85
  I.B. Nadel, 637(VS):Summer86-651
Cocteau, J. Beauty and the Beast.
  617(TLS):15Aug86-899
Cocteau, J. Le Passé defini. (Vol 1)
(P. Chanel, ed)
  A.D. Ketchum, 207(FR):Feb86-472
  M. Sheringham, 617(TLS):18Jul86-783
Cocteau, J. Le Passé defini. (Vol 2)
(P. Chanel, ed)
  M. Sheringham, 617(TLS):18Jul86-783
Code, M. Order and Organism.
  L.S. Ford, 543:Mar86-559
Cody, L. Head Case.
  T.J. Binyon, 617(TLS):3Jan86-11
  M. Laski, 362:9Jan86-30
Coe, M. Islands in the Bush.
  W. George, 617(TLS):8Aug86-860
Coe, M. - see "Oxford Illustrated Encyclo-
pedia"
Coe, R.D. and C.K. Wilbur, eds. Capital-
ism and Democracy.
  W. Nelson, 185:Jul86-881
Coe, R.N. When the Grass Was Taller.*
  R. Coles, 115:Summer85-372
  K. Goodwin, 538(RAL):Winter85-612
  P. Lewis, 565:Spring85-43
  I.B. Nadel, 637(VS):Summer86-651
  S. Neuman, 598(SoR):Spring86-407
  A.E. Stone, 481(PQ):Fall85-598
  295(JML):Nov85-412

Coerver, D.M. and L.B. Hall. Texas and
the Mexican Revolution.
  L. Milazzo, 584(SWR):Spring85-262
Coetzee, J.M. Foe.
  G. Dyer, 362:2Oct86-25
  P.N. Furbank, 617(TLS):12Sep86-995
Coffey, T.M. Iron Eagle.
  R. Sherrod, 441:5Oct86-36
Coffin, L. - see Akhmatova, A.
Coffman, M.E. French Vocabulary.
  B. Ebling 2d, 207(FR):Oct85-170
Coggeshall, R. Traffic, With Ghosts.*
  P. Stitt, 219(GaR):Spring85-188
  639(VQR):Spring85-56
Coggins, C.C. and O.C. Shane 3d, eds.
Cenote of Sacrifice.
  M.D. Coe, 263(RIB):Vol35No2-211
  M. Schevill, 2(AfrA):Aug85-94
Cogman, P. Hugo: "Les Contemplations."
  M. Gatti-Taylor, 446(NCFS):Spring-
  Summer86-363
Cogswell, F., ed. The Atlantic Anthology.
(Vol 1)
  I. Huggan, 526:Summer85-79
Cogswell, F. Pearls.* Selected Poems.
  L. Welch, 198:Spring85-93
Cogswell, F. - see Nelligan, E.
Cohen, A. Les Étangs de la Reine Blanche.
  F. de Martinoir, 450(NRF):Apr85-90
Cohen, A. Guardian Angel.
  R. Hill, 617(TLS):25Apr86-454
Cohen, A. and L.E. Miller, comps. Music
in the Paris Academy of Sciences 1666-
1793.
  412:May84-149
Cohen, A.A. Herbert Bayer.
  J.R. Guilfoyle, 507:Jan/Feb85-114
  N. Whiteley, 324:Mar86-269
Cohen, A.P., ed and trans. Tales of Venge-
ful Souls.
  J.L. Scott, 302:Vol21No1-59
Cohen, B.J. In Whose Interest?
  E.L. Morse, 441:21Dec86-11
Cohen, C.L. God's Caress.
  P.F. Gura, 165(EAL):Fall86-177
Cohen, D. Theft in Athenian Law.*
  M. Gagarin, 303(JoHS):Vol 105-214
  M. Nouhaud, 555:Vol59fasc1-107
Cohen, D. and C. Eisdorfer. The Loss of
Self.
  B. Gastel, 441:23Mar86-47
Cohen, D.S. The Folklore and Folklife of
New Jersey.*
  S.R. Sherman, 292(JAF):Apr/Jun85-211
Cohen, E.A. Citizens and Soldiers.
  P. Gold, 129:Feb86-66
  639(VQR):Autumn85-133
Cohen, E.R. Human Rights in the Israeli-
occupied Territories 1967-1982.
  B. Wasserstein, 617(TLS):10Oct86-1123
Cohen, H.F. Quantifying Music.
  M. Fend, 410(M&L):Jul85-289
  J.C. Kassler, 308:Fall85-328
Cohen, I.B. Revolution in Science.*
  I. Hacking, 453(NYRB):27Feb86-21
Cohen, L. Book of Mercy.*
  R. Smith, 102(CanL):Spring85-155
Cohen, L.J. The Dialogue of Reason.
  J. Dancy, 617(TLS):26Dec86-1452
Cohen, M. Life on This Planet.
  E. Tallent, 441:16Feb86-10
Cohen, M. The Pathless Way.
  B. Devall, 649(WAL):May85-69

Coles, R. Walker Percy.
  V.A. Makowsky, 536(Rev):Vol7-305
Coles, R. - see "Dorothea Lange: Photo-
graphs of a Lifetime"
Colesanti, M., ed. Il romanzo barocco tra
Italia e Francia.
  L.C. Pennarola, 475:Vol 12No22-293
Colesanti, M. Stendhal.
  K. Ringger, 547(RF):Band97Heft4-479
Colet, J. John Colet's Commentary on
First Corinthians. (B. O'Kelly and
C.A.L. Jarrott, eds and trans)
  A. Hamilton, 617(TLS):26Sep86-1074
Colette. Flowers and Fruit. (R. Phelps,
ed)
  G. Greer, 441:1Jun86-31
  442(NY):21Jul86-95
Colette. Oeuvres.* (Vol 1) (C. Pichois,
ed)
  R.D. Cottrell, 207(FR):Mar86-623
  D. Coward, 208(FS):Jul85-363
Coletti, V. Parole dal pulpito.
  A.M. Perrone Capano Compagna,
  379(MedR):Apr85-135
Colgan, P. Comparative Social Recognition.
  D.A. Chant, 529(QQ):Summer85-418
Colin, G., ed. De libris compactis miscel-
lanea.
  D. McKitterick, 617(TLS):3Jan86-24
Coll, A.R. The Wisdom of Statecraft.
  J. Luxmoore, 617(TLS):6Jun86-614
Coll, S. The Deal of the Century.
  S. Kinsley, 441:23Nov86-13
Collard, E. Nineteenth-Century Pottery
and Porcelain in Canada.
  T.A. Lockett, 324:May86-415
  G. Wills, 39:Apr85-284
Collard, E. The Potters' View of Canada.
  G. Wills, 39:Mar85-210
Colledge, E. and J. Walsh - see Julian of
Norwich
Colledge, M.A.R. The Art of Palmyra.
  E.W. Gray, 313:Vol175-280
Colledge, M.A.R. Parthian Art.
  E.W. Gray, 313:Vol175-280
Collet, P., ed. Les Romanciers français
et le Canada (1842-1981).
  C.A. Demharter, 207(FR):Dec85-312
Collet, G-P. - see Blanche, J-É.
Collett, B. Italian Benedictine Scholars
and the Reformation.
  A. Hamilton, 617(TLS):22Aug86-922
Collett, P. An Elgar Travelogue.*
  M. Kennedy, 410(M&L):Jan85-60
Colletti, L. Le déclin du marxisme.
  R. Gervais, 154:Winter85-732
Colley, A.C. Tennyson and Madness.*
  D.F. Goslee, 637(VS):Winter85-358
  P. Sharp, 85(SBHC):Vol 13-124
  H.F. Tucker, 405(MP):Feb86-321
Colli, G. and M. Montinari - see Nietzsche,
F.
Collie, M. George Borrow: Eccentric.*
  A.F.T. Lurcock, 541(RES):Feb85-109
Collie, M. and A. Fraser. George Borrow.*
  W.J. Keith, 627(UTQ):Summer85-419
  B. Lake, 78(BC):Summer85-244
Collier, C. and J.L. Decision in Philadel-
phia.
  J.H. Hutson, 441:2Mar86-19

Collier, S., H. Blakemore and T.E. Skid-
more, eds. The Cambridge Encyclopedia
of Latin America and the Caribbean.
  E. Best, 617(TLS):16May86-522
Collin, F. Theory and Understanding.
  R. Harré, 617(TLS):11Apr86-399
Collin, P. and others - see "Harrap's
Shorter French and English Dictionary"
Collin, R.H. Theodore Roosevelt, Culture,
Diplomacy, and Expansion.
  R. Caplan, 441:26Jan86-21
Collinet, J-P. - see Racine, J.
Collini, S., D. Winch and J. Burrow. That
Noble Science of Politics.
  T.W. Heyck, 637(VS):Autumn85-156
Collins, A., ed. CIV/n.*
  J. Mulvihill, 102(CanL):Fall85-139
Collins, A.W. Thought and Nature.
  S. Brown, 617(TLS):5Sep86-962
Collins, F., Jr., with R.F. Cook and R.
Harmon, eds. A Medieval Songbook.*
  G.A. Bond, 545(RPh):Aug85-147
Collins, G.R. and J. Bassegoda Nonell.
The Designs and Drawings of Antonio
Gaudí.*
  K.L. Hilton, 161(DUJ):Jun84-277
Collins, J. Hollywood Husbands.
  K. Olson, 441:2Nov86-26
Collins, J. The Omega Workshops.
  M. Goldstein, 569(SR):Fall85-624
Collins, J. Spinoza on Nature.
  G.S., 185:Oct85-220
Collins, J.T. The Historical Relation-
ships of the Languages of Central Maluku,
Indonesia.
  R. Blust, 350:Jun86-471
Collins, L. Going to See the Leaves.
  J.D. Bellamy, 441:9Mar86-27
Collins, M. and E.K. Kirk, eds. Opera and
Vivaldi.*
  D. Arnold, 410(M&L):Jul85-286
  S. Pinegar, 143:Issue37/38-214
  M. Talbot, 415:Jul85-411
Collins, M.A. A Shroud for Aquarius.
  N. Callendar, 441:26Jan86-40
Collins, M.A. and J.L. Traylor. One
Lonely Knight.
  B.H., 395(MFS):Summer85-425
Collins, R. Early Medieval Spain.
  P. Freedman, 589:Jul85-737
Collins, R.A. and H.D. Pearce, eds. The
Scope of the Fantastic — Theory, Tech-
nique, Major Authors.
  L. Basney, 395(MFS):Winter85-848
Collins, R.G., ed. Critical Essays on
John Cheever.*
  G.F. Manning, 106:Summer85-237
Collins, R.G. Tolerable Levels of Vio-
lence.*
  L. Rogers, 102(CanL):Winter84-126
Collins, S. Selfless Persons.*
  J.P. McDermott, 318(JAOS):Apr-Jun84-
  344
Collins, T.J. - see Browning, R.
"Collins Pocket French Dictionary." (P-H.
Cousin, comp)
  M-N. Lamy, 208(FS):Apr85-244
Collison, R.L. A History of Foreign-
Language Dictionaries.
  E.A. Ebbinghaus, 215(GL):Vol25No1-57
"Colloque Patrice de La Tour du Pin (Sor-
bonne 21 et 22 nov. 1981)."
  G. Cesbron, 535(RHL):Sep/Oct85-895

"Colloquio Internazionale AIEGL: Bartol-
omeo Borghesi."
  M. Crawford, 123:Vol35No1-227
Colls, R. and P. Dodd, eds.  Englishness.
  C. Townshend, 617(TLS):28Nov86-1335
Collura, M-E.L.  Winners.
  A. Kertzer, 102(CanL):Fall85-117
Colman, J.  John Locke's Moral Philosophy.*
  C. Stewart, 319:Jan86-127
de Colombí-Monguió, A.  Petrarquismo peru-
ano.
  E.F. Stanton, 304(JHP):Fall85-83
Colombo, J.R.  Canadian Literary Landmarks.
  W.J. Keith, 627(UTQ):Summer85-429
Colombo, J.R., ed.  Friendly Aliens.
Years of Light.
  D. Ketterer, 561(SFS):Mar85-91
Colombo, J.R., ed.  Songs of the Indians.*
  R.J. Merrett, 529(QQ):Spring85-177
Colombo, J.R. - see Faludy, G.
Colombo, U., ed.  Vita e processo di suor
Virginia Maria de Leyva Monaca di Monza.
  D. Robey, 617(TLS):31Jan86-122
Colón, A.  La syntaxe de Louis Meigret à
travers "L'histoire de C. Crispe Saluste
touchant la coniuration de L. Serge
Catelin" (1547).
  F.J. Hausmann, 475:Vol 12No22-300
Colón, E.  Lecturas fáciles: Ritmos y
melodías.  (J. Olivio Jiménez, ed)
  L.S. Glaze, 399(MLJ):Spring85-108
Coltman, P.  A Momentary Stay.
  P. Gross, 493:Oct85-67
Colum, P.  The King of Ireland's Son.
  P. Craig, 617(TLS):3Oct86-1119
Colussi, G.  Ricerche sulla lingua del
Duecento e primo Trecento.
  A.L. Lepschy, 545(RPh):Feb86-359
Colvert, J.B.  Stephen Crane.
  E. Solomon, 27(AL):Oct85-507
Colville, J.  The Fringes of Power.*
  A. Cooke, 442(NY):3Mar86-98
Colvin, H.  Calke Abbey, Derbyshire.
  J.D. Hunt, 617(TLS):3Jan86-16
Colwin, L.  Another Marvelous Thing.
  R.F. Dew, 441:13Apr86-14
Comanzo, C.  Le David inachevé.
  J. Ducruet, 605(SC):15Jul86-362
Comella, A.  Il deposito votivo presso
l'Ara della Regina.
  J. Champeaux, 555:Vol59fasc1-160
  F.R.S. Ridgway, 123:Vol35No1-166
Comerford, R.V.  The Fenians in Context.
  M.E. Daly, 272(IUR):Spring85-104
  D. Fitzpatrick, 617(TLS):31Jan86-108
"Commedie e comicità nel cinquecento fran-
cese."
  R. Aulotte, 535(RHL):Sep/Oct85-852
Compagnon, A.  Ferragosto.
  R. Buss, 617(TLS):21Mar86-306
Compagnon, A.  La Troisième République
des lettres, de Flaubert à Proust.*
  M. Bertrand, 704(SFR):Summer85-255
  P. France, 402(MLR):Jan85-174
  N. Furman, 446(NCFS):Fall-
Winter85/86-173
  A. Roche, 535(RHL):May/Jun85-517
Comparot, A.  Amour et Vérité.*
  G. Nakam, 535(RHL):May/Jun85-484
Comparot, A.  Augustinisme et aristotél-
isme.
  M. Adam, 542:Jul-Sep85-311

Compitello, A.M.  Ordering the Evidence.
  F. Carenas, 552(REH):May85-139
  R. Manteiga, 238:Mar85-69
Compton, M.D.  Ricardo Palma.*
  R.K. Britton, 402(MLR):Apr85-483
Comte, A.  Correspondance générale et con-
fessions.  (Vol 4 ed by P.E. Berrêdo
Carneiro and P. Arnaud; Vol 5 ed by P.E.
Berrêdo Carneiro and P. Arbousse-Bastide)
  A. Petit, 535(RHL):Mar/Apr85-318
Comte-Sponville, A.  Le mythe d'Icare.
  M. Adam, 542:Jan-Mar85-79
  J-M. Gabaude, 542:Jan-Mar85-80
Comyns, B.  The Skin Chairs.
  P. Craig, 617(TLS):19Dec86-1428
Conacher, D.J.  Aeschylus' "Prometheus
Bound."
  W.J. Verdenius, 394:Vol38fasc3/4-408
Conan Doyle, A.  The Unknown Conan Doyle.
(J.M. Gibson and R.L. Green, eds)
  H. Greene, 362:27Feb86-23
Conati, M., ed.  Interviews and Encounters
with Verdi.
  W. Dean, 410(M&L):Apr85-178
de la Concha, V.G. - see under García de
la Concha, V.
Conche, M. - see Heraclitus
Condé, M.  Ségou.
  C. Zimra, 207(FR):Feb86-484
Conder, J.J.  Naturalism in American Fic-
tion.
  T.A. Gullason, 395(MFS):Winter85-745
  G. Hendrick, 26(ALR):Spring/Autumn85-
291
  R. Lehan, 445(NCF):Dec85-360
  J.R. McElrath, Jr., 27(AL):Dec85-681
  M. Sidone, 590:Dec85-125
  W.B. Stone, 573(SSF):Fall85-493
de Condillac, É.B.  Condillac: "La langue
des calculs."*  (A-M. Chouillet and S.
Auroux, eds)
  F. Duchesneau, 154:Summer85-355
de Condillac, É.B.  Les Monades.  (L.L.
Bongie, ed)
  F. Duchesneau, 154:Summer85-372
Condit, J.  Music of the Korean Renais-
sance.
  A. Dick, 415:Mar85-158
  R.C. Provine, 410(M&L):Apr85-138
Condon, A.G.  The Envy of the American
States.
  J. Errington, 529(QQ):Winter85-847
  E. Jones, 298:Fall85-149
Condon, R.  Prizzi's Family.
  J. Breslin, 441:28Sep86-13
  442(NY):17Nov86-152
Condren, C.  The Status and Appraisal of
Classic Texts.
  A.S.M., 185:Jul86-900
  639(VQR):Autumn85-122
Cone, J.F.  First Rival of the Metropol-
itan Opera.
  J.B., 412:Aug/Nov84-300
Conesa, G.  Le Dialogue moliéresque.
  A. Blanc, 535(RHL):May/Jun85-486
  Q.M. Hope, 207(FR):Dec85-294
Confucius.  The Analects.  (D.C. Lau,
trans)
  R.E. Hegel, 116:Jul84-204
Congdon, L.  The Young Lukács.*
  D. Barnouw, 221(GQ):Fall85-593
  G. Woodcock, 569(SR):Summer85-457

Congreve, W.  Congreve: Comedies.  (P.
Lyons, ed)
   R. Selden, 447(N&Q):Mar84-127
Congreve, W.  The Double-Dealer.  (J.C.
Ross, ed)
   H. Love, 402(MLR):Jan85-125
   K. Robinson, 447(N&Q):Mar84-91
Conisbee, P.  Chardin.
   G. Steiner, 442(NY):17Nov86-144
Conley, V.A.  Hélène Cixous.
   I. de Courtivron, 207(FR):Apr86-800
   A.A. Jardine, 546(RR):Nov85-450
Conlon, J.J.  Walter Pater and the French
Tradition.*
   R.Z. Temple, 149(CLS):Summer85-274
Conlon, P.M.  Le siècle des lumières.*
(Vol 1)
   C.J. Betts, 402(MLR):Jan85-165
   P. Jansen, 535(RHL):Sep/Oct85-876
   A. Rosenberg, 627(UTQ):Summer85-458
   L.S. Thompson, 70:Mar/Apr85-124
Conlon, P.M.  Le siècle des lumières.
(Vol 2)
   A. Rosenberg, 627(UTQ):Summer85-458
   L.S. Thompson, 70:Mar/Apr85-124
Conlon, P.M.  Le siècle des lumières.
(Vol 3)
   L.S. Thompson, 70:Mar/Apr85-124
Conn, J.E.  Red Shoes in the Rain.
   D. O'Rourke, 102(CanL):Fall85-138
Conn, P.  The Divided Mind.*
   J. Bibber, 366:Spring85-135
Connell, C.  They Gave Us Shakespeare.*
   J.M.B., 179(ES):Feb85-73
Connell, E.S.  Son of the Morning Star.*
   E.S. Twining, 152(UDQ):Fall85-124
Connell, J.  The New Maginot Line.
   W.J. Lynn, 441:21Dec86-9
Connell, R.J.  William James on the Cour-
age to Believe.
   P.K. Dooley, 619:Fall85-569
Connelly, T.L.  Will Campbell and the Soul
of the South.
   F. Hobson, 577(SHR):Summer85-245
Conner, P.  Michael Angelo Rooker 1746-
1801.*
   W. Joll, 39:May85-359
Connolly, C.  Cyril Connolly: Journal and
Memoir.  (D. Pryce-Jones, ed)
   295(JML):Nov85-460
Connolly, J.  The Book Quiz Book.
   S. Silvers, 364:Mar86-112
Connolly, J.  Modern First Editions.*
   N. Burwood, 364:Jul85-103
Connolly, P., ed.  Literature and the
Changing Ireland.
   W.E. Hall, 637(VS):Autumn84-191
Connor, S.  Charles Dickens.*
   R. Maxwell, 637(VS):Summer86-646
Connor, W.R.  Thucydides.
   V. Hunter, 487:Summer85-167
   P.J. Rhodes, 123:Vol35No2-385
   T. Scanlon, 124:Jan-Feb86-203
   H.D. Westlake, 303(JoHS)Vol 105-184
Connors, J.  The Robie House of Frank
Lloyd Wright.
   P.E. Sprague, 658:Winter85-281
Connors, R.J., L.S. Ede and A. Lunsford,
eds.  Essays on Classical Rhetoric and
Modern Discourse.
   J.J. Murphy, 126(CCC):Feb85-105
Conover, R.L. - see Loy, M.

Conquest, R.  The Harvest of Sorrow.
   C.R. Whitney, 441:26Oct86-11
Conquest, R.  Inside Stalin's Secret
Police.
   P. Johnson, 362:30Jan86-22
Conrad, B.  Referring and Non-Referring
Phrases.*
   A.M. Zwicky, 350:Sep86-682
Conrad, B. - see Dostojewskaya, A.G.
Conrad, J.  The Collected Letters of Jo-
seph Conrad.* (Vol 1) (F.R. Karl and L.
Davies, eds)
   J. Batchelor, 541(RES):Nov85-593
   T.K. Bender, 141:Fall85-425
   P. Goetsch, 72:Band222Heft2-418
   W.H. Pritchard, 249(HudR):Winter86-673
   M. Ray, 148:Winter85-77
   G. Ward, 97(CQ):Vol 14No3-257
Conrad, J.  The Collected Letters of
Joseph Conrad.  (Vol 2) (F.R. Karl
and L. Davies, eds)
   P. Kemp, 362:21Aug86-23
   J. Lucas, 617(TLS):29Aug86-931
   M. Thorpe, 176:Nov86-51
Conrad, J.  Conrad: Oeuvres.  (Vol 2) (S.
Monod, general ed)
   J. Taylor, 136:Vol 18No1-59
Conradi, P.  John Fowles.
   K. Watson, 447(N&Q):Jun84-281
Conrart, V.  Lettres à Lorenzo Magalotti.*
(G. Berquet and J-P. Collinet, eds)
   B. Bray, 549(RLC):Jan-Mar85-90
   C.N. Smith, 208(FS):Oct85-469
Conroy, F.  Stop-time.
   T.D. Adams, 145(Crit):Spring86-153
Conroy, H., S.T.W. Davis and W. Patterson,
eds.  Japan in Transition.
   M.W. Steele, 407(MN):Winter85-440
Conroy, M.  Modernism and Authority.
   P.B. Armstrong, 136:Vol 18No1-64
   D.W. Ross, 395(MFS):Winter85-793
   G.L. Ulmer, 454:Spring86-275
Conroy, P.  The Prince of Tides.
   G. Godwin, 441:12Oct86-14
"Conservation et Mise en Valeur des Fonds
Anciens, Rare et Precieux des Biblio-
thèques Françaises."
   78(BC):Summer85-145
Constant, D.  Aux Sources du Reggae.
   P. O'Gorman, 187:Winter86-159
Constantine, D.  Davies.
   T. Dooley, 617(TLS):24Jan86-82
Constantine, K.C.  The Man Who Liked to
Look at Himself.
   T.J. Binyon, 617(TLS):25Apr86-454
Constantinides, C.N.  Higher Education in
Byzantium in the Thirteenth and Early
Fourteenth Centuries (1204-ca. 1310).
   J.W. Barker, 589:Jan85-139
Conta, G.  Asculum II.
   T.W. Potter, 123:Vol35No1-219
Contejean, C.  Glossaire du patois de Mont-
béliard.  (new ed rev by M. Thom)
   J. Chaurand, 209(FM):Apr85-141
"Contemporary Canadian Photography."
   W.N., 102(CanL):Fall85-184
Contini, G. - see Dante Alighieri
Contoni, M-H.  L'Exégèse du Nouveau Testa-
ment dans la philosophie française du
dix-huitième siècle.
   J. Macary, 546(RR):May85-337

Contreras, B.R. Tradition and Innovation in New Deal Art.
F.V. O'Connor, 127:Winter84-393
Contreras, H. and J. Klausenburger, eds. Proceedings of the Tenth Anniversary Symposium on Romance Linguistics.
D.J. Napoli, 545(RPh):Aug84-71
Contrucci, J. Comme un cheval fourbu.
M.A. Fitzpatrick, 207(FR):Feb86-485
Coogan, R. - see "Babylon on the Rhone"
Cook, A. Figural Choice in Poetry and Art.
J.D. Carney, 290(JAAC):Summer86-414
Cook, A.J. The Privileged Playgoers of Shakespeare's London, 1576-1642.*
L. Potter, 402(MLR):Jul85-691
Cook, B. Brecht in Exile.*
R. Mueller, 609:Spring86-76
Cook, B. Disorderly Elements.
N. Callendar, 441:17Aug86-20
Cook, B.F. The Elgin Marbles.
90:Mar85-172
Cook, D. Missing Persons.
L. Taylor, 617(TLS):8Aug86-862
Cook, D. and M. Okenimkpe. Ngugi wa Thiong'o.
D. Maughan-Brown, 538(RAL):Summer85-283
Cook, E-D. A Sarcee Grammar.
V. Golla, 350:Jun86-444
K.D. Rice, 320(CJL):Summer85-232
Cook, E-D. and D.B. Gerdts, eds. The Syntax of Native American Languages.
R.D. Van Valin, Jr., 350:Mar86-178
Cook, H.J. The Decline of the Old Medical Regime in Stuart London.
R. Porter, 617(TLS):11Jul86-755
Cook, J. Greene's "Tu Quoque" or, "The Cittie Gallant." (A.J. Berman, ed)
J. Egan, 568(SCN):Fal185-34
Cook, J.M. The Persian Empire.
A. Kuhrt, 303(JoHS):Vol 105-211
Cook, M., ed. Contes révolutionnaires.*
D.M. Bickerton, 208(FS):Apr85-215
Cook, M. The Management of Information from Archives.
D. Vaisey, 617(TLS):1Aug86-851
Cook, M.L. Mystery, Detective, and Espionage Magazines.
P.Z. Du Bois, 87(BB):Dec85-215
F. Erisman, 534(RALS):Spring83-109
Cook, M.L. Mystery Fanfare.* Dime Novel Roundup.
P.Z. Du Bois, 87(BB):Dec85-215
Cook, P., ed. The Cinema Book.
Z. Leader, 617(TLS):6Jun86-610
Cook, R.F. "Chanson d'Antioche," chanson de geste.
P. Ménard, 545(RPh):Nov85-256
Cook, T.H. Elena.
J. Knowles, 441:5Jan86-23
Cooke, A. The Patient Has the Floor.
P-L. Adams, 61:Jun86-84
B. Avishai, 441:1Jun86-7
S. Hearst, 362:15May86-27
C. Hitchens, 617(TLS):11Jul86-757
442(NY):30Jun86-88
Cooke, D. An Index to "Acadiensis," 1901-1908.
D.W. McLeod, 470:Vol23-112
Cooke, D. Vindications.*
R.L.J., 412:Feb83-57

Cooke, M.G. Afro-American Literature in the Twentieth Century.*
N.Y. McKay, 659(ConL):Summer86-270
C. Scruggs, 27(AL):Dec85-692
Cooke, O.A. The Canadian Military Experience 1867-1983. (2nd ed)
R.V. Cupido, 470:Vol123-103
Cookshaw, M. Personal Luggage.
C. Wiseman, 102(CanL):Summer85-188
Cookson, J.E. The Friends of Peace.
C. Woodring, 340(KSJ):Vol134-199
Cookson, P.W., Jr. and C.H. Persell. Preparing for Power.
T.S. Purdum, 441:16Feb86-17
Cookson, W. A Guide to "The Cantos" of Ezra Pound.
W.S. Milne, 4:Autumn-Winter85/86-147
Cooley, D. Fielding.*
R. Stevenson, 628(UWR):Fall-Winter85-83
Cooley, E. Trimotor and Trail.
S. Jenkins, 649(WAL):May85-80
Coombes, A.J. The Collingridge Dictionary of Plant Names.
A. Room, 424:Dec85-275
Coomer, J. A Flatland Fable.
442(NY):3Nov86-165
Cooney, R. Run for Your Wife.
D. Devlin, 157:No156-49
Cooney, T.J. Telling Right from Wrong.*
J.W.D., 185:Jul86-890
Coonts, S. Flight of the Intruder.
M.S. Kaplan, 441:14Dec86-25
Cooper, B. The End of History.
H.S. Harris, 154:Winter85-739
Cooper, C.L., ed. Improving Interpersonal Relations.
J. Turner, 617(TLS):11Jul86-751
Cooper, D. The Gunge File.
P. Black, 362:23Oct86-23
Cooper, D. The Road to Mingulay.
D.A.N. Jones, 362:6Mar86-25
D. Profumo, 617(TLS):15Aug86-887
Cooper, D. Theatre Year 1984.
O. Trilling, 157:No156-51
Cooper, D.E. Authenticity and Learning.
G.M. Brodsky, 543:Jun85-883
S.L. Gilman, 221(GQ):Spring85-312
N.A. Szorenyi, 63:Mar85-99
Cooper, H. The Structure of the "Canterbury Tales."
D.C. Baker, 191(ELN):Jun86-57
N.F. Blake, 179(ES):Apr85-170
A.J. Minnis, 184(EIC):Jul85-265
P. Neuss, 541(RES):Aug85-408
P.G. Ruggiers, 589:Oct85-958
Cooper, H.A. Winslow Homer Watercolors.
P-L. Adams, 61:Jun86-83
A. Stevens, 441:11May86-25
Cooper, J. How to Survive Christmas.
B. Bainbridge, 617(TLS):26Dec86-1453
Cooper, J. Ruth.
B. Tonkin, 362:4Dec86-25
Cooper, J.C. A Piece of Mine.
J. Winterson, 617(TLS):22Aug86-921
Cooper, J.F. The Last of the Mohicans.*
(J.A. Sappenfield and E.N. Feltskog, eds) Gleanings in Europe: England.* (J.P. Elliott, K.W. Staggs and R.D. Madison, eds) Wyandotté, or The Hutted Knoll.* (T. and M. Philbrick, eds)
B. Lawson-Peebles, 541(RES):May85-311

Cooper, L. and A. Synge, eds. Beyond the Far Pavilions.
  A.L. Le Quesne, 617(TLS):5Sep86-987
Cooper, M. and H. Chalfant. Subway Art.
  C. Hess, 507:Mar/Apr85-105
Cooper, P.L. Signs and Symptoms.*
  S.E. Grace, 106:Winter85-483
Cooper, R. Quantification and Syntactic Theory.
  A. Cormack, 297(JL):Mar85-209
  R. May, 350:Dec86-902
  J.C. Moreno Cabrera, 548:Jan-Jun85-232
Cooper, W.J. Liberty and Slavery.
  H.E. Amos, 9(AlaR):Jan85-75
Cooper, W.J., M.F. Holt and J. McCardell, eds. A Master's Due.
  P.J. Parish, 617(TLS):13Jun86-660
Cooter, R. The Cultural Meaning of Popular Science.
  G. Cantor, 617(TLS):3Jan86-10
  R. Yeo, 637(VS):Summer86-620
Coover, R. Gerald's Party.*
  P-L. Adams, 61:Feb86-88
  D. Montrose, 617(TLS):2May86-478
  R. Towers, 453(NYRB):24Apr86-38
Coover, R. In Bed One Night and Other Brief Encounters.
  M.J. Wenckus, 532(RCF):Spring85-147
Cope, W. Making Cocoa for Kingsley Amis.
  D. Davis, 362:10Apr86-27
  B. O'Donoghue, 617(TLS):6Jun86-616
Copeau, J. Registres IV.
  B.V. Daniels, 610:Autumn85-251
Copeland, A. Earthen Vessels.
  A.S. Brennan, 198:Winter85-114
  T. Middlebro', 102(CanL):Summer85-173
  J. Parks, 99:Aug/Sep85-32
Copeland, J.E., ed. New Directions in Linguistics and Semiotics.*
  R.A. Champagne, 399(MLJ):Autumn85-312
Copeland, J.G., R. Kite and L. Sandstedt. Intermediate Spanish. (3rd ed)
  E. Spinelli, 399(MLJ):Winter85-435
Copland, A. and V. Perlis. Copland: 1900 through 1942.*
  P. Dickinson, 415:Mar85-159
  J. Harbison, 414:Vol71No1-95
  R. Holloway, 607:Mar85-45
Copley, S., ed. Literature and the Social Order in Eighteenth-Century England.
  D.C. Payne, 566:Autumn85-94
Copp, D. and S. Wendell, eds. Pornography and Censorship.*
  J.E. Bickenbach, 154:Summer85-330
Copp, D. and D. Zimmerman, eds. Morality, Reason and Truth.
  M. Baron, 185:Jul86-878
Coppenger, M. Bioethics.
  J.G.H., 185:Jul86-917
Corballis, R. Stoppard.
  J. Morris, 615(TJ:)Dec85-523
  P. Storfer, 157:No158-47
Corbett, G.G. Hierarchies, Targets and Controllers.*
  R. Beard, 574(SEEJ):Spring85-116
  C.V. Chvany, 279:Vol29-156
  V.M. Du Feu, 402(MLR):Jan85-247
Corbin, A. The Foul and the Fragrant.
  R.M. Adams, 453(NYRB):20Nov86-24
  J.W. Scott, 441:2Nov86-11
Corbineau-Hoffmann, A. and A. Gier, eds. Aspekte der Literatur des fin-de-siècle
[continued]

in der Romania.*
  H. Felten, 52:Band20Heft3-322
Corcoran, N. The Song of Deeds.
  W. Blissett, 627(UTQ):Winter85/86-212
  K.H. Staudt, 659(ConL):Fall86-409
  C. Wilcockson, 541(RES):May85-300
Corcoran, P.E., ed. Before Marx.
  B. Rigby, 208(FS):Apr85-219
Cordero, N-L. Les deux chemins de Parménide.
  D. Babut, 542:Jul-Sep85-297
Cordes, G. and D. Möhn, eds. Handbuch zur niederdeutschen Sprach- und Literaturwissenschaft.
  G. Krogerus, 439(NM):1985/3-414
  W.G. Moulton, 355(LSoc):Sep85-403
Coren, A. Something for the Weekend.
  B. Bainbridge, 617(TLS):26Dec86-1453
Coren, M. Theatre Royal.
  A. Vivis, 157:No156-50
Cork, R. Art Beyond the Gallery in Early 20th Century England.*
  A. Causey, 90:Nov85-816
  D. Farr, 39:Oct85-320
  E. Silber, 324:Oct86-765
Cormack, R. Writing in Gold.
  J. Herrin, 617(TLS):17Oct86-1172
Corman, C. - see Niedecker, L.
Cormeau, C. - see Kuhn, H.
Cormeau, C. and W. Störmer. Hartmann von Aue.
  B. Haupt, 72:Band222Heft2-355
Corn, A. Notes from a Child of Paradise.*
  455:Mar85-64
Corn, J.J. The Winged Gospel.*
  L. Goldstein, 385(MQR):Fall86-736
Cornazani, A. Fraudiphila. (S. Pittaluga, ed and trans)
  A. Stäuble, 228(GSLI):Vol 162fasc518-276
Cornazano, A. The Book on the Art of Dancing.
  R.M., 412:Feb83-53
Corneille, P. Théâtre complet. (Pt 1) (A. Niderst, ed)
  M. Margitić, 207(FR):Apr86-780
  D.A. Watts, 475:Vol 12No23-732
Corneille, T. Ariadne. (O. Mandel, ed and trans)
  J. Moravcevich, 475:Vol 12No22-337
  D.A. Watts, 535(RHL):Jan/Feb85-89
Cornet, J. Art Royal Kuba.
  J. Mack, 59:Sep85-391
Cornford, J. Collected Writings. (J. Galassi, ed)
  H. Francis, 362:17Jul86-25
  D.D. Gilmore, 441:8Jun86-44
Cornwell, B. Sharpe's Regiment.
  S. Altinel, 617(TLS):18Jul86-793
Cornwell, N., ed. Irish-Russian Contacts.
  W.F. Ryan, 575(SEER):Oct85-603
Cornwell, N. V.F. Odoyevsky.
  S. Karlinsky, 617(TLS):26Sep86-1067
Coromines, J. Diccionari etimològic i complementari de la llengua catalana. (Vols 1-4)
  H. Meier, 547(RF):Band97Heft2/3-279
Corr, C.A. - see Wolff, C.
Correa, G. Antología de la poesía española (1900-1980).
  R. Warner, 86(BHS):Apr85-210
"Les Correspondances."
  A. Schweiger, 535(RHL):Nov/Dec85-1087

82

Corrie, J. Plays, Poems and Theatre Writ-
ings. (L. Mackenney, ed)
D. Devlin, 157:No158-45
Corrigan, F. Helen Waddell.
P. Craig, 617(TLS):28Mar86-334
V. Glendinning, 362:27Mar86-31
Corrigan, T. Coleridge, Language, and
Criticism.
R.L. Brett, 541(RES):Feb85-106
Corrigan, T. New German Film.*
B.A. Murray, 221(GQ):Spring85-323
Corsinovi, G. Pirandello.
G. Singh, 276:Autumn85-265
de Cortázar, C.S. - see under Sabor de
Cortázar, C.
Cortázar, J. Around the Day in Eighty
Worlds.
J. Krich, 441:4May86-9
442(NY):16Jun86-121
Cortázar, J. Cuaderno de bitácora de
"Rayuela." (A.M. Barrenechea, ed)
J. Alazraki, 240(HR):Autumn85-518
Cortazzi, H., ed. Mitford's Japan.
J. McMullen, 617(TLS):4Apr86-368
Cortazzi, H. Dr. Willis in Japan 1862-
1877.
J. McMullen, 617(TLS):4Apr86-368
Cortés, J., ed. El Corán.
C. López-Morillas, 318(JAOS):Apr-Jun84-
384
Cortesi Bosco, F. Gli affreschi dell'-
Oratorio Suardi.
P. Reutersward, 341:Vol54No1-39
Cortez, J. Coagulations.
M. Kumin, 219(GaR):Spring85-169
Corti, M. - see "Letture Classensi"
Corvin, M. and others. Théâtres du XIXe
siècle.
J. Emelina, 535(RHL):Jan/Feb85-106
Cosby, B. Fatherhood.
P-L. Adams, 61:Jul86-79
K. Ray, 441:11May86-25
Cosentino, C. and W. Ertl. Zur Lyrik
Volker Brauns.
U. Brandes, 222(GR):Fall85-145
S. Hoefert, 564:Nov85-315
Cosentino, D. Defiant Maids and Stubborn
Farmers.*
J. Knappert, 203:Vol96No1-134
Coser, L.A. Refugee Scholars in America.*
42(AR):Spring85-256
Coseriu, E. Introducción a la lingüística.
R. Martin, 553(RLiR):Jul-Dec85-447
Cosslett, T., ed. Science and Religion in
the Nineteenth Century.*
C.B. Jones, 506(PSt):May85-82
Cosslett, T. The "Scientific Movement"
and Victorian Literature.
R.L. Brett, 541(RES):Aug85-441
J. Paradis, 637(VS):Winter86-328
Costa, C.D.N. Lucretius, "De Rerum Natura
V."
G.B. Townend, 123:Vol35No2-273
Costa, R.H. H.G. Wells.
J.R. Reed, 395(MFS):Winter85-805
da Costa Fontes, M., ed. Romanceiro
português dos Estados Unidos.* (Vol 1)
C. Slater, 545(RPh):Aug84-120
de Costa Fontes, M., ed. Romanceiro por-
tuguês dos Estados Unidos. (Vol 2)
D.W. Foster, 292(JAF):Jul/Sep85-353
H. Kröll, 547(RF):Band97Heft2/3-345

Costantini, H. The Gods, the Little Guys,
and the Police.
S. White, 448:Vol23No3-150
Costantini, H. The Long Night of Fran-
cisco Sanctis.*
J. Updike, 442(NY):22Sep86-111
Costello, D.P. Fellini's Road.
G. Marrone, 276:Summer85-137
Costello, J. Virtue Under Fire.
W. Karp, 441:17Aug86-24
Costello, J.R. Syntactic Change and Syn-
tactic Reconstruction.*
J. Algeo, 159:Spring85-105
D.G. Lockwood, 660(Word):Aug85-186
Costigliola, F. Awkward Dominion.
639(VQR):Summer85-82
Côté, P.R. Les Techniques picturales chez
Malraux.
D. O'Connell, 207(FR):Mar86-624
Cott, J. Pipers at the Gates of Dawn.
S. Pickering, 569(SR):Spring85-xxxvi
Cotterill, R. The Cambridge Guide to the
Material World.*
J. Taylor, 324:Apr86-342
Cottingham, J., R. Stoothoff and D.
Murdoch - see Descartes, R.
Cottom, D. The Civilized Imagination.
S. Soupel, 189(EA):Oct-Dec86-463
Cottrell, A. Social Classes in Marxist
Theory.
J.C.I., 185:Apr86-677
Cottrell, A.P. Goethe's View of Evil and
the Search for a New Image of Man in Our
Time.
H. Eichner, 406:Winter85-469
H. Knust, 301(JEGP):Jul85-407
Couchoud, M-T.A. Kierkegaard ou l'instant
paradoxal.
L.R. Wilkinson, 563(SS):Summer85-333
Coudrette. Le Roman de Mélusine ou His-
toire de Lusignan.* (E. Roach, ed)
P. Rickard, 208(FS):Oct85-451
J.H.M. Taylor, 382(MAE):1985/2-339
Coughlin, T.G. The Hero of New York.
D. Smith, 441:21Sep86-43
442(NY):29Sep86-135
Coulet, N., A. Planche and F. Robin. Le
roi René.
D. Angers, 589:Jan85-219
Coupry, F. Le Rire du pharaon.
S. Wolitz, 207(FR):Dec85-332
Courchay, C. Retour à Malaveil.
M.I. Madden, 207(FR):Oct85-147
Courdy, J-C. The Japanese.*
K.A. Grossberg, 293(JASt):May85-615
Coursen, H.R. The Leasing Out of England.*
D. Evett, 702:Vol 17-266
Court, A. Puck of the Droms.*
G. Mangan, 617(TLS):30May86-584
Courter, G. Code Ezra.
E. Fishel, 441:25May86-14
Courtney-Clarke, M. Ndebele.
G. Packer, 441:3Aug86-19
Cousin, P-H. - see "Collins Pocket French
Dictionary"
Cousins, N. Albert Schweitzer's Mission.
D. Cupitt, 617(TLS):5Sep86-964
N. Miller, 441:5Jan86-17
Coustillas, P. - see Gissing, G.
Couton, G. Corneille et la tragédie poli-
tique.
J. Morel, 475:Vol 12No22-302

Couturier, M. and R. Durand. Donald Bar-
thelme.
  R. Gray, 447(N&Q):Dec84-572
Couzyn, J., ed. The Bloodaxe Book of Con-
temporary Women Poets.*
  E. Longley, 493:Apr85-39
  J. Mole, 176:Jan86-58
Couzyn, J. Life by Drowning.*
  J. Mole, 176:Jan86-58
  L. Thompson, 102(CanL):Summer85-136
Covell, C. The Redefinition of Conserva-
tism.
  J. Dunn, 617(TLS):4Apr86-347
  A. Ryan, 362:30Jan86-23
Covell, J.C., with S. Yamada. Unraveling
Zen's Red Thread.
  T.J. Kodera, 293(JASt):Aug85-838
Cowan, B. Exiled Waters.*
  M. Bickman, 27(AL):Dec85-661
Cowan, J.C., ed. D.H. Lawrence.* (Vol 1)
  G.J. Zytaruk, 40(AEB):Vol8No3-212
Cowan, P. An Orphan in History.
  R. Leiter, 390:Jan85-63
Coward, D. Marivaux: "La Vie de Marianne"
and "Le Paysan parvenu."*
  A. Goodden, 402(MLR):Apr85-464
  G.E. Rodmell, 83:Autumn85-245
Coward, H.G. Bhartṛhari.
  F. Blackwell, 314:Winter-Spring85-245
Coward, H.G. - see Murti, T.R.V.
Coward, N. Autobiography.
  H. Carpenter, 617(TLS):9May86-507
Cowart, D. Arches and Light.*
  K. Tölölyan, 301(JEGP):Oct85-534
Cowden, M.H. Russian Bolshevism and Brit-
ish Labor, 1917-1921.
  F.M. Leventhal, 550(RusR):Jul85-311
  T.E. O'Connor, 104(CASS):Spring85-79
Cowdrey, A.E. This Land, This South.*
  N.L. Christensen, 579(SAQ):Winter85-
  109
Cowdrey, C. and J. Smith. Good Enough?
  A.L. Le Quesne, 617(TLS):5Sep86-987
Cowdrey, H.E.J. The Age of Abbot Desid-
erius.*
  G. Constable, 377:Jul84-105
  D.J. Osheim, 589:Oct85-960
Cowie, A.P. and R. Mackin. Oxford Diction-
ary of Current Idiomatic English.* (Vol
1)
  B.S. Sutton, 399(MLJ):Summer85-217
Cowie, A.P., R. Mackin and I.R. McCaig.
Oxford Dictionary of Current Idiomatic
English.* (Vol 2)
  B.S. Sutton, 399(MLJ):Summer85-217
Cowie, P. Ingmar Bergman.
  R. Wright, 563(SS):Winter85-94
Cowie, V. Games.
  J. Kaufman, 441:13Apr86-22
Cowler, R. - see Pope, A.
Cowley, M. The Flower and the Leaf.*
(D.W. Faulkner, ed)
  H. Bak, 219(GaR):Fall85-649
Cowley, M., ed. Writers at Work. (1st
Ser)
  M. Mudrick, 249(HudR):Winter86-648
Cowley, R.L.S. Hogarth's "Marriage A-la-
mode."*
  P. Brückmann, 627(UTQ):Spring85-293
  F.H. Dowley, 405(MP):Nov85-192

Cowling, M. Religion and Public Doctrine
in Modern England. (Vol 2)
  P. Clarke, 617(TLS):14Mar86-271
  S.R. Letwin, 362:23Jan86-29
  H.R. Trevor-Roper, 453(NYRB):13Mar86-7
Cowper, T. Relative Strangers.
  D. Devlin, 157:No158-45
Cowper, W. The Letters and Prose Writings
of William Cowper.* (Vol 2) (J. King
and C. Ryskamp, eds)
  P.M. Spacks, 301(JEGP):Oct85-559
Cowper, W. The Letters and Prose Writings
of William Cowper.* (Vol 3) (J. King
and C. Ryskamp, eds)
  P. Danchin, 179(ES):Dec85-561
  P.M. Spacks, 301(JEGP):Oct85-559
Cowper, W. The Letters and Prose Writings
of William Cowper. (Vol 4) (J. King and
C. Ryskamp, eds)
  P. Danchin, 179(ES):Dec85-561
  V. Newey, 506(PSt):Dec85-95
  P.M. Spacks, 301(JEGP):Oct85-559
Cox, A. Art-as-Politics.
  D. Craven, 59:Dec85-499
Cox, C.B. Two-Headed Monster.
  D. Davis, 362:10Apr86-27
  T. Dooley, 617(TLS):1Aug86-839
Cox, C.B. and D.J. Palmer, eds. Shake-
speare's Wide and Universal Stage.
  R. Berry, 570(SQ):Autumn85-367
Cox, D.R., ed. Sexuality and Victorian
Literature.*
  N. Armstrong, 637(VS):Spring86-483
Cox, G. Tyrant and Victim in Dostoevsky.
  E. Egeberg, 172(Edda):1985/6-372
  I. Naginsky, 104(CASS):Summer85-221
  L.M. Porter, 395(MFS):Winter85-824
  G. Rosenshield, 574(SEEJ):Winter85-473
Cox, I. Montesquieu and the History of
French Laws.
  J.F. Jones, Jr., 207(FR):Feb86-466
  M.H. Waddicor, 208(FS):Jan85-76
Cox, J. The English Churches in a Secular
Society.
  J.H.Y. Briggs, 637(VS):Spring85-546
Cox, J.R. and C.A. Willard, eds. Advances
in Argumentation Theory and Research.
  M. Cooper, 480(P&R):Vol 18No3-193
  C.W., 185:Oct85-211
Cox, M. M.R. James.*
  J.P.T. Bury, 637(VS):Winter86-324
Cox, M. and R.A. Gilbert, eds. The Oxford
Book of English Ghost Stories.
  P. Craig, 617(TLS):21Nov86-1324
Cox, P. Biography in Late Antiquity.*
  T.D. Barnes, 123:Vol35No1-197
Cox, T.R. and others. The Well-Wooded
Land.
  D. Murray, 441:16Mar86-21
Cox-Rearick, J. Dynasty and Destiny in
Medici Art.*
  C. Dempsey, 90:Nov85-808
  C. Gould, 39:Jun85-434
Coye, M.J., J. Livingston and J. Highland.
China Yesterday and Today.
  D. Murray, 293(JASt):May85-580
Cozzens, J.G. Selected Notebooks 1960-
1967. (M.J. Bruccoli, ed)
  J. Braham, 395(MFS):Winter85-740
Crabbe, G. Selected Letters and Journals
of George Crabbe. (T.C. Faulkner, ed)
  M. Butler, 617(TLS):3Jan86-3

Crick, M. The March of Militant.
 P. Clarke, 617(TLS):7Nov86-1240
Crider, B. Too Late to Die.
 N. Callendar, 441:7Sep86-17
Crimmins, J.C. and M. Keil. Enterprise in
 the Nonprofit Sector.
 E.A. Prieve, 476:Summer84-91
Crippa, M.A. Carlo Scarpa.
 A. McIntyre, 46:Mar85-83
Crisp, J., comp. Jessie Fothergill, 1851-
 1891.*
 S. Mitchell, 635(VPR):Spring85-40
Crispin, E. Fen Country.
 362:4Dec86-32
Crispin, J. Quest for Wholeness.
 A. Carreño, 238:Dec85-778
Crist, S. The Horse Traders.
 J. Quinlan, 441:11May86-25
 442(NY):16Jun86-122
Cristofani, M. L'arte degli Etruschi.
 N. Spivey, 313:Vol75-270
Critchfield, R. Those Days.
 H. Nissenson, 441:23Mar86-1
Crittall, E. - see Hunt, W.
Croce, B. Poetry and Literature. (G.
 Gullace, ed and trans)
 M.A. Finocchiaro, 543:Dec84-383
Crocker, D.A. Praxis and Democratic
 Socialism.
 D.C., 185:Oct85-215
 L. Outlaw, 543:Sep85-144
Croft, J. Their Solitary Way.
 P. Smelt, 617(TLS):20Jun86-682
Croft, P.J. - see Sidney, R.
Croissant, F. Les Protomés féminines
 archaïques.
 J. Boardman, 123:Vol35No1-153
de la Croix, J. Les Dits de Lumière et
 d'Amour.
 G. Quinsat, 450(NRF):Dec85-91
Croke, B. and A.M. Emmett, eds. History
 and Historians in Late Antiquity.
 T.D. Barnes, 123:Vol35No2-398
Croll, E. The Family Rice Bowl.
 G.E. Johnson, 293(JASt):Feb85-363
Crompton, A. The Man Who Drew Tomorrow.
 R. McLean, 617(TLS):7Mar86-243
Crompton, D. A View from the Spire.
 G. Klaus, 189(EA):Oct-Dec86-471
Crompton, L. Byron and Greek Love.*
 K. Walker, 364:Aug-Sep85-151
"Cronaca di Novalesa." (G.C. Alessio, ed)
 P. Frassica, 545(RPh):Nov84-268
Crone, M. A Period of Confinement.
 B. Harvey, 441:31Aug86-12
Cronin, A. Dead as Doornails.
 617(TLS):10Oct86-1147
Cronin, A. Letter to an Englishman.
 T. Dooley, 617(TLS):21Nov86-1325
Cronin, J. The Anglo-Irish Novel. (Vol 1)
 R.A. Cave, 541(RES):Feb85-136
Cronley, J. Funny Farm.
 D. Guy, 441:26Jan86-20
Crook, D.P. Benjamin Kidd.
 G. Mariz, 637(VS):Spring86-480
Crook, J., ed. The Wainscot Book.
 S.J., 90:Sep85-631
Crook, J.M. and C.A. Lennox-Boyd. Axel
 Haig and the Victorian Vision of the
 Middle Ages.*
 R. O'Donnell, 90:Sep85-630
Crooke, W. - see Yule, H. and A.C. Burnell
Crooks, D.Z. - see Praetorius, M.

Cros, E. Ideología y genética textual.*
 M. Cavillac, 92(BH):Jul-Dec84-537
Crosby, A.W. Ecological Imperialism.
 B. Fell, 441:19Oct86-20
Crosby, J. Take No Prisoners.
 N. Callendar, 441:26Jan86-40
Crosland, M. Piaf.*
 E. Cameron, 364:Mar86-101
Cross, A.G. and G.S. Smith. Eighteenth
 Century Russian Literature, Culture and
 Thought.
 I.R. Titunik, 550(RusR):Jan85-113
Cross, J.E. and T.D. Hill, eds. The
 "Prose Solomon and Saturn" and "Adrian
 and Ritheus."*
 C. Sisam, 541(RES):Nov85-549
Cross, N. The Common Writer.
 A. Bell, 617(TLS):14Feb86-171
 J.L.W. West 3d, 517(PBSA):Vol79No4-591
Cross, N., ed. Developments in Design
 Methodology.
 B. Russell, 46:Sep85-81
Cross, T. Painting the Warmth of the Sun.*
 E.H. Ramsden, 39:Apr85-283
Cross, W.L. The Development of the En-
 glish Novel.
 W.J. Palmer, 158:Sep85-98
Crossley, C. Musset: "Lorenzaccio."
 W.D. Howarth, 208(FS):Jul85-353
 P.J. Siegel, 446(NCFS):Spring-Summer86-
 403
Crossley, C. Edgar Quinet (1803-1875).*
 D.G. Burnett, 210(FrF):Jan85-113
 R.T. Denommé, 207(FR):Apr86-792
Crossley-Holland, K., ed. Folk-Tales of
 the British Isles.
 C. Causley, 362:16Oct86-22
 J. Westwood, 617(TLS):28Nov86-1347
Crossley-Holland, K., ed. The Oxford Book
 of Travel Verse.
 D. Davis, 617(TLS):17Oct86-1154
Crossley-Holland, K. Time's Oriel.*
 J. Saunders, 565:Spring85-72
Crossley-Holland, K. Waterslain and Other
 Poems.
 S. Rae, 617(TLS):19Dec86-1423
Crotty, K. Song and Action.*
 A. Burnett, 122:Apr85-176
 M. Williamson, 303(JoHS):Vol 105-181
Crouch, A.R. Scholars' Guide to China
 Mission Resources in the Libraries and
 Archives of the United States (Fascicle
 I: Pennsylvania).
 K-C. Yip, 293(JASt):May85-582
Crouch, D. The Beaumont Twins.
 R.H.C. Davis, 617(TLS):18Jul86-796
Crouch, M. and R. Porter, eds and trans.
 Understanding Soviet Politics Through
 Literature.
 M.K. Frank, 399(MLJ):Spring85-102
 J.M. Mills, 574(SEEJ):Spring85-100
Crouchett, L.J. Filipinos in California.
 A.B. Chen, 293(JASt):May85-660
Croussy, G. Le Sphinx.
 J.O. Lowrie, 207(FR):Dec85-333
Crouzet, F. De la Supériorité de l'Angle-
 terre sur la France.
 P.K. O'Brien, 617(TLS):12Sep86-1000
 S. Soupel, 189(EA):Oct-Dec86-454
Crouzet, M. Stendhal et l'Italianité.
 G. Strickland, 208(FS):Jan85-84

Crouzet, M. Stendhal: Quatre études sur Lucien Leuwen.
  W.A. Guentner, 446(NCFS):Fall-Winter85/86-168
  V.D.L., 605(SC):15Jul86-360
Crovitz, G. Europe's Siberian Gas Pipeline.
  D. Wilson, 550(RusR):Apr85-211
Crow, C. Carl Crow's Handbook for China. (H.J. Lethbridge, ed)
  R. Harris, 617(TLS):6Jun86-617
Crow, J. - see Chappuzeau, S.
Crow, J.A. and G.D. Panorama de Las Américas. (6th ed)
  R. Ruiz, 399(MLJ):Autumn85-321
Crow, M., ed. Woman Who Has Sprouted Wings.
  A.M. Pasero, 238:Dec85-790
Crow, T.E. Painters and Public Life in Eighteenth-Century Paris.*
  W. Olander, 441:9Mar86-21
  C. Ratcliff, 62:Jan86-14
Crowl, P.A. The Intelligent Traveller's Guide to Historic Scotland.
  D. Walker, 617(TLS):24Oct86-1199
Crowley, D.J. African Myth and Black Reality in Bahian Carnaval.
  D. Cosentino, 2(AfrA):Nov84-22
Crowley, E.T., ed. Reverse Acronyms, Initialisms, and Abbreviations Dictionary. (8th ed) (Vol 3)
  K.B. Harder, 424:Sep85-204
Crowley, J.W. The Black Heart's Truth.
  B. Morton, 617(TLS):1Aug86-838
Crowne, J. The Comedies of John Crowne. (B.J. McMullin, ed)
  J. Milhous, 612(ThS):May85-95
Crozier, B. The Andropov Deception.
  N. Callendar, 441:28Dec86-15
Crozier, L. The Weather.*
  J. Bayly, 526:Summer85-86
  M. Fiamengo, 102(CanL):Winter84-133
Crozier, M. The Trouble with America.*
  S. Tichy, 219(GaR):Fall85-670
Crucitti Ullrich, F.E. Apollo tra le dune.
  P. Jourdan, 535(RHL):Mar/Apr85-324
Cruickshank, C. SOE in the Far East.
  R.H. Taylor, 293(JASt):Feb85-460
Cruickshank, D. A Guide to the Georgian Buildings of Britain and Ireland.*
  J. Summerson, 46:Dec85-98
Cruickshank, J. Pascal: "Pensées."*
  R. Maber, 161(DUJ):Jun85-274
  E. Moles, 402(MLR):Oct85-940
Crump, M. and M. Harris, eds. Searching the Eighteenth Century.*
  H. Amory, 517(PBSA):Vol79No1-128
de la Cruz, J. La prosa de los anglosajones.
  P. Tejada, 548:Jul-Dec85-456
de la Cruz, J.I. Inundación castálida. (G. Sabat de Rivers, ed)
  R.M. Price, 402(MLR):Apr85-481
de la Cruz, R. Sainetes, I.* (J. Dowling, ed)
  I.L. McClelland, 86(BHS):Oct85-408
de la Cruz, S.J. - see under San Juan de la Cruz
Cua, A.S. Ethical Argumentation.
  J. Marshall, 543:Mar86-561

Cuartero Sancho, M.P. Fuentes clásicas de la literatura paremiológica española del siglo XVI.
  R.W. Truman, 86(BHS):Oct85-406
Cubells, M. La Provence des Lumières.
  O. Ranum, 173(ECS):Summer86-545
Cubillo de Aragon, A. Auto sacramental de la muerte de Frislan. (M.F. Schmidt, ed)
  J.A. Madrigal, 345(KRQ):Vol132No4-430
"Cuckolds, Clerics, and Countrymen."*
  (J. Du Val, trans; R. Eichmann, ed)
  M.J. Schenck, 545(RPh):May85-548
Čudakova, M.O. Poètika Michaila Zoščenko.
  W. Busch, 688(ZSP):Band45Heft1-185
de la Cuesta, A.R. - see under Ruiz de la Cuesta, A.
Cuevas, C., ed. Fray Luis de León y la escuela salmantina.*
  D.G. Walters, 86(BHS):Apr85-198
Cuevas García, C. - see de Zabaleta, J.
Cugusi, P. Evoluzione e forme dell'epistolografia latina nella tarda repubblica e nei primi due secoli dell'impero.
  A.N. Sherwin-White, 313:Vol175-308
Čukovskaja, L. Pamjati detitva.
  E. Sokol, 574(SEEJ):Winter85-486
Culicover, P.W. and W.K. Wilkins. Locality in Linguistic Theory.
  M-L. Rivero, 320(CJL):Fall85-396
Cullen, P. and T.P. Roche, Jr. - see "Spenser Studies"
Culler, A.D. The Victorian Mirror of History.
  R. Altick, 617(TLS):25Apr86-441
Culler, J. Barthes.*
  S. Rendall, 478:Apr85-111
  J.F. Solomon, 405(MP):Aug85-101
Culler, J. On Deconstruction.*
  N. Cotton, 435:Spring85-100
  D.H. Hirsch, 569(SR):Summer85-465
  T.J. Reiss, 107(CRCL):Sep85-422
  H. Staten, 400(MLN):Sep85-871
Culler, J. The Pursuit of Signs.*
  T.J. Reiss, 107(CRCL):Sep85-422
Culley, M., ed. A Day at a Time.
  P-L. Adams, 61:Mar86-112
  P. Hampl, 441:16Mar86-19
Cullhed, A. "Tiden söker sin röst."*
  L. Thompson, 562(Scan):Nov85-240
Cullingford, E. - see Yeats, W.B.
Culver, C.M. and B. Gert. Philosophy in Medicine.*
  J.E. Thomas, 154:Spring85-168
Cummer, W.W. and E. Schofield - see under Willson Cummer, W. and E. Schofield
Cumming, R.D. Starting Point.
  D.C. Hoy, 311(JP):Sep85-489
Cumming, W. Sketchbook.
  M.S. Young, 39:Aug85-162
Cummings, E.E. IS5. (G.J. Firmage, ed)
  639(VQR):Autumn85-132
Cummings, M. The Lives of the Buddha in the Art and Literature of Asia.
  R. Morris, 318(JAOS):Jul-Sep84-601
Cummings, T. Gopher Hills.
  G. Noonan, 102(CanL):Winter84-116
Cummins, R. The Nature of Psychological Explanation.*
  R. Harré, 449:Sep85-473
Cunningham, E.V. The Wabash Factor.
  N. Callendar, 441:23Mar86-16
  442(NY):10Mar86-124
Cunningham, J.S. - see Marlowe, C.

Cunningham, M. Golden States.
C.L. Crow, 649(WAL):May85-92
Cunningham, M., with J. Lesschaeve. The Dancer and the Dance.*
H. Moss, 453(NYRB):13Mar86-36
Cunningham, V., ed. Spanish Front.
H. Francis, 362:17Jul86-25
442(NY):13Oct86-157
Cunninghame Graham, R.B. The Scottish Sketches of R.B. Cunninghame Graham.* (J. Walker, ed)
C. Watts, 541(RES):Feb85-117
Cupaiuolo, G., ed. Bibliografia terenziana (1470-1983).
S.M. Goldberg, 121(CJ):Dec85/Jan86-175
Cupaiuolo, G., ed and trans. Evanzio, De fabula.
D. Holwerda, 394:Vol38fasc3/4-434
Cupitt, D. Life Lines.
D.Z. Phillips, 617(TLS):26Dec86-1446
Curb, R. and N. Manahan, eds. Breaking Silence.
M. Lefkowitz, 617(TLS):25Apr86-438
Curley, E. - see Spinoza, B.
Curran, J., ed. Bending Reality.
362:7Aug86-26
Current, R.N. Northernizing the South.
M.E. Bradford, 392:Fall85-495
T.L. Seip, 9(AlaR):Apr85-141
Currie, D.P. The Constitution in the Supreme Court.
J.P. Dougherty, 543:Jun86-760
Currie, E. Available Light.
T. Gertler, 441:2Mar86-15
Currie, G. Frege.*
R.H. Stoothoff, 63:Mar85-101
Curry, D.P. James McNeill Whistler at the Freer Gallery of Art.*
D. Sutton, 39:Jan85-71
Curry, J. The River's in My Blood.*
J. Lauber, 106:Spring85-47
Curry, J.L., ed. Dissent in Eastern Europe.
P. Petro, 104(CASS):Spring85-103
Curry, R.J. and S. Kirk. Philip Webb in the North.
M. Chase, 326:Winter85/86-26
Curtis, J. - see Wordsworth, W.
Curtis, J.M. Solzhenitsyn's Traditional Imagination.*
R. Russell, 575(SEER):Jul85-446
Curtis, L.A. The Elusive Daniel Defoe.
S. Sim, 83:Autumn85-242
Curtis, T. Letting Go.
J. Cobley, 376:Mar85-161
Curtis, T., ed. Wales.
N. Thomas, 617(TLS):13Jun86-658
Curtius Rufus, Q. Quintus Curtius Rufus: The History of Alexander. (J. Yardley, trans; W. Heckel, ed)
A.M. Devine, 487:Autumn85-297
Lord Curzon. Travels with a Superior Person. (P. King, ed)
A. Harvey, 441:1Jun86-14
J. Ure, 617(TLS):4Apr86-368
442(NY):19May86-122
Cusa, N. Tunnicliffe's Birdlife.
T. Halliday, 617(TLS):21Mar86-314
Cushman, S. William Carlos Williams and the Meanings of Measure.
P. Lagayette, 189(EA):Oct-Dec86-484
Cussler, C. Cyclops.
R. Nalley, 441:16Feb86-16

Cutler, A. and D.R. Ladd, eds. Prosody.*
A. Cruttenden, 297(JL):Mar85-226
Cutler, P. The Public Landscape of the New Deal.
G. Jellicoe, 324:Aug86-627
Cutrer, T.W. Parnassus on the Mississippi.*
W.C. Havard, 639(VQR):Summer85-537
R.B. Heilman, 569(SR):Spring85-330
J.H. Justus, 578:Spring86-123
R.S. Moore, 27(AL):May85-347
Cutts, P. and R. Curr. Creative Techniques in Stage and Theatrical Photography.
J.M. Burian, 615(TJ):Mar85-125
Cutts, S. Pianostool Footnotes.
J. Saunders, 565:Spring85-72
Čvani, E.N. and S. Ljubenskaja - see Vakar, G.
Cybulska, M.E. Wacław Iwaniuk Poeta.
Z. Folejewski, 497(PolR):Vol30No3-305
Saint Cyprian. The Letters of Saint Cyprian. (G.W. Clarke, ed and trans)
R.P.C. Hanson, 123:Vol35No2-394
Czerniawski, A. - see Różewicz, T.
Czucka, E. Idiom der Entstellung.
R.W. Williams, 402(MLR):Jan85-231
Czyba, L. Mythes et idéologie de la femme dans les romans de Flaubert.*
K. Zappel, 627(UTQ):Spring85-312

Daalder, J. - see Seneca
Daan, J. and H. Heikens. Dialectresistentie bij kleuters en eersteklassertjes.
G. Van der Elst, 685(ZDL):2/1985-264
Dabney, V. Virginius Dabney's Virginia.
A. Friesinger, 441:14Dec86-25
Dąbrowa, E. L'Asie Mineure sous les Flaviens.
B. Levick, 313:Vol75-301
Dąbrowa, E. La politique de l'état parthe à l'égard de Rome.
M.A.R. Colledge, 313:Vol75-321
Dabydeen, C. Elephants Make Good Stepladders.
P.K. Smith, 526:Spring85-88
Dabydeen, D., ed. The Black Presence in English Literature.
D. Walder, 617(TLS):13Jun86-663
Dach, K. Polsko-rumuńska współpraca polityczna w latach 1831-1852.
A.A. Hetnal, 497(PolR):Vol30No3-295
D'Achille, P. and C. Giovanardi. La letteratura volgare e i dialetti di Roma e del Lazio. (Vol 1)
A. Castelvecchi, 708:Vol 11fasc1-129
Dachy, M. Persévérance.
B. Beaulieu, 102(CanL):Summer85-153
Dadson, T.R. The Genoese in Spain.
W.F. King, 405(MP):Feb86-310
Dafydd ap Gwilym. Dafydd ap Gwilym: A Selection of Poems. (R. Bromwich, ed and trans)
N. Jacobs, 382(MAE):1985/1-150
D.N. Klausner, 627(UTQ):Spring85-284
G. Ruddock, 617(TLS):6Jun86-624
Dafydd ap Gwilym. Dafydd ap Gwilym: The Poems. (R.M. Loomis, trans)
N. Jacobs, 382(MAE):1985/1-150
D.N. Klausner, 627(UTQ):Spring85-284
[continued]

Dafydd ap Gwilym. Dafydd ap Gwilym: The Poems. [continuing]
  D.F. Melia, 589:Apr85-476
  J. Rowland, 112:Vol 16-201
Daglish, R. Coping with Russia.
  R. Hattersley, 617(TLS):7Feb86-147
Dagognet, F. Philosophie de l'image.
  C. Debru, 98:Jun-Jul85-731
D'Agostino, P. and A. Muntadas, eds. The Un/Necessary Image.
  M. Reese, 127:Fall85-269
D'Aguiar, F. Mama Dot.
  P. Gross, 493:Oct85-67
  C. Rawson, 617(TLS):7Feb86-137
  W. Scammell, 364:Dec85/Jan86-119
Dahl, E. Die Entstehung der Phantastischen Kinder- und Jugend-erzählung in England.
  B. Alderson, 617(TLS):31Oct86-1231
Dahl, L. Stormy Weather.*
  D.A. Handy, 91:Spring85-117
  J.K. Skipper, Jr., 498:Vol 10No1-78
Dahl, N.O. Practical Reason, Aristotle and Weakness of Will.
  D.B., 185:Jan86-456
  D. Charles, 518:Oct85-209
  P. Corrigan, 543:Dec85-349
Dahl, R. Controlling Nuclear Weapons.
  R.H., 185:Apr86-694
Dahl, R. Going Solo.
  A. Ross, 617(TLS):12Sep86-996
  G. Wilson, 441:12Oct86-12
Dahl, R.A. Dilemmas of Pluralist Democracy.*
  M.W. Howard, 543:Jun86-761
Dahl, R.A. A Preface to Economic Democracy.
  J.K., 185:Jul86-892
Dahl, W. Norges litteratur II.
  R. Eide, 172(Edda):1985/3-187
Dahlerup, P. Det moderne gennembruds kvinder.*
  A. Jensen, 562(Scan):May85-84
Dahlhaus, C. Between Romanticism and Modernism.*
  H.B.R., 412:Feb84-72
Dahlhaus, C. Foundations of Music History.*
  H.B.R., 412:May84-147
Dahlhaus, C. and H. de la Motte-Haber, eds. Systematische Musikwissenschaft.
  B. Bujić, 410(M&L):Apr85-135
Dahlie, H. Brian Moore.*
  D. Staines, 402(MLR):Apr85-449
Dahlke, H. - see Feuchtwanger, L.
Dahlmann, H. Zu Fragmenten römischer Dichter.
  N. Horsfall, 123:Vol35No1-186
Dahmus, J. Dictionary of Medieval Civilization.*
  C.T. Wood, 589:Oct85-967
Dahmus, J. Seven Decisive Battles of the Middle Ages.
  J. Beeler, 589:Jul85-737
Dahnke, H-D., with others, eds. Parallelen und Kontraste.
  H. Finze, 654(WB):12/1985-2095
Dahrendorf, R. and T.C. Sorensen. A Widening Atlantic?
  F. Sauzey, 441:4May86-41
Daiber, H. Aetius Arabus.
  E.K. Rowson, 318(JAOS):Apr-Jun84-387

Daiches, D. Edinburgh.
  A.J. Youngson, 617(TLS):24Oct86-1199
Daiches, D. God and the Poets.
  J. Dedes, 134(CP):Vol 18No1/2-150
  M.R. Konvitz, 390:Aug/Sep85-47
  D.M. Rosenberg, 115:Summer85-379
Daigle, J.O. A Dictionary of the Cajun Language.
  M.P. Trenkle, 207(FR):Apr86-836
Dailey, J. The Great Alone.
  C.L. Mithers, 441:17Aug86-22
Dainard, A. and others - see Helvétius, C-A.
Daitch, S. L.C.
  L. Marcus, 617(TLS):20Jun86-682
  J. Turner, 362:7Aug86-25
Daiyun, Y. and C. Wakeman - see under Yue Daiyun and C. Wakeman
Dakubu, M.E.K. One Voice.
  D.M. Warren, 538(RAL):Fall85-423
The Dalai Lama VII. Selected Works of the Dalai Lama VII: Songs of Spiritual Change. (2nd ed) (G.H. Mullin, trans)
  D.S. Lopez, Jr., 469:Vol 11No3-118
Dalby, R. Bram Stoker.
  S. Grider, 517(PBSA):Vol79No3-450
Dalcourt, G. The Methods of Ethics.
  B.G., 185:Jan86-435
d'Alcripe, P. La Nouvelle Fabrique des excellents traicts de verité.* (F. Joukovsky, ed)
  T. Thomson, 402(MLR):Oct85-933
Daleski, H.M. The Divided Heroine.*
  R. Gagnier, 637(VS):Autumn85-159
  J. Gindin, 401(MLQ):Sep84-305
  J. Pickering, 395(MFS):Summer85-375
D'Alfonso, A. Black Tongue.*
  L. Welch, 198:Summer85-84
Dalgish, G.M. A Dictionary of African-isms.*
  M.H. Morgan, 355(LSoc):Sep85-427
Dalla Palma, G. Le strutture narrative dell'"Orlando Furioso."
  A.R. Ascoli, 551(RenQ):Winter85-751
  B. Guthmüller, 547(RF):Band97Heft4-489
Dallet, J-M. Paradis, paradis.
  M. Herz, 207(FR):May86-991
Dallmayr, F.R. Polis and Praxis.
  R.J. Bernstein, 543:Dec85-350
  N.S.L., 185:Apr86-666
Dalpé, J.M. Et d'ailleurs.
  B. Beaulieu, 102(CanL):Summer85-153
d'Alpuget, B. Winter in Jerusalem.
  A. Boston, 617(TLS):10Oct86-1130
  R. Samuel, 441:8Jun86-15
Dalton, H. The Second World War Diary 1940-45. (B. Pimlott, ed)
  J. Grigg, 362:6Mar86-24
  M. Pugh, 617(TLS):21Mar86-296
Daly, I. Ellen.
  P. Craig, 617(TLS):7Mar86-256
Daly, L.W. - see Philoponus, I.
Daly, P.M., ed. The European Emblem.
  K.J. Höltgen, 179(ES):Oct85-474
Dalziel, M. Janet Frame.
  P. Quartermaine, 447(N&Q):Dec84-575
D'Amato, A. Jurisprudence.
  G.J. Postema, 185:Jan86-420
Dameron, J.L. and J.W. Mathews, eds. No Fairer Land.
  L.D. Rubin, Jr., 165(EAL):Fall86-173

89

Damiani, B.M. "La Diana" of Montemayor as
Social and Religious Teaching.*
  T.A. Perry, 551(RenQ):Spring85-151
  E. Urbina, 568(SCN):Winter85-68
Damiani, B.M. Jorge de Montemayor.
  S.G. Dahlgren, 238:Sep85-513
Damiani, B.M. Montemayor's "Diana," Music,
and the Visual Arts.*
  B.W. Ife, 86(BHS):Oct85-391
Damiani, B.M. - see López de Ubeda, F.
Damiani Indelicato, S. Piazza pubblica e
palazzo nella Creta minoica.
  D.J.I. Begg, 487:Summer85-163
  J.L. Fitton, 303(JoHS):Vol 105-219
  H. Waterhouse, 123:Vol35No1-151
Damico, H. Beowulf's Wealhtheow and the
Valkyrie Tradition.
  M.C. Ross, 563(SS):Autumn85-465
D'Amico, J.F. Renaissance Humanism in
Papal Rome.*
  R. Catani, 278(IS):Vol40-127
  T. Deutscher, 539:Nov85-294
  M.L. Kuntz, 589:Apr85-389
Damrosch, L., Jr. Symbol and Truth in
Blake's Myth.*
  J.M.Q. Davies, 161(DUJ):Jun84-300
Dance, S. The World of Count Basie.
  E.J. Hobsbawm, 453(NYRB):16Jan86-3
"Dance and Music in South Asian Drama —
Chhau, Mayākālī pyākhan, and Yakshagāna."
  H. Chung, 187:Fall86-582
  A. Dick, 415:Mar85-158
  P.B. Zarrilli, 293(JASt):Feb85-419
Danchev, A. Balgarska transkripcija ang-
lijski imena. (2nd ed)
  E.D. Lawson, 424:Dec85-273
Danchin, P., ed. The Prologues and Epi-
logues of the Restoration 1660-1700.*
(Pt 1)
  H. Love, 402(MLR):Jan85-124
Danchin, P., ed. The Prologues and Epi-
logues of the Restoration 1660-1700.*
(Pt 2)
  A.H. Scouten, 611(TN):Vol39No3-155
  J.P. Vander Motten, 179(ES):Dec85-557
Dandamaev, M.A. Slavery in Babylonia from
Nabopolassar to Alexander the Great
(626-331 BC). (rev) (M.A. Powell and
D.B. Weisberg, eds)
  P. Briant, 617(TLS):17Oct86-1173
D'Andrea, A. Il nome della storia.*
  A. Bonadeo, 276:Summer85-142
  E. Bonora, 228(GSLI):Vol 162fasc517-
  130
Danell, K.J. Remarques sur la construc-
tion dite causative.
  H.B-Z. Shyldkrot, 545(RPh):Aug84-81
Danesi, M. A Guide to Puzzles and Games
in Second Language Pedagogy.
  R.A. Hartzell, 207(FR):Apr86-802
Danforth, L.M. The Death Rituals of Rural
Greece.*
  R. Hague, 24:Fall85-390
D'Angelo, R.M. Fra trimetro e senario
giambico.
  H.D. Jocelyn, 123:Vol35No2-262
Dania, L. Fortunato Duranti.
  D.B., 90:Nov85-820
Daniel, A. - see under Arnaut Daniel
Daniel, G. Some Small Harvest.
  D. Cupitt, 362:4Dec86-22
  P. Fowler, 617(TLS):21Nov86-1300

Daniel, L. and P. Christensen, eds. Ride
Off to Any Horizon.
  M. Fee, 376:Mar85-162
  G.P. Greenwood, 526:Summer85-81
Daniel, N. Heroes and Saracens.
  T. Hunt, 402(MLR):Jan85-156
  J-L. Picherit, 207(FR):Feb86-455
Daniel, P. Breaking the Land.
  639(VQR):Autumn85-115
Daniel, S.H. John Toland.*
  E. Talmor, 319:Oct86-562
Daniele, A. and L. Renzi - see Mussafia, A.
Danieli, M. Zum Problem der Tradition-
saneignung bei Aristoteles.
  R.W. Jordan, 123:Vol35No2-403
Daniels, A. Coups and Cocaine.
  J. Ure, 617(TLS):20Jun86-674
Daniels, B.C. Dissent and Conformity on
Narragansett Bay.*
  J.M. Sosin, 106:Fall85-301
Daniels, B.V. Revolution in the Theatre.
  N. King, 610:Summer85-179
Daniels, J. Places/Everyone.
  P. Stitt, 441:4May86-22
Daniels, K. The White Wave.*
  M. Boruch, 460(OhR):No36-123
  M. Kumin, 219(GaR):Spring85-169
  455:Mar85-64
  639(VQR):Winter85-26
Danielsen, N. and others, eds. Friser-
studier.
  T.L. Markey, 260(IF):Band90-351
Danielson, D.R. Milton's Good God.*
  A. Low, 403(MLS):Fall85-332
Danielson, H., ed and trans. Ādiśeṣa.
  K.G. Zysk, 318(JAOS):Oct-Dec84-784
Danielsson, B. - see Smith, T.
"Dänisch-Deutsche Kontrastive Grammatik."
(Report No 4)
  R. Baudusch, 682(ZPSK):Band38Heft2-185
Dankleff, R. Westerns.
  F.L. Lee, 649(WAL):Feb86-359
Danky, J.P., with M.E. Hady and A. Bowles,
eds. Native American Periodicals and
Newspapers 1828-1982.
  V.S. Salabiye, 635(VPR):Winter85-151
Danky, J.P., M.E. Hady and R.J. Morris,
eds. Native American Press in Wisconsin
and the Nation.
  B.R. Johnson, 517(PBSA):Vol79No4-611
Dann, P. Mermaids.
  M-A.T. Smith, 441:12Oct86-50
Dannhauer, H-M. and others, comps. Wörter-
buch zu Friedrich Hölderlin. (Pt 1)
  D. Constantine, 402(MLR):Jan85-217
Danon, R. Work in the English Novel.
  N. Berry, 617(TLS):21Mar86-312
Danon, S. and S.N. Rosenberg - see "Ami
and Amile"
Danson, L. The Harmonies of "The Merchant
of Venice."
  K. Schlüter, 38:Band103Heft3/4-482
Dante Alighieri. Dante's Inferno.* (T.
Phillips, trans and illustrator)
  J.R.B., 148:Autumn85-93
  J.R. Woodhouse, 324:Dec85-69
Dante Alighieri. Dante's Paradise. (M.
Musa, ed and trans)
  G.C. Di Scipio, 276:Summer85-143
  A.R.C. Duncan, 529(QQ):Autumn85-645
  M.U. Sowell, 589:Jul85-669

Dante Alighieri. Dante's Purgatory. (M. Musa, ed and trans)
    P. Hainsworth, 447(N&Q):Jun84-256
Dante Alighieri. The Divine Comedy. (C.H. Sisson, trans)
    C.C. Park, 396(ModA):Fall85-361
Dante Alighieri. The Divine Comedy.* (Vol 2: Purgatorio.) (A. Mandelbaum, trans)
    P. Hainsworth, 447(N&Q):Jun84-256
Dante Alighieri. The Divine Comedy.* (Vol 3: Paradiso.) (A. Mandelbaum, trans)
    A.R.C. Duncan, 529(QQ):Autumn85-645
Dante Alighieri. "Il Fiore" e "Il Detto d'Amore" attribuibili a Dante Alighieri. (G. Contini, ed)
    L. Vanossi, 228(GSLI):Vol 162fasc519-453
D'Antuono, N.L. Boccaccio's "Novelle" in the Theater of Lope de Vega.*
    D.J. Hill, 345(KRQ):Vol132No4-438
Danuser, H. Die Musik des 20. Jahrhunderts.
    D. Jarman, 410(M&L):Apr85-172
Dao, B. - see under Bei Dao
Daoud, H.S. and A. Al-Rawi. Flora of Kuwait. (Vol 1)
    M. Jebb, 617(TLS):10Jan86-47
Darby, M. John Pollard Seddon.
    R. O'Donnell, 90:Oct85-725
de Dardel, R. Esquisse structurale des subordonnants conjonctionnels en roman commun.
    J. Vizmuller-Zocco, 547(RF):Band97 Heft1-52
    R. Wright, 545(RPh):Feb86-338
Dardess, J.W. Confucianism and Autocracy.
    J.F. Handlin, 293(JASt):May85-583
de Dargies, G. - see under Gautier de Dargies
Darling, S. Chicago Furniture.*
    S. Jervis, 39:Mar85-212
Darmon, P. Damning the Innocent.
    R. Darnton, 453(NYRB):9Oct86-15
    L. Stone, 441:23Mar86-41
Darmon, P. Trial by Impotence.*
    H.G. Pitt, 364:Apr/May85-136
Darnton, R. The Great Cat Massacre.*
    C.N. Davidson, 115:Summer84-261
    G. Lewis, 208(FS):Oct85-483
    J. Richetti, 533:Summer85-128
    P. Stewart, 173(ECS):Winter85/86-260
Darragon, E. Manierisme en crise.
    E.A. Carroll, 551(RenQ):Spring85-140
d'Arras, J. - see under Jean d'Arras
Daruwalla, K.N. The Keeper of the Dead.*
    D. McDuff, 565:Winter84/85-73
Darwall, S.L. Impartial Reason.
    E.J. Bond, 518:Oct85-232
    T.E. Hill, Jr., 185:Apr86-604
    J.P. Sterba, 449:Sep85-470
Darweesh, M. Sand, and other Poems.
    B. Morton, 362:4Dec86-28
Darwent, B. - see Saroyan, W.
Darwin, E. The Letters of Erasmus Darwin. (D. King-Hele, ed)
    C. Bush, 677(YES):Vol 15-306
Dary, D. Entrepreneurs of the Old West.
    R.F. Snow, 441:31Aug86-13
Das, M.M. Thomas Hardy.
    H.L. Weatherby, 569(SR):Winter85-162

Dasenbrock, R.W. The Literary Vorticism of Ezra Pound and Wyndham Lewis.
    R. Lewis, 432(NEQ):Dec85-607
    L. Mackinnon, 617(TLS):21Mar86-292 639(VQR):Autumn85-124
Dasilva, F., A. Blasi and D. Dees. The Sociology of Music.
    M. Bolling, 187:Spring/Summer86-348
Dassin, J., ed. Torture in Brazil.
    A. Stepan, 441:23Nov86-22
Dassonville, M. Ronsard: Etude historique et littéraire. (Vol 4)
    U. Langer, 546(RR):Jan85-118
Dassoucy, C. Adventures in the Age of Louis XIV. (C.E. Scruggs, ed and trans)
    R. Parish, 208(FS):Jul85-333
Datar, K.K. Malaysia.
    C. Hirschman, 293(JASt):May85-664
Dathorne, O.R., ed. The Afro World.
    L.A. Johnson, 538(RAL):Fall85-435
d'Aubigné, A. Histoire universelle.* (Vols 1 and 2) (A. Thierry, ed)
    K. Cameron, 208(FS):Apr85-194
Dauenhauer, B.P. Silence.
    G.J. Agich, 323:Jan85-105
Dauer, A.M. Blues aus 100 Jahren.
    A. Prévos, 91:Spring85-115
Dauge, Y.A. Le Barbare.
    J.M. Alonso-Núñez, 123:Vol35No2-411
Daunton, M.J. House and Home in the Victorian City.
    D. Englander, 637(VS):Autumn85-179
Dauses, A. Das Imperfekt in den Romanischen Sprachen.
    B. Schlieben-Lange, 547(RF):Band97 Heft4-434
Dautel, K. Zur Theorie des Literarischen Erbes in der "Entwickelten Sozialistischen Gesellschaft" der DDR.
    W. Müller, 406:Summer85-247
Davenport, M. and others, eds. Current Topics in English Historical Linguistics.
    J.T. Jensen, 350:Mar86-211
Davenport, W.A. Fifteenth-Century English Drama.*
    G. Bourquin, 189(EA):Jan-Mar86-90
    P. Gradon, 447(N&Q):Jun84-258
    A.A. MacDonald, 179(ES):Apr85-162
    D. Staines, 589:Jul85-738
Davey, F. Margaret Atwood.
    L. Scheier, 99:May85-31
Davey, F. Edward and Patricia.*
    P.M. St. Pierre, 102(CanL):Summer85-183
Davey, F. Surviving the Paraphrase.*
    S. Gingell, 102(CanL):Spring85-112
Daviau, D. Der Mann von Übermorgen.
    A.W. Barker, 402(MLR):Apr85-502
Daviau, D., J.B. Johns and J.B. Berlin - see Zweig, S.
David, D. and M. Slabbert, eds. Crime and Power in South Africa.
    J.E. Spence, 617(TLS):15Aug86-882
David, E. Aristophanes and Athenian Society of the Early Fourth Century B.C.
    D.G. Kyle, 124:May-Jun86-333
David II. The Acts of David II, King of Scots, 1329-1371. (B. Webster, ed)
    W.E. Kapelle, 589:Oct85-962
David-Neel, A. My Journey to Lhasa.
    A. Harvey, 441:1Jun86-14
Davidoff, L. The Best Circles.
    617(TLS):19Dec86-1434

91

Davidsen, L. The Sardine Deception.
E. Pall, 441:4May86-40
Davidson, A.E. Conrad's Endings.
C.R. La Bossière, 268(IFR):Summer86-98
295(JML):Nov85-460
Davidson, A.E. Mordecai Richler.*
C. Thomas, 395(MFS):Summer85-431
Davidson, B. The Story of Africa.
G. Wheatcroft, 617(TLS):14Nov86-1285
Davidson, C. From Creation to Doom.
L.M. Clopper, 589:Oct85-964
J.W. Robinson, 130:Winter85/86-365
Davidson, C., ed. A Middle English Trea-
tise on the Playing of Miracles.*
A.H. Nelson, 402(MLR):Jan85-115
Davidson, C., C.J. Gianakaris and J.H.
Stroupe, eds. The Drama of the Middle
Ages.*
A.A. MacDonald, 179(ES):Apr85-162
Davidson, C.N. The Experimental Fictions
of Ambrose Bierce.
L.I. Berkove, 26(ALR):Spring/Autumn85-
263
M.E. Grenander, 395(MFS):Summer85-399
J.R. Vitelli, 27(AL):May85-339
295(JML):Nov85-450
Davidson, D. Inquiries into Truth and
Interpretation.*
J. Bennett, 393(Mind):Oct85-601
D. Gorman, 478:Oct85-258
S.D. Guttenplan, 483:Jul85-408
J. Heal, 483:Jul85-405
Davidson, H.M. Blaise Pascal.*
E. Morot-Sir, 207(FR):Dec85-293
Davidson, J.H.C.S. and H. Cordell, eds.
The Short Story in Southeast Asia.
D.G. Fernandez, 293(JASt):Aug85-884
Davidson, M. Hugger Mugger.
M. Seymour, 617(TLS):8Aug86-863
Davie, C.T. Musical Structure and Design.
A.F.L.T., 412:Aug/Nov84-304
Davie, D. Collected Poems 1970-1983.*
Dissentient Voice.
D.E. Richardson, 569(SR):Fall85-634
Davie, D. Czeslaw Milosz and the Insuffi-
ciency of Lyric.
J. Bayley, 617(TLS):21Nov86-1295
Davie, D., ed. The New Oxford Book of
Christian Verse.
D.E. Richardson, 569(SR):Fall85-634
Davie, D. These the Companions.
W. Bedford, 4:Autumn-Winter85/86-99
Davie, D. Trying to Explain.
R. McDowell, 249(HudR):Autumn85-508
Davie, E. A Traveller's Room.*
J.A.S. Miller, 571(ScLJ):Winter85-67
P. Parker, 364:Jun85-107
Davie, G.E. The Crisis of the Democratic
Intellect.
P. Drew, 617(TLS):24Oct86-1201
Davie, M. The Titanic.
E.S. Turner, 617(TLS):10Oct86-1129
Davies, A. An Annotated Critical Bibliog-
raphy of Modernism.
J.A. Varsava, 541(RES):Nov85-626
Davies, A., C. Criper and A.P.R. Howatt,
eds. Interlanguage.
S.N. Gynan, 399(MLJ):Winter85-423
J. Heath, 350:Dec86-962
Davies, H. Catching the Conscience.
D.W. Ross, 395(MFS):Summer85-452

Davies, J.A. John Forster.*
R. Bennett, 541(RES):Nov85-586
R.L. Patten, 158:Jun85-58
H. Stone, 637(VS):Spring85-541
Davies, J.G., ed. A New Dictionary of
Liturgy and Worship.
G. Irvine, 617(TLS):10Oct86-1146
Davies, K. At Home in Manhattan.
C.L. Venable, 658:Winter85-315
Davies, N. God's Playground.* (Vols 1
and 2)
G. Gömöri, 497(PolR):Vol30No2-203
Davies, N. Heart of Europe.
S. Bóbr-Tylingo, 497(PolR):Vol30No3-
277
639(VQR):Spring85-52
Davies, P. The Last Election.
J.K.L. Walker, 617(TLS):14Feb86-162
Davies, P. Splendours of the Raj.
M. Archer, 39:Aug85-162
J.M. Richards, 46:Oct85-76
Davies, P.R. The Damascus Covenant.
J.A. Sanders, 318(JAOS):Oct-Dec84-773
Davies, R. The Mirror of Nature.*
L.W. Conolly, 178:Jun85-260
B. Kalikoff, 637(VS):Autumn85-184
J. Noonan, 616:Fall/Winter85-48
Davies, R. The Papers of Samuel March-
banks.
J.K. Galbraith, 441:3Aug86-9
442(NY):15Sep86-121
Davies, R. What's Bred in the Bone.*
W. Balliett, 442(NY):27Jan86-96
D.J. Enright, 453(NYRB):27Feb86-16
S. French, 617(TLS):28Feb86-215
M. Hulse, 176:Sep/Oct86-57
A. Huth, 362:27Feb86-26
B. Morton, 362:16Oct86-22
F. Sutherland, 99:Dec85-22
T.W., 111:Fall86-11
Davies, S. Images of Kingship in "Para-
dise Lost."*
J.S. Bennett, 551(RenQ):Spring85-185
B.M. Berry, 401(MLQ):Sep84-295
G. Christopher, 301(JEGP):Jan85-120
Davies, S. Paris and the Provinces in
Eighteenth-Century Prose Fiction.*
G. Bremner, 208(FS):Jan85-82
J. Dunkley, 402(MLR):Jan85-166
Davies, W. Wales in the Early Middle Ages.
P.K. Ford, 589:Jan85-141
F. Kelly, 112:Vol 16-201
Davies, W. - see Hardy, T.
Davies, W.D. and L. Finkelstein, eds. The
Cambridge History of Judaism. (Vol 1)
S.J.D. Cohen, 124:Mar-Apr86-280
Davies, W.H. Selected Poems.* (J. Barker,
ed)
W.H., 148:Summer85-93
"Juan Davila: Hysterical Tears." (P.
Taylor, ed)
L. Ellmann, 617(TLS):18Jul86-791
Davis, B.D. Storm Over Biology.
E.O. Wilson, 129:Nov86-78
Davis, B.H. Thomas Percy.*
D.C. Mell, Jr., 402(MLR):Jul85-698
Davis, C. Joseph and the Old Man.
M. Stout, 441:17Aug86-22
Davis, C. W.S. Merwin.
R. Pooley, 402(MLR):Apr85-452
Davis, C.T. Black Is the Color of the
Cosmos.
N.Y. McKay, 659(ConL):Summer86-270

92

Davis, C.T. Dante's Italy and Other
Essays.
  J.K. Hyde, 366:Autumn85-300
Davis, C.T. and M. Fabre. Richard Wright.
  J. Mason, 392:Winter84/85-87
Davis, D. The Covenant.*
  J. Lanchester, 493:Apr85-60
  W. Scammell, 364:Jul85-80
  G. Szirtes, 148:Summer85-51
Davis, D. Wisdom and Wilderness.*
  A. Gelpi, 27(AL):Dec85-653
  T. Parkinson, 405(MP):Aug85-94
Davis, D.B. From Homicide to Slavery.
  L.D. Rubin, Jr., 441:5Oct86-27
Davis, D.B. Slavery and Human Progress.*
  C.N. Degler, 656(WMQ):Apr85-259
  A. MacIntyre, 185:Jan86-429
Davis, E. Graham Greene.
  D.J. Dooley, 627(UTQ):Summer85-424
Davis, J. Talking Heads.
  J. Fleming, 441:28Sep86-27
Davis, J.E. The Spanish of Argentina and
Uruguay.
  B.R. Lavandera, 355(LSoc):Dec85-569
Davis, K.S. FDR: The New Deal Years, 1933-
1937.
  I. Howe, 441:28Sep86-3
  442(NY):27Oct86-144
Davis, K.S. FDR: The New York Years, 1928-
1933.*
  R.C. Wade, 441:19Jan86-33
Davis, L. Break It Down.
  F. Howe, 441:28Sep86-16
Davis, L.J. Factual Fictions.*
  M. Irwin, 541(RES):Aug85-430
  J.E. Young, 125:Winter85-219
Davis, L.J. Onassis.
  L. Wayne, 441:3Aug86-19
Davis, L.M. English Dialectology.*
  G. Bailey, 35(AS):Fall85-254
Davis, N. The Last Two Years of Salvador
Allende.* (British title: The Last
Years of Salvador Allende.)
  A.H. Bernstein, 129:Jul86-64
Davis, P. Memory and Writing.
  D. Ellis, 97(CQ):Vol 14No2-174
  J. Saunders, 161(DUJ):Jun85-278
Davis, P., with M.S. Foster. Home Front.
  E.R. Lipson, 441:9Mar86-24
Davis, P.J. and R. Hersh. Descartes'
Dream.
  D. Gorenstein, 441:5Oct86-45
Davis, R. The English Rothschilds.
  639(VQR):Winter85-10
Davis, R.C. and R. Schleifer, eds. Rhet-
oric and Form.
  P. O'Donnell, 400(MLN):Dec85-1144
Davis, R.J. Augustus Thomas.
  I.H. Herron, 26(ALR):Spring/Autumn85-
296
Davis, R.M. A Catalogue of The Evelyn
Waugh Collection at The Humanities
Research Center, The University of
Texas at Austin.
  M. Stannard, 402(MLR):Jan85-136
Davis, S.D. and P.D. Beidler, eds. The
Mythologizing of Mark Twain.*
  G. Rotella, 587(SAF):Autumn85-254
Davis, T. Playing the Changes.
  C. Hernton, 472:Spring/Summer/Fall/
Winter85-518

Davis, W. The Serpent and the Rainbow.
  P-L. Adams, 61:Mar86-110
  J. Gleason, 617(TLS):4Jul86-725
  J. Haskins, 441:2Mar86-25
Davis, W.E. The Celebrated Case of Esther
Waters.
  E. Gilcher, 177(ELT):Vol28No3-318
  M. Levin, 174(Éire):Summer85-156
Davis-Friedmann, D. Long Lives.
  A. Sankar, 293(JASt):Feb85-365
Davison, P. "Hamlet."
  B.W. Kliman, 130:Winter85/86-383
Davison, P. Popular Appeal in English
Drama to 1850.
  J.L. Levenson, 570(SQ):Autumn85-380
Davison, P. Praying Wrong.*
  M. Hulse, 493:Feb86-50
  J.D. McClatchy, 249(HudR):Spring85-157
  R. Mitchell, 491:Jan86-227
  R. Saner, 152(UDQ):Summer85-107
  639(VQR):Summer85-98
Davison, P., ed. Sheridan: Comedies.
  T.O. Treadwell, 617(TLS):18Jul86-789
Davison, P. - see Orwell, G.
Dawber, D. Cankerville.
  F. Cogswell, 529(QQ):Winter85-845
Dawe, D. Organists of the City of London
1666-1850.
  W.J. Gatens, 410(M&L):Apr85-150
Dawe, R.D. - see Sophocles
Dawkins, L. Natives and Strangers.*
  442(NY):10Feb86-113
Dawkins, R. The Blind Watchmaker.
  S.R.L. Clark, 617(TLS):26Sep86-1047
  M.T. Ghiselin, 441:14Dec86-18
  H. Lawson, 362:9Oct86-27
Dawson, A.C. and L.M. Dicho y hecho.
(2nd ed)
  M.E. Beeson, 238:Dec85-798
Dawson, P. Virginia Dare.*
  I. Malin, 532(RCF):Fall85-194
Dawson, P.M.S. The Unacknowledged Legisla-
tor.*
  W. Keach, 533:Fall85-120
  H.N. Rohloff, 38:Band103Heft1/2-225
Day, D. The Animals Within.
  M.T. Lane, 198:Winter85-106
Day, D.B. Index to the Science-Fiction
Magazines, 1926-50.
  R.M.P., 561(SFS):Jul85-225
Day, R.C. When in Florence.
  R. Hansen, 441:19Jan86-20
Dayan, Y. My Father, His Daughter.*
  D. Casse, 129:Mar86-66
Daydí-Tolson, S. Voces y ecos en la
poesía de José Angel Valente.
  T.R. Franz, 238:Sep85-521
Dazai Osamu. Return to Tsugaru.* (J.
Westerhoven, trans)
  A.V. Heinrich, 407(MN):Winter85-438
d'Azevedo, W.L., ed. Straight with the
Medicine.
  T. Buckley, 469:Vol 11No1-92
Deacon, G. John Clare and the Folk Tradi-
tion.*
  J. Lucas, 637(VS):Spring85-538
  I. Russell, 203:Vol96No1-126
Deacon, R. The Cambridge Apostles.
  M. Le Fanu, 362:20Feb86-27
Deal, S.S. The Dark is a Door.
  H.W. Stauffer, 649(WAL):Feb86-355
Dean, E., ed. Africa beyond Africa.
  D. Dabydeen, 538(RAL):Fall85-437

93

Dean, M.R. Les Jardins secrets.
T. Dey, 450(NRF):Jun85-94
Dean, S.F.X. Death and the Mad Heroine.
T.J. Binyon, 617(TLS):8Aug86-863
Dean, W. Bizet. (3rd ed)
A.F.L.T., 412:Aug/Nov84-304
Dean, W. - see Dent, E.J.
Deane, S. Celtic Revivals.*
R. Imhof, 272(IUR):Autumn85-250
Dearing, A.P. The Elegant Inn.
A. Heckscher, 441:29Jun86-41
Dearlove, J.E. Accommodating the Chaos.
J. Pilling, 447(N&Q):Jun84-280
Deathridge, J. and C. Dahlhaus. The New
Grove Wagner.*
R. Anderson, 415:Feb85-93
A. Whittall, 410(M&L):Apr85-170
Deb Roy, H.L. A Tribe in Transition.
C. Lindholm, 293(JASt):May85-634
Debicki, A.P. Poetry of Discovery.*
D. Harris, 86(BHS):Apr85-211
J.C. Wilcox, 240(HR):Spring85-257
De Blois, A.D. and A. Metallic. Micmac
Lexicon.
J. Hewson, 320(CJL):Fall85-363
P. Proulx, 269(IJAL):Apr85-243
Debord, P. Aspects sociaux et économiques
de la vie religieuse dans l'Anatolie
gréco-romaine.
S.R.F. Price, 313:Vol75-264
Debreczeny P., ed. American Contribu-
tions to the Ninth International Con-
gress of Slavists (Kiev, September
1983).* (Vol 2)
R. Reid, 402(MLR):Oct85-1005
Debreczeny, P. The Other Pushkin.*
J-L.B., 549(RLC):Oct-Dec85-471
A.D.P. Briggs, 402(MLR):Apr85-509
Debreczeny, P. - see Pushkin, A.S.
Debrie, R. Glossaire du moyen picard.
G. Roques, 553(RLiR):Jul-Dec85-501
De Carlo, A. Vögel in Käfigen und Voli-
eren. Creamtrain.
M. Rutschky, 384:Nov85-1020
Décaudin, M., ed. Anthologie de la poésie
française du XXe siècle.
G.D. Martin, 402(MLR):Apr85-469
Décaudin, M. - see Apollinaire, G.
Décaudin, M. - see Verlaine, P.
Dechert, H.W., M. Brüggemeier and D. Füt-
terer, comps. Transfer and Interference
in Language.
M. Heller, 350:Sep86-730
Decker, J. and R. Crease - see Taminiaux,
J.
Decleva Caizzi, F. Pirrone: "Testimoni-
anze."*
J.D.G. Evans, 303(JoHS):Vol 105-190
W. Görler, 53(AGP):Band67Heft3-320
De Coster, C. - see de Alarcón, P.A.
Décote, G. - see Cazotte, J.
De Deckker, P. - see Pritchard, G.
Dedner, B. Carl Sternheim.
R.W. Williams, 402(MLR):Jan85-229
Deeken, A. "Seine Majestät das Ich."
C.F. Lorenz, 602:Band16Heft2-304
Deely, J.N., with R.A. Powell - see Poin-
sot, J.
Deen, L.W. Conversing in Paradise.*
M.L. Johnson, 88:Winter85/86-107
A. Lincoln, 541(RES):Nov85-576
V. Myers, 301(JEGP):Jan85-141

Dees, A., ed. Actes du IVe Colloque inter-
national sur le Moyen Français.
G. Roques, 553(RLiR):Jul-Dec85-425
Dees, A. Atlas des formes et de construc-
tions des chartes françaises du 13e
siècle.*
N.L. Corbett, 545(RPh):May85-506
L. Wolf, 685(ZDL):2/1985-272
Dees, J.S. Sir Thomas Elyot and Roger
Ascham.
J. McConica, 402(MLR):Oct85-900
Deese, J. American Freedom and the Social
Sciences.
639(VQR):Autumn85-132
Deese, J. Thought into Speech.*
A. Cutler, 307:May85-72
N.J. Spencer, 35(AS):Summer85-166
Defaux, G. Le curieux, le glorieux et la
sagesse du monde dans la première moitié
du XVIe siècle.*
C. Clark, 208(FS):Jul85-325
Defaux, G., ed. Montaigne.*
F. Gray, 535(RHL):Jan/Feb85-76
S. Rendall, 153:Summer85-44
"The Defence Implications of the Future of
Westland plc."
J. Turner, 617(TLS):22Aug86-904
Deford, F. The Spy in the Deuce Court.
N. Callendar, 441:17Aug86-20
Deforges, R. La Bicyclette bleue (3).
D.B. Brautman, 207(FR):Mar86-643
De Francis, J. The Chinese Language.
M.Y. Chen, 350:Sep86-690
Degenhart, B. and A. Schmitt. Jacopo Bel-
lini.*
F. Ames-Lewis, 90:Apr85-235
Deguise, A. Trois femmes.*
G. Van de Louw, 549(RLC):Jan-Mar85-104
Deguy, M. Gisants.*
D. Leuwers, 450(NRF):Sep85-75
Deguy, M. Given Giving.
S. Romer, 617(TLS):26Sep86-1050
De Hart, S. The Meininger Theater: 1776-
1926.
M. Carlson, 612(ThS):May85-89
Deichmann, F.W., with J. Kramer and U.
Peschlow. Corpus der Kapitelle der
Kirche von San Marco zu Venedig.
D.M. Ebitz, 589:Jan85-144
Deighton, L. London Match.*
T.J. Binyon, 617(TLS):30May86-588
M. Laski, 362:9Jan86-30
442(NY):27Jan86-100
Deist, W., ed. The German Military in the
Age of Total War.
G. Best, 617(TLS):10Jan86-32
De Jean, J. Libertine Strategies.*
J. Campbell, 208(FS):Apr85-200
De Jean, J. Literary Fortifications.
G. May, 546(RR):Nov85-449
P.H. Meyer, 207(FR):Mar86-617
De Kervasdoue, J., J.R. Kimberly and V.G.
Rodwin. The End of an Illusion.
S.K., 185:Jul86-919
Dekeyser, X. and others. Foundations of
English Grammar.
H. Ulherr, 38:Band103Heft1/2-112
Dekker, G., ed. Donald Davie and the
Responsibilities of Literature.
S. Black, 175:Spring85-80
D.E. Richardson, 569(SR):Fall85-634
De Koven, M. A Different Language.*
C.N. Pondrom, 659(ConL):Spring86-98

De Krey, G.S. A Fractured Society.
  V. Pearl, 617(TLS):14Feb86-169
Deladrière, R. - see Kalâbâdhî
Delahunty, R.J. Spinoza.
  S. Brown, 617(TLS):31Jan86-119
  D.E.G., 185:Jul86-910
De Lamarter, R.T. Big Blue.
  S. Kinsley, 441:23Nov86-13
Delano, S.F. "The Harbinger" and New
  England Transcendentalism.*
  D.F. Warders, 534(RALS):Spring83-58
De-la-Noy, M. Elgar.*
  I.P., 412:Feb84-62
De-la-Noy, M. - see Welch, D.
Delany, S.R. Stars In My Pocket Like
  Grains of Sand.*
  S. Scobie, 376:Mar85-159
Delatte, L. and others. Aristoteles,
  "Metaphysica," Index verborum, Listes
  de fréquence.
  J.L. Ackrill, 123:Vol35No2-386
Delaty, S. - see de Heredia, J-M.
De Laurentiis, A. Marx' und Engels' Rezep-
  tion der Hegelschen Kantkritik.
  G-W. Küsters, 342:Band76Heft3-353
Delbanco, N. The Beaux Arts Trio.*
  R. Anderson, 415:Nov85-673
  S. Baron, 385(MQR):Summer86-600
Delbanco, N. - see Gardner, J.
Delblanc, S. Waldstein. Speranza. Kas-
  traten. Samuels Buch.
  G. Sammet, 384:Mar85-243
Delbouille, P. Poésie et sonorités II.
  R. Arveiller, 209(FM):Oct85-247
  J.P. Houston, 207(FR):May86-968
Deledalle, G. La Philosophie américaine.
  P.L. Bourgeois, 619:Spring85-286
  P. Engel, 542:Jan-Mar85-82
Deledda, G. After the Divorce.*
  D.J. Enright, 364:Mar86-104
Delesalle, J. and T. Van Toan. Quand
  l'amour éclipse Dieu.
  M. Adam, 542:Oct-Dec85-573
Deleuze, G. Cinéma I.
  A. Thiher, 207(FR):Dec85-308
Deleuze, G. Kant's Critical Philosophy.
  S.E., 185:Apr86-686
Deleuze, G. and F. Guattari. Mille pla-
  teaux.
  A. Villani, 98:Apr85-331
Delevoy, R.L. Symbolists and Symbolism.
  R. Nasgaard, 127:Summer85-155
Delgado Martins, M.R. Aspects de l'accent
  en portugais.
  J. Klare, 682(ZPSK):Band38Heft2-193
Delhez-Sarlet, C. and M. Catani, eds.
  Individualisme et autobiographie en
  Occident.
  J. Gaulmier, 549(RLC):Jul-Sep85-323
  M. Schmeling, 547(RF):Band97Heft2/3-
  285
De Liguori, S.A.M. Brevi avvertimenti di
  grammatica e aritmetica. (R. Librandi,
  ed)
  L. Serianni, 708:Vol 11fasc2-292
De Lillo, D. White Noise.*
  D. Flower, 249(HudR):Summer85-308
  R. Kaveney, 617(TLS):17Jan86-56
  42(AR):Fall85-503
De Lio, T. Circumscribing the Open Uni-
  verse.*
  P. Dickinson, 415:Jun85-349

Delius, H. Self-Awareness.*
  B. Smith, 484(PPR):Sep85-170
Dell, G. The Earth Abideth.
  K. Ray, 441:21Dec86-14
Della Neva, J.A. Song and Counter-Song.*
  D. Fenoaltea, 210(FrF):Jan85-110
  I.D. McFarlane, 208(FS):Jan85-66
  N. Mann, 402(MLR):Apr85-457
Dellheim, C. The Face of the Past.*
  M.S. Gaskell, 366:Spring85-148
Del Litto, V. - see Stendhal
Del Litto, V. and K. Ringer, with others,
  eds. Stendhal et le romantisme.*
  L. Le Guillou, 535(RHL):Sep/Oct85-881
Delman, D. Death of a Nymph.
  T.J. Binyon, 617(TLS):28Nov86-1357
Del Mar, N. Anatomy of the Orchestra.
  D. Charlton, 410(M&L):Jul85-269
  A.F.L.T., 412:Aug/Nov84-304
Deloche, J. La circulation en Inde, avant
  la révolution des transports.
  L. Rocher, 318(JAOS):Jul-Sep84-598
Deloffre, F. and M. Menemencioglu - see
  Challe, R.
De Long, L.R. Nature's Forms/Nature's
  Forces.
  L. Milazzo, 584(SWR):Spring85-262
Deloria, V., Jr., ed. American Indian
  Policy in the Twentieth Century.
  L. Milazzo, 584(SWR):Autumn85-547
Deloria, V., Jr., ed. A Sender of Words.
  P. Wild, 649(WAL):May85-79
Delphy, F. Emily Dickinson.
  D. Porter, 189(EA):Oct-Dec86-480
Del Río, C.M. Jorge Luis Borges y la
  ficción.
  T. Lyon, 238:Sep85-527
Deluc, Y. and H. Rück. Prisunic.
  P.A. Berger, 399(MLJ):Spring85-87
De Maddalena, A. and H. Kellenbenz, eds.
  Finanze e ragion di Stato in Italia e in
  Germania nella prima Età moderna.
  M.M. Bullard, 551(RenQ):Winter85-714
De Mallie, R.J. - see Black Elk
Demandt, A. Die Auflösung des römischen
  Reiches im Urteil der Nachwelt: Der Fall
  Roms.
  P.R. Ghosh, 313:Vol75-256
  P. Gottfried, 121(CJ):Feb/Mar86-261
  A. Heuss, 384:Jan85-65
De Marinis, R. Under the Wheat. The Burn-
  ing Women of Far Cry.
  J. Shaw, 441:14Dec86-26
Dembkowski, H.E. The Union of Lublin.*
  P.B. Brown, 497(PolR):Vol30No4-437
Dembowski, P.F. Jean Froissart and His
  "Meliador."
  G.T. Diller, 589:Apr85-392
  A.H. Diverres, 402(MLR):Jan85-159
  N. Wilkins, 208(FS):Apr85-185
  M.E. Winters, 207(FR):Mar86-604
Demerson, G. Dorat e son temps.
  L.V.R., 568(SCN):Fall85-53
Demerson, G., ed. La Notion de genre à la
  Renaissance.
  F. Rigolot, 551(RenQ):Summer85-343
Demetriades, V. Topographia tēs Thessalon-
  ikēs kata tēn epochē tēs Tourkokratias
  1430-1912.
  G.P. Henderson, 303(JoHS):Vol 105-251
Demetz, P. After the Fires.
  J. Ryan, 441:28Dec86-23

Demiri-Prodromidou, E., D. Nicolaidou-Nestora and N. Tryphona-Antonopoulou. Ē Glōssa tōn Idiōtismōn kai tōn Ekphraseōn.
J.E. Rexine, 399(MLJ):Spring85-97
Demorest, J.J. and L. Leibacher-Ouvrard, eds. Pascal; Corneille; désert, retraite, engagement.
J.L. Pallister, 568(SCN):Spring-Summer85-19
Demosthenes. Scholia Demosthenica. (Vol 1) (M.R. Dilts, ed)
D.M. MacDowell, 303(JoHS):Vol 105-188
De Mott, R.J. Steinbeck's Reading.*
T. Ludington, 534(RALS):Spring83-105
De Mouy, J.K. Katherine Anne Porter's Women.*
E. Mills, 392:Spring85-139
Dempsey, H.A., ed. The CPR West.
J.R. Miller, 298:Fall185-156
Dempster, B. Real Places and Imaginary Men.
A.S. Brennan, 198:Winter85-114
M. Darling, 102(CanL):Summer85-149
M. Dyment, 526:Spring85-97
Demski, E. Dead Alive.
G. Marcus, 441:2Nov86-31
Demus, O., with R.M. Kloos and K. Weitzmann. The Mosaics of San Marco in Venice.*
E. Kitzinger, 90:Jan85-40
W. Sauerländer, 453(NYRB):26Jun86-30
Denapoli, A.J. and S.L. Levy. Diálogos Simpáticos.
E.D. Keyser, 399(MLJ):Autumn85-322
Denby, E. The Complete Poems. (R. Padgett, ed)
G. Dickerson, 441:2Nov86-28
Dendinger, L.N., ed. E.E. Cummings: The Critical Reception.
N. Friedman, 534(RALS):Spring83-10
Dendle, B.J. and J. Schraibman - see Pérez Galdós, B.
Denecke, L., ed. Brüder Grimm Gedenken. (Vol 4)
C.L. Gottzmann, 684(ZDA):Band114Heft4-151
Deneckere, M. Benedetto Croce et la linguistique.
R.A. Hall, Jr., 350:Mar86-207
De Neef, A.L. Spenser and the Motives of Metaphor.*
J. van Dorsten, 179(ES):Oct85-467
L. Geller, 301(JEGP):Jul85-421
De Negri, E. Tra filosofia e letteratura.
A. Franceschetti, 276:Winter85-313
Denham, B. Two Thyrdes.
N. Callendar, 441:23Mar86-16
Denholtz, E. Playing for High Stakes.
A.R. Hochschild, 441:11May86-15
Denis, H. Logique hégélienne et systèmes économiques.
O. Clain, 154:Winter85-735
Denis, J-J. Le Trésor.
P.A. Berger, 399(MLJ):Spring85-87
Denisoff, R.S. Waylon.*
M.R. Winchell, 585(SoQ):Spring86-91
Denk, R. "Musica getutscht."
T. Binkley, 589:Apr85-394
Denker, H. Judge Spencer Dissents.
N. Ramsey, 441:6Apr86-22

Denkler, H., ed. Romane und Erzählungen des Bürgerlichen Realismus.
N.A. Kaiser, 406:Spring85-108
Dennerline, J. The Chia-ting Loyalists.
R.V. Des Forges, 318(JAOS):Jul-Sep84-564
A.Y-C. Lui, 302:Vol21No1-56
Dennett, D.C. Elbow Room.*
G. Dworkin, 185:Jan86-423
J.L. McGregor, 529(QQ):Winter85-865
Denning, C. Adventures with Julia.
R. Cohen, 441:14Dec86-24
Dennis, C. The Near World.*
V. Shetley, 491:Feb86-294
639(VQR):Autumn85-129
Dennis, R. English Industrial Cities of the Nineteenth Century.
R. Lawton, 637(VS):Spring86-491
Dennison, G. Luisa Domic.*
A. Bloom, 434:Summer86-513
Dennison, P. Pelham Humfrey.
C. Price, 617(TLS):26Dec86-1444
Dennison, S. [Alternative] Literary Publishing.
J.R. Millichap, 395(MFS):Winter85-864
295(JML):Nov85-372
Dennison, S. Scandalize My Name.
B. Harrah-Conforth, 187:Winter86-187
De Nonno, M., ed. La grammatica dell' "Anonymus Bobiensis" (G.L., I, 533-565 Kiel).*
P. Flobert, 555:Vol59fasc1-143
Dent, E.J. The Rise of Romantic Opera. (W. Dean, ed)
A.F.L.T., 412:Aug/Nov84-304
Dent, P. From the Flow.
R. Pybus, 565:Summer85-62
Dent, R.W. Shakespeare's Proverbial Language.
G.K. Hunter, 402(MLR):Jan85-118
Dentan, M. Le Texte et son lecteur.*
P. Carrard, 210(FrF):May85-245
Dentinger, J. First Hit of the Season.
T.J. Binyon, 617(TLS):13Jun86-646
Denton, M. Evolution.*
P. Zaleski, 469:Vol 11No3-112
442(NY):15Sep86-121
Den Uyl, D.J. and D.B. Rasmussen, eds. The Philosophic Thought of Ayn Rand.*
L. Lewis, 395(MFS):Summer85-413
Denvir, B. The Early Nineteenth Century.
D. Jeremiah, 324:Dec85-71
Déon, M. Bagages pour Vancouver.
A. Bosquet, 450(NRF):Nov85-94
J. Ducruet, 605(SC):15Apr86-270
D'Epiro, P. A Touch of Rhetoric.
J. Brogunier, 468:Fall84-303
Depland, D. La Sirène de Redcliff.
L.K. Penrod, 207(FR):Feb86-486
De Prospo, R.C. Theism in the Discourse of Jonathan Edwards.
D.B. Shea, 165(EAL):Winter86/87-268
Derfler, L. President and Parliament.
S.P. Kramer, 579(SAQ):Spring85-227
Derolez, A. Lambertus qui librum fecit.
P. Meyvaert, 589:Jul85-740
De Rosa, P.L. and S.W. McGuire. A Concordance to the Works of Jane Austen.*
G.E. Bentley, Jr., 627(UTQ):Fall84-119
B. Roth, 594:Summer85-224
Derouet, C. and J. Boissel. Kandinsky.
P. Vergo, 59:Dec85-496

De Vries, J.E.   Race and Kinship in a Mid-
western Town.
  H.A. Reed, 115:Spring85-268
De Vries, P.   Peckham's Marbles.
  P-L. Adams, 61:Nov86-139
  E. Stumpf, 441:2Nov86-26
  442(NY):8Dec86-153
De Vries, P.   The Prick of Noon.*
  G. Ewart, 617(TLS):24Jan86-82
  R. Jones, 362:8May86-26
Dew, R.F.   The Time of Her Life.
  W.H. Pritchard, 249(HudR):Spring85-122
Dewar, A.   Geometry.
  J. Mole, 176:Jan86-61
Dewar, J. and others, eds.   Nuclear Weap-
ons, the Peace Movement and the Law.
  D. Pannick, 617(TLS):28Nov86-1337
Dewey, J.   The Collected Works of John
Dewey. (Vols 2 and 3)
  R.D. Boisvert, 619:Spring85-292
Dewey, J.   Types of Thinking.*
  R.J. Roth, 258:Sep85-333
Dewhurst, C.K., B. MacDowell and M. Mac-
Dowell.   Religious Folk Art in America.
  T.D. Carroll, 292(JAF):Apr/Jun85-232
  R.T. Teske, 650(WF):Apr85-141
De Woskin, K.J.   A Song for One or Two.*
  M.J. Pearson, 293(JASt):May85-585
  B.M. Wilson, 485(PE&W):Apr85-219
Dews, P. - see Habermas, J.
Dexter, P.   Deadwood.
  P-L. Adams, 61:May86-100
  R. Hansen, 441:20Apr86-9
Dezalay, A.   L'Opéra des Rougon-Macquart.
  D. Baguley, 535(RHL):May/Jun85-511
Dezon-Jones, E.   Proust et l'Amérique.*
  R. Bales, 208(FS):Jul85-362
  J-Y. Tadié, 535(RHL):Jan/Feb85-128
d'Haussy, C.   La Vision du monde chez G.K.
Chesterton.
  B. Reynolds, 677(YES):Vol 15-334
Dhavamony, M.   Classical Hinduism.
  F. Podgorski, 485(PE&W):Jan85-105
  L. Rocher, 318(JAOS):Apr-Jun84-335
Dhôtel, A.   Histoire d'un fonctionnaire.
  T. Dey, 450(NRF):Mar85-88
Diamond, E. and S. Bates.   The Spot.
  J. Beerman, 42(AR):Summer85-366
Diamonstein, B.   American Architecture Now
II.
  A. Barnet, 441:9Feb86-25
Diamonstein, B.   Remaking America.
  J.V. Iovine, 441:7Dec86-69
Dias, E.M. - see under Mayone Dias, E.
Díaz, J.S. - see under Simón Díaz, J.
Dibba, E.   Chaff on the Wind.
  R. Brain, 617(TLS):5Sep86-977
Di Benedetto, V.   Sofocle.
  J.C. Kamerbeek, 394:Vol38fasc3/4-409
Dibon, P. and F. Waquet.   Johannes Fred-
ericus Gronovius, Pèlerin de la Répub-
lique des Lettres.
  P. Wolfe, 475:Vol 12No23-694
Dick, M.   Der junge Heinse in seiner Zeit.
  M.L. Baeumer, 406:Spring85-101
Dick, P.K.   I Hope I Shall Arrive Soon.
  C. Greenland, 617(TLS):7Feb86-150
Dick, P.K.   In Milton Lumky Territory.
  J. Clute, 617(TLS):17Jan86-56
Dick, P.K.   Radio Free Albemuth.
  G. Jonas, 441:12Jan86-22
Dick, S. - see Woolf, V.

Dickason, O.P.   The Myth of the Savage and
the Beginnings of French Colonialism in
the Americas.
  D.B. Smith, 656(WMQ):Jul85-403
Dickel, G. and H. Speer, comps.   Deutsches
Rechtswörterbuch. (Vol 7)
  R. Schmidt-Wiegand, 680(ZDP):
  Band104Heft3-465
Dickens, A.G. and J.M. Tonkin.   The Refor-
mation in Historical Thought.
  J. Bossy, 617(TLS):1Aug86-847
Dickens, C.   American Notes. Pictures
from Italy.
  D. Walder, 617(TLS):31Jan86-125
Dickens, C.   The Cricket on the Heath.
  D. Paroissien, 158:Dec85-144
Dickens, C.   A December Vision. (N.
Philip and V. Neuberg, eds)
  D. Walder, 362:18/25Dec86-52
Dickens, C.   Dining with Dickens.
  D. and E. Parker, 155:Spring85-57
Dickens, C.   The Letters of Charles Dick-
ens.* (Vol 5) (G. Storey and K.J.
Fielding, eds)
  D. Mehl, 38:Band103Heft3/4-508
Dickens, C.   Martin Chuzzlewit.* (M. Card-
well, ed)
  D. Mehl, 38:Band103Heft3/4-508
  S. Shatto, 158:Mar85-22
Dickens, C.   Selected Letters of Charles
Dickens. (D. Paroissien, ed)
  S. Monod, 189(EA):Oct-Dec86-465
Dickens, C.   Un Albero di Natale. (V.
Poggi-Chigi, trans)
  R. Glancy, 107(CRCL):Sep85-548
Dickens, C. and M. Haz.   Un Albero di
Natale.
  D. Paroissien, 158:Dec85-144
"Dickens Studies Annual." (Vol 9) (M.
Timko, F. Kaplan and E. Guiliano, eds)
  S.M. Smith, 677(YES):Vol 15-317
"Dickens Studies Annual."* (Vols 10-12)
(M. Timko, F. Kaplan and E. Guiliano,
eds)
  H.S. Nelson, 637(VS):Autumn85-164
Dickey, C.   With the Contras.
  A. Brumberg, 441:26Jan86-3
  D. Hughes, 362:9Oct86-25
  P. Kemble, 129:May86-64
  A. Neier, 453(NYRB):10Apr86-3
  442(NY):17Feb86-103
Dickey, J.   The Central Motion.
  P. Christensen, 472:Spring/Summer86-
  202
  J. Parini, 617(TLS):24Jan86-95
Dickey, W.   Brief Lives.
  R.I. Scott, 648(WCR):Oct85-66
Dickie, G.   The Art Circle.
  J. Wieand, 290(JAAC):Fall85-80
Dickie, M.   On the Modernist Long Poem.
  A.W. Litz, 617(TLS):10Oct86-1142
Dickinson, A. and M.L. Todd.   Austin and
Mabel.* (P. Longsworth, ed)
  M.E.K. Bernhard, 432(NEQ):Mar85-131
Dickinson, C.   Crows.*
  G.C., 569(SR):Spring85-xxxix
Dickinson, M. and S. Street.   Cinema and
State.
  J. Terry, 707:Summer85-224
Dickinson, P.   Tefuga.
  D. Johnson, 441:20Apr86-1
  J. Melmoth, 617(TLS):16May86-536
  442(NY):12May86-127

"Dictionary of American Regional English."*
(Vol 1) (F.G. Cassidy, chief ed)
H. Kenner, 617(TLS):9May86-490
J.G. Pival, 70:May/Jun86-157
"Dictionary of Canadian Biography/Diction-
naire Biographique du Canada." (Vol 5)
(F.G. Halpenny, ed)
529(QQ):Summer85-436
"The Dictionary of National Biography 1971-
1980." (Lord Blake and C.S. Nicholls,
eds)
A. Bell, 362:27Nov86-26
R. Davenport-Hines, 617(TLS):14Nov86-
1263
"Dictionnaire du français langue étrangère,
Niveau 1." "Dictionnaire du français
langue étrangère, Niveau 2."
D.E. Corbin, 399(MLJ):Summer85-176
Diderot, D. Jack the Fatalist and His
Master. (W.D. Camp, trans)
S. Diaconoff, 399(MLJ):Summer85-173
Diderot, D. Lettres à Sophie Volland.
(J. Varloot, ed)
S. Baudiffier, 535(RHL):Sep/Oct85-877
P. France, 208(FS):Jan85-79
Diderot, D. Salons. (2nd ed) (Vol 3) (J.
Seznec, ed)
C. Sherman, 207(FR):Feb86-466
Didi-Huberman, G. L'invention de l'hys-
térie.
J-M. Gros, 98:Aug-Sep85-889
Didi-Huberman, G. La Peinture incarnée.
T. Cordellier, 450(NRF):Jun85-80
Diefendorf, B.B. Paris City Councillors
in the Sixteenth Century.*
R. Mettam, 161(DUJ):Dec84-102
de Diéguez, M. Jésus.
M. Adam, 542:Oct-Dec85-564
de Diéguez, M. L'idole monothéiste.
J-L. Cherlonneix, 192(EP):Oct-Dec85-
554
Diehl, G. Nicolas Tarkhoff.
N. Powell, 39:Jul85-78
Dierks, K. Handlungsstrukturen im Werk
von Charles Dickens.
K. Tetzeli von Rosador, 72:Band222
Heft2-415
Dierks, M. Autor — Text — Leser.*
D. Sevin, 133:Band17Heft3/4-380
Diersch, M. and H. Orłowski. Annäherung
und Distanz.
D. Ignasiak, 654(WB):2/1985-344
Dieseldorff, H.Q. X Balam Q'ué, el pájaro
sol.
M. Schevill, 37:Nov-Dec85-59
Dieter, W. The Cactus Garden.
442(NY):14Jul86-83
Dietze, J. Frequenzwörterbuch zur Synod-
alhandschrift der Ersten Novgoroder
Chronik. Frequenzwörterbuch zur jün-
geren Redaktion der Ersten Novgoroder
Chronik. Frequenzwörterbuch zur
Vierten Novgoroder Chronik.
G. Neweklowsky, 559:Vol9No1-112
Dietzsch, S. - see Schelling, F.W.J.
Díez, G.M. and F. Rodríguez - see under
Martínez Díez, G. and F. Rodríguez
Digby, A. Madness, Morality and Medicine.
M. Neve, 617(TLS):28Mar86-335
Digges, D. Vesper Sparrows.
J. Graham, 441:28Sep86-32
Diggle, J. - see Euripides

Diggory, T. Yeats and American Poetry.*
M. O'Neill, 161(DUJ):Dec84-129
J. Ronsley, 529(QQ):Spring85-173
Di Giovanni, C.M., ed. Italian Canadian
Voices.
V. Comensoli, 102(CanL):Fall85-84
Di Girolamo, C. A Critical Theory of Lit-
erature.
G. Costa, 545(RPh):Aug84-96
A. Wordsworth, 541(RES):Aug85-458
Di Girolamo, C., ed. Libru di lu transitu
et vita di misser sanctu Iheronimu.
A.G. Mocciaro, 545(RPh):Aug85-133
Dihle, A. Der Prolog der "Bacchen" und
die antike Überlieferungsphase des
Euripides-Textes.
J. Wilkins, 123:Vol35No1-10
Dihle, A. The Theory of Will in Classical
Antiquity.*
A.W.H. Adkins, 122:Oct85-364
Dihoff, I.R., ed. Current Approaches to
African Linguistics. (Vol 1)
D.K. Nylander, 320(CJL):Fall85-377
van Dijk, T.A. and W. Kintsch. Strategies
of Discourse Comprehension.
D. Biber, 350:Sep86-664
J.J. Staczek, 399(MLJ):Summer85-171
Diker, G. Perceptual Knowledge.
F. Recanati, 192(EP):Oct-Dec85-550
Dilks, D. Neville Chamberlain.* (Vol 1)
P.V. O'Dea, 637(VS):Summer86-641
Dillard, A. Encounters with Chinese
Writers.
J. Eis, 219(GaR):Winter85-906
Dillard, A. Living by Fiction.
B. McHale, 107(CRCL):Mar85-138
Dillard, A. Teaching a Stone to Talk.*
R.T. Smith, 577(SHR):Winter85-94
Dillenberger, J. The Visual Arts and
Christianity in America: The Colonial
Period Through the Nineteenth Century.
J.H. Gill, 290(JAAC):Winter85-202
Diller, A-M. La pragmatique des questions
et des réponses.
R. Declerck, 361:Dec85-334
R. Martin, 553(RLiR):Jul-Dec85-449
Diller, G.T. Attitudes chevaleresques et
réalités politiques chez Froissart.
N.J. Lacy, 207(FR):Feb86-456
Dillman, K.J. The Subject in Rimbaud.
J.P. Houston, 446(NCFS):Spring-
Summer86-369
Dillon, G.L. Constructing Texts.
B.E. Brown, 126(CCC):Feb85-108
Dillon, J. Shakespeare and the Solitary
Man.*
A. Brissenden, 447(N&Q):Mar84-118
Dillon, M. - see Bowles, J.
Dillow, H.C. Orts and Scantlings.
J.V. Hicks, 647:Winter85-109
M. Turner, 102(CanL):Spring85-151
Dilman, I. Freud and Human Nature.
G.D. Marino, 185:Oct85-198
M. Midgley, 483:Oct85-544
Dilman, I. Freud and the Mind.
J-M. Gabaude, 542:Jan-Mar85-61
G.D. Marino, 185:Oct85-198
M. Midgley, 483:Oct85-544
R.M. Restak, 567:Vol55No3/4-303
Dilman, I. Quine on Ontology, Necessity
and Experience.
D. Bolton, 483:Jan85-142

Dilthey, W. Selected Works. (Vol 5) (R.A. Makkreel and F. Rodi, eds and trans)
G. Steiner, 617(TLS):3Oct86-1104
Dilts, M.R. - see Demosthenes
Dilworth, C. Scientific Progress.
D. Shrader, 84:Jun85-221
Dilworth, T. - see Jones, D.
Diman, R.C. and L.W. Winget - see Alfonso X
Di Marco, V. "Piers Plowman."
M-J. Arn, 179(ES):Feb85-78
Dimen, M. Surviving Sexual Contradictions.
P. McBroom, 441:2Nov86-41
Dimitroff, P. Boris III of Bulgaria.
S. Runciman, 617(TLS):12Sep86-999
Dimler, G.R. - see Spee, F.
Dimmendaal, G.J. The Turkana Language.
C.A. Creider, 361:Mar85-270
Dinan, J.A. The Pulp Western.
M.T. Marsden, 649(WAL):May85-67
Diner, S. and others, eds. The Wave-Particle Dualism.
S.P. Gudder, 486:Mar85-169
Dinesen, I. On Modern Marriage.
S. Gubar, 441:21Dec86-8
442(NY):22Dec86-92
Dinesen, I. Out of Africa [and] Shadows on the Grass.
R. Baker, 469:Vol 11No2-86
"Isak Dinesen's Africa."*
R. Baker, 469:Vol 11No2-86
Dinesen, R. and H. Müssener - see Sachs, N.
Dingley, J. The Peripheral Plural Endings of Nouns in Petrine Sermons.
G. Hüttl-Folter, 279:Vol29-166
Ding Ling. Miss Sophie's Diary and Other Stories.
P. Link, 441:6Jul86-16
Di Noto, A. Art Plastic.*
J.L. Meikle, 658:Winter85-320
Dintenfass, M. A Loving Place.
A. Hoffman, 441:23Feb86-9
Diogenes of Apollonia. Diogène d'Apollonie, la dernière cosmologie présocratique.* (A. Laks, ed and trans)
J-F. Duvernoy, 192(EP):Jul-Sep85-419
Dionigi, I. Lucio Anneo Seneca, "De otio (dial. VIII)."
H.M. Hine, 123:Vol35No2-393
Dionne, R., ed. Le Québécois et sa littérature.
P. Collet, 627(UTQ):Summer85-474
Diophantus. Diophante, "Les Arithmétiques." (Vols 3 and 4) (R. Rashed, ed)
I. Bulmer-Thomas, 123:Vol35No2-255
Dircks, R.J. Henry Fielding.
S. Varey, 566:Spring86-201
Dirven, R. and others. The Scene of Linguistic Action and Its Perspectivization by "Speak," "Talk," "Say" and "Tell."*
S. Thomas, 355(LSoc):Dec85-547
Dirven, R. and G. Radden, eds. Issues in the Theory of Universal Grammar.
P. Sgall, 361:Jan85-161
Di Salvo, J. War of Titans.*
J. Blondel, 189(EA):Jan-Mar86-97
R.F. Gleckner, 88:Spring86-146
Disch, T. Here I Am, There You Are, Where Were We.
M. O'Neill, 493:Jan85-61
J. Saunders, 565:Autumn85-73

"Discursos leídos ante la Real Academia de Bellas Artes de San Fernando en la recepción pública del Excelentísimo Señor Don Jesús Aguirre y Ortiz de Zárate, Duque de Alba, el día 5 de marzo."
J. Brown, 240(HR):Summer85-367
Diski, J. Nothing Natural.
L. Heron, 362:24Jul86-26
N. Shulman, 617(TLS):4Jul86-732
Dispaux, G. La logique et le quotidien.
M. Meyer, 540(RIPh):Vol39fasc1/2-188
Disterheft, D. The Syntactic Development of the Infinitive in Indo-European.
K.R. McCone, 112:Vol 16-179
Dittmaier, H. Die linksrheinischen Orts-namen auf -dorf und -heim.
R. Bauer, 685(ZDL):1/1985-120
Diwo, J. Les Dames du faubourg.
R.J. Golsan, 207(FR):Dec85-336
Dixon, G. Carissimi.
D. Stevens, 617(TLS):9May86-496
Dixon, R.M.W. and J. Godrich. Blues and Gospel Records, 1902-1943. (3rd ed)
J.T. Titon, 187:Fall86-557
Diz, M.A. Patronio y Lucanor.
P.N. Dunn, 304(JHP):Winter85-167
Djebar, A. L'Amour, la fantasia.
M. Le Clézio, 207(FR):Apr86-811
Djilas, M. Of Prisons and Ideas.
A. Boyer, 441:14Dec86-25
Djilas, M. Rise and Fall.*
639(VQR):Summer85-79
Djuretić, V. Saveznici i jugoslovenska ratna drama.
C. Cviić, 176:Apr86-56
Djwa, S. and R.S. MacDonald, eds. On F.R. Scott.*
T. Goldie, 102(CanL):Winter84-146
Dmytryshyn, B. and E.A.P. Crownhart-Vaughan - see Golovin, P.
Dobat, K-D. Musik als romantische Illusion.
H.M.K. Riley, 133:Band18Heft2-174
Döblin, A. A People Betrayed [and] The Troops Return.* Karl and Rosa.
S.S. Prawer, 617(TLS):26Dec86-1457
Dobroszycki, L., ed. The Chronicle of the Lodz Ghetto, 1941-1944.*
J. Rothenberg, 390:Oct85-52
D. Stone, 287:Jun-Jul85-30
639(VQR):Winter85-8
Dobson, C. and J. Miller. The Day They Almost Bombed Moscow.
R. Nalley, 441:12Oct86-29
H. Szamuely, 617(TLS):12Sep86-999
Dobson, C. and R. Payne. War Without End.
C. Townshend, 617(TLS):29Aug86-928
Dobson, C.R. Masters and Journeymen.
M. Rediker, 656(WMQ):Apr85-267
Dobson, R. The Three Fates and Other Poems.
P. Carter, 381:Mar85-48
J. Tulip, 581:Mar85-45
Dobyns, S. Black Dog, Red Dog.*
J. Elledge, 491:Aug85-297
M. Karr, 29(APR):Mar/Apr86-20
455:Mar85-64
639(VQR):Winter85-26
Dobyns, S. Cold Dog Soup.*
442(NY):10Feb86-113
Dobyns, S. Saratoga Headhunter.*
T.J. Binyon, 617(TLS):27Jun86-711

Donnell, D. Settlements.*
   J. Orange, 102(CanL):Winter84-103
Donnell-Kotzrozo, C. Critical Essays on
Post-Impressionism.*
   90:Aug85-546
Donnelly, J. The Concept of Human Rights.
T.M.R., 185:Jul86-888
Donnelly, S. Eve Names the Animals.
   M. Jarman, 249(HudR):Summer85-333
Donoghue, D. We Irish.
   R. Boyers, 441:21Sep86-13
   442(NY):27Oct86-146
Donoghue, D. - see Blackmur, R.P.
Donohue, A.M. Hawthorne.
   J.L. Idol, Jr., 573(SSF):Fall85-488
Donoso, A. Julián Marías.
   J. Labanyi, 86(BHS):Oct85-410
Donovan, P.J., ed. Cywyddau Serch y Tri
Bedo.
   J. Rowland, 112:Vol 16-202
Donyo, V. - see Twain, M.
Doody, M.A. The Daring Muse.
   H. Erskine-Hill, 617(TLS):14Mar86-280
   P. Lewis, 364:Oct85-110
   H. Love, 566:Spring86-187
Dooley, J. and J. Tanis, eds. Bookbinding
in America, 1680-1910, from the Collec-
tion of Frederik E. Maser.
   P. Morgan, 40(AEB):Vol8No2-126
Dooley, T. The Interrupted Dream.
   P. Gross, 493:Oct85-67
   J. Mole, 176:Jan86-61
   C. Rawson, 617(TLS):7Feb86-137
Dooling, D.M., ed. A Way of Working.
   J. Bruchac, 469:Vol 11No2-114
Doolittle, J., ed. Eight Plays for Young
People.
   R. Skene, 108:Fall85-140
van Doorn, J. Javanese Society in
Regional Perspective.
   R.R. Jay, 293(JASt):Aug85-883
Döpp, S. Zeitgeschichte in Dichtungen
Claudians.
   J.B. Hall, 123:Vol35No2-291
Dor, J. Introduction à la lecture de
Lacan. (Vol 1)
   A. Reix, 542:Jul-Sep85-352
Dorat, C-J. Les Malheurs de l'inconstance.
   C. Bonfils, 535(RHL):May/Jun85-490
"Gustave Doré, 1832-1883."
   M.D., 90:Aug85-545
Dorfman, A. Widows.
   S. White, 448:Vol23No2-106
Dorian, N.C. The Tyranny of Tide.
   J.C. McClure, 571(ScLJ):Autumn85-1
Dormann, G. Amoureuse Colette.
   C. Slawy-Sutton, 207(FR):May86-984
Dormann, G. Colette.
   R.P. Sinkler, 441:29Jun86-25
   442(NY):21Jul86-95
Dorment, R. Alfred Gilbert.*
   R. Jefferies, 324:May86-414
Dormer, P. and D. Cripps. Alison Britton
in Studio. Elizabeth Fritsch in Studio.
   T.A. Lockett, 324:Jun86-470
Dormer, P. and R. Turner. The New Jew-
elry.*
   A. Mahler, 139:Dec85/Jan86-45
d'Ormesson, J. Le Vent du soir.
   A. Bosquet, 450(NRF):Oct85-92

Dorn, K. Players and Painted Stage.*
   B. Dolan, 305(JIL):May85-76
   M.K. Fielder, 615(TJ):Oct85-394
   N. Grene, 610:Summer85-185
   P. van de Kamp, 272(IUR):Spring85-108
Dorpalen, A. German History in Marxist
Perspective.
   G.A. Craig, 453(NYRB):25Sep86-62
Dorson, R.M. Man and Beast in American
Comic Legend.*
   B. af Klintberg, 64(Arv):Vol39-216
Dorter, K. Plato's "Phaedo."*
   J.L. Ackrill, 123:Vol35No1-65
Doskow, M. William Blake's "Jerusalem."*
   D. John, 541(RES):Aug85-434
Doss-Quinby, E. Les Refrains chez les
trouvères du XIIe siècle au début du
XIVe.
   D.A. Fein, 207(FR):May86-972
Dostoevsky, F. The Karamazov Brothers.
   (J. Katzer, trans)
   J.E.A. Woodbury, 399(MLJ):Autumn85-317
Dostoevsky, F. The Village of Stepanchi-
kovo and Its Inhabitants. (I. Avsey,
trans)
   A. McMillin, 575(SEER):Jan85-115
Dostojewskaya, A.G. Tagebücher. (B. Con-
rad, ed and trans)
   R. Görner, 176:May86-52
Dothan, M. Hammath Tiberias.
   E.M. Meyers, 318(JAOS):Jul-Sep84-577
Dothan, T. The Philistines and Their
Material Culture.
   R.R. Stieglitz, 318(JAOS):Jul-Sep84-
584
Dotsekno, P.S. The Struggle for a Democ-
racy in Siberia, 1917-1920.*
   C.F. Smith, 550(RusR):Jan85-108
Doubrovsky, S. La Vie l'instant.
   M. Naudin, 207(FR):Apr86-812
Doucet, C. John Coe's War.
   G. Drolet, 102(CanL):Fall85-148
Doucette, L.E. Theatre in French Canada:
Laying the Foundations 1606-1867.
   R. Plant, 529(QQ):Winter85-740
   D. Rubin, 99:May85-34
   A. Wagner, 102(CanL):Fall85-142
Dougherty, C. Ideal, Fact, and Medicine.
   R.B.M., 185:Jul86-917
Dougherty, D.M. and E.B. Barnes, eds. Le
"Galien" de Cheltenham.
   P.F. Dembowski, 545(RPh):May85-537
   W.G. van Emden, 208(FS):Apr85-181
Doughtie, E., ed. Liber Lilliati.
   K. Duncan-Jones, 617(TLS):28Feb86-228
Douglas, A. Last Rights.
   T.J. Binyon, 617(TLS):27Jun86-711
Douglas, C. - see Khlebnikov, V.
Douglas, G.H. Edmund Wilson's America.*
   R.H. Costa, 395(MFS):Winter85-751
   J.R. Fargnoli, 115:Summer85-378
Douglas, K. A Prose Miscellany.* (D.
Graham, comp)
   V. Cunningham, 493:Aug85-13
Douglas, M., ed. Food in the Social Order.
   R.V., 185:Apr86-675
Douglas, M. and B. Isherwood. The World
of Goods.
   M. Herzfeld, 567:Vol56No1/2-153
Douglas, P.M. - see Hotteterre, J-M.
Douin, J-L., ed. La Nouvelle Vague 25
ans après.
   H.A. Garrity, 207(FR):May86-1026

102

Dournon, G.  Guide for the Collection of
Traditional Musical Instruments.
  E. Koskoff, 187:Winter85-168
Dove, R.  Museum.*
  C. Hernton, 472:Spring/Summer/Fall/
  Winter85-518
Dove, R.  Thomas and Beulah.
  H. Vendler, 453(NYRB):23Oct86-47
Dowden, W.S., with B.G. Bartholomew and
J.L. Linsley - see Moore, T.
Dowell, R.W., J.L.W. West 3d and N.M. West-
lake - see Dreiser, T.
Dower, J.W.  War Without Mercy.
  I. Buruma, 453(NYRB):14Aug86-23
  D.W. Plath, 441:29Jun86-19
Dower, J.W. and J. Junkerman, eds.  The
Hiroshima Murals.
  P-L. Adams, 61:Sep86-104
Dowling, D.  Bloomsbury Aesthetics and the
Novels of Forster and Woolf.*
  D.F. Gillespie, 177(ELT):Vol28No3-312
  295(JML):Nov85-377
Dowling, J. - see de la Cruz, R.
Dowling, M.  Humanism in the Age of Henry
VIII.
  C. Cross, 617(TLS):18Apr86-427
Dowling, W.C.  Language and Logos in
Boswell's "Life of Johnson."
  D.C. Mell, Jr., 402(MLR):Jul85-700
Downar, J.  The Empire of Light.*
  T. Dooley, 617(TLS):7Feb86-138
Downes, D.A.  The Great Sacrifice.
  J. Bump, 637(VS):Summer85-690
Downes, W.  Language and Society.
  I. Smith, 350:Jun86-474
Downie, J.A.  Jonathan Swift.*
  J.S. Cunningham, 506(PSt):Dec85-84
  H.T. Dickinson, 366:Autumn85-306
  V. Rumbold, 184(EIC):Jan85-82
  P.J. Schakel, 173(ECS):Spring86-417
Downie, M.A. and B. Robertson, comps.  The
New Wind Has Wings.
  J.C. Stott, 526:Winter85-75
Downing, A.B. and B. Smoker, eds.  Volun-
tary Euthanasia.
  I. McGilchrist, 617(TLS):7Nov86-1251
Downs, R.B., with E.C. Downs.  British and
Irish Library Resources.
  R.J. Roberts, 447(N&Q):Jun84-252
Dowson, E.  New Letters from Ernest Dowson.
  (D. Flower, ed)
  I. Fletcher, 177(ELT):Vol28No3-323
Dowty, A.  Middle East Crisis.
  A. Watson, 617(TLS):14Feb86-160
Dowty, D.R., R.E. Wall and S. Peters.
Introduction to Montague Semantics.
  P. Dau, 316:Sep85-856
Doyle, A.C. - see under Conan Doyle, A.
Doyle, B.  Angel Square.
  P. Nodelman, 102(CanL):Fall85-122
Doyle, E.G. - see Sedulius Scottus
Doyle, J.  Altered Harvest.
  T. Monmaney, 441:16Mar86-21
Doyle, J.  North of America.
  P. Buitenhuis, 102(CanL):Spring85-167
  J-M. Lacroix, 189(EA):Oct-Dec86-477
  M.A. Peterman, 627(UTQ):Summer85-431
Doyle, M.  A Steady Hand.*
  I. Sowton, 102(CanL):Fall85-112
Doyle, M.W.  Empires.
  A. Sykes, 617(TLS):5Sep86-982

Dpal-khang Lo-tsā-ba.  Dag-yig ngag-sgron-
gyi rtsa-ba dang de'i 'grel-pa.
  L.W.J. van der Kuijp, 259(IIJ):Jul85-
  214
Drabble, M., ed.  The Oxford Companion to
English Literature.*  (5th ed)
  G.B. Tennyson, 445(NCF):Sep85-249
  O. Trilling, 157:No158-49
  566:Spring86-223
Drabeck, B.A. and H.E. Ellis - see
"Archibald MacLeish: Reflections"
Drache, S.  The Mikveh Man and Other
Stories.*
  M. Darling, 102(CanL):Summer85-149
  J.K. Keefer, 198:Winter85-95
Drachman, V.G.  Hospital with a Heart.
  J.W. Estes, 432(NEQ):Jun85-285
Drage, C.L.  Russian and Church Slavonic
Books 1701-1800 in United Kingdom Lib-
raries.
  W.F. Ryan, 575(SEER):Jul85-434
Draine, B.  Substance under Pressure.*
  N. Bradbury, 541(RES):Nov85-600
Drakakis, J., ed.  Alternative Shake-
speares.
  I-S. Ewbank, 617(TLS):25Apr86-451
Drakakis, J., ed.  British Radio Drama.
  P. Davison, 677(YES):Vol 15-362
Drake, F.C.  The Empire of the Seas.
  R.R. Swartout, Jr., 293(JAst):Aug85-
  793
Draper, C.G., ed.  Great American Stories
I.
  P. Markham, 399(MLJ):Autumn85-329
Dreher, M.  Sophistik und Polisentwicklung.
  G.B. Kerferd, 123:Vol35No1-62
Dreiser, T.  An Amateur Laborer.*  (R.W.
  Dowell, J.L.W. West 3d and N.M. Westlake,
  eds)
  D. Pizer, 534(RALS):Spring83-55
Dreiser, T.  Theodore Dreiser: American
Diaries, 1902-1926.*  (T.P. Riggio,
J.L.W. West 3d and N.M. Westlake, eds)
  P.L. Gerber, 534(RALS):Autumn83-229
Dreiser, T.  Selected Magazine Articles of
Theodore Dreiser.  (Y. Hakutani, ed)
  H. McNeil, 617(TLS):21Feb86-181
Dreisziger, N.F., ed.  Mobilization for
Total War.
  P. Brown, 106:Spring85-107
Drescher, H.W., ed.  Lexikon der eng-
lischen Literatur.
  W.G. Müller, 38:Band103Heft3/4-523
Dresner, S.H. - see Heschel, A.J.
Dressler, W.U.  Morphonology.
  F. Chevillet, 189(EA):Oct-Dec86-492
Dressler, W.U. and O.E. Pfeiffer - see
"Phonologica 1976"
Dretske, F.I.  Knowledge and the Flow of
Information.
  J-M. Gabaude, 542:Jan-Mar85-69
  J.C. Maloney, 449:Jun85-299
Drew, B., ed.  Hard-Boiled Dames.
  M. Stasio, 441:20Jul86-18
Drew, P.  Leaves of Iron — Glenn Murcutt.
  R. Spence, 46:Dec85-96
Drew, P.  The Meaning of Freedom.
  J.W. Saunders, 541(RES):Feb85-137
Drewal, H.J. and M.T. Gẹlẹdẹ.*
  K. Götrick, 538(RAL):Fall85-449
  J. Mack, 59:Sep85-391

Drewes, G.W.J., ed and trans. Two Achehnese Poems.
　J.T. Siegel, 293(JASt):Feb85-462
Drewry, G., ed. The New Select Committees.*
　W. Plowden, 617(TLS):11Apr86-376
Drews, P. Die slawische Avantgarde und der Westen.*
　J.T. Baer, 574(SEEJ):Spring85-96
　R.B. Pynsent, 575(SEER):Jul85-440
Drews, R. Basileus.*
　D. Stockton, 123:Vol35No2-418
Drexler, K.E. Engines of Creation.
　T. Monmaney, 441:10Aug86-8
Dreyer, E.L. Early Ming China.
　P. Huang, 293(JASt):Nov84-161
Dreyfus, H.L. and P. Rabinow. Michel Foucault.* (2nd ed)
　I. Hacking, 311(JP):May85-273
　M. Jarrety, 450(NRF):Feb85-99
Dreyfus, J. Aspects of French Eighteenth Century Typography.
　E. Harris, 517(PBSA):Vol79No2-248
Dreyfus, K. - see Grainger, P.
van Driel, G. and others, eds. Zikir Šumim.
　R.D. Biggs, 318(JAOS):Apr-Jun84-366
Drinka, G.F. The Birth of Neurosis.
　C.K. Warsh, 529(QQ):Winter85-878
Drinkwater, J.F. Roman Gaul.*
　R. Chevallier, 487:Summer85-188
Driscoll, J. The China Cantos of Ezra Pound.
　J.J. Nolde, 468:Winter84-465
Driscoll, J.P. and J.K. Howat. John Frederick Kensett.
　M.S. Young, 39:Dec85-506
Drogin, M. Anathema!*
　L.K. Little, 589:Oct85-1045
Dronke, P. The Medieval Poet and His World.
　E. Vance, 617(TLS):21Mar86-311
Drossard, W. Das Tagalog als Repräsentant des aktivischen Sprachbaus.
　G. Bossong, 353:Vol23No3-490
Drost, W. - see Giusti, V.
von Droste-Hülshoff, A. Annette von Droste-Hülshoff: Historisch-kritische Ausgabe.* (Vol 4, Pt 1 and Vol 6, Pt 1) (W. Woesler, ed)
　E. Care, 402(MLR):Oct85-996
Drucker, P.F. The Frontiers of Management.
　D. Diamond, 441:26Oct86-39
Drummond de Andrade, C. The Minus Sign.*
　F.G. Williams, 238:Mar85-81
Drüppel, C.J. Altfranzösische Urkunden und Lexikologie.
　M-J. Deggeller, 553(RLiR):Jul-Dec85-478
Drury, A. Pentagon.
　W. Schott, 441:26Oct86-18
Drury, J. The Parables in the Gospels.
　S. Medcalf, 617(TLS):25Jul86-824
Drury, N. Dictionary of Mysticism and the Occult.
　639(VQR):Autumn85-135
Drury, W. Norton I.
　J. Moore, 441:20Jul86-19
Druskin, M. Igor Stravinsky.*
　J.B., 412:Feb84-68
　S. Karlinsky, 550(RusR):Jul85-281
Dryden, E. Anna's Room.
　D. Devlin, 157:No157-50

Dryden, J. The Beauties of Dryden. (D. Hopkins and T. Mason, eds)
　566:Autumn85-89
Dryden, J. Dryden: Poems and Prose.
　S.W.R. Smith, 566:Spring86-220
Dryden, K. The Game.
　D. Daymond, 102(CanL):Spring85-115
Du, N. The Tale of Kieu. (H.S. Thong, ed and trans)
　T.B. Lam, 293(JASt):May85-666
Duarte, J.N., with D. Page. Duarte.
　J. Morley, 453(NYRB):4Dec86-15
　L. Robinson, 441:2Nov86-18
Duarte i Montserrat, C. and A. Alsina i Keith. Gramàtica històrica del català. (Vol 1)
　E. Blasco Ferrer, 379(MedR):Apr85-148
Dube, W-D. Expressionists and Expressionism.*
　J. Lloyd, 59:Mar85-128
Du Bellay, J. The Regrets. (C.H. Sisson, trans)
　G.H. Tucker, 208(FS):Oct85-458
Dubie, N. The Springhouse.
　J. Graham, 441:28Sep86-32
Dubinski, R.R. - see Brome, A.
Dubnick, R.K. The Structure of Obscurity.*
　C.N. Pondrom, 659(ConL):Spring86-98
Du Boff, L.D. Art Law in a Nutshell.
　J. Kaufman, 476:Fall84-99
Du Boff, L.D. The Law (in Plain English) for Craftspeople. (M. Scott, ed)
　C.A. Hecker, 476:Fall85-73
Dubois, P. L'Acte photographique. La Chronophotographie.
　F. de Mèredieu, 450(NRF):Oct85-116
Dubois, P. L'Oeuvre de Berkeley.
　L. Dechery, 540(RIPh):Vol139fasc3-272
Du Bois, W.E.B. Writings. (N. Huggins, ed)
　E.J. Sundquist, 129:Dec86-62
Duboy, P. Lequeu.
　J. Rykwert, 617(TLS):26Dec86-1439
Dubreuil, G. La Jeunesse est lente à mourir.
　C.F. Coates, 207(FR):Mar86-644
Dubrow, H. Genre.
　R.J. Dingley, 447(N&Q):Dec84-555
Dubuisson, P. Atlas linguistique et ethnographique du Centre. (Vol 3)
　W. Dahmen, 553(RLiR):Jul-Dec85-516
Dubus, A. The Last Worthless Evening.
　C. Sigal, 441:21Dec86-12
Dubus, A. Voices from the Moon.*
　W.H. Pritchard, 249(HudR):Spring85-129
Duby, G. The Knight, the Lady and the Priest.
　R. Mayne, 176:Jul/Aug86-48
Duby, G. William Marshal.
　G. Garrett, 441:2Feb86-7
　M. Keen, 453(NYRB):16Jan86-39
　G. Steiner, 442(NY):26May86-103
Du Camp, M. Souvenirs littéraires.
　A. Clerval, 450(NRF):Mar85-86
Ducháček, O. L'Évolution de l'articulation linguistique du domaine esthétique du latin au français contemporain.
　D. Justice, 545(RPh):May85-503
Duchêne, R. Françoise de Grignan ou le mal d'amour.
　M-O. Sweetser, 207(FR):Feb86-508

Duchêne, R. L'Imposture littéraire dans les "Provinciales" de Pascal.*
  A.J. Krailsheimer, 208(FS):Oct85-466
  C. Meurillon, 475:Vol 12No23-697
Duchêne, R. Ninon de Lenclos.*
  N. Aronson, 475:Vol 12No22-304
Duchet, C. and J. Neefs, eds. Balzac.
  O. Heathcote, 208(FS):Jan85-86
Dückert, J. and G. Kempcke, eds. Wörterbuch der Sprachschwierigkeiten.
  B. Matzke, 682(ZPSK):Band38Heft6-779
Duckworth, D. The Influence of Biblical Terminology and Thought on Wolfram's "Parzival."
  E.S. Dick, 406:Spring85-92
Ducornet, R. Entering Fire.
  H. Kureishi, 617(TLS):21Feb86-198
Ducrot, O. and others. Les mots du discours.
  N.C.W. Spence, 208(FS):Jan85-120
Dudden, F.E. Serving Women.
  B. Todd, 106:Fall85-329
Dudek, L. Ideas for Poetry.
  P.M. St. Pierre, 102(CanL):Summer85-183
"Duden Deutsches Universalwörterbuch."
  W. Christian, 399(MLJ):Summer85-185
Dudzinskaia, E.A. Slavianofily v obshchestvennoi bor'be.
  A. Gleason, 550(RusR):Oct85-417
Duff, R.A. Trials and Punishments.
  N. Lacey, 617(TLS):18Jul86-779
Duffy, C. The Military Life of Frederick the Great.
  G.A. Craig, 441:2Feb86-10
  J. Keegan, 453(NYRB):13Feb86-9
Duffy, C.A. Standing Female Nude.
  J. Lanchester, 493:Feb86-58
  C. Rawson, 617(TLS):7Feb86-137
Duffy, M.J., ed. The Episcopal Diocese of Massachusetts, 1784-1984.
  J.M. O'Toole, 432(NEQ):Dec85-616
Dufournet, J., ed. Etudes sur le "Roman de la Rose" de Guillaume de Lorris.
  M. Lecco, 379(MedR):Aug85-296
  L. Löfstedt, 439(NM):1985/4-603
Dufournet, J. - see Villon, F.
Dufournet, J. and A. Méline, eds and trans. Le Roman de Renart 1-2.
  E. Suomela-Härmä, 439(NM):1985/4-606
Dufty, A.R. Morris Embroideries: The Prototypes.
  B.J. Morris, 326:Winter85/86-23
Dufwa, J. Winds from the East.
  R.T., 90:Aug85-545
Duggan, J.J. A Guide to Studies on the "Chanson de Roland."
  A. Vanderheyden, 356(LR):Aug85-223
Duhaime, A. Visions outaouaises/Ottawax.
  B. Beaulieu, 102(CanL):Summer85-153
Duhamel, P. Les Fourmis de Dieu.
  R.T. Cargo, 207(FR):Oct85-148
Duiker, W.J. Vietnam.
  G. Porter, 293(JASt):Feb85-463
Duke, D.C. Distant Obligations.*
  R.A. Martin, 115:Summer84-255
Dukes, P. A History of Europe 1648-1948.
  M.S. Anderson, 617(TLS):5Sep86-982
Dukore, B.F. American Dramatists 1918-1945 Excluding O'Neill.
  B. Grantham, 157:No156-50
Dull, J.L. - see Hsu, C-Y.

Dull, J.R. A Diplomatic History of the American Revolution.
  P. Marshall, 617(TLS):6Jun86-612
Dulles, A. The Catholicity of the Church.
  P. Hebblethwaite, 617(TLS):16May86-541
Duman, D. The English and Colonial Bars in the Nineteenth Century.
  D. Philips, 637(VS):Autumn85-161
Dumas, A. Le Corricolo.*
  J. Aeply, 450(NRF):Jan85-92
Dumas, A. Lettres d'Alexandre Dumas à Mélanie Waldor. (C. Schopp, ed)
  F. Bassan, 535(RHL):Mar/Apr85-314
Dumas, C. Delightful The Hague.
  E. Schrijver, 39:Jun85-437
Dumas, J-L. Vivre et philosopher au grand siècle.
  M. Adam, 542:Jul-Sep85-317
Dumas, M-C. Robert Desnos ou l'exploration des limites.
  A.M. Russo, 546(RR):Mar85-227
Dumbach, A.E. and J. Newborn. Shattering the German Night.
  S.M. Halpern, 441:17Aug86-10
Dumbleton, W.A. Ireland.
  K. Danaher, 305(JIL):Sep85-114
Dumenil, L. Freemasonry and American Culture, 1880-1930.*
  639(VQR):Spring85-53
Dumestre, G. La geste de Ségou racontée par des griots bambara.
  T.A. Hale, 538(RAL):Fall85-407
Dumézil, G. L'Oubli de l'homme et l'honneur des dieux.
  H. Cronel, 450(NRF):Jul-Aug85-162
  B. Lincoln, 617(TLS):3Oct86-1107
Dumézil, G. The Stakes of the Warrior. (J. Puhvel, ed)
  E.C. Polomé, 292(JAF):Jan/Mar85-103
Duminil, M-P. Le Sang, les vaisseaux, le coeur dans la Collection hippocratique.*
  J.T. Vallance, 123:Vol35No2-426
Dümling, A. Lasst euch nicht verführen.
  J. Willett, 617(TLS):3Oct86-1106
Dumont, L. Affinity as Value.
  P. Kolenda, 293(JASt):Nov84-226
Dumoulin, B. Recherches sur le premier Aristote.*
  C.J. Rowe, 303(JoHS):Vol 105-188
Dunaway, J.M. Jacques Maritain.
  J. Flower, 208(FS):Apr85-230
Dunbar, R.G. Forging New Rights in Western Waters.
  J.P. Reid, 250(HLQ):Winter85-89
Duncan, A. American Art Deco.
  P. Goldberger, 441:7Dec86-17
Duncan, E. Those Giants: Let Them Rise!
  B.F. Williamson, 441:16Mar86-21
Duncan, E. Unless Soul Clap Its Hands.*
  S.C., 219(GaR):Summer85-458
Duncan, J.A., ed. L'Époque symboliste et le monde proustien à travers la correspondance de Paul Adam (1884-1920).
  T.M.P. Lima, 535(RHL):Jan/Feb85-129
Duncan, R. Ground Work: Before the War.*
  T. Gardner, 30:Winter86-90
  K. Irby, 138:No7-261
Duncan, R. Working with Britten.
  J.B., 412:Aug/Nov83-294
Duncan, S.J. The Pool in the Desert.*
  C. Gerson, 102(CanL):Fall85-104
Dundes, A., ed. Cinderella.*
  R. Wehse, 196:Band26Heft3/4-353

Dundes, A. Life is Like a Chicken Coop
Ladder.*
  N. Tucker, 203:Vol96No2-262
Dundes, A., ed. Sacred Narrative.*
  C. Goldberg, 121(CJ):Oct/Nov85-71
Dunlap, R. - see Hunt, L.
Dunlay, T.W. Wolves for the Blue Soldiers.
  B.W. Dippie, 106:Spring85-31
Dunleavy, J.E., ed. George Moore in
Perspective.*
  I. Fletcher, 637(VS):Summer85-693
  J.W. Weaver, 177(ELT):Vol28No2-195
Dunlop, I. Royal Palaces of France.
  442(NY):13Jan86-88
Dunlop, J.B. The Faces of Contemporary
Russian Nationalism.*
  S.R. Burant, 104(CASS):Spring85-82
  S. Garnett, Jr., 550(RusR):Jan85-111
Dunlop, L., ed and trans. A Late Chrysan-
themum.
  G. O'Brien, 441:10Aug86-7
Dunlop, S. Not Exactly a Brahmin.
  N. Callendar, 441:9Feb86-27
Dunmore, T. Soviet Politics, 1945-53.
  A. Kemp-Welch, 575(SEER):Oct85-636
Dunn, D. Elegies.*
  H. Lomas, 364:Apr/May85-117
  B. O'Donoghue, 493:Apr85-49
  W. Scammell, 148:Winter85-65
Dunn, D. Secret Villages.*
  J. Mellors, 364:Apr/May85-145
  639(VQR):Autumn85-124
Dunn, J. Locke.
  J.C., 185:Jan86-455
  R.W. Dyson, 83:Spring85-112
  M.A. Stewart, 319:Apr86-273
Dunn, J. Rethinking Modern Political
Theory.*
  D. Miller, 617(TLS):24Jan86-90
Dunn, J. Timor.
  M. Picken, 453(NYRB):4Dec86-44
Dunn, M. Engraved on Air.
  J. Carter, 219(GaR):Summer85-432
Dunn, R.D. - see Camden, W.
Dunn, R.E. The Adventures of Ibn Battuta.
  R. Irwin, 617(TLS):12Dec86-1398
Dunn, S. Local Time.
  A. Brumer, 441:6Jul86-23
  H. Vendler, 453(NYRB):23Oct86-47
Dunn, S. Not Dancing.*
  J. Holden, 651(WHR):Summer85-155
  G. Kuzma, 460(OhR):No36-98
  455:Mar85-65
Dunn, S.P. The Fall and Rise of the Asi-
atic Mode of Production.
  L. Stillman, 318(JAOS):Oct-Dec84-767
Dunn, T.P. and R.D. Erlich, eds. The
Mechanical God.*
  C.C. Smith, 395(MFS):Summer85-462
  S. Thomason, 161(DUJ):Jun84-312
Dunne, C. Black Ice.
  M. Laski, 362:3Jul86-32
Dunne, J.G. Dutch Shea, Jr.
  M.R. Winchell, 577(SHR):Summer85-283
Dunne, S., ed. Poets of Munster.
  B. O'Donoghue, 493:Feb86-65
Dunnett, D. Niccolò Rising.
  R. Goodman, 441:19Oct86-30
Dünnhaupt, G. Bibliographisches Handbuch
der Barockliteratur.* (Pts 1-3)
  K-H. Habersetzer, 224(GRM):Band35Heft3-
  352

[continued]

[continuing]
  F. van Ingen, 680(ZDP):Band104Heft2-
  278
Dünnhaupt, G. and K-H. Habersetzer - see
Gryphius, A.
Dunning, A., ed. Visitatio organorum.
  A. Bond, 415:Dec85-756
Dunphy, W. - see Siger de Brabant
Dunthorne, H. and H.M. Scott. Early Mod-
ern European History, c. 1492-1789.
  D.J.F., 83:Spring85-126
Dupèbe, J. - see Nostradamus
Dupin, J-M. Opus incertum.
  R. Bréchon, 98:Nov85-1133
Du Plessis, R.B. Writing beyond the End-
ing.
  L.L. Doan, 395(MFS):Winter85-866
  J.E. Kennard, 659(ConL):Fall86-396
Dupont, F. - see Mazarin, J.
Dupont-Roc, R. and J. Lallot - see Aris-
totle
Dupré, F. La "solution" du passage à
l'acte.
  J-M. Gabaude, 542:Jul-Sep85-355
Dupré, L. Marx's Social Critique of Cul-
ture.
  J.S. Morgan, 543:Sep84-117
  W. Stafford, 366:Autumn85-305
Du Pree, D.K. - see Harrison, C.
Duque, A.J.M. - see under Martin Duque,
A.J.
Duque de Estrada, D. Comentarios del
desengañado de sí mismo.
  R.D. Pope, 304(JHP):Spring85-264
Duquesne, T. and E. Goodman. Britain.
  C. Townshend, 617(TLS):28Nov86-1335
Duran, E. Latin America and the World
Recession.
  S. Strange, 617(TLS):6Jun86-613
Durand, F. Influssi greci nel dialetto
ligure (con particolare riferimento alla
parlata di Val d'Arroscia).
  H. and R. Kahane, 545(RPh):Nov85-206
Durand, G. La foi du cordonnier.
  M. Adam, 542:Jul-Sep85-368
Durand, M.M. and N.T. Huan. An Introduc-
tion to Vietnamese Literature. (D.M.
Hawke, ed and trans)
  D.G. Marr, 617(TLS):19Sep86-1022
Durand, R. Les campagnes portugaises
entre Douro et Tage aux XIIe et XIIIe
siècles.
  L.H. Nelson, 589:Jul85-671
Durant, A. Ezra Pound.*
  A. Easthope, 366:Spring85-151
  A. Ross, 468:Spring85-137
Duranti, A. The Samoan "fono."
  T. Huebner, 355(LSoc):Sep85-387
Duranti, F. The House on Moon Lake.
  O. Conant, 441:9Nov86-32
  442(NY):8Dec86-153
Durantini, M.F. The Child in Seventeenth-
Century Dutch Painting.
  W. Franits, 54:Dec85-695
  I.G., 90:Feb85-110
Duranton, H., ed. Correspondance littér-
aire du Président Bouhier, no 10.
  P. Rétat, 535(RHL):Mar/Apr85-299
Duranton, H. - see Hotman, F.
Duranty, L-E. La Cause du beau Guillaume.
  P. Trémolières, 450(NRF):Oct85-91

Eckman, F.R., L.H. Bell and D. Nelson, eds.
Universals of Second Language Acquisi-
tion.
    E. Bialystok, 399(MLJ):Spring85-77
    R. Young, 355(LSoc):Dec85-558
Eco, U.  Art and Beauty in the Middle Ages.
    E. Kolb, 441:19Oct86-31
Eco, U.  Faith in Fakes.
    G. Adair, 617(TLS):26Sep86-1061
    D. Caute, 362:28Aug86-21
Eco, U.  The Name of the Rose.*  (Italian
title: Il nome della rosa; French title:
Le nom de la rose.)
    P. Lewis, 565:Winter84/85-42
Eco, U.  Postscript to "The Name of the
Rose."*  (British title: Reflections on
"The Name of the Rose.")
    P. Lewis, 565:Summer85-50
    S. Scobie, 376:Sep85-145
Eco, U.  Semiotics and the Philosophy of
Language.*
    R.L. Bogue, 478:Oct85-245
Eco, U.  Travels in Hyperreality.
    P-L. Adams, 61:Jun86-83
    G. Garrett, 441:27Jul86-7
    J. Updike, 442(NY):18Aug86-70
Eco, U. and T.A. Sebeok, eds.  The Sign of
Three.
    E.S. Lauterbach, 395(MFS):Summer85-382
"Ecrire l'amour."
    P. Smart, 627(UTQ):Summer85-492
"Les Écrivains et l'Affaire Dreyfus."
    C. Becker, 535(RHL):May/Jun85-515
Eddings, D.W., ed.  The Naiad Voice.
    P.F. Quinn, 495(PoeS):Jun85-13
Ede, J.  A Way of Life: Kettle's Yard.*
    R. Demarco, 592:Vol 198No1009-52
Edel, A.  Aristotle and His Philosophy.*
    T.M. Olshewsky, 319:Oct86-548
Edel, L.  Stuff of Sleep and Dreams.*
    V.A. Makowsky, 284:Spring85-204
Edel, L. - see James, H.
Edel, L. - see Wilson, E.
Edel, L. and D.H. Laurence, with J. Ram-
beau, eds.  A Bibliography of Henry
James.* (3rd ed)
    L.H. Powers, 534(RALS):Autumn83-223
Edel, L. and L.H. Powers - see James, H.
Edel, L., with M. Wilson - see James, H.
Edelman, B.  La maison de Kant.
    A. Stanguennec, 542:Jul-Sep85-328
Edelman, M.  Democratic Theories and the
Constitution.
    O.J., 185:Jan86-438
Edelson, J.  No News Is Good.
    J. McCulloch, 441:8Jun86-36
Edelson, M.  Hypothesis and Evidence in
Psychoanalysis.*
    R.A. Paskauskas, 529(QQ):Summer85-416
Edelstein, S.J.  The Sickled Cell.
    J. Deaton, 441:5Oct86-54
Eden, D.  Gilbert and Sullivan.
    A. Jacobs, 617(TLS):11Jul86-764
Eden, P.T. - see Seneca
Eden, R.  Political Leadership and Nihil-
ism.
    C.S., 185:Oct85-217
Eder, D.  Three Writers in Exile.
    295(JML):Nov85-402
Edgan, N.L. and W.Y. Ma, eds.  Travel in
Asia.
    H-W. Lee, 87(BB):Mar85-44

Edgar, W.B., ed.  A Southern Renascence
Man.
    L. Casper, 651(WHR):Winter85-366
    J.H. Justus, 578:Spring86-123
    V. Strandberg, 579(SAQ):Autumn85-441
Edgell, Z.  Beka Lamb.
    R. Deveson, 617(TLS):24Oct86-1187
Edgerton, C.  Raney.*
    G.C., 569(SR):Spring85-xxxix
Edgerton, S.Y., Jr.  Pictures and Punish-
ment.
    F. Gilbert, 453(NYRB):9Oct86-43
    J. Hale, 617(TLS):28Mar86-322
    639(VQR):Summer85-100
Edgeworth, M.  Belinda.
    J. Bayley, 617(TLS):27Jun86-695
Edmond, L.  Selected Poems.
    S. Rae, 617(TLS):1Aug86-839
Edmonds, F.  Another Bloody Tour.
    S. Fry, 362:18/25Dec86-55
Edmondson, A.  How to be a Complete Bas-
tard.
    B. Bainbridge, 617(TLS):26Dec86-1453
Edmondson, L.H.  Feminism in Russia, 1900-
1917.*
    C. Johansen, 104(CASS):Spring85-74
    J. Sanders, 550(RusR):Apr85-207
    R. Stites, 575(SEER):Jan85-134
Edmonson, M.S., with P.A. Andrews, eds.
Supplement to the Handbook of Middle
American Indians.  (Vol 2)
    K.M. Kensinger, 263(RIB):Vol35No3-327
Saint Edmund of Abingdon.  "Mirour de
Seinte Eglyse."* (A.D. Wilshere, ed)
    B. Merrilees, 382(MAE):1985/2-332
    W. Rothwell, 208(FS):Oct85-449
Edmunds, L. and A. Dundes, eds.  Oedipus.*
    G.K. Beynen, 292(JAF):Jul/Sep85-340
    C.K. Callanan, 196:Band26Heft1/2-144
    J. Wall, 64(Arv):Vol39-213
Edmunds, R.D.  Tecumseh and the Quest for
Indian Leadership.
    G.W., 102(CanL):Winter84-189
Edric, R.  A New Ice Age.
    C. Hawtree, 617(TLS):25Jul86-818
Edwardes, M.  The Myth of the Mahatma.
    I. Jack, 617(TLS):10Oct86-1144
Edwards, A.  Katharine Hepburn.
    P. Oakes, 617(TLS):9May86-507
Edwards, A.  A Remarkable Woman.*
    B. Weeks, 18:Mar86-65
Edwards, A.S.G.  Stephen Hawes.
    E.R. Harvey, 447(N&Q):Sep84-425
Edwards, D.  Rhapsody. Winter Sonata.
    P. Craig, 617(TLS):18Jul86-792
Edwards, G.  The Discreet Art of Luis
Buñuel.
    P.W. Evans, 86(BHS):Jul85-322
Edwards, G.  El teatro de Federico García
Lorca.
    R.G. Sánchez, 240(HR):Summer85-376
Edwards, H. and T. Zanetta.  Stardust.
    M. Miles, 441:24Aug86-19
Edwards, J.  Christian Córdoba.*
    D.W. Lomax, 86(BHS):Jan85-139
Edwards, J.  Language, Society and Iden-
tity.
    J.E. Joseph, 350:Dec86-955
Edwards, J., ed.  Linguistic Minorities.
    T.C. Frazer, 300:Oct85-195

Edwards, J. The Works of Jonathan Edwards. (Vols 1-6) (P. Miller and J.E. Smith, general eds)
  A. Heimert, 165(EAL):Winter85/86-256
Edwards, J. The Works of Jonathan Edwards. (Vol 7) (N. Pettit, ed)
  N. Fiering, 432(NEQ):Jun85-295
  A. Heimert, 165(EAL):Winter85/86-256
Edwards, J.C. Ethics without Philosophy.*
  M. Malherbe, 192(EP):Oct-Dec85-555
Edwards, L.R. Psyche as Hero.
  N. Baym, 27(AL):Mar85-162
  J.E. Kennard, 659(ConL):Fall86-396
Edwards, M. Towards a Christian Poetics.*
  J. Blondel, 189(EA):Apr-Jun86-188
  295(JML):Nov85-413
Edwards, M.U., Jr. Luther's Last Battles.
  J.M. Estes, 539:Nov85-289
Edwards, N. Mud.
  A. Haverty, 617(TLS):20Jun86-682
Edwards, O. The Time of Christ.
  J.D.M. Derrett, 617(TLS):27Jun86-718
Edwards, P. Heidegger and Death.
  S. Paluch, 323:Jan85-99
Edwards, P. The Lake.
  I. Fonseca, 617(TLS):18Apr86-416
Edwards, P. Shakespeare.
  K. Brown, 617(TLS):22Aug86-917
Edwards, P. - see Shakespeare, W.
Edwards, P. and others. The Revels History of Drama in English. (Vol 4)
  A. Gurr, 677(YES):Vol 15-288
Edwards, P.D., comp. Edmund Yates, 1831-1894.*
  S. Mitchell, 635(VPR):Spring85-40
Edwards, S.H. Critics and Composers.
  R. Anderson, 415:Sep85-538
van Eeghen, I.H. "In mijn journaal gezet," Amsterdam 1805-1808.
  E. van Uitert, 600:Vol 15No3/4-236
Eekman, T. and D. Worth, eds. Russian Poetics.*
  J. Graffy, 575(SEER):Jul85-435
  D.L. Plank, 402(MLR):Jan85-255
van Effenterre, H. Le palais de Mallia et la cité minoenne.
  D.J.I. Begg, 487:Summer85-163
Effinger, G.A. The Bird of Time.
  G. Jonas, 441:8Jun86-23
Efremova, N.N. Ministerstvo Iustitsii Rossiiskoi Imperii, 1802-1917 gg. Istorikopravovoe issledovanie.
  B.F. Adams, 550(RusR):Jan85-107
Egan, D. Collected Poems.
  T. Eldeman, 305(JIL):Jan85-55
Egan, J. The Inward Teacher.
  T.N. Corns, 677(YES):Vol 15-290
Egan, M. - see "The Vidas of the Troubadours"
Egan, S. Patterns of Experience in Autobiography.
  S. Neuman, 598(SoR):Spring86-407
Eggebrecht, H.H., ed. Handwörterbuch der musikalischen Terminologie. (Pt 10)
  J. Caldwell, 410(M&L):Apr85-147
Eggum, A. Edvard Munch.*
  E. Prelinger, 55:Sep85-23
  J.B. Smith, 39:May85-355
Egremont, M. Dear Shadows.
  V. Bogdanor, 362:17Apr86-28
  T. Fitton, 617(TLS):28Mar86-342

Ehlert, F.W. and others. Patés and Terrine.
  W. and C. Cowen, 639(VQR):Spring85-68
Ehrenburg, I. and K. Simonov. In One Newspaper.
  T.G. Butson, 441:2Mar86-25
Ehrenpreis, I. Swift.* (Vol 3)
  J.S. Cunningham, 506(PSt):Dec85-84
  F. Rosslyn, 83:Spring85-107
  V. Rumbold, 184(EIC):Jan85-82
  L. Speirs, 179(ES):Dec85-558
Ehrenreich, B., E. Hess and G. Jacobs. Re-Making Love.
  P. Rose, 61:Sep86-100
  J. Viorst, 441:14Sep86-9
Ehrenstein, D. and B. Reed. Rock on Film.
  R.S. Denisoff, 493:Vol9No4-67
Ehrenwald, J. Anatomy of Genius.
  R.M. Restak, 567:Vol55No3/4-303
Ehrlich, C. The Music Profession in Britain since the Eighteenth Century.
  A. Jacobs, 617(TLS):18Apr86-422
Ehrlich, G. The Solace of Open Spaces.*
  442(NY):17Mar86-111
Ehrlich, H., ed. Light Rays.
  R. Pearce, 329(JJQ):Spring86-370
Ehrlich, L. Christian Dietrich Grabbe.
  D. Horton, 402(MLR):Jan85-219
Ehrlich, P.R. The Machinery of Nature.
  E. Dobb, 441:29Jun86-25
Ehrlichman, J. The China Card.
  O. Schell, 441:22Jun86-13
Ehrman, J. The Younger Pitt.*
  W.K. Hackmann, 173(ECS):Spring86-433
Eibl-Eibesfeldt, I. Die Biologie des menschlichen Verhaltens.
  J. Herbig, 384:Apr85-329
von Eichborn, R., ed. Cambridge-Eichborn German Dictionary.
  M. Burkhard, 301(JEGP):Apr85-299
  70:May/Jun85-165
von Eichendorff, J. Ahnung und Gegenwart. (G. Hoffmeister, ed)
  E. Schwarz, 133:Band18Heft2-173
Eichmann, R. - see "Cuckolds, Clerics, and Countrymen"
Eichner, H. and N. Lelless - see Schlegel, F.
Eicker, H.J., with others. Straelener Mundart.
  H. Niebaum, 685(ZDL):3/1985-390
Eidelberg, M., ed. Eva Zeisel.
  T.A. Lockett, 324:Jun86-470
Eigeldinger, F. and G. Schaeffer, eds. Table de concordances rythmique et syntaxique des "Poésies" d'Arthur Rimbaud.* (Vol 1)
  C. Chadwick, 208(FS):Jul85-356
Eigeldinger, M. Lumières du mythe.
  L. Forestier, 535(RHL):May/Jun85-521
Eigeldinger, M. - see Gautier, T.
"The Eighteenth Century: A Current Bibliography." (Vol 3: 1977 and Vol 4: 1978) (R.R. Allen, ed)
  P.R. Backscheider, 402(MLR):Jul85-681
"The Eighteenth Century: A Current Bibliography." (Vol 5: 1979) (P.J. Korshin, ed)
  L. Versini, 535(RHL):Mar/Apr85-305
"The Eighteenth Century: A Current Bibliography." (Vol 7: 1981)(J.S. Borck, ed)
  566:Spring86-202
Eigler, G. - see Plato

Eigner, E.M. and G.J. Worth, eds. Victor-
ian Criticism of the Novel.
  P. Boumelha, 617(TLS):10Oct86-1141
Eiko Ishioka. Eiko by Eiko.
  M. Nesbit, 59:Mar85-132
Eisele, U. Die Struktur des modernen
deutschen Romans.
  J.H. Petersen, 680(ZDP):Band104Heft4-
  625
Eisenberg, D. Romance of Chivalry in the
Spanish Golden Age.*
  F. Márquez Villanueva, 545(RPh):Feb85-
  415
Eisenberg, D. Transactions in a Foreign
Currency.
  N. Shack, 617(TLS):4Jul86-733
  B. Shacochis, 441:9Mar86-19
  R. Towers, 453(NYRB):26Jun86-32
Eisenhower, D. Eisenhower: At War 1943-
1945.
  T. Draper, 453(NYRB):25Sep86-30
  T. Draper, 453(NYRB):9Oct86-34
  T. Draper, 453(NYRB):23Oct86-61
  A. Schlesinger, Jr., 441:14Sep86-1
  R.F. Weigley, 61:Aug86-85
Eisenhower, D.D. Ike's Letters to a
Friend, 1941-1958.* (R. Griffith, ed)
  J.E. Ferling, 377:Nov85-211
Eisenhower, J.N. Pat Nixon.
  J. Woodruff, 441:30Nov86-12
Eisenmeier, E. Adalbert-Stifter-Biblio-
graphie. (Vol 2)
  P.H. Zoldester, 301(JEGP):Oct85-611
Eisenmeier, E. Adalbert-Stifter-Biblio-
graphie. (Vol 3)
  L.D. Wells, 400(MLN):Apr85-702
  P.H. Zoldester, 301(JEGP):Oct85-611
Eisenstadt, S.N. The Transformation of
Israeli Society.
  B. Wasserstein, 617(TLS):10Oct86-1123
Eisenstadt, S.N. and O. Ahimeir, eds. The
Welfare State and Its Aftermath.*
  K-K.T., 185:Jul86-916
Eisenstein, S.M. Immoral Memories.*
  L. Landrum, 115:Spring85-275
  R. Taylor, 617(TLS):27Jun86-716
Eisenstein, S.M. On the Composition of
the Short Fiction Scenario. Eisenstein
2. Eisenstein 3. (J. Leyda, ed of last
two)
  R. Taylor, 617(TLS):27Jun86-716
Eisinger, E.M. and M.W. McCarty, eds.
Colette.
  D. Coward, 208(FS):Jul85-363
Eisler, B. Private Lives.
  A. Barnet, 441:6Jul86-15
Eisner, R. How Real Is the Federal
Deficit?
  J.H. Makin, 441:17Aug86-15
  J. Tobin, 453(NYRB):25Sep86-43
Eiximenis, F. Lo libre de les dones.* (F.
Naccarato, ed; rev by C. Wittlin and A.
Comas)
  C.B. Faulhaber, 545(RPh):Aug84-124
van Ek, J.A. and N.J. Robat. The Stu-
dent's Grammar of English.
  L.V. Zuck, 351(LL):Dec85-585
Ekstrom, M. Death's Midwives.
  J. Humphreys, 441:16Feb86-29
Elam, K. Shakespeare's Universe of Dis-
course.
  D. Birch, 610:Autumn85-239
                            [continued]

[continuing]
  B.G. Lyons, 533:Spring86-147
  A.L. Magnusson, 539:May86-229
  J.A. Porter, 570(SQ):Winter85-505
Elbaum, B. and W. Lazonick, eds. The
Decline of the British Economy.
  D. Carlton, 617(TLS):24Oct86-1184
Elbert, S.H. and M.K. Pukui. Hawaiian
Grammar.
  G.F. Meier, 682(ZPSK):Band38Heft6-756
Elder, W.V. 3d and L. Bartlett. John Shaw.
  C.V. Hershey, 658:Spring85-86
Elderfield, J. The Drawings of Henri
Matisse.*
  J. Klein, 127:Winter85-359
Eldredge, N. Time Frames.*
  B. Halstead, 362:22May86-31
Eldridge, C.C., ed. British Imperialism
in the Nineteenth Century.
  J. Springhall, 637(VS):Summer86-633
Elert, C-C., I. Johansson and E. Strangert,
eds. Nordic Prosody III.*
  I. Lehiste, 361:Sep85-92
Elgin, D.D. The Comedy of the Fantastic.
  L. Basney, 395(MFS):Winter85-848
  G.K. Wolfe, 561(SFS):Nov85-334
Elgin, S.H. The Gentle Art of Verbal Self-
Defense.
  J.L. Colson, 351(LL):Jun85-315
Eliade, M. Briser le toit de la maison.
  A.M. Piatigorsky, 617(TLS):26Sep86-
  1074
Eliade, M. A History of Religious Ideas.
(Vol 3)
  J. Loudon, 469:Vol 11No3-94
  A.M. Piatigorsky, 617(TLS):26Sep86-
  1074
Elias, A.C., Jr. Swift at Moor Park.*
  C. Rawson, 541(RES):May85-385
Elias, J.A. Plato's Defence of Poetry.
  R. McKim, 124:Jan-Feb86-208
Elias, N. The Court Society.
  R. Helgerson, 551(RenQ):Autumn85-557
Eliasson, S., ed. Theoretical Issues in
Contrastive Phonology.
  B.J. Wenk, 353:Vol23No1-173
Eliav-Feldon, M. Realistic Utopias.*
  T.R. Knox, 568(SCN):Spring-Summer85-12
  R. Robbins, 447(N&Q):Jun84-262
Eliot, G. The Lifted Veil.
  G. Levine, 441:13Apr86-12
Eliot, G. Selections from George Eliot's
Letters.* (G.S. Haight, ed)
  R. Benvenuto, 115:Summer85-385
Elkhadem, S. The York Companion to Themes
and Motifs of World Literature: Mythol-
ogy, History and Folklore.
  M. Hugues, 549(RLC):Jan-Mar85-83
Elkin, S. Early Elkin.
  R. Cohen, 441:18May86-24
Elkin, S. Stanley Elkin's The Magic King-
dom.*
  M. Martone, 152(UDQ):Summer85-118
  42(AR):Fal185-503
Elkington, J. The Gene Factory.*
  T. Monmaney, 441:9Feb86-25
Elledge, S. E.B. White.*
  295(JML):Nov85-568
Ellerbee, L. "And So It Goes."
  N. Hollander, 441:11May86-9
Elliot, A. On the Appian Way.*
  M. O'Neill, 493:Jan85-61

Elliott, A.G., ed and trans. Seven
Medieval Latin Comedies.
R.P. Sonkowsky, 124:Mar-Apr86-281
Elliott, A.G. The "Vie de Saint Alexis"
in the Twelfth and Thirteenth Centuries.
A. Foulet, 589:Jul85-741
T.D. Hemming, 208(FS):Jul85-317
Elliott, D.W.P., ed. The Third Indochina
Conflict.
D. Pike, 302:Vol21No1-98
Elliott, E., ed. American Writers of the
Early Republic.
E. Emerson, 165(EAL):Winter86/87-276
Elliott, E. Revolutionary Writers.*
J. Tyler, 447(N&Q):Mar84-141
Elliott, I.M. Batik.*
B. Scott, 39:Dec85-504
Elliott, J. Dr. Gruber's Daughter.
M. Stimpson, 617(TLS):19Sep86-1029
Elliott, J.H. The Count-Duke of Olivares.
R. Carr, 453(NYRB):20Nov86-39
H. Kamen, 617(TLS):28Nov86-1352
H. Stone, 441:16Nov86-25
Elliott, J.P., K.W. Staggs and R.D.
Madison - see Cooper, J.F.
Elliott, M. Partners in Revolution.*
D.B. Smith, 174(Éire):Spring85-156
Elliott, M. The Willow Street Kids.
M. Warnock, 617(TLS):31Oct86-1212
Elliott, R.W.V. Thomas Hardy's English.*
M. Bath, 637(VS):Winter86-319
K. Sørensen, 179(ES):Aug85-375
Elliott, T.G. Ammianus Marcellinus and
Fourth Century History.
J. Szidat, 487:Spring85-92
Ellis, A.T. Home Life.
C. Brown, 617(TLS):27Jun86-719
Ellis, A.T. and T. Pitt-Aikens. Secrets
of Strangers.
C. Rycroft, 617(TLS):19Dec86-1418
Ellis, B.E. Less than Zero.*
A. Jenkins, 617(TLS):28Feb86-216
D. Pinckney, 453(NYRB):29May86-30
Ellis, C. Age of Exploration.
M. Harmon, 272(IUR):Autumn85-234
Ellis, J.M. One Fairy Story Too Many.*
R.B. Bottigheimer, 221(GQ):Winter85-
144
G.K. Zalazar, 590:Dec85-127
Ellis, K. Cuba's Nicolás Guillén.*
E. Busto Ogden, 240(HR):Autumn85-514
M.P. Predmore, 627(UTQ):Summer85-504
Ellis, P.J. The Poetry of Emilio Prados.*
D.K. Benson, 400(MLN):Mar85-436
Ellis, R. and W. Cronkite. North by North-
east.
P-L. Adams, 61:Oct86-103
Ellis, S. The Borzoi Control.
N. Callendar, 441:28Dec86-15
Ellis, S. Dante and English Poetry.
C.P. Brand, 278(IS):Vol40-113
Ellison, D.R. The Reading of Proust.*
F.C. St. Aubyn, 207(FR):Feb86-471
Ellison, H.J., ed. Soviet Policy toward
Western Europe.
A. Stent, 550(RusR):Apr85-216
Ellison, J. Emerson's Romantic Style.*
G.M. Johnson, 27(AL):Oct85-491
J. Michael, 223:Fall85-304
J. Myerson, 432(NEQ):Sep85-471
Ellison, J. A Fine Excess.*
H. Benedict, 441:8Jun86-36

Ellison, R. Going to the Territory.
P-L. Adams, 61:Aug86-91
G.S. Johnston, 129:Dec86-71
J.E. Wideman, 441:3Aug86-15
Ellison, R.C. Bibb County, Alabama: The
First Hundred Years, 1818-1918.
G.W. Hubbs, 9(AlaR):Apr85-136
Ellmann, R. Samuel Beckett.
A. Jenkins, 617(TLS):14Nov86-1281
Ellmann, R. James Joyce.* (rev)
C. Owens, 174(Éire):Summer85-150
H. Pyle, 541(RES):May85-312
Ellroy, J. Suicide Hill.
N. Callendar, 441:6Jul86-21
Ellul, J. Perspectives on our Age.
H.T. Wilson, 488:Sep85-349
Ellwein, T., T. Herrmann and K. Stapf -
see Stachowiak, H.
Elman, B.A. From Philosophy to Philology.
J. Spence, 453(NYRB):16Jan86-41
Elmessiri, A.M., ed and trans. The Pales-
tinian Wedding.
D. Hopwood, 294:Vol 16-146
Elon, F. Self-Made.*
M. O'Neill, 493:Apr85-54
van Els, T. and others. Applied Linguis-
tics and the Learning and Teaching of
Foreign Languages.
M.E. Call, 399(MLJ):Winter85-426
P. Westney, 257(IRAL):Aug85-255
El Saffar, R. Beyond Fiction.*
P.N. Dunn, 238:May85-300
R.D. Pope, 240(HR):Autumn85-488
639(VQR):Winter85-16
Elsen, A.E. Rodin's "Thinker" and the
Dilemmas of Modern Public Sculpture.
"The Gates of Hell" by Auguste Rodin.
T. Hilton, 617(TLS):28Mar86-324
Elshtain, J.B. Public Man, Private Woman.*
P. Allen, 543:Sep84-118
Elster, J. Making Sense of Marx.*
A. Ryan, 617(TLS):25Apr86-437
Elster, J. Sour Grapes.*
J. Bishop, 63:Jun85-245
Elstun, E.N. Richard Beer-Hoffman.*
M. Sonnenfeld, 221(GQ):Summer85-466
Elsworth, J.D. Andrey Bely.*
V.H. Bennett, 558(RLJ):Fall84-292
S.J. Rabinowitz, 104(CASS):Summer85-
217
A. Steinberg, 575(SEER):Jul85-439
R.D.B. Thomson, 402(MLR):Jan85-252
Elton, G.R. F.W. Maitland.*
N. Annan, 453(NYRB):13Feb86-31
R. Jann, 637(VS):Summer86-648
R. Mayne, 176:Jul/Aug86-48
S.F.C. Milsom, 617(TLS):28Feb86-225
H.G. Pitt, 364:Oct85-96
Éluard, P. Anthologie Éluard. (C. Scott,
ed)
R. Adamson, 402(MLR):Apr85-473
R. Cardinal, 208(FS):Jan85-108
Éluard, P. Lettres à Gala.
R. Cardinal, 617(TLS):26Dec86-1440
J-C. Gateau, 450(NRF):Feb85-78
Éluard, P. and J. Miró. A Toute Épreuve.
J.H. Matthews, 593:Spring85-75
Elvers, R. - see Mendelssohn, F.
Elvin, L. Bishop and Son, Organ Builders.
N. Thistlethwaite, 415:Apr85-240
Elwert, T.W. Italienische Metrik. (2nd
ed)
R. Baehr, 547(RF):Band97Heft4-488

Emad, P. Heidegger and the Phenomenology
of Values.*
S.W. Davis, 321:Vol 19No3-247
Emanuel, L. Hotel Fiesta.
A. Hudgins, 434:Summer86-526
G. Schulman, 491:Nov85-112
639(VQR):Winter85-28
Embree, L. - see Gurwitsch, A.
Emeneau, M.B. Toda Grammar and Texts.*
S.B. Steever, 353:Vol23No3-510
Emerson, C. - see Bakhtin, M.
Emerson, E. The Authentic Mark Twain.*
E.N. Harbert, 587(SAF):Autumn85-246
J.S. Leonard, 392:Fall85-471
J. Steinbrink, 432(NEQ):Mar85-142
J.S. Tuckey, 395(MFS):Summer85-395
639(VQR):Winter85-12
Emerson, E.T. The Letters of Ellen Tucker
Emerson.* (E.E.W. Gregg, ed) The Life
of Lidian Jackson Emerson. (D.B.
Carpenter, ed)
P. Cole, 591(SIR):Fall85-413
Emerson, E.W. Nervous Laughter.
N. Callendar, 441:16Mar86-31
Emerson, G.J. John Dewey's Concept of
Education as a Growth Process.
M.L. Simmons, Jr., 619:Summer85-455
Emerson, K.L. Wives and Daughters.
C.R. Swift, 551(RenQ):Summer85-358
Emerson, R.L., G. Girard and R. Runte, eds.
Man and Nature/L'Homme et la nature.*
P. Rogers, 541(RES):Aug85-431
Emerson, R.W. The Collected Works of
Ralph Waldo Emerson.* (Vol 3) (J.
Slater, A.R. Ferguson and J.F. Carr, eds)
P.F. Gura, 534(RALS):Autumn83-218
Emerson, R.W. Emerson in His Journals.*
(J. Porte, ed)
J.S. Martin, 106:Summer85-205
Emerson, R.W. Essays and Lectures. (J.
Porte, ed)
529(QQ):Summer85-438
Emerson, R.W. The Journals and Miscella-
neous Notebooks. (Vols 15 and 16)
D. Robinson, 534(RALS):Spring83-1
Emiliani, A. Federico Barocci (Urbino
1535-1612).
N. Penny, 617(TLS):26Sep86-1059
Emmerick, R.E. The Siddhasāra of Ravigup-
ta. (Vol 2)
J.W. de Jong, 259(IIJ):Jul85-226
Emmerick, R.E. and P.O. Skjaervø. Studies
in the Vocabulary of Khotanese I.
M.J. Dresden, 318(JAOS):Oct-Dec84-770
O. von Hinüber, 259(IIJ):Apr85-139
Emmerig, T. Joseph Riepel (1709-1782).
N.R. Knouse, 143:Issue37/38-221
Emmerson, R.K. Antichrist in the Middle
Ages.
J.A. Nelson, 345(KRQ):Vol32No3-331
Emmet, D. The Effectiveness of Causes.*
L.B. McHenry, 543:Dec85-351
Emmons, T. The Formation of Political
Parties and the First National Elections
in Russia.*
G.A. Hosking, 575(SEER):Apr85-305
Empedocles. The Extant Fragments.* (M.R.
Wright, ed and trans)
C. Emlyn-Jones, 303(JoHS):Vol 105-183
G.L. Koniaris, 24:Summer85-242
W.J. Verdenius, 394:Vol38fasc3/4-400

Empson, W. Essays on Shakespeare. (D.B.
Pirie, ed)
A.P. Slater, 617(TLS):14Nov86-1271
Empson, W. The Royal Beasts and Other
Works. (J. Haffenden, ed)
I. Hamilton, 617(TLS):14Nov86-1272
Empson, W. The Structure of Complex Words.
Seven Types of Ambiguity. Some Versions
of Pastoral. Essays on Shakespeare.
A.S. Byatt, 176:Nov86-48
Empson, W. Using Biography.*
D. Fuller, 161(DUJ):Jun85-290
C. Norris, 577(SHR):Summer85-285
P. Robinson, 175:Autumn85-270
A. Shelston, 148:Spring85-71
Emsley, K. and C.M. Fraser. The Courts of
the County Palatinate of Durham.
P. Rushton, 161(DUJ):Jun85-259
Ende, M. Mirror in the Mirror.
L. Heron, 362:24Jul86-26
Engberg, R. - see Muir, J.
Engberg-Pedersen, T. Aristotle's Theory
of Moral Insight.*
P. Corrigan, 543:Dec84-384
A.R. Mele, 482(PhR):Apr85-273
M. Woods, 123:Vol35No1-73
Engel, B.A. Mothers and Daughters.*
D. Field, 550(RusR):Apr85-208
Engel, E. and M.F. King. The Victorian
Novel before Victoria.
C. Gallagher, 637(VS):Spring86-463
G.B. Tennyson, 445(NCF):Jun85-117
Engel, M., ed. The Guardian Book of
Cricket.
S. Fry, 362:18/25Dec86-55
Engel, M. The Tattooed Woman.
A. Boston, 617(TLS):18Jul86-792
Engelberg, E. Bismarck, Urpreusse und
Reichsgründer.
G.A. Craig, 453(NYRB):25Sep86-62
Engelkamp, J. and H.D. Zimmer. Dynamic
Aspects of Language Processing.*
P. Erdmann, 257(IRAL):Nov85-336
Engell, J., ed. Johnson and his Age.*
J. Abbott, 324:Nov86-843
A. McDermott, 148:Winter85-86
Engell, J. and W.J. Bate - see Coleridge,
S.T.
Engen, R. Richard Doyle.
R.T. Matthews, 635(VPR):Winter85-157
Engen, R.K. Dictionary of Victorian Wood
Engravers.
L.J. De Freitas, 617(TLS):24Jan86-96
T. Russell-Cobb, 324:Jul86-537
England, J., ed. Hispanic Studies in Hon-
our of Frank Pierce Presented by Former
and Present Members of the Department of
Hispanic Studies in the University of
Sheffield.
G.A. Davies, 86(BHS):Apr85-191
Englander, D. Landlord and Tenant in
Urban Britain 1838-1918.
P.H.J.H. Gosden, 637(VS):Spring85-550
Engle, M.M. Tzintzuntzan.
V. Provenzano, 404:Winter-Spring85-71
Engman, J. Keeping Still, Mountain.
L. Forestier, 496:Winter86-245
Engman, M. St. Petersburg och Finland.*
J.G. Rice, 563(SS):Spring85-201
Enkvist, N.E., ed. Coherence and Composi-
tion.
K. Allan, 350:Sep86-734

Euripides. Euripidis Fabulae. (Vol 1)
(J. Diggle, ed)
  J. Irigoin, 555:Vol59fasc1-101
"European Bibliography of Soviet, East
European and Slavonic Studies." (Vol 5)
(M. Armand and M. Aymard, eds)
  J. Freeman, 575(SEER):Jul85-476
von Euw, A. and J.M. Polotzek. Die Hand-
schriften der Sammlung Ludwig.
  P. Verdier, 589:Jan85-203
Evanier, D. The One-Star Jew.*
  N. Yood, 390:Nov85-57
Evans, A.C. Sutton Hoo Ship Burial.
  J. Graham-Campbell, 617(TLS):12Sep86-
1008
Evans, B.L. and G. - see Lloyd Evans, B.
and G.
Evans, C. Frontier Theatre.*
  R. Plant, 529(QQ):Winter85-740
Evans, C.S. Kierkegaard's Fragments and
Postscript.
  J.W. Elrod, 543:Sep84-120
Evans, G. Collected Papers.
  M. Sainsbury, 617(TLS):7Mar86-253
Evans, G. John Grierson and the National
Film Board.
  D. Clandfield, 627(UTQ):Summer85-523
  E. Sussex, 707:Winter84/85-72
Evans, G. Nightvision.
  J. Penberthy, 617(TLS):18Apr86-430
Evans, G. The Varieties of Reference.*
(J. McDowell, ed)
  M. Devitt, 63:Jun85-216
  R.M. Sainsbury, 393(Mind):Jan85-120
Evans, G.B. - see Shakespeare, W.
Evans, G.R. Alan of Lille.
  J. Jolivet, 542:Apr-Jun85-245
Evans, G.R. Augustine on Evil.
  D.M. Johnson, 529(QQ):Spring85-209
Evans, H. The Patio Garden.
  S. Brownmiller, 441:1Jun86-31
Evans, J. - see White, E.W.
Evans, J.L. Russia and the Khanates of
Central Asia to 1865. Mission of N.P.
Ignat'ev to Khiva and Bukhara, 1858.
  A. Bodger, 575(SEER):Oct85-604
Evans, J.M. The Road from Horton.*
  A-L. Scoufos, 179(ES):Aug85-368
Evans, M., ed. Black Women Writers (1950-
1980).
  K. Byerman, 395(MFS):Winter85-730
Evans, N. The East Anglian Linen Industry.
  J. Fisher, 637(VS):Summer86-644
Evans, P. Ari.
  A. Howard, 617(TLS):19Sep86-1027
  L. Wayne, 441:15Jun86-21
Evans, S.M. and H.C. Boyte. Free Spaces.
  B.R. Barber, 441:9Mar86-15
Evans, T. Prairie.
  A. Grundberg, 441:7Dec86-21
Even, L. Maine de Biran: Critique de
Locke.
  J. Bernhardt, 319:Jul86-413
  M. Phillips, 192(EP):Oct-Dec85-556
  A. Reix, 542:Jan-Mar85-35
Everest, K., ed. Shelley Revalued.*
  J. Buxton, 541(RES):Nov85-582
  D. Hughes, 591(SIR):Winter85-565
  W. Keach, 661(WC):Fall85-193
Everett, B. Poets in Their Time.
  P. Porter, 617(TLS):26Dec86-1441

Everitt, A. Landscape and Community in
England.
  D.M. Palliser, 617(TLS):1Aug86-846
"Everyday American English Dictionary."
  T. Goldstein, 35(AS):Fall85-258
Ewart, G. The Ewart Quarto.*
  T. Eagleton, 565:Winter84/85-68
Ewart, G. The Gavin Ewart Show.
  B. Bennett, 441:17Aug86-26
Ewart, G. The Young Pobble's Guide to his
Toes.*
  B. Bennett, 441:17Aug86-26
  N. Jenkins, 493:Apr85-52
  H. Lomas, 364:Jun85-89
Ewert, C. Spanisch-Islamiche Systeme sich
kreuzender Bögen. (Vol 3)
  R. Hillenbrand, 59:Jun85-265
Ewert, M. Die problematische Kritik der
Ideologie.
  W. van Reijen, 342:Band76Heft2-225
Ewing, J.H. Canada Home. (M.H. and T.E.
Blom, eds)
  F. Cogswell, 178:Sep85-366
  C. MacMillan, 198:Spring85-91
Ewing, W.A. The Photographic Art of
Hoyningen-Huene.
  A. Grundberg, 441:7Dec86-21
Ezekiel. Ezechiel: The "Exagoge" of
Ezekiel. (H. Jacobson, ed and trans)
  W.G. Arnott, 303(JoHS):Vol 105-192
Ezergailis, I. Women Writers.*
  S.D. Shattuck, 538(RAL):Winter85-607
Ezerskaia, B. Mastera.
  L. Loseff, 550(RusR):Apr85-198


F.A.D.C. Triste deleytaçión. (R. Rohland
de Langbehn, ed)
  E.M. Gerli, 304(JHP):Winter85-169
Fabbri, P. Tre secoli de musica a Ravenna.
  D. Arnold, 410(M&L):Jul85-275
Fabian, B. Buch, Bibliothek und geistes-
wissenschaftliche Forschung.*
  78(BC):Summer85-145
Fabian, B., ed. Friedrich Nicolai 1733-
1811.
  W. Albrecht, 654(WB):8/1985-1399
  P.M. Mitchell, 301(JEGP):Oct85-605
Fabian, M.H. Joseph Wright, American
Artist, 1756-1793.
  K. Manthorne, 127:Winter85-375
Fabiny, T., ed. Shakespeare and the
Emblem.
  R.M. Frye, 130:Spring85-89
"Fables from Old French."* (N.R. Shapiro,
trans; H. Needler, ed)
  M.J. Schenck, 545(RPh):May85-548
Fabre, G. Drumbeats, Masks, and Metaphor.*
  H.S. Anderson, 529(QQ):Spring85-170
Fabricant, C. Swift's Landscape.*
  F. Doherty, 541(RES):Nov85-572
Faerch, C., K. Haastrup and R. Phillipson.
Learner Language and Language Learning.
  M. Saville-Troike, 399(MLJ):Spring85-
78
Fagundes Telles, L. Tigrela and Other
Stories.
  R. Burgin, 441:4May86-40
Fähnrich, H., ed. Sprachen Kaukasiens.
  B.G. Hewitt, 361:Apr85-333
Fåhraeus, A-M. Two Kinds of Syntactic-
Semantic Value-Loading in English.
  M. Viel, 189(EA):Apr-Jun86-198

116

Fehérvári, G. and Y.H. Safadi. 1400 Years of Islamic Art.
  R. Hillenbrand, 59:Jun85-265
Fehn, A.C. - see Benn, G.
Fehr, K. Conrad Ferdinand Meyer.*
  G. Vitt-Maucher, 133:Band17Heft3/4-353
Feierstein, R. Escala uno en cincuenta.
  A. Avellaneda, 238:Dec85-787
Feigin, L., ed. Russian Jazz.
  L. Birnbaum, 441:13Jul86-19
  J. Škvorecký, 617(TLS):16May86-534
Feijoo, L.I. - see under Iglesias Feijoo, L.
Feilchenfeldt, K. - see Varnhagen, R.L.
Fein, D.A. A Reading of Villon's "Testament."
  M.R. Blakeslee, 207(FR):Mar86-606
  J. Fox, 208(FS):Jan85-64
Fein, R. Medical Care, Medical Costs.
  R. Pear, 441:16Nov86-22
Feinberg, B. and R. Kasrils. Bertrand Russell's America. (Vol 2)
  N. Griffin, 556:Summer85-72
Feingold, M. The Mathematicians' Apprenticeship.*
  A.G. Debus, 551(RenQ):Summer85-335
Feinstein, H.M. Becoming William James.
  S. Haack, 432(NEQ):Mar85-139
  H.S. Levinson, 619:Summer85-449
  D.J. Murray, 529(QQ):Autumn85-606
  L. Willson, 569(SR):Spring85-279
Feirstein, B. Nice Guys Sleep Alone.
  B. Lovenheim, 441:21Sep86-27
Fekete, É. and É. Karádi. Georg Lukács.
  D. Löffler, 654(WB):4/1985-694
Felber, A. A Reverse Index of Patristic Greek.
  A. Pourkier, 555:Vol59fasc1-129
Feld, A.J., M. O'Hare and J.M.D. Schuster. Patrons Despite Themselves.
  F.V. O'Connor, 127:Winter84-393
  P. Swords, 476:Summer84-82
Feldbrugge, F. and W. Simon, eds. Perspectives on Soviet Law for the 1980s.
  E. Huskey, 550(RusR):Oct85-403
Feldhaus, A. The Religious System of the Mahānubhāva Sect.
  B.G. Gokhale, 293(JASt):Feb85-422
Feldman, E. Conjugal Rites.
  E. Abeel, 441:16Feb86-20
Feldman, I. All of Us Here.
  D. Kirby, 441:12Oct86-32
Feldman, L.H. Josephus and Modern Scholarship (1937-1980).
  J.N. Birdsall, 123:Vol35No1-24
Feldman, M. Morton Feldman Essays. (W. Zimmermann, ed)
  C. Newman and H. Skempton, 607:Sep85-41
Feldman, S., ed. Take Two.
  B. Testa, 627(UTQ):Summer85-527
Felix, Z., ed. Erich Heckel, 1883-1970.
  S. Rainbird, 90:Oct85-726
Fell, A. Every Move You Make.
  P. Lewis, 565:Winter84/85-42
Fell, M. The Persistence of Memory.*
  E. Butscher, 496:Spring85-47
Fellini, F. Moraldo in the City and A Journey with Anita. (J.C. Stubbs, ed and trans)
  G. Marrone, 276:Summer85-137
Fellows, J. Ruskin's Maze.*
  M. Hardman, 677(YES):Vol 15-321

Fellows, R.A. Sir Reginald Blomfield.*
  J. Frew, 324:Mar86-272
Felman, S. Writing and Madness.
  B.L. Knapp, 446(NCFS):Spring-Summer86-405
  M. Steig, 529(QQ):Winter85-857
Femia, J.V. Gramsci's Political Thought.*
  W. Hartley, 275(IQ):Summer/Fall84-216
"Une Femme à la recherche d'une illusion et cinq autres nouvelles." (M. Orange, trans)
  D. Bouchez, 293(JASt):Feb85-414
Fenady, A.J. The Summer of Jack London.
  D.L. Walker, 649(WAL):Feb86-361
Fender, S. American Literature in Context 1620-1830.
  H. Cohen, 617(TLS):21Nov86-1302
Fénelon. Letter to the French Academy. (B. Warnick, ed and trans)
  J-P. Dens, 207(FR):Oct85-129
Fénelon. Oeuvres I. (J. Le Brun, ed)
  J. Lafond, 535(RHL):Sep/Oct85-873
Fenger, H. Kierkegaard, the Myths and their Origins.
  H.A. Durfee, 543:Dec84-387
Fenley, G.W. Compositions illustrées.
  C.F. Demaray, 207(FR):Feb86-495
Fennelly, T. The Glory Hole Murders.
  N. Callendar, 441:19Jan86-17
Fenoaltea, D. "Si haulte Architecture."*
  H.H. Glidden, 188(ECr):Spring85-88
  F. Lecercle, 535(RHL):May/Jun85-482
Fenton, J. - see May, S.
Feo, M. - see "Quaderni petrarcheschi"
Fera, V. Una ignota "Expositio Suetoni" del Poliziano.
  M.L. Doglio, 228(GSLI):Vol162fasc519-458
Ferber, R. Platos Idee des Guten.
  J. Barnes, 520:Vol130No2-211
  D. Frede, 543:Dec85-353
  Y. Lafrance, 154:Winter85-749
Fergus, J. Jane Austen and the Didactic Novel.*
  B. Roth, 594:Summer85-223
Ferguson, C.A. and S.B. Heath, eds. Language in the U.S.A.*
  J.C. Beal, 402(MLR):Oct85-896
Ferguson, K.E. The Feminist Case Against Bureaucracy.
  S.K. Foss, 583:Winter86-184
Ferguson, M.W. Trials of Desire.
  T. Cave, 131(CL):Spring85-182
  K. Duncan-Jones, 541(RES):Nov85-560
  J. Timpane, 405(MP):Aug85-67
Ferguson, N. Bars of America.
  R. Kaveney, 617(TLS):22Aug86-920
  J. Turner, 362:7Aug86-25
Ferguson, R.A. Law and Letters in American Culture.*
  T. Wortham, 445(NCF):Dec85-369
  L. Ziff, 432(NEQ):Mar85-117
Ferguson, R.H. Laforgue y Lugones.
  G. Meo Zilio, 547(RF):Band97Heft1-121
  P. Verdevoye, 92(BH):Jul-Dec84-576
Ferguson, T. Onyx John.
  C. Rooke, 376:Jun85-126
Ferguson, T. and J. Rogers. Right Turn.
  A. Clymer, 441:14Sep86-30
Ferguson, W. Freedom and Other Fictions.
  R.M. Davis, 573(SSF):Summer85-358

119

Ferguson, W.M., with J.Q. Royce. Maya Ruins of Mexico in Color.
R. Okey, 37:Sep-Oct85-58
Fergusson, P. Architecture of Solitude.
M.H. Caviness, 377:Jul85-122
D. Clelland, 46:May85-80
C.R. Dodwell, 39:May85-351
L. Grant, 90:May85-306
Ferlinghetti, L. Over All Obscene Boundaries.
S. Scobie, 376:Jun85-131
Fermor, P.L. Between the Woods and the Water.
P. Binding, 362:11Dec86-23
J. Ure, 617(TLS):17Oct86-1154
Fernald, D. The Hans Legacy.*
T.A. Sebeok, 567:Vol57No1/2-117
Fernández, A., R. Munoa and J. Rabasco. Enciclopedia de la plata española y virreinal americana.
M.J. Sanz, 48:Apr-Jun85-167
Fernández, J. Lecturas fáciles: Abra su propio negocio. (J. Olivio Jiménez, ed)
L.S. Glaze, 399(MLJ):Spring85-108
Fernández, J.U. and J.C. Brasas - see under Urrea Fernández, J. and J.C. Brasas
Fernández, L.S. - see under Suárez Fernández, L.
Fernández, M.T.G.D. - see under González de Garay Fernández, M.T.
Fernández, P.H. Ideario etimológico de Miguel de Unamuno.
N.R. Orringer, 552(REH):Oct85-148
Fernández, R.G. La vida es un special $1/3Ø.75.*
A. Fernández-Vázquez, 140(CH):Vol7No2-175
Fernández-Cañadas de Greenwood, P. Pastoral Poetics.
R. Early, 552(REH):Jan85-146
Fernández Cifuentes, L. Teoría y mercado de la novela en España.
C.A. Longhurst, 86(BHS):Jul85-312
Ferrand, M. and M. González - see Arquillo Torres, F. and others
Ferrante, J.M. The Political Vision of the "Divine Comedy."
P. Shaw, 617(TLS):31Jan86-122
Ferraro, G.A., with L.B. Francke. Ferraro: My Story.*
J.R. Adams, 129:Feb86-34
Ferrars, E.X. I Met Murder.
442(NY):18Aug86-76
Ferrater Mora, J. Modos de hacer filosofía.
A. Reix, 542:Oct-Dec85-550
Ferrell, R.H. - see Hagerty, J.C.
Ferreras, J.I. La estructura paródica del "Quijote."
P. Waley, 86(BHS):Apr85-200
Ferreras, J.I. and others. Narrativa de la Restauración.
V.A. Chamberlin, 238:May85-303
Ferreyrolles, G. Pascal et la raison du politique.
M. Adam, 542:Jul-Sep85-318
F. Assaf, 475:Vol 12No23-701
Ferreyrolles, G. Blaise Pascal — "Les Provinciales."
F. Assaf, 475:Vol 12No23-701
L.A. MacKenzie, Jr., 207(FR):Oct85-128

Ferris, P. Dylan Thomas.
C. Rawson, 617(TLS):2May86-475
Ferris, P. - see Thomas, D.
Ferris, S.V. and E.S. Hoppe. Scalpels and Sabers.
L. Milazzo, 584(SWR):Autumn85-547
Ferris, W., ed. Afro-American Folk Art and Crafts.
T. Harris, 650(WF):Jan85-52
Ferruolo, S.C. The Origins of the University.
D.E. Luscombe, 617(TLS):10Jan86-46
Ferry, A. The "Inward" Language.*
J.K. Gardiner, 301(JEGP):Apr85-259
R.L. Levao, 551(RenQ):Spring85-177
W. Weiss, 156(ShJW):Jahrbuch1985-213
Ferry, L. and A. Renaut. La Pensée 68.
A. Besançon, 176:Jul/Aug86-33
Fessaguet, C. L'Héritier.
R. Knee, 207(FR):Apr86-813
R. de Martinoir, 450(NRF):May85-83
Festa-McCormick, D. Proustian Optics of Clothes.*
R. Bales, 402(MLR):Oct85-948
C.G.H. Mann, 67:May85-76
J.P. Plottel, 446(NCFS):Spring-Summer86-385
J.T. Rosasco, 546(RR):Mar85-222
Fet, A. I Have Come to You to Greet You.* (J. Greene, ed and trans)
R.F. Gustafson, 550(RusR):Jan85-97
Fetzer, G. Wertungsprobleme in der Trivialliteraturforschung.
K. Hasselbach, 406:Spring85-91
Fetzer, J.F. Clemens Brentano.
R.C. Conard, 406:Summer85-226
Fetzer, J.H. Scientific Knowledge.
M. Tiles, 518:Jan85-39
Feuchtwanger, L. Dramen. (H. Dahlke, ed)
K. Kändler, 654(WB):6/1985-1044
Feuer, J., P. Kerr and T. Vahimagi, eds. MTM: "Quality Television."
E. Taylor, 18:Oct85-78
Feuerbach, L. Gesammelte Werke. (Vol 17) (W. Schuffenhauer, ed)
S. Dietzsch, 489(PJGG):Band92Heft2-438
"Feydeau, First to Last."
D. Devlin, 157:No155-49
Feyerabend, P. Wissenschaft als Kunst.
J. Koepp, 384:Apr85-334
Feynman, R.P. QED.
442(NY):24Mar86-125
Feynman, R.P., with R. Leighton. "Surely You're Joking, Mr. Feynman."* (E. Hutchings, ed)
P. Davies, 617(TLS):17Jan86-64
Ffinch, M. G.K. Chesterton.
H. Spurling, 617(TLS):15Aug86-885
Fichte, J.G. Fondement du droit naturel selon les principes de la doctrine de la science (1796-1797). (A. Renaut, ed and trans)
M. Adam, 542:Jul-Sep85-334
Fichte, J.G. Gesamtausgabe der Bayerischen Akademie der Wissenschaften.* (Pt 1, Vol 6 and Pt 2, Vol 6) (R. Lauth and H. Gliwitzky, with others, eds)
K. Gloy, 687:Apr-Jun85-314
Fichter, A. Poets Historical.*
C.P. Brand, 131(CL):Winter85-73
H. Cooper, 447(N&Q):Mar84-108
W.J. Kennedy, 403(MLS):Spring85-82
[continued]

[continuing]
K.M. Lea, 541(RES):May85-254
S. Weiner, 405(MP):Aug85-62
Fido, M. Murder Guide to London.
P.D. James, 617(TLS):9May86-508
Field, A. Nabokov.
D. Flower, 249(HudR):Spring85-152
Field, A. VN.
P-L. Adams, 61:Dec86-104
J. Conarroe, 441:2Nov86-7
Field, J. A Life of One's Own. An Exper-
iment in Leisure.
L. Gerend, 617(TLS):19Dec86-1418
Field, L. - see Wolfe, T.
Field, T. Maurice Barrès.
S. Wilson, 208(FS):Jul85-359
Fieldhouse, H. Good English Guide.
A. Tellier, 189(EA):Apr-Jun86-194
Fielding, G. The Women of Guinea Lane.
J.K.L. Walker, 617(TLS):29Aug86-933
Fielding, H. Amelia. (M.C. Battestin, ed)
C. Rawson, 83:Spring85-105
H. Reinhold, 38:Band103Heft3/4-502
P. Rogers, 402(MLR):Apr85-430
L. Speirs, 179(ES):Oct85-404
S. Varey, 566:Autumn85-70
Fielding, S. Remarks on Clarissa.
S. Soupel, 189(EA):Oct-Dec86-493
D. Womersley, 617(TLS):21Mar86-312
Fielding, X. - see Brenan, G. and R. Par-
tridge
Fields, K.E. Revival and Rebellion in
Colonial Central Africa.
R. Gray, 617(TLS):4Jul86-726
Figes, E. The Seven Ages.
M. Seymour, 617(TLS):16May86-535
Figes, E. Sex and Subterfuge.*
P. Boumelha, 541(RES):Feb85-101
Filin, F.P., ed. Russkij jazyk.
D.S. Worth, 279:Vol29-169
Fill, H. Katalog der Handschriften des
Benediktinerstiftes Kremsmünster. (Pt 1)
70:May/Jun85-170
Fillion, J. Pourquoi cracher sur la lune?
P. Merivale, 102(CanL):Winter84-101
Fillion, J. Un An de sursis pour Timi.
E. Cobley, 102(CanL):Winter84-108
Filliozat, J., ed and trans. Yogaśataka.
K.G. Zysk, 318(JAOS):Oct-Dec84-782
della Fina, G.M. Le antichità a Chiusi.*
N. Spivey, 313:Vol75-270
Finch, A. Stendhal, "La Chartreuse de
Parme."*
F.W.J. Hemmings, 402(MLR):Jul85-717
K.G. McWatters, 208(FS):Apr85-221
K. Ringger, 547(RF):Band97Heft2/3-323
Finch, K. and C. Putnam. The Care and
Preservation of Textiles.
B. Scott, 324:Nov86-847
Finch, S. Triad.
G. Jonas, 441:10Aug86-29
Findlay, J.M. People of Chance.
A. Boyer, 441:13Apr86-23
Findley, T. Dinner Along the Amazon.*
E. Thompson, 198:Autumn85-103
G. Woodcock, 102(CanL):Spring85-140
Findley, T. Not Wanted on the Voyage.*
D. Barbour, 102(CanL):Fall85-161
W.J. Keith, 198:Autumn85-82
C. Rooke, 376:Mar85-158
Fine, A. The Killjoy.
G. Mangan, 617(TLS):13Jun86-646

Fine, D., ed. Los Angeles in Fiction.
R.L. Buckland, 573(SSF):Fall85-492
J. Helbert, 649(WAL):Feb86-363
W.J. Palmer, 395(MFS):Winter85-755
Fine, E.C. The Folklore Text.
B. Grisch and A. Schwarz, 196:Band26
Heft3/4-354
Fine, G.A. Shared Fantasy.
B. Ellis, 292(JAF):Jul/Sep85-337
Fine, S. Frank Murphy: The Washington
Years.
C.W. McCurdy, 385(MQR):Winter86-141
Finegold, H. A Midrash on American Jewish
History.
M.W. Kiel, 287:Feb85-28
Fineman, J. Shakespeare's Perjured Eye.
R.M. Adams, 453(NYRB):6Nov86-50
de Finetti, B. Wahrscheinlichkeitstheorie.
D. Zittlau, 679:Band16Heft1-176
Finger, J.R. The Eastern Band of Chero-
kees 1819-1900.
H.L. Martin, 9(AlaR):Jan85-72
Fink, M. Pindarfragmente.*
J. Söring, 52:Band20Heft1-91
Finkelman, P. Slavery in the Courtroom.
70:May/Jun85-174
Finkelstein, M.J. The American Academic
Profession.*
A. Hacker, 453(NYRB):13Feb86-35
Finkielkraut, A. La sagesse de l'amour.
S. Plourde, 154:Autumn85-554
Finlayson, I. The Sixth Continent.
E. Toynton, 441:23Nov86-20
Finley, G. George Heriot.*
J. Murray, 529(QQ):Summer85-388
Finley, M.I. Ancient History.
S. Hornblower, 617(TLS):25Apr86-456
M. Lefkowitz, 441:30Mar86-12
Finley, M.I. L'Invention de la politique.
M. Jarrety, 450(NRF):Jul-Aug85-165
Finley, M.I. Politics in the Ancient
World.
R. Seager, 123:Vol35No1-103
Finley, M.I., D. Mack Smith and C.J.H.
Duggan. A History of Sicily.
I. Thomson, 362:4Dec86-26
Finn, C.E., Jr., D. Ravitch and R.T. Fan-
cher, eds. Against Mediocrity.
R. Berman, 289:Winter85-115
Finn, D. and C. Houser. Greek Monumental
Bronze Sculpture.
R. Higgins, 39:Jan85-68
Finné, J. La litterature Fantastique.
R. Cardinal, 529(QQ):Autumn85-549
Finnegan, W. Crossing the Line.
N. Rush, 441:21Sep86-7
L. Thompson, 453(NYRB):23Oct86-3
Finneran, R.J., ed. Recent Research on
Anglo-Irish Writers.*
H. Adams, 40(AEB):Vol8No3-220
Finneran, R.J. - see Yeats, W.B.
Finneran, R.J. - see "Yeats Annual"
Finney, B. - see Lawrence, D.H.
Finney, B.R. and E.M. Jones, eds.
Interstellar Migration and the Human
Experience.
D. King-Hele, 617(TLS):30May86-603
Finney, G. The Counterfeit Idyll.
B. Seaton, 446(NCFS):Fall-Winter85/86-
188
Finnis, J. Fundamentals of Ethics.*
G. Brown, 479(PhQ):Apr85-210
I.G. McFetridge, 393(Mind):Jan85-158

Finocchiaro, M. and S. Sako. Foreign Language Testing.
K.A. Mullen, 399(MLJ):Winter85-402
Finscher, L., ed. Ludwig van Beethoven.
B. Cooper, 410(M&L):Apr85-152
Fiore, R.L. Lazarillo de Tormes.
A. Blackburn, 238:Mar85-65
H. Mancing, 304(JHP):Winter85-175
Fiorentino, F. Dalla geografia all'autobiografia.
E. Balmas, 535(RHL):Mar/Apr85-302
Firchow, P.E. The End of Utopia.
A. Dommergues, 189(EA):Oct-Dec86-495
S.M. Fjellman, 561(SFS):Jul85-222
H.H. Watts, 395(MFS):Summer85-343
Firmage, G.J. - see Cummings, E.E.
Firmat, G.P. - see under Pérez Firmat, G.
Firmicus. Firmicus Maternus, "L'Erreur des Religions Païennes." (R. Turcan, ed)
J. Harries, 123:Vol35No1-50
Firpo, L., F. Francioni and G. Gaspari - see Beccaria, C.
Firpo, M. and D. Marcatto, eds. Il processo inquisitoriale del Cardinal Giovanni Morone. (Vol 2)
P.F. Grendler, 551(RenQ):Autumn85-523
Fischer, A., ed. English-Xhosa Dictionary.
J. Peires, 617(TLS):9May86-512
Fischer, B. Literatur und Politik.
P.M. Lützeler, 221(GQ):Winter85-125
Fischer, C. Italian Drawings in the J.F. Willumsen Collection.*
D. De Grazia, 380:Winter84-452
Fischer, D. Preventing War in the Nuclear Age.*
S.L., 185:Jan86-457
Fischer, H. Ehre, Hof und Abenteuer in Hartmanns "Iwein."
D.H. Green, 402(MLR):Apr85-484
Fischer, H., ed. Die Philosophie der Antike. (Vol 3)
H. Kuhn, 489(PJGG):Band92Heft1-178
Fischer, H. Sound-Producing Instruments in Oceania.
M. McLean, 187:Fall86-593
Fischer, H. Studien zur deutschen Märendichtung. (2nd ed rev by J. Janota)
J. Heinzle, 684(ZDA):Band114Heft2-53
S.L. Wailes, 133:Band17Heft3/4-314
Fischer, K-D. and D. Najock, eds. In "Pelagonii" Artem Veterinariam Concordantiae.
P. Flobert, 555:Vol59fasc1-147
Fischer, M. Does Deconstruction Make Any Difference?*
L. Stern, 290(JAAC):Spring86-295
Fischer, M.S. Nationale Images als Gegenstand Vergleichender Literaturgeschichte.*
V. Hell, 107(CRCL):Sep85-476
Fischer, M.S. Probleme internationaler Literaturrezeption.
A. Purdy, 107(CRCL):Sep85-561
Fischer, U. Der Einfluss des Englischen auf den deutschen Wortschatz im Bereich von Essen und Trinken.
K. Kehr, 685(ZDL):3/1985-408
Fischer-Lichte, E. Semiotik des Theaters.*
T. Kowzan, 567:Vol53No1/3-227
Fish, S. Is There a Text in This Class?*
L. Milic, 599:Fall85-385
Fisher, A. Africa Adorned.*
J. Distefano, 2(AfrA):May85-23

Fisher, C. and D. Richardson. August Strindberg: "Hemsöborna."*
C.S. McKnight, 563(SS):Spring85-224
Fisher, D. Morality and the Bomb.
L. Stevenson, 479(PhQ):Oct85-437
Fisher, L. Constitutional Conflicts between Congress and the President.*
A.S., 185:Jul86-913
Fisher, M. The Bright Face of Danger.
T.J. Binyon, 617(TLS):29Aug86-948
Fisher, P. Hard Facts.*
G. Davenport, 569(SR):Summer85-499
42(AR):Summer85-370
Fisher, P. Making Up Society.*
R. Ashton, 541(RES):May85-288
Fisher, R. A Furnace.
R. Sheppard, 617(TLS):20Jun86-677
Fisher, S. and R.L. Pretend the World is Funny and Forever.
W.F. Fry, Jr., 616:Fall/Winter85-50
Fishkin, J.S. Beyond Subjective Morality.
I.M. Fowlie, 518:Jul85-176
D. Little, 185:Oct85-187
A. Taylor, 543:Sep85-146
Fishkin, S.F. From Fact to Fiction.
H. McNeil, 617(TLS):21Feb86-181
T. Wortham, 445(NCF):Dec85-370
Fishlock, T. The State of America.
A. Dannatt, 362:19Jun86-27
Fishwick, M.W. Common Culture and the Great Tradition.
H.F. Smith, 106:Winter85-451
Fisiak, J., ed. Contrastive Linguistics.
R.K. Herbert, 350:Mar86-166
J. Vizmuller-Zocco, 320(CJL):Winter85-506
S. Woinicki, 355(LSoc):Dec85-570
Fisiak, J., ed. Historical Syntax.
F. Chevillet, 189(EA):Apr-Jun86-195
R.J. Jeffers, 159:Fall85-245
D. Lightfoot, 350:Jun86-439
Fisiak, J., ed. Papers and Studies in Contrastive Linguistics. (Vol 18)
F. Chevillet, 189(EA):Apr-Jun86-193
Fisk, E.K. and H. Osman-Rani, eds. The Political Economy of Malaysia.
T.R. Leinbach, 293(JASt):Nov84-242
Fiske, D. Academic Murder.
N. Callendar, 441:23Feb86-32
Fiske, E.B. Selective Guide to Colleges.
A. Hacker, 453(NYRB):13Feb86-35
Fisse, B. and J. Braithwaite. The Impact of Publicity on Corporate Offenders.
T.D., 185:Oct85-225
Fitch, B.T., ed. Albert Camus, 10.
J. Sarocchi, 535(RHL):Jan/Feb85-130
Fitch, B.T., ed. Albert Camus, 11.
G. Cesbron, 535(RHL):Jan/Feb85-131
Fitch, B.T. Monde à l'envers, texte réversible.
F. Marmande, 535(RHL):Sep/Oct85-901
Fitch, B.T. The Narcissistic Text.
D. Moutote, 535(RHL):Jan/Feb85-133
Fitch, N.R. Sylvia Beach and the Lost Generation.*
D. Seed, 97(CQ):Vol 14No1-72
Fitch, R.E. The Poison Sky.*
A.W.B., 506(PSt):May85-99
S. Gurney, 396(ModA):Summer85-269
R. Hewison, 541(RES):May85-289
Fitting, M. Proof Methods for Modal and Intuitionistic Logics.
R.A. Bull, 316:Sep85-855

122

Fitton, J.L., ed. Cycladica.
R. Higgins, 39:Jul85-79
Fittschen, K. and P. Zanker. Katalog der
römischen Porträts in den Capitolin-
ischen Museen und den anderen kommunalen
Sammlungen der Stadt Rom. (Vol 3)
R.R.R. Smith, 313:Vol75-209
G.B. Waywell, 123:Vol35No1-211
Fitzgerald, C.P. China.
617(TLS):21Nov86-1327
Fitz Gerald, F. Cities on a Hill.
C.N. Degler, 441:12Oct86-11
Fitzgerald, F.S. Lettres à Zelda et
autres correspondances.
J. Aeply, 450(NRF):Jun85-86
Fitz Gerald, G. Hunting the Yahoos.
J.R. Clark, 616:Fall/Winter85-47
Fitzgerald, J. Beneath the Skin of Para-
dise.*
S. Hutchison, 102(CanL):Spring85-164
Fitzgerald, J., ed. Un Dozen.
B. Pell, 102(CanL):Spring85-136
Fitzgerald, J.T. and L.M. White. The
Tabula of Cebes.
M.B. Trapp, 123:Vol35No2-387
Fitzgerald, K. With O'Leary in the Grave.
A. Haverty, 617(TLS):19Dec86-1433
Fitzgerald, M.J. Rope Dancer.
C. Kino, 617(TLS):7Nov86-1254
Fitzgerald, P. Innocence.
A. Duchêne, 617(TLS):12Sep86-995
Fitzgerald, R. Enlarging the Change.*
P.C. Hogan, 70:May/Jun85-154
Fitzgerald, R. From the Dreaming to 1915.
From 1915 to the Early 1980s.
G. Duncan, 381:Sep85-311
Fitzgerald, S. - see O'Connor, F.
Fitzsimons, M.S. The Past Recaptured.
M. Flynn, 125:Winter85-234
Flach, B. Kafkas Erzählungen.
E. Schlant, 221(GQ):Summer85-428
Flaherty, G. Filthy the Man.
C. Hardesty, 455:Sep85-70
Flaherty, G. Opera in the Development of
German Critical Thought.
M. Gilbert, 406:Spring85-100
412:Aug/Nov83-300
Flam, J. Matisse.
J. Perl, 441:28Dec86-13
Flanagan, O.J., Jr. The Science of Mind.
J. Owens, 185:Oct85-195
Flanagan, T. Riel and the Rebellion.
K. Turnbull, 529(QQ):Winter85-801
Flanders, W.A. Structures of Experience.*
J. Richetti, 173(ECS):Fall85-135
M. Schonhorn, 566:Spring86-189
Flanner, K. Wiener Neustadt im Stände-
staat.
F.L. Carsten, 575(SEER):Jan85-157
Flasch, K. Augustin.
E. Zum Brunn, 192(EP):Oct-Dec85-557
Flasche, H. Geschichte der spanischen Lit-
eratur. (Vol 1)
M.P.A.M. Kerkhof, 72:Band222Heft2-459
Flasche, H. Geschichte der spanischen Lit-
eratur. (Vol 2)
A. Porqueras-Mayo, 149(CLS):Winter85-
541
F.M.A. Robben, 72:Band222Heft2-460
Flasche, H. and G. Hofmann. Konkordanz zu
Calderón.
J.E. Varey, 86(BHS):Oct85-393
Flashar, H. - see Ueberweg, F.

Flater, L., A. van Herk and R. Wiebe, eds.
West of Fiction.
I. Huggan, 526:Summer85-79
Flaubert, G. The Letters of Gustave
Flaubert 1857-1880. (F. Steegmuller, ed)
W.H., 148:Spring85-94
Flaubert, G. La Tentation de Saint
Antoine. (C. Gothot-Mersch, ed)
A. Fairlie, 208(FS):Jan85-90
Flaubert, G. and G. Sand. Correspondence
Flaubert-Sand. (A. Jacobs, ed)
E.F. Gray, 207(FR):Oct85-135
Flaubert, G. and I.S. Turgenev. Flaubert
and Turgenev. (B. Beaumont, ed and
trans)
A. Fitzlyon, 364:Mar86-109
V.S. Pritchett, 442(NY):10Feb86-111
"Flaubert et Maupassant écrivains nor-
mands."
B. Bray, 549(RLC):Jan-Mar85-108
Flay, J.C. Hegel's Quest for Certainty.
W.D. Ludwig, 543:Sep85-148
M. Westphal, 319:Jul86-420
Fleck, J. Character and Context.
S. Pinsker, 395(MFS):Summer85-457
Fleck, L. Genesis and Development of a
Scientific Fact.
N. Tilley, 488:Sep85-380
Fleck, P. Polychronicon.
L. Boone, 102(CanL):Fall85-111
Fleeman, J.D. A Preliminary Handlist of
Copies of Books Associated with Dr.
Samuel Johnson.
A. Reddick, 517(PBSA):Vol79No2-250
Fleeman, J.D. - see Johnson, S.
Fleetwood, H. A Dangerous Place.
R.J. Meislin, 441:20Apr86-24
Fleetwood, H. Paradise.
K. Milne, 617(TLS):28Mar86-342
Fleischer, M.P. Späthumanismus in
Schlesien.
P. Schaeffer, 551(RenQ):Spring85-118
Fleischer, R. Der Klagefrauensarkophag
aus Sidon.
G.B. Waywell, 123:Vol35No1-157
Fleischman, S. The Future in Thought and
Language.
O. Gsell, 545(RPh):Nov84-226
R. Martin, 553(RLiR):Jul-Dec85-460
I. Short, 208(FS):Jan85-116
Fleishman, A. Figures of Autobiography.*
P.J. Eakin, 637(VS):Spring85-534
R. Fréchet, 549(RLC):Oct-Dec85-450
L. Hartveit, 179(ES):Apr85-180
A.F.T. Lurcock, 541(RES):Nov85-613
S. Neuman, 506(PSt):May85-94
Fleishman, L. Boris Pasternak v tridt-
satye gody.*
R.D.B. Thomson, 104(CASS):Summer85-207
Flejšman, L., R. X'juz and O. Raevskaja-
X'juz. Russkij Berlin, 1921-1923.
T.R. Beyer, Jr., 574(SEEJ):Summer85-
212
Fleming, A. The Letters of Ann Fleming.*
(M. Amory, ed)
P. Johnson, 362:31Oct85-29 [inadvert-
ently deleted from last vol]
D. Melville, 364:Dec85/Jan86-149
Fleming, G. Hitler and the Final Solu-
tion.*
L.L. Langer, 385(MQR):Winter86-127
Fleming, G.H. Murderer's Row.
639(VQR):Summer85-99

Fleming, J.V. From Bonaventure to Bellini.*
  M. Harvey, 161(DUJ):Dec84-95
Fleming, J.V. Reason and the Lover.
  T.D. Hill, 589:Oct85-973
Fleming, S. The Exile of Sergeant Nen.
  W.W. Larsen, 441:16Nov86-33
Fleming-Williams, I. and L. Parris. The Discovery of Constable.*
  G. Reynolds, 39:May85-359
Fletcher, A. and J. Stevenson. Order and Disorder in Early Modern England.
  J.A. Sharpe, 617(TLS):18Apr86-427
Fletcher, H. Bluestocking.
  617(TLS):6Jun86-631
Fletcher, I. - see Johnson, L.
Fletcher, J. Alain Robbe-Grillet.
  J. Alter, 207(FR):Apr86-798
  D.P. Deneau, 577(SHR):Summer85-287
Fletcher, P. Gardens and Grim Ravines.
  D. Birch, 184(EIC):Jan85-87
  A. London, 541(RES):Nov85-583
  L.R. Pratt, 637(VS):Winter85-339
Fletcher, R.A. Saint James's Catapult.
  J.E. Salisbury, 589:Oct85-977
Fletcher, T. 100 Years of the Negro in Show Business.
  D.E. McGinty, 91:Fall85-227
Abbon de Fleury. Questions grammaticales.
  (A. Guerreau-Jalabert, ed and trans)
  P. Flobert, 555:Vol59fasc1-144
Flexner, J.T. An American Saga.
  M. Moran, 556:Winter85/86-175
Flieger, W., M.K. Abenoja and A.C. Lim. On the Road to Longevity.
  J.S. Parsons, 293(JASt):May85-678
Flieger, W. and I. Pagtolun-an. An Assessment of Fertility and Contraception in Seven Philippine Provinces: 1975.
  J.S. Parsons, 293(JASt):May85-678
Flikeid, K. La variation phonétique dans le parler acadien du nord-est du Nouveau-Brunswick.
  H.R. Runte, 207(FR):Feb86-478
  A. Thomas, 320(CJL):Spring85-109
Flisfish, E. Kantonisty.
  E.K. Wirtschafter, 550(RusR):Apr85-204
Flon, C., ed. The World Atlas of Archaeology.
  N. Hammond, 617(TLS):10Oct86-1145
Flook, M. Reckless Wedding.
  455:Mar85-65
Flora, J.M., ed. The English Short Story, 1880-1945.
  M. Rohrberger, 395(MFS):Winter85-802
Flora, J.M. Hemingway's Nick Adams.*
  J. Meyers, 50(ArQ):Winter85-370
Florby, G. The Painful Passage to Virtue.*
  J.N. Brown, 447(N&Q):Jun84-263
  L. Potter, 161(DUJ):Dec84-114
Florenskij, P. La prospettiva rovesciata e altri scritti. (N. Misler, ed and trans)
  A. Lawton, 574(SEEJ):Winter85-479
Florentini, B. Candelabrum. (G.C. Alessio, ed)
  C. de Nigris, 379(MedR):Apr85-123
Flores, A., ed. Designing for Safety.
  D.O., 185:Oct85-226
Flores, E., ed. Dall'epigramma ellenistico all'elegia romana.
  J. Chomarat, 555:Vol59fasc1-136

Flores, R. The Rhetoric of Doubtful Authority.*
  R. Chambers, 301(JEGP):Jul85-410
  B. Duyfhuizen, 435:Fall85-67
  J.D. Lyons, 478:Oct85-229
Flores, R.M. Sancho Panza through Three Hundred Seventy-five Years of Continuations, Imitations, and Criticism, 1605-1980.*
  J.J. Allen, 131(CL):Fall85-371
  F. Pierce, 402(MLR):Jan85-194
Flower, D. - see Dowson, E.
Flower, J.E. Literature and the Left in France.*
  H. Davies, 208(FS):Oct85-491
  H. Peyre, 207(FR):Oct85-138
Flowers, A.R. Demojo Blues.
  J. Haskins, 441:19Jan86-20
Fluck, W., J. Peper and W.P. Adams, eds. Forms and Functions of History in American Literature.*
  H.F. Smith, 106:Winter85-451
Flügge, M. Verweigerung oder Neue Ordnung.*
  I. Galster, 72:Band222Heft1-232
Flury-Lemberg, M. and K. Stolleis, eds. Documenta Textilia.
  A. Rapp, 683:Band48Heft4-582
Flusin, B. Miracle et histoire dans l'oeuvre de Cyrille de Scythopolis.
  D.D. Abrahamse, 589:Apr85-396
  P. Pattenden, 123:Vol35No1-185
Flusser, V. Ins Universum der technischen Bilder.
  H. Pross, 384:Sep/Oct85-917
Flydal, E. Oljespråk.
  R. Burling, 355(LSoc):Mar85-117
Flynn, E.P. My Country Right or Wrong?
  J.M., 185:Apr86-697
Flynn, T.R. Sartre and Marxist Existentialism.
  J.P. Fell, 319:Jan86-139
Flys, M.J. - see Cernuda, L.
Foa, V. La Gerusalemme rimandata.
  S. Woolf, 617(TLS):7Feb86-134
Foakes, R.A. - see Shakespeare, W.
Fodor, A. Tolstoy and the Russians.
  G.R. Jahn, 574(SEEJ):Fall85-348
Fodor, J.A. The Modularity of Mind.
  R. Cummins, 482(PhR):Jan85-101
  C. Pléh, 206(FoLi):Vol 19No3/4-539
Fogarasi, M. Grammatica Italiana del Novecento. (2nd ed)
  A. Castelvecchi, 708:Vol 11fasc1-130
Fogel, J.A. Politics and Sinology.*
  L. Grove, 293(JASt):Aug85-806
Fogel, R.W. and G.R. Elton. Which Road to the Past?
  W.H. Dray, 529(QQ):Spring85-189
  M. Flynn, 125:Fall84-91
  C. Parker, 366:Autumn85-288
Fogelin, R.J. Hume's Skepticism in the "Treatise of Human Nature."*
  C.C., 185:Jul86-909
Fogelin, R.J. Understanding Arguments. (2nd ed)
  C. Plantin, 540(RIPh):Vol139fasc4-467
Fogelquist, J.D. El "Amadis" y el género de la historia fingida.
  J.R. Green, 238:Sep85-512
Fokkelman, J.P. Narrative Art and Poetry in the Books of Samuel. (Vol 1)
  M. Fishbane, 318(JAOS):Apr-Jun84-375

Forgacs, D., ed. Rethinking Italian Fascism.
  P. McCarthy, 617(TLS):26Sep86-1052
Forgacs, D. and G. Nowell-Smith - see Gramsci, A.
Forisha, B.L. and B.H. Goldman, eds. Outsiders on the Inside.
  S.K. Foss, 583:Spring86-289
Forkel, J.N. Vie de Johann-Sebastian Bach. (A. Dürr, ed)
  S. Daw, 415:Mar85-156
Forlati Tamaro, B. Iscrizioni lapidarie latine del Museo Civico di Oderzo.
  M.H. Crawford, 313:Vol75-319
Forment Giralt, E. Fenomenología descriptiva del lenguaje.
  A. Reix, 542:Jan-Mar85-89
Forment Giralt, E. Introducción a la metafísica.
  A. Reix, 542:Oct-Dec85-551
Formigari, L., ed. Teorie e pratiche linguistiche nell'Italia del Settecento.
  A. Castelvecchi, 708:Vol 11fasc1-143
Fornara, C.W. The Nature of History in Ancient Greece and Rome.
  J. Glazewski, 124:Mar-Apr86-278
  K. Moors, 543:Dec85-355
  L. Pearson, 24:Summer85-254
  G.S. Shrimpton, 487:Winter85-395
  F.W. Walbank, 303(JoHS):Vol 105-211
  T.E.J. Wiedemann, 313:Vol75-307
  T.P. Wiseman, 123:Vol135No1-109
Forssman, B. - see Wackernagel, J.
Forster, E.M. E.M. Forster's "Commonplace Book." (P. Gardner, ed)
  A.S. Byatt, 617(TLS):7Mar86-258
  S. Spender, 441:23Feb86-11
Forster, E.M. "The Hill of Devi" and Other Indian Writings.* (E. Heine, ed)
  T. Brown, 541(RES):Aug85-451
Forster, E.M. Selected Letters of E.M. Forster.* (Vol 1) (M.M. Lago and P.N. Furbank, eds)
  J. Batchelor, 541(RES):Nov85-593
  M. Goldstein, 569(SR):Fall85-624
  F.P.W. McDowell, 177(ELT):Vol28No1-81
  V.N. Paananen, 115:Spring84-151
Forster, E.M. Selected Letters of E.M. Forster.* (Vol 2) (M.M. Lago and P.N. Furbank, eds)
  W.H. Pritchard, 249(HudR):Winter86-673
Forster, E.M. - see Fay, E.
Forster, J. Music-Lab.
  P. Standford, 415:Nov85-674
Forster, L., ed. Studien zur europäischen Rezeption deutscher Barockliteratur.
  G. Hoffmeister, 107(CRCL):Sep85-522
Forster, M. Private Papers.
  L. Duguid, 617(TLS):7Mar86-256
  K.C. O'Brien, 362:1May86-30
Forster, P.G. The Esperanto Movement.*
  J. Knobloch, 685(ZDL):2/1985-261
Forster, T.E. Quine's New Foundations.
  U. Oswald, 316:Jun85-547
Forsyth, A. A Natural History of Sex.
  Y. Baskin, 441:13Jul86-19
Forsyth, K. "Ariadne auf Naxos" by Hugo von Hofmannsthal and Richard Strauss.*
  J.B., 412:Feb83-591
Forsyth, M. Buildings for Music.*
  S. Cantacuzino, 617(TLS):25Apr86-457

Fortassier, R. Le Roman français au XIXe siècle.
  A. Tooke, 208(FS):Apr85-220
Forti Grazzini, N. L'arazzo ferrarese.
  C. Adelson, 90:May85-307
Fortin, C. L'Ombre des cibles.
  N. Bishop, 102(CanL):Spring85-132
Fortún, C. Animales Legendarios. Artes Populares.
  V. Benmaman, 399(MLJ):Summer85-210
Fortuna, J.L., Jr. "The Unsearchable Wisdom of God."
  F. Rau, 38:Band103Heft3/4-500
Fortune, S.A. Merchants and Jews.
  J. Walvin, 656(WMQ):Jul85-413
Forty, A. Objects of Desire.
  D. Murray, 441:20Apr86-23
  S. Rose, 324:Oct86-762
Foshay, E.M. Reflections of Nature.
  F. Kelly, 658:Winter85-305
Foss, S.K., K.A. Foss and R. Trapp. Contemporary Perspectives on Rhetoric.
  J.C. Roundtree 3d, 583:Fall85-85
Foster, B.L. Commerce and Ethnic Differences.
  A. Pongsapich, 293(JASt):Nov84-243
Foster, C. and A. Valdman, eds. Haiti — Today and Tomorrow.
  J-M. Salien, 207(FR):Mar86-626
Foster, D.W., comp. Jorge Luis Borges.
  S.I. Bellman, 573(SSF):Fall85-490
  M.E. Filer, 238:May85-320
  J. Tyler, 263(RIB):Vol35No3-328
  A.R. Williams, 37:Jul-Aug85-56
Foster, D.W., comp. Cuban Literature.
  K. Müller-Bergh, 263(RIB):Vol35No1-64
Foster, E.H. William Saroyan.
  A. Ronald, 649(WAL):May85-55
Foster, H., ed. The Anti-Aesthetic.*
  G. Banks, 592:Vol 198No1009-54
Foster, J. A.J. Ayer.
  A. O'Hear, 617(TLS):25Apr86-455
Foster, J. The Case for Idealism.*
  I. Hinckfuss, 63:Mar85-88
Foster, J. and H. Robinson, eds. Essays on Berkeley.
  G. Warnock, 617(TLS):7Mar86-253
Foster, J.B., Jr. Heirs to Dionysus.*
  G. Gillespie, 131(CL):Winter85-85
  G. Good, 107(CRCL):Sep85-556
Foster, K. Petrarch.
  P. Hainsworth, 278(IS):Vol40-116
Foster, M.K., J. Campisi and M. Mithun, eds. Extending the Rafters.
  B. Graymont, 656(WMQ):Jul85-410
Foster, M.L. and S.H. Brandes, eds. Symbol as Sense.
  M. Herzfeld, 567:Vol56No1/2-153
Foster, S.C., ed. Dada/Dimensions.
  G. Marcus, 62:Jan86-13
Foster, S.C. and R.E. Kuenzli, eds. Dada Spectrum.
  S. Scobie, 107(CRCL):Sep85-442
Fothergill, B. The Strawberry Hill Set.
  F. Doherty, 83:Spring85-104
Foti, F. La critica letteraria. (Vol 2)
  E. Chevallier, 549(RLC):Jul-Sep85-351
Foucart, J. Les Peintures de Rembrandt au Louvre.
  I.G., 90:Mar85-173
Foucault, M. The Foucault Reader.* (P. Rabinow, ed)
  42(AR):Spring85-253

Foucault, M.  Histoire de la Sexualité.
(Vol 3)
  M. Lefkowitz, 473(PR):Vol52No4-460
Foucault, M.  Language, Counter-Memory,
  Practice.
  S. Richmond, 488:Sep85-369
Foucault, M.  This Is Not A Pipe.*  (J.
  Harkness, ed and trans)
  M. Van de Pitte, 154:Winter85-742
Foucault, M.  The Use of Pleasure.*
  (French title: Histoire de la Sexualité.
  (Vol 2)).
  M. Lefkowitz, 473(PR):Vol52No4-460
  G.E.R. Lloyd, 453(NYRB):13Mar86-24
  G. Steiner, 442:17Mar86-105
Fouché, P.  Au Sans Pareil.
  D.A. Steel, 402(MLR):Oct85-948
Fougère, J.  Destinee City.
  M.B. Yoken, 207(FR):May86-993
Foulkes, A.P.  Literature and Propaganda.*
  W.L. Adamson, 478:Oct85-230
  J.S. Dean, 125:Winter85-227
Foulkes, R.  The Shakespeare Tercentary of
  1864.
  P. Hyland, 610:Autumn85-238
"Four Failures: A Report on the UN Special
  Rapporteurs on Human Rights in Chile,
  Guatemala, Iran and Poland."
  M. Kempton, 453(NYRB):13Feb86-34
Fourastie, J. and B. Bazil.  Pourquoi les
  prix baissent.
  P. Adam, 98:Dec85-1206
de Fournival, R. - see under Richard de
  Fournival
Fowke, E. - see Kane, A.
Fowler, A.  Kinds of Literature.*
  B. Corman, 627(UTQ):Fall84-101
  D. Robey, 541(RES):May85-308
Fowler, D.  S.J. Perelman.
  A.L. Cooke, 70:Nov/Dec84-62
Fowler, D. and A.J. Abadie, eds.  Faulkner.
  S.M. Ross, 395(MFS):Winter85-737
Fowler, D. and A.J. Abadie, eds.  Faulkner
  and Humor.
  M. Grimwood, 578:Fall86-100
Fowler, D. and A.J. Abadie, eds.  New
  Directions in Faulkner Studies.
  M. Grimwood, 578:Fall86-100
  639(VQR):Spring85-45
Fowler, M.  Redney.*
  C. Gerson, 102(CanL):Winter84-78
  T. Tausky, 298:Summer85-159
Fowler, V.C.  Henry James's American Girl.*
  C.B. Cox, 27(AL):Oct85-501
  P.J. Eakin, 445(NCF):Sep85-240
  D.M. Fogel, 26(ALR):Spring/Autumn85-
  279
  M. Graulich, 651(WHR):Autumn85-275
  M. Jacobson, 577(SHR):Summer85-269
  G.D. Smith, 594:Winter85-435
  C. Wegelin, 395(MFS):Summer85-391
  295(JML):Nov85-500
Fowles, J.  A Maggot.*
  D.J. Taylor, 176:Jun86-55
Fowles, J. and J. Draper.  Thomas Hardy's
  England.
  A. Shelston, 148:Summer85-84
Fowlie, W.  Aubade.*
  E. Current-Garcia, 577(SHR):Summer85-
  278
Fowlkes, F.  Majendie's Cat.
  442(NY):15Sep86-122

Fox, A.  German Intonation.
  C. Hoequist, 353:Vol23No1-165
Fox, A.  Thomas More.*
  E. McCutcheon, 77:Winter85-83
Fox, A. and J. Guy.  Reassessing the Henri-
  cian Age.
  G.R. Elton, 176:Jul/Aug86-37
  P. Williams, 617(TLS):5Dec86-1381
Fox, D.M.  Health Policies, Health Pol-
  itics.
  C. Webster, 617(TLS):7Nov86-1253
Fox, J.  Villon: Poems.
  M.J. Freeman, 208(FS):Oct85-454
  382(MAE):1985/2-347
Fox, K.  Metropolitan America.
  P. Hall, 617(TLS):30May86-581
Fox, M.A.  The Case for Animal Experimenta-
  tion.
  J. Koslow, 441:30Mar86-19
Fox, M.A. and L. Groarke, eds.  Nuclear
  War.
  R.H., 185:Apr86-694
Fox, P.  A Servant's Tale.*
  L. Taylor, 617(TLS):21Feb86-199
Fox, R.G.  Lions of the Punjab.
  C.A. Bayly, 617(TLS):13Jun86-654
Fox, R.L.  Better Gardening.
  S. Brownmiller, 441:1Jun86-30
Fox, R.W.  Reinhold Niebuhr.
  H. Cox, 441:5Jan86-1
  D.B. Davis, 453(NYRB):13Feb86-7
  W.E. Leuchtenburg, 61:Jan86-93
  R.J. Neuhaus, 129:Mar86-58
  442(NY):24Mar86-125
Fox, S.  The Mirror Makers.
  R. Draper, 453(NYRB):26Jun86-14
  W. Leach, 533:Summer85-138
Foxell, N.  Loving Emma.
  R. Porter, 617(TLS):5Dec86-1380
Foy, G.  Coaster.
  P-L. Adams, 61:Feb86-87
  M.M. Thomas, 441:2Mar86-19
Foye, R. - see Wieners, J.
Fracastoro, G.  Fracastoro's "Syphilis."
  (G. Eatough, ed and trans)
  J.W. Binns, 123:Vol35No1-228
  C. Kallendorf, 568(SCN):Fall85-54
Frago, A.V. - see under Viñao Frago, A.
Fraisse, S. - see Péguy, C.
Fraistat, N.  The Poem and the Book.*
  C.E. Lloyd, 70:May/Jun86-160
Fraistat, R.A.C.  Caroline Gordon as Novel-
  ist and Woman of Letters.
  E. Ammons, 27(AL):Mar85-169
  S. Pinsker, 577(SHR):Summer85-265
  W.J. Stuckey, 395(MFS):Summer85-400
Fralin, F., ed.  The Indelible Image.
  C. Hagen, 62:Jan86-14
Frame, J.  An Angel at My Table.
  L. Jones, 49:Oct85-127
Frame, J.  The Envoy from Mirror City.*
  F. Adcock, 617(TLS):10Jan86-42
Frame, J.  To the Is-land.
  L. Jones, 49:Oct85-127
  P. Lewis, 565:Winter84/85-42
Frame, R.  A Long Weekend With Marcel
  Proust.
  W. Brandmark, 362:11Mar86-22
  M. Casserley, 617(TLS):17Oct86-1169
Frame, R.  Watching Mrs. Gordon.*
  P. Parker, 364:Jun85-107
Frame, R.  Winter Journey.
  442(NY):14Jul86-83

Frampton, K., ed. Tadao Ando.
  B. Bognar, 505:May85-251
France, J. and M. McConnell. Incident at
  Big Sky.
  A. Friesinger, 441:3Aug86-19
France, P. Diderot.
  S. Baudiffier, 535(RHL):Sep/Oct85-877
  J. Chouillet, 208(FS):Apr85-211
  R. Niklaus, 83:Spring85-115
France, P. Poets of Modern Russia.*
  L. O'Bell, 574(SEEJ):Spring85-106
Franchi, A. La svolta politico-ecclesias-
  tica tra Roma e Bisanzio (1249-1254).
  D.J. Granakoplos, 589:Apr85-478
di Francia, G.T. - see under Toraldo di
  Francia, G.
Francis, C. Red Crystal.
  M. Laski, 362:9Jan86-30
Francis, D. Break In.
  P-L. Adams, 61:Apr86-131
  T.J. Binyon, 617(TLS):25Apr86-454
  A. Ross, 364:Feb86-108
  M. Stasio, 441:16Mar86-7
  442(NY):14Apr86-112
Francis, D. A Jockey's Life.
  J. Quinlan, 441:120ct86-29
Francis, R. Pot Shots at Poetry.
  R. McDowell, 249(HudR):Autumn85-517
Francis, R. Swansong.
  L. Heron, 362:21Aug86-24
Francis, W.N. Dialectology.*
  J.K. Chambers, 361:Jan85-155
  W.G. Moulton, 355(LSoc):Dec85-563
  P. Mühlhäusler, 541(RES):Nov85-544
  W. Viereck, 300:Oct85-184
Francis, W.N. and H. Kučera, with A.W.
  Mackie. Frequency Analysis of English
  Usage.
  R. Burchfield, 300:Apr85-64
Franck, D. La Dame du soir.
  S. Keane, 207(FR):Apr86-812
Francks, P. Technology and Agricultural
  Development in Pre-War Japan.
  W.W. Kelly, 407(MN):Autumn85-372
François, C. André Marissel.
  M. Cranston, 207(FR):Apr86-800
François, F., ed. J'cause français, non?
  J-P. Colin, 209(FM):Apr85-138
François, F., C. Hudelot and E. Sabeau-
  Jouannet. Conduites linguistiques chez
  le jeune enfant.
  A. Reix, 542:Jul-Sep85-356
François Ier. Oeuvres poétiques.* (J.E.
  Kane, ed)
  R. Salminen, 439(NM):1985/4-607
  J. Sproxton, 402(MLR):Oct85-934
  C.H. Winn, 547(RF):Band97Heft4-466
  M-C. Wrage, 207(FR):Apr86-779
Francome, J. Born Lucky.
  A. Ross, 364:Feb86-107
de Francovich, G. Persia, Siria, Bisanzio
  e il Medioevo artistico Europeo.
  J.M. Rogers, 90:Nov85-819
Franić, A. Hrvatski putopisi romantizma.
  C. Taylor-Skarica, 574(SEEJ):Spring85-
  115
von Frank, A.J. The Sacred Game.
  D. Penrice, 617(TLS):25Apr86-436
Frank, A.P. Einführung in die britische
  und amerikanische Literaturkritik und
  -theorie.
  P. Goetsch, 38:Band103Heft3/4-520

Frank, D.H. The Arguments "From the Sci-
  ences" in Aristotle's "Peri Ideon."
  J. Barnes, 520:Vol30No1-102
  R.W. Jordan, 123:Vol35No2-402
  J. Kung, 319:Apr86-263
Frank, E. Louise Bogan.*
  K. Osborne, 152(UDQ):Fall85-138
  K. Pollitt, 676(YR):Summer85-596
  42(AR):Summer85-370
  295(JML):Nov85-451
  639(VQR):Autumn85-118
Frank, F. and F. Anshen. Language and the
  Sexes.*
  C.C. Eble, 300:Oct85-198
Frank, H., ed. Faschistische Architek-
  turen.
  I.B. Whyte, 617(TLS):4Apr86-362
Frank, J. Dostoevsky: The Seeds of Revolt,
  1821-1849.
  M. Gorra, 249(HudR):Spring85-140
Frank, J. Dostoevsky: The Stir of Libera-
  tion 1860-1865.
  V.S. Pritchett, 453(NYRB):25Sep86-11
  H. Robinson, 441:31Aug86-8
Frank, J. Dostoevsky: The Years of Ordeal,
  1850-1859.*
  M. Gorra, 249(HudR):Spring85-140
  R.E. Matlaw, 574(SEEJ):Spring85-103
  R.F. Miller, 104(CASS):Summer85-224
  S. Monas, 473(PR):Vol52No4-452
  R.A. Peace, 31(ASch):Winter84/85-133
  P. Roazen, 639(VQR):Summer85-551
  G. Woodcock, 569(SR):Spring85-293
Frank, K. A Voyager Out.
  E. Langer, 441:30Nov86-28
Frank, L. Charles Dickens and the Roman-
  tic Self.*
  R.A. Levine, 594:Winter85-423
  S. Tick, 637(VS):Spring86-475
  D. Walder, 617(TLS):31Jan86-125
Frank, S.L. The Unknowable.
  K.R. Hill, 543:Jun86-763
Frank, T., ed. The Origins and Original-
  ity of American Culture.
  G-J. Forgue, 189(EA):Oct-Dec86-489
Franklin, B. The Autobiography of Benja-
  min Franklin.* (J.A.L. Lemay and P.M.
  Zall, eds)
  J. Griffith, 165(EAL):Fall86-166
Franklin, B. The Papers of Benjamin Frank-
  lin. (Vols 20-23) (W.B. Willcox, ed)
  J.N. Rakove, 656(WMQ):Oct85-530
Franklin, B. The Papers of Benjamin Frank-
  lin. (Vol 24) (W.B. Willcox, ed)
  J.N. Rakove, 656(WMQ):Oct85-530
  639(VQR):Summer85-81
Franklin, B., ed. The Rights of Children.
  M. Warnock, 617(TLS):31Oct86-1212
Franklin, J. and A. Doelp. Not Quite a
  Miracle.
  S. Wolfe, 529(QQ):Autumn85-624
Franklin, J.H. George Washington Wil-
  liams.*
  J. Olney, 598(SoR):Spring86-428
Franklin, P. The Idea of Music.
  D. Jarman, 617(TLS):7Feb86-143
Franklin, R. The Defender.
  N. Kristof, 441:27Jul86-19
Franks, R. What's in a Nickname?
  E.D. Lawson, 424:Dec85-276
Franksen, O.I. Mr. Babbage's Secret.
  S. Alderson, 324:Mar86-270
  D.K. Stein, 637(VS):Spring86-496

Franz, E. Pierre Michel d'Ixnard, 1723-
1795.
  W. Schirmer, 43:Band15Heft1-97
von Franz, M-L. On Dreams and Death.
  C. Zaleski, 469:Vol 11No4-99
Franzen, W. Die Bedeutung von "wahr" und
"Wahrheit."*
  M.S. Gram, 543:Mar85-623
Frappier, J. Chrétien de Troyes.*
  E.J. Burns, 545(RPh):Nov84-261
  N.J. Lacy, 403(MLS):Summer85-89
Frascina, F., ed. Pollock and After.
  D. Carrier, 90:Nov85-817
  J. Gardner, 129:Aug86-60
Fraser, A. The Weaker Vessel.*
  B.G. Carson, 658:Winter85-295
  C. Clark, 615(TJ):Oct85-379
Fraser, C.M. and K. Emsley, eds. The
Court Rolls of the Manor of Wakefield
from October 1639 to September 1640.
  A.R. De Windt, 589:Jan85-146
Fraser, F. Beloved Emma.
  R. Porter, 617(TLS):5Dec86-1380
Fraser, G. René Lévesque and the Parti
Québécois in Power.
  G.W., 102(CanL):Fall85-186
Fraser, G.M. Flashman and the Dragon.*
  S. Schiff, 441:4May86-19
Fraser, I.H.C. The Heir of Parham.
  A. Bell, 617(TLS):1Aug86-849
Fraser, J.T. The Genesis and Evolution of
Time.
  R.S. Brumbaugh, 543:Sep84-121
Fraser, K. Foreign Affairs.
  B. Draine, 99:Feb86-37
Fraser, P.M. - see Butler, A.J.
Frauenlob (Heinrich von Meissen). Leichs,
Sangsprüche, Lieder.* (K. Stackmann and
K. Bertau, eds)
  I. Glier, 221(GQ):Winter85-108
  B. Wachinger, 684(ZDA):Band114Heft4-
119
Frawley, W., ed. Linguistics and Literacy.
  V. John-Steiner and C. Panofsky, 350:
Jun86-480
Frazier, I. Dating Your Mom.
  M. Richler, 441:5Jan86-5
Frazier, K., ed. Science Confronts the
Paranormal.
  617(TLS):15Aug86-899
Freccero, J. Dante. (R. Jacoff, ed)
  P. Shaw, 617(TLS):12Sep86-997
Frederic, H. The Damnation of Theron Ware,
or Illumination. (C. Dodge, ed)
  R. Asselineau, 189(EA):Oct-Dec86-483
  W. French, 26(ALR):Spring/Autumn85-277
Frédéric, M. La répétition.
  B. Johnstone, 350:Dec86-960
Frédéric, M. La répétition et ses struc-
tures dans l'oeuvre poétique de Saint-
John Perse.
  P. Van Rutten, 209(FM):Oct85-248
Frederick, W.H., ed. Reflections on Rebel-
lion.
  P.B. Henry, 293(JASt):Feb85-464
Fredericks, C. The Future of Eternity.
  L. Hatfield, 128(CE):Mar85-275
Frederickson, G.M. White Supremacy.
  G. Vandal, 106:Spring85-41
Frederiksen, A.R. Love and Guilt.
  G. Davenport, 598(SoR):Winter86-210
Frederiksen, M. Campania.
  J.P. Vallat, 313:Vol75-232

Fredrikson, K. American Rodeo.
  L. Milazzo, 584(SWR):Spring85-262
Fredriksson, G. Bertrand Russell.
  S. Andersson, 556:Winter85/86-169
Freeborn, R. The Russian Revolutionary
Novel.*
  R. Cockrell, 402(MLR):Jan85-250
Freed, L. Home Ground.
  C. Hope, 617(TLS):9May86-499
  J.T. Hospital, 441:17Aug86-7
Freedberg, S.J. Circa 1600.*
  J. Gash, 59:Jun85-249
von Freeden, J. Oikia Kyrrēstou.*
  R.R.R. Smith, 303(JoHS):Vol 105-230
Freeden, M. Liberalism Divided.
  M. Campbell, 617(TLS):21Nov86-1298
Freedman, F.B. William Douglas O'Connor.
  R. Asselineau, 646:Spring86-39
Freedman, L. The Price of Peace.
  M. MccGwire, 617(TLS):31Oct86-1214
Freedman, S. and C.A. Taylor. Roland
Barthes.
  J. Culler, 107(CRCL):Sep85-492
Freely, M. The Life of the Party.*
  639(VQR):Summer85-92
Freeman, B. Harbour Thieves.
  A. Kertzer, 102(CanL):Fall85-117
Freeman, C. Seasons of the Heart.
  M. Wexler, 441:27Apr86-23
Freeman, D. A Hollywood Education.
  R. Rosen, 441:24Aug86-24
Freeman, E., ed. The Relevance of Charles
Peirce.
  P. Ochs, 619:Winter85-121
Freeman, F.W. Robert Fergusson and the
Scots Humanist Compromise.
  L. Hartveit, 179(ES):Jun85-279
  A.H. MacLaine, 571(ScLJ):Autumn85-5
Freeman, G.D. Midnight and Noonday.
  L. Milazzo, 584(SWR):Winter85-130
Freeman, J.A. Milton and the Martial
Muse.*
  J.M. Steadman, 677(YES):Vol 15-292
Freeman, J.W. Metropolitan Opera.
  E. Forbes, 415:Sep85-538
Freeman, M.A. The Poetics of "Translatio
Studii" and "Conjointure."
  J.L. Grigsby, 545(RPh):Aug84-53
Freemantle, B. The Blind Run.
  N. Callendar, 441:7Sep86-17
  442(NY):21Jul86-95
Freemantle, B. The Kremlin Kiss.
  M. Laski, 362:3Jul86-32
Freese, P., ed. Growing Up Black in
America.
  M. Diedrich, 72:Band222Heft2-427
Freeze, G.L. The Parish Clergy in Nine-
teenth-Century Russia.*
  P.G. Pera, 575(SEER):Jan85-128
Frege, G. Collected Papers on Mathematics,
Logic and Philosophy. (B. McGuinness,
ed)
  C.J. Hookway, 518:Apr85-90
Frei, N. Theodore Fontane.
  M. Totten, 406:Spring85-113
Freiberg, M., ed. Journals of the House
of Representatives of Massachusetts,
1776. (Vol 51, Pt 3)
  J.A. Schutz, 432(NEQ):Mar85-155
Freile, J.R. - see under Rodríguez Freile,
J.
Frénaud, A. La Sorcière de Rome.
  G. Cookson, 402(MLR):Apr85-477

French, A.P. and P.J. Kennedy, eds. Niels Bohr.
  B. Pippard, 617(TLS):25Apr86-443
A.R. Ubbelohde, 324:Aug86-623
French, D. Salt-Water Moon.
  P. Walsh, 108:Winter85-143
French, M. Beyond Power.*
  A. Clare, 362:13Feb86-29
  M. Warnock, 617(TLS):24Jan86-90
French, P.A. Collective and Corporate Responsibility.
  D. Copp, 185:Apr86-636
French, Y. Blue Guide London.
  D. Piper, 617(TLS):9May86-508
Frenz, H. and S. Tuck, eds. Eugene O'Neill's Critics.
  J.R. Bryer, 397(MD):Dec85-688
  M.U. Burns, 615(TJ):May85-248
  J.H. Raleigh, 678(YCGL):No34-149
  J.H. Stroupe, 130:Spring85-92
  G.J. Williams, 610:Summer85-188
Frère, J. Les Grecs et le désir de l'Etre des préplatoniciens à Aristote.*
  J. Moreau, 542:Apr-Jun85-232
Frescoln, W. - see Guillaume le Clerc
Frescura, M.S. - see under Sassu Frescura, M.
Freud, S. The Complete Letters of Sigmund Freud to Wilhelm Fliess, 1887-1904.*
  (J.M. Masson, ed and trans)
  R. Fuller, 364:Aug-Sep85-136
  P. Loewenberg, 617(TLS):7Feb86-145
  J. Mann, 152(UDQ):Fall85-84
Frewin, L., ed. The Boundary Book, Second Innings.
  S. Fry, 362:18/25Dec86-55
Frey, R.G. Rights, Killing, and Suffering.*
  D.H. Bennett, 63:Dec85-571
  L. Francis, 529(QQ):Winter85-870
  A. Soble, 185:Oct85-192
Freyer, G. W.B. Yeats and the Anti-Democratic Tradition.*
  W.E. Hall, 637(VS):Autumn84-191
Freytag, H. Die Theorie der allegorischen Schriftdeutung und die Allegorie in deutschen Texten besonders des 11. und 12. Jahrhunderts.*
  C.S. Jaeger, 589:Apr85-398
Frézouls, E., ed. Les villes antiques de la France. (Vol 1, Pt 1)
  J.F. Drinkwater, 313:Vol75-292
Friday, A. and D.S. Ingram, eds. The Cambridge Encyclopedia of Life Sciences.
  D. Macdonald, 617(TLS):20Jun86-685
Fried, M. Absorption and Theatricality.*
  P. Joannides, 97(CQ):Vol 14No3-240
Frieden, N.M. Russian Physicians in an Era of Reform and Revolution, 1856-1905.
  W. Harrison, 161(DUJ):Jun84-291
Friedenreich, K., ed. "Accompaninge the Players."
  M. Kiniry, 551(RenQ):Summer85-373
Friedland, B. - see Barzun, J.
Friedlander, M.R. Sadat and Begin.
  S.F. Singer, 129:Oct86-81
Friedländer, S. Reflections of Nazism.
  A.H. Rosenfeld, 390:Oct85-63
  J. Rury, 42(AR):Winter85-117
Friedman, A.J. and C.C. Donley. Einstein as Myth and Muse.
  A. Saunders, 617(TLS):12Dec86-1407

Friedman, A.W. William Faulkner.
  M. Grimwood, 578:Fall86-100
  H. McNeil, 617(TLS):27Jun86-704
Friedman, B.J. Let's Hear It for a Wonderful Guy.
  W. Peden, 651(WHR):Autumn85-269
Friedman, J-A. Home Health Care.
  A.E. Johnson, 441:23Mar86-47
Friedman, L.M. A History of American Law. (2nd ed)
  C. Woodard, 441:16Feb86-31
Friedman, M. The Confirmation of Otherness.
  K.N. Cissna, 583:Fall85-88
Friedman, M. Paper Phoenix.
  N. Callendar, 441:1Jun86-46
Friedman, M. The Utopian Dilemma.
  L.S. Dawidowicz, 129:Jun86-73
Friedman, M.A. Jewish Marriage in Palestine.
  J. Neusner, 318(JAOS):Oct-Dec84-776
Friedman, P. Serious Trouble.
  R. Cohen, 441:19Oct86-30
Friedman, R., ed. The Poet and the Historian.
  J. Van Seters, 318(JAOS):Oct-Dec84-774
Friedman, S.S. Psyche Reborn.
  J. Retallack, 472:Spring/Summer/Fall/Winter85-67
Friedman, T. James Gibbs.
  E. Denby, 324:Dec85-68
  K. Downes, 90:May85-311
  J.M. Robinson, 39:Apr85-282
  566:Spring86-214
Friedrich, O. City of Nets.
  N. Gabler, 441:23Nov86-12
Friedrichsmeyer, E. Die satirische Kurzprosa Heinrich Bölls.*
  H. Müssener, 406:Fall85-376
Friel, B. Selected Plays.
  D. Devlin, 157:No156-49
  C. Murray, 272(IUR):Autumn85-244
Friel, G. The Boy Who Wanted Peace.
  J.A.S. Miller, 571(ScLJ):Winter85-67
Friendly, F. and M. Elliott. The Constitution.
  639(VQR):Winter85-21
Fries, M.S. The Changing Consciousness of Reality.
  S.L. Cocalis, 406:Spring85-114
Friesen, G. The Canadian Prairies.
  J.R. Miller, 298:Fall85-156
Friesen, V.C. The Spirit of the Huckleberry.
  R. Sattelmeyer, 183(ESQ):Vol31No3-190
Friis, E.J. - see Allardt, E. and others
Friis-Jensen, K., ed. Saxo Grammaticus.*
  W.F. Hansen, 563(SS):Summer85-335
Frings, M.S. - see Heidegger, M.
Frisch, W. Brahms and the Principle of Developing Variation.*
  R. Anderson, 415:May85-285
  M. Musgrave, 317:Fall85-628
Frisch, W., ed. Schubert.
  G. Abraham, 617(TLS):26Sep86-1066
Frisé, A. - see Musil, R.
Fritschi, G. Africa and Gutenberg.
  N.J. Schmidt, 538(RAL):Winter85-572
Fritz, R. Die Gefässe aus Kokosnuss in Mitteleuropa 1250-1800.*
  R.W. Lightbown, 39:Jun85-438
Fritzmann, A. Friedrich von Logau.
  G.R. Hoyt, 221(GQ):Summer85-452

Frohock, F.M. Special Care.
P.J.A. Hillard, 441:5Oct86-54
"From the Classroom to the Workplace."
C.Ü. Grosse, 399(MLJ):Summer85-165
Froman, W. Merleau-Ponty.
R.E. Innis, 543:Jun85-887
Froment-Meurice, M. Sartre et l'existen-
tialisme.
C. Attuel, 542:Jan-Mar85-50
Fromentin, E. Dominique.
D. Coward, 617(TLS):6Jun86-625
Fromentin, E. and P. Bataillard. Étude
sur l'"Ahasvérus" d'Edgar Quinet. (B.
Wright and T. Mellors, eds)
E. Knecht, 535(RHL):Jan/Feb85-104
Frommel, C.L. and others. Raffaello
architetto.
D. Howard, 90:Oct85-721
Frommer, S.H. Murder in C Major.
N. Callendar, 441:5Oct86-28
Frongia, G. Guida alla letteratura su
Wittgenstein.
M.A. Finocchiaro, 543:Dec84-388
Frongia, G. Wittgenstein, regole e
systema.
P. Engel, 542:Jan-Mar85-50
Froning, H. Marmor-Schmuckreliefs mit
griechischen Mythen im 1. Jahrhundert v.
Chr.
R. Ling, 313:Vol75-277
Frost, R. Prose Jottings of Robert Frost.
(E.C. Lathem and H. Cox, eds)
W.G. Heath, 106:Fall85-345
Frost, S.B. McGill University. (Vol 2)
L.R., 102(CanL):Spring85-183
Froula, C. To Write Paradise.*
L.S. Rainey, 405(MP):May86-441
H. Witemeyer, 191(ELN):Jun86-66
295(JML):Nov85-541
Fruchtman, J., Jr. The Apocalyptic
Politics of Richard Price and Joseph
Priestley.
M. Fitzpatrick, 83:Autumn85-236
A.H. Williamson, 319:Jul86-418
Fruin, W.M. Kikkoman.
T.B. Lifson, 293(JASt):Feb85-395
Sugiyama Shinya, 407(MN):Winter85-459
Frutkin, M. The Growing Dawn.
E. McNamara, 102(CanL):Winter84-113
Fry, C.B. Life Worth Living.
M. Imlah, 617(TLS):10Oct86-1128
Fry, H.T. A History of the Mountain Prov-
ince.
B. Cruikshank, 293(JASt):May85-668
Fry, P.H. The Poet's Calling in the
English Ode.*
N. Teich, 477(PLL):Winter85-88
Fry, P.H. The Reach of Criticism.*
H.R. Elam, 290(JAAC):Fall85-85
C. Nelson, 301(JEGP):Apr85-243
Fry, P.S. - see under Somerset Fry, P.
Fry, P.S. and F.S. - see under Somerset
Fry, P. and F.
Fryckstedt, M.C. Elizabeth Gaskell's
"Mary Barton" and "Ruth."
T.R. Wright, 161(DUJ):Dec84-126
Frye, N. Northrop Frye on Shakespeare.
(R. Sandler, ed)
R.M. Adams, 453(NYRB):6Nov86-50
S. Schoenbaum, 441:30Nov86-15
Frye, N. The Great Code.
N. Smith, 541(RES):May85-302
K. Williamson, 447(N&Q):Jun84-288

Frye, N. The Myth of Deliverance.*
R.P. Knowles, 178:Jun85-237
Frye, R.M. The Renaissance "Hamlet."*
R. Battenhouse, 125:Spring85-335
B.G. Lyons, 551(RenQ):Winter85-764
A.M. McLean, 615(TJ):Dec85-512
Frye, R.M. Shakespeare.
K. Muir, 677(YES):Vol 15-278
Fryer, J. Felicitous Space.
L. Auchincloss, 453(NYRB):17Jul86-31
Fryer, M.B. John Walden Myers.
W. Baker, 102(CanL):Winter84-69
Frymer, B. Jewish Horizons.
N. Guttman, 287:Apr85-26
Fu-ch'ing, H. - see under Huang Fu-ch'ing
Fubini, E. Les philosophes et la musique.
M-A. Lescourret, 98:Jun-Jul85-744
Fuchs, V. - see "Oxford Illustrated Ency-
clopedia"
Fudge, E.C. English Word-Stress.
L. Guierre, 297(JL):Sep85-518
J.T. Jensen, 320(CJL):Winter85-491
D.R. Ladd, 350:Mar86-170
Fuegi, J., G. Bahr and J. Willett, eds.
Beyond Brecht.
R. Ley, 397(MD):Dec85-690
de Fuentes, Á.G. - see under Galmés de
Fuentes. Á.
Fuentes, C. The Good Conscience.
I. Fonseca, 617(TLS):26Dec86-1456
Fuentes, C. The Old Gringo.*
S. French, 617(TLS):4Jul86-733
J. Mellors, 362:12Jun86-29
J. Updike, 442(NY):24Feb86-102
Fuentes, C. Where the Air is Clear.
S. French, 617(TLS):4Jul86-733
362:3Jul86-34
Fuentes, N. Hemingway in Cuba.
G. Johnson, 219(GaR):Spring85-212
J. Meyers, 395(MFS):Summer85-406
M.S. Reynolds, 27(AL):May85-343
Fuertes, G. Off the Map.
H.J.F. De Aguilar, 472:Spring/Summer/
Fall/Winter85-369
Fues, W.M. Mystik als Erkenntnis?
F.J. Tobin, 406:Summer85-216
Fühmann, F. Vor Feuerschlünden.
D.P. Lotze, 403(MLS):Fall85-372
Führer, B. Das Berlinische im Tages-
schrifttum von 1848/49.
D. Stellmacher, 685(ZDL):3/1985-383
Führer, C. The Mysteries of Montreal. (P.
Ward, ed)
L. Good, 529(QQ):Winter85-848
Fujii, T. Humor and Satire in Early
English Comedy and Japanese Kyōgen Drama.
S.L. Leiter, 615(TJ):May85-257
Fukuda, N., ed. Japanese History: A Guide
to Survey Histories. (Pt 1)
M.W. Steele, 407(MN):Summer85-234
Fukuda, N. Survey of Japanese Collections
in the United States 1979-1980.
H.C. Li, 302:Vol21No1-93
Fukumoto, N., Noboru Harano and Satoru
Suzuki - see under Naoyuki Fukumoto,
Noboru Harano and Satoru Suzuki
Fuller, C.J. Servants of the Goddess.
P. Price, 293(JASt):Aug85-854
Fuller, E. - see Royster, V.
Fuller, E.E. Milton's Kinesthetic Vision
in "Paradise Lost."*
G. Christopher, 301(JEGP):Jan85-120
[continued]

Fuller, E.E. Milton's Kinesthetic Vision in "Paradise Lost." [continuing]
P. Stevens, 627(UTQ):Spring85-285
J.S. Tanner, 70:Nov/Dec85-61
Fuller, F. The Translator's Handbook.
M.S. Peden, 238:Sep85-541
Fuller, J. The Adventures of Speedfall.
J. Mellors, 362:9Jan86-29
D. Sexton, 617(TLS):10Jan86-35
Fuller, J. Flying to Nowhere.
P. Wolfe, 502(PrS):Spring85-105
Fuller, J. Mass.*
M. Laski, 362:9Jan86-30
Fuller, J. Selected Poems 1954-1982.
D. Davis, 362:30Jan86-24
H. Haughton, 617(TLS):28Feb86-213
Fuller, J. - see Gay, J.
Fuller, K. Radical Aristocrats.
P. Renshaw, 617(TLS):30May86-600
Fuller, M. The Letters of Margaret Fuller.* (Vols 1 and 2) (R.N. Hudspeth, ed)
P.F. Gura, 639(VQR):Spring85-351
A. Kolodny, 301(JEGP):Apr85-289
E.S. Watts, 115:Spring84-150
Fuller, M. The Letters of Margaret Fuller. (Vol 3) (R.N. Hudspeth, ed)
M. Banta, 27(AL):Oct85-496
Fuller, P. Images of God.*
P. Faulkner, 326:Winter85/86-21
I. Jeffrey, 364:Jul85-87
Fuller, P. Marches Past.
M. Jones, 362:27Mar86-34
T. Phillips, 617(TLS):11Apr86-379
Fuller, P. The Naked Artist.* Aesthetics after Modernism.*
A. Harrison, 89(BJA):Autumn85-401
Fuller, R. New and Collected Poems 1934-84.*
D. Davis, 362:30Jan86-24
H. Lomas, 364:Oct85-78
J. Mole, 176:Jan86-55
P. Reading, 493:Oct85-64
W. Scammell, 148:Winter85-65
Fuller, R. Subsequent to Summer.
P. Reading, 617(TLS):25Apr86-450
Fuller, T.D. and others. Migration and Development in Modern Thailand.
E.B. Ayal, 293(JASt):May85-668
Fuller, W.C., Jr. Civil-Military Conflict in Imperial Russia 1881-1914.
F. Kazemzadeh, 441:16Feb86-13
M. Raeff, 617(TLS):30May86-601
Fullinwider, R.K., ed. Conscripts and Volunteers.
A.C., 185:Jan86-465
Fulton, A. Dance Script With Electric Ballerina.*
S.C. Behrendt, 502(PrS):Summer85-115
Fulton, R. - see Smith, I.C.
Fulton, R.D. and C.M. Colee, eds. Union List of Victorian Serials.
K. Chittick, 635(VPR):Winter85-149
Fulwiler, T. and A. Young, eds. Language Connections.
B.C. Mallonee, 126(CCC):May85-243
Fumaroli, M., ed. Le Statut de la littérature.*
D. Bellos, 208(FS):Apr85-242
Fung, E.S.K. The Military Dimension of the Chinese Revolution.
S.R. MacKinnon, 293(JASt):Feb85-368

Funke, H-G. Studien zur Reiseutopie der Frühaufklärung.* Fontenelle.
E.D. James, 208(FS):Jul85-339
Funkhouser, E. Natural Affinities.*
M. Kumin, 219(GaR):Spring85-169
von Fürer-Haimendorf, C. Tribal Populations and Cultures of the Indian Subcontinent.
N.J. Allen, 617(TLS):10Jan86-30
Furet, F., ed. Jules Ferry.
S. Englund, 617(TLS):26Sep86-1070
Furet, F. La Gauche et la Révolution française au milieu du XIXe siècle.
T. Judt, 617(TLS):26Sep86-1069
J-F. Revel, 176:Nov86-32
Furet, F. Marx et la Révolution française.
T. Judt, 617(TLS):26Sep86-1069
J-F. Revel, 176:Nov86-34
Furet, F. 1789 — Vom Ereignis zum Gegenstand der Geschichtswissenschaft.
W. Scott, 384:Jan86-60
Furetière, A. Le Roman bourgeois. (J. Prévot, ed)
H.T. Barnwell, 208(FS):Apr85-202
Furgurson, E.B. Hard Right.
S. Neal, 441:2Nov86-37
Furia, P. Pound's Cantos Declassified.
B. Raffel, 27(AL):Oct85-516
Furlong, M. Genuine Fake.
M. Pye, 617(TLS):9May86-507
Furman, L. Tuxedo Park.
F. Taliaferro, 441:28Sep86-14
Furness, R. Wagner and Literature.*
M. Gilbert, 406:Winter85-496
Furst, L.R. Fictions of Romantic Irony in European Narrative, 1760-1857.*
L. Metzger, 678(YCGL):No34-140
Furtwangler, A. The Authority of Publius.*
R.A. Ferguson, 27(AL):May85-327
M.P. Kramer, 173(ECS):Spring86-450
R.J. Morgan, 656(WMQ):Apr85-296
Fusek, L. - see "Among the Flowers: The Hua-chien chi"
Fusi, J.P. Franco.
P. Preston, 617(TLS):3Oct86-1093
Fussell, P. - see Sassoon, S.
Fuszek, R.M. Piano Music in Collections.
A.F.L.T., 412:Feb83-67
Futrell, A.W. and C.B. Wordell - see Maurer, D.W.

Gaál, K. and G. Neweklowsky, eds. Erzählgut der Kroaten aus Stinatz im südlichen Burgenland.
M. Bošković-Stulli, 196:Band26Heft3/4-356
Gaan, M. White Poppy.
S. Altinel, 617(TLS):18Jul86-793
El-Gabalawy, S., ed and trans. Three Pioneering Egyptian Novels.
V.J. Ramraj, 268(IFR):Summer86-107
Gabbay, D.M. and F. Guenthner, eds. Handbook of Philosophical Logic.* (Vol 1)
L. Humberstone, 63:Sep85-369
Gabel, G.U. Répertoire bibliographique des thèses françaises (1885-1975) concernant la littérature française des origines à nos jours.
H.T. Barnwell, 208(FS):Jul85-372
Gabin, R.J., ed. Cancionero del Bachiller Jhoan Lopez, Manuscrito 3168 de la Biblioteca [continued]

lioteca Nacional de Madrid.
A. Carreño, 304(JHP):Fall85-80
Gabler, H.W., with W. Steppe and C. Melchior - see Joyce, J.
Gablik, S. Has Modernism Failed?*
D.J. Drier, 55:Mar85-33
F. Frascina, 59:Dec85-515
P. Fuller, 90:Aug85-542
I. Jeffrey, 364:Jun85-109
Gabor, M. The Illustrated History of Girlie Magazines.
M. Distad, 635(VPR):Summer85-78
Gabriel, N. Peter Handke und Österreich.*
T.F. Barry, 221(GQ):Fall85-639
D.G. Daviau, 133:Band18Heft3-278
Gabriel, R.A. Military Incompetence.*
J.K. Simon, 129:Apr86-74
Gabriel, R.A. Operation Peace for Galilee.
D. Spanier, 176:Apr86-60
Gabriel, T.H. Third Cinema in the Third World.
R. Cancel, 2(AfrA):Aug85-97
Gabriel, Y. Freud and Society.
A. Dunn, 367(L&P):Vol32No1-57
Gächter, O. Hermeneutics and Language in Pūrva Mīmāṃsā.
J. Taber, 485(PE&W):Apr85-215
Gadamer, H-G. The Idea of the Good in Platonic-Aristotelian Philosophy.
A. Nehamas, 441:22Jun86-29
Gadamer, H-G. Philosophical Apprenticeships.*
M. Rosen, 617(TLS):16May86-520
Gadamer, H-G. Reason in the Age of Science.*
B. Cowan, 543:Mar85-626
Gadda, C.E. La connaissance de la douleur. Il tempo e le opere.
P. Lombardo, 98:Jun-Jul85-644
Gadda, C.E. That Awful Mess on Via Merulana.
D.J. Enright, 364:Mar86-104
Gaddis, W. Carpenter's Gothic.*
M. Gorra, 249(HudR):Winter86-663
A. Hislop, 617(TLS):28Feb86-215
R. Kelly, 138:No8-238
P. Kemp, 362:13Mar86-28
Gaddis, W. The Recognitions. JR.
P. Kemp, 362:13Mar86-28
Gadney, R. Cry Hungary! Uprising 1956.
442(NY):8Dec86-154
Gage, J.T. In the Arresting Eye.*
M. Perloff, 677(YES):Vol 15-344
Gagnon, J.C. Essaime.
R. Giroux, 102(CanL):Spring85-124
Gailey, A. Rural Houses of the North of Ireland.
T. Carter, 292(JAF):Oct/Dec85-492
Gaillard, C. Le Portugal sous Philippe III.
P. Loupes, 92(BH):Jul-Dec84-572
Gaines, J.F. Social Structures in Molière's Theater.
G. Defaux, 207(FR):Mar86-611
J-P. Dens, 356(LR):Aug85-229
Gair, R. The Children of Paul's.*
A. Gurr, 570(SQ):Summer85-248
P. Hollindale, 541(RES):Feb85-80
Gairdner, W.D. The Critical Wager.
E. Jewinski, 628(UWR):Fall-Winter85-78

Gaiser, K. Platone come scrittore filosofico.
J. Annas, 123:Vol35No2-401
Gala, A. Los verdes campos del Edén.
P. Zatlin, 552(REH):May85-150
Galan, F.W. Historic Structures.
J. Graffy, 617(TLS):2May86-477
M.E. Schaffer, 350:Sep86-735
M. Sprinker, 400(MLN):Dec85-1110
Galán, P.C. - see under Cerezo Galán, P.
Galanter, M. Competing Equalities.
M.R. Barnett, 293(JASt):Aug85-855
Galarza, E. Barrio Boy.
R. Saldívar, 153:Fall85-25
Galassi, J. - see Cornford, J.
Galay, T. After Baba's Funeral/Sweet and Sour Pickles.
A. Filewod, 108:Spring85-145
Galbraith, J.K. A View from the Stands. (A.D. Williams, ed)
T. De Pietro, 441:21Dec86-15
Galdós, B.P. - see under Pérez Galdós, B.
Galdós, B.P. and J. de Cubas - see under Pérez Galdós, B. and J. de Cubas
Gale, P. Ease.
P. Morrice, 441:14Dec86-24
Gale, R.L. Will Henry/Clay Fisher (Henry W. Allen).
J.D. Nesbitt, 649(WAL):May85-66
Galey, M. Marguerite Yourcenar.
A. Cismaru, 395(MFS):Summer85-441
Galford, E. The Fires of Bride.
R. Kaveney, 617(TLS):7Nov86-1255
Galich, A. Alexander Galich: Songs and Poems. (G.S. Smith, ed and trans)
V. Frumkin and M. Reichert, 550(RusR):Apr85-197
J. Graffy, 575(SEER):Jul85-447
Galisson, R. Des mots pour communiquer.*
J-P. Colin, 209(FM):Oct85-262
Galisson, R. and others. D'autres voies pour la didactique des langues étrangères.
E. Bautier-Castaing, 209(FM):Apr85-133
Gall, S.M. Ramon Guthrie's "Maximum Security Ward."*
M. Cowley, 569(SR):Winter85-ii
Gall, S.M. - see Guthrie, R.
Gallacher, T. The Jewel Maker.
G. Mangan, 617(TLS):2May86-478
Gallagher, C. The Industrial Reformation of English Fiction.
N. Berry, 617(TLS):21Mar86-312
J. Wallen, 400(MLN):Dec85-1183
Gallagher, D. - see Waugh, E.
Gallagher, S.F., ed. Woman in Irish Legend, Life and Literature.*
J. Mitchell, 178:Sep85-370
Gallagher, T. John Ford.
G. Johnson, 441:14Sep86-31
Gallagher, T. The Lover of Horses.
B. Pesetsky, 441:28Sep86-9
Gallagher, T. Under Stars. Instructions to the Double.
V. Karp, 472:Spring/Summer/Fall/Winter85-407
Gallagher, T. Willingly.*
J. Elledge, 491:Aug85-300
V. Karp, 472:Spring/Summer/Fall/Winter85-407
Gallais, P. Dialectique de récit médiéval (Chrétien de Troyes et l'hexagone
[continued]

133

García Márquez, G. and P. Apuleyo Mendoza. El olor de la guayaba.
    S. Karsen, 403(MLS):Fall85-365
García Montoro, A. El león y el azor.
    T. Montgomery, 545(RPh):May86-524
García-Posada, M. Lorca.
    C.B. Morris, 240(HR):Autumn85-506
García-Posada, M. - see Lorca, F.G.
Gardam, J. Crusoe's Daughter.*
    B. Coleman, 441:27Apr86-39
Garde, P., ed. IIIe Colloque de linguistique russe.*
    J.M. Kirkwood, 575(SEER):Jan85-110
Gardeazábal, G.A. - see under Alvarez Gardeazábal, G.
Garden, R.W. Modern Logic and Quantum Mechanics.
    R. Healey, 486:Dec85-642
Gardes, R. Un écrivain au travail.
    H. Godin, 208(FS):Jan85-108
Gardette, P. Etudes de géographie linguistique.
    H. Meier, 72:Band222Heft2-435
    R. Morgan, Jr., 207(FR):Feb86-477
Gardezi, H. and J. Rashid, eds. Pakistan.
    B.R. Rubin, 293(JASt):Feb85-422
Gardiner, S.C. Old Church Slavonic.
    W.R. Schmalstieg, 104(CASS):Summer85-231
Gardner, J. The Art of Fiction.*
    M. Lopez, 115:Summer85-384
Gardner, J. Nobody Lives Forever.
    J. Kaufman, 441:13Jul86-19
Gardner, J. On Becoming a Novelist.*
    E. Guereschi, 395(MFS):Summer85-428
    J.M. Howell, 403(MLS):Fall85-382
Gardner, J. Stillness [and] Shadows. (N. Delbanco, ed)
    P-L. Adams, 61:Aug86-92
    R. Gilman, 441:20Jul86-11
Gardner, P. Kingsley Amis.*
    J.L. Halio, 402(MLR):Jan85-148
Gardner, P. - see Forster, E.M.
Gardner, P.W. The Lost Elementary Schools of Victorian England.
    D.P. Leinster-Mackay and D.W. Collin, 637(VS):Summer86-635
Garebian, K. Hugh Hood.*
    M. Fee, 102(CanL):Winter84-121
Garelli, J. La gravitation poétique. Le recel et la dispersion. Artaud et la question du lieu. Le temps des signes.
    S. Meitinger, 98:Apr85-353
Garelli, P. Breton de los Herreros e la sua "formula comica."
    J-L. Picoche, 92(BH):Jan-Jun84-251
Garfield, E. Citation Indexing.
    P. Urbach, 488:Mar85-101
Garfield, J.L. and P. Hennessey, eds. Abortion.*
    J.C., 185:Jan86-467
Garfield, S. Expensive Habits.
    N. Berry, 617(TLS):17Oct86-1174
    D. Rimmer, 362:11Dec86-25
Gargan, W. and S. Sharma, eds. Find That Tune.
    B.L. Cooper, 498:Vol9No4-74
Garín Ortiz de Taranco, F.M. and others. Catálogo Monumental de la Ciudad de Valencia.
    D. Angulo Íñiguez, 48:Jan-Mar85-91
Garlén, C. Svenskans fonologi.
    C-C. Elert, 452(NJL):Vol8No2-233

Garlick, R. and R. Mathias, eds. Anglo-Welsh Poetry 1480-1980.
    W.H., 148:Summer85-93
    J. Saunders, 565:Autumn85-74
Garner, H. The Children's Bach.
    P. Craven, 381:Jun85-209
    K. Kramer, 441:7Dec86-79
    442(NY):29Sep86-135
Garner, H. Monkey Grip. Honour and Other People's Children.
    P. Craven, 381:Jun85-209
Garner, H. Postcards from Surfers.
    K. Kramer, 441:7Dec86-79
Garner, J.S. The Model Company Town.*
    K.C. Parsons, 432(NEQ):Dec85-639
Garner, P. Emile Gallé.*
    639(VQR):Winter85-10
Garner, S.N., C. Kahane and M. Sprengnether, eds. The (M)other Tongue.
    L.E. Buchanan, 367(L&P):Vol32No3-60
Garner, W. Zones of Silence.
    M. Laski, 362:3Jul86-32
Garnett, A. Deceived with Kindness.*
    295(JML):Nov85-373
Garnett, H. Family Skeletons.
    P. Craig, 617(TLS):12Dec86-1408
    J. Mellors, 362:20Nov86-28
Garnham, B.G. Robbe-Grillet: "Les Gommes" and "Le Voyeur."
    V. Minogue, 402(MLR):Jan85-180
    C. Rigolot, 207(FR):Apr86-799
Garnsey, P., K. Hopkins and C.R. Whittaker, eds. Trade in the Ancient Economy.*
    M.M. Austin, 303(JoHS):Vol 105-210
    T.T. Renner, 124:Sep-Oct85-57
Garnsey, P. and C.R. Whittaker, eds. Trade and Famine in Classical Antiquity.*
    M.M. Austin, 303(JoHS):Vol 105-209
    G.E. Rickman, 123:Vol35No1-105
Garr, W.R. Dialect Geography of Syria-Palestine, 1000-586 B.C.E.
    A.S. Kaye, 350:Sep86-726
Garrard, J. Leadership and Power in Victorian Industrial Towns, 1830-80.
    M.J. Winstanley, 637(VS):Spring85-561
Garrard, J., ed. The Russian Novel from Pushkin to Pasternak.*
    N.O. Warner, 550(RusR):Jan85-95
Garraty, J.A. The Great Depression.
    M. Olson, 441:26Oct86-29
Garrett, G. The Collected Poems of George Garrett.*
    J. Holden, 651(WHR):Summer85-155
    D.R. Slavitt, 385(MQR):Fall86-771
Garrett, G. An Evening Performance.*
    D.R. Slavitt, 385(MQR):Fall86-771
Garrett, G. James Jones.*
    J.R. Giles, 651(WHR):Autumn85-285
    C.P. Wilson, 27(AL):May85-349
Garrett, G. Poison Pen.
    H. Pekar, 441:5Oct86-25
Garrick, D. David Garrick: Selected Verse.* (J.D. Hainsworth, ed)
    C. Price, 447(N&Q):Mar84-96
    P. Rogers, 677(YES):Vol 15-303
Garrick, D. The Plays of David Garrick.* (Vols 3 and 4) (H.W. Pedicord and F.L. Bergmann, eds)
    J. Donohue, 402(MLR):Jan85-127
Garrido Garrido, J.M. Documentación de la catedral de Burgos (804-1183 & 1184-1222).
    D. Gifford, 304(JHP):Fall85-72

135

Garrison, D. - see Vorse, M.H.
Garrow, D.J. Bearing the Cross.
    H. Raines, 441:30Nov86-1
Gartner, C.B. Rachel Carson.
    J. Wexler, 405(MP):Feb86-330
Garton, T. Early Romanesque Sculpture in
    Apulia.
    P.W., 90:Aug85-546
Garulo Muñoz, T. Les arabismos en el
    léxico andaluz.
    K.I. Kobbervig, 545(RPh):May86-497
Garvey, S., with S. Rozin. Garvey.
    R. Litke, 441:11May86-24
Garvi, P.A. Zapiski sotsial-demokrata,
    1906-1921.*
    D.C.B. Lieven, 575(SEER):Jan85-137
Garvie, A.F. - see Aeschylus
Garvin, H.R. and J.M. Heath, eds. Litera-
    ture, Arts, and Religion.*
    W.L. Stull, 478:Oct85-233
Garvin, H.R. and S. Mailloux, eds. Rhet-
    oric, Literature and Interpretation.
    R.J. Fertel, 478:Oct85-236
Gascar, P. Le Diable à Paris.
    J. Blot, 450(NRF):Jun85-67
Gascoigne, B. Cod Streuth.
    P. Reading, 617(TLS):30May86-588
Gascoigne, B. and J. Ditchburn. Images of
    Twickenham.
    G.S. Rousseau, 579(SAQ):Winter85-99
Gascoigne, G. George Gascoigne, The Green
    Knight. (R. Pooley, ed)
    A.E.W., 148:Autumn85-91
Gash, J. The Tartan Ringers.
    T.J. Binyon, 617(TLS):8Aug86-863
Gash, J. The Tartan Sell.
    N. Callendar, 441:6Jul86-21
Gaskin, C. The Ambassador's Women.
    K. Ray, 441:18May86-24
Gaskin, J.C.A. The Quest for Eternity.*
    D. Brown, 393(Mind):Apr85-298
Gasparov, B. Poetika "Slova o polku
    Igoreve."
    H. Birnbaum, 104(CASS):Summer85-205
    T. Romanyk, 575(SEER):Oct85-579
de Gaspé fils, P.A. - see under Aubert de
    Gaspé fils, P.
Gass, S.M. and L. Selinker, eds. Language
    Transfer in Language Learning.
    J. Arabski, 351(LL):Sep85-489
    D. Masny, 399(MLJ):Summer85-166
    J. Vizmuller-Zocco, 320(CJL):Spring85-
    118
Gass, W.H. Habitations of the Word.*
    42(AR):Summer85-370
Gasset, J.O. - see under Ortega y Gasset,
    J.
Gasteyger, C., ed. The Future for Euro-
    pean Energy Security.
    P. McDonald, 617(TLS):25Jul86-820
Gaston, A-M. Śiva in Dance, Myth, and
    Iconography.
    C.R. Jones, 293(JASt):Feb85-424
Gaston, G.M.A. The Pursuit of Salvation.
    E. Davis, 268(IFR):Summer86-106
Gaston, J.C. London Poets and the Amer-
    ican Revolution.
    R. Morton, 106:Spring85-197
Gaston, P.M. Women of Fair Hope.
    639(VQR):Spring85-45

Gateau, J-C. Paul Éluard et la peinture
    surréaliste (1910-1939).*
    M-C. Dumas, 535(RHL):Mar/Apr85-324
    A.M. Russo, 188(ECr):Summer85-98
Gateau, J-C. Éluard, Picasso et la pein-
    ture (1936-1952).
    A.M. Russo, 188(ECr):Summer85-98
Gates, D. The Spanish Ulcer.
    D. Chandler, 617(TLS):4Jul86-742
    D. Middleton, 441:29Jun86-26
Gates, H.L., ed. Our Nig.
    B. Brown, 95(CLAJ):Mar86-378
Gates, H.L., Jr., ed. Black Literature
    and Literary Theory.*
    J. Weixlmann, 659(ConL):Spring86-48
Gathorne-Hardy, J. The City Beneath the
    Skin.
    J. Melmoth, 617(TLS):18Jul86-793
Gati, C. Hungary and the Soviet Bloc.
    A.J. McAdams, 441:14Dec86-34
Gauger, H-M. Untersuchungen zur span-
    ischen und französischen Wortbildung.
    A.S. Allen, 545(RPh):Nov85-246
Gauger, H-M., W. Oesterreicher and R.
    Windisch. Einführung in die romanische
    Sprachwissenschaft.*
    H-H. Körner, 603:Vol9No2-291
Gauguin, P. Correspondance de Paul Gau-
    guin. (Vol 1) (V. Merlhès, ed)
    R. Pickvance, 90:Jun85-394
Gaulmier, J., with J. Boissel - see de
    Gobineau, A-J.
Gaulmier, J., with P. Lesetieux and V.
    Monteil - see de Gobineau, A-J.
Gault, P. Golden Rod.
    D. Pope, 526:Spring85-93
Gaur, A. A History of Writing.*
    G. James, 324:Jul86-536
Gauthier, G. Initiation à la sémiologie
    de l'image. (new ed)
    S. Fischer, 207(FR):Oct85-180
Gauthier, H. L'Image de l'homme intérieur
    chez Balzac.*
    G.R. Besser, 207(FR):May86-981
    P. Somville, 542:Jul-Sep85-349
Gauthier, Y. Théorétiques.
    F. Lepage, 154:Spring85-101
    R. Nadeau, 154:Spring85-115
Gautier, T. Correspondance générale.
    (Vols 1 and 2) (C. Lacoste-Veysseyre and
    P. Laubriet, eds)
    V. Brombert, 617(TLS):26Sep86-1051
Gautier, T. Mademoiselle Dafné. (M.
    Eigeldinger, ed)
    U. Döring, 547(RF):Band97Heft4-482
    A.G. Gann, 446(NCFS):Spring-Summer86-
    355
Gautier, T. Poésies. (H. Cockerham, ed)
    J. Van Eerde, 446(NCFS):Spring-
    Summer86-357
"Théophile Gautier, l'art et l'artiste."*
    H.P. Lund, 535(RHL):Mar/Apr85-312
Gautier de Dargies. Poesie. (A.M. Raugei,
    ed)
    L.J. Friedman, 545(RPh):Feb85-393
Gavin, T. The Last Film of Emile Vico.
    N. Johnson, 441:1Jun86-23
Gay, J. John Gay: Dramatic Works.* (J.
    Fuller, ed)
    R.D. Hume, 301(JEGP):Apr85-271
    I. Simon, 179(ES):Apr85-178
    C. Winton, 569(SR):Fall85-1xxxv

Gay, J. John Gay: L'Opera du Gueux (The Beggar's Opera).* (J. Michon, ed and trans)
D.J.F., 83:Spring85-126
Gay, P. The Bourgeois Experience. (Vol 1)
R.J. Helmstadter, 635(VPR):Summer85-72
L.D. Nachman, 560:Winter-Spring85-171
Gay, P. The Bourgeois Experience. (Vol 2)
N. Annan, 453(NYRB):20Nov86-8
R. Jenkyns, 617(TLS):8Aug86-855
P. Kemp, 362:19Jun86-25
P. Robinson, 441:16Mar86-6
442(NY):21Apr86-125
Gay, P. Education of the Senses.
V.L. Bullough, 637(VS):Summer85-682
Gay, P. Freud for Historians.*
E. Gellner, 617(TLS):24Jan86-79
Gayet, C. The Intellectual Development of Henry David Thoreau.
R.E. Spiller, 677(YES):Vol 15-319
Gaylin, W. Rediscovering Love.
D. Goldstine, 441:12Oct86-45
P. Rose, 61:Sep86-100
Gayraud, M. Narbonne antique des origenes à la fin du IIIe siècle.*
J.F. Drinkwater, 313:Vol75-292
Gazdar, G., E. Klein and G.K. Pullum, eds. Order, Concord and Constituency.*
R. Salkie, 297(JL):Mar85-231
"Gazette officielle du Québec: Répertoire toponymique du Québec."
M. O'Nan, 424:Sep85-181
Gealt, A. Domenico Tiepolo: The Punchinello Drawings.
P-L. Adams, 61:Oct86-104
J. Russell, 441:7Dec86-73
Geanakoplos, D.J. Byzantium.
J.E. Rexine, 551(RenQ):Winter85-712
Gearhart, S. The Open Boundary of History and Fiction.*
G.P. Bennington, 208(FS):Oct85-483
F.M. Keener, 173(ECS):Summer86-557
P.H. Meyer, 207(FR):Apr86-784
Geary, J. Goethe's "Faust": The Making of Part I.
E. Bahr, 564:Feb85-64
Geary, J.S., C.B. Faulhaber and D.C. Carpenter, eds. Florilegium Hispanicum.
J. Snow, 545(RPh):Nov84-270
M.T. Ward, 240(HR):Summer85-363
Geary, R. Policing Industrial Disputes, 1893-1985.
M.B. Carter, 617(TLS):10Jan86-29
Gebauer, G., ed. Das Laokoon-Projekt.
H.B. Nisbet, 402(MLR):Oct85-988
Gebhard, D. Santa Barbara.
K.J. Weitze, 576:May85-188
Gebhard, D. and R. Winter. Architecture in Los Angeles.
505:Sep85-238
Gebhard, W. Nietzsche's Totalismus.
L.J. Elders, 543:Sep85-149
Gebhard, W. "Der Zusammenhang der Dinge."
G. Finney, 221(GQ):Fall85-619
Gébler, C. August in July.
J. Melmoth, 617(TLS):28Mar86-342
Gébler, C. The Eleventh Summer.*
M. Koenig, 272(IUR):Spring85-112
Geddes, G., ed. The Inner Ear.
B. Pell, 102(CanL):Spring85-136
Geddes, G. The Terracotta Army.
P. Jasper, 99:Dec85-24
S. Scobie, 376:Jan86-124

Geddes, P. A State of Corruption.*
N. Callendar, 441:8Jun86-34
Gedge, P. Stargate.
V. Broege, 198:Summer85-91
Gedge, P. The Twelfth Transforming.
N. Golfman, 102(CanL):Fall85-98
Geduld, H.M., ed. Charlie Chaplin's Own Story.
D. Robinson, 617(TLS):27Jun86-716
Geduld, H.M. The Definitive "Dr. Jekyll and Mr. Hyde" Companion.
R.A. Boyle, 637(VS):Autumn84-196
Gee, M. Light Years.*
G. Johnson, 441:13Apr86-22
P. Lewis, 364:Oct85-90
Geelhaar, C. and H.J. Jans. Stravinsky: Sein Nachlass.
A. Whittall, 410(M&L):Jul85-260
Geering, R.G. - see Stead, C.
Geerts, G. and others, eds. Algemene Nederlandse Spraakkunst.
J.G. Kooij, 204(FdL):Sep85-224
Geerts, G. and A. Hagen, eds. Sociolinguïstische studies, 1.
J. Vromans, 685(ZDL):1/1985-104
Gehring, W.D. Charlie Chaplin.
D. McKenzie, 615(TJ):May85-248
Geiger, G.L. Filippino Lippi's Caraffa Chapel.
C. Hope, 617(TLS):19Sep86-1038
Geiger, R.L. To Advance Knowledge.
J.M. Banner, Jr., 441:26Oct86-24
Geille, A. Une Femme amoureuse.
G.R. Besser, 207(FR):Oct85-150
Geiser, C. Wüstenfahrt.*
H. Graf, 384:Mar85-248
Geisst, C.R. The Political Thought of John Milton.
G.M. Ridden, 391:Mar85-23
Gelb, N. The Berlin Wall.
I. McDougall, 362:7Aug86-24
Gelb, N. Scramble.*
P-L. Adams, 61:Feb86-87
van Gelder, G.J.H. Beyond the Line.
A. Hamori, 318(JAOS):Apr-Jun84-385
Geldof, B., with P. Vallely. Is That It?
H. Kureishi, 617(TLS):8Aug86-874
Gelfand, E.D. Imagination in Confinement.*
L. Ezdinli, 210(FrF):Sep85-370
S. Rava, 207(FR):Feb86-452
Gelfant, B.H. Women Writing in America.
C. Cole, 395(MFS):Summer85-467
295(JML):Nov85-379
Gelles, B.J. Peshat and Derash in the Exegesis of Rashi.
F. Talmage, 318(JAOS):Jul-Sep84-576
Gelling, M. Place-Names in the Landscape.
F. Chevillet, 189(EA):Apr-Jun86-200
W.F.H. Nicolaisen, 424:Mar-Jun85-100
Gellman, B. Contending with Kennan.*
S.L., 185:Jan86-461
Gellner, E. Nations and Nationalism.*
J. Breuilly, 488:Mar85-65
Gellner, E. Relativism in the Social Sciences.
D.L.H., 185:Jul86-898
Gellrich, J.M. The Idea of the Book in the Middle Ages.
A.J. Minnis, 617(TLS):10Jan86-46
Gémar, J-C. Les Trois états de la politique linguistique du Québec.
T.R. Wooldridge, 627(UTQ):Summer85-487

Gendre, A., C-T. Gossen and G. Straka, eds. Mélanges d'Études Romanes du Moyen Age et de la Renaissance offerts à Monsieur Jean Rychner.
P.H. Stäblein, 545(RPh):Feb85-330
Gendreau-Massaloux, M. and P. Laurens, eds and trans. La pointe ou l'art du génie.
F. Graziani, 549(RLC):Oct-Dec85-464
Gendron, F. La Jeunesse sous Thermidor.
W. Scott, 384:Jan85-60
Genet, J. - see Yeats, W.B.
Genicot, L. L'économie rurale namuroise au bas moyen âge. (Vol 3)
B. Lyon, 589:Jan85-149
Genoud, C. and Takao Inoue. Buddhist Wall-Painting of Ladakh.*
S. Aryan, 60:Jul-Aug85-128
Gentili, B. Poesia e pubblico nella Grecia antica.
W. Donlan, 124:Sep-Oct85-63
Gentilini, G., ed. Il teatro umanistico veneto: La commedia.
A. Stäuble, 228(GSLI):Vol 162fasc518-276
Gentry, F.G., ed. German Medieval Tales.
R.W. Walker, 399(MLJ):Summer85-185
George, A.L., ed. Managing U.S.-Soviet Rivalry.
D.E. Powell, 550(RusR):Jul85-271
George, M. The Autobiography of Henry VIII.
B. Tritel, 441:12Oct86-28
George, N. Where Did Our Love Go?
L. Birnbaum, 441:30Mar86-19
George of Trebizond. Collectanea Trapezuntiana. (J. Monfasani, ed)
N.G. Wilson, 551(RenQ):Summer85-312
Georgeault, P. Conscience linguistique des jeunes Québécois.
M. Heller, 355(LSoc):Jun85-267
Georgiev, V. La lingua e l'origine degli Etruschi.
G.F. Meier, 682(ZPSK):Band38Heft6-760
Gephart, R.M., ed. Revolutionary America, 1763-1789.
D. Higginbotham, 579(SAQ):Autumn85-444
Geraci, G. Genesi della provincia romana d'Egitto.
A.K. Bowman, 313:Vol75-285
Geraghty, P.A. The History of the Fijian Languages.*
J. Lynch, 215(GL):Vol25No1-34
Gérard, J. L'Exclamation en français.
N.C.W. Spence, 208(FS):Jan85-120
Gerato, E.G. Guido Gozzano.
K.J. Jewell, 276:Autumn85-266
Gerber, A. Les Jours de vin et de roses.
J. Moss, 207(FR):Apr86-814
Gerber, D.E., ed. Greek Poetry and Philosophy.
H. Lloyd-Jones, 487:Autumn85-275
Gerber, D.E. Pindar's "Olympian One."*
R. Scodel, 122:Jul85-266
Gerber, M. and others, eds. Studies in GDR Culture and Society, 2.
A.D. Langdon, 221(GQ):Winter85-151
Gerber, M.J. Honeymoon.*
R.F. Dew, 344:Spring86-122
Gerber, P.L., ed. Critical Essays on Robert Frost.
W.G. Heath, 106:Fall85-345
Gerdin, I. The Unknown Balinese.
J.L. Ecklund, 293(JASt):Feb85-456

Gerhardi, G.C. Geld und Gesellschaft im Theater des Ancien Régime.
W. Henning, 547(RF):Band97Heft4-467
D. Ziegler, 475:Vol 12No22-318
Gerlach, J. Toward the End.
J.V. Hagopian, 27(AL):Dec85-690
W.C. Hamlin, 395(MFS):Winter85-721
Gerlaud, B. - see Triphiodorus
Gerli, E.M., ed. Triste deleytación.*
A. Gargano, 304(JHP):Fall85-77
Gerli, M. - see de Berceo, G.
Gerlovina, R. and others. Russian Samizdat Art.
C. Lyon, 441:23Nov86-25
German, T.J. Hamann on Language and Religion.*
W.M. Alexander, 301(JEGP):Jul85-405
Germán Romer, M. - see Rodríguez Freile, J.
Germer, H. The German Novel of Education from 1764 to 1792.
M. Swales, 402(MLR):Jul85-753
Germond, P. Sekhmet et la protection du monde.
J.H. Johnson, 318(JAOS):Apr-Jun84-361
Gerndt, H., K. Roth and G.R. Schroubek, eds. Dona Ethnologica Monacensia.
C. Daxelmüller, 196:Band26Heft1/2-149
Gernet, J. China and the Christian Impact.
D.E. Mungello, 441:7Sep86-32
Gernet, J. A History of Chinese Civilization.
J.L. Dull, 293(JASt):Nov84-165
Gerols, J. Le Roman québécois en France.
D.M. Hayne, 627(UTQ):Summer85-469
Gerould, D. and others, eds. Polish Plays in Translation.
L. Hecht, 574(SEEJ):Spring85-99
Gershon, K. The Bread of Exile.*
C. Goodrich, 441:16Feb86-16
Gerson, K. Hard Choices.
A. Hacker, 453(NYRB):14Aug86-26
Gerson, L.P., ed. Graceful Reason.*
M.D. Jordan, 589:Oct85-1047
Gerstenberger, D. Richard Hugo.
D.E. Wylder, 649(WAL):Aug85-187
Gerstler, A. White Marriage and Recovery.
T. Martin, 703:No13-152
Gervais, C.H. Public Fantasy.
M. Fiamengo, 102(CanL):Winter84-133
Gervers, M. The Cartulary of the Knights of St. John of Jerusalem in England, Secunda Camera: Essex.
W.T. Reedy, 589:Oct85-979
Gerz, R. Bertolt Brecht und der Faschismus.
P.L. Parmalee, 221(GQ):Fall85-628
Gessel, V.C. and Tomone Matsumoto, eds. The Showa Anthology.
H. Sato, 441:9Feb86-12
442(NY):12May86-126
Getchell, C. - see Benchley, R.
Gethin, D. Dane's Testament.
M. Laski, 362:17Apr86-29
Gethner, P. and E. Campion - see Du Ryer, P.
Getsi, L.C. Teeth Mother Letters.
J. McGowan, 236:Spring-Summer85-35
Getty, I.A.L. and A.S. Lussier, eds. As Long as the Sun Shines and Water Flows.
M. Bowering, 102(CanL):Spring85-170
Getty, J.A. Origins of the Great Purge.
R. Conquest, 617(TLS):9May86-503

Getz, W.  Sam Patch.
  B. Coleman, 441:2Nov86-26
Geuenich, D., R. Neumüllers-Klauser and K.
  Schmid.  Die Altarplatte von Reichenau-
  Niederzell.
  P.J. Geary, 589:Jul85-675
Geyer, I.  Die deutsche Mundart von
  Tischelwang (Timau) in Karnien (Ober-
  italien).
  H. Scheer, 350:Dec86-946
Ghatage, A.M., general ed.  An Encyclopae-
  dic Dictionary of Sanskrit on Historical
  Principles.  (Vol 2, Pts 2 and 3)
  O. von Hinüber, 259(IIJ):Apr85-135
Ghedini, F. and G. Rosada.  Sculture
  greche e romane del museo provinciale di
  Torcello.
  R. Adam, 555:Vol59fascl-162
Ghidetti, E.  Il caso Svevo.
  E. Saccone, 400(MLN):Jan85-188
Ghose, Z.  Figures of Enchantment.
  R. Hoffman, 441:27Jul86-18
Ghosh, A.  The Circle of Reason.
  A. Burgess, 441:6Jul86-6
  J. Mellors, 364:Mar86-98
  N. Shack, 617(TLS):11Apr86-382
Ghosh, D.  Translations of Bengali Works
  into English.
  J. Katz, 617(TLS):29Aug86-951
Giacolone, G.  Il Viaggio in Alamagna di
  F. Vettori e i miti del Rinascimento.
  E. Chevallier, 549(RLC):Jul-Sep85-335
Giacometti, M., ed.  The Sistine Chapel.
  C. Hope, 617(TLS):12Dec86-1399
Giamatti, A.B., ed.  Dante in America.
  R.B. Herzman, 589:Jul85-678
  L.R. Rossi, 276:Summer85-145
Giamatti, A.B.  Exile and Change in Renais-
  sance Literature.*
  C. Cairns, 278(IS):Vol40-126
  L. Potter, 161(DUJ):Jun85-267
Giardina, A. and A. Schiavone, eds.  Soci-
  età romana e produzione schiavistica.
  M.S. Spurr, 123:Vol35Nol-123
Gibans, N.F.  The Community Arts Council
  Movement.
  V.E. Whitfield, 476:Summer83-90
Gibault, F.  Céline.  (Vol 2)
  P. McCarthy, 617(TLS):6Jun86-625
Gibb, R.  The White House.
  455:Mar85-64
Gibbon, D. and H. Richter, eds.  Intona-
  tion, Accent and Rhythm.
  W. Cichocki, 350:Jun86-461
Gibbons, B.  Jacobean City Comedy.  (2nd
  ed)
  D.W. Pearson, 568(SCN):Spring-Summer85-
  14
Gibbons, R.W.  The CCFCS Collection of
  Musical Instruments.  (Vol 1)
  J.D.A. Widdowson, 203:Vol96Nol-131
Gibbs, A.M.  The Art and Mind of Shaw.*
  B.F. Dukore, 397(MD):Sep85-506
Gibbs, R.  A Mouth Organ for Angels.
  J.K. Keefer, 198:Summer85-107
Gibian, G. - see Seifert, J.
Gibian, G. and S.J. Parker, eds.  The
  Achievements of Vladimir Nabokov.*
  M. Couturier, 189(EA):Oct-Dec86-488
  D.B. Johnson, 574(SEEJ):Summer85-218
  E. Pifer, 550(RusR):Jul85-322

Gibson, A.M.  The Santa Fe and Taos
  Colonies.
  L. Horne, 106:Summer85-221
Gibson, J.M. and R.L. Green - see Conan
  Doyle, A.
Gibson, M.  Long Walks in the Afternoon.
  R. Mitchell, 460(OhR):No36-106
Gibson, M., ed.  To Breathe Freely.
  R.E.G., 185:Jul86-921
Gibson, R.W.  As It Comes.
  J.D.A. Widdowson, 203:Vol96Nol-131
Gibson, S.  More Than an Island.
  W.N., 102(CanL):Fal185-168
Gibson, W.  Count Zero.
  C. Greenland, 617(TLS):20Jun86-683
Gibson, W.M. and C.K. Lohmann - see
  Howells, W.D.
Gid, D.  Catalogue des reliures françaises
  estampées à froid (XVe-XVIe siècle) de
  la Bibliothèque Mazarine.
  A. Hobson, 617(TLS):3Jan86-24
Giddan, J.J. and N.S.  Teaching Language
  with Pictures.
  A.S. Kaye, 350:Mar86-231
Giddens, A.  A Contemporary Critique of
  Historical Materialism.*  (Vol 1)
  R.S. Gottlieb, 142:Winter86-87
Giddens, A.  A Contemporary Critique of
  Historical Materialism.  (Vol 2)
  B. Anderson, 617(TLS):28Mar86-333
Giddings, R., ed.  The Changing World of
  Charles Dickens.*
  B. Lecker, 150(DR):Winter84/85-800
  N.D. Miller, 158:Dec85-140
  H.S. Nelson, 637(VS):Autumn85-164
Giddings, R.  Musical Quotes and Anecdotes.
  K. Spence, 415:Apr85-226
Giddins, G.  Rhythm-a-ning.*
  R.M. Swann, 455:Sep85-74
Giddins, G.  Riding on a Blue Note.
  J.T. Titon, 187:Fal186-557
Gide, A.  Corydon.
  M. Stimpson, 617(TLS):7Mar86-254
Gide, A.  Travels in the Congo.
  617(TLS):25Apr86-459
Gide, A. and J. Last.  Correspondance
  (1934-1950).  (C.J. Greshoff, ed)
  P-L. Rey, 450(NRF):Oct85-87
Gidley, C.  The Believer.
  S. Altinel, 617(TLS):26Dec86-1456
Giedymin, J.  Science and Convention.
  J.R. Brown, 486:Mar85-168
Giegerich, H.J.  Metrical Phonology and
  Phonological Structure.
  D. Bates, 350:Sep86-706
Gier, N.F.  Wittgenstein and Phenomenol-
  ogy.*
  G. Hottois, 540(RIPh):Vol39fascl/2-184
Gierlich, H. - see von Saar, F.
Gifford, B. and L. Lee.  Saroyan.
  G. Haslam, 649(WAL):Feb86-370
Gifford, D.  The Complete Catalogue of
  British Comics.
  F. Barker, 364:Dec85/Jan86-156
Gifford, H.  Pasternak.
  A. Kerrigan, 569(SR):Spring85-312
Gifford, H.  Poetry in a Divided World.
  J. Bayley, 617(TLS):21Nov86-1295
Gifford, N.L.  When in Rome.*
  M. Smithurst, 518:Apr85-94
Gifford, T.  Where's The Justice?
  362:7Aug86-26

139

Gigante, M.  Scetticismo e Epicureismo.
  D. Fowler, 466:Vol2-237
Gilbert, A.  The Long Shadow.
  639(VQR):Autumn85-126
Gilbert, B.  In God's Countries.
  M.E. Ackerman, 649(WAL):May85-65
Gilbert, C.  Across the Mutual Landscape.*
  639(VQR):Spring85-56
Gilbert, E.L. - see Kipling, R.
Gilbert, G.N. and M. Mulkay.  Opening Pan-
  dora's Box.
  J-P. Courtial, 542:Jan-Mar85-70
Gilbert, J.  A Cycle of Outrage.
  N. Sayre, 441:18May86-35
Gilbert, J.A.  Clear Speech.*
  B.L. Ervin, 399(MLJ):Spring85-118
Gilbert, M.  Winston S. Churchill.  (Vol 7)
  W.F. Kimball, 441:14Dec86-12
Gilbert, M.  The Holocaust.
  R.K. Angress, 617(TLS):23May86-566
  G.A. Craig, 453(NYRB):10Apr86-7
  T.S. Hamerow, 129:May86-78
  A.J. Sherman, 441:9Feb86-7
  M. Warnock, 362:6Feb86-27
  442(NY):5May86-133
Gilbert, M.  Jerusalem.*
  R.C. Smail, 453(NYRB):10Apr86-42
  442(NY):24Mar86-127
Gilbert, M.  The Jews of Hope.*
  A. Wohl, 390:May85-62
Gilbert, M., ed.  The Oxford Book of Legal
  Anecdotes.
  P. Devlin, 617(TLS):8Aug86-869
  D. Pannick, 362:24Apr86-29
Gilbert, M.  Shcharansky.
  P. Reddaway, 453(NYRB):25Sep86-13
  D.K. Shipler, 441:25May86-8
  442(NY):30Jun86-88
Gilbert, P.  Dire l'Ineffable, lecture du
  "Monologion" de saint Anselme.
  J. Jolivet, 542:Apr-Jun85-246
Gilbert, S.M.  Emily's Bread.
  J. Penberthy, 617(TLS):18Apr86-430
  V. Shetley, 491:Apr85-45
Gilbert, S.M. and S. Gubar.  The Madwoman
  in the Attic.*
  D. Schneider, 38:Band103Heft1/2-233
Gilbert, S.M. and S. Gubar, eds.  The
  Norton Anthology of Literature by Women.*
  M. Perloff, 703:No14-132
Gilbert, W.S. and A.S. Sullivan.  The Anno-
  tated Gilbert and Sullivan.*  (I. Brad-
  ley, ed)
  J.B., 412:May83-143
Gilboa, Y.A.  A Language Silenced.
  J.V. Mallow, 362:Jan85-25
Gilborn, C.  Durant.
  S. Satterthwaite, 576:May85-192
Gilchrist, E.  Drunk with Love.
  W. Lesser, 441:5Oct86-18
Gilchrist, E.  Victory over Japan.*
  D. Flower, 249(HudR):Summer85-313
  P. Lewis, 364:Aug-Sep85-147
  J. Mellors, 362:16Jan86-30
  W. Peden, 651(WHR):Autumn85-269
  C. Rooke, 376:Sep85-141
Gildea, J. - see Peter of Waltham
Gildin, H.  Rousseau's Social Contract.*
  H.K., 185:Jan86-454
Gildner, G.  Blue Like The Heavens.
  F. Allen, 496:Fall85-179
  S. Scobie, 376:Jun85-131

Gildner, G.  The Crush.*
  C. Hagen, 448:Vol23Nol-114
Giles, F.  Sundry Times.
  A. Chancellor, 617(TLS):19Sep86-1026
Giles, G.J.  Students and National Social-
  ism in Germany.
  A.J. Nicholls, 617(TLS):27Jun86-703
Giles, M.  Rough Translations.*
  639(VQR):Autumn85-126
Giles of Rome.  On Ecclesiastical Power.
  (R.W. Dyson, ed and trans)
  O. Chadwick, 617(TLS):9May86-494
Gilissen, J.  La coutume.
  S.D. White, 589:Jan85-151
Gilkes, M.  The West Indian Novel.*
  J. King, 402(MLR):Jan85-151
Gill, A.  The Early Mallarmé.  (Vol 2)
  A. Raitt, 617(TLS):31Oct86-1226
Gill, B.  McGarr and the Legacy of a Woman
  Scorned.
  N. Callendar, 441:6Jul86-21
Gill, D., ed.  The Book of the Piano.
  412:May83-142
Gill, D., ed.  The Book of the Violin.
  R. Stowell, 415:Jul85-407
Gill, M.M., B. Wegmann and T. Méndez-Faith
  - see under McVey Gill, M., B. Wegmann
  and T. Méndez-Faith
Gillam, S.G., ed.  The Douce Legacy.
  P.R. Harris, 354:Jun85-191
Gillan, G.  From Sign to Symbol.
  R. McLure, 323:Jan85-91
Gillespie, G. and G. Spellerberg, eds.
  Studien zum Werk Daniel Caspers von
  Lohenstein anlässlich der 300. Wieder-
  kehr des Todesjahres.
  J.P. Aiken, 222(GR):Fall85-147
  B. Asmuth, 133:Band18Heft2-168
  J. Hardin, 221(GQ):Summer85-450
Gillespie, M.A.  Hegel, Heidegger, and the
  Ground of History.
  R. Beiner, 529(QQ):Autumn85-628
  D.A. Kolb, 319:Oct86-569
  W.S., 185:Oct85-216
  639(VQR):Summer85-84
Gillespie, M.P.  Inverted Volumes Improper-
  ly Arranged.
  C. Barrow, 174(Éire):Fall85-152
  C. Hart, 354:Sep85-287
Gillett, M. and K. Sibbald, eds.  A Fair
  Shake.
  R. Nemser, 102(CanL):Summer85-175
Gilliatt, P.  They Sleep Without Dreaming.*
  J. Mellors, 362:16Jan86-30
Gillies, M.  No Promises.
  J. Caird, 571(ScLJ):Autumn85-14
Gillis, C.M.  The Paradox of Privacy.*
  I. Grundy, 566:Autumn85-72
Gillis, P.  Days Like This.
  B. Ehrenreich, 441:27Jul86-8
Gillman, P. and L.  Alias David Bowie.
  C.S. Murray, 617(TLS):17Oct86-1174
  P. York, 362:9Oct86-23
Gillon, A.  Joseph Conrad.
  K. Williamson, 447(N&Q):Jun84-275
Gillon, W.  A Short History of African Art.
  J. Vansina, 2(AfrA):Aug85-21
Gilman, S.L.  Jewish Self-Hatred.
  R.K. Angress, 617(TLS):26Sep86-1068
Gilman, S.L.  On Blackness without Blacks.*
  W.F. Feuser, 538(RAL):Spring85-123
Gilman, S.L.  Wahnsinn, Text und Kontext.
  R.S. Struc, 107(CRCL):Sep85-503

Gilmont, J-F. Bibliographie des éditions de Jean Crespin, 1550-1572.* Jean Crespin.
  D.J. Shaw, 354:Sep85-274
Gilmore, M.T. Early American Literature.
  R. Morton, 106:Summer85-197
Gilot, M. and J. Sgard, eds. Le Vocabulaire du sentiment dans l'oeuvre de J-J. Rousseau.
  D. Williams, 208(FS):Jul85-348
Giloy-Hirtz, P. Deformation des Minnesangs.*
  I. Bennewitz-Behr, 684(ZDA): Band14Heft4-114
Gilpin, W. Trois essais sur le beau pittoresque, sur les voyages pittoresques et sur l'art d'esquisser les paysages.
  J-R. Mantion, 98:Oct85-989
Gilroy, B. Frangipani House.
  R. Deveson, 617(TLS):24Oct86-1187
Gils, P-M., with others - see Aquinas, T.
Gilson, D. A Bibliography of Jane Austen.*
  W.A. Craik, 541(RES):Aug85-439
  J.D.F., 447(N&Q):Mar84-138
  D.L. Vander Meulen, 517(PBSA):Vol79No3-435
Gimbernat de González, E. Paradiso.
  J.C. Ulloa, 238:Mar85-74
Gimello, R.M. and P.N. Gregory, eds. Studies in Ch'an and Hua-yen.
  D.L. Overmyer, 293(JASt):May85-586
Gimpel, R. Diary of an Art Dealer.
  617(TLS):15Aug86-899
Ginet, C. and S. Shoemaker, eds. Knowledge and Mind.*
  J.W.R. Cox, 518:Jan85-31
Gingell, S. - see Pratt, E.J.
Gingher, M. Bobby Rex's Greatest Hit.
  E. Pall, 441:14Dec86-27
Gingras, R. Syncope.
  R. Benson, 102(CanL):Spring85-171
Ginsberg, A. Collected Poems 1947-1980.*
  E. Butscher, 496:Winter86-234
  L. Hamalian, 363(LitR):Spring86-376
  M. Jarman, 249(HudR):Summer85-330
  W.G. Regier, 502(PrS):Winter85-105
  R. Tillinghast, 472:Spring/Summer86-193
  H. Vendler, 442(NY):13Jan86-77
  A. Williamson, 703:No14-159
  639(VQR):Summer85-97
Ginsberg, E.K. and L.M. Gottlieb, eds. Virginia Woolf.
  L. Blanchard, 594:Spring85-95
  M.M. Rowe, 395(MFS):Summer85-349
Ginsberg, W. The Cast of Character.*
  J.B. Friedman, 301(JEGP):Jul85-411
  R.W. Hanning, 589:Apr85-404
Ginsburg, N. and B.A. Lalor, eds. China.
  R.J. Latham, 293(JASt):May85-587
Ginsburgs, G. The Citizenship Law of the USSR.
  E. Huskey, 550(RusR):Oct85-403
Ginzburg, C. The Enigma of Piero.
  D. Summers, 617(TLS):23May86-570
  H. Trevor-Roper, 362:20Mar86-30
Ginzburg, C. The Night Battles.*
  P.H. Jobe, 539:Aug86-307
  W. Shumaker, 551(RenQ):Spring85-130
  A. Stone, 203:Vol196No2-267
Ginzburg, L. O starom i novom.
  S. Lubensky, 550(RusR):Jul85-320

Ginzburg, N. The Little Virtues.*
  K. Simon, 441:16Nov86-15
Gioia, D. Daily Horoscope.*
  T. Swiss, 441:30Nov86-17
Gioia, D. - see Kees, W.
Gioia, G. Ateismo e trascendenza.
  M. Adam, 542:Jan-Mar85-96
Giordano, F.R., Jr. "I'd Have My Life Unbe."
  R.K. Anderson, 395(MFS):Winter85-795
  M. Bath, 637(VS):Winter86-319
  K. Brady, 177(ELT):Vol28No2-206
  G.B. Tennyson, 445(NCF):Jun85-121
Gioscio, J. Il dialetto lucano di Calvello.
  D.J. Napoli, 350:Sep86-719
Giraldo, J.J.M. - see under Montes Giraldo, J.J.
Giraldo, J.J.M. and L. Flórez - see under Montes Giraldo, J.J. and L. Flórez
Giraldo, J.J.M. and M.L. Rodríguez de Montes - see under Montes Giraldo, J.J. and M.L. Rodríguez de Montes
Giralt, E.F. - see under Forment Giralt, E.
Girardet, F. The Cuisine of Fredy Girardet.
  W. and C. Cowen, 639(VQR):Spring86-67
Girardet, K.M. Die Ordnung der Welt.*
  E. Rawson, 313:Vol75-310
Girardot, N.J. Myth and Meaning in Early Taoism.*
  R.C. Neville, 485(PE&W):Oct85-431
Giraud, Y., ed. L'Emblème à la Renaissance.*
  C. Lauvergnat-Gagnière, 535(RHL): Sep/Oct85-854
Giraudoux, J. Théâtre complet.* (J. Body and others, eds)
  J. Voisine, 549(RLC):Jul-Sep85-367
Girgus, S.B. The New Covenant.*
  S.I. Bellman, 27(AL):May85-356
  M.J. Friedman, 587(SAF):Spring85-114
  M. Shapiro, 125:Winter85-216
Girke, W., H. Jachnow and J. Schrenk. Handbibliographie zur slavistischen und allgemeinen Linguistik in Osteuropa. (Vol 2)
  J. Udolph, 260(IF):Band90-366
Girling, R. Sprigg's War.
  442(NY):12May86-126
Girling, R., ed. The Sunday Times Travel Book.*
  442(NY):24Mar86-126
"Girodet."
  R. Wrigley, 90:Jun85-393
Girouard, M. Cities and People.*
  D. Bowen, 324:Jan86-127
  R. Harbison, 46:Nov85-102
  J. Summerson, 90:Dec85-904
Girouard, M. Robert Smythson and the Elizabethan Country House.*
  K. Downes, 90:Feb85-98
Girouard, M. Victorian Pubs.
  B.N., 636(VP):Summer85-222
Giroud, F. Marie Curie.
  T. Monmaney, 441:28Dec86-19
Giroux, R. The Book Known as Q.*
  W. Weiss, 156(ShJW):Jahrbuch1985-213
Giroux, R. - see Bishop, E.
Giscard d'Estaing, V. Démocratie Française. (A. Clark, ed)
  J. Howorth, 208(FS):Jan85-112

Gish, R.  Paul Horgan.*
  J.M. Day, 649(WAL):Nov85-265
Gissing, G.  A Life's Morning.  Workers in
  the Dawn.  (P. Coustillas, ed of both)
  S. Monod, 189(EA):Apr-Jun86-227
Gitelman, Z.  Becoming Israelis.
  E.R. Frankel, 550(RusR):Apr85-219
Gitler, I.  Swing to Bop.*
  A.V. Hewat, 617(TLS):8Aug86-874
Gittings, R. and J. Manton.  Dorothy Words-
  worth.*
  B. Ruddick, 148:Winter85-45
del Giudice, D.  Atlante occidentale.
  P.N. Furbank, 617(TLS):15Aug86-893
Giudice, F.  I pittori della classe di
  Phanyllis.  (Vol 1)
  T.H. Carpenter, 123:Vol35No2-419
  E.A. Moignard, 303(JoHS):Vol 105-236
Giusti, V.  Opere drammatiche.  (W. Drost,
  ed)
  F-J. Albersmeier, 547(RF):Band97
  Heft2/3-340
Given-Wilson, C.  The Royal Household and
  the King's Affinity.
  J.R. Maddicott, 617(TLS):18Jul86-796
Givner, J.  Tentacles of Unreason.*
  R.F. Dew, 344:Spring86-122
Givón, T.  Syntax.  (Vol 1)
  S. Carroll, 320(CJL):Fall85-343
  J. Heath, 350:Mar86-160
  J. Van der Auwera, 297(JL):Sep85-503
  J.W.M. Verhaar, 204(FdL):Jun85-149
Givón, T., ed.  Topic Continuity in Dis-
  course.
  P. Chen, 355(LSoc):Sep85-410
  A. Tellier, 189(EA):Jan-Mar86-87
Gladkij, A.V. and I.A. Mel'čuk.  Elements
  of Mathematical Linguistics.*  (J.
  Lehrberger, ed)
  S.G. Pulman, 297(JL):Mar85-262
Gladney, F.Y.  Handbook of Polish.
  L.R. Micklesen, 279:Vol29-160
  C.A. Wertz, 574(SEEJ):Summer85-231
Gladstein, M.R.  The Ayn Rand Companion.
  L. Lewis, 395(MFS):Summer85-413
Gladstone, W.E.  The Gladstone Diaries.
  (Vol 11) (H.C.G. Matthew, ed)
  C. Patten, 362:12Jun86-24
Glaeser, G. - see Brecht, B.
Glanville, B., ed.  The Joy of Football.
  S. Gilligan, 362:25Sep86-24
Glare, P.G.W. - see "Oxford Latin Diction-
  ary"
Glaser, G.  Das Tun ohne Bild.
  C. Jamme, 489(PJGG):Band92Heft2-408
Glasgow, E.  Barren Ground.
  P. Craig, 617(TLS):19Dec86-1428
Glasheen, A.  Third Census of "Finnegans
  Wake."
  R.D. Newman, 577(SHR):Spring85-185
Glass, J.M.  Delusion.
  T.M.R., 185:Apr86-695
Glasser, R.  Growing Up in the Gorbals.
  D. Craig, 362:25Sep86-23
Glassman, P.  J.S. Mill.
  J.N. Gray, 617(TLS):4Apr86-367
Glassman, R. and V. Murvar, eds.  Max
  Weber's Political Sociology.
  K.S., 185:Jul86-904
Glatzer, N.N.  The Loves of Franz Kafka.
  G. Josipovici, 617(TLS):4Jul86-738

Glauser, J.  Isländische Märchensagas.
  R. Cook, 563(SS):Spring85-197
  H. Engster, 196:Band26Heft1/2-151
  A. Heinrichs, 684(ZDA):Band114Heft2-46
  M.E. Kalinke, 402(MLR):Jan85-244
  H. Pálsson, 562(Scan):Nov85-225
Glaze, A.J.  Art and Death in a Senufo
  Village.
  J. Mack, 59:Sep85-391
Glazer, M., ed.  Flour from Another Sack,
  and Other Proverbs, Folk Beliefs, Tales,
  Riddles and Recipes.*
  G. Boyes, 203:Vol96No1-126
  S.R. Sherman, 292(JAF):Apr/Jun85-211
Gleckner, R.F.  Blake's Prelude.*
  D. John, 541(RES):Aug85-434
  D.M. Welch, 401(MLQ):Sep84-301
Gledson, J.  The Deceptive Realism of
  Machado de Assis.*
  D.T. Haberly, 238:Mar85-79
Glei, R.  Die Batrachomyomachie.
  M.L. West, 123:Vol35No2-379
Gleize, J-M.  Poésie et figuration.
  G. Cesbron, 535(RHL):Sep/Oct85-908
Glen, H.  Vision and Disenchantment.*
  J.R. Bennett, 627(UTQ):Spring85-299
  M.H. Friedman, 661(WC):Fall85-160
Glen, R.  Urban Workers in the Early Indus-
  trial Revolution.
  D. Nicholls, 637(VS):Summer85-687
Glendinning, R.J. and H. Bessason, eds.
  Edda.*
  M. Ciklamini, 301(JEGP):Jan85-103
  H. Kratz, 221(GQ):Spring85-272
Glendinning, V.  Edith Sitwell.
  V. Shaw, 677(YES):Vol 15-351
Glendinning, V.  Vita.*
  S. Pickering, 569(SR):Fall85-632
  M.M. Rowe, 395(MFS):Winter85-815
Glenmore, J.S. and W. Leman.  Cheyenne Top-
  ical Dictionary.
  D.G. Frantz, 269(IJAL):Jul85-325
Glenn, C.W.  Jim Dine: Drawings.*
  B. Schwabsky, 62:Jan86-14
Glennon, R.J.  The Iconoclast as Reformer.
  639(VQR):Summer85-96
Glenny, M. - see Lakshin, V.
Glickman, R.L.  Russian Factory Women.
  H. Reichman, 550(RusR):Oct85-421
Glickman, S.  Complicity.*
  L. Weir, 102(CanL):Winter84-105
Gligo, A.  María Luisa.
  L. Guerra-Cunningham, 263(RIB):
  Vol35No3-329
Glimcher, A. and M. - see Picasso, P.
Glissant, E.  Pays rêvé, pays réel.
  J. Silenieks, 207(FR):May86-995
Gloag, J.  Blood for Blood.*
  J. Mellors, 364:Jun85-102
Gloag, J.  Only Yesterday.
  C. Hawtree, 617(TLS):26Sep86-1058
Glock, W.S.  Eighteenth-Century English
  Literary Studies.
  566:Spring86-203
Glorieux, J-P.  Novalis dans les lettres
  françaises à l'époque et au lendemain
  du symbolisme (1885-1914).*
  R. Leroy, 133:Band18Heft1-89
"Glossaire des patois de la Suisse
  romande."  (fasc 76 and 77)
  P. Swiggers, 353:Vol23No4-644
Glover, D.  The Love Island.*
  C. Goodrich, 441:27Apr86-22

142

Goldberg, B. The Mirror and Man.
J. Zaleski, 469:Vol 11No2-110
Goldberg, E.L. Patterns in Late Medici
Art Patronage.*
M. Chiarini, 90:Sep85-628
Goldberg, J. James I and the Politics of
Literature.*
R.L. Greaves, 125:Fall84-87
R. Helgerson, 551(RenQ):Spring85-180
Goldberg, J. Rich and Poor.
T. De Pietro, 441:30Mar86-27
Goldberg, L. A Commentary on Plato's
"Protagoras."
C.C.W. Taylor, 123:Vol35No1-67
S. Umphrey, 543:Jun86-765
Goldberg, M.K. and J.P. Seigel - see
Carlyle, T.
Goldberg, R. Sex and Enlightenment.
D.J. Adams, 161(DUJ):Jun85-275
M. Blondel, 189(EA):Oct-Dec86-460
P. Rogers, 208(FS):Jul85-344
Goldberg, S.M. The Making of Menander's
Comedy.
P.G.M. Brown, 123:Vol35No1-18
Goldberg, V. Margaret Bourke-White.
T. Foote, 441:20Jul86-7
Goldberger, P. The Houses of the Hamptons.
V. Geibel, 441:10Aug86-19
Goldblatt, R. Axiomatising the Logic of
Computer Programming.
M. Wand, 316:Sep85-854
Golden, J.L., G.F. Berquist and W.E. Cole-
man. The Rhetoric of Western Thought.
(2nd ed)
C. Plantin, 540(RIPh):Vol39fasc4-459
Golden, M. A Woman's Place.
J. Wilson, 441:14Sep86-30
Golden, R.M. The Godly Rebellion.
R. Mettam, 208(FS):Apr85-199
Goldenberg, S. Trading.
J.H.C. Leach, 617(TLS):25Jul86-820
Goldensohn, L. The Tether.*
C. Wright, 448:Vol23No1-118
Goldhill, S. Language, Sexuality, Narra-
tive.*
E.S. de Angeli, 124:Jul-Aug86-419
M. Heath, 123:Vol35No2-243
Goldhill, S. Reading Greek Tragedy.
J. Gould, 617(TLS):26Sep86-1071
Golding, A.S. Classicistic Acting.
K. Neiiendam, 610:Spring85-74
Golding, R. Idiolects in Dickens.
S. Monod, 189(EA):Oct-Dec86-466
Golding, W. Äquatortaufe.
G. Seehase, 654(WB):9/1985-1533
Golding, W. An Egyptian Journal.*
C. Boyle, 364:Aug-Sep85-142
Goldman, E.A. Visions, Images, and Dreams.
F. Burko, 287:Mar85-27
Goldman, J. James Rosenquist.
A.B. Sandback, 62:Dec85-15
Goldman, L. Lights, Camera, Action!
G. Flatley, 441:13Jul86-18
Goldman, L.H. Saul Bellow's Moral Vision.
J. Braham, 395(MFS):Winter85-740
Goldman, M. Acting and Action in Shake-
spearean Tragedy.*
P.C. McGuire, 615(TJ):Dec85-511
Goldman, N. and L. Szymanski. English
Grammar for Students of Latin. (J.
Morton, ed)
D.N. Lacey, 399(MLJ):Winter85-422

Goldman, R.P. and S.J. Sutherland - see
"The Rāmāyaṇa of Vālmīki"
Goldmann, B. Wolf Heinrich Graf Baudissin.
J.K. Fugate, 406:Summer85-227
Goldsborough, R. Murder in E Minor.
N. Callendar, 441:18May86-38
Goldschläger, A. Simone Weil et Spinoza.
A. Roche, 535(RHL):Sep/Oct85-898
Goldschmidt, H., ed. Zu Beethoven, 2.
B. Cooper, 415:Aug85-463
Goldsmith, B. Strange Ailments; Uncertain
Cures.
C.L. Mithers, 441:28Dec86-18
Goldsmith, D. Nemesis.
442(NY):24Feb86-106
Goldsmith, J. - see Spender, S.
Goldsmith, R.W. The Financial Development
of India, Japan, and the United States.
The Financial Development of India, 1860-
1977. The Financial Development of
Japan, 1868-1977.
V.V. Bhatt, 293(JASt):Aug85-795
Goldsmith, U.K. and D. Goldschmidt - see
Weigand, H.J.
Goldstein, D. Hebrew Incunables in the
British Isles: A Preliminary Census.
D. McKitterick, 617(TLS):28Feb86-229
Goldstein, D. A la Russe.
W. and C. Cowen, 639(VQR):Spring85-67
Goldstein, I. My World As a Jew.
M.R. Konvitz, 390:Feb85-60
Goldstein, K.S. and N.V. Rosenberg, eds.
Folklore Studies in Honour of Herbert
Halpert.
R.D. Bethke, 650(WF):Jan85-68
Goldstein, L. The Flying Machine and Mod-
ern Literature.
C. Baldick, 617(TLS):14Nov86-1273
Goldstrom, J.M. and L.A. Clarkson, eds.
Irish Population, Economy, and Society.
272(IUR):Autumn85-257
Goldthorpe, R. Sartre.
C. Baldick, 617(TLS):14Nov86-1273
C. Howells, 323:May85-210
L.S. Roudiez, 546(RR):May85-339
B. Stoltzfus, 395(MFS):Winter85-829
42(AR):Spring85-252
295(JML):Nov85-551
Goldwasser, T. Family Pride.
S. Prokesch, 441:26Oct86-39
Goldwater, R. Symbolism.
R. Nasgaard, 127:Summer85-155
Goldwin, D. Les Nouvelles Françaises ou
les divertissements de la Princesse
Aurélie de Segrais.
R. Godenne, 475:Vol 12No22-322
Gole, S. India Within the Ganges.
J.E. Schwartzberg, 293(JASt):Feb85-425
Golinenko, O.A. and others - see Tolstoya,
S.
Golitsyn, A. New Lies for Old.*
M. Heller, 390:Jan85-50
Golla, V. - see Sapir, E. and A. Kroeber
Gollin, J. The Verona Passamezzo.
442(NY):10Feb86-116
Gollin, R.K. Portraits of Nathaniel Haw-
thorne.
C. Higgins, 658:Spring85-92
B. Jones, 27(AL):May85-334
Golovin, P.N. Civil and Savage Encoun-
ters.* (B. Dmytryshyn and E.A.P.
Crownhart-Vaughan, eds and trans)
G. Lewinson, 575(SEER):Oct85-606

Golub, S. Evreinov.
S.M. Carnicke, 574(SEEJ):Fall85-349
L. Senelick, 615(TJ):Mar85-131
Gom, L. NorthBound.*
J. Ditsky, 649(WAL):Nov85-256
Gombrich, E.H. The Image and the Eye.*
R.N. MacGregor, 289:Winter85-118
Gombrich, E.H. Tributes.*
M. Stein, 39:Jul85-77
R. Woodfield, 89(BJA):Autumn85-389
Gombrich, E.H. Aby Warburg.
J. Russell, 441:7Dec86-73
Gomery, D. The Hollywood Studio System.
L. Braudy, 18:May86-59
Gómez, I.M. - see under Mateo Gómez, I.
Gómez Asencio, J.J. Gramática y categor-
ías verbales en la tradición española
(1771-1847).
J.R. Craddock, 545(RPh):Feb85-381
Gómez Moreno, M. Las Águilas del Renaci-
miento español.
M. Estella, 48:Jul-Sep85-314
Gómez Moreno, M. Catálogo monumental de
la provincia de Ávila. (rev by Á. de la
Morena and T. Pérez de Higuera)
M. Estella, 48:Apr-Jun85-165
Gompers, S. The Samuel Gompers Papers.
(Vol 1) (S.B. Kaufman, ed)
J. McCartin, 441:6Jul86-15
Gong, G.W., A.E. Stent and R.V. Strode.
Areas of Challenge for Soviet Foreign
Policy in the 1980s.
639(VQR):Summer85-94
Gong, V., ed. Understanding AIDS.
J. Lieberson, 453(NYRB):16Jan86-43
Gonick, J. Mostly True Confessions.
M.F. Coburn, 441:14Sep86-18
Gontard, M. Violence du texte.
E. Sellin, 538(RAL):Spring85-106
González, A. La crónica modernista his-
panoamericana.
O. Rivera-Rodas, 238:Dec85-782
I.A. Schulman, 263(RIB):Vol35No4-464
González, C. "El Cavallero Zifar" y el
regno lejano.*
P. Cherchi, 379(MedR):Apr85-153
González, C., ed. "Libro del Caballero
Zifar."
J. González Muela, 240(HR):Autumn85-
482
L.O. Vasvari, 238:Sep85-510
González, E. La persona y el relato.
G. Pérez Firmat, 140(CH):Vol7No2-176
de González, E.G. - see under Gimbernat de
González, E.
González, J.J.M. - see under Martín Gon-
zález, J.J.
González Boixo, J.C. Claves narrativas de
Juan Rulfo. (2nd ed)
L.H. Peña, 238:Mar85-75
Gonzalez-Crussi, F. Three Forms of Sudden
Death.
I. Poliski, 441:5Oct86-55
González de Garay Fernández, M.T. Intro-
ducción a la obra poética de Francisco
López de Zárate.
C. Maurer, 240(HR):Spring85-244
González Echevarría, R. Isla a su vuelo
fugitiva.
P.B. Dixon, 395(MFS):Winter85-775
N. Lindstrom, 238:Mar85-78
J. Perez, 573(SSF):Spring85-255

González-Montes, Y. Pasión y forma en
"Cal y canto" de Rafael Alberti.
J. Bernardo Pérez, 552(REH):Oct85-140
González Muela, J., ed. Libro del Cabal-
lero Zifar.
C. González, 240(HR):Autumn85-483
González-Palacios, A. Il Tempio del Gusto.
H. Honour, 90:Nov85-813
Gonzalo, I.O. - see under Oceja Gonzalo, I.
Gooch, G., with A. Lee. Out of the Wilder-
ness.
A. Ross, 617(TLS):3Jan86-21
Good, I.J. Good Thinking.
C.L. Byrne, 543:Dec84-390
Goodacre, S.H. - see Carroll, L.
Goodall, J. The Chimpanzees of Gombe.
J.H. Crook, 441:24Aug86-12
Goodden, A. Actio and Persuasion.
J.H. Mason, 617(TLS):30May86-598
Goodenough, J.B. Dower Land.
W. Zander, 363(LitR):Spring86-379
Goodheart, E. The Skeptic Disposition in
Contemporary Criticism.*
G.S. Jay, 223:Fall85-297
L. Lane, Jr., 150(DR):Summer85-293
639(VQR):Summer85-89
Goodich, M. Vita perfecta.
P.J. Geary, 589:Apr85-406
Goodin, G. The Poetics of Protest.
M. Sperber, 395(MFS):Winter85-844
Gooding, D. and F.A.J.L. James, eds. Fara-
day Rediscovered.
J. Calado, 617(TLS):30May86-603
Goodkin, R.E. The Symbolist Home and the
Tragic Home.
C. de Dobay Rifelj, 446(NCFS):Spring-
Summer86-370
Goodman, D.S.G., ed. Beijing Street
Voices.
J. Saunders, 565:Autumn85-74
Goodman, M. State and Society in Roman
Galilee, A.D. 132-212.
L.J. Archer, 313:Vol75-303
M. Smith, 124:Jan-Feb86-202
Goodman, N. Of Mind and Other Matters.*
J. Bruner and C.F. Feldman, 453(NYRB):
27Mar86-46
M. Hanen, 518:Jul85-153
C. Lyas, 479(PhQ):Jul85-318
R.A. Sharpe, 89(BJA):Summer85-285
Goodman, N. Weisen der Welterzeugung.
J. Koepp, 384:Apr85-336
Goodrick-Clarke, N. The Occult Roots of
Nazism.
I. Kershaw, 617(TLS):19Dec86-1416
Goodstein, P.H. The Theory of the General
Strike from the French Revolution to
Poland.
W. Westergard-Thorpe, 104(CASS):
Spring85-104
Goodwin, D.W. Anxiety.
G. Butler, 617(TLS):16May86-542
Goodwin-Gill, G.S. The Refugee in Inter-
national Law.
A.E.S., 185:Apr86-658
Goodyear, F.H., Jr. Welliver.*
R. Bass, 55:Dec85-32
Goonatilake, S. Crippled Minds.
L.D. Wurgaft, 293(JASt):Feb85-434
Gooneratne, Y. Relative Merits.
S.R. Weisman, 441:21Sep86-43

Goonetileke, H.A.I. A Bibliography of Ceylon (Sri Lanka). (Vols 4 and 5)
K.S. Diehl, 293(JASt):Nov84-227
Goossen, E.C. Herbert Ferber.
M. Welish, 473(PR):Vol52No3-299
Goossens, J. De kwestie Lambertus "li Beges" (†1177).
D. Nicholas, 589:Oct85-982
Goossens, J., ed. Die Reynaert-Ikonographie.*
D. Blamires, 402(MLR):Jul85-749
Goossens, J., ed. Reynaerts Historie.*
D. Blamires, 402(MLR):Jul85-749
N.F. Palmer, 447(N&Q):Sep84-421
Göpfert, H.G., ed. Das Bild Lessings in der Geschichte.
C.O. Sjögren, 406:Summer85-220
Goppel-Meinke, B. Ein projektiver Lösungsversuch.
A. Grewe, 72:Band222Heft2-455
Gorbunow, W. Der Beitrag Lenins zur marxistischen Kulturtheorie.
J. Hertrampf, 654(WB):9/1985-1565
Gorceix, P. Le Symbolisme en Belgique.*
H. Felten, 52:Band20Heft1-100
Gordett, M. Freeze Tag.
M. Boruch, 460(OhR):No36-123
J.D. McClatchy, 249(HudR):Spring85-160
Gordillo, A.A.S. - see under Sánchez Gordillo, A.A.
Gordimer, N. Something Out There.*
639(VQR):Spring85-62
Gordon, A. The Evolution of Labor Relations in Japan.
R. Dore, 617(TLS):27Jun86-698
Gordon, C. The Southern Mandarins.* (S. Wood, ed)
E. Ammons, 27(AL):Mar85-169
H. Bevington, 579(SAQ):Summer85-332
Gordon, H. and J. Bloch, eds. Martin Buber.
W. Kluback, 390:May85-60
Gordon, I. and F. Weitzenhoffer - see Rewald, J.
Gordon, K.E. The Transitive Vampire.
T. De Pietro, 219(GaR):Spring85-207
Gordon, L. Robert Coover.*
R. Andersen, 577(SHR):Summer85-289
Gordon, L. Virginia Woolf.*
D. Gervais, 175:Autumn85-266
Gordon, M. Final Payments.
S. Gilead, 145(Crit):Summer86-213
Gordon, M. Men and Angels.*
W. Lesser, 249(HudR):Autumn85-471
Gordon, M. and A.C. Swinburne. The Children of the Chapel.* (R.E. Lougy, ed)
T.A.J. Burnett, 541(RES):Aug85-448
L.M. Findlay, 447(N&Q):Dec84-536
Gordon, M.M. - see Reid, B.J.
Gordon, N. The Physician.
J. Fast, 441:17Aug86-22
Gordon, S. A Talent for Tomorrow.
C. Hope, 364:Feb86-63
Gordon, W.T. A History of Semantics.*
R.H. Robins, 361:Dec85-329
Gorenstein, F. Psaume.
J. Blot, 450(NRF):Mar85-113
Gores, J. Come Morning.
N. Callendar, 441:30Mar86-22
Gori, F., ed. Pensiero e azione politica di Lev Trockij.
I. Getzler, 575(SEER):Apr85-307

Görlach, M., ed. Wilhelm Busch, Max und Moritz.
K. Kehr, 685(ZDL):2/1985-274
Görlach, M., ed. The Gestes of Mak and Morris.
T. Turville-Petre, 402(MLR):Oct85-898
Gorman, E. Murder Straight Up.
N. Callendar, 441:21Sep86-36
Gorman, L. beautiful chance.
A. Rotella, 404:Winter-Spring85-73
Gorman, L. Heart's Garden.
R. Willmot, 404:Summer85-47
Gormley, G. A Dolphin Summer.
B. Webster, 441:29Jun86-25
Gornick, V. Women in Science.
639(VQR):Winter85-29
van Gorp, H. and others, eds. Lexicon van literaire termen.
P.F. Schmitz, 204(FdL):Mar85-79
Goscilo, H. - see Nagibin, Y.
Gosling, J.C.B. and C.C.W. Taylor. The Greeks on Pleasure.*
J. Dybikowski, 122:Oct85-358
C.A. Freeland, 123:Vol35No1-77
R. Kraut, 482(PhR):Apr85-265
G. Neal, 303(JoHS):Vol 105-206
J.O. Urmson, 466:Vol2-209
A.M. Wiles, 543:Mar85-627
Gossett, P. and others. Masters of Italian Opera.*
D. Arnold, 410(M&L):Jan85-60
J.N. Black, 278(IS):Vol140-148
Gossett, P. and C. Rosen, eds. Early Romantic Opera.
W. Ashbrook, 317:Fall85-622
Gossman, L. Orpheus Philologus.
N.D. Smith, 125:Fall84-116
Gothot-Mersch, C. - see Flaubert, G.
Gotlieb, S. Wife of ...
F. King, 441:26Jan86-41
Gottlieb, S. - see Jenner, T.
Gottschalk, H.B. Heraclides of Pontus.
J. Mansfeld, 394:Vol38fasc1/2-202
Gottschalk, L. American Toy Cars and Trucks, 1894-1942.
W. Novak, 441:7Dec86-68
Gottsched, J.C. Ausgewählte Werke. (Vol 5, Pts 1 and 2) (P.M. Mitchell, ed)
H. Eichner, 301(JEGP):Jan85-82
Gottzmann, G.J. Njáls saga.
W.I. Miller, 563(SS):Winter85-84
Götze, H. Castel del Monte.
P.W., 90:Aug85-546
Goubault, C. La Critique musicale dans la Presse française de 1870 à 1914.
J-M. Bailbé, 537:Vol71No1/2-216
Gouk, P. - see Walker, D.P.
Gould, C. Bernini in France.*
R.M. Adams, 453(NYRB):8May86-9
Gould, C. and R.P. Morgan. South Carolina Imprints 1731-1800.
B. Franklin 5th, 365:Summer85-43
Gould, D. The Black and White Medicine Show.
I. McGilchrist, 617(TLS):7Nov86-1251
Gould, E., ed. The Sin of the Book.*
[shown in prev under Jabès, E.]
W.F. Motte, Jr., 400(MLN):Dec85-1193
Gould, G. The Glenn Gould Reader.* (T. Page, ed)
E. Ronsheim, 42(AR):Summer85-366
Gould, J. The Wines of Pentagoet.
J. Dodson, 441:28Sep86-44

Gould, P. Kitty Collins.
  E. Jarolim, 441:13Apr86-22
Gould, P. A Peasant of El Salvador.
  D. Devlin, 157:No156-49
Gould, M.S. A Cast of Hawks.
  B. Shulgasser, 441:16Feb86-17
Gould, S.J. The Flamingo's Smile.*
  M. Neve, 617(TLS):6Jun86-607
Gould, S.J. Quand les poules auront des
  dents.
  P. Pellegrin, 542:Jan-Mar85-71
Gould, W.B. Japan's Reshaping of American
  Labor Law.
  J.O. Haley, 293(JASt):May85-617
Gouldner, A.W. Against Fragmentation.*
  639(VQR):Autumn85-133
Goulet, A. Giovanni Papini juge d'André
  Gide.
  C. Angelet, 535(RHL):Jul/Aug85-696
Gourévitch, D-J., M-F. Forestier and J.
  Gourévitch. La Bonne lecture.
  J.T. Mitchell, 399(MLJ):Summer85-181
Gourley, E. The M Poems.
  A. Munton, 198:Winter85-100
  T. Whalen, 102(CanL):Winter84-75
Gouws, J. - see Greville, F.
Goux, J-P. Lamentations des ténèbres.
  J. Pfeiffer, 450(NRF):Jan85-94
Govier, K. Fables of Brunswick Avenue.
  A. Boston, 617(TLS):18Jul86-792
Govier, T. A Practical Study of Argument.
  C. Plantin, 540(RIPh):Vol39fasc4-474
Gowans, A. The Comfortable House.
  P. Goldberger, 441:7Dec86-16
Gowers, E. The Complete Plain Words.
  A. Burgess, 617(TLS):9May86-489
Gowing, L. The Originality of Thomas
  Jones.
  J.B. Shaw, 617(TLS):28Mar86-328
  A. Whittick, 324:Sep86-697
Goy, R.J. Chioggia and the Villages of
  the Venetian Lagoon.
  S. Pepper, 617(TLS):17Jan86-67
Goyard-Fabre, S. L'interminable querelle
  du contrat social.
  J. Boulad-Ayoub, 154:Spring85-166
Gozzano, G. La Signorina Felicita ovvero
  la felicità. (E. Esposito, ed)
  M. Bacigalupo, 402(MLR):Oct85-956
Gozzi, R., ed. Thoreau's Psychology.
  R. Sattelmeyer, 183(ESQ):Vol31No3-190
Grab, W. Heinrich Heine als politischer
  Dichter.
  G.F. Peters, 406:Spring85-106
  C. Prignitz, 224(GRM):Band35Heft3-358
Grabar, A. L'iconoclasme byzantin. (2nd
  ed)
  A. Reix, 542:Apr-Jun85-233
Grabar, O. The Illustrations of the
  Maqâmât.
  B. Gray, 39:Jun85-433
Grabar, O. - see "Muqarnas"
Grabes, H. The Mutable Glass.*
  D. Kay, 541(RES):Aug85-398
  G. Schmitz, 72:Band222Heft2-409
Grabo, N.S. The Coincidental Art of
  Charles Brockden Brown.*
  B. Christophersen, 651(WHR):Spring85-
  77
Grabow, S. Christopher Alexander.
  R. Banham, 617(TLS):3Jan86-15
Grace, S.E. The Voyage that Never Ends.*
  J. Kertzer, 178:Mar85-117

Gracia, J.J.E. and others, eds. Philosoph-
  ical Analysis in Latin America.
  J.E.K. Secada, 483:Oct85-550
Gracian, B. Art et figures de l'esprit.
  (B. Pelegrin, ed and trans)
  F. Graziani, 549(RLC):Oct-Dec85-464
Gracq, J. La Forme d'une ville.*
  F. de Martinoir, 450(NRF):Jul-Aug85-
  147
Gracq, J. The Opposing Shore.
  E. Cardonne-Arlyck, 441:22Jun86-9
Grade, C. My Mother's Sabbath Days.
  H. Gold, 441:16Nov86-12
Grade, C. Rabbis and Wives.*
  C. Leviant, 390:Feb85-54
Grady, J. Hard Bargains.
  N. Callendar, 441:2Mar86-28
Graebner, N.A. America as a World Power.
  639(VQR):Spring85-59
Graeffe, E. Untersuchungen zur Verwaltung
  und Geschichte der Institution der Gott-
  esgemahlin des Amun vom Beginn des Neuen
  Reiches bis zur Spätzeit.
  K.A. Kitchen, 318(JAOS):Oct-Dec84-765
Graff, G. and R. Gibbons, eds. Criticism
  in the University.
  D. Bialostosky, 454:Winter86-164
de Graffigny, F. Correspondance de Madame
  de Graffigny. (Vol 1) (E. Showalter,
  with others, eds)
  M. Gutwirth, 173(ECS):Summer86-542
Grafton, A. Joseph Scaliger.* (Vol 1)
  W. den Boer, 394:Vol38fasc3/4-456
  M.D. Feld, 517(PBSA):Vol79No3-457
  P.O. Kristeller, 31(ASch):Summer85-428
  C.G. Nauert, Jr., 551(RenQ):Spring85-
  107
Graham, C. Historical Explanation
  Reconsidered.
  H. Palmer, 518:Jan85-63
Graham, D. Cowboys and Cadillacs.
  P.A. Hutton, 649(WAL):Aug85-188
Graham, D. and S. Bidwell. Tug of War.
  H. Goodman, 441:17Aug86-23
Graham, D. and P. Clarke. The New Enlight-
  enment.
  C. Johnson, 617(TLS):19Dec86-1420
Graham, D., J.W. Lee and W.T. Pilkington,
  eds. The Texas Literary Tradition.*
  D.C. Grover, 50(ArQ):Summer85-189
Graham, G. Politics in its Place.
  D. Miller, 617(TLS):27Jun86-702
Graham, J. Erosion.*
  S.C. Behrendt, 502(PrS):Summer85-115
  A. Hudgins, 434:Summer85-526
  A. Melnyczuk, 472:Spring/Summer/Fall/
  Winter85-588
Graham, J.F., ed. Difference in Transla-
  tion.
  R. Greene, 400(MLN):Dec85-1126
Graham, M.B.W. RCA and the Videodisc.
  D.E. Sanger, 441:5Oct86-55
Graham, N. Seven Robins.
  S. Kamboureli, 102(CanL):Winter84-138
Graham, P.W. - see Hobhouse, J.C.
Graham, R. Spain.*
  639(VQR):Summer85-96
Graham, R.B.C. - see under Cunninghame
  Graham, R.B.
Graham-Yooll, A. A State of Fear.
  E. Crawley, 617(TLS):15Aug86-883
Grainger, J.H. Patriotisms.
  A. Sykes, 617(TLS):14Nov86-1264

Grainger, M. - see Clare, J.

Grainger, P. The Farthest North of Humanness. (K. Dreyfus, ed)
   P. O'Connor, 617(TLS):12Dec86-1394

Gram, M.S. Direct Realism.
   B. Mauud, 63:Dec85-538

Gram, M.S., ed. Interpreting Kant.
   A.C. Genova, 543:Mar85-629

Grambs, D. Words about Words.
   42(AR):Winter85-123

Gramsci, A. History, Philosophy and Culture in the Young Gramsci. (P. Cavalcanti and P. Piccone, eds)
   W. Graham, 275(IQ):Summer/Fall84-183

Gramsci, A. Selections from Cultural Writings. (D. Forgacs and G. Nowell-Smith, eds)
   R.S. Dombroski, 275(IQ):Summer/Fall84-167

Granaas, R.C. and others. Kvinnesyn — tvisyn.
   Å.H. Lervik, 172(Edda):1985/3-191

Grandi, D. Il mio paese.
   A. Lyttelton, 617(TLS):30ct86-1099

de Grandmont, É. First Secrets and Other Poems.
   K.W. Meadwell, 526:Spring85-78

Grandy, R.E. and R. Warner, eds. Philosophical Grounds of Rationality.
   J. Bennett, 617(TLS):24Oct86-1196

Granger, B. Hemingway's Notebook.
   A.P. Harris, 441:19Jan86-20

Granger, L. and B. The Magic Feather.
   P-L. Adams, 61:Nov86-140
   J. Perlez, 441:7Dec86-36

Granger, S. The Be + Past Participle Construction in Spoken English (with Special Emphasis on the Passive).*
   F.R. Palmer, 297(JL):Mar85-256

Grannes, A., A. Lillehammer and E. Pettersen. Documents russes sur la pêche et le commerce russes en Norvège au XVIIIe siècle.
   W.F. Ryan, 575(SEER):Jul85-429

Gransden, A. Historical Writing in England. (Vol 2)
   F.A.C. Mantello, 589:Apr85-408

Gransden, K.W. Virgil's "Iliad."*
   S.Q. Katz, 124:Jul-Aug86-415

Grant, G.P. English-speaking Justice.*
   A.S., 185:Apr86-697

Grant, M., ed. T.S. Eliot: The Critical Heritage.*
   R.Z. Temple, 536(Rev):Vol7-329

Grant, M. The History of Ancient Israel.
   M.M. Eisman, 124:Sep-Oct85-65

Grant, S.A. Scholars' Guide to Washington, D.C. for Russian/Soviet Studies. (2nd ed rev by B.P. Johnson and M.H. Teeter)
   J.E.O. Screen, 575(SEER):Apr85-317

Grant-Adamson, L. Guilty Knowledge.
   J. Mellors, 362:20Nov86-28

Grant-Adamson, L. Patterns in the Dust. The Face of Death.
   P. Craig, 617(TLS):19Dec86-1428

Granzotto, G. Christopher Columbus.*
   F. Fernandez-Armesto, 617(TLS):18Apr86-408

Grappin, P., ed. Actes du colloque Stefan Zweig.
   R. Dumont, 549(RLC):Jul-Sep85-366

Grass, G. Die Rättin.
   G.P. Butler, 617(TLS):4Apr86-355

Grasselli, M.M. and P. Rosenberg, with N. Parmantier. Watteau 1684-1721.
   P. Conisbee, 59:Sep85-359
   J. Sweetman, 324:Dec85-66

Grassi, E. Heidegger and the Question of Renaissance Humanism.
   B. Casper, 489(PJGG):Band92Heft1-211
   E.F. Hirsch, 319:Jan86-122
   L.V.R., 568(SCN):Spring-Summer85-28

Grassnick, M., ed. Materialien zur Baugeschichte.* (Vol 1) [entry in prev was of Vols 1-4]
   W.W. Wurster, 43:Band15Heft2-199

Grattan-Guinness, I., ed. From Calculus to Set Theory, 1630-1910.
   R. Jones, 486:Sep84-519

Grau, S.A. Nine Women.
   J. Canfield, 598(SoR):Autumn86-904
   M. Cantwell, 441:9Feb86-17

Grauer, N.A. Wits and Sages.
   E.L. Galligan, 569(SR):Spring85-283

de Grauwe, L. De Wachtendonckse Psalmen en Glossen.
   B.J. Koekkoek, 301(JEGP):Oct85-593

Gravell, T.L. and G. Miller. A Catalogue of Foreign Watermarks Found on Paper Used in America 1700-1835.
   P.S. Koda, 517(PBSA):Vol79No4-598

Graver, S. George Eliot and Community.*
   L. Lefkovitz, 454:Fall85-86
   F.C. Thomson, 445(NCF):Jun85-108
   R.T. Van Arsdel, 594:Spring85-105
   H. Witemeyer, 637(VS):Winter86-317

Graves, R. Rhetoric and Composition. (2nd ed)
   A.R. Gere, 128(CE):Jan85-58

Graves, R.J. Flamenca.
   S. Fleischman, 545(RPh):Nov85-274
   L.E. Jones, 589:Oct85-984

Graves, R.P. The Brothers Powys.*
   M. Buning, 179(ES):Jun85-280
   C. Lock, 447(N&Q):Dec84-545

Graves, R.P. Robert Graves. (Vol 1)
   D. Hibberd, 617(TLS):21Nov86-1299

Graves, R.P. A.E. Housman.
   P.G. Naiditch, 121(CJ):Apr/May86-365

Gravili, A.D. - see under de Vaucher Gravili, A.

Gray, A. The Fall of Kelvin Walker.*
   L. McCaffery, 441:21Dec86-7
   442(NY):22Sep86-116

Gray, A. Lanark.*
   J. Thielemans, 532(RCF):Spring85-154

Gray, A.S. Edwardian Architecture.*
   J.S. Curl, 324:Jul86-539

Gray, A.X.D. Memoirs of Many in One. (P. White, ed)
   J. Baumbach, 441:26Oct86-12
   B. Maddox, 362:3Apr86-28

Gray, B., general ed. The Arts of the Book in Central Asia.
   R. Hillenbrand, 59:Jun85-265

Gray, B. Sung Porcelain and Stoneware.
   Cheng te-K'un, 324:Aug86-630

Gray, D. and E.G. Stanley, eds. Middle English Studies Presented to Norman Davis in Honour of his Seventieth Birthday.*
   R. Dahood, 377:Mar85-46
   M. Rigby, 541(RES):Nov85-553

Gray, E.A., ed. Cath Maige Tuired.
   F. Kelly, 112:Vol 17-185

Gray, F.  John Arden.*
   A.P. Hinchliffe, 148:Spring85-87
Gray, F. and M. Tetel, eds.  Textes et
   intertextes.
   E. Kushner, 535(RHL):May/Jun85-475
Gray, J.  City in Revolt.
   H. Butler, 617(TLS):21Mar86-297
Gray, J.  Dazzled.
   L.K. Mackendrick, 102(CanL):Fall85-146
Gray, J.  Hayek on Liberty.
   P. Franco, 185:Apr86-651
Gray, J.C., ed.  Mirror up to Shakespeare.
   J. Baxter, 627(UTQ):Summer85-405
Gray, J.M. - see Tennyson, A.
Gray, M.K. - see Oliphant, M.
Gray, N.  Happy Families.
   D.J. Taylor, 176:Jan86-53
Gray, P.  Honey From a Weed.
   J. Grigson, 617(TLS):26Dec86-1454
Gray, R., ed.  American Fiction.*
   D. Seed, 541(RES):Nov85-605
Gray, R.  Cardinal Manning.*
   J. Clais, 189(EA):Oct-Dec86-468
   I. Ker, 617(TLS):7Feb86-136
Gray, R.  The Skylight.
   G. Bitcon, 581:Sep85-352
Gray, R.  Writing the South.
   P. Binding, 362:25Sep86-21
Gray, S.  Sex and Death to the Age 14.
   D. Guy, 441:4May86-32
Gray, S.  Swimming to Cambodia.
   L. Zeidner, 441:12Jan86-20
Gray, S.  An Unnatural Pursuit and Other
   Pieces.*
   M. Gussow, 441:6Apr86-23
   M. Meyer, 364:Oct85-106
Grayling, A.C.  Berkeley.
   J. Foster, 617(TLS):2May86-482
Grayling, A.C.  An Introduction to Philo-
   sophical Logic.
   S. Haack, 316:Jun85-553
Grayson, R.  Death en Voyage.
   M. Laski, 362:3Jul86-32
Graziano, C.  Dialoghi Simpatici.
   G. Jackson, 399(MLJ):Winter85-420
Graziano, F., ed.  Georg Trakl.*
   D. McDuff, 565:Winter84/85-73
Grazzini, N.F. - see under Forti Grazzini,
   N.
Greacen, R.  A Bright Mask.
   M. Harmon, 272(IUR):Autumn85-234
Gréban, A.  Le Mystère de la Passion.*
   (Vol 2) (O. Jodogne, ed)
   D. Smith, 356(LR):Aug85-226
Greciano-Grabner, G.  Signification et
   dénotation en allemand.
   F. Schanen, 680(ZDP):Band104Heft3-472
Greco, F.G., ed.  Spenser at Kalamazoo,
   1983.
   D.W. Pearson, 568(SCN):Spring-Summer85-
   4
"Greek Lyric."*  (Vol 1) (D.A. Campbell,
   trans)
   A.M. Bowie, 303(JoHS):Vol 105-198
Greeley, A.M.  Angels of September.
   M.L. Polak, 441:30Mar86-10
Greeley, A.M.  Confessions of a Parish
   Priest.
   S.A. Toth, 441:14Sep86-14
Greeley, A.M.  God Game.
   G. Jonas, 441:21Sep86-31
Green, C.  The Human Evasion.  (2nd ed)
   M. Adam, 542:Jul-Sep85-370

Green, D.  Bunter Sahib.*
   P. Parker, 364:Oct85-101
Green, D.  The Music of Love.
   G. Turner, 71(ALS):May85-132
Green, D.H.  The Art of Recognition in
   Wolfram's "Parzival."*
   I. Glier, 224(GRM):Band35Heft4-464
   J.F. Poag, 589:Oct85-1048
   K. Smits, 680(ZDP):Band104Heft3-454
Green, G.  East and West.
   H. Knight, 441:13Jul86-29
Green, G.  Literary Criticism and the
   Structures of History.*
   A.R. Evans, Jr., 131(CL):Winter85-90
   D.H. Hirsch, 569(SR):Summer85-465
Green, G.M.  No Picnic.
   D. Devlin, 157:No158-45
Green, H.  Fit for America.
   W. Bennett, 441:23Mar86-32
Green, J.  American Photography.
   H. Martin, 507:Jan/Feb85-114
Green, J.  Newspeak.
   D.J. Enright, 176:Jun86-63
Green, J.  Paris.
   L.A. MacKenzie, Jr., 207(FR):Apr86-830
Green, J.  The Slang Thesaurus.
   A. Burgess, 617(TLS):5Dec86-1373
Green, J.  The Small Theatre Handbook.
   B. Whiteman, 476:Spring82-68
Green, J. and D. Miller.  AIDS.
   D. Widgery, 362:4Sep86-21
Green, J.P.  Edmund Thornton Jenkins.
   E. Southern, 91:Spring85-119
Green, L.W.  The Silence of Snakes.
   W. Sullivan, 569(SR):Fall85-649
Green, M.  The Great American Adventure.
   M.G. De Jong, 27(AL):Mar85-155
Green, M.  Mountain of Truth.
   J. Joll, 453(NYRB):26Jun86-19
   J. Lucas, 362:18Sep86-23
   J. Seigel, 441:29Jun86-32
Green, M., ed.  The Old English Elegies.
   C. Chase, 589:Jul85-980
   D.A.H. Evans, 597(SN):Vol57No2-259
   T.A. Shippey, 179(ES):Jun85-272
Green, M. and J. Katsell - see Olesha, Y.
Green, M. and J. Swan.  The Triumph of
   Pierrot.
   W. Kendrick, 441:13Jul86-25
Green, M.D.  Black Women Composers.
   E. Southern, 91:Spring85-122
Green, P.  Retrieving Democracy.*
   J.K., 185:Jul86-893
Green, R.  Max Papart.
   R. Bass, 55:Nov85-29
Green, R.F.  Poets and Princepleasers.*
   D.R. Shore, 178:Dec85-491
Green, S.  Taking Sides.
   M. Rubner, 390:May85-59
Green, T.A.  Verdict According to Con-
   science.
   A.W.B. Simpson, 617(TLS):31Jan86-120
Green, V. - see Pattison, M. and M. Brad-
   ley
Greenbaum, S., ed.  The English Language
   Today.*
   W.N. Francis, 350:Dec86-942
Greenberg, A.  The Man in the Cardboard
   Mask.*
   P. Glasser, 455:Dec85-75
Greenberg, C.  The Collected Essays and
   Criticism.  (J. O'Brian, ed)
   J. Russell, 441:7Dec86-11

149

Greenberg, C. Mid-Century Modern.
J.V. Iovine, 45:Mar85-77
Greenberg, J. Simple Gifts.
M. Childress, 441:12Oct86-38
Greenberg, M. Detours of Desire.
C. Rolfe, 208(FS):Jan85-70
G. Verdier, 207(FR):Mar86-609
P. Zoberman, 546(RR):Jan85-119
Greenberg, M. Ezekiel, 3-20.
J.W. Wevers, 318(JAOS):Oct-Dec84-772
Greenberg, M.H. and A.R. Norton, eds.
Touring Nam.
639(VQR):Summer85-93
Greenberg, M.H. and B. Pronzini, eds.
Academy Mystery Novellas. (Vol 1)
P. Craig, 617(TLS):19Dec86-1428
Greenberger, E. and L. Steinberg. When
Teenagers Work.
M. Kaus, 441:26Oct86-30
Greenblatt, S., ed. The Power of Forms in
the English Renaissance.*
M.G. Brennan, 541(RES):Nov85-561
Greenburg, D. Confessions of a Pregnant
Father.
K. Davis, 441:23Mar86-44
Greene, D. - see Johnson, S.
Greene, D.B. Mahler, Consciousness and
Temporality.
P. Franklin, 410(M&L):Jul85-271
F.E. Maus, 451:Spring86-234
M. Taylor, 607:Mar85-43
J.W., 412:Aug/Nov84-296
Greene, D.B. Temporal Processes in
Beethoven's Music.*
F.E. Maus, 451:Spring86-234
S.D. Miller, 289:Fall85-118
Greene, G. The Tenth Man.*
C. Hawtree, 364:Apr/May85-143
639(VQR):Autumn85-126
Greene, J. Small Change for the Long Haul.
F. Chappell, 472:Spring/Summer86-237
Greene, J. - see Fet, A.
Greene, J.C. American Science in the Age
of Jefferson.
S.G. Kohlstedt, 656(WMQ):Jul85-420
Greene, J.P., ed. Encyclopedia of Amer-
ican Political History.
70:May/Jun85-166
Greene, J.P. and J.R. Pole, eds. Colonial
British America.
M.B. Norton, 656(WMQ):Jan85-119
Greene, N. The Papers of Nathanael Greene.
(Vol 2) (R.K. Showman, ed)
J.C. Cavanagh, 656(WMQ):Jan85-149
Greene, N. The Papers of Nathanael Greene.
(Vol 3) (R.K. Showman, ed)
J.C. Cavanagh, 656(WMQ):Jan85-149
A.J. Hayter, 83:Autumn85-223
Greene, T.M. The Light in Troy.*
G. Gueudet, 535(RHL):Mar/Apr85-285
D. Javitch, 131(CL):Winter85-69
W.J. Kennedy, 403(MLS):Spring85-82
J. Rees, 541(RES):Feb85-73
J. Roe, 447(N&Q):Jun84-261
A. Scaglione, 545(RPh):Aug84-99
Greenfield, T.N. The Eye of Judgment.*
J. van Dorsten, 179(ES):Oct85-467
N. Lindheim, 405(MP):Aug85-69
J. Robertson, 541(RES):Feb85-77
Greengrass, M. France in the Age of Henri
IV.
M. Heath, 208(FS):Jul85-330

Greenleaf, S. Beyond Blame.
N. Callendar, 441:30Mar86-22
442(NY):17Mar86-112
Greenway, D., C. Holdsworth and J. Sayers,
eds. Tradition and Change.
H. Lawrence, 617(TLS):5Sep86-984
Greenwood, J. Mosley Went to Mow.
R. Hill, 617(TLS):25Apr86-454
de Greenwood, P.F-C. - see under Fernández-
Cañadas de Greenwood, P.
Greenya, J. and A. Urban. The Real David
Stockman.
J.K. Galbraith, 453(NYRB):26Jun86-3
P.T. Kilborn, 441:18May86-17
Greer, B. Time Loves a Hero.
A. Gelb, 441:18May86-24
Greer, G. Sex and Destiny.*
J. Beerman, 42(AR):Winter85-117
T. McCormack, 529(QQ):Summer85-251
Greer, G. Shakespeare.
J. Bayley, 362:20Mar86-27
K. Brown, 617(TLS):22Aug86-917
A.S. Byatt, 176:Nov86-49
Greger, D. And.
J. Graham, 441:28Sep86-32
Gregg, E.E.W. - see Emerson, E.T.
Gregg, L. Alma.
J.D. McClatchy, 441:16Mar86-12
Gregg, R.B. Symbolic Inducement and Know-
ing.
L.W. Rosenfield, 480(P&R):Vol 18No4-
264
Gregor, B. Genuszuordnung.*
B. Carstensen, 38:Band103Heft1/2-133
Gregor, D.B. Romontsch — Language and
Literature.
E. Diekmann, 72:Band222Heft1-220
Gregor, I. The Great Web.
P. Coustillas, 189(EA):Jan-Mar86-106
Gregor-Dellin, M. Richard Wagner.*
R.L.J., 412:Aug/Nov83-291
T.E. Willey, 529(QQ):Spring85-213
Gregori, A., ed. I Campi.
E. Young, 39:Dec85-504
"Gregorii Ariminiensis, 'Lecture super
Primum et Secundum Sententiarum.'" (A.D.
Trapp, ed)
J. Jolivet, 192(EP):Oct-Dec85-565
di Gregorio, M.A. T.H. Huxley's Place in
Natural Science.*
E. Block, Jr., 637(VS):Spring86-468
Gregory, D. and J. Urry, eds. Social
Relations and Spatial Structures.
P. Jackson, 617(TLS):6Jun86-626
Gregory, S. The Cormorant.
P. Reading, 617(TLS):25Jul86-819
Gregory, S. Private Investigations.
P.B. McElwain, 590:Dec85-129
P. Wolfe, 395(MFS):Winter85-769
Gregory, W. The Shallow Grave.
H. Francis, 362:17Jul86-25
St. Gregory of Nazianzus. Grégoire de
Nazianze, "Discours 4-5 (Contre Julien)."
(J. Bernardi, ed and trans)
É. des Places, 555:Vol159fasc1-131
Greif, H.K. Historia de nacimientos.*
D.K. Benson, 400(MLN):Mar85-438
Greimas, A.J. Structural Semantics.*
C. Norris, 307:Dec85-186
Greiner, D.J. John Updike's Novels.
R.E. Burkholder, 580(SCR):Fall85-116
C.B. Harris, 659(ConL):Summer86-279
[continued]

Grimm, G.E. Literatur und Gelehrtentum in Deutschland.
J. Hardin, 564:Feb85-62
K.F. Otto, Jr., 301(JEGP):Oct85-601
Grimm, J. Das avantgardistische Theater Frankreichs, 1895-1930.*
W. Asholt, 535(RHL):May/Jun85-505
Grimm, J. Molière.
C. Abraham, 475:Vol 12No23-705
Grimm, J. and W. Brüder Grimm: Kinder- und Hausmärchen.* (Vols 1-3) (H. Rölleke, ed)
J.M. McGlathery, 406:Spring85-103
Grimm, J. and W. Märchen aus dem Nachlass der Brüder Grimm. (3rd ed) (H. Rölleke, ed)
J. Zipes, 133:Band18Heft2-178
Grimshaw, M.E. Pre-Victorian Silver School Medals Awarded to Girls in Great Britain.
P.A. Clayton, 324:Mar86-274
Grimsted, P.K., comp. Archives and Manuscript Repositories in the USSR: Estonia, Latvia, Lithuania, and Belorussia.
A. Ezergailis, 104(CASS):Summer85-237
Grindea, C., ed. Tensions in the Performance of Music.
P.J.P., 412:Aug/Nov83-304
Grindle, J. and S. Gatrell - see Hardy, T.
Grinspoon, L., ed. The Long Darkness.
E. Rhodes, 441:12Oct86-29
"Gripla." (Vol 5) (J. Kristjánsson, ed)
T.M. Andersson, 563(SS):Winter85-109
Grisanti, M.L. Rare Earth.
A. Krystal, 441:9Mar86-24
Grisman, A. The Winning Streak.*
442(NY):6Jan86-87
Grize, J-B. De la logique à l'argumentation.
R. Arnaud, 355(LSoc):Dec85-550
Grizzard, I. My Daddy was a Pistol and I'm a Son of a Gun.
E. Zotti, 441:19Oct86-31
Grizzard, L. Shoot Low, Boys — They're Ridin' Shetland Ponies.
A. Schmitz, 441:9Feb86-25
Grmek, M.D. Les maladies à l'aube de la civilisation occidentale.
P. Pellegrin, 542:Apr-Jun85-234
Groce, N. The Hammered Dulcimer in America.
A. Smith, 292(JAF):Jul/Sep85-368
Groce, N.E. Everyone Here Spoke Sign Language.
O. Sacks, 453(NYRB):27Mar86-23
Grodecki, L., with C. Brisac. Gothic Stained Glass: 1200-1300.
D.J.R. Bruckner, 441:2Feb86-16
Groenewegen, P. and J. Halevi, eds. Altro Polo: Italian Economics Past and Present.
A. Cigno, 278(IS):Vol40-141
Grojnowski, D. - see Laforgue, J.
de Grolier, E., ed. Glossogenetics.*
R.A. Hall, Jr., 205(ForL):Aug84-172
R.W. Wescott, 355(LSoc):Mar85-127
"The Grolier Club 1884-1984."
D.F. McKenzie, 517(PBSA):Vol79No4-579
Gronau, K. Literarische Form und gesellschaftliche Entwicklung.
R. Rumold, 406:Spring85-88
Grønbech, B. Hans Christian Andersen.
G.C. Schoolfield, 563(SS):Winter85-72

Gronemeyer, R. Zigeuner in Osteuropa.
T.F. Magner, 574(SEEJ):Summer85-200
van Groningen, B.A. Euphorion.
K.J. McKay, 394:Vol38fasc3/4-416
Grønvik, O. Runene på Tunesteinen.*
H. Beck, 301(JEGP):Apr85-297
R.L. Morris, 563(SS):Winter85-92
Groom, W. Forrest Gump.
J. Baumbach, 441:9Mar86-31
Groos, A. and R. Parker. Giacomo Puccini: "La bohème."
J. Budden, 617(TLS):24Oct86-1194
Grootes, E.K. Het literaire leven in de zestiende eeuw.
P.F. Schmitz, 204(FdL):Mar85-78
Groover, D.L. and C.C. Conner, Jr. Skeletons from the Opera Closet.
442(NY):22Dec86-92
Grosjean, F. Life With Two Languages.*
F. Nuessel, 361:Jul85-267
Grosjean, J. Jonas.
C. Dis, 450(NRF):May85-74
Grosrichard, A. Structure du sérail.
P. Saint-Amand, 188(ECr):Fall85-95
Gross, H. A Theory of Criminal Justice.
R. Birmingham, 449:Mar85-129
Grossberg, M. Governing the Hearth.
I. Marcus, 441:23Feb86-23
Grosseteste, R. Templum Dei Edited from MS. 27 of Emmanuel College, Cambridge. (J. Goering and F.A.C. Mantello, eds)
E.B. King, 589:Oct85-1048
Grosshans, H. Hitler and the Artists.*
S.L. Gilman, 221(GQ):Winter85-149
Grossholtz, J. Forging Capitalist Patriarchy.
V. Samaraweera, 293(JASt):Aug85-857
Grosskurth, P. Melanie Klein.
R. Dinnage, 453(NYRB):8May86-15
M. Jones, 362:10Jul86-30
S. Turkle, 441:18May86-14
Grosskurth, P. - see Symonds, J.A.
Grossman, J.D.. Valery Bryusov and the Riddle of Russian Decadence.
T.J. Binyon, 617(TLS):9May86-505
Grossman, M. Com es parla a l'Alguer?
M. Iliescu, 553(RLiR):Jan-Jun85-213
Grossman, R. The Animals.*
J. Saunders, 565:Spring85-72
Grossman, S. Julien Gracq et le surréalisme.
R. Cardinal, 208(FS):Apr85-229
Grossman, V. Forever Flowing.
M. Wandor, 362:16Oct86-25
Grossman, V. Life and Fate.*
A. Fitzlyon, 364:Oct85-94
R. Hingley, 441:9Mar86-1
S. Markish, 129:Apr86-39
J. Skvorecky, 453(NYRB):17Jul86-46
Grote, D. Script Analysis.
B. Kiralyfalvi, 615(TJ):Oct85-398
Grout, P.B. and others, eds. The Legend of Arthur in the Middle Ages.
J.M. Cowen, 447(N&Q):Dec84-528
P.J.C. Field, 541(RES):Aug85-410
Grove, F.P. Fanny Essler. (A.W. Riley and D.O. Spettigue, eds)
E.D. Blodgett, 102(CanL):Fall85-152
P. Hjartarson, 627(UTQ):Summer85-440
R. Mathews, 99:Apr85-35
Grove, F.P. The Genesis of Grove's "The Adventure of Leonard Broadus."* (M.
[continued]

[continuing]
Rubio, ed)
  P. Nodelman, 102(CanL):Winter84-149
Groves, D. - see Hogg, J.
Gruber, B. and M. Vedder. Kunst und
  Video.
  L. Zippay, 127:Fall85-263
Gruen, E.S. The Hellenistic World and the
  Coming of Rome.*
  K.R. Bradley, 121(CJ):Dec85/Jan86-167
  E.D. Carney, 124:Jan-Feb86-196
Gruending, D. Emmett Hall.
  B.H. Barlow, 647:Winter85-105
Gruenwald, I. Apocalyptic and Merkavah
  Mysticism.
  P. Schäfer, 318(JAOS):Jul-Sep84-537
Grundmann, S. Die Stadt.
  W. Schubert, 654(WB):9/1985-1572
"Grundriss der romanischen Literaturen des
  Mittelalters." (Vol 2, Pt 1, fasc 5)
  W.D. Paden, 589:Jan85-153
Grundtvig, N.F.S. A Grundtvig Anthology.
  (N.L. Jensen, ed)
  B. Baldwin, 563(SS):Spring85-223
Grundy, I., ed. Samuel Johnson.*
  J. Gray, 150(DR):Summer85-300
  W.H., 148:Autumn85-91
  A. Pailler, 189(EA):Apr-Jun86-218
Grundy, K.W. The Militarization of South
  African Politics.
  J.E. Spence, 617(TLS):15Aug86-882
Grünendahl, R. Hochschulschriften zu Süd-
  und Südostasien.
  P. Gaeffke, 318(JAOS):Oct-Dec84-780
Grunwald, L. Summer.
  C. Bancroft, 441:26Jan86-20
Grushow, I. The Imaginary Reminiscences
  of Sir Max Beerbohm.*
  H-P. Breuer, 395(MFS):Summer85-338
  C. Markgraf, 177(ELT):Vol28No3-315
  42(AR):Spring85-251
  295(JML):Nov85-448
Gryphius, A. Absurda Comica Oder Herr
  Peter Squentz Schimpfspiel. (G. Dünn-
  haupt and K-H. Habersetzer, eds)
  R.E. Schade, 133:Band17Heft3/4-325
Gryphius, A. Die Übersetzungen der Erbau-
  ungsschriften Sir Richard Bakers. (H.
  Powell, ed)
  V. Meid, 301(JEGP):Oct85-604
Grzimek, M. Heartstop.
  S. Pinsker, 573(SSF):Summer85-354
Gu Hua. Pagoda Ridge and Other Stories.
  P. Link, 441:6Jul86-16
Gualdo Rosa, L. La fede nella "paideia."
  J. Hankins, 551(RenQ):Autumn85-517
"The Guardian."* (J.C. Stephens, ed)
  [shown in prev under Steele, R.]
  J.D.F., 447(N&Q):Mar84-93
  C. Rawson, 541(RES):Feb85-96
Guarini, E.F., ed. Prato. (Vol 2)
  S. Woolf, 617(TLS):3Oct86-1098
Guback, D. Français commercial.*
  D. O'Connell, 207(FR):Dec85-313
Gubern, R. La censura.
  J-L. Marfany, 86(BHS):Apr85-212
Gudmudsson, F.G. Stephan G. Stephansson
  in Retrospect.
  E.S. Firchow, 563(SS):Spring85-208
Guégan, G. Pour toujours.
  P.A. Mankin, 207(FR):Dec85-337

Guenancia, P. Descartes et l'ordre poli-
  tique.*
  G. Ferreyrolles, 192(EP):Apr-Jun85-261
Guenther, R.J. - see Orlova, A.
Guérard, M. Michel Guérard's Cuisine for
  Home Cooks.
  W. and C. Cowen, 639(VQR):Spring85-68
Guérin de Bouscal, D. Le Gouvernement de
  Sanche Pansa. (C.E.J. Caldicott, ed)
  C.N. Smith, 208(FS):Jul85-336
Guerlac, R. - see Hutton, J.
Guernsey, P. Unhallowed Ground.
  C. Goodrich, 441:21Sep86-27
Gueroult, M. Descartes' Philosophy Inter-
  preted According to the Order of Reasons.
  (Vol 1)
  J. Cottingham, 518:Jul85-140
Guerra, L. Más allá de las máscaras.
  M.J. Treacy, 238:Dec85-788
Guerreau-Jalabert, A. - see Abbon de
  Fleury
Guery, F., ed. L'idée de la ville.
  E-E. Schmitt, 542:Oct-Dec85-552
Guest, B. Herself Defined.
  F.D. Crawford, 536(Rev):Vol7-215
  A. Morris, 271:Spring-Summer85-195
  J. Retallack, 472:Spring/Summer/Fall/
    Winter85-67
  295(JML):Nov85-468
Guest, H. The Emperor of Outer Space.
  J. Saunders, 565:Spring85-72
Guest, H. Lost and Found.
  T. Eagleton, 565:Winter84/85-68
Guest, I. Jules Perrot.
  S.A. Manning, 612(ThS):Nov85-205
Guez Ricord, C.G. La Mort a ses images.
  M. Hutchinson, 617(TLS):26Sep86-1050
Guha, A-A. Ende.
  G. Dyer, 362:3Jul86-34
"Francesco Guicciardini, 1483-1983."
  D.J. Wilcox, 551(RenQ):Summer85-323
Guichemerre, R. La Tragi-Comédie.*
  C.N. Smith, 208(FS):Jan85-112
Guichemerre, R. - see Scarron, F.
"A Guide to the Modern Literary Manu-
  scripts in the Special Collections of
  the Washington University Libraries."
  M.A. O'Donnell, 365:Summer85-41
"Guidelines for Journal Editors and Con-
  tributors." [MLA]
  M. West, 128(CE):Nov85-726
Guidicelli, C. Le Point de fuite.
  R. Knee, 207(FR):Dec85-338
Guidotti, C.R. - see under Ravanelli
  Guidotti, C.
Guidotti, G.C. - see under Cantini Gui-
  dotti, G.
Guiffrey, J. André le Nostre.
  J. Summerson, 617(TLS):28Nov86-1353
Guignon, C. Heidegger and the Problem of
  Knowledge.
  D.P. Michelfelder, 543:Sep85-150
  T.R. Schatzki, 262:Jun85-273
Guigonnat, H. Daemon in Lithuania.*
  I. Malin, 532(RCF):Fall85-189
Guilbaut, S. How New York Stole the Idea
  of Modern Art.*
  D. Craven, 59:Dec85-499
  B. Grosskurth, 627(UTQ):Summer85-507
  G. van Hensbergen, 90:Dec85-912
Guild, T.S. and H.L. Carter. Kit Carson.
  C.E. Trafzer, 649(WAL):Feb86-372

153

Guilherm, J-P. and others. Le Miroir des
Femmes. (Vol 1)
    Y. Bellenger, 549(RLC):Jul-Sep85-334
Guiliano, E. and J.R. Kincaid, eds. Soar-
ing with the Dodo.
    J. Bump, 637(VS):Winter85-316
Guillaume, G. Foundations for a Science
of Language.
    L.G. Kelly, 320(CJL):Winter85-493
Guillaume, G. and J-P. Chauveau, with R.
Lagrange-Barreteau. Atlas linguistique
et ethnographique de la Bretagne romane,
de l'Anjou et du Maine. (Vol 2)
    J. Chaurand, 209(FM):Oct85-256
    P. Rézeau, 553(RLiR):Jul-Dec85-512
Guillaume, J. and C. Pichois. Gérard de
Nerval.
    A. Du Bruck, 446(NCFS):Fall-
    Winter85/86-170
Guillaume, J. and C. Pichois, with others -
see de Nerval, G.
Guillaume, O. Fouilles d'Aï Khanoum.
(Vol 2)
    R.A. Tomlinson, 303(JoHS):Vol 105-229
Guillaume, P., J-M. Lacroix and P. Spriet,
eds. Canada et Canadiens.*
    W.N., 102(CanL):Fall85-185
"Guillaume de Machaut: Poète et composi-
teur."
    D. Ingenschay, 547(RF):Band97Heft2/3-
    302
    N. Wilkins, 382(MAE):1985/1-142
Guillaume le Clerc. The Romance of Fer-
gus.* (W. Frescoln, ed)
    K. Busby, 382(MAE):1985/2-333
    A.J. Holden, 402(MLR):Jul85-710
Guillebaud, J-C. L'Ancienne Comédie.
    T. Dey, 450(NRF):Feb85-91
    T.P. Fraser, 207(FR):May86-996
de Guillebon, R.D. La porcelaine à Paris
sous le Consulat et l'Empire.
    T. Préaud, 90:Oct85-723
Guillemin, H. L'Engloutie.
    J. Aeply, 450(NRF):May85-97
Guilleragues, G.D. Histoire d'Ali, prince
de Tunis. (G. Turbet-Delof, ed)
    F. Assaf, 475:Vol 12No22-389
    J-P. Leroy, 549(RLC):Jul-Sep85-343
    Z. Youssef, 535(RHL):Jan/Feb85-95
Guillermit, L. Le réalisme de F.H. Jacobi.
    A. Stanguennec, 542:Jul-Sep85-327
Guillory, J. Poetic Authority.*
    J. van Dorsten, 179(ES):Oct85-467
    R.S. Ide, 536(Rev):Vol7-89
    G.F. Waller, 125:Fal184-104
Guilloux, L. L'Herbe d'oubli.* (F.
Lambert, ed)
    J. Blot, 450(NRF):Apr85-79
Guimarães, C. Um Ato de Resistência.
    S.J. Albuquerque, 352(LATR):Spring86-
    127
Guinness, A. Blessings in Disguise.*
    P-L. Adams, 61:Apr86-131
    C. James, 453(NYRB):27Mar86-21
    M. Seldes, 441:6Apr86-14
    442(NY):24Mar86-124
Guitart, J. and J. Zamora Munné. Dialec-
tología hispanoamericana.
    H. Ruiz, 238:May85-332
Guitarte, G.L. Siete estudios sobre el
español de América.
    H. Meier, 547(RF):Band97Heft2/3-275

Guittard, J-M. Catalogue du fonds ancien
de la bibliothèque de l'Institut
d'Études Hispaniques de Paris.*
    T.S. Beardsley, Jr., 240(HR):Winter85-
    94
Guitton, E. - see Bernardin de Saint-
Pierre, J.H.
Gulati, L. Profiles in Female Poverty.
    H. Papanek, 293(JASt):Nov84-127
Gulden, A. Et es neme wíít frej wôôa.
    K. Kehr, 685(ZDL):2/1985-276
Gullace, G. - see Croce, B.
Gullick, J. Malaysia.
    R.O. Tilman, 293(JASt):May85-670
Gulliford, A. America's Country Schools.
    D. Medd, 46:Jul85-78
Gullón, G. La novela como acto imagina-
tivo.
    T.R. Franz, 240(HR):Winter85-106
Gullón, R. La novela lírica.
    R. Kirsner, 238:May85-310
Gumpel, L. Metaphor Reexamined.
    T.R. Austin, 350:Dec86-960
Gumperz, J.J. Discourse Strategies.
    N. Bruss, 608:Mar86-111
    B. Wald, 355(LSoc):Mar85-81
Gunatilleke, G., N. Tiruchelvam and R.
Coomaraswamy. Ethical Dilemmas of
Development in Asia.
    J.R. Macy, 293(JASt):May85-569
von Gunden, H. The Music of Pauline
Oliveros.*
    G.D.P., 412:Aug/Nov84-301
Gundermann, H. Einführung in die Praxis
der Logopädie.
    K-P. Becker, 682(ZPSK):Band38Heft4-443
Gungwu, W., M. Guerrero and D. Marr, eds.
Society and the Writer.
    I.V. Peterson, 318(JAOS):Jul-Sep84-608
Gunn, C.E. Workers' Self-Management in
the United States.
    D.C., 185:Oct85-213
Gunn, E.M., ed. Twentieth-Century Chinese
Drama.*
    P. Clark, 293(JASt):May85-602
Gunn, G., ed. The Bible and American Art
and Letters.
    K.R.R. Gros Louis, 149(CLS):Winter85-
    561
Gunn, J.A.W. Beyond Liberty and Property.*
    F. Dreyer, 529(QQ):Autumn85-638
Gunn, N.M. The Atom of Delight.
    617(TLS):21Nov86-1327
Gunn, T. The Occasions of Poetry.
    W.S. Di Piero, 569(SR):Winter85-140
Gunnars, K. The Night Workers of Ragnarök.
    S. Scobie, 376:Jan86-125
Guntermann, C.G., ed. Contemporary Latin
American Culture.
    C.M. Cherry, 399(MLJ):Autumn85-323
Günther, G. and H. Zeilinger. Wieland-
Bibliographie.*
    H. Schelle, 680(ZDP):Band104Heft2-296
    W.D. Wilson, 133:Band18Heft3-274
Gunther, J.D. Riverside County, Cali-
fornia, Place Names.
    K.B. Harder, 424:Dec85-274
Gupte, P. Vengeance.*
    D. Hiro, 617(TLS):18Jul86-782
Gura, P.F. A Glimpse of Sion's Glory.*
    S. Bush, Jr., 27(AL):May85-326
    E. Elliott, 432(NEQ):Mar85-104
    639(VQR):Winter85-7

154

Gura, P.F. and J. Myerson, eds. Critical
Essays on American Transcendentalism.*
  J.R. Reaver, 577(SHR):Spring85-178
Guralnick, E., ed. Vikings in the West.
  D.J. Shepherd, 563(SS):Spring85-210
Gurney, I. Collected Poems of Ivor Gurney.
  (P.J. Kavanagh, ed)
  A.H. Ashe, 161(DUJ):Jun84-308
Gurney, I. Ivor Gurney War Letters.
  (R.K.R. Thornton, ed)
  A.H. Ashe, 161(DUJ):Jun84-308
  S. Banfield, 410(M&L):Apr85-128
Guroff, G. and F.V. Carstensen, eds.
Entrepreneurship in Imperial Russia and
the Soviet Union.*
  M. Falkus, 575(SEER):Jul85-453
Gurr, A. - see Shakespeare, W.
Gürsel, N. Les Lapins du Commandant.
  L. Kovacs, 450(NRF):Nov85-111
Gurwitsch, A. Marginal Consciousness. (L.
Embree, ed)
  A.H. Vigneron, 543:Dec85-356
Gusdorf, G. Fondements du savoir roman-
tique.*
  S. Guerlac, 400(MLN):Sep85-887
Gusdorf, G. L'homme romantique.*
  M. Adam, 542:Jul-Sep85-332
Gusdorf, G. Du néant à Dieu dans le
savoir romantique.
  M. Adam, 542:Jan-Mar85-36
Güse, E.G., ed. Auguste Rodin, Drawings
and Watercolours.
  T. Hilton, 617(TLS):28Mar86-324
Gusmani, R. Lydisches Wörterbuch. (Supp,
Pt 2)
  A. Heubeck, 260(IF):Band90-295
Gussenhoven, C. On the Grammar and Seman-
tics of Sentence Accents.*
  J. Hirschberg and G. Ward, 350:Sep86-
707
  C.E. Keijsper, 204(FdL)Sep85-237
Gustafson, J.M. Ethics from a Theocentric
Perspective. (Vol 2)
  D. Sturm, 185:Apr86-654
Gustafson, R. At the Ocean's Verge.*
  F. Candelaria, 648(WCR):Oct85-63
  P.J.M. Robertson, 529(QQ):Winter85-838
Gustafson, R. Impromptus. Directives of
Autumn.
  F. Candelaria, 648(WCR):Oct85-63
Gustafson, R. and W.W.E. Ross. A Literary
Friendship. (B. Whiteman, ed)
  F. Candelaria, 648(WCR):Oct85-63
  A. Mortifee, 105:Fall/Winter85-105
Gustafsson, L. Stories of Happy People.
  E.O. Johannesson, 441:7Sep86-18
Gustafsson, L. The Tennis Players.*
  J. Byrne, 532(RCF):Spring85-152
Gútemberg Bohórquez C., J. Concepto de
"americanismo" en la historia del
español.
  P.M. Boyd-Bowman, 238:Sep85-537
"Gutenberg-Jahrbuch 1985." (H-J. Koppitz,
ed)
  J.L. Flood, 617(TLS):4Apr86-371
Gütersloh, A.P. Sonne und Mond. Der
Lügner unter Bürgern. Eine sagenhafter
Figur. Die Fabel von der Freundschaft.
  J. Adler, 617(TLS):30ct86-1087
Guthke, K.S. Der Mythos der Neuzeit.*
  D.C. Riechel, 221(GQ):Summer85-488
  W. Schatzberg, 301(JEGP):Jan85-95

Guthrie, R. Maximum Security Ward and
Other Poems.* (S.M. Gall, ed)
  M. Cowley, 569(SR):Winter85-ii
Gutiérrez Mouat, R. José Donoso.
  P. Bacarisse, 86(BHS):Jul85-325
Gutmanis, J. Na Pule Kahiko.
  W. Derden, 292(JAF):Jul/Sep85-367
Gutmann, A. and D. Thompson, eds. Ethics
and Politics.
  E. Bardach, 185:Oct85-206
Gutowski, A., A.A. Arnaudo and H-E.
Scharrer. Financing Problems of
Developing Countries.
  D. Delamaide, 617(TLS):28Feb87-222
Gutteridge, W., ed. The New Terrorism.
  P. Johnson, 617(TLS):29Aug86-929
Guttridge, L.F. Icebound.
  P-L. Adams, 61:Oct86-104
  R. Huntford, 441:10Aug86-11
Gutzwiller, A. Die Shakuhachi der Kinko-
Schule.
  R.K. Lee and G. Groemer, 187:Spring/
Summer86-353
Guy, A. Histoire de la philosophie
espagnole.
  M. Adam, 542:Oct-Dec85-553
Guy, A.J. Oeconomy and Discipline.*
  J. Black, 566:Spring86-231
Guy, J.A. The Public Career of Sir Thomas
More.
  E. McCutcheon, 77:Winter85-83
Gvozdanović, J. Tone and Accent in
Standard Serbo-Croatian.
  P. Rehder, 685(ZDL):2/1985-259
Gwaltney, J.L. The Dissenters.
  D. Nathan, 441:14Sep86-31
ap Gwilym, D. - see under Dafydd ap Gwilym
Gwyn, R. The 49th Paradox.
  R. Mathews, 99:Jan86-34
Gwyn, S. The Private Capital.
  H.B. Neatby, 102(CanL):Fall85-154
Gwynn, R.D. Huguenot Heritage.*
  R. Weinstein, 90:Jun85-393
Gwynne, S.C. Selling Money.
  M.M. Thomas, 441:26Oct86-28
Gysin, B. The Last Museum.
  M. Sanderson, 617(TLS):19Dec86-1428
362:4Sep86-30
Gysin, B. and T. Wilson. Here to Go.
  J. Campbell, 617(TLS):24Jan86-76


H.D. Collected Poems, 1912-1944.* (L.L.
Martz, ed)
  C. Doyle, 529(QQ):Summer85-310
  T. Eagleton, 565:Winter84/85-68
  A. Morris, 271:Spring-Summer85-195
  J. Retallack, 472:Spring/Summer/Fall/
Winter85-67
H.D. Helen in Egypt.* End in Torment.
Hermetic Definition.
  J. Retallack, 472:Spring/Summer/Fall/
Winter85-67
H.D. Nights.
  E. Jarolim, 441:10Aug86-18
H.D. Tribute to Freud.*
  L.M. Freibert, 50(ArQ):Spring85-96
  J. Retallack, 472:Spring/Summer/Fall/
Winter85-67
Haag-Higuchi, R. Untersuchungen zu einer
Sammlung persischer Erzählungen.
  U. Marzolph, 196:Band26Heft3/4-361

155

Haak, B. The Golden Age.*
C. Ford, 59:Jun85-234
P. Hecht, 90:Nov85-812
A. Washton, 55:Mar85-35
Haak, B. Hollandse schilders in de gouden
eeuw.
E. de Jongh, 600:Vol 15No1-65
Haake, K. No Reason on Earth.
B.F. Williamson, 441:28Sep86-26
Haaland, R. and P. Shinnie, eds. African
Iron Working.
M. McLeod, 617(TLS):6Jun86-629
de Haan, G. and W. Zonneveld, eds. Formal
Parameters of Generative Grammar, I.
T.F. Shannon, 350:Dec86-940
Haar, C.M. and D.W. Fessler. The Wrong
Side of the Tracks.
R. Dworkin, 61:Mar86-107
L.G. Forer, 441:13Apr86-15
Haar, M., ed. Martin Heidegger.
M.D. Villela-Petit, 192(EP):Apr-Jun85-
263
Haarder, A. and others, eds. The Medieval
Legacy.
R.G. Finch, 562(Scan):Nov85-227
Haas, A.M. and H. Stirnimann, eds. Das
"einig Ein."
B. McGinn, 406:Spring85-96
Haas, W. and H. Taylor. Sprechen wir
darüber.
J.L. Cox, 399(MLJ):Summer85-186
Haase, G. Dresdener Möbel des 18. Jahr-
hunderts.
G. Himmelheber, 683:Band48Heft4-575
Habachi, R. Le moment de l'homme.
B. Feillet, 192(EP):Oct-Dec85-560
Habegger, A. Gender, Fantasy and Realism
in American Literature.*
B. Pitz, 106:Fall85-317
Haberly, D.T. Three Sad Races.*
S.S. Kellum, 345(KRQ):Vol32No4-434
M. Silverman, 240(HR):Winter85-117
R. Wasserman, 141:Fall85-434
Habermas, J. Autonomy and Solidarity. (P.
Dews, ed)
M. Jay, 441:9Nov86-26
Habermas, J. Philosophical-Political Pro-
files.*
K.L. Schultz, 478:Oct85-256
L. Spencer, 323:May85-212
Habermas, J. Theorie des kommunikativen
Handelns.
K-H. Nusser, 687:Oct-Dec85-590
Habermas, J. The Theory of Communicative
Action. (Vol 1)
S.B. Smith, 185:Apr86-638
Habib, J.S. Ibn Saᶜud's Warriors of Islam.
R. Colman, 318(JAOS):Apr-Jun84-388
Habiby, E. The Secret Life of Saeed The
Pessoptimist.*
R. Irwin, 617(TLS):18Jul86-793
Habich, R.D. Transcendentalism and the
"Western Messenger."
S. Fender, 617(TLS):21Feb86-182
27(AL):Oct85-529
von Habsburg-Lothringen, G. Gold Boxes
from the Collection of Rosalinde and
Arthur Gilbert.
A.K. Snowman, 39:Feb85-136
Hachey, T.E. Britain and Irish Separatism.
S. Cronin, 174(Éire):Fall85-154

Hacker, M. Assumptions.*
P. Filkins, 363(LitR):Spring86-362
S.M. Gilbert, 491:Dec85-167
R. Saner, 152(UDQ):Summer85-107
P. Stitt, 344:Fall86-128
639(VQR):Autumn85-129
Hackett, J. The Profession of Arms.
G. Best, 176:Jun85-48
Hackett, N. XIX Century British Working-
Class Autobiographies.
I.B. Nadel, 637(VS):Summer86-651
Hacking, I. Representing and Intervening.*
J. De Groot, 543:Jun86-766
Y. Gauthier, 154:Spring85-162
J. Leplin, 486:Jun85-314
P. Menzies, 63:Dec85-540
M. Tiles, 483:Jan85-133
C. Wright, 518:Jan85-37
Hackl, U. Senat und Magistratur in Rom
von der Mitte des 2. Jahrhunderts v. Chr.
bis zur Diktatur Sullas.*
A. Lintott, 313:Vol75-237
Hadas, R. Slow Transparency.*
455:Mar85-65
Haddad, F.I. and E.S. Kennedy - see "ᶜAlī
ibn Sulaymān al-Hāshimī"
Hadfield, J. Every Picture Tells a Story.
E. Esdaile, 324:Sep86-698
Hadjadj, D. Parlers en contact aux con-
fins de l'Auvergne et du Forez.
J-P. Chambon, 553(RLiR):Jul-Dec85-509
N. Gueunier, 209(FM):Oct85-254
Hadley, A.T. The Straw Giant.
D. Middleton, 441:13Jul86-7
Hadot, P. Exercices spirituels et philos-
ophie antique.
R. Imbach, 98:Mar85-275
D.J. O'Meara, 543:Mar85-631
Hadrovics, L. and A. Hollós - see "Hungaro-
Slavica, 1983"
Haentjens, B. and J.M. Dalpe. 1932, la
Ville du Nickel.
J. Moss, 102(CanL):Fall85-145
Haffenden, J., ed. W.H. Auden: The Criti-
cal Heritage.*
A. Haberer, 189(EA):Jan-Mar86-110
Haffenden, J. The Life of John Berryman.*
R.M. Philmus, 106:Winter85-491
R. Pooley, 677(YES):Vol 15-364
Haffenden, J. - see Empson, W.
Hagarty, B. The Day the World Turned Blue.
B.L. Cooper, 498:Vol9No4-76
Hage, P. and F. Harary. Structural Models
in Anthropology.
E. Koskoff, 187:Winter86-167
Hageman, E.H. Robert Herrick.*
Z. Stribrny, 568(SCN):Spring-Summer85-
8
Hagemann, E.R. A Comprehensive Index to
Black Mask, 1920-1951.
P.Z. Du Bois, 87(BB):Dec85-216
Hagerty, J.C. The Diary of James C. Hag-
erty: Eisenhower in Mid-Course, 1954-
1955. (R.H. Ferrell, ed)
J.O. Robertson, 106:Winter85-465
Hägg, T. The Novel in Antiquity.*
A. Billault, 487:Summer85-186
G.N. Sandy, 303(JoHS):Vol 105-202
G. Schmeling, 24:Winter85-530
Haggard, V. My Life with Chagall.
S. Gablik, 441:17Aug86-6
Haggard, W. The Martello Tower.
M. Laski, 362:3Jul86-32

Haggenmacher, P. Grotius et la doctrine de la guerre juste.
S. Goyard-Fabre, 154:Winter85-717
A. Reix, 542:Jul-Sep85-314
Hagiwara, M.P. and F. de Rocher. Thème et variations. (3rd ed)
R.E. Hiedemann, 399(MLJ):Winter85-412
K.E. Kintz, 207(FR):Feb86-496
Haglund, D.G. Latin America and the Transformation of U.S. Strategic Thought, 1936-1940.
G. Frank, 263(RIB):Vol35No1-65
Hague, A. Iris Murdoch's Comic Vision.
J. Pickering, 395(MFS):Summer85-375
Hahl-Koch, J. - see Schoenberg, A. and W. Kandinsky
Hahn, M. Nāgārjuna's Ratnāvalī. (Vol 1)
C. Lindtner, 259(IIJ):Oct85-302
Hahn, N.L., ed. Medieval Mensuration.
B.S. Hall, 589:Apr85-409
Hahn, R. and others, eds. Die Lietung und Planung der kulturell-sozialen Bereiche.
P. Biermann, 654(WB):8/1985-1396
Hähnel, I., J. Rähmer and M. Dau, eds. Auswahl 84.
H. Riedel, 654(WB):12/1985-2055
Hähnel, K-D. Rainer Maria Rilke.
H. Nalewski, 654(WB):11/1985-1926
Haien, J. The All of It.
J. McCulloch, 441:19Oct86-30
442(NY):15Dec86-128
Haig, A. The Victorian Clergy.*
J.L. Altholz, 637(VS):Autumn86-321
Haig, S. Flaubert and the Gift of Speech.
C. Baldick, 617(TLS):14Nov86-1273
Haight, G.S. - see Eliot, G.
Haight, G.S. and R.T. Van Arsdel, eds. George Eliot.*
B. Hardy, 541(RES):Feb85-143
Hailey, E.F. Joanna's Husband and David's Wife.
R.D. MacDougall, 441:23Feb86-22
Hailperin, T. Boole's Logic and Probability.
N.T. Gridgeman, 316:Sep85-851
Hain, P. Political Strikes.
V. Bogdanor, 617(TLS):27Jun86-699
Haines, J. Living Off the Country.
R. McDowell, 249(HudR):Autumn85-509
Haines, V.Y. The Fortunate Fall of Sir Gawain.*
M. Furrow, 150(DR):Spring85-139
C. Gauvin, 189(EA):Jan-Mar86-89
T.A. Shippey, 447(N&Q):Sep84-418
Haining, P., ed. LBW — Laughter Before Wicket!
S. Fry, 362:18/25Dec86-55
Hains, M. The "Sacrestia della Messe" of the Florentine Cathedral.
C. Gould, 39:Feb85-137
Hainsworth, G.B. and others, eds. Southeast Asia.
E.C.K. Johnson, 293(JASt):May85-671
Hainsworth, J.B. and G.A. Privitera - see Homer
Hainsworth, J.D. - see Garrick, D.
Hajek, F. Selbstzeugnisse der Afroamerikaner.
H. Wüstenhagen, 654(WB):3/1985-523
Hájek, H.J. T.G. Masaryk Revisited.
Z.A.B. Zeman, 575(SEER):Jan85-131

Ḥājib, Y.K. Widsom of Royal Glory (Kutadgu Bilig).
R.W. Bulliet, 589:Jul85-743
Håkanson, L., ed. Declamationes XIX maiores Quintiliano falso ascriptae.
D.A. Russell, 123:Vol35No1-43
al Hakim, T. The Return of Consciousness.
P.J. Vatikiotis, 617(TLS):14Feb86-159
Hakuta, K. Mirror of Language.
H. Gardner, 453(NYRB):23Oct86-36
A. Levitt, 441:25May86-15
P.O. Tabors, 608:Dec86-752
Hakutani, Y., ed. Critical Essays on Richard Wright.
J. Mason, 392:Winter84/85-87
Hakutani, Y. - see Dreiser, T.
Halberstam, D. The Reckoning.
J.K. Galbraith, 441:26Oct86-1
442(NY):27Oct86-147
Halbfass, W. Studies in Kumārila and Śaṅkara.
J. Taber, 485(PE&W):Jul85-311
Halbrook, S.P. That Every Man Be Armed.
J.O., 185:Jan86-463
Haldane, D. Mamluk Painting.
R. Hillenbrand, 59:Jun85-265
Hale, A. Research on Tibeto-Burman Languages.
D.H., 355(LSoc):Dec85-573
Hale, J.C. The Jailing of Cecelia Capture.*
L. Owens, 649(WAL):Feb86-375
Hales, C. January Fire.
J. Carter, 219(GaR):Summer85-432
Hales, P.B. Silver Cities.
B.R. Kahler, 658:Winter85-308
R. Kimball, 45:Feb85-83
C. McShane, 432(NEQ):Jun85-306
Haley, J.L. Texas.
L. Milazzo, 584(SWR):Summer85-415
Haley, K.H.D. An English Diplomat in the Low Countries.
J. Kenyon, 617(TLS):11Jul86-755
Haley, S.C. A Nest of Singing Birds.
M. Stone, 150(DR):Spring85-129
Halford, M-B. Illustration and Text in Lutwin's "Eva und Adam."
T.R. Jackson, 402(MLR):Apr85-491
Halfpenny, P. Positivism and Sociology.
H. Bakker, 488:Jun85-224
Halimi, S. Aspects de la vie des campagnes dans le roman anglais de 1740 à 1780.
P. Wheatley, 541(RES):May85-278
Halka, C.S. Melquíades, Alchemy and Narrative Theory.
G. Pontiero, 86(BHS):Jul85-324
Halkin, J. Kenya.
M. Bowden, 441:31Aug86-12
Halkin, L-E. Erasmus ex Erasmo.*
H.R. Guggisberg, 517(PBSA):Vol79No3-460
Hall, A.R. Philosophers at War.
F. Duchesneau, 154:Summer85-365
Hall, D. Fathers Playing Catch With Sons.*
G. Ewart, 364:Feb86-110
J. Hildebidle, 434:Winter84-252
Z. Leader, 617(TLS):21Feb86-203
Hall, D. Goatfoot, Milktongue, Twinbird.
R. McDowell, 249(HudR):Autumn85-517

157

Hall, D., ed. The Oxford Book of Children's Verse in America.*
  J. Hollander, 676(YR):Summer85-xiii
  639(VQR):Autumn85-130
Hall, D. The Weather for Poetry.
  W.S. Di Piero, 569(SR):Winter85-140
  R. McDowell, 249(HudR):Autumn85-517
Hall, D. and C.C. Olds. Winter.
  P-L. Adams, 61:Apr86-132
Hall, D.D. and D.G. Allen, eds. Seventeenth-Century New England.
  R. Thompson, 432(NEQ):Dec85-602
Hall, D.J. Robert Frost.*
  P.L. Gerber, 659(ConL):Spring86-134
  W.G. Heath, 106:Fall85-345
  G. Rotella, 30:Spring86-91
Hall, D.L. Eros and Irony.
  A.L. Herman, 485(PE&W):Jan85-97
Hall, H.G. Comedy in Context.
  M-F. Hilgar, 207(FR):Mar86-612
  C.N. Smith, 208(FS):Apr85-205
  M-O. Sweetser, 475:Vol 12No23-708
Hall, H.G. A Critical Bibliography of French Literature.* (Vol 3A: The Seventeenth Century, Supplement)
  R. Rancoeur, 535(RHL):Mar/Apr85-296
Hall, H.W. SFBRI: Science Fiction Book Review Index. (Vol 14)
  R.M.P., 561(SFS):Jul85-225
Hall, H.W., ed. Science/Fiction Collections.
  L. Hatfield, 128(CE):Mar85-275
Hall, J.C. Selected and New Poems.
  W. Scammell, 364:Dec85/Jan86-119
Hall, J.M., ed. John Dryden.
  S. Archer, 568(SCN):Fall85-43
  J.D. Canfield, 566:Spring86-201
Hall, J.T.D., ed. The Tounis College.
  G. Donaldson, 617(TLS):24Oct86-1200
Hall, M. Harrison Birtwhistle.
  P. Griffiths, 415:Aug85-463
  D. Lancaster, 607:Mar85-35
  A. Whittall, 410(M&L):Jul85-277
Hall, M.G. Österreichische Verlagsgeschichte 1918-1938.
  E. Timms, 617(TLS):3Oct85-1089
Hall, M.G. and others. Die Muskete.
  F. Achberger, 221(GQ):Spring85-317
Hall, N.J. - see "Browning Institute Studies"
Hall, N.J. - see Trollope, A.
Hall, P. A Minor Operation.*
  S. Kamboureli, 102(CanL):Winter84-138
  S. Scobie, 376:Jun85-131
Hall, R.A., Jr. Proto-Romance Morphology.*
  H. van den Bussche, 361:Jul85-225
Hall, T.H. The Enigma of Daniel Home.
  F.B. Smith, 637(VS):Summer86-613
Hallahan, W.H. Foxcatcher.
  N. Callendar, 441:11May86-32
Hallam, E.M. Domesday Book. Domesday Heritage.
  H.R. Loyn, 617(TLS):16May86-526
von Hallberg, R. American Poetry and Culture 1945-1980.*
  J.G. Kronick, 659(ConL):Summer86-265
  L. Mackinnon, 617(TLS):9May86-506
  M. Perloff, 191(ELN):Jun86-61
  V. Shetley, 676(YR):Spring86-429
von Hallberg, R., ed. Canons.
  W.V. Harris, 568(SCN):Winter85-61
Halle, K. - see Churchill, W.S.

Halle, L.J. The Elements of International Strategy.
  M.T., 185:Jan86-459
Halle, M., ed. Roman Jakobson.
  G.S. Smith, 575(SEER):Oct85-582
Haller, H., ed. Il Panfilo veneziano.
  P. Trovato, 379(MedR):Apr85-137
Haller, J.S., Jr. American Medicine in Transition, 1840-1910.
  C.D. Howell, 106:Fall85-339
Haller, R., ed. Schlick und Neurath, ein Symposion.
  P. Engel, 542:Jul-Sep85-339
Halleran, M.R. Stagecraft in Euripides.*
  N.W. Slater, 124:Jul-Aug86-418
Hallett, C.A. and E.S. The Revenger's Madness.*
  R.A. Foakes, 677(YES):Vol 15-274
Hallett, J.P. Fathers and Daughters in Roman Society.*
  K.R. Bradley, 487:Winter85-404
  J. Glazewski, 124:Jul-Aug86-422
Halley, L. Abiding City.
  L. Caldecott, 441:21Sep86-29
Halliburton, D. Poetic Thinking.*
  D.H. Hirsch, 569(SR):Summer85-465
Halliday, F. The Making of the Second Cold War.
  G. Amyot, 529(QQ):Autumn85-650
Halliday, T. and K. Adler, eds. The Encyclopaedia of Reptiles and Amphibians.
  T.J.C. Beebee, 617(TLS):5Sep86-986
Hallin, D.C. The "Uncensored War."
  A. Barnett, 362:25Sep86-20
  M. Miner, 441:8Jun86-37
Halliwell, L. Seats in All Parts.
  R. Caplan, 441:23Feb86-23
Hallman, B.M. Italian Cardinals, Reform, and the Church as Property, 1492-1563.
  D.S. Chambers, 617(TLS):11Jul86-756
Hallon, J. Apartheid's Second Front.
  362:6Nov86-36
Halloran, R. To Arm a Nation.
  A. Tonelson, 441:30Nov86-7
Hallowell, J.H. Main Currents in Modern Political Thought.
  R. Williamson, 396(ModA):Fall85-369
Halman, T.S. - see Faik, S.
Halmøy, J-O. Le Gérondif.
  M-F. Mortureux, 209(FM):Apr85-96
  G. Price, 545(RPh):Aug85-77
Halpenny, F.G. - see "Dictionary of Canadian Biography/Dictionnaire Biographique du Canada"
Halper, N. Studies in Joyce.
  Z. Bowen, 329(JJQ):Winter86-233
Halperin, D.J. The Merkabah in Rabbinic Literature.
  P. Schäfer, 318(JAOS):Jul-Sep84-537
Halperin, J. Gissing.*
  R. Barrow, 541(RES):Feb85-119
Halperin, J. The Life of Jane Austen.*
  M.A. Doody, 445(NCF):Sep85-225
  C.S. Green, 577(SHR):Summer85-263
  C. Heilbrun, 454:Winter86-183
  R.J. Merrett, 150(DR):Spring85-122
  J. Nardin, 152(UDQ):Fall85-117
  P.M. Spacks, 219(GaR):Spring85-182
Halperin, J. C.P. Snow.
  J.V. Knapp, 395(MFS):Summer85-363
Halperin, J., ed. Trollope Centenary Essays.*
  S.M. Smith, 541(RES):Feb85-110

158

Hansen, V. Thomas Mann.
H. Siefken, 402(MLR):Oct85-999
Hansen, V. and G. Heine - see Mann, T.
Hansen, W.F. Saxo Grammaticus and the
Life of "Hamlet."*
J.D. Dorst, 292(JAF):Jan/Mar85-105
M. Mack, Jr., 405(MP):Nov85-187
K. Pulmer, 196:Band26Heft1/2-154
J. Reibetanz, 539:Nov85-284
Hanslick, E. Vom Musikalisch-Schönen;
Aufsätze; Musikkritiken. (K. Mehner, ed)
G.P., 412:Feb84-74
Hanson, K., ed. An Everyday Story.*
M.L. Shogren, 563(SS):Summer85-360
Hanson, K.O. Lighting the Night Sky.
B.P. Kelly, 448:Vol23No2-74
Hanson, V.D. Warfare and Agriculture in
Classical Greece.
D. Whitehead, 123:Vol35No1-121
Hansson, K. The Warped Universe.
G.A. Wilkes, 581:Jun85-243
Hansson, S. Afsatt på Swensko.
G.C. Schoolfield, 563(SS):Spring85-192
Hantos, T. Das römische Bundesgenossen-
system in Italien.
J. Briscoe, 123:Vol35No1-133
Hantrais, L. Contemporary French Society.
A.G. Hargreaves, 208(FS):Jul85-369
Happe, P., ed. Medieval English Drama.
C. Gauvin, 189(EA):Apr-Jun86-202
Harari, J.V. and D.F. Bell - see Serres, M.
Harasymiw, B. Political Elite Recruitment
in the Soviet Union.*
R.F. Miller, 575(SEER):Oct85-628
Harbert, E.N. - see Adams, H.
Harbert, E.N. and R.A. Rees, eds. Fifteen
American Authors before 1900.* (rev)
J.A.L. Lemay, 365:Winter/Spring85-53
D. Van Leer, 534(RALS):Spring83-53
Harbutt, F.J. The Iron Curtain.
C.S. Maier, 441:7Sep86-13
Härd, J.E. Studien zur Struktur mehrglied-
riger deutscher Nebensatzprädikate.
B. Haftka, 682(ZPSK):Band38Heft4-444
A. Lötscher, 685(ZDL):2/1985-269
Hardacre, H. Lay Buddhism in Contemporary
Japan.
R. Ellwood, 407(MN):Spring85-118
Murakami Shigeyoshi, 285(JapQ):Apr-
Jun85-211
Harden, E. Maria Edgeworth.
K. Danaher, 305(JIL):Sep85-114
Harden, E. Thackeray's "English Humour-
ists" and "Four Georges."
J. Sutherland, 617(TLS):14Nov86-1283
Harder, H-B., ed. Landesbeschreibungen
Mitteleuropas vom 15. bis 17. Jahr-
hundert.
F.W. Carter, 575(SEER):Jul85-450
Hardesty, S. and N. Jacobs. Success and
Betrayal.
W. Kaminer, 441:26Oct86-43
Hardie, A. Statius and the "Silvae."*
E. Courtney, 122:Oct85-371
P. White, 487:Winter85-408
Hardie, P.R. Virgil's "Aeneid."
N. Horsfall, 617(TLS):29Aug86-943
Hardin, J. Johann Beer.
G. Dünnhaupt, 301(JEGP):Jul85-403
Harding, A.J. Coleridge and the Inspired
Word.
R. Ashton, 617(TLS):19Sep86-1035

Harding, B. American Literature in Con-
text II, 1830-1865.
R. Mason, 447(N&Q):Jun84-282
Harding, H., ed. China's Foreign Rela-
tions in the 1980s.
J.R. Townsend, 293(JASt):May85-588
Harding, J. Agate.
B. Nightingale, 617(TLS):11Apr86-383
E.S. Turner, 362:3Apr86-30
Harding, N., ed. Marxism in Russia.*
G.R. Swain, 575(SEER):Apr85-302
Harding, S. and M.B. Hintikka, eds. Dis-
covering Reality.
S. Haack, 483:Apr85-265
Harding, S.F. Remaking Ibieca.*
639(VQR):Spring85-54
Hardt, U.H. - see Wollstonecraft, M.
Harduf, D.M. Biblical Proper Names.
E.D. Lawson, 424:Sep85-186
Hardy, A. La Belle Egyptienne. (B.B.
Caravaggi, ed)
J. Descrains, 535(RHL):Sep/Oct85-860
A. Gable, 208(FS):Jul85-333
M-O. Sweetser, 207(FR):Oct85-126
P. Tomlinson, 475:Vol 12No22-276
Hardy, A. Panthée. (P. Ford, ed)
J. Descrains, 535(RHL):Sep/Oct85-861
A. Gable, 208(FS):Jul85-333
R. Guichemerre, 475:Vol 12No22-307
Hardy, B. Forms of Feeling in Victorian
Fiction.*
M. Moseley, 569(SR):Summer85-485
B. Ruddick, 148:Autumn85-86
Hardy, B. The Moral Art of Dickens.
D. Cottom, 594:Winter85-424
Hardy, B. Particularities.*
I. Adam, 541(RES):Feb85-112
Hardy, D. and C. Ward. Arcadia for All.
N. Wates, 46:Mar85-83
Hardy, E. Emma Hardy: Diaries. (R.
Taylor, ed)
B. Jones, 364:Oct85-84
Hardy, J. Jane Austen's Heroines.*
D.R. Anderson, 594:Fall85-315
J. McMaster, 445(NCF):Mar86-476
Hardy, J. and A. McCredie, eds. The
Classical Temper in Western Europe.
R. Anderson, 415:Aug85-462
P. le Huray, 410(M&L):Oct85-396
Hardy, P., ed. Science Fiction.
T. Vahimagi, 707:Spring85-148
Hardy, T. The Collected Letters of
Thomas Hardy. (Vol 2) (R.L. Purdy and
M. Millgate, eds)
T.R.M. Creighton, 541(RES):May85-294
H.L. Weatherby, 569(SR):Winter85-162
Hardy, T. The Collected Letters of Thomas
Hardy.* (Vol 3) (R.L. Purdy and M. Mill-
gate, eds)
T.R.M. Creighton, 541(RES):May85-294
M. Ray, 148:Winter85-77
H.L. Weatherby, 569(SR):Winter85-162
M. Williams, 447(N&Q):Jun84-273
Hardy, T. The Collected Letters of Thomas
Hardy.* (Vol 4) (R.L. Purdy and M. Mill-
gate, eds)
P. Coustillas, 189(EA):Jan-Mar86-103
T.R.M. Creighton, 541(RES):May85-294
J. Halperin, 395(MFS):Summer85-336
M. Ray, 148:Winter85-77
M. Thorpe, 179(ES):Jun85-282
H.L. Weatherby, 569(SR):Winter85-162

Harrison, M.  A Study in Surmise.
   E.S. Lauterbach, 177(ELT):Vol28No3-321
Harrison, M., C. Fox and E. Thacker.  The
   Essential Jazz Records.  (Vol 1)
   A. Shipton, 415:Jul85-413
Harrison, N.  Winnie Mandela.*
   J.M. Coetzee, 453(NYRB):8May86-3
   S.J. Ungar, 441:27Apr86-17
Harrison, R.  Bentham.
   J. Dunphy, 63:Dec85-576
   H.L.A. Hart, 393(Mind):Jan85-153
   B. Parekh, 637(VS):Summer85-701
   F. Rosen, 483:Apr85-272
   J. Skorupski, 479(PhQ):Jul85-320
Harrison, R.  Death of a Dancing Lady.
   R. Hill, 617(TLS):25Apr86-454
Harrison, R.  Death of an Honourable
   Member.
   639(VQR):Summer85-91
Harrison, S.R.  The Etchings of Odilon
   Redon.
   J. Russell, 441:1Jun86-11
Harrison, T.  Dramatic Verse 1973-1985.
   O. Murray, 617(TLS):6Jun86-615
Harrison, T.  The Mysteries.
   B. O'Donoghue, 493:Oct85-61
Harrison, T.  Selected Poems.*
   W. Scammell, 364:Jul85-80
Hart, C.  The Prehistory of Flight.*
   D. King-Hele, 617(TLS):16May86-524
Hart, D.A.  Through the Open Door.*
   B. Murray, 395(MFS):Summer85-380
Hart, G., with W.S. Lind.  America Can Win.
   A.H. Bernstein, 129:Oct86-76
   M.A. Uhlig, 441:8Jun86-30
Hart, H.L.A.  Essays in Jurisprudence and
   Philosophy.*
   J. Waldron, 393(Mind):Apr85-281
Hart, H.L.A.  Essays on Bentham.*
   G.J. Postema, 482(PhR):Oct85-571
Hart, K.  Your Shadow.
   G. Bitcon, 581:Sep85-352
Hart, L.  The Complete Lyrics of Lorenz
   Hart.  (D. Hart and R. Kimball, eds)
   B. Short, 441:7Dec86-12
Hart, R.  Position of Trust.
   N. Callendar, 441:20Apr86-32
Hart, T.R. - see Vicente, G.
Hart-Davis, D.  Hitler's Games.
   G.A. Craig, 441:15Jun86-11
Hart-Davis, D. - see Lascelles, A.
Hart-Davis, R. - see Sassoon, S.
Hart-Davis, R. - see Wilde, O.
Hartcup, J. and A.  Spello.
   A. Cornelisen, 617(TLS):7Feb86-147
Harter, E.  The Wink.
   A.P. Harris, 441:28Dec86-18
Harter, P.  In the Broken Curve.
   J. Winke, 404:Summer85-51
Hartford, B., A. Valdman and C.R. Foster,
   eds.  Issues in International Bilingual
   Education.
   H. Dahlbäck, 596(SL):Vol39No1-87
Hartford, D. and others.  How to Be a
   Mogul.
   K. Arenson, 441:26Oct86-38
Harth, E.  Ideology and Culture in Seven-
   teenth-Century France.*
   M.S. Koppisch, 115:Summer84-266
Harth, H. - see Poggio Bracciolini, G.F.
Harth, P., A. Fisher and R. Cohen.  New
   Homage to John Dryden.*
   A. Poyet, 189(EA):Jan-Mar86-95

Hartjen, C.A. and S. Priyardarsini.  Delin-
   quency in India.
   R.D. Lambert, 293(JASt):Aug85-859
Hartle, A.  The Modern Self in Rousseau's
   "Confessions."*
   S.H., 185:Oct85-219
Hartley, L.P.  The Complete Short Stories
   of L.P. Hartley.
   J. Parini, 441:14Dec86-14
Hartley, L.P.  Eustace and Hilda.
   M. North, 441:5Oct86-26
Hartman, C.O.  Free Verse.
   H.M. Dennis, 677(YES):Vol 15-262
Hartman, E.  French Romantics on Progress.
   S. Dunn, 207(FR):Apr86-788
   J.P. Gilroy, 446(NCFS):Fall-
   Winter85/86-165
Hartman, G.H., ed.  Bitburg in Moral and
   Political Perspective.
   A. Kenny, 617(TLS):12Sep86-1001
   E. O'Shaughnessy, 441:31Aug86-13
Hartmann, R.R.K., ed.  Lexicography.
   C.L. Barnhart, 660(Word):Aug85-183
   J. Vizmuller-Zocco, 320(CJL):Spring85-
   117
Hartnett, D.W.  A Signalled Love.
   D. Davis, 362:10Apr86-27
   P. Gross, 493:Oct85-67
   C. Rawson, 617(TLS):7Feb86-137
Hartnett, M.  Collected Poems.  (Vol 1)
   T. Eagleton, 493:Aug85-64
   M. Harmon, 272(IUR):Autumn85-234
Hartog, H.  Public Property and Private
   Power.
   H.A. Johnson, 656(WMQ):Oct85-551
de Hartog, J.  The Commodore.
   J. Koslow, 441:24Aug86-18
   442(NY):15Sep86-120
Hartshorne, C.  Creativity in American
   Philosophy.
   M.C. Miller, 619:Summer85-435
   A.J.R., 185:Apr86-669
Hartshorne, C.  Insights and Oversights
   of Great Thinkers.*
   S. Connair, 543:Sep85-154
Hartshorne, C.  Omnipotence and Other
   Theological Mistakes.*
   P. Helm, 518:Jan85-52
   M. Vorobej, 154:Winter85-759
Hartung, H., ed.  Gedichte und Interpreta-
   tionen.  (Vol 5)
   M. Winkler, 133:Band17Heft3/4-361
Hartwieg-Hiratsuka, K.  Saigyō-Rezeption.
   M. Ury, 407(MN):Winter85-428
Hartwig, J.  Shakespeare's Analogical
   Scene.*
   W.M. Jones, 130:Fall85-281
   B.W. Kliman, 70:Nov/Dec84-59
   J.W. Velz, 401(MLQ):Dec84-404
Harvey, A.  Burning Houses.  (British
   title: Burning Homes.)
   V. Cunningham, 617(TLS):6Jun86-622
   A. Josephs, 441:18May86-17
Harvey, A.  No Diamonds, No Hat, No Honey.*
   R. Mitchell, 491:Jan86-228
Harvey, A.D.  English Literature and the
   Great War with France.*
   P. Marshall, 677(YES):Vol 15-309
Harvey, A.E., ed.  Alternative Approaches
   to New Testament Study.
   S. Medcalf, 617(TLS):25Jul86-824

Harvey, E.R., ed.  The Court of Sapience.
  B. Cottle, 301(JEGP):Jul85-417
  H. Spiegel, 589:Jul85-744
Harvey, I.E.  Derrida and the Economy of
  Différance.
  M. Rosen, 617(TLS):5Dec86-1383
Harvey, J.  Coup d'état.
  G. Strickland, 97(CQ):Vol 14No3-266
Harvey, N.  A History of Farm Buildings in
  England and Wales.
  G. Darley, 46:Mar85-83
Harwood, J.T.  Critics, Values and Restora-
  tion Comedy.*
  D.F. Hills, 447(N&Q):Mar84-125
Harwood, R., ed.  The Ages of Gielgud.*
  T. Minter, 157:No156-52
Hashim, W. - see under Wan Hashim
"ʿAlī ibn Sulaymān al-Hāshimī."  (F.I.
  Haddad and E.S. Kennedy, trans)
  B.R. Goldstein, 318(JAOS):Apr-Jun84-
  392
Hashmi, A.  This Time in Lahore.
  D. McDuff, 565:Summer85-72
Haskell, B.  Blam!
  L. Cooke, 90:Jun85-395
Haskins, L.  Castings.
  S. Meats, 389(MQ):Winter86-256
Haslam, J.  Soviet Foreign Policy, 1930-33.
  R.K. Debo, 550(RusR):Jan85-110
von Haslau, K. - see under Konrad von
  Haslau
Hasler, K.  Studien zu Wesen und Wert des
  Geldes in der römischen Kaiserzeit von
  Augustus bis Severus Alexander.
  M.H. Crawford, 313:Vol175-320
Hasler, L., ed.  Schelling.
  T.F. O'Meara, 543:Sep85-155
Hass, R.  Twentieth Century Pleasures.*
  M. Boruch, 219(GaR):Spring85-205
  R. Earle, 110:Fall85-73
  J. Matthias, 598(SoR):Spring86-391
Hassan, I.  The Dismemberment of Orpheus.
  (2nd ed)
  C. Brooke-Rose, 549(RLC):Jul-Sep85-377
Hasse, J.E., ed.  Ragtime.*
  C. Fox, 617(TLS):24Jan86-98
Hassel, J.W., Jr.  Middle French Proverbs,
  Sentences and Proverbial Phrases.
  G. Roques, 553(RLiR):Jan-Jun85-250
Hassler, D.M.  Comic Tones in Science Fic-
  tion.
  G.K. Wolfe, 395(MFS):Summer85-458
Hastings, A.  A History of English Chris-
  tianity, 1920-1985.
  P. Hebblethwaite, 617(TLS):28Nov86-
  1339
Hastings, M., ed.  The Oxford Book of Mil-
  itary Anecdotes.*
  G. Ewart, 364:Dec85/Jan86-150
Hastings, M. and G. Stevens.  Victory in
  Europe.*
  R.W. Lewis, 234:Spring86-50
Hastings, S.  Nancy Mitford.*
  G. Annan, 453(NYRB):14Aug86-3
  W. McBrien, 441:17Aug86-8
  P. Parker, 364:Nov85-98
"The Hastings Hours."
  C.R., 90:Jul85-471
Hasubek, P., ed.  Fabelforschung.
  E.A. Metzger, 222(GR):Winter85-32
Hasubek, P. and others, eds.  Die Fabel.
  F. Hassauer, 196:Band26Heft1/2-158
  A. Otten, 406:Fall85-350

Hatch, R.M.  Major John André.
  R. Walters, 441:27Apr86-23
Hathaway, W.  Fish, Flesh, and Fowl.
  R. Mitchell, 491:Jan86-230
Hattaway, M.  Elizabethan Popular Theatre.*
  T.W. Craik, 161(DUJ):Jun85-273
  A. Gurr, 541(RES):Feb85-79
Hattori, S. and K. Inoue, eds.  Pro-
  ceedings of the XIIIth International
  Congress of Linguists.
  B. Peeters, 320(CJL):Summer85-218
Hauerwas, S.  Responsibility for Devalued
  Persons.
  D.O., 185:Oct85-222
Haugeland, J.  Artificial Intelligence.
  A. Hodgkin, 617(TLS):1Aug86-835
Haugen, E.  Ole Edvart Rölvaag.*
  I.R. Kongslien, 562(Scan):Nov85-232
  H.S. Naess, 563(SS):Spring85-212
Haupt, J.  Natur und Lyrik.
  A. Vieregg, 67:Nov85-255
Hauptfleisch, T. and I. Steadman, eds.
  South African Theatre.
  M. Banham, 610:Autumn85-261
Hauptman, L.M.  The Iroquois and the New
  Deal.
  D.W. Dippie, 106:Spring85-31
Hauptman, R.  The Pathological Vision.*
  J. Byrne, 532(RCF):Fall85-193
Hauptmann, G.  Notiz-Kalender 1889 bis
  1891.*  (M. Machatzke, ed)
  P. Skrine, 402(MLR):Jan85-222
Hauser, M.  The Memoirs of the Late Mr.
  Ashley.
  S. Trachtenberg, 441:28Sep86-26
Hausmann, F.J.  Louis Meigret.
  P. Swiggers, 353:Vol23No4-650
Hausmann, F.J. - see Meigret, L.
Hausmann, R. and K. Schwitters.  Pin und
  die Geschichte von Pin.
  P. Reading, 617(TLS):4Jul86-738
Haussherr, R.  Convenevolezza.
  A. von Ajkay, 341:Vol54No2-93
Havard, W.C.  The Recovery of Political
  Theory.
  639(VQR):Summer85-94
Havel, V.  The Anatomy of a Reticence.
  T.G. Ash, 453(NYRB):9Oct86-45
Havel, V. and others.  The Power of the
  Powerless.  (J. Keane, ed)
  T.G. Ash, 453(NYRB):9Oct86-45
Haverkamp, A., ed.  Theorie der Metapher.
  D. Moutote, 535(RHL):Nov/Dec85-1089
  H.A. Pausch, 564:Nov85-303
Haward, B.  Nineteenth-Century Norfolk
  Stained Glass.*
  M. Archer, 90:Feb85-104
  R. Mander, 39:Apr85-285
Hawes, J.M. and N.R. Hiner, eds.  American
  Childhood.
  G. Avery, 617(TLS):11Apr86-386
Hawke, D.M. - see Durand, M.M. and N.T.
  Huan
Hawkes, A.D.  A World of Vegetable Cookery.
  W. and C. Cowen, 639(VQR):Autumn85-141
Hawkes, E.  Feminism on Trial.
  M. Orth, 441:22Jun86-12
Hawkes, J.  Adventures in the Alaskan Skin
  Trade.*
  J. Daynard, 138:No8-250
  P. Lewis, 364:Feb86-100
  L. Marcus, 617(TLS):28Feb86-216
Hawkes, J. - see Tristan, F.

165

Hawkes, T. That Shakespeherian Rag.
  R.M. Adams, 453(NYRB):6Nov86-50
  K. Brown, 617(TLS):22Aug86-917
Hawkins, G. and F.E. Zimring, eds. The
  Pursuit of Criminal Justice.
  J.O., 185:Jan86-463
Hawkins, H. The Devil's Party.
  R.M. Adams, 453(NYRB):6Nov86-50
  I-S. Ewbank, 617(TLS):25Apr86-451
Hawkins, J.N. Education and Social Change
  in the People's Republic of China.
  J. Kwong, 293(JASt):Feb85-369
Hawkins, P. Children at Risk.
  D. Griego, 441:19Oct86-45
Hawkins, P. Introducing Phonology.
  F. Chevillet, 189(EA):Apr-Jun86-199
  P. Hagiwara, 399(MLJ):Autumn85-312
Hawkins, P.S. The Language of Grace.*
  J. Cunningham, 577(SHR):Summer85-297
Hawley, J.S. Krishna, The Butter Thief.
  A. Feldhaus, 293(JASt):Feb85-426
  R.S. McGregor, 318(JAOS):Jul-Sep84-602
Hawley, J.S. Sur Das.
  L.A. Siegel, 617(TLS):24Jan86-78
Hawthorn, J., ed. Criticism and Critical
  Theory.
  M.A.R. Habib, 89(BJA):Autumn85-404
  D. Morton, 395(MFS):Winter85-842
Hawthorn, J. Multiple Personality and the
  Disintegration of Literary Character.
  E. Kafalenos, 149(CLS):Winter85-555
Hawthorne, N. The House of the Seven
  Gables. (M.R. Stern, ed)
  R. Snape, 161(DUJ):Jun84-304
Hawthorne, N. Tales and Sketches.* (R.H.
  Pearce, ed) Novels. (M. Bell, ed)
  529(QQ):Summer85-438
Hawthorne, N. The Letters, 1813-1843.
  The Letters, 1843-1853. (T. Woodson,
  L.N. Smith and N.H. Pearson, eds)
  B. Nevius, 445(NCF):Mar86-482
Hawtree, C., ed. Night and Day.*
  J. Le Bas, 364:Dec85/Jan86-152
  R. Craft, 453(NYRB):24Apr86-17
Hawtrey, R.S.W. Commentary on Plato's
  "Euthydemus."*
  G.J. de Vries, 394:Vol38fasc1/2-197
Haxton, B. Dominion.
  D. Kirby, 441:12Oct86-32
Hay, M.V. The Life of Robert Sidney, Earl
  of Leicester (1563-1626).*
  T. Cogswell, 377:Jul85-130
  K. Duncan-Jones, 551(RenQ):Autumn85-
  567
Hay, S.H. Story Hour.*
  F.C. Rosenberger, 50(ArQ):Autumn85-
  276
Haycraft, J. Italian Labyrinth.
  A. Lyttelton, 617(TLS):25Apr86-439
Hayden, D. Redesigning the American Dream.
  A. Betsky, 505:Aug85-123
Hayes, A.W. Roberto Arlt.*
  P. Verdevoye, 92(BH):Jul-Dec84-577
Hayes, J. The Landscape Paintings of
  Thomas Gainsborough.*
  D.H. Solkin, 54:Sep85-507
Hayes, J.P. James A. Michener.
  295(JML):Nov85-527
Hayes, J.W. Greek, Roman, and Related
  Metalware in the Royal Ontario Museum.
  C.C. Mattusch, 487:Summer85-180
Hayes, L.D. Politics in Pakistan.
  A.H. Syed, 293(JASt):Aug85-860

Hayles, N.K. The Cosmic Web.*
  D.D. Elgin, 395(MFS):Winter85-852
  K. Tölölyan, 400(MLN):Dec85-1174
Hayman, D. "Ulysses." (rev)
  V. Mahon, 677(YES):Vol 15-336
Hayman, R. Brecht.*
  C.R. Mueller, 615(TJ):May85-255
Hayman, R. Bertolt Brecht: The Plays.
  R. Mueller, 609:Spring86-75
Hayman, R. Writing Against.
  R. Goldthorpe, 617(TLS):12Dec86-1404
  A. Ryan, 362:23Oct86-25
Hayne, P.H. A Man of Letters in the Nine-
  teenth-Century South. (R.S. Moore, ed)
  A. Bendixen, 534(RALS):Autumn83-220
Hayward, J. The State and the Market
  Economy.
  D.S. Bell, 617(TLS):27Jun86-700
Hayward, M. Writers in Russia, 1917-1978.*
  (P. Blake, ed)
  A. Kerrigan, 569(SR):Spring85-312
  S. Monas, 473(PR):Vol52No3-292
Hazai, G. Kurze Einführung in das Studium
  der türkischen Sprache.
  E. Birnbaum, 318(JAOS):Apr-Jun84-379
Hazan, M. Marcella's Italian Kitchen.
  F. Fabricant, 441:7Dec86-17
Hazard, J.N. Managing Change in the USSR.
  G.B. Smith, 104(CASS):Spring85-87
  R. Walker, 575(SEER):Oct85-623
Hazard, J.N. Recollections of a Pioneer-
  ing Sovietologist.*
  G.G. Weickhardt, 550(RusR):Apr85-203
Hazleton, L. Jerusalem, Jerusalem.
  C. Samuels, 441:22Jun86-27
Head, R. The Indian Style.
  M. Girouard, 617(TLS):11Jul86-763
Head, W.P. America's China Sojourn.
  S.I. Levine, 293(JASt):May85-590
Headington, C. The Bodley Head History of
  Western Music. (new ed)
  H.T.E.M., 412:Aug/Nov83-289
Headley, G. and W. Meulenkamp. Follies.
  D. Watkin, 617(TLS):8Aug86-872
Heald, G. and R.J. Wybrow. The Gallup
  Survey of Britain.
  G. Townshend, 617(TLS):28Nov86-1335
Heald, T. Red Herrings.
  T.J. Binyon, 617(TLS):20Jun86-683
Healey, E. Wives of Fame.
  M. Jones, 362:29May86-23
  A.L. Le Quesne, 617(TLS):27Jun86-719
Healey, J. The Staked Goat.
  N. Callendar, 441:23Mar86-16
  442(NY):12May86-128
Healy, D. Fighting With Shadows, or
  Sciamachy.*
  M. Koenig, 272(IUR):Spring85-112
Healy, J.F. Blunt Darts.*
  J. Symons, 617(TLS):14Mar86-266
Heaney, S. Station Island.*
  A. Frazier, 174(Éire):Winter85-134
  M. Harmon, 272(IUR):Spring85-93
  J.D. McClatchy, 249(HudR):Spring85-170
  B. O'Donoghue, 493:Jan85-57
  R.B. Shaw, 676(YR):Summer85-581
  D. Smith, 491:Oct85-35
Heaney, S. Sweeney Astray.*
  E.G. Ingersoll, 174(Éire):Spring85-150
Heanue, J. - see Meinong, A.
Heap, N.A. A Word List from Bucks County,
  Pennsylvania, 1850-1876.
  G.R. Wood, 35(AS):Summer85-171

166

Hearder, H. Italy in the Age of Risorgimento 1790-1870.
C. Seton-Watson, 278(IS):Vol40-145
Hearn, L. Writings from Japan.* (F. King, ed)
J. Haylock, 364:Apr/May85-154
Hearn, M.F. Romanesque Sculpture.*
C. Christofides, 589:Jan85-155
Hearne, V. Adam's Task.
P-L. Adams, 61:Oct86-103
Y-F. Tuan, 441:7Sep86-10
Hearne, V. In the Absence of Horses.
W. Logan, 472:Spring/Summer/Fall/Winter85-463
J. Saunders, 565:Autumn85-73
Heath, C.D. The Pronunciation of English in Cannock, Staffordshire.*
K. Dietz, 72:Band222Heft1-173
Heath, J. Functional Grammar of Nunggubuyu. Nunggubuyu Myths and Ethnographic Texts. Nunggubuyu Dictionary.
J. Haiman, 350:Sep86-654
Heath, M.J. - see de Lucinge, R.
Heath, S. Questions of Cinema.
D. Polan, 81:Winter/Spring85-157
M. Turim, 567:Vol58No1/2-185
Heath, S.B. Ways with Words.*
D. Brandt, 128(CE):Feb85-128
D. Christian, 35(AS):Spring85-70
Heath, T. Method in Architecture.
B. Russell, 46:Sep85-81
Heath-Stubbs, J. The Immolation of Aleph.*
S. Rae, 617(TLS):20Jun86-677
Hebblethwaite, P. In the Vatican.
M. Walsh, 617(TLS):20Jun86-670
Hebblethwaite, P. Pope John XXIII.*
J. Pollard, 278(IS):Vol40-159
Hebblethwaite, P. Synod Extraordinary.
M. Santer, 617(TLS):21Mar86-313
Hebden, M. Pel and the Paris Mob.
T.J. Binyon, 617(TLS):3Oct86-1115
Hébert, A. In the Shadow of the Wind.
E-M. Kroller, 102(CanL):Winter84-129
Hébert, M. Inventaires des Gravures des Ecoles du Nord.
A.G., 90:Apr85-243
Hébert, P. and S. Meurant. Etienne et Sara.
C.A. Demharter, 207(FR):May86-995
Hébert, R. The Questing Beast.
L. Rogers, 102(CanL):Winter84-126
Hecht, A. Obbligati.
L. Menand, 441:7Sep86-19
442(NY):8Dec86-154
Hecht, A. A Summoning of Stones. The Hard Hours. Millions of Strange Shadows. The Venetian Vespers.
B. Leithauser, 453(NYRB):13Feb86-11
Hecht, W. Brecht. (2nd ed)
H. Claus, 610:Autumn85-257
Heckel, W. - see Curtius Rufus, Q.
Hecker, B. - see Macho, J.
Heckscher, G. The Welfare State and Beyond.
B.J. Nordstrom, 562(Scan):Nov85-246
Hector of Chartres. La vie de la forêt normande à la fin du moyen âge. (A. Roquelet, ed)
R.K. Berlow, 589:Oct85-1050
Hedges, I. Languages of Revolt.*
R. Pearce, 115:Summer84-256

Hedin, T. The Sculpture of Gaspard and Balthazard Marsy.*
T. Hodgkinson, 90:May85-310
Hedrick, J.D. Solitary Comrade.
J. Tavernier-Courbin, 587(SAF):Spring85-115
Heed, S.Å. Le Coco du Dada.*
D. Bradby, 208(FS):Oct85-498
Heelan, P.A. Space-Perception and the Philosophy of Science.
H.I. Brown, 486:Mar85-159
Heerding, A. The History of N.V. Philips' Gloeilampenfabrieken. (Vol 1)
R. Davenport-Hines, 617(TLS):29Aug86-946
Heffernan, J.A.W. The Re-Creation of the Landscape.*
J. Barrell, 90:Nov85-815
M.C. Brennan, 219(GaR):Fall85-672
639(VQR):Summer85-88
Heffernan, T.F. Stove by a Whale.
H. Beaver, 402(MLR):Jan85-131
Heffernan, W. Acts of Contrition.
N. Callendar, 441:30Nov86-20
Hegel, G.W.F. Gesammelte Werke. (Vol 9) (W. Bonsiepen and R. Heede, eds)
M. Westphal, 125:Summer85-448
Hegel, G.W.F. Hegel: The Letters.* (C. Butler and C. Seiler, trans)
S.S., 185:Jan86-453
639(VQR):Summer85-80
Hegel, G.W.F. Philosophie des Rechts. (D. Henrich, ed)
K. Hartmann, 53(AGP):Band67Heft3-338
H. Kincaid, 449:Sep85-475
L.S. Stepelevich, 543:Mar85-634
Hegenbarth-Rösgen, A. Soziale Normen und Rollen im Roman.
A. Gier, 72:Band222Heft2-451
Hegyi, O., ed. Cinco leyendas y otros relatos moriscos (Ms. 4953 de la Bibl. Nac. Madrid).*
A. Gier, 553(RLiR):Jan-Jun85-215
Heichelheim, F.M., C.A. Yeo and A.M. Ward. A History of the Roman People. (2nd ed)
A.P. Dobsevage, 124:May-Jun86-350
Heid, M., ed. New Yorker Werkstattgespraech 1982.
J.K. Swaffar, 399(MLJ):Summer85-163
Heidegger, M. Les Cahiers de l'Herne: Martin Heidegger.
C. Piché, 98:Oct85-954
Heidegger, M. Parmenides. (M.S. Frings, ed)
C. Jamme, 489(PJGG):Band92Heft2-408
Heidegger, M. Les Problèmes fondamentaux de la phénoménologie.
T. Cordellier, 450(NRF):Sep85-88
Heidegger, M. Schelling's Treatise on the Essence of Human Freedom.
M.A.G., 185:Jul86-906
Heike, A.E. and E. Lattey. Using Idioms.
W. Paprotté, 257(IRAL):Feb85-71
Heil, J. Perception and Cognition.*
C.C., 185:Apr86-659
D.W. Hamlyn, 393(Mind):Apr85-297
J. Russell, 518:Apr85-105
Heilbron, J.L. The Dilemmas of an Upright Man.
R. Peierls, 453(NYRB):20Nov86-56
C.A. Russell, 617(TLS):12Dec86-1407

Heilbron, J.L.  Physics at the Royal Soci-
ety during Newton's Presidency.*
  R.A. Hatch, 173(ECS):Fall85-101
  J. Kenny, 568(SCN):Winter85-71
Heilbroner, R.L.  The Nature and Logic of
Capitalism.*
  A. Ryan, 617(TLS):16May86-521
Heilbut, A.  Exiled in Paradise.*
  E.L. Jurist, 390:Dec85-55
Heilman, S.  The Gate Behind the Wall.*
  B. Levine, 287:Jun-Jul85-27
Heilmann, W.  Ethische Reflexion und
römische Lebenswirklichkeit in Ciceros
Schrift "De Officiis."
  M. Griffin, 313:Vol75-311
  H.M. Hine, 123:Vol35No2-300
Heimel, C.  But Enough About You.
  L. Shapiro, 441:2Nov86-12
Heimert, A. and A. Delbanco, eds.  The
Puritans in America.*
  H. Cohen, 617(TLS):21Nov86-1302
  639(VQR):Summer85-89
Hein, C.  Horns Ende.
  M. Hofmann, 617(TLS):14Feb86-173
Heine, B., T.C. Schadeberg and E. Wolff,
eds.  Die Sprachen Afrikas.
  S. Brauner, 682(ZPSK):Band38Heft2-177
Heine, E. - see Forster, E.M.
Heinekamp, A. - see Müller, K.
Heineman, H.  Restless Angels.*
  L. Chambers-Schiller, 637(VS):Winter85-
  338
Heinerman, J. and A. Shupe.  The Mormon
Corporate Empire.
  W. Turner, 441:6Apr86-17
Heinrich, A.  Bach's "Die Kunst der Fuge."
  S. Daw, 415:Mar85-156
Heinrich, D. and W. Iser, eds.  Funktionen
des Fiktiven.
  J.H. Petersen, 52:Band20Heft1-72
Heinrich von Meissen - see under Frauenlob
Heintze, M.R.  Private Black Colleges in
Texas, 1865-1954.
  L. Milazzo, 584(SWR):Summer85-415
Heinz, M.  Zeitlichkeit und Temporalität.
  C. Jamme, 489(PJGG):Band92Heft1-204
Heiple, D.L.  Mechanical Imagery in
Spanish Golden Age Poetry.*
  W. Ferguson, 240(HR):Autumn85-494
Heisig, J.W. - see Takeuchi Yoshinori
Heitsch, E.  Antiphon aus Rhamnus.
  M. Gagarin, 124:Jul-Aug86-416
Helbo, A.  Les mots et les gestes.
  M. Carlson, 567:Vol56No3/4-309
  T. Kowzan, 567:Vol55No1/2-125
van Helden, A.  Measuring the Universe.
  J. North, 617(TLS):7Feb86-131
Heldmann, K.  Antike Theorien über Entwick-
lung und Verfall der Redekunst.
  E. Fantham, 122:Jul85-278
Helgason, J., ed.  Íslenzk Fornkvaeði.
  B.R. Jonsson, 64(Arv):Vol39-218
Helgerson, R.  Self-Crowned Laureates.*
  R.S. Ide, 536(Rev):Vol7-89
Hellberg, F.  Walter Mehring.
  K. Petersen, 133:Band17Heft3/4-369
Heller, A.  A Radical Philosophy.
  W. Suchting, 63:Dec85-568
Heller, E.  In the Age of Prose.
  C.S. Brown, 569(SR):Spring85-288
Heller, J.  God Knows.*
  J.S. Beerman, 42(AR):Spring85-249
                                [continued]

[continuing]
  P. Lewis, 565:Spring85-43
  W.H. Pritchard, 249(HudR):Spring85-121
Heller, J. and S. Vogel.  No Laughing
Matter.
  P. Buckman, 362:18Sep86-24
  A. Burgess, 441:16Feb86-8
  N.S. Sutherland, 617(TLS):14Nov86-1266
Heller, M.  Conviction's Net of Branches.
  B. Morrow, 138:No7-267
Heller, M. and A. Nekrich.  Utopia in
Power.
  D. Holloway, 441:21Sep86-15
  442(NY):27Oct86-148
Heller, M.A.  A Palestinian State.
  M. Nisan, 390:Mar85-63
Heller, R.  Munch.*
  E. Prelinger, 55:Sep85-23
  J.B. Smith, 39:May85-355
  42(AR):Winter85-122
Heller, S., ed.  Innovators of American
Illustration.
  A. Anderson, 441:30Nov86-23
Hellerstedt, K.J.  Gardens of Earthly
Delight.
  J. Summerson, 617(TLS):28Nov86-1353
Hellerstein, D.  Battles of Life and Death.
  M. Oppenheim, 441:23Mar86-46
Hellholm, D., ed.  Apocalypticism in the
Mediterranean World and the Near East.
  R. Seaford, 123:Vol35No1-203
Hellinga, L.  Caxton in Focus.
  M.L. Turner, 382(MAE):1985/1-139
  J.E. Walsh, 517(PBSA):Vol79No1-146
Hellmann, J.  American Myth and the Legacy
of Vietnam.
  P. French, 617(TLS):6Jun86-610
Hellmann, M., ed.  Handbuch der Geschichte
Russlands.  (Vol 1, fasc 10 and 11)
  D.C. Waugh, 589:Jan85-222
Hellmuth, L.  Gastfreundschaft und Gast-
recht bei den Germanen.
  N. Wagner, 684(ZDA):Band114Heft4-103
Hellström, P. and T. Thieme.  Labraunda:
Swedish Excavations and Researches.*
  (Vol 1, Pt 3)
  J.J. Coulton, 123:Vol35No1-209
Hellwig, D.  Adikia in Platons "Politeia."
  H-J. Horn, 53(AGP):Band67Heft3-292
Hellwig, F., W. Reiniger and K. Stopp.
Landkarten der Pfalz am Rhein 1513-1803.
  70:May/Jun85-175
Helmholz, R.H. and T.A. Green.  Juries,
Libel and Justice.*
  G.M. Townend, 566:Spring86-226
Helsinger, E.K.  Ruskin and the Art of the
Beholder.*
  A.W.B., 506(PSt):May85-98
  R. Hewison, 541(RES):May85-289
  G. Wihl, 627(UTQ):Fall85-109
Helterman, J.  Symbolic Action in the
Plays of the Wakefield Master.*
  A.C. Cawley, 541(RES):Feb85-72
Helvétius, C-A.  Correspondance générale
d'Helvétius.*  (Vol 1)  (A. Dainard and
others, eds)
  J-L. Lecercle, 535(RHL):May/Jun85-488
Helvétius, C-A.  Correspondance générale
d'Helvétius.  (Vol 2)  (A. Dainard and
others, eds)
  W. Hanley, 627(UTQ):Summer86-433

168

Henry, F.G. Le Message humaniste des "Fleurs du mal."
J.C. McLaren, 446(NCFS):Fall-Winter85/86-175
Henry, G.C. Logos.
H.A. Durfee, 543:Dec85-359
Henry, J.F. Early Maritime Artists of the Pacific Northwest Coast, 1741-1841.
M.S. Young, 39:Jun85-438
Henry, M. Généalogie de la psychanalyse.
F. Roustang, 98:Dec85-1172
Henry, P. A Hamlet of His Time: Vsevolod Garshin.*
A.R. Durkin, 574(SEEJ):Spring85-105
D. Lowe, 550(RusR):Apr85-190
R. Reid, 402(MLR):Jul85-765
Henry, W. Will Henry's West. (D.L. Walker, ed)
E. Labor, 649(WAL):Nov85-267
Hensellek, W. Sprachstudien an Augustins "De vera religione."
J. den Boeft, 394:Vol38fasc1/2-241
Hensley, J.L. Robak's Fire.
N. Callendar, 441:30Nov86-20
Henson, S. The Impossible Jigsaw.
P. Gross, 493:Oct85-67
C. Rawson, 617(TLS):7Feb86-137
Hentoff, N. Boston Boy.
D. Wakefield, 441:27Apr86-34
442(NY):19May86-121
Heny, F. and B. Richards, eds. Auxiliaries and Related Puzzles.
S. Steele, 603:Vol9No3-395
Heny, F. and B. Richards, eds. Linguistic Categories.* (Vols 1 and 2)
R. Salkie, 297(JL):Sep85-471
Henze, H.W. Music and Politics.*
G.D.P., 412:Feb83-64
Henze, P. The Plot to Kill the Pope.
B.T. Lupack, 497(PolR):Vol30No1-123
Hepburn, R.W. "Wonder" and Other Essays.*
P. Crowther, 89(BJA):Autumn85-394
Hepokoski, J.A. Giuseppe Verdi: "Falstaff."*
J.B., 412:Aug/Nov84-300
J.N. Black, 278(IS):Vol40-149
F.W. Sternfeld, 410(M&L):Oct85-386
Heraclitus. Héraclite: Fragments. (M. Conche, ed)
J. Barnes, 617(TLS):26Sep86-1072
Hérail, R.J. and E.A. Lovatt, eds. Dictionary of Modern Colloquial French.*
S. Haig, 207(FR):Oct85-165
V.L. Remillard, 399(MLJ):Winter85-413
Herbers, J. The New Heartland.
A. Hacker, 441:16Nov86-20
Herbert, E.W. Red Gold of Africa.
R.A. Silverman, 2(AfrA):Feb85-18
Herbert, J. Moon.
A. Postman, 441:16Nov86-24
Herbert, Z. Barbarian in the Garden.*
S. Gardiner, 364:Oct85-107
R. Kimball, 617(TLS):19Sep86-1020
Herbert, Z. Report from the Besieged City and Other Poems.*
J. Bayley, 617(TLS):31Jan86-103
S. Birkerts, 703:No15-154
E. Hoffman, 441:16Feb86-14
G.T. Kapolka, 497(PolR):Vol30No4-452
Herbert, Z. Selected Poems.*
J. Bayley, 617(TLS):31Jan86-103

Herbst, H.L. and H. Sturges 2d. Encore une fois.
M. Lavallée-Williams, 399(MLJ): Summer85-182
M. Shockey, 207(FR):Dec85-313
Herbstrith, W. Edith Stein.
D. Ackerman, 441:2Mar86-16
Hercus, L.A. and others, eds. Indological and Buddhist Studies.
O. von Hinüber, 259(IIJ):Jan85-49
L. Rocher, 318(JAOS):Apr-Jun84-335
Herde, P. Cölestin V. (1294).
C.T. Davis, 589:Jan85-156
Herdeg, K. The Decorated Diagram.*
K. Crossman, 106:Winter85-443
C.F. Otto, 31(ASch):Winter84/85-141
Herding, K. and K. Schmidt. Les voyages secrets de Monsieur Courbet.
P. ten-Doesschate Chu, 380:Winter84-455
Herdmann, U. Die südlichen Poeme A.S. Puškins.
M. Colin, 549(RLC):Jul-Sep85-353
de Heredia, J-M. Oeuvres poétiques complètes de José-Maria de Heredia. (Vol 2) (S. Delaty, ed)
V.L. de Vivero, 446(NCFS):Spring-Summer86-171
Herf, J. Reactionary Modernism.*
G.A. Craig, 453(NYRB):30Jan86-20
Hériau, M. Le verbe impersonnel en français moderne.
J. Chaurand, 209(FM):Apr85-104
Herington, J. Aeschylus.
J.H.C. Leach, 617(TLS):29Aug86-943
Herington, J. Poetry into Drama.
J. Gould, 617(TLS):3Jan86-18
A. Shaw, 385(MQR):Fall86-750
Heriot, A. The Castrati in Opera.
A.F.L.T., 412:Aug/Nov84-304
Herlihy, D. Medieval Households.
A. Boyer, 441:25May86-15
Herlihy, D. and C. Klapisch-Zuber. Tuscans and Their Families.*
F. Gilbert, 453(NYRB):90ct86-43
Herlin, H. The Last Spring in Paris.*
P. Lewis, 565:Summer85-50
Herlinger, J. - see de' Beldomandi, P.
Herman, A.L. An Introduction to Buddhist Thought.
H. Cruise, 63:Sep85-378
Hermanns, W. Einstein and the Poet in Search of the Cosmic Man.
R. Titlebaum, 390:Nov85-62
Hermans, T. The Structure of Modernist Poetry.*
295(JML):Nov85-434
Hermerén, G. Aspects of Aesthetics.*
M.R. Lagerlöf, 341:Vol54No1-42
E. Schaper, 518:Jul85-171
Hernández, J. Martín Fierro. (R. Navas Ruiz, ed)
D.C. Scroggins, 240(HR):Spring85-260
Hernández, J.A. Studien zum religiös-ethischen Wortschatz der deutschen Mystik.
G.J. Lewis, 564:Nov85-306
Hernandez, K. and M. Bryan. If At First.
J. Howe, 441:18May86-25
Hernández Pina, F. Teorías psicolingüísticas y su aplicación a la adquisición del español como lengua materna.
J.M. Lipski, 238:Sep85-538

Herndon, M. and N. McLeod. Field Manual for Ethnomusicology.
  N.A. Jairazbhoy, 187:Spring/Summer86-341
  P. Sonnichsen, 292(JAF):Apr/Jun85-216
Hero, A.C. - see Akindynos, G.
Héroët, A. La Parfaicte Amye.* (C.M. Hill, ed)
  A. Moss, 208(FS):Apr85-192
Herren, M.W., ed. Insular Latin Studies.
  H. Gneuss, 38:Band103Heft3/4-440
Herrick, E.M. Sociolinguistic Variation.
  W.M. Christie, 660(Word):Dec85-249
  R. Schreyer, 205(ForL):Dec84-274
Herriman, G. Krazy Kat. (P. McDonnell, K. O'Donnell and G.R. de Havenon, eds)
  A. Gopnik, 453(NYRB):18Dec86-19
  G. Weales, 441:25May86-15
  442(NY):2Jun86-108
Herring, R. McCampbell's War.
  442(NY):13Oct86-155
Herring, R.J. Land to the Tiller.
  M. Sharma, 293(JASt):Nov84-228
Herrmann, D. S.J. Perelman.
  J. Lahr, 441:7Sep86-3
Herrmann, H. Martin Luther.
  F. Posset, 77:Fall85-356
Herrmann, W. Laugier and Eighteenth-Century French Theory.
  617(TLS):10Oct86-1147
Herrmann, W. Gottfried Semper.
  B. Bergdoll, 45:Jun85-91
  R. Bletter, 617(TLS):24Jan86-97
  H.F. Mallgrave, 576:May85-187
  A. Saint, 46:Aug85-66
Herrmann-Fiore, K. Disegni degli Alberti.
  J.B. Shaw, 90:Feb85-96
Hersey, G.L. Architecture, Poetry, and Number in the Royal Palace at Caserta.*
  A.A. Jensen, 505:Nov85-135
Hersh, S.M. The Price of Power.* (British title: Kissinger: The Price of Power.)
  N. Schmitz, 529(QQ):Winter85-785
Hersh, S.M. "The Target Is Destroyed."
  A.M. Codevilla, 129:Dec86-68
  T. Powers, 441:21Sep86-3
  B. Woffinden, 362:23Oct86-26
  442(NY):13Oct86-158
Herstein, S.R. A Mid-Victorian Feminist, Barbara Leigh Smith Bodichon.
  G. Beer, 617(TLS):15Aug86-886
Hertel, H. and S.M. Kristensen, eds. The Activist Critic.*
  G.C. Schoolfield, 221(GQ):Spring85-265
Hertz, R. More Equal Than Others.
  W. Kaminer, 441:26Oct86-43
Hervey, E. Into the Valley of Death.
  T.J. Binyon, 617(TLS):28Nov86-1357
Hervier, J. Entretiens avec Ernst Jünger.
  J. Théodoridès, 605(SC):15Apr86-273
Herz, J. Vom Überleben.
  H. Pross, 384:Sep/Oct85-921
Herzel, R. The Original Casting of Molière's Plays.
  C.E.J. Caldicott, 535(RHL):Mar/Apr85-294
Herzfeld, M. The Poetics of Manhood.
  P. Loizos, 617(TLS):11Apr86-399
Herzhaft, G. Le blues. Nouvelle encyclopédie du blues.
  A. Prévos, 91:Spring85-115

Herzog, C. Le passé simple dans les journaux du XXe siècle.*
  H. Meier, 547(RF):Band97Heft2/3-269
  S.F. Noreiko, 208(FS):Apr85-243
Herzog, D. Without Foundations.
  W.A. Galston, 185:Jul86-880
Herzog, K. Women, Ethnics, and Exotics.*
  M. Lopez, 115:Summer84-258
Heschel, A.J. The Circle of the Baal Shem Tov. (S.H. Dresner, ed)
  L. Jacobs, 617(TLS):16May86-541
Hesiod. Hesiodi "Theogonia," "Opera et Dies," "Scutum," Fragmenta Selecta.* (2nd ed) (F. Solmsen, R. Merkelbach and M.L. West, eds)
  R.L. Fowler, 124:Sep-Oct85-55
Heskes, I., comp. The Resource Book of Jewish Music.
  E. Koskoff, 187:Spring/Summer86-344
Hess, J. Strangled Prose.
  N. Callendar, 441:16Mar86-31
Hess, K., J. Brustkern and W. Lenders. Maschinenlesbare deutsche Wörterbücher.
  F.E. Knowles, 361:Mar85-259
Hesse, E.W. Theology, Sex and the Comedia.
  J. Escobar, 345(KRQ):Vol32No4-437
Hesse, E.W., H.H. Orjuela and T.D. Terrell. Spanish Review. (6th ed)
  D.P. Hill, 399(MLJ):Summer85-208
Hesse, M.G. Gabrielle Roy.
  P.G. Lewis, 207(FR):Feb86-453
Hester, M.B. Sensibility and Criticism.
  M.R. Haight, 89(BJA):Summer85-290
  M.A. McCloskey, 63:Dec85-560
Hester, M.T. Kinde Pitty and Brave Scorn.*
  H. Peters, 541(RES):May85-263
"Het Lumineuze Beeld/The Luminous Image."
  L. Zippay, 127:Fall85-263
"Het nieuwe bouwen."
  R. Padovan, 46:Jan85-4
"Het nieuwe bouwen in Rotterdam."
  R. Padovan, 46:Jan85-4
Hetherington, A. News, Newspapers and Television.
  P. Smith, 617(TLS):21Feb86-189
Hetherington, M.S. The Beginnings of Old English Lexicography.*
  S. Cooper, 382(MAE):1985/2-291
Heubeck, A. and G. Neumann, eds. Res Mycenaeae.
  G.R. Hart, 123:Vol35No1-213
Heubeck, A. and G.A. Privitera - see Homer
Heubner, H. - see Tacitus
Heussler, R. Completing a Stewardship.
  R.O. Tilman, 293(JASt):Aug85-888
Hewat, A.V. Lady's Time.*
  G. Mangan, 617(TLS):21Feb86-199
Hewett, C. English Cathedral and Monastic Carpentry.
  J.N. White, 324:Jun86-469
Hewett, C., ed. The Living Curve.*
  H. Guest, 503:Autumn84-141
Hewett, E. and W.F. Axton. Convivial Dickens.*
  P. Schlicke, 158:Mar85-26
Hewison, R. Footlights!
  A. Masters, 157:No155-49
Hewison, R. In Anger.
  G. Reeves, 402(MLR):Oct85-921
Hewison, R., ed. New Approaches to Ruskin.*
  J. Clegg, 541(RES):Feb85-113

Hoffmann, H., ed. Die Chronik von Monte-cassino.
  F. Newton, 589:Apr85-412
Hoffmann, H., ed. Das Lehenbuch des Fürst-bischofs Albrecht von Hohenlohe 1345-1372.
  J.B. Freed, 589:Jan85-159
Hoffmann, L. Kommunikation vor Gericht.
  C. Dechert, 355(LSoc):Dec85-540
Hoffmann, L-F. Le Français en français.
  S. Hecht, 207(FR):Oct85-172
Hoffmann-Axthelm, D. Sinnesarbeit.
  M.R. Becher, 384:Sep/Oct85-935
Hoffmannová, J. Sémantické a pragmatické aspekty koherence textu.
  D. Short, 575(SEER):Oct85-576
Hoffmeister, D.L. The Theater of Confine-ment.
  M. Silberman, 221(GQ):Winter85-143
Hoffmeister, G. Byron und der europäische Byronismus.*
  F. Garber, 678(YCGL):No34-146
Hoffmeister, G., ed. German Baroque Liter-ature.*
  J.P. Aikin, 221(GQ):Winter85-110
  J. Hardin, 301(JEGP):Jan85-79
  L.P. Johnson, 400(MLN):Apr85-679
Hoffmeister, G. Goethe und die euro-päische Romantik.
  M. Mayer, 680(ZDP):Band104Heft2-300
Hoffmeister, G. - see von Eichendorff, J.
Höfler, M. Dictionnaire des anglicismes.
  R. de Gorog, 545(RPh):May85-475
Höfler, M., H. Vernay and L. Wolf, eds. Kurt Baldinger zum 60. Geburtstag.
  H. Meier, 72:Band222Heft2-430
Hofmann, G. The Parable of the Blind.
  D.J. Enright, 453(NYRB):14Aug86-37
  L. Hafrey, 441:26Jan86-27
  442(NY):17Feb86-103
Hofmann, G. The Spectacle at the Tower.
  M. Hulse, 364:Jun85-106
Hofmann, J. Kritisches Handbuch des west-deutschen Theaters.
  T. Reber, 193(ELit):Spring-Summer85-206
Hofmann, M. Nights in the Iron Hotel.*
  J. Saunders, 565:Autumn85-74
Hofstadter, D.R. Metamagical Themas.*
  M. MacBeath, 617(TLS):18Apr86-411
  C. Taylor, 42(AR):Summer85-365
  639(VQR):Autumn85-124
Hogan, D. A New Shirt.
  T. Dooley, 617(TLS):12Dec86-1407
  B. Tonkin, 362:20ct86-23
Hogan, R. "Since O'Casey" and Other Essays on Irish Drama.*
  J.C. Countryman, 615(TJ):Mar85-134
Hogan, R. and R. Burnham. The Art of the Amateur: 1916-1920.
  M.K. Fielder, 615(TJ):Oct85-394
Hogan, R.S., L. Sawin and L.L. Merrill, eds. A Concordance to the Poetry of George Meredith.
  S. Brown, 354:Dec85-382
Hogarth, P. Arthur Boyd Houghton.
  C.F., 90:Sep85-632
"The Hogarth Letters."
  H. Stevens, 364:Dec85/Jan86-157
Hogg, J. James Hogg: Selected Stories and Sketches. (D.S. Mack, ed)
  D. Oakleaf, 588(SSL):Vol20-306

Hogg, J. Tales of Love and Mystery. (D. Groves, ed)
  G. Mangan, 617(TLS):8Aug86-870
Hogrefe, J. "Wholly Unacceptable."
  D.C. McGill, 441:18May86-15
Hogwood, C. Handel.*
  D. Burrows, 415:Feb85-90
  A. Suied, 450(NRF):Nov85-113
Hogwood, C. and R. Luckett, eds. Music in Eighteenth-Century England.*
  C.M.B., 412:Feb83-55
  G.S. Rousseau, 566:Spring86-222
Hohendahl, P.U. Literarische Kultur im Zeitalter des Liberalismus 1830-1870.
  J. Hermand, 406:Winter85-491
Hohendahl, P.U., ed. Literaturkritik. (Vol 4)
  H. Steinecke, 680(ZDP):Band104Heft4-618
Holba, H., G. Knorr and P. Spiegel. Reclams deutsches Filmlexikon.
  H-J. Greif, 193(ELit):Spring-Summer85-207
Holbo, P.S. Tarnished Expansion.*
  J. Braeman, 106:Fall85-353
Holcombe, L. Wives and Property.
  M.L. Shanley, 637(VS):Spring85-528
Holcroft, M.H. The Way of a Writer.
  L. Jones, 49:Oct85-127
Holden, J. Falling from Stardom.*
  S.C. Behrendt, 502(PrS):Spring85-100
  C. Guilford, 649(WAL):Aug85-176
Holden, R. Bursting with Feelings.
  S.L. Cuba, 497(PolR):Vol30No1-105
Holden, U. Tin Toys.
  C. Rumens, 617(TLS):18Apr86-415
Hölderlin, F. Hymns and Fragments. (R. Sieburth, trans)
  M. Perloff, 472:Spring/Summer86-144
Hölderlin, F. Sämtliche Werke. (Vols 4 and 5) (D.E. Sattler and M. Knaupp, eds)
  G. Stanitzek, 384:Apr85-341
Holderness, G. D.H. Lawrence.*
  V. Mahon, 541(RES):Feb85-127
Holderness, G. Shakespeare's History.
  I-S. Ewbank, 617(TLS):25Apr86-451
Holdheim, W.W. The Hermeneutic Mode.*
  M. Danahy, 446(NCFS):Spring-Summer86-348
  L.M. Findlay, 150(DR):Spring85-135
  G. Green, 678(YCGL):No34-133
  V. Nemoianu, 400(MLN):Dec85-1148
Holes, C. Colloquial Arabic of the Gulf and Saudi Arabia.
  D.R. Magrath, 399(MLJ):Spring85-85
Holisky, D.A. Aspect and Georgian Medial Verbs.
  J. Nichols, 350:Jun86-468
van Holk, A.G.F., ed. Dutch Contributions to the Ninth International Congress of Slavists, Kiev, September 6-14, 1983: Linguistics.*
  J.I. Press, 402(MLR):Jan85-246
Holk, I., ed. Tegnverden.
  N. Ingwersen, 563(SS):Winter85-102
Holland, N.N. The I.
  A. Brink, 529(QQ):Winter85-876
  L. Keyes, 367(L&P):Vol32No2-55
Holland, P. - see Wycherley, W.
Holland, W.E. Let a Soldier Die.
  L.T. Lemon, 502(PrS):Spring85-109
Hollander, J. Vision and Resonance.
  617(TLS):28Mar86-343

Holleman, J.F. - see van Vollenhoven, C.
Holliday, B., with W. Dufty. Lady Sings
the Blues.
  A. Shipton, 415:Apr85-227
Hollier, D. Politique de la prose.*
  P. Collier, 208(FS):Jan85-110
Hollingsworth, J. Unspeakable Acts.
  G. Collins, 441:14Dec86-21
Hollis, C.C. Language and Style in
"Leaves of Grass."*
  C. Bedient, 569(SR):Spring85-273
  E. Folsom, 481(PQ):Spring85-294
  J. Gatta, 183(ESQ):Vol31No4-272
Hollis, M. and S. Lukes, eds. Rationality
and Relativism.*
  R. Phillips, 63:Sep85-361
Holloway, J. The Slumber of Apollo.
  D.W.L., 506(PSt):May85-96
  N. Miller, 42(AR):Winter85-119
Hollqvist, H. The Use of English in Three
Large Swedish Companies.
  J. Pauchard, 189(EA):Apr-Jun86-240
Holly, M.A. Panofsky and the Foundations
of Art History.*
  A. Harrison, 90:Oct85-727
  C. Landauer, 290(JAAC):Fall85-82
Holm, J., ed. Central American English.*
  F.W. Gester, 72:Band222Heft2-379
  G.G. Gilbert, 35(AS):Fall85-261
  E.W. Schneider, 685(ZDL):2/1985-245
  L. Todd, 260(IF):Band90-343
Holm, J.A., with A.W. Shilling. Diction-
ary of Bahamian English.
  M. Görlach, 38:Band103Heft1/2-157
Holmberg, E.J. A Mycenaean Chamber Tomb
near Berbati in Argolis.
  P. Warren, 123:Vol35No1-207
Holmes, J.C. Gone in October.
  K. Knight, 532(RCF):Fall85-191
  H. Nuwer, 580(SCR):Fall85-120
Holmes, J.D. and B.W. Bickers. A Short
History of the Catholic Church.
  P. Crane, 161(DUJ):Jun84-318
Holmes, J.E. The Mood/Interest Theory of
American Foreign Policy.
  639(VQR):Autumn85-135
Holmes, L.D. Quest for the Real Samoa.
  S. Silverman, 441:9Nov86-24
Holmes, N. Designer's Guide to Creating
Charts and Diagrams.
  T. Reese, 507:Jul/Aug85-316
Holmes, N., with R. De Neve. Designing
Pictorial Symbols.
  C. Hess, 507:Nov/Dec85-118
Holmes, R. Acts of War.
  E.N. Luttwak, 441:23Mar86-13
Holmes, R. Footsteps.*
  R.M. Adams, 453(NYRB):10Apr86-36
  442(NY):7Apr86-106
Holmes, W.C. "La Statira" by Pietro Otto-
boni and Alessandro Scarlatti.*
  W. Dean, 410(M&L):Apr85-165
Holmgren, O. Kärlek och ära.
  K. Hallind, 563(SS):Winter85-89
Holmlander, I. Zur Distribution und Leis-
tung des Pronominaladverbs.
  A. Lötscher, 685(ZDL):1/1985-116
Holt, H. and H. Pym - see Pym, B.
Holt, J.C. Robin Hood.*
  R.W. Kaeuper, 382(MAE):1985/1-137
Holt, S. One of Us Is Wrong.
  N. Callendar, 441:31Aug86-14

Holtby, W. Poor Caroline.
  P. Craig, 617(TLS):18Jul86-792
Holter, K., ed. Der goldene Psalter
"Dagulf-Psalter."
  L. Nees, 54:Dec85-681
Holthaus, G. Circling Back.
  J.R. Saucerman, 649(WAL):Feb86-351
Holthusen, H.E. Gottfried Benn.
  M. Hofmann, 617(TLS):26Sep86-1055
Holton, G. The Advancement of Science,
and Its Burdens.
  J. Trefil, 441:5Oct86-50
Holton, G. and R.S. Morison, eds. Limits
of Scientific Inquiry.
  D.A. Bantz, 486:Sep84-522
Holton, S.W. Down Home and Uptown.*
  K. Byerman, 395(MFS):Winter85-730
  M.N. Simmons, 355(LSoc):Sep85-398
Holtus, G. and E. Radtke, eds. Varietäten-
linguistik des Italienischen.*
  G. Lepschy, 545(RPh):May86-492
Holtz, L. Donat et la tradition de
l'enseignement grammatical.
  A.P. Orbán, 394:Vol38fasc1/2-243
Holub, M. On the Contrary.
  M. Hofmann, 493:Jan85-59
  G. Szirtes, 148:Summer85-51
Holub, R.C. Reception Theory.*
  A. Bony, 189(EA):Apr-Jun86-188
  M. Eckert, 141:Summer85-310
  G. Herlt and J.J. White, 402(MLR):
  Jul85-673
  C. Koelb, 149(CLS):Winter85-554
  T. Kontje, 222(GR):Fall85-146
Holum, K.G. Theodosian Empresses.
  J.H.W.G. Liebeschuetz, 123:Vol35No1-
  146
Holz, H. and E. Wolf-Gazo, eds. Whitehead
und der Prozessbegriff.
  K. Hartmann, 687:Oct-Dec85-651
Holz-Mänttäri, J. Translatorisches
Handeln.
  C. Hall, 439(NM):1985/3-424
Holzbauer, H., ed. Johann Anton Fils
(1733-1760).
  R. Halton, 410(M&L):Oct85-401
Holzberg, N. - see Pirckheimer, W.
Holzel, T. and A. Salkeld. The Mystery of
Mallory and Irvine.
  R. Huntford, 362:13Nov86-24
Holzer, H., G.S. Boritt and M.E. Neely, Jr.
The Lincoln Image.*
  F.S. Voss, 658:Spring85-91
Holzhey, H. and J-P. Leyvraz, eds. Ration-
alitätskritik und neue Mythologien.
  A. Reix, 542:Jan-Mar85-92
Homan, S. Beckett's Theaters.
  G. Armstrong, 610:Autumn85-262
  H.L. Baldwin, 191(ELN):Mar86-71
  V. Cooke, 529(QQ):Winter85-863
  A. Roche, 577(SHR):Fall85-384
  295(JML):Nov85-447
Homan, S. When the Theater Turns to
Itself.*
  R. Warren, 677(YES):Vol 15-277
Home, R. City of Blood Revisited.
  D. Killingray, 637(VS):Summer85-703
Home, R.W., ed. Science Under Scrutiny.
  R. Nola, 63:Dec85-553
Home, R.W. - see Aepinus, F.U.T.
"Homenaje al Prof. Tomás Buesa Oliver."
  H. Guiter, 553(RLiR):Jul-Dec85-436

177

Hough, J., Jr. The Conduct of the Game.
  J. Lardner, 442(NY):16Jun86-120
  J.W. Poses, 441:18May86-28
Hough, R. Ace of Clubs.
  J. Morgan, 617(TLS):26Dec86-1455
Hough, R. The Greatest Crusade.
  442(NY):24Feb86-106
Houlden, J.L. Connections.
  P. Baelz, 617(TLS):25Jul86-824
Houm, P. En mann forut for vår tid.
  Ø. Rottem, 562(Scan):May85-59
Hounshell, D.A. From the American System
  to Mass Production 1800-1932.
  B.D. Palmer, 529(QQ):Autumn85-594
Hountondji, P.J. African Philosophy.*
  A. Appiah, 529(QQ):Winter85-873
Hourcade, B. Le Siècle des légendes.
  J.L. Pallister, 207(FR):Apr86-816
House, J. and A. Distel, with others.
  Renoir.
  K. Adler, 59:Sep85-374
Household, G. Arrows of Desire.
  J. Sullivan, 441:2Feb86-16
Householder, F.W. The Syntax of Apollon-
  ius Dyscolus.
  D.M. Schenkeveld, 394:Vol38fasc3/4-424
Houseman, J. Entertainers and the Enter-
  tained.
  P. Dunne, 18:Sep86-69
  B. Shulgasser, 441:30Nov86-22
Housley, N. The Avignon Papacy and the
  Crusades 1305-1378.
  M. Barber, 617(TLS):7Nov86-1259
Houston, D. With the Offal Eaters.
  F. Adcock, 617(TLS):7Nov86-1256
Houston, J.P. The Rhetoric of Poetry in
  the Renaissance and Seventeenth Century.*
  M.G. Brennan, 541(RES):Nov85-561
  L. Carrive, 549(RLC):Oct-Dec85-463
  R.F., 391:Dec85-115
  H. Rusche, 604:Winter85-6
  A. Sununu, 569(SR):Summer85-liii
  A.E. Watson, 148:Summer85-85
Houston, J.P. The Shape and Style of
  Proust's Novel.*
  E.J. Hughes, 208(FS):Jul85-362
  P. Newman-Gordon, 210(FrF):Jan85-117
Houston, R. The Nation Thief.
  P. Wild, 649(WAL):May85-93
Houtzagers, H.P. The Čakavian Dialect of
  Orlec on the Island of Cres.
  S.G. Thomason, 350:Sep86-725
Houzeau, J-C. My Passage at the New
  Orleans "Tribune." (D.C. Rankin, ed)
  J.J. Perret, 207(FR):Mar86-629
Hovdhaugen, E. Foundations of Western Lin-
  guistics.
  P. Swiggers, 353:Vol23No4-646
Hoving, T. Masterpiece.
  L. Weschler, 441:19Oct86-18
Howard, C.M. Les Fortunes de Madame de
  Sévigné au XVIIème et au XVIIIème
  siècles.*
  A.G. Suozzo, Jr., 210(FrF):May85-241
Howard, J. Margaret Mead.
  A.S. Grossman, 77:Summer85-265
Howard, J.A., ed. Wunderparlich und selt-
  same Historien Til Eulen Spiegels.
  J.W. Thomas, 133:Band17Heft3/4-323
Howard, J.E. Shakespeare's Art of Orches-
  tration.
  J. Coakley, 130:Winter85/86-378
  J.L. Styan, 612(ThS):Nov85-200

Howard, J.H., ed. Belief, Faith and
  Reason.
  R. Williamson, 396(ModA):Spring85-179
Howard, M. Expensive Habits.
  K. Bucknell, 617(TLS):12Dec86-1409
  G. Wolff, 441:8Jun86-9
Howard, M. Grace Abounding.
  P. Iyer, 473(PR):Vol52No3-286
Howard, P., ed. Benjamin Britten: "The
  Turn of the Screw."
  C. Matthews, 617(TLS):21Feb86-197
Howard, P. C.W. von Gluck, "Orfeo."
  J.B., 412:May84-146
Howard, R., ed. La Bibliothèque et le
  laboratoire de Guy de la Brosse au
  Jardin des Plantes à Paris.
  P. Wolfe, 475:Vol 12No22-323
Howard, R. Brave New Workplace.*
  J. Fallows, 61:May86-96
Howard, R. Lining Up.*
  M.E. Gibson, 472:Spring/Summer86-220
Howard, R., with E. Skjei. What Makes the
  Crops Rejoice.
  S. Brownmiller, 441:1Jun86-30
Howard, W. John Clare.*
  P.M. Ball, 677(YES):Vol 15-312
Howarth, D. Lord Arundel and his Circle.
  J. Buxton, 617(TLS):14Mar86-272
  442(NY):5May86-135
Howarth, D. Pursued by a Bear.
  P. Oakes, 617(TLS):7Mar86-243
Howarth, W. The Book of Concord.*
  R.H. Du Pree, 577(SHR):Winter85-67
  R. Sattelmeyer, 183(ESQ):Vol31No3-190
Howarth, W. - see Thoreau, H.D.
Howarth, W.D. Anouilh: "Antigone."*
  D.B. Parsell, 207(FR):Apr86-794
Howarth, W.D. Molière.*
  M. Cuénin, 535(RHL):Nov/Dec85-1064
Howat, R. Debussy in Proportion.*
  R. Nichols, 415:Jun85-349
  R.S. Parks, 308:Fall85-315
  R.L. Smith, 617(TLS):13Jun86-638
Howe, A. The Cotton Masters, 1830-1860.*
  R. Church, 637(VS):Spring86-485
Howe, F. Myths of Coeducation.*
  E. Toth, 115:Fall85-484
Howe, I. The American Newness.
  B. De Mott, 441:29Jun86-17
  442(NY):26May86-107
Howe, I. A Margin of Hope.
  E.S. Shapiro, 396(ModA):Spring85-173
Howe, I. Socialism and America.*
  C.V. Woodward, 453(NYRB):30Jan86-26
Howe, J. Marlowe, Tamburlaine and Magic.
  G.W. O'Brien, 111:Spring86-4
Howe, R.W. Mata Hari.
  C. Andrew, 441:8Jun86-13
Howe, S. My Emily Dickinson. Defenestra-
  tion of Prague.
  M. Perloff, 29(APR):Jul/Aug86-12
Howell, C. Land, Family and Inheritance
  in Transition.
  M.K. McIntosh, 589:Jan85-222
Howell, D. Blind Victory.
  B. Anderson, 362:26Jun86-22
  C. Moore, 617(TLS):22Aug86-904
Howell, D. British Workers and the
  Independent Labour Party 1888-1906.
  J. Schneer, 637(VS):Spring85-532
Howell, M. and P. Ford. The Beetle of
  Aphrodite.
  P-L. Adams, 61:Mar86-111

Howells, W.D. Selected Letters. (Vol 1
ed by G. Arms and others; Vol 2 ed by G.
Arms and C.K. Lohmann)
  B. Pitz, 106:Fall85-317
Howells, W.D. Selected Letters of W.D.
Howells. (Vol 6) (W.M. Gibson and C.K.
Lohmann, eds)
  G.C. Carrington, Jr., 70:Sep/Oct85-28
  J. Katz, 579(SAQ):Winter85-114
Howells, W.D. and others. The Whole Fam-
ily.
  442(NY):21Jul86-94
Howson, G. Thief-Taker General.
  42(AR):Fall85-501
Howson, M. - see Barthel, M.
Hoy, D.C. The Critical Circle.*
  J.F. Brown, 438:Spring85-246
Hoy, H., ed. Modern English-Canadian
Prose.*
  W.N., 102(CanL):Winter84-190
Hoyle, F. and C. Wickramasinghe. Archae-
opteryx, the Primordial Bird.
  A. Charig, 617(TLS):31Oct86-1213
Hoyle, P. Brantwood.
  P-L. Adams, 61:Oct86-103
  L. Duguid, 617(TLS):3Oct86-1115
  G. Dyer, 362:28Aug86-22
Hoyt, E.P. Japan's War.
  D. Murray, 441:6Apr86-23
Hoyt, R. The Dragon Portfolio.
  S. McCauley, 441:21Dec86-14
Hribal, C.J. Matty's Heart.
  W.D. Everman, 455:Jun85-62
Hryciuk, M. this is hilarious.
  W. Swist, 404:Autumn85-59
Hsi K'ang. Philosophy and Argumentation
in Third Century China. (R.G. Henricks,
trans)
  A.S. Cua, 543:Sep85-157
Hsia, R.P-C. Society and Religion in
Münster, 1535-1618.
  J.A. Vann, 551(RenQ):Spring85-120
Hsiang-hsiang, W. - see under Wu Hsiang-
hsiang
Hsieh Ping-ying. Autobiography of a Chi-
nese Girl.
  442(NY):30Jun86-89
Hsien-yung, P. - see under Pai Hsien-yung
Hsu, C-Y. Han Agriculture.* (J.L. Dull,
ed)
  D. Grafflin, 293(JASt):Nov84-169
Hsü, R.S.W. The Style of Lu Hsün.
  W.A. Lyell, 302:Vol21No1-76
Hsü, T-C. The Chinese Conception of the
Theatre.
  C. Mackerras, 617(TLS):5Sep86-958
Hsüan-chih, Y. - see under Yang Hsüan-chih
Hsün Yüeh. Hsün Yüeh and the Mind of Late
Han China. (C-Y. Ch'en, ed and trans)
  W.G. Crowell, 318(JAOS):Apr-Jun84-349
Hua, G. - see under Gu Hua
Hua Yin. Class and Communalism in
Malaysia.
  C. Hirschman, 293(JASt):May85-664
Huang Fu-ch'ing. Chin-tai Jih-pen tsai-
Hua wen-hua chi she-hui shih-yeh chih
yen-chiu.
  J.A. Fogel, 293(JASt):Feb85-371
Huang, P.C.C. The Peasant Economy and
Social Change in North China.
  J. Spence, 453(NYRB):16Jan86-41
Huang, R. 1587, A Year of No Significance.
  T. Fisher, 302:Vol21No1-60

Hubbard, D.G. Winning Back the Sky.
  G. James, 441:16Feb86-17
Hubbard, E. Clwyd.
  J. Harris, 617(TLS):27Jun86-713
Hubbard, F.A. Theories of Action in
Conrad.
  A.E. Davidson, 136:Vol 18No3-233
  295(JML):Nov85-461
Hubbard, L.R. The Invaders Plan.
  G. Jonas, 441:12Jan86-22
Hubbell, S. A Country Year.
  P. Hagan, 441:13Apr86-20
Huber, L. and J.J. White, eds. Musil in
Focus.*
  E. Boa, 402(MLR):Apr85-499
Huber, T.M. The Revolutionary Origins of
Modern Japan.
  H. Bolitho, 244(HJAS):Dec85-667
Hubka, T.C. Big House, Little House, Back
House, Barn.
  P. Chase-Harrell, 432(NEQ):Sep85-477
Hübler, A. Understatements and Hedges in
English.
  F.L. Smith, 350:Jun86-462
Hübner, K. and J. Vuillemin, eds. Wissen-
schaftliche und nichtwissenschaftliche
Rationalität.
  K. Gloy, 687:Jan-Mar85-137
Huchel, P. Gesammelte Werke. (A. Vieregg,
ed)
  P. Brady, 617(TLS):10Jan86-33
Huchet, J-C. Le Roman médiéval.
  G.R. Mermier, 207(FR):May86-971
Huchon, M. Rabelais grammairien.
  F. Charpentier, 535(RHL):Mar/Apr85-286
Huddle, D. Only the Little Bone.
  M.S. Willis, 441:14Sep86-40
Huddleston, J. Sarah Grand, 1854-1943.
  S. Mitchell, 635(VPR):Spring85-40
Huddleston, R. Introduction to the Gram-
mar of English.
  R. Salkie, 353:Vol23No4-640
Hudgins, A. Saints and Strangers.
  P. Stitt, 441:4May86-22
Hudson, A., ed. English Wycliffite Ser-
mons.* (Vol 1)
  J. Frankis, 541(RES):Aug85-404
  R. Hanna 3d, 589:Apr85-416
  E. Wilson, 382(MAE):1985/2-311
Hudson, H. Criminal Trespass.*
  J. Winterson, 617(TLS):22Aug86-921
Hudson, L. Night Life.*
  M.V. Miller, 441:9Mar86-17
Hudson, R. The Allemande, the Balletto
and the Tanz.
  I. Fenlon, 617(TLS):26Dec86-1444
Hudson, R. Invitation to Linguistics.
  A.S. Kaye, 350:Dec86-976
Hudson, R. Word Grammar.*
  R.W. Langacker, 350:Mar86-157
Hudson, R. and S. Davidson. Rock Hudson.
  J. Kearney, 441:20Jul86-13
Hudson, R., D. Rhind and H. Mounsey. An
Atlas of EEC Affairs.
  J. Creedy, 161(DUJ):Dec84-101
Hudson, R.V. The Writing Game.
  A. Bendixen, 534(RALS):Autumn83-239
Hudson, W.H. Far Away and Long Ago.
  F. Gallix, 189(EA):Apr-Jun86-229
Hudspeth, R.N. - see Fuller, M.

Huelsenbeck, R.  Reise bis ans Ende der
Freiheit.  (U. Karthaus and H. Krueger,
eds)
  A. Otten, 42(AR):Spring85-247
Huenemann, R.W.  The Dragon and the Iron
Horse.
  T.R. Gottschang, 293(JASt):Nov84-170
Huerta, J.A.  Chicano Theater.*
  J. Bruce-Novoa, 352(LATR):Fall85-107
Hufbauer, K.  The Formation of the German
Chemical Community (1720-1795).*
  M.C. Usselman, 486:Mar85-165
Huff, C.  British Women's Diaries.
  I.B. Nadel, 637(VS):Summer86-651
Huffman, F.E. and Im Proum.  Cambodian-
English Glossary.
  P.N. Jenner, 293(JASt):Aug85-889
Hug, M.  La distribution des phonèmes en
français/Die Phonemverteilung im
Deutschen.
  K. Heger, 685(ZDL):1/1985-99
Huggan, I.  The Elizabeth Stories.
  K. Chittick, 198:Autumn85-91
  J. Giltrow, 102(CanL):Summer85-163
Huggins, N. - see Du Bois, W.E.B.
Hughes, A. and D. Porter, eds.  Current
Developments in Language Testing.
  P.J. Angelis, 399(MLJ):Autumn85-293
Hughes, B.B. - see Jordanus de Nemore
Hughes, D.  But for Bunter.*
  P. Parker, 364:Oct85-101
Hughes, D.  Dryden's Heroic Plays.
  M.E. Novak, 402(MLR):Oct85-906
Hughes, D.  The Joke of the Century.
  J. Cantor, 441:9Nov86-15
Hughes, D., ed.  Winter's Tales.  (New
Ser, Vol 1)
  J.N. Shaw, 441:2Mar86-17
Hughes, D. and G. Gordon, eds.  Best Short
Stories 1986.
  C. Hawtree, 617(TLS):21Nov86-1324
Hughes, E.J.  Marcel Proust.*
  295(JML):Nov85-545
Hughes, G.  Barns of Rural Britain.*
  J.N. White, 324:Feb86-207
Hughes, G., ed.  Papers Given at the First
Conference of the James Hogg Society
(Stirling, 1983).
  R. MacLachlan, 571(ScLJ):Autumn85-10
Hughes, G.  The Poetry of Francisco de la
Torre.
  C.P. Thompson, 447(N&Q):Sep84-428
Hughes, G.E. - see Buridan, J.
Hughes, G.R.  Emerson's Demanding Opti-
mism.*
  G.M. Johnson, 27(AL):Oct85-491
  J. Myerson, 432(NEQ):Sep85-471
Hughes, H.S.  Prisoners of Hope.*
  E.M. Schächter, 278(IS):Vol40-156
Hughes, J. and W.S. Ramson.  Poetry of the
Stewart Court.
  A.A. MacDonald, 179(ES):Oct85-462
  H.M. Shire, 588(SSL):Vol20-267
Hughes, L.  The Big Sea.
  617(TLS):25Apr86-459
Hughes, L.A.J.  Russia and the West.
  A. McKinnon, 550(RusR):Jan85-103
Hughes, M.  My Name is Paula Popowich!
  M. Rubio, 102(CanL):Fall85-115
Hughes, M. and M. Kennedy.  New Futures.
  F. Cairncross, 617(TLS):4Apr86-349
Hughes, S.  Hashknife Cowboy.
  L. Milazzo, 584(SWR):Winter85-130

Hughes, T.  River.*
  P. Lagayette, 189(EA):Jan-Mar86-112
  J. Saunders, 565:Spring85-72
Hughes, T.  Gabrielle Roy et Margaret
Laurence.*
  J-A. Elder, 102(CanL):Winter84-89
Hugo, R.  Making Certain It Goes On.*
  P. Stitt, 472:Spring/Summer86-169
Hugues, E.J.  Marcel Proust.
  J-Y. Tadié, 535(RHL):Jan/Feb85-126
Huguet, M.  L'ennui et ses discours.
  J-M. Gabaude, 542:Jul-Sep85-356
Huisman, D., ed.  Dictionnaire des philo-
sophes.
  Y. Brès, 542:Jan-Mar85-74
Huld, M.E.  Basic Albanian Etymology.
  G. Bevington, 350:Mar86-219
  V.A. Friedman, 574(SEEJ):Winter85-494
Hulliung, M.  Citizen Machiavelli.*
  F. Chiappelli, 551(RenQ):Winter85-736
Hulme, K.  The Bone People.*
  D.J. Enright, 453(NYRB):27Feb86-16
  C.K. Stead, 49:Oct85-101
  442(NY):3Feb86-105
Hulse, C.  Metamorphic Verse.*
  J.R. Brink, 702:Vol 17-278
  J. van Dorsten, 179(ES):Oct85-467
Hulse, M.  Propaganda.*
  J. Lanchester, 493:Oct85-66
  S. Rae, 364:Aug-Sep85-129
van der Hulst, H.  Syllable Structure and
Stress in Dutch.
  R. van Zonneveld, 204(FdL):Sep85-229
Hult, G.  Bronze Age Ashlar Masonry in the
Eastern Mediterranean.
  E.J. Peltenburg, 303(JoHS):Vol 105-223
Hulton, P., ed.  America 1585.*
  C. Rainwater, 568(SCN):Winter85-66
  M.S. Young, 39:Jan85-70
Humbach, N.A. and others.  Spanish Today.
  K.R. Westinghouse, 399(MLJ):Spring85-
110
Humber, J.M. and R.F. Almeder - see "Bio-
medical Ethics Reviews: 1984"
Humbert, M-T.  Le Volkameria.
  P.J.T. Gormally, 207(FR):May86-997
von Humboldt, W.  Brief am M. Abel-Rémusat.
  P. Swiggers, 350:Jun86-456
von Humboldt, W.  Izbrannye trudy po jazy-
koznaniju.
  R. Lötzsch, 682(ZPSK):Band38Heft5-612
von Humboldt, W.  Über die Sprache.  (J.
Trabant, ed)
  W. Neumann, 682(ZPSK):Band38Heft5-611
Hume, A.  Edmund Spenser.*
  J.N. King, 551(RenQ):Summer85-365
  R.D.S., 604:Spring-Summer85-30
Hume, K.  Fantasy and Mimesis.
  L. Basney, 395(MFS):Winter85-848
  R.H.C., 125:Winter85-231
  O.M. Meidner, 89(BJA):Autumn85-408
Hume, L.P., ed.  The National Union of
Women's Suffrage Societies 1897-1914.
  J.H. Dalgleish, 637(VS):Autumn85-166
Hume, R.D., ed.  The London Theatre World,
1660-1800.
  R. Halsband, 570(SQ):Summer85-250
Hummel, D.  The Collector's Guide to the
American Musical Theatre.*
  D.E. McGinty, 91:Fall85-227

182

Hummer, T.R. The Passion of the Right-
Angled Man.
  S. Burris, 569(SR):Fall85-lxxxii
  R. McDowell, 249(HudR):Winter86-690
Humphrey, C. Karl Marx Collective.
  A. Wood, 575(SEER):Apr85-313
Humphrey, J. Roman Circuses.
  J.J. Wilkes, 617(TLS):12Sep86-1012
Humphrey, N. and R.J. Lifton, eds. In a
Dark Time.
  G. Best, 176:Jun85-49
Humphrey, W. The Collected Stories of
William Humphrey.*
  T.O. Treadwell, 617(TLS):1Aug86-844
Humphries, A. - see Shakespeare, W.
Humphreys, E. An Absolute Hero.
  V. Bogdanor, 362:20Feb86-28
Humphreys, E. The Taliesin Tradition.
  N. Thomas, 176:May86-59
Humphreys, J. Dreams of Sleep.*
  P. Parker, 364:Apr/May85-152
Humphreys, S.C. The Family, Women and
Death.*
  P.J. Rhodes, 303(JoHS):Vol 105-210
Humphries, J. Metamorphoses of the Raven.
  W.L. Andrews, 659(ConL):Summer86-257
  B.L. Knapp, 594:Fall85-317
Humphries, J. The Otherness Within.*
  J. Anzalone, 207(FR):May86-969
Humphries, M., comp. Not Love Alone.
  L. Wheel, 493:Feb86-61
Humphry, D. and A. Wickett. The Right to
Die.
  M. Cranston, 362:18Sep86-24
  E.E. Shelp, 441:14Sep86-32
Huneke, D.K. The Moses of Rovno.
  A. Schmitz, 441:19Jan86-21
Huneker, J.G. Americans in the Arts, 1890-
1920. (A.T. Schwab, ed)
  K. Beckson, 365:Winter/Spring85-55
"Hungaro-Slavica, 1983." (Vol 9) (L. Had-
rovics and A. Hollós, eds)
  V.M. Du Feu, 575(SEER):Jan85-105
Hunger, H. Prochoras Kydones, Übersetzung
von acht Briefen des Hl. Augustinus.
  D.M. Nicol, 123:Vol35No2-428
  É. des Places, 555:Vol59fasc1-131
Hunt, D.C. and M.V. Gallagher - see "Karl
Bodmer's America"
Hunt, E.D. Holy Land Pilgrimage in the
Later Roman Empire A.D. 312-460.
  K.G. Holum, 122:Oct85-377
Hunt, J.D. Garden and Grove.
  J. Summerson, 617(TLS):28Nov86-1353
Hunt, L. Captain Sword and Captain Pen.
(R. Dunlap, ed)
  M. Baron, 155:Summer85-118
  R.N. MacKenzie, 635(VPR):Winter85-160
Hunt, L. Politics, Culture and Class in
the French Revolution.*
  S.H., 185:Oct85-214
  N. Hampson, 173(ECS):Winter85/86-297
Hunt, V. The Return of the Good Soldier.*
(R. and M. Secor, eds)
  J. Wiesenfarth, 594:Winter85-437
Hunt, W. The Justicing Notebook of
William Hunt 1744-1749. (E. Crittall,
ed)
  D.G. Vaisey, 447(N&Q):Mar84-118
Hunter, A. The Chelsea Ghost.
  T.J.B., 617(TLS):21Feb86-198

Hunter, A. Joseph Conrad and the Ethics
of Darwinism.*
  R.G. Hampson, 175:Autumn85-259
  B.E. Teets, 637(VS):Spring85-558
Hunter, J. Edwardian Fiction.*
  B. Tippett, 366:Spring85-152
Hunter, J. - see Murdoch, J.
Hunter, J. and C. Maclean. Skye.
  D. Profumo, 617(TLS):24Oct86-1200
Hunter, J.E., comp. Concise Dictionary of
Modern Japanese History.
  C. Gluck, 407(MN):Winter85-449
Hunter, J.M., ed. The Trail Drivers of
Texas.
  L. Milazzo, 584(SWR):Summer85-415
Hunter, R. Wait till the Sun Shines,
Nellie.
  R. Christiansen, 617(TLS):11Jul86-764
Hunter, R.L., ed. Eubulus: The Fragments.*
  S.M. Goldberg, 24:Winter85-518
Hunter, R.L. A Study of "Daphnis and
Chloe."
  K. Dowden, 123:Vol35No1-184
  G.N. Sandy, 303(JoHS):Vol 105-202
Hunter, R.L. and V.L. Living Dogs and
Dead Lions.
  N. Proffitt, 441:11May86-14
Hunter, S. Victorian Idyllic Fiction.
  G.B. Tennyson, 445(NCF):Jun85-120
  E. Wright, 637(VS):Spring86-479
Hunter, V.J. Past and Process in Herod-
otus and Thucydides.*
  D. Lateiner, 122:Jan85-69
Hunter, W.B., Jr. Milton's "Comus."
  J.G. Demaray, 551(RenQ):Spring85-187
  R. Flannagan, 391:Oct85-87
  P. Stevens, 539:Nov85-302
  M. Treip, 610:Summer85-174
Huntford, R. Shackleton.
  P-L. Adams, 61:Feb86-87
  J.C. Batchelor, 441:2Feb86-11
  R. Fox, 362:9Jan86-26
  T. Gibbs, 442(NY):24Mar86-118
Huntington, S.L. The "Pāla-Sena" Schools
of Sculpture.
  G. Bhattacharya, 463:Winter85/86-440
Huntington, S.L. and J.C. The Art of
Ancient India.
  S. Digby, 617(TLS):11Jul86-763
Huntley, F.L. Bishop Joseph Hall and
Protestant Meditation in Seventeenth-
Century England.
  R.P. Lessenich, 38:Band103Heft1/2-213
  R.A. McCabe, 541(RES):May85-265
Hurford, J.R. and B. Heasley. Semantics.
  K. Allan, 67:May85-74
Huriet, M. La Grande muraille du Japon.
  J. Kirkup, 617(TLS):21Mar86-306
Hurlebusch, K. and K.L. Schneider - see
Stadler, E.
Hürlimann, M., ed. Musiker-Handschriften
aus fünf Jahrhunderten von Monteverdi
bis Britten.
  70:May/Jun85-174
Hurst, A., O. Reverdin and J. Rudhardt.
Papyrus Bodmer XXIX.
  J.N. Birdsall, 123:Vol35No2-384
Hurston, Z.N. Dust Tracks on a Road.*
(2nd ed) (R.E. Hemenway, ed)
  K. Byerman, 395(MFS):Winter85-730
  A. Maja-Pearce, 617(TLS):2May86-479

Hurston, Z.N.  Their Eyes Were Watching God.
  A. Maja-Pearce, 617(TLS):2May86-479
Hurt, H.  Reasonable Doubt.
  H. Brogan, 617(TLS):27Jun86-701
  A. Clymer, 441:23Feb86-16
Husain, S.S.A.  The Indianness of Rudyard Kipling.
  R.W. Reising, 599:Summer85-292
Huse, D., ed.  Spinner. (Vol 3)
  E.W. Hall, 432(NEQ):Sep85-479
Huse, N.L.  The Survival Tales of John Hersey.*
  J.H. Justus, 27(AL):Mar85-174
Hussain, A.  Islamic Iran.
  C. Heywood, 617(TLS):21Mar86-293
Husserl, E.  Ideas Pertaining to a Pure Phenomenology and to a Phenomenological Philosophy.* (Vol 1) (F. Kersten, trans)
  L. Embree, 484(PPR):Dec85-348
Husserl, E.  Idées directrices pour une phénoménologie.
  T. Cordellier, 450(NRF):Oct85-99
Husserl, E.  Studien zur Arithmetik und Geometrie. (I. Strohmeyer, ed)
  R. Sokolowski, 543:Mar85-639
  U. Will, 687:Apr-Jun85-325
Hussey, E. - see Aristotle
Hussey, S.S.  The Literary Language of Shakespeare.*
  M. de Grazia, 570(SQ):Winter85-507
  A.C. Partridge, 156(ShJW):Jahrbuch1985-240
Hutcheon, L.  Formalism and the Freudian Aesthetic.
  T.H. Adamowski, 627(UTQ):Summer85-457
  R. Macksey, 400(MLN):Dec85-1203
  W.F. Motte, Jr., 207(FR):Apr86-793
Hutcheon, L.  Narcissistic Narrative.*
  A. Jefferson, 208(FS):Apr85-235
  R.R. Wilson, 107(CRCL):Jun85-292
  295(JML):Nov85-426
Hutcheon, L.  A Theory of Parody.*
  P. Chipchase, 607:Sep85-41
  S. Scobie, 376:Jan86-128
Hutchings, B.  The Poetry of William Cowper.*
  P. Danchin, 179(ES):Aug85-369
Hutchings, E. - see Feynman, R.P., with R. Leighton
Hutchings, R.  The Soviet Budget.*
  W. Moskoff, 104(CASS):Spring85-88
Hutchinson, I.G.C.  A Political History of Scotland 1832-1924.
  C. Harvie, 617(TLS):2May86-467
Hutchinson, P.  Games Authors Play.*
  A. Bony, 549(RLC):Oct-Dec85-453
  S.D. Harasym, 107(CRCL):Jun85-359
  J. Osborne, 402(MLR):Jul85-676
Hutchinson, S.  Henry James.*
  N. Bradbury, 541(RES):May85-296
  R.P. Hoople, 106:Spring85-57
  D. Kirby, 639(VQR):Winter85-175
  R.B. Yeazell, 536(Rev):Vol7-43
Hutchison, R.  The Politics of the Arts Council.
  R. Berman, 289:Fall85-124
Hutchison, R.A.  Off the Books.
  D. Diamond, 441:18May86-25
Hutt, M.  Chouannerie and Counter-Revolution.*
  M. Elliott, 83:Autumn85-234

Hüttl-Folter, G.  Die trat/torot-Lexeme in den altrussischen Chroniken.*
  H. Leeming, 575(SEER):Jan85-104
Hutton, J.  Themes of Peace in Renaissance Poetry.* (R. Guerlac, ed)
  639(VQR):Summer85-88
Hutton, R.  The Royalist War Effort, 1642-1646.*
  M.G. Finlayson, 539:Nov85-299
Hutton, W.  The Revolution that Never Was.
  J. Eatwell, 362:11Sep86-21
Huxley, E.  The African Poison Murders.
  P. Craig, 617(TLS):18Jul86-792
Huxley, E.  Out in the Midday Sun.
  R. Baldock, 617(TLS):31Jan86-107
Huxley, J.  Leaves of the Tulip Tree.
  A. Duchêne, 617(TLS):15Aug86-885
Huyler, S.P.  Village India.
  C. Allen, 617(TLS):24Jan86-78
Huyser, R.E.  Mission to Tehran.
  T. Jacoby, 617(TLS):5Dec86-1367
Hyde, D.  New-found Voices.
  N. Temperley, 415:Jul85-408
Hyde, D.O.  Don Coyote.
  S. Laschever, 441:27Jul86-19
Hyde, E.  Her Native Colors.
  M. Corrigan, 441:25May86-14
Hyde, L.  The Gift.*
  V. Nemoianu, 125:Spring85-311
Hyde, L., ed.  On the Poetry of Allen Ginsberg.*
  W.G. Regier, 502(PrS):Winter85-105
  R. Tillinghast, 472:Spring/Summer86-193
Hyde, M.J., ed.  Communication Philosophy and the Technological Age.
  C. Marvin, 480(P&R):Vol 18No2-127
  H.T. Wilson, 488:Sep85-349
Hyde, R.  A Home in This World.
  L. Jones, 49:Oct85-127
Hyer, R.  Riceburner.
  N. Callendar, 441:9Nov86-25
Hyland, G.  Street of Dreams.
  F. Zichy, 102(CanL):Fall85-134
Hyland, P.  The Stubborn Forest.
  M. O'Neill, 493:Jan85-61
Hyman, L.M.  A Theory of Phonological Weight.
  D. Odden, 350:Sep86-669
Hyman, V.D.  Han Dynasty Impressions 206 B.C. - 221 A.D.
  U. Roberts, 60:Jul-Aug85-127
Hymes, D.H.  Essays on the History of Linguistic Anthropology.
  B.G. Blount, 355(LSoc):Mar85-121
  R.H. Robins, 297(JL):Sep85-517
Hyneman, C.S. and D.S. Lutz, comps.  American Political Writing During the Founding Era: 1760-1805.*
  G.W. Carey, 396(ModA):Winter85-71
Hynes, S. - see Hardy, T.
Hyvernaud, G.  La Peau et les os.
  L. Arénilla, 450(NRF):Jun85-64


"ISIS Cumulative Bibliography 1966-1975." (J. Neu, ed)
  J. Henry, 617(TLS):9May86-513
Iacocca, L., with W. Novak.  Iacocca.*
  J.K. Galbraith, 453(NYRB):10Apr86-11
Iannace, G.A.  Interferenza linguistica ai confini fra Stato e Regno.
  E. Radtke, 72:Band222Heft1-218

Ibargüengoitia, J. The Lightning of
August.
  A. Dorfman, 441:23Feb86-30
Ibn Buṭlān. Das Ärztebankett. (F. Klein-
Francke, trans)
  C. Boot, 589:Jul85-745
Ibn Gabirol, S. La couronne royale.
  A. Reix, 542:Apr-Jun85-240
de Icaza, F.A. Efímeras & Lejanías.
(R.A. Cardwell, ed)
  C. Davies, 402(MLR):Jul85-740
Ichiro Nakano, ed and trans. 101 Favorite
Songs Taught in Japanese Schools.
  U. Eppstein, 407(MN):Autumn85-374
Ickler, T. Deutsch als Fremdsprache.
  R.A. Fowkes, 660(Word):Apr85-86
"Iconographie et littérature: D'un art à
l'autre."
  N. Boulestreau, 535(RHL):Nov/Dec85-
  1085
  R.N. Nicolich, 678(YCGL):No34-152
Ide, R.S. and J. Wittreich, eds. Compos-
ite Orders.
  R.L. Entzminger, 577(SHR):Fall85-362
Iden, P. Die Schaubühne am Halleschen
Ufer 1970-1979.
  A. Désilets, 193(ELit):Spring-Summer85-
  208
Iffland, J. Quevedo and the Grotesque.*
(Vol 2)
  P.J. Smith, 402(MLR):Jan85-195
Iffland, J., ed. Quevedo in Perspective.*
  D.W. Bleznick, 552(REH):Jan85-144
  B.W. Ife, 86(BHS):Apr85-202
Ifrah, G. From One to Zero.*
  442(NY):6Jan86-86
Ifri, P.A. Proust et son narrataire dans
"A la recherche du temps perdu."*
  A. Corbineau-Hoffmann, 547(RF):Band97
  Heft1-102
  W.L. Hodson, 402(MLR):Jan85-176
  J. Murray, 207(FR):Dec85-304
Iglesias Feijoo, L. La trayectoria dramá-
tica de Antonio Buero Vallejo.
  M.E.W. Jones, 140(CH):Vol7No1-92
  J.W. Kronik, 240(HR):Spring85-254
Ignatow, D. Leaving the Door Open.*
  J. Elledge, 491:Aug85-295
  P. Filkins, 363(LitR):Spring86-362
Ignatow, D. Open Between Us.* (R.J.
Mills, Jr., ed)
  R. McDowell, 249(HudR):Autumn85-512
Ihde, D. Existential Technics.
  M. Harney, 63:Dec85-520
Ihle, S.N. Malory's Grail Quest.*
  S. Dannenbaum, 545(RPh):Aug85-107
  P.J.C. Field, 541(RES):Aug85-410
  C. Gauvin, 189(EA):Jan-Mar86-88
  G. Zaganelli, 547(RF):Band97Heft2/3-
  294
Ihrie, M. Skepticism in Cervantes.*
  J.G. Weiger, 345(KRQ):Vol32No2-219
Ikeda, D. La vie à la lumière du boudd-
hisme.
  A. Reix, 542:Oct-Dec85-555
Ikegami, T., ed. The Lyfe of Ipomydon.
(Vol 1)
  R. Beadle, 354:Sep85-272
Ikels, C. Aging and Adaptation.
  J.K. Kallgren, 293(JASt):Feb85-373
Iknayan, M. The Concave Mirror.
  M.E. Birkett, 210(FrF):Jan85-114
    [continued]

[continuing]
  R. Lloyd, 402(MLR):Jul85-716
  E.J. Talbot, 207(FR):Feb86-468
  P.A. Ward, 446(NCFS):Spring-Summer86-
  350
Iles, F. Malice Aforethought.
  362:6Nov86-36
"I'll Buy That!"
  R. Plunket, 441:7Dec86-69
Illiano, A. Metapsichica e letteratura in
Pirandello.
  F. Firth, 402(MLR):Oct85-958
Illich, I. H$_2$O and the Waters of Forget-
fulness.
  D.P. Slattery, 435:Fall85-81
Ilson, R., ed. Lexicography.
  P. Rogers, 617(TLS):9May86-487
Ilting, K-H. Naturrecht und Sittlichkeit.
  R. Zimmer, 489(PJGG):Band92Heft2-396
"Images de La Rochefoucauld."
  A.H.T. Levi, 208(FS):Oct85-467
"Images of the Spanish Civil War."
  H. Francis, 362:17Jul86-25
Imbert, P. Roman Québécois contemporain
et clichés.*
  V. Harger-Grinling, 102(CanL):Summer85-
  171
Imgalrea, T. and others. Cev'armuit
Qanemciit Qulirait-Llu. (A.C. Woodbury,
ed)
  J.R. Sheppard, 292(JAF):Jul/Sep85-368
Imhof, R., ed. Alive-Alive O!
  M. Mortimer, 617(TLS):1Aug86-845
Impey, O. and A. MacGregor. The Origins
of Museums.
  S. Piggott, 617(TLS):25Jul86-808
"Impressionism and Post-Impressionism."
  J. Russell, 441:1Jun86-12
Inada, K.K. and N.P. Jacobson, eds. Bud-
dhism and American Thinkers.
  K.P. Pedersen, 485(PE&W):Oct85-447
  W.L. Reese, 619:Winter85-152
Inagaki, H., with P.G. O'Neill, comps. A
Dictionary of Japanese Buddhist Terms.
  G.J. Tanabe, Jr., 407(MN):Summer85-253
Inboden, G. and T. Kellein. Ad Reinhardt.
  C. Scherrmann, 384:Sep/Oct85-941
"Incipit."* (Vols 1-3)
  K. Kohut, 547(RF):Band97Heft4-501
"Incunabula in Dutch Libraries."
  J.C.T. Oates, 354:Sep85-268
Indelicato, S.D. - see under Damiani
Indelicato, S.
"Index of Manuscripts in the British Lib-
rary."* (Vols 1-10)
  A. Bell, 617(TLS):29Aug86-951
Inez, C. Eight Minutes from the Sun.
  P. Hasty, 502(PrS):Fall85-115
Infante, G.C. - see under Cabrera Infante,
  G.
Ing, N., ed and trans. Summer Glory.
  J.L. Faurot, 293(JASt):Nov84-172
Ing, N., ed. Winter Plum.
  J.L. Faurot, 293(JASt):Nov84-172
Ingalls, R. I See a Long Journey.
  A. Bernays, 441:31Aug86-9
Ingalls, R. Mrs. Caliban.
  M. Dorris, 441:28Dec86-7
Ingalls, R. The Pearlkillers.
  P. Kemp, 617(TLS):9May86-499
Ingalls, R. Theft.
  P. Craig, 617(TLS):19Dec86-1428

185

Ingalls, R.  Three of a Kind.*
  J. Mellors, 362:16Jan86-30
Ingarden, R.  Man and Value.
  M. Adam, 542:Oct-Dec85-556
  G. Casey, 543:Dec84-391
Ingdahl, K.  The Artist and the Creative
  Act.
  A. Barratt, 575(SEER):Oct85-589
  M. Numano, 550(RusR):Jan85-93
van Ingen, F. - see von Zesen, P.
Ingham, K.  Jan Christian Smuts.
  L. Thompson, 617(TLS):14Nov86-1286
Inglis, B.  The Hidden Power.
  P. Forbes, 362:24Jul86-23
Inglis, F.  Radical Earnestness.
  J.W. Saunders, 541(RES):Nov85-595
Ingoldby, G.  Last Dance With You.
  E. Barry, 617(TLS):7Mar86-256
  K.C. O'Brien, 362:27Feb86-27
Ingram, A.  Boswell's Creative Gloom.*
  I.D. McGowan, 447(N&Q):Mar84-98
Ingrams, R.  John Stewart Collis.
  D. Profumo, 617(TLS):14Nov86-1266
Ingrams, R. and J. Wells.  The Best of
  Dear Bill.
  B. Bainbridge, 617(TLS):26Dec86-1453
Inkster, I. and J. Morrell, eds.  Metrop-
  olis and Province.
  J. Paradis, 637(VS):Winter86-328
Inman, A.C.  The Inman Diary.*  (D. Aaron,
  ed)
  J. Symons, 617(TLS):10Jan86-41
Innes, C.  Edward Gordon Craig.*
  R.C. Beacham, 611(TN):Vol39No2-86
  R. Jackson, 72:Band222Heft2-420
  A. Rood, 610:Spring85-83
Innes, H.  High Stand.
  J. Sullivan, 441:21Dec86-14
Innis, R.E., ed.  Semiotics.
  S. Scobie, 376:Jan86-128
"International Who's Who in Music and
  Musicians Directory."
  N. Goodwin, 415:Jul85-412
"An Inventory of the Historical Monuments
  in the County of Northampton."  (Vol 6)
  A. Gomme, 617(TLS):14Feb86-168
"Involvement in Learning."
  A. Hacker, 453(NYRB):13Feb86-35
van Inwagen, P.  An Essay on Free Will.*
  M. Adam, 542:Oct-Dec85-557
  M. Slote, 311(JP):Jun85-327
  G. Watson, 484(PPR):Mar86-507
Inwood, B.  Ethics and Human Action in
  Early Stoicism.
  J. Barnes, 520:Vol30No2-215
  T. Engberg-Pedersen, 617(TLS):18Apr86-
  424
  G. Verbeke, 543:Mar86-566
Inwood, M.J.  Hegel.*
  F. Craig, 393(Mind):Apr85-319
  K.R. Dove, 319:Apr86-281
  D.R. Knowles, 479(PhQ):Apr85-199
  A.W. Wood, 482(PhR):Oct85-574
Ioffe, O.S. and P.B. Maggs.  Soviet Law in
  Theory and Practice.
  H.J. Berman, 550(RusR):Jan85-72
Ioppolo, A.M.  Aristone di Chio e lo Stoi-
  cismo Antico.
  J. Mansfeld, 394:Vol38fasc1/2-209
  N. White, 466:Vol13-289
Ireland, A.  A Certain Mr. Takahashi.
  S. Posesorski, 441:15Jun86-20

Irick, R.L.  Ch'ing Policy Toward the
  Coolie Trade 1847-1878.
  G. Mahood, 302:Vol21No1-71
Irigaray, L.  Ethique de la différence
  sexuelle.
  E. Berg, 188(ECr):Summer85-102
Irigaray, L.  Speculum of the Other Woman.
  This Sex Which Is Not One.
  M.E. Papke, 367(L&P):Vol32No1-53
Irizarry, E.  Writer-Painters of Contempor-
  ary Spain.
  J.P. Gabriele, 140(CH):Vol7No2-180
  H.T. Young, 238:May85-310
Irmscher, J. and R. Müller, eds.  Aristo-
  teles als Wissenschaftstheoretiker.
  L. Judson, 123:Vol135No1-200
Irving, C.  Comrades.
  T. Miller, 441:24Aug86-18
Irving, J.  The Cider House Rules.*
  J. Mellors, 364:Jul85-97
Irving, J.A.  The Public in Your Woods.
  J. Cripps, 324:Apr86-343
Irving, W.  Journals and Notebooks.  (Vol
  4)  (W.R. Kime and A.B. Myers, eds)
  D.A. Ringe, 70:Mar/Apr85-123
Irwin, J., ed.  Sacred Sound.
  K.K. Shelemay, 187:Winter86-176
Irwin, R.  The Limits of Vision.
  S. Dobyns, 441:24Aug86-7
  J. Winterson, 617(TLS):25Apr86-453
Irwin, R.  The Middle East in the Middle
  Ages.
  C.F. Petry, 617(TLS):25Jul86-826
Isaacs, N.E.  Untended Gates.
  K.J. Turner, 441:2Feb86-34
Isaacs, R.R.  Walter Gropius.*
  J. Rykwert, 617(TLS):2May86-463
Isaacson, W. and E. Thomas.  The Wise Men.
  R. Steel, 441:2Nov86-3
Isbister, J.N.  Freud.
  P. Lomas, 617(TLS):3Jan86-9
Iscla Rovira, L.  Spanish Proverbs.
  L. Martin, 238:May85-335
Isdebsky-Pritchard, A.  The Art of Mikhail
  Vrubel, 1856-1910.*
  M.H., 90:Nov85-821
Isella, D. - see Montale, E.
Isenbart, H-H. and E.M. Bührer.  The Impe-
  rial Horse.
  A.S. Barnes, 441:7Dec86-69
Isherwood, R.M.  Farce and Fantasy.
  A.J. Plattus, 441:15Jun86-26
Ishida, T.  Japanese Political Culture.
  B-A. Shillony, 293(JASt):Nov84-202
Ishiguro, K.  An Artist of the Floating
  World.
  A. Chisholm, 617(TLS):14Feb86-162
  J. Mellors, 364:Feb86-97
  B. Morton, 362:16Oct86-22
  K. Morton, 441:8Jun86-19
  442(NY):10Nov86-144
Ishimoto, S.  Facing Two Ways.
  T.S. Lebra, 407(MN):Summer85-245
Ishioka, E. - see under Eiko Ishioka
San Isidoro de Sevilla.  Etimologías.  (J.
  Oroz Reta and M-A. Marcos Casquero, eds
  and trans)
  R. Wright, 86(BHS):Jan85-127
Isitt, D.  Crazic, Menty and Idiotal.*
  G. Cannon, 353:Vol23No3-494

Islam, M.N., R. Morse and M.H. Soesastro,
eds. Rural Energy to Meet Development
Needs.
  I. Tinker, 293(JASt):Aug85-796
Islam, S., ed. Exploring the Other Half.
  H. Papanek, 293(JASt):Nov84-127
"Islam in India." (Vol 1) (C.W. Troll, ed)
  G. Böwering, 293(JASt):Feb85-448
"Islands at the Edge."
  L.R., 102(CanL):Fall85-184
Isler, H.P. and others. Der Tempel der
Aphrodite.
  R.A. Tomlinson, 303(JoHS):Vol 105-229
Isorni, J. Mémoires, 1911-1945.
  R.M. Webster, 207(FR):Apr86-834
Israel, J.I. The Dutch Republic and the
Hispanic World 1606-1661.*
  P. Williams, 86(BHS):Jul85-303
Israel, J.I. European Jewry in the Age of
Mercantilism.
  T.K. Rabb, 617(TLS):26Sep86-1068
Israel, M., ed. National Unity.
  A.T. Embree, 293(JASt):Feb85-450
Israel, M. and N.K. Wagle, eds. Islamic
Society and Culture.
  W. Fusfeld, 293(JASt):Feb85-428
Israeli, R. Man of Defiance.
  D. Spanier, 176:Apr86-61
  P.J. Vatikiotis, 617(TLS):14Feb86-159
Israeli, R., ed. PLO in Lebanon.
  N. Frankel, 390:Feb85-62
Issatschenko, A. Geschichte der russi-
schen Sprache. (Vol 2)
  H. Galton, 361:Apr85-340
Itälä, M-L. Die lokosemantischen Inter-
relationen zwischen Verb und Lokativ-
bestimmung.
  H. Nikula, 439(NM):1985/4-595
"Italia Judaica."
  A.V., 379(MedR):Aug85-301
Iteanu, A. La ronde des échanges.
  M. Houseman, 98:Nov85-1053
"Itinéraires." (Vol 1)
  E.E. John, 538(RAL):Spring85-100
"Itinéraires et contacts de cultures."
(Vol 2)
  E. Sellin, 538(RAL):Spring85-103
Itkonen, E. Causality in Linguistic
Theory.
  K. Arnold, 320(CJL):Winter85-473
  T. Pateman, 297(JL):Sep85-481
Ival, M-M., ed and trans. Beufves de
Hantonne.
  G. Roques, 553(RLiR):Jul-Dec85-529
Iversen, G., ed. Research on Tropes.
  C.M. Atkinson, 589:Jul85-684
Iverson, P. Carlos Montezuma and the
Changing World of American Indians.
  D.W. Dippie, 106:Spring85-31
Ives, E.D. The Tape-Recorded Interview.
(rev)
  R.I. McDavid, Jr., 300:Apr85-54
Ives, V.A., ed. The Rich Papers.
  W.J. Scheick, 568(SCN):Winter85-65
Ivry, A.L. - see al-Kindī, Y.I.
Iyayi, F. The Contract.
  A. Maja-Pearce, 364:Mar86-50
Iyayi, F. Violence.
  A. Maja-Pearce, 364:Mar86-57
Iyer, S.S. Sanskrit Dramas.
  H. Heifetz, 314:Winter-Spring85-248
"Izbornik Svjatoslava 1073 goda."
  R. Marti, 559:Vol9No1-117

Izumo, T. and others - see under Takeda
Izumo and others

Jabès, E. - see under Gould, E.
Jaccottet, P. À travers un verger.
  C. Dis, 450(NRF):Feb85-84
Jachnow, H., with K. Hartenstein and W.
Jachnow, eds. Handbuch des Russisten.
  P. Swiggers, 353:Vol23No6-1008
Jack, D. Me Too.
  D. Daymond, 102(CanL):Spring85-115
Jack, I. The Poet and his Audience.
  J. Blondel, 189(EA):Apr-Jun86-189
  P.W. Martin, 366:Autumn85-293
  C.T. Probyn, 67:Nov85-260
  J.S., 636(VP):Summer85-222
  566:Spring86-213
Jack, I. and M. Smith - see Browning, R.
Jack, R.D.S. and R.J. Lyall - see Urquhart,
T.
Jack, R.D.S. and A. Noble, eds. The Art
of Robert Burns.*
  D. Murison, 447(N&Q):Mar84-136
Jackel, E. and J. Rohwer, eds. Der Mord
an den Juden im Zweiten Weltkrieg.
  I. Kershaw, 617(TLS):7Nov86-1242
Jackendoff, R. Semantics and Cognition.
  S.E. Boer, 482(PhR):Jan85-111
  J. Haiman, 320(CJL):Spring85-90
Jackson, D. Voyages of the Steamboat Yel-
low Stone.*
  442(NY):13Jan86-85
Jackson, D.P. and J.A. Tibetan Thangka
Painting.
  U. Roberts, 60:May-Jun85-134
Jackson, F. Perception.
  D.M. Rosenthal, 311(JP):Jan85-28
Jackson, F. Sir Raymond Unwin.
  A. Saint, 617(TLS):28Feb86-221
Jackson, H. Analyzing English. (2nd ed)
  F.W. Gester, 72:Band222Heft2-373
  D. Mindt, 38:Band103Heft1/2-113
Jackson, H.J., ed. Samuel Taylor Cole-
ridge.
  R. Ashton, 617(TLS):19Sep86-1035
Jackson, H.J., ed. Editing Polymaths.*
  W.J.B. Owen, 627(UTQ):Summer85-415
Jackson, J. The Politics or Depression in
France 1932-1936.
  D. Johnson, 617(TLS):26Sep86-1052
Jackson, J.B. The Essential Landscape.
  L. Milazzo, 584(SWR):Autumn85-547
Jackson, J.E. La Mort Baudelaire.*
  P. Pelckmans, 535(RHL):Jul/Aug85-690
Jackson, J.R.D. - see Coleridge, S.T.
Jackson, K.T. Crabgrass Frontier.
  G. Clay, 441:27Apr86-14
Jackson, M. Allegories of the Wilderness.*
  R. Cancel, 538(RAL):Fall85-388
  J. Knappert, 203:Vol96No1-130
Jackson, M. Barawa.
  J.I. Guyer, 469:Vol 11No4-106
  F.R. Vivelo, 441:8Jun86-36
Jackson, M.H. Guide to Correspondence in
Spanish.
  L.J. Walker, 399(MLJ):Winter85-437
Jackson, P. and J. Lockhart, eds. The
Cambridge History of Iran. (Vol 6)
  R. Irwin, 617(TLS):12Sep86-998
Jackson, R. Fantasy.*
  R. Cardinal, 529(QQ):Autumn85-549

Jackson, R. - see Jones, H.A.
Jackson, R.A.  Vive le Roi!*
  J.R. Major, 377:Jul85-123
Jackson, R.L., ed.  Dostoevsky.
  G. Woodcock, 569(SR):Spring85-293
Jackson, W.  Vision and Re-Vision in Alexander Pope.*
  R.D. Lund, 403(MLS):Fall85-342
Jackson, W.T.H.  The Hero and the King.*
  W. McConnell, 400(MLN):Apr85-680
Jackson-Stops, G., ed.  The Treasure Houses of Britain.*
  J. Steer, 324:Feb86-204
Jacob, A.  Cheminements, de la dialectique à l'éthique.
  J-J. Goux, 704(SFR):Spring85-111
Jacob, J.R.  Henry Stubbe, Radical Protestantism and the Early Enlightenment.
  R.H. Popkin, 319:Apr86-270
Jacob, M. and J., eds.  The Origins of Anglo-American Radicalism.
  J. Black, 161(DUJ):Jun85-260
Jacobi, F.H.  Briefwechsel.  (Ser 1, Vol 1 ed by M. Brüggen and others; Ser 1, Vol 2 ed by P. Bachmaier and others)  David Hume über den Glauben oder Idealismus und Realismus.
  D. Breazeale, 319:Apr86-278
Jacobowitz, E.S. and S.L. Stepanek.  The Prints of Lucas van Leyden and His Contemporaries.
  G. Harbison, 54:Jun85-331
Jacobs, A.  Arthur Sullivan.*
  R. Sherr, 317:Fall85-637
Jacobs, A. - see Flaubert, G. and G. Sand
Jacobs, E.M., ed.  Soviet Local Politics and Government.*
  R.C. Gripp, 104(CASS):Spring85-86
Jacobs, J.  Cities and the Wealth of Nations.*
  A. Betsky, 505:Aug85-123
Jacobs, J.  Cooking for All It's Worth.
  W. and C. Cowen, 639(VQR):Spring85-69
Jacobs, J.  Fokus und Skalen.
  E. König, 257(IRAL):May85-165
Jacobs, M.  Precautions Against Death.
  M. Madoff, 102(CanL):Winter84-141
Jacobs, W.G., J. Jantzen and W. Schieche - see Schelling, F.W.J.
Jacobson, A.  Women in Charge.
  A. Hacker, 453(NYRB):14Aug86-26
Jacobson, G. and J. Hillkirk.  Xerox.
  D.E. Sanger, 441:22Jun86-18
Jacobson, H.  Peeping Tom.*
  P. Lewis, 565:Summer85-50
Jacobson, H.  Redback.
  G. Mangan, 617(TLS):31Oct86-1225
Jacobson, H. - see Ezekiel
Jacobson, M.  Henry James and the Mass Market.*
  J.F. Blackall, 301(JEGP):Jul85-463
  S. Carlson, 481(PQ):Winter85-150
  D.D. Stone, 577(SHR):Spring85-180
Jacobson, S.  Preverbal Adverbs and Auxiliaries.*
  R. Zimmermann, 38:Band103Heft1/2-125
Jacoby, R.  The Repression of Psychoanalysis.
  E.W. Holland, 560:Winter-Spring85-155
  R.A. Paskauskas, 529(QQ):Summer85-416
Jacoff, R. - see Freccero, J.
Jacques, D.  Georgian Gardens.*
  P. Martin, 566:Autumn85-82

Jaeger, J.W.  Humor und Satire in der DDR.
  M. Wedel, 654(WB):11/1985-1929
Jaeger, P. and R. Lüthe, eds.  Distanz und Nähe.
  B. Smith, 323:Oct85-320
Jaffe, A. and others.  Alaska.
  P-L. Adams, 61:Sep86-104
Jaffe, H.  Beasts.
  A. Mobilio, 441:4May86-40
Jäger, L., ed.  Erkenntnistheoretische Grundfragen der Linguistik.
  D. Stellmacher, 685(ZDL):3/1985-357
Jagersma, H.  A History of Israel in the Old Testament Period.
  P.E. Dion, 318(JAOS):Oct-Dec84-763
Jaggar, A.M.  Feminist Politics and Human Nature.*
  S. Lovibond, 393(Mind):Jan85-151
Jagger, B.  A Song Twice Over.
  S. Altinel, 617(TLS):9May86-498
Jagger, P.J.  Clouded Witness.
  J.L. Altholz, 637(VS):Winter86-320
Jagger, P.J., ed.  Gladstone, Politics and Religion.
  M. Lynch, 637(VS):Spring86-489
Jagu, A. - see Musonius Rufus
Jaguer, E.  Les Mystères de la chambre noire.
  J.H. Matthews, 403(MLS):Summer85-85
Jahr, E.H.  Talemålet i skolen.
  E. Haugen, 355(LSoc):Jun85-259
  P. Trudgill, 562(Scan):Nov85-248
"Jahrbuch der deutschen Shakespeare-Gesellschaft West (1984)."
  D. Meyer-Dinkgraefe, 610:Autumn85-242
"Jahrbuch zur Literatur in der DDR, 3."  (P.G. Klussmann and H. Mohr, eds)
  U. Brandes, 221(GQ):Spring85-308
Jain, D., with N. Singh and M. Chand.  Women's Quest for Power.
  H. Papanek, 293(JASt):Nov84-127
Jákfalvi-Leiva, S.  Traducción, escritura y violencia colonizadora.
  A.M. Armendáriz Zabalza, 552(REH): May85-145
Jakle, J.A.  The Tourist.
  639(VQR):Summer85-101
Jakobson, R.  The Poetry of Grammar and the Grammar of Poetry.
  T.G. Winner, 279:Vol30-159
Jakobson, R.  Russian and Slavic Grammar.*  (L.R. Waugh and M. Halle, eds)
  E. Battistella, 350:Jun86-464
  K.L. Black, 399(MLJ):Autumn85-318
Jakobson, R.  Selected Writings, III.
  I. Fónagy, 361:Nov85-251
Jakobson, R.  Verbal Art, Verbal Sign, Verbal Time.  (K. Pomorska and S. Rudy, eds)
  B. Hollander, 703:No15-177
Jakobson, R. and K. Pomorska.  Dialogues.
  S. Raval, 402(MLR):Apr85-400
  G.S. Smith, 575(SEER):Oct85-582
Jakubec, D., ed.  Nouvelles de Suisse Française/Nouvellas dalla Svizra Franzosa.
  J. Van Eerde, 207(FR):Mar86-646
Jallat, J.  Introduction aux figures valéryennes.*
  W.N. Ince, 208(FS):Oct85-495
  R. Pietra, 535(RHL):Jul/Aug85-693
James, B.  The Bill James Baseball Abstract 1986.
  R. Strauss, 441:4May86-41

Janson, H.W. History of Art. (3rd ed)
(A.F. Janson, ed)
  J. Russell, 441:1Jun86-12
Janson, H.W. Nineteenth-Century Sculpture.*
  M. Jordan, 617(TLS):24Jan86-96
  M. Yorke, 324:May86-416
Janson, S. and B., eds. Forsmarks bruk.
  S. Karling, 341:Vol54No1-40
Janson, T. Mechanisms of Language Change
in Latin.
  H. Pinkster, 394:Vol38fasc3/4-431
Janssen, F.A. - see Wardenaar, D.
Janvier, Y. La Géographie d'Orose.
  J.M. Alonso-Núñez, 123:Vol35No1-193
Janz, C.P. Nietzsche: Biographie II.
  C. Cordellier, 450(NRF):Apr85-92
Janz, D.R. Luther and Late Medieval
Thomism.
  M.L. Führer, 589:Jul85-686
Jao Tsung-i and Tseng Hsien-t'ung. Yun-
meng Ch'in-chien jih-shu yen-chiu.
  C-Y. Hsu, 293(JASt):Feb85-374
Japp, U. Theorie der Ironie.
  K. Peter, 221(GQ):Winter85-95
Jarausch, K.H. Students, Society and
Politics in Imperial Germany.
  W.R. Ward, 161(DUJ):Jun84-289
Jardin, C. Comme une amie ...
  D. O'Connell, 207(FR):Mar86-647
Jardine, A.A. Gynesis.
  C.J. Stivale, 207(FR):May86-967
Jardine, N. The Birth of History and
Philosophy of Science.
  E. Rosen, 322(JHI):Jul-Sep85-449
  J. Worrall, 479(PhQ):Jul85-311
Jarman, A.O.H. and E.D. Jones, eds. Llyfr
du Caerfyrddin.
  D. Johnston, 112:Vol 16-203
Jarman, D. Derek Jarman's Caravaggio.
  L. Gowing, 617(TLS):25Apr86-448
Jarrard, M.E.W. and P.R. Randall. Women
Speaking.
  B. Davis, 35(AS):Summer85-175
Jarrell, R. Randall Jarrell's Letters.*
(M. Jarrell, ed)
  P. Beer, 362:13Feb86-25
  F. Hobson, 344:Winter86-119
  M. Hofmann, 617(TLS):11Jul86-759
  J. Mole, 176:Nov86-63
  295(JML):Nov85-505
Jarvis, G.A. and others. Passeport. (2nd
ed)
  R.J. Melpignano, 399(MLJ):Spring85-88
Jasmin, E. and C. Deux Mats une Galère.
  M. Lacombe, 102(CanL):Winter84-81
Jason, K. - see Landolfi, T.
Jastrow, M. Looking Back.
  A. Paolucci, 441:Jul86-19
Jastrow, R. How to Make Nuclear Weapons
Obsolete.*
  G.F. Chapline, 473(PR):Vol52No4-471
  M. MccGwire, 617(TLS):31Oct86-1214
  Lord Zuckerman, 453(NYRB):30Jan86-32
Jauss, H.R. Aesthetic Experience and Lit-
erary Hermeneutics.* (German title:
Ästhetische Erfahrung und literarische
Hermeneutik.)
  R. Zimmer, 53(AGP):Band67Heft3-343
Jauss, H.R. Towards an Aesthetic of Recep-
tion.*
  G. Herlt and J.J. White, 402(MLR):
  Jul85-673

Jay, E., ed. The Evangelical and Oxford
Movements.*
  W. Bies, 72:Band222Heft1-185
  A.O.J. Cockshut, 447(N&Q):Dec84-534
Jay, M. Adorno.
  W.M. McClay, 31(ASch):Spring85-268
  M. Rosen, 410(M&L):Apr85-161
Jay, M. Marxism and Totality.
  T. Ball, 185:Oct85-200
Jay, M. Permanent Exiles.
  J. Joll, 617(TLS):27Jun86-703
Jay, P. Being in the Text.*
  R. Gagnier, 141:Spring85-195
Jay, R., ed. A Crack in the Mirror.
  E. Leach, 567:Vol53No1/3-169
Jay, R. Learned Pigs and Fireproof Women.
  J. Randi, 441:14Dec86-1
Jaye, M.C. and A.C. Watts, eds. Litera-
ture and the American Urban Experience.*
  A.J. Weitzman, 541(RES):May85-304
Jayne, R. Erkenntnis und Transzendenz.
  E. Schlant, 221(GQ):Summer85-428
  J.J. White, 402(MLR):Oct85-1000
Jaynes, E.T. Papers on Probability, Sta-
tistics and Statistical Physics. (R.D.
Rosenkrantz, ed)
  D.A. Lavis and P.J. Milligan, 84:Jun85-
  193
Jayyusi, L. Categorization and the Moral
Order.
  M. Douglas, 185:Apr86-633
Jean d'Arras. Le Roman de Mélusine, ou
l'histoire des Lusignan. (M. Perret,
trans)
  B. Cazelles, 545(RPh):Feb85-390
Jeannet, A.M., ed. Parliamo Dell'Italia.
  J. Siracusa, 399(MLJ):Winter85-421
Jech, J., ed. Tschechische Volksmärchen.
(2nd ed)
  H-J. Uther, 196:Band26Heft1/2-164
Jechova, H. L'image poétique dans le
mouvement romantique slave.
  O. Scherer, 549(RLC):Jan-Mar85-105
Jędrzejewicz, W. Piłsudski.
  W.M. Drzewieniecki, 497(PolR):Vol30No1-
  113
Jeffares, A.N. Anglo-Irish Literature.
  J.C. Beckett, 402(MLR):Jul85-685
  R.A. Cave, 541(RES):Feb85-136
Jeffares, A.N. A New Commentary on the
Poems of W.B. Yeats.*
  R.J. Finneran, 536(Rev):Vol7-163
  D.T. O'Hara, 659(ConL):Summer86-285
Jeffares, A.N. - see Yeats, W.B.
Jefferson, A. and D. Robey, eds. Modern
Literary Theory.*
  F. Berry, 541(RES):Feb85-139
Jefferson, D. and G. Martin, eds. The
Uses of Fiction.
  K.M. Hewitt, 541(RES):Nov85-611
Jefferson, L. The John Foster Dulles Book
of Humor.
  M. Russell, 441:13Jul86-15
Jeffery, K., ed. The Divided Provinces.
  R. Fréchet, 189(EA):Oct-Dec86-475
Jeffery, K. - see Wilson, H.
Jeffrey, D.K., ed. A Grit's Triumph.
  L. Butts, 577(SHR):Winter85-77
Jeffrey, F. Jeffrey's Criticism. (P.F.
Morgan, ed)
  D.W. Pitre, 588(SSL):Vol20-315
  B. Ruddick, 148:Spring85-86

Jeffrey, R.C.  The Logic of Decision.
(2nd ed)
   B. Skyrms, 316:Mar85-247
Jeffreys, S.  The Spinster and Her Enemies.
   P. Grosskurth, 617(TLS):21Mar86-298
Jeffreys-Jones, R. and B. Collins, eds.
The Growth of Federal Power in American
History.
   G.S. Smith, 529(QQ):Summer85-297
Jeffri, J.  Arts Money.
   A.B. Harris, 476:Fall83-80
Jehasse, J. and B. Yon - see de Balzac,
J-L.G.
Jehenson, M.Y.  The Golden World of the
Pastoral.
   A.V. Ettin, 402(MLR):Jul85-687
Jelavich, B.  Russia and the Formation of
the Romanian National State 1821-1878.
   D. MacKenzie, 104(CASS):Spring85-69
Jelavich, P.  Munich and Theatrical Modern-
ism.
   J. Osborne, 617(TLS):30May86-598
Jeletsky, T.F., ed.  Russian Canadians.
   G.W., 102(CanL):Winter84-186
Jelinek, Y.A.  The Lust for Power.*
   Z.A.B. Zeman, 575(SEER):Apr85-311
Jellicoe, A.  The Knack and The Sport of
My Mad Mother.
   D. Devlin, 157:No157-50
Jenkin, L.  New Jerusalem.
   K. Tucker, 441:23Mar86-12
Jenkins, A. and others.  New Chatto Poets.
   F. Adcock, 617(TLS):7Nov86-1256
Jenkins, B. and S. Krane.  Hollis Frampton.
   P.A. Sitney, 18:Apr86-67
Jenkins, D. and M.E. Owen, eds.  The Welsh
Law of Women.
   F. Kelly, 112:Vol 16-199
Jenkins, H. - see Shakespeare, W.
Jenkins, I.  Greek and Roman Life.
   P. Levi, 176:Jul/Aug86-45
Jenkins, J.H.  Basic Texas Books.*
   W.S. Reese, 517(PBSA):Vol79No1-141
Jenkins, J.H.  Printer in Three Republics.
   D. Farmer, 517(PBSA):Vol79No3-455
Jenkins, M., ed.  Islamic Art in the
Kuwait National Museum.
   A. Schimmel, 318(JAOS):Oct-Dec84-778
Jenkins, P.  Across China.
   M. Howard, 441:7Dec86-14
Jenkins, R.  Truman.
   H. Brogan, 362:20Feb86-24
   K.S. Davis, 453(NYRB):4Dec86-28
   J.F. Martin, 441:9Nov86-31
   H.G. Pitt, 364:Feb86-84
   D. Seideman, 617(TLS):14Mar86-268
   442(NY):15Dec86-129
Jenner, T.  The Emblem Books of Thomas
Jenner.  (S. Gottlieb, ed)
   M. Bath, 541(RES):Nov85-568
Jenner, W.J.  Memories of Loyang.
   D.R. Knechtges, 318(JAOS):Apr-Jun84-
   347
Jennings, E.  Collected Poems.
   M. O'Neill, 617(TLS):28Nov86-1355
Jennings, E.  Extending the Territory.
   S. Rae, 617(TLS):30May86-586
Jennings, F.  The Ambiguous Iroquois
Empire.
   J.W. Bradley, 432(NEQ):Jun85-292
   S.S. Webb, 656(WMQ):Jan85-123

Jennings, F. and others, eds.  The History
and Culture of Iroquois Diplomacy.
   D.H. Kent, 656(WMQ):Oct85-539
Jennings, H.  Pandaemonium.*  (M-L. Jen-
nings and C. Madge, eds)
   E. Rhode, 176:May86-47
   A. Singer, 362:1May86-28
   E. Toynton, 441:26Jan86-39
Jennings, L.  White Lies.
   J. Carter, 219(GaR):Summer85-432
Jennings, L.B.  Justinus Kerners Weg nach
Weinsberg (1809-1819).*
   B. Fischer, 221(GQ):Fall85-611
Jens, W.  In Sachen Lessing.
   P.M. Lützeler, 133:Band18Heft3-271
Jensen, J.F. and others.  Dansk littera-
turhistorie.*  (Vol 4)
   B. Glienke, 562(Scan):May85-72
Jensen, J.F. and others.  Dansk litteratur-
historie.  (Vol 5)
   B. Glienke, 562(Scan):Nov85-228
Jensen, L.  Shelter.*
   S. Friebert, 199:Spring86-93
   J. Nower, 448:Vol23No3-138
Jensen, M.A.  Love's $weet Return.
   M. Fee, 376:Sep85-146
Jensen, N.L. - see Grundtvig, N.F.S.
Jensen, P.J.  J.N. Madvig.
   P. Flobert, 555:Vol59fasc1-175
Jensen, S.  Under faelles ansvar.
   G.S. Argetsinger, 563(SS):Spring85-217
Jeppesen, B.H.  Johannes V. Jensen og den
hvide mands byrde.
   A. Heitmann, 562(Scan):May85-90
Jeppsson, A-L.  Tankar till salu.
   V. Zuck, 563(SS):Winter85-81
Jernakoff, N., J.E. Bowlt and T.E. Bird,
eds.  On Russian Art.
   J.R. Stapanian, 550(RusR):Apr85-194
Jernakoff, N., A.E. Klimoff and E.L.
Magerovsky - see "Transactions of the
Association of Russian-American Scholars
in USA"
Jersild, P.C.  After the Flood.
   A. Cheuse, 441:5Jan86-17
Jersild, P.C.  Children's Island.
   J.L. Sensibar, 441:21Dec86-26
Jervis, R.  The Illogic of American
Nuclear Strategy.*
   R.H. Falls, 529(QQ):Winter85-886
   S.L., 185:Jan86-459
Jervis, R. and others.  Psychology and
Deterrence.
   D.C. Unger, 441:18May86-37
Jervis, S.  The Penguin Dictionary of
Design and Designers.*
   N. Powell, 39:May85-358
   A.W-C., 90:Sep85-631
Jesenská, M.  Alles ist Leben.
   G. Sammet, 384:Aug85-701
Jesi, F.  Kultur von rechts.
   G. Hartung, 654(WB):7/1985-1222
Jetter, D.  Geschichte des Hospitals.
(Vol 4)
   F. Marías, 48:Jul-Sep85-314
Jevons, M.  The Fatal Equilibrium.*
   M. Laski, 362:9Jan86-30
Jewell, H.M., ed.  The Court Rolls of the
Manor of Wakefield from September 1348
to September 1350.
   A.R. De Windt, 589:Jan86-146
Jewett, M.Z.  Coit Tower, San Francisco.
   F.V. O'Connor, 127:Winter84-393

191

Jha, R.  Gandhian Thought and Indo-Anglian Novelists.
R.J. Lewis, 293(JASt):May85-635
Jhabvala, R.P.  Out of India.
R. Godden, 441:25May86-1
Jiajin, Z. - see under Zhu Jiajin
Jian, G. and R. Hester.  Découverte et création.  (4th ed)
G.R. Montbertrand, 207(FR):May86-1021
Jiles, P.  Celestial Navigation.
D. O'Rourke, 102(CanL):Fall85-138
Jimack, P.  Rousseau: "Emile."*
J.H. Bloch, 83:Autumn85-249
M. Carroll, 402(MLR):Oct85-943
Jiménez, J.O. - see under Olivio Jiménez, J.
Jiménez, J.R.  Poesías últimas escojidas (1918-1958).  (A. Sánchez Romeralo, ed)
H.T. Young, 240(HR):Winter85-112
Jiménez, J.R. - see under Rubio Jiménez, J.
Jiménez-Fajardo, S. and J.C. Wilcox, eds.  At Home and Beyond.*
F. López-Criado, 552(REH):May85-141
M.H. Persin, 345(KRQ):Vol32No3-333
Jiménez Lozano, J. - see San Juan de la Cruz
Joas, H.  G.H. Mead.
D. Wrong, 617(TLS):24Jan86-91
Jobe, B. and M. Kaye.  New England Furniture.
C.A. Hammond, 432(NEQ):Jun85-297
Jodogne, O., ed.  Miracle de Saint Nicolas et d'un Juif.
L. Muir, 208(FS):Jul85-322
G. Pinkernell, 72:Band222Heft1-224
Jodogne, O. - see Gréban, A.
Johannes Teutonicus.  Apparatus glossarum in Compilationem tertiam.  (Vol 1) (K. Pennington, ed)
J. Tarrant, 589:Oct85-985
Johannsen, R.W.  To the Halls of the Montezumas.*
L. Milazzo, 584(SWR):Summer85-415
Johansen, H.F.  Fri mands tale.
E. Kraggerud, 172(Edda):1985/4-257
Johansen, H.F. and E.W. Whittle.  Aeschylus: "The Suppliants."
W.J. Verdenius, 394:Vol38fasc3/4-407
Johansen, J.D. and E. Nielsen, eds.  Litteraer Vaerdi og Vurdering.
F. Conrad, 562(Scan):Nov85-244
John, A.V.  Unequal Opportunities.
F. Cairncross, 617(TLS):4Apr86-349
John, N., ed.  English National Opera Guides.  (Vol 1) [compilation of first four booklets]
A.F.L.T., 412:Aug/Nov83-296
John, N.  English National Opera Guides.  (No 9-12)
J.B., 412:Feb83-59
John, N., ed.  English National Opera Guides.*  (No 29-32)
R. Anderson, 415:Aug85-465
John, S.B.  Anouilh: "L'Alouette" and "Pauvre Bitos."
D.B. Parsell, 207(FR):Apr86-794
John of Salisbury.  Le "Policraticus" de Jean de Salisbury.  (Bk 4) (D. Foulechat, trans; C. Brucker, ed)
G. Roques, 553(RLiR):Jul-Dec85-526
Johns, C. and T. Potter.  The Thetford Treasure: Roman Jewellery and Silver.
M.A.R. Colledge, 123:Vol35No1-220

Johns, E., T. Petersen and H. Sonne, eds.  Studier i skandinavistik I.
E. Haugen, 563(SS):Spring85-223
Johnson, A.  Roman Forts of the First and Second Centuries AD in Britain and the German Provinces.
M.R. Werner, 124:May-Jun86-337
Johnson, B.  Pottery from Karanis.
R. Reece, 123:Vol35No1-221
Johnson, B.  True Correspondence.*
M. Childers, 141:Fall85-422
P. Coustillas, 189(EA):Jan-Mar86-105
N. Page, 637(VS):Spring85-545
D.R. Schwarz, 301(JEGP):Jan85-148
Johnson, B.C.  Lost in the Alps.
D. McKitterick, 617(TLS):28Feb86-229
Johnson, B.P. and M.H. Teeter - see Grant, S.A.
Johnson, B.S.  House Mother Normal.*
J. Marcus, 441:29Jun86-24
Johnson, C.  The Sorcerer's Apprentice.
P-L. Adams, 61:Apr86-130
M. Ventura, 441:30Mar86-7
442(NY):5May86-132
Johnson, C.B.  Madness and Lust.*
E.H. Friedman, 552(REH):Jan85-143
N. Holland, 240(HR):Spring85-238
Johnson, D.  Fiskadoro.*
G. Dyer, 362:3Jul86-34
Johnson, D.  Dashiell Hammett.*
P. Wolfe, 395(MFS):Winter85-769
Johnson, D.  Scottish Fiddle Music in the 18th Century.
R.C. Provine, 83:Autumn85-251
Johnson, D.  The Stars at Noon.
C. James, 441:28Sep86-7
Johnson, D., A. Tyson and R. Winter.  The Beethoven Sketchbooks.  (D. Johnson, ed)
W. Drabkin, 617(TLS):18Apr86-422
H.C. Schonberg, 441:26Jan86-18
Johnson, D.B.  Worlds in Regression.
M. Couturier, 189(EA):Oct-Dec86-488
Johnson, D.G.  Computer Ethics.
K.L.S., 185:Jul86-923
Johnson, D.G. and K.M. Brooks.  Prospects for Soviet Agriculture in the 1980s.
W.A.D. Jackson, 104(CASS):Spring85-92
E. Schinke, 550(RusR):Jan85-83
Johnson, D.G. and J.W. Snapper, eds.  Ethical Issues in the Use of Computers.
K.L.S., 185:Jul86-923
Johnson, D.R.  Yuarn Music Dramas.
B. Yung, 187:Spring/Summer86-349
Johnson, E.  Dreams of Roses and Fire.
L. Desertrain, 563(SS):Spring85-222
Johnson, E.D.H.  Paintings of the British Social Scene.
J. Wilson, 441:19Oct86-31
Johnson, E.J., ed.  Charles Moore.
P. Goldberger, 441:7Dec86-16
Johnson, G.  Emily Dickinson.
A.H. Petry, 357:Spring86-72
Johnson, G.  Machinery of the Mind.
G. Krist, 441:5Oct86-54
Johnson, H. and H. Simons.  The Landing.
P. Andrews, 441:13Jul86-12
Johnson, J.H. and C.G. Pooley, eds.  The Structure of Nineteenth Century Cities.
R. Lawton, 637(VS):Spring85-564
Johnson, J.L.  Mark Twain and the Limits of Power.*
J.M. Cox, 587(SAF):Autumn85-250
J. Lauber, 106:Spring85-47

Johnson, K. and D. Porter, eds. Perspectives in Communicative Language Teaching.
S.S. Magnan, 399(MLJ):Autumn85-293
Johnson, K.A. Women, the Family, and Peasant Revolution in China.*
E. Honig, 293(JASt):Feb85-329
Johnson, L. The Collected Poems of Lionel Johnson. (2nd ed) (I. Fletcher, ed)
R. Crawford, 447(N&Q):Dec84-540
Johnson, L. and others, eds. Towards Defining the African Aesthetic.
R. Fraser, 538(RAL):Spring85-115
Johnson, L.K. A Season of Inquiry.
S.J. Ungar, 441:21Dec86-3
Johnson, L.M. Wordsworth's Metaphysical Verse.*
A. McWhir, 178:Mar85-94
Johnson, L.S. The Voice of the "Gawain"-Poet.
R.W. Hanning, 401(MLQ):Dec84-395
Johnson, M. Here On Earth.
R. Pybus, 565:Summer85-62
Johnson, M.K., ed and trans. Recycling the Prague Linguistic Circle.
G. Lepschy, 545(RPh):Feb85-362
Johnson, M.P. and J.L. Roark. Black Masters.*
639(VQR):Spring85-50
Johnson, N. Tender Offer.
A. McDermott, 441:19Jan86-7
Johnson, P. Marxist Aesthetics.
A. Skillen, 89(BJA):Autumn85-396
Johnson, P. Modern Times.
R.A. Cooper, 390:Jun/Jul85-58
Johnson, P. November Greeting.
J. MacVean, 4:Autumn-Winter85/86-104
Johnson, P., ed. The Oxford Book of Political Anecdotes.
R. Jenkins, 617(TLS):17Oct86-1157
E. Pearce, 362:9Oct86-26
Johnson, P. Saving and Spending.
J. Burnett, 617(TLS):30May86-600
Johnson, P.E., ed. Sigrid Undset i dag.
R. Eide, 562(Scan):May85-93
Johnson, R. The American Table.
W. and C. Cowen, 639(VQR):Spring85-65
Johnson, R. Ark 50: Spires 34-50.
E. Butscher, 496:Spring85-47
Johnson, R. Cinema Novo x 5.*
R.M. Levine, 263(RIB):Vol35No1-66
Johnson, R.K. Neil Simon.
F. Pettinelli, 615(TJ):May85-262
Johnson, R.W. Shootdown.
J. Brinkley, 441:20Jul86-21
P. Windsor, 617(TLS):20Jun86-669
B. Woffinden, 362:23Oct86-26
Johnson, S. Johnson's Juvenal. (N. Rudd, ed)
J. Woodruff, 447(N&Q):Mar84-97
Johnson, S. A Journey to the Western Islands of Scotland. (J.D. Fleeman, ed)
A. Pailler, 189(EA):Oct-Dec86-458
Johnson, S. The Oxford Authors: Samuel Johnson.* (D. Greene, ed)
A. Pailler, 189(EA):Apr-Jun86-217
Johnson, S. Rasselas Principe d'Abissinia. (G. Miglietta, trans)
J.D.F., 447(N&Q):Mar84-135
"Samuel Johnson, writer."
A. Reddick, 517(PBSA):Vol79No2-262
Johnson, T.O. Synge.*
H. Pyle, 541(RES):Aug85-450

Johnson, W. The Girl Who Would Be Russian.
E.J. Kenney, Jr., 441:9Mar86-22
442(NY):7Apr86-102
Johnson, W. Poetry and Speculation of the Ṛg Veda.
K.G. Zysk, 318(JAOS):Oct-Dec84-783
Johnson, W.R. The Idea of Lyric.*
P. Alpers, 122:Oct85-374
G. Bedetti, 223:Spring85-101
Johnson, W.S. Sons and Fathers.
G.B. Tennyson, 445(NCF):Mar86-492
Johnson, W.S. - see "Browning Institute Studies"
Johnston, A.J.B. Religion in Life at Louisbourg, 1713-1758.
J. Axtell, 656(WMQ):Apr85-281
Johnston, C. Jack London — An American Radical?
S.S. Baskett, 395(MFS):Summer85-398
D.L. Walker, 649(WAL):Nov85-255
Johnston, C. Selected Poems.
C. Boyle, 364:Nov85-79
Johnston, D. Design Protection.
J. Thackara, 617(TLS):25Jul86-807
Johnston, D. Irish Poetry after Joyce.
M. Hofmann, 617(TLS):30May86-585
Johnston, G. The Cruising Auk. Home Free. Happy Enough. Ask Again.
H. De Roo, 648(WCR):Oct85-49
Johnston, J. The Railway Station Man.*
M. Koenig, 272(IUR):Spring85-112
Johnston, J.H. The Poet and the City.*
W.H., 148:Winter85-90
566:Spring86-224
Johnston, K.R. Wordsworth and "The Recluse."
M. Baron, 175:Summer85-157
P.J. Manning, 661(WC):Fall85-153
P. Morgan, 179(ES):Dec85-567
Johnston, M. Takeover.
A.M. Solomon, 441:26Oct86-27
Jöhrens, G. Der Athenahymnus des Ailios Aristides mit einem Anhang zum Höhenkult der Athena und Testimonien zur allegorischen Deutung des Athena.
N.G. Devlin, 123:Vol3No1-182
P.R. Hardie, 303(JoHS):Vol 105-194
Jolivet, J. and R. Rashed, eds. Etudes sur Avicenne.
M. Amir-Moezzi, 542:Jul-Sep85-305
Jollès, B. - see Aquinas, T.
Jolley, E. Foxybaby.*
L. Chamberlain, 617(TLS):13Jun86-645
Jolley, E. Milk and Honey.*
P. Ackroyd, 441:15Jun86-12
442(NY):4Aug86-86
Jolley, E. Miss Peabody's Inheritance.* Mr. Scobie's Riddle.*
42(AR):Summer85-373
Jolley, E. Palomino.*
P. Lewis, 364:Apr/May85-148
Jolley, E. The Well.
R. Coover, 441:16Nov86-1
P. Craig, 617(TLS):15Aug86-894
Jolley, E. Woman in a Lampshade.
R. Coover, 441:16Nov86-1
Jolley, N. Leibniz and Locke.*
F. Duchesneau, 154:Autumn85-562
S.E., 185:Oct85-219
G.A.J. Rogers, 319:Oct86-556
Joly, A. and W.H. Hirtle, eds. Langage et Psychomécanique du langage.
A. Lorian, 545(RPh):Aug85-44

Joly, M.   La Bourle et son interprétation.*
   F. Delpech, 92(BH):Jan-Jun84-235
   J.R. Jones, 86(BHS):Oct85-392
Jonas, H.   The Imperative of Responsibility.
   H.K., 185:Jan86-437
   J.C. McCarthy, 543:Dec85-362
Jonas of Orléans.   The "De institutione regia." (R.W. Dyson, trans)
   K.F. Morrison, 589:Apr85-481
Jonassaint, J.   La Déchirure du (corps) texte et autres brèches.
   N. Bishop, 102(CanL):Spring85-132
Jonassen, C.T.   Value Systems and Personality in a Western Civilization.
   R.F. Tomasson, 563(SS):Autumn85-452
Jones.   Jack and Jill in Toronto.
   R. Stevenson, 102(CanL):Spring85-148
Jones.   Two Cops Kissing.
   W. Swist, 404:Autumn85-59
Jones, A.   Britain's Economy.
   R. Floud, 617(TLS):14Feb86-161
Jones, A.J.I.   Communication and Meaning.*
   D.H. Helman, 482(PhR):Jul85-421
Jones, B.   The Children of Separation.
   G. Lindop, 617(TLS):28Nov86-1355
   H. Lomas, 364:Mar86-87
Jones, B.B.   Edwin Romanzo Elmer, 1850-1923.
   M.B. Péladeau, 432(NEQ):Mar85-148
Jones, B.W.   The Emperor Titus.
   J.C. Traupman, 124:May-Jun86-333
Jones, C., ed.   Party and Management in Parliament 1660-1784.
   H.T. Dickinson, 566:Autumn85-93
Jones, C. and M. Brenton - see "The Year Book of Social Policy in Britain 1984-5"
Jones, C. and G. Holmes - see Nicolson, W.
Jones, D.   Inner Necessities. (T. Dilworth, ed)
   W. Blissett, 627(UTQ):Winter85/86-212
   K.H. Staudt, 659(ConL):Fall86-409
Jones, D.C.   Roman.
   T. Nolan, 441:13Jul86-18
Jones, D.G.   Brave New People. (rev)
   R.B.M., 185:Jul86-918
Jones, D.R.   Great Directors at Work.
   R. Brustein, 441:27Jul86-11
Jones, E.T.   Following Directions.
   A. Vivis, 157:No158-47
Jones, G.   Escape Plans.
   J. Clute, 617(TLS):28Nov86-1357
Jones, G.   The Norse Atlantic Saga. (rev)
   617(TLS):10Oct86-1147
Jones, G.F.   The Salzburger Saga.
   H.E. Davis, 656(WMQ):Apr85-284
Jones, G.I.   The Art of Eastern Nigeria.
   J. Boston, 2(AfrA):May85-12
Jones, G.M.   That Reminds Me.
   E.O. de Bary, 392:Fall85-488
Jones, G.S.   Languages of Class.
   S. Meacham, 637(VS):Autumn85-162
Jones, H.A.   Plays by Henry Arthur Jones.* (R. Jackson, ed)
   S. Gatrell, 541(RES):Feb85-115
Jones, J.   Come come.
   P. Lewis, 565:Winter84/85-42
Jones, J.   Dostoevsky.*
   D. Rayfield, 402(MLR):Jul85-764
   G. Woodcock, 569(SR):Spring85-293
Jones, J.   Union Man.
   D. Smith, 362:18Sep86-22
   J. Turner, 617(TLS):5Sep86-965

Jones, J. and J.   Canadian Fiction.
   D. Staines, 402(MLR):Apr85-449
Jones, J. and J.   New Zealand Fiction. Australian Fiction.
   S.F.D. Hughes, 395(MFS):Summer85-471
Jones, J.P. and G.A. Nance.   Philip Roth.
   J.L. Halio, 677(YES):Vol 15-359
Jones, J.T.   Wayward Skeptic.
   C. Baldick, 617(TLS):14Nov86-1273
Jones, K.   As Soon as it Rains.
   J. House, 441:9Mar86-24
Jones, K.   Simulations in Language Teaching.
   J.M. Purcell, 399(MLJ):Spring85-79
Jones, L./A. Baraka.   The Autobiography of Le Roi Jones/Amiri Baraka.*
   S. Krim, 364:Apr/May85-102
Jones, L. and C. Von Baeyer.   Functions of American English.*
   M.J. Cashel-Cordo, 351(LL):Jun85-319
Jones, L.E.   Sad Clowns and Pale Pierrots.
   R. Chambers, 208(FS):Jul85-360
   G. May, 207(FR):Mar86-619
   R. Sorensen, 67:Nov85-258
   R. Storey, 446(NCFS):Fall-Winter85/86-179
Jones, L.M.   The Life of John Hamilton Reynolds.*
   P.F. Morgan, 661(WC):Fall85-202
Jones, M.   Coming Home.
   J. Mellors, 362:29May86-25
Jones, M.   Failure in Palestine.
   W.R. Louis, 617(TLS):8Aug86-857
Jones, M.   Holding On.
   P. Craig, 617(TLS):19Dec86-1428
Jones, M.P.   Conrad's Heroism.
   J. Hawthorn, 637(VS):Spring86-492
   S. Pinsker, 136:Vol 18No2-147
   295(JML):Nov85-461
Jones, M.S.   "Der Sturm."
   M. Kuxdorf, 221(GQ):Fall85-622
Jones, M.V. and G.M. Terry, eds.   New Essays on Dostoyevsky.*
   W.J. Leatherbarrow, 402(MLR):Jan85-248
Jones, N.   Strikes and the Media.
   R. Hattersley, 362:8May86-22
Jones, P.   Hume's Sentiments.*
   T. Penelhum, 154:Autumn85-515
   M.A. Stewart, 518:Oct85-217
Jones, P.M.   Medieval Medical Miniatures.
   W. Schupbach, 90:Oct85-720
Jones, P.M.   Politics and Rural Society.
   C. Jones, 617(TLS):21Mar86-310
Jones, R.E.   Provincial Development in Russia.*
   W.R. Augustine, 104(CASS):Spring85-68
   R.P. Bartlett, 575(SEER):Jul85-456
Jones, R.W.   Saving Grace.
   M. Laski, 362:17Apr86-29
Jones, S.   Two Centuries of Overseas Trading.
   A. Briggs, 362:3Jul86-31
Jones, S. - see Takeda Izumo and others
Jones, S.A.   Thoreau amongst Friends and Philistines and Other Thoreauviana. (G. Hendrick, ed)
   R. Sattelmeyer, 183(ESQ):Vol31No3-190
Jones, W.F.   Nature and Natural Science.*
   J.P. Anton, 319:Jul86-427
Jones, W.G.   Tove Jansson.
   T. Lundell, 563(SS):Autumn85-456
Jones, W.G.   Nikolay Novikov.*
   R.P. Bartlett, 575(SEER):Oct85-602

194

de Jong, E.D., ed. Spreektal.
  J.B. Berns, 685(ZDL):2/1985-263
de Jong, W.R. The Semantics of John
  Stuart Mill.*
  C.F. Kielkopf, 543:Mar85-643
de Jonge, A. Stalin.
  A. Austin, 441:27Apr86-23
de Jonge, A. Stalin and the Shaping of
  the Soviet Union.
  J. Keep, 617(TLS):24Oct86-1182
  442(NY):12May86-127
de Jonge, H.J. - see Erasmus
de Jonge, M., ed. Outside the Old Testa-
  ment.
  G. Vermes, 617(TLS):27Jun86-718
Jonnes, J. We're Still Here.
  R. Curvin, 441:16Feb86-25
Jónsdóttir, S., S. Karlsson and S. Tómas-
  son - see Bergr Sokkason
Jonson, B. Volpone, or The Fox.* (R.B.
  Parker, ed)
  D. Fuller, 541(RES):Aug85-427
"Ben Jonson." (I. Donaldson, ed)
  A.J. Smith, 617(TLS):11Jul86-765
Joost, U. and A. Schöne - see Lichtenberg,
  G.C.
Joppien, R. and B. Smith. The Art of Cap-
  tain Cook's Voyages.*
  B.A.L. Cranstone, 617(TLS):28Mar86-326
  N. Powell, 39:Dec85-501
Jordan, D.P. The Revolutionary Career of
  Maximilien Robespierre.*
  H. Brogan, 362:28Aug86-23
Jordan, J.E. - see Wordsworth, W.
Jordan, L., B. Kortländer and F. Nies, eds.
  Interferenzen — Deutschland and Frank-
  reich.*
  R. Dumont, 549(RLC):Jul-Sep85-365
  E. Reichel, 72:Band222Heft2-479
Jordan, M.P. Rhetoric of Everyday English
  Texts.*
  M. Viel, 189(EA):Apr-Jun86-199
Jordan, R.W. Plato's Arguments for Forms.
  R. Heinaman, 303(JoHS):Vol 105-185
  M. Woods, 123:Vol35No1-29
Jordan, T.G. American Log Buildings.
  P. Johnson, 292(JAF):Oct/Dec85-491
Jordanova, L.J., ed. Languages of Nature.
  G.S. Rousseau, 441:14Dec86-42
Jordanus de Nemore. De numeris datis.
  (B.B. Hughes, ed and trans)
  J.V. Wagner, 543:Mar85-641
Jorden, W.J. Panama Odyssey.*
  639(VQR):Winter85-21
Jorgens, E.B. The Well-Tun'd Word.*
  H.B.R., 412:May83-143
Jorgensen, P.A. William Shakespeare: The
  Tragedies.
  K. Brown, 617(TLS):22Aug86-917
Jorgensen-Dahl, A. Regional Organization
  and Order in Southeast Asia.
  L.D. Howell, 293(JASt):Feb85-465
Jose, N. Ideas of the Restoration in En-
  glish Literature, 1660-1671.*
  N.K. Maguire, 568(SCN):Winter85-60
  G. Reedy, 173(ECS):Fall85-98
  J. Strugnell, 67:May85-67
Josefson, E-K. La Vision citadine et
  sociale dans l'oeuvre d'Émile Verhaeren.*
  I. Higgins, 208(FS):Jul85-357
Joselow, B. The April Wars.
  W. Zander, 363(LitR):Spring86-379

Joseph, B. A Shakespeare Workbook.
  G.L. Voth, 570(SQ):Summer85-245
Joseph, B.D. The Synchrony and Diachrony
  of the Balkan Infinitive.*
  R. Alexander, 574(SEEJ):Spring85-118
  J. Haiman, 320(CJL):Winter85-488
Joseph, C.M. Stravinsky and the Piano.
  A. Whittall, 410(M&L):Apr85-127
Joseph, G. - see "Browning Institute
  Studies"
Joseph, J., ed. Applied Language Study.
  T. Piper, 320(CJL):Fall85-391
  R.V. Teschner, 238:Sep85-536
Joseph, J. Persephone.
  J-A. Goodwin, 617(TLS):29Aug86-932
Joseph, J.R. Crébillon fils.
  P. Stewart, 207(FR):Mar86-616
Joseph, W.A. The Critique of Ultra-Left-
  ism in China, 1958-1981.
  R. Kraus, 293(JASt):May85-593
Josephides, L. The Production of Inequal-
  ity.
  A. Weiner, 617(TLS):28Feb86-224
Josephs, A. White Wall of Spain.*
  E. Current-Garcia, 577(SHR):Fall85-378
  E. Gascón Vera, 552(REH):Oct85-141
  H.T. Young, 240(HR):Winter85-92
Josephus. Flavius Josèphe: "La guerre des
  Juifs."* (P. Savinel, trans)
  M. Canto, 98:Jun-Jul85-618
Josipovici, G. Contre-Jour.
  E. Feinstein, 617(TLS):25Jul86-819
Josipovici, G. Conversations in Another
  Room.
  C. Baranger, 189(EA):Apr-Jun86-234
Jost, M. Practice, Interpretation, Per-
  formance.
  J. Methuen-Campbell, 415:May85-288
Jost, W. Räume der Einsamkeit bei Marcel
  Proust.
  A. Corbineau-Hoffmann, 72:Band222Heft2-
  453
  E. Eells-Ogée, 535(RHL):Jan/Feb85-122
Jouan, F. - see Euripides
Jouannet, F. Le Français au Rwanda.
  A. Valdman, 207(FR):Mar86-653
Joubert, E. Poppie Nongena.
  442(NY):24Feb86-104
Joubert, J. Essais, 1779-1821. (R.
  Tessonneau, ed)
  J.M. Cocking, 208(FS):Apr85-214
  A.J. Steele, 402(MLR):Jan85-169
Joukovsky, F. Le regard intérieur.*
  K. Ley, 547(RF):Band97Heft1-83
Joukovsky, F. - see d'Alcripe, P.
Jouve, N.W. Baudelaire.
  J.M. Cocking, 208(FS):Jul85-355
Jover, A.A. - see under Arqués Jover, A.
Jowell, J. and D. Oliver, eds. The Chang-
  ing Constitution.
  J. Waldron, 617(TLS):18Apr86-410
Jowitt, D. The Dance in Mind.*
  S.J. Cohen, 290(JAAC):Winter85-199
  E. Zimmer, 151:Dec85-97
Joyce, H. The Decoration of Walls, Ceil-
  ings and Floors in Italy in the Second
  and Third Centuries A.D.
  P.C. Finney, 54:Dec85-679
  R. Ling, 313:Vol75-277
Joyce, J. Ulisse: Telemachia. (G.
  Melchiori, ed)
  C.D. Lobner, 329(JJQ):Fall85-95

Joyce, J.  Ulysses.*  (H.W. Gabler, with W. Steppe and C. Melchior, eds)
M. Amis, 61:Sep86-96
Z. Bowen, 305(JIL):Jan85-53
R. Bush, 250(HLQ):Spring85-187
J. Hunter, 249(HudR):Summer85-315
K. Lawrence, 651(WHR):Winter85-362
R. Lewis, 184(EIC):Jul85-276
J.J. McGann, 141:Summer85-283
M. Magalaner, 395(MFS):Winter85-782
R.D. Newman, 577(SHR):Fall85-379
C. Owens, 272(IUR):Spring85-99
D. Seed, 40(AEB):Vol8No3-173
529(QQ):Summer85-434
Joyce, J.J.  The Monodies of Sigismondo d'India.
N.C.F., 410(M&L):Oct85-376
Joyce, M.  The War Outside Ireland.
M. Stephens, 532(RCF):Spring85-153
Joyce, R.O.  A Woman's Place.
J.S. Powell, 650(WF):Apr85-149
Joyce, W.L. and others, eds.  Printing and Society in Early America.*
T.R. Adams, 517(PBSA):Vol79No4-567
Joyner, C.  Down By The Riverside.
J. Minton, 292(JAF):Jul/Sep85-358
F. Shivers, 577(SHR):Summer85-273
Jrade, C.L.  Rubén Darío and the Romantic Search for Unity.*
D.L. Shaw, 402(MLR):Apr85-482
San Juan de la Cruz.  Cántico espiritual. (E. Pacho, ed)
C.P. Thompson, 86(BHS):Jul85-300
San Juan de la Cruz.  Poesía. (J. Jiménez Lozano, ed)
C.G. Peale, 240(HR):Winter85-100
M. Wilson, 86(BHS):Oct85-407
Jubert, P.  Repertoire automatisé des livres du XVIe siècle conservés à la Bibliothèque Municipale de Rouen (1501-1550). (E. Bayle and others, eds)
78(BC):Spring85-9
Judd, D.  Alison Uttley.
N. Tucker, 617(TLS):5Dec86-1378
Judge, A. and F.G. Healey.  A Reference Grammar of Modern French.*
R. Wakely, 402(MLR):Jan85-152
Judt, T.  Marxism and the French Left.
J. Hayward, 617(TLS):18Jul86-782
Juergens, G.  New from the White House.
J. Braeman, 106:Fall85-353
Juhász, J., ed.  Kontrastive Studien Ungarisch-Deutsch.
M. Katzschmann, 685(ZDL):2/1985-254
Juhasz, S., ed.  Feminist Critics Read Emily Dickinson.*
G. Monteiro, 26(ALR):Spring/Autumn85-250
Juhasz, S.  The Undiscovered Continent.*
W. Barker, 26(ALR):Spring/Autumn85-247
Juilland, A.  Transformational and Structural Morphology.
K. Klingebiel, 545(RPh):Feb86-323
Julian, J.  Ellen Bray.
C.D. Kennedy, 441:9Nov86-32
Julian of Norwich.  A Book of Showings to the Anchoress Julian of Norwich.  (E. Colledge and J. Walsh, eds)
A.V.C. Schmidt, 447(N&Q):Mar84-100
Julliard, J.  La faute à Rousseau.
J-F. Revel, 176:Apr86-39
Julyan, R.H.  Mountain Names.
K.B. Harder, 424:Mar-Jun85-105

Jung, C.G.  Dream Analysis.  (W. McGuire, ed)
P. Seligman, 154:Spring85-155
Jung, H.  Thronende und sitzende Götter.
J. Boardman, 123:Vol35No2-419
Jünger, E.  Soixante-dix s'efface.* (Vol 2)
L. Kovacs, 450(NRF):Jul-Aug85-174
Junghans, H., ed.  Leben und Werk Martin Luthers von 1526 bis 1546.
F. Posset, 77:Fall85-356
Jungraithmayr, H. and W.J.G. Möhlig, eds.  Lexikon der Afrikanistik, Afrikanische Sprachen und ihre Erforschung.
S. Brauner, 682(ZPSK):Band38Heft6-766
Jupp, P.  Lord Grenville 1759-1834.
J. Cannon, 617(TLS):2May86-466
Juranville, A.  Lacan et la philosophie.
J.F. Marquet, 542:Jan-Mar85-53
Juretschke, H. - see Schlegel, F.
Jurgensen, M., ed.  Bernhard: Annäherungen.
M. Adams, 67:Nov85-261
W. Riemer, 301(JEGP):Jan85-97
Jurgensen, M.  Deutsche Frauenautoren der Gegenwart.
M. Adams, 67:Nov85-262
Juškevič, A.P. and R. Taton - see Euler, L.
Just, A.  Meissen Porcelain in the Art Nouveau Period.
I.L., 90:Oct85-728
Just, W.  The American Blues.
639(VQR):Winter85-23
Justeson, J.S. and others.  The Foreign Impact on Lowland Mayan Language and Script.
B. Love, 350:Sep86-727
Justeson, J.S. and L. Campbell, eds.  Phoneticism in Mayan Hieroglyphic Writing.
V.R. Bricker, 350:Sep86-694
Justice, D.  Platonic Scripts.
R. Wertime, 676(YR):Summer85-602
"Justification de l'éthique."
M. Adam, 542:Jan-Mar85-88
Jutikkala, E., Y. Kaukianen and S-E. Åström, eds.  Suomen taloushistoria I.
S. Oakley, 562(Scan):May85-65

Kabal, A.M.  The Adversary.
M. Laski, 362:17Apr86-29
Kabir.  The Bījak of Kabir.  (L. Hess and S. Singh, trans)
J. Cort, 314:Winter-Spring85-249
Kabira, W.M.  The Oral Artist.
C.A. Kratz, 538(RAL):Fall85-427
Kacewicz, G.  Great Britain, the Soviet Union and the Polish Government-in-Exile (1939-1945).
R.A. Walawender, 497(PolR):Vol30No2-215
Kachru, B.B., ed.  The Other Tongue.
A.C. Purves, 128(CE):Apr85-419
Kaczmarczyk, A. and R.E.M. Hedges.  Ancient Egyptian Faience.
E.J. Peltenberg, 303(JoHS):Vol 105-238
Kadaré, I.  Invitation à un concert officiel et autres récits.
L. Kovacs, 450(NRF):Jun85-93
Kadatz, H-J. and G. Murza.  Georg Wenzeslaus von Knobelsdorff.
J. Rykwert, 617(TLS):4Apr86-362

Kamenetz, R. Terra Infirma.
   J. Olney, 598(SoR):Spring86-428
Kamin, D. Charlie Chaplin's One-Man Show.
   A. Lust, 615(TJ):Dec85-526
Kaminsky, A.P. The India Office, 1880-
   1910.
   K. Ballhatchet, 617(TLS):19Dec86-1431
Kaminsky, A.R. The Victim's Song.
   R. Abrams, 129:Jan86-78
Kaminsky, H. Simon de Cramaud and the
   Great Schism.*
   F. Oakley, 589:Jul85-688
Kamm-Kyburz, C. Der Arkitekt Ottavio Ber-
   totti Scamozzi 1719-1790.
   C.M. Sicca, 90:Jul85-463
Kammen, M. A Machine That Would Go of
   Itself.
   D.M. Kennedy, 441:14Sep86-11
Kampf, A. Jewish Experience in the Art of
   the Twentieth Century.*
   S.S. Schwarzschild, 55:Jan85-35
Kamuf, P. Fictions of Feminine Desire.*
   N. Homad-Sultan, 549(RLC):Jul-Sep85-
   328
   J.F. MacCannell, 591(SIR):Summer85-275
   M. Myers, 173(ECS):Fall85-107
   S.I. Spencer, 577(SHR):Winter85-71
"Kandinsky in Russland und am Bauhaus 1915-
   1933."
   P. Vergo, 59:Dec85-496
Kane, A. Songs and Sayings of an Ulster
   Childhood.* (E. Fowke, ed)
   D. Kodish, 292(JAF):Apr/Jun85-229
Kane, G. Chaucer.*
   M. Dodsworth, 175:Summer85-183
Kane, J.E. - see François Ier
Kane, M. Roman africain et tradition.
   C.L. Dehon, 207(FR):Mar86-603
   T. El-Miskin, 538(RAL):Winter85-570
Kane, P.M. and P.A. Short. Entretiens
   avec les mots.*
   M. Lavallée-Williams, 399(MLJ):
   Summer85-182
Kanellos, N., ed. Hispanic Theatre in the
   United States.
   J.W. Brokaw, 352(LATR):Fall85-109
Kanellos, N., ed. Mexican American
   Theatre.
   J.I. Bissett, 238:May85-325
K'ang, H. - see under Hsi K'ang
Kanigel, R. Apprentice to Genius.
   C.R. Herron, 441:50ct86-55
Kanitscheider, B., ed. Moderne Natur-
   philosophie.
   G. Böhme, 687:Oct-Dec85-639
Kannemeyer, J.C. Geskiedenis van die
   Afrikaanse Literatuur.
   M. Trump, 538(RAL):Spring85-141
Kanowski, M.G. Containers of Classical
   Greece.
   R.M. Cook, 303(JoHS):Vol 105-234
Kant, I. Critique of Pure Reason.* (W.
   Schwarz, ed and trans)
   M.J. Gregor, 543:Sep84-124
Kant, I. Gelecekte bilim olarak ortaya
   cikabilecek her metafiziğe. (J. Kuçur-
   adi, ed)
   A.J. Bucher, 342:Band76Heft2-225
Kant, I. Kant's Latin Writings. (L.W.
   Beck, ed)
   E. Förster, 617(TLS):11Jul86-754

Kantaris, S. The Sea at the Door.
   C. Boyle, 364:Nov85-79
W. Scammell, 148:Winter85-65
Kantra, R.A. All Things Vain.
   R.A. Anselment, 301(JEGP):Oct85-557
   R. Smolkin, 566:Autumn85-90
Kapferer, B. A Celebration of Demons.
   H.L. Seneviratne, 293(JASt):May85-636
Kaplan, E.A. Women and Film.
   J. Nelson, 529(QQ):Summer85-432
Kaplan, E.K. - see Michelet, J.
Kaplan, F. Thomas Carlyle.*
   J.A.V. Chapple, 366:Spring85-147
   J.P. Farrell, 637(VS):Spring85-530
   C.R. Harland, 529(QQ):Summer85-408
   R.L. Patten, 158:Jun85-58
   M. Peckham, 579(SAQ):Autumn85-435
   R.L. Tarr, 536(Rev):Vol7-239
   G.B. Tennyson, 506(PSt):May85-86
   C.R. Vanden Bossche, 401(MLQ):Sep84-
   303
Kaplan, F. - see Pascal, B.
Kaplan, J. - see Whitman, W.
Kaplan, M. Science, Language and the
   Human Condition.
   D.D. Laitin, 185:Jul86-884
Kaplan, R.B. - see "Annual Review of
   Applied Linguistics 1983"
Kaplan, S.L. Provisioning Paris.*
   639(VQR):Summer85-86
Kappeler, S. The Pornography of Represen-
   tation.
   W. Smith, 441:28Dec86-19
Kappeler, S. and N. Bryson, eds. Teaching
   the Text.*
   C. Norris, 577(SHR):Winter85-95
Kapr, A. The Art of Lettering.
   J. Kelly, 517(PBSA):Vol79No3-448
Kapschutschenko, L. El laberinto en la
   narrativa hispanoamericana contempor-
   ánea.*
   J.M. Labanyi, 402(MLR):Jan85-203
Kapsner, O.L., comp. A Benedictine Bibli-
   ography. (1st Supp)
   A. Groos, 589:Jan85-223
Kapur, R.A. Sikh Separatism.
   I. Jack, 617(TLS):1Aug86-832
Kapuscinski, R. Shah of Shahs.*
   639(VQR):Summer85-94
Karadagli, T. Fabel und Ainos.
   J. Vaio, 123:Vol35No2-397
Karageorghis, V. Palaepaphos-Skales, an
   Iron Age Cemetery in Cyprus.
   M. Popham, 123:Vol35No2-337
Karageorghis, V. and M. Demas. Pyla-
   Kokkinokremos.
   S. Hood, 123:Vol35No2-416
Karátson, A. and J. Bessière. Déracine-
   ment et littérature.*
   R. Robin, 535(RHL):Jul/Aug85-705
Karch, D. Monographien 13.
   H. Tatzreiter, 685(ZDL):3/1985-392
Karetzky, S. The Canons of Journalism.
   N. Frankel, 390:Jun/Jul85-57
Karius, I. Die Ableitung der denominalen
   Verben mit Nullsuffigierung im Englis-
   chen.
   R. Beard, 350:Sep86-715
Karl, F.R. American Fictions, 1940-1980.*
   G. Davenport, 569(SR):Summer85-499
   T. Schaub, 577(SHR):Summer85-291
Karl, F.R. and L. Davies - see Conrad, J.

Karlin, D.  The Courtship of Robert Brown-
ing and Elizabeth Barrett.
  B. Hardy, 617(TLS):7Feb86-136
  442(NY):31Mar86-83
Karling, S.  Kalmar domkyrka och Nikodemus
Tessin d.ä.
  I. Rosell, 341:Vol54No2-95
Karlinger, F. and E. Turczynski, eds.
Rumänische Sagen und Sagen aus Rumänien.
  H. Stein, 196:Band26Heft3/4-363
Karlinsky, S.  Russian Drama from its
Beginnings to the Age of Pushkin.
  A.G. Cross, 617(TLS):14Feb86-156
Karlinsky, S.  Marina Tsvetaeva.
  R. Hingley, 617(TLS):11Jul86-768
Karlinsky, S. - see Nabokov, V. and E.
Wilson
Karlsen, C.F. and L. Crumpacker - see Burr,
E.E.
Karlsson, K.E.  Syntax and Affixation.
  G. Price, 208(FS):Jan85-122
Karnow, S.  Vietnam.
  E.E. Moise, 293(JASt):Feb85-343
Karski, J.  The Great Powers and Poland,
1919-1945.
  J.K. Zawodny, 497(PolR):Vol30No4-413
Kartašova, L.A., ed.  Učebnyj russko-
malagasijski slovar.
  B. Schmidt, 682(ZPSK):Band38Heft2-182
Karthaus, U. and H. Krueger - see Huelsen-
beck, R.
Kartomi, M., ed.  Five Essays on the Indo-
nesian Arts.
  M. Adams, 293(JASt):Feb85-467
Karumanchiri, L.P. and J. Vizmuller-Zocco -
see under Polesini Karumanchiri, L. and
J. Vizmuller-Zocco
Kasang, D.  Wilhelminismus und Expression-
ismus.
  W.D. Elfe, 406:Summer85-242
Kaspranskij, R.R.  Očerk teoretičeskoj i
normativnoj fonetiki.
  F. Häusler, 682(ZPSK):Band38Heft2-183
Kassel, R. and C. Austin, eds.  Poetae
Comici Graeci.*  (Vol 4)
  J.T.M.F. Pieters, 394:Vol38fasc3/4-412
Kasserman, D.R.  Fall River Outrage.
  E. Fox-Genovese, 441:10Aug86-20
Kastan, D.S.  Shakespeare and the Shapes
of Time.*
  P.C. Alley, 570(SQ):Winter85-504
  P. Bement, 541(RES):Feb85-82
Kasten, L. and J. Nitti, eds.  Concor-
dances and Texts of the Fourteenth-
Century Aragonese Manuscripts of Juan
Fernández de Heredia.  Concordances and
Texts of the Royal Scriptorium Manu-
scripts of Alfonso X, el Sabio.
  J.R. Craddock, 545(RPh):May86-462
Kastner, R.  Geistlicher Rauffhandel.*
  R.W. Brednich, 196:Band26Heft1/2-165
Kaston, C.  Imagination and Desire in the
Novels of Henry James.
  E. Carton, 445(NCF):Sep85-243
  C.B. Cox, 27(AL):Oct85-501
  J. Freedman, 432(NEQ):Jun85-323
  J.E. Funston, 594:Winter85-425
  295(JML):Nov85-501
Kateb, G.  Hannah Arendt.*
  A. Taylor, 543:Mar85-645
Kater, M.H.  The Nazi Party.
  J. Caplan, 529(QQ):Spring85-66
  P. Milbouer, 221(GQ):Spring85-319

Kates, J.A.  Tasso and Milton.*
  A.R. Cirillo, 551(RenQ):Summer85-376
  C.S. Ross, 405(MP):Feb86-305
Katō Hidetoshi - see Kuwabara Takeo
Kato, S.  A History of Japanese Literature
(Nihon bungakushi).  [vol unknown]
  S. Heine, 485(PE&W):Jan85-101
Kattán-Ibarra, J. and T. Connell.  Spanish
for Business.
  D.E. Rivas, 399(MLJ):Autumn85-324
Katz, H. - see Lewy, E.
Katz, J.  The Darker Side of Genius.
  J. Deathridge, 617(TLS):14Nov86-1270
Katz, J.  From Prejudice to Destruction.
  R.S. Wistrich, 390:Apr85-48
Katz, J.  The Silent World of Doctor and
Patient.
  A.L. Wax, 31(ASch):Summer85-419
Katz, J.J.  Language and Other Abstract
Objects.*
  S. Davis, 484(PPR):Dec85-339
  S. McConnell-Ginet, 482(PhR):Oct85-590
Katz, M.B.  In the Shadow of the Poorhouse.
  A. Grimes, 441:2Nov86-26
Katz, M.R.  Dreams and the Unconscious in
Nineteenth-Century Russian Fiction.*
  J.D. Clayton, 104(CASS):Summer85-216
  S.S. Lottridge, 574(SEEJ):Fall85-342
Katz, N., ed.  Buddhist and Western Philos-
ophy.
  W. Halbfass, 318(JAOS):Oct-Dec84-787
Katz, S.  Plastics.
  J.L. Meikle, 658:Winter85-320
Katz, S.  Weir and Pouce.*
  138:No8-253
Katz, W.W.  Witchery Hill.
  P. Nodelman, 102(CanL):Fall85-122
Katzner, K.  English-Russian Russian-
English Dictionary.
  D.J. Birnbaum, 550(RusR):Apr85-187
  M. Heim, 574(SEEJ):Summer85-225
  S. Lubensky, 399(MLJ):Summer85-195
Kauffeldt, R.  Erich Mühsam.
  P.K. Jansen, 405(MP):Nov85-209
Kauffman, J.  Collaborators.
  U. Hegi, 441:20Apr86-17
Kauffman, J.  Places in the World a Woman
Could Walk.*
  G.L. Morris, 502(PrS):Spring85-108
Kauffmann, C.M.  John Varley 1778-1842.*
  W. Joll, 39:May85-359
Kaufman, B.I.  The Korean War.
  D.S. Zagoria, 441:7Sep86-20
Kaufman, B.I.  Trade and Aid.
  J.O. Robertson, 106:Winter85-465
Kaufman, G.  Inside the Promised Land.
  B. Wasserstein, 617(TLS):100ct86-1123
Kaufman, G.D.  Theology for a Nuclear Age.
  R.B.M., 185:Jul86-924
Kaufman, H.  Interest Rates, the Markets
and the New Financial World.
  T. Congdon, 617(TLS):7Nov86-1250
Kaufman, L. and K. Mallory, eds.  The Last
Extinction.
  D. Sagan, 441:30Nov86-39
Kaufman, S.  Claims.
  M. Jarman, 249(HudR):Summer85-328
  639(VQR):Spring85-54
Kaufman, S.B. - see Gompers, S.
Kaufman, W.  Musikgeschichte in Bildern.
(Vol 2)
  J. Kuckertz, 187:Spring/Summer86-351

Kaufmann, E., Jr., with C. Little and T.A. Heinz. Fallingwater.
  P. Goldberger, 441:7Dec86-16
Kaufmann, G. My Life in the Silver Screen.
  C. Hawtree, 364:Dec85/Jan86-147
Kaufmann, W. Discovering the Mind.
  R. Lüthe, 342:Band76Heft3-352
Kavaler, R. Tigers in the Wood.
  S. Tanenhaus, 441:21Sep86-26
Kavan, R. Freedom at a Price.
  T.G. Ash, 617(TLS):24Jan86-77
  J. Laber, 441:10Aug86-22
Kavanagh, D. Putting the Boot In.
  T.J. Binyon, 617(TLS):13Jun86-646
  M. Bream, 364:Aug-Sep85-156
Kavanagh, J.H. Emily Brontë.*
  S. Davies, 148:Autumn85-35
Kavanagh, P.J. Only by Mistake.
  G. Dyer, 362:28Aug86-22
Kavanagh, P.J. - see Gurney, I.
Kawalilak, R. Wilderness Dances.
  P.K. Smith, 526:Spring85-88
Kawin, B.F. The Mind of the Novel.*
  J. Phelan, 405(MP):Aug85-98
Kawin, B.F. - see Faulkner, W.
Kay, N.M. Martial Book XI.
  N. Horsfall, 617(TLS):28Mar86-337
Kay, S. Legacy.
  S. Altinel, 617(TLS):21Feb86-198
  M. Rubin, 441:11May86-24
Kayden, X. and E. Mahe, Jr. The Party Goes On.
  T.B. Edsall, 453(NYRB):24Apr86-3
Kaye, H.J. The British Marxist Historians.
  F.M.L. Thompson, 617(TLS):23May86-572
Kayne, R. Connectedness and Binary Branching.
  G. Longobardi, 297(JL):Sep85-477
Kazhdan, A., with S. Franklin. Studies on Byzantine Literature of the Eleventh and Twelfth Centuries.
  P. Magdalino, 575(SEER):Jul85-432
Kazhdan, A.P. and A.W. Epstein. Change in Byzantine Culture in the Eleventh and Twelfth Centuries.
  C. Mango, 617(TLS):17Oct86-1172
Kazin, A. An American Procession.*
  G. Johnson, 639(VQR):Winter85-146
  E.J. Sundquist, 651(WHR):Winter85-379
  L. Ziff, 27(AL):May85-322
  295(JML):Nov85-416
Keach, W. Elizabethan Erotic Narratives.
  W. Weiss, 38:Band103Heft3/4-480
Keal, P. Unspoken Rules and Superpower Dominance.
  D.E. Powell, 550(RusR):Jul85-271
Keane, J., ed. The Power of the Powerless.
  E. Gellner, 617(TLS):3Oct86-1090
Keane, J. Public Life and Late Capitalism.
  C.R.S., 185:Apr86-678
Keane, J. - see Havel, V. and others
Kearney, R. Dialogues with Contemporary Continental Thinkers.
  W. Desmond, 543:Sep85-160
  D. Moran, 323:Oct85-307
Kearney, R., ed. The Irish Mind.*
  M.E. Daly, 272(IUR):Spring85-101
Kearney, R. Poétique du possible.
  J. Macquarrie, 323:Oct85-310
Kearns, J.T. Using Language.
  F.L. Smith, 350:Jun86-476

Kearns, L. Convergences.
  D. Gutteridge, 529(QQ):Winter85-840
  A. Pritchard, 102(CanL):Spring85-157
Keates, J. Handel.*
  D. Burrows, 415:Dec85-731
Keating, F. Gents and Players.
  A.L. Le Quesne, 617(TLS):5Sep86-987
Keating, F. High, Wide and Handsome.
  A. Ross, 617(TLS):11Jul86-770
Keating, H.R.F. Mrs. Craggs.
  T.J. Binyon, 617(TLS):17Jan86-57
Keating, H.R.F. Under a Monsoon Cloud.
  T.J. Binyon, 617(TLS):13Jun86-646
  M. Laski, 362:17Apr86-29
Keating, H.R.F., ed. Whodunit?*
  L.O. Sauerberg, 447(N&Q):Dec84-560
Keats, J. The Poems of John Keats. (J. Stillinger, ed)
  R. Sharrock, 447(N&Q):Jun84-270
Keats, V. Chessmen for Collectors.
  T. Russell-Cobb, 324:May86-418
Keaveney, A. Sulla.*
  J. Briscoe, 313:Vol75-238
Kechris, A.S., D.A. Martin and Y.N. Moscho-vakis, eds. Cabal Seminar 77-79.
  T. Jech, 316:Sep85-849
Kechris, A.S. and Y.N. Moschovakis, eds. Cabal Seminar 76-77.
  T. Jech, 316:Sep85-849
Keddie, N.R., ed. Religion and Politics in Iran.
  C. Heywood, 617(TLS):21Mar86-293
Kee, H.C. Miracle in the Early Christian World.*
  M. Beard, 123:Vol35No1-202
  J.A.S. Evans, 529(QQ):Summer85-340
  I.N. Wood, 313:Vol75-267
Kee, R. Trial and Error.
  A.W.B. Simpson, 617(TLS):5Dec86-1365
Keeble, B. - see Raine, K.
Keeble, N.H. Richard Baxter.*
  N. Smith, 447(N&Q):Mar84-123
Keefe, T. Simone de Beauvoir.*
  A. Cismaru, 395(MFS):Summer85-441
Keefe, T. French Existentialist Fiction.
  P. Thody, 617(TLS):14Nov86-1280
Keegan, J. and R. Holmes, with J. Gau. Soldiers.*
  E.N. Luttwak, 441:23Mar86-13
Keel, A. Innovation und Restauration.
  P. Hallberg, 563(SS):Winter85-87
Keele, A.F. The Apocalyptic Vision.
  A.A. Kuzniar, 400(MLN):Apr85-685
  R.K. Shirer, 405(MP):Feb86-333
Keen, M. Chivalry.
  R.C. McCoy, 551(RenQ):Summer85-361
Keenan, D.J. The Catholic Church in Nineteenth-Century Ireland.*
  W. Schoenl, 637(VS):Autumn85-171
Keenan, E.L. and L.M. Faltz. Boolean Semantics for Natural Language.
  J. van Benthem, 350:Dec86-908
Keene, D. Dawn to the West.*
  E. McClellan, 244(HJAS):Dec85-703
  M. Ueda, 407(MN):Spring85-107
Keener, F.M. The Chain of Becoming.*
  L.K. Barnett, 677(YES):Vol 15-301
  J.A. Dussinger, 301(JEGP):Jan85-126
  P. Rogers, 541(RES):Aug85-431
  R.C. Rosbottom, 173(ECS):Fall85-120
Keep, J.L.H. Soldiers of the Tsar.
  M. Raeff, 617(TLS):30May86-601

Keery, S. The Streets of Laredo.
    P. Craig, 617(TLS):26Sep86-1058
Kees, W. The Ceremony and Other Stories.*
    (D. Gioia, ed)
    R.E. Knoll, 502(PrS):Summer85-111
    R. Scheele, 584(SWR):Spring85-271
Kees, W. Two Prose Sketches.
    R.E. Knoll, 502(PrS):Summer85-111
Kefala, A. The First Journey. The Island.
    J. Brett, 381:Mar85-125
Keillor, G. Lake Wobegon Days.*
    D. Sexton, 617(TLS):7Mar86-257
Keith, A. Three Came Home.
    617(TLS):31Jan86-127
Keith, W.J. Canadian Literature in
    English.
    G. Woodcock, 627(UTQ):Spring86-302
Keith, W.J. Epic Fiction.
    J. Thieme, 49:Jul85-102
Keith, W.J., ed. A Voice in the Land.*
    J. Thieme, 49:Jul85-102
Kejzlar, R. Literatur und Neutralität.
    B. Nolin, 562(Scan):Nov85-239
Kelikian, A.A. Town and Country under
    Fascism.
    T. Abse, 617(TLS):30ct86-1099
Kelland, G. Crime in London.
    L. Taylor, 362:11Dec86-23
Kellenberger, J. The Cognitivity of Reli-
    gion.
    J. Coulson, 617(TLS):28Mar86-336
Keller, B. Black Wolf.*
    J. Polk, 102(CanL):Fall85-120
Keller, E.F. A Feeling for the Organism.
    S. Bernstein, 42(AR):Spring85-242
    C.R. Grontkowski, 486:Jun85-323
Keller, E.F. Reflections on Gender and
    Science.*
    P.S.M., 185:Jul86-895
Keller, H. The Great Haydn Quartets.
    W. Mellers, 617(TLS):5Sep86-957
Keller, J.E. and R.P. Kinkade. Iconog-
    raphy in Medieval Spanish Literature.
    H. Goldberg, 238:Mar85-64
    S.G. Nichols, 304(JHP):Winter85-163
Keller, U. - see "August Sander: Citizens
    of the Twentieth Century"
Keller-Bauer, F. Metaphorisches Verstehen.
    J-P. Van Noppen, 353:Vol23No3-502
Kellerman, J. Shrunken Heads.
    T.J. Binyon, 617(TLS):13Jun86-646
Kelletat, A.F. Herder und die Weltliter-
    atur.
    N. Gabriel, 52:Band20Heft3-311
Kelley, K. His Way.
    J. Crace, 617(TLS):31Oct86-1228
    B.G. Harrison, 441:2Nov86-13
Kelley, M. - see Milton, J.
Kelley, P. and B.A. Coley, comps. The
    Browning Collections.*
    A. Allsop, 503:Autumn84-143
    T. Hofmann, 78(BC):Spring85-107
    M. Smith, 541(RES):Aug85-445
Kelling, H.D. and C.L. Preston. A KWIC
    Concordance to Jonathan Swift's "A Tale
    of a Tub," "The Battle of the Books,"
    and "A Discourse Concerning the Mechani-
    cal Operation of the Spirit, A Fragment."
    M. Shinagel, 566:Spring86-197
Kellner, D. Herbert Marcuse and the
    Crisis of Marxism.
    T.B., 185:Apr86-681

Kellogg, F.R. The Formative Essays of
    Justice Holmes.
    J.D. Moreno, 619:Winter85-147
Kelly, D. Chrétien de Troyes.
    A. Vanderheyden, 356(LR):Aug85-224
Kelly, F.J. and H.M. What They Really
    Teach You at the Harvard Business School.
    K. Conlin, 441:26Oct86-38
Kelly, H.A. Canon Law and the Archpriest
    of Hita.
    J.K. Walsh, 238:Dec85-767
Kelly, J. Women, History and Theory.
    G.R. Elton, 31(ASch):Autumn85-549
    V. Held, 185:Apr86-652
Kelly, J., with E. Domville - see Yeats,
    W.B.
Kelly, J.N.D. The Oxford Dictionary of
    Popes.
    O. Chadwick, 617(TLS):9May86-494
Kelly, O. Community, Art and the State.
    B. Roberts, 381:Dec85-548
Kelly, R. George Du Maurier.
    L. Ormond, 637(VS):Winter85-342
Kelly, R.G., ed. Children's Periodicals
    of the United States.
    E. Keyser, 534(RALS):Spring83-79
Kelly, S. A Long Way from Heaven.
    S. Altinel, 617(TLS):21Feb86-198
Kelly, W.P. Plotting America's Past.
    J.F. Beard, 27(AL):Mar85-157
Kelly, W.W. Deference and Defiance in
    Nineteenth-Century Japan.
    A. Waswo, 617(TLS):22Aug86-908
Kelman, J., A. Owens and A. Gray. Lean
    Tales.*
    D.J. Taylor, 176:Jan86-54
Kelsall, M. Christopher Marlowe.*
    J. Weil, 402(MLR):Oct85-904
Kelsay, I.T. Joseph Brant, 1743-1807.
    R. Aquila, 656(WMQ):Jul85-415
    F.P. Prucha, 377:Mar85-53
Kelton, E. Stand Proud.
    D.C. Grover, 649(WAL):Aug85-180
Kelton, E. The Time It Never Rained.
    L. Clayton, 649(WAL):Feb86-362
Kelvin, N. - see Morris, W.
Kelvin, P. and J.E. Jarrett. Unemployment.
    R.E. Pahl, 617(TLS):14Mar86-284
Kemal, Y. Das Lied der Tausand Stiere.
    S. Kleinmichel, 654(WB):1/1985-119
Kemal, Y. Salman le Solitaire.
    H. Cronel, 450(NRF):Feb85-110
Kemal, Y. The Sea-Crossed Fisherman.*
    J. Mellors, 364:Jul85-97
    J. Updike, 442(NY):6Jan86-84
Kemble, F.A. Journal of a Residence on a
    Georgian Plantation in 1838-1839. (J.A.
    Scott, ed)
    T. Bonner, Jr., 392:Fall85-477
Kemp, B.J. and R.S. Merrillees, with E.
    Edel. Minoan Pottery in Second Millen-
    nium Egypt.
    P. Warren, 123:Vol35No1-147
Kemp, I. Tippett.
    P. Dickinson, 410(M&L):Jul85-245
    M. Hayes, 607:Mar85-33
    J. Warrack, 415:Jan85-28
Kemp, J.R. - see "Lewis Hine: Photographs
    of Child Labor in the New South"
Kemp, P. Binding Twine.*
    B. Pirie, 102(CanL):Summer85-181
Kemp, P. The Strauss Family.
    A. Lamb, 415:Dec85-733

[continued]

Kevles, B. Females of the Species.
R. Cherry, 441:5Oct86-52
S.J. Gould, 453(NYRB):25Sep86-47
442(NY):21Jul86-94
Keyes, C.F. and E.V. Daniel, eds. Karma.*
P. Richman, 293(JASt):Feb85-429
Keyes, D. Unveiling Claudia.
J. Quinlan, 441:24Aug86-19
Keyes, G.S. Esaias van de Velde 1587-1630.*
K.J. Hellerstedt, 600:Vol 15No3/4-231
Keyes, R. Surimono.
U. Roberts, 60:Mar-Apr85-127
de Keyser, E. Degas.
A.A. McLees, 207(FR):Apr86-831
R.T., 90:Aug85-545
Keyser, S.J., ed. Recent Transformational
Studies in European Languages.
N.L. Corbett, 545(RPh):Aug85-80
Keyssar, A. Out of Work.
M. Kazin, 617(TLS):17Oct86-1170
A. Kessler-Harris, 441:4May86-36
Keyssar, H. Feminist Theatre.*
J. Breslauer, 609:Winter85-89
Kezich, L. Composition with Dark Centre.
J. Davies, 617(TLS):14Nov86-1290
Khachikyan, M.L. Khurritskij i Urartskij
Jazyki.
J.A.C. Greppin, 617(TLS):21Nov86-1305
Khammaan Khonkhai. The Teachers of Mad
Dog Swamp.
H.L. Lefferts, Jr., 293(JASt):Feb85-468
Kharma, N. A Contrastive Analysis of the
Use of Verb Forms in English and Arabic.*
M.R. Zughoul, 257(IRAL):Nov85-338
Khawam, R.R. - see "Les Aventures de Sind-
bad le marin"
Khlebnikov, V. The King of Time.* (C.
Douglas, ed)
P. France, 617(TLS):11Jul86-768
M. Perloff, 29(APR):Jan/Feb86-37
Imam Khomeini. Islam and Revolution.*
(H. Algar, ed and trans)
C. Heywood, 617(TLS):21Mar86-293
Khonkhai, K. - see under Khammaan Khonkhai
Kiam, V. Going for It!
M. Walton, 441:8Jun86-37
von Kibéd, A.V. - see under Varga von
Kibéd, A.
Kibler, W.W. An Introduction to Old
French.
R.F. Cook, 399(MLJ):Autumn85-306
D.A. Kibbee, 207(FR):May86-1016
Kibler, W.W. - see Chrétien de Troyes
Kidder, T. House.*
D. Johnson, 453(NYRB):4Dec86-3
Kido Takayoshi. The Diary of Kido Takayo-
shi.* (Vol 1)
M.W. Steele, 293(JASt):May85-613
Kieckhefer, R. Unquiet Souls.
U. Stargardt, 481(PQ):Fall85-593
Kiefer, F. Fortune and Elizabethan Trag-
edy.*
C.A. Hallett, 301(JEGP):Jul85-426
J. Margeson, 405(MP):Feb86-307
E. Pechter, 401(MLQ):Jun84-196
Kielland, A.L. Redaktør Alexander L. Kiel-
land — en svøpe for byen. (E.O. Risa,
ed)
F. Hermundsgaard, 563(SS):Autumn85-459
Kiely, B. Nothing Happens in Carmincross.*
C.C. O'Brien, 453(NYRB):8May86-42

Kienast, D. Augustus: Prinzeps und Mon-
arch.
A. Wallace-Hadrill, 313:Vol75-245
Kierans, E. Globalism and the Nation-
State.
G.W., 102(CanL):Winter84-189
Kierimo, K. Observationes de Latinitate
Porthaniana.
B. Löfstedt, 439(NM):1985/1-143
Kiernan, B., ed. Burchett Reporting the
Other Side of the World 1939-1983.
J. Luxmoore, 617(TLS):19Dec86-1419
Kiernan, R.F. American Writing Since 1945.
S.E. Grace, 106:Winter85-483
Kiersh, E. Where Are You Now, Bo Diddley?
P. Pullman, 441:2Nov86-27
Kieser, R. Erzwungene Symbiose.*
A. Arnold, 564:Sep85-240
"A Kikuyu Market Literature." (P.R.
Bennett, trans)
S. Gikandi, 538(RAL):Winter85-633
Kilian, L. Zum Ursprung der Indogermanen.
W.P. Schmid, 260(IF):Band90-278
Killingley, S-Y. The Grammatical Hier-
archy of Malayan Cantonese.
S. De Lancey, 350:Mar86-223
Killy, W. Schreibweisen — Leseweisen.
J. Kiermeier-Debre, 224(GRM):Band35
Heft4-466
K.E. Webb, 221(GQ):Spring85-269
Killy, W. and C. Perels, eds. Die
deutsche Literatur. (Vol 4, Pt 2)
M. Oehme, 654(WB):8/1985-1405
Kilroy, J.F., ed. The Irish Short Story.
F. Kersnowski, 573(SSF):Spring85-246
K. Marre, 395(MFS):Summer85-377
Kilroy-Silk, R. Hard Labour.
P. Clarke, 617(TLS):7Nov86-1240
Kiltz, H. Das erotische Mahl.
U. Schulz-Buschhaus, 52:Band20Heft1-95
Kilvert, R.F. Kilvert's Diary: 1870-1879.
(W. Plomer, ed)
M. Howard, 441:7Dec86-14
Kim, J-S. Franz Kafka.
E. Schlant, 221(GQ):Summer85-428
Kimball, M. Firewater Pond.
A. Mobilio, 441:9Feb86-24
Kimbell, D.R.B. Verdi in the Age of Ital-
ian Romanticism.*
412:Aug/Nov83-292
Kime, W.R. and A.B. Myers - see Irving, W.
Kincaid, J. Annie John.*
639(VQR):Summer85-93
Kincaid, J.R. and A.J. Kuhn, eds. Victor-
ian Literature and Society.*
D. Hawes, 155:Summer85-117
W.A. Madden, 637(VS):Autumn85-155
Kindelan, M.V. - see under Valasco Kinde-
lan, M.
Kinder, A.G. Spanish Protestants and
Reformers in the Sixteenth Century.*
C.P. Thompson, 86(BHS):Jul85-295
Kindermann, G-K., ed. Sun Yat-sen.
F.G. Chan, 293(JASt):Nov84-174
Kindermann, H. Das Theaterpublikum der
Renaissance. (Vol 1)
G. Flaherty, 610:Summer85-162
al-Kindī, Y.I. Al-Kindī's Metaphysics.
(A.L. Ivry, ed)
H.H. Biesterfeldt, 318(JAOS):Jul-Sep84-595
Kindler, A. The Coinage of Bostra.
C.E. King, 123:Vol35No2-424

Kindstrand, J.F. The Stylistic Evaluation of Aeschines in Antiquity.*
   D.M. MacDowell, 123:Vol35No1-182
Kindstrand, J.F. - see Koolmeister, R. and T. Thalmeister
King, B. Seventeenth-Century English Literature.
   J.D. Canfield, 566:Spring86-208
   R. Ellrodt, 189(EA):Apr-Jun86-241
King, B. Women of the Future.*
   V. Aarons, 395(MFS):Summer85-470
King, D.Y. Interest Groups and Political Linkage in Indonesia, 1800-1965.
   D. Hindley, 293(JASt):Nov84-246
King, F. One is a Wanderer.*
   J. Mellors, 362:9Jan86-29
   R. Robinson, 441:2Mar86-24
   D.J. Taylor, 176:Jun86-54
King, F., ed. Twenty Stories.*
   D.J. Taylor, 176:Jan86-54
King, F. - see Hearn, L.
King, J. William Cowper.
   W.B. Carnochan, 617(TLS):11Jul86-765
King, J. and C. Ryskamp - see Cowper, W.
King, J.N. English Reformation Literature.*
   P. Collinson, 366:Spring85-137
   N.H. Keeble, 447(N&Q):Mar84-107
   D. Norbrook, 541(RES):Feb85-74
King, K. Trial by Jury.
   H. Krasnick, 608:Sep86-545
King, L.L. None But a Blockhead.
   R. Rosen, 441:23Feb86-20
King, M.L. Venetian Humanism in an Age of Patrician Dominance.
   B.S. Pullan, 617(TLS):22Aug86-922
King, M.L. and A. Rabil, Jr., eds. Her Immaculate Hand.
   B.G. Kohl, 551(RenQ):Spring85-109
   J. Krochalis, 377:Mar85-48
King, M.L., Jr. A Testament of Hope. (J.M. Washington, ed)
   C. Sitton, 441:16Feb86-16
   442(NY):24Feb86-105
King, N. Abel Gance.*
   J. Forbes, 208(FS):Apr85-240
King, P. The Viceroy's Fall.
   P. Johnson, 362:5Jun86-24
   J. Ure, 617(TLS):27Jun86-714
King, P. - see Lord Curzon
King, S. It.
   T.R. Edwards, 453(NYRB):18Dec86-58
   R. Kaveney, 617(TLS):5Dec86-1368
   L. Rose, 61:Sep86-102
   W. Wager, 441:24Aug86-9
King, W.N. Hamlet's Search for Meaning.*
   J.L. Halio, 702:Vol 17-280
King-Hele, D. Erasmus Darwin and the Romantic Poets.
   G. Beer, 617(TLS):19Sep86-1036
King-Hele, D. - see Darwin, E.
Kingson, M.H. The Woman Warrior.
   J. Rothfork, 448:Vol23No2-122
Kingston-Mann, E. Lenin and the Problem of Marxist Peasant Revolution.*
   D.A.J. Macey, 550(RusR):Jan85-109
Kinmonth, E.H. The Self-Made Man in Meiji Japanese Thought.
   W.D. Kinzley, 293(JASt):Aug85-840
Kinnaird, J. William Hazlitt.
   J.C. Robinson, 536(Rev):Vol7-65

Kinnell, G. The Past.
   H. Beaver, 441:2Mar86-14
   M. Oliver, 344:Summer86-129
Kinnell, G. Walking Down the Stairs.
   R. McDowell, 249(HudR):Autumn85-514
Kinney, A.F. Flannery O'Connor's Library.
   R.H. Brinkmeyer, Jr., 392:Spring85-143
   M.J. Friedman, 268(IFR):Winter86-32
   W.J. Stuckey, 395(MFS):Winter85-749
Kinsella, T., ed and trans. The New Oxford Book of Irish Verse.
   D. Davis, 362:10Jul86-31
Kinsella, T. Songs of the Psyche. Her Vertical Smile.
   M. Hofmann, 617(TLS):30May86-585
Kinsella, T. - see "The Táin"
Kinsella, W.P. The Alligator Report.
   H. Marten, 441:5Jan86-16
Kinsella, W.P. The Iowa Baseball Confederacy.
   E. Asinof, 441:20Apr86-15
Kinsella, W.P. The Moccasin Telegraph and Other Stories.
   F.W. Kaye, 502(PrS):Spring85-103
Kinsella, W.P. The Thrill of the Grass.
   K. Kealy, 102(CanL):Summer85-168
   P. Lanthier, 99:Aug/Sep85-29
   R. Maggs, 198:Autumn85-106
Kinsey, M. Living Masters of Netsuke.
   V.G. Atchley, 60:Sep-Oct85-131
Kintgen, E.R. The Perception of Poetry.*
   R. Carter, 307:Dec85-210
Kintzler, C. Jean-Philippe Rameau.*
   C. Verba, 317:Spring85-169
Kiparsky, P. Explanation in Phonology.
   T. Bynon, 603:Vol9No2-283
   B.G. Hewitt, 361:Sep85-87
Kiple, K.F. The Caribbean Slave.
   J. Ward, 617(TLS):17Jan86-66
Kipling, R. Early Verse by Rudyard Kipling, 1879-99. (A. Rutherford, ed)
   P. Johnson, 362:3Apr86-26
Kipling, R. Kipling's India. (T. Pinney, ed)
   P-L. Adams, 61:Apr86-130
   N. Andrew, 362:2Jan86-24
   G. Tindall, 617(TLS):31Jan86-107
Kipling, R. "O Beloved Kids." (E.L. Gilbert, ed)
   H-P. Breuer, 395(MFS):Summer85-338
   N. Page, 177(ELT):Vol28No3-308
Király, G. Dosztojevskij és az orosz próza.
   L. Tikos, 574(SEEJ):Winter85-476
Király, G. and Á. Kovács, comps. Poetika.
   J. Graffy, 575(SEER):Apr85-286
Kirby, H.L., Jr., ed. Selected Proceedings: The Third Louisiana Conference on Hispanic Languages and Literatures: 1982.
   E.T. Aylward, 238:Dec85-780
Kirby, W.C. Germany and Republican China.
   P.M. Coble, Jr., 293(JASt):May85-594
Kirchhoff, B. Mexikanische Novelle.
   W. Winkler, 384:Jun85-522
Kirchhoff, F. John Ruskin.*
   J. Loesberg, 506(PSt):May85-91
   F.G. Townsend, 637(VS):Winter86-342
Kiriakopoulos, G.C. Ten Days to Destiny.*
   D. Hunt, 617(TLS):30May86-582
Kirk, G.S., J.E. Raven and M. Schofield. The Presocratic Philosophers. (2nd ed)
   A. Barker, 84:Dec85-465

[continued]

Klausenburger, J. French Liaison and Linguistic Theory.
D.J. Napoli, 350:Sep86-721
Klausenburger, J. Morphologization.
J.L. Bybee, 545(RPh):Feb85-355
Klee, E., ed. Dokumente zur "Euthanasie."
H. Pross, 384:Sep/Oct85-914
Klee, E. "Euthanasie" im NS-Staat.
H. Pross, 384:Sep/Oct85-914
Klein, A.M. Beyond Sambation.* (M.W. Steinberg and U. Caplan, eds)
M.S. Madoff, 178:Mar85-102
L. Shohet, 102(CanL):Spring85-117
Klein, C. The Heart in the Casket.
A.M. Davidon, 441:20Apr86-22
Klein, D. and W. Lloyd, eds. The History of Glass.*
G. Wills, 39:Jan85-70
Klein, E. Semantic and Pragmatic Indeterminacy in English Non-Finite Verb Complementation.
P. Sgall, 361:Jan85-174
Klein, F-J. Lexematische Untersuchungen zum französischen Verbalwortschatz im Sinnbezirk von Wahrnehmung und Einschätzung.*
R. Martin, 553(RLiR):Jul-Dec85-491
Klein, H.S. African Slavery in Latin America and the Caribbean.
V.P. Franklin, 441:23Nov86-24
Klein, M. The Life and Legend of Jay Gould.
L. Auchincloss, 453(NYRB):29May86-35
J. Train, 441:29Jun86-29
Klein, M.L. The Fragment-Targums of the Pentateuch According to their Extant Sources.
E.G. Clarke, 318(JAOS):Apr-Jun84-373
Klein, P. Endzeiterwartung und Ritterideologie.
P. Binski and G. Henderson, 90:Sep85-625
Klein, P.D. Certainty.*
J. Harrison, 479(PhQ):Jan85-95
Klein, R., ed and trans. Die Romrede des Aelius Aristides.*
L. Pernot, 555:Vol59fasc1-122
Klein, W. William Klein: Photographs.
M. Nesbit, 59:Mar85-132
Klein, W. Zweitspracherwerb.
G.A. Everett, Jr., 399(MLJ):Summer85-187
Klein-Andreu, F., ed. Discourse Perspectives on Syntax.*
B. Comrie, 350:Mar86-163
Kleinbauer, M. Montaigne.
L. van Delft, 535(RHL):Jan/Feb85-79
Kleinbaum, A.W. The War Against the Amazons.
W. Schleiner, 149(CLS):Winter85-558
Kleine, G. Ninon und Hermann Hesse.
M. Boulby, 301(JEGP):Jan85-93
R. Koester, 133:Band17Heft3/4-370
Kleine, P. Zur Figurencharakteristik in Shakespeares "Henry VI."
H-J. Weckermann, 72:Band222Heft1-184
Kleinfield, S. A Machine Called Imdomitable.
G. Fjermedal, 441:9Feb86-20
Kleinfield, S. Staying at the Top.
E. Bailey, 441:26Oct86-31

Kleinman, A. and B. Good, eds. Culture and Depression.
R. Littlewood, 617(TLS):16May86-542
von Kleist, H., L. Tieck and E.T.A. Hoffmann. Six German Romantic Tales. (R. Taylor, trans)
S. Plaice, 617(TLS):19Sep86-1036
"Kleist-Jahrbuch 1980."* "Kleist-Jahrbuch 1981/82."* "Kleist-Jahrbuch 1983." (H.J. Kreutzer, ed of all)
D.C. Riechel, 680(ZDP):Band104Heft2-301
Klemm, I. Fiktionale Rede als Problem der sprachanalytischen Philosophie.
A. Schwarz, 196:Band26Heft3/4-364
Klemp, P.J. - see Sheppard, S.
Klenin, E. Animacy in Russian.*
C.V. Chvany, 279:Vol29-185
G. Corbett, 402(MLR):Apr85-506
F.E. Knowles, 575(SEER):Jul85-431
Klett, M. and others. Second View.
L. Milazzo, 584(SWR):Spring85-262
Klibbe, J.H. Lorda's "Impresiones y paisajes."*
L.T. González-del-Valle, 240(HR):Winter85-113
Kligman, G. Căluş.*
T. Buckland, 203:Vol96No1-129
Klima, L. Je suis la Volonté Absolue (Métaphilosophiques).
T. Cordellier, 450(NRF):Feb85-95
Klimov, A. Veilleurs de nuit.
C. Gratton, 154:Spring85-165
Klimov, G.A. Principy kontensivnoj tipologii.
W.R. Schmalstieg, 215(GL):Vol25No1-60
Kline, G.C. The Last Courtly Lover.*
P. van de Kamp, 272(IUR):Spring85-108
Kline, M. Mathematics and the Search for Knowledge.*
D. Pedge, 529(QQ):Winter85-883
Klinkenborg, V. Making Hay.
S. Hubbell, 441:12Oct86-20
Klinkott, M. Islamische Baukunst in Afghanisch-Sīstān.*
R. Hillenbrand, 59:Jun85-265
Klinkowitz, J. The Self-Apparent Word.*
M.J. Friedman, 27(AL):Mar85-184
S.G. Kellman, 395(MFS):Summer85-449
Klinkowitz, J. and J. Knowlton. Peter Handke and the Postmodern Transformation.*
T.H. Falk, 115:Spring85-277
R. Voris, 221(GQ):Summer85-483
Klitgaard, R. Choosing Elites.*
639(VQR):Autumn85-134
Kłoczowski, J., ed. The Christian Community of Medieval Poland.
P.W. Knoll, 497(PolR):Vol30No4-449
Kloetzli, R. Buddhist Cosmology.
P. Richman, 293(JASt):Nov84-231
Kloocke, K. Benjamin Constant.*
U. Schulz-Buschhaus, 547(RF):Band97Heft1-96
Klopstock, F.G. Werke und Briefe. (Werke IV, Vol 4) (E. Höpker-Herberg, ed)
H.T. Betteridge, 402(MLR):Apr85-497
Klose, K. Russia and the Russians.*
P. Reddaway, 617(TLS):3Jan86-7
Klosko, G. The Development of Plato's Political Theory.
T.J. Saunders, 617(TLS):15Aug86-881

Kloss, W. Treasures from the National Museum of American Art.
S.M. Halpern, 441:27Apr86-22
Klotz, H. Die Ornamentik der Klavier- und Orgelwerke von Johann Sebastian Bach.
P. Williams, 401(M&L):Oct85-402
Klotz, H., ed. Postmodern Visions.
A. Plattus, 441:16Mar86-20
Kluge, G., ed. Studien zur Dramatik in der Bundesrepublik Deutschland.
L.D. Lindsay, 221(GQ):Spring85-307
Kluger, R., with P. Kluger. The Paper.
D. Shaw, 441:26Oct86-13
442(NY):17Nov86-153
Klussmann, P.G. and H. Mohr, eds. Deutsche Misere einst und jetzt.
D. Sevin, 133:Band17Heft3/4-376
Klussmann, P.G. and H. Mohr - see "Jahr- buch zur Literatur in der DDR, 3"
Knaän, D. Towards a Definition of Art.
L. Aagaard-Mogensen, 290(JAAC): Summer86-419
Knape, J. "Historie" im Mittelalter und früher Neuzeit.
D.R. Kelley, 589:Oct85-987
Knapp, B.L. Andrée Chedid.*
R. Linkhorn, 188(ECr):Spring85-95
S. Petit, 345(KRQ):Vol32No1-108
C. Slawy-Sutton, 207(FR):May86-988
M.J. Worton, 402(MLR):Jan85-178
Knapp, B.L. Edgar Allan Poe.
J.A.L. Lemay, 445(NCF):Mar86-487
Knapp, B.L. Word/Image/Psyche.
M.T. Braun, 446(NCFS):Fall-Winter85/86- 181
Knapp, B.L. - see Mumford, L. and D. Lieb- owitz
Knapp, P.A. - see "Assays"
Knapp, P.A. and M.A. Stugrin - see "Assays"
Knapp, R.C. Roman Córdoba.*
N. Mackie, 313:Vol75-288
Knapp, S. Personification and the Sublime.
R. Ashton, 617(TLS):19Sep86-1035
Knapp-Potthoff, A. and K. Knapp. Fremd- sprachenlernen und -lehren.*
F. Abel, 547(RF):Band97Heft4-454
Knecht, H.H. La logique chez Leibniz.
M. Imbeault, 154:Spring85-181
P. Schulthess, 706:Band17Heft1-108
Knepler, H. and M., eds. Crossing Cul- tures.
M. Kiniry, 126(CCC):Dec85-501
Knerr, A.D. - see Shelley, P.B.
Knigge, A. Puškins Verserzählung "Der Eherne Reiter" in der russischen Kritik.
A. McMillin, 575(SEER):Oct85-584
W. Vickery, 279:Vol30-187
Knight, A.E. Aspects of Genre in Late Medieval French Drama.*
K.M. Ashley, 589:Apr85-420
Knight, G.W. Shakespeare's Dramatic Chal- lenge.
K. Tetzeli von Rosador, 156(ShJW): Jahrbuch1985-229
Knight, N. and S. Priebatsch. Ndebele Images.
M. Adams, 2(AfrA):Nov84-88
Knight, S. Arthurian Literature and Soci- ety.
M. Lambert, 402(MLR):Oct85-893
R. Morse, 382(MAE):1985/2-347

Knight, S. Form and Ideology in Crime Fiction.*
W.W. Stowe, 107(CRCL):Sep85-433
Knightley, P. The Second Oldest Profes- sion.
K. Jeffrey, 362:20Nov86-28
Knights, L.C. Selected Essays in Criti- cism.*
C. Belsey, 677(YES):Vol 15-265
Knilli, F. and others. Jud Süss.
M. Silbermann, 221(GQ):Summer85-490
Knobel, L. The Faber Guide to Twentieth- Century Architecture: Britain and Northern Europe.*
J.M. Richards, 46:Nov85-104
Knobloch, E., I.S. Louhivaara and J. Winkler, eds. Zum Werk Leonhard Eulers.
H-J. Hess, 706:Band17Heft1-87
Knobloch, J. Sprache und Religion. (Vol 1, Pts 1 and 2)
R. Kahane, 545(RPh):Aug85-90
Knopf, J. Brecht-Handbuch: Lyrik, Prosa, Schriften.
J. Milfull, 67:May85-72
Knorr-Cetina, K. Die Fabrikation von Erkenntnis.
J. Koepp, 384:Apr85-338
Knorr-Cetina, K.D. The Manufacture of Knowledge.*
T.V. Upton, 543:Mar85-647
Knott, A. It's Knott Cricket.
A. Ross, 617(TLS):3Jan86-21
Knott, K. My Sweet Lord.
A.D. Jones, 617(TLS):23May86-558
Knowland, A.S. W.B. Yeats.
B. Dolan, 305(JIL):May85-76
Knowles, A.V. - see Turgenev, I.S.
Knowles, C. Les Enseignements de Théodore Paléologue.*
W. Rothwell, 208(FS):Oct85-450
Knowles, J. The Private Life of Axie Reed.
W. Schott, 441:11May86-19
Knox, C. The House Party.*
455:Mar85-64
Knox, D. The Korean War.
D. Middleton, 441:2Feb86-17
Knox, G. Piazzetta.*
A. Binion, 380:Winter84-450
K. Garlick, 39:Jan85-69
D. Irwin, 83:Spring85-122
Knühl, B. Die Komik in Heinrich Witten- wilers "Ring" im Vergleich zu den Fastnachtspielen des 15. Jahrhunderts.
O. Ehrismann, 224(GRM):Band35Heft1-103
Knust, H. Bertolt Brecht: Leben des Galilei.*
R.C. Reimer, 406:Fall85-378
Kobal, V. People Will Talk.
B. Shulgasser, 441:9Feb86-9
D. Thomson, 18:Jun86-61
Kobler, J.F. Ernest Hemingway.
295(JML):Nov85-494
Koblitz, A.H. A Convergence of Lives.*
B. Engel, 550(RusR):Jul85-303
Koc, R.A. The German Gesellschaftsroman at the Turn of the Century.
H-G. Richert, 133:Band18Heft1-90
Koch, C.J. The Doubleman.*
C. Fein, 441:23Feb86-22
P. Lewis, 364:Apr/May85-148
P. Lewis, 565:Summer85-50
S. McKernan, 381:Dec85-432

Koch, D.M.  Malfalda y sus amigos.
   V. Benmaman, 399(MLJ):Summer85-210
Koch, E.I., with W. Rauch.  Politics.*
   E.M. Breindel, 129:Mar86-70
Koch, G.M.  Zum Verhältnis von Dichtung
   und Geschichtsschreibung.
   D. Mehl, 156(ShJW):Jahrbuch1985-259
Koch, H.C.  Introductory Essay on Composi-
   tion.  (C.V. Palisca, ed)
   E.R. Sisman, 308:Fall85-341
   P. Whitmore, 410(M&L):Apr85-149
Koch, K.  On the Edge.
   J. Ash, 441:20Apr86-19
Koch, K.  Selected Poems, 1950-1982.
   J. Hollander, 676(YR):Summer85-vi
   R. McDowell, 249(HudR):Winter86-683
   P. Stitt, 219(GaR):Fall85-635
Koch, L.  Gli scaldi.
   F.R. Psaki, 563(SS):Autumn85-461
Koch, M.  Wird und Linguistik der Bedeu-
   tung gerecht?
   L. Seppänen, 439(NM):1985/4-593
Koch, S.  The Bachelors' Bride.
   E. Fishel, 441:23Nov86-11
   A.H.G. Phillips, 617(TLS):3Oct86-1114
   442(NY):13Oct86-156
Koch, U.E. and P-P. Sagave.  "Le Chari-
   vari."
   A. Kleinert, 224(GRM):Band35Heft4-469
Kochan, T.A., H.C. Katz and R.B. McKersie.
   The Transformation of American Indus-
   trial Relations.
   G. Easterbrook, 441:26Oct86-34
Kochanek, S.A.  Interest Groups and Devel-
   opment.
   L. Ziring, 293(JASt):May85-639
Kochman, T.  Black and White Styles in
   Conflict.*
   D.L. Lawton, 205(ForL):Aug84-176
Kocka, J.  Facing Total War.
   G. Best, 617(TLS):10Jan86-32
Kockel, V.  Die Grabbauten von dem Herkul-
   aner Tor in Pompeji.*
   D.E.E. and F.S. Kleiner, 576:Mar85-82
Kockelmans, J.J.  Heidegger on Art and Art
   Works.
   R. Lilly, 290(JAAC):Summer86-411
Kocks, D.  Jean-Baptiste Carpeaux.
   D. Irwin, 161(DUJ):Jun84-278
Kocourek, R.  La Langue Française de la
   Technique et de la Science.*
   J. Heslot, 209(FM):Apr85-124
Koda, P.S. - see Walker, E.
Koda, R. - see under Rohan Koda
Kodjo, J.  ... Et demain, l'Afrique.
   H. Cronel, 450(NRF):Sep85-101
Koebner, T., ed.  Zwischen den Weltkriegen.
   K.H. Kiefer, 343:Heft11-112
Koelb, C.  The Incredulous Reader.*
   W.E. Broman, 478:Apr85-113
   C.S. Brown, 569(SR):Spring85-288
   R. Chambers, 301(JEGP):Oct85-538
   R. Craig, 290(JAAC):Winter85-197
   B. Duyfhuizen, 435:Fall85-67
   R.C. Holub, 149(CLS):Winter85-551
   R.B. Kershner, Jr., 219(GaR):Winter85-
   892
Koen, K.  Through a Glass Darkly.
   P-L. Adams, 61:Nov86-140
   E. Jong, 441:7Sep86-13
Koenig, J-P.  Malagasy Customs and Pro-
   verbs.
   L. Haring, 538(RAL):Fall85-420

Koenig, Y., ed and trans.  Le Papyrus
   Boulaq 6.
   V.L. Davis, 318(JAOS):Apr-Jun84-359
Koerner, K., ed.  Linguistics and Evolu-
   tionary Theory.
   P. Beade, 320(CJL):Spring85-77
Koestler, A. and C.  Stranger on the
   Square.
   J. Russell, 396(ModA):Summer85-257
Koethe, J.  The Late Wisconsin Spring.*
   M. Jarman, 249(HudR):Summer85-337
   P. Stitt, 219(GaR):Summer85-414
   639(VQR):Spring85-57
Kogan, V.  The Flowers of Fiction.*
   E. Smyth, 535(RHL):May/Jun85-519
Koh, J-M.  Major Themes in the Contempor-
   ary American Novel.
   Y. Park, 395(MFS):Summer85-433
Kohák, E.  The Embers and the Stars.*
   T.F. Murphy, 258:Dec85-435
   P.H. Spader, 543:Jun85-888
Kohansky, M.  The Disreputable Profession.
   J. Beryl, 615(TJ):May85-251
Kohfeldt, M.L.  Lady Gregory.*
   M.R. Callaghan, 305(JIL):Jan85-50
   W.E. Hall, 637(VS):Spring86-493
   T. West, 272(IUR):Autumn85-249
Kohl-Larsen, L., comp and trans.  Das Haus
   der Trolle.
   L. Bäckman, 64(Arv):Vol39-217
Köhler, E.  Literatursoziologische Per-
   spektiven.  (H. Krauss, ed)
   W. Rothwell, 208(FS):Apr85-187
Kohler, K.J.  Einführung in die Phonetik
   des Deutschen.
   M. Philipp, 685(ZDL):2/1985-229
Köhler, L. and H. Saner - see Arendt, H.
   and K. Jaspers
Kohli, M. and G. Robert, eds.  Biographie
   und soziale Wirklichkeit.
   H. Elbeshausen, 462(OL):Vol40No2-171
   A. Lehmann, 196:Band26Heft1/2-167
   M. Ruthe, 654(WB):11/1985-1932
Kohlmaier, G. and B. von Sartory.  Houses
   of Glass.
   P. Goldberger, 441:7Dec86-16
Kohnen, J.  Theodor Gottlieb von Hippel,
   1741-1796.
   T.F. Sellner, 221(GQ):Spring85-278
Kohrt, M.  Phonetik, Phonologie und die
   "Relativität der Verhältnisse."
   B.J. Koekkoek, 350:Jun86-457
   E.F.K. Koerner, 660(Word):Dec85-258
Kojo Laing, B.  Search Sweet Country.
   B. Tonkin, 362:4Sep86-22
"Kokinshū."*  (L.R. Rodd, with M.C. Hen-
   kenius, eds and trans)
   T.H. Rohlich, 407(MN):Autumn85-352
Kokoschka, O.  Briefe.  (Vols 1 and 2)  (O.
   Kokoschka and H. Spielmann, eds)
   N. Lynton, 617(TLS):3Oct86-1086
Kokoschka, O.  Mirages du passé.
   R. Millet, 450(NRF):May85-102
Kolakowski, L.  Religion: If there is no
   God ...
   G.D. Marino, 543:Sep84-126
Kolb, F.  Die Stadt im Altertum.
   N.B. Rankov, 123:Vol135No2-406
Kolb, P. - see Proust, M.
Kolbenhoff, W.  Schellingstrasse 48.
   H. Schwab-Felisch, 384:May85-430

Kolin, P.C., ed.  Shakespeare in the South.*
  R.C. Fulton, 570(SQ):Autumn85-362
  J.S. Mebane, 583:Winter86-182
  P.D. Shaw, 615(TJ):Oct85-391
  M.R. Winchell, 580(SCR):Fall85-119
Kolker, R.P.  Bernardo Bertolucci.
  P. Brunette, 18:Jul/Aug86-75
  G. Johnson, 441:25May86-15
Kolko, G.  Anatomy of a War.  (British title: Vietnam.)
  D.M. Oshinsky, 441:19Jan86-8
  C. Thorne, 617(TLS):19Sep86-1021
Koller, A.M.  The Theatre Duke.*
  M. Carlson, 612(ThS):May85-89
  R.K. Sarlós, 615(TJ):May85-240
  A. Vivis, 157:No156-50
  S. Williams, 610:Autumn85-249
Kolodny, A.  The Land Before Her.*
  M.K. Brady, 651(WHR):Winter85-376
  U. Brumm, 165(EAL):Winter85/86-271
  C.N. Davidson, 115:Fall84/Winter85-144
  M. Graulich, 649(WAL):Feb86-356
  C.L. Karcher, 301(JEGP):Apr85-286
Koltès, B-M.  La Fuite à cheval, très loin dans la ville.
  N.S. Hellerstein, 207(FR):Mar86-648
Koltès, B-M.  Night Just Before the Forest [and] Struggle of the Dogs and the Black.
  S. Dieckman, 615(TJ):Mar85-123
Kolve, V.A.  Chaucer and the Imagery of Narrative.*
  J.A. Burrow, 184(EIC):Jan85-76
  R. Edwards, 219(GaR):Winter85-871
  J.H. Fisher, 301(JEGP):Jul85-415
  B. McMullen, 191(ELN):Dec85-69
  M. Mudrick, 249(HudR):Spring85-133
  L. Patterson, 639(VQR):Autumn85-727
  D. Pearsall, 179(ES):Feb85-80
  N.P. Pope, 377:Nov85-193
  E.S. Sklar, 141:Summer85-312
  M. Stevens, 401(MLQ):Sep84-287
Komanecky, M. and V. Butero, eds.  The Folding Image.
  A.A. McLees, 207(FR):Dec85-323
Komarovsky, M.  Women in College.*
  639(VQR):Autumn85-134
Komesu, O.  The Double Perspective of Yeats's Aesthetics.
  P. van de Kamp, 272(IUR):Spring85-108
Komlos, J.  The Habsburg Monarchy as a Customs Union.
  M.E.F. Jones, 161(DUJ):Dec84-106
Koné, A., G.D. Lezou and J. Mlanhoro, eds.  Anthologie de la littérature ivoirienne.
  R. Pageard, 549(RLC):Jul-Sep85-373
Koneski, B.  A Historical Phonology of the Macedonian Language.
  C. Kramer, 574(SEEJ):Summer85-233
König, E.  Form und Funktion.
  H. Janssen, 260(IF):Band90-334
König, E.  Französische Buchmalerei um 1450.
  J.J.G. Alexander, 354:Jun85-179
König, H.  Die Spur führt nach Bayern.  Das mysteriöse Konzert.
  H. Taylor, 399(MLJ):Summer85-188
Koning, H.  Acts of Faith.
  P. Smelt, 617(TLS):25Apr86-453
Konishi, J.  A History of Japanese Literature.  (Vol 1) (E. Miner, ed)
  D.E. Mills, 407(MN):Autumn85-355
  M. Ury, 293(JASt):Aug85-842

Konka, R.  Histoire de la littérature camerounaise.
  E.O. Ako, 538(RAL):Winter85-628
Konrád, G.  Antipolitics.
  T.G. Ash, 453(NYRB):9Oct86-45
Konrad von Haslau.  Der Jüngling.  (W. Tauber, ed)
  W. Hofmeister, 602:Band16Heft2-281
Konstan, D.  Roman Comedy.*
  E. Segal, 124:Jan-Feb86-206
Konstantinović, Z., W. Anderson and W. Dietze, eds.  Classical Models in Literature/Les Modèles Classiques dans les Littératures/Klassische Modelle in der Literatur.*
  F. Meregalli, 107(CRCL):Sep85-481
Kontorini, V.  Inscriptions inédites relatives à l'histoire et aux cultes de Rhodes au IIe et au Ie av. J.C.: Rhodiaka I.
  L. Migeotte, 487:Winter85-400
Kontzi, R., ed.  Substrate und Superstrate in den romanischen Sprachen.*
  H. Meier, 72:Band222Heft1-206
  H-J. Niederehe, 159:Spring85-111
van der Kooi, J.  Volksverhalen in Friesland.
  H-J. Uther, 196:Band26Heft1/2-168
Koolmeister, R. and T. Thalmeister, comps.  An Index to Dio Chrysostomus.  (J.F. Kindstrand, ed)
  D.M. Schenkeveld, 394:Vol38fasc1/2-217
Koon, H.  Colley Cibber.
  P. Rogers, 617(TLS):18Jul86-789
Koontz, D.R.  Strangers.
  D. Kirk, 441:15Jun86-20
Koopman, A.  Misschien schrijk ik straks nog wel een klein versje.
  P.F. Schmitz, 204(FdL):Mar85-77
Koopmann, H.  Der klassisch-moderne Roman in Deutschland.
  S. Schürer, 221(GQ):Summer85-469
Koopmann, H.  Schiller-Forschung 1970-1980.
  A.J. Camigliano, 406:Fall85-356
Koopmans, J., ed.  Quatre Sermons Joyeux.
  G. Roques, 553(RLiR):Jan-Jun85-249
Kopanev, A.I.  Krest'ianstvo russkogo severa v XVI v.  Krest'iane russkogo severa v XVII v.
  D.H. Kaiser, 550(RusR):Jul85-296
Köpcke, K-M.  Untersuchungen zum Genussystem der deutschen Gegenwartssprache.
  T.F. Shannon, 350:Dec86-943
"Kopenhagener Beiträge zur Germanistischen Linguistik."  (Vols 3-14)
  H.H. Munske, 685(ZDL):2/1985-267
Kopff, E.C. - see Otis, B.
Köpke, W.  Lion Feuchtwanger.*
  M. Goth, 221(GQ):Fall85-630
Kopp, D.  Geschichte und Gesellschaft in den Dramen Christian Dietrich Grabbes.
  R.C. Cowen, 406:Fall85-361
Kopp, R. - see von Saar, F.
Koppen, E. and R. von Tiedemann, eds.  Wege zur Komparatistik.
  J. Strutz, 602:Band16Heft2-292
Kopper, J.  Die Stellung der "Kritik der reinen Vernunft" in der neueren Philosophie.
  J. Ferrari, 192(EP):Apr-Jun85-266
Koppisch, M.S.  The Dissolution of Character.
  L. van Delft, 535(RHL):Mar/Apr85-295

Koppitz, H-J. - see "Gutenberg-Jahrbuch 1985"
Körber, J., ed. Bibliographisches Lexikon der utopisch-phantastischen Literatur. (1st supp)
   R. Krämer, 196:Band26Heft3/4-365
Korboński, S. Polskie państwo podziemne. Between the Hammer and the Anvil.
   I. Nagurski, 497(PolR):Vol30No1-118
Korczak, J. King Matt the First.
   442(NY):21Apr86-124
"Korean Literary Works."
   D.R. McCann, 293(JASt):May85-625
Korff, F.W. Der komische Kierkegaard.
   L.J. Elders, 543:Mar85-649
   L.R. Wilkinson, 563(SS):Summer85-333
Korg, J. Browning and Italy.
   I.G., 506(PSt):Dec85-101
   P. Honan, 637(VS):Spring85-563
   J. Maynard, 536(Rev):Vol7-297
Korkhmazian, E., I. Drampian and G. Hakobian. Armenian Miniatures of the 13th and 14th Centuries from the Matenadaran Collection, Yerevan.
   T.F. Mathews, 90:Oct85-720
Korman, G. No Coins, Please.
   A. Kertzer, 102(CanL):Fall85-117
Korn, M. Ezra Pound.*
   W. Baumann, 468:Winter84-469
Korn, Y. Jews at the Crossroads.
   B. Frymer, 287:Mar85-25
Korner, S. Metaphysics.
   D.E.B., 185:Jan86-446
   R. Hanna, 543:Dec85-364
   A.R. White, 518:Oct85-255
Kornicki, P.F. The Reform of Fiction in Meiji Japan.
   J.A. Walker, 407(MN):Winter85-433
Koroleva, N.G. Pervaia rossiiskaia revoliutsiia i tsarizm.
   A.M. Verner, 550(RusR):Jul85-305
Korpi, W. The Democratic Class Struggle.
   M.W., 185:Apr86-662
Korshin, P.J. Typologies in England, 1650-1820.*
   M.I. Lowance, 173(ECS):Winter85/86-271
   G. Midgley, 541(RES):Nov85-569
   W. Walling, 340(KSJ):Vol34-201
Korshin, P.J. - see "The Eighteenth Century: A Current Bibliography"
Korsten, F.J.M. Roger North (1651-1734) Virtuoso and Essayist.*
   P. Rogers, 677(YES):Vol 15-298
Kortekaas, G.A.A. Historia Apollonii Regis Tyri.
   W. Maaz, 196:Band26Heft1/2-170
Korthals-Altes, S.W. The Aerospace Plane.
   J. Fallows, 453(NYRB):18Dec86-34
Korzenik, D. Drawn to Art.
   R. Gernand, 441:2Mar86-25
Kosegarten, A.M. Sienesische Bildhauer am Duomo Vecchio.
   J. White, 59:Dec85-484
Koselleck, R. Vergangene Zukunft.
   C. Piché, 98:Oct85-954
Kosicki, J. and D. Gerould. A Life of Solitude.
   L. Chamberlain, 617(TLS):19Sep86-1020
   D. Edgar, 362:4Sep86-23
Koskenniemi, K. Two-Level Morphology.
   G. Gazdar, 353:Vol23No4-597
Kosnik, A.M. A Escribir.
   G.A. Olivier, 399(MLJ):Autumn85-325

Koss, S. The Rise and Fall of the Political Press in Britain. (Vol 2)
   P. Stansky, 635(VPR):Spring85-37
Kossick, S.G. - see Martienssen, H.
Kostelanetz, R. The Old Poetries and the New.
   R. McDowell, 249(HudR):Autumn85-515
Kostiainen, A. Santeri Nuorteva — Kansanvälinen suomalainen.
   D. Kirby, 575(SEER):Oct85-611
Kostof, S. A History of Architecture.*
   A. Betsky, 505:Sep85-235
   R. Kimball, 45:Nov85-85
   A. Saint, 617(TLS):14Feb86-168
Kotei, S.I.A. The Book Today in Africa.
   T.C. Nwosu, 538(RAL):Spring85-112
Kotlowitz, R. Sea Changes.
   G. Motola, 441:14Dec86-20
Kottje, R. Die Bussbücher Halitgars von Cambrai und des Hrabanus Maurus.
   P.A. Breatnach, 112:Vol 17-163
Koukoules, M. Loose-Tongued Greeks.
   E. Orso, 292(JAF):Jan/Mar85-117
Kouwenhoven, J.A. Half a Truth is Better Than None.*
   H.F. Smith, 106:Winter85-451
Kouwenhoven, J.K. Apparent Narrative as Thematic Metaphor.*
   J.H. Anderson, 301(JEGP):Jul85-423
   M. Evans, 161(DUJ):Jun85-269
   P.J. Klemp, 604:Spring-Summer85-32
Kovács, I., ed. Les Lumières en Hongrie, en Europe Centrale et en Europe Orientale.
   G.F. Cushing, 575(SEER):Oct85-601
Kovtun, G.J. Czech and Slovak Literature in English.
   M. Croucher, 574(SEEJ):Winter85-491
   R.B. Pynsent, 575(SEEJ):Jul85-475
Kowalk, W. Alexander Pope.*
   C.J. Rawson, 677(YES):Vol 15-302
Kozer, J. Bajo este cien.
   K. Schwartz, 238:Dec85-790
Kozlik, F.C. L'Influence de l'anthroposophie sur l'oeuvre d'Andréi Biélyi.
   V.E. Alexandrov, 574(SEEJ):Spring85-109
Kozlovskij, V. Sobranie russkix vorovskix slovarej.
   A. Karpovič, 558(RLJ):Fall84-275
Kozol, J. Illiterate America.*
   J. Ashcroft, 186(ETC.):Summer85-180
   R. Ohmann, 126(CCC):Dec85-491
Kra, S. Aging Myths.
   B. Lindeman, 441:23Mar86-47
Kraehe, E.E. Metternich's German Policy. (Vol 2)
   D. McKay, 575(SEER):Apr85-301
Kraggerud, E. - see Vergil
Krajewski, W., ed. Polish Essays in the Philosophy of the Natural Sciences.
   B. Mundy, 486:Mar85-166
Krakovitch, O. Hugo censuré.
   F. Bassan, 446(NCFS):Spring-Summer86-401
Krakowski, S. The War of the Doomed.
   J. Stanley, 497(PolR):Vol30No4-459
Král, P. Le Burlesque ou morale de la tarte à la creme.
   P. Hammond, 707:Spring85-148

Krall, H. Shielding the Flame.
    A. Brumberg, 441:19Oct86-11
    N. Davies, 453(NYRB):20Nov86-21
    442(NY):15Dec86-128
Kralt, P. Door Nacht en Ontijd.
    P.F. Schmitz, 204(FdL):Mar85-77
Kramarae, C. Women and Men Speaking.
    P.R. Randall, 35(AS):Spring85-81
Kramer, B., C. Römer and D. Hagedorn, eds.
    Kölner Papyri 4.*
    W.E.H. Cockle, 123:Vol35No2-362
Kramer, D. - see Hardy, T.
Kramer, G. - see "Das Nibelungenlied"
Krämer, H. Plädoyer für eine Rehabilitie-
    rung der Individualethik.
    B. Taureck, 687:Jul-Sep85-467
Krämer, H. Platone e i fondamenti della
    metafisica.*
    N. Gulley, 303(JoHS):Vol 105-185
Kramer, H. The Revenge of the Philis-
    tines.*
    N. Rosenthal, 362:14Aug86-22
Kramer, J. Deutsch und Italienisch in
    Südtirol.
    R. Damerau-Neustadt, 72:Band222Heft1-
    219
Kramer, L. A Lifelong House.*
    J. Saunders, 565:Autumn85-74
Kramer, L. Music and Poetry.*
    R. Arnheim, 414:Vol71No3-378
    B.N., 636(VP):Summer85-226
Kramer, L. and A. Mitchell, eds. The
    Oxford Anthology of Australian Litera-
    ture.
    P. Conrad, 617(TLS):19Dec86-1421
    N. Potter, 441:9Feb86-24
Kramer, S.N. In the World of Sumer.
    J. Maier, 469:Vol 11No3-115
Krampen, M. and others. Die Welt als
    Zeichen.
    I. Rauch, 567:Vol55No3/4-227
Krannich, R.L. and C.R. The Politics of
    Family Planning in Thailand.
    J.S. Parsons, 293(JASt):May85-678
Krantz, F., ed. History from Below.
    T. Judt, 617(TLS):26Sep86-1069
Krantz, J. I'll Take Manhattan.
    L. Shapiro, 441:4May86-15
Kranz, G. Das Bildgedicht.
    J. Becker, 600:Vol 15No3/4-225
Krapf, G. Bach: Improvised Ornamentation
    and Keyboard Cadenzas.
    C.M.B., 412:Feb84-61
    P. Williams, 415:Sep85-536
Krapf, L. and C. Wagenknecht, eds. Stutt-
    garter Hoffeste.
    F. Baron, 406:Spring85-97
Krása, J. The "Travels" of Sir John Mande-
    ville.*
    J. Folda, 589:Jul85-693
Krashen, S.D. The Input Hypothesis.
    K.R. Gregg, 608:Mar86-116
Krasin, V. Sud.
    P. Reddaway, 617(TLS):3Jan86-7
Krasnov, V. Soviet Defectors.
    J.G. Pilon, 129:Sep86-64
Kratins, O. The Dream of Chivalry.*
    R. Copeland, 545(RPh):Nov84-256
    F. Goldin, 589:Apr85-423
    W. McConnell, 400(MLN):Apr85-686
    A.G. Martin, 406:Summer85-215

Kratochwill, D., A. Mühlböck and P. Wind.
    Die deutschen Handschriften des Mittel-
    alters der Erzabtei St. Peter zu Salz-
    burg.
    I. Glier, 301(JEGP):Apr85-300
Kratzenstein, M. and J. Hamilton. Four
    Centuries of Organ Music.
    A. Bond, 415:Mar85-179
Krätzer, A. Studien zum Amerikabild in
    der neueren deutschen Literatur.*
    D. Caldwell, 221(GQ):Summer85-481
von Kraus, C. Des Minnesangs Frühling.
    (Vols 1 and 2) (H. Tervooren and H.
    Moser, eds)
    P.W. Tax, 301(JEGP):Jul85-398
Kraus, D. and H. Las sillerías góticas
    españolas.
    I. Mateo, 48:Jan-Mar85-90
Kraus, J. Hans Erich Nossack.
    C. Poore, 406:Fall85-375
Kraus, J.W. A History of Way and Williams.
    J.C. Nelson, 517(PBSA):Vol79No2-255
Kraus, K. Half-Truths and One-and-a-Half
    Truths. (H. Zohn, ed and trans)
    D.J. Enright, 453(NYRB):6Nov86-46
    G. Steiner, 442(NY):21Jul86-90
Kraus, K. In These Great Times.* (H.
    Zohn, ed)
    D.J. Enright, 453(NYRB):6Nov86-46
Kraus, O. and L.L. McAllister - see Bren-
    tano, F.
Krause, D. The Profane Book of Irish Com-
    edy.*
    V. Cooke, 529(QQ):Spring85-201
Krause, J. "Märtyrer" und "Prophet."
    R. Furness, 402(MLR):Oct85-998
Krauss, E.S., T.P. Rohlen and P.G. Stein-
    hoff, eds. Conflict in Japan.
    S.B. Hanley, 407(MN):Summer85-238
Krauss, H., ed. Europäisches Hochmittel-
    alter.*
    U. Schöning, 224(GRM):Band35Heft1-111
Krauss, H. - see Köhler, E.
Krauss, M. How NATO Weakens the West.
    M. Helprin, 441:9Nov86-11
Krauss, R.E. The Originality of the Avant-
    Garde and Other Modernist Myths.
    Y-A. Bois, 127:Winter85-369
    D. Carrier, 90:Nov85-817
    R. McRae, 529(QQ):Winter85-820
Krausser, P. Kants Theorie der Erfahrung
    und Erfahrungswissenschaft.
    P. Rohs, 342:Band76Heft4-457
Kraut, R. Socrates and the State.
    T.H. Irwin, 185:Jan86-400
    D. Kagan, 377:Nov84-171
    K. Masugi, 543:Jun85-890
    P.P. Nicholson, 518:Oct85-207
    J.M. Queen, 150(DR):Spring85-141
    M.G. Sollenberger, 124:Jan-Feb86-193
    C.C.W. Taylor, 123:Vol35No1-63
    M.D. Yaffe, 319:Jan86-113
Krauthammer, C. Cutting Edges.*
    L.D. Nachman, 129:Feb86-79
Krautheimer, R. The Rome of Alexander VII
    1655-1667.
    A. Braham, 617(TLS):24Oct86-1198
    442(NY):24Feb86-107
Krautschick, S. Cassiodor und die Politik
    seiner Zeit.
    W. Goffart, 589:Oct85-989

Kroker, A. Technology and the Canadian Mind.*
  R.M. Campbell, 298:Winter85/86-158
  M. Freiman, 627(UTQ):Summer85-448
  A. Rotstein, 99:Aug/Sep85-34
Kroll, B.M. and R.J. Vann, eds. Exploring Speaking-Writing Relationships.
  H. Bonheim, 677(YES):Vol 15-258
Krömer, W. Dichtung und Weltsicht des 19. Jahrhunderts.*
  R.D. Hacken, 406:Spring85-104
  H.H. Wetzel, 72:Band222Heft2-350
Kronenberg, A. and W., eds and trans. Nubische Märchen.
  E. Ettlinger, 203:Vol96No1-133
Kronick, J.G. American Poetics of History.
  G.W. Allen, 27(AL):May85-353
Kropfinger, K. - see Wagner, R.
Kross, J. The Evolution of an American Town.*
  J.M. Sosin, 106:Fall85-301
Krueger, M.C. Authors and the Opposition.
  J. Osinski, 52:Band20Heft3-329
  U. Rainer, 406:Fall85-374
Krulik, D. and B. Zaffran. English with a Smile.
  D.E. Eskey, 399(MLJ):Summer85-218
Krüll, M. Freud and His Father.
  M. Ignatieff, 453(NYRB):12Jun86-22
  S. Minuchin, 441:17Aug86-13
Krull, W. Prosa des Expressionismus.
  N.A. Donahue, 564:Nov85-313
Krummel, D.W. Bibliographies.
  R.C. Alston, 354:Mar85-76
Krummel, R.F. Nietzsche und der deutsche Geist. (Vol 2)
  R. Furness, 402(MLR):Oct85-998
  S.L. Gilman, 221(GQ):Spring85-312
Krupat, E. People in Cities.
  P. Hall, 617(TLS):30May86-581
Krupnick, M., ed. Displacement.*
  T. Bahti, 125:Fall84-106
Krupnick, M. Lionel Trilling and the Fate of Cultural Criticism.
  R. Boyers, 441:13Apr86-19
  A.S. Byatt, 176:Nov86-46
  J. Symons, 617(TLS):5Sep86-959
Kruse, H.H. Mark Twain and "Life on the Mississippi."*
  A. Gribben, 49:Jan85-99
  J. Lauber, 106:Spring85-47
  R. Sattelmeyer, 27(AL):Dec85-671
Krysinski, W. Carrefours de signes.
  B. McHale, 107(CRCL):Mar85-138
Krzyżanowski, L. and I. Nagurski, with K. Olszer - see Zimmer, S.K.
Kubalkova, V. and A. Cruickshank. Marxism and International Relations.
  G. Frost, 617(TLS):9May86-504
Kübler, G. Die soziale Aufsteigerin.
  P.A. Herminghouse, 406:Fall85-363
Kucich, J. Excess and Restraint in the Novels of Charles Dickens.*
  S. Monod, 402(MLR):Apr85-443
Kuçuradi, I. - see Kant, I.
Kuehl, J. and S. Moore, eds. In Recognition of William Gaddis.*
  I. Malin, 532(RCF):Spring85-150
  A. Nadel, 395(MFS):Summer85-417
Kuenzli, R. and others. New York Dada.
  C. Lyon, 441:20Jul86-19

Kugelmass, J. The Miracle of Intervale Avenue.
  M. Klass, 441:21Sep86-15
Kugelmass, J. and J. Boyarin, eds and trans. From a Ruined Garden.
  N. Benoit-Lapierre, 98:Nov85-1112
  M. Zoltan, 287:Apr85-27
Kuhlmann, W. Reflexive Letztbegründung.
  J. Habermas, 384:Sep/Oct85-904
Kuhn, A. The Power of the Image.
  C. Kraus, 441:13Apr86-23
Kuhn, H. Minnelieder Walthers von der Vogelweide.* (C. Cormeau, ed)
  A. Groos, 589:Jan85-224
Kuhn, H. - see Neckel, G.
Kuhn, R. Corruption in Paradise.
  G. Avery, 447(N&Q):Dec84-553
Kuhn, R. Komposition und Rhythmus.
  M.P., 90:Jan85-52
Kuhn, S.M. Studies in the Language and Poetics of Anglo-Saxon England.
  W.A.K., 300:Apr85-89
Kuhn, S.M. - see "Middle English Dictionary"
Kuhn, S.M. and J. Reidy - see "Middle English Dictionary"
Kühn, W. Das Prinzipienproblem in der Philosophie des Thomas von Aquin.
  J. Owens, 543:Sep84-129
Kühne, W. Die Politik der Sowjetunion in Afrika.
  E.K. Valkenier, 550(RusR):Jan85-82
Kühnel, J. and others, eds. Mittelalter-Rezeption II.
  W.C. McDonald, 406:Summer85-217
Kühnel-Kunze, I. Bergung — Evakuierung — Rückführung.
  G. Himmelheber, 683:Band48Heft2-275
Kuhns, R. Psychoanalytic Theory of Art.*
  M. Cavell, 482(PhR):Oct85-596
Kuhoff, W. Quellen zur Geschichte der Alamannen.
  E.A. Thompson, 123:Vol135No2-414
Kuhoff, W. Studien zur zivilen senator-ischen Laufbahn im 4. Jahrhundert n. Chr. Ämter und Amtsinhaber in Clarissimat und Spektabilität.
  A.R. Birley, 123:Vol135No1-206
Kuhse, H. and P. Singer. Should the Baby Live?
  R.G. Frey, 617(TLS):18Apr86-431
Kuipers, G. Verzamellijst van recensies en vermeldingen van buitenlandse litera-tuur in de Nederlandse periodieke pers gedurende het tijdvak 1830 tot en met 1839.
  T. Janssen and K. Korevaart, 204(FdL): Mar85-75
Kuist, J.M. The Nichols File of "The Gentleman's Magazine."*
  J.D. Fleeman, 541(RES):Feb85-99
Kuklick, B. Churchmen and Philosophers.
  P.F. Gura, 27(AL):Dec85-655
Kulik, G., R. Parks and T.Z. Penn, eds. The New England Mill Village, 1790-1860.
  529(QQ):Summer85-437
Kully, E., ed. Codex Weimar Q565.*
  L.S., 382(MAE):1985/1-148
Kumiega, J. The Theatre of Grotowski.
  M. Hunter, 609:Summer/Fall86-104
  M. Wolf, 157:No158-47
Kumin, M. The Long Approach.
  H. Beaver, 441:2Mar86-14

214

Kumin, M.  Our Ground Time Here Will Be
Brief.
  B. Crenshaw, 472:Spring/Summer/Fall/
  Winter85-432
Kumin, M.  To Make a Prairie.
  R. McDowell, 249(HudR):Autumn85-513
Kümmel, H.M.  Familie, Beruf und Amt im
spätbabylonischen Uruk.
  D.B. Weisberg, 318(JAOS):Oct-Dec84-739
Kundera, M.  Life is Elsewhere.
  B. Tonkin, 362:4Dec86-25
Kunert, G.  Windy Times.  (A. Stein, ed
and trans)
  A. Otten, 42(AR):Spring85-248
Küng, H.  Vie éternelle?
  T. Dey, 450(NRF):Jul-Aug85-154
Kung, L.  Factory Women in Taiwan.
  E. Honig, 293(JASt):Aug85-808
Kunisch, H.  Von der "Reichsunmittelbar-
keit der Poesie."
  F. Seewald, 224(GRM):Band35Heft2-235
Kunitz, S.  Next-to-Last Things.
  R.W. Flint, 441:6Apr86-24
  M. Oliver, 344:Summer86-129
Kunitzsch, P.  Glossar der arabischen
Fachausdrücke in der mittelalterlichen
europäischen Astrolabliteratur.
  D. Pingree, 589:Apr85-482
Kunnas, T.  Nietzsches Lachen.
  H. Weinmann, 154:Autumn85-551
Künne, W.  Abstrakte Gegenstände.
  J. Habermas, 384:Sep/Oct85-899
Kunsmann, P. and O. Kuhn, eds.  Welt-
sprache Englische in Forschung und Lehre.
  H. Ulherr, 38:Band103Heft3/4-418
Kunstler, J.H.  Blood Solstice.
  A.S. Grossman, 441:11May86-24
Kuntz, M.L.  Guillaume Postel, Prophet of
the Restitution of All Things.
  B.M. Damiani, 543:Mar85-651
  T.W., 111:Fall86-10
Kuntz, P.G.  Alfred North Whitehead.
  L.S. Ford, 543:Jun85-891
Kunze, E.  Finnische Literatur in deutsch-
er Übersetzung 1675-1975.*
  G.C. Schoofield, 133:Band17Heft3/4-388
Kunze, E.  Friedrich Ruckert und Finnland.*
  G.C. Schoolfield, 133:Band17Heft3/4-
  386
Kunze, K., ed.  Die Elsässische "Legenda
aurea."*  (Vol 2)
  N.F. Palmer, 402(MLR):Jul85-747
  H-G. Richert, 133:Band17Heft3/4-315
  R. Schenda, 196:Band26Heft1/2-172
Kuo, W.  Teaching Grammar of Thai.
  R.J. Bickner, 293(JASt):Aug85-890
Kuper, A. and J., eds.  The Social Science
Encyclopedia.
  D. Papineau, 617(TLS):9May86-492
Kuper, L.  Genocide.
  B.J. Berman, 529(QQ):Spring85-133
Kuper, L.  The Prevention of Genocide.
  A. Ryan, 617(TLS):27Jun86-702
Kupferberg, H.  Amadeus.
  K. Gann, 441:27Jul86-19
Kupferschmid, G.S.  Al tanto.
  M.J. Cousino, 399(MLJ):Autumn85-326
  P.S. Finch, 238:Mar85-86
Küpper, R.  Shakespeare im Unterricht.
  J.L. Gunther, 570(SQ):Summer85-240

Kupperman, J.J.  The Foundations of Moral-
ity.*
  J.M. Day, 518:Oct85-229
  P.T. Mackenzie, 483:Oct85-552
Kuppner, F.  A Bad Day for the Sung
Dynasty.*
  D. McDuff, 565:Summer85-72
  W. Scammell, 364:Jul85-80
Kuralt, C., with I. Glusker.  Southerners.
  P. Laws, 441:7Dec86-69
Kureishi, H.  My Beautiful Laundrette [and]
The Rainbow Sign.
  M. Gorra, 441:4May86-26
  I. Jack, 617(TLS):2May86-470
Kurmacheva, M.D.  Krepostnaia intelli-
gentsiia Rossii (vtoraia polovina
XVIII- nachalo XIX veka).
  M.J. Okenfuss, 550(RusR):Jan85-104
Kuroda, K.  Keiko's Haiku Poems.
  R. Spiess, 404:Winter-Spring85-74
Kürschner, W. and R. Vogt, with S. Siebert-
Nemann, eds.  Sprachtheorie, Pragmatik,
Interdisziplinäres.
  G. Kleiber, 553(RLiR):Jul-Dec85-421
Kurtén, B.  Singletusk.
  P-L. Adams, 61:Sep86-104
  A. Parson, 441:21Sep86-26
Kurtz, D., ed.  Beazley and Oxford.
  M. Beard, 617(TLS):12Sep86-1013
Kurtz, L.R.  Evaluating Chicago Sociology.
  D. Wrong, 617(TLS):24Jan86-91
Kurtz, P., ed.  Sidney Hook.
  N. Glick, 176:Jun85-28
Kurtz, P.  In Defense of Secular Humanism.
  42(AR):Spring85-254
Kurz, D. - see Plato
Kurz, G.  Metapher, Allegorie, Symbol.
  H. Slessarev, 406:Fall85-351
Kurzke, H.  Romantik und Konservatismus.
  S. Friedrichsmeyer, 221(GQ):Spring85-
  283
  N. Saul, 402(MLR):Oct85-992
Kurzman, D.  Day of the Bomb.
  L. Lamont, 441:12Jan86-31
Kushner, E., ed.  Actes du Colloque
international: Renouvellements dans la
théorie de l'histoire littéraire/Proceed-
ings of the International Colloquium:
Renewals in the Theory of Literary
History.
  F. Jost, 149(CLS):Summer85-285
Kushner, H.S.  When All You've Ever Wanted
Isn't Enough.
  A. Boyer, 441:22Jun86-27
Kuspit, D.  The Critic Is Artist.
  D. Carrier, 55:Jan85-38
Kuspit, D.  Leon Golub.
  J. Yau, 703:No15-162
Küster, B.  Die Literatur des 19. Jahr-
hunderts im Urteil von Émile Montégut.*
  P. Berthier, 535(RHL):May/Jun85-499
Kutscher, E.Y.  A History of the Hebrew
Language.
  E.J. Revell, 318(JAOS):Oct-Dec84-772
  P. Wexler, 350:Sep86-687
von Kutschera, F.  Grundfragen der Erkennt-
nistheorie.
  E. Bencivenga, 543:Dec84-395
Kuttert, R.  Syntaktische und semantische
Differenzierung der spanischen Tempusfor-
men der Vergangheit perfecto simple,
perfecto compuesto, und imperfecto.
  M.B. Harris, 545(RPh):Feb85-379

215

Kuwabara Takeo. Japan and Western Civiliz-
ation. (Katō Hidetoshi, ed)
  K.A. Grossberg, 293(JASt):May85-615
Kuwayama, G., ed. The Great Bronze Age of
China.
  V.C. Kane, 293(JASt):Aug85-810
Kuyk, D., Jr. Threads Cable-Strong.*
  295(JML):Nov85-475
Kuz'minskij, K.K. and G.L. Kovalev, eds.
Antologija novejšej russkoj pozzii u
Goluboj laguny/The Blue Lagoon Anthol-
ogy of Modern Russian Poetry. (Vols 1,
2A, 4A and 4B)
  I.R. Titunik, 574(SEEJ):Summer85-203
Kvam, S. Linksverschachtelung im Deut-
schen und Norwegischen.
  T.F. Shannon, 350:Jun86-463
Kyburg, H.E. Theory and Measurement.
  P. Smith, 518:Oct85-240
Kyle, D. The Dancing Men.
  W.J. Harding, 441:19Oct86-30
Kyrris, K.P. To Byzantion chata ton ID
aiōna, 1.
  A.E. Laiou, 589:Apr85-483
Kyvig, D.E. and M.A. Marty. Nearby His-
tory.*
  R. Schwegler, 126(CCC):Dec85-504


Labarca, A. and J.M. Hendrickson. Our
Global Village.
  F.E. Winfield, 399(MLJ):Autumn85-330
Labarrière, P-J. Le discours de l'altér-
ité.
  C. Chalier, 192(EP):Oct-Dec85-561
de La Boëtie, É. Mémoire sur la pacifica-
tion des troubles. (M. Smith, ed)
  D. Maskell, 208(FS):Oct85-462
  G. Schrenck, 535(RHL):Nov/Dec85-1057
  J. Supple, 402(MLR):Oct85-936
Labor, E. - see London, J.
La Bossière, C., ed. Translation in
Canadian Literature.
  R.A. Cavell, 102(CanL):Fall85-108
Laboucheix, H. Richard Price as Moral
Philosopher and Political Theorist.
  M. Fitzpatrick, 83:Autumn85-236
de La Bretonne, R. - see under Restif de
La Bretonne
Labrie, R. James Merrill.
  R.K. Martin, 178:Dec85-502
Labrousse, E. Bayle.*
  W.E. Rex, 319:Apr86-269
La Capra, D. History and Criticism.
  H. Kellner, 400(MLN):Dec85-1114
  H. White, 617(TLS):31Jan86-109
La Capra, D. "Madame Bovary" on Trial.*
  D. Knight, 208(FS):Jan85-91
La Capra, D. A Preface to Sartre.
  H.A. Durfee, 543:Sep84-131
La Capra, D. Rethinking Intellectual His-
tory.
  A.C. Goodson, 115:Fall84/Winter85-145
  C. Parker, 366:Autumn85-288
  S. Pierson, 131(CL):Fall85-359
  L. Shiner, 125:Fall84-102
La Capria, R. L'armonia perduta.
  J. Burnham, 617(TLS):30Oct85-1098
de La Ceppède, J. From the Theorems of
Master Jean de La Ceppède.* (K. Bosley,
ed and trans)
  J. Mayes, 161(DUJ):Dec84-113

Lacey, R. Ford.
  R. Davenport-Hines, 617(TLS):19Sep86-
1023
  J.K. Galbraith, 453(NYRB):14Aug86-17
  P. Lennon, 362:10Jul86-28
  T. Morgan, 441:13Jul86-1
  442(NY):8Sep86-137
Lachapelle, R. and J. Henripin. The Demo-
linguistic Situation in Canada.
  A. Hull, 35(AS):Spring85-85
La Charité, R.C., ed. A Critical
Bibliography of French Literature:
The Sixteenth Century. (rev) (Vol 2)
  M. Tetel, 207(FR):Feb86-457
de La Chaussée, P.C.N. L'Ecole des Mères,
Comédie (1744). (I. Bernard, ed)
  W. Henning, 72:Band222Heft1-228
  W.D. Howarth, 208(FS):Apr85-208
  J-M. Thomasseau, 535(RHL):Jan/Feb85-98
de La Chesnaye des Bois, A. Lettre à
Madame la Comtesse d'... (D.J. Adams,
ed)
  E.D. James, 208(FS):Apr85-208
Lachmann, R., ed. Slavische Barocklitera-
tur II.*
  A.R. Hippisley, 575(SEER):Jan85-113
  J.P. Mozur, 574(SEEJ):Summer85-205
Lachtman, H. - see London, J.
Laclau, E. and C. Mouffe. Hegemony and
Socialist Strategy.
  P. Rumble, 275(IQ):Summer/Fall84-210
"Laclos et le libertinage, 1782-1982."*
  G.E. Rodmell, 402(MLR):Apr85-466
Lacoste-Veysseyre, C. and P. Laubriet -
see Gautier, T.
Lacoue-Labarthe, P. and J-L. Nancy.
L'Absolu littéraire.
  S. Guerlac, 400(MLN):Sep85-887
Lacroix, R. and F. Vaillancourt. Les
revenus et la langue au Québec (1970-
1978).
  M. Heller, 355(LSoc):Mar85-144
Lacy, A. Farther Afield.
  S. Brownmiller, 441:1Jun86-30
Lacy, N., ed. L'Istoyre de Jehan Coquault.
  R.F. Cook, 446(NCFS):Fall-Winter85/86-
162
Lacy, N.J. The Arthurian Encyclopaedia.
  T.A. Shippey, 617(TLS):30May86-583
Laderman, C. Wives and Midwives.
  P. Van Esterik, 293(JASt):Aug85-892
Ladis, A. Taddeo Gaddi.*
  B. Cole, 589:Jan85-169
  C. Lloyd, 447(N&Q):Sep84-422
Ladner, B., ed. The Humanities in Precol-
legiate Education.
  R. Berman, 289:Winter85-115
Ladrière, J. L'articulation du sens.
  A. Reix, 542:Oct-Dec85-559
Lafarga, F. Voltaire en España (1734-
1835).*
  R. Álvarez, 240(HR):Spring85-246
  T.E.D. Braun, 207(FR):Oct85-132
  P. Juan i Tous, 52:Band20Heft2-209
La Favia, L.M. The Man of Sorrows.
  R. Goffen, 589:Jan85-167
Madame de Lafayette. Zaïde, histoire
espagnole. (J.A. Kreiter, ed)
  J. Chupeau, 535(RHL):Jan/Feb85-94
La Feber, W. Inevitable Revolutions.
  R.T. Peterson, 115:Fall84/Winter85-158
Laffi, U. Asculum II.
  T.W. Potter, 123:Vol35No1-219

Lambton, L.  Beastly Buildings.
  B. Brophy, 617(TLS):11Apr86-401
  M. Levine, 441:6Jul86-15
Laminger-Pascher, G.  Beiträge zu den
  griechischen Inschriften Lykaoniens.
  P.M. Fraser, 123:Vol35No2-422
Lamiroy, B.  Les Verbes de mouvement en
  français et espagnol.*
  S. Fleischman, 545(RPh):May86-473
Lamm, R.D. and G. Imhoff.  The Immigration
  Time Bomb.
  J. Rosenthal, 441:5Jan86-14
Lammel, I.  Arbeitermusikkultur in Deutsch-
  land 1844-1945.
  H. Groschopp, 654(WB):10/1985-1756.
Lämmert, E., ed.  Erzählforschung.
  H. Bausinger, 196:Band26Heft1/2-173
  I. Diersen, 654(WB):1/1985-160
Lamming, G.  In the Castle of my Skin.
  R. Deveson, 617(TLS):24Oct86-1187
Lamming, R.M.  In the Dark.*
  S. Vogan, 441:9Mar86-12
L'Amour, L.  Last of the Breed.
  A. Gelb, 441:6Jul86-14
Lampe, G.W.  Ohne Subjektivität.
  P. Stenberg, 564:Feb85-68
Lampert, H.  Behind Closed Doors.
  M.M. Thomas, 441:26Oct86-28
Lampert, V. and others.  Modern Masters.
  G. Lewis, 415:Mar85-160
Lamphere, R.J. and T. Shachtman.  The FBI-
  KGB War.
  J. Bamford, 441:3Aug86-9
  H. Klehr, 129:Nov86-83
Lamping, D.  Der Name in der Erzählung.
  W.R. Maurer, 221(GQ):Winter85-104
Lamport, F.J.  Lessing and the Drama.*
  C.J. Wickham, 406:Summer85-222
Lamprecht, A.  Relationale Satzanalyse.
  P. Erdmann, 257(IRAL):May85-170
Lampugnani, V.M. - see under Magnano
  Lampugnani, V.
Lamy, S.  Quand je lis je m'invente.
  P. Smart, 627(UTQ):Summer85-492
Lamy, S. and I. Pagès.  Féminité, sub-
  version, écriture.
  P. Smart, 627(UTQ):Summer85-492
Lan, D.  Guns and Rain.
  A.D. Jones, 617(TLS):3Jan86-8
Lana, R.G.Z. - see Du Ryer, P.
Lancashire, I.  Dramatic Texts and Records
  of Britain: A Chronological Topography
  of Britain to 1558.
  L.M. Clopper, 589:Oct85-992
  R.W. Ingram, 627(UTQ):Summer85-404
"Lancelot: Roman en prose du XIIIe
  siècle."*  (Vols 1-9) (A. Micha, ed)
  E. Kennedy, 382(MAE):1985/2-327
Land, S.K.  Paradox and Polarity in the
  Fiction of Joseph Conrad.
  R.K. Anderson, 395(MFS):Winter85-795
  M. Bock, 136:Vol 18No1-77
  C.R. La Bossière, 268(IFR):Winter86-44
  295(JML):Nov85-462
Landau, B. and L. Gleitman.  Language and
  Experience.
  J.N. Bohannon 3d, 350:Jun86-446
Landau, E.G.  Artists for Victory.
  F.V. O'Connor, 127:Winter84-393
Landau, N.  The Justices of the Peace,
  1679-1760.*
  H.T. Dickinson, 566:Spring86-229

Landau, S.I.  Dictionaries.*
  J. Algeo, 35(AS):Winter85-357
Landau, Z. and J. Tomaszewwski.  The
  Polish Economy in the Twentieth Century.*
  B. Mieczkowski, 497(PolR):Vol30No3-308
Landes, D.S.  Revolution in Time.
  S.G. Wolf, 658:Summer/Autumn85-191
Landgraf, W.  Martin Luther.
  J. Rosellini, 406:Fall85-354
Landgrebe, L.  Faktizität und Individua-
  tion.*
  H.A. Durfee, 543:Mar85-652
Landheer, R.  Aspects linguistiques et
  pragma-rhétoriques de l'ambiguïté.
  A. Moerdijk, 204(FdL):Jun85-153
Landman, F. and F. Veltman, eds.  Vari-
  eties of Formal Semantics.
  M.J. Cresswell, 353:Vol123No4-626
  D.F. Farkas, 350:Jun86-415
Landolfi, T.  Un amour de notre temps.
  C. Dis, 450(NRF):Mar85-111
Landolfi, T.  Words in Commotion.  (K.
  Jason, ed and trans)
  A. Cancogni, 441:30Nov86-37
Landon, H.C.R.  Handel and his World.*
  D. Burrows, 415:Feb85-90
Landon, H.C.R.  Mozart and the Masons.*
  J.M., 412:Feb83-56
Landow, G.P.  Ruskin.*
  E.K. Helsinger, 637(VS):Summer86-614
Landsman, N.C.  Scotland and Its First
  American Colony, 1683-1765.
  B. Aspinwall, 617(TLS):17Jan86-66
Lane, B.G.  The Altar and the Altar-Piece.
  C. Harbison, 600:Vol 15No3/4-221
  P. Humfrey, 324:May86-413
  F. Lewis, 90:Mar85-164
Lane, C.W.  Evelyn Waugh.*
  M. Stannard, 402(MLR):Jan85-136
Lane, E.  Hear the Other Side.
  D. Pannick, 362:9Jan86-27
Lane, F.C. and R.C. Mueller.  Money and
  Banking in Medieval and Renaissance
  Venice.  (Vol 1)
  B.S. Pullan, 617(TLS):17Jan86-67
Lane, H., ed.  The Deaf Experience.
  C.B. Roy, 350:Dec86-963
  O. Sacks, 453(NYRB):27Mar86-23
Lane, H.  When the Mind Hears.
  O. Sacks, 453(NYRB):27Mar86-23
Lane, P.  A Linen Crow, A Caftan Magpie.
  S. Scobie, 376:Sep85-142
Lane, P.  Passing into Storm.
  J. Owens, 102(CanL):Winter84-93
Lang, B.  Philosophy and the Art of Writ-
  ing.
  G. Shapiro, 290(JAAC):Fall85-88
Lang, B., W. Sacksteder and G. Stahl, eds.
  The Philosopher in the Community.
  D.L., 185:Jan86-436
Lang, G.E. and K.  The Battle for Public
  Opinion.
  J. Braeman, 106:Fall85-353
Lang, J.  Sprache im Raum.
  H. Goebl, 547(RF):Band97Heft1-69
Lang, M.L.  Herodotean Narrative and Dis-
  course.
  J.A.S. Evans, 639(VQR):Summer85-556
  D. Lateiner, 124:Mar-Apr86-289
  G.S. Shrimpton, 487:Spring85-80
de Langbehn, R.R. - see under Rohland de
  Langbehn, R.

Lange, C.H., C.L. Riley and E.M. Lange - see Bandelier, A.F.
"Dorothea Lange: Photographs of a Lifetime." (text by R. Coles)
J.C. Curtis, 658:Winter85-317
Lange, O. The Devil at Home.
D. Finkle, 441:25May86-14
Lange, V. The Classical Age of German Literature 1740-1815.*
B. Bjorklund, 400(MLN):Apr85-688
P. Boerner, 301(JEGP):Oct85-606
W. Leppmann, 131(CL):Summer85-282
L. Sharpe, 402(MLR):Jan85-215
Langedijk, K. The Portraits of the Medici, 15th-18th Centuries.* (Vols 1 and 2)
M. Campbell, 90:Jun85-386
Langenbucher, W.R., R. Rytlewski and B. Weyergraf, eds. Kulturpolitisches Wörterbuch.
A. von Bormann, 224(GRM):Band35Heft4-457
K-H. Schoeps, 301(JEGP):Jul85-397
Langendoen, D.T. and P.M. Postal. The Vastness of Natural Languages.
B. Abbott, 350:Mar86-154
Langer, E. Josephine Herbst.
N. Weyl, 390:Dec85-54
42(AR):Spring85-252
295(JML):Nov85-496
Langham, I. The Building of British Social Anthropology.
S.R. Barrett, 488:Mar85-103
Langhammer, W. Bertrand Russell.
H. Ruja, 556:Summer85-93
Langhans, E.A. Restoration Promptbooks.
J. Wilders, 541(RES):Aug85-465
Langland, E. Society in the Novel.*
H. Anderson, 115:Fall85-486
J. Colmer, 67:Nov85-253
J.M. Lennon, 395(MFS):Winter85-855
Langland, W. Piers Plowman: The Z Version. (A.G. Rigg and C. Brewer, eds)
J.O. Fichte, 38:Band103Heft3/4-468
R.F. Green, 40(AEB):Vol8No2-129
G. Kane, 589:Oct85-910
D. Pearsall, 72:Band222Heft1-181
Langley, B. Autumn Tiger.
N. Callendar, 441:14Sep86-38
Langley, L.D. The Banana Wars.
W.G. Lovell, 529(QQ):Summer85-396
Lanham, R.A. Analyzing Prose.
R.A. Eden, 599:Summer85-282
Lanham, R.A. Literacy and the Survival of Humanism.
D. Rygiel, 577(SHR):Summer85-252
Lanne, J-C. Velimir Khlebnikov: poète futurien.*
J. Graffy, 575(SEER):Oct85-567
R. Vroon, 550(RusR):Oct85-409
"L'année 1768 à travers la presse traitée par ordinateur."
J. Lough, 208(FS):Jan85-82
Lanner, R.M. Trees of the Great Basin.
T.J. Lyon, 649(WAL):May85-63
Lanning, J. and J., eds. Texas Cowboys.*
E. West, 585(SoQ):Spring86-88
Lansbury, C. Elizabeth Gaskell.
E. Wright, 637(VS):Spring86-479
Lansbury, C. The Reasonable Man.*
V. Shaw, 402(MLR):Oct85-914
Lansbury, C. Ringarra.
M. Rubin, 441:23Mar86-25

Lansdale, J.R. The Magic Wagon.
A. Roston, 441:14Dec86-24
Lansdown, A. Windfalls.
G. Bitcon, 581:Sep85-352
Lanser, S.S. The Narrative Act.*
J. Frank, 569(SR):Summer85-493
U. Margolin, 107(CRCL):Sep85-498
S.R. Suleiman, 131(CL):Winter85-67
Lansing, K.M. and A.E. Richards. The Elementary Teacher's Art Handbook.
W.L. Brittain, 289:Fall85-121
Lantz, K.A. - see Leskov, N.
Lanzara, V.G. - see Callimachus
Lao She. Crescent Moon and Other Stories.
P. Link, 441:6Jul86-16
Laourdas, B. and L.G. Westerink - see Photius
Lapidge, M. and H. Gneuss, eds. Learning and Literature in Anglo-Saxon England.
P. Godman, 617(TLS):10Jan86-46
Lapierre, D. The City of Joy.*
I. Buruma, 453(NYRB):29May86-19
Lapointe, F.H. Georg Lukács and His Critics.
P. Breines, 40(AEB):Vol8No2-142
L. De Lowry-Fryman, 87(BB):Mar85-46
Laporte, R. Une Vie.
J. Sturrock, 617(TLS):3Oct86-1111
Lapp, J.C. La Fenêtre ouverte sur la création. (C.B. Kerr, ed)
P.A. Wadsworth, 207(FR):Oct85-122
Lapping, B. End of Empire.
J. Morris, 176:Feb86-54
Laprevotte, G. Science et poésie de Dryden à Pope.
P. Rogers, 83:Spring85-125
Laqueur, W. World of Secrets.*
R. Cecil, 617(TLS):26Sep86-1076
Laqueur, W. and R. Breitman. Breaking the Silence.
H.A. Turner, 441:22Jun86-19
442(NY):15Sep86-121
Larbaud, V. La Prose du Monde. (J. Bessiere and J. Darras, eds)
S. Taylor-Horrex, 208(FS):Oct85-498
Lardy, N.R. Agriculture in China's Modern Economic Development.
J.E. Nickum, 293(JASt):Aug85-813
"L'area del 'santuario siriaco del Gianicolo.'"
J. Champeaux, 555:Vol59fasc1-163
Large, A. The Artificial Language Movement.
G. Sampson, 617(TLS):4Jul86-740
Large, D.C. and W. Weber, eds. Wagnerism in European Culture and Politics.*
R. Anderson, 415:Jul85-407
Large, S.S. Organized Workers and Socialist Politics in Interwar Japan.
D. Pong, 302:Vol21No1-89
Larkin, E. The Historical Dimensions of Irish Catholicism.
S. Cronin, 174(Éire):Fall85-154
Larkin, P. High Windows.
D. Young, 199:Spring86-103
Larminie, V.M. The Godly Magistrate.
D.G. Vaisey, 447(N&Q):Mar84-118
La Rocca, E. L'età d'oro di Cleopatra.
R. Ling, 303(JoHS):Vol 105-244
Larochette, J. Le langage et la réalité II.*
P. Wunderli, 209(FM):Apr85-90

de La Roque, S-G. Poésies.* (G. Mathieu-
Castellani, ed)
  N. Clerici Balmas, 535(RHL):Jul/Aug85-
  678
Larouche-Thibault, M. Quelle douleur!
  E. Dansereau, 102(CanL):Fall85-106
de Larra, M.J. Artículos sociales, políti-
cos y de crítica literaria. (J. Cano
Ballesta, ed)
  A.D. Inglis, 86(BHS):Jul85-311
de Larra, M.J. Las palabras, artículos y
ensayos.* (J.L. Varela, ed)
  J. Spencer, 552(REH):May85-146
Larre, C. Le traité VII du Houai Nan Tseu.
  D.D. Leslie, 302:Vol21No1-65
Larreya, P. Le possible et le nécessaire.
  L. Goossens, 353:Vol23No6-998
Larsen, J.K. and E.M. Rogers. Silicon
Valley Fever.
  362:7Aug86-26
Larsen, S.E. Sémiologie littéraire.
  S. Jansen, 462(OL):Vol40No4-380
Larsen, W.W. and Tran Thi Nga. Shallow
Graves.
  L. Abrams, 441:15Jun86-14
Larson, G.O. The Reluctant Patron.*
  E. Arian, 476:Summer83-87
  F.V. O'Connor, 127:Winter84-393
Larson, J.L. Dickens and the Broken Scrip-
ture.
  S. Monod, 189(EA):Oct-Dec86-467
Larson, M.L. Meaning-Based Translation.
  E.A. Nida, 205(ForL):Dec84-265
"L'art décoratif à Rome à la fin de la
république et au début du principat:
Table ronde organisée par l'École fran-
çaise de Rome (Rome, 10-11 mai 1979)."
  R. Ling, 313:Vol75-277
Larthomas, P. - see de Beaumarchais, P.A.C.
La Rue, J. Guidelines for Style Analysis.
  L.D., 412:May84-150
Laruelle, F. Une biographie de l'homme
ordinaire.*
  P. Petit, 540(RIPh):Vol39fasc4-465
Larwood, L., A.H. Stromberg and B. Gutek -
see "Women and Work"
La Salle, P. Strange Sunlight.
  A. Weir, 649(WAL):Feb86-374
Lasater, D. Falfurrias.
  L. Milazzo, 584(SWR):Summer85-415
Lascault, G. and N. Alquin. Coutumes des
vents.
  O. Juilliard, 450(NRF):May85-76
Lascelles, A. End of an Era. (D. Hart-
Davis, ed)
  I. Colegate, 617(TLS):19Sep86-1026
Lasch, A. Ausgewählte Schriften zur
Niederdeutschen Philologie. (R. Peters
and T. Sodmann, eds)
  E. Seebold, 685(ZDL):3/1985-379
Lasch, C. The Minimal Self.*
  H. Wagschal, 99:Aug/Sep85-35
Lascoumes, P. and H. Zander. Marx: du
"vol de vois" à la critique du droit.
  R. Gervais, 154:Spring85-187
Lasdun, D. Architecture in an Age of
Scepticism.
  C. Davies, 46:Sep85-97
  E. Denby, 324:Jul86-539
Lasdun, J. Delirium Eclipse and Other
Stories.
  J. Penner, 441:3Aug86-12

Lasdun, J. The Silver Age.*
  M. Hulse, 176:Sep/Oct86-61
  P. Lewis, 364:Aug-Sep85-147
Lasker-Schüler, E. Your Diamond Dreams
Cut Open My Arteries.*
  K. Weissenberger, 133:Band17Heft3/4-
  363
de Lasry, A. "Carlos Maynes" and "La
enperatrís de Roma."* [title may be:
Two Romances.]
  M.S. Brownlee, 400(MLN):Mar85-424
Lasserre, F. - see "Strabon, 'Géographie'"
Lassiter, M. Our Names, Our Selves.
  E.D. Lawson, 424:Dec85-286
Lassus, J. La forteresse byzantine de
Thamugadi: Fouilles à Timgad 1938-1956,
I.
  P. Gros, 555:Vol59fasc1-169
Lathem, E.C. and H. Cox - see Frost, R.
Lathrop, T.A. Curso de gramática histór-
ica española.
  B.A. Lafford, 238:May85-330
Lathrop, T.A. The Evolution of Spanish.*
  E. Blasco Ferrer, 379(MedR):Apr85-151
Latimer, M. Two Cities.
  E.C. Cromley, 576:Oct85-289
La Tourette, A. Cry Wolf.
  A. Haverty, 617(TLS):11Jul86-766
La Tourette, A. Ice Dancing.
  I. Scholes, 617(TLS):12Dec86-1409
Latrobe, B.H. The Correspondence and
Miscellaneous Papers of Benjamin Henry
Latrobe. (Vol 1) (J.C. Van Horne and
L.W. Formwalt, eds)
  D. Stroud, 90:Oct85-723
Lau, D.C. - see "Tao Te Ching"
Lau, J.S.M., ed. The Unbroken Chain.
  J.L. Faurot, 116:Jul84-196
  E.C. Knowlton, Jr., 573(SSF):Summer85-
  367
Laube, J. Dialektik der absoluten Vermitt-
lung.
  J.W. Heisig, 407(MN):Spring85-115
Laucirica, J.C. - see under Camarena
Laucirica, J.
Laudan, L., ed. Mind and Medicine.*
  M. Lavin, 486:Jun85-321
Laudan, L. Science and Hypothesis.*
  J.R. Milton, 84:Mar85-89
  T.V. Upton, 543:Mar85-653
Laudan, L. Science and Values.
  D.M., 185:Jan86-449
Laudan, R., ed. The Nature of Technolog-
ical Knowledge.
  J. Forge, 63:Dec85-551
Laudizi, G. D. Giunio Giovenale: Il fram-
mento Winsted.
  R.C.T. Parker, 123:Vol35No2-391
Lauer, Q. Hegel's Concept of God.*
  D.R. Knowles, 479(PhQ):Apr85-199
Laughlin, J. Selected Poems, 1935-1985.
  G. Dickerson, 441:2Nov86-28
Laughton, B. The Euston Road School.
  F. Spalding, 617(TLS):5Dec86-1364
Laurence, D.H. Bernard Shaw: A Bibliog-
raphy.*
  C.A. Berst, 177(ELT):Vol28No2-188
Laurence, D.H. - see Shaw, G.B.
Laurence, D.H. and M. Quinn - see Shaw,
G.B.
Laurence, D.H. and J. Rambeau - see Shaw,
G.B.

de Lauretis, T. Alice Doesn't.*
H. Rapaport, 223:Spring85-89
Laurich, C. Der französische Malerroman.
H.P. Lund, 535(RHL):Sep/Oct85-890
U. Schützenberger, 602:Band16Heft1-172
Lauter, E. Women as Mythmakers.*
K. Lokke, 659(ConL):Spring86-85
Lauter, W. Hildegard-Bibliographie.
G.J. Lewis, 564:Nov85-305
Lauterstein, I. Vienna Girl.
M. Robinson, 441:11May86-7
Lauth, R. and H. Gliwitzky, with others -
see Fichte, J.G.
Lauth, R., E. Heller and K. Hiller - see
Reinhold, K.L.
Lauxerois, R. Le bas Vivarais à l'époque
romaine.
J.F. Drinkwater, 313:Vol75-292
Lavagetto, M. - see Baratto, M. and others
Lavandera, B.R. Variación y significado.
F. Nuessel, 361:Nov85-265
A.K. Spears, 350:Mar86-225
Lavender, D. River Runners of the Grand
Canyon.
L. Milazzo, 584(SWR):Autumn85-547
Lavers, A. Roland Barthes.*
J.F. Solomon, 405(MP):Aug85-101
Lavers, N. The Northwest Passage.*
E.K. Garber, 455:Mar85-71
Laverty, M. No More Than Human.
P. Craig, 617(TLS):19Dec86-1428
Lavin, I. Bernini and The Unity of the
Visual Arts.
G. Pochat, 341:Vol154No4-181
Lavin, I., ed. Drawings by Gianlorenzo
Bernini from the Museum der Bildenden
Künste, Leipzig, German Democratic Repub-
lic.
G. Pochat, 341:Vol154No4-183
Lavis, G. and M. Stasse. Les Chansons de
Thibaut de Champagne.
N. Wilkins, 208(FS):Jan85-61
Lavoie, P. Pour suivre le théâtre au
Québec.
C. Barrett, 193(ELit):Winter85-239
A. Wagner, 108:Fall85-139
Law, A.H. and P. Goslett, eds. Soviet
Plays in Translation.
L. Hecht, 574(SEEJ):Spring85-99
Law, V. The Insular Latin Grammarians.*
P.A. Breatnach, 112:Vol 16-182
H. Gneuss, 38:Band103Heft3/4-440
R. Sharpe, 541(RES):Aug85-390
Lawrence, D.H. The Letters of D.H. Law-
rence.* (Vol 3) (J.T. Boulton and A.
Robertson, eds)
J.M. Coetzee, 453(NYRB):16Jan86-33
D. Mehl, 72:Band222Heft2-421
J. Meyers, 395(MFS):Summer85-357
W.H. Pritchard, 249(HudR):Winter86-673
D.R. Schwarz, 177(ELT):Vol28No3-298
Lawrence, D.H. The Lost Girl.* (J.
Worthen, ed)
J. Lane, 402(MLR):Jul85-706
Lawrence, D.H. Mr. Noon.* (L. Vasey, ed)
M. Dodsworth, 141:Spring85-69
C. Fuller, 565:Autumn85-25
J. Meyers, 395(MFS):Winter85-710
R.G. Walker, 177(ELT):Vol28No4-425
Lawrence, D.H. Mornings in Mexico.
617(TLS):25Apr86-459

Lawrence, D.H. St. Mawr and Other Stor-
ies.* (B. Finney, ed)
K.M. Hewitt, 541(RES):Nov85-598
Lawrence, D.H. The White Peacock.* (A.
Robertson, ed) The Prussian Officer and
Other Stories.* (J. Worthen, ed)
J.M. Coetzee, 453(NYRB):16Jan86-33
K.M. Hewitt, 541(RES):Nov85-598
Lawrence, D.H. Study of Thomas Hardy and
Other Essays.* (B. Steele, ed)
J.M. Coetzee, 453(NYRB):16Jan86-33
Lawrence, D.H. Women in Love. (C.L. Ross,
ed)
J. Newman, 161(DUJ):Jun84-308
Lawrence, K. The Life of Helen Alone.
J. Humphreys, 441:12Oct86-22
Lawrence, K.R. Maud Gone.
L. Liebmann, 441:21Sep86-32
Lawrence, K.R. The Odyssey of Style in
"Ulysses."*
M.H. Begnal, 480(P&R):Vol 18No1-60
V. Mahon, 677(YES):Vol 15-336
Lawrence, R.D. In Praise of Wolves.
P-L. Adams, 61:Jun86-83
N. Stoyen, 441:22Jun86-27
Lawrence, T.E. Crusader Castles.
S. Pepper, 617(TLS):17Oct86-1167
Lawson, A. Irvin S. Cobb.
J.W. Grinnell, 573(SSF):Spring85-251
Lawson, E.T. Religions of Africa.
J.S. La Fontaine, 617(TLS):10Jan86-45
Lawson, H. Reflexivity.
D.E. Cooper, 617(TLS):7Feb86-148
Lawson, L.A. Another Generation.
T.J. Fleming, 396(ModA):Summer85-265
D.R. Noble, 392:Fall85-483
W.J. Stuckey, 395(MFS):Summer85-400
Lawson, P. George Grenville.
J.J. Hecht, 173(ECS):Summer86-576
Lawson, R., with M. Naison, eds. The
Tenant Movement in New York City, 1904-
1984.
R. Caplan, 441:14Sep86-31
Lawson, S. The Archibald Paradox.
D. Green, 381:Jun85-193
W.M. Maidment, 71(ALS):May85-137
Lawton, D. Chaucer's Narrators.
A. Wawn, 617(TLS):28Nov86-1356
Lawton, D.A., ed. "Joseph of Arimathea."
P. Gradon, 541(RES):Nov85-558
J. Noble, 589:Apr85-427
Lawton, D.A., ed. Middle English Allitera-
tive Poetry and its Literary Background.*
C. Clark, 179(ES):Aug85-361
H.N. Duggan, 589:Jan85-170
E.D. Kennedy, 38:Band103Heft3/4-465
Lawton, M. Some Survived.*
B. Skardon, 580(SCR):Fall85-115
Laxalt, R. A Cup of Tea in Pamplona.
J. Sullivan, 441:18May86-25
Layman, R. Shadow Man.*
J.S. Whitley, 677(YES):Vol 15-353
Layton, E.T., with R. Pineau and J.
Costello. "And I Was There."
N. Bliven, 442(NY):14Apr86-105
R.H. Spector, 441:5Jan86-9
Layton, R. Sibelius. (2nd ed)
A.F.L.T., 412:Aug/Nov84-304
Lazarus, M. The Neighborhood Watch.
R. Goodman, 441:2Mar86-24

Lee, C-S. Revolutionary Struggle in Man-
churia.
  S.I. Levine, 293(JASt):Feb85-375
Lee, D. Jelly Belly.
  P. Nodelman, 102(CanL):Winter84-149
Lee, D., ed. The New Canadian Poets (1970-
1985).
  P.K. Smith, 99:Feb86-38
Lee, D.S. Native North American Music and
Oral Data.
  A.F.L.T., 412:Feb83-67
Lee, E. To the Bitter End.
  P. Warwick, 617(TLS):14Mar86-270
Lee, H. Heroes, Villains and Ghosts.
  T.J. Gordon, 649(WAL):Nov85-268
Lee, H. Philip Roth.
  R. Gray, 447(N&Q):Dec84-572
Lee, H., ed. The Secret Self.
  P. Craig, 617(TLS):18Jul86-792
Lee, H. - see Bowen, E.
Lee, H. - see Smith, S.
Lee, J.G. Philadelphians and the China
Trade, 1784-1844.
  A.L. Jensen, 656(WMQ):Jan85-158
Lee, L. and B. Gifford. Saroyan.
  T.K. Meier, 27(AL):Dec85-687
  D.W. Petrie, 395(MFS):Winter85-727
  295(JML):Nov85-551
Lee, L.O-F. - see Prusek, J.
Lee, M. The Road to Revolution.
  D. Stevenson, 617(TLS):13Jun86-636
Lee, M.L.R. - see under Rodríguez Lee,
M.L.
Lee, O-Y. Smaller Is Better.
  J. Abrams, 407(MN):Summer85-246
Lee, S. Law and Morals.
  A.M. Smith, 362:27Nov86-27
Lee, S.E. The Sketchbook of Hiroshige.*
  G. McNamee, 469:Vol 11No1-118
Lee, T-S. Die griechische Tradition der
aristotelischen Syllogistik in der
Spätantike.
  H. Maconi, 520:Vol30No1-92
Lee Yee, ed. The New Realism.
  J.C. Kinkley, 293(JASt):May85-596
Leech, G.N. Explorations in Semantics and
Pragmatics.
  U. Fries, 38:Band103Heft1/2-148
Leech, G.N. Principles of Pragmatics.*
  J. Verschueren, 297(JL):Sep85-459
Leech, G.N. and M.H. Short. Style in Fic-
tion.*
  H. Bonheim, 677(YES):Vol 15-261
  R. Carter, 447(N&Q):Dec84-558
  Z. Szabó, 599:Spring85-141
Leeman, F.W.G. Alciatus' Emblemata.
  H. Miedema, 600:Vol 15No2-151
Leerssen, J.T. Komparatistik in Grossbrit-
annien 1800-1950.
  J. Fletcher, 343:Heft12-120
  E.S. Shaffer, 678(YCGL):No34-156
Lees, A. Cities Perceived.
  P. Hall, 617(TLS):30May86-581
Lees, R.A. The Negative Language of the
Dionysian School of Mystical Theology.
  R. Bradley, 589:Jul85-695
Lees-Milne, A., ed. The Englishman's Room.
  D. Johnson, 453(NYRB):4Dec86-3
Lees-Milne, J. The Earls of Creation.
  617(TLS):15Aug86-899
Lees-Milne, J. The Enigmatic Edwardian.
  J. Grigg, 617(TLS):28Nov86-1334

Lees-Milne, J. and D. Ford. Images of
Bath.
  G.S. Rousseau, 579(SAQ):Winter85-99
Leetch, B. and P. Grundlehner. ¿Qué pasa?*
  D.R. Whitmore, 399(MLJ):Spring85-112
Le Faye, D. - see Austen, C.
Lefebure, M. The Bondage of Love.
  N. Fruman, 617(TLS):22Aug86-910
  D. Punter, 362:31Jul86-25
Lefebvre, C., H. Magloire-Holly and N.
Piou, eds. Syntaxe de l'haïtien.*
  H. Wise, 208(FS):Jul85-376
Lefkowitz, M.R. Women in Greek Myth.
  H. King, 617(TLS):18Jul86-1430
Lefort, J. Villages de Macédoine.* (Vol
1)
  R. Morris, 303(JoHS):Vol 105-251
Legaré, C. Pierre la fève et autres
contes de la Mauricie [suivi de] Le
statut sémiotique du motif en ethnolit-
térature.
  P. Imbert, 403(MLS):Fall85-374
Légaré, C. and A. Bougaïeff. L'Empire du
sacre québécois.
  L.B. Mignault, 627(UTQ):Summer85-485
Legge, M. Flowers and Fables.
  G. Wills, 39:Apr85-284
Leggett, J. Making Believe.
  P. West, 441:11May86-45
Leggett, W. Democratick Editorials.
  L.G., 185:Oct85-218
Le Goff, J. L'Imaginaire médiéval.
  A. Murray, 617(TLS):20Jun86-671
Le Goff, J. and B. Köpeczi, eds. Objets
et méthodes de l'histoire de la culture.
  É. Martonyi-Horváth, 535(RHL):Jul/
  Aug85-700
Legrand, M. Psychanalyse, science,
société.
  J-M. Gabaude, 542:Jan-Mar85-61
Le Guern, M. L'Image dans l'oeuvre de
Pascal.
  G. Molinié, 535(RHL):Sep/Oct85-871
Le Guin, U.K. Always Coming Home.*
  E. Jahner, 469:Vol 11No1-100
Lehman, D. and C. Berger, eds. James
Merrill.
  C. Nelson, 27(AL):Oct85-524
  D. Seed, 447(N&Q):Dec84-573
Lehmann, A. Erzählstruktur und Lebens-
lauf.*
  S. Lundin, 64(Arv):Vol39-211
Lehmann, A.G. The European Heritage.
  D. Thistlewood, 89(BJA):Summer85-295
Lehmann, C. Der Relativsatz.
  P. Ramat, 206(FoLi):Vol 19No3/4-523
Lehmann, H. and D. Lohmeier, eds. Aufklä-
rung und Pietismus in dänischen Gesamt-
staat 1770-1820.
  P.M. Mitchell, 301(JEGP):Apr85-306
Lehmann, J. New and Selected Poems.
  N. Jenkins, 617(TLS):1Aug86-839
Lehmann, J. and R. Fuller, eds. The Pen-
guin New Writing 1940-1950.*
  J. Symons, 364:Nov85-101
Lehmann, J.M. Italienische, französische
und spanische Gemälde des 16. bis 18.
Jahrhunderts.
  E. Schleier, 90:Sep85-626
Lehmann, W. Gesammelte Werke in acht
Bänden. (Vol 1) (H.D. Schäfer, ed)
  K. Weissenberger, 133:Band17Heft3/4-
  362

Lehmann, W.P. and Y. Malkiel, eds. Perspectives on Historical Linguistics.*
N.E. Collinge, 320(CJL):Spring85-79
Lehmann-Haupt, C. Me and DiMaggio.
D. Hall, 441:14Sep86-12
Lehni, E.R.R. - see under Rowedder Lehni, E.R.
Lehrberger, J. - see Gladkij, A.V. and I.A. Mel'čuk
Lehrer, A. Wine and Conversation.
J.B. Gatewood, 355(LSoc):Sep85-429
Leibnitz, T., ed. Katalog der Sammlung Anthony van Hoboken in der Musiksammlung der Österreichischen Nationalbibliothek, iii.
O. Neighbour, 410(M&L):Oct85-402
Leibniz, G.W. Escritos Filosóficos. (E. de Olaso, ed)
A. Guillermo Ranea, 706:Band17Heft2-225
Leibniz, G.W. New Essays on Human Understanding.* (P. Remnant and J. Bennett, eds and trans)
B. Mates, 449:Jun85-306
Leibniz, G.W. Renlei Lizhi Xin Lun. (Chen Xiuzhai, trans)
Wei Hsiung, 706:Band17Heft1-126
Leibniz, G.W. Sočinenija v četōrjoch tomach. (Vol 1) (V.V. Sokolov, ed)
M. Kõiv and P. Müürsepp, 706:Band17Heft2-220
Leidecker, K. Zauberklänge der Phantasie.
R. Brandl, 196:Band26Heft1/2-176
Leigh, R.A., ed. Rousseau after Two Hundred Years.*
C.J. Betts, 208(FS):Jan85-78
E. Gans, 591(SIR):Fall85-433
Leighton, A. Shelley and the Sublime.
S.M. Smith, 89(BJA):Summer85-281
C. Walker, 340(KSJ):Vol34-184
Leighton, L.G., ed. Studies in Honor of Xenia Gąsiorowska.*
J. Graffy, 575(SEER):Oct85-581
Leighton, L.G. - see Chukovksy, K.I.
Leims, T., with I. Chlan and L. Pavlicek. Kabuki, Holzschnitt, Japonismus.
D. Schauwecker, 407(MN):Summer85-247
Leinbaugh, H.P. and J.D. Campbell. The Men of Company K.
D. Murray, 441:19Jan86-21
Leinieks, V. The Plays of Sophokles.*
G. Gellie, 67:May85-80
Leinsdorf, E. The Composer's Advocate.*
P.J.P., 412:Aug/Nov83-304
A.F.L.T., 412:Aug/Nov84-304
Leiris, M. Francis Bacon.*
A. Woods, 97(CQ):Vol 14No2-145
Leiss, W., S. Kline and S. Jhally. Social Communication in Advertising.
R. Draper, 453(NYRB):26Jun86-14
J. Rosen, 362:27Nov86-28
Leitch, D. Family Secrets.
P. Ackroyd, 441:13Jul86-9
Leitch, V.B. Deconstructive Criticism.*
D.H. Hirsch, 569(SR):Summer85-465
A. Wordsworth, 541(RES):Aug85-458
Leiter, S. Akhmatova's Petersburg.*
W. Rosslyn, 402(MLR):Jan85-251
Leites, E. The Puritan Conscience and Modern Sexuality.
A.K. Offit, 441:16Mar86-35
Leith, D. A Social History of English.*
J. Algeo, 215(GL):Vol25No4-273

Leithauser, B. Cats of the Temple.
R. Tillinghast, 441:13Jul86-35
H. Vendler, 453(NYRB):23Oct86-47
Leithauser, B. Equal Distance.*
D. Pinckney, 453(NYRB):29May86-30
W.H. Pritchard, 249(HudR):Spring85-130
Leitner, G. BBC English und der BBC.
M. Uesseler, 682(ZPSK):Band38Heft2-188
Leki, I. Alain Robbe-Grillet.
J. Alter, 207(FR):Oct85-144
K. Racevskis, 345(KRQ):Vol32No1-105
Leland, M. The Killeen.
C. Verderese, 441:16Nov86-24
Lelièvre, C. and E. Walter. La Presse picarde, mémoire de la République.
R. Waller, 83:Spring85-117
Lelyveld, J. Move Your Shadow.*
E. Hahn, 442(NY):24Nov86-139
J. Levine, 676(YR):Summer86-610
C.C. O'Brien, 617(TLS):14Mar86-269
Lem, S. One Human Minute.
G. Jonas, 441:9Feb86-39
Lemann, N. Out of the Forties.*
J. Guimond, 219(GaR):Winter86-876
Lemay, J.A.L. The Canon of Benjamin Franklin, 1722-1776.
J. Griffith, 165(EAL):Fall86-166
Lemay, J.A.L. "New England's Annoyances."
27(AL):Dec85-699
Lemay, J.A.L. and P.M. Zall - see Franklin, B.
Lemerle, P. Les plus anciennes recueils des miracles de saint Démétrius et la pénétration des Slaves dans les Balkans.
R. Browning, 303(JoHS):Vol 105-246
Lemerle, P. and others. Actes de Lavra.* (Pt 4)
K. Snipes, 589:Jul85-697
Lemire, M. and others. Dictionnaire des oeuvres littéraires du Québec, IV, 1960-1969.
B-Z. Shek, 627(UTQ):Summer85-471
Lemm, U. Die literarische Verarbeitung der Träume Gottfried Kellers in seinem Werk.
L.A. Rickels, 221(GQ):Winter85-132
Lemmon, D. Ken McEwan.
A. Ross, 617(TLS):3Jan86-21
Lemon, R. The Probity Chorus.
B. Harvey, 441:6Apr86-22
442(NY):14Apr86-109
Le Moncheck, L. Dehumanizing Women.
P.S. Mann, 185:Jul86-885
Lencek, R.L. and H.R. Cooper, Jr., eds. Papers in Slavic Philology.* (Vol 2)
T. Eekman, 574(SEEJ):Winter85-493
Leneman, L. Living in Atholl.
B. Lenman, 617(TLS):24Oct86-1200
Lenger, M-T. Corpus des Ordonnances des Ptolémées (C. Ord. Ptol.).
W. Clarysse, 394:Vol38fasc3/4-455
Lenk, E. Die unbewusste Gesellschaft.
A. Allkemper, 680(ZDP):Band104Heft4-629
Lennon, J. Skywriting by Word of Mouth.
442(NY):8Dec86-154
Lennon, N. Alfred Jarry.*
295(JML):Nov85-506
Lennon, T.M., J.M. Nicholas and J.W. Davis, eds. Problems of Cartesianism.*
J-R. Armogathe, 192(EP):Apr-Jun85-267

225

Lesko, D. James Ensor.
  R. Cardinal, 617(TLS):11Apr86-379
Leskov, N. Five Tales.* (M. Sholton, ed
  and trans) The Enchanted Wanderer.
  G. Annan, 617(TLS):28Mar86-340
Leskov, N. The Sealed Angel and Other
  Stories. (K.A. Lantz, ed and trans)
  J. Muckle, 402(MLR):Oct85-1007
Lesky, A. Greek Tragic Poetry.*
  A. Bradshaw, 161(DUJ):Jun85-256
  K.J. Dover, 447(N&Q):Sep84-410
Leslau, W. Gurage Folklore.
  J. Knappert, 203:Vol96No2-265
Leslie, M. Spenser's "Fierce Warres and
  Faithfull Loves."
  R.C. McCoy, 551(RenQ):Summer85-361
Lesser, M. Clarkey.*
  A-C. Stoltzfus, 446(NCFS):Spring-
  Summer86-394
Lessing, D. The Good Terrorist.*
  P. Lewis, 364:Oct85-90
"Lessing Yearbook." (Vol 14 ed by E.P.
  Harris and W. Wuckerpfennig; Vol 15 ed
  by E.P. Harris)
  J.W. Van Cleve, 221(CQ):Winter85-113
Lester, G.A. Sir John Paston's "Grete
  Boke."
  A.S.G. Edwards, 589:Jul85-699
  A. Payne, 354:Jun85-182
Lester, G.A., ed. Three Late Medieval
  Morality Plays.*
  M. Axton, 402(MLR):Jul85-686
Lester, R.K. "Trivialneger."*
  H.D. Osterle, 406:Winter85-503
Lestringant, F. - see Thevet, A.
Lesure, F., ed. Querelle des Gluckistes
  et des Piccinnistes.
  J. Rushton, 410(M&L):Oct85-400
Lesy, M. Visible Light.
  442(NY):3Mar86-106
Lesy, M. Wisconsin Death Trip. Real Life.
  Time Frames. Bearing Witness.
  F. Brunet, 98:Aug-Sep85-878
Letarouilly, P-M. Edifices de Rome
  Moderne.
  C. Matheu, 45:Oct85-109
Lethbridge, H.J. - see Crow, C.
Lethbridge, R. Maupassant: "Pierre et
  Jean."
  M. Donaldson-Evans, 446(NCFS):Spring-
  Summer86-376
Lethist, M. Poèmes de la mémoire.
  S.L. Rosenstreich, 207(FR):May86-999
Letsch, H. Der Alltag und die Dinge um
  uns.
  M. Hofmann, 654(WB):9/1985-1569
Lett, Z. Anaesthesia in Hong Kong.
  G.H. Choa, 302:Vol21No1-108
"Letteratura popolare di espressione fran-
  cese dall''Ancien Régime' all'Ottocento/
  Roland Barthes e il suo metodo critico."
  F. Assaf, 475:Vol 12No22-273
  J.G. Rosso, 535(RHL):Sep/Oct85-891
"Letture Classensi." (Vol 13) (M. Corti,
  ed)
  Z.G. Barański, 402(MLR):Jul85-728
Leuchtenburg, W.E. In the Shadow of FDR.
  G.S. Smith, 529(QQ):Summer85-297
Leuci, B. Odessa Beach.
  N. Callendar, 441:19Jan86-17
Leunig, M. A Piece of Cake.
  B. Bainbridge, 617(TLS):26Dec86-1453

van Leuven-Zwart, K.M. Vertaling en
  origineel.
  C. van der Voort, 204(FdL):Sep85-221
Leuwers, D., ed. Pierre-Jean Jouve I.*
  M. Callander, 208(FS):Jul85-365
Levack, D.J.H. Amber Dreams.
  G.K. Wolfe, 561(SFS):Mar85-102
Léveillé, J.R. Plage.
  J.M. Paterson, 102(CanL):Spring85-159
"Levend Nederlands." (rev)
  E.S. Randall, 399(MLJ):Autumn85-304
Levenson, C.B. Le chemin de Lhassa.
  J-F. Revel, 176:Jan86-36
Levenson, L. and J.H. Natterstad. Hanna
  Sheehy-Skeffington.
  M. Tax, 441:7Sep86-15
Levenson, M.H. A Genealogy of Modernism.
  A.W. Litz, 617(TLS):10Oct86-1142
  D. Schier, 569(SR):Summer85-lxv
  295(JML):Nov85-373
Lever, E. Louis XVI.
  J. Rogister, 617(TLS):24Jan86-85
Lever, H. and C. Huhne. Debt and Danger.
  J.E. Spero, 441:18May86-23
Lever, J. Architects' Designs for Furni-
  ture.
  L.B., 90:Sep85-632
Lever, W. and C. Moore, eds. The City in
  Transition.
  N. Deakin, 617(TLS):7Nov86-1239
Levere, T.H. Poetry Realized in Nature.*
  T. Corrigan, 403(MLS):Fall85-355
Levernier, J.A. and D.R. Wilmes, eds.
  American Writers before 1800.*
  N.S. Grabo, 173(ECS):Fall85-130
  P.J. Lindholdt, 568(SCN):Spring-
  Summer85-18
  W.P. Wenska, 656(WMQ):Apr85-273
Levertov, D. Oblique Prayers.*
  S. Scobie, 376:Mar85-162
  639(VQR):Spring85-56
Lévesque, C. and C.V. McDonald, eds.
  L'Oreille de l'autre.*
  J.M. Todd, 131(CL):Fall85-361
Levi, I. The Enterprise of Knowledge.*
  P. Maher, 486:Dec84-690
Levi, P. The Echoing Green.*
  J. Saunders, 565:Autumn85-74
Levi, P. If Not Now, When?*
  C. Chanteau, 362:15May86-30
  M. Hulse, 176:Sep/Oct86-59
  A.L. Lepschy, 617(TLS):22Aug86-923
Levi, P. Moments of Reprieve.
  D. Evanier, 441:23Feb86-24
  M. Wandor, 362:16Oct86-25
  442(NY):31Mar86-84
Levi, P. The Monkey's Wrench.
  P-L. Adams, 61:Dec86-103
  A. Kazin, 441:12Oct86-1
Levi, P., ed. The Penguin Book of English
  Christian Verse.
  H. Clucas, 4:Autumn-Winter85/86-51
Levi, P. The Periodic Table.*
  M.A. Abidor, 287:Nov-Dec85-30
  S. Bernstein, 42(AR):Summer85-364
  P. Collier, 364:Nov85-99
  N. Lewis, 362:2Jan86-22
  639(VQR):Summer85-100
Lévi-Strauss, C. La Potière Jalouse.
  M. Bloch, 617(TLS):21Mar86-299
Levin, B. Hannibal's Footsteps.*
  442(NY):17Nov86-154

Lewis, H.D.  The Elusive Self.*
  E.T. Long, 543:Mar85-655
Lewis, H.D.  Freedom and Alienation.
  E.T. Long, 543:Mar86-571
Lewis, J.  The Twentieth Century Book.*
  C. Hess, 507:Mar/Apr85-104
Lewis, J.D. and R.L. Smith.  American
  Sociology and Pragmatism.
  E. Matthews, 488:Jun85-197
Lewis, M.  The Monk.  (D.P. Varma, ed)
  P-G. Boucé, 189(EA):Jan-Mar86-116
Lewis, M.A.  Afro-Hispanic Poetry, 1940-
  1980.*
  M.K. Cobb, 238:May85-324
Lewis, N.  Jackdaw Cake.
  J. Mellors, 364:Oct85-105
Lewis, N.  Life in Egypt under Roman Rule.*
  J. Rowlandson, 123:Vol35No1-140
Lewis, N.  Within the Labyrinth.
  A. Cornelisen, 441:15Jun86-12
Lewis, P.  John le Carré.
  B. Morrison, 617(TLS):11Apr86-381
Lewis, P., ed.  Radio Drama.
  P. Davison, 677(YES):Vol 15-362
Lewis, P.G.  The Literary Vision of Gab-
  rielle Roy.
  T. Quigley, 268(IFR):Winter86-58
Lewis, R.  Slings and Arrows.
  H.K. Chinoy, 615(TJ):Mar85-117
Lewis, R.  A Trout in the Milk.
  N. Callendar, 441:28Sep86-28
Lewis, R. and J.B. Easson.  Publishing and
  Printing at Home.
  D. Chambers, 503:Winter84-192
Lewis, R.E. - see "Middle English Diction-
  ary"
Lewis, R.E. and A. McIntosh.  A Descrip-
  tive Guide to the Manuscripts of the
  "Prick of Conscience."*
  S.J. Ogilvie-Thomson, 541(RES):Feb85-
  142
Lewis, S.  Art Out of Agony.
  L. Shohet, 102(CanL):Spring85-117
Lewis, W.  A bas la France, Vive la France.
  (B. Lafourcade, ed)
  V.D.L., 605(SC):15Apr86-274
Lewis-Williams, J.D.  The Rock Art of
  Southern Africa.
  D. Brokensha, 2(AfrA):Nov84-87
Lewontin, R.C., S. Rose and L.J. Kamin.
  Not In Our Genes.*
  N.S. Lehrman, 390:Nov85-61
Lewy, C. - see Broad, C.D.
Lewy, E.  Tscheremissisches Wörterbuch.
  (Vol 3) (H. Katz, ed)
  J. Gulya, 260(IF):Band90-377
Lewytzkyj, B.  Politics and Society in
  Soviet Ukraine, 1953-1980.
  I. Stebelsky, 104(CASS):Spring85-94
"Lexikon des frühgriechischen Epos."
  (Pt 10) (E-M. Voigt, ed)
  B. Forssman, 260(IF):Band90-302
"Lexikon des Mittelalters."  (Vol 1, Pts
  9 and 10; Vol 2, Pts 1-6)
  H. Beck, 680(ZDP):Band104Heft1-143
"Lexikon des Mittelalters."  (Vol 2) (G.
  Avella-Wildhalm, L. Lutz and U. and R.
  Mattejiet, eds)
  P. Dinter, 52:Band20Heft3-305
  R. Schenda, 196:Band26Heft1/2-179
Ley, A.C.  A Reputation Dies.
  639(VQR):Summer85-92
Leyda, J. - see Eisenstein, S.M.

Leyda, J. and Z. Voynow.  Eisenstein at
  Work.*
  R. Taylor, 617(TLS):27Jun86-716
von Leyden, W.  Aristotle on Equality and
  Justice.
  T.J. Saunders, 617(TLS):7Feb86-149
Leyner, M., C. White and T. Glynn.  Amer-
  ican Made.
  J.D. O'Hara, 441:21Sep86-46
Leys, C.  Politics in Britain.
  A. King, 529(QQ):Winter85-833
  C. Townshend, 617(TLS):28Nov86-1335
Leys, S.  The Burning Forest.*  (French
  title: La Forêt en feu.)
  442(NY):10Feb86-113
Lézy, D.  Dans le Métro.
  P.A. Berger, 399(MLJ):Spring85-87
Lhote, H.  Les Chars Rupestres Sahariens.
  M. Posnansky, 2(AfrA):Feb85-91
Li Ang.  The Butcher's Wife.
  R. Burgin, 441:28Dec86-18
Li, Z.Y. and others - see under Zheng Yi
  Li and others
Liang Heng and J. Shapiro.  After the
  Nightmare.
  J.K. Fairbank, 453(NYRB):17Jul86-33
  C. Wakeman, 441:22Jun86-7
Liang Ssu-ch'eng.  A Pictorial History of
  Chinese Architecture.*  (W. Fairbank, ed)
  42(AR):Winter85-123
Libby, A.  Mythologies of Nothing.*
  M. Dickie, 115:Fall84/Winter85-152
Liberman, A. - see Lermontov, M.
Liberman, A. - see Propp, V.
Libert, B.  Parades.
  S.L. Rosenstreich, 207(FR):May86-1000
Libin, L.  American Musical Instruments.
  L. Charlton, 441:23Feb86-22
Librandi, R. - see De Liguori, S.A.M.
Lichtenberg, G.C.  Briefwechsel.  (Vol 1)
  (U. Joost and A. Schöne, eds)
  D.C.G. Lorenz, 301(JEGP):Apr85-307
Lichtenberg, G.C.  Schriften und Briefe.
  (F.H. Mautner, ed)
  W. Goetschel, 221(GQ):Summer85-453
Lida de Malkiel, M.R.  Juan de Mena poeta
  del prerrenacimiento español.  (2nd ed)
  A.V., 379(MedR):Aug85-302
Liddell, R.  Elizabeth and Ivy.
  A. Hayter, 617(TLS):21Feb86-201
  M. Jones, 362:16Jan86-29
  H. Stevens, 364:Mar86-109
Lidtke, V.L.  The Alternative Culture.
  L.D. Stokes, 150(DR):Summer85-320
Lieb, H-H.  Integrational Linguistics.
  (Vol 1)
  J. Pogonowski, 361:Jul85-274
Lieb, M.  Poetics of the Holy.*
  G. Campbell, 402(MLR):Oct85-905
Liebanensis, B. and Eterius Oxomensis -
  see under Beatus Liebanensis and Eterius
  Oxomensis
Lieber, M.  Street Life.
  K.Q. Warner, 95(CLAJ):Jun86-493
Lieberman, E.J.  Acts of Will.*
  Z. Leader, 617(TLS):3Jan86-9
Lieberman, L.  The Mural of Wakeful Sleep.
  R. McDowell, 249(HudR):Winter86-689
  D. Smith, 491:Oct85-37
  P. Stitt, 344:Fall86-128
Liebeschütz, H.  Synagoge und Ecclesia.
  G.I. Langmuir, 589:Apr85-430

Lingenfelter, R.E.  Death Valley and the Amargosa.
  J. van der Zee, 441:24Aug86-15
Linggard, R.  Electronic Synthesis of Speech.
  W.S-Y. Wang, 350:Sep86-705
Lings, M.  The Secrets of Shakespeare.
  R. Kift, 157:No157-51
"Lingua e storia in Puglia." (fasc 13-22)
  E. Radtke, 553(RLiR):Jan-Jun85-189
"Linguística e letteratura."
  G. Lepschy, 545(RPh):Nov84-234
Linhart, S. and F. Wöss.  Old Age in Japan.
  M. Cooper, 407(MN):Summer85-243
Link, G.  Montague-Grammatik.
  G.F. Meier, 682(ZPSK):Band38Heft2-190
Link, P., ed.  Roses and Thorns.*
  F.P. Brandauer, 293(JASt):Aug85-815
Link, P., ed.  Stubborn Weeds.*
  H. Siu, 293(JASt):Feb85-377
Link, P. - see Liu Binyan
Linke, H.G.  Das zarische Russland und der Erste Weltkrieg.
  M. Perrins, 575(SEER):Jan85-132
Linklater, M. and D. Leigh.  Not With Honour.
  J. Turner, 617(TLS):22Aug86-904
Linse, U.  Barfüssige Propheten.
  R. Rudolph and C. Ford, 59:Mar85-125
Linsky, L.  Oblique Contexts.
  D.H. Helman, 393(Mind):Jan85-149
Linthout, G. and H. Schatz.  Deutsch Aktuell.
  B.J. Koekkoek, 399(MLJ):Spring85-93
Lintvelt, J.  Essai de typologie narrative.*
  A. Jefferson, 208(FS):Jan85-115
Lioure, M.  Le Théâtre religieux en France.
  A. Viala, 535(RHL):Mar/Apr85-331
Lipman, J.  Frank Lloyd Wright and the Johnson Wax Buildings.
  E. Zotti, 441:22Jun86-27
Lipman, J., E.V. Warren and R. Bishop.  Young America.
  442(NY):27Oct86-150
Lipman, S.  The House of Music.
  R.S. Clark, 249(HudR):Spring85-106
Lipow, A.  Authoritarian Socialism in America.*
  H.P. Segal, 26(ALR):Spring/Autumn85-262
Lippard, L.R.  Ad Reinhardt.
  C. Scherrmann, 384:Sep/Oct85-942
Lippolis, E.  La necropoli del palazzone di Perugia.
  M.H. Crawford, 313:Vol75-319
Lipset, S.M., ed.  Unions in Transition.
  G. Easterbrook, 441:26Oct86-34
Lipski, J.J.  KOR.
  T.G. Ash, 453(NYRB):9Oct86-45
  A. Brumberg, 617(TLS):3Oct86-1091
Lipson, C.  Standing Guard.
  D. Lal, 617(TLS):2May86-469
Lipstadt, D.E.  Beyond Belief.*
  D. Casse, 129:Apr86-70
  G.A. Craig, 453(NYRB):10Apr86-7
Lipton, L.  A Truthful Likeness.
  K. Manthorne, 127:Winter85-375
Liscinsky, R.N., ed.  Le Fais et Conc-questes du noble roy Alexandre.*
  L.J. Friedman, 545(RPh):Feb85-398

Lish, G.  Peru.
  S. Dobyns, 441:2Feb86-7
  442(NY):10Mar86-123
Lish, G.  What I Know So Far.
  R. Stevens, 573(SSF):Spring85-245
Lispector, C.  Family Ties.*
  S. White, 448:Vol23No2-106
Lispector, C.  The Foreign Legion.
  J. Gledson, 617(TLS):30May86-587
Lispector, C.  The Hour of the Star.
  J. Gledson, 617(TLS):30May86-587
  A.J. MacAdam, 441:18May86-27
Liss, S.B.  Marxist Thought in Latin America.
  M.C. Needler, 263(RIB):Vol35No2-212
List, G.  Music and Poetry in a Colombian Village.
  G. Béhague, 317:Summer85-399
  D.A. Olsen, 650(WF):Jan85-62
  P. Poveda, 292(JAF):Jan/Mar85-109
Lister, R.  The Paintings of Samuel Palmer.
  K.Z. Cieszkowski, 324:Nov86-847
Lister, R.  Prints and Printmaking.
  S. Houfe, 39:Mar85-211
Littell, R.  The Sisters.
  P. Andrews, 441:2Feb86-9
  T.R. Edwards, 453(NYRB):8May86-12
  M. Laski, 362:17Apr86-29
"La littérature chinoise au temps de la guerre de résistance contre le Japon (de 1937 à 1945)."*
  P. Bady, 549(RLC):Jul-Sep85-368
Little, G.C.  Endless Waves.
  V. Provenzano, 404:Summer85-49
Little, J.  Comedy and the Woman Writer.*
  C. Heilbrun, 301(JEGP):Jan85-110
Little, J.P.  Samuel Beckett: "En attendant Godot" and "Fin de partie."
  J. Knowlson, 208(FS):Apr85-233
Little, R.  Études sur Saint-John Perse.
  A. Berrie, 208(FS):Oct85-499
Little, R.  Rimbaud: "Illuminations."*
  C. Chadwick, 208(FS):Jan85-99
  F.S. Heck, 207(FR):Apr86-791
Littlefield, D.F., Jr. and J.W. Parins.  American Indian and Alaska Native Newspapers and Periodicals, 1826-1924.
  V.S. Salabiye, 635(VPR):Winter85-151
Littlefield, M.G., ed.  Biblia Romanceada I.I.8.*
  D.W. Lomax, 86(BHS):Jan85-134
Littlejohn, D.  Architect.
  W. Hubbard, 45:Jan85-73
Littlejohn, G.  A Sociology of the Soviet Union.
  B. Kerblay, 575(SEER):Jul85-472
Littlewood, I.  The Writings of Evelyn Waugh.*
  D. Gallagher, 67:May85-65
Littlewood, W.  Foreign and Second Language Learning.
  W. Acton, 351(LL):Jun85-323
  H.J. Siskin, 207(FR):Oct85-173
Littrup, L.  Subbureaucratic Government in China in Ming Times.
  J. Lacey, 293(JASt):Nov84-180
Littwin, S.  The Postponed Generation.
  P. Weiss, 441:2Mar86-25
"Liturgie et musique (IXe-XIVe s.)."
  M.K. McGrory, 589:Oct85-1051
Litvack, F.E.P.  "Le Droit du seigneur" in European and American Literature (From
                                    [continued]

Lockwood, M., ed. Moral Dilemmas in Modern Medicine.
  I. McGilchrist, 617(TLS):7Nov86-1251
Lockwood, W.B. The Oxford Book of British Bird Names.*
  L.R.N. Ashley, 424:Dec85-298
Lockwood, Y.R. Text and Context.
  M. Alexiou, 575(SEER):Oct85-591
  D.E. Bynum, 104(CASS):Spring85-112
  R.O. Joyce, 292(JAF):Apr/Jun85-215
Lodder, C. Russian Constructivism.*
  J. Kennedy, 550(RusR):Jan85-89
  P. Wood, 59:Mar85-105
Loderecker, P. Dictionarium septem diversarum linguarum. (A. Mestan, ed)
  Z. Salzmann, 350:Mar86-219
Lodge, D. Out of the Shelter.*
  P. Lewis, 565:Summer85-50
Lodge, D. Small World.*
  J.R. Banks, 148:Spring85-79
  J. Klinkowitz, 532(RCF):Spring85-151
  W. Lesser, 249(HudR):Autumn85-465
  639(VQR):Summer85-92
Lodge, D. Write On.
  C. Baldick, 617(TLS):12Dec86-1393
Lodge, K.R. Studies in the Phonology of Colloquial English.
  A.R. James, 361:Sep85-89
Loeb, P.R. Hope in Hard Times.
  P. La Farge, 441:19Oct86-32
Loescher, G. and J.A. Scanlan. Calculated Kindness.
  M.S. Teitelbaum, 441:12Oct86-34
"L'Oeuvre de Louis Couturat (1878-1914)."
  A.C. Lewis, 556:Winter85/86-184
Loew, E.A. The Beneventan Script. (V. Brown, ed)
  P. Meyvaert, 589:Jul85-748
Loewenberg, P. Decoding the Past.*
  H.R. Coursen, 125:Fall84-93
Loewenstein, J. Responsive Readings.
  T. Minter, 157:No157-51
Löfstedt, B. - see Beatus Liebanensis and Eterius Oxomensis
Logan, F.D. The Vikings in History.*
  R.T. Farrell, 589:Apr85-433
Logan, G.M. The Meaning of More's "Utopia."*
  M.F. Dixon, 178:Jun85-233
  R.W. Dyson, 161(DUJ):Jun84-313
  W.S. Hill, 405(MP):Nov85-184
Logan, J. A Ballet for the Ear. (A. Poulin, Jr., ed)
  R. McDowell, 249(HudR):Autumn85-509
Logan, W. Difficulty.
  B. Ruddick, 148:Autumn85-79
  R. Tillinghast, 441:13Jul86-35
Logan, W. Moorhen.
  J.D. McClatchy, 249(HudR):Spring85-168
Loggins, O.S. Tenderfoot Trail.
  G. Noonan, 102(CanL):Winter84-116
Logue, C., comp. The Children's Book of Children's Rhymes.
  G. Szirtes, 617(TLS):4Jul86-746
Logue, C.M. - see McGill, R.
Loh, W.D. Social Research in the Judicial Process.
  B.G.H., 185:Jul86-913
Löhken, H. Ordines Dignitatum.
  A.R. Birley, 123:Vol35No1-205
Lohmander, I. Old and Middle English Words for "Disgrace" and "Dishonour."*
  S. Ohlander, 597(SN):Vol57No1-117

Lohmann, H-M., ed. Psychoanalyse und Nationalsozialismus.
  C. Neubaur, 384:May85-427
Lohnes, W.F.W. and E.A. Hopkins, eds. The Contrastive Grammar of English and German.
  B. Carstensen, 685(ZDL):3/1985-402
  A. Fill, 224(GRM):Band35Heft4-474
Lohrmann, D. Kirchengut im nördlichen Frankreich.
  C.V. Graves, 589:Apr85-434
Lökkös, A. Catalogue des incunables imprimés à Genève 1478-1500.
  D.J. Shaw, 354:Sep85-274
Lomas, H. Fire in the Garden.*
  M. O'Neill, 493:Jan85-61
Lomas, H. Letters in the Dark.
  G. Lindop, 617(TLS):3Oct86-1118
Lombard, L.B. Events.
  J.E. Tiles, 617(TLS):25Apr86-455
Lombardi, L. Conversazioni con Petrassi.
  J.C.G. Waterhouse, 410(M&L):Oct85-383
Lombardi, S. Jean Fouquet.
  90:Apr85-243
Lomnitzer, H. - see Neidhart von Reuenthal
London, J. A Klondike Trilogy. (E. Labor, ed)
  D.L. Walker, 26(ALR):Spring/Autumn85-266
London, J. Young Wolf. (H. Lachtman, ed)
Jack London's Tales of Hawaii.
  F. Buske, 649(WAL):May85-74
Londré, F.H. Federico García Lorca.
  J. Ortega, 125:Winter85-228
Loney, G., ed. Musical Theatre in America.
  G. Maschio, 615(TJ):May85-237
Long, F.A., D. Hafner and J. Boutwell, eds. Weapons in Space.
  M. MccGwire, 617(TLS):31Oct86-1214
  N. Wade, 441:8Jun86-37
Long, M. Marvell, Nabokov.*
  C.S. Brown, 131(CL):Fall85-369
  M. Couturier, 189(EA):Oct-Dec86-488
  A. Gibson, 175:Spring85-88
  G.M. Hyde, 97(CQ):Vol 14No1-68
  E.P. Walkiewicz, 568(SCN):Fall85-42
  295(JML):Nov85-530
Long, R. Javanese Shadow Theater.*
  M. Hatch, 187:Winter86-182
Long, R.E. Henry James: The Early Novels.
  J.W. Tuttleton, 26(ALR):Spring/Autumn85-256
Long, R.E. Barbara Pym.
  C. Barr, 362:31Jul86-24
  A.S. Byatt, 617(TLS):8Aug86-862
Longeon, C. - see Dolet, É.
Longford, E. The Pebbled Shore.
  V. Glendinning, 617(TLS):29Aug86-930
  A. Howard, 441:26Oct86-16
Longford, F. The Bishops.
  J. Whale, 617(TLS):7Nov86-1238
Longley, E. - see Durcan, P.
Longley, E. - see Thomas, E.
Longley, M. Poems 1963-1983.*
  D. Davis, 362:30Jan86-24
  T. Eagleton, 565:Autumn85-69
  P. McDonald, 493:Jan85-14
  J. Mole, 176:Jan86-57
"Longman Dictionary of the English Language."
  H. Käsmann, 38:Band103Heft3/4-426

Lucas, J.   Moderns and Contemporaries.
    D. Sexton, 617(TLS):9May86-506
Lucas, J.R.   Space, Time and Causality.
    A.W. Moore, 617(TLS):17Jan86-68
Lucas, P.R.   American Odyssey, 1607-1789.
    C. Ubbelohde, 656(WMQ):Jul85-407
Lucci, V.   Etude phonétique du français
    contemporain à travers la variation
    situationnelle.
    P. Léon, 207(FR):Oct85-167
Luce, T.J., ed-in-chief.   Ancient Writers:
    Greece and Rome.*   (Vol 1) [entry in
    prev was Vols 1 and 2]
    T. Van Nortwick, 24:Spring85-122
Luce, T.J., ed-in-chief.   Ancient Writers:
    Greece and Rome.*   (Vol 2)
    E.J. Kenney, 24:Spring85-124
Lucente, G.L.   The Narrative of Realism
    and Myth.
    A. Arnold, 107(CRCL):Sep85-558
    G. Cecchetti, 276:Autumn85-267
    L.M. Gunzberg, 400(MLN):Dec85-1190
Luchetti, C., with C. Olwell.   Women of
    the West.
    R. Whitaker, 649(WAL):May85-63
Luciano, R. and D. Fisher.   The Fall of
    the Roman Umpire.
    J. Michalak, 441:3Aug86-19
Lucie-Smith, E.   American Art Now.   Art of
    the 1930s.
    A. Ross, 364:Dec85/Jan86-126
de Lucinge, R.   De la naissance, durée et
    chute des estats.   (M.J. Heath, ed)
    J.J. Supple, 208(FS):Jul85-329
Ludden, D.   Peasant History in South India.
    J. Brow, 617(TLS):19Sep86-1040
Lüderitz, G.   Corpus jüdischer Zeugnisse
    aus der Cyrenaika.
    M.D. Goodman, 313:Vol75-284
Ludlum, R.   The Bourne Supremacy.
    T.R. Edwards, 453(NYRB):8May86-12
    D. Wiltse, 441:9Mar86-12
Ludlum, R.   The Aquitaine Progression.*
    (French title: La Progression Aquitaine.)
    L. Kovacs, 450(NRF):Apr85-107
Lüdtke, H., ed.   Kommunikationstheore-
    tische Grundlagen des Sprachwandels.*
    O. Werner, 260(IF):Band90-268
Ludvigson, S.   The Swimmer.
    V. Shetley, 491:Apr85-41
    639(VQR):Winter85-26
Lüger, H-H.   Pressesprache.
    B.J. Koekkoek, 221(GQ):Spring85-271
Lühning, H.   "Titus"-Vertonungen im 18.
    Jahrhundert.
    R. Monelle, 410(M&L):Jul85-248
Lühr, R.   Studien zur Sprache des Hilde-
    brandliedes.
    R. d'Alquen, 406:Winter85-480
    D.H. Green, 402(MLR):Jan85-203
    H. Tiefenbach, 260(IF):Band90-358
Luis, W., ed.   Voices from Under.
    J. Ariza Gonzalez, 263(RIB):Vol35No2-
    212
    C. Werner, 395(MFS):Summer85-420
Lukács, G.   Essays on Realism.   (R. Living-
    stone, ed)   The Historical Novel.
    G. Woodcock, 569(SR):Summer85-457
Lukacs, J.   Outgrowing Democracy.
    J.P. Diggins, 31(ASch):Winter84/85-138
    E. Genovese, 560:Summer85-198
    W.M. McClay, 639(VQR):Winter85-162

Lukas, J.A.   Common Ground.*
    J.Q. Wilson, 129:Jan86-68
Lukas, R.C.   Forgotten Holocaust.
    G.A. Craig, 453(NYRB):10Apr86-7
Luke, M.   The Nine Days Queen.
    J. Kaufman, 441:21Sep86-30
Lukes, S.   Marxism and Morality.*
    E. Kamenka, 441:2Feb86-20
Lukes, S. and I. Galnoor.   No Laughing
    Matter.
    A. Hodgkin, 617(TLS):30May86-580
Lumiansky, R.M. and D. Mills, with R.
    Rastall.   The Chester Mystery Cycle.*
    S. Carpenter, 541(RES):Aug85-412
    A.H. Nelson, 402(MLR):Jan85-115
"Les Lumières en Hongrie, en Europe
    centrale et en Europe orientale."
    D-H. Pageaux, 549(RLC):Jan-Mar85-92
Lummis, T.   Occupation and Society.
    R. Blythe, 617(TLS):24Jan86-94
Lund, H.P.   La critique du siècle chez
    Nodier.*
    O.R. Trinik, 475:Vol 12No22-329
Lund-Baer, K.   The Orphan.*
    K. Robinson, 447(N&Q):Mar84-91
Lundahl, M. and E. Wadensjö.   Unequal
    Treatment.
    J.L.H., 185:Apr86-676
Lundin, J. and D.P. Dolson, eds.   Studies
    on Immersion Education.
    W.E. De Lorenzo, 399(MLJ):Spring85-80
Lundstrom, R.F.   William Poel's Hamlets.
    C.M. Mazer, 615(TJ):Oct85-388
Lunn, E.   Marxism and Modernism.*
    D. Barnouw, 221(GQ):Fall85-593
Lunn, K., ed.   Race and Labour in
    Twentieth-Century Britain.
    J. Rex, 617(TLS):13Jun86-656
Lunt, J.   "A Hell of a Licking."
    M. Carver, 617(TLS):21Mar86-294
Lupaş, L. and Z. Petre.   Commentaire aux
    "Sept contre Thèbes" d'Eschyle.*
    W.J. Verdenius, 394:Vol38fasc3/4-404
Lupica, M.   Dead Air.
    A. Krystal, 441:25May86-14
Lupinin, N.   Religious Revolt in the
    XVIIth Century.
    A.V. Muller, 104(CASS):Summer85-238
Luplow, C.   Isaac Babel's Red Cavalry.
    M. Friedberg, 550(RusR):Jan85-91
    E.R. Sicher, 575(SEER):Jan85-99
Lupson, J.P.   Guide to German Idioms.
    R.H. Buchheit, 399(MLJ):Winter85-416
Lurati, O.   Natura e cultura nei nomi di
    luogo di Castel San Pietro e del Monte
    Generoso.
    J-P. Chambon, 553(RLiR):Jan-Jun85-212
Lurati, O. and I. Pinana.   Le parole di
    una valle.*
    J-P. Chambon, 553(RLiR):Jan-Jun85-209
Luria, S.E.   A Slot Machine, A Broken Test
    Tube.
    S. Bernstein, 42(AR):Spring85-242
Lurie, A.   Foreign Affairs.*
    W.H. Pritchard, 249(HudR):Spring85-127
Lurie, A.T. and A. Percy.   Bernardo Caval-
    lino of Naples 1616-1656.
    C. Dempsey, 617(TLS):7Mar86-245
Luschei, M.   The Sovereign Wayfarer.
    V.A. Makowsky, 536(Rev):Vol7-305

Maas, P. Manhunt.
  T. Powers, 441:27Apr86-7
Maase, K. Lebensweise der Lohnarbeiter in
  der Freizeit.
  H. Hanke, 654(WB):7/1985-1219
Mabberley, D.J. Jupiter Botanicus.
  W. George, 617(TLS):11Apr86-400
Maber, R.G. The Poetry of Pierre Le Moyne
  (1602-1671).*
  B. Nicholas, 402(MLR):Jan85-164
  G. de Rocher, 345(KRQ):Vol32No4-429
Maber, R.G. - see "Malherbe, Théophile de
  Viau, and Saint-Amant"
Mabey, R. The Frampton Flora.*
  442(NY):22Sep86-118
McAdam, R. Life in Glass.
  B. Whiteman, 529(QQ):Winter85-842
McAdams, A.J. East Germany and Détente.
  G.A. Craig, 453(NYRB):25Sep86-62
Macafee, C. Glasgow.*
  R.K.S. Macaulay, 355(LSoc):Sep85-407
McAleavey, D. Holding Obsidian.
  L. Forestier, 496:Winter86-245
McAleer, J. Ralph Waldo Emerson.
  C. Bode, 432(NEQ):Mar85-122
  G.M. Johnson, 27(AL):Oct85-491
McAlester, V. and L. A Field Guide to
  American Houses.
  P. Kaufman, 576:Mar85-81
  R. Kimball, 45:Sep85-71
  D. Upton, 658:Summer/Autumn85-211
McAlister, L. The Development of Franz
  Brentano's Ethics.*
  J-M. Gabaude, 542:Jan-Mar85-38
McAllister, P.A. Umsindleko.
  D. Coplan, 538(RAL):Fall85-412
McAlpin, M.B. Subject to Famine.*
  R.C. Michie, 161(DUJ):Dec84-100
Macandrew, H. Dutch Church Painters.
  W. Liedtke, 90:Mar85-164
McArthur, B. Actors and American Culture,
  1880-1920.*
  S.M. Archer, 651(WHR):Autumn85-281
  D.B. Wilmeth, 612(ThS):Nov85-193
McArthur, L.A. Oregon Geographic Names.
  (5th ed rev by L.L. McArthur)
  K.H., 424:Dec85-300
McArthur, T. A Foundation Course for Lan-
  guage Teachers.*
  J.T. Chamberlain, 399(MLJ):Spring85-81
  J.N. Lacasa, 238:Dec85-796
McArthur, T. Worlds of Reference.
  A. Rosenheim, 617(TLS):9May86-492
McArthur, T. and P. Waddell. The Secret
  Life of John Logie Baird.
  N. Moss, 362:27Feb86-24
Macary, J. - see de Voltaire, F.M.A.
Macaulay, M. and others, eds. Proceedings
  of the Eighth Annual Meeting of the
  Berkeley Linguistics Society.
  M.W. Wheeler, 545(RPh):May85-496
McBain, E. Another Part of the City.
  D. Lehman, 441:11May86-21
  442(NY):4Aug86-88
McBain, E. Cinderella.
  D. Lehman, 441:11May86-21
McBain, E. Eight Black Horses.
  T.J. Binyon, 617(TLS):17Jan86-57
MacBeth, G. Dizzy's Woman.
  B. Tonkin, 362:4Sep86-22
  J.K.L. Walker, 617(TLS):31Oct86-1225
MacBeth, G. The Lion of Pescara.*
  J. Giovannini, 441:18May86-29

MacBeth, G. The Long Darkness.
  M. O'Neill, 493:Jan85-61
  R. Pybus, 565:Summer85-62
McBride, W.L. and C.O. Schrag, eds.
  Phenomenology in a Pluralistic Context.
  D.G., 185:Jan86-447
McBroom, P.A. The Third Sex.
  A. Hacker, 453(NYRB):14Aug86-26
  A.R. Hochschild, 441:11May86-15
McCabe, B. The Lipstick Circus.
  D. Montrose, 617(TLS):10Jan86-35
McCabe, C. The Face on the Cutting-Room
  Floor.
  362:7Aug86-26
MacCabe, C., ed. James Joyce.*
  C. Barrow, 174(Éire):Winter85-144
  V. Mahon, 677(YES):Vol 15-336
McCabe, C. Theoretical Essays.
  C. Butler, 617(TLS):14Feb86-170
MacCabe, C. and O. Stewart, eds. The BBC
  and Public Service Broadcasting.
  N. Annan, 617(TLS):12Sep86-991
McCabe, R.A. Joseph Hall.*
  J.M. Wands, 541(RES):Feb85-86
McCabe, W.H. An Introduction to the
  Jesuit Theater.* (L.J. Oldani, ed)
  P. Brady, 611(TN):Vol39No2-90
  S. Gossett, 551(RenQ):Spring85-160
  J. Schwartz, 568(SCN):Fall85-36
McCaffery, L. The Metafictional Muse.*
  G.F. Manning, 106:Summer85-237
McCaffery, S. Knowledge Never Knew.*
  P.M. St. Pierre, 102(CanL):Summer85-
  183
MacCaig, N. Collected Poems.
  A. Bold, 493:Oct85-58
  H. Lomas, 364:Feb86-76
  J. Mole, 176:Jan86-56
McCallum, P. Literature and Method.*
  L. Findlay, 49:Jan85-101
  J.A. Varsava, 577(SHR):Fall85-373
McCalman, J. Struggletown.
  K. Tsokhas, 381:Jun85-170
McCanles, M. The Discourse of "Il Prin-
  cipe."*
  B. Richardson, 402(MLR):Oct85-954
McCann, T.J., ed. The Correspondence of
  the Dukes of Richmond and Newcastle
  1724-1750.
  J. Black, 83:Autumn85-227
McCarriston, L. Talking Soft Dutch.
  M. Kumin, 219(GaR):Spring85-169
  V. Shetley, 491:Apr85-38
McCart, N. 20th Century Passenger Ships
  of the P&O.
  P.S. Bagwell, 324:Sep86-699
McCarthy, A. and J.G. Muskie. One Woman
  Lost.
  M. Dowd, 441:12Oct86-15
McCarthy, C. Blood Meridian.*
  W. Sullivan, 569(SR):Fall85-649
MacCarthy, D. Desmond MacCarthy: The Man
  and His Writings.* (D. Cecil, ed)
  J.A. Stein, 31(ASch):Winter84/85-135
MacCarthy, D. Sailing with Mr. Belloc.
  T.J. Binyon, 617(TLS):26Dec86-1442
McCarthy, J.A. and A.A. Kipa, eds. Auf-
  nahme — Weitergabe.
  H. Eichner, 406:Winter85-469
McCarthy, M. Occasional Prose.*
  D. Johnson, 617(TLS):31Jan86-111
McCarthy, M.Q. David R. Williams.
  L. Milazzo, 584(SWR):Summer85-415

McCarthy, M.S. Balzac and His Reader.*
G.R. Besser, 207(FR):Dec85-298
McCarthy, P. A Second Skin.
P. Levi, 4:Autumn-Winter85/86-62
C. Rawson, 617(TLS):7Feb86-137
McCarthy, T. The Non-Aligned Storyteller.
T. Eagleton, 565:Autumn85-69
M. Harmon, 272(IUR):Autumn85-234
H. Lomas, 364:Apr/May85-117
B. O'Donoghue, 493:Apr85-58
G. Szirtes, 148:Summer85-51
McCarthy, W. Hester Thrale Piozzi.
D. Nokes, 617(TLS):18Apr86-414
442(NY):14Apr86-110
MacCarthy-Morrogh, M. The Munster Planta-
tion.
L.M. Cullen, 617(TLS):19Sep86-1039
McCarty, M. The Transforming Principle.*
J. Secord, 617(TLS):16May86-524
MacCary, W.T. Childlike Achilles.*
C. Gill, 303(JoHS):Vol 105-176
McCash, W.B. Thomas R.R. Cobb (1823-1862).
A.P. McDonald, 9(AlaR):Jan85-77
McCaughey, R.A. International Studies and
Academic Enterprise.
C. Johnson, 293(JASt):Feb85-359
McCauley, M. The German Democratic Repub-
lic since 1945.
R. Woods, 575(SEER):Jan85-152
McCauley, M. Octobrists to Bolsheviks.
B. Williams, 575(SEER):Jan85-135
McCauley, M., ed. The Soviet Union after
Brezhnev.
P. Frank, 575(SEER):Jan85-149
McCawley, J.D. Thirty Million Theories of
Grammar.*
S. Romaine, 603:Vol9No1-154
Macchia, G. Le rovine di Parigi.
B. Craveri, 617(TLS):30ct86-1097
McClain, J.L. Kanazawa.
J.C. Baxter, 293(JASt):Feb85-397
McClatchy, J.D. Stars Principal.
R. Tillinghast, 441:13Jul86-35
McClintock, A. Drama for Mentally Handi-
capped Children.
P. Jones, 157:No155-52
McCloskey, D.N. The Rhetoric of Economics.
J. Coates, 617(TLS):1Aug86-834
R.L. Heilbroner, 453(NYRB):24Apr86-46
McCloskey, H.J. Ecological Ethics and
Politics.*
S.R.L. Clark, 518:Jul85-184
R. Elliot, 63:Dec85-499
McClosky, H. and A. Brill. Dimensions of
Tolerance.
J.L. Hochschild, 185:Jan86-386
McClung, N. Duenda.
P.K. Smith, 526:Spring85-88
McClung, W.A. The Architecture of Para-
dise.*
M.M. Gwin, 577(SHR):Summer85-295
H. Petroski, 579(SAQ):Winter85-102
McClure, J. Cop World.*
639(VQR):Summer85-95
McClure, J.D., ed. Scotland and the Low-
land Tongue.*
H. Utz, 588(SSL):Vol20-276
Maccoby, H. The Mythmaker.
D. Cupitt, 362:27Mar86-28
J.L. Houlden, 617(TLS):28Mar86-336
J.L. Martyn, 441:20Jul86-8
J. Pelikan, 129:Nov86-76

MacColl, E. and P. Seeger. Till Doomsday
in the Afternoon.
A. Smith, 617(TLS):30May86-584
McColley, D.K. Milton's Eve.*
R.J. Du Rocher, 577(SHR):Summer85-267
G.R. Evans, 541(RES):Nov85-623
C. Heilbrun, 301(JEGP):Jan85-110
McConkey, J. To a Distant Island.
295(JML):Nov85-458
McConnell, W. The Nibelungenlied.
F.H. Bäuml, 400(MLN):Apr85-690
W. Hoffmann, 133:Band18Heft1-76
McConville, M. Ascendancy to Oblivion.
R. Foster, 617(TLS):5Sep86-982
McCoola, R. Theatre in the Hills.
S. Rosenfeld, 611(TN):Vol39No3-157
McCord, W. and A. Paths to Progress.
P.D. Bell, 441:28Sep86-22
McCorkle, M. Johannes Brahms.
E. Sams, 415:Jul85-406
McCormack, W.J. Ascendancy and Tradition
in Anglo-Irish Literary History from
1789 to 1939.*
R. Tracy, 637(VS):Summer86-619
McCormack, W.J. and A. Stead, eds. James
Joyce and Modern Literature.*
V. Mahon, 677(YES):Vol 15-336
McCormick, E.A., ed. Germans in America.*
C.L. Dolmetsch, 221(GQ):Fall85-647
MacCormick, N. H.L.A. Hart.*
M.P. Golding, 311(JP):Aug85-440
McCormick, R.A. Notes on Moral Theology:
1981 through 1984.
D.S., 185:Apr86-683
McCorquodale, R. Dansville.
A.S. Grossman, 441:12Jan86-20
McCourt, J. Kaye Wayfaring in "Avenged."
I. Malin, 532(RCF):Spring85-151
McCown, R.A., ed. The Life and Times of
Leigh Hunt.
W. St. Clair, 617(TLS):18Apr86-428
McCoy, E. The Second Generation.
K.J. Weitze, 576:May85-188
McCracken, C.J. Malebranche and British
Philosophy.*
K. Haakonssen, 63:Dec85-574
T.M. Lennon, 482(PhR):Apr85-275
McCracken, D. Wordsworth and the Lake
District.*
D. Oakleaf, 178:Sep85-361
McCracken, K.H. Connie Hagar.
B. Webster, 441:50ct86-40
McCrea, B. Henry Fielding and the Pol-
itics of Mid-Eighteenth-Century England.*
S. Varey, 402(MLR):Apr85-432
McCrum, R., W. Cran and R. MacNeil. The
Story of English.
R. Harris, 617(TLS):26Sep86-1062
Maccubbin, R.P. and P. Martin, eds.
British and American Gardens in the
Eighteenth Century.
J.G. Turner, 566:Autumn85-80
D.S. Wilson, 656(WMQ):Jul85-405
McCullagh, C.B. Justifying Historical Des-
criptions.
J.L. Gorman, 518:Oct85-246
H. White, 617(TLS):31Jan86-109
McCulloch, I. The Moon of Hunger.*
L. Boone, 102(CanL):Winter84-136
McCullough, J.W. Living Pictures on the
New York Stage.
A.K. Koger, 615(TJ):May85-250
D.B. Wilmeth, 612(ThS):May85-100

Macfarlane, L.J.  William Elphinstone and the Kingdom of Scotland 1431-1514.
  G. Donaldson, 617(TLS):6Jun86-628
Macfarlane, L.J.  The Theory and Practice of Human Rights.*
  M.D., 185:Jul86-889
MacFarquhar, R.  The Origins of the Cultural Revolution.*  (Vol 2)
  D. Bachman, 293(JASt):May85-601
McFerren, M.  Get Me Out of Here.
  639(VQR):Summer85-98
McFie, H., M.R. Menocal and L. Sera.  Primavera.*
  A.G. Dente, 276:Winter85-319
McGahern, J.  High Ground.*
  J. Mellors, 362:9Jan86-29
McGann, J.J.  The Beauty of Inflections.*
  C. Bernstein, 703:No15-146
  J. Lucas, 617(TLS):10Oct86-1141
McGann, J.J.  A Critique of Modern Textual Criticism.*
  C. Bernstein, 703:No15-146
  J.M. Robson, 354:Dec85-357
McGann, J.J., ed.  Historical Studies and Literary Criticism.
  C. Falck, 617(TLS):30May86-599
McGann, J.J.  The Romantic Ideology.*
  C. Bernstein, 703:No15-146
  W.H. Galperin, 301(JEGP):Jan85-135
  M. Levinson, 661(WC):Fall85-171
  M.B. Ross, 405(MP):Nov85-204
  F.W. Shilstone, 577(SHR):Spring85-176
McGee, H.  On Food and Cooking.*
  P. Levy, 617(TLS):26Dec86-1454
McGill, P.  The Navvy Poet.
  T. Eldeman, 305(JIL):Jan85-55
McGill, R.  No Place to Hide.  (C.M. Logue, ed)
  R. Overstreet, 583:Spring86-285
McGill, R.  Southern Encounters.  (C.M. Logue, ed)
  D.W. Hollis 3d, 9(AlaR):Apr85-151
MacGillivray, R.  The House of Ontario.
  K.L. Morrison, 102(CanL):Winter84-73
McGinn, C.  The Subjective View.*
  E.W. Averill, 482(PhR):Apr85-296
  G. Stock, 479(PhQ):Jan85-109
McGinn, D.J.  Thomas Nashe.
  E.D. Mackerness, 677(YES):Vol 15-284
McGlathery, J.M.  Desire's Sway.
  R.K. Angress, 221(GQ):Spring85-286
  J.M. Ellis, 301(JEGP):Jan85-87
  J.D. Prandi, 222(GR):Summer85-116
McGonigle, T.  In Patchogue.
  J. Byrne, 532(RCF):Fall85-185
Macgoye, M.O.  Coming to Birth.
  A. Maja-Pearce, 617(TLS):5Sep86-977
McGrath, D.F. - see "Bookman's Price Index"
McGrath, M.  Etienne Gilson.
  J.P. Dougherty, 543:Sep84-132
McGrath, R.D.  Gunfighters, Highwaymen, and Vigilantes.
  W.E. Hollon, 649(WAL):May85-62
McGrath, T.  Echoes Inside the Labyrinth.
  S.I. Bellman, 649(WAL):Aug85-174
McGrath, W.J.  Freud's Discovery of Psychoanalysis.
  P. Gay, 617(TLS):30ct86-1085
  L. Goldberger, 441:19Jan86-34
  M. Ignatieff, 453(NYRB):12Jun86-22
McGraw, P.A.  Monographien 12.
  H. Tatzreiter, 685(ZDL):3/1985-393

McGreevy, J., ed.  Glenn Gould.
  J.H. Kaplan, 102(CanL):Spring85-122
McGregor, A.  Greg Chappell.
  S. Rae, 617(TLS):11Jul86-770
MacGregor, I.  The Enemies Within.
  M. Crick, 617(TLS):24Oct86-1184
  N. Jones, 362:2Oct86-22
MacGregor, R.  The Last Season.*
  D. Daymond, 102(CanL):Spring85-115
McGuane, T.  To Skin a Cat.
  E. Tallent, 441:19Oct86-13
McGuckian, M.  Venus and the Rain.*
  C. Benfey, 472:Spring/Summer/Fall/Winter85-500
  J.D. McClatchy, 249(HudR):Spring85-170
McGuiness, T.  So You Want To Be A Rock 'n Roll Star?
  D. Rimmer, 362:11Dec86-25
McGuinness, B. - see Frege, G.
McGuire, J.E. and M. Tamny - see Newton, I.
McGuire, M.C.  Milton's Puritan Masque.*
  C.C. Brown, 551(RenQ):Summer85-380
  R.S. Ide, 536(Rev):Vol7-89
  P. Stevens, 539:Nov85-302
  M. Treip, 610:Summer85-174
McGuire, P.C.  Speechless Dialect.
  K. Brown, 617(TLS):22Aug86-917
McGuire, W. - see Jung, C.G.
McGuirk, C.  Robert Burns and the Sentimental Era.
  P. Sabor, 529(QQ):Winter85-861
  639(VQR):Autumn85-122
McGurk, P. and others, eds.  An Eleventh-Century Anglo-Saxon Illustrated Miscellany.
  H. Gneuss, 38:Band103Heft3/4-455
  J. Morrish, 405(MP):Feb86-298
  W. Provost, 70:May/Jun85-153
Machado, A.  Antonio Machado: Selected Poems.  (A.S. Trueblood, ed and trans)
  P.R. Olson, 403(MLS):Fall85-363
Machado de Assis, J.M.  The Devil's Church and Other Stories.  (J. Schmitt and L. Ishimatsu, eds and trans)  Epitaph of a Small Winner.
  J. Gledson, 617(TLS):3Jan86-11
Machado de Assis, J.M.  Helena.  (H. Caldwell, trans)
  R.E. Dimmick, 37:Jan-Feb85-54
  P.B. Dixon, 238:May85-328
  J. Gledson, 617(TLS):3Jan86-11
Machan, T.R. and M.B. Johnson, eds.  Rights and Regulation.
  P.A. Danielson, 154:Summer85-361
McHaney, T.L. - see Ohashi, K. and K. Ono
Machatzke, M. - see Hauptmann, G.
Machiavelli, N.  The Prince.  (P. Bondanella, ed)
  B. Richardson, 278(IS):Vol40-129
Macho, J.  Ésope.  (B. Hecker, ed)
  G. Demerson, 535(RHL):May/Jun85-483
McHugh, R.  The "Finnegans Wake" Experience.*
  R.D. Newman, 577(SHR):Spring85-185
McHugh, R.  Annotations to "Finnegans Wake."*
  R.D. Newman, 577(SHR):Spring85-185
McInerney, J.  Ransom.*
  D. Pinckney, 453(NYRB):29May86-30
  G. Strawson, 617(TLS):18Apr86-415
McInerny, R.  Leave of Absence.
  M. Malone, 441:28Sep86-11

MacInnes, C. England, Half English.
J. Neville, 617(TLS):7Nov86-1254
362:7Aug86-26
MacInnes, C. To the Victors the Spoils.
All Day Saturday. June in Her Spring.
J. Neville, 617(TLS):7Nov86-1254
McInnes, E. Das deutsche Drama des 19.
Jahrhunderts.*
S. Hoefert, 133:Band17Heft3/4-351
I.F. Roe, 402(MLR):Jul85-760
McInnes, G. Humping My Bluey.
J. Neville, 617(TLS):7Nov86-1254
McIntire, C.T. England Against the Papacy
1858-1861.
W.L. Arnstein, 637(VS):Spring85-552
MacIntyre, A. After Virtue.*
B. Haller, 489(PJGG):Band92Heft2-431
J-F. Spitz, 98:Dec85-1137
F.S. Troy, 418(MR):Winter85-615
Macintyre, S. Militant.
K. Tsokhas, 381:Jun85-170
Mack, D.S. - see Hogg, J.
Mack, M. Collected in Himself.*
M.R. Brownell, 541(RES):May85-276
R.D. Lund, 403(MLS):Fall85-342
Mack, M. Alexander Pope.*
R.M. Adams, 453(NYRB):13Mar86-29
P-G. Boucé, 189(EA):Jan-Mar86-78
F. Eberstadt, 129:Aug86-42
P. Lewis, 364:Jul85-93
C. Ricks, 176:Jan86-38
J. Wain, 441:2Mar86-11
442(NY):7Apr86-105
Mack, M. - see Pope, A.
Mack, M. and J.A. Winn. Pope.
P. Dixon, 447(N&Q):Mar84-94
Mack Smith, D. - see under Smith, D.M.
McKane, R., ed and trans. The Shalford
Book of 20th Century Russian Poetry.
R. Milner-Gulland, 617(TLS):31Oct86-
1222
McKay, A. ... sometimes in a certain light.
404:Autumn85-60
MacKay, A. and D.S. Severin, eds. Cosas
sacadas de la Historia del Rey Don Juan
el Segundo.*
N.G. Round, 402(MLR):Apr85-480
Mackay, J.A. The Burns Federation 1885-
1985.
G.R.R., 588(SSL):Vol20-329
McKay, J.H. Narration and Discourse in
American Realistic Fiction.*
R.P. Hoople, 106:Spring85-57
McKay, N.Y. Jean Toomer, Artist.*
S.B. Garren, 392:Spring85-136
A. Shucard, 27(AL):Mar85-173
J. Weixlmann, 659(ConL):Spring86-48
C. Werner, 395(MFS):Summer85-420
295(JML):Nov85-562
McKay, P. Inside Private Eye.
S. Fry, 362:6Nov86-23
McKay, S., ed. Composing in a Second Lan-
guage.
M.E. Call, 399(MLJ):Spring85-82
H.J. Siskin, 207(FR):Apr86-803
Mackay, S. Redhill Rococo.
A. Duchêne, 617(TLS):14Feb86-163
K.C. O'Brien, 362:27Feb86-27
McKay, T. Infinitival Complements in Ger-
man.
T.F. Shannon, 350:Dec86-945

McKee, E.A. John Calvin on the Diaconate
and Liturgical Almsgiving.
R.M. Kingdon, 551(RenQ):Autumn85-527
MacKendrick, L.K., ed. Probable Fictions.
E-M. Kroller, 102(CanL):Winter84-128
M.S. Madoff, 628(UWR):Fall-Winter85-88
McKendrick, M., ed. Golden Age Studies in
Honour of A.A. Parker.
J.A. Parr, 238:Sep85-516
McKendrick, N., J. Brewer and J.H. Plumb.
The Birth of a Consumer Society.
P. Borsay, 83:Autumn85-235
McKenna, W.R. Husserl's "Introductions to
Phenomenology."
E. Kohák, 543:Sep85-163
K. Schuhmann, 687:Jan-Mar85-150
Mackenney, L. - see Corrie, J.
Mackensen, L. Die Nibelungen.
T.M. Andersson, 589:Oct85-1053
O. Ehrismann, 224(GRM):Band35Heft4-461
McKenzie, A.T. Thomas Gray.
R. Lonsdale, 402(MLR):Jan85-126
McKenzie, A.T., ed. A Grin on the Inter-
face.
G.F. Freije, 365:Winter/Spring85-57
McKenzie, D.F. Oral Culture, Literacy and
Print in Early New Zealand.
G. Palmer, 617(TLS):24Oct86-1203
Mackenzie, J. The Children of the Souls.
D.A.N. Jones, 617(TLS):25Jul86-823
Mackenzie, J.G. A Lexicon of the 14th-
Century Aragonese Manuscripts of Juan
Fernández de Heredia.
R. af Geijerstam, 304(JHP):Winter85-
153
Mackenzie, J.M. Propaganda and Empire.
J.M. Carland, 635(VPR):Summer85-75
D.C. Ellinwood, 637(VS):Winter86-323
Mackenzie, M.M. Plato on Punishment.
C. Gill, 466:Vol 1-211
MacKenzie, N. and J. - see Webb, B.
McKenzie, R. James FitzGibbon.
W. Baker, 102(CanL):Winter84-69
Mackerras, C., ed. Chinese Theatre from
its Origins to the Present Day.
P. Clark, 293(JASt):May85-602
Mackie, J.L. The Miracle of Theism.*
G. Gutting, 449:Sep85-456
J.F. Ross, 543:Mar85-657
R. Swinburne, 311(JP):Jan85-46
Mackie, J.L. Selected Papers. (J. and P.
Mackie, eds)
B. Stroud, 617(TLS):18Apr86-424
McKie, R. Panic.
D. Widgery, 362:4Sep86-21
Mackiewicz, W. Providenz und Adaptation
in Defoes "Robinson Crusoe."
W. Pache, 402(MLR):Oct85-908
MacKillop, I. The British Ethical Socie-
ties.
P. Clarke, 617(TLS):23May86-564
A. Kenny, 362:27Mar86-27
McKinley, M.B. Words in a Corner.*
A. Compagnon, 535(RHL):Mar/Apr85-291
MacKinnon, C. Finding Hoseyn.
N. Callendar, 441:16Mar86-31
442(NY):24Nov86-148
MacKinnon, E.M. Scientific Explanation
and Atomic Physics.*
J. Brennan, 543:Mar85-660
A. Franklin, 486:Sep85-481

MacKinnon, S.R.  Power and Politics in
Late Imperial China.
    M.B. Rankin, 293(JASt):Nov84-185
McKinsey, E.  Niagara Falls.
    R. Paulson, 617(TLS):28Mar86-325
    W.B. Scott, 344:Winter86-131
    27(AL):Dec85-699
McKitterick, D.  Four Hundred Years of
University Printing and Publishing in
Cambridge, 1584-1984.*
    P. Morgan, 354:Dec85-378
McKnight, B.E.  The Quality of Mercy.
    K-C. Yip, 302:Vol21No1-69
MacLaine, A.H.  Allan Ramsay.
    F.W. Freeman, 571(ScLJ):Winter85-52
Maclaren, A.  The Fairy Family.
    H. Morgan, 326:Winter85/86-18
McLaren-Turner, P., ed.  Canadian Studies.
    B. Whiteman, 470:Vol23-105
MacLaverty, B.  Secrets and Other Stories.*
    D. Flower, 249(HudR):Summer85-301
    W. Peden, 651(WHR):Autumn85-271
MacLean, A.  The Lonely Sea.
    M. Buck, 441:15Jun86-20
McLean, D.  1885.
    K. Turnbull, 529(QQ):Winter85-801
MacLean, D., ed.  The Security Gamble.
    J.M., 185:Jan86-458
McLean, G.F.  Man and Nature.
    H.A. Durfee, 543:Sep84-133
MacLean, R.  In a Canvas Tent.
    K. Meadwell, 102(CanL):Summer85-140
"Archibald MacLeish: Reflections."  (B.A.
Drabeck and H.E. Ellis, eds)
    R.G. Davis, 441:10Aug86-14
McLeish, K.  Longman Guide to Shake-
speare's Characters.
    I-S. Ewbank, 617(TLS):25Apr86-451
McLeish, K.  Myths and Folk Stories of
Britain and Ireland.
    J. Westwood, 617(TLS):28Nov86-1347
McLendon, W., ed.  L'Hénaurme Siècle.
    B.L. Murphy, 446(NCFS):Spring-Summer86-
    346
McLendon, W.L.  Une ténébreuse carrière
sous l'Empire et la Restauration.*
    J. Carleton, 446(NCFS):Fall-
    Winter85/86-171
Macleod, C.  Collected Essays.  (O. Taplin,
ed)
    S.H. Braund, 313:Vol75-316
    J. Griffin, 123:Vol35No2-372
Macleod, C.W. - see Homer
McLeod, D.W. and A.V. Miller, comps.
Medical, Social, and Political Aspects
of the AIDS Crisis.
    J. Lieberson, 453(NYRB):16Jan86-43
McLeod, J.  Greendream.*
    L. Boone, 102(CanL):Winter84-136
McLeod, M. and L. Wevers, eds.  Women's
Work.
    J. Perlez, 441:22Jun86-26
MacLeod, N.  Womanculture.
    F. Allen, 496:Fall85-179
McLeod, P.N.  Daffodils in Winter.  (J.
Murray, ed)
    H. Kirkwood, 99:Oct85-32
McLeod, R.C., ed.  Reminiscences of a
Bungle by One of the Bunglers.
    H. Prest, 102(CanL):Winter84-151
McLoughlin, W.G.  Cherokees and Mission-
aries, 1789-1839.*
    K.L. Valliere, 9(AlaR):Jan85-71

McLuhan, T.C.  Dream Tracks.*
    442(NY):17Feb86-105
MacLulich, T.D.  Hugh MacLennan.*
    P. Goetsch, 268(IFR):Winter86-34
    F.W. Watt, 102(CanL):Spring85-138
Maclure, S.  Educational Development and
School Building.
    C. Boyne, 46:Apr85-83
McLynn, F.J.  The Jacobite Army in England,
1745.*
    L.K.J. Glassey, 566:Autumn85-93
McMahan, E., ed.  Critical Approaches to
Mark Twain's Short Stories.*
    J. Lauber, 106:Spring85-47
McMahon, J., with B. Verdi.  McMahon!
    J.P. Calagione, 441:2Nov86-27
MacMillan, C., ed.  The Proceedings of the
Sir Charles C.D. Roberts Symposium.
    G. Lynch, 105:Fall/Winter85-95
McMillan, I.  Now it can be told.
    J. Saunders, 565:Spring85-72
McMinn, J.R.B.  Against the Tide.
    O. MacDonagh, 617(TLS):21Mar86-297
McMullen, L.  An Odd Attempt in a Woman.
    M.J. Edwards, 173(ECS):Spring86-430
    J. Giltrow, 627(UTQ):Summer85-429
    D. Seed, 83:Autumn85-242
    T. Tausky, 298:Summer85-159
    C. Thomas, 178:Jun85-251
MacMullen, R.  Christianizing the Roman
Empire (A.D. 100-400).*
    G.P. Corrington, 124:Mar-Apr86-277
    R.P.C. Hanson, 123:Vol35No2-335
McMullen, R.  Degas.*
    F. Haskell, 453(NYRB):27Mar86-7
    A.A. McLees, 207(FR):Apr86-831
McMullin, B.J. - see Crowne, J.
McMullin, N.  Buddhism and the State in
Sixteenty-Century Japan.
    Wakita Osamu, 285(JapQ):Oct-Dec85-437
McMurtry, J.  English Language, English
Literature.*
    D.P. Leinster-Mackay and D.W. Collin,
    637(VS):Summer86-635
McMurtry, L.  The Desert Rose.
    C.L. Adams, 649(WAL):Aug85-167
McNab, T.  The Fast Men.
    362:6Nov86-36
McNair, J.M.  Education for a Changing
Spain.
    L.T. Valdivieso, 238:Sep85-540
McNair, W.  The Faces of Americans in
1853.*
    455:Mar85-64
McNamara, E.  Call It A Day.*
    S. Martindale, 526:Autumn85-92
McNamara, R.  Blundering into Disaster.
    L. Freedman, 441:16Nov86-7
McNamee, K.  Abbreviations in Greek Liter-
ary Papyri and Ostraca.
    J. Moore-Blunt, 123:Vol35No1-223
McNeil, F.  All Kinds of Magic.
    P. Nodelman, 102(CanL):Fall85-122
McNeil, F.  Barkerville.
    A. Parkin, 102(CanL):Spring85-161
    S. Scobie, 376:Jun85-132
McNeil, H.  Emily Dickinson.
    P. Kemp, 362:24Apr86-33
MacNeill, M.  The Festival of Lughnasa.
    T. Ó Cathasaigh, 112:Vol 17-184
McNerney, K.  "Tirant lo Blanc" Revisited.
    J.B. Avalle-Arce, 589:Oct85-997

Magnusson, M-L., ed. Bogen i Sovjet.
   E. Egeberg, 172(Edda):1985/5-322
Magnusson, W. and others. The New Reality.
   R.M. Campbell, 298:Winter85/86-158
Magocsi, P.R. Galicia.*
   P. Longworth, 575(SEER):Jan85-121
Magocsi, P.R. The Rusyn-Ukrainians of
Czechoslovakia.*
   A. Baran, 575(SEER):Jul85-452
Magocsi, P.R. and F. Zapletal. Holz-
kirchen in den Karpaten/Wooden Churches
in the Carpathians.
   M. Winokur, 574(SEEJ):Fall85-363
Magraw, R. France 1815-1914.
   W.H.C. Smith, 208(FS):Jan85-100
Magrini, T. and G. Bellosi. Vi do la
buonasera.
   M.S. Keller, 187:Fall86-563
Maguire, H. Art and Eloquence in Byzan-
tium.
   L-A. Hunt, 303(JoHS):Vol 105-250
   G.A. Press, 480(P&R):Vol 18No1-65
Maher, J. Biography of Broken Fortunes.
   P-L. Adams, 61:Aug86-92
   A. Morgan, 441:10Aug86-19
Maheu, P. Un Parti pris révolutionnaire.
   P. Smart, 627(UTQ):Summer85-492
Mahler, G. and R. Strauss. Gustav Mahler,
Richard Strauss: Correspondence 1888-
1911.* (H. Blaukopf, ed)
   M. Carner, 415:Apr85-226
   M. Kennedy, 410(M&L):Oct85-394
   D. Matthews, 607:Mar85-41
   E.R. Reilly, 451:Spring86-248
Mahler, R. Hasidism and the Jewish
Enlightenment.
   L. Jacobs, 617(TLS):16May86-541
Mahmoudian, M., ed. Linguistique fonction-
nelle.
   W.J. Ashby, 545(RPh):Nov85-229
Mahon, D. Antarctica.
   M. Hofmann, 617(TLS):30May86-585
Mahon, R. The Politics of Industrial
Restructuring.
   R.M. Campbell, 298:Winter85/86-158
Mahoney, J.L. The Whole Internal Universe.
   H. Erskine-Hill, 617(TLS):26Dec86-1441
Mahr, J. Eisenbahnen in der deutschen
Dichtung.
   I.M. Goessl, 406:Winter85-498
Mahyère, E. I Will Not Serve.
   P. Lewis, 565:Winter84/85-42
Mailer, N. Tough Guys Don't Dance.*
   L.K. Miller, 152(UDQ):Fall85-144
Maillet, A. Crache à Pic.
   C.R. La Bossiere, 102(CanL):Summer85-
   169
Maillet, M. Histoire de la littérature
acadienne III.
   A.B. Chartier, 207(FR):Oct85-122
   L.E. Doucette, 627(UTQ):Summer85-460
Main, G.L. Tobacco Colony.*
   G. Morgan, 161(DUJ):Jun85-260
Mainer, J-C. Regionalismo, burguesía y
cultura.
   J-L. Marfany, 86(BHS):Jul85-314
Maiorano, R. and V. Brooks. Balanchine's
Mozartiana.*
   M. Mudrick, 249(HudR):Autumn85-520
Mair, V.H., ed. Experimental Essays on
Chuang-tzu.
   R. Eno, 293(JASt):Feb85-379
   J. Fleming, 485(PE&W):Jul85-315

Mairs, N. Plaintext.
   P. Klass, 441:27Apr86-21
Mais, R. Listen, The Wind and Other
Stories.
   R. Deveson, 617(TLS):24Oct86-1187
Maitland, S. Vesta Tilley.
   P. Kemp, 362:24Apr86-33
Maitland, S. Virgin Territory.
   J. Eidus, 441:29Jun86-24
Maitre, R.A. Blue Barometers.
   F. Adcock, 617(TLS):7Nov86-1256
Major, C. My Amputations.
   R. Perry, 441:28Sep86-30
Major, J-L. Entre l'écriture et la parole.
   N.B. Bishop, 627(UTQ):Summer85-484
Major, K. Thirty-Six Exposures.
   A. Kertzer, 102(CanL):Fall85-117
Major, R. Le discernement.
   A. Reix, 542:Jul-Sep85-357
Major-Poetzl, P. Michel Foucault's Arche-
ology of Western Culture.
   G.F. Waller, 152(UDQ):Summer85-126
Majorano, M., ed. Il Roman des Eles di
Raoul de Houdenc.*
   K. Varty, 382(MAE):1985/2-329
Makdisi, G. The Rise of Colleges.
   N. Daniel, 318(JAOS):Jul-Sep84-586
"Making Space."
   K. Macintosh, 46:Feb85-84
Makkreel, R.A. and F. Rodi - see Dilthey,
W.
Malaj, L. Regeneración (Ibergus).
   G.F. Waldman, 352(LATR):Spring86-131
Malamat, A. Das davidische und salomon-
ische Königreich und seine Beziehungen
zu Ägypten und Syrien.
   J.A. Soggin, 318(JAOS):Oct-Dec84-766
Malandain, P. Delisle de Sales, philo-
sophe de la nature, 1741-1816.*
   J. Lough, 208(FS):Oct85-477
Malavieille, S. Reliures et cartonnages
d'éditeur en France au XIXe siècle:
1815-1865.*
   C. Allix, 354:Dec85-385
Malaxecheverria, I. Le Bestiaire médiéval
et l'archétype de la féminité.
   K. Varty, 208(FS):Jul85-324
Malcolm, A.H. Final Harvest.
   C.D.B. Bryan, 441:20Apr86-7
   442(NY):12May86-127
Malcolm, J. The Gwen John Sculpture.*
   N. Callendar, 441:8Jun86-34
   442(NY):21Jul86-95
Malcolm, J. In the Freud Archives.*
   J. Mann, 152(UDQ):Fall85-84
Malcolm, J. Whistler in the Dark.
   T.J. Binyon, 617(TLS):27Jun86-711
Malcolm, N. Soviet Political Scientists
and American Politics.*
   R.J. Hill, 575(SEER):Jul85-473
   D.E. Powell, 550(RusR):Oct85-435
Malcolm, W.K. A Blasphemer and Reformer.*
   J.B. Caird, 571(ScLJ):Autumn85-11
   A.T. McKenzie, 395(MFS):Winter85-816
Malcolmson, R.W. Life and Labour in
England, 1700-1780.
   M. Rediker, 656(WMQ):Apr85-267
Malcolmson, R.W. Nuclear Fallacies.
   G. Amyot, 529(QQ):Autumn85-649
Mâle, É. Religious Art in France: The
Thirteenth Century.
   W. Sauerländer, 617(TLS):30May86-594

de Malebranche, N. Oeuvres. (Vol 1) (G.
Rodis-Lewis, with G. Malbreil, eds)
I.W. Alexander, 208(FS):Jan85-73
Maley, A. and A. Duff. Drama Techniques
in Language Learning. (2nd ed)
J.L. Fox, 399(MLJ):Spring85-81
Maley, C.A. Dans le vent. (2nd ed)
M.J. Baker, 207(FR):Dec85-315
Malherbe, J-F. Le langage théologique à
l'âge de la science.
A. Reix, 542:Jul-Sep85-341
"Malherbe, Théophile de Viau, and Saint-
Amant." (R.G. Maber, ed)
J. Marmier, 475:Vol 12No22-332
C. Rolfe, 208(FS):Jul85-330
C. Smith, 161(DUJ):Jun85-271
Malik, Y.K., ed. Politics, Technology,
and Bureaucracy in South Asia.
B.R. Nayar, 293(JASt):May85-642
Malitz, J. Die "Historien" des Posei-
donius.
P. Pédech, 555:Vol59fasc1-116
E. Rawson, 123:Vol35No1-107
de Malkiel, M.R.L. - see under Lida de
Malkiel, M.R.
Malkiel, Y. From Particular to General
Linguistics.*
D.H., 355(LSoc):Jun85-275
R. Martin, 553(RLiR):Jul-Dec85-427
J. Vizmuller-Zocco, 361:Sep85-85
de Mallac, G. Boris Pasternak.
A. Kerrigan, 569(SR):Spring85-312
Mallarmé, S. Correspondance. (Vols 6 and
7) (H. Mondor and L.J. Austin, eds)
A. Fongaro, 535(RHL):Jan/Feb85-116
Mallarmé, S. Correspondance.* (Vols 9
and 10) (H. Mondor and L.J. Austin, eds)
U. Franklin, 207(FR):Oct85-140
Mallarmé, S. Correspondance.* (Vol 11)
(H. Mondor and L.J. Austin, eds)
E. Souffrin-Le Breton, 208(FS):Oct85-
486
Mallarmé, S. Igitur. (R.G. Cohn, ed)
Y-A. Favre, 535(RHL):Jul/Aug85-691
Mallarmé, S. Oeuvres complètes. (Vol 1)
(C.P. Barbier and C.G. Millan, eds)
J. Kearns, 402(MLR):Jul85-719
Mallett, A. Trumper.
P. Sutcliffe, 617(TLS):3Jan86-21
Mallett, M.E. and J.R. Hale. The Military
Organization of a Renaissance State.
C.H. Clough, 278(IS):Vol40-123
F. Gilbert, 551(RenQ):Summer85-325
Mallinson, G.J. The Comedies of Cor-
neille.*
N. Ekstein, 210(FrF):May85-240
W.O. Goode, 207(FR):Feb86-462
M. Greenberg, 568(SCN):Spring-Summer85-
20
D.L. Rubin, 401(MLQ):Dec84-410
M-O. Sweetser, 475:Vol 12No22-333
M-O. Sweetser, 535(RHL):Sep/Oct85-865
Malliol, W. Slave.
C.R. Larson, 441:20Jul86-18
Mallon, T. A Book of One's Own.*
B. Duyfhuizen, 454:Winter86-171
J. Symons, 617(TLS):10Jan86-41
Mallory, N.A. - see under Ayala Mallory, N.
Malmberg, B. Analyse du langage au XXe
siècle.
W.J. Ashby, 207(FR):Feb86-478
D. Nehls, 257(IRAL):Feb85-77

Malmgren, C.D. Fictional Space in the
Modernist and Postmodernist American
Novel.
A. Nadel, 395(MFS):Winter85-759
Malone, B.C. Country Music.
L. Milazzo, 584(SWR):Autumn85-547
Malone, B.C. Southern Music: American
Music.
F.W. Childrey, Jr., 585(SoQ):Spring86-
89
Malone, M. Handling Sin.
A.C. Greene, 441:13Apr86-11
442(NY):5May86-132
Malone, M.P., ed. Historians and the Amer-
ican West.*
D.J. Pisani, 250(HLQ):Winter85-98
"The Malone Society: Collections." (Vol
12)
P. Bement, 541(RES):Aug85-413
Maloney, J. Marshall, Orthodoxy and the
Professionalisation of Economics.
T.W. Hutchison, 617(TLS):14Mar86-285
Malory, T. Caxton's Malory. (J.W. Spisak
and W. Matthews, eds)
N.F. Blake, 179(ES):Aug85-358
B. Cottle, 301(JEGP):Apr85-252
P.J.C. Field, 354:Dec85-366
Malouf, D. Antipodes.*
J. Mellors, 362:9Jan86-29
Malouf, D. 12 Edmonstone Street.
I. Thomson, 362:13Feb86-28
Malter, R. and E. Staffa. Kant in Königs-
berg seit 1945.
R. Lüthe, 342:Band76Heft3-355
Maltzoff, N. Everyday Conversations in
Russian.
K.L. Black, 399(MLJ):Spring85-103
Malzahn, M. Aspects of Identity.
C. Craig, 571(ScLJ):Winter85-56
T.C. Richardson, 588(SSL):Vol20-319
Mamet, D. Writing in Restaurants.
G. Johnson, 441:14Dec86-25
de Man, P. Allegories of Reading.
A. Stoekl, 153:Fall85-36
de Man, P. Blindness and Insight.* (2nd
ed)
B. Bjorklund, 221(GQ):Winter85-100
R. Machin, 89(BJA):Autumn85-407
B.F. Scholz, 343:Heft12-117
de Man, P. The Rhetoric of Romanticism.
N. Frye, 617(TLS):17Jan86-51
D.T. O'Hara, 659(ConL):Summer86-285
S. Simpkins, 363(LitR):Spring86-392
Manceron, G. - see Segalen, V. and H.
Manceron
Mancini, M. La gaia scienza dei trova-
tori.*
W. Hülk, 547(RF):Band97Heft4-464
de Mandach, A., ed and trans. Le Jeu des
trois rois de Neuchâtel.*
N. Wilkins, 208(FS):Jul85-322
Maṇḍala, P., ed. Guru-Kṛipa ou la grâce
du guru.
A. Reix, 542:Jan-Mar85-94
Mandel, D. The Petrograd Workers and the
Fall of the Old Regime. The Petrograd
Workers and the Soviet Seizure of Power.
M. McAuley, 575(SEER):Jul85-462
D.J. Raleigh, 550(RusR):Jul85-309
Mandel, E. and A. Freeman, eds. Ricardo,
Marx, Sraffa.
J.C.I., 185:Apr86-677

Mandel, M. The Collected Poems of Miriam Mandel. (S. Watson, ed)
S. Scobie, 376:Sep85-143
Mandel, O. - see Corneille, T.
Mandela, W. Part of My Soul Went With Him.* (A. Benjamin, ed; adapted by M. Benson)
J.M. Coetzee, 453(NYRB):8May86-3
442(NY):27Jan86-98
Mandell, R.D. Sport.
B. Lowrey, 639(VQR):Autumn85-732
Mandelstam, O. Selected Poems. (C. Brown and W.S. Merwin, trans)
J. Aleshire, 434:Winter84-272
Mandelstam, O. Voyage en Arménie.
J-M. le Sidaner, 450(NRF):Apr85-103
Manderscheid, H. Die Skulpturenausstattung der kaiserzeitlichen Thermenanlagen.
R. Ling, 313:Vol75-277
Mandlich, A.M. Una Rivista Italiana in Lingua Francese.
R. Pouilliart, 356(LR):Aug85-235
Manessy, G. and P. Wald. Le Français en Afrique noire.
M. Wieland, 207(FR):Mar86-656
Manganaro, A. Mario Pomilio.
U. Mariani, 275(IQ):Winter/Spring/Summer85-264
Manganelli, M. Il linguaggio nel pensiero di H. Bergson. Il segno nel pensiero di Antonio Rosmini.
M. Adam, 542:Jan-Mar85-56
Manger, K. Literarisches Leben in Strassburg während der Prädikatur Johann Geilers von Kayserberg (1478-1510).
F.L. Borchardt, 221(GQ):Spring85-275
Manger, K. Das "Narrenschiff."
M.K. Kremer, 564:May85-150
"Manger et Boire au Moyen Age."
G. Roques, 553(RLiR):Jul-Dec85-414
Mangin, M. Alesia.
J.F. Drinkwater, 313:Vol75-292
Mango, C. Byzantium and its Image.
J.W. Barker, 377:Jul84-103
Manguel, A., ed. Black Water.
R. Cardinal, 529(QQ):Autumn85-549
Manguel, A., ed. Other Fires.
W. Brandmark, 362:7Aug86-26
M. Morris, 441:4May86-35
A. Vaux, 617(TLS):24Oct86-1188
Manhire, B. Zoetropes.
H. Lomas, 364:Jun85-89
Manin, D. and G. Boerio. Carteggio Daniele Manin — Giuseppe Boerio. (A. Caracciolo Aricò, ed)
P. Zolli, 708:Vol 11fasc1-146
Manion, M.M. and V.F. Vines. Medieval and Renaissance Illuminated Manuscripts in Australian Collections.
C. Reynolds, 90:Apr85-233
Manlove, C.N. The Gap in Shakespeare.
R.A. Foakes, 402(MLR):Oct85-901
M.R.G. Spiller, 161(DUJ):Jun84-296
Manlove, C.N. The Impulse of Fantasy Literature.*
L. Hatfield, 128(CE):Mar85-275
M.H. Parkinson, 447(N&Q):Dec84-554
S. Prickett, 541(RES):Nov85-625
Manlove, C.N. Science Fiction.
J. Clute, 617(TLS):31Oct86-1223
Mann, B. The Secular Madrigals of Filippo di Monte 1521-1603.
D. Arnold, 410(M&L):Apr85-175

Mann, J. V kružke Stankeviča.
L. Koehler, 574(SEEJ):Summer85-207
Mann, K.B. The Language That Makes George Eliot's Fiction.*
J.D. Benson, 637(VS):Summer85-704
D.E. Nord, 651(WHR):Spring85-86
J. Wiesenfarth, 594:Fall85-321
Mann, M. The Sources of Social Power. (Vol 1)
P. Anderson, 617(TLS):12Dec86-1405
Mann, N. Petrarch.
P. Hainsworth, 278(IS):Vol40-116
Mann, R.G. El Greco and his Patrons.
C. Gould, 324:Nov86-844
P. Troutman, 617(TLS):23May86-570
Mann, T. Aufsätze, Reden, Essays.* (Vols 1 and 2) (H. Matter, ed)
K.W. Jonas, 221(GQ):Fall85-624
T.J. Reed, 402(MLR):Jan85-234
Mann, T. Frage und Antwort. (V. Hansen and G. Heine, eds)
J. Rieckmann, 221(GQ):Winter85-137
H. Siefken, 402(MLR):Oct85-999
Mann, T. Thomas Mann, Pro and Contra Wagner. (A. Blunden, ed and trans)
J. Joll, 453(NYRB):27Mar86-18
M. Tanner, 617(TLS):21Mar86-300
Mann, T. Reflections of a Nonpolitical Man.*
W.F. Michael, 221(GQ):Winter85-138
Mann, T. Tagebücher 1940-1943.* (P. de Mendelssohn, ed)
F. Rau, 224(GRM):Band35Heft3-359
Mann, T. The Yale "Zauberberg"-Manuscript.* (J.F. White, ed)
T.J. Reed, 402(MLR):Jan85-234
Mannari, H. and H. Befu, eds. The Challenge of Japan's Internationalization.*
J.H. Bailey, 293(JASt):May85-621
Mannheim, K. Structures of Thinking. (D. Kettler, V. Meja and N. Stehr, eds)
R.A. Morrow, 488:Dec85-507
Manni, E. Geografia fisica e politica della Sicilia antica.*
R.J.A. Wilson, 313:Vol75-296
Manning, E. Marble and Bronze.*
M. Stocker, 637(VS):Winter85-347
Manning, F.E., ed. The Celebration of Society.
D.J. Crowley, 650(WF):Apr85-136
B.J. Stoeltje, 292(JAF):Jan/Mar85-119
Manning, P. Electronic and Computer Music.*
R. Samuels, 607:Dec85-52
Manning, P. Hirohito.
D. Murray, 441:15Jun86-21
442(NY):19May86-121
Mannoni, M., ed. Travail de la métaphore.
A. Reix, 542:Jan-Mar85-63
Mannoni, O. Prospero et Caliban.
F. Trémolières, 450(NRF):Sep85-97
Manns, P. and H.N. Loose. Martin Luther.
F. Posset, 77:Fall85-356
Manoliu-Manea, M., ed. The Tragic Plight of a Border Area.
D. Deletant, 575(SEER):Jan85-125
Mansbridge, J.J. Why We Lost the ERA.
B. Ehrenreich, 61:Oct86-98
A. Hacker, 453(NYRB):14Aug86-26
K. Luker, 441:19Oct86-7
Manselli, R. Nos qui cum eo fuimus.
P. Dinzelbacher, 684(ZDA):Band114Heft1-32

Manser, A. and G. Stock, eds. The Philos-
ophy of F.H. Bradley.
P. Dubois, 542:Jan-Mar85-57
P.F., 185:Apr86-682
D. Lamb, 323:May85-206
Manser, A.R. Bradley's Logic.*
M.J. Cresswell, 482(PhR):Jan85-139
P. Dubois, 542:Jan-Mar85-58
A.P. Martinich, 319:Apr86-285
P.M. Simons, 479(PhQ):Jan85-107
Mansfield, H.C., Jr. Machiavelli's New
Modes and Orders.
N. Wood, 488:Mar85-45
Mansfield, H.C., Jr. - see Burke, E.
Mansfield, K. The Collected Letters of
Katherine Mansfield.* (Vol 1) (V.
O'Sullivan and M. Scott, eds)
M. Moran, 556:Winter85/86-175
295(JML):Nov85-526
639(VQR):Spring85-48
Mansfield, K. Short Stories. (C. Tomalin,
ed)
G. Bas, 189(EA):Apr-Jun86-243
Mansingh, S. India's Search for Power.
A.G. Rubinoff, 293(JASt):May85-643
Mansion, S. Etudes aristotéliciennes.
P. Pellegrin, 542:Jul-Sep85-303
Manso, P., ed. Mailer.*
27(AL):Dec85-703
295(JML):Nov85-525
Manteiga, R.C., D.K. Herzberger and M.A.
Compitello, eds. Critical Approaches to
the Writings of Juan Benet.
J.W. Kronik, 240(HR):Summer85-381
J. Ortega, 238:May85-307
J. Sandarg, 395(MFS):Summer85-446
Mantel, H. Vacant Possession.
C. Hawtree, 617(TLS):20Jun86-682
Mantsuo, T. - see under Takahashi Mantsuo
Manuel, J. Juan Manuel: A Selection. (I.
MacPherson, ed)
P.O. Gericke, 545(RPh):Aug84-117
Manuelian, A. - see Livy
Manuliu-Manea, M. Tipología e historia.
M-L. Rivero, 320(CJL):Winter85-501
"El manuscrito de la Academia de Murillo."
D. Angulo Íñiguez, 48:Jan-Mar85-92
Manzini, P. Giovanni Gabrieli.
D. Arnold, 410(M&L):Oct85-399
Map, W. De nugis curialium.* (M.R.
James, ed and trans; rev by C.N.L.
Brooke and R.A.B. Mynors)
A.G. Rigg, 589:Jan85-179
Mappen, E. Helping Women at Work.
S.G. Bell, 637(VS):Summer86-627
F. Cairncross, 617(TLS):4Apr86-349
Maquet, J. The Aesthetic Experience.
T. Phillips, 617(TLS):15Aug86-897
F. Schier, 441:6Apr86-29
Marantz, A.P. On the Nature of Grammat-
ical Relations.
R. Clark, 350:Sep86-674
Maras, R.J. Innocent XI, Pope of Chris-
tian Unity. (Vol 1)
F.J. Coppa, 377:Nov85-201
Marc, D. Demographic Vistas.*
J.G. Cawelti, 658:Summer/Autumn85-219
"Gabriel Marcel et les injustices de ce
temps."
M. Adam, 542:Jan-Mar85-57
Marcel, O. Une Éducation française.
P. Desan, 207(FR):Oct85-159

Marc'hadour, G. and R. Galibois. Erasme
de Rotterdam et Thomas More Correspon-
dance.
M. Lebel, 539:Aug86-305
Marchand, R. Advertising the American
Dream.*
R. Draper, 453(NYRB):26Jun86-14
Marchant, E.C. - see Xenophon
Marchant, R. A Picture of Shakespeare's
Tragedies [and] Tragedy against Psychol-
ogy.
H. Mills, 175:Autumn85-279
Marchello-Nizia, C. Dire le vrai.
G. Kleiber, 553(RLiR):Jul-Dec85-472
Marcheschi, D., ed. Ingiurie, improperi,
contumelie, ecc.*
S. Fornasiero, 228(GSLI):Vol 162
fasc520-613
Marchessault, J. Saga of the Wet Hens.
R.P. Knowles, 198:Spring85-84
Marchett, M.R. - see under Ruggeri Mar-
chett, M.
Marchi, M. and C. Menotti. Il cristiane-
simo come profezia in Mario Pomilio.
F. Zangrilli, 275(IQ):Winter/Spring/
Summer85-262
Marcialis, M.T. Filosofia e psicologia
animale da Rerario a Leroy.
A.J. Bingham, 149(CLS):Summer85-271
Marcil-Lacoste, L. La thématique contemp-
oraine de l'égalité.
J. Boulad-Ayoub, 154:Autumn85-566
Marco, J. and J. Pont, eds. La nova
poesia catalana.
A. Terry, 86(BHS):Apr85-217
Marcos, J.M. Roa Bastos, precursor del
post-boom.
S.K. Ugalde, 238:May85-321
Marcos, M.M.E. - see under Estella Marcos,
M.M.
Marcos Marín, F., ed. Introducción plural
a la gramática histórica.
R. Wright, 86(BHS):Oct85-406
Marcos Marín, F. Metodología del español
como segunda lengua.
C. Hernández González, 548:Jan-Jun85-
238
Marcovich, M. Three-Word Trimeter in
Greek Tragedy.
J. Diggle, 123:Vol35No1-12
Marcus, E. Ausgewählte Schriften II. (G.
Martin and G.H. Lübben, eds)
W. Steinbeck, 342:Band76Heft1-116
Marcus, J., ed. Virginia Woolf.*
L. Blanchard, 594:Spring85-95
M. Childers, 141:Spring85-221
J. Hayes, 177(ELT):Vol128No2-211
A. Jardine, 301(JEGP):Oct85-572
M.M. Rowe, 395(MFS):Summer85-349
Marcus, P.L., W. Gould and M.J. Sidnell -
see Yeats, W.B.
Marcus-Tar, J. Thomas Mann und Georg
Lukács.
E. Middell, 654(WB):4/1985-699
Marel, H. and A. Cadet. 100 ans après
"Germinal."
C. Becker, 535(RHL):May/Jun85-510
Marenbon, J. Early Medieval Philosophy
(480-1150).*
P.V. Spade, 449:Sep85-467
G.L. Stengren, 589:Apr85-436
L.J. Thro, 377:Nov84-172

Marenzio, L.  The Secular Works.  (Vol 6)
(P. Myers, ed)
    J. Chater, 317:Summer85-376
Margadant, B.  The Swiss Poster:  1900-1983.
    T. Reese, 507:Jul/Aug85-314
de Margerie, D.  Le Ressouvenir.
    B.L. Knapp, 207(FR):May86-992
Margolies, D.  Novel and Society in Eliza-
bethan England.*
    J.C. Beasley, 594:Fall85-303
Margolin, J-C.  L'humanisme en Europe au
temps de la Renaissance.
    P. Magnard, 192(EP):Oct-Dec85-562
Margolis, J., ed.  The Worlds of Art and
the World.
    G.R. Holmes, 89(BJA):Autumn85-395
Marguerite de Navarre.  Dialogue en forme
de vision nocturne.  (R. Salminen, ed)
    H. Vernay, 553(RLiR):Jul-Dec85-527
Marguerite de Navarre.  The Heptameron.
(P.A. Chilton, trans)
    J. Harris, 208(FS):Jul85-324
Marguerite de Valois.  Memoirs of Marguer-
ite de Valois.  (L. Dieckmann, trans)
    L.C. Locey, 568(SCN):Spring-Summer85-
22
Margulis, L. and D. Sagan.  Microcosmos.
    P-L. Adams, 61:Jul86-80
    M. Konner, 441:13Jul86-13
MARHO.  Visions of History.
    C. Parker, 366:Autumn85-288
Mariani, P.  Prime Mover.
    P. Stitt, 344:Fall86-128
Marías, J.  Ortega: Las trayectorias.*
Ortega: Circumstancia y vocación.
    N.R. Orringer, 240(HR):Autumn85-504
Mariategui, J.C.  Correspondencia (1915-
1930).  (A. Melis, ed)
    D. Wise, 263(RIB):Vol35No4-466
Marienstras, R.  New Perspectives on the
Shakespearean World.
    I-S. Ewbank, 617(TLS):25Apr86-451
Marín, F.M. - see under Marcos Marín, F.
Marín, J.L.M. - see under Morales y Marín,
J.L.
Marin, L.  Le Portrait du roi.*
    J.L. Logan, 188(ECr):Spring85-89
Marín, N. - see de Vega Carpio, L.
Marinetti, A.  Le Iscrizioni Sudpicene, I.
    P. Baldi, 350:Sep86-718
Mariño Veiras, D.  Señorio de Santa Maria
de Meira (de 1150 a 1525).
    C. Estow, 589:Jul85-701
Marius, R.  Thomas More.*
    W. Allen, 569(SR):Winter85-xiii
Mark, R.  Experiments in Gothic Structure.*
    A.J. Durelli, 576:Oct85-295
    O. von Simson, 576:Oct85-292
Marker, F.J. and L-L.  Edward Gordon Craig
and "The Pretenders."*
    A.M. Nagler, 402(MLR):Oct85-919
Marker, G.  Publishing, Printing, and the
Origins of Intellectual Life in Russia,
1700-1800.
    A.G. Cross, 617(TLS):7Mar86-239
Markey, T.L.  Frisian.*
    P. Swiggers, 260(IF):Band90-345
Markgraf, H.  Das Schreckliche in den
Tragödien Crébillons.
    F. Baasner, 547(RF):Band97Heft1-92
Markham, E.A.  Living in Disguise.  Some-
thing Unusual.
    C. Rumens, 617(TLS):24Oct86-1186

Markham, E.J.  Saibara.*
    A. Dick, 415:Mar85-158
    S.G. Nelson, 407(MN):Spring85-122
Markley, R. and L. Finke, eds.  From Ren-
aissance to Restoration.
    P. Hyland, 568(SCN):Fall85-29
    M. Neill, 223:Spring85-82
Markov, V.  Russian Imagism: 1919-1924.
    D.M. Bethea, 574(SEEJ):Spring85-112
Markov, V. and D.S. Worth, eds.  From Los
Angeles to Kiev.*
    D. Ward, 559:Vol9No1-81
    F.C.M. Wigzell, 575(SEER):Apr85-285
Markovič, M.  Dialectical Theory of Mean-
ing.
    W.L.M., 185:Apr86-681
Marks, E.R.  Coleridge on the Language of
Verse.*
    S.M. Tave, 402(MLR):Jul85-704
Marks, G.A. and C.B. Johnson - see "Har-
rap's Slang Dictionary: English-French/
French-English"
van Marle, J.  On the Paradigmatic Dimen-
sion of Morphological Creativity.
    T.F. Shannon, 350:Sep86-708
Marling, K.A.  Tom Benton and His Drawings.
    G. Glueck, 441:12Jan86-28
Marling, K.A.  Wall-to-Wall America.
    F.V. O'Connor, 127:Winter84-393
Marling, W.  William Carlos Williams and
the Painters, 1909-1923.
    V.M. Kouidis, 577(SHR):Fall85-386
Marlis, S.  Red Tools.
    R. Robbins, 649(WAL):Aug85-177
Marlow, E. and V. Morrison.  A la page:
grammaire.
    B. Ebling 2d, 207(FR):Mar86-663
Marlowe, C.  The Complete Works of Christo-
pher Marlowe.  (2nd ed) (F. Bowers, ed)
Tamburlaine the Great.  (J.S. Cunningham,
ed)
    E. Jones, 447(N&Q):Mar84-109
Marmo, V.  Dalle fonti alle forme.
    D.C. Clarke, 589:Oct85-1054
Marmura, M.E., ed.  Islamic Theology and
Philosophy.
    F. Rosenthal, 589:Apr85-484
Marotin, F., ed.  Frontières du conte.
    K. Sasse, 547(RF):Band97Heft4-456
Marotta, K.  A Piece of Earth.*
    639(VQR):Summer85-90
Marotzki, W.  Subjektivität und Negativi-
tät als Bildungsproblem.
    A.K.D. Lorenzen, 489(PJGG):Band92Heft2-
429
Marqués, M.M. - see under Mena Marqués, M.
Márquez, G.G. - see under García Márquez,
G.
Márquez, G.G. and P. Apuleyo Mendoza - see
under García Márquez, G. and P. Apuleyo
Mendoza
Márquez-Villanueva, F., ed.  Harvard Uni-
versity Conference in Honor of Gabriel
Miró (1879-1930).
    F. García Sarriá, 86(BHS):Jul85-314
Marquis, A.G.  Hopes and Ashes.
    S.D. Stark, 441:28Dec86-7
Marqusee, M.  Slow Turn.
    S. Rae, 617(TLS):5Sep86-977
Marr, D.  Vision.
    R. Schwartz, 482(PhR):Jul85-411

Marr, D.G. Vietnamese Tradition on Trial, 1920-1945.
  S.L. Popkin, 293(JASt):Feb85-349
Marranca, B. Theatrewritings.
  R. Simard, 397(MD):Sep85-503
  T.J. Taylor, 615(TJ):Dec85-520
Marrey, B. and J-P. Monnet. La Grande histoire des serres et des jardins d'hiver en France, 1780-1900.
  J.C. Garcias, 46:Sep85-81
Marrow, J.H. Passion Iconography in Northern European Art of the Late Middle Ages and Early Renaissance.
  R. Haussherr, 683:Band48Heft2-265
Marrus, M.R. The Unwanted.*
  N. Ascherson, 453(NYRB):27Feb86-5
  M. Burns, 441:2Feb86-17
  L.D. Nachman, 129:Jun86-76
Marsack, R. The Cave of Making.
  R.G. Thomas, 541(RES):May85-301
Marsden, P. Roman London.
  S.E. Cleary, 123:Vol35No1-221
Marsh, D. and J. Swenson, eds. The New Rolling Stone Record Guide. (rev)
  B. Allan, 529(QQ):Winter85-810
Marsh, J. Pre-Raphaelite Sisterhood.*
  R.W., 326:Winter85/86-28
Marsh, M. A Matter of Personal Survival.
  A. Shalom, 543:Dec85-366
Marsh, P. and P. Collett. Driving Passion.
  S. Hey, 362:27Nov86-28
Marshall, A. The Brass Bed.
  S. Hearon, 441:12Jan86-20
Marshall, A. The German Naturalists and Gerhart Hauptmann.
  R.C. Cowen, 406:Fall85-364
Marshall, B.A. A Historical Commentary on Asconius.
  J.S. Ruebel, 124:Jul-Aug86-424
Marshall, E. and L. Watkins. Paperweight.
  404:Summer85-59
Marshall, H. Masters of the Soviet Cinema.
  L. Hecht, 574(SEEJ):Winter85-484
  J.C. Troncale, 615(TJ):May85-246
Marshall, P. Praisesong for the Widow.
  A.A. Scarboro, 268(IFR):Winter86-53
Marshall, P.H. William Godwin.*
  J.P. Clark, 141:Summer85-320
  M.K. Stocking, 661(WC):Fall85-190
  B.J. Tysdahl, 173(ECS):Spring86-435
  G.W., 185:Jan86-453
Marshall, R.C. Collective Decision Making in Rural Japan.
  D.W. Plath, 407(MN):Winter85-457
Marshall, W. Head First.
  T.J. Binyon, 617(TLS):17Oct86-1169
Marteau, R. Mount Royal. Interlude.
  M. Fee, 102(CanL):Spring85-120
Martel, G. Le Messianisme de Louis Riel (1844-1885).
  J.R. Miller, 298:Fall85-156
Martello, P.J. Teatro. (H.S. Noce, ed)
  P. Cherchi, 405(MP):May86-430
Martens, K. Negation, Negativität und Utopie im Werk von Wallace Stevens.
  U. Horstmann, 38:Band103Heft1/2-257
Martens, L. The Diary Novel.
  B. Duyfhuizen, 454:Winter86-171
Marthan, J. Le vieillard amoureux dans l'oeuvre cornélienne.
  A. Gabriel, 546(RR):Nov85-444

Martienssen, H. Insights. (S.G. Kossick, ed)
  J. Carman, 89(BJA):Autumn85-400
Martin, A., ed. Anthologie du conte en France, 1750-1799.*
  D. Fletcher, 208(FS):Jan85-83
Martin, A. The Knowledge of Ignorance.
  E. Said, 617(TLS):30May86-599
Martin, A. Tillie Olsen.
  A. Ronald, 649(WAL):May85-55
Martin, A.Y. and R.F., eds. Theory and History of Folklore.
  42(AR):Winter85-122
Martin, B.F. The Hypocrisy of Justice in the Belle Epoque.*
  639(VQR):Winter85-8
Martin, C.E. Hollybush.
  T.A. Adler, 658:Summer/Autumn85-207
Martin, D. and P. Mullen, eds. No Alternative.
  L. Lerner, 402(MLR):Oct85-896
Martin, D. and P. Mullen, eds. Unholy Warfare.
  T.D., 185:Apr86-662
Martin, E. Canadian Fairy Tales.
  E. Greene, 526:Winter85-77
Martín, E. - see Lorca, F.G.
Martin, E.A. H.L. Mencken and the Debunkers.*
  C. Scruggs, 27(AL):Oct85-509
  639(VQR):Spring85-44
Martin, G. and G.H. Lübben - see Marcus, E.
Martin, G.R.R. Nightflyers.
  G. Jonas, 441:12Jan86-22
Martin, H. Cult and Canon.
  B. Womack, 293(JASt):Nov84-189
Martin, H-J. and R. Chartier, eds. L'Histoire de l'Édition française. (Vol 3)
  E. Weber, 617(TLS):2May86-483
Martin, H-J. and R. Chartier, with J-P. Vivet, eds. Histoire de l'édition française. (Vols 1 and 2)
  78(BC):Spring85-9
Martin, J. Style and Substance.
  P-L. Adams, 61:Dec86-104
  L. Zeidner, 441:9Nov86-9
  442(NY):8Dec86-153
Martin, J.B. It Seems Like Only Yesterday.
  L. Bernstein, 441:12Oct86-16
Martin, J.E. Feudalism to Capitalism.
  S. Fenoaltea, 589:Jul85-703
Martin, J-P. Description Lexicale du Français Parlé en Vallée d'Aoste.
  B.J. Wenk, 353:Vol23No3-518
Martin, J.R. Reclaiming a Conversation.
  M. Nussbaum, 453(NYRB):30Jan86-7
Martin, J.W. The Golden Age of French Cinema: 1929-1939.
  Y.V. Karageorge, 207(FR):Oct85-181
Martín, L. Daughters of the Conquistadores.
  B. Mujica, 37:Mar-Apr85-50
Martin, M. Vatican.
  M. Boland, 441:2Feb86-16
Martin, M.K., ed. Self-Deception and Self-Understanding.
  D. Sachs, 185:Jul86-882
Martin, P.G. Everyday Conversations in French.
  R.A. Hartzell, 207(FR):Apr86-802
Martin, P.M. L'idée de royauté à Rome. (Vol 1)
  J. Champeaux, 555:Vol159fasc1-151

249

Martin, R.  Cowboy.*
  D. Graham, 584(SWR):Winter85-138
Martin, R.  Pour une logique du sens.
  S.F. Noreiko, 208(FS):Apr85-247
  P. Swiggers, 567:Vol56No3/4-347
Martin, R.  To be Free!
  K. Ray, 441:14Sep86-30
Martin, R. and M. Barasch, eds.  Writers
  of the Purple Sage.
  P. Wild, 649(WAL):Aug85-185
Martin, R. and J. Wallace.  Working Women
  in Recession.
  F. Cairncross, 617(TLS):4Apr86-349
Martin, R.M.  Mind, Modality, Meaning, and
  Method.
  S.B. Rosenthal, 543:Dec85-367
Märtin, R-P.  Wunschpotentiale.*
  C.F. Lorenz, 602:Band16Heft2-304
  B. Steinbrink, 52:Band20Heft3-315
Martin, S.  California Writers.*
  A. Frietzsche, 649(WAL):May85-60
Martin, S.  Wagner to "The Waste Land."*
  P. Murphy, 541(RES):Aug85-466
Martín, V.T. - see under Tovar Martín, V.
Martin, W.  An American Triptych.*
  U. Brumm, 165(EAL):Winter85/86-271
  K.Z. Derounian, 568(SCN):Fall85-45
  C. Keyes, 357:Spring86-74
  M. Kumin, 219(GaR):Spring85-169
  P.J. McAlexander, 577(SHR):Summer85-
  262
Martin, W.  Cracknrigg.
  R. Pybus, 565:Summer85-62
Martin, W.E., Jr.  The Mind of Frederick
  Douglass.*
  W.L. Andrews, 392:Winter84/85-91
Martín Cea, J.C.  El campesinado castel-
  lano de la cuenca del Duero.
  C. Estow, 589:Oct85-996
Martín Duque, A.J.  Documentacion medieval
  de Leire (siglos IX a XII).
  B. Leroy, 92(BH):Jul-Dec84-532
Martín González, J.J.  Escultura barroca
  en España, 1600-1770.
  M. Estella, 48:Jul-Sep85-311
Martín Nogales, J.L.  Los cuentos de
  Ignacio Aldecoa.
  F. Arrojo, 238:Sep85-520
  M. Casado Velarde, 140(CH):Vol7No2-181
  F.D. López-Herrera, 552(REH):May85-140
Martine, B.J.  Individuals and Individual-
  ity.
  W. Desmond, 543:Mar86-572
Martineau, H.  Harriet Martineau's Letters
  to Fanny Wedgwood.*  (E.S. Arbuckle, ed)
  L. Chambers-Schiller, 637(VS):Winter85-
  338
Martínez, E.B. - see under Bermejo Mar-
  tínez, E.
Martínez, R.C. - see under Camacho Mar-
  tínez, R.
Martínez Díez, G. and F. Rodríguez, eds.
  La colección canónica hispana, 3.
  F.X. Murphy, 589:Oct85-1055
Martínez Nadal, R.  Cuatro lecciones sobre
  Federico García Lorca.
  G. Connell, 86(BHS):Apr85-209
Martínez Nadal, R.  Españoles en la Gran
  Bretaña.
  J.M. Naharro, 240(HR):Winter85-115
Martínez Nadal, R. - see Lorca, F.G.

Martinique, E.  Chinese Traditional Book-
  binding.
  E.S. Rawski, 293(JASt):Nov84-187
Martins, H.  Do Barroco a Guimarães Rosa.
  M.L. Daniel, 238:May85-327
Martins, J.V.D. - see under de Pina Mar-
  tins, J.V.
Martins, M.R.D. - see under Delgado Mar-
  tins, M.R.
Martius-von Harder, G.  Women in Rural
  Bangladesh.
  H. Papanek, 293(JASt):Nov84-127
Martorell, J. and M.J. de Galba.  Tirant
  lo Blanc.  (D.H. Rosenthal, trans)
  A. Gullón, 240(HR):Autumn85-479
  639(VQR):Winter85-24
Marty, E.  L'écriture du jour.
  P. Schnyder, 547(RF):Band97Heft4-483
Martz, E.M., with R.K. McClure and W.T.
  La Moy - see Walpole, H.
Martz, L.L. - see H.D.
Marún, G.  Orígenes del costumbrismo ético-
  social.
  P.L. Ullman, 238:Dec85-773
Maruya, S.  Singular Rebellion.
  R. Wiley, 441:7Sep86-14
Marx, L.  Benny Andersen.
  F. Hugus, 563(SS):Spring85-200
Marx, W.  Gibt es auf Erden ein Mass?
  B. Casper, 489(PJGG):Band92Heft2-406
  K. Düsing, 687:Jul-Sep85-464
  D.F. Krell, 323:May85-196
Marx, W., ed.  Heidegger Memorial Lectures.
  A.G. Pleydell-Pearce, 323:Jan85-97
Marx, W.  The Philosophy of F.W.J. Schell-
  ing.
  W. Desmond, 543:Jun86-778
Marzaduri, M., ed and trans.  Dada Russo.
  A. Lawton, 574(SEEJ):Winter85-479
Marzolph, U.  Typologie des persischen
  Volksmärchens.
  H-J. Uther, 196:Band26Heft1/2-180
Marzolph, U.  Der weise Narr Buhlūl.
  A. Schimmel, 196:Band26Heft3/4-371
Marzys, Z. - see de Vaugelas, C.F.
Masahide, S. - see under Shibusawa Masa-
  hide
Masheck, J.  Historical Present.
  D. Carrier, 55:Jan85-38
Masi, M.  Boethian Number Theory.*
  I. Bulmer-Thomas, 123:Vol35No1-86
Maskiell, M.  Women Between Cultures.
  M. Borthwick, 293(JASt):Aug85-864
Maslow, J.E.  Bird of Life, Bird of Death.
  G. Gibson, 441:9Mar86-13
  J.A.C. Greppin, 617(TLS):15Aug86-887
  H. O'Shaughnessy, 362:31Jul86-24
Maso, C.  Ghost Dance.
  M.S. Willis, 441:20Jul86-18
  442(NY):15Sep86-120
Mason, A.  Ports of Entry.
  W.R. Slager, 399(MLJ):Autumn85-332
Mason, B.A.  In Country.*
  A. Bloom, 434:Summer86-513
  A. Boston, 617(TLS):18Apr86-416
Mason, C.  The Poet Robert Browning and
  his Kinsfolk by his Cousin Cyrus Mason.*
  (W.C. Turner, ed)
  T.J. Collins, 637(VS):Winter85-322
Mason, H.  Cyrano de Bergerac: "L'Ature
  Monde."
  M. Alcover, 207(FR):Apr86-782
  P.M. Harry, 208(FS):Apr85-203

Mason, H.A.   To Homer through Pope.
617(TLS):31Jan86-127
Mason, H.A.   The Tragic Plane.
J. Gould, 617(TLS):5Sep86-981
C. Lacassagne, 189(EA):Oct-Dec86-492
Maspero, F.   Cat's Grin.
H.R. Lottman, 441:18May86-19
442(NY):24Nov86-149
Massa, A.   American Literature in Context
IV, 1900-1930.
R. Mason, 447(N&Q):Jun84-282
Massel, D.P.   The Vikings Who Came to Fly.
P.K. Smith, 526:Spring85-88
Massie, A.   Augustus.
S. Altinel, 617(TLS):30ct86-1115
B. Tonkin, 362:20ct86-23
Massie, A.   The Caesars.
J.C. Traupman, 124:Jan-Feb86-197
Massignon, L.   The Passion of al-Ḥallāj.
S.H. Nasr, 589:Jan85-183
Massingham, B.   A Century of Gardeners.
M.L. Simo, 637(VS):Winter85-334
Massip, R.   Douce lumière.
F. de Martinoir, 450(NRF):Sep85-81
Masson, J.M.   The Assault on Truth.*
E.W. Holland, 560:Winter-Spring85-155
Masson, J.M.   Was hat man dir, du armes
Kind, getan?
C. Neubaur, 384:May85-426
Masson, J.M. - see Freud, S.
Masson, P.   André Gide: Voyage et écriture.
P. Schnyder, 224(GRM):Band35Heft4-439
Masterman, L., ed.   Television Mythologies.
D. Wilson, 707:Summer85-225
Masters, B.   Killing for Company.*
J. Quinlan, 441:13Jul86-19
Masters, B.   The Swinging Sixties.
J. Stokes, 617(TLS):28Mar86-338
Masters, H.   Clemmons.*
G.C., 569(SR):Spring85-xxxix
Masters, H.   Hammertown Tales.
C. Ames, 441:20Apr86-22
Mastrocinque, A.   Manipolazione della
storia in età ellenistica: i Seleucidi e
Roma.
E.S. Gruen, 303(JoHS):Vol 105-218
Mastromarco, G.   The Public of Herondas.
I.C. Cunningham, 123:Vol35No2-384
Mastronarde, D.J. and J.M. Bremer.   The
Textual Tradition of Euripides'
"Phoinissai."*
P.G. Mason, 303(JoHS):Vol 105-183
J.M. Wilkins, 123:Vol35No2-382
Mat-Hasquin, M.   Voltaire et l'antiquité
grecque.*
M.H. Waddicor, 208(FS):Jul85-346
Matarasso, P.   The Redemption of Chivalry.
J.L. Grigsby, 545(RPh):Aug84-53
Mateo Gómez, I.   Juan Correa de Vivar.*
J.M. Serrera, 48:Jan-Mar85-89
Materassi, A.   Corrispondenza italiana.
J. Vizmuller-Zocco, 276:Spring85-84
Materassi, G. and E. Fornaini.   Grammatica
italiana.  (Vol 1)
J. Vizmuller-Zocco, 276:Spring85-84
Materer, T. - see Pound, E. and W. Lewis
Mathabane, M.   Kaffir Boy.
L. Thomas, 441:27Apr86-23
Mather, J. and H.H. Speitel, eds.   The
Linguistic Atlas of Scotland (Scots
Sections).  (Vol 3)
A.J. Aitken, 617(TLS):9May86-491

Mather, J.R.   The Birds of Yorkshire.
E. Dunn, 617(TLS):5Dec86-1385
Mathes, J., ed.   Prosa des Jugendstils.
W.E. Yates, 402(MLR):Jul85-762
Mathews, A.C.   Minding Ruth.*
T. Eagleton, 565:Autumn85-69
Mathews, H.   Country Cooking.
I. Malin, 532(RCF):Spring85-144
Mathews, H.   The Sinking of the Odradek
Stadium.
K. Burke, 532(RCF):Fall85-186
J. Clute, 617(TLS):7Nov86-1254
Mathews, N.M., ed.   Cassatt and Her Circle.
F. Spalding, 90:Apr85-237
Mathews, R.   Blood Ties.
J.K. Keefer, 198:Winter85-95
Mathiesen, T.J. - see Aristides Quintil-
ianus
Mathieu, J-C.   La Poésie de René Char, ou
Le Sel de la Splendeur.
M.A. Caws, 546(RR):Mar85-230
E. Marty, 98:Jun-Jul85-719
Mathieu, P-L.   Gustave Moreau: The Water-
colours.
P. Conisbee, 617(TLS):18Apr86-423
Mathieu-Castellani, G.   Mythes de l'éros
baroque.
G. Gillespie, 107(CRCL):Sep85-518
Mathieu-Castellani, G. - see de La Roque,
S-G.
Matić, D.   Bagdala.
L. Kovacs, 450(NRF):Feb85-113
Matich, O. and M. Heim, eds.   The Third
Wave.
S.F. Orth, 574(SEEJ):Winter85-488
G.N. Slobin, 550(RusR):Apr85-193
Matilal, B.K.   Perception.
J.N. Mohanty, 617(TLS):10Oct86-1143
Matossian, N.   Xenakis.
P. Griffiths, 617(TLS):4Jul86-739
Matras, D.   Proverbes.  (I. Kjaer, ed)
U. Palmenfelt, 64(Arv):Vol39-220
Matras-Troubetzkoy, J. and C. Taillard,
eds.   Cheminements.
A.T. Rambo, 293(JASt):Aug85-798
Matson, J.L. and T.M. Di Lorenzo.   Punish-
ment and Its Alternatives.
J.M.O., 185:Apr86-673
Matsumara, T.   The Labour Aristocracy
Revisited.
D. Englander, 637(VS):Summer85-694
Matsunaga, S.M.   The Mars Project.
W.J. Broad, 441:28Sep86-27
Matte, E.J.   Histoire des modes phoné-
tiques du français.*
J. Klausenburger, 545(RPh):Feb85-324
Matter, H. - see Mann, T.
Mattesini, E. - see Nomi, F.
Matthee, D.   Fiela's Child.
F. Levy, 441:27Jul86-10
Matthes, L.   Vaudeville.
W.D. Howarth, 208(FS):Jan85-88
Matthew, H.C.G. - see Gladstone, W.E.
Matthews, D.   Beethoven.
W. Drabkin, 617(TLS):31Jan86-118
Matthews, G.   Heart of the Country.
S. Altinel, 617(TLS):21Feb86-198
D. Fitzpatrick, 441:4May86-52
Matthews, J.   Crazy Women.*
L.K. Abbott, 460(OhR):No37-123
P. Glasser, 455:Dec85-75
Matthews, J.H.   Joyce Mansour.
B.L. Knapp, 593:Spring85-74

251

Matthews, J.T.  The Play of Faulkner's
Language.*
  J.S. Whitley, 447(N&Q):Dec84-570
Matthews, P.H.  Syntax.
  N. Burton-Roberts, 402(MLR):Apr85-413
  U. Fries, 38:Band103Heft1/2-109
  A. Radford, 545(RPh):Feb85-346
Matthews, W.  A Happy Childhood.*
  R. Jackson, 502(PrS):Winter85-109
  W. Scammell, 148:Winter85-65
  D. Wojahn, 491:Jun85-178
Matthiessen, P.  Indian Country.
  M. Abley, 617(TLS):21Mar86-299
  J. Reed, 364:Feb86-111
  J.C. Rice, 649(WAL):May85-59
Matthiessen, P.  Men's Lives.
  P-L. Adams, 61:Sep86-104
  R. Hughes, 453(NYRB):23Oct86-21
  J. Raban, 441:22Jun86-1
Matthiessen, P.  Nine-Headed Dragon River.
  R. Fields, 469:Vol 11No4-113
  J. van de Wetering, 441:6Apr86-23
  442(NY):21Apr86-125
Mattison, C.  Snakes of the World.
  M. O'Shea, 617(TLS):4Jul86-745
Mattoso, K.M.D. - see under de Queirós Mat-
toso, K.M.
Maturo, G.  La literatura hispanoamericana.
  N. Holland, 238:May85-319
Matusow, A.J.  The Unraveling of America.
  G.S. Smith, 529(QQ):Summer85-297
Matzat, W.  Dramenstruktur und Zuschauer-
rolle.*
  V. Kapp, 475:Vol 12No23-721
  F. Moureau, 535(RHL):Jan/Feb85-91
Mauduit, A-M. and J.  La France contre la
France.
  D. O'Connell, 207(FR):May86-1013
Maulpoix, J-M.  Dans la paume du rêveur.
  M. Le Bot, 450(NRF):Apr85-76
Mauquoy-Hendrickx, M.  Les Estampes des
Wierix.*
  S. Boorsch, 551(RenQ):Autumn85-535
Maurel, J-P.  Le Haut Vol.
  A. Nabarra, 207(FR):Oct85-152
Maurel, S. - see Tirso de Molina
Maurer, A. - see Siger de Brabant
Maurer, A.A.  About Beauty.
  F.J. Kovach, 543:Mar85-662
Maurer, D.W.  Language of the Underworld.*
  (A.W. Futrell and C.B. Wordell, eds)
  B.M.H. Strang, 677(YES):Vol 15-259
Maurer, N.Q.  Les démons sont petits.*
  J. Le Hardi, 98:Dec85-1200
Mauron, C., ed and trans.  Lou Proucez de
Carementran.
  C. Rostaing, 553(RLiR):Jul-Dec85-529
Mautner, F.H. - see Lichtenberg, G.C.
Mautner, G.  Lovers and Fugitives.
  J. Marcus, 441:2Mar86-24
Mauzi, R., M. Delon and S. Menant.  Littér-
ature française.  (Vol 6)
  D.C. Charlton, 208(FS):Apr85-214
Mavrodina, P.M.  Kievskaia Rus' i koche-
vniki.
  E.S. Hurwitz, 550(RusR):Jan85-102
Maxim, J.R.  Time Out of Mind.
  F. Taliaferro, 441:9Feb86-11
Maxwell, A.E.  The Frog and the Scorpion.
  N. Callendar, 441:20Jul86-20

Maxwell, D.E.S.  A Critical History of
Modern Irish Drama 1891-1980.
  B. Grantham, 157:No156-50
  C. Murray, 272(IUR):Autumn85-244
Maxwell, J.C.  Maxwell on Saturn's Rings.
  (S.G. Brush, C.W.F. Everitt and E. Gar-
ber, eds)
  D.B. Wilson, 637(VS):Spring85-539
Maxwell, K.B.  Bemba Myth and Ritual.
  D. Henige, 538(RAL):Fall85-409
Maxwell, N.  From Knowledge to Wisdom.*
  M. Adam, 542:Oct-Dec85-567
  J. Kekes, 262:Sep85-388
Maxwell, W.  Time Will Darken It.
  J. Armstrong, 389(MQ):Winter86-252
May, D.  Hannah Arendt.
  362:3Jul86-34
May, E., ed.  Musics of Many Cultures.
  A. Dick, 415:Mar85-158
May, H.F.  Ideas, Faiths, and Feelings.*
  P. Merkley, 529(QQ):Autumn85-598
May, J.  A Pliocene Companion.
  S.L. Nickerson, 561(SFS):Mar85-101
May, P., with M. Melford.  A Game Enjoyed.
  P. Sutcliffe, 617(TLS):3Jan86-21
May, P. and M. Tuckson.  The Traditional
Pottery of Papua New Guinea.
  J. Povey, 2(AfrA):Nov84-87
May, R.J. and F. Nemenzo, eds.  The
Philippines After Marcos.
  I. Buruma, 453(NYRB):16Jan86-27
May, S.  Cambodian Witness.  (J. Fenton,
ed)
  A. Barnett, 362:6Nov86-26
  D. Chandler, 617(TLS):19Dec86-1419
Mayakovsky, V.  Love is the Heart of Every-
thing.  (B. Jangfeldt, ed)
  P. France, 617(TLS):9May86-505
Mayer, C.J. and G.A. Riley.  Public Domain,
Private Dominion.
  W. Green, 441:6Apr86-22
Mayer, D. and M. Scott, eds.  Four Bars of
"Agit."*
  M. Sands, 611(TN):Vol39No3-158
Mayer, F.H.  Ancient Tales in Modern Japan.
  C. Mulhern, 407(MN):Autumn85-367
Mayer, H.  Outsiders.*
  G. Woodcock, 569(SR):Summer85-457
Mayer, J.  A Son of Thunder.
  S. Wilentz, 441:3Aug86-17
Mayer, R., ed.  Lucan: "Civil War" VIII.*
  G.W.M. Harrison, 24:Spring85-138
Mayer, R.  The Search.
  M.S. Kaplan, 441:9Feb86-24
Mayes, F.  Hours.
  F. Allen, 496:Fall85-179
  M. Kumin, 219(GaR):Spring85-169
  455:Mar85-65
Maynard, J.  Charlotte Brontë and Sexual-
ity.*
  N. Armstrong, 637(VS):Spring86-483
  S. Davies, 148:Autumn85-35
  R. Keefe, 445(NCF):Sep85-228
  H.W., 636(VP):Summer85-224
Maynard, W.  Elizabethan Lyric Poetry and
Its Music.
  D. Wulstan, 617(TLS):31Oct86-1229
Mayne, R., ed.  Handbooks to the Modern
World: Western Europe.
  V. Bogdanor, 176:Sep/Oct86-52
Mayo, J.K.  The Hunting Season.
  T.J. Binyon, 617(TLS):17Jan86-57
  W. Smith, 441:11May86-24

252

Mayone Dias, E., ed. Cantares de além-mar.*
  C. Slater, 545(RPh):Aug84-120
Mayor, A.H. Artists and Anatomists.
  W. Schupbach, 90:Oct85-720
Mayr-Harting, H. and R.I. Moore, eds.
  Studies in Medieval History Presented to
  R.H.C. Davis.
  W.L. Warren, 617(TLS):25Apr86-442
Mayrhofer, M., M. Peters and O.E. Pfeiffer,
  eds. Lautgeschichte und Etymologie.
  J. Udolph, 260(IF):Band90-246
Mayröcker, F. Reise durch die Nacht. Das
  Herzzereissende der Dinge.
  J. Adler, 617(TLS):4Jul86-738
Maza, S.C. Servants and Masters in Eigh-
  teenth-Century France.*
  J. Dunkley, 83:Autumn85-232
  D.K. Van Kley, 173(ECS):Fall85-83
Mazarin, J. Bréviaire des politiciens.
  (F. Dupont, ed and trans)
  S. Boulbina, 98:Dec85-1211
Mažiulis, V. Prūsų kalbos paminklai.
  R. Eckert, 682(ZPSK):Band38Heft5-614
Mazlish, B. The Meaning of Karl Marx.*
  D.M., 185:Apr86-670
Mazrui, A.A. The Africans.
  G. Packer, 441:16Nov86-24
  G. Wheatcroft, 617(TLS):14Nov86-1285
Mazur, B.W. Colloquial Polish.*
  R.A. Rothstein, 399(MLJ):Summer85-193
Mazzini, I. De observantia ciborum.
  V. Nutton, 123:Vol35No2-396
Mazzoni, G. On the Defense of the Comedy
  of Dante.
  J.J. Guzzardo, 276:Winter85-321
Mazzotta, G. Dante, Poet of the Desert.
  V. Tripodi, 345(KRQ):Vol32No4-431
Mazzotta, G. The World at Play in Boccac-
  cio's "Decameron."
  M. Verdicchio, 107(CRCL):Jun85-365
Mead, L.M. Beyond Entitlement.*
  J. Cohn, 129:May86-74
Mead, S.M. and B. Kernot, eds. Art and
  Artists of Oceania.
  J. Povey, 2(AfrA):Nov84-89
Meades, J. Filthy English.
  P. Lewis, 565:Winter84/85-42
Meadows, J. Space Garbage.
  J. North, 617(TLS):7Feb86-131
Mechanicus, P. Waiting for Death.
  R. Sherer, 287:Oct85-27
Mecklenburg, N. Erzählte Provinz.*
  A.C. Ulmer, 406:Fall85-373
Mečkovskaja, N.B. Rannie vostočnoslav-
  janskie grammatiki. (A.E. Supruna, ed)
  L. Ďurovič, 559:Vol9No1-92
Medaglia, S.M. Note di esegesi archilo-
  chea.
  D. Arnould, 555:Vol59fasc1-100
Medawar, P. Memoir of a Thinking Radish.
  A.J. Ayer, 362:3Apr86-27
  J. Calado, 617(TLS):21Nov86-1300
  A. Fels, 441:15Jun86-15
"Mededelingen van de Nijmeegse Centrale
  voor Dialect- en Naamkunde." (Vol 16)
  J.B. Berns, 685(ZDL):2/1985-265
Medhurst, M.J. and T.W. Benson, eds.
  Rhetorical Dimensions in Media.
  S. Osborn, 583:Fall85-87
"Medieval and Renaissance Studies." (Vol
  9) (F. Tirro, ed)
  J.D. Burnley, 541(RES):Feb85-70

Medina, J., C. Morali and A. Senik. La
  philosophie comme débat entre les textes.
  M. Adam, 542:Jan-Mar85-78
Medvedev, I.P., ed. Vizantiiskii zemled-
  el'cheskii zakon.
  D.H. Kaiser, 550(RusR):Jan85-99
Medvedev, R. All Stalin's Men.
  A. Kemp-Welch, 575(SEER):Jan85-145
Medvedev, R. China and the Superpowers.
  J. Mirsky, 617(TLS):11Apr86-377
  A.E. Stent, 441:15Jun86-19
Medvedev, R. Khrushchev.*
  L. Good, 529(QQ):Summer85-390
Medvedev, Z.A. Gorbachev.
  A. Brown, 617(TLS):18Jul86-781
  D. Holloway, 453(NYRB):12Jun86-18
  S. Schmemann, 441:20Jul86-9
Meehan, E.M. Women's Rights at Work.
  F. Cairncross, 617(TLS):4Apr86-349
Meehan, P. Frank Lloyd Wright.
  M. Ison, 576:Mar85-75
Meehan, P.J. - see Wright, F.L.
Meehan-Waters, B. Autocracy and Aristoc-
  racy.*
  I. de Madariaga, 575(SEER):Apr85-297
Meek, M.R.D. In Remembrance of Rose.
  T.J. Binyon, 617(TLS):17Oct86-1169
Meek, M.R.D. The Split Second.
  T.J.B., 617(TLS):28Feb86-216
Meeks, W.A. The First Urban Christians.*
  D. Kyrtatus, 313:Vol75-265
van der Meer, J.H. Musikinstrumente.
  M.H. Schmid, 683:Band48Heft3-396
Meggs, P.B. A History of Graphic Design.*
  P.P. Piech, 503:Winter83-185
Megill, A. Prophets of Extremity.*
  D. Cook, 529(QQ):Winter85-874
Mehendale, M.A. Avesta rendered into San-
  skrit.
  B. Schlerath, 259(IIJ):Apr85-157
Mehl, D. Die Tragödien Shakespeares.*
  K.P. Steiger, 156(ShJW):Jahrbuch1985-
  228
Mehner, K. - see Hanslick, E.
Mehra, M. Die Bedeutung der Formel "Offen-
  bares Geheimnis" in Goethes Spätwerk.
  J.D. Simons, 221(GQ):Winter85-118
Mehta, V. Sound-Shadows of the New World.
  H. Kureishi, 617(TLS):30May86-589
  C. Sternhell, 441:9Mar86-14
Meier, G.M. Emerging from Poverty.
  P. Bauer, 453(NYRB):20Nov86-51
Meier, H. Notas críticas al "Diccionario
  crítico etimológico castellano e hispán-
  ico."
  J. Mondéjar, 547(RF):Band97Heft4-412
Meier, H. - see Rousseau, J-J.
Meier, R., comp. Richard Meier, Architect
  1964/1984.*
  W. James, 505:Jun85-149
Meiggs, R. Trees and Timber in the
  Ancient Mediterranean World.*
  M.W. Mikesell, 122:Oct85-385
Meigret, L. Le Traité de la Grammaire
  française (1550) — Le Menteur de Lucien
  Aus Lecteurs (1548). (F.J. Hausmann, ed)
  P. Swiggers, 353:Vol123No4-650
Meigs, M. The Medusa Head.
  L. Weir, 102(CanL):Winter84-105
Meijer, B.W. Rembrandt nel seicento Tos-
  cano.
  I.G., 90:Mar85-173

Meijer, B.W. and C. van Tuyll. Disegni
italiani del Teylers Museum Haarlem.*
   D. De Grazia, 380:Winter84-452
Meinig, D.W.  The Shaping of America.
   (Vol 1)
   W. Cronon, 441:17Aug86-12
Meininger, A-M. - see Stendhal
Meinong, A.  On Assumptions.  (J. Heanue,
ed and trans)
   N. Griffin, 154:Winter85-726
Meinsma, K.O.  Spinoza et son cercle.
   R. Israël, 192(EP):Oct-Dec85-563
Meisel, M.  Realizations.*
   R.D. Altick, 301(JEGP):Apr85-278
   G. Ashton, 39:Sep85-237
   V. Emeljanow, 529(QQ):Summer85-400
   L. James, 635(VPR):Summer85-74
   D. Mayer, 610:Autumn85-246
   M. Vicinus, 637(VS):Spring85-527
   H.W., 636(VP):Summer85-221
   D.J. Watermeier, 615(TJ):May85-236
   S. Williams, 612(ThS):May85-85
Meisel, P. and W. Kendrick - see Strachey,
J. and A.
Meisner, M.  Marxism, Maoism, and Utopian-
ism.
   B. Womack, 293(JASt):Nov84-189
Meister, M.W., ed.  Discourses on Śiva.
   P. Mitter, 617(TLS):24Jan86-78
Meister, M.W., with M.A. Dhaky, eds.  Ency-
clopaedia of Indian Temple Architecture.*
   (Vol 1, Pts 1 and 2)
   J.C. Harle, 463:Autumn85-309
   P. Mitter, 576:Oct85-297
Meister, W.  Sprachführer Deutsch-Portu-
giesisch.
   J. Klare, 682(ZPSK):Band38Heft4-424
Meixner, H. and S. Vietta, eds.  Expres-
sionismus — sozialer Wandel und Kunstle-
rische Erfahrung.
   B. Chołuj, 597(SN):Vol57No2-263
Meja, V. and N. Stehr, eds.  Der Streit um
die Wissensoziologie.
   R.A. Morrow, 488:Dec85-507
Melanchthon, P.  Melanchthons Brief-
wechsel.  (Vol 4) (H. Scheible and W.
Thüringer, eds)
   S.H. Hendrix, 551(RenQ):Winter85-732
"Mélanges sur la littérature de la Renais-
sance à la mémoire de V-L. Saulnier."
   L.K. Donaldson-Evans, 551(RenQ):
Autumn85-540
Melchiori, B.A.  Terrorism in the Late
Victorian Novel.
   S. Collini, 617(TLS):31Jan86-125
Melchiori, G., ed.  Joyce in Rome.*
   J. Kidd, 617(TLS):5Sep86-980
   C.D. Lobner, 329(JJQ):Fall85-91
Melchiori, G. - see Joyce, J.
Mel'čuk, I. and others.  Dictionnaire
explicatif et combinatoire du français
contemporain.
   D.A. Kibbee, 399(MLJ):Summer85-175
Mel'čuk, I. and A. Žolkovskij.  Tolkovo-
kombinatornyj slovar' sovremennogo russ-
kogo jazyka.
   A. Wierzbicka, 350:Sep86-684
Meldrum, B.H.  Sophus K. Winther.
   D.E. Wylder, 649(WAL):Aug85-187
Melfi, M.  A Bride in Three Acts.
   V. Comensoli, 102(CanL):Fall85-84

Melikian-Chirvani, A.S.  Islamic Metalwork
from the Iranian World, 8th-18th Centur-
ies.
   R. Hillenbrand, 59:Jun85-265
Melillo, J.V., ed.  Market the Arts!*
   S. Roschwalb, 476:Winter84-80
Melis, A. - see Mariategui, J.C.
Mellers, W.  Angels of the Night.
   B. Case, 617(TLS):7Nov86-1245
   R. Christiansen, 362:30Oct86-27
Mellers, W.  Beethoven and the Voice of
God.*
   412:Aug/Nov84-293
Mellers, W.  A Darker Shade of Pale.*
   A. Shipton, 415:Jul85-413
Mellick, J.S.D.  The Passing Guest.*
   W.H. Scheuerle, 637(VS):Autumn85-167
   G.A. Wilkes, 581:Jun85-244
Mellini, G.L., ed.  Canova: Disegni.
   L. Vertova, 39:Sep85-239
Mellinkoff, R.  The Mark of Cain.
   R.F. Hardin, 107(CRCL):Sep85-509
   J. Milgrom, 318(JAOS):Jul-Sep84-585
Mellon, S. and T. Crawford.  The Artist-
Gallery Partnership.
   M.E. Vetrocq, 476:Fall82-67
Mellor, D.H.  Real Time.*
   L.N. Oaklander, 449:Mar85-105
Mellow, J.R.  Invented Lives.*
   B. Straight, 395(MFS):Summer85-404
   295(JML):Nov85-479
Melly, G.  It's All Writ Out For You.
   A. Gray, 617(TLS):14Mar86-277
Melman, C.  Nouvelles études sur l'hys-
térie.
   A. Reix, 542:Jul-Sep85-357
Melman, Y.  The Master Terrorist.
   J. Kifner, 441:14Sep86-14
Meltzer, D.J., D.D. Fowler and J.A. Sab-
loff, eds.  American Archaeology Past
and Future.
   C. Chippindale, 617(TLS):12Sep86-1008
Melville, H.  Typee, Omoo, Mardi.*  Red-
burn, White-Jacket, Moby-Dick.  (T.
Tanselle, ed of both)
   529(QQ):Summer85-438
Melzer, G.  Wolfgang Bauer.
   R. Voris, 221(GQ):Spring85-310
Memmi, A.  Dependence.
   K.S., 185:Jul86-894
Mena Marqués, M.  Dibujos Italianos de los
siglos XVII y XVIII en la Biblioteca
Nacional.*
   D. Angulo Íñiguez, 48:Jan-Mar85-92
   J.B. Shaw, 90:Jan85-46
"Le Menagier de Paris."*  (G.E. Brereton
and J.M. Ferrier, eds)
   E. Kennedy, 382(MAE):1985/2-337
Menander.  Aspis to Epitrepontes.  (W.G.
Arnott, ed and trans)
   J. Blundell, 303(JoHS):Vol 105-190
Menander.  Samia.*  (D.M. Bain, ed and
trans)
   R. Hamilton, 124:Sep-Oct85-54
Ménard, G.  L'Accent Aigu.
   R. Beaudoin, 102(CanL):Spring85-130
Ménard, M.  Balzac et le comique dans "La
Comédie humaine."
   L. Weinstein, 704(SFR):Summer85-253
Ménard, P.  Les Fabliaux, contes à rire du
moyen âge.*
   M-A. Bossy, 589:Apr85-439
                              [continued]

[continuing]
N.J. Lacy, 403(MLS):Fall85-337
B.J. Levy, 382(MAE):1985/2-334
Mende, F. Heinrich Heine.
    M. Geisler, 221(GQ):Fall85-613
    H.H.F. Henning, 406:Fall85-359
    D. Kliche, 654(WB):10/1985-1753
Mende, H-W. Sprachvermittlung im Dienste
  der Entwicklungspolitik.
    P. Herzberger-Fofana, 343:Heft11-130
Mende, M. Dürer in Dublin.
    A.G., 90:Mar85-172
Mendelsohn, E. The Jews of East Central
  Europe Between the World Wars.
    A.L. Kagedan, 287:Jun-Jul85-28
Mendelson, D. Metaphor in Babel's Short
  Stories.
    M. Friedberg, 550(RusR):Jan85-91
    E.R. Sicher, 575(SEER):Jan85-99
Mendelssohn, F. Felix Mendelssohn: A Life
  in Letters. (R. Elvers, ed)
    K. Gann, 441:21Dec86-15
Mendelssohn, M. Gesammelte Schriften.
  (Vol 6, Pts 1 and 2) (A. Altmann, E.J.
  Engel and F. Bamberger, eds)
    M.B. de Launay, 192(EP):Jul-Sep85-420
de Mendelssohn, P. - see Mann, T.
Mendl, W. Western Europe and Japan.
  Takayanagi Sakio, 285(JapQ):Jan-Mar85-
  83
de Mendoza, Í.L. - see under López de
  Mendoza, Í.
Menéndez Onrubia, C. Introducción al
  teatro de Benito Pérez Galdós.
    S. Finkenthal, 240(HR):Autumn85-502
    T.A. Sackett, 238:Dec85-774
Menéndez Pelayo, M. Epistolario. (Vols
  1 and 2) (M. Revuelta Sañudo, ed)
    A. Baron, 92(BH):Jul-Dec84-561
    A.H. Clarke, 86(BHS):Apr85-205
Menéndez Pidal, R., ed. Historia de
  España. (Vol 2, Pts 1 and 2) (2nd ed)
    J.C. Edmondson, 313:Vo175-286
Ménétra, J-L. Journal of My Life.
  (French title: Journal de ma vie.)
  (D. Roche, ed)
    R. Birn, 173(ECS):Spring86-404
    S. Hanley, 441:3Aug86-12
    442(NY):10Nov86-147
Menger, P-M. Le paradoxe du musicien.
    J-R. Julien, 537:Vo171No1/2-218
Mengham, R. The Idiom of the Time.*
    J. Tyler, 447(N&Q):Dec84-546
Menikoff, B. Robert Louis Stevenson and
  "The Beach of Falesá."*
    H-P. Breuer, 395(MFS):Summer85-338
    K. Gelder, 588(SSL):Vo120-311
    J. Meckier, 445(NCF):Mar86-489
Menna Sconamiglio, C. Commedie di Molière
  in veste napoletana, e in particolare
  "La Scola de li marite e de la mmogliere,
  overo chi sputa ncielo nface le torna"
  di Tofano Rotontiano.
    E. de Gennaro, 475:Vol 12No22-341
Mennell, S. All Manners of Food.
    B.A. Henisch, 441:16Mar86-22
Menton, S. Magic Realism Rediscovered.
    D. Scrase, 149(CLS):Summer85-281
Menuhin, M. The Menuhin Saga.
    N. Goodwin, 415:May85-287
Menuhin, Y. The Compleat Violinist.
    K. Gann, 441:20Jul86-18

de Meo, C. Lingue tecniche del latino.
    J.N. Adams, 123:Vol35No1-96
Meo-Zilio, G. and S. Mejía. Diccionario
  de gestos. (Vol 1)
    R. de Gorog, 545(RPh):May85-475
    M. Wandruszka, 547(RF):Band97Heft2/3-
    277
Meo-Zilio, G. and S. Mejía. Diccionario
  de gestos. (Vol 2)
    M. Wandruszka, 547(RF):Band97Heft2/3-
    277
Mercado, J. La seguidilla gitana.
    J. Greco, 240(HR):Summer85-373
Mercer, G.E. The Cole Papers.
    W.M. Stern, 324:Sep86-695
Merchant, C. The Death of Nature.
    W.T. Griffith, 142:Summer85-101
Merchant, I. Indian Cuisine.
    F. Fabricant, 441:7Dec86-17
Mercier, L-S. Parallèle de Paris et de
  Londres. (C. Bruneteau and B. Cottret,
  eds)
    J. Gillet, 549(RLC):Jul-Sep85-349
    R. Waller, 83:Spring85-116
Meredith, C. This.
    S. O'Brien, 617(TLS):16May86-540
    M. O'Neill, 493:Apr85-54
Meredith, G. The Notebooks of George
  Meredith. (G. Beer and M. Harris, eds)
    S. Brown, 354:Dec85-382
Meredith, M. The First Dance of Freedom.
    G. Wheatcroft, 617(TLS):14Nov86-1285
Meredith, M. - see Browning, R.
Meredith, P. and J.E. Tailby, eds. The
  Staging of Religious Drama in Europe in
  the Later Middle Ages.*
    A.E. Knight, 589:Oct85-998
    P. Neuss, 611(TN):Vol39No1-43
Mérimée, P. Carmen.
    P.A. Berger, 399(MLJ):Spring85-87
Merino-Morais, J. Différence et répéti-
  tion dans les "Contes" de La Fontaine.*
    R. Danner, 210(FrF):Jan85-112
    M. Defrenne, 475:Vol 12No22-343
    J. Grimm, 547(RF):Band97Heft4-470
Meriwether, J.B. - see Faulkner, W.
Merkin, D. Enchantment.
    P. Hampl, 441:5Oct86-7
Merkin, R. Zombie Jamboree.
    L. McCaffery, 441:3Aug86-16
Merkl, H. Ein Kult der Frau und der
  Schönheit.
    M. Gsteiger, 52:Band20Heft1-101
Merklinger, E. Indian Islamic Architec-
  ture.
    A. Schimmel, 318(JAOS):Apr-Jun84-391
Merle, R. Le Prince que voilà.
    R.D. Frye, 207(FR):Apr86-817
Merlhès, V. - see Gauguin, P.
Mermall, T. Las alegorías del poder en
  Francisco Ayala.
    M. Bieder, 238:Sep85-519
Mermet, G. Francoscopie — Les Français.
    A. Prévos, 207(FR):Feb86-511
Mermin, D. The Audience in the Poems.
    L.K. Hughes, 637(VS):Winter85-312
    P.J. McCarthy, 301(JEGP):Jul85-451
Méron, E. Tendre et cruel Corneille.
    R.C. Knight, 208(FS):Oct85-463
Merquior, J.G. Foucault.
    C. Gordon, 617(TLS):6Jun86-626
Merquior, J.G. From Prague to Paris.
    A. Jefferson, 617(TLS):21Nov86-1306

Merquior, J.G.  Western Marxism.
 J. Gray, 617(TLS):5Sep86-965
Merrell, F.  Semiotic Foundations.*
 J. Fronek, 307:Dec85-197
Merrett, R.J., ed.  Man and Nature/L'Homme
 et la nature.
 A. Morvan, 189(EA):Apr-Jun86-221
Merrill, J.  The Changing Light at Sand-
 over.
 E. Butscher, 496:Spring85-47
 J.H. Harrison 3d, 577(SHR):Winter85-86
Merrill, J.  From the First Nine.
 J.H. Harrison 3d, 577(SHR):Winter85-86
Merrill, J.  Late Settings.*
 D.W. Hartnett, 617(TLS):7Feb86-138
 R. McDowell, 249(HudR):Winter86-686
 V. Shetley, 491:Feb86-301
 639(VQR):Autumn85-129
Merriman, M. and W. Lerude.  American
 Commander in Spain.
 D.D. Gilmore, 441:8Jun86-44
Merriman, M.P.  Giuseppe Maria Crespi.
 D.C. Miller, 54:Jun85-339
Merson, A.  Communist Resistance in Nazi
 Germany.
 F.L. Carsten, 617(TLS):18Apr86-412
Mertens, P.  Perdre.
 J. Sojcher, 98:Apr85-376
Mertian, I.  Allgemeine Sprachkunde.
 P. Swiggers, 350:Jun86-455
Mertner, E.  Rudyard Kipling und seine
 Kritiker.
 M. Draudt, 38:Band103Heft1/2-237
Merton, R.K.  On the Shoulders of Giants.
 S. French, 617(TLS):25Jul86-807
de Mesa, J. and T. Gisbert.  Historia de
 la Pintura Cuzqueña.
 D. Angulo, 48:Jan-Mar85-86
Messenger, J.C.  An Anthropologist at Play.
 A.G. Barrand, 292(JAF):Apr/Jun85-230
Messent, P.B., ed.  Literature of the
 Occult.*
 R. Cardinal, 529(QQ):Autumn85-549
Messer Leon, J.  The Book of the Honey-
 comb's Flow.*  (I. Rabinowitz, ed and
 trans)
 J.J. Murphy, 589:Jan85-161
Messerli, D. - see Barnes, D.
Messmer, P. and A. Larcan.  Les écrits
 militaires de Charles de Gaulle.
 G. Best, 617(TLS):3Oct86-1109
Mestan, A. - see Loderecker, P.
Mészáros, L.  Italien sieht Dürer.
 U.F., 90:Mar85-173
Metcalf, B.D.  Islamic Revival in British
 India.
 A. Schimmel, 318(JAOS):Apr-Jun84-378
Metcalf, B.D., ed.  Moral Conduct and
 Authority.
 C.W. Troll, 293(JASt):Aug85-865
Metcalf, E., comp.  The Penguin Dictionary
 of Modern Humorous Quotations.
 D.J. Enright, 617(TLS):26Sep86-1079
Meter, J.H.  The Literary Theories of
 Daniel Heinsius.
 A.L. Van Gastel, 568(SCN):Winter85-57
"Metropolitan Museum Journal."  (Vol 19/20)
 J. Russell, 441:1Jun86-11
Metscher, T.  Der Friedensgedanke in der
 europäischen Literatur.
 U. Heukenkamp, 654(WB):6/1985-1034

Mettinger, T.N.D.  The Dethronement of
 Sabaoth.
 R.P. Knierim, 318(JAOS):Oct-Dec84-775
Mews, S., ed.  "The Fisherman and His
 Wife."
 O. Durrani, 402(MLR):Jan85-242
Mewshaw, M.  Blackballed.
 J. House, 441:30Nov86-22
Meyer, B. and B. O'Riordan, eds.  In Their
 Words.
 S. Kane, 627(UTQ):Summer85-426
 C. Rooke, 376:Sep85-148
Meyer, F.  Gso-ba rig-pa.
 P. Kvaerne, 259(IIJ):Jan85-52
Meyer, H.  Bibliographie der Buch- und
 Bibliotheksgeschichte.*  (Vols 1 and 2)
 B.J. McMullin, 517(PBSA):Vol79No2-260
Meyer, J.  Vom elsässischen Kunstfrühling
 zur utopischen Civitas Hominum.
 H.F. Pfanner, 406:Summer85-243
Meyer, M.  Meaning and Reading.
 D.E.B. Pollard, 89(BJA):Autumn85-406
Meyer, M.  Strindberg.*
 H. Lomas, 364:Aug-Sep85-138
Meyer, M. - see Casebeer, E.
Meyer, M.C.  Water in the Hispanic South-
 west.
 J.P. Reid, 250(HLQ):Winter85-89
Meyer, P. - see Bitov, A.
Meyer, S.  The Dynamics of Nuclear Prolif-
 eration.
 A.C., 185:Apr86-686
Meyer, S. 3d.  The Five Dollar Day.
 N. Faires, 385(MQR):Spring86-468
Meyer, W.J.  Modalverb und semantische
 Funktion.*
 G. Held, 547(RF):Band97Heft1-66
 R. Martin, 209(FM):Apr85-103
Meyers, J., ed.  The Craft of Literary
 Biography.*
 C.W. White, 637(VS):Summer86-631
Meyers, J.  Disease and the Novel, 1880-
 1960.*
 P. Stevick, 395(MFS):Winter85-838
Meyers, J.  Hemingway.*
 J.R. Bryer, 454:Spring86-270
 J. Campbell, 617(TLS):1Aug86-837
 W. Sheed, 453(NYRB):12Jun86-5
Meyers, J., ed.  Hemingway: The Critical
 Heritage.*
 D. Seed, 677(YES):Vol 15-354
Meyers, J.  D.H. Lawrence and the Exper-
 ience of Italy.*
 I.C., 506(PSt):May85-97
 D.I. Janik, 405(MP):Aug85-82
 A. Wilkin, 278(IS):Vol40-153
Meyrowitz, J.  No Sense of Place.
 R. Silverstone, 617(TLS):2May86-471
von Meysenbug, M.  Briefe an Joanna und
 Gottfried Kinkel 1849-1885.  (S. Rossi,
 ed) Der Maikäfer.  (U. Brandt and
 others, eds)
 G. Häntzschel, 602:Band16Heft1-151
Mianney, R.  Maurice Rollinat, poète et
 musicien du fantastique.*
 G. Cesbron, 535(RHL):May/Jun85-507
Miao, R.C.  Early Medieval Chinese Poetry.
 J. Larsen, 293(JASt):May85-604
Micewski, A.  Cardinal Wyszyński.
 S. Kosmicki, 497(PolR):Vol30No4-445
Micha, A.  Etude sur le "Merlin" de Robert
 de Boron, roman du XIIIe siècle.*
 A.M. Colby-Hall, 545(RPh):Nov85-258

Micha, A. - see "Lancelot: Roman en prose du XIIIe siècle"
Michael, C.V. Choderlos de Laclos.*
    J.H. Bloch, 208(FS):Jan85-80
    D. Coward, 40(AEB):Vol8No2-147
Michael, D.P.M. The Mapping of Monmouth-shire.
    R. Hyde, 617(TLS):17Jan86-71
Michael, J. Private Affairs.
    R. Grant, 441:2Mar86-24
Michael, W.F. Das deutsche Drama der Reformationszeit.
    R.E. Schade, 221(GQ):Fall85-604
Michaels, B. Shattered Silk.
    R. Grant, 441:9Nov86-32
Michaels, J.E. Anarchy and Eros.
    D.O. Hoffmann, 221(GQ):Fall85-623
Michaels, W.B. and D.E. Pease, eds. The American Renaissance Reconsidered.
    J. Myerson, 27(AL):Dec85-663
Michaud, Y. Hume et la fin de la philosophie.*
    D. Sauvé, 154:Spring85-183
Michaux, J-P., ed. George Gissing.*
    S.M. Smith, 677(YES):Vol 15-328
Michel, A. La Parole et la beauté.
    G. Declercq, 535(RHL):Jul/Aug85-702
Michel, J. Liturgie de la lumière nocturne dans les récits de Henri Bosco.
    J. Onimus, 535(RHL):Jul/Aug85-698
Michel, L. A travers la vie et la mort. (D. Armogathe and M. Piper, eds)
    E. Schulkind, 208(FS):Apr85-225
Michel, L.P. Die "Literaturnaja gazeta" A.A. Del'vigs (1830-1831).
    W. Busch, 688(ZSP):Band45Heft1-194
Michel, M., ed. La théologie à l'épreuve de la vérité.
    A. Reix, 542:Oct-Dec85-560
Michel, M.R. Lajoue et l'Art Rocaille.
    P. Conisbee, 59:Sep85-359
    D. Irwin, 83:Spring85-122
    M. Levey, 90:Apr85-236
Michel, M.R. Watteau.*
    H. Opperman, 90:Dec85-913
    J. Sweetman, 324:Dec85-66
Michel, P., with others, eds. Montaigne et les "Essais."
    J. Bailbé, 535(RHL):Jan/Feb85-73
    M. Hugues, 549(RLC):Jul-Sep85-337
    G. Schrenck, 475:Vol 12No23-687
di Michele, M., ed. Anything is Possible.
    L. Dudek, 99:Apr85-29
di Michele, M. Necessary Sugar.*
    J. Bayly, 526:Summer85-86
Michelet, J. Mother Death.* (E.K. Kaplan, ed and trans)
    L. Gossman, 125:Winter85-209
Michelini, A.N. Tradition and Dramatic Form in the "Persians" of Aeschylus.*
    M. McCall, 303(JoHS):Vol 105-178
Michell, G., with T. Santra and Z. Haque. Brick Temples of Bengal.
    C.B. Asher, 293(JASt):Feb85-431
    R. Hillenbrand, 90:Jan85-50
Michelson, A. - see Vertov, D.
Michie, J. New and Selected Poems.
    J. Saunders, 565:Spring85-72
Michler, C. Le Somme abregiet de Theologie. (H. Ripelins, trans)
    M. Bambeck, 72:Band222Heft2-447

Michnik, A. Letters from Prison.
    T.G. Ash, 453(NYRB):9Oct86-45
    N. Davies, 441:5Oct86-11
    442(NY):10Nov86-146
Michnik, A. Takie czasy ... Rzecz o kompromisie.
    T.G. Ash, 453(NYRB):9Oct86-45
Michon, J. Emile Nelligan.
    D.M. Hayne, 627(UTQ):Summer85-468
Michon, J. - see Gay, J.
Micone, M. Addolorata.
    L. Forni, 102(CanL):Fall85-82
Micone, M. Voiceless People.
    V. Comensoli, 102(CanL):Fall85-84
Mićunović, V. Moscow Diary. Moskovske Godine, 1969/71.
    D. Floyd, 176:Mar86-69
"Middle English Dictionary." (Plan and Bibliography, Supp 1; Pt Q; and Pt R.1) (R.E. Lewis, ed-in-chief)
    H. Käsmann, 38:Band103Heft3/4-424
"Middle English Dictionary." (Pts M1-M3 ed by S.M. Kuhn and J. Reidy; Pts M4-P7 ed by S.M. Kuhn)
    M. Wakelin, 382(MAE):1985/2-292
Middleton, B.C. The Restoration of Leather Bindings. (rev)
    F. Broomhead, 503:Autumn84-144
Middleton, R. Towards the Managed Economy.
    R. Skidelsky, 617(TLS):20Jun86-684
Middleton, S. An After-Dinner's Sleep.
    L. Duguid, 617(TLS):23May86-553
    J. Mellors, 362:29May86-25
Middleton Murry, K. Beloved Quixote.
    P.N. Furbank, 362:20Mar86-26
    H. Spurling, 617(TLS):4Apr86-352
Midgley, M. Animals and Why They Matter.*
    A. Soble, 185:Oct85-192
Midgley, M. Evolution as a Religion.
    P. Corsi, 617(TLS):14Mar86-282
    R.M. Young, 441:23Mar86-22
Midgley, M. Wickedness.
    R.M. McCleary, 185:Jan86-418
Midwinter, E. Fair Game.
    P. Smith, 617(TLS):11Jul86-770
Miedema, H. Karel van Manders "Leven der Moderne, oft Dees-Tijtsche Doorluchtighe Italiaensche Schilders en hun bron."
    C. Ford, 90:Dec85-908
Mieder, W. International Proverb Scholarship.*
    L. Röhrich, 196:Band26Heft1/2-181
    H. Rölleke, 133:Band17Heft3/4-382
    H. Sauer, 38:Band103Heft1/2-165
Mieder, W., ed. Mädchen, pfeif auf den Prinzen.
    J. Zipes, 133:Band17Heft3/4-381
Mieder, W. - see Petri, F.
Miemietz, B. Kontrastive Linguistik Deutsch-Polnisch 1965-1980.
    F. Keller, 688(ZSP):Band35Heft1-207
Miething, C. Saint-Sartre oder der autobiographische Gott.
    I. McLeod, 208(FS):Apr85-233
Migliorini, B. The Italian Language. (rev by T.G. Griffith)
    A. Aquilecchia, 278(IS):Vol40-107
    V. Lucchesi, 402(MLR):Oct85-952
Miguet-Ollagnier, M. La Mythologie de Marcel Proust.*
    A. Henry, 535(RHL):Jan/Feb85-123
Mihailović, D. Bonne nuit, Fred.
    L. Kovacs, 450(NRF):Dec85-103

Mihailovich, V.D. and M. Matejic. A Comprehensive Bibliography of Yugoslav Literature in English, 1593-1980.
G.M. Terry, 575(SEER):Oct85-637
Mihály, H. Hungarian-English, English-Hungarian Dictionary of Christian Names.
W.H. Finke, 424:Dec85-272
Mihm, M.T. - see Raoul de Houdenc
Mijuskovic, B. Contingent Immaterialism.
J-M. Gabaude, 542:Oct-Dec85-561
Mikalson, J.D. Athenian Popular Religion.*
R. Parker, 123:Vol135No1-90
Mikhail, E.H. Sean O'Casey and His Critics.
R.E. Ward, 174(Éire):Winter85-154
Milanini, C. - see Saba, U.
Milbank, C.R. Couture.*
442(NY):10Feb86-115
Milbauer, A.Z. Transcending Exile.
T. Billy, 136:Vol 18No3-231
Mileck, J. Hermann Hesse.*
H. Wittman, 627(UTQ):Summer85-500
Mileham, J.W. The Conspiracy Novel.*
C. Massol-Bedoin, 535(RHL):Jul/Aug85-687
Miles, H. and M. Salisbury. Kingdom of the Ice Bear.
S. Mills, 617(TLS):4Apr86-370
Miles, J. Collected Poems 1930-83.*
J. Penberthy, 617(TLS):18Apr86-430
C.H. Taylor, 649(WAL):Aug85-171
Miles, J., ed. The Women's Project 2.
S. Weinberg, 615(TJ):Oct85-380
Miles, M.R. Image as Insight.
D. Auchincloss, 469:Vol 11No4-109
R. Minkoff, 441:9Feb86-25
P. Partner, 453(NYRB):10Apr86-38
Mileur, J-P. Vision and Re-Vision.*
L. Lockridge, 403(MLS):Winter85-92
S.J. Wolfson, 141:Spring85-198
Milgate, W. - see Donne, J.
Milhous, J. and R.D. Hume. Producible Interpretation.
D.C. Payne, 566:Spring86-198
Milhous, J. and R.D. Hume - see Coke, T.
Millar, F. and E. Segal, eds. Caesar Augustus: Seven Aspects.
R.J. Penella, 124:Mar-Apr86-287
A. Wallace-Hadrill, 313:Vol75-245
Millar, M. Spider Webs.
N. Callendar, 441:26Oct86-47
Millar, T.B., ed. International Security in the Southeast Asian and Southwest Pacific Region.
D.K. Crone, 293(JASt):Nov84-247
Millard, P. - see North, R.
Miller, A. and I. Morath. "Salesman" in Beijing.*
R. Kift, 157:No155-52
R.A. Martin, 397(MD):Sep85-513
295(JML):Nov85-527
Miller, B., ed. Women in Hispanic Literature.*
A. McDermott, 86(BHS):Jul85-291
Miller, B.D. The Endangered Sex.
H. Papanek, 293(JASt):Nov84-127
Miller, C.H. and others - see More, T.
Miller, C.L. Blank Darkness.
J.A. Ferguson, 617(TLS):22Aug86-907
Miller, C.R. Technical and Cultural Prerequisites for the Invention of Printing in China and the West.
E.S. Rawski, 293(JASt):Nov84-187

Miller, D. Anarchism.*
L. Kolakowski, 384:Sep/Oct85-906
Miller, D. Philosophy and Ideology in Hume's Political Thought.*
J. Bricke, 543:Mar85-632
Miller, D.G. Homer and the Ionian Epic Tradition.*
A. Heubeck, 260(IF):Band90-298
Miller, D.G. Improvisation, Typology, Culture, and "The New Orthodoxy."
J.M. Bremer, 303(JoHS):Vol 105-177
Miller, G. John Irving.
G.F. Manning, 106:Summer85-237
Miller, G.A. Language and Speech.
O.D. Gensler, 545(RPh):Aug84-65
Miller, H. Fiction and Repetition.
K. Carabine, 447(N&Q):Dec84-559
Miller, H. Henry VIII and the English Nobility.
P. Williams, 617(TLS):7Nov86-1258
Miller, I. Husserl, Perception, and Temporal Awareness.
K. Ameriks, 482(PhR):Jul85-414
S. Cunningham, 543:Mar85-665
Miller, J. Rousseau.*
M. Cranston, 208(FS):Oct85-475
J-L. Lecercle, 535(RHL):Nov/Dec85-1069
H. Payne, 173(ECS):Spring86-395
B.J.S., 185:Jul86-908
639(VQR):Winter85-18
Miller, J. Subsequent Performances.
R. Osborne, 617(TLS):5Sep86-958
Miller, J. Women Writing About Men.
A.S. Grossman, 617(TLS):26Sep86-1077
A. Huth, 362:30Jan86-26
Miller, J.A. Running in Place.
M. Tolchin, 441:15Jun86-21
442(NY):5May86-134
Miller, J.D.B. Norman Angell and the Futility of War.
K.G. Robbins, 617(TLS):3Oct86-1109
Miller, J.E. The United States and Italy 1940-1950.
H.S. Hughes, 617(TLS):12Sep86-1001
Miller, J.H. Fiction and Repetition.*
P. Alden, 403(MLS):Winter85-91
P. Davis, 97(CQ):Vol 14No1-60
R. Posnock, 599:Spring85-134
Miller, J.H. The Linguistic Moment.
W. Jackson, 344:Summer86-120
Miller, K. Doubles.*
M. Duperray, 189(EA):Oct-Dec86-452
D. Grant, 148:Winter85-59
Miller, K.A. Emigrants and Exiles.*
O. MacDonagh, 617(TLS):18Jul86-776
Miller, L. John Milton and the Oldenburg Safeguard.
R. Lejosne, 189(EA):Oct-Dec86-457
Miller, L.B., with S. Hart, eds. The Selected Papers of Charles Willson Peale and His Family. (Vol 1)
J.A.L. Lemay, 658:Winter85-297
K. Silverman, 656(WMQ):Jan85-153
J.V. Turano, 16:Winter85-87
Miller, M.E. The Murals of Bonampak.
W. Bray, 617(TLS):5Dec86-1382
Miller, M.R. Place-Names of the Northern Neck of Virginia from John Smith's 1606 Map to the Present.*
S.M. Embleton, 355(LSoc):Mar85-145
Miller, N., ed. Bilingualism and Language Disability.
M.W. Salus, 350:Mar86-230

Minchinton, W., C. King and P. Waite, eds. Virginia Slave-Trade Statistics, 1698-1775.
D.M. Sweig, 656(WMQ):Oct85-537
Miner, E. - see Konishi, J.
Miner, E., Hiroko Odagiri and R.E. Morrell. The Princeton Companion to Classical Japanese Literature.
J. McMullen, 617(TLS):9May86-510
Miner, M.M. Insatiable Appetites.*
L. Pannill, 70:Jan/Feb85-95
Miner, V. Winter's Edge.
J. Jackson, 441:19Jan86-20
Minervini, V. Il "Libro di Sidrac."
F. Fery-Hue, 554:Vol 105No2/3-384
Mineur, W.H. Callimachus, "Hymn to Delos."
N. Hopkinson, 123:Vol35No2-249
Ming-hsuan, S. - see under Shang Ming-hsuan
Mingay, G.E. The Transformation of Britain 1830-1939.
J. Burnett, 617(TLS):5Sep86-961
Minhinnick, R. The Dinosaur Park.
T. Curtis, 493:Feb86-62
Minichiello, S. Retreat from Reform.
S.M. Garon, 293(JASt):Aug85-844
B-A. Shillony, 407(MN):Spring85-113
Minnis, A.J. Chaucer and Pagan Antiquity.*
V.J. Di Marco, 38:Band103Heft1/2-189
P.J. Mroczkowski, 541(RES):Aug85-406
A.G. Rigg, 447(N&Q):Jun84-258
W. Wetherbee, 589:Apr85-440
H. White, 382(MAE):1985/2-305
Minnis, A.J. Medieval Theory of Authorship.
C.D. Benson, 191(ELN):Jun86-74
N.F. Blake, 179(ES):Feb85-82
Minogue, K. Alien Powers.*
E. Pearce, 129:Jan86-76
Minor, J. A Measure of Light.
404:Summer85-60
Minot, S. Monkeys.
K. Bucknell, 617(TLS):5Sep86-978
A.R. Gurney, Jr., 441:27Apr86-1
R. Towers, 453(NYRB):26Jun86-32
Minot, S. Surviving the Flood.
W. Herbert, 441:27Jul86-18
Minot, W.S. Rhetoric.
R.J. Connors, 126(CCC):Feb85-110
Minsky, M. and M. Machlin. Minsky's Burlesque.
G.J. Goldberg, 441:30Mar86-11
Minton, H. The Canal Bed.
639(VQR):Summer85-97
Mintz, J.R. The Anarchists of Casas Viejas.
J.E. Limón, 292(JAF):Jan/Mar85-116
Mintz, M. At Any Cost.
J.K. Galbraith, 453(NYRB):10Apr86-11
T. Lewin, 441:12Jan86-27
Mintz, S. A Prison of Expectations.
J.A. Banks, 637(VS):Winter85-310
T.C. Barker, 366:Autumn85-310
Mintz, S.W. Sweetness and Power.*
J. Ward, 617(TLS):29Aug86-946
Miola, R.S. Shakespeare's Rome.*
A.M. French, 366:Spring85-137
M.B. Rose, 536(Rev):Vol7-19
Miquel, A. Laylâ, ma raison.
P.J.T. Gormally, 207(FR):Dec85-340
F. de Martinoir, 450(NRF):Feb85-89
Miquet, J., ed. Fierabras.
G. Roques, 553(RLiR):Jan-Jun85-242

della Mirandola, G.P. - see under Pico della Mirandola, G.
Mirbeau, O. Le Journal d'une femme de chambre. (N. Arnaud, ed)
R. Carr, 208(FS):Jul85-358
de Mirimonde, A.P. Astrologie et Musique.
M.M., 412:May83-150
"Le miroir et l'image."
G.M. Fondi, 475:Vol 12No22-348
Mirollo, J.V. Mannerism and Renaissance Poetry.
R.J. Rodini, 276:Winter85-322
Miscall, P.D. The Workings of Old Testament Narrative.
R.T. Anderson, 115:Fall85-480
"Miscel·lània Sanchis Guarner I."
H. Guiter, 553(RLiR):Jul-Dec85-428
Mischakoff, A. Khandoshkin and the Beginning of Russian String Music.
C. Brown, 410(M&L):Oct85-385
Mischiati, O. Indici, cataloghi e avvisi degli editori e librai musicali italiani dal 1591 al 1798.
R. Andrewes, 415:Aug85-466
von Mises, L. L'action humaine.
A. Reix, 542:Jul-Sep85-364
Mishler, E.G. The Discourse of Medicine.
M. Heller, 350:Dec86-958
Misler, N. - see Florenskij, P.
Misler, N. and J.E. Bowlt, eds. Pavel Filonov.*
D. Goldstein, 550(RusR):Apr85-196
G.J. Janecek, 574(SEEJ):Winter85-481
N.D. Lobanov, 39:Apr85-284
C. Lodder, 90:Oct85-726
Misra, B.B. District Administration and Rural Development.
H. Tinker, 293(JASt):Aug85-868
Mistral, F. The Memoirs of Frédéric Mistral.
D. Shapiro, 441:30Nov86-23
Mitcham, A. The Northern Imagination.*
R. Davis, 102(CanL):Winter84-144
Mitchell, A. Victors and Vanquished.
S.C. Hause, 377:Jul85-129
Mitchell, B. and F.C. Robinson. A Guide to Old English.* (rev)
J. Roberts, 447(N&Q):Jun84-253
E.G. Stanley, 541(RES):Feb85-141
Mitchell, D. Britten and Auden in the Thirties: The Year 1936.*
D. Pond, 396(ModA):Summer85-272
J.H. Sutcliffe, 414:Vol71No2-225
Mitchell, D. Living Upcountry.
E. Hebert, 441:26Oct86-20
Mitchell, D. Gustav Mahler. (Vol 3)
D.B. Greene, 617(TLS):17Jan86-53
Mitchell, J. Sometimes You Could Die.*
N. Callendar, 441:8Jun86-34
Mitchell, P.M. - see Gottsched, J.C.
Mitchell, R. The Leaning Towel of Babel.
R.F. Gregory, 128(CE):Apr85-421
Mitchell, R.H. Censorship in Imperial Japan.*
R.H. Minear, 293(JASt):Feb85-399
Mitchell, S. Dinah Mulock Craik.
P. Marks, 635(VPR):Winter85-153
Mitchell, S. A Dictionary of British Equestrian Artists.
J. Egerton, 39:Dec85-506
Mitchell, S. - see Rilke, R.M.
Mitchell, S. - see Wood, Mrs. H.

Mitchell, W.J.T. Iconology.
R. Arnheim, 617(TLS):27Jun86-712
Mitchell, W.J.T., ed. The Politics of
Interpretation.*
D.J.G., 185:Apr86-661
O. Kenshur, 678(YCGL):No34-128
Mitchell, W.O. Since Daisy Creek.*
F.W. Kaye, 102(CanL):Fall85-126
"Mitchell/Giurgola Architects."
S. Lavin, 505:Dec85-99
Mitchison, N. Among You Taking Notes . . .*
(D. Sheridan, ed)
362:4Sep86-30
Mitford, N., ed. Noblesse Oblige.
G. Annan, 453(NYRB):14Aug86-3
Mitford, N. A Talent to Annoy. (C.
Mosley, ed)
A. Chisholm, 617(TLS):19Sep86-1026
Mitford, N. The Water Beetle.
G. Annan, 453(NYRB):14Aug86-3
Mitford, T.B. and O. Masson. The Syllabic
Inscriptions of Rantidi-Paphos.
W.C. Brice, 303(JoHS):Vol 105-245
P.M. Fraser, 123:Vol35No1-225
Mitias, M.H. Moral Foundation of the
State in Hegel's Philosophy of Right.
A. Reix, 542:Jan-Mar85-38
Mitra, A., L.P. Pathak and S. Mukherji.
The Status of Women.
H. Papanek, 293(JASt):Nov84-127
Mitroff, I.I. and R.O. Mason. Creating a
Dialectical Social Science.
P. Diesing, 488:Jun85-232
Mittelholzer, E. My Bones and My Flute.
R. Deveson, 617(TLS):24Oct86-1187
Mitterand, H. Le Discours du roman.*
J.M. Cocking, 208(FS):Jan85-114
Mitterand, H. - see Zola, É.
Mittman, B.G. Spectators on the Paris
Stage in the Seventeenth and Eighteenth
Centuries.
J.F. Gaines, 207(FR):Dec85-320
Miyagawa, S. and C. Kitagawa, eds.
Studies in Japanese Language Use.
C. Ross, 399(MLJ):Summer85-192
Mo, T. An Insular Possession.
D.J. Enright, 617(TLS):9May86-498
R. Scott, 362:8May86-25
Mo, T. Sour Sweet.*
M. Gorra, 249(HudR):Winter86-670
Moberg, U.T. Gunnar Ekelöfs non-figura-
tion och situationspoesi.
J. Lutz, 563(SS):Winter85-91
"Mobilising Against AIDS."
D. Widgery, 362:4Sep86-21
Mochulsky, K. Aleksandr Blok.
G. Pirog, 651(WHR):Autumn85-277
Modarressi, T. The Book of Absent People.
J.T. Hospital, 441:9Feb86-21
442(NY):10Mar86-122
Modell, J.S. Ruth Benedict.
H.A. Freund, 650(WF):Jan85-60
Modiano, P. Dimanches d'Août.
N. Irving, 617(TLS):30Oct86-1112
Modiano, P. Quartier perdu.*
C. Dis, 450(NRF):Apr85-82
L. Ferrara, 207(FR):Feb86-489
Modiano, R. Coleridge and the Concept of
Nature.
R. Ashton, 617(TLS):19Sep86-1035
Modleski, T. Loving with a Vengeance.
C. Baranger, 189(EA):Apr-Jun86-239
Modlin, C.E. - see Anderson, S.

Moelleken, W.W., ed. Dialectology, Lin-
guistics, Literature.
B.J. Koekkoek, 221(GQ):Fall85-598
Moeller, J. and H. Liedloff. Deutsch
heute. (3rd ed)
J.F. Lalande 2d, 399(MLJ):Winter85-418
Moeran, B. Lost Innocence.
R. Barnard, 139:Oct/Nov85-50
Moerk, E.L. The Mother of Eve as a Lan-
guage Teacher.
C.B. Cazden, 355(LSoc):Jun85-276
Moffat, L.N. Norman Rockwell.
P-L. Adams, 61:Dec86-104
A.C. Danto, 441:28Sep86-12
Moffett, C.S. The New Painting.
P-L. Adams, 61:May86-99
P. Conisbee, 617(TLS):22Aug86-916
Moffett, J. James Merrill.
W.J. Scheick, 30:Fall85-89
V. Shetley, 659(ConL):Spring86-138
Moffett, J. Whinney Moor Crossing.*
S.C. Behrendt, 502(PrS):Summer85-115
R. Saner, 152(UDQ):Summer85-107
Moggach, D. To Have and to Hold.
L. Duguid, 617(TLS):2May86-479
Moglen, H. Charlotte Brontë.
E.J. Higgins, 95(CLAJ):Mar86-368
Mohanty, J.N. Husserl and Frege.*
C. Hill, 543:Jun85-894
G. Küng, 484(PPR):Dec85-344
Mohr, C.L. On the Threshold of Freedom.
J. Haskins, 441:15Jun86-21
Möhren, F. Le renforcement affectif de la
négation par l'expression d'une valeur
minimale en ancien français.
N.L. Corbett, 545(RPh):Feb85-366
Mohrt, M. La Guerre civile.
R. Buss, 617(TLS):18Jul86-783
Moignet, G. Etudes de psycho-systématique
française. Systématique de la langue
française.
A. Lorian, 545(RPh):Aug85-44
Moir, A., ed. Old Master Drawings from
the Feitelson Collection.
D. De Grazia, 380:Winter84-452
Moisan, C. A Poetry of Frontiers.
R. Davis, 102(CanL):Winter84-144
Moise, E.E. Modern China.
D. Wilson, 617(TLS):8Aug86-873
Mojares, R.B. Origins and Rise of the
Filipino Novel.
A.M.B. Nabi Baksh, 395(MFS):Summer85-
475
Mojsisch, B. Meister Eckhart, Analogie,
Univozität und Einheit.
J-F. Courtine, 192(EP):Jul-Sep85-421
O. Langer, 684(ZDA):Band14Heft2-70
Mojtabai, A.G. Blessed Assurance.
J.A. Lukas, 441:8Jun86-7
Mokyr, J. Why Ireland Starved.
S. Clark, 637(VS):Spring86-477
M.E. Daly, 272(IUR):Spring85-104
Moldanova, S.P., E.A. N'omysova and V.N.
Remezanova. Slovar' Khantijsko-Russkij
i Russko-Khantijskij.
Y.A. Tambovtsev, 320(CJL):Spring85-107
Moldea, D.E. Dark Victory.
J. Gerth, 441:19Oct86-30
Mole, J. In and Out of the Apple.*
M. O'Neill, 493:Jan85-61
Mole, J. The Monogamist.
T. Fitton, 617(TLS):17Oct86-1168

Mora, P. and L. Andrinal. Diplomatari del
monestir de Santa Maria de La Real de
Mallorca. (Vol 1)
 J.N. Hillgarth, 589:Jan85-185
Morace, R.A. John Gardner.
 L.C. Butts, 573(SSF):Summer85-369
Morain, M., ed. Bridging Worlds Through
General Semantics.
 S.B. Gibson, 186(ETC.):Spring85-78
Morales, J.L.O. - see under Onieva Morales,
J.L.
Morales y Marín, J.L. Diccionario de
términos artéisticos.
 A. Bustamante García, 48:Jul-Sep85-311
Moran, M.H. Margaret Drabble.*
 B. Dixson, 577(SHR):Summer85-266
Moran, W.R. Nellie Melba.
 J. Steane, 617(TLS):21Feb86-197
Moraña, M. Literatura y cultura nacional
en Hispanoamérica (1910-1940).
 A. Blasi, 238:Sep85-526
Morantz, R.M., C.S. Pomerleau and C.H.
Fenichel, eds. In Her Own Words.
 C.D. Howell, 106:Fall85-339
Morantz-Sanchez, R.M. Sympathy and
Science.
 L. Gordon, 441:12Jan86-14
Moravcevich, J. Jean Racine's "Andro-
maque."
 H.T. Barnwell, 208(FS):Jul85-338
 J. Morel, 475:Vol 12No22-345
Moravia, A. Erotic Tales.*
 A. Cancogni, 441:5Jan86-6
 J. Mellors, 362:9Jan86-29
Moravia, A. The Voyeur.
 B. Tonkin, 362:4Dec86-25
 R. Wells, 617(TLS):14Nov86-1290
Morch, D.T. Winter's Child.
 A.M. Davidon, 441:24Aug86-18
Mordden, E. Broadway Babies.
 G. Maschio, 615(TJ):May85-237
Mordden, E. One Last Waltz.
 J. Hendin, 441:28Sep86-18
More, T. The Complete Works of St. Thomas
More.* (Vol 3, Pt 2: Latin Poems.)
(C.H. Miller and others, eds)
 L.V. Ryan, 551(RenQ):Winter85-743
Moreau, A. Dialogues sympathiques.
 C.F. Demaray, 207(FR):Mar86-665
Moreau, F. Un Aspect de l'imagination
créatrice chez Rabelais.*
 D.G. Coleman, 208(FS):Apr85-190
Moreau, F. L'Image littéraire.*
 M. Le Guern, 535(RHL):Mar/Apr85-327
Moreau, H. and A. Tournon - see Béroalde
de Verville
Moreau, M-L. and M. Richelle. L'Acquisi-
tion du langage.
 J-P. Corneille, 209(FM):Apr85-136
Moreau, T. Le Sang de l'histoire, Miche-
let, l'histoire et l'idée de la femme au
XIXe siècle.
 H. Lafon, 535(RHL):Jan/Feb85-107
Morel, J-P. Le Roman insupportable.
 W. Redfern, 617(TLS):30ct86-1110
Morello, K.B. The Invisible Bar.
 R.E. Hauser, 441:9Nov86-28
de la Morena, Á. and T. Pérez de Higuera -
see Gómez Moreno, M.
Moreno, J.D. and B. Glassner. Discourse
in the Social Sciences.
 C.M. Watson, 488:Mar85-114
Moreno, M.G. - see under Gómez Moreno, M.

Moreton, E. and G. Segal, eds. Soviet
Strategy Towards Western Europe.
 M.J. Bradshaw, 104(CASS):Spring85-95
Morford, M. Persius.
 C. Cowherd, 124:Jan-Feb86-197
Morgan, B.L.G. The Food and Drug Inter-
action Guide.
 R. Lingeman, 441:23Mar86-46
Morgan, E. Grafts/Takes.
 C. Milton, 571(ScLJ):Winter85-59
Morgan, E. Selected Poems.
 A. Bold, 493:Oct85-58
 K. McCarra, 571(ScLJ):Winter85-64
Morgan, E. Sonnets from Scotland.*
 S.J. Boyd, 493:Apr85-58
Morgan, F. The Fountain and Other Fables.
 639(VQR):Autumn85-129
Morgan, H. Symbols of America.
 K. Coleman, 441:9Feb86-24
Morgan, J. Godly Learning.
 P. Collinson, 617(TLS):15Aug86-884
Morgan, J. and M. Rinvolucri. Once Upon a
Time.
 E. André, 399(MLJ):Spring85-83
Morgan, J.V. Stanislavski's Encounter
with Shakespeare.
 S.M. Carnicke, 574(SEEJ):Winter85-483
Morgan, N.J. The Medieval Painted Glass
of Lincoln Cathedral.
 M.H. Caviness, 90:Feb85-95
Morgan, P.F. Literary Critics and Review-
ers in Early 19th-Century Britain.*
 R.D. Fulton, 637(VS):Winter86-336
Morgan, P.F. - see Jeffrey, F.
Morgan, R.G. Kenneth Patchen.
 C.F. Terrell, 659(ConL):Spring86-115
Morgan, S. and L.J. Sears, eds. Aesthetic
Tradition and Cultural Transition in
Java and Bali.
 R. Long, 293(JASt):Aug85-893
Morgan, T. Churchill, 1874-1915.
 M. Brock, 637(VS):Winter85-327
Morgan, T. FDR.*
 M. Cranston, 617(TLS):23May86-550
 A. Howard, 362:27Mar86-30
Morgan, W. The Almighty Wall.*
 A. Betsky, 505:Feb85-171
 D. Gebhard, 576:Mar85-79
 M.N. Woods, 45:Sep85-67
Morgana, S.S. - see under Scotti Morgana,
S.
Morganstern, J. The Byzantine Church at
Dereagzi and Its Decoration.
 R.W. Edwards, 589:Oct85-1001
Morinis, E.A. Pilgrimage in the Hindu Tra-
dition.
 B.N. Aziz, 293(JASt):Aug85-869
Morino, A., ed. Indici degli Studi di
Filologia Italiana, volumi I-XXXV (1927-
1977).
 M. Pozzi, 228(GSLI):Vol 162fasc520-591
Morison, R. Humanist Scholarship and
Public Order. (D.S. Berkowitz, ed)
 L.H. Carlson, 551(RenQ):Summer85-353
Morison, W.L. John Austin.
 D. Philips, 637(VS):Summer86-629
Morita, A., with E.M. Reingold and M. Shi-
momura. Made in Japan.
 J. Fallows, 441:26Oct86-41
Moritz, A.F. The Visitation.
 J. Orange, 102(CanL):Winter84-103
Morlang, W. and B. Echte - see Walser, R.

264

Morley, H.  To Hold in My Hand.
  J. Elledge, 491:Aug85-293
  T. Enslin, 138:No7-269
  M. Kumin, 219(GaR):Spring85-169
  J. Penberthy, 617(TLS):18Apr86-430
Morley, H.  What Are Winds and What Are
  Waters.
  T. Enslin, 138:No7-269
Morley, J.  The Making of the Royal Pavil-
  ion, Brighton.*
  J.M. Robinson, 39:Feb85-135
Morley, J.D.  Pictures from the Water
  Trade.*
  J.R.B., 148:Autumn85-93
  J. Burnham, 617(TLS):3Jan86-20
  C. Rooke, 376:Jan86-121
Morley, J.T.  Secular Socialists.
  G.L. Caplan, 529(QQ):Autumn85-610
Morley, J.W., ed.  The China Quagmire.
  L. Grove, 407(MN):Summer85-231
Morley, J.W., ed.  Japan Erupts.
  I. Nish, 407(MN):Winter85-446
Morley, P.  Margaret Laurence.
  D. Staines, 402(MLR):Apr85-449
Morley-Fletcher, H., ed.  Techniques of
  the World's Great Masters of Pottery and
  Ceramics.
  G. Wills, 39:Jul85-79
Mörner, M.  The Andean Past.
  T.M. Davies, Jr., 263(RIB):Vol35No4-
  467
Mornin, E.  Kunst und Anarchismus.
  S. Hoefert, 564:May85-152
Morowitz, H.J.  Mayonnaise and the Origin
  of Life.
  E. Dobb, 441:19Jan86-21
Morozowa, O.  Bronisław Szwarce.
  A.A. Hetnal, 497(PolR):Vol30No2-227
Morrell, J. and A. Thackray, eds.  Gentle-
  men of Science.
  D.K. Stein, 637(VS):Spring86-496
Morriconi, V.  Arrows of Longing.
  R. Kaveney, 617(TLS):7Mar86-256
Morris, B. - see Shakespeare, W.
Morris, D.  The Art of Ancient Cyprus.
  R. Higgins, 39:Oct85-320
Morris, D.B.  Alexander Pope.*
  M.R. Brownell, 566:Autumn85-68
  W. Hutchings, 148:Autumn85-73
  C. Koralek, 175:Spring85-60
  A.D. Nuttall, 301(JEGP):Jul85-437
  D.L. Patey, 639(VQR):Winter85-152
Morris, G.L.  A World of Order and Light.*
  J. Henderson, 27(AL):Mar85-175
Morris, H.  Dream Palace.
  J.D. McClatchy, 441:16Mar86-12
Morris, H.  Last Things in Shakespeare.
  K. Brown, 617(TLS):22Aug86-917
Morris, H.  The Henry Morris Collection.
  (H. Rée, ed)
  J. Holloway, 97(CQ):Vol 14No3-251
Morris, H.  Peru.
  A. Hudgins, 434:Summer86-526
Morris, J.  The Matter of Wales.*
  N. Thomas, 176:May86-60
Morris, J.P. and L.H. Warner - see Harper,
  A.S.
Morris, K.L.  The Image of the Middle Ages
  in Romantic and Victorian Literature.
  R. Dellamora, 637(VS):Spring86-471
Morris, M.R.  Mieux écrire en français.
  P. Verdaguer, 207(FR):Feb86-498

Morris, P.  The Film Companion.
  D. Clandfield, 627(UTQ):Summer85-521
Morris, R.  The Captain's Lady.*
  M. Meyer, 364:Nov85-104
Morris, R.  The Character of King Arthur
  in Medieval Literature.
  P.J.C. Field, 382(MAE):1985/2-323
  K.H. Göller, 72:Band222Heft2-389
  D. Maddox, 589:Jan85-186
  J. Rider, 405(MP):Nov85-181
Morris, R.  The Nature of Reality.
  S. Boxer, 441:5Oct86-54
Morris, R. and F.  Scottish Healing Wells.
  T. Brown, 203:Vol96No1-128
Morris, S.P.  The Black and White Style.
  B. Cohen, 124:May-Jun86-337
  J.M. Cook, 303(JoHS):Vol 105-236
Morris, T.V.  Understanding Identity State-
  ments.
  E.J. Lowe, 518:Oct85-252
Morris, W.  A Cloak of Light.*
  J. Braham, 395(MFS):Winter85-740
  J.J. Wydeven, 649(WAL):Feb86-373
  639(VQR):Summer85-80
Morris, W.  The Collected Letters of Wil-
  liam Morris.*  (Vol 1)  (N. Kelvin, ed)
  F.S. Boos, 637(VS):Summer85-684
  P. Faulkner, 161(DUJ):Jun85-281
  P. Fuller, 90:Feb85-103
  E. Norwich, 139:Aug/Sep85-46
  C. Silver, 636(VP):Spring85-105
Morris, W.  Collected Stories 1948-1986.
  R. Brown, 441:14Dec86-7
Morrisey, W.  Reflections on Malraux.
  B. Stoltzfus, 395(MFS):Winter85-829
Morrison, B.  Dark Glasses.*
  T. Eagleton, 565:Autumn85-69
  M. O'Neill, 493:Apr85-54
  G. Szirtes, 148:Summer85-51
Morrison, B.  Seamus Heaney.
  K. Watson, 447(N&Q):Jun84-281
Morrison, K.  Canters and Chronicles.*
  A.R. Braunmuller, 401(MLQ):Jun84-217
Morrison, M.A. and D.I. Owen, eds.
  Studies on the Civilization and Culture
  of Nuzi and the Hurrians, in Honor of
  E.R. Lacheman.
  S. Greengus, 318(JAOS):Apr-Jun84-364
Morrison, T.  Song of Solomon.  Tar Baby.
  J.P. Campbell, 149(CLS):Fall85-394
Morrissette, B.  Novel and Film.
  P.J. Schwartz, 268(IFR):Winter86-48
Morrissey, R.J.  La Rêverie jusqu'à
  Rousseau.
  L.W. Lynch, 207(FR):May86-970
Morrow, B. - see Rexroth, K.
Morrow, J.  This is the Way the World Ends.
  G. Jonas, 441:10Aug86-29
Morsbach, P.  Isaak Babel' auf der sowjet-
  ischen Bühne.
  E.R. Sicher, 575(SEER):Jan85-99
Morse, R.A., ed.  The Limits of Reform in
  China.
  J.C. Oi, 293(JASt):Nov84-192
Morse, S.F.B.  Lectures on the Affinity of
  Painting with the Other Fine Arts.*  (N.
  Cikovsky, Jr., ed)
  G.W. Linden, 289:Fall85-115
  P. Staiti, 54:Mar85-163
Morselli, P. and G. Corti.  La chiesa di
  Santa Maria delle Carceri in Prato.*
  L. Pellecchia, 576:May85-184

Morson, G.S. The Boundaries of Genre.
  R.L. Jackson, 131(CL):Winter85-80
Mortier, R. L'Originalité.*
  A. Becq, 535(RHL):Jan/Feb85-102
Mortimer, G.L. Faulkner's Rhetoric of
  Loss.*
  B. Foley, 27(AL):Mar85-161
  N. Polk, 594:Spring85-106
  S.M. Ross, 70:Nov/Dec84-60
  N. Schwartz, 141:Winter85-106
Mortimer, J. Paradise Postponed.*
  W. Lesser, 441:30Mar86-1
  V.S. Pritchett, 442(NY):11Aug86-83
Mortimer, P. Queen Elizabeth.
  P. Beer, 362:13Mar86-27
  S. Gotlieb, 441:29Jun86-12
  K.O. Morgan, 617(TLS):4Apr86-351
Morton, B., ed. Halley's Comet, 1755-
  1984.
  J. North, 617(TLS):7Feb86-131
Morton, J. - see Goldman, N. and L. Szyman-
  ski
Morton, M. and F. Chocolate.
  B. Plain, 441:10Aug86-19
Morton, N. The Journey Is Home.
  E.A. Matter, 441:20Apr86-23
Morton, P. The Vital Science.
  E. Block, Jr., 637(VS):Spring86-468
  S. Lavabre, 189(EA):Apr-Jun86-227
Morwood, J. The Life and Works of Richard
  Brinsley Sheridan.
  T.O. Treadwell, 617(TLS):18Jul86-789
Moscato, M. and L. Le Blanc, eds. The
  United States of America v. One Book
  Entitled "Ulysses" by James Joyce.*
  J.A. Quinn, 628(UWR):Fall-Winter85-92
  J. Sutherland, 250(HLQ):Spring85-195
  T. Wright, 161(DUJ):Jun85-285
Moscovici, S. The Age of the Crowd. (Ger-
  man title: Das Zeitalter der Massen.)
  M. Banton, 617(TLS):10Jan86-28
  H. Pross, 384:Sep/Oct85-917
Moseley, W.M., G. Emmons and M.C. Emmons.
  Spanish Literature, 1500-1700.
  D.B. Drake, 238:Sep85-523
  D. Eisenberg, 304(JHP):Spring85-255
  J.A. Parr, 399(MLJ):Winter85-442
Moser, G. and M. Ferreira, comps.
  Bibliografia das literaturas africanas
  de expressão portuguesa.
  A. Segal, 538(RAL):Spring85-111
Moser, H., I. Schröbler and S. Grosse -
  see Paul, H.
Moser-Raph, E. "Lustige Gesellschaft."
  H. Lixfeld, 196:Band26Heft3/4-372
Moses, C.G. French Feminism in the Nine-
  teenth Century.*
  M. Yalom, 446(NCFS):Spring-Summer86-
  397
Moses, J. The Novelist as Comedian.*
  R.M. De Graaff, 637(VS):Winter85-355
  S-J. Spånberg, 541(RES):Aug85-447
Moses, L.G. The Indian Man.
  C.E. Trafzer, 649(WAL):Feb86-352
Mosey, D. Botham.
  S. Fry, 362:18/25Dec86-55
Mosher, S.W. Broken Earth.
  N. Diamond, 293(JASt):Aug85-785
Moskalew, W. Formular Language and Poetic
  Design in the "Aeneid."
  R.R. Schlunk, 24:Spring85-135

Moskalskaja, O.I. Grammatik der deutschen
  Gegenwartssprache. (3rd ed)
  H. Meier, 682(ZPSK):Band38Heft6-771
Mosley, C. - see Mitford, N.
Mosley, L. Disney's World.
  P.T. O'Conner, 441:26Jan86-21
Mosley, L. The Real Walt Disney.
  S. Schoenbaum, 617(TLS):11Jul86-758
Mosley, N. Judith.
  C. Brown, 617(TLS):15Aug86-894
  L. Heron, 362:21Aug86-24
Mosley, N. Rules of the Game. Beyond the
  Pale.
  J. Byrne, 532(RCF):Spring85-136
Moss, A. Ovid in Renaissance France.*
  H. Lamarque, 535(RHL):May/Jun85-478
  P. Sharratt, 402(MLR):Apr85-458
Moss, A. Poetry and Fable.*
  G. Castor, 208(FS):Jul85-328
  J.C. Nash, 207(FR):Apr86-778
Moss, A. and C. Holder. Improving Student
  Writing.
  E. Strenski, 126(CCC):May85-247
Moss, E. Part of the Pattern.
  P. Pearce, 617(TLS):11Apr86-391
Moss, H. Minor Monuments.
  W. Woessner, 441:2Nov86-27
Moss, H. New Selected Poems.*
  V. Shetley, 491:Feb86-299
Moss, H. Rules of Sleep.*
  639(VQR):Autumn85-130
Moss, R. The Game of the Pink Pagoda.
  P. Reading, 617(TLS):15Aug86-894
  J. Turner, 362:7Aug86-25
Moss, R. Moscow Rules.*
  639(VQR):Spring85-63
Moss, R.F. Rudyard Kipling and the Fic-
  tion of Adolescence.
  P.A. Dunae, 637(VS):Spring85-566
Moss, S.P. Charles Dickens' Quarrel with
  America.
  D. Walder, 617(TLS):31Jan86-125
  C.A. Wegelin, 27(AL):Dec85-666
Mossberg, B.A.C. Emily Dickinson.*
  W. Barker, 26(ALR):Spring/Autumn85-247
Mossman, C.A. The Narrative Matrix.
  S. Haig, 207(FR):Mar86-620
  A. Jefferson, 208(FS):Oct85-485
  L. Parks, 446(NCFS):Spring-Summer86-
  353
Mossman, E. - see Pasternak, B. and O.
  Freidenberg
Motion, A. Dangerous Play.*
  S. Rae, 364:Aug-Sep85-129
  G. Szirtes, 148:Summer85-51
Motion, A. The Lamberts.
  R. Blythe, 362:1May86-25
  V. Glendinning, 617(TLS):2May86-465
Mott, M.C. The Seven Mountains of Thomas
  Merton.*
  P. Hebblethwaite, 617(TLS):23May86-559
  P.F. Knitter, 344:Winter86-128
  K. Quinlan, 219(GaR):Summer85-448
Mottahedeh, R. The Mantle of the Prophet.*
  F. Halliday, 617(TLS):20Jun86-667
  E. Mortimer, 453(NYRB):30Jan86-13
Motte, W., Jr. The Poetics of Experiment.
  D. Bellos, 402(MLR):Oct85-951
Motto, N. Mined With a Motion.
  L. Adey, 637(VS):Winter86-322
  J. Bump, 636(VP):Winter85-419
  D.G. Riede, 301(JEGP):Oct85-567

Möttölä, K., O.N. Bykov and I.S. Korolev, eds. Finnish-Soviet Economic Relations.
  G. Maude, 575(SEER):Oct85-633
Mottram, R. Inner Landscapes.*
  G. Burk, 615(TJ):Oct85-385
M. Hinden, 659(ConL):Fall86-400
Motz, L. The Wise One of the Mountain.
  A. Liberman, 563(SS):Spring85-215
  J. Simpson, 203:Vol96No1-135
Mouat, R.G. - see under Gutiérrez Mouat, R.
Moukanos, D.D. Ontologie der "Mathematika" in der Metaphysik des Aristoteles.
  J. Annas, 123:Vol35No1-200
du Moulin, H.S. - see under Schmitz du Moulin, H.
Mouloud, N. and J-M. Vienne, eds. Langages, Connaissance et Pratique.
  M. Dominicy, 540(RIPh):Vol39fasc4-447
Moulton, G.E., ed. Atlas of the Lewis and Clark Expedition.*
  R.E. Robinson, 649(WAL):May85-58
Moulton, G.E. - see Ross, J.
Mouré, E. Domestic Fuel.
  R. Donovan, 526:Autumn85-97
Moureau, F. Le "Mercure Galant" de Dufresny (1710-1714) ou le journalisme à la mode.*
  J. Lough, 208(FS):Oct85-471
  P. Rétat, 535(RHL):Jan/Feb85-97
  W. Wrage, 207(FR):Oct85-131
Moureau, F. and R. Bernouilli. Autour du "Journal de Voyage" de Montaigne, 1580-1980.
  C. Dédéyan, 535(RHL):Jan/Feb85-82
Mouron, H. A.M. Cassandre.
  S. Heller, 441:30Mar86-19
Mousnier, R. The Institutions of France Under the Absolute Monarchy, 1598-1789.* (Vol 2)
  R. Birn, 173(ECS):Fall85-140
Mowat, F. My Discovery of America.*
  442(NY):6Jan86-86
Mowat, F. Sea of Slaughter.*
  A. Purdy, 102(CanL):Fall85-132
Mowl, T. and B. Earnshaw. Trumpet at a Distant Gate.*
  E. Denby, 324:Oct86-767
  J.M. Robinson, 39:Oct85-317
Mowry, H-Y.L. Chinese Love Stories from "Ch'ing-shih."
  C. Swatek, 116:Jul84-191
Moxon, I.S., J.D. Smart and A.J. Woodman, eds. Past Perspectives.
  S. Hornblower, 617(TLS):1Aug86-848
Moyes, P. Night Ferry to Death.
  T.J. Binyon, 617(TLS):20Jun86-683
Moyles, R.G. The Text of "Paradise Lost."*
  R. Flannagan, 391:Mar85-22
Moynihan, D.P. Family and Nation.
  B. Dworkin, 441:2Mar86-9
  G.C. Loury, 129:Jun86-21
  442(NY):7Apr86-105
Moynihan, E.B. Paradise as a Garden in Persia and Mughal India.
  R. Hillenbrand, 59:Jun85-265
Możejko, E. Yordan Yovkov.
  P. Matejic, 104(CASS):Summer85-234
Mozet, N. La Ville de province dans l'oeuvre de Balzac.*
  H.W. Wardman, 208(FS):Apr85-221
Mrosovsky, K. Hydra.
  I. Fonseca, 617(TLS):28Nov86-1358

Mucchielli, A. and A. Vexliard, eds. L'Homme et ses potentialités.
  J-M. Gabaude, 542:Jan-Mar85-64
Mudra, J. and J. Petr. Učebnik verxnelužickogo jazyka.
  G. Stone, 575(SEER):Apr85-316
Muela, J.G. - see under González Muela, J.
Mueller, J.M. The Native Tongue and the Word.*
  A.S.G. Edwards, 589:Oct85-1056
  A.D. Hall, 551(RenQ):Autumn85-561
  639(VQR):Spring85-43
Mueller, M. Les Idées politiques dans le roman héroïque de 1630 à 1670.
  M. Bannister, 208(FS):Oct85-469
Mueller, M. "The Iliad."
  W.H., 148:Spring85-94
  P.W. Rose, 124:Mar-Apr86-291
Abbé Mugnier. Journal de l'abbé Mugnier (1879-1930). (M. Billot, ed)
  J. Aeply, 450(NRF):Oct85-86
  J. Ducruet, 605(SC):15Jan86-178
Mühlberg, D. Woher wir wissen, was Kultur ist.
  L. Parade, 654(WB):8/1985-1392
Muir, E. Edwin Muir: Uncollected Scottish Criticism.* (A. Noble, ed)
  E. Longley, 447(N&Q):Jun84-279
Muir, J. John Muir: Summering in the Sierra. (R. Engberg, ed)
  B. Devall, 649(WAL):May85-69
Muir, K., ed. "King Lear": Critical Essays.
  B.S. Hammond, 610:Autumn85-231
Muir, K. Shakespeare.
  J. Pitcher, 617(TLS):18Jul86-790
Muir, K. - see Shakespeare, W.
Muir, K., J.L. Halio and D.J. Palmer, eds. Shakespeare, Man of the Theater.*
  J.R. Mulryne, 402(MLR):Jul85-690
Muir, L.R. Literature and Society in Medieval France.
  D.D.R. Owen, 617(TLS):16May86-538
Muir, R. The Stones of Britain.
  P. Levi, 176:Jul/Aug86-42
Mujica, B., R. Woehr and F. Vergara. Pasaporte, First-Year Spanish. (2nd ed)
  V. Arizpe, 399(MLJ):Spring85-113
Mukherjee, B. Darkness.
  H. Cooke, 441:12Jan86-14
  A. Desai, 364:Dec85/Jan86-143
  C. Rooke, 376:Jan86-123
Mukherjee, S.N., ed. India.
  R.W. Lariviere, 293(JASt):Feb85-432
  L. Rocher, 318(JAOS):Jul-Sep84-597
Muldoon, P., ed. The Faber Book of Contemporary Irish Poetry.
  D. Davis, 362:10Jul86-31
  M. Hofmann, 617(TLS):30May86-585
Muldoon, P. The Wishbone.
  M. Hofmann, 617(TLS):30May86-585
Mulhallen, K., D. Bennett and R. Brown, eds. Tasks of Passion.*
  T. Goldie, 102(CanL):Winter84-146
Mulisch, H. The Assault.*
  J. Mellors, 364:Dec85/Jan86-140
  J. Updike, 442(NY):6Jan86-83
Mullard, C. Race, Power and Resistance.
  J. Stone, 617(TLS):13Jun86-656
Mullen, E.J. and J.F. Garganigo. El cuento hispánico.
  M.L. Bretz, 238:Sep85-543

267

Muray, P.  Le 19e siècle à travers les
âges.*
    J-F. Fourny, 704(SFR):Winter85-437
    C. Prendergast, 617(TLS):16May86-538
Murdoch, I.  Acastos.
    D.A.N. Jones, 362:5Jun86-25
    M. Nussbaum, 617(TLS):15Aug86-881
Murdoch, I.  The Good Apprentice.*
    H. Bloom, 441:12Jan86-1
    P. Lewis, 364:Oct85-90
    H. Moss, 453(NYRB):12Jun86-39
    J. Updike, 442(NY):12May86-123
Murdoch, I.  The Sovereignty of Good.
    483:Oct85-559
Murdoch, J.  For the People's Cause.  (J.
    Hunter, ed)
    D. Profumo, 617(TLS):24Oct86-1200
Mure, D.  The Last Temptation.
    M.R.D. Foot, 176:Jun85-63
Murfin, R.C., ed.  Conrad Revisited.
    J. Hawthorn, 637(VS):Spring86-492
    F.P.W. McDowell, 136:Vol 18No3-237
    D.W. Ross, 395(MFS):Winter85-793
Murfin, R.C.  The Poetry of D.H. Lawrence.
    K. Cushman, 301(JEGP):Jan85-151
Murphy, A.  The Restless Factor.
    M. Harmon, 272(IUR):Autumn85-234
Murphy, D.  Full Tilt.
    A. Harvey, 441:1Jun86-14
    442(NY):5May86-135
Murphy, G.R.  Brecht and the Bible.*
    S. Hoefert, 406:Summer85-246
Murphy, H.  Murder for Lunch.
    N. Callendar, 441:30Mar86-22
Murphy, J.  Realités Françaises.
    E.G. Lombeida, 207(FR):Oct85-174
    J.W. Zdenek, 399(MLJ):Summer85-175
Murphy, J.G.  Evolution, Morality, and the
    Meaning of Life.*
    L.J. Splitter, 63:Mar85-115
Murphy, J.J., ed.  Critical Essays on
    Willa Cather.
    J. Lloyd, 649(WAL):Aug85-185
Murphy, J.J., ed.  Renaissance Eloquence.
    E.S. Donno, 551(RenQ):Summer85-315
    A. Tomarken, 354:Jun85-186
    D.R. Woolf, 529(QQ):Autumn85-640
Murphy, J.J., ed.  The Rhetorical Tradi-
    tion and Modern Writing.
    R. Hoffpauir, 107(CRCL):Sep85-494
    D. Seed, 447(N&Q):Dec84-556
Murphy, N.T.P.  In Search of Blandings.
    D. Cannadine, 617(TLS):8Aug86-861
Murphy, P.  Summer Island.
    M. Thorpe, 198:Winter85-87
Murphy, R.  The Price of Stone.*
    T. Eagleton, 493:Aug85-64
    H. Lomas, 364:Jun85-89
    J. Mole, 176:Jan86-59
    W. Scammell, 148:Winter85-65
Murrah, D.J.  The Pitchford Land and
    Cattle Company.
    L. Milazzo, 584(SWR):Winter85-130
Murray, A.C.  Germanic Kinship Structure.
    B.S. Bachrach, 589:Oct85-1003
Murray, D.R. and R.A.  The Prairie Builder.
    J.R. Miller, 298:Fall85-156
Murray, I. and B. Tait.  Ten Modern Scot-
    tish Novels.
    C. Craig, 571(ScLJ):Winter85-56
    F.R. Hart, 588(SSL):Vol20-282
    A.T. McKenzie, 395(MFS):Winter85-816
    A. Stevenson, 161(DUJ):Jun85-286

Murray, J.  The Best of the Group of Seven.
    D. Farr, 529(QQ):Autumn85-604
Murray, J.  Kin.
    J. Mellors, 362:20Nov86-28
Murray, J.  Samarkand.
    J. Mellors, 364:Jun85-102
Murray, J. - see McLeod, P.N.
Murray, L.  Michelangelo.*
    E.H. Ramsden, 39:Jan85-68
Murray, L.A., ed.  The New Book of Austra-
    lian Verse.
    P. Conrad, 617(TLS):19Dec86-1421
Murray, L.A.  The People's Otherworld.*
    R. Pybus, 565:Summer85-62
Murray, L.A.  Selected Poems.
    N. Corcoran, 617(TLS):22Aug86-919
Murray, M.J.  The Development of Capital-
    ism in Colonial Indochina (1870-1940).
    S.L. Popkin, 293(JASt):Feb85-349
Murray, P., ed.  The Deer's Cry.
    D. Davis, 362:10Jul86-31
Murray, W.  Luftwaffe.
    R.J. Overy, 617(TLS):10Jan86-32
Murru, F. and G. Pessolano Filos.  Alla
    riscoperta della didattica del latino in
    Italia nel settecento e nell'ottocento.
    P. Flobert, 555:Vol59fasc1-175
    O. Wenskus, 260(IF):Band90-330
Murry, K.M. - see under Middleton Murry, K.
Murti, T.R.V.  Studies in Indian Thought.
    (H.G. Coward, ed)
    D. Allen, 293(JASt):May85-632
Musa, M. - see Dante Alighieri
Musacchio, E.  Amore, ragione e follia.
    P.D. Wiggins, 276:Winter85-326
Muscatine, D., M.A. Amerine and B. Thomp-
    son, eds.  Book of California Wine.
    J. Ronsheim, 42(AR):Spring85-248
Muscetta, C., ed.  Francesco De Sanctis
    nella storia della cultura.
    P. De Marchi, 228(GSLI):Vol 162fasc520-
    598
Muschamp, H.  Man About Town.*
    K. Crossman, 106:Winter85-443
Muschg, A.  Bayoun ou le voyage en Chine.
    L. Kovacs, 450(NRF):Jan85-111
Musco, A. - see Barone, G. and others
"Il Museo dell'Accademia Ligustica di
    Belle Arti — La Pinacoteca."
    C. Thiem, 683:Band48Heft2-277
"The Museum of Modern Art, New York: The
    History of the Collection."
    G.V., 90:Jun85-397
"Museums for a New Century."
    E.H. Brown, 476:Fall85-75
    A.S. Weller, 289:Summer85-143
Musgrave, M.  The Music of Brahms.
    E. Sams, 617(TLS):7Mar86-244
Musgrave, P.W.  From Brown to Bunter.
    A.L. Le Quesne, 617(TLS):11Apr86-386
Mushkat, M.  The Making of the Hong Kong
    Administrative Class.
    H.C. Kuan, 302:Vol21No1-109
"Music Competitions: A Report."
    P. Standford, 415:Jan85-29
Musil, R.  Five Women.
    J.M. Coetzee, 453(NYRB):18Dec86-10
Musil, R.  Gesammelte Werke.  (Vol 8)
    (A. Frisé, ed)
    G. Kortian and N. Nercessian, 98:Apr85-
    321

Musil, R.  On Mach's Theories.
  K. Harries, 543:Mar85-668
  J.A. Wiesheipl, 438:Spring85-228
Muske, C.  Wyndmere.*
  S.M. Gilbert, 491:Dec85-163
  A. Turner, 199:Spring86-85
  639(VQR):Autumn85-131
Musonius Rufus.  Entretiens et fragments.
  (A. Jagu, ed and trans)
  J. Ecole, 192(EP):Apr-Jun85-271
  D.J. O'Meara, 543:Mar85-640
Mussafia, A.  Scritti di filologia e
  linguistica.  (A. Daniele and L. Renzi,
  eds)
  M. Pozzi, 228(GSLI):Vol 162fasc517-142
Müssener, H., ed.  Aspekte des Kultur-
  austausches zwischen Schweden und dem
  deutsprachigen Mitteleuropa nach 1945.
  H. Uecker, 52:Band20Heft2-219
Muyskens, J.L.  The Sufficiency of Hope.
  A. Rocque, 154:Winter85-720
Muzzarelli, M.G.  Ebrei e città d'Italia
  in età di transizione.
  S. Cohn, Jr., 589:Oct85-1004
Mwanzi, H.  Notes on Grace Ogot's "Land
  without Thunder."
  B.F. Berrian, 538(RAL):Winter85-595
"Carl Mydans: Photojournalist."*
  M. Ignatieff, 617(TLS):3Jan86-5
Myer, V.G., ed.  Laurence Sterne.*
  L. Graves, 594:Winter85-430
  S. Soupel, 189(EA):Apr-Jun86-222
Myers, A.R.  Crown, Household and Parlia-
  ment in Fifteenth Century England.
  J.R. Maddicott, 617(TLS):14Mar86-272
Myers, J., ed.  A Trout in the Milk.
  P.J. Lindholdt, 577(SHR):Winter85-81
Myers, K.  Understains.
  J. Rosen, 362:7Aug86-22
Myers, P.  Deadly Cadenza.
  T.J. Binyon, 617(TLS):28Nov86-1357
Myers, P.  Deadly Variations.
  N. Callendar, 441:22Jun86-25
Myers, P. - see Marenzio, L.
Myers, R. and M. Harris, eds.  Development
  of the English Book Trade, 1700-1899.
  J.D.F., 447(N&Q):Mar84-128
Myers, R. and M. Harris, eds.  Sale and
  Distribution of Books from 1700.*
  J.D.F., 447(N&Q):Mar84-129
Myers, R.H. and M.R. Peattie, eds.  The
  Japanese Colonial Empire, 1895-1945.
  C.I.E. Kim, 407(MN):Summer85-227
Myers, R.L.  Racine's "La Thébaïde."
  A. Gable, 208(FS):Jan85-75
Myers, W.  The Teaching of George Eliot.
  E. Wright, 637(VS):Spring86-479
Myerscough, J., ed.  Funding the Arts in
  Europe.
  J. Press, 176:Mar86-51
Myerson, J.  Emily Dickinson.
  R.W. Franklin, 517(PBSA):Vol79No1-133
  D.H. Keller, 87(BB):Dec85-217
Myerson, J., ed.  The Transcendentalists.
  W. Glick, 534(RALS):Spring85-89
Mylius, K.  Die vier edlen Wahrheiten.
  J.M. Verpoorten, 259(IIJ):Oct85-304
Mylius-Erichsen, L., ed.  Vagten (1899-
  1900).
  B. Glienke, 562(Scan):May85-89
Myrdal, J.  Return to a Chinese Village.
  N. Diamond, 293(JASt):Aug85-785

Myres, J.N.L.  The English Settlements.
  D. Dumville, 617(TLS):4Jul86-741
"Le Mythe du héros."
  P. Rogers, 677(YES):Vol 15-297
"Mythes, Images, Représentations."*
  D-H. Pageaux, 107(CRCL):Sep85-485
  D-H. Pageaux, 549(RLC):Jul-Sep85-319

Nababan, P.W.J.  A Grammar of Toba-Batak.
  S. Cumming, 350:Jun86-470
Nabhan, G.P.  Gathering the Desert.
  D. Mabberley, 617(TLS):9May86-515
Nabholtz, J.R.  "My Reader My Fellow-
  Labourer."
  C. Baldick, 617(TLS):14Nov86-1273
Nabokov, V.  The Enchanter.
  L. Rose, 61:Nov86-133
  J. Updike, 442(NY):15Dec86-125
  E. White, 441:19Oct86-7
Nabokov, V.  Lectures on Russian Litera-
  ture.*  Lectures on Literature.
  Lectures on "Don Quixote."  (F. Bowers,
  ed of all)
  D. Flower, 249(HudR):Spring85-148
Nabokov, V. and E. Wilson.  The Nabokov-
  Wilson Letters, 1940-1971.  (S. Karlin-
  sky, ed)
  D. Flower, 249(HudR):Spring85-151
Naccarato, F. - see Eiximenis, F.
Nadal, R.M. - see under Martínez Nadal, R.
"Nadar."  (A. Jammes, ed)  "Nadar, photo-
  graphies."  (Vol 1)  "Nadar, dessins et
  écrits."  (Vol 2)
  E. Darragon, 98:Aug-Sep85-860
Nadeau, J.  Le Fruit noir.
  N.B. Bishop, 102(CanL):Fall85-166
Nadeau, R. and J. Désautels.  Epistemology
  and the Teaching of Science.
  F. Lepage, 154:Summer85-313
  J. Van Evra, 154:Summer85-321
Nadeau, R.L.  Reading from the New Book
  of Nature.
  D. Seed, 402(MLR):Oct85-923
  M.M. Van de Pitte, 599:Spring85-144
Nadel, I.B.  Biography.*
  S. Neuman, 598(SoR):Spring86-407
  C.W. White, 637(VS):Summer86-631
Nadel, I.B.  Jewish Writers of North Amer-
  ica.
  M.F. Schulz, 402(MLR):Jan85-142
Nader, R. and W. Taylor.  The Big Boys.
  M. Singer, 441:22Jun86-24
Naef-Hinderling, A.  The Search for the
  Culprit.*
  L. Hartveit, 179(ES):Apr85-181
Naess, H.  Knut Hamsun.
  S. Lyngstad, 563(SS):Summer85-345
  R.N. Nettum, 562(Scan):Nov85-233
Nag, M. and F. Pettersen.  Reise gjennom
  vår egen tid.
  D. Buttry, 563(SS):Summer85-354
Nagai, T.  The Bells of Nagasaki.
  J. Kirkup, 364:Apr/May85-109
Nagel, B.  Kafka und die Weltliteratur.
  R. Jayne, 52:Band20Heft3-324
  G. Müller, 597(SN):Vol57No2-251
Nagel, G.  The Structure of Experience.*
  M. Kuehn, 154:Autumn85-507
  E. Schaper, 323:Oct85-311

Nagel, G.L.  Critical Essays on Sarah Orne Jewett.*
S.B. Smith, 26(ALR):Spring/Autumn85-253
Nagel, J., ed.  Ernest Hemingway.*
R.E. Fleming, 234:Spring86-52
J.J. Martine, 587(SAF):Spring85-117
R.S. Nelson, 268(IFR):Winter86-39
M.S. Reynolds, 534(RALS):Spring83-115
Nagel, T.  The View from Nowhere.
A. Kenny, 441:23Feb86-14
C. Taylor, 617(TLS):5Sep86-962
Nagibin, J.  Reka Geraklita.
M. Sendich, 558(RLJ):Fall84-302
Nagibin, Y.  The Peak of Success and Other Stories.  (H. Goscilo, ed)
J.H. Billington, 441:5Oct86-24
Nagl-Docekal, H.  Die Objektivität der Geschichtswissenschaft.
K. Röttgers, 687:Jan-Mar85-140
Nagy, G.  The Best of Achaeans.
W.J. Verdenius, 394:Vol38fascl/2-180
Nahem, J.  Psychology and Psychiatry Today.
M. Smith, 488:Jun85-216
van Nahl, A.  Originale Riddarasögur als Teil altnordischer Sagaliteratur.
A. Heinrichs, 684(ZDA):Band114Heft2-46
Nail, N.  Nachrichten aus Köln, London, Moskau und Prag.
H-R. Fluck, 685(ZDL):1/1985-121
Naimark, N.  Terrorists and Social Democrats.*
R. Service, 575(SEER):Oct85-609
Naipaul, S.  Beyond the Dragon's Mouth.*
J. Crace, 617(TLS):12Sep86-996
639(VQR):Autumn85-136
Naipaul, S.  An Unfinished Journey.
J. Crace, 617(TLS):12Sep86-996
N. Mosley, 362:14Aug86-25
Naipaul, V.S.  Finding the Centre.*
529(QQ):Summer85-435
Naipaul, V.S.  Une Maison pour Monsieur Biswas.
H. Cronel, 450(NRF):Dec85-101
Nairn, A., ed.  Essays on Van Dyck.
I.G., 90:Feb85-109
Nairn, B. and G. Serle, eds.  Australian Dictionary of Biography.  (Vol 10)
R. Davenport-Hines, 617(TLS):14Nov86-1263
Naito, M.  Tokyo 1970-1985.
M. Holborn, 62:Jan86-15
Najarian, P.  Daughters of Memory.
R. Hadas, 441:21Sep86-21
Najder, Z.  Joseph Conrad.*
J. Batchelor, 541(RES):Nov85-592
T.K. Bender, 141:Fall85-425
F.J.M. Blom, 179(ES):Apr85-182
M. Ray, 148:Winter85-77
G. Ward, 97(CQ):Vol 14No3-257
L. Williams, 396(ModA):Fall85-374
Najder, Z., ed.  Conrad Under Familial Eyes.*
T.K. Bender, 141:Fall85-425
K. Carabine, 136:Vol 18No1-48
D.L. Higdon, 177(ELT):Vol28No1-88
G. Ward, 97(CQ):Vol 14No3-257
Najemy, J.M.  Corporatism and Consensus in Florentine Electoral Politics, 1280-1400.*
F.W. Kent, 551(RenQ):Winter85-703

Nakagawa, H.  Félicité et salut chez Jean-Jacques Rousseau.
A. Suwa, 535(RHL):Nov/Dec85-1069
Nakam, G.  Les "Essais" de Montaigne.*
M.C. Horowitz, 551(RenQ):Autumn85-546
Nakam, G.  Montaigne et son temps.*
R.E. Leake, 207(FR):Mar86-610
Nakamura, H.  Ansätze modernen Denkens in den Religionen Japans.
A. Schwade, 407(MN):Summer85-250
Nakamura, H.  Indian Buddhism.
C. Lindtner, 259(IIJ):Oct85-298
Nakano, I. - see under Ichiro Nakano
Nalbantian, S.  Seeds of Decadence in the Late Nineteenth-Century Novel.*
J. Stokes, 402(MLR):Jan85-108
Nalty, B.C.  Strength for the Fight.
R.F. Weigley, 441:22Jun86-15
442(NY):4Aug86-87
Nam, J-H.  America's Commitment to South Korea.
L. Freedman, 617(TLS):8Aug86-857
Namjoshi, S.  From the Bedside Book of Nightmares.
M.T. Lane, 198:Winter85-106
L.M. York, 102(CanL):Summer85-190
Nammalvar.  Hymns for the Drowning.  (A.K. Ramanujan, trans)
S. Viswanathan, 293(JASt):Nov84-237
Ñaṇamoli, B., ed and trans.  The Path of Discrimination (Paṭisambhidā-magga).
(rev by A.K. Warder)
L.S. Cousins, 259(IIJ):Jul85-209
Nance, J.J.  Blind Trust.
R. Witkin, 441:19Jan86-10
Nancy, J-L.  L'Impératif catégorique.*
P. Fenves, 400(MLN):Dec85-1136
Nanda, B.R.  The Nehrus.
N. Mansergh, 617(TLS):10Jan86-30
Nandy, A.  The Intimate Enemy.
L.D. Wurgaft, 293(JASt):Feb85-434
Naoyuki Fukumoto, Noburo Harano and Satoru Suzuki - see "La Roman de Renart"
Napier, A.D.  Masks, Transformation, and Paradox.
D.F. Pocock, 617(TLS):19Sep86-1040
Napier, P.  A Late Beginner.
617(TLS):31Jan86-127
"Napoli e la Francia."
V.D.L., 605(SC):15Apr86-272
Narayan, R.K.  Talkative Man.
G. Mangan, 617(TLS):3Oct86-1113
J. Mellors, 362:20Nov86-28
Narayan, R.K.  A Tiger for Malgudi.
D.W. Atkinson, 314:Winter-Spring85-237
Narayan, R.K.  Under the Banyan Tree and Other Stories.*
M. Gorra, 249(HudR):Winter86-669
Nardin, T.  Law, Morality, and the Relations of States.*
S. Wein, 150(DR):Spring85-143
Narten, J.  Die Amǝša Spǝntas im Avesta.
B. Schlerath, 259(IIJ):Apr85-152
Narvarte, C.  Nihilismo y violencia.
A. Reix, 542:Jul-Sep85-342
Narveson, J., ed.  Moral Issues.*
J.E. Bickenbach, 154:Summer85-283
J.N. Kaufmann, 154:Summer85-265
Nash, R.  Settlement in a School of Whales.*
P.M. St. Pierre, 102(CanL):Summer85-183

Nash, S. Paul Valéry's "Album des vers anciens."*
  L.M. Porter, 446(NCFS):Fall-Winter85/86-177
Nash, W. The Language of Humor.
  F. Chevillet, 189(EA):Apr-Jun86-201
  R. Machin, 349:Spring85-215
Nassauer, R. Kramer's Goats.
  L. Chamberlain, 617(TLS):17Oct86-1169
Nastase, I. Break Point.
  N. Callendar, 441:7Sep86-17
Nasution, A. Financial Institutions and Policies in Indonesia.
  P.C.I. Ayre, 293(JASt):May85-680
Natali, C. La Scuola dei filosofi, scienza ed organizzazione istitutionale della Scuola di Aristotele.
  A. Bélis, 555:Vol59fasc1-104
Nathan, G.J. My Very Dear Sean. (R.G. Lowery and P. Angelin, eds)
  B. Dolan, 305(JIL):Jan85-52
Nathan, M. Le Ciel des fouriéristes.*
  P. Desan, 207(FR):May86-1007
"National Video Festival, 1984."
  L. Zippay, 127:Fall85-263
Natkiel, R. and A. Preston. The Weidenfeld Atlas of Maritime History.
  G.V. Scammell, 617(TLS):19Sep86-1039
Natov, N. Mikhail Bulgakov.
  V. Terras, 268(IFR):Winter86-35
Natsolim. Enduring Poles.
  S.L. Cuba, 497(PolR):Vol30No1-105
Nattiez, J-J. Proust Musicien.*
  M. Cooper, 208(FS):Apr85-226
Nattiez, J-J. - see Boulez, P.
Naudé, G. Lettres de Gabriel Naudé à Jacques Dupuy (1632-1652).* (P. Wolfe, ed)
  J-F. Battail, 597(SN):Vol57No1-127
Naudeau, O., ed. La Passion de Sainte Catherine d'Alexandrie par Aumeric.
  G.A. Runnalls, 545(RPh):Feb85-407
Naughton, J.T. The Poetics of Yves Bonnefoy.*
  E.K. Kaplan, 207(FR):May86-986
  B.L. Knapp, 345(KRQ):Vol32No1-112
  S. Lawall, 188(ECr):Summer85-101
"Naughty Dots."
  B. Bainbridge, 617(TLS):26Dec86-1453
Naumann, H-P. Sprachstil und Textkonstitution.
  M. Jacoby, 685(ZDL):2/1985-251
Nava, M. The Little Death.
  N. Callendar, 441:10Aug86-23
de Navarre, M. - see under Marguerite de Navarre
Navarre, Y. Romances sans paroles.
  H. Le Mansec, 207(FR):Oct85-153
Navarre, Y. Swimming Pools at War.
  S. Dieckman, 615(TJ):Mar85-123
Navarro Talegón, J. Plateros zamoranos de los siglos XVI y XVII.
  C. Esteras, 48:Apr-Jun85-163
Navas Ruiz, R. - see Hernández, J.
Nayar, B.R. India's Quest for Technological Independence. (Vols 1 and 2)
  D.K. Vajpeyi, 293(JASt):May85-645
Naylor, G. The Bauhaus Reassessed.
  C.J. Child, 324:Oct86-762
Naylor, G. The Women of Brewster Place.
  E. Ward, 381:Mar85-80
Naylor, P. Unexpected Pleasures.
  E.J. Kenney, Jr., 441:2Nov86-16

Ndebele, N. Fools.
  F. Tuohy, 441:14Sep86-36
Neal, E. The Natural History of Badgers.
  H. Kruuk, 617(TLS):5Sep86-986
Neale, R.S. Writing Marxist History.
  S. Pollard, 617(TLS):23May86-572
Neale-Silva, E., R. Webster and M.K. Hellerman. Salsa y salero.
  V.E. Sherer, 399(MLJ):Summer85-206
"Neat Pieces."
  M.Y. Frye, 658:Summer/Autumn85-181
Neckel, G., ed. Edda.* (Vol 1) (5th ed rev by H. Kuhn)
  K. Grimstad, 301(JEGP):Jul85-409
Nectoux, J-M. - see Fauré, G.
Nedjalkov, V.P., ed. Tipologija rezul'tativnyx konstrukcij (rezul'tativ, stativ, passiv, perfekt).*
  W.D. Kaliuscenko and N.A. Lutsenko, 353:Vol23No1-147
Nee, V. and D. Mozingo, eds. State and Society in Contemporary China.
  J.C. Oi, 293(JASt):Nov84-192
Needham, J. China and the Origins of Immunology.
  K.F. Shortridge, 302:Vol21No1-107
Needham, P. The Printer and the Pardoner.
  G.D. Painter, 617(TLS):19Sep86-1043
Needle, J. and P. Thomson. Brecht.*
  R. Meuller, 609:Spring86-75
Needleman, J. The Heart of Philosophy.
  M. Deutscher, 63:Sep85-375
Needleman, J. Sorcerers.
  442(NY):8Dec86-153
Needler, H. - see "Fables from Old French"
Neely, C.T. Broken Nuptials in Shakespeare's Plays.
  I-S. Ewbank, 617(TLS):25Apr86-451
Ne'eman, Y. and Y. Kirsh. The Particle Hunters.
  C. Ronan, 617(TLS):12Dec86-1407
de Neeve, P.W. Colonus.
  D.W. Rathbone, 123:Vol35No2-329
Nef, F. L'analyse logique des langues naturelles.
  G. Kleiber, 553(RLiR):Jan-Jun85-189
Nehamas, A. Nietzsche.
  K. Harries, 441:19Jan86-14
  M. Tanner, 617(TLS):16May86-519
Neher, A. Jérusalem, vécu juif et message.
  A. Reix, 542:Jan-Mar85-95
  S. Zac, 192(EP):Apr-Jun85-267
Neher, A. L'essence du prophétisme.
  A. Reix, 542:Jan-Mar85-95
Nehru, J. Glimpses of World History.
  N. Mansergh, 617(TLS):10Jan86-30
Neidhart von Reuenthal. Die Lieder Neidharts. (E. Wiessner, ed; 4th ed rev by P. Sappler) Lieder. (H. Lomnitzer, ed and trans)
  J.W. Thomas, 133:Band18Heft1-81
Neidpath, J. The Singapore Naval Base and the Defense of Britain's Eastern Empire, 1919-1941.
  T.J. Bellows, 293(JASt):Aug85-885
Neiger, A. Il Poeta e la parola.
  C. Muller, 553(RLiR):Jul-Dec85-465
Neil, B. As We Forgive.
  J. McCulloch, 441:9Feb86-24
Neil, J.M., ed. Will James.
  L. Milazzo, 584(SWR):Autumn85-547
Neill, A.S. A Dominie's Log.
  617(TLS):25Apr86-459

Neill, S. A History of Christianity in India 1707-1858.
  P.J. Marshall, 617(TLS):18Apr86-426
Neilson, K. Strategy and Supply.
  R.K. Debo, 104(CASS):Spring85-76
  L.L. Farrar, Jr., 550(RusR):Apr85-209
Neises, C.P., ed. The Beatles Reader.
  B.L. Cooper, 498:Vol9No4-80
Neizvestnyj, E. Govorit Neizvestnyj.
  J. Kennedy, 550(RusR):Jan85-88
  A. Leong, 574(SEEJ):Winter85-487
Neizvestnyj, E. O sinteze v iskusstve/On Synthesis in Art.*
  J. Kennedy, 550(RusR):Jan85-88
Nekrylova, A.F. Russkie narodnye gorodskie prazdniki, uveselenija i zreliŝca.
  R. Bowie, 574(SEEJ):Winter85-496
Nelligan, E. The Complete Poems of Emile Nelligan.* (F. Cogswell, ed and trans)
  L. Welch, 198:Spring85-93
Nelson, A. Murder under Two Flags.
  L. Rohter, 441:28Dec86-19
Nelson, A.L. Cabrera Infante in the Menippean Tradition.*
  A.M. Hernández de López, 552(REH):May85-147
Nelson, B. The Last Campfire.
  L. Milazzo, 584(SWR):Winter85-130
Nelson, B. Émile Zola.*
  C. Becker, 535(RHL):Jan/Feb85-114
Nelson, B. Zola and the Bourgeoisie.*
  D. Baguley, 535(RHL):May/Jun85-510
  R.D. Fulton, 594:Spring85-108
  B.L. Murphy, 188(ECr):Winter85-117
  P. Walker, 207(FR):Feb86-470
Nelson, C. Our Last First Poets.*
  R. Pooley, 677(YES):Vol 15-364
Nelson, H. Robert Bly.
  D.D. Kummings, 125:Winter85-232
  C. Molesworth, 141:Summer85-324
  W.J. Scheick, 30:Fall85-89
Nelson, H.S. Charles Dickens.*
  J. Larson, 637(VS):Winter85-318
  S. Monod, 402(MLR):Apr85-442
Nelson, M.C. Masters of Western Art.
  P.A. Tackabury, 649(WAL):May85-51
Nelson, P.D. Anthony Wayne.
  J.M. Elukin, 441:16Feb86-17
Nelson, R. Pascal.
  S.E. Melzer, 149(CLS):Summer85-268
Nelson, R. Kenneth Patchen and American Mysticism.
  C.F. Terrell, 659(ConL):Spring86-115
  D. Wakoski, 115:Fall85-482
  295(JML):Nov85-539
Nelson, R.K. Make Prayers to the Raven.*
  D.W. Dippie, 106:Spring85-31
Nelson, V., ed. A Myrour to Lewde Men and Wymmen.*
  V. Gillespie, 382(MAE):1985/2-313
  A. Hudson, 402(MLR):Oct85-898
Nelton, S. In Love and in Business.
  J. Kaufman, 441:26Oct86-38
Nemerov, H. Inside the Onion.*
  P. Filkins, 271:Fall85-166
  W. Prunty, 569(SR):Fall85-646
Nemerov, H. New and Selected Essays.
  G. Johnson, 219(GaR):Fall85-661
  R. Wertime, 676(YR):Summer85-602
Nemeth, T. Gramsci's Philosophy.
  W. Hartley, 275(IQ):Summer/Fall84-218

Nemoianu, V. The Taming of Romanticism.*
  G. Hoffmeister, 678(YCGL):No34-145
  L. Metzger, 661(WC):Fall85-175
  639(VQR):Spring85-44
de Nemore, J. - see under Jordanus de Nemore
Nencioni, G. Tra grammatica e retorica.
  P. Manni, 708:Vol 11fasc1-137
Nepveu, P. Mahler et autres matières.
  R. Giroux, 102(CanL):Spring85-124
Nerlich, G. The Shape of Space.
  P. Horwich, 311(JP):May85-269
Nerlich, U., ed. The Soviet Asset.
  D.E. Powell, 550(RusR):Jul85-271
Nersessian, N.J. Faraday to Einstein.
  P. Enfield, 486:Dec85-641
de Nerval, G. Oeuvres complètes. (Vol 2) (J. Guillaume and C. Pichois, with others, eds)
  J-L. Steinmetz, 535(RHL):Sep/Oct85-886
"Gérard de Nerval et la Bibliothèque Nationale."
  G. Malandain, 535(RHL):Sep/Oct85-888
Netanyahu, B., ed. Terrorism.
  S. Bakhash, 453(NYRB):14Aug86-12
  M. Clark, 362:21Aug86-22
  C. Townshend, 617(TLS):29Aug86-928
  M. Zonis, 441:18May86-7
Nettl, B. The Study of Ethnomusicology.*
  N. Deshane, 529(QQ):Summer85-409
  K. Lornell, 292(JAF):Jan/Mar85-107
Nettl, B., with others. The Western Impact on World Music.
  R.B. Qureshi, 187:Fall86-574
Neu, J. - see "ISIS Cumulative Bibliography 1966-1975"
"Neues aus der Wezel-Forschung." (Vols 1 and 2)
  G. Hoffmeister, 221(GO):Winter85-115
Neugroschel, J., comp and trans. The Great Works of Jewish Fantasy and Occult.
  M.S. Kaplan, 441:6Jul86-14
Neuhaus, R.J. Dispensations.
  J.M. Coetzee, 453(NYRB):8May86-3
  S.P. Huntington, 129:Sep86-70
Neuhaus, V. Der zeitgeschichtliche Sensationsroman in Deutschland 1855-1878.
  N.A. Kaiser, 406:Spring85-110
Neuman, S. and R. Wilson. Labyrinths of Voice.*
  B. Edwards, 107(CRCL):Sep85-566
  K. Gelder, 49:Jan85-96
  T. Whalen, 526:Autumn85-99
Neumann, B. Gottfried Keller.*
  L.B. Jennings, 406:Fall85-362
  P. Schäublin, 680(ZDP):Band104Heft2-307
Neumann, F. Ornamentation in Baroque and Post-Baroque Music.
  A.F.L.T., 412:Aug/Nov84-304
Neusner, J. - see "The Talmud of the Land of Israel"
Neuss, P., ed and trans. The Creacion of the World.*
  R. Longsworth, 589:Apr85-486
Neustadt, R.E. and E.R. May. Thinking in Time.
  J. Chace, 441:16Mar86-11
  P. Kennedy, 61:Jul86-76
  L.D. Nachman, 129:Dec86-74
  R. Steel, 453(NYRB):6Nov86-39
  442(NY):7Jul86-83

273

Olivier, L. On Acting.
   P-L. Adams, 61:Dec86-104
   F. Weaver, 441:16Nov86-14
   442(NY):15Dec86-130
Olivio Jiménez, J. José Martí, poesía y
existencia.
   C. Ripoll, 238:May85-315
   I.A. Schulman, 240(HR):Summer85-388
Olivio Jiménez, J. - see Arenas, R.
Olivio Jiménez, J. - see Cañas, D.
Olivio Jiménez, J. - see Colón, E.
Olivio Jiménez, J. - see Fernández, J.
Ollard, R. and P. Tudor-Craig, eds. For
Veronica Wedgwood.
   B. Worden, 617(TLS):1Aug86-846
Oller, J.W., Jr., ed. Issues in Language
Testing Research.
   M. Pennock-Román, 355(LSoc):Jun85-277
Ollivier, E. Mère-solitude.
   E-M. Kroller, 102(CanL):Winter84-129
Olmstead, A. Roger Sessions and His
Music.
   L. Starr, 513:Spring-Summer85-216
Olofsson, A. Relative Junctions in
Written American English.*
   U. Carls, 682(ZPSK):Band38Heft4-428
Olsen, D.J. The City as a Work of Art.
   M. Girouard, 453(NYRB):18Dec86-8
   D. Watkin, 441:19Oct86-36
Olsen, J. Give a Boy a Gun.
   B. Lancaster, 441:12Jan86-21
Olsen, M.A., ed. "Libro del Cauallero
Cifar."
   L.A. Vasvari, 238:Sep85-510
Olshan, J. Clara's Heart.*
   H. Kureishi, 617(TLS):16May86-536
Olson, C. The Maximus Poems.* (G.F.
Butterick, ed)
   A. Golding, 405(MP):Nov85-212
Olson, E. Last Poems.
   M. Jarman, 249(HudR):Summer85-327
   J. Penberthy, 617(TLS):18Apr86-430
Olson, G. Literature as Recreation in the
Later Middle Ages.*
   S.P. Coy, 545(RPh):Aug84-105
   P. Gradon, 541(RES):Feb85-69
   D. Pearsall, 447(N&Q):Mar84-89
   J.F. Poag, 221(GQ):Fall85-601
   J. Ruud, 125:Fall84-114
Olson, S. John Singer Sargent.
   P-L. Adams, 61:Aug86-91
   J. Grigg, 362:29May86-25
   R. Kimball, 441:24Aug86-2
   A. Staley, 617(TLS):22Aug86-916
   442(NY):23Jun86-99
Olson, T. We Are the Fire.
   B. Christophersen, 50(ArQ):Autumn85-
   286
Olson, T. The Woman Who Escaped from
Shame.
   R. Kelly, 441:1Jun86-25
Olsson, A. Ekelöfs nej.
   L. Thompson, 562(Scan):Nov85-242
Oltolina, C. I salmi di tradizione orale
delle Valli Ossolane.
   M.S. Keller, 292(JAF):Jul/Sep85-356
Omaggio, A.C., ed. Proficiency, Curricu-
lum, Articulation.
   E.C. Knox, 207(FR):Oct85-157
Omaggio, A.C. and others. Kaléidoscope.*
   J. Labat, 399(MLJ):Spring85-89
O'Malley, M. Doctors.
   S. Wolfe, 529(QQ):Autumn85-624

Omari, M.S. From the Inside to the Out-
side.
   J. Bettelheim, 2(AfrA):Feb85-92
O'Meara, D.J., ed. Neoplatonism and Chris-
tian Thought.
   W. Beierwaltes, 53(AGP):Band67Heft2-
   185
O'Meara, P. K.F. Ryleev.
   L.G. Leighton, 550(RusR):Jul85-301
Omond, R. The Apartheid Handbook. (2nd
ed)
   J.E. Spence, 617(TLS):15Aug86-882
Ondaatje, M. Secular Love.*
   J. Kertzer, 102(CanL):Fall85-163
   S. Scobie, 376:Mar85-163
O'Neil, D.C., ed. Life: The Second Decade,
1946-1955.
   J. Guimond, 219(GaR):Winter85-876
   C. Hess, 507:Jul/Aug85-314
O'Neill, F. Agents of Sympathy.
   T.J.B., 617(TLS):31Jan86-113
   M. Laski, 362:9Jan86-30
O'Neill, J. Essaying Montaigne.*
   F. Rigolot, 535(RHL):Mar/Apr85-292
O'Neill, J. Five Bodies.
   D. O'Keeffe, 617(TLS):10Jan86-28
Ong, W.J. Orality and Literacy.*
   G. Bourquin, 189(EA):Jan-Mar86-86
   T.J. Farrell, 126(CCC):Oct85-363
   K. Reichl, 38:Band103Heft1/2-172
   A. Squires, 161(DUJ):Jun84-294
   T.J. Taylor, 541(RES):May85-245
Onieva Morales, J.L. Cómo dominar el
análisis gramatical básico.
   A. Terker, 238:Dec85-800
Önnerfors, A. - see Tacitus
"Onomastique et dialectologie."
   J. Chaurand, 209(FM):Oct85-259
Onrubia, C.M. - see under Menéndez Onrubia,
C.
"Ontario Universities: Options and
Futures."
   B. Neatby, 298:Spring85-153
Onuf, P.S. The Origins of the Federal
Republic.
   J.P. Kaminski, 656(WMQ):Jan85-151
Oomen, I. Determination bei generischen,
definiten und indefiniten Beschreibungen
im Deutschen.
   P. Wagener, 260(IF):Band90-362
Oots, K.L. A Political Organization
Approach to Transnational Terrorism.
   C. Townshend, 617(TLS):29Aug86-928
Openshaw, S. Nuclear Power.
   M. Warnock, 617(TLS):17Oct86-1155
Opie, I. and P., eds. The Oxford Book of
Narrative Verse.*
   C. Clausen, 569(SR):Winter85-157
Opitz, M. Gesammelte Werke. (Vol 2, Pts
1 and 2) (G. Schulz-Behrend, ed)
   C. Wagenknecht, 133:Band18Heft2-165
Opland, J. Anglo-Saxon Oral Poetry.*
   K. Reichl, 38:Band103Heft1/2-172
Opland, J. Xhosa Oral Poetry.
   D.P. Biebuyck, 292(JAF):Oct/Dec85-486
Opolka, U. and others - see Bloch, E.
Opp, K.D. Die Entstehung sozialer Normen.
   A. Oberschall, 185:Apr86-649
Oppenheim, J. The Other World.
   A.L. Le Quesne, 617(TLS):4Apr86-353
   F.B. Smith, 637(VS):Summer86-613
Oppenheimer, J. and J. Vitek. Idol.
   J. Kearney, 441:20Jul86-13

Oppenlander, E.A.  Dickens' "All the Year Round."
  S. Monod, 189(EA):Apr-Jun86-224
Orange, D.M.  Peirce's Conception of God.
  M.B. Mahowald, 619:Summer85-430
  R.J. Roth, 258:Jun85-213
Orange, M. - see "Une Femme à la recherche d'une illusion et cinq autres nouvelles"
Orbach, S.  Hunger Strike.
  D. Breen, 617(TLS):25Apr86-438
  J. Moore, 441:23Mar86-41
Ord-Hume, A.W.J.G.  Restoring Pianolas and Other Self-playing Pianos.  Pianola.
  H. Schott, 415:Nov85-673
Orderic Vitalis.  Ecclesiastical History. (Vol 1, Bks 1 and 2)
  R.B. Patterson, 589:Jan85-225
Orduna, G. - see López de Ayala, P.
O'Reilly, B.  "Tiger" O'Reilly.
  S. Rae, 617(TLS):11Jul86-770
Orel, H., ed.  Kipling: Interviews and Recollections.*
  M.N. Cohen, 579(SAQ):Summer85-334
  V.N. Paananen, 115:Summer84-265
Orel, H.  Victorian Literary Critics.
  R.D. Fulton, 637(VS):Winter86-336
  A. Johnson, 177(ELT):Vol28No3-306
Oren, D.A.  Joining the Club.
  G.G. Rose, 129:Sep86-63
  A.J. Sherman, 617(TLS):8Aug86-858
Orengo, F. and V.  Il romanzo del canto popolare piemontese.
  M.S. Keller, 292(JAF):Jul/Sep85-356
Oresick, P.  An American Peace.
  J. Carter, 219(GaR):Summer85-432
Orfanidis, N.  I politiki diastasi tis pyisis tou Giorgou Seferi.
  H. Gifford, 617(TLS):12Dec86-1391
"Organizacion de los Estados Americanos."
  H. Gros Espiell, 263(RIB):Vol35No3-330
Orians, G.H.  Blackbirds of the Americas.
  E. Dunn, 617(TLS):4Jul86-745
Origo, I.  A Need to Testify.*
  E.A. Miller, 278(IS):Vol40-155
O'Riordan, J.  A Guide to O'Casey's Plays.*
  M. Kahan, 157:No157-52
Orledge, R.  Debussy and the Theatre.*
  C.S. Brown, 131(CL):Summer85-277
  A.G. Engstrom, 207(FR):Oct85-137
  A.W., 412:Feb83-63
Orlova, A.  Musorgsky's Days and Works.* (R.J. Guenther, ed)
  J. Warrack, 410(M&L):Apr85-142
Orme, N.  From Childhood to Chivalry.*
  S.E. Lehmberg, 551(RenQ):Winter85-708
Ormerod, B.  An Introduction to the French Caribbean Novel.
  S. Crosta, 95(CLAJ):Jun86-497
Ormerod, R.  Dead Ringer.*
  N. Callendar, 441:14Sep86-38
Ormsby, F.  A Northern Spring.
  W. Scammell, 617(TLS):21Nov86-1325
Ornstein-Galicia, J., ed.  Form and Function in Chicano English.
  G.M. Blanco, 399(MLJ):Autumn85-328
  H.T. Trueba, 355(LSoc):Jun85-255
  P.R. Turner, 269(IJAL):Jul85-324
O'Rourke, A.P.  The Red Banner Mutiny.
  A. Krystal, 441:22Jun86-26
O'Rourke, B., ed and trans.  Blas Meala.
  M. Harmon, 272(IUR):Autumn85-234
Oroz Reta, J. and M-A. Marcos Casquero - see San Isidoro de Sevilla

Orrell, J.  Fallen Empires.
  R. Plant, 529(QQ):Winter85-740
Orrell, J.  The Quest for Shakespeare's Globe.*
  W.H. Allison, 536(Rev):Vol7-153
  R.C. Kohler, 702:Vol 17-292
  D.F. Rowan, 627(UTQ):Summer86-424
Orrell, J.  The Theatres of Inigo Jones and John Webb.*
  T. Minter, 157:No158-50
  J. Summerson, 90:Jul85-463
Orrieux, C.  Les papyrus de Zénon.
  D.J. Thompson, 303(JoHS):Vol 105-216
Orsi, R.A.  The Madonna of 115th Street.
  V. Crapanzano, 617(TLS):13Jun86-652
  M. Gottlieb, 441:6Jul86-15
Ortas, F.M.  The Last Pharaoh.
  B. Tonkin, 362:4Sep86-22
Ortega, J.  Poetics of Change.
  P.B. Dixon, 395(MFS):Winter85-775
  J. Tittler, 238:May85-317
Ortega y Gasset, J.  Historical Reason.
  H. White, 617(TLS):31Jan86-109
Ortega y Gasset, J.  The Revolt of the Masses.
  A. Dobson, 617(TLS):12Dec86-1404
  R.J. Neuhaus, 129:Jul86-53
Orth, D.J.  Official Authorities and Other Organizations Involved with Geographic Names — 1984: United States, Canada, Mexico.
  K.B. Harder, 424:Mar-Jun85-102
Orth, D.J. and R.L. Payne.  The National Geographic Names Data Base: Phase II Instructions.
  K.B. Harder, 424:Mar-Jun85-103
Orth, E.W., ed.  Zeit und Zeitlichkeit bei Husserl und Heidegger.
  C. Jamme, 489(PJGG):Band92Heft1-204
Ortí, V.C. - see under Cárcel Ortí, V.
Ortiz, A.  Eighteenth-Century Reforms in the Caribbean.
  M. Monteón, 83:Spring85-99
Ortiz, S.J.  Fightin'.
  R. Salisbury, 448:Vol23No2-113
Ortiz Armengol, P.  El año que vivió Moratín en Inglaterra 1792-1793.
  N. Glendinning, 617(TLS):21Nov86-1304
Ortmann, W.D.  Sprechsilben im Deutschen.
  G.F. Meier, 682(ZPSK):Band38Heft4-445
Ortmann, W.D.  Wortbildung und Morphemstruktur eines deutschen Gebrauchswortschatzes.
  B.J. Koekkoek, 221(GQ):Summer85-446
  C. Römer, 682(ZPSK):Band38Heft4-446
Ortolá, M-S.  Un estudio del "Viaje de Turquía."
  R.D. Pope, 240(HR):Autumn85-486
Orton, J.  The Orton Diaries.  (J. Lahr, ed)
  T. Gould, 617(TLS):14Nov86-1266
  S. Townsend, 362:13Nov86-23
Orwell, G.  Down and Out in Paris and London.  Homage to Catalonia.  A Clergyman's Daughter.
  D.J. Enright, 362:10Apr86-24
Orwell, G.  Nineteen Eighty-Four.* (B. Crick, ed)
  M. Doughty, 366:Autumn85-311
  J. Meyers, 627(UTQ):Fall85-117
Orwell, G.  "Nineteen Eighty-Four": The Facsimile of The Extant Manuscript.*
[continued]

(P. Davison, ed)
J. Meyers, 627(UTQ):Fall85-117
Orwell, G. George Orwell: The War Commentaries. (M.J. West, ed)
E. O'Shaughnessy, 441:9Nov86-33
J. Symons, 617(TLS):3Jan86-6
442(NY):3Nov86-167
Orwen, G.P. Jean-François Regnard.
B. Griffiths, 208(FS):Apr85-207
van Os, H., with K. van der Ploeg. Sienese Altarpieces, 1215-1460.* (Vol 1)
H. Belting, 683:Band48Heft4-567
C.G. von Teuffel, 90:Jun85-391
J. White, 59:Dec85-484
Osamu, D. - see under Dazai Osamu
Osbey, B.M. Ceremony for Minneconjoux.
C. Hernton, 472:Spring/Summer/Fall/Winter85-518
C. Wright, 448:Vol23No1-118
Osborn, C. The Fields of Memory.*
R.M. Davis, 573(SSF):Fall85-487
Osborn, M. - see "Beowulf"
Osborn, R. - see Wordsworth, W.
Osborne, C. Giving It Away.
J. Falk, 362:30Oct86-28
B. Morrison, 617(TLS):31Oct86-1210
Osborne, C. Schubert and His Vienna.
J. Machlis, 441:5Jan86-11
442(NY):10Feb86-114
Osborne, C. The World Theatre of Wagner.
D. Unruh, 615(TJ):May85-259
Osborne, F. The True Tragicomedy Formerly Acted at Court. (L. Potter, ed)
J. Limon, 179(ES):Apr85-176
Osborne, J. Meyer or Fontane?
G.W. Field, 564:Feb85-75
H.R. Klieneberger, 402(MLR):Apr85-498
R. Koc, 222(GR):Spring85-78
M.T. Peischl, 221(GQ):Fall85-617
H-G. Richert, 133:Band17Heft3/4-355
Osborne, M. Before Kampuchea.
M. Smithies, 302:Vol21No1-95
Osborne, M.J. Naturalization in Athens.*
(Vols 1-3)
D.M. MacDowell, 123:Vol35No2-317
Osborne, R. Rossini.
J. Rosselli, 617(TLS):26Sep86-1066
Osborne, T.R. A Grande École for the Grands Corps.
F. Healey, 208(FS):Jan85-103
Oseth, J.M. Regulating U.S. Intelligence Operations.
639(VQR):Autumn85-134
O'Shaughnessy, E. Pasaquina.
E. Pall, 441:10Aug86-18
O'Shea, E. A Descriptive Catalog of W.B. Yeats's Library.
R.E. Ward, 174(Éire):Winter85-154
Osiatyński, W. Contrasts.
639(VQR):Spring85-57
Osinski, J. Über Vernunft und Wahnsinn.
S.L. Gilman, 222(GR):Winter85-36
Osinski, Z. Grotowski and His Laboratory.
(L. Vallee and R. Findlay, eds and trans)
R. Brustein, 441:27Jul86-11
M. Hunter, 609:Summer/Fall86-104
Osler, M.J. and P.L. Farber, eds. Religion, Science and Worldview.
P.W. Atkins, 617(TLS):1Aug86-836
Osmond, J., ed. The National Question Again.*
N. Thomas, 176:May86-58

Osmond-Smith, D. Playing on Words.*
M. Smith, 607:Jun85-42
Osmond-Smith, D. - see Berio, L., with R. Delmonte and B. András Varga
Ossola, C. - see Ungaretti, G.
Østbo, J. Expressionismus und Montage.
K. Menges, 406:Winter85-499
von der Osten, G. Hans Baldung Grien, Gemälde und Dokumente.
J.E. von Borries, 90:Feb85-97
Oster, D. Monsieur Valéry.
W.N. Ince, 208(FS):Jul85-361
Østerud, E. Det borgerlige subjekt.
J. Haugan, 562(Scan):May85-78
Osterwalder, P. Das althochdeutsche Galluslied Ratperts und seine lateinischen Übersetzungen durch Ekkehart IV.
J. Splett, 680(ZDP):Band104Heft1-150
Östman, J-O. You Know — A Discourse-Functional Approach.
U. Oomen, 38:Band103Heft1/2-150
Östör, Á., L. Fruzzetti and S. Barnett, eds. Concepts of Person.
M.J. Leaf, 293(JASt):Feb85-438
Ostriker, A. Writing Like a Woman.
R. McDowell, 249(HudR):Autumn85-516
Ostriker, A.S. Stealing the Language.
M. Perloff, 29(APR):Jul/Aug86-12
L. Rosenberg, 441:20Jul86-21
Ostwald, P.F. Schumann.*
A. Storr, 415:Nov85-671
O'Sullivan, N., ed. Terrorism, Ideology and Revolution.
P. Kennedy, 617(TLS):14Nov86-1268
O'Sullivan, V. and M. Scott - see Mansfield, K.
Otero, A.D. - see under de Santos Otero, A.
Otis, B. Cosmos and Tragedy.* (E.C. Kopff, ed)
A.M. van Erp Taalman Kip, 394:Vol138 fascl/2-194
O'Toole, J. The Trouble with Advertising.
R. Draper, 453(NYRB):26Jun86-14
O'Toole, L.M. Structure, Style and Interpretation in the Russian Short Story.*
K.D. Kramer, 558(RLJ):Fall84-295
Ott, N.H. Rechtspraxis und Heilsgeschichte.
H.B. Willson, 301(JEGP):Oct85-595
Ottaviani, G. L'Attore e lo Sciamano.
L. Richards, 610:Autumn85-253
Otten, H. Die Apologie Hattusilis III.
G. Neumann, 260(IF):Band90-288
Ottman, R.W. Advanced Harmony.
P. Standford, 415:Aug85-464
Oudot, S. and D.L. Gobert. La France.
D. O'Connell, 207(FR):Apr86-807
Ouellet, R. Sur Lahontan.
P. Berthiaume, 535(RHL):Sep/Oct85-875
Ouellette-Michalska, M. La Maison Trestler, ou le 8e jour d'Amérique.
T. La Fontaine, 102(CanL):Winter84-125
Oughton, J. Gearing of Love.
L.M. York, 102(CanL):Summer85-190
Ould, C. A Kind of Sleep.
W. Brandmark, 362:11Mar86-22
Oumano, E. Film Forum.*
E. de Antonio, 18:Nov85-72
Oumano, E. Sam Shepard.
S. Laschever, 441:9Mar86-25
Ouy, G. and V. Gerz-von Büren, eds. Le Catalogue de la bibliothèque de l'abbaye
[continued]

Packard, G.R. and A.D. Wilhelm, Jr., eds.
China Policy for the Next Decade.
M. Schaller, 293(JASt):Aug85-806
Packard, W. Saturday Night at San Marcos.
R. Weinreich, 441:2Feb86-16
Packer, B.L. Emerson's Fall.*
J.R. Reaver, 577(SHR):Winter85-65
Packman, D. Vladimir Nabokov.*
P. Miles, 447(N&Q):Dec84-548
Paddock, H. A Dialect Survey of Carbonear,
Newfoundland.
J. Tucker, 178:Dec85-484
Padel, J.O. Beroul's Geography and Patron-
age.
G. Raynaud de Lage, 554:Vol 105No2/3-
382
Paden, W.D., T. Sankovitch and P.H.
Stäblein - see Bertran de Born
Padgett, R. - see Denby, E.
Padley, G.A. Grammatical Theory in West-
ern Europe 1500-1700.*
R.H. Robins, 353:Vol23No1-170
Padoch, C. Migration and Its Alternatives
Among the Iban of Sarawak.
R.E. Seavoy, 293(JASt):Nov84-249
Paetzold, H. - see Baumgarten, A.G.
Pagagno, G. and A. Quondam, eds. La Corte
e lo Spazio.
L. Lockwood, 551(RenQ):Winter85-726
Pagano, M., ed. "Dit des Cornetes."*
A.G. Elliott, 545(RPh):Aug85-124
W. Rothwell, 208(FS):Oct85-450
G. Zaganelli, 547(RF):Band97Heft2/3-
301
Pagden, A. The Fall of Natural Man.
B.W. Ife, 402(MLR):Oct85-961
Page, M. John Arden.*
R.L. Calder, 178:Sep85-381
Page, M. Britain's Unknown Genius.
R.V. Holdsworth, 148:Summer85-89
Page, N., ed. William Golding: Novels,
1954-67.
G. Klaus, 189(EA):Oct-Dec86-469
P. Reading, 617(TLS):17Oct86-1153
Page, N. A.E. Housman.*
P.G. Naiditch, 121(CJ):Apr/May86-362
G. Williams, 637(VS):Autumn85-170
Page, N., ed. Henry James.
M. Jacobson, 534(RALS):Spring83-68
C. Wegelin, 395(MFS):Summer85-391
Page, N. A Kipling Companion.
D. Duffy, 627(UTQ):Summer85-423
Page, N. - see "Thomas Hardy Annual"
Page, P.K. The Glass Air.
E. Tihanyi, 99:Mar86-37
Page, T. - see Gould, G.
Pageaux, D-H., ed. La Recherche en littér-
ature générale et comparée en France.
M.G. Rose, 678(YCGL):No34-160
Paget, B. and others, eds. Kvinnor och
skapande.
A. Jensen, 562(Scan):May85-100
Pagnoni-Sturlese, M.R. and L. Sturlese -
see Berthold von Moosburg
Pai Hsien-yung. Wandering in the Garden,
Waking from a Dream.
L.S. Robinson, 116:Jul84-200
Paikeday, T.M. The Native Speaker Is Dead!
W.A.K., 300:Oct85-203
Pailin, D.A. Attitudes to Other Reli-
gions.*
G.E. Pruett, 566:Spring86-227

Paillet, J-P. and A. Dugas. Approaches to
Syntax.
P.H. Matthews, 361:Nov85-259
D.K. Nylander, 320(CJL):Fall85-384
Painter, C. Into the Mother Tongue.
L. Menn, 350:Sep86-729
Painter, P. Getting to Know the Weather.*
R.F. Dew, 344:Spring86-122
Pais, A. "Subtle is the Lord ... "*
K.W. Lake, 529(QQ):Winter85-829
Pakenham, M. - see Nouveau, G.
Pakenham, V. Out in the Noonday Sun.*
(British title: The Noonday Sun.)
J. Rose, 441:5Jan86-16
Pakula, H. The Last Romantic.*
639(VQR):Summer85-80
Pal, P. Art of Tibet.*
D.A. Jayasundera, 293(JASt):May85-605
Pal, P. Court Paintings of India, 16th-
19th Centuries.
S.H. Safrani, 60:Mar-Apr85-128
Pal, P. and V. Dehejia. From Merchants to
Emperors.
S.C. Welch, 453(NYRB):9Oct86-41
Palacios, J.M. El Idealismo Transcenden-
tal.
M.P.M. Caimi, 342:Band76Heft3-340
Palagia, O. O Glyptos Diakosmos tou
Parthenona.
B.F. Cook, 123:Vol35No1-207
Palencia-Roth, M. Gabriel García Márquez,
la línea, el círculo y las metamorfosis
del mito.
S. Menton, 240(HR):Summer85-389
Palencia-Roth, M., ed. Perspectives on
Faust.
L. Bailey, 602:Band16Heft2-299
O. Durrani, 402(MLR):Jan85-216
Paley, G. Later the Same Day.*
B. Lyons, 573(SSF):Fall85-484
C.C. Park, 249(HudR):Autumn85-481
Paley, G. Leaning Forward.
S. Friebert, 199:Spring86-93
Paley, M. Bad Manners.
S. Braudy, 441:26Jan86-7
Paley, M.D. The Continuing City.*
J. Bogan, 651(WHR):Spring85-90
V.A. De Luca, 88:Fall85-76
D. Fuller, 541(RES):Nov85-577
N. Hilton, 401(MLQ):Dec84-413
Paley, V.G. Mollie is Three.
P. Leach, 441:6Jul86-8
Palisca, C.V. - see Koch, H.C.
Palisca, C.V. - see Zarlino, G.
Pallasmaa, J., with others, eds. Alvar
Aalto Furniture.
T.W. Booth, 576:Dec85-397
Palley, J. The Ambiguous Mirror.
W.R. Blue, 238:Mar85-71
Pallottino, M. Storia della prima Italia.
D. Ridgway, 617(TLS):17Jan86-67
Palm, K. Vom Boykott zur Anerkennung.
B. Zimmermann, 133:Band18Heft1-95
Palmer, A. An Encyclopaedia of Napoleon's
Europe.
639(VQR):Summer85-84
Palmer, C., ed. The Britten Companion.*
J.H. Sutcliffe, 414:Vol71No2-222
Palmer, F.R. Grammar. (2nd ed)
J. Aitchison, 353:Vol23No3-489
Palmer, G. Biographical Sketches of Loyal-
ists of the American Revolution.
P. Marshall, 617(TLS):9May86-494

Palmer, J. Thrillers.
W.W. Stowe, 107(CRCL):Sep85-433
Palmer, K. - see Shakespeare, W.
Palmer, M. First Figure.*
M. Jarman, 249(HudR):Summer85-336
A. Lauterbach, 138:No8-255
Palmer, M.F. Paul Tillich's Philosophy of Art.
M. Austin, 89(BJA):Summer85-283
C.W. Kegley, 543:Jun85-896
Palmer, N.D. The United States and India.
S. Mansingh, 293(JASt):Aug85-873
Palmer, N.F. Visio Tnugdali.
J.L. Flood, 447(N&Q):Mar84-102
F. Shaw, 402(MLR):Apr85-489
Palmer, R. Deep Blues.
J.T. Titon, 187:Fall86-557
Palmer, R., ed. The Oxford Book of Sea Songs.
H. Wackett, 362:12Jun86-25
Palmer, R. The Rolling Stones.
B. Allan, 529(QQ):Summer85-265
Palmer, R.C. The Whilton Dispute, 1264-1380.
M. Prestwich, 161(DUJ):Jun85-258
Palmer, R.R. The Improvement of Humanity.*
G. Kates, 173(ECS):Summer86-551
Paloma, J.A., ed. Romancer català.
S.G. Armistead, 545(RPh):Aug85-145
Pálsson, H. Sagnagerð.
P. Hallberg, 562(Scan):May85-68
Pancake, J.S. This Destructive War.
G. Palmer, 617(TLS):4Jul86-742
Pancrazi, J-N. L'Heure des adieux.
F. de Martinoir, 450(NRF):Jun85-69
Pandey, S.M. The Hindi Oral Epic Loriki. The Hindi Oral Epic Canainī.
K. Schomer, 293(JASt):May85-649
Pandit, G.L. The Structure and Growth of Scientific Knowledge.
R.J. Blackwell, 543:Mar85-673
Pankey, E. For the New Year.
M. Jarman, 249(HudR):Summer85-339
P. Stitt, 219(GaR):Summer85-414
Pannick, D. Sex Discrimination Law.
K. O'Donovan, 617(TLS):18Jul86-779
Pannick, G.J. Richard Palmer Blackmur.
C. Norris, 402(MLR):Jan85-138
Panter-Downes, M. One Fine Day.
P. Craig, 617(TLS):18Jul86-792
Paolo Ciardi, R. and L. Tongiorgi Tomasi. Le pale della Crusca.
M. Pozzi, 228(GSLI):Vol 162fasc520-591
J.R. Woodhouse, 402(MLR):Jul85-732
Paolucci, A. and R. Warwick - see "Review of National Literatures"
Paolucci, A.A. Sepia Tones.
N. Forbes, 441:16Feb86-16
Papas, L.S. New American Chef.
W. and C. Cowen, 639(VQR):Autumn85-139
Papastratis, P. British Policy towards Greece during the Second World War, 1941-1944.
S. Wichert, 575(SEER):Jul85-467
Pape, H. - see Peirce, C.S.
Pape-Müller, S. Textfunktionen des Passivs.
G. Koller, 685(ZDL):2/1985-237
Papert, S. Mindstorms.
D. Woods, 351(LL):Mar85-131
Papin, J. La voie du yoga.
A. Reix, 542:Apr-Jun85-236

Paquet, A. Prophecies.
M. Sonnenfeld, 221(GQ):Fall85-629
Paquette, D. L'Instrument de musique dans la céramique de la Grèce antique.
M.L. West, 303(JoHS):Vol 105-209
"Paradigmes de théologie philosophique."
M. Adam, 542:Jan-Mar85-96
Parain-Vial, J. Philosophie des sciences de la nature.*
M. Gagnon, 543:Jun85-898
Páral, V. Válka s mnohozvířetem.
I. Hajek, 617(TLS):7Feb86-150
Parameswaran, U., ed. The Commonwealth in Canada.
A. Hashmi, 314:Winter-Spring85-250
Parant, R. L'affaire Sinouhé.
E.S. Meltzer, 318(JAOS):Apr-Jun84-363
Paratore, E. Studi su Corneille.
C. Dédéyan, 535(RHL):Sep/Oct85-866
Parekh, B. Marx's Theory of Ideology.
A. Eshete, 482(PhR):Apr85-281
Pareles, J. and P. Romanowski, eds. The Rolling Stone Encyclopedia of Rock and Roll.
B. Allan, 529(QQ):Winter85-810
Parenti, M. Inventing Reality.
M. Pollan, 441:6Apr86-26
Paret, P., with G.A. Craig and F. Gilbert, eds. Makers of Modern Strategy.
J. Gooch, 441:13Apr86-34
J. Keegan, 453(NYRB):17Jul86-38
Paretsky, S. Killing Orders.*
T.J. Binyon, 617(TLS):20Jun86-683
M. Laski, 362:17Apr86-29
Parezo, N.J. Navajo Sandpainting.
C.R. Farrer, 292(JAF):Apr/Jun85-218
Parfit, D. Reasons and Persons.*
A.H. Goldman, 262:Sep85-373
D. Gordon, 258:Sep85-327
S. Shoemaker, 393(Mind):Jul85-443
P. Simpson, 543:Dec85-370
Parfit, M. South Light.
P-L. Adams, 61:Mar86-110
K. Bouton, 441:9Mar86-19
Parfitt, G. English Poetry of the Seventeenth Century.*
R.C. Richardson, 366:Autumn85-285
Pariente, Á., ed. Góngora.
A.P. Debicki, 240(HR):Autumn85-496
van Parijs, P. Evolutionary Explanation in the Social Sciences.
M. Verdon, 488:Mar85-53
Parini, J. The Patch Boys.
J.D. Bloom, 441:28Dec86-18
Paris, E. Unhealed Wounds.
J.R. Saul, 441:25May86-17
Paris, J. Noctuelles suivi de Planctus.
M. Fougères, 207(FR):Apr86-818
Park, H. At a Certain Age.
J. Snead, 441:11May86-24
Park, J. Learning to Dream.*
G. Millar, 707:Winter84/85-71
Park, J.W. Rafael Núñez and the Politics of Colombian Regionalism, 1863-1886.
C. Abel, 617(TLS):15Aug86-883
Park, K. Doctors and Medicine in Early Renaissance Florence.*
F. Gilbert, 453(NYRB):9Oct86-43
Park, M. and G.E. Markowitz. Democratic Vistas.*
J.V. Turano, 16:Spring85-90

Partridge, C. The Making of New Cultures.
J.M. Labanyi, 402(MLR):Jul85-677
Partridge, D. Deer in the Haystacks.
R. Henigan, 649(WAL):Nov85-269
M. Kumin, 219(GaR):Spring85-169
Partridge, F. Everything to Lose.*
C. James, 441:4May86-21
Pascal, B. Les "Pensées" de Pascal.* (F.
Kaplan, ed)
D. Descotes, 535(RHL):Sep/Oct85-870
Pascal, R. Kafka's Narrators.*
G. Benda, 406:Fall85-367
P.W. Nutting, 221(GQ):Winter85-140
A. Stephens, 67:Nov85-266
Pascale, R.T. and A.G. Athos. The Art of
Japanese Management.
J. Turner, 617(TLS):11Jul86-751
Pascall, R., ed. Brahms.*
M.T.R., 412:May84-139
Pascoli, G. Dai Canti di Castelvecchio.
(M. Perugi, ed)
M. Bacigalupo, 402(MLR):Oct85-956
Pascoli, G. Poesie famigliari. (C. Gar-
boli, ed)
F. Donini, 617(TLS):18Jul86-784
"Giovanni Pascoli poesia e poetica."
F. Donini, 617(TLS):18Jul86-784
Pasini, M. Thomas Burnet.
J. Beaude, 192(EP):Apr-Jun85-269
Paskievich, J. A Voiceless Song/Un chant
muet.
M. Braun, 99:Apr85-33
Pasnak, W. In the City of the King.
J. Walker, 102(CanL):Summer85-186
Pasolini, P.P. The Ragazzi.
I. Thomson, 617(TLS):14Nov86-1290
Pasolini, P.P. Roman Nights.
P. Brunette, 441:30Nov86-12
Pasolini, P.P. Selected Poems.
A. Formis, 402(MLR):Oct85-959
Pasolini, P.O. A Violent Life.*
M. Berger, 62:Dec85-16
Pasquazi, S., ed. San Francesco e il
francescanesimo nella Letteratura
italiana del Novecento.
P. Baldan, 228(GSLI):Vol 162fasc518-
299
Passalacqua, M. Tre testi grammaticali
Bobbiesi (GL V 555-566; 634-654; IV 207-
216 Kiel).*
P. Flobert, 555:Vol59fasc1-144
Passmore, J. Recent Philosophers.
483:Jul85-417
Passuth, K. Moholy-Nagy.*
S. Bodine, 62:Jan86-12
P. Overy, 592:Vol 198No1011-54
F. Whitford, 90:Nov85-815
Pasternak, B. Selected Poems.*
J. Aleshire, 434:Winter84-272
Pasternak, B. The Voice of Prose. (Vol 1)
(C. Barnes, ed and trans)
P. France, 617(TLS):9May86-505
Pasternak, B. and O. Freidenberg. The
Correspondence of Boris Pasternak and
Olga Freidenberg. (E. Mossman, ed and
trans)
A. Kerrigan, 569(SR):Spring85-312
Pasternak, B., M. Tsvetayeva and R.M.
Rilke. Letters: Summer 1926.* (Y.
Pasternak, Y. Pasternak and K.M.
Azadovsky, eds)
R. Hingley, 617(TLS):11Jul86-768

Pasternak, L. The Memoirs of Leonid Pas-
ternak.
J. Kennedy, 550(RusR):Jan85-87
Pastner, S. and L. Flam, eds. Anthro-
pology in Pakistan.
P. Jeffery, 293(JASt):Nov84-234
Pastor Boomer, B. El discurso narrativo
de la conquista de América.
I.M. Zuleta, 263(RIB):Vol35No1-70
Pastoureau, M. Les atlas français, XVIe-
XVIIe siècles.
H.P. Shoemaker, 70:May/Jun85-156
Paszkiewicz, H. The Rise of Moscow's
Power.*
E. Levin, 589:Jul85-705
Patai, D. The Orwell Mystique.*
E. Gottlieb, 150(DR):Winter84/85-807
R.J. Voorhees, 395(MFS):Winter85-810
295(JML):Nov85-537
Patchen, K. What Shall We Do Without Us?
H. Carruth, 138:No7-270
C.F. Terrell, 659(ConL):Spring86-115
Paterculus, V. - see under Velleius Pater-
culus
Paterson, A. The Floating World.
S. O'Brien, 617(TLS):10Jan86-34
Paterson, N. The China Run.
S. Altinel, 617(TLS):26Dec86-1456
Patey, D.L. Probability and Literary
Form.*
L. Manley, 566:Spring86-218
E. Rothstein, 173(ECS):Spring86-421
W. Stafford, 366:Autumn85-307
Patey, D.L. and T. Keegan, eds. Augustan
Studies.
D. Nokes, 617(TLS):7Nov86-1257
Patnaik, J.N. The Aesthetics of New Criti-
cism.
G. Wihl, 150(DR):Spring85-134
Patnaik, N. A Second Paradise.*
L. Nicholson, 617(TLS):1Aug86-832
Paton, W. Man and Mouse.*
A.R., 185:Apr86-689
Patrides, C.A., ed. Approaches to Sir
Thomas Browne.*
F. Berry, 541(RES):May85-268
N.H. Keeble, 447(N&Q):Mar84-119
K.D. Weeks, 568(SCN):Winter85-61
Patrides, C.A., ed. George Herbert: The
Critical Heritage.
F. Dinshaw, 541(RES):Nov85-566
Patrides, C.A. Premises and Motifs in
Renaissance Thought and Literature.*
H. Cooper, 447(N&Q):Mar84-106
T.M. Greene, 570(SQ):Autumn85-378
M.R.G. Spiller, 161(DUJ):Jun84-295
Patrides, C.A. - see Donne, J.
Patrides, C.A. and J. Wittreich, eds.
The Apocalypse in English Renaissance
Thought and Literature.
F. Kermode, 551(RenQ):Autumn85-554
Patterson, A. Censorship and Interpreta-
tion.*
S. Soupel, 189(EA):Apr-Jun86-215
566:Autumn85-88
Patterson, A., ed. Roman Images.*
E.S. de Angeli, 124:Sep-Oct85-66
Patterson, D.W. Gift Drawing and Gift
Song.
J. Neal, 650(WF):Apr85-143
J.M. Vlach, 292(JAF):Apr/Jun85-222
Patterson, D.W. The Shaker Spiritual.
412:Aug/Nov83-301

Patterson, J. Black Market.
  N. Callendar, 441:20Jul86-20
Patterson, M. The Revolution in German
  Theatre 1900-1933.
  A. Vivis, 157:No155-53
Patterson, M.C. Literary Research Guide.
  (2nd ed)
  G.A. Thompson, Jr., 107(CRCL):Sep85-
  473
Patterson, O. The Children of Sisyphus.
  R. Deveson, 617(TLS):24Oct86-1187
Patterson, R.P. The Seed of Sally Good'n.
  I. Duffield, 617(TLS):17Oct86-1170
Patterson, W.T. The Genealogical Struc-
  ture of Spanish.*
  R.M. Barasch, 399(MLJ):Winter85-440
  B. Pottier, 92(BH):Jul-Dec84-580
Pattison, M. and M. Bradley. Love in a
  Cool Climate. (V. Green, ed)
  J. Clive, 617(TLS):18Apr86-413
Pattison, R. On Literacy.*
  D. Brandt, 128(CE):Feb85-128
  E. Finegan, 35(AS):Winter85-354
  A. Pitts, 577(SHR):Winter85-91
Patton, M. Historic Buildings, Groups of
  Buildings, Areas of Architectural
  Importance in Bangor (and Groomsport).
  M. Bence-Jones, 324:Sep86-697
Patton, P. Open Road.
  K.A. Marling, 441:29Jun86-15
Paul, D.W. Politics, Art and Commitment
  in the East European Cinema.
  J.C. Troncale, 615(TJ):May85-246
Paul, G.M. A Historical Commentary on
  Sallust's "Bellum Jugurthinum."
  M. Morford, 124:May-Jun86-352
Paul, H. Mittelhochdeutsche Grammatik.
  (22nd ed) (H. Moser, I. Schröbler and S.
  Grosse, eds)
  E. Seidelmann, 685(ZDL):2/1985-225
Paul of Venice. Logica Magna. (Pt 1,
  fasc 7) (P. Clarke, ed and trans)
  I. Angelelli, 543:Dec84-399
de Paula Pombar, M.N. Contribución al
  estudio de la aposición en español
  actual.
  A. Manteca Alonso-Cortés, 547(RF):
  Band97Heft2/3-274
Paulaharju, S. Arctic Twilight.
  V. Zuck, 563(SS):Spring85-227
Pauley, B.F. Hitler and the Forgotten
  Nazis.
  G.A. Craig, 453(NYRB):9Oct86-3
Paulhan, J. Choix de Lettres. (Vol 1) (D.
  Aury, J-C. Zylberstein and B. Leuilliot,
  eds)
  P. Fawcett, 617(TLS):26Dec86-1440
Paulhan, J. and F. Ponge. Correspondance
  1923-1968. (C. Boaretto, ed)
  P. Fawcett, 617(TLS):26Dec86-1440
Paulin, B. and others, eds. Bonheur inviv-
  able?
  J-M. Racault, 189(EA):Apr-Jun86-191
Paulin, R. Ludwig Tieck.
  S.S. Prawer, 617(TLS):14Feb86-172
Paulin, T., ed. The Faber Book of Polit-
  ical Verse.
  D. Davis, 362:29May86-24
  G. Steiner, 617(TLS):23May86-547
Paulin, T. Ireland and the English
  Crisis.*
  A. Haberer, 189(EA):Apr-Jun86-238
                              [continued]

[continuing]
  P. Hamilton, 493:Apr85-20
  R. Imhof, 272(IUR):Autumn85-250
Paulos, J.A. I Think, Therefore, I Laugh.
  G. Turcotte, 616:Fall/Winter85-59
Paulsen, W. and H.G. Hermann, eds. Sinn
  aus Unsinn.*
  K. Weissenberger, 133:Band17Heft3/4-
  364
Paulson, R. Book and Painting.*
  K. Garlick, 541(RES):Aug85-424
Paulson, R. Literary Landscape: Turner
  and Constable.*
  L. Lerner, 131(CL):Spring85-169
  M. Meisel, 591(SIR):Summer85-267
  J.R. Peters-Campbell, 403(MLS):
  Winter85-84
Paulson, R. Representations of Revolution
  (1789-1820).*
  N. Bryson, 90:Feb85-102
  W.B. Carnochan, 405(MP):Aug85-80
  F.V. Randel, 173(ECS):Winter85/86-268
  W. Ruddick, 366:Spring85-143
  P. Wagner, 72:Band222Heft2-477
  W. Walling, 340(KSJ):Vol34-201
  W. Walling, 678(YCGL):No34-143
  H. Witemeyer, 401(MLQ):Jun84-204
  J. Wordsworth, 541(RES):Nov85-581
Paulston, C.B. and others. Writing.
  F.J. Bosco, 399(MLJ):Spring85-119
Paulus, R. and G. Kolter. Der Lyriker
  Karl Krolow.
  V.B. Profit, 133:Band17Heft3/4-374
Paulus Venetus. Logica Parva. (A.R. Per-
  reiah, ed and trans)
  S.F. Brown, 319:Oct86-554
  J. Jolivet, 542:Apr-Jun85-242
Pauly, T.H. An American Odyssey.*
  G. Petrie, 106:Winter85-475
  L. Simon, 579(SAQ):Summer85-335
Pavlović, M. Singing at the Whirlpool.*
  M. Fee, 102(CanL):Spring85-120
Pavone, M.A. and V. Pavelli, eds. Enciclo-
  pedia Bernardiniana, II.
  90:May85-313
Pawel, E. The Nightmare of Reason.*
  C. Koelb, 395(MFS):Winter85-822
  W. Phillips, 473(PR):Vol52No4-444
  295(JML):Nov85-513
Pawle, G. R.E.S. Wyatt.
  P. Sutcliffe, 617(TLS):3Jan86-21
Pawling, C., ed. Popular Fiction and
  Social Change.
  J.M. Lennon, 395(MFS):Winter85-855
Paxton, J. Companion to Russian History.
  D.L. Schlafly, Jr., 377:Jul84-117
Payen, J-C., ed. La légende arthurienne
  et la Normandie.
  M. Boulton, 589:Jul85-707
Payen, J.C. Le moyen âge.
  N.J. Lacy, 589:Jul85-750
Payen, J-C. Le Prince d'Aquitaine.
  T.H. Newcombe, 208(FS):Jan85-59
Payne, A. Frank Bridge.*
  T. Bray, 410(M&L):Jul85-280
Payne, H.C. - see "Studies in Eighteenth-
  Century Culture"
Payne, K.B. Strategic Defense.
  M. MccGwire, 617(TLS):31Oct86-1214
Paysan, C. Le Rendez-vous de Strasbourg.
  M-N. Little, 207(FR):Mar86-650

Peirce, C.S. Charles S. Peirce: Phänomen und Logik der Zeichen. (H. Pape, ed and trans)
  B. Kirstein, 619:Fall85-576
Peirce, C.S., ed. Studies in Logic by Members of the Johns Hopkins University (1883).*
  J.L. Esposito, 567:Vol53No1/3-165
Peirce, C.S. Textes anticartésiens. (J. Chenu, ed and trans)
  C. Chauviré, 98:Apr85-402
Peirce, C.S. Writings of Charles S. Peirce.* (Vol 1) (E.C. Moore and others, eds)
  M.A. Bonfantini, 567:Vol55No3/4-251
Peirce, C.S. Writings of Charles S. Peirce.* (Vol 2) (E.C. Moore and others, eds)
  T.A. Goudge, 319:Jan86-132
  M.G. Murphey, 567:Vol55No3/4-259
  I.K. Skrupskelis, 619:Spring85-271
de Peiresc, N.C.F. Peiresc: Lettres à Naudé (1629-1637).* (P. Wolfe, ed)
  F. Assaf, 475:Vol 12No23-755
  R. Zuber, 535(RHL):Mar/Apr85-293
Pekar, H. American Splendor.
  D. Rosenthal, 441:11May86-44
Pekkilä, E., ed. Suomen Antropologi, 4.
  P. Hopkins, 187:Spring/Summer86-336
Pelayo, M.M. - see under Menéndez Pelayo, M.
Pelc, J. Jan Kochanowski.
  R.H. Stone, 574(SEEJ):Winter85-489
Pelc, J. and others, eds. Sign, System and Function.
  P.H. Salus, 350:Mar86-234
Pelckmans, P. Le Sacre du père.*
  P. Hoffmann, 547(RF):Band97Heft2/3-313
  J-P. Sermain, 535(RHL):May/Jun85-491
Pelczynski, Z.A., ed. The State and Civil Society.*
  G.G.B., 185:Apr86-688
Pelegrin, B. Éthique et Esthétique du Baroque (L'Espace jésuitique de Baltasar Gracián).
  T. Cordellier, 450(NRF):Jul-Aug85-160
Pelegrin, B. Le fil perdu du "Criticón" de Baltasar Gracián.
  U. Schulz-Buschhaus, 547(RF):Band97 Heft4-493
Pelegrin, B. - see Gracian, B.
Pelikan, J. Jesus through the Centuries.*
  J.M. Cameron, 453(NYRB):13Feb86-21
  K.B. Osborne, 344:Spring86-130
Pellandra, C. Seicento francese e strategie di compensazione.
  E. De Gennaro, 475:Vol 12No23-735
  J. Morel, 549(RLC):Oct-Dec85-468
Pellegrin, P. La classification des animaux chez Aristote.*
  D. Pralon, 542:Apr-Jun85-236
Pellegrini, A. and T. Yawkey, eds. The Development of Oral and Written Language in Social Contexts.
  W. Frawley, 350:Mar86-227
Pellegrini, R.G. - see de Scudéry, G.
Pellegrini, S. and G. Marroni. Nuovo repertorio bibliografico della prima lirica galegoportoghese (1814-1977).
  D. Woll, 547(RF):Band97Heft1-113
Pelletier, C. The Funeral Makers.
  P-L. Adams, 61:Jul86-79
  S. Kenney, 441:1Jun86-7

Pelletier, F. Imaginaires du cinématographe.
  I. Hedges, 207(FR):Feb86-503
Pelletier, F.J. and J. King-Farlow, eds. New Essays on Aristotle.
  J. Barnes, 520:Vol30No2-212
Pelletier, Y., with others - see Aristotle
Pelorson, J-M. Les "letrados" juristes castillans sous Philippe III.
  F. Márquez Villanueva, 240(HR): Spring85-201
Peltason, T. Reading "In Memoriam."
  A.S. Byatt, 617(TLS):14Nov86-1274
Pelzer, K.J. Planters Against Peasants.
  J.R. Bowen, 293(JASt):Feb85-469
Peña, M. The Texas-Mexican Conjunto.
  J.H. Cowley, 617(TLS):24Jan86-98
  D.W. Dickey, 187:Fall86-553
Peña Pérez, F.J. Documentación del monasterio de San Juan de Burgos (1091-1400).
  D. Gifford, 304(JHP):Fall85-72
Penavin, O., ed. Jugoszláviai magyar népmesék.
  K. Horn, 196:Band26Heft1/2-187
Penelhum, T. Butler.
  R. Swinburne, 617(TLS):21Feb86-202
Penelhum, T. God and Skepticism.
  W.P. Alston, 482(PhR):Oct85-599
  J.C.A. Gaskin, 518:Apr85-124
  B. Langtry, 63:Dec85-579
  R. Swinburne, 311(JP):Jan85-46
Peng, F.C.C., ed. Towards a Neurology of Language.
  M. Humes-Bartlo, 350:Dec86-963
Peng Zeyi. Shijiu shiji houbanqi de Zhongguo caizheng yu jingji.
  W.T. Rowe, 293(JASt):May85-607
Penkower, M.N. The Jews Were Expendable.*
  E. Matz, 390:Apr85-55
Pennachioni, I. La Nostalgie en images.
  J. Paulhan, 207(FR):Feb86-504
Penner, J. Private Parties.
  R.L. Johnson, 573(SSF):Fall85-481
Pennington, E.C. William Edward West, 1788-1857.
  K. Manthorne, 127:Winter85-375
Pennington, K. Pope and Bishops.
  R.H. Helmholz, 589:Oct85-1011
  B. Lyon, 377:Jul85-120
Pennington, K. - see Johannes Teutonicus
Pennington, R. A Descriptive Catalogue of the Etched Work of Wenceslaus Hollar 1607-1677.
  S.T. Fisher, 570(SQ):Winter85-510
  S. Tyacke, 354:Sep85-280
Pennock, J.R. and J.W. Chapman, eds. NOMOS XXV.
  C. Pateman, 185:Jan86-375
Penny, N., ed. Reynolds.
  F. Haskell, 453(NYRB):27Mar86-7
  P. Rogers, 617(TLS):31Jan86-117
Penrose, A. The Lives of Lee Miller.*
  M. Ignatieff, 617(TLS):3Jan86-5
  D. Thomas, 362:2Jan86-24
Pensado Ruiz, C. El orden histórico de los fonológicos.
  M. Torreblanca, 240(HR):Spring85-229
Pensom, R. Literary Technique in the "Chanson de Roland."*
  W.W. Kibler, 545(RPh):Aug85-117

Pentland, D.H. and H.C. Wolfart. Bibliography of Algonquian Linguistics.*
  R. Dominique, 320(CJL):Winter85-484
  K.B. Harder, 424:Dec85-285
Pepicello, W.J. and T.A. Green. The Language of Riddles.*
  J.H. McDowell, 292(JAF):Oct/Dec85-483
Pepper, L. Caught in Amber.
  R. Potter, 526:Summer85-84
Pepper, S. China's Universities.
  S. Rosen, 293(JASt):Aug85-817
Pepys, S. Journal.
  J. Aeply, 450(NRF):Apr85-101
Pequigney, J. Such is My Love.
  R.M. Adams, 453(NYRB):6Nov86-50
Peradotto, J. and J.P. Sullivan, eds. Women in the Ancient World.
  J. O'Brien, 124:May-Jun86-336
Percival, W.K. A Grammar of the Urbanised Toba-Batak of Medan.
  S. Cumming, 350Jun86-470
Percy, C. and J. Ridley - see Lutyens, E.
Percy, T. and J. Pinkerton. The Correspondence of Thomas Percy and John Pinkerton. (H.H. Wood, ed)
  P. Morère, 189(EA):Oct-Dec86-462
Percy, W. Lost in the Cosmos.
  E. Current-Garcia, 577(SHR):Spring85-191
Percy, W. The Moviegoers. The Last Gentleman. The Second Coming.
  L. Mackinnon, 617(TLS):16May86-536
Perdue, C., ed. Second Language Acquisition by Adult Immigrants.*
  W.E. Rutherford, 399(MLJ):Autumn85-297
  L. Selinker, 351(LL):Dec85-567
Perec, G. Penser, classer.
  J-L. Coatalem, 450(NRF):Dec85-82
Pereira, J.E.L. - see under Lopez Pereira, J.E.
Perelmuter Pérez, R. Noche intelectual.*
  M-C. Bénassy-Berling, 140(CH):Vol7No1-85
Perelomov, L.S. Konfutsianstvo i Legism v Politicheskoi Istorii Kitaya.
  D. Bodde, 293(JASt):Aug85-821
Pereña, L. and others - see Suarez, F.
Perera, V. Rites.
  S. Kellerman, 441:13Jul86-19
  J. Ure, 617(TLS):19Sep86-1027
Pérez, F.J.P. - see under Peña Pérez, F.J.
Pérez, J. Gonzalo Torrente Ballester.
  S. Miller, 238:May85-305
Pérez, J-C. La trayectoria novelística de Juan Goytisolo.
  G. Navajas, 238:May85-308
Pérez, R.P. - see under Perelmuter Pérez, R.
Pérez de Hita, G. Guerras civiles de Granada.* (S.M. Bryant, ed)
  M. Turón, 552(REH):May85-143
Pérez Firmat, G. Idle Fictions.*
  G. Navajas, 86(BHS):Jul85-316
Pérez Galdós, B. Los artículos políticos en la "Revista de España" 1871-1872. (B.J. Dendle and J. Schraibman, eds)
  E. Rodgers, 86(BHS):Apr85-206
Pérez Galdós, B. Misericordia.* (L. García Lorenzo, with C. Menéndez Onrubia, eds)
  B. Entenza de Solare, 547(RF):Band97 Heft1-115

Pérez Galdós, B. Torquemada.
  P. Ward, 441:30Nov86-26
Pérez Galdós, B. and J. de Cubas. Cartas sobre teatro (1893-1912). (C. de Zuleta, ed)
  J. Lowe, 86(BHS):Oct85-409
Pérez-Gómez, A. Architecture and the Crisis of Science.
  P. Tabor, 46:Apr85-83
Pérez-Ramos, B. Intelligenz und Politik im spanischen Bürgerkrieg, 1936-39.
  J.M. López de Abiada, 86(BHS):Jul85-318
Périlleux, G. Stig Dagerman et L'Existentialisme.
  L. Thompson, 563(SS):Winter85-85
Perina, R.M. Onganía. Levingston. Lanusse.
  G.W. Wynia, 263(RIB):Vol35No1-72
Perinbanayagam, R.S. The Karmic Theatre.
  S. Kemper, 293(JASt):Nov84-235
Perkins, E. - see Harpur, C.
Perkins, M.L. Diderot and the Time-Space Continuum.*
  D.J. Adams, 208(FS):Apr85-212
  A. Strugnell, 402(MLR):Jan85-168
Perkins, M.R. Modal Expressions in English.*
  J. Coates, 353:Vol23No4-625
  L. Hermerén, 320(CJL):Summer85-212
  H. Wekker, 297(JL):Sep85-520
Perkins, R.L., ed. History and System.
  D.R. Knowles, 479(PhQ):Apr85-199
Perkins, V.P. Film as Film.
  617(TLS):21Nov86-1327
Perkins, W.H., ed. Hearing Disorders. Language Handicaps in Children.
  M.W. Salus, 350:Jun86-478
Perkins, W.H., ed. Stuttering Disorders.
  N.F. Shepard, 350:Jun86-478
Perkyns, R., ed. Major Plays of the Canadian Theatre 1934-1984.
  C. Johnson, 108:Spring85-147
  D. Rubin, 99:Dec85-25
Perl, J.M. The Tradition of Return.*
  W.F. Cain, 125:Spring85-341
  295(JML):Nov85-419
Perl, M., ed. Estudios sobre el léxico del español en América.
  D. Gifford, 86(BHS):Apr85-193
Perle, G. The Operas of Alban Berg.* (Vol 1: Lulu.)
  J. Ronsheim, 42(AR):Fall85-496
  C. Spies, 414:Vol17No4-520
Perlina, N. Varieties of Poetic Utterance.
  C.J.G. Turner, 104(CASS):Summer85-228
Perlmutter, D.M. and C.G. Rosen, eds. Studies in Relational Grammar 2.
  R.C. De Armond, 320(CJL):Fall85-352
Perloff, M. The Dance of the Intellect.
  A.W. Litz, 617(TLS):10Oct86-1142
Perloff, M. The Poetics of Indeterminacy.*
  J.X. Cooper, 49:Jan85-91
  S. Neuman, 107(CRCL):Sep85-553
Perlot, J-N. Gold Seeker.* (H.R. Lamar, ed)
  J. Seelye, 617(TLS):6Jun86-612
Permjakov, G.L., ed. Paremiologičeskie issledovanija.
  W. Mieder, 574(SEEJ):Fall85-356
Pernot, L. Les "Discours siciliens" d'Aelius Aristide (Or. 5-6).*
  M.D. Macleod, 123:Vol35No2-254

Perosa, S. American Theories of the Novel, 1793-1903.*
J.E. Bassett, 141:Spring85-219
J.T. Matthews, 223:Spring85-95
Perosa, S. Teorie americane del romanzo, 1800-1900.
R. Asselineau, 189(EA):Oct-Dec86-494
Perowne, S. Hadrian.
617(TLS):28Mar86-343
Perreiah, A.R. - see Paulus Venetus
Perrie, M., ed. Protokoly pervogo s"ezda Partii sotsialistov-revoliutsionerov.
M. Melancon, 550(RusR):Oct85-424
Perrier, F. Voyages extraordinaires en Translacanie.
F. George, 98:Nov85-1084
Perrot, J-C. and S.J. Woolf. State and Statistics in France, 1789-1815.
A. Forrest, 617(TLS):21Mar86-310
Perrot, M. Jeunesse de la grève.
R.T. Denommé, 207(FR):May86-1011
Perrot, M. - see de Tocqueville, A.
Perrow, C. Norman Accidents.
T.D., 185:Oct85-226
Perry, D. Life Above the Jungle Floor.
R.B. Swain, 441:5Oct86-45
Perry, E.J., ed. Chinese Perspectives on the Nien Rebellion.*
E.S.K. Fung, 302:Vol21No1-74
Perry, G. The Great British Picture Show. (2nd ed)
D. Robinson, 617(TLS):17Jan86-69
Perry, L. Intellectual Life in America.
J. Campbell, 619:Summer85-425
J.C. Dawson, 658:Summer/Autumn85-196
Perry, R. The Celebrated Mary Astell.
M.A. Lourie, 441:2Nov86-24
Perry, R. - see Ballard, G.
Perry, R. and M.W. Brownley, eds. Mothering the Mind.
J.E. Hartman, 219(GaR):Winter85-899
M. Myers, 173(ECS):Fall85-107
Perry, S. and J. Dawson. Nightmare.*
J.K. Galbraith, 453(NYRB):10Apr86-11
Perryman, J., ed. The King of Tars.*
M. Mills, 382(MAE):1985/2-301
Perse, S. Anabase.* (A. Henry, ed)
M.A. Caws, 207(FR):Feb86-475
The Earl of Perth, ed. A Tour in Scotland 1863.
A. Bell, 617(TLS):17Jan86-71
Pertschuk, M. Giant Killers.
D. Murray, 441:28Dec86-19
Pertwee, M. Do Not Disturb.
D. Devlin, 157:No155-49
Perugi, M. - see Pascoli, G.
Pérus, F. Historia y crítica literaria.
P. Hulme, 86(BHS):Apr85-219
Peschel, R.E. and E.R. When a Doctor Hates a Patient.
Y. Baskin, 441:5Oct86-54
Pesenti, T. Professori e promotori di medicina nello Studio di Padova dal 1405 al 1509.
H.S. Matsen, 551(RenQ):Winter85-718
Peset, J.L. and E. Hernández Sandoica. Estudiantes de Alcalá.
M. Cavillac, 92(BH):Jul-Dec84-571
Peshkin, A. God's Choice.
K. Leishman, 61:Nov86-135
T. Teachout, 129:Sep86-66
Pessen, E. The Log Cabin Myth.*
617(TLS):10Oct86-1147

Pessoa, F. Selected Poems. (2nd ed)
J. Parker, 86(BHS):Apr85-215
Peter, L.J. The Peter Pyramid.
J. Kaufman, 441:2Feb86-17
Peter of Waltham. "Remediarium conversorum." (J. Gildea, ed)
C. Straw, 589:Oct85-1058
Péteri, G. Effects of World War I.
639(VQR):Summer85-84
Peters, A. Cabinetmaking.
R. Carter, 46:Jul85-78
R. Grant, 324:May86-417
Peters, A.K., ed. Jean Cocteau and the French Scene.
R. Craft, 453(NYRB):13Feb86-28
Peters, E. The Raven in the Foregate.
T.J. Binyon, 617(TLS):30Oct86-1115
Peters, E. Torture.*
P. Singer, 453(NYRB):27Feb86-27
Peters, F.E. Children of Abraham.
M. Swartz, 318(JAOS):Jul-Sep84-592
Peters, F.E. Jerusalem.*
R.C. Smail, 453(NYRB):10Apr86-42
Peters, H. Das mittelenglische Wortfeld "schlecht/böse" Synchronisch-diachronische Darstellung seiner semantischen Struktur.
E.G. Stanley, 447(N&Q):Sep84-419
Peters, J. From Time Immemorial.*
Y. Porath, 453(NYRB):16Jan86-36
D. Stone, 390:Jan85-60
Peters, M. Mrs. Pat.
R. Jackson, 610:Spring85-80
C.M. Mazer, 612(ThS):Nov85-207
K. Worth, 611(TN):Vol39No2-88
Peters, R. and T. Sodmann - see Lasch, A.
Peters, S. Los objetivos de la teoría lingüística.
J.C. Moreno Cabrera, 548:Jan-Jun85-225
Peters, S. and E. Saarinen, eds. Processes, Beliefs and Questions.
J. Groenendijk and M. Stokhof, 603: Vol9No3-409
Peters, U. Literatur in der Stadt.
F.H. Bäuml, 301(JEGP):Apr85-302
E. Kleinschmidt, 680(ZDP):Band104Heft3-444
H. Parigger, 684(ZDA):Band114Heft2-55
Peters, U.H. Hölderlin.
R. Reschke, 654(WB):1/1985-152
Petersen, K. Die "Gruppe 1925."
A. Lixl, 406:Fall85-368
G.B. Pickar, 133:Band17Heft3/4-365
Petersmann, G. Themenführung und Motiventfaltung in der Monobiblos des Properz.
J.H. Brouwers, 394:Vol38fasc1/2-231
Peterson, A. Victorian Masters of Mystery.
E.S. Lauterbach, 395(MFS):Summer85-382
G.B. Tennyson, 445(NCF):Jun85-118
Peterson, L.H. Victorian Autobiography.
A.O.J. Cockshut, 617(TLS):1Aug86-849
Peterson, L.S., ed. Greening Wheat.
C.M. Wright, 649(WAL):Feb86-366
Peterson, M. Mercy Flights.
L.Z. Bloom, 573(SSF):Fall85-485
Peterson, N. Photographic Art.
R. Woodfield, 89(BJA):Summer85-292
Peterson, R.F. William Butler Yeats.*
K. Williamson, 447(N&Q):Jun84-275
Peterson, R.S. Imitation and Praise in the Poems of Ben Jonson.*
B. Gibbons, 677(YES):Vol 15-285

Peterson, S. Lucy M. Lewis.
  L.K. New, 139:Feb/Mar85-52
Peterson, W.S. A Bibliography of the
  Kelmscott Press.*
  D. McKitterick, 78(BC):Summer85-241
Peterson, W.S. - see "Browning Institute
  Studies"
Petersson, O. Folkstyrelse och statsmakt
  i Norden.
  B.J. Nordstrom, 562(Scan):Nov85-247
Petit, J., ed. Barbey d'Aurevilly, II.
  P.J. Yarrow, 208(FS):Jul85-351
"Petit Larousse illustré 1984."
  J.E. Joseph, 399(MLJ):Winter85-415
Petitmengin, P. and others. Pélagie la
  Pénitente.
  P. Meyvaert, 589:Oct85-1013
Petrarch. Francesco Petrarca: "Letters on
  Familiar Matters." (A.S. Bernardo,
  trans)
  T.G. Bergin, 545(RPh):Feb85-410
  L.V.R., 568(SCN):Spring-Summer85-27
Petras, R. and K. Inside Track.
  S. Salisbury, 441:4May86-41
Petri, F. Der Teutschen Weissheit. (W.
  Mieder, ed)
  L. Röhrich, 196:Band26Heft1/2-188
Petrie, G. Hollywood Destinies.
  S.S. Prawer, 617(TLS):21Feb86-200
  H. Rubin, 441:8Jun86-37
Petrie, J. Petrarch: The Augustan Poets,
  the Italian Tradition and the Canzoniere.
  J.C. Barnes, 402(MLR):Jul85-731
  A.S. Bernardo, 551(RenQ):Summer85-320
  A. de Colombí-Monguió, 545(RPh):Feb86-
  401
  K. Foster, 278(IS):Vol40-118
Petrone, G. Teatro antico e inganno.*
  M. Hammond, 124:Sep-Oct85-66
  F. Muecke, 67:May85-81
Petrone, P., ed. First People, First
  Voices.*
  L.R., 102(CanL):Winter84-186
Petroni, F. Svevo.
  E. Saccone, 400(MLN):Jan85-188
Petruck, P.R., ed. The Camera Viewed.
  Y. Michaud, 98:Aug-Sep85-761
Petrushevsky, I.P. Islam in Iran.
  F. Halliday, 617(TLS):20Jun86-667
Petry, A. The Street.
  A. Maja-Pearce, 617(TLS):2May86-479
Pettersson, O. and H. Åkerberg. Interpret-
  ing Religious Phenomena.
  E. Barker, 488:Mar85-88
Pettigrew, E. The Silent Enemy.
  W.N., 102(CanL):Spring85-184
Pettigrew, J. - see Browning, R.
Pettijohn, F.J. Memoirs of an Unrepentant
  Field Geologist.
  M. Corlett, 529(QQ):Summer85-420
Pettinelli, R.A. - see under Alhaique Pet-
  tenelli, R.
Pettit, N. - see Edwards, J.
Pettiward, R. The Last Cream Bun.
  M. Bream, 364:Oct85-104
Petzold, B. Goethe und der Mahayana Bud-
  dhismus. (J.P. Strelka, ed and trans)
  H. Eichner, 406:Winter85-469
Petzold, D. Das englische Kunstmärchen im
  neunzehnten Jahrhundert.
  A. Klein, 38:Band103Heft1/2-231
Pevear, R. Exchanges.
  A. Hudgins, 434:Summer86-526

Peyramaure, M. Le Printemps des pierres.
  D. Festa-McCormick, 207(FR):Oct85-154
Peytard, J. and others. Littérature et
  classe de langue.
  E. Bautier-Castaing, 209(FM):Apr85-131
Pfaelzer, J. The Utopian Novel in America,
  1886-1896.
  D. Ketterer, 26(ALR):Spring/Autumn85-
  285
Pfaff, F. The Cinema of Ousmane Sembene.
  C. Taylor, 18:Oct85-77
Pfanner, H.F. Exile in New York.*
  A. Arnold, 564:Sep85-240
  R.F. Bell, 133:Band18Heft2-184
Pfeffer, J.A., ed. Studies in Descriptive
  German Grammar.
  W.P. Ahrens, 350:Mar86-217
Pfeffer, L. Religion, State, and the
  Burger Court.
  42(AR):Summer85-367
Pfeiffer, E. - see Andreas-Salomé, L.
Pfeil, F. Goodman 2020.
  G. Jonas, 441:20Apr86-27
Pfister, M. and B. Schulte-Middelich, eds.
  Die "Nineties."
  L. Hönnighausen, 72:Band222Heft1-195
Pflaum, H.G. and H.H. Prinzler. Le film
  en République Fédérale d'Allemagne.
  H-J. Greif, 193(ELit):Spring-Summer85-
  209
Phaneuf, R. Ille.
  R. Giroux, 102(CanL):Spring85-124
Phelan, J. Worlds from Words.*
  J. Frank, 569(SR):Summer85-493
Phelan, N. The Voice Beyond the Trees.
  J. Crace, 617(TLS):31Jan86-112
Phelps, J.K. and A.E. Nourse. The Hidden
  Addiction.
  D. Breo, 441:23Mar86-46
Phelps, R. - see Colette
Philbrick, T. and M. - see Cooper, J.F.
Philip, I. The Bodleian Library in the
  Seventeenth and Eighteenth Centuries.*
  J.C.T. Oates, 354:Jun85-189
Philip, N. and V. Neuberg - see Dickens, C.
Philipp, W. - see Schmidt, C.D., with
  others
Philippidis, D., ed. Griechische tradi-
  tionelle Architektur. (Vols 1 and 2)
  H.J. Kienast, 43:Band15Heft1-94
Philips, M., ed. Philosophy and Science
  Fiction.
  W.M. Schuyler, Jr., 561(SFS):Jul85-225
Phillip, W. Ausgewählte Schriften. (H-J.
  Torke, ed)
  R.P. Bartlett, 575(SEER):Apr85-295
Phillips, K.C. Language and Class in Vic-
  torian England.*
  F. Austin, 179(ES):Dec85-564
  R.B. Le Page, 353:Vol123No1-167
Phillips, A. - see Lamb, C.
Phillips, B. Peterwell.
  G. William, 83:Autumn85-224
Phillips, C. A State of Independence.
  V. Bogdanor, 362:17Apr86-28
Phillips, D. Ella.
  R. Kaveney, 617(TLS):23May86-553
Phillips, D.E. Student Protest, 1960-
  1970. (rev)
  J.R. Cox, 583:Spring86-286

Phillips, G. The Imagery of the "Libro de Buen Amor."*
G.B. Gybbon-Monypenny, 86(BHS):Jan85-136
Phillips, G. and N. Whiteside. Casual Labour.
P.J. Waller, 617(TLS):7Feb86-134
Phillips, H. - see Chaucer, G.
Phillips, J., with J. Jerome. Papa John.
D. Finkle, 441:17Aug86-3
Phillips, J.A. Machine Dreams.*
639(VQR):Winter85-23
Phillips, J.C. A Natural History of the Ducks.
N. Bryant, 441:7Dec86-68
Phillips, K.P. Staying on Top.*
639(VQR):Spring85-58
Phillips, L.W. - see Hemingway, E.
Phillips, M. California Dreamin'.
D. Finkle, 441:17Aug86-3
Phillips, M.M. Erasmus and the Northern Renaissance.
M.J. Heath, 447(N&Q):Jun84-260
Phillips, N. Sijobang.*
J.L. Peacock, 355(LSoc):Mar85-146
Phillips, P. The Adventurous Muse.
J. Chalker, 597(SN):Vol57No1-122
I. Simon, 179(ES):Dec85-554
Phillips, P.T. The Sectarian Spirit.*
J. Kenyon, 635(VPR):Winter85-155
Phillips, R. - see Schwartz, D.
Phillips, R. - see Welch, D.
Phillips, R.C., Jr. Struthers Burt.
D.E. Wylder, 649(WAL):Aug85-187
Phillips, R.L. War and Justice.
S.L., 185:Jan86-457
Phillips, S.S., D. Travis and W.J. Naef. André Kertész.*
A. Anderson, 62:Dec85-14
H. Martin, 507:Nov/Dec85-118
Phillips, W. A Partisan View.*
L. Mellichamp, 396(ModA):Spring85-177
Phillipson, M. Painting, Language, and Modernity.
S. Bann, 617(TLS):7Feb86-144
J.C. Gilmour, 290(JAAC):Spring86-297
Philombe, R. Tales from Cameroon.
T. Ngenge, 538(RAL):Fall85-397
Philoponus, I. On the Accent of Homonyms. (L.W. Daly, ed)
B. Baldwin, 589:Apr85-418
"Philosophies de l'Université."
A. Villani, 192(EP):Apr-Jun85-272
Phipps, C. - see Villiers, A.
Pholien, G. Les deux "Vie de Jésus" de Renan.
K. Gore, 208(FS):Jan85-92
"Phonologica 1976." (W.U. Dressler and O.E. Pfeiffer, eds)
P. Swiggers, 260(IF):Band90-239
Photius. Epistulae et Amphilochia. (Vol 1) (B. Laourdas and L.G. Westerink, eds)
R. Browning, 303(JoHS):Vol 105-247
Piaia, G. Vestigia philosophorum.
B. Faes de Mottoni, 319:Apr86-266
Piana, C. Il "Liber Secretus Iuris Caesarei" dell' Università di Bologna (1451-1500).
H.S. Matsen, 551(RenQ):Winter85-718
Pianu, G. Ceramiche etrusche sovradipinte.
R. Rebuffat, 555:Vol59fasc1-158
F.R.S. Ridgway, 123:Vol35No1-166

Piattelli-Palmarini, M., ed. Language and Learning.* (French title: Théories de l'apprentissage. Spanish title: Teorías del lenguaje, teorías del aprendizaje.)
F. Abad, 548:Jul-Dec85-469
Picard, H.R. Dichtung und Religion.
G. Kranz, 52:Band20Heft1-77
Picasso, P. Je Suis le Cahier. (A. and M. Glimcher, eds)
T. Hilton, 617(TLS):19Sep86-1034
R. Johnson, 441:7Dec86-72
Picchio, L.S. - see under Stegagno Picchio, L.
Picchio, R. and H. Goldblatt, eds. Aspects of the Slavic Language Question. (Vol 1)
M.J. Elson, 574(SEEJ):Fall85-338
D.A. Frick, 350:Jun86-466
Picchio, R. and H. Goldblatt, eds. Aspects of the Slavic Language Question. (Vol 2)
D.A. Frick, 350:Jun86-466
G.Y. Shevelov, 279:Vol30-173
Picchio Simonelli, M. Figure foniche dal Petrarca ai petrarchisti.
A.L. Lepschy, 545(RPh):Nov85-269
Piccone, P. Italian Marxism.
S. Aronowitz, 275(IQ):Summer/Fall84-205
Pichois, C. - see Colette
Pichois, C. and V., with A. Brunet, eds. Album Colette.
D. Coward, 208(FS):Jul85-363
Picken, L., ed. Musica Asiatica 4.
T.E. Miller, 187:Winter86-175
Pickens, R.T., ed. The Sower and His Seed.*
E.J. Burns, 400(MLN):Sep85-905
A.H. Diverres, 208(FS):Oct85-448
H. Klüppelholz, 72:Band222Heft2-444
Pickering, A. Constructing Quarks.
J.T. Cushing, 486:Dec85-640
Pickering, P. Perfect English.
T. Fitton, 617(TLS):31Oct86-1225
Pickering, R. Paul Valéry: poète en prose.*
P. Collier, 402(MLR):Jan85-177
Pickering, S.F., Jr. A Continuing Education.
G.C., 569(SR):Fall85-xcii
Pickford, C.E. and R. Last, eds. The Arthurian Bibliography.* (Vol 1)
M. Lambert, 402(MLR):Oct85-893
Pickford, C.E., R. Last and C.R. Barker, eds. The Arthurian Bibliography. (Vol 2)
F. Alexander, 541(RES):Feb85-143
J.M. Cowen, 447(N&Q):Dec84-528
P.J.C. Field, 382(MAE):1985/2-346
M. Foley, 589:Jul85-751
M. Lambert, 402(MLR):Oct85-893
Pickowicz, P.G. Marxist Literary Thought in Chinese.
L. Feigon, 293(JASt):Aug85-818
T. Huters, 116:Jul84-125
Pickthall, M. Said the Fisherman.
M. Ruthven, 617(TLS):5Sep86-964
Pico della Mirandola, G. Über die Vorstellung/De imaginatione. (E. Kessler, ed and trans)
M. Lentzen, 547(RF):Band97Heft2/3-339
B. Pinchard, 192(EP):Oct-Dec85-567

Picone, M., G. Di Stefano and P.D. Stewart, eds. La nouvelle.
  V. Marmo, 379(MedR):Aug85-291
Pidal, R.M. - see under Menéndez Pidal, R.
Pieiller, É. Eldorado et cavaliers.
  F. de Martinoir, 450(NRF):Apr85-88
Pielke, R.G. You Say You Want a Revolution.
  J. Fleming, 441:17Aug86-23
Pierce, C.E., Jr. The Religious Life of Samuel Johnson.*
  N.J. Hudson, 447(N&Q):Jun84-266
Pierce, F. Alonso de Ercilla y Zúñiga.
  J.B. Avalle-Arce, 240(HR):Autumn85-512
Pierce, R.A. - see "The Russian-American Company"
Piercy, M. My Mother's Body.
  S.M. Gilbert, 491:Dec85-159
Piercy, M. Parti-Colored Blocks for a Quilt.
  R. McDowell, 249(HudR):Autumn85-514
Piercy, M. Stone, Paper, Knife.*
  A. Hudgins, 434:Summer86-526
Piercy, M. Woman on the Edge of Time.
  C. Cramer, 145(Crit):Summer86-229
Pierret, J-M. Phonétique du français.
  A.W. Grundstrom, 207(FR):Oct85-168
Pierrot, J. The Decadent Imagination.
  A. Demaitre, 577(SHR):Summer85-276
Pierson, R.H. Guide to Spanish Idioms/Guía de Modismos Españoles.
  H. Ruiz, 399(MLJ):Winter85-440
Pierssens, M. Lautréamont.
  J-P. Barou, 98:Oct85-1020
Pietrangeli, C. and others. The Sistine Chapel.
  J. Russell, 441:7Dec86-11
Pietrow, B. Stalinismus Sicherheit Offensive.
  H. Hanak, 575(SEER):Oct85-617
Pifer, A. and L. Bronte, eds. Our Aging Society.
  G. Collins, 441:25May86-14
Pigeot, J. and K. Kosugi - see "Le Chrysanthème solitaire"
Piggott, G.L. and A. Grafstein, eds. An Ojibway Lexicon.
  R. Rhodes, 320(CJL):Winter85-453
Pigman, G.W. 3d. Grief and English Renaissance Elegy.
  A.L. Prescott, 604:Fall85-61
Pignatti, T. and G. Romanelli. Drawings from Venice.
  F. Russell, 324:Jan86-130
Piirainen, I.T., comp. Frühneuhochdeutsche Bibliographie.
  E. Neuss, 685(ZDL):3/1985-363
Piirainen, I.T. Das Iglauer Bergrecht nach einer Handschrift aus Schemnitz.
  E. Neuss, 685(ZDL):3/1985-369
Pike, B. The Image of the City in Modern Literature.*
  A. Gelley, 149(CLS):Summer85-284
Pike, D. Lukács and Brecht.
  639(VQR):Autumn85-122
Pike, K.L. Linguistic Concepts.*
  E. Ternes, 685(ZDL):1/1985-90
Pikoulis, J. The Art of William Faulkner.*
  J.J. Tucker, 106:Spring85-83
  J.S. Whitley, 447(N&Q):Dec84-570
Pileggi, N. Wiseguy.
  P-L. Adams, 61:Jun86-84

[continued]

[continuing]
  M. Kempton, 453(NYRB):8May86-43
  V. Patrick, 441:26Jan86-7
  442(NY):17Feb86-104
Pilger, J. Heroes.
  P. Barker, 617(TLS):11Jul86-757
Pilgrim, R. You Precious Winners All.
  K. Brown, 617(TLS):22Aug86-917
Pilkington, J. Stark Young.
  R.C. Petersen, 585(SoQ):Spring86-86
Pillar, P.R. Negotiating Peace.
  C. Debenedetti, 529(QQ):Spring85-162
Pilleux, M. Formación de palabras en español.
  F. Nuessel, 239:Vol 1No1-139
Pimlott, B. - see Dalton, H.
Pina, F.H. - see under Hernández Pina, F.
de Pina-Cabral, J. Sons of Adam, Daughters of Eve.
  J. du Boulay, 617(TLS):5Sep86-963
de Pina Martins, J.V. - see de Carvalho, J.
Pinault, M. Dessin et Science.
  90:Dec85-917
Pinborg, J. Medieval Semantics.
  P.O. Lewry, 589:Apr85-488
Pincher, C. Too Secret Too Long.*
  N. Weyl, 390:Jun/Jul85-54
  639(VQR):Summer85-94
Pinches, T.G. Cuneiform Texts from Babylonian Tablets in the British Museum, #55, #56, and #57. (I.L. Finkel, ed)
  G. Frame, 318(JAOS):Oct-Dec84-745
Pincus-Witten, R. Eye to Eye.*
  D. Carrier, 55:Jan85-38
Pindar. Selections from Pindar.* (G. Kirkwood, ed)
  R. Scodel, 122:Jul85-266
Pineda, C. Frieze.
  D. Mason, 441:23Nov86-24
Ping-ying, H. - see under Hsieh Ping-ying
Pinget, R. Baga.
  C. Dis, 450(NRF):Jul-Aug85-150
Pinget, R. Someone.
  J. Byrne, 532(RCF):Fall85-184
  R.A. Champagne, 399(MLJ):Autumn85-307
Pinguet, M. La Mort volontaire au Japon.
  J-P. Guinle, 450(NRF):Feb85-101
  C. Thomas, 98:Apr85-382
Pinkerton, H. Poems, 1946-1976.
  D.E. Stanford, 385(MQR):Summer86-607
Pinkney, D. Decisive Years in France 1840-1847.
  T. Judt, 617(TLS):26Sep86-1069
Pinkus, B. The Soviet Government and the Jews, 1948-1967.*
  L. Hirszowicz, 575(SEER):Oct85-625
Pinnells, J. Style and Structure in the Novel.
  P-G. Boucé, 189(EA):Oct-Dec86-452
  S.G. Kellman, 395(MFS):Summer85-449
Pinney, T. - see Kipling, R.
Pinoteau, H. Vingt-cinq ans d'études dynastiques.
  E.A.R. Brown, 589:Jan85-227
Pinsky, R. History of My Heart.*
  S.C., 219(GaR):Spring85-213
  R. Mitchell, 491:Jan86-236
Pinto, E. Edgar Poe et l'art d'inventer.*
  A. Moeglin-Delcroix, 192(EP):Oct-Dec85-568
Pinto, J.A. The Trevi Fountain.
  F. Haskell, 617(TLS):15Aug86-892

Pinxten, R., I. van Dooren and F. Harvey. The Anthropology of Space.*
  M.K. Brady, 292(JAF):Jul/Sep85-339
Pioletti, A. Forme del racconto arturiano.
  C. Lee, 379(MedR):Aug85-288
Piper, D., general ed. A-Z of Arts and Artists.
  E. Young, 39:Jun85-436
Piperek, K. Zeichen und Grammatik.
  H-G. Ruprecht, 320(CJL):Summer85-238
Pirazzoli-t'Serstevens, M. The Han Dynasty.
  J.L. Dull, 293(JASt):May85-608
Pirckheimer, W. Eckius dedolatus. (N. Holzberg, ed)
  T.W. Best, 133:Band17Heft3/4-323
Pirie, D.B. William Wordsworth.*
  R. Sharrock, 447(N&Q):Mar84-143
Pirie, D.B. - see Empson, W.
Pirog, G. Aleksandr Blok's "Ital'ianskie Stikhi."*
  M. Banjanin, 574(SEEJ):Spring85-107
  J. Graffy, 402(MLR):Jul85-766
  A. Pyman, 575(SEER):Apr85-290
Piron, A. Alexis Piron épistolier.* (G. von Proschwitz, ed)
  H-G. Funke, 547(RF):Band97Heft1-93
  H.G. Hall, 208(FS):Oct85-477
Pironon, J. Le Temps figé et l'inexprimable distance.
  I. Simon, 189(EA):Apr-Jun86-213
Pirro, A. L'ésthétique de Jean-Sébastien Bach.
  S. Daw, 415:Mar85-156
Pirrotta, N. Music and Culture in Italy from the Middle Ages to the Baroque.* (L. Lockwood and C. Wolff, eds)
  I. Fenlon, 415:Jul85-411
  L.L. Perkins, 551(RenQ):Autumn85-529
  F.W. Sternfeld, 410(M&L):Oct85-397
de Pisan, C. - see under Christine de Pisan
Pisano, R.G. A Leading Spirit in American Art.
  N. Cikovsky, Jr., 658:Winter85-304
Pistorius, G. Marcel Proust und Deutschland.
  H. Grauerholz-Heckmann, 72:Band222 Heft1-230
Pitkin, H.F. Fortune is a Woman.*
  D.R. Kelley, 551(RenQ):Summer85-321
Pitou, S. The Paris Opéra.* (Vol 1)
  P. Danchin, 612(ThS):May85-90
  W. Dean, 617(TLS):10Oct86-1138
  C.B. Schmidt, 317:Summer85-385
Pitou, S. The Paris Opéra. (Vol 2)
  W. Dean, 617(TLS):10Oct86-1138
Pitt, D.G. E.J. Pratt: The Truant Years 1882-1927.*
  B.N.S. Gooch, 376:Mar85-165
  A. McAuliffe, 150(DR):Winter84/85-804
  I.B. Nadel, 627(UTQ):Summer85-442
  C.M. Pfaff, 102(CanL):Fall85-89
  295(JML):Nov85-544
Pitt, J.C., ed. Philosophy in Economics.
  L.A. Boland, 488:Mar85-108
Pitt-Kethley, F. Sky Ray Lolly.
  A. Haverty, 617(TLS):1Aug86-839
Pittaluga, M.P. L'évolution de la langue commerciale.
  F. Martin-Berthet, 209(FM):Oct85-252
Pittaluga, S. - see Cornazani, A.

"I Pittori Bergamaschi dal XIII al XIX secolo: Il seicento II."
  K. Garlick, 39:Jan85-69
  E. Langmuir, 90:Feb85-99
Pivano, F. Hemingway.
  V. Meyers, 395(MFS):Winter85-735
Pizarro, F.A. - see under Astorquiza Pizarro, F.
Pizer, D., ed. Critical Essays on Theodore Dreiser.
  D. Seed, 677(YES):Vol 15-332
Pizer, D. Realism and Naturalism in Nineteenth-Century American Literature. (rev)
  E.N. Harbert, 587(SAF):Spring85-112
  G. Hendrick, 26(ALR):Spring/Autumn85-291
Pizzorusso, A. Analisi e Variazioni.*
  C. Dédéyan, 535(RHL):Mar/Apr85-332
Plain, B. The Golden Cup.
  N. Ramsey, 441:28Sep86-27
Plank, F., ed. Ergativity.
  M.S. Dryer, 320(CJL):Summer85-207
Plank, F. Morphologische (Ir-)Regularität-en.
  J.S. Barbour, 603:Vol9No1-146
Plank, F., ed. Objects.
  R.M.W. Dixon, 350:Jun86-437
Plant, R. Hegel.* (2nd ed)
  D.R. Knowles, 479(PhQ):Apr85-199
Plant, R., ed. The Penguin Book of Modern Canadian Drama. (Vol 1)
  C. Johnson, 108:Spring85-147
  D. Rubin, 99:Dec85-25
Plant, R. The Pink Triangle.
  S. Salisbury, 441:16Nov86-25
Plante, D. The Catholic.*
  J. Moynahan, 441:13Apr86-13
Plante, R. Le Train sauvage.
  J.M. Paterson, 102(CanL):Spring85-159
Plantinga, A. and N. Wolterstorff, eds. Faith and Rationality.*
  R. Swinburne, 311(JP):Jan85-46
Plantinga, L., ed. Anthology of Romantic Music.
  H. Macdonald, 415:Oct85-602
Plantinga, L. Romantic Music.
  C. Hatch, 143:Issue37/38-187
  H. Macdonald, 415:Oct85-602
Plate, B., ed. Gregorius auf dem Stein.
  H. Freytag, 680(ZDP):Band104Heft3-447
Plater, A. The Beiderbecke Tapes.
  T.J. Binyon, 617(TLS):27Jun86-711
Plath, D.W., ed. Work and Lifecourse in Japan.*
  D. Kondo, 293(JASt):Nov84-206
Plato. The Being of the Beautiful.* (S. Benardete, ed and trans)
  R.G.M., 185:Jul86-912
  V. Tejera, 319:Jan86-115
Plato. Hippias Major.* (P. Woodruff, ed and trans)
  C. Kahn, 466:Vol3-261
Plato. Phaidros, Parmenides, Briefe. (G. Eigler, ed) (Vol 5 ed by D. Kurz)
  E. Martens, 489(PJGG):Band92Heft1-217
Plato. Plato's "Euthyphro." (I. Walker, ed)
  R.J. Cavalier, 124:Jul-Aug86-421
Plato. Two Comic Dialogues. (P. Woodruff, trans)
  J.F. Finamore, 124:Sep-Oct85-50

Pontaut, A. Madame Jocaste.
  R. Benson, 102(CanL):Spring85-171
Pontévia, J-M. La Peinture, masque et
  miroir.
  F. Wybrands, 450(NRF):Jan85-104
Ponting, C. Whitehall.
  M., 176:Jun86-26
  O.R. McGregor, 617(TLS):4Apr86-348
  M. Parris, 362:20Mar86-25
  362:4Dec86-32
Poole, F. and M. Fanzi. Revolution in the
  Philippines.
  I. Buruma, 453(NYRB):16Jan86-27
  T.C. Holyoke, 42(AR):Winter85-118
Poole, M. The Wood Engravings of John
  Farleigh.
  D. Chambers, 503:Spring85-43
Pooley, R. - see Gascoigne, G.
Poortvliet, R. Noah's Ark.
  S.R. Sanders, 441:7Dec86-68
Poovey, M. The Proper Lady and the Woman
  Writer.*
  J.V. Catano, 599:Fall85-403
  K. Fowler, 661(WC):Fall85-199
  A.G. Fredman, 340(KSJ):Vol34-190
  S. Morgan, 141:Winter85-100
  E.L. Pugh, 125:Winter85-222
  M.E.S., 506(PSt):Dec85-100
  J. Wilt, 405(MP):May86-434
Popadić, H. Deutsche Seidlungsmundarten
  aus Slawonien/Jugoslawien.
  F. Patocka, 685(ZDL):1/1985-112
Pope, A. The Last and Greatest Art.* (M.
  Mack, ed)
  V. Carretta, 173(ECS):Summer86-560
Pope, A. Pope: Poems.
  S.W.R. Smith, 566:Spring86-220
Pope, A. The Prose Works of Alexander
  Pope. (Vol 2) (R. Cowler, ed)
  R. Halsband, 441:5Oct86-20
Pope, D. Galleon.
  S. Altinel, 617(TLS):18Jul86-793
Pope, D. Ramage's Challenge.
  S. Altinel, 617(TLS):21Feb86-198
Pope, D. A Separate Vision.
  V.F. Harris, 30:Fall85-91
  S. Juhasz, 115:Summer85-377
  L.W. Wagner, 27(AL):Mar85-147
Pope-Hennessy, J. Cellini.*
  S.B. Butters, 617(TLS):28Mar86-319
  C. Hope, 453(NYRB):29May86-7
  G. Steiner, 442(NY):7Apr86-96
Popelar, I. - see Baldinger, K.
"Popol vuh."* (D. Tedlock, ed and trans)
  G. Brotherston, 617(TLS):18Apr86-407
Popova, O. Russian Illuminated Manu-
  scripts.
  W.F. Ryan, 78(BC):Winter85-526
Popovac, G. Wet Paint.
  J. Marcus, 441:28Dec86-24
Popovic, A. and G. Weinstein, eds. Les
  Ordres mystiques dans l'Islam.
  J. Baldick, 617(TLS):26Sep86-1073
Popovsky, M. The Vavilov Affair.* Delo
  Akademika Vavilova.
  Y.M. Rabkin, 550(RusR):Jul85-312
Poppe, A. The Rise of Christian Russia.
  S. Franklin, 575(SEER):Jul85-448
Popper, K.R. Die beiden Grundprobleme der
  Erkenntnistheorie. (T.E. Hansen, ed)
  J. Wettersten, 488:Dec85-487

Popper, K.R. The Open Universe.* (W.W.
  Bartley 3d, ed)
  M. Sachs, 488:Jun85-205
Popper, K.R. Postscript to The Logic of
  Scientific Discovery.* (Vol 1) (W.W.
  Bartley 3d, ed)
  N. Capaldi, 543:Jun85-900
  J.N. Hattiangadi, 488:Dec85-461
  A. O'Hear, 393(Mind):Jul85-453
Popper, K.R. Postscript to The Logic of
  Scientific Discovery.* (Vol 2) (W.W.
  Bartley 3d, ed)
  A. O'Hear, 393(Mind):Jul85-453
Popper, K.R. Postscript to The Logic of
  Scientific Discovery.* (Vol 3) (W.W.
  Bartley 3d, ed)
  A. O'Hear, 393(Mind):Jul85-454
  M. Sachs, 488:Sep85-321
Poppi, A., ed. Scienza e filosofia all'-
  Università di Padova nel Quattrocento.
  N.G. Siraisi, 551(RenQ):Summer85-309
Pops, M. Home Remedies.
  P. West, 560:Summer85-212
Por, P. Epochenstil.
  A. Hartmann, 549(RLC):Jan-Mar85-85
  I. Hoesterey, 343:Heft11-121
Porath, Y. In Search of Arab Unity 1930-
  1945.
  A. Hourani, 617(TLS):21Nov86-1297
Porcher, M-C. Figures de style en san-
  skrit.
  K. Bhattacharya, 318(JAOS):Apr-Jun84-
  339
Porrmann, M. Grabbe — Dichter für das
  Vaterland.
  G. Piens, 654(WB):5/1985-873
Porta, G. - see Anonimo romano
Porte, J., ed. Emerson.
  B.L. Packer, 591(SIR):Winter85-575
Porte, J. - see Emerson, R.W.
Porter, A. Hidden Agenda.
  D.E. Westlake, 441:27Apr86-35
Porter, A., M. Spence and R. Thompson.
  The Energy Fix.
  M. Warnock, 617(TLS):17Oct86-1155
Porter, B.D. The USSR in Third World Con-
  flicts.*
  S.N. MacFarlane, 104(CASS):Spring85-99
Porter, C.M. The Eagle's Nest.
  N. Eldredge, 441:19Oct86-39
Porter, D. The Pursuit of Crime.*
  W.W. Stowe, 107(CRCL):Sep85-433
Porter, J., ed. The Ballad Image.*
  G. Boyes, 203:Vol96No1-125
  D.M. Dugaw, 292(JAF):Jan/Mar85-112
  P. Tyler, 650(WF):Jan85-66
  N. Würzbach, 196:Band26Heft1/2-193
Porter, L. Lester Young.
  G. Giddins, 617(TLS):11Apr86-402
Porter, P. Fast Forward.*
  H.S. Bhabra, 493:Apr85-62
Porter, R., ed. Patients and Practition-
  ers.
  L. Jordanova, 617(TLS):19Sep86-1024
Porter, T.M. The Rise of Statistical
  Thinking.
  M. Kline, 441:5Oct86-47
"Portrait of Mr. B."*
  M. Mudrick, 249(HudR):Autumn85-520
Porush, D. The Soft Machine.
  R.A. Schwartz, 561(SFS):Nov85-331

Posch, S. P. Ovidius Naso, "Tristia I."
(Vol 1)
E.J. Kenney, 123:Vol35No2-284
Posidonius. Poseidonios: Die Fragmente.*
(W. Theiler, ed)
É. des Places, 555:Vol59fasc1-114
Posner, D. Antoine Watteau.
P. Conisbee, 59:Sep85-359
D. Irwin, 83:Spring85-122
H. Opperman, 90:Dec85-913
Posner, G.L. and J. Ware. Mengele.
I. Hilton, 362:16Oct86-23
Posner, R. Rational Discourse and Poetic
Communication.*
B.M. Scherer, 679:Band16Heft2-375
Posner, R.A. The Federal Courts.*
639(VQR):Summer85-95
Posnock, R. Henry James and the Problem
of Robert Browning.*
T.J. Collins, 637(VS):Summer86-637
R.E. Gridley, 85(SBHC):Vol 13-117
C.D. Ryals, 27(AL):Oct85-505
F. Wegener, 432(NEQ):Dec85-622
Pospielovsky, D. The Russian Church Under
the Soviet Regime, 1917-1982.
P. Valliere, 104(CASS):Spring85-80
Pospíšil, I. Ruská románová kronika.
R. Porter, 575(SEER):Oct85-586
Post, J.F.S. Henry Vaughan.*
C.C. Brown, 541(RES):May85-272
O. Johnson, 447(N&Q):Mar84-120
Postlethwaite, D. Making It Whole.*
G.B. Tennyson, 445(NCF):Dec85-364
R. Yeo, 637(VS):Summer86-620
Postlewait, T. - see Archer, W.
Postman, N. Amusing Ourselves to Death.*
A. Howard, 617(TLS):21Feb86-189
D. Sexton, 364:Mar86-96
Poteat, P.L. Walker Percy and the Old Mod-
ern Age.
R.H. Brinkmeyer, Jr., 578:Spring86-132
L. Mackinnon, 617(TLS):16May86-536
W.J. Stuckey, 395(MFS):Winter85-749
Potel, J-Y., ed. L'État de la France et
de ses habitants.
A. Prévos, 207(FR):Feb86-511
Potok, A. My Life With Goya.
J. Neugeboren, 441:7Sep86-22
442(NY):27Oct86-144
Potter, D. Ticket to Ride.
W.S. Gilbert, 362:2Oct86-23
P. Smelt, 617(TLS):17Oct86-1169
Potter, D. Waiting for the Boat.
A. Rissik, 157:No158-46
Potter, J. The Liberty We Seek.*
L.D. Cress, 106:Fall85-307
G. Stewart, 529(QQ):Autumn85-593
Potter, J. The Taking of Agnes.*
P. Parker, 364:Apr/May85-152
Potter, J. To a Violent Grave.
P-L. Adams, 61:Jan86-95
R. Kimball, 441:2Feb86-15
Potter, J., P. Stringer and M. Wetherell.
Social Texts and Context.
J. Brown and H. Giles, 307:Aug85-134
Potter, J.A. Dalhart Windberg.
L. Milazzo, 584(SWR):Spring85-262
Potter, J.H. Five Frames for the "Decam-
eron."*
A.K. Cassell, 589:Jan85-190
J.M. Ferrante, 545(RPh):Aug85-130

Potter, K.H., ed. Advaita Vedānta up to
Śaṃkara and His Pupils.* Indian Meta-
physics and Epistemology.
J.W. de Jong, 259(IIJ):Jul85-218
Potter, L. "Twelfth Night."
A. Goolden, 617(TLS):3Jan86-19
M. Willems, 189(EA):Apr-Jun86-209
Potter, L. - see Osborne, F.
Potter, S. The Complete Upmanship.
617(TLS):10Oct86-1147
Pottle, F.A. James Boswell: The Earlier
Years, 1740-1769.*
42(AR):Winter85-120
Pottle, F.A. Pride and Negligence.
F.V. Bogel, 588(SSL):Vol20-294
Poucet, J. Les Origines de Rome.
T.J. Cornell, 617(TLS):1Aug86-848
de Pougy, L. My Blue Notebooks.
617(TLS):28Mar86-343
Poulin, A., Jr. - see Logan, J.
Poulin, G. All the Way Home.
B.N.S. Gooch, 102(CanL):Fall85-157
Poulin, G. Les Mensonges d'Isabelle.
R. Beaudoin, 102(CanL):Spring85-130
Poulin, J. Volkswagen Blues.
B. Melancon, 102(CanL):Winter84-111
Poulsen, R.C. The Pure Experience of
Order.
S.R. Sherman, 650(WF):Apr85-137
Pound, E. and F.M. Ford. Pound/Ford.* (B.
Lindberg-Seyersted, ed)
M. King, 659(ConL):Spring86-127
Pound, E. and W. Lewis. Pound/Lewis.*
(T. Materer, ed)
C.J. Fox, 364:Feb86-92
R. Humphreys, 4:Autumn-Winter85/86-137
R. Lewis, 432(NEQ):Dec85-607
W.H. Pritchard, 249(HudR):Winter86-673
B. Raffel, 363(LitR):Spring86-384
138:No8-254
Pound, E. and D. Shakespear. Ezra Pound
and Dorothy Shakespear: Their Letters
1909-1914.* (O. Pound and A.W. Litz,
eds)
M. Alexander, 4:Autumn-Winter85/86-131
D. Anderson and W.S. Flory, 468:
Spring85-143
M. King, 659(ConL):Spring86-127
M. North, 27(AL):Oct85-518
295(JML):Nov85-542
639(VQR):Spring85-46
Pound, E. and J. Theobald. Ezra Pound/
John Theobald: Letters.* (D. Pearce and
H. Schneidau, eds)
C. McDowell, 468:Fall/Winter85-489
295(JML):Nov85-543
Pounds, N.J.G. An Historical Geography of
Europe 1800-1914.
P.K. O'Brien, 617(TLS):25Apr86-440
Pountain, C.J. Structures and Transforma-
tions.*
S.N. Dworkin, 238:May85-331
C. Lyons, 278(IS):Vol40-108
Poupard, D., ed. Literature Criticism
from 1400 to 1800. (Vol 1)
S. Soupel, 189(EA):Oct-Dec86-453
Poupard, P., ed. Dictionnaire des reli-
gions.
A. Reix, 542:Oct-Dec85-563
"Pour une philosophie chrétienne."
M. Adam, 542:Jan-Mar85-96
Pow-Key, S. - see under Sohn Pow-Key

Powe, B.W. A Climate Charged.
D. Daymond, 102(CanL):Summer85-159
J. Robinson, 627(UTQ):Summer85-427
Powe, E.L. Hausa Studies.
G. Furniss, 538(RAL):Fall85-463
Powell, A. The Fisher King.
G. Craig, 617(TLS):4Apr86-356
J. Espey, 441:19Oct86-30
G. Millar, 362:3Apr86-28
442(NY):20Oct86-130
Powell, B. Epic and Chronicle.*
D. Hook, 402(MLR):Jan85-192
I. Michael, 86(BHS):Jan85-128
Powell, D. The Wisdom of the Novel.
566:Autumn85-90
Powell, G. Yvor Winters.
R. Hoffpauir, 178:Sep85-379
Powell, H. - see Gryphius, A.
Powell, I. Writers and Society in Modern
Japan.
N. Twine, 407(MN):Winter85-436
Powell, J. Restoration Theatre Production.
J.M.B., 179(ES):Jun85-283
T. Minter, 157:No158-50
C. Price, 410(M&L):Oct85-369
Powell, J. Risk, Ruin and Riches.
A. Scardino, 441:26Oct86-38
Powell, L.C. El Morro.
P. Wotipka, 649(WAL):May85-86
Powell, M. Fabula Docet.*
D. Fox, 589:Jul85-710
M. Fries, 301(JEGP):Jan85-118
A.A. MacDonald, 179(ES):Oct85-461
Powell, M. A Life in Movies.
C. Barr, 362:30Oct86-26
A. Walker, 617(TLS):31Oct86-1210
Powell, M.A. and D.B. Weisberg - see
Dandamaev, M.A.
Powell, P. Edisto.*
L. Simon, 502(PrS):Summer85-122
Powell, R.B. Catalogue of Portrait Minia-
tures in the Fitzwilliam Museum, Cam-
bridge.
B. Allen, 90:Aug85-538
Powell, S., ed. The Advent and Nativity
Sermons from a Fifteenth-Century Revi-
sion of John Mirk's Festial.*
A. Hudson, 402(MLR):Oct85-898
Power, M.S. The Killing of Yesterday's
Children.*
R. Lourie, 441:6Apr86-28
Power, M.S. Lonely the Man Without Heroes.
J. Melmoth, 617(TLS):6Jun86-622
Power, V. The Town of Ballymuck.
C.C. Ward, 174(Éire):Fall85-148
Powers, L.H. Faulkner's Yoknapatawpha
Comedy.
H-W. Schaller, 38:Band103Heft1/2-260
Powers, R. Three Farmers on Their Way to
a Dance.*
D. Baker, 138:No8-255
Powers, R. White Town Drowsing.
R. Reed, 441:30Nov86-25
442(NY):29Dec86-96
Powers, R.H. The Dilemma of Education in
a Democracy.
C.D. Murphy, 396(ModA):Winter85-79
Powledge, F. Fat of the Land.
639(VQR):Winter85-20
Powys, J.C. Powys to Knight. (R. Black-
more, ed)
P. McClure, 161(DUJ):Dec84-131

Pozzi, G. La Parola dipinta.
F. Graziani, 549(RLC):Jan-Mar85-88
Pozzi, L. De Ramus a Kant.
M. Dominicy, 540(RIPh):Vol39fasc3-273
Pradier, J. Correspondance.* (Vol 1) (D.
Siler, ed)
C. Crossley, 208(FS):Jul85-352
Prado, C.G. Making Believe.
G. Bouchard, 154:Autumn85-543
S.G. Kellman, 395(MFS):Summer85-449
K. Kolenda, 478:Oct85-251
42(AR):Winter85-121
Prado, M. Practical Spanish Grammar.*
More Practical Spanish Grammar.*
J.E. Ackerman, 238:Mar85-85
Prados, J. Presidents' Secret Wars.
S.J. Ungar, 441:21Dec86-3
Praetorius, M. Syntagma Musicum II. (D.Z.
Crooks, ed and trans)
D. Fallows, 617(TLS):9May86-496
Swami Prajnanananda. A Historical Study
of Indian Music. (2nd ed)
W. Howard, 318(JAOS):Apr-Jun84-345
Prakasa Rao, V.L.S. Urbanization in India.
J.E. Brush, 293(JASt):Feb85-440
Prakash, O. The Dutch East India Company
and the Economy of Bengal 1630-1720.
K.N. Chaudhuri, 617(TLS):23May86-571
Prandi, J.D. Spirited Women Heroes.
H.M.K. Riley, 133:Band18Heft3-276
Prange, G.W. Target Tokyo.
639(VQR):Spring85-50
Prange, G.W., with D.M. Goldstein and K.V.
Dillon. Pearl Harbor.
N. Bliven, 442(NY):14Apr86-105
R.H. Spector, 441:5Jan86-9
Prantera, A. The Cabalist.*
J. Marcus, 441:7Sep86-22
Prat, M-A. Cercle et carré.
Y-A. Bois, 98:Jun-Jul85-741
Prater, D. A Ringing Glass.
M. Hofmann, 441:21Sep86-18
T. Ziolkowski, 617(TLS):14Nov86-1265
Pratt, A., with others. Archetypal Pat-
terns in Women's Fiction.
A.J. Wiemer, 107(CRCL):Sep85-505
Pratt, E.J. E.J. Pratt on His Life and
Poetry.* (S. Gingell, ed)
A. McAuliffe, 150(DR):Winter84/85-804
L.K. MacKendrick, 178:Sep85-372
Pratt, G. The Dynamics of Harmony.
P. Standford, 415:Aug85-604
Pratt, J. - see "Harrap's Slang Dictionary:
English-French/French-English"
Pratt, N.T. Seneca's Drama.*
R.J. Tarrant, 123:Vol35No2-287
H. Zehnacker, 555:Vol59fasc1-140
Pratt, S. Russian Metaphysical Romanti-
cism.
R. Lane, 575(SEER):Jul85-437
E.D. Sampson, 574(SEEJ):Winter85-471
J. Zeldin, 104(CASS):Summer85-203
Pratt, S. The Semantics of Chaos in
Tjutčev.
B. Bilokur, 574(SEEJ):Winter85-472
R. Lane, 575(SEER):Jul85-437
Prauss, G. Kant über Freiheit als Autono-
mie.*
K. Ameriks, 543:Sep84-136
W. Marx, 342:Band76Heft3-344
Prawer, S.S. Heine's Jewish Comedy.
H. Reiss, 133:Band17Heft3/4-349
J.L. Sammons, 221(GQ):Winter85-127

Prior, J.  A Balance of Power.
  J. Critchley, 362:6Nov86-27
  J. Lloyd, 617(TLS):10Oct86-1128
Prior, W.J.  Unity and Development in
  Plato's Metaphysics.
  J. Barnes, 520:Vol30No2-211
Pritchard, G.  The Aggressions of the
  French at Tahiti and Other Islands of
  the Pacific.  (P. De Deckker, ed)
  K. O'Connor, 617(TLS):27Jun86-714
Pritchard, W.H.  Frost.*
  S.S. Baskett, 115:Fall85-481
  P. Bland, 364:Apr/May85-134
  P.L. Gerber, 659(ConL):Spring86-134
  D.G. Sheehy, 432(NEQ):Jun85-320
  639(VQR):Summer85-79
Pritchett, V.S.  A Man of Letters.*
  D. Donoghue, 453(NYRB):26Jun86-7
  P.N. Furbank, 362:23Jan86-31
  W. Maxwell, 442(NY):9Jun86-108
  W.H. Pritchard, 441:4May86-12
Pritchett, W.K.  Studies in Ancient Greek
  Topography.*  (Vols 3 and 4)
  J.B. Salmon, 123:Vol35No1-100
Pritsak, O.  The Origin of Rus'.*  (Vol 1)
  G.D. Knysh, 104(CASS):Spring85-54
  "Problemy istočnikovedčeskogo izučenija
  rukopisnyh i staropečatnyh tondov."
  C. and M. Mervaud, 535(RHL):Jul/Aug85-
  685
Probst, G.F. and J.F. Bodine, eds.  Per-
  spectives on Max Frisch.*
  E. Schürer, 221(GQ):Summer85-479
Proclus.  Commentaire sur le Parménide de
  Platon.*  (Vol 1) (Guillaume de Moerbeke,
  trans; C. Steel, ed)
  K. Bormann, 53(AGP):Band67Heft3-299
Proctor, D.  The Experience of Thucydides.
  J.A.S. Evans, 529(QQ):Spring85-185
Proctor, N.  Garden Birds.
  S. Brownmiller, 441:1Jun86-30
Proffer, E.  Bulgakov.*
  D.M. Fiene, 574(SEEJ):Summer85-215
  M.L. Hoover, 615(TJ):May85-245
  P.W. Powell and B. Beatie, 395(MFS):
  Summer85-438
  B. Sharratt, 104(CASS):Summer85-219
Proffer, E., ed.  A Pictorial Biography of
  Mikhail Bulgakov.
  P.W. Powell and B. Beatie, 395(MFS):
  Summer85-438
  B. Sharratt, 104(CASS):Summer85-219
Proffitt, N.  The Embassy House.
  J. Klein, 441:29Jun86-8
  442(NY):18Aug86-74
Profumo, D. and G. Swift, eds.  The Magic
  Wheel.*
  J. Reed, 364:Mar86-111
Prokopp, M.  Italian Trecento Influence on
  Murals in East Central Europe, Particu-
  larly Hungary.
  A.S., 90:Apr85-243
Prokosch, F.  The Asiatics.*  (French
  title: Les Asiatiques.)
  R. Millet, 450(NRF):Jun85-90
Prokosch, F.  Voices.*
  E. Guereschi, 395(MFS):Summer85-428
Pronko, L.C.  Eugène Labiche and Georges
  Feydeau.*
  E. Fallaize, 208(FS):Jan85-88
Pronzini, B. and M.H. Greenberg, eds.  The
  Reel West.
  L. Milazzo, 584(SWR):Winter85-130

Pronzini, B. and M.H. Greenberg, eds.  The
  Second Reel West.
  L. Milazzo, 584(SWR):Autumn85-547
Propertius.  Sexti Properti "Elegiarum"
  Libri IV.  (P. Fedeli, ed)
  S.J. Heyworth, 123:Vol35No2-281
Propp, V.  Theory and History of Folklore.
  (A. Liberman, ed)
  F.J. Oinas, 279:Vol30-189
  A.H. Marschall, 400(MLN):Dec85-1123
Propp, V.J.  Russkaja skazka.
  P. Grzybek, 196:Band26Heft3/4-377
  A. Liberman, 292(JAF):Jul/Sep85-347
von Proschwitz, G. - see Piron, A.
von Proschwitz, G. - see Tessin, C.G.
Prosdocimi, A.L.  Le tavole Iguvine, I.
  P. Baldi, 350:Sep86-717
  D. Briquel, 555:Vol59fasc1-132
Prose, F.  Bigfoot Dreams.
  S.A. Toth, 441:25May86-8
  442(NY):27Oct86-144
Proust, M.  Correspondance de Marcel
  Proust.  (Vol 13) (P. Kolb, ed)
  F. Steegmuller, 617(TLS):30May86-597
Proust, M.  Pleasures and Regrets.
  P.N. Furbank, 362:26Jun86-23
  F. Steegmuller, 617(TLS):30May86-597
Proust, M.  A Search for Lost Time.  (Vol
  1) (J. Grieve, trans)
  G. Craig, 402(MLR):Jul85-724
Provine, W.B.  Sewall Wright and Evolution-
  ary Biology.
  M.W. Feldman, 441:5Oct86-52
Prucha, F.P.  The Great Father.
  M.S. Ball, 219(GaR):Winter85-889
  R.M. Utley, 250(HLQ):Winter85-97
Prucha, F.P.  The Indians in American
  Society.
  B. Fisher, 441:20Apr86-23
Prudhomme, P.  Chef Paul Prudhomme's Lou-
  isiana Kitchen.
  W. and C. Cowen, 639(VQR):Spring85-65
Prunty, W.  What Women Know, What Men
  Believe.
  J. Wingard, 598(SoR):Summer86-658
Prusek, J.  The Lyrical and the Epic.
  (L.O-F. Lee, ed)
  T. Huters, 116:Jul84-125
Pryce-Jones, D.  The Afternoon Sun.
  A. Beevor, 617(TLS):23May86-554
  J. Mellors, 362:10Apr86-28
  A.R.G. Solmssen, 441:23Nov86-18
Pryce-Jones, D. - see Connolly, C.
Pryde, D.  Nunaga.
  617(TLS):28Mar86-343
Prys Williams, A.G.  Applicable Inductive
  Logic.
  D.E. Over, 518:Jan85-43
Pryse, M. and H.J. Spillers, eds.  Conjur-
  ing.
  R.G. O'Meally, 441:30Mar86-18
Pseudo-Dionysius.  Pseudo-Dionysius Aero-
  pagite, The Divine Names and Mystical
  Theology.  (J.D. Jones, trans)
  S. Gersh, 438:Spring85-231
Pucci, M.  La rivolta ebraica al tempo di
  Traiano.
  T. Rajak, 123:Vol35No1-204
Puffett, D.  The Song Cycles of Othmar
  Schoeck.
  A.W., 412:Feb84-63

Pugh, A. The Composition of Pascal's Apologia.
  E. Moles, 208(FS):Oct85-465
Pugh, A.C. Simon: "Histoire."
  M. Evans, 208(FS):Jan85-111
  C. Rigolot, 207(FR):Apr86-799
Pugh, M. The Tories and the People 1880-1935.
  A. Sykes, 617(TLS):31Jan86-106
Puhvel, J. Hittite Etymological Dictionary.*
  N. Oettinger, 159:Fall85-255
Puhvel, J. - see Dumézil, G.
Puig, M. Blood of Requited Love.
  D. Flower, 249(HudR):Summer85-307
Puig, M. Pubis Angelical.
  S. Erickson, 441:28Dec86-9
  R. Towers, 453(NYRB):18Dec86-29
Puig, M. Under a Mantle of Stars.
  R.K. Reading, 352(LATR):Spring86-129
Pujol, J. and N. West. Garbo.
  M.R.D. Foot, 617(TLS):7Mar86-240
Pujol, J., with N. West. Operation Garbo.
  C.C. Davis, 441:23Nov86-25
Pulgram, E., ed. Romanitas.
  M.E. Schaffer, 350:Sep86-718
Pullan, B.S. The Jews of Europe and the Inquisition of Venice, 1550-1670.
  M.J.C. Lowry, 278(IS):Vol40-132
  G. Ruggiero, 551(RenQ):Spring85-126
Pullen, J.J. Comic Relief.*
  M. Moseley, 534(RALS):Spring83-95
Pulman, S.G. Word Meaning and Belief.*
  T. Pateman, 307:May85-71
  B. Peeters, 320(CJL):Summer85-226
Punter, D. Blake, Hegel and Dialectic.*
  J. Williams, 366:Spring85-142
Punter, D. The Literature of Terror.
  R. Cardinal, 529(QQ):Autumn85-549
Punyavijayaji, M.S. - see "Rāmacandra's Mallikāmakarandanāṭaka"
Pupo-Walker, E. La vocación literaria del pensamiento histórico en América.*
  P. Verdevoye, 92(BH):Jul-Dec84-573
Purcell, G.R. Reference Sources in Library and Information Sciences.
  M. Gaylord, 87(BB):Dec85-218
Purcell, R.W. and S.J. Gould. Illuminations.
  A. Grundberg, 441:7Dec86-21
Purdy, A. Morning and It's Summer.*
  C. McLay, 102(CanL):Summer85-144
Purdy, A. Piling Blood.
  M.T. Lane, 198:Winter85-106
  S. Scobie, 376:Jun85-132
  P.K. Smith, 99:Aug/Sep85-34
  G. Woodcock, 102(CanL):Summer85-192
Purdy, D.H. Joseph Conrad's Bible.*
  R. Davis, 395(MFS):Winter85-798
  E.K. Hay, 445(NCF):Jun85-112
  D.R. Schwarz, 177(ELT):Vol28No1-91
Purdy, J. The House of the Solitary Maggot.
  V. Bogdanor, 362:20Feb86-28
Purdy, J. In the Hollow of His Hand.
  L. Smith, 441:19Oct86-15
Purdy, R.L. and M. Millgate - see Hardy, T.
Puri, H.K. Ghadar Movement.
  J. Singh, 293(JASt):Nov84-236
Purkis, J. A Preface to George Eliot.
  J. Adlard, 617(TLS):26Sep86-1078

Pusch, L.F. Kontrastive Untersuchungen zum italienischen "gerundio."
  G. Ernst, 547(RF):Band97Heft1-77
  G. Lepschy, 545(RPh):Feb86-361
Puschmann, R. Magisches Quadrat und Melancholie in Thomas Manns "Doktor Faustus."
  W.R. Berger, 52:Band20Heft1-104
Pushkin, A.S. Complete Prose Fiction.* (P. Debreczeny, ed and trans)
  A.D.P. Briggs, 402(MLR):Apr85-509
Pushkin, A.S. The Tales of Belkin [with] The History of the Village of Goryukhino.* (G. Aitken and D. Budgen, trans)
  A. McMillin, 575(SEER):Jan85-115
Pushkin, A.S. and M. Lermontov. Narrative Poems by Alexander Pushkin and by Mikhail Lermontov.* (C. Johnston, trans)
  P. Debreczeny, 550(RusR):Jan85-98
  D. McDuff, 565:Summer85-72
Pusztay, J. Die Pur-Mundart des Waldjurakischen.
  B. Comrie, 350:Mar86-222
Putnam, H. Realism and Reason.*
  M. Espinoza, 542:Jul-Sep85-344
  J.J.C. Smart, 63:Dec85-533
Putnam, H. Reason, Truth and History.* (German title: Vernunft, Wahrheit und Geschichte. French title: Raison, vérité et histoire.)
  J. Habermas, 384:Sep/Oct85-904
  P. Jacob, 98:Jun-Jul85-593
  M. Jarrety, 450(NRF):Mar85-105
  K. Okruhlik, 486:Dec84-692
Putnam, M.C.J. Essays on Latin Lyric, Elegy and Epic.
  A.M. Bowie, 161(DUJ):Jun84-280
Putt, S.G. The Golden Age of English Drama.*
  J.L. Levenson, 570(SQ):Autumn85-380
Puttfarken, T. Roger de Piles' Theory of Art.
  J. Steer, 324:Nov86-846
  R. Wollheim, 617(TLS):28Mar86-327
Putzel, M. Genius of Place.*
  A.F. Kinney, 27(AL):Dec85-688
  H. McNeil, 617(TLS):27Jun86-704
  S.M. Ross, 395(MFS):Winter85-737
  295(JML):Nov85-476
  639(VQR):Summer85-86
Putzer, O. Konjunktionale Nebensätze und äquivalente Strukturen in der Heinrich von Langenstein zugeschriebenen "Erkenntnis der Sünde."
  H. von Gadow, 685(ZDL):1/1985-117
Puzo, M. The Sicilian.*
  T.J. Binyon, 617(TLS):13Jun86-646
Py, M. L'"oppidum" des castels à Nages (Gard).
  J.F. Drinkwater, 313:Vol75-292
Pye, L.W., with M.W. Pye. Asian Power and Politics.
  L.I. Rudolph, 441:9Feb86-34
Pyenson, L. The Young Einstein.
  J. Calado, 617(TLS):14Mar86-283
Pyle, E. Ernie's War. (D. Nichols, ed)
  J.D. Atwater, 441:5Oct86-16
  442(NY):27Oct86-147
Pym, B. An Academic Question.
  C. Barr, 362:31Jul86-24
  A.S. Byatt, 617(TLS):8Aug86-862
  M. Rubin, 441:7Sep86-25
  442(NY):3Nov86-165

Rabinow, P. - see Foucault, M.
Rabinowitz, H.N., ed. Southern Black Leaders of the Reconstruction Era.*
  G. Vandal, 106:Spring85-41
Rabinowitz, I. - see Messer Leon, J.
Rabkin, E.S., M.H. Greenberg and J.D. Olander, eds. The End of the World.*
  C.C. Smith, 395(MFS):Summer85-462
Rable, G.C. But There Was No Peace.
  M.M. Hennessey, 9(AlaR):Apr85-152
Racevskis, K. Michel Foucault and the Subversion of Intellect.*
  D.M. Kercher, 478:Oct85-260
  G.F. Waller, 152(UDQ):Summer85-126
  R. Young, 208(FS):Apr85-239
Rachel, H. Das Nietzsche-Bild im George-Kreis.
  S.L. Gilman, 221(GQ):Spring85-312
Rachels, J. The End of Life.
  I. McGilchrist, 617(TLS):7Nov86-1251
  A.H. Malcolm, 441:29Jun86-20
Rachman, O-A. Un Périodique libéral sous la Restauration.
  A. Nabarra, 207(FR):May86-980
  M. Tilby, 208(FS):Apr85-218
Racine, J. Théâtre complet. (Vol 2) (J-P. Collinet, ed)
  R.W. Tobin, 475:Vol 12No22-298
Rackham, O. The History of the Countryside.
  J. Buxton, 617(TLS):5Sep86-986
Rader, D. Tennessee.*
  W.K. Holditch, 598(SoR):Autumn86-892
al-Radi, S.M.S. Phlamoudhi Vounari.*
  D.M. Buitron, 303(JoHS):Vol 105-225
Radic, T. G.W.L. Marshall-Hall.
  A-M.H.F., 412:May84-145
Radice, B. Memphis.
  K.D. Stein, 45:Jul85-79
Radley, P.J. My Blue-Checker Corker and Me.
  E. Gleick, 441:30Nov86-22
Radley, P.J. Jack Rivers and Me.
  K. Weber, 441:16Mar86-20
Radway, J.A. Reading the Romance.*
  C.N. Davidson, 27(AL):Oct85-526
Radzinowicz, M.A., ed. American Colonial Prose.
  N.H. Keeble, 506(PSt):May85-79
Rae, C. Edith Wharton's New York Quartet.
  T.A. Gullason, 395(MFS):Winter85-745
Raeburn, J. Fame Became of Him.*
  S.F. Beegel, 234:Fall85-49
  K.G. Johnston, 27(AL):Mar85-152
  R.F. Lucid, 536(Rev):Vol7-113
  M.S. Reynolds, 534(RALS):Spring83-115
  295(JML):Nov85-494
Raeder, J. Die statuarische Ausstattung der Villa Hadriana bei Tivoli.
  D.C. Bellingham, 313:Vol175-274
Raeff, M. Understanding Imperial Russia.*
  N.V. Riasanovsky, 550(RusR):Jul85-295
Raelin, J.A. The Clash of Cultures.
  R. Krulwich, 441:14Dec86-14
Raffaele da Verona. Aquilon de Bavière.
  L. Bartolucci, 72:Band222Heft2-470
Raffat, D. The Prison Papers of Bozorg Alavi.
  F. Halliday, 617(TLS):20Jun86-667
Raffel, B. Ezra Pound, Prime Minister of Poetry.*
  295(JML):Nov85-543

Raftis, J.A. A Small Town in Late Medieval England.
  P.R. Hyams, 589:Apr85-451
Ragaz, L. Signs of the Kingdom. (P. Bock, ed and trans)
  R.L., 185:Oct85-215
Ragland-Sullivan, E. Jacques Lacan and the Philosophy of Psychoanalysis.
  E. Wright, 617(TLS):15Aug86-880
Ragon, M. L'Architecture des gares.
  J. Duvignaud, 450(NRF):Oct85-115
Ragonese, G. Da Manzoni a Fogazzaro.
  E. Gerato, 276:Summer85-153
Ragsdale, K.B. Wings Over the Border.
  L. Milazzo, 584(SWR):Spring85-262
Raguin, V.C. Stained Glass in Thirteenth Century Burgundy.
  M.H. Caviness, 589:Apr85-454
  C.R. Dodwell, 39:May85-351
  F. Gatouillat, 90:Aug85-535
Rähmer, J. Bekenntnisse eines Einfältigen.
  W. Jehser, 654(WB):8/1985-1370
Rai, S.M. Legislative Politics and the Freedom Struggle in the Punjab, 1897-1947.
  D. Gilmartin, 293(JASt):Aug85-876
Raidt, E.H. Einführung in Geschichte und Struktur des Afrikaans.
  R. Leclercq, 684(ZDA):Band114Heft4-147
Raifeartaigh, T.O., ed. The Royal Irish Academy.
  M. Harmon, 272(IUR):Autumn85-252
Raimes, A. Techniques in Teaching Writing.
  M.E. Call, 399(MLJ):Spring85-82
Raine, C. Rich.*
  T. Eagleton, 565:Autumn85-69
  A. Haberer, 189(EA):Apr-Jun86-235
Raine, K. The Human Face of God.
  B.O. Lindberg, 88:Spring86-151
Raine, K. The Inner Journey of the Poet. (B. Keeble, ed)
  E. Longley, 447(N&Q):Dec84-562
Rainer, F. Intensivierung im Italienischen.
  J. Albrecht, 547(RF):Band97Heft4-446
Raison, L., ed. The South of France.
  A. Harvey, 441:1Jun86-14
Raitiere, M.N. Faire Bitts.*
  J. van Dorsten, 551(RenQ):Winter85-759
Raitt, L.N.R.C. Garrett and the English Muse.
  N.J. Lamb, 86(BHS):Oct85-403
Raizis, M.B. From Caucasus to Pittsburgh.
  R. Trousson, 549(RLC):Jul-Sep85-329
Rajak, T. Josephus.
  J.N. Birdsall, 123:Vol35No1-22
Rajchman, J. Michel Foucault.
  C. Gordon, 617(TLS):6Jun86-626
Rajic, N. The Master of Strappado.
  M. Thorpe, 198:Winter85-87
Rakosi, C. Spiritus, 1.
  J. Saunders, 565:Spring85-72
Raleigh, D.J. Revolution on the Volga.
  J. Keep, 617(TLS):12Sep86-999
Rama, A. La ciudad letrada.
  K. Müller-Bergh, 238:Sep85-530
"Rāmacandra's Mallikāmakarandanāṭaka." (M.S. Punyavijayaji, ed)
  E. Bender, 318(JAOS):Oct-Dec84-789
Ramage, C.T. Ramage in South Italy. (E. Clay, ed)
  M. Howard, 441:7Dec86-14

Ramaiah, L.S. and T.V.P. Chandra. Noam Chomsky.
  B.D. Joseph, 350:Sep86-710
Ramallo Asensio, G. Luis Fernández de la Vega, escultor asturiano del siglo XVII.
  M. Estella, 48:Oct-Dec85-434
Ramaswamy, U. Work, Union, and Community.
  J. Lessinger, 293(JASt):May85-651
Ramat, P. Linguistica tipologica.
  M. Harris, 361:Nov85-263
Ramati, A. And the Violins Stopped Playing.
  R. Smith, 441:12Oct86-28
"The Rāmāyaṇa of Vālmīki." (Vol 1) (R.P. Goldman and S.J. Sutherland, eds)
  W.G. Regier, 400(MLN):Dec85-1151
Ramazani, R.K. Revolutionary Iran.
  E. Mortimer, 441:28Dec86-1
Ramboz, I.W. Spanish Verbs and Essentials of Grammar.
  J.W. Brown, 399(MLJ):Winter85-439
Ramirez, A.G. Bilingualism Through Schooling.
  R. Otheguy, 399(MLJ):Autumn85-300
Ramírez, J.A. Edificios y sueños (Ensayos sobre Arquitectura y Utopía).
  F. Marías, 48:Jan-Mar85-85
Ramírez de Arellano y Lynch, R.W. La poesía cortesano del siglo XV y el "Cancionero de Vindel."
  A. Deyermond, 86(BHS):Jan85-140
Ramišvili, G. Enis energet'uli teoriis sak'itxebi.
  G.F. Meier, 682(ZPSK):Band38Heft5-613
Ramón, F.R. - see under Ruiz Ramón, F.
Ramos, D. and others. Francisco de Vitoria y la escuela de Salamanca.
  A. Reix, 542:Jul-Sep85-316
Ramos-Horta, J. "Funu."
  M. Picken, 453(NYRB):4Dec86-44
Rampersad, A. The Life of Langston Hughes. (Vol 1)
  G. Brooks, 441:12Oct86-7
Rampton, D. Vladimir Nabokov.*
  M. Couturier, 189(EA):Oct-Dec86-488
  B. Jones, 104(CASS):Summer85-227
  J.J. White, 575(SEER):Oct85-590
  295(JML):Nov85-531
Ramraj, V.J. Mordecai Richler.*
  F.W. Watt, 102(CanL):Spring85-138
Ramsay, P. The Fickle Glass.
  W. Weiss, 156(ShJW):Jahrbuch1985-213
Ramsden, H. Baroja: "La busca." Pío Baroja: "La busca" 1903 to "La busca" 1904.
  J. Alberich, 86(BHS):Oct85-398
  B. Ciplijauskaité, 403(MLS):Fall85-367
  C.A. Longhurst, 402(MLR):Jan85-199
Ramsden, H. - see Lorca, F.G.
Ramsey, J. Reading the Fire.*
  K.M. Roemer, 115:Summer84-259
  B. Toelken, 650(WF):Jan85-46
Ramsey, J.T. Sallust's "Bellum Catilinae."
  M. Winterbottom, 123:Vol35No1-188
Ramsey, L.C. Chivalric Romances.
  G.D. Economou, 377:Mar85-45
  A.B. Friedman, 589:Jul85-712
  C. Platt, 366:Spring85-136
Ramsey, P.A., ed. Rome in the Renaissance.
  V. Comensoli, 403(MLS):Fall85-339
  C. Valone, 377:Nov85-198
"C.F. Ramuz: Études ramuziennes."
  G. Cesbron, 535(RHL):Sep/Oct85-896

Ranade, A.D. On Music and Musicians of Hindoostan.
  J.L. Erdman, 293(JASt):Aug85-876
Rancière, J. Le philosophe et ses pauvres.
  G.L., 185:Apr86-657
Rand, P. Paul Rand: A Designer's Art.*
  J. Thackara, 617(TLS):16May86-528
Randall, D.B.J. Gentle Flame.*
  M.J.M. Ezell, 568(SCN):Spring-Summer85-16
Randall, W.S. A Little Revenge.*
  E.K. Ginsberg, 27(AL):Dec85-657
  P.H. Smith, 656(WMQ):Oct85-534
Randers-Pehrson, J.D. Barbarians and Romans.
  G.M. Woloch, 121(CJ):Oct/Nov85-77
Randle, J., with M. Watanabe. Coping with Japan.
  R. Hattersley, 617(TLS):7Feb86-147
Randolph, M. The Virginia House-Wife.
  W. and C. Cowen, 639(VQR):Spring85-64
Ranelagh, E.L. Men on Women.
  A.S. Grossman, 617(TLS):26Sep86-1077
  A. Huth, 362:30Jan86-26
Ranelagh, J. The Agency.
  J. Bamford, 441:13Jul186-11
Rangel, C. Third World Ideology and Western Reality.
  S. McConnell, 129:Oct86-78
Ranger, T. Peasant Consciousness and Guerrilla War in Zimbabwe.
  M. Crowder, 617(TLS):4Jul86-726
Ranhofer, C. The Epicurean.
  W. and C. Cowen, 639(VQR):Autumn85-138
Prince Ranjitsinhji. With Stoddart's Team in Australia.
  D. Durrant, 364:Nov85-110
  T.D. Smith, 617(TLS):21Feb86-203
Rankin, D.C. - see Houzeau, J-C.
Rankin, H.D. Sophists, Socratics and Cynics.
  J.L. Creed, 123:Vol35No1-198
Rankin, I. The Flood.
  I. Bamforth, 617(TLS):2May86-478
Rankka, E., ed. Li Ver del Juïse.*
  P. Gehrke, 545(RPh):May86-513
  B. Levy, 208(FS):Jan85-60
Ransom, J.C. Selected Essays of John Crowe Ransom.* (T.D. Young and J. Hindle, eds)
  639(VQR):Winter85-16
Ransom, J.C. Selected Letters of John Crowe Ransom.* (T.D. Young and G. Core, eds)
  A. Brown, 639(VQR):Autumn85-708
  W. Harmon, 578:Fall86-92
  F. Hobson, 344:Winter86-119
  J.H. Justus, 578:Spring86-123
  295(JML):Nov85-547
Rao, K.B. Paul Scott.*
  J. Newman, 161(DUJ):Jun84-305
Rao, V.L.S.P. - see under Prakasa Rao, V.L.S.
Raoul de Houdenc. The Songe d'Enfer of Raoul de Houdenc. (M.T. Mihm, ed)
  D.D.R. Owen, 208(FS):Jul85-319
  G. Roques, 553(RLiR):Jan-Jun85-238
Rapaport, H. Milton and the Postmodern.*
  R.J. Du Rocher, 577(SHR):Fall85-359
  R.B. Rollin, 301(JEGP):Jul85-433
Raphael, C. The Road from Babylon.
  B. Segal, 176:Apr86-51
  R.M. Seltzer, 129:Aug86-58

Ray, E. - see Acton, E.
Ray, G.N. H.G. Wells and Rebecca West.
N. Steffen-Fluhr, 561(SFS):Nov85-311
Ray, J.L. The Future of American-Israeli
Relations.
B. Wasserstein, 617(TLS):10ct86-1123
Ray, R. Bloody Murdock.
N. Callendar, 441:5Oct86-28
Ray, R., ed. Words on Music.
K. Spence, 415:Apr85-226
Ray, R.B. A Certain Tendency of the Holly-
wood Cinema, 1930-1980.*
V. Konieczny, 648(WCR):Apr86-70
Ray, W. Literary Meaning.*
F. Albers, 204(FdL):Dec85-314
A. Easthope, 366:Spring85-130
A. Kennedy, 150(DR):Summer85-314
Raygor, A.L. and R.D. Effective Reading.
B.A. Beatie, 399(MLJ):Winter85-404
Raymond, F. and D. Compère. Le développe-
ment des études sur Jules Verne (domaine
français).
J. Hansel, 356(LR):Aug85-232
Raymond, J.C., ed. Literacy as a Human
Problem.
A. Pitts, 577(SHR):Winter85-91
Raymond, J.G. A Passion for Friends.
V. Miner, 441:7Sep86-23
Raymond, M. Romantisme et rêverie.
Y. Vadé, 535(RHL):Mar/Apr85-329
Raymond, M.B. and M.R. Sullivan - see
Browning, E.B.
Raynor, H. Music in England.
T.H., 412:Aug/Nov83-290
Raz, J. Audience and Actors.
J.R. Brandon, 407(MN):Autumn85-360
Razzell, M. Snow Apples.
P. Nodelman, 102(CanL):Fall85-122
Rea, J.R. The Oxyrhynchus Papyri. (Vol
51)
B. Kramer, 123:Vol35No2-360
Read, F. '76: One World and "The Cantos"
of Ezra Pound.*
P. Makin, 677(YES):Vol 15-349
Read, G. Style and Orchestration.
D.C., 412:Aug/Nov83-306
Read, P.P. The Free Frenchman.
D. Johnson, 617(TLS):10ct86-1131
J. Turner, 362:25Sep86-22
Read, W.A. Indian Place Names in Alabama.
(rev)
M.M. Bryant, 424:Dec85-287
M.J. McDaniel, 9(AlaR):Oct85-309
Reading, P. C.*
D. O'Driscoll, 493:Apr85-15
G. Szirtes, 148:Summer85-51
Reading, P. Ukelele Music.
C. Boyle, 364:Nov85-79
N. Jenkins, 493:Oct85-69
J. Mole, 176:Jan86-60
S. Rae, 617(TLS):10Jan86-34
W. Scammell, 148:Winter85-65
Real, Á.M. - see under Madruga Real, Á.
Real, H.J. and H.J. Vienken. Jonathan
Swift: "Gulliver's Travels."
C.S. Durer, 149(CLS):Winter85-546
E. Kreutzer, 72:Band222Heft2-476
W. Zach, 566:Spring86-139
Real, W., ed. Racism in America.
M. Diedrich, 72:Band222Heft2-427
Reale, G. The Systems of the Hellenistic
Age.
J. Barnes, 520:Vol30No2-216

Reale, M. Le Ragioni della politica.
G. Bremner, 208(FS):Oct85-474
Rearick, C. Pleasures of the Belle Epoque.
M. Burns, 441:19Jan86-11
R. Shattuck, 453(NYRB):18Dec86-66
Reaves, W.W., ed. American Portrait
Prints.
J.V. Turano, 16:Winter85-90
H. Wright, 658:Summer/Autumn85-198
Rebell, M.A. and A.R. Block. Equality and
Education.
A.L. Goldman, 441:24Aug86-19
Reboul, O. La rhétorique.
P. Somville, 542:Jul-Sep85-350
Récanati, F. Les Énoncés Performatifs.*
S.L. Tsohatzidis, 603:Vol9No2-271
Rectanus, M., G. Humphreys and H. Spence.
Deutschland und Amerika.
J.F. Lalande 2d, 399(MLJ):Spring85-93
Rector, L. The Sorrow of Architecture.*
455:Mar85-64
Red Hawk. Journey of the Medicine Man.
639(VQR):Spring85-55
Redfern, J. Basic Terms of Business and
Finance.
M.G. Elton, 207(FR):Apr86-808
Redfern, W. Puns.*
B. Richards, 184(EIC):Oct85-357
Redgrove, P. The Man Named East and Other
New Poems.*
N. Jenkins, 493:Aug85-28
H. Lomas, 364:Jun85-89
J. Rasula, 703:No15-184
Redgrove, P. The Working of Water.*
N. Jenkins, 493:Aug85-28
Redlich, S. Propaganda and Nationalism in
Wartime Russia.*
A.L. Kagedan, 287:Apr85-24
Redmond, J., ed. Drama, Dance and Music.*
A. Kernan, 402(MLR):Apr85-407
Redner, H. In the Beginning Was the Deed.
R. Nicholls, 131(CL):Winter85-82
Redon, O. Uomini e comunità del contado
senese nel duecento.
J.C. Brown, 589:Jul85-714
Redondo, A., ed. Les problèmes de
l'exclusion en Espagne (XVI-XVII siècles:
idéologie et discours).
M. Cavillac, 92(BH):Jul-Dec84-541
R.L. Kagan, 551(RenQ):Spring85-129
Redwood, C., ed. A Delius Companion.
A.F.L.T., 412:Aug/Nov84-304
Redwood, C., ed. An Elgar Companion.
E.W.A., 412:May83-136
S. Banfield, 410(M&L):Apr85-169
Rée, H. - see Morris, H.
Ree, J. Proletarian Philosophers.
D.M., 185:Apr86-665
Reed, A. Romantic Weather.*
J.P. Houston, 207(FR):Dec85-301
P. Jay, 301(JEGP):Apr85-273
W.T. Jones, 478:Apr85-114
Reed, A., ed. Romanticism and Language.*
P.M.S. Dawson, 148:Summer85-67
V. Nemoianu, 400(MLN):Dec85-1177
S. Simpkins, 599:Summer85-289
Reed, F. A Friend in Need.
S. Silvers, 364:Dec85/Jan86-159
Reed, H.H. The New York Public Library.
R.F. Shepard, 441:28Dec86-19
Reed, I. Reckless Eyeballing.
B. Staples, 441:23Mar86-11

Reilly, R.  The God of Mirrors.
    G. Levine, 441:2Mar86-17
Reilly, R., ed.  The Transcendent Adven-
    ture.
    D.D. Elgin, 395(MFS):Winter85-852
    H. Kaminsky, 561(SFS):Nov85-330
Reiner, H.  Duty and Inclination.
    N. Potter, 543:Sep85-165
Reiner, R.  The Politics of the Police.
    M.B. Carter, 617(TLS):10Jan86-29
Reinert, C.  Unzumutbare Wahrheiten?
    S. Bauschinger, 221(GQ):Summer85-477
Reinhard, D.W.  The Republican Right Since
    1945.
    G.S. Smith, 529(QQ):Summer85-297
Reinhard, K. and U.  Musik der Türkei.
    I. Markoff, 187:Fall86-555
Reinhardt, A.  Schriften und Gespräche.
    C. Scherrmann, 384:Sep/Oct85-938
Reinhart, T.  Anaphora and Semantic Inter-
    pretation.*
    D. Bouchard, 320(CJL):Winter85-475
    L. Hellan, 603:Vol9No1-140
    R. Maclaran, 297(JL):Mar85-221
    R.R. van Oirsouw, 307:Dec85-205
Reinharz, J.  Chaim Weizmann.*
    W. Kluback, 390:Nov85-60
Reinharz, J. and W. Schatzberg, eds.  The
    Jewish Response to German Culture.
    R.K. Angress, 617(TLS):26Sep86-1068
Reinhold, K.L.  Korrespondenzausgabe der
    Österreichischen Akademie der Wissen-
    schaften.*  (Vol 1)  (R. Lauth, E. Heller
    and K. Hiller, eds)
    S. Dietzsch, 489(PJGG):Band92Heft1-199
Reinhold, M.  Classica Americana.
    M.E. Bradford, 121(CJ):Apr/May86-355
    S.F. Wiltshire, 124:Jan-Feb86-198
Reinhold, M.  Diaspora, the Jews Among the
    Greeks and Romans.
    L.J. Sanders, 487:Spring85-94
Reino, J.  Karl Shapiro.
    R. Pooley, 402(MLR):Apr85-452
Reischauer, E.O.  My Life Between Japan
    and America.
    R.C. Christopher, 441:24Aug86-8
Reischauer, H.M.  Samurai and Silk.
    W.G. Beasley, 617(TLS):27Jun86-698
    I. Buruma, 441:30Mar86-13
Reiser, S.J. and M. Anbar, eds.  The
    Machine at the Bedside.
    M.B., 185:Apr86-675
Reisinger, R.  Die Rolle des Schweigens in
    der Dichtungstheorie von Rimbaud bis
    Valéry.*
    S. Siegrist, 547(RF):Band97Heft1-100
Reisner, M.  Cadillac Desert.
    G. Hill, 441:14Sep86-40
Reiss, K. and H.J. Vermeer.  Grundlegung
    einer allgemeinen Translationstheorie.*
    R.R.K. Hartmann, 257(IRAL):Aug85-256
Reiss, T.J.  The Discourse of Modernism.*
    K. Cochrane, 541(RES):May85-309
    R. Elbaz, 107(CRCL):Mar85-154
Reiter, N.  Nationalbewegungen auf dem
    Balkan.  Ziele und Wege der Balkanlin-
    guistik.
    D. Deletant, 575(SEER):Jul85-458
Reitmajer, V.  Der Einfluss des Dialekts
    auf die standardsprachlichen Leistungen
    von bayrischen Schülern in Vorschule,
    Grundschule und Gymnasium.
    H.H. Menge, 685(ZDL):1/1985-108

Reitmann, K.  Language from Nine to Five.
    D.R. Magrath, 399(MLJ):Winter85-448
"Les Relations entre juifs et musulmans
    en afrique du nord, XIXe-XXe siècles."
    H. Toledano, 318(JAOS):Jul-Sep84-588
"Relazioni storiche e culturali fra
    l'Italia e la Bulgaria."
    P.G. Pera, 575(SEER):Jan85-120
"Religion et culture dans la cité
    italienne de l'antiquité à nos jours."
    H.W. Wittschier, 547(RF):Band97Heft1-
    112
Remak, H.H.H.  Novellistische Struktur.
    R. Dumont, 549(RLC):Jul-Sep85-358
    J. Leibowitz, 678(YCGL):No34-138
Remnant, P. and J. Bennett - see Leibniz,
    G.W.
Rémy, P-J.  Comédies italiennes.
    J.A. Yeager, 207(FR):Apr86-820
Remys, E.  Hermann Hesse's Das Glasperlen-
    spiel.
    J. Mileck, 221(GQ):Spring85-301
"Renaissance Drama."  (Vol 14)  (L. Barkan,
    ed)
    W. Godshalk, 130:Fall85-270
Renan, E.  Judaïsme et Christianisme.  (A.
    de Benoist, ed)
    M. Bernal, 208(FS):Jan85-92
Renard, J-C.  Toutes les îles sont sec-
    rètes.
    Y-A. Favre, 450(NRF):Jun85-61
Renaud, B.  The Cat in the Cathedral.
    M. Rubio, 102(CanL):Fall85-115
Renaud, M.  Pour une lecture du "Moyen de
    Parvenir" de Beroalde de Verville.
    S. Bamforth, 161(DUJ):Jun85-268
    N. Kenny, 208(FS):Apr85-196
Renaut, A. - see Fichte, J.G.
Rendell, R.  Live Flesh.
    M. Laski, 362:17Apr86-29
    442(NY):20Oct86-132
Rendell, R.  The New Girl Friend.
    442(NY):31Mar86-82
Rendell, R.  The Tree of Hands.*
    639(VQR):Summer85-91
Rennert, J.  Hoher Mond.
    D. von Törne, 654(WB):6/1985-993
Rennick, R.M.  Kentucky Place Names.
    L.E. Seits, 424:Dec85-271
Renouard, P.  Imprimeurs et libraires
    parisiens du XVIe siècle.  (Vol 3)
    (U. Baurmeister and others, eds)
    78(BC):Spring85-9
Renwick, J.  Voltaire et Morangiès, 1772-
    1773, ou les Lumières l'ont échappé
    belle.*
    G. Gargett, 208(FS):Jul85-345
    J. Marchand, 535(RHL):Jan/Feb85-101
Renz, H. and F.W. Graf, eds.  Troeltsch-
    Studien.  (Vol 3)
    W.R. Ward, 161(DUJ):Jun85-294
Renza, L.A.  "A White Heron" and the Ques-
    tion of Minor Literature.*
    E. Ammons, 115:Summer85-375
    J.M. Lennon, 395(MFS):Winter85-855
    M. Pryse, 27(AL):Oct85-506
    S.B. Smith, 26(ALR):Spring/Autumn85-
    253
    295(JML):Nov85-507
"Répertoire des troupes de Trois-Rivières."
    L.E. Doucette, 627(UTQ):Summer85-464

"Répertoire du Centre d'essai des auteurs dramatiques."
 J-M. Larue, 193(Elit):Winter85-240
"Répertoire littéraire de l'Ouest canadien."
 A.B. Chartier, 207(FR):Dec85-285
"Report to the President by the Presidential Commission on the Space Shuttle Challenger Accident."
 J. Fallows, 453(NYRB):18Dec86-34
Reps, J.W. Views and Viewmakers of Urban America.
 E. Hulse, 470:Vol23-117
 T.J. Schlereth, 658:Summer/Autumn85-205
Rescher, N. Leibniz's Metaphysics of Nature.*
 D. Weissman, 543:Mar85-679
Rescher, N. The Riddle of Existence.
 J. Leslie, 486:Sep85-485
Rescher, N. Risk.
 W.A. Davis, 543:Mar86-579
Reshef, O. Guerre, mythes et caricature.
 B.T. Cooper, 207(FR):Apr86-833
Resnick, M.C. Interact in Spanish.
 G. Valdés, 238:Dec85-797
Resnick, M.C. Introducción a la historia de la lengua española.*
 S. Saporta, 239:Vol 1No1-142
Resnick, P. Parliament vs. People.
 R.M. Campbell, 298:Winter85/86-158
Restak, R.M. The Infant Mind.
 A.E. Johnson, 441:30Nov86-30
Restif de La Bretonne. Les Nuits de Paris. (J. Varloot and M. Delon, eds) My Father's Life. (R. Veasey, trans)
 D. Coward, 617(TLS):31Oct86-1226
Restivo, S. The Social Relations of Physics, Mysticism, and Mathematics.
 R.S. Brumbaugh, 543:Mar85-682
 A. Pickering, 84:Jun85-226
Reta, J.O. and M-A. Marcos Casquero - see under Oroz Reta, J. and M-A. Marcos Casquero
Retallack, J. Circumstantial Evidence.
 R. McDowell, 249(HudR):Winter86-684
Cardinal de Retz. Oeuvres. (M-T. Hipp and M. Pernot, eds)
 R. Zuber, 535(RHL):Nov/Dec85-1063
von Reuenthal, N. - see under Neidhart von Reuenthal
"Fritz Reuter im Urteil der Literaturkritik seiner Zeit."
 R. Fasold, 654(WB):1/1985-168
Reuter, H-H. Dichters Lande im Reich der Geschichte.
 P. Goldammer, 654(WB):2/1985-348
"Review of National Literatures." (Vol 10) (A. Paolucci and R. Warwick, eds)
 J.A. Ramsaran, 402(MLR):Jan85-141
"Review of the Public Health Service's Response to AIDS."
 J. Lieberson, 453(NYRB):16Jan86-43
"Review of the State-of-the-Art of Educational Technologies Implemented in Programs Serving LEP Students."
 R.E. Le Mon, 608:Jun86-331
Revuelta Sañudo, M. - see Menéndez Pelayo, M.
Rewald, J. Cézanne.
 J. Golding, 617(TLS):5Dec86-1363
 J. Russell, 441:7Dec86-11

Rewald, J. Paul Cézanne: The Watercolours.*
 L. Gowing, 90:Feb85-105
 C. Hartley, 39:May85-353
Rewald, J. Studies in Impressionism. Studies in Post-Impressionism. (I. Gordon and F. Weitzenhoffer, eds of both)
 A. Bowness, 617(TLS):28Mar86-324
 J. Russell, 441:1Jun86-11
Rexroth, K. Selected Poems. (B. Morrow, ed)
 M. Gibson, 30:Winter86-86
 S. Hamill, 29(APR):May/Jun86-9
Rey, A. - see Robert, P.
Rey, A. and others. Lexique 2: Le dictionnaire.
 E. Zöfgen, 547(RF):Band97Heft1-63
Rey, J.A.L. - see under León Rey, J.A.
Rey-Flaud, B. La Farce ou la machine à rire.
 D. Stone, Jr., 551(RenQ):Winter85-749
Rey-von Allmen, M. Apprentissage de l'orthographe française élémentaire par des adolescents non francophones enfants de travailleurs migrants.
 J-P. Beaujot, 209(FM):Oct85-260
Reydellet, M. La royauté dans la littérature latine de Sidoine Apollinaire à Isidore de Séville.
 M. Banniard, 555:Vol59fasc1-155
Reynen, H. "Eychesthai" und seine Derivate bei Homer.
 J-L. Perpillou, 555:Vol59fasc1-98
Reynolds, B., ed. Cambridge/Signorelli Dizionario Italiano-Inglese/Inglese-Italiano.
 G. Lepschy, 617(TLS):9May86-512
Reynolds, C. The Vigil.
 G. Krist, 441:16Feb86-16
Reynolds, G. The Later Paintings and Drawings of John Constable.*
 L. Parris and I. Fleming-Williams, 90:Mar85-164
 M. Warner, 324:Apr86-341
Reynolds, J. Aphrodisias and Rome.*
 C.P. Jones, 24:Summer85-262
Reynolds, J. Birket Foster.*
 M. Warner, 90:Oct85-725
Reynolds, L.D., ed. Texts and Transmission.
 S. Schierling, 377:Mar85-42
Reynolds, M. The Young Hemingway.
 J.R. Bryer, 454:Spring86-270
 J. Campbell, 617(TLS):1Aug86-837
 J. Chamberlain, Jr., 441:9Mar86-24
 W. Sheed, 453(NYRB):12Jun86-5
Reynolds, M.S., ed. Critical Essays on Hemingway's "In Our Time."*
 J. Meyers, 50(ArQ):Winter85-370
Reynolds, M.T. Joyce and Dante.*
 H. Shankland, 161(DUJ):Jun84-306
Reynolds, O. Skevington's Daughter.*
 P. Gross, 493:Oct85-67
 C. Rawson, 617(TLS):7Feb86-137
 W. Scammell, 364:Dec85/Jan86-119
Reynolds, S. The Vision of Simeon Solomon.
 M. Bence-Jones, 324:Dec85-68
 L. Lambourne, 90:Aug85-541
Rézeau, P. Dictionnaire des régionalismes de l'Ouest entre Loire et Gironde.*
 C. Verreault, 320(CJL):Winter85-503

Riegl, A. Late Roman Art Industry.
  A. Cutler, 124:Jul-Aug86-425
Rielo, F. Teoría del Quijote.
  J. Rodríguez-Luis, 240(HR):Autumn85-490
Riemenschneider, D., ed. The History and Historiography of Commonwealth Literature.
  S.H. Arnold, 678(YCGL):No34-125
Riemer, A.P. Antic Fables.
  M. Gilbert, 570(SQ):Autumn85-375
Ries, G. Prolog und Epilog in Gesetzen des Altertums.
  C. Williamson, 313:Vol75-257
Rieselbach, H.F. Conrad's Rebels.
  295(JML):Nov85-463
Riffaterre, M. Sémiotique de la poésie.
  F. Rastier, 209(FM):Apr85-143
Rigby, A. Initiation and Initiative.
  T.A. Emmert, 104(CASS):Summer85-235
Rigby, P. Persistent Pastoralists.
  T. Ingold, 617(TLS):2May86-481
Rigby, T.H. and B. Harasymiw, eds. Leadership Selection and Patron-Client Relations in the USSR and Yugoslavia.
  R.C. Gripp, 104(CASS):Spring85-93
  S.S. Vosper, 575(SEER):Jan85-146
Rigg, A.G. and C. Brewer - see Langland, W.
Riggio, T.P., J.L.W. West 3d and N.M. Westlake - see Dreiser, T.
Riggs, D. Keelhauled.
  T. Gibbs, 441:17Aug86-17
Righetti, A. Il ritratto, l'epitaffio, il clavicordo.
  M. del Sapio, 402(MLR):Oct85-913
Rigolot, F. Le Texte de la Renaissance.*
  G. Defaux, 546(RR):Jan85-116
  U. Langer, 400(MLN):Sep85-901
Rigoni Stern, M. L'anno della vittoria.
  A.L. Lepschy, 617(TLS):15Aug86-893
Rijlaarsdam, J.C. Platon über die Sprache.
  G. Lepschy, 545(RPh):Feb86-336
Riley, A.W. and D.O. Spettigue - see Grove, F.P.
Riley, E.C. "Don Quixote."
  A.J. Close, 617(TLS):28Nov86-1352
Riley, H.M.K. Das Bild der Antike in der deutschen Romantik.
  J. Ryan, 406:Summer85-229
Riley, T. The Price of a Life.
  N. Robertson, 441:13Apr86-32
Riley-Smith, J. The First Crusade and the Idea of Crusading.
  H.E.J. Cowdrey, 617(TLS):25Jul86-826
Rilke, R.M. Letters on Cézanne.* (C. Rilke, ed)
  H. Moss, 442(NY):7Jul86-80
  J. Russell, 441:1Jun86-11
Rilke, R.M. Lettres à une amie vénitienne.
  L. Kovacs, 450(NRF):Oct85-84
Rilke, R.M. Lettres françaises à Merline, 1919-1922.
  M. Jarrety, 450(NRF):Apr85-77
Rilke, R.M. New Poems. (E. Snow, trans)
  639(VQR):Summer85-99
Rilke, R.M. Poems 1912-1926.* (M. Hamburger, ed) The Selected Poetry of Rainer Maria Rilke.* (S. Mitchell, ed and trans) Selected Poems of Rainer Maria Rilke. (R. Bly, ed and trans) Letters to a Young Poet. (S. Mitchell, trans)
  C.S. Brown, 569(SR):Fall85-656
  M. Goldstein, 569(SR):Fall85-624

Rilke, R.M. Rodin and Other Prose Pieces.
  617(TLS):25Apr86-459
Rilke, R.M. The Sonnets to Orpheus.
  M. Hofmann, 441:21Sep86-18
Rilke, R.M. The Unknown Rilke.*
  J.T. Brewer, 399(MLJ):Summer85-188
  C.S. Brown, 569(SR):Fall85-656
Rimbaud, A. Stixi (Poésies).
  J.L. Backès, 549(RLC):Jul-Sep85-361
Rimler, W. Not Fade Away.
  J.K. Skipper, Jr., 498:Vol9No4-81
Rimmon-Kenan, S. Narrative Fiction.*
  W. Leith, 307:May85-74
  O. Scherer, 549(RLC):Oct-Dec85-455
"Il Rinascimento: Interpretazioni e problemi."
  A. Buck, 72:Band222Heft2-472
Rincón García, W. Un siglo de escultura en Zaragoza (1808-1908).
  M. Estella, 48:Oct-Dec85-435
Ring, B. Let Virtue Be a Guide to Thee.
  D.L.F. Affleck, 432(NEQ):Mar85-113
Ring, F.K. Against the Current.
  442(NY):13Jan86-87
Ringger, K. L'Ame et la page.*
  A. Pizzorusso, 405(MP):May86-437
Rio, M. Parrot's Perch.*
  P. Smelt, 617(TLS):30May86-597
Ríos, A. Five Indiscretions.
  C. Muske, 441:9Feb86-28
Rioux, J-P. La France de la Quatrième République, 2.
  J. Howorth, 208(FS):Jul85-369
Ripley, J. "Julius Caesar" on Stage in England and America, 1599-1973.
  T. Pughe, 179(ES):Apr85-184
Ripoll, R. Réalité et Mythe chez Zola.*
  R. Lethbridge, 208(FS):Apr85-226
Riquelme, J.P. Teller and Tale in Joyce's Fiction.*
  J.H. Maddox, 329(JJQ):Fall85-101
Riquelme, J.P. - see Senn, F.
Risa, E.O. - see Kielland, A.L.
Rischbieter, H., ed. Theater-Lexikon.
  R. Engle, 615(TJ):Dec85-515
Rischin, M. - see Cahan, A.
Riseboro, B. The Story of Western Architecture.
  42(AR):Fall85-502
Ristori, R. - see Poggio Bracciolini, G.F.
Ritchie, D.A. James M. Landis.
  G.F. Goodwin, 106:Spring85-95
Ritchie, J.M. German Literature under National Socialism.*
  H. Ridley, 402(MLR):Jan85-237
  A. Stephan, 222(GR):Summer85-117
Ritchie, R.C. Captain Kidd and the War against the Pirates.
  P. Earle, 617(TLS):12Dec86-1397
  J. Haskins, 441:190ct86-31
Rittaud-Hutinet, J. La Vision d'un Futur.
  M. de Rougemont, 610:Spring85-76
Ritter, A. Bibliographie zu Pierre Corneille von 1958 bis 1983.
  W.L., 475:Vol 12No22-361
Ritter, E. Urban Scrawl.
  W.N., 102(CanL):Spring85-183
  C. Rooke, 376:Mar85-166
Ritter-Schaumburg, H. Die Nibelungen zogen nordwärts.
  G. Müller, 597(SN):Vol57No1-105

Roddewig, M. Dante Alighieri, Die gött-
liche Komödie; vergleichende Bestandauf-
nahme der Commedia-Handschriften.
  M. Bosch, 70:May/Jun85-157
Roderick, G.W. and M.D. Stephens. Post
School Education.
  D.P. Leinster-Mackay and D.W. Collin,
  637(VS):Summer86-635
Rodes, R.E., Jr. Lay Authority and Reform-
ation in the English Church: Edward I to
the Civil War.
  M.C. Burson, 589:Jul85-715
  R.A. Houlbrooke, 382(MAE):1985/2-296
Rodewald, J.D. Reviewing German Grammar.
  M.W. Conner, 399(MLJ):Autumn85-309
Rodger, N.A.M. The Wooden World.
  R. Morriss, 617(TLS):12Dec86-1397
Rodgers, P.H., C. Sullivan and others. A
Photographic History of Cambridge.
  B.A. Norton, 432(NEQ):Sep85-474
Rodin, A.E. and J.D. Key. Medical Case-
book of Doctor Arthur Conan Doyle.
  E.S. Lauterbach, 395(MFS):Summer85-382
Rodini, R.J. and S. Di Maria. Ludovico
Ariosto.
  E. Bigi, 228(GSLI):Vol 162fasc519-462
  C.P. Brand, 276:Winter85-327
  P.D. Wiggins, 539:Aug86-301
Rodinis, G.T. - see under Toso Rodinis, G.
Rodis-Lewis, G. Descartes.
  J. Bernhardt, 542:Jul-Sep85-320
Rodis-Lewis, G., with G. Malbreil - see de
Malebranche, N.
Rodley, L. Cave Monasteries of Byzantine
Cappadocia.
  A. Bryer, 617(TLS):14Nov86-1288
Rodman, F.R. Keeping Hope Alive.
  D. Sobel, 441:23Mar86-47
Rodríguez, E. and A. Tordera. Calderón y
la obra corta dramática del siglo XVII.
  J-M. Díez Borque, 304(JHP):Winter85-
  178
  T.A. O'Connor, 238:Mar85-66
Rodríguez, E. and A. Tordera - see Cal-
derón de la Barca, P.
Rodríguez, R. Hunger of Memory.*
  R. Saldívar, 153:Fall85-25
Rodríguez Freile, J. El Carnero. (M.
Germán Romer, ed)
  J.J. Alstrum, 238:Sep85-524
Rodríguez Lee, M.L. Juegos sicológicos en
la narrativa de Vargas Llosa.
  E. McCracken, 238:Sep85-528
Rodríguez López-Vázquez, A. - see de Clara-
monte, A.
Rodríguez-Luis, J. Novedad y ejemplo de
la Novelas de Cervantes.
  E.H. Friedman, 552(REH):May85-153
Rodríguez M. Montalvo, S. - see Alfonso X
Rodríguez-Peralta, P. Tres poetas en la
poesía peruana.
  J.M. Naharro, 552(REH):Oct85-144
Rodríguez-Seda de Laguna, A. Shaw en el
mundo hispánico.
  R.A. Young, 107(CRCL):Sep85-559
Roe, S.A. Matter, Life and Generation.
  P.R. Sloan, 84:Mar85-94
Roeck, B. Elias Holl, Architekt einer
europäischen Stadt.
  W. Schirmer, 43:Band15Heft1-97
Roeder, G.H., Jr. Forum of Uncertainty.
  D. Anfam, 59:Jun85-261

Roegiest, E. Les Prépositions A et DE en
espagnol contemporain.*
  R. Wright, 545(RPh):May85-523
Roegiest, E. and L. Tasmowski, eds. Verbe
et phrase dans les langues romanes.
  M. Iliescu, 553(RLiR):Jan-Jun85-191
Roethel, H.K. and J.K. Benjamin. Kandin-
sky: Catalogue Raisonné of the Oil Paint-
ings.* (Vol 1)
  P. Overy, 592:Vol 198No1011-55
Roethel, H.K. and J.K. Benjamin. Kandin-
sky, Catalogue Raisonné of the Oil Paint-
ings.* (Vol 2)
  P. Overy, 592:Vol 198No1011-55
  S.A. Stein, 90:Apr85-239
  F. Thürlemann, 683:Band48Heft1-126
  P. Vergo, 59:Dec85-496
Roetzer, H.G. Traditionalität und Modern-
ität in der europäischen Literatur.
  P. Kapitza, 224(GRM):Band35Heft2-228
Roger, A. Les Plaisirs et les noms.
  P-L. Rey, 450(NRF):Apr85-95
Rogers, J. Her Living Image.
  B. Tritel, 441:17Aug86-22
Rogers, J.N. The Country Music Message.
  B.L. Cooper, 498:Vol 10No1-77
Rogers, J.S. Stage by Stage.
  P. Cotes, 324:Nov86-848
Rogers, K.M. Feminism in Eighteenth-
Century England.*
  M. Gutwirth, 403(MLS):Fall85-353
  M. Myers, 173(ECS):Fall85-107
  J. Richetti, 131(CL):Spring85-190
  J. Simons, 541(RES):Aug85-432
  J. Spencer, 447(N&Q):Mar84-130
  C. Wellbery, 149(CLS):Summer85-270
Rogers, M. Blue Guide Museums and Gal-
leries of London. (2nd ed)
  D. Piper, 617(TLS):9May86-508
Rogers, P. Eighteenth-Century Encounters.*
Literature and Popular Culture in
Eighteenth-Century England.*
  P. Lewis, 364:Jun85-98
Rogers, P. - see Swift, J.
Rogers, W.E. The Three Genres and the
Interpretation of Lyric.*
  G. Bedetti, 223:Spring85-101
  J. Voelker, 577(SHR):Fall85-363
Rogerson, J. Atlas of the Bible.
  P-L. Adams, 61:Jan86-96
Rogerson, J. Old Testament Criticism in
the Nineteenth Century.
  J.L. Altholz, 637(VS):Spring86-474
Rogger, H. Russia in the Age of Modernisa-
tion and Revolution, 1881-1917.
  R. Wortman, 550(RusR):Jul85-299
Rogin, M.P. Subversive Genealogy.*
  M.R. Patterson, 594:Winter85-432
  M.M. Sealts, Jr., 579(SAQ):Spring85-
  225
Rogow, A.A. Thomas Hobbes.
  A.A. Rhodes, 441:13Jul86-19
Rohan, C. Down by the Dockside.
  442(NY):8Sep86-136
Rohan Koda. Pagoda, Skull and Samurai.
  G. O'Brien, 441:30Mar86-18
"Mies van der Rohe: Architect as Educator."
  M. Filler, 453(NYRB):12Jun86-26
Rohland de Langbehn, R. - see F.A.D.C.
Rohland de Langbehn, R. - see Scrivá, L.
Rohlfs, G. Antroponimia e Toponomastica
nelle lingue neolatine.
  J-P. Chambon, 553(RLiR):Jul-Dec85-464

319

Rohlfs, G. Romanische Lehnübersetzungen aus germanischer Grundlage (Materia romana, spirito germanico).*
H. Lausberg, 547(RF):Band97Heft2/3-263
Rohlfs, G. Von Rom zur Romania.*
E.F. Tuttle, 545(RPh):Nov85-234
Ro'i, Y., ed. The USSR and the Muslim World.
S. Akiner, 575(SEER):Oct85-630
A.S. Donnelly, 104(CASS):Spring85-97
Roig, M. Ramona, adiós. Tiempo de cerezas. La hora violeta.
P. Zatlin-Boring, 241:May85-117
Rojas Nieto, C. Las construcciones coordinadas sindéticas en el español hablado culto de la Ciudad de México.
S. Plann, 545(RPh):Nov85-253
Rojo, G. and E. Montero Cartelle. La Evolución de los esquemas condicionales (Potenciales e irreales desde el poema del Cid hasta 1400).
M.B. Harris, 545(RPh):Feb86-354
Rolant, E. Gwaith Owain ap Llywelyn ab y Moel.
T.A. Watkins, 112:Vol 17-170
Roli, R. and G. Sestieri. I disegni italiani del settecento.*
D.C. Miller, 90:Apr85-236
Rolland, B.J. and E. O'Connor. Initiation aux affaires.
E. Doss-Quinby, 207(FR):Dec85-316
B. Muller, 399(MJL):Summer85-178
Rollason, D.W. The Mildrith Legend.*
E. Mason, 382(MAE):1985/1-135
Rölleke, H. "Nebeninschriften."
J.M. McGlathery, 406:Spring85-103
Rölleke, H. - see Grimm, J. and W.
Rolley, C. Les vases de bronze de l'archaïsme récent en Grande-Grèce.
P. Cartledge, 303(JoHS):Vol 105-238
Rollinger, C-R., ed. Probleme des (Text-) Verstehens.
A. Jameson, 353:Vol23No4-637
Rollins, J. Between Women.
W. Kaminer, 441:2Feb86-17
Rollins, J.D. A History of Swahili Prose. (Pt 1)
J. Knappert, 538(RAL):Winter85-630
Rollyson, C.E., Jr. Uses of the Past in the Novels of William Faulkner.
P.H. Gallert, 392:Summer85-383
Rolph, C.H. As I Was Saying.
L. Taylor, 617(TLS):18Jul86-779
Rolston, H. Religious Inquiry.
M. Adam, 542:Oct-Dec85-564
Rølvaag, O.E. When the Wind is in the South and Other Stories. (S. Zempel, ed and trans)
E. Haugen, 563(SS):Summer85-358
Romaine, S. The Language of Children and Adolescents.
B. Johnstone, 350:Dec86-927
Romaine, S., ed. Sociolinguistic Variation in Speech Communities.
R.W. Fasold, 355(LSoc):Dec85-515
G. Radden, 257(IRAL):Feb85-74
"La Roman de Renart." (Naoyuki Fukumoto, Noboru Harano and Satoru Suzuki, eds)
G. Roques, 553(RLiR):Jul-Dec85-519
"Le roman romantique latino-américain et ses prolongements."
B. Lavallé, 92(BH):Jul-Dec84-575

Romanell, P. John Locke and Medicine.
C. Walton, 319:Oct86-558
Romano, A. - see under Anonimo romano
"Il romanzo in discussione."
E. Smyth, 535(RHL):Jul/Aug85-699
Rombach, H. Welt und Gegenwelt.
B. Casper, 489(PJGG):Band92Heft2-405
Romeiser, J.B., ed. Red Flags, Black Flags.
S.G. Thacker, 345(KRQ):Vol32No4-442
Romeo-Mark, A. Two Faces, Two Phases.
A. Sistrunk-Krakue, 95(CLAJ):Sep85-106
Römer, G. and F. Patzer, eds. Abraham a Sancta Clara.
F. Gaede, 406:Winter85-482
Romer, M.G. - see under Germán Romer, M.
Romer, S. Idols.
F. Adcock, 617(TLS):7Nov86-1256
Romeralo, A.S. - see under Sánchez Romeralo, A.
Romeralo, A.S. and others - see under Sánchez Romeralo, A. and others
de Romilly, J. A Short History of Greek Literature.
W.E. McCulloh, 344:Summer86-135
Romulo, C.P., with B.D. Romulo. Forty Years.
E. Sciolino, 441:9Nov86-33
Ronan, R. Narratives From America. A Radiance Like Wind or Water.
M. Scates, 448:Vol23No3-124
Ronchi, G. - see Ariosto, L.
Ronen, O. An Approach to Mandelštam.
J.E. Malmstad, 550(RusR):Jul85-319
D.M. West, 402(MLR):Jul85-767
Ronneberger-Sibold, E. Sprachverwendung — Sprachsystem.
E. Beneš, 685(ZDL):1/1985-94
Ronzeaud, P., ed. Le Roman Historique (XVIIe-XXe Siècles).
P. Hourcade, 475:Vol 12No22-366
Rood, D.S., ed. 1983 Mid-American Linguistics Conference Papers.
W. Bright, 350:Sep86-698
Rooke, L. A Bolt of White Cloth.
A. Dawson, 102(CanL):Fall85-155
B. Dempster, 99:Apr85-31
Rooke, L. Shakespeare's Dog.
A.B. Dawson, 102(CanL):Spring85-109
Rooke, L. Sing Me No Love Songs, I'll Say You No Prayers.*
C.A. Howells, 102(CanL):Summer85-165
Rooks, G. Can't Stop Talking.
D. Danielson, 399(MLJ):Spring85-120
Room, A. A Concise Dictionary of Modern Place-Names in Great Britain and Ireland.*
E.G. Stanley, 447(N&Q):Dec84-530
Rooney, C.J., Jr. Dreams and Visions.
D. Ketterer, 26(ALR):Spring/Autumn85-285
C.P. Wilson, 594:Winter85-434
295(JML):Nov85-383
Roose-Evans, J. Experimental Theatre.*
T. Dunn, 157:No156-51
Roosevelt, E. The Hyde Park Murder.
T.J. Binyon, 617(TLS):7Mar86-256
Ropars-Wuilleumier, M-C. Le texte divisé.
D.N. Rodowick, 153:Spring85-34
Roquelet, A. - see Hector of Chartres
Roqueta, M. Grünes Paradies.
G. Kremnitz, 72:Band222Heft2-457

Rorem, P.  Biblical and Liturgical Symbols
within the Pseudo-Dionysian Synthesis.
W.J. Carroll, 543:Mar86-580
Rorty, R.  Consequences of Pragmatism.*
    J. Habermas, 384:Sep/Oct85-905
    P. Jacob, 98:Jun-Jul85-593
    D. Mannison, 63:Mar85-96
    S. Raval, 50(ArQ):Summer85-183
Rorty, R., J.B. Schneewind and Q. Skinner.
Philosophy in History.
    A. Montefiore, 617(TLS):17Jan86-68
    A. O'Hear, 262:Dec85-455
Rosa, A.  Salem, Transcendentalism, and
Hawthorne.
    B.J., 27(AL):May85-360
Rosa, J.G.  They Called Him Wild Bill.
    L. Horne, 106:Summer85-221
Rosa, L.G. - see under Gualdo Rosa, L.
von Rosador, K.T. - see under Tetzeli von
Rosador, K.
Rosanvallon, P.  Le Moment Guizot.
    J-P. Guinle, 450(NRF):Sep85-94
Rosasco, J.T.  Voies de l'imagination
proustienne.
    M. Muller, 546(RR):Mar85-223
Rose, E.  Blick nach Osten.  (I. Schuster,
ed)
    S.L. Gilman, 107(CRCL):Sep85-542
Rose, I.  Werner Drewes.
    N. Powell, 39:Jun85-436
Rose, J.  The Case of Peter Pan, or the
Impossibility of Children's Fiction.
    M. Bal, 204(FdL):Jun85-151
Rose, M.  Writer's Block.
    L.M. Schultz, 126(CCC):Dec85-497
Rose, M.A.  Marx's Lost Aesthetic.
    R. Taylor, 89(BJA):Summer85-282
Rose, N.  Chaim Weizmann.
    B. Wasserstein, 441:23Nov86-12
Rose, S.J.  The American Profile Poster.
    R. Lekachman, 441:4May86-39
Rose, W.  El pastor de la muerte.*
    A. de Toro, 547(RF):Band97Heft2/3-331
Rosecrance, B.  Forster's Narrative
Vision.*
    T. Brown, 541(RES):Aug85-451
Rosecrance, R.  The Rise of the Trading
State.*
    P. Kennedy, 441:5Jan86-7
Rösel, H.  Wörterbuch zu den tschechischen
Schriften des J.A. Comenius.*
    J. Daňhelka, 688(ZSP):Band45Heft1-214
    A. Měšťan, 688(ZSP):Band45Heft1-218
Roseliep, R.  The Earth We Swing On.
    R. Spiess, 404:Winter-Spring85-67
Rosellini, J.  Volker Braun.
    M. Eifler, 221(GQ):Fall85-635
Rosen, B.M., ed.  Iran Since the Revolu-
tion.
    F. Halliday, 617(TLS):20Jun86-667
Rosen, C.  Plays of Impasse.*
    M.G. Rose, 130:Summer85-187
Rosen, C.  Schoenberg.
    A.F.L.T., 412:Aug/Nov84-304
Rosen, C. and H. Zerner.  Romanticism and
Realism.*
    A. Brookner, 90:Aug85-540
    J-C. Lebensztejn, 98:Mar85-225
Rosen, D. and A. Porter, eds.  Verdi's
"Macbeth."*
    D.R.B. Kimbell, 410(M&L):Oct85-391
    W. Dean, 415:May85-284
                              [continued]

[continuing]
    G. Schmidgall, 130:Winter85/86-387
    K. Tetzeli von Rosador, 156(ShJW):
    Jahrbuch1985-260
Rosen, D. and S.  Death and Blintzes.
    N. Callendar, 441:26Jan86-40
Rosen, G.  The Structure of American Med-
ical Practice, 1875-1941.  (C. Rosenberg,
ed)
    C.D. Howell, 106:Fall85-339
Rosén, H.B.  East and West.  (Pt 2)
    M. O'Connor, 350:Dec86-950
Rosen, K.  Ammianus Marcellinus.
    T.D. Barnes, 123:Vol35No1-48
    J-P. Callu, 555:Vol59fasc1-145
Rosen, M.  Hegel's Dialectic and its Criti-
cism.*
    D.R. Knowles, 479(PhQ):Apr85-199
Rosen, R.  Fadeaway.
    442(NY):24Nov86-151
Rosen, S.  Plato's "Sophist."*
    L. Brown, 123:Vol35No1-69
    D.C. Lindenmuth, 543:Sep85-167
    P. Seligman, 154:Spring85-158
Rosenbaum, A., M.N. Rosenbaum and B.
Foltin, Jr.  Folk Visions and Voices.
    W.E. Lightfoot, 292(JAF):Jul/Sep85-351
Rosenbaum, J.  Film.
    B. Allen, 529(QQ):Autumn85-618
Rosenberg, A.  Nicolas Gueudeville and his
Work (1652-172?).*
    E. Labrousse, 535(RHL):Jul/Aug85-684
Rosenberg, A.  Sociobiology and the Pre-
emption of Social Science.
    E. Sober, 488:Mar85-89
Rosenberg, A.  The Structure of Biological
Science.
    D.L.H., 185:Jul86-899
Rosenberg, B. and E. Goldstein.  Creators
and Disturbers.
    H. Merker, 390:Jan85-61
Rosenberg, C. - see Rosen, G.
Rosenberg, D.M.  Oaten Reeds and Trumpets.
    A. Rudrum and J. Sturrock, 677(YES):
    Vol 15-289
Rosenberg, H.  Art and Other Serious
Matters.*
    R. Boyers, 617(TLS):18Jul86-791
    D. Carrier, 90:Nov85-817
Rosenberg, H.  The Case of the Baffled
Radical.
    R. Boyers, 617(TLS):18Jul86-791
    442(NY):24Feb86-104
von Rosenberg, I.  Alan Sillitoe: "Satur-
day Night and Sunday Morning."
    D. Mehl, 72:Band222Heft2-423
Rosenberg, J.F.  Thinking Clearly about
Death.*
    J. Harris, 518:Jul85-188
Rosenberg, L.  The Fire Music.
    A. Brumer, 441:6Jul86-23
Rosenberg, N. and L.E. Birdzell, Jr.  How
the West Grew Rich.
    D.S. Landes, 453(NYRB):29May86-46
    D.N. McCloskey, 441:9Feb86-18
    B. Supple, 617(TLS):12Sep86-1000
Rosenberg, P.  Tout l'oeuvre peint de Char-
din.
    P. Conisbee, 90:Feb85-100
Rosenberg, P. and U. Van de Sandt.  Pierre
Peyron 1744-1814.
    P. Bordes, 54:Mar85-158


321

Rosenberg, S.E. The Real Jewish World.
  J. Riemer, 390:Aug/Sep85-55
Rosenberg, S.N. and H. Tischler, eds.
  Chanter m'estuet.
  I. Short, 208(FS):Apr85-183
Rosenberg, W.G., ed. Bolshevik Visions.
  L. Mally, 550(RusR):Jul85-316
Rosenblum, M. Mission to Civilize.
  W.R. Carlson, 441:21Dec86-20
Rosenblum, N. A World History of Photog-
  raphy.
  H. Martin, 507:Mar/Apr85-104
Rosenblum, R. and H.W. Janson. 19th Cen-
  tury Art.* (British title: Art of the
  Nineteenth Century.)
  K. Baker, 55:May85-29
Rosendahl, P.J. Han Ola og han Per — en
  norsk-amerikansk tegne-serie. (J.
  Buckley and E. Haugen, eds)
  K. Smemo, 563(SS):Summer85-341
Rosenfeld, A.H. Imagining Hitler.*
  L.L. Langer, 385(MQR):Winter86-127
Rosenfeld, S. Georgian Scene Painters and
  Scene Painting.
  M. Jones, 447(N&Q):Mar84-95
Rosenfeld, S. The Georgian Theatre of
  Richmond Yorkshire.*
  F.A. Langhans, 612(ThS):May85-97
  C. Willmott, 611(TN):Vol39No2-91
Rosenfel, W. The Practical Specifier.
  T. Fisher, 505:Dec85-101
Rosenfield, L.C., ed. Condorcet Studies I.
  J. Popkin, 319:Jul86-414
Rosengarten, T. Tombee.
  E.D. Genovese, 441:20Jul86-1
  442(NY):18Aug86-74
Rosenkrantz, R.D. - see Jaynes, E.T.
Rosenmeyer, T.G. The Art of Aeschylus.*
  M. Gagarin, 131(CL):Spring85-178
  D.A. Lupher, 24:Winter85-515
Rosenplenter, L. Zitat und Autoritäten-
  berufung im Renner Hugo von Trimberg.
  W.H. Jackson, 402(MLR):Oct85-978
Rosenthal, B., ed. Critical Essays on
  Charles Brockden Brown.
  B. Christophersen, 651(WHR):Spring85-
  77
  E. Wagenknecht, 402(MLR):Jan85-129
Rosenthal, C. Loop's Progress.
  W. Grimes, 441:16Nov86-24
Rosenthal, E. The Calculus of Murder.
  N. Callendar, 441:28Dec86-15
Rosenthal, M. The Character Factory.
  J. Gathorne-Hardy, 441:1Jun86-7
  T. Nairn, 362:28Aug86-22
  D. Pryce-Jones, 617(TLS):19Dec86-1431
  G. Wheatcroft, 453(NYRB):26Jun86-11
  442(NY):23Jun86-98
Rosenthal, M. Constable.*
  D.H. Solkin, 54:Sep85-507
Rosier, I. La grammaire spéculative des
  modistes.*
  W.E. McMahon, 589:Jul85-716
Rosińska, G. Scientific Writings and
  Astronomical Tables in Cracow (XIVth-
  XVIth Centuries).
  P.W. Knoll, 497(PolR):Vol30No2-225
  R.B. Thomson, 589:Oct85-1060
Roskell, J.S. The Impeachment of Michael
  de la Pole, Earl of Suffolk, in 1836 in
  the Context of the Reign of Richard II.
  J.L. Gillespie, 589:Jul85-718
  G.B. Stow, 377:Jul85-125

Roskill, M. The Interpretation of Cubism.
  P. Daix, 90:Dec85-909
Roskill, M. and D. Carrier. Truth and
  Falsehood in Visual Images.*
  M. Austin, 89(BJA):Winter85-81
  J. Hunter, 639(VQR):Winter85-170
Rosman, D. Evangelicals and Culture.
  J. Seed, 366:Spring85-154
Ross, A. Blindfold Games.
  A. Massie, 362:30Jan86-25
  P. Oakes, 617(TLS):21Feb86-201
Ross, A. The Emissary.
  M. Bose, 362:18Sep86-22
Ross, A. and D. Woolley - see "Jonathan
  Swift"
Ross, C. Richard III.*
  J.M.W. Bean, 551(RenQ):Winter85-710
Ross, C.L. - see Lawrence, D.H.
Ross, C.S. Vladimir Nabokov.
  J.P. Levine, 268(IFR):Summer86-104
  J.P. Shute, 395(MFS):Winter85-757
Ross, G., ed. The Foreign Office and the
  Kremlin.
  F.S. Northedge, 575(SEER):Jul85-468
Ross, G.M. Leibniz.
  J. Egan, 568(SCN):Winter85-69
  P.J. Fitz Patrick, 83:Spring85-110
Ross, I.C. - see Sterne, L.
Ross, J. Beaton in Vogue.
  A. Grundberg, 441:7Dec86-21
  442(NY):13Oct86-159
Ross, J. The Papers of Chief John Ross.
  (G.E. Moulton, ed)
  M. Abley, 617(TLS):21Mar86-299
Ross, J. - see Congreve, W.
Ross, J.F. Portraying Analogy.*
  D. Burrell, 438:Summer85-347
  W.A. Frank, 543:Dec84-401
  J.N. Pankhurst, 307:Aug85-130
  M.L. Raposa, 438:Spring85-233
  E. Wierenga, 484(PPR):Jun86-692
Ross, M., ed. The Arts.
  P. Abbs, 89(BJA):Winter85-72
Ross, M. Lohengrin.
  M. Laski, 362:3Jul86-32
Ross, P. Hovey's Deception.
  N. Callendar, 441:17Aug86-20
Ross, S.D., ed. Art and Its Significance.
  D. Collinson, 89(BJA):Winter85-76
Ross, V. Fisherwoman.
  J.K. Keefer, 198:Summer85-107
Rossabi, M., ed. China among Equals.
  R.W. Dunnell, 293(JASt):Nov84-194
Rossel, A. Le Faux Grand Siècle (1604-
  1715).
  N. Aronson, 475:Vol 12No22-374
Rossel, S.H. Johannes V. Jensen.
  A. Heitmann, 562(Scan):May85-90
Rosselli, J. The Opera Industry in Italy
  from Cimarosa to Verdi.*
  J. Allitt, 278(IS):Vol40-146
  C. Duggan, 410(M&L):Apr85-155
  K. Neely, 615(TJ):May85-239
Rosset, C. La Force majeure.*
  E. Blondel, 542:Jan-Mar85-41
Rossi, F. Ceramica geometrica apula nella
  collezione Chini del Museo Civico di
  Bassano del Grappa.
  J-P. Morel, 555:Vol59fasc1-159
Rossi, P. The Dark Abyss of Time.*
  R. Laudan, 486:Dec85-644
Rossi, S. - see von Meysenbug, M.

Rossiliano, E.L. My Sins.
  S.L. Cuba, 497(PolR):Vol30No1-105
Rossini, G. L'edizione critica delle
  opere di Gioachino Rossini. (Vol 1)
  (B. Cagli, P. Gossett and A. Zedda, eds)
  R. Osborne, 415:Feb85-92
"Rossiya i SShA."
  J.M. Hartley, 575(SEER):Oct85-595
Rosslyn, F. - see Homer
Rosslyn, W. The Prince, the Fool and the
  Nunnery.
  B. Heldt, 402(MLR):Apr85-511
  L. Tlusty, 575(SEER):Apr85-293
Rossman, C., D. Stark and P. Brown.
  Enchanted Rock.
  L. Milazzo, 584(SWR):Spring85-262
Rössner, M. and B. Wagner, eds. Aufstieg
  und Krise der Vernunft.
  P.V. Zima, 602:Band16Heft2-287
Rosso, C. Pagine al vento.*
  E. Chevallier, 549(RLC):Jul-Sep85-371
Rostand, E. Cyrano de Bergerac. (P.
  Besnier, ed)
  W.D. Howarth, 208(FS):Oct85-491
Rostow, W.W. The United States and the
  Regional Organization of Asia and the
  Pacific, 1965-1985.
  S. Krasner, 441:4May86-18
Roszak, T. The Cult of Information.
  P. Forbes, 362:16Oct86-24
  J. Gleick, 441:22Jun86-21
Rotella, A. Closing the Circle.
  404:Autumn85-57
Rotella, A. Polishing the Ladybug.
  404:Summer85-58
Rotella, A. Rearranging Light.
  404:Summer85-50
Rotenstreich, N. Jews and German Philos-
  ophy.
  J.G.H., 185:Apr86-667
Rotenstreich, N. Man and His Dignity.
  G. Graham, 543:Sep85-169
Roth, H. Touching the Stone Ax.
  C. Brickley, 404:Winter-Spring85-69
Roth, J. Tarabas.
  L. Kovacs, 450(NRF):Sep85-107
Roth, L.M. McKim, Mead and White, Archi-
  tects.*
  B. Donham, 505:Jan85-173
  C.F. Otto, 31(ASch):Spring85-276
  L. Wodehouse, 658:Spring85-94
Roth, M.P., ed. Perspectives on Faust.
  D. Vincent, 564:Nov85-307
Roth, P. The Prague Orgy.*
  N. Berry, 176:May86-56
  A.R. Tintner, 390:Dec85-49
Roth, P. Reading Myself and Others.
  617(TLS):6Jun86-631
Roth, P. Zuckerman Bound.*
  M. Gorra, 249(HudR):Winter86-664
Rothe, H. Religion und Kultur in den
  Regionen des russischen Reiches im 18.
  Jahrhundert — Erster Versuch einer
  Grundlegung.
  L. Hughes, 402(MLR):Apr85-508
  M.J. Okenfuss, 104(CASS):Spring85-67
Rothenberg, J., ed. Technicians of the
  Sacred. (2nd ed)
  M. Perloff, 29(APR):Jan/Feb86-37
Rothenberg, J. and D., eds. Symposium of
  the Whole.*
  J. Bruchac, 538(RAL):Fall85-440

Röther, K. Die Germanistenverbände und
  ihre Tagungen.
  H. Schmidt, 682(ZPSK):Band38Heft4-426
Rothermund, D. and J. Simon. Education
  and the Integration of Ethnic Minorities.
  S. Nasta, 617(TLS):13Jun86-658
Rothman, E.K. Hands and Hearts.
  J.W. Crowley, 432(NEQ):Dec85-619
Rothstein, E. Restoration and Eighteenth-
  Century Poetry 1660-1780.*
  J. Sitter, 677(YES):Vol 15-295
Rothwell, K.S. A Mirror for Shakespeare.
  G.L. Voth, 570(SQ):Summer85-245
Rotili, M. Arte bizantina in Calabria e
  in Basilicata.
  R.C., 90:May85-313
Rotroff, S.I. The Athenian Agora.* (Vol
  22)
  J. Dillon, 487:Winter85-418
Rotrou, J. Cosroès.* (D.A. Watts, ed)
  W.L., 475:Vol 12No22-396
Rotstein, A. Rebuilding From Within.
  R.M. Campbell, 298:Winter85/86-158
Roty, M. Dictionnaire russe-français des
  termes en usage dans l'église russe.
  (1st ed)
  M. Winokur, 574(SEEJ):Summer85-227
Roty, M. Dictionnaire russe-français des
  termes en usage dans l'église Russe.
  (2nd ed)
  R.M. Cleminson, 575(SEER):Apr85-284
Roubaud, J. Quelque chose noir.
  M. Edwards, 617(TLS):26Sep86-1050
Rouben, L. - see Bussy-Rabutin
Roudiez, L.S. - see Kristeva, J.
Roueché, B. Sea to Shining Sea.
  J. Schnedler, 441:26Jan86-21
Rousseau, F. La croissance solidaire des
  droits de l'homme.
  E.L. Fortin, 543:Mar85-683
Rousseau, J-J. Diskurs über die Ungleich-
  heit. (H. Meier, ed)
  J. Jurt, 547(RF):Band97Heft4-471
Rousseau, P. Pachomius.
  H. Chadwick, 617(TLS):14Nov86-1288
Rousseau-Dujardin, J. L'Excursion.
  J.P. Gilroy, 207(FR):Feb86-491
Roustang, F. Le Bal masqué de Giacomo
  Casanova.
  A. Clerval, 450(NRF):Sep85-99
  P. Saint-Amand, 400(MLN):Sep85-882
Rouy, F. L'Esthétique du traité moral
  d'après les oeuvres d'Alain Chartier.
  B. Cazelles, 545(RPh):Nov85-264
Rovira, C. Sears: lista de encabezamien-
  tos de materia. (12th ed) (B.M. Westby,
  ed)
  I.L. Sontag, 263(RIB):Vol35No3-331
Rovira, L.I. - see under Iscla Rovira, L.
Rowe, A.P. Costumes and Featherwork of
  the Lords of Chimor.
  J. Mefford, 2(AfrA):Nov84-88
Rowe, C.J. Plato.*
  J. Annas, 123:Vol35No2-400
  R.G.M., 185:Apr86-684
Rowe, J.C. The Theoretical Dimensions of
  Henry James.*
  N. Baym, 115:Summer85-371
  W.R. Macnaughton, 27(AL):Dec85-677
  G.D. Smith, 594:Winter85-435
  J.A. Ward, 395(MFS):Winter85-723
  295(JML):Nov85-502

Rowe, W.T. Hankow.
D.D. Buck, 293(JASt):Aug85-819
Rowedder Lehni, E.R. Studien zu Lorenzo
Santi (1783-1839).
R.M., 90:Mar85-173
Rowell, G. Theatre in the Age of Irving.
M.R. Booth, 402(MLR):Jul85-705
Rowell, G. The Vision Glorious.
J.J. Hughes, 637(VS):Spring85-554
Rowell, G. and A. Jackson. The Repertory
Movement.
A. Vivis, 157:No156-50
Rowell, L. Thinking About Music.
M. Musgrave, 89(BJA):Winter85-90
R.A.S., 412:May84-151
J.O. Urmson, 410(M&L):Jul85-249
Rowen, H.H. John de Witt.
J. Kenyon, 617(TLS):11Jul86-755
Rowlands, J. Holbein.
P. Humfrey, 324:Jun86-466
Rowley, A., ed. Sprachliche Orientierung
I.
K. Rein, 685(ZDL):1/1985-107
Rowse, A.L. Reflections on the Puritan
Revolution.
P. Collinson, 617(TLS):15Aug86-884
Rowse, A.L. Shakespeare's Self-Portrait.
I-S. Ewbank, 617(TLS):25Apr86-451
Rowse, A.L. - see Shakespeare, W.
Roxborough, I. Unions and Politics in
Mexico.
K.M. Coleman, 263(RIB):Vol35No4-469
Roxman, S. Guilt and Glory.
J. Pickering, 395(MFS):Summer85-375
Roy, A. The Islamic Syncretistic Tradi-
tion in Bengal.
R.M. Eaton, 293(JASt):Feb85-442
Roy, C.D., ed. Iowa Studies in African
Art.
M.J. Arnoldi, 2(AfrA):Aug85-93
Roy, G. La Détresse et l'enchantement.
R. Robidoux, 627(UTQ):Summer85-478
Roy, G.R. - see Burns, R.
Roy, G.R. - see "Studies in Scottish
Literature"
Roy, H.L.D. - see under Deb Roy, H.L.
Roy, R. Gandhi.
D. Dalton, 293(JASt):May85-653
Royer, J. Ecrivains Contemporains. (Vol
2)
P. Collet, 627(UTQ):Summer85-474
R. Sarkonak, 102(CanL):Winter84-84
Royle, T. The Best Years of Their Lives.
A. Protheroe, 362:30Oct86-29
Royle, T. The Kitchener Enigma.*
N. Ascherson, 453(NYRB):6Nov86-43
Royster, V. The Essential Royster.* (E.
Fuller, ed)
639(VQR):Autumn85-136
Rozett, M.T. The Doctrine of Election and
the Emergence of Elizabethan Tragedy.*
P. Sahel, 189(EA):Apr-Jun86-203
Różewicz, T. Conversations with the
Prince and other Poems. (A. Czerniawski,
ed and trans)
J.T. Baer, 497(PolR):Vol30No2-232
Rozman, G., ed. Soviet Studies of Pre-
modern China.
D. Dodde, 293(JASt):Aug85-821
Ru Zhijuan. Lilies and Other Stories.
P. Link, 441:6Jul86-16
Ruark, G. Keeping Company.*
R. Mitchell, 460(OhR):No36-106

Ruas, C. Conversations with American
Writers.*
B.H., 395(MFS):Winter85-763
M. Mudrick, 249(HudR):Winter86-648
Rubach, J. Cyclic and Lexical Phonology.
F.Y. Gladney, 361:Dec85-337
E. Gussmann, 353:Vol23No4-609
G.S. Nathan, 350:Jun86-467
Rubens, B. Mr. Wakefield's Crusade.*
S. Lardner, 442(NY):10Mar86-121
Rubens, G. William Richard Lethaby.
C. Frayling, 617(TLS):12Dec86-1394
J. Summerson, 362:1May86-26
de Rubercy, E. and D. Le Buhan. Douze
questions posées à Jean Beaufret à
propos de Martin Heidegger.
J. Hervier, 549(RLC):Jul-Sep85-380
Rubin, G.R. and D. Sugarman, eds. Law,
Economy and Society, 1750-1914.
D. Philips, 637(VS):Summer86-629
Rubin, J. Injurious to Public Morals.*
R.H. Minear, 293(JASt):Feb85-399
Rubin, L.B. Quiet Rage.
K. Johnson, 441:19Oct86-31
Rubin, L.D., Jr. and others, eds. The
History of Southern Literature.*
A.E. Stone, 344:Fall86-125
Rubin, T.I. Lisa and David Today.
E.H. Baruch, 441:27Apr86-30
Rubin, W., ed. "Primitivism" in 20th Cen-
tury Art.*
G. Kortian and N. Nercessian, 98:Apr85-
321
D.W. Penney, 2(AfrA):Aug85-27
Rubino, C.A. and C.W. Shelmerdine, eds.
Approaches to Homer.
R.B. Rutherford, 447(N&Q):Sep84-409
Rubinsohn, W.Z. Der Spartakus-Aufstand
und die sowjetische Geschichtsschrei-
bung.
J.G. Griffith, 123:Vol35No2-325
Rubinstein, A. The Zionist Dream Revis-
ited.
H.A. Addison, 287:May85-21
Rubinstein, C.S. American Women Artists
from Early Indian Times to the Present.
P.A. Tackabury, 649(WAL):May85-51
Rubinstein, F. A Dictionary of Shake-
speare's Sexual Puns and Their Signifi-
cance.
J.L. Halio, 570(SQ):Autumn85-373
Rubinstein, H. Provincial French Cooking.
W. and C. Cowen, 639(VQR):Spring85-68
Rubinstein, N. Nela's Cookbook.
W. and C. Cowen, 639(VQR):Spring85-66
Rubio, M. - see Grove, F.P.
Rubio Jiménez, J. Ideología y teatro en
España: 1890-1900.
R.G. Sánchez, 240(HR):Winter85-110
Rücker, G. Herr von Oe/Hilde das Dienst-
mädchen.
M. Lange, 601(SuF):Mar-Apr85-405
Rucker, R. Infinity and the Mind.
J. Shipman, 316:Mar85-246
Rückert, I. The Touch of Sympathy.
G. Schmitz, 72:Band222Heft1-200
Ruckman, J.A. The Moscow Business Elite.
J.H. Bater, 104(CASS):Spring85-71
A.J. Rieber, 550(RusR):Apr85-205
Rudavsky, T., ed. Divine Omniscience and
Omnipotence in Medieval Philosophy.
B. Kent, 543:Jun86-783
Rudd, N. - see Johnson, S.

Rush, N. Whites.
L.M. Silko, 441:23Mar86-7
Rushdie, S. Shame.*
G. Davenport, 569(SR):Spring85-321
Rushton, J. W.A. Mozart: "Don Giovanni."*
J.B., 412:May84-146
Rushton, J. The Musical Language of
Berlioz.
P. Banks, 410(M&L):Jul85-268
P. Friedheim, 317:Spring85-178
Rusiecki, J. Adjectives and Comparison in
English.
K. Allan, 350:Sep86-716
Russ, J.M. German Festivals and Customs.
I.F. Riester, 133:Band17Heft3/4-383
Russell, B. The Collected Papers of Bert-
rand Russell.* (Vol 1: Cambridge Essays,
1888-1899.) (K. Blackwell and others,
eds)
J. Couture, 154:Summer85-364
T. Sprigge, 518:Jan85-23
Russell, B. The Collected Papers of Bert-
rand Russell. (Vol 7: Theory of Knowl-
edge.) (E.R. Eames, ed)
H.W. Noonan, 518:Apr85-93
Russell, B. and J.C. Powys. Is Modern
Marriage a Failure?
M. Kohl, 556:Winter85/86-162
Russell, C. Poets, Prophets, and Revolu-
tionaries.
D. Coward, 617(TLS):9May86-506
R. Shattuck, 453(NYRB):18Dec86-66
Russell, C.A. Cross-Currents.
P. Byrne, 617(TLS):14Mar86-282
Russell, D.A. Greek Declamation.
A.T. Edwards, 124:May-Jun86-334
M.J. Edwards, 303(JoHS):Vol 105-201
J. Fairweather, 123:Vol35No1-54
Russell, D.E.H. The Secret Trauma.
R. Dinnage, 453(NYRB):4Dec86-39
S.L. Pettus, 441:8Jun86-37
Russell, D.W. Anne Hébert.
J-A. Elder, 102(CanL):Winter84-89
Russell, F., ed. Richard Rogers Archi-
tects.
J.M. Richards, 617(TLS):2May86-464
Russell, J. Explaining Mental Life.
K.V. Wilkes, 393(Mind):Oct85-639
Russell, J.B. Satan.
J. Boswell, 589:Apr85-458
Russell, M. The Blessings of a Good Thick
Skirt.
J. Ure, 617(TLS):12Dec86-1398
Russell, N. The Novelist and Mammon.
D. Grylls, 617(TLS):26Sep86-1078
Russell, P.A. Lay Theology in the Reforma-
tion.
A. Hamilton, 617(TLS):1Aug86-847
Russell, P.E. Cervantes.
A.J. Close, 617(TLS):28Nov86-1352
Russell-Gebbett, P., N.G. Round and A.H.
Terry, eds. Belfast Spanish and Portu-
guese Papers.
J.L. Brooks, 86(BHS):Apr85-190
"The Russian-American Company." (R.A.
Pierce, trans)
N.N. Bolkhovitinov, 550(RusR):Oct85-
415
"Russian-English/English-Russian Military
Dictionary." "Russian-English Military
Dictionary."
M.K. Launer, 574(SEEJ):Spring85-120

Russo, C.F. Aristofane. (2nd ed)
R.L. Hunter, 123:Vol35No2-383
Russo, R. Mohawk.
G. Johnson, 441:12Oct86-28
Russo, V. Con le Muse in Parnaso.
J. Usher, 402(MLR):Oct85-953
Rutherford, A. - see Kipling, R.
Rutherford, M. Catharine Furze. Clara
Hopgood.
S. Bennison, S. Ledger and J. Porteous,
366:Autumn85-281
Rutherford, P. A Victorian Authority.*
J.A. Wiseman, 470:Vol23-116
Ruthven, K.K. Feminist Literary Studies.
G. Castro, 189(EA):Apr-Jun86-239
Ruthven, K.K. Feminist Literary Theory.
S. Gunew, 67:Nov85-223
L. Johnson, 67:Nov85-229
P. Maclean, 67:Nov85-232
P. Rothfield, 67:Nov85-234
Ruthven, M. Traveller Through Time.
M. Howard, 441:7Dec86-14
442(NY):8Dec86-155
Rutkoff, P.M. and W.B. Scott. New School.
N. Glazer, 441:31Aug86-6
Rutman, D.B. and A.H. A Place in Time.*
T.H. Breen, 656(WMQ):Apr85-251
R.E. Gallman, 656(WMQ):Apr85-255
J. Kukla, 658:Winter85-292
Rutsala, V. Backtracking.
L. Rector, 249(HudR):Winter86-697
Rutten, R. Women Workers of Hacienda
Milagros.
F.E. McCarthy, 293(JASt):Feb85-470
van Ruusbroec, J. Opera omnia.* (Vols 1
and 2) (G. de Baere, ed)
K. Emery, Jr., 589:Jan85-192
Ruwet, N. Grammaire des insultes et
autres études.*
U. Teleman, 596(SL):Vol39No1-84
Ruyer, R. Le sceptique résolu ...
R. Prévost, 192(EP):Apr-Jun85-271
Ružičková, E. Slovesá pohybu v slovenčine
a angličtine.
R. Sussex, 575(SEER):Jul85-429
Ryals, C.D. Becoming Browning.
T.J. Collins, 637(VS):Winter85-322
J. Maynard, 536(Rev):Vol7-297
529(QQ):Summer85-438
Ryan, A. Property and Political Theory.*
T.D. Campbell, 518:Oct85-223
M. Hollis, 393(Mind):Oct85-630
D. Knowles, 479(PhQ):Oct85-433
A.J. Skillen, 483:Oct85-554
Ryan, A.A., Jr. Quiet Neighbors.
639(VQR):Spring85-58
Ryan, G. Manners of an Astronaut.
J. Leonard, 381:Sep85-413
Ryan, J. The Uncompleted Past.*
S.L. Gilman, 564:Feb85-65
H. Wagener, 221(GQ):Winter85-141
Ryan, M., ed. The Derrynaflan Hoard I.
S. Connelly, 174(Éire):Fall85-145
Ryan, M. Filling Out a Life.
C. Wright, 448:Vol23No1-118
Ryan, M. Marxism and Deconstruction.*
D.H. Hirsch, 569(SR):Summer85-465
C. Norris, 577(SHR):Spring85-159
Ryan, M.J. The Túngara Frog.
T. Halliday, 617(TLS):30May86-602
Ryan, R. and S. van Zyl, eds. An Intro-
duction to Contemporary Literary Theory.
T. Hawkes, 447(N&Q):Dec84-557

Rybakov, B.A. and others, eds. Izbornik
Svjatoslava 1073 goda.
  H.G. Hunt, 279:Vol29-164
Rybczynski, W. Home.
  P-L. Adams, 61:Oct86-102
  W.H. Gass, 441:3Aug86-1
  D. Johnson, 453(NYRB):4Dec86-3
  J. Lukacs, 442(NY):1Sep86-96
Rychner, J. Genève et ses typographes vus
de Neuchâtel 1770-1780.
  D. McKitterick, 617(TLS):9May86-513
  D. Smith, 173(ECS):Spring86-429
Ryden, M. The English Plant Names in the
"Grete Herball" (1526).
  K.H., 424:Dec85-299
Ryder, F.G. and R.M. Browning, eds. Ger-
man Literary Fairy Tales.
  E. Diller, 399(MLJ):Spring85-94
Rydland, K. Vowel Systems and Lexical-
Phonemic Patterns in South-East Cumbria.*
  W. Elmer, 38:Band103Heft1/2-153
Ryken, L. and J.H. Sims, eds. Milton and
Scriptural Tradition.
  R.J. Du Rocher, 577(SHR):Fall85-359
Rykwert, J. and A. The Brothers Adam.*
  S. Gardiner, 362:6Feb86-28
Ryley, R.M. William Warburton.
  J. Freehafer, 566:Autumn85-84
Rymut, K., ed. Proceedings of the
Thirteenth International Congress of
Onomastic Sciences.
  M.R. Miller, 300:Apr85-75
Rževskij, L. Zvezdopad.
  J.T. Baer, 558(RLJ):Fall84-282
Rzhevsky, N. Russian Literature and
Ideology.*
  L. Koehler, 574(SEEJ):Fall85-345

el-Saadawi, N. God Dies by the Nile.
  B. Mukherjee, 441:27Jul86-14
el-Saadawi, N. Two Women in One.
  N. Keddie, 441:7Sep86-22
von Saar, F. Kritische Texte und Deutun-
gen. (K.K. Polheim, general ed) (Vol 1
ed by R. Kopp; Vol 2 ed by H. Gierlich)
  J. Strelka, 133:Band17Heft3/4-359
von Saar, F. Sündenfall und andere Erzäh-
lungen. (K.K. Polheim, ed)
  J. Strelka, 133:Band18Heft2-180
Saavedra, M.D. - see under de Cervantes
Saavedra, M.
Saba, U. Coi miei occhi. (C. Milanini,
ed)
  M. Bacigalupo, 402(MLR):Oct85-956
Sabais, H.W. The People and the Stones.
  D. McDuff, 565:Winter84/85-73
Sabarsky, S., with others. George Grosz:
The Berlin Years.
  P-L. Adams, 61:Jul86-78
  J. Russell, 441:1Jun86-11
Sabat de Rivers, G. - see de la Cruz, J.I.
Sabatine, J. The Actor's Image.
  B. Rolfe, 615(TJ):Dec85-525
Sabato, L.J. PAC Power.
  F. Barnes, 639(VQR):Summer85-546
Sabbah, G., ed. Médecins et médecine dans
l'Antiquité.
  J.T. Vallance, 123:Vol35No2-425
Sabini, J. and M. Silver. Moralities of
Everyday Life.
  C.H. Sommers, 543:Mar85-686
el Sabio, A. - see under Alfonso el Sabio

Sabor, P. Horace Walpole.
  M. McCarthy, 627(UTQ):Summer85-414
Sabor, P. - see Cleland, J.
Sabor de Cortázar, C. - see de Vega Carpio,
L.
Šabršula, J. Substitution, représentation,
diaphore.
  H. Bonnard, 209(FM):Oct85-267
Sachar, A.L. The Redemption of the
Unwanted.*
  A.J. Lelyveld, 287:Jan85-22
Sachs, H. Hans Sachs: Selections. (M.
Beare, ed)
  C.D. Cossar, 402(MLR):Jan85-212
Sachs, N. Briefe der Nelly Sachs. (R.
Dinesen and H. Müssener, eds)
  N. Gabriel, 680(ZDP):Band104Heft2-312
Sachs, V. The Game of Creation.
  R. Mason, 447(N&Q):Jun84-285
Sack, V. Die Inkunabeln der Universitäts-
bibliothek und anderer öffentlichen
sammlungen in Freiburg im Breisgau und
Umgebung.
  L.S. Thompson, 70:May/Jun86-158
Sacks, O. A Leg to Stand On.
  A.L. Wax, 31(ASch):Summer85-419
Sacks, O. The Man Who Mistook His Wife
For a Hat.*
  P-L. Adams, 61:Mar86-112
  J.C. Marshall, 441:2Mar86-3
  C. Rycroft, 453(NYRB):13Mar86-11
  J.K. Wing, 617(TLS):7Feb86-146
Sacks, P. The English Elegy.
  M. Zeiger, 400(MLN):Dec85-1165
Sackville-West, V. The Letters of Vita
Sackville-West to Virginia Woolf.*
  (L. De Salvo and M.A. Leaska, eds)
  M. Goldstein, 569(SR):Fall85-624
  N. Miller, 42(AR):Winter85-119
Saddington, D.B. The Development of the
Roman Auxiliary Forces from Caesar to
Vespasian (49 B.C. - A.D. 79).
  A.K. Bowman, 123:Vol35No1-137
  J.J. Wilkes, 313:Vol75-239
Saddlemyer, A. - see Synge, J.M.
Saddlemyer, A. - see Yeats, W.B., Lady
Gregory and J.M. Synge
Sadek, M.M. The Arabic "Materia Medica"
of Dioscorides.
  C.S.F. Burnett, 123:Vol35No2-427
Sadie, S., ed. The New Grove Dictionary
of Musical Instruments.*
  W.P. Malm, 187:Spring/Summer86-337
  R.E. Mannering, 70:May/Jun85-155
  J. Montagu, 415:Apr85-223
Sadji, U., ed. Entdeckungsreisen nach
Indien und Amerika.
  E.J. Morrall, 402(MLR):Oct85-979
Sadler, B. and A. Carlson, eds. Environ-
mental Aesthetics.*
  A. Whittick, 89(BJA):Winter85-74
Sadlier, D.J. Imagery and Theme in the
Poetry of Cecília Meireles.
  S. Schnepf, 552(REH):Oct85-147
Sadlier, D.J., ed. New Perspectives in
Brazilian Literary Studies.
  C. Slater, 238:Sep85-534
Sadoff, D.F. Monsters of Affection.*
  N. Auerbach, 403(MLS):Winter85-88
Sa'edi, G-H. Fear and Trembling.
  S. El-Gabalawy, 268(IFR):Summer86-104
Saeed, J.I. Central Somali.
  F. Serzisko, 361:May85-110

Sáenz, P. The Life and Works of Eugenio d'Ors.
  P.H. Dust, 238:Dec85-775
Sáez-Godoy, L., ed. Estudios lingüísticos en memoria de Gastón Carrillo Herrera.
  A. Manteca Alonso-Cortés, 547(RF): Band97Heft2/3-261
Safarik, A. and G. Torselli. La Galleria Doria Pamphilj a Roma.
  S. Pepper, 90:Aug85-537
  F. Russell, 324:Aug86-631
Safley, T.M. Let No Man Put Asunder.
  J.O. Newman, 551(RenQ):Spring85-122
Safranski, R. E.T.A. Hoffmann.
  B. Naumann, 384:Jun85-525
Sagan, C. Contact.*
  C. Greenland, 617(TLS):31Oct86-1224
Sagan, E. At the Dawn of Tyranny.*
  A. de Jasay, 617(TLS):14Nov86-1269
  W.G. Runciman, 453(NYRB):18Dec86-64
Sagan, F. The Still Storm.
  442(NY):5May86-132
Sagan, M. Aegean Doorway.
  B. Raffel, 152(UDQ):Fall85-131
  W. Zander, 363(LitR):Spring86-379
Sagar, K., ed. The Achievement of Ted Hughes.*
  R. Marsack, 541(RES):Aug85-454
Sagar, K., ed. A D.H. Lawrence Handbook.
  K.M. Hewitt, 541(RES):Feb85-125
Sagar, K. D.H. Lawrence: Life into Art.*
  J.M. Coetzee, 453(NYRB):16Jan86-33
Sager, S. The Parliamentary System of Israel.
  B. Wasserstein, 617(TLS):10Oct86-1123
Sagovsky, N. Between Two Worlds.
  M.J. Weaver, 637(VS):Spring85-551
Sagvari, A., ed. Capitals of Europe.
  M. Ison, 576:Mar85-75
Sahel, P. La Pensée politique dans les drames historiques de Shakespeare.
  M.C. Bradbrook, 189(EA):Apr-Jun86-204
Sahgal, N. Plans for Departure.*
  A. Haverty, 617(TLS):21Feb86-198
  J. Mellors, 364:Mar86-98
  442(NY):13Jan86-85
Sahgal, N. Rich Like Us.*
  A. Becker, 441:6Jul86-14
  J. Mellors, 364:Aug-Sep85-144
Sahlins, M. Islands of History.*
  P. Gathercole, 617(TLS):28Feb86-224
Said, E.W. Covering Islam.
  D. Spanier, 176:Apr86-61
Said, E.W. The World, the Text, and the Critic.*
  R.W. Dasenbrock, 435:Spring85-92
  W.A. Johnsen, 115:Spring84-148
Said, E.W. and J. Mohr. After the Last Sky.
  R.B. Cramer, 441:9Nov86-27
  J. Mantle, 362:6Nov86-36
Saidel, R.G. The Outraged Conscience.
  H. Fein, 390:Apr85-61
Saif, L.A. - see under Abou Saif, L.
Saiko, G. Sämtliche Werke in fünf Bänden. (Vols 2 and 4)
  J. Adler, 617(TLS):3Oct86-1087
Sainsbury, K. The Turning Point.*
  A. Verrier, 176:Feb86-56
Saint, A. The Image of the Architect.*
  C. Burroughs, 59:Sep85-380

Saint-Amand, P. Diderot, le labyrinthe de la relation.
  A. Vartanian, 173(ECS):Winter85/86-276
St. Armand, B.L. Emily Dickinson and Her Culture.*
  W. Barker, 432(NEQ):Sep85-459
  J. Burbick, 357:Spring86-69
  D. Davis, 617(TLS):17Jan86-58
  L. Lane, Jr., 150(DR):Winter84/85-802
  R. Miller, 385(MQR):Fall86-760
  B.R. Voloshin, 27(AL):Dec85-669
St. Clair, P. At the Tent of Heaven.
  R. Henigan, 649(WAL):Nov85-269
St. Clair, W. Lord Elgin and the Marbles. (rev)
  C. Collard, 123:Vol35No1-213
Saint-Denis, A. L'Hôtel-Dieu de Laon 1150-1300.
  S.F. Roberts, 589:Jul85-721
de Saint-Exupéry, A. Wartime Writings 1939-1944.
  N. Balakian, 441:31Aug86-9
de Saint-Gelais, O. La Chasse d'Amours. (M.B. Winn, ed)
  T. Thomson, 402(MLR):Oct85-937
"St. Ives 1939-64."
  I. Hunter, 592:Vol 198No1011-50
St. John, D. No Heaven.*
  V. Shetley, 491:Feb86-295
St. John-Stevas, N. - see Bagehot, W.
Monsieur de Saint-Lambert. Principles of the Harpsichord.* (R. Harris-Warwick, ed and trans)
  H. Wilcox, 83:Autumn85-250
de Saint-Martin, L-C. Le Philosophe inconnu, Les nombres. (R. Amadou, ed)
  A. Reix, 542:Jan-Mar85-98
Saint-Pierre, A. and R. Vien, eds. Répertoire littéraire de l'Ouest canadien.
  L.E. Doucette, 627(UTQ):Summer85-460
de Saint-Pierre, I. Une Croisière en enfer.
  M. Cottenet-Hage, 207(FR):Apr86-819
de Saint-Pierre, J.H.B. - see under Bernardin de Saint-Pierre, J.H.
Duc de Saint-Simon. Mémoires 1701-1707. (Vol 2) (Y. Coirault, ed)
  D. van der Cruysse, 535(RHL):Mar/Apr85-298
Sainte-Beuve, C.A. Correspondance générale. (Vol 19) (J. and A. Bonnerot, eds)
  J. Gaulmier, 535(RHL):May/Jun85-492
Sainte-Beuve, C.A. Volupté. (M. Regard, ed)
  L. Le Guillou, 535(RHL):Sep/Oct85-884
  R. Lloyd, 208(FS):Jul85-350
de Ste. Croix, G.E.M. The Class Struggle in the Ancient Greek World.*
  G.J.D. Aalders H. Wzn., 394:Vol38 fascl/2-248
Saitoti, T.O. The Worlds of a Maasai Warrior.
  J.P. Calagione, 441:12Jan86-20
Sajous, M. - see Beffroy de Reigny, L-A.
Sakata, H.L. Music in the Mind.
  J. Baily, 187:Winter86-173
Sakellariou, M.B. Les Proto-Grecs.
  C.J. Ruijgh, 394:Vol38fascl/2-166
Sakowski, H. Wie ein Vogel im Schwarm.
  R. Bernhardt, 654(WB):4/1985-647
  I. Siefert, 601(SuF):Mar-Apr85-412

Sala, M. and others. El Español de
América.* (vol 1)
    M. Perl, 682(ZPSK):Band38Heft6-773
Salaman, N. Falling Apart.
    A. Hislop, 617(TLS):23May86-554
    J. Mellors, 362:24Apr86-34
Salamanca, J.R. Southern Light.
    J. Daynard, 441:30Mar86-18
Salamun, K. Karl Jaspers.
    J. Habermas, 384:Sep/Oct85-902
Salazar, R. Spectator.
    C. Colman, 441:22Jun86-26
Salbstein, M.C.N. The Emancipation of the
Jews in Britain.
    J. von Arx, 637(VS):Summer85-691
Saldívar, R. Figural Language in the
Novel.
    G.L. Lucente, 400(MLN):Mar85-425
    P. O'Donnell, 594:Spring85-110
Salgado, G. "King Lear."
    M. Willems, 189(EA):Apr-Jun86-209
Salisbury, C.Y. Long March Diary.
    R.O. Boorstin, 441:11May86-25
Salisbury, H.E. The Long March.*
    D. Wilson, 617(TLS):21Mar86-294
Sallese, N.F. and L.B. Fernández. Pan y
mantequilla. (3rd ed)
    J.E. McKinney, 399(MLJ):Summer85-212
Sallmann, N. - see Censorinus
Salmen, W. Der Spielmann im Mittelalter.
    M. Dobozy, 589:Jul85-723
    R. Rastall, 410(M&L):Apr85-176
Salminen, J. Gränsland.
    G.C. Schoolfield, 563(SS):Autumn85-469
Salminen, J. Snellman i urval.
    G.C. Schoolfield, 563(SS):Winter85-79
Salminen, R. - see Marguerite de Navarre
Salmon, C., comp. Literature in Malay by
the Chinese of Indonesia.
    S. Tiwon, 293(JASt):Feb85-471
Salmon, E., ed. Bernhardt and the Theatre
of her Time.
    N. Auerbach, 637(VS):Autumn85-178
Salmon, J.B. Wealthy Corinth.
    P. Cartledge, 123:Vol35No1-115
Salmon, N. Frege's Puzzle.
    D. Freedman, 617(TLS):19Dec86-1429
Salmon, W.C. Scientific Explanation and
the Causal Structure of the World.
    T.J.C., 185:Apr86-682
    J. Forge, 63:Dec85-546
    J.F. Hanna, 543:Mar86-582
Salmond, J.A. A Southern Rebel.
    W.D. Barnard, 9(AlaR):Apr85-147
    G.C. Fite, 579(SAQ):Winter85-108
    F. Hobson, 577(SHR):Summer85-245
Salomon, N. Realidad, ideología y litera-
tura en el "Facundo" de D.F. Sarmiento.
    G. Marún, 547(RF):Band97Heft1-120
Salon, A. L'Action culturelle de la
France dans le monde.
    J. Laroche, 207(FR):Mar86-631
Salter, E. Fourteenth Century English Po-
etry.* (D. Pearsall and N. Zeeman, eds)
    A. Middleton, 589:Oct85-1060
    A. Squires, 161(DUJ):Dec84-112
    E. Wilson, 541(RES):May85-251
Salter, M.J. Henry Purcell in Japan.*
    W. Logan, 472:Spring/Summer/Fall/
    Winter85-463
    G. Schulman, 491:Nov85-104
    W. Shear, 389(MQ):Summer86-518
    639(VQR):Autumn85-130

Saltykov-Shchedrin, M.E. The Golovlevs.
The Pompadours.
    D.J. Enright, 617(TLS):29Aug86-947
Salutin, R. Marginal Notes.
    A.B. Dawson, 628(UWR):Fall-Winter85-75
    M. Fee, 376:Sep85-148
    G.W., 102(CanL):Spring85-184
Salvaggio, R. Dryden's Dualities.*
    J.V. Guerinot, 568(SCN):Fall85-43
    A. Poyet, 189(EA):Jan-Mar86-95
Salwak, D. Interviews with Britain's
Angry Young Men.
    R.C. Schweik, 395(MFS):Summer85-365
Salwak, D. John Wain.*
    J.L. Halio, 402(MLR):Oct85-922
Saly, A. Edition critique du "Meliacin"
de Girart d'Amiens accompagnée d'une
étude historique et littéraire.
    G. Roques, 553(RLiR):Jul-Dec85-524
Salzman, P. English Prose Fiction, 1558-
1700.
    J.C. Beasley, 594:Fall85-303
Sambrook, J. - see Thomson, J.
Sammons, J.L. Heinrich Heine: A Selected
Critical Bibliography of Secondary Lit-
erature, 1956-1980.*
    H.H.F. Henning, 406:Fall85-359
Sampson, A. and S., eds. The Oxford Book
of Ages.*
    J. Silverlight, 176:Mar86-55
Sampson, D. The Double Genesis.
    L. Rector, 249(HudR):Winter86-695
Sampson, G. Writing Systems.
    J.T. Hooker, 617(TLS):14Mar86-278
Sampson, R. Yesterday's Faces. (Vol 2)
    B.H., 395(MFS):Summer85-425
Sampson, S.L. National Integration
through Socialist Planning.
    I.M. Matley, 104(CASS):Spring85-115
Sams, E., ed. Shakespeare's Lost Play:
Edmund Ironside.
    I-S. Ewbank, 617(TLS):25Apr86-451
Sams, E. The Songs of Hugo Wolf.* (2nd
ed)
    D. Puffett, 410(M&L):Apr85-168
Sams, F. The Whisper of the River.
    G.C., 569(SR):Spring85-xxxix
Samson, J. The Music of Chopin.
    J. Warrack, 617(TLS):7Mar86-244
Samuels, R.J. The Politics of Regional
Policy in Japan.
    Funaba Masatomi, 285(JapQ):Jan-Mar85-
    90
    S.R. Reed, 293(JASt):Nov84-208
Samuelson, A. With Hemingway.*
    J. Meyers, 395(MFS):Summer85-406
    M.S. Reynolds, 27(AL):Oct85-511
Sanchez, R. Chicano Discourse.*
    H.T. Trueba and C. Delgado-Gaitan,
    355(LSoc):Jun85-257
Sánchez Álvarez, M., ed. El manuscrito
misceláneo 774 de la Biblioteca Nacional
de París.
    L. López-Baralt, 545(RPh):Aug85-136
Sánchez Gordillo, A.A. Religiosas esta-
ciones que frecuentaba la religiosidad
sevillana. (J. Bernales Ballestero, ed)
    D. Angulo Íñiquez, 48:Jan-Mar85-91
Sánchez Romeralo, A. - see Jiménez, J.R.
Sánchez Romeralo, A. and others, eds. Bib-
liografía del romancero oral, 1.*
    M.E. Barrick, 545(RPh):Feb85-418
Sánchez Vidal, A. - see Buñuel, L.

Sancho, M.P.C. - see under Cuartero Sancho, M.P.
Sand, G. Correspondance.* (Vol 17) (G. Lubin, ed)
    J. Gaulmier, 535(RHL):Mar/Apr85-322
Sand, G. Lucrezia Floriani.* (J. Eker, trans)
    42(AR):Fall85-503
Sandbach, F.H. Aristotle and the Stoics.
    J. Barnes, 520:Vol30No2-213
    D.J. O'Meara, 543:Mar86-585
Sandback, A.B., ed. Looking Critically.
    D.F. Stalker, 290(JAAC):Spring86-305
Sandburg, C. Ever the Winds of Chance.
    J.T. Flanagan, 534(RALS):Spring83-103
Sandeen, E.J. - see Bourne, R.
Sandel, C. Cora Sandel: Selected Short Stories.
    B.L. Clark, 441:23Feb86-22
Sandel, M.J., ed. Liberalism and Its Critics.
    J.F., 185:Apr86-672
Sandel, M.J. Liberalism and the Limits of Justice.*
    N.S. Care, 449:Sep85-459
"August Sander: Citizens of the Twentieth Century." (Text by U. Keller; G. Sander, ed)
    B. Newhall, 441:28Sep86-44
Sander, R., ed. Der Karibische Raum zwischen Selbst- und Fremdbestimmung.
    R. Ventura, 343:Heft11-122
Sanders, A. Charles Dickens, Resurrectionist.
    J. Larson, 637(VS):Winter85-318
Sanders, C.R. - see Carlyle, T. and J.W.
Sanders, C.R. and K.J. Fielding - see Carlyle, T. and J.W.
Sanders, D. and L. Lovallo. The Agatha Christie Companion.
    E.S. Lauterbach, 395(MFS):Summer85-382
Sanders, J.T. Ben Sira and Demotic Wisdom.
    M. Lichtheim, 318(JAOS):Oct-Dec84-768
Sanders, L. The Eighth Commandment.
    M. Watkins, 441:10Aug86-18
Sanders, N. - see Shakespeare, W.
Sanders, S.R. Fetching the Dead.
    J.L. Halio, 573(SSF):Spring85-241
    S. Watson, 219(GaR):Summer85-426
Sanders, S.W. Mexico.
    A. Riding, 441:7Dec86-30
    L. Weiner, 129:Dec86-76
Sanders, W. Sachsensprache, Hansesprache, Plattdeutsch.
    J. Schildt, 682(ZPSK):Band38Heft3-335
    P. Wagener, 260(IF):Band90-356
Sandford, J. Landscape and Landscape Imagery in R.M. Rilke.
    R. Delphendahl, 406:Summer85-244
Sandkuhler, H.J., ed. Natur und geschichtlicher Prozess.
    J-M. Gabaude, 542:Jan-Mar85-42
Sandler, I. and A. Newman - see Barr, A.H., Jr.
Sandler, K.W. and S. Whitebook. Tour de Grammaire. (2nd ed)
    M-N. Little, 207(FR):Feb86-499
Sandler, L.F. The Psalter of Robert De Lisle in the British Library.*
    J. Alexander, 90:Feb85-94
Sandler, R. - see Frye, N.
Sandoz, M. Les Lagrenée. (Vol 1)
    P. Conisbee, 90:Nov85-814

Sandqvist, S. Notes textuelles sur le "Roman de Tristan" de Béroul.
    G. Roques, 553(RLiR):Jan-Jun85-237
Sandqvist, S., ed. Trois Contes Français au XIVe siècle tirés du recueil intitulé "Le Tombel de Chartrose."
    T. Hobbs, 382(MAE):1985/2-336
Sandred, K.I. Good or Bad Scots?*
    C. Macafee, 597(SN):Vol57No2-261
    J.D. McClure, 571(ScLJ):Winter85-50
Sandvoss, E.R. Bertrand Russell in Selbstzeugnissen und Bilddokumenten.
    H. Ruja, 556:Summer85-95
Sanesi, R. In Visible Ink. (R. Burns, ed)
    D. McDuff, 565:Winter84/85-73
Sanford, C.B. The Religious Life of Thomas Jefferson.
    C.L. Albanese, 656(WMQ):Apr85-294
    A.O. Aldridge, 27(AL):May85-329
Sanford, J. The Winters of That Country.
    J. Napora, 532(RCF):Fall85-194
Sänger, M. Die kategoriale Systematik in den "Metaphysischen Anfangsgründen der Rechtslehre."
    G. Geismann, 687:Oct-Dec85-649
Sanger, P. The America Reel.
    A. Munton, 198:Winter85-100
Sangster, C. The St. Lawrence and the Saguenay and Other Poems. (rev) (F.M. Tierney, ed)
    T. Ware, 105:Fall/Winter85-92
Sangsue, D. - see Nodier, C.
San Juan de la Cruz - see under Juan
Sankoff, G. The Social Life of Language.*
    S. Poplack, 350:Mar86-189
Sankovitch, T. Jodelle et la création du masque.
    B.C. Bowen, 545(RPh):Feb86-364
Sanouillet, M. and D. Baudoin, eds. Dada.
    R. Sheppard, 208(FS):Oct85-497
Sansone, G.E., ed. La poesia dell'antica Provenza. (Vol 1)
    D. Rieger, 547(RF):Band97Heft1-80
de Santerre, H.G. - see under Gallet de Santerre, H.
Santí, E.M. Pablo Neruda.*
    M. García Pinto, 405(MP):Aug85-91
Santini, R. A Swell Style of Murder.
    A. Gottlieb, 441:11May86-24
Santmyer, H.H. ...And Ladies of the Club.*
    R.F. Fleissner, 95(CLAJ):Jun86-486
Santoli, A. To Bear Any Burden.*
    639(VQR):Autumn85-133
de Santos Otero, A. Die handschriftliche Überlieferung der altslavischen Aprokryphen. (Vol 2)
    F.J. Thomson, 575(SEER):Jan85-73
Sanua, V.D., ed. Fields of Offerings.
    H. Lenowitz, 390:Oct85-54
Sañudo, M.R. - see under Revuelta Sañudo, M.
Sapargaliiev, G. and V. Diakov. Polacy w Kazachstanie w XIX w.
    A.A. Hetnal, 497(PolR):Vol30No3-310
Sapergia, B. Lokkinen.
    A. Filewod, 108:Spring85-145
Sapir, E. and A. Kroeber. The Sapir-Kroeber Correspondence. (V. Golla, ed)
    L. Campbell, 350:Mar86-183
Sapolsky, H.M., ed. Consuming Fears.
    W.F. Allman, 441:12Oct86-29
Sappenfield, J.A. and E.N. Feltskog - see Cooper, J.F.

Sappler, P. - see Neidhart von Reuenthal
Sarduy, S. Colibrí.
R. Prieto, 140(CH):Vol7No2-184
Sargent, M.G. James Grenehalgh as Textual
Critic.
S.S. Hussey, 354:Sep85-265
Sargent-Baur, B.N. and R.F. Cook. "Aucas-
sin et Nicolete."*
N.B. Smith, 589:Jul85-753
Sargeson, F. Sargeson. More than Enough.
Never Enough!
L. Jones, 49:Oct85-127
Sarkar, H. A Theory of Method.
A. Chalmers, 84:Jun85-228
D. Garber, 486:Jun85-315
K. Harrison, 63:Jun85-244
Sarkisyanz, M. Die Kulturen Kontinental-
Südostasiens.
F.K. Lehman, 293(JASt):Aug85-898
Sarkonak, R., ed. The Language of Differ-
ence.
S. Ross, 150(DR):Spring85-137
Sarmiento, R., ed. Gramática de la lengua
castellana (1771) de la Real Academia
Española.
P. Swiggers, 350:Sep86-701
Saroyan, W. The New Saroyan Reader. (B.
Darwent, ed) Births.
E.H. Foster, 649(WAL):Feb86-369
Sarraute, N. Childhood.*
P. Lewis, 565:Spring85-43
Sarraute, N. Paul Valéry et l'enfant
d'éléphant. Flaubert le précurseur.
P. Thody, 617(TLS):11Apr86-396
Sarton, M. At Seventy.
639(VQR):Winter85-10
Sarton, M. The Magnificent Spinster.*
J.L. Slonczewski, 344:Fall86-120
Sartori, G., ed. Social Science Concepts.
J.F., 185:Oct85-212
Sartre, J-P. Critique de la raison
dialectique.
A.C. Danto, 617(TLS):11Jul86-753
Sartre, J-P. The Freud Scenario. (J-B.
Pontalis, ed)
G. Millar, 362:16Jan86-28
J. Sturrock, 441:12Oct86-15
Sartre, M. Inscriptions grecques et
latines de la Syrie. (Vol 13, fasc 1)
G.W. Bowersock, 24:Spring85-139
P.M. Fraser, 123:Vol35No1-226
Sarźvelaźe, Z. Kartuli saliţeraţuro enis
istoriis šesavali.
H. Fähnrich, 682(ZPSK):Band38Heft6-775
Saslow, J.M. Ganymede in the Renaissance.
C. Hope, 453(NYRB):29May86-7
M. Warner, 617(TLS):19Sep86-1038
Saslow, J.M. and J.F. Mongillo. English
in Context.
S.J. Sacco, 399(MLJ):Autumn85-333
Sassoon, A.S., ed. Approaches to Gramsci.
P. Rumble, 275(IQ):Summer/Fall84-210
Sassoon, S. Diaries 1915-1918.* (R. Hart-
Davis, ed)
M. Thorpe, 179(ES):Feb85-86
Sassoon, S. Siegfried Sassoon's Long
Journey.* (P. Fussell, ed)
S.S. Baskett, 115:Summer84-264
Sassu Frescura, M. Interferenze lessicali.
P. Friedrich, 399(MLJ):Spring85-98

Sattelmeyer, R. and J.D. Crowley, eds.
One Hundred Years of "Huckleberry Finn."
W. Baker, 42(AR):Summer85-365
S. Pinsker, 219(GaR):Winter85-891
Sattin, A. - see Tytler, H.
Sattler, D.E. and M. Knaupp - see Hölder-
lin, F.
Sauer, G. - see Steinitz, W.
Sauer, H., ed and trans. The Owl and the
Nightingale.
H. Reichl, 38:Band103Heft3/4-464
Sauer, L. Marionetten, Maschinen, Auto-
maten.*
M. Brunkhorst, 343:Heft11-126
G. Vitt-Maucher, 221(GQ):Winter85-122
Sauer, T.G. A.W. Schlegel's Shakespear-
ean Criticism in England, 1811-1846.*
W. Bies, 52:Band20Heft1-87
Saul, J.R. The Next Best Thing.
S. Dobyns, 441:28Sep86-20
Saulnier, C. L'armée et la guerre chez
les peuples samnites (VIIe-IVe siècle).
E. Rawson, 313:Vol75-268
Saulnier, L. and N. Stratford. La sculp-
ture oubliée de Vézelay.
P. Williamson, 90:Feb85-94
Saulnier, V-L. Rabelais II.
C. Clark, 208(FS):Apr85-189
Saunders, H.H. The Other Walls.
B. Gwertzman, 441:16Mar86-36
Saunders, H.N. All the Astrolabes.
H.D. Howse, 324:Feb86-205
Saunders, J. Fall.
D. Devlin, 157:No158-45
Sauneron, S. Esna VIII.
R.S. Bianchi, 318(JAOS):Apr-Jun84-360
de Saussure, F. Course in General Linguis-
tics. (R. Harris, ed and trans)
G. Lepschy, 297(JL):Mar85-250
Saussy, G.S. 3d. The Penguin Dictionary
of Curious and Interesting Words.
617(TLS):19Dec86-1434
Savarin, J.J. Lynx.
N. Callendar, 441:21Sep86-37
Savary, C. and C. Panaccio, eds. L'idéolo-
gie et les stratégies de la raison.
J. Boulad-Ayoub, 154:Summer85-333
Savary, R. Ordre langagier, champ spatial
et emplois "figurés."
G. Kleiber, 553(RLiR):Jan-Jun85-197
Saville, R., ed. The Economic Development
of Modern Scotland 1950-1980.
C. Harvie, 617(TLS):4Jul86-744
Savitzkaya, E. Les Morts sentent bon.
A. Otten, 532(RCF):Fall85-191
Savoca, G. Concordanza di tutte le poesie
di Guido Gozzano.
C. Muller, 553(RLiR):Jan-Jun85-207
Savona, J.L. Jean Genet.
M.A.F. Witt, 207(FR):May86-985
Savory, J. and P. Marks. The Smiling Muse.
C.S.C., 636(VP):Summer85-224
E. Guiliano, 85(SBHC):Vol 13-121
Savoy, A.A., ed. Cajun Music. (Vol 1)
A. Prévos, 207(FR):Mar86-629
Saw Swee-Hock. Population Control for
Zero Growth in Singapore.
R. Hassan, 293(JASt):Feb85-472
Sawadogo, E. Contes de jadis.
E. Julien, 538(RAL):Fall85-406
Sawicki, S. and P. Nowaczyński, eds.
Polska liryka religijna.
D.A. Frick, 497(PolR):Vol30No2-229

331

Sawka, J. A Book of Fiction.
    D. McGill, 441:7Dec86-69
Sawyer, H. Soviet Perceptions of the Oil
    Factor in U.S. Foreign Policy.
    D. Wilson, 550(RusR):Apr85-211
Sawyer, P., ed. Domesday Book.
    H.R. Loyn, 617(TLS):16May86-526
Sawyer, P.H. Kings and Vikings.*
    J. Lindow, 563(SS):Winter85-110
Sawyer, P.L. Ruskin's Poetic Argument.
    E.K. Helsinger, 637(VS):Summer86-614
Sawyer, R. Casement.
    T.E. Hachey, 637(VS):Winter86-341
Sawyer, R. Slavery in the Twentieth Cen-
    tury.
    D. Henshaw, 362:13Nov86-25
Sawyer, R. - see "Harrap's Concise German
    and English Dictionary"
Saxon, A.H. - see Barnum, P.T.
Saxton, J. Little Tours of Hell.
    J-A. Goodwin, 617(TLS):21Nov86-1324
Sayce, O. The Medieval German Lyric 1150-
    1300.*
    S.L. Clark, 481(PQ):Winter85-146
    F.G. Gentry, 406:Winter85-481
    I. Glier, 447(N&Q):Sep84-420
Sayce, R.A. and D. Maskell. A Descriptive
    Bibliography of Montaigne's "Essais,"
    1580-1700.*
    I. Maclean, 402(MLR):Apr85-460
Sayers, S. Reality and Reason.
    C. Janaway, 617(TLS):4Apr86-367
Sayre, H.M. The Visual Text of William
    Carlos Williams.*
    V.M. Kouidis, 577(SHR):Fall85-386
    G.W. Linden, 289:Fall85-115
    W. Marling, 401(MLQ):Dec84-416
Sayre, K. Plato's Late Ontology.*
    M. Matthen, 482(PhR):Jul85-395
Sayre, R.F. - see Thoreau, H.D.
Sayres, S. and others, eds. The 60s, With-
    out Apology.*
    T. De Pietro, 219(GaR):Winter85-903
Saywell, S. Women in War.
    M. Woodall, 441:5Jan86-17
Sbarbaro, C. L'opera in versi e in prosa.
    (G. Lagorio and V. Scheimiller, eds)
    P. Hainsworth, 617(TLS):18Jul86-784
Sbarbaro, C. Pianissimo. (L. Polato, ed)
    M. Bacigalupo, 402(MLR):Oct85-956
Scaglione, A., ed. The Emergence of
    National Languages.*
    E.A. Ebbinghaus, 215(GL):Vol25No3-199
Scalapino, L. that they were at the beach —
    aeolotropic series.
    M. Perloff, 29(APR):Jan/Feb86-37
Scalapino, R.A. The Early Japanese Labor
    Movement.
    S.S. Large, 407(MN):Winter85-454
Scalapino, R.A. and J. Wanandi, eds.
    Economic, Political, and Security Issues
    in Southeast Asia in the 1980s.
    D.K. Crone, 293(JASt):Nov84-247
Scalvini, M.L. and M.G. Sandri. L'imma-
    gine storiografica dell'architettura
    contemporanea da Platz a Giedion.
    J.P. Bonta, 290(JAAC):Spring86-300
Scammell, M. Solzhenitsyn.*
    S. Monas, 550(RusR):Oct85-397
    R. Porter, 364:Apr/May85-132
    295(JML):Nov85-555

Scammell, W. Jouissance.*
    N. Jenkins, 493:Apr85-61
    H. Lomas, 364:Jun85-89
    J. Mole, 176:Jan86-61
    G. Szirtes, 148:Summer85-51
Scanlan, J.P. Marxism in the USSR.
    S. Krancberg, 617(TLS):3Jan86-7
Scanlon, J.P. Marxism in the USSR.
    I.S., 185:Jul86-901
Scanlon, P.A., ed. Stories from Central
    and Southern Africa.
    D. Williams, 49:Apr85-102
Scarfe, G. Scarfe by Scarfe.
    B. Bainbridge, 617(TLS):26Dec86-1453
Scarisbrick, D. Il valore dei gioielli e
    degli orologi da collezione — Antique
    Jewellery and Watch Values.
    H.H., 90:Sep85-631
    A.K. Snowman, 39:Apr85-280
Scarisbrick, D. Jewellery.*
    B. Scott, 39:Mar85-209
Scarisbrick, J.J. The Reformation and the
    English People.
    S.E. Lehmberg, 551(RenQ):Summer85-333
Scarron, P. L'Héritier ridicule ou la
    dame intéressée. (R. Guichemerre, ed)
    F. Moureau, 535(RHL):Sep/Oct85-868
    M-O. Sweetser, 207(FR):Apr86-781
Scarron, P. Le Roman comique. (R. Gara-
    pon, ed)
    H.T. Barnwell, 208(FS):Apr85-202
Scarron, P. Il Romanzo del Comici di Cam-
    pagna.
    C. Dédéyan, 535(RHL):Jan/Feb85-88
Scarry, E. The Body in Pain.
    A.S. Byatt, 617(TLS):13Jun86-637
    P. Singer, 453(NYRB):27Feb86-27
    S.R. Suleiman, 441:5Jan86-20
Scattergood, V.J. and J.W. Sherborne, eds.
    English Court Culture in the Later
    Middle Ages.*
    J. Griffiths, 382(MAE):1985/2-299
Ščedrov, A. Forcing and Classifying Topoi.
    P.T. Johnstone, 316:Sep85-852
Schaap, E. and others. Dutch Tiles.
    G. Wills, 39:Jun85-438
Schaar, C. "The Full-Voic'd Quire Below."*
    A. Burnett, 447(N&Q):Mar84-122
Schach, P. Icelandic Sagas.
    T.M. Andersson, 589:Oct85-1017
Schachermeyr, F. Griechische Früh-
    geschichte.
    J.T. Hooker, 303(JoHS):Vol 105-220
    J. Rutter, 124:Sep-Oct85-62
Schachermeyr, F. Die griechische Rücker-
    innerung im Lichte neuer Forschungen.
    J.T. Hooker, 303(JoHS):Vol 105-220
Schacht, R. Classical Modern Philosophers.
    G.S., 185:Apr86-670
Schacht, R. Nietzsche.*
    N. Davey, 323:Oct85-316
    J.T. Wilcox, 449:Jun85-294
Schaeder, B. Lexikographie als Praxis und
    Theorie.
    D. Herberg, 682(ZPSK):Band38Heft2-194
Schaefer, J. Shane. (J.C. Work, ed)
    J.H. Maguire, 649(WAL):May85-78
Schaeffer, S.F. The Injured Party.
    S. Ballantyne, 441:16Nov86-15
    J.H. Korelitz, 617(TLS):12Dec86-1409
Schaeffer, S.F. Mainland.*
    A. Kavounas, 617(TLS):17Jan86-56

Schäfer, F. Untersuchungen zur Reflexivität im Alttschechischen.
  D. Short, 575(SEER):Oct85-572
Schäfer, H.D. - see Lehmann, W.
Schäfer, H-W. Indipohdi und der weisse Heiland.
  R.C. Cowen, 406:Summer85-239
  P. Skrine, 402(MLR):Jan85-222
Schäfer, J., ed. Commonwealth-Literatur.*
  W. Pache, 402(MLR):Jul85-708
Schäfer, J. Documentation in the O.E.D.
  A.C. Partridge, 156(ShJW):Jahrbuch1985-240
Schäfer, P., with M. Schlüter and H.G. von Mutius. Synopse zur Hekhalot-Literatur.
  D.J. Halperin, 318(JAOS):Jul-Sep84-543
Schäfer, W.E. Johann Michael Moscherosch.*
  F. Gaede, 406:Fall85-354
Schakel, P.J. Reason and Imagination in C.S. Lewis.
  B. Murray, 395(MFS):Summer85-380
Schalk, E. From Valor to Pedigree.
  J. Powis, 617(TLS):4Jul86-729
Schaller, G.B. and others. The Giant Pandas of Wolong.*
  H. Kruuk, 617(TLS):11Apr86-400
Schanze, F. Meisterliche Liedkunst zwischen Heinrich von Mügeln und Hans Sachs. (Vol 1)
  W.C. McDonald, 301(JEGP):Oct85-598
Schanze, F. Meisterliche Liedkunst zwischen Heinrich von Mügeln und Hans Sachs. (Vol 2)
  C. Petzsch, 72:Band222Heft2-361
Schaper, E., ed. Pleasure, Preference and Value.*
  M.A. McCloskey, 63:Dec85-560
  M. Stchedroff, 518:Jan85-55
  D.D. Todd, 154:Autumn85-552
Schaper, E. and W. Vossenkuhl, eds. Bedingungen der Möglichkeit.
  W. Kersting, 687:Oct-Dec85-643
Schapiro, B.A. The Romantic Mother.*
  W.H. Galperin, 577(SHR):Spring85-174
  K. Swann, 591(SIR):Fall85-424
Scharf, A. Art and Photography. (rev)
  E. Darragon, 98:Aug-Sep85-825
Scharnhorst, G. and J. Bales. The Lost Life of Horatio Alger, Jr.*
  D.W. Petrie, 395(MFS):Winter85-727
Scharrer, M. Die Spaltung der deutschen Arbeiterbewegung.
  F.L. Carsten, 575(SEER):Apr85-310
Schaya, L. La création en Dieu à la lumière du judaïsme, du christianisme et de l'Islam.
  A. Reix, 542:Jan-Mar85-99
Schebera, J. Kurt Weill.
  S. Hinton, 410(M&L):Oct85-393
Scheckner, P. Class, Politics and the Individual.
  J.M. Coetzee, 453(NYRB):16Jan86-33
Schefer, J-L. L'Homme ordinaire du cinéma.
  T. Conley, 153:Spring85-4
Scheffers, H. Höfische Konvention und die Aufklärung.*
  M. Kruse, 547(RF):Band97Heft1-88
Scheffler, S. The Rejection of Consequentialism.*
  R.G. Frey, 393(Mind):Jan85-146
  B.R. Gross, 484(PPR):Jun86-696

Schehadé, G. Le Nageur d'un seul amour.
  D. Gascoyne, 617(TLS):26Sep86-1050
  D. Leuwers, 450(NRF):Jun85-60
Scheible, H. and W. Thüringer - see Melanchthon, P.
Scheibler, I. Griechische Töpferkunst.
  R.M. Cook, 303(JoHS):Vol 105-234
Scheick, W.J. The Splintering Frame.
  H.H. Watts, 395(MFS):Summer85-343
Scheier, C-A. Analytischer Kommentar zu Hegels Phänomenologie des Geistes.
  D. Dahlstrom, 543:Sep84-139
Schein, S.L. The Mortal Hero.
  J.H. Dee, 124:Jan-Feb86-200
  É. des Places, 555:Vol59fasc1-99
  W.C. Scott, 121(CJ):Oct/Nov85-68
  O. Taplin, 453(NYRB):13Mar86-39
Schele, L. and M.E. Miller. The Blood of Kings.
  B. Welsh, 617(TLS):26Sep86-1075
Scheler, M. Der englische Wortschatz.
  K. Reichl, 72:Band222Heft2-377
Scheler, M. Shakespeares Englisch.
  N.F. Blake, 72:Band222Heft1-177
  J. Schäfer, 156(ShJW):Jahrbuch1985-243
Schelle, H., ed. Christoph Martin Wieland.
  M. Dufner, 173(ECS):Spring86-445
  H. Jaumann, 680(ZDP):Band104Heft4-608
Schelling, F.W.J. Clara [ou] Du lien de la nature au monde des spirits.
  F. Wybrands, 450(NRF):May85-86
Schelling, F.W.J. Historisch-Kritische Ausgabe.* (1st Ser, Vol 1 ed by W.G. Jacobs, J. Jantzen and W. Schieche; Vol 2 ed by H. Buchner and J. Jantzen; Vol 3 ed by H. Buchner, W.G. Jacobs and A. Pieper)
  S. Smid, 489(PJGG):Band92Heft1-182
Schelling, F.W.J. Texte zur Philosophie der Kunst.* (W. Beierwaltes, ed) Über das Verhältnis der bildenen Künste zu der Natur. (L. Sziborsky, ed) Schriften 1804-1812. (S. Dietzsch, ed)
  H. Paetzold, 489(PJGG):Band92Heft1-188
Schemann, H. Die portugiesischen Verbalperiphrasen.
  J. Schmidt-Radefeldt, 547(RF):Band97 Heft1-75
Schemann, H. and L. Schemann-Dias. Die portugiesischen Verbalperiphrasen und ihre deutschen Entsprechungen.
  J. Schmidt-Radefeldt, 547(RF):Band97 Heft1-75
Schemmel, B. - see Hoffmann, E.T.A.
Schena, O. Le leggi palatine di Pietro IV d'Aragona.
  J.N. Hillgarth, 589:Oct85-1062
Scher, S.P., ed. Literatur und Musik.
  J-L. Cupers, 52:Band20Heft3-302
Scherer, C. Comédie et société sous Louis XIII.*
  G.J. Mallinson, 402(MLR):Jan85-162
  L. Picciola, 535(RHL):Sep/Oct85-864
Scherer, D. and T. Attig, eds. Ethics and the Environment.
  A. Carlson, 154:Winter85-755
Scherer, H.S. Sprechen im situativen Kontext.
  C. Schäffner, 682(ZPSK):Band38Heft4-432
Scherer, J. Le théâtre de Corneille.
  A. Niderst, 475:Vol 12No23-747

Scherf, W.  Lexikon der Zaubermärchen.
   J.M. McGlathery, 406:Winter85-483
Scherfer, P.  Funktionale Sprachvarianten.
   J. Albrecht, 685(ZDL):2/1985-252
Scherner, M.  Sprache als Text.
   B.J. Koekkoek, 221(GQ):Spring85-270
Scherwinsky, F.  Die Neologismen in der
   modernen französischen Science-Fiction.*
   M. Jackson, 545(RPh):Feb86-341
Scheuer, J.  Śiva dans le Mahābhārata.
   J.W. de Jong, 259(IIJ):Jul85-222
   B.M. Sullivan, 293(JASt):Aug85-878
Scheuermann, B.  Titel und Text.
   L.H. Hoek, 535(RHL):Jan/Feb85-109
Schick, F.  Having Reasons.*
   D-H. Ruben, 518:Apr85-108
   D. MacIntosh, 529(QQ):Autumn85-630
Schickel, R.  The Disney Version.  (rev)
   S. Schoenbaum, 617(TLS):11Jul86-758
Schiedlausky, G.  Kühlkugel und Wärmapfel.
   I.S. Weber, 683:Band48Heft1-124
Schiefen, R.J.  Nicholas Wiseman and the
   Transformation of English Catholicism.*
   L. Mahoney, 377:Nov85-204
Schiendorfer, M.  Ulrich von Singenberg,
   Walther und Wolfram.
   D.H. Green, 402(MLR):Apr85-487
   H. Kratz, 133:Band18Heft1-78
   W. McConnell, 221(GQ):Winter85-107
Schier, K., ed.  Märchen aus Island.*
   D. Erlingsson, 301(JEGP):Jan85-108
Schiff, B.N.  International Nuclear Tech-
   nology Transfer.
   D.H., 185:Apr86-661
Schiff, D.  The Music of Elliott Carter.*
   R.D. Morris, 317:Spring85-183
Schiff, E.  From Stereotype to Metaphor.*
   H. Kreisel, 107(CRCL):Sep85-563
   N. Stiller, 403(MLS):Fall85-376
Schiff, Z.  A History of the Israeli Army.
   A.H. Cordesman, 441:20Apr86-25
Schiff, Z. and E. Ya'ari.  Israel's Leba-
   non War.*
   D. Spanier, 176:Apr86-59
   D. Stone, 390:Mar85-62
Schiff, Z. and E. Ya'ari.  Israel's Leba-
   non War.  (new ed)
   B. Wasserstein, 617(TLS):10Oct86-1123
Schiffer, E.  Zwischen den Zeilen.*
   T.J. Reed, 402(MLR):Jan85-234
Schiffler, L.  Pour un enseignement inter-
   actif des langues étrangères.
   L.K. Martin, 399(MLJ):Winter85-405
Schiffman, H.F.  A Reference Grammar of
   Spoken Kannada.*
   R.V. Miranda, 293(JASt):May85-654
Schiffman, J.  Harlem Heyday.
   D.E. McGinty, 91:Fall85-227
von Schilcher, F. and N. Tennant.  Philos-
   ophy, Evolution and Human Nature.
   F. Gifford, 482(PhR):Oct85-602
   A. O'Hear, 518:Jan85-45
   F. Schier, 479(PhQ):Apr85-205
Schildt, G.  Alvar Aalto: The Early Years.
   C.L. Hancock, 45:Aug85-75
   W.C. Miller, 505:Mar85-169
   M. Spens, 46:May85-79
Schilpp, M.G. and S.M. Murphy.  Great
   Women of the Press.
   M.A. Gardner, 115:Summer84-262
Schimmel, A.  Calligraphy and Islamic Cul-
   ture.
   G.G., 90:May85-312

Schimmel, J.  The Art and Life of W. Her-
   bert Dunton, 1878-1936.
   L. Milazzo, 584(SWR):Spring85-262
Schimmelpfennig, J.P., ed.  Uneeda Review.
   O.W. Ferguson, 579(SAQ):Summer85-337
Schinke-Llano, L. and R.A. Spears.  Build-
   ing Dictionary Skills in English.
   T. Goldstein, 35(AS):Fall85-258
   S. Klopp, 399(MLJ):Winter85-446
Schinz, M. and S. Littlefield.  Visions of
   Paradise.*
   R.I. Ross, 617(TLS):16May86-543
Schippan, T.  Lexikologie der deutschen
   Gegenwartssprache.
   J. Bahns, 257(IRAL):Nov85-331
Schipper, M.  Afrikaanse letterkunde.
   J.M. Coetzee, 538(RAL):Winter85-616
Schippmann, K.  Grundzüge der parthischen
   Geschichte.
   E.W. Gray, 313:Vol75-250
Schirer, T.  Mark Twain and the Theatre.
   H.G. Baetzhold, 27(AL):May85-338
Schirmacher, W.  Technik und Gelassenheit.
   D. Dahlstrom, 543:Mar85-688
   R. Margreiter, 489(PJGG):Band92Heft1-
   208
Schirmer, W.F.  Geschichte der englischen
   und amerikanischen Literatur.*  (Vols 1
   and 2) (6th ed) (U. Broich and others,
   eds)
   W. Füger and J. Schäfer, 38:Band103
   Heft1/2-199
Schlee, A.  Rhine Journey.
   A. Lohrey, 381:Mar85-94
Schlegel, F.  Gemälde alter Meister.  (H.
   Eichner and N. Lelless, eds)
   R. Immerwahr, 301(JEGP):Oct85-609
Schlegel, F.  Obras selectas.  (H. Jure-
   tschke, ed; M.A. Vega Cernuda, trans)
   F. Meregalli, 52:Band20Heft1-99
Schleiner, L.  The Living Lyre in English
   Verse.
   A. Shaw, 385(MQR):Fall86-750
   639(VQR):Summer85-88
Schlemmer, G.  Die Rolle des germanischen
   Superstrats in der Geschichte der roman-
   ischen Sprachwissenschaft.
   H. Meier, 547(RF):Band97Heft1-54
Schlenstedt, D.  Egon Erwin Kisch.
   J. Schebera, 654(WB):6/1985-1041
Schlenstedt, S.  Stephan Hermlin.
   K. Werner, 654(WB):12/1985-2105
Schlenstedt, S. and others, eds.  Wer
   schreibt, handelt.
   T. Rietzschel, 654(WB):6/1985-1037
Schlesinger, A.M., Jr.  The Cycles of Amer-
   ican History.
   B.R. Barber, 441:16Nov86-13
   G.F. Kennan, 453(NYRB):6Nov86-3
   442(NY):17Nov86-152
Schlesinger, G.N.  Metaphysics.*
   M. Adam, 542:Oct-Dec85-567
   P. Menzies, 63:Mar85-103
Schless, H.H.  Chaucer and Dante.
   D.C. Baker, 191(ELN):Dec85-71
   B. Nolan, 377:Nov85-195
   D.J. Ransom, 107(CRCL):Sep85-514
   W. Wetherbee, 405(MP):May86-419
Schlicke, P.  Dickens and Popular Enter-
   tainment.
   S. Monod, 189(EA):Oct-Dec86-466

Schmookler, A.B.   The Parable of the
Tribes.
   42(AR):Spring85-253
Schnackenberg, G.   The Lamplit Answer.*
   S.M. Gilbert, 491:Dec85-165
   J. Hollander, 676(YR):Summer85-xi
   W. Logan, 472:Spring/Summer/Fall/
   Winter85-463
   R. McDowell, 249(HudR):Winter86-685
   J. Mole, 176:Nov86-58
   P. Stitt, 219(GaR):Summer85-414
Schnädelbach, H.   Philosophy in Germany,
1831-1933.  (German title: Philosophie
in Deutschland 1831-1933.)
   J. Habermas, 384:Sep/Oct85-898
   M. Mandelbaum, 319:Oct86-566
   H. Sluga, 84:Dec85-469
Schnädelbach, H.   Rationalität.
   J.C.E., 185:Apr86-691
Schneeberger, P-F.   The Baur Collection,
Geneva: Japanese Lacquer.
   J. Earle, 90:Apr85-242
   "Skipjack," 463:Autumn85-310
Schneer, J.   Ben Tillett.
   P. Williamson, 161(DUJ):Jun84-293
   P.R. Ziegler, 637(VS):Winter85-343
Schneider, A.   Entrances.
   M. Esslin, 441:26Jan86-14
   442(NY):7Apr86-104
Schneider, D.J.   D.H. Lawrence.*
   W.K. Buckley, 594:Spring85-112
Schneider, E.W.   Morphologische und syntak-
tische Variablen im amerikanischen Early
Black English.
   M. Görlach, 685(ZDL):2/1985-244
Schneider, F.   Aufklärung und Politik.
   K. Dicke, 489(PJGG):Band92Heft2-436
Schneider, G.   Probensprache der Oper.*
   B.J. Koekkoek, 221(GQ):Spring85-270
Schneider, J. - see Buridan, J.
Schneider, J. and J. Delaigue.  La Fugue
d'Isabelle.
   P.A. Berger, 399(MLJ):Spring85-87
Schneider, O.   Tanz-Lexikon.
   70:May/Jun85-175
Schneider, P.   Matisse.*
   J. Klein, 127:Winter85-359
   J.H. Neff, 55:May85-29
   D. Vallier, 98:Jun-Jul85-677
Schneider, U.   Einführung in den Buddhis-
mus.
   C. Lindtner, 259(IIJ):Oct85-296
Schneider, U.   Grundzüge einer Philosophie
des Glücks bei Nietzsche.
   R. Furness, 402(MLR):Oct85-998
   S.L. Gilman, 221(GQ):Spring85-312
Schneiderman, S.   Jacques Lacan.*
   M. Clark, 405(MP):Nov85-218
Schneiders, W.   Aufklärung und Vorurteils-
kritik.
   S. Carboncini, 706:Band17Heft1-118
   H-J. Engfer, 687:Jan-Mar85-143
Schneiders, W., ed.   Christian Wolff 1679-
1754.
   S. Carboncini, 706:Band17Heft1-111
Schnell, R.   Andreas Capellanus.*
   P. Cherchi, 545(RPh):May86-504
Schnerb-Lièvre, M., ed.   Le Songe du Verg-
ier.*
   K. Daly, 382(MAE):1985/1-143
Schnitzler, A.   Plays and Stories.  (E.
Schwarz, ed)
   D. Hunsberger, 399(MLJ):Spring85-95

Schnitzler, A.   Tagebuch 1909-1912.*  (W.
Welzig and others, eds)
   J.B. Berlin, 406:Summer85-237
   H. Thomé, 462(OL):Vol40No1-88
Schnitzler, A.   Tagebuch 1913-1916.*  (W.
Welzig and others, eds)
   A. Obermayer, 564:Nov85-310
   U.S. Rettig, 222(GR):Fall85-149
   H. Thomé, 462(OL):Vol40No1-88
Schnitzler, A.   Vienne au crépuscule.
   A. Clerval, 450(NRF):Jul-Aug85-172
Schober, R.   Abbild, Sinnbild, Wertung.
   E. Ibsch, 52:Band20Heft2-202
Schobert, W. and others.  Fischer Film
Almanach 1984.
   W. Schwarz, 193(ELit):Spring-Summer85-
   211
Schoblin, R.C., ed.   The Aesthetics of Fan-
tasy Literature and Art.
   L. Hatfield, 128(CE):Mar85-275
Schoell, K.   Die französische Komödie.
   W. Asholt, 72:Band222Heft2-441
Schoeman, F.D., ed.   Philosophical Dimen-
sions of Privacy.
   C.F. Cranor, 185:Apr86-643
Schoenbaum, S.   Shakespeare and Others.
   I-S. Ewbank, 617(TLS):25Apr86-451
   G. Schmidgall, 250(HLQ):Autumn85-385
Schoenberg, A.   Structural Functions of
Harmony.  (rev)  (L. Stein, ed)
   A.F.L.T., 412:Aug/Nov84-304
Schoenberg, A. and W. Kandinsky.  Arnold
Schoenberg — Wassily Kandinsky: Letters,
Pictures and Documents.*  (J. Hahl-Koch,
ed)
   R. Arnheim, 414:Vol71No1-92
   R. Craft, 453(NYRB):13Feb86-30
   P. Vergo, 90:Jan85-49
   H. Wood, 415:Feb85-94
Schoenl, W.J.   The Intellectual Crisis in
English Catholicism.
   J.L. Altholz, 637(VS):Winter86-320
Schoenstein, R.   Every Day Is Sunday.
   L. Thomas, 441:9Mar86-25
Schofield, J.   The Building of London from
the Conquest to the Great Fire.
   K. Biddick, 589:Oct85-1063
Schofield, M., M. Burnyeat and J. Barnes,
eds.  Doubt and Dogmatism.
   M.J. White, 53(AGP):Band67Heft3-314
Schofield, M. and M.C. Nussbaum, eds.  Lan-
guage and Logos.*
   J. Sisson, 518:Jul85-134
Schofield, M. and G. Striker, eds.  The
Norms of Nature.
   C. Rowe, 617(TLS):4Jul86-730
Schofield, M.A.   Quiet Rebellion.*
   M. Myers, 173(ECS):Fall85-107
Scholar, N.  Anaïs Nin.
   B.L. Knapp, 385(MQR):Summer86-622
Scholberg, K.R.   Introducción a la poesía
de Gómez Manrique.*
   J. Gimeno Casalduero, 240(HR):Summer85-
   361
Scholefield, A.   King of the Golden Valley.
   442(NY):23Jun86-98
Scholes, R.   Semiotics and Interpretation.
   C. Bremond, 567:Vol53No1/3-215
   N. Cotton, 435:Spring85-99
   A. Easthope, 366:Spring85-130
Scholes, R.   Textual Power.*
   G. Graff, 454:Winter86-179
   S. Scobie, 376:Jan86-128

336

Scholtes, G. Umgebungsstrukturen von
Verben im Shakespeare-Corpus.
 J. Schäfer, 156(ShJW):Jahrbuch1985-243
Schöne, A. Götterzeichen — Liebeszauber —
Satanskult.*
 H. Eichner, 406:Winter85-469
Schönert, J., ed. Literatur und Kriminal-
ität.*
 J. Schmidt, 268(IFR):Winter86-33
Schönherr, M. Lanner, Strauss, Ziehrer.
 A. Lamb, 410(M&L):Apr85-164
Schönzeler, H-H. Dvořák.
 J. Clapham, 415:Mar85-157
Schoolfield, G.C. Edith Södergran.*
 W.G. Jones, 562(Scan):Nov85-236
Schöpflin, G., ed. Handbooks to the Mod-
ern World: The Soviet Union and Eastern
Europe.
 V. Bogdanor, 176:Sep/Oct86-52
Schopp, C. - see Dumas, A.
Schor, N. Breaking the Chain.
 P. Kamuf, 400(MLN):Sep85-908
 L.W. Rabine, 454:Winter86-186
Schor, N. and H.F. Majewski, eds. Flau-
bert and Postmodernism.
 B. Fleming, 546(RR):Jan85-120
 R. Griffin, 210(FrF):May85-243
 L.M. Porter, 446(NCFS):Fall-
Winter85/86-174
 E.D. Sullivan, 345(KRQ):Vol32No1-110
Schorr, J.L. The Life and Works of Justus
van Effen.
 L. Gasbarrone, 207(FR):Dec85-296
Schøsler, L. La déclinaison bicasuelle de
l'ancien français.
 G. Roques, 553(RLiR):Jul-Dec85-470
 M.E. Winters, 350:Mar86-209
Schoterman, J.A., ed and trans. The
Ṣaṭsāhasrasaṃhitā. (Chapters 1-5)
 A. Padoux, 259(IIJ):Apr85-140
 K.G. Zysk, 318(JAOS):Jul-Sep84-606
Schott, P.S. A Little Ignorance.
 R. Grant, 441:6Jul86-14
Schott, R.L. and D.S. Hamilton. People,
Positions, and Power.*
 J.O. Robertson, 106:Winter85-465
Schouls, P.A. The Imposition of Method.*
 F. Duchesneau, 154:Summer85-327
Schöwerling, R. Chapbooks.
 N. Würzbach, 38:Band103Heft3/4-491
Schrader, F.O. Kleine Schriften. (J.F.
Sprockhoff, ed)
 J.W. de Jong, 259(IIJ):Jul85-224
Schrader, L., ed. Augusto Roa Bastos.
 L. Pollmann, 547(RF):Band97Heft4-505
Schramm, G. Eroberer und Eingesessene.
 J. Udolph, 260(IF):Band90-317
Schrecker, E.W. No Ivory Tower.
 D.M. Oshinsky, 441:28Sep86-15
 C.V. Woodward, 453(NYRB):25Sep86-3
Schreiber, B. La Descente au Berceau.
 D. Aury, 450(NRF):Mar85-92
Schreiber, B. L'Organeau.
 T. Greene, 207(FR):Oct85-155
Schreier-Hornung, A. Spielleute, Fahrende,
Aussenseiter.
 U. Meves, 224(GRM):Band35Heft2-229
Schrey, H. Anglistisches Kaleidoskop.
 G. Haenicke, 72:Band222Heft2-428
Schrock, N.C., ed. Architectural Records
in Boston.
 M. Ison, 576:Mar85-75

Schröder, P., ed. Vernunft — Erkenntnis —
Sittlichkeit.
 A. Rocque, 154:Winter85-745
Schröder, W. "Arabel"-Studien II.
 M. Resler, 133:Band18Heft1-82
Schroedel, J.R. Alone in a Crowd.*
 A. Hacker, 453(NYRB):14Aug86-26
Schroeder, M.R., ed. Speech and Speaker
Recognition.
 W.S-Y. Wang, 350:Sep86-706
Schroeder, W.R. Sartre and his Predeces-
sors.
 L.C., 185:Jul86-902
 P.S. Morris, 323:Oct85-313
Schroll-Fleischer, N.O. Der Gottesgedanke
in der Philosophie Kants.*
 D. Dahlstrom, 543:Mar85-690
Schuck, P.H. and R.M. Smith. Citizenship
Without Consent.
 N. Glazer, 617(TLS):13Jun86-655
Schudson, M. Advertising.
 R. Draper, 453(NYRB):26Jun86-14
 J. Richetti, 533:Summer85-138
Schuffenhauer, W. - see Feuerbach, L.
Schuh, W. Richard Strauss: A Chronicle
of the Early Years 1864-1898.
 J.B., 412:Feb83-59
Schuhmann, K. and J. Möller. Jonathan
Swift.*
 E. Kreutzer, 72:Band222Heft2-411
Schuller, G. Early Jazz.
 617(TLS):21Nov86-1327
Schuller, G. Musings.
 C.J. Oja, 441:16Feb86-10
Schulman, G. Hemispheres.*
 S.M. Gilbert, 491:Dec85-161
 J.D. McClatchy, 249(HudR):Spring85-167
Schulthess, P. Relation und Funktion.*
 R. Finster, 706:Band17Heft1-122
Schultz, J.A. The Shape of the Round
Table.
 D.H. Green, 402(MLR):Jul85-744
 T.L. Markey, 133:Band17Heft3/4-310
 J. Rider, 589:Jan85-195
 B. Thoran, 680(ZDP):Band104Heft1-144
Schultz, J.W. Bear Chief's War Shirt.
(W.W. Betts, ed)
 D.R. Miller, 649(WAL):Feb86-354
Schultz, J.W. My Life as an Indian.
 L.D. Clark, 649(WAL):May85-85
Schultz, P. Deep Within the Ravine.*
 E. Butscher, 496:Spring85-47
 V. Shetley, 491:Apr85-43
 P. Stitt, 219(GaR):Spring85-188
 639(VQR):Winter85-28
Schulz, G. Die deutsche Literatur
zwischen Französischer Revolution und
Restauration. (Pt 1)
 K.L. Berghahn, 221(GQ):Fall85-585
 G. Hoffmeister, 406:Winter85-485
Schulz, M.F. Paradise Preserved.
 S. Soupel, 189(EA):Oct-Dec86-464
Schulz, W. Die aufgehobene Zeit.
 J. Glenn, 221(GQ):Spring85-306
Schulz-Behrend, G. - see Opitz, M.
Schulz-Hoffman, C. and J.C. Weiss, eds.
Max Beckmann.*
 J.B. Smith, 39:Nov85-400
Schulze, F. Mies van der Rohe.*
 M. Filler, 453(NYRB):12Jun86-26
 H. Muschamp, 62:Dec85-15

Schulze, L. and W. Wetzel, eds. Litera-
ture and History.
    H. Reiss, 133:Band17Heft3/4-306
Schulze, M. and W. Simon - see Luther, M.
Schumacher, L. Servus Index.
    T. Wiedemann, 123:Vol35No1-135
Schuman, H., C. Steeh and L. Bobo. Racial
Attitudes in America.
    N. Glazer, 617(TLS):13Jun86-655
Schuon, F. Le Soufisme, voile et quintes-
sence.
    A. Schimmel, 318(JAOS):Oct-Dec84-777
Schupbach, R.D. Lexical Specialization
in Russian.
    E. Klenin, 574(SEEJ):Fall85-355
    A. Mustajoki, 559:Vol9No1-88
    J.I. Press, 575(SEER):Oct85-573
Schürmann, R. Le principe d'anarchie.*
    J. Llewelyn, 323:May85-208
Schurre, J. Currier and Ives Prints.
(rev)
    J.V. Turano, 16:Winter85-91
Schuster, G. - see Benn, G.
Schuster, I. - see Rose, E.
Schütrumpf, E. Die Analyse der Polis
durch Aristoteles.*
    J.B. Skemp, 303(JoHS):Vol 105-189
Schutte, W. Index of Recurrent Elements
in James Joyce's "Ulysses."*
    R.D. Newman, 577(SHR):Spring85-185
Schütte, W. Klassenverhältnisse.
    W. Schwarz, 193(ELit):Spring-Summer85-
212
Schutz, B.M. All the Old Bargains.
    N. Callendar, 441:9Feb86-27
Schutz, H. The Prehistory of Germanic
Europe.
    H. Joldersma, 564:Feb85-73
Schützeichel, R. Althochdeutsches Wörter-
buch. (3rd ed)
    E. Seebold, 685(ZDL):3/1985-363
Schützeichel, R. Codex Pal. lat. 52.*
    W. Haubrichs, 684(ZDA):Band114Heft1-9
Schuyler, J. A Few Days.
    D. Revell, 152(UDQ):Spring/Summer86-
185
Schwab, A.T. - see Huneker, J.G.
Schwab, R. The Oriental Renaissance.
    W. Halbfass, 293(JASt):Aug85-799
    639(VQR):Spring85-52
Schwab, R.N., with W.E. Rex. Inventory
of Diderot's "Encyclopédie." (Vol 7)
    G. Bremner, 208(FS):Oct85-473
Schwan, W. Goethes "Wahlverwandtschaften."
    H. Dunkle, 221(GQ):Spring85-282
Schwantes, C. Coxey's Army.*
    P-L. Adams, 61:Jan86-95
Schwarte, K-H. Der Ausbruch des zweiten
punischen Krieges — Rechtsfrage und
Überlieferung.
    J.W. Rich, 123:Vol35No1-131
    E.S. Staveley, 313:Vol75-234
Schwartz, B. The Battle for Human Nature.
    D.H. Wrong, 441:6Jul86-10
Schwartz, B. Swann's Way.
    L. Greenhouse, 441:11May86-25
Schwartz, B. and H. Lacey. Behaviorism,
Science, and Human Nature.
    T.L. Smith, 486:Dec84-696
Schwartz, B.I. The World of Thought in
Ancient China.*
    A.C. Graham, 617(TLS):18Jul86-795

Schwartz, B.M. Travels Through the Third
World.
    N. Barley, 617(TLS):19Sep86-1041
Schwartz, B.M. A World of Villages.
    J. Koslow, 441:21Sep86-27
Schwartz, D. The Ego is Always at the
Wheel. (R. Phillips, ed)
    442(NY):4Aug86-87
Schwartz, D. The Letters of Delmore
Schwartz.* (R. Phillips, ed)
    F. Hobson, 344:Winter86-119
    R. Leiter, 249(HudR):Autumn85-503
Schwartz, D. Portrait of Delmore. (E.
Pollet, ed)
    P-L. Adams, 61:Sep86-104
    S. Moss, 441:19Oct86-12
Schwartz, G. Rembrandt.
    J. Nash, 617(TLS):9May86-495
    J. Snyder, 441:9Mar86-9
Schwartz, H. Never Satisfied.
    J. O'Reilly, 441:7Dec86-18
Schwartz, J. The Sexual Politics of Jean-
Jacques Rousseau.*
    M. Cranston, 173(ECS):Fall85-78
    T.M. Kavanagh, 400(MLN):Sep85-877
Schwartz, L.S. Disturbances in the
Field.*
    G. Davenport, 569(SR):Spring85-321
Schwartz, M.F., A.S. Moraczewski and J.A.
Monteleone. Sex and Gender.
    A.S., 185:Apr86-696
Schwartz, R.B. Daily Life in Johnson's
London.
    M. Byrd, 88:Winter85/86-110
    D. Jarrett, 83:Autumn85-239
Schwartz, S. The Matrix of Modernism.
    A.W. Litz, 617(TLS):10Oct86-1142
    R. Shattuck, 453(NYRB):18Dec86-66
Schwartz, S. To Leningrad in Winter.
    C. Hardesty, 455:Sep85-70
Schwarz, B. Great Masters of the Violin.
    C. Brown, 410(M&L):Jul85-250
    M. Campbell, 415:Jul85-407
Schwarz, D.R. Conrad: The Later Fiction.*
    T.C. Moser, 637(VS):Winter85-329
Schwarz, E. Dichtung, Kritik, Geschichte.
    B.L. Bradley, 133:Band18Heft2-181
Schwarz, E. - see Schnitzler, A.
Schwarz, E.A. and R. Ezawa. Everyday
Japanese.
    D.R. McCreary, 399(MLJ):Autumn85-310
Schwarz, J.A. The Speculator.
    G.F. Goodwin, 106:Spring85-95
Schwarz, J.E. America's Hidden Success.
    G.S. Smith, 529(QQ):Summer85-297
Schwarz, W. Guitar Bibliography.
    M. Criswick, 415:Jun85-350
Schwarz, W. - see Kant, I.
Schwarz, W.F. Drama der russischen und
tschechischen Avantgarde als szenischer
Text.
    R.B. Pynsent, 575(SEER):Oct85-587
Schwarz-Bart, S. Pluie et vent sur
Télumée Miracle. Ti Jean L'horizon.
    J.P. Campbell, 149(CLS):Fall85-394
Schwarzbaum, H. The "Mishle Shu'alim"
(Fox Fables) of Rabbi Berechiah Ha-
Nakdan.
    H. Goldberg, 545(RPh):Aug84-41
Schwarze, C., ed. Analyse des préposi-
tions.*
    K-H. Körner, 72:Band222Heft1-150

Scruton, R.  Sexual Desire.
  S.R. Letwin, 362:15May86-28
  M. Nussbaum, 453(NYRB):18Dec86-49
  R.A. Shweder, 441:23Mar86-38
  G. Strawson, 617(TLS):28Feb86-207
  J. Weightman, 176:Sep/Oct86-46
Scruton, R.  Thinkers of the New Left.
  J. Dunn, 617(TLS):4Apr86-347
  A. Ryan, 362:30Jan86-23
de Scudéry, G.  Poésies diverses.  (Vol 1)
  (R.G. Pellegrini, ed)
  C. Abraham, 207(FR):Oct85-127
  M. Bertaud, 475:Vol 12No22-309
  R. Maber, 402(MLR):Jul85-714
  A. Niderst, 535(RHL):Jul/Aug85-680
Scupham, P.  Out Late.
  N. Corcoran, 617(TLS):19Dec86-1423
Scupham, P.  Winter Quarters.*
  J. Cobley, 376:Jun85-132
Seabrook, J.  Landscapes of Poverty.
  G. Tindall, 617(TLS):14Feb86-161
Seagrave, S.  The Soong Dynasty.*
  639(VQR):Autumn85-118
Seal, A., P. Bryant and C. Hall.  Full and
  Short Entry Catalogues.
  J. Somers, 87(BB):Dec85-218
Seale, D.  Vision and Stagecraft in
  Sophocles.*
  D.J. Mastronarde, 122:Apr85-179
Seale, W.  The President's House.
  P. Goldberger, 441:7Dec86-16
Sealock, R.B., M.M. Sealock and M.S.
  Powell.  Bibliography of Place-Name Lit-
  erature, United States and Canada.  (3rd
  ed)
  T. Algeo, 35(AS):Spring85-79
Sealts, M.M., Jr.  Pursuing Melville, 1940-
  1980.*
  R. Mason, 447(N&Q):Jun84-285
Sealy, R.J.  The Palace Academy of Henry
  III.*
  J.B. Atkinson, 207(FR):Dec85-288
Searle, J.  Minds, Brains and Science.*
  R.G.M., 185:Apr86-668
  639(VQR):Summer85-99
Searle, J.R.  Intentionality.*
  R.E. Aquila, 484(PPR):Sep85-159
Searle, R.  To the Kwai — and Back.
  B. Mauldin, 441:10Aug86-9
  D. Thomas, 362:13Mar86-28
  442(NY):30Jun86-89
Searles, G.J.  The Fiction of Philip Roth
  and John Updike.
  C.B. Harris, 659(ConL):Summer86-279
  W.T.S., 395(MFS):Summer85-415
  295(JML):Nov85-404
Seaver, P.S.  Wallington's World.
  A. Woolrych, 617(TLS):11Apr86-380
Sebba, A.  Enid Bagnold.
  A. Chisholm, 617(TLS):26Dec86-1442
  N. Williams, 362:13Nov86-26
"The Second Link."
  L. Zippay, 127:Fall85-263
Secor, R.  John Ruskin and Alfred Hunt.*
  D. Birch, 447(N&Q):Dec84-579
Secor, R. and D. Moddelmog, comps.  Joseph
  Conrad and American Writers.
  C.R. La Bossière, 268(IFR):Summer86-98
Secor, R. and M. - see Hunt, V.
Secrest, M.  Kenneth Clark.*
  639(VQR):Summer85-81
Secrest, M.  Salvador Dali.
  G. Glueck, 441:30Nov86-9

Secretan, P.  L'analogie.
  M. Adam, 542:Jan-Mar85-101
Seddon, G. and A. Bicknell.  The Complete
  Guide to Conservatory Gardening.
  S. Brownmiller, 441:1Jun86-31
Sedelow, W.A., Jr. and S.Y. Sedelow, eds.
  Computers in Language Research 2.*
  S.M. Embleton, 320(CJL):Spring85-83
  D.H., 355(LSoc):Jun85-278
Sedgwick, E.K.  Between Men.
  C.C. Hollis, 646:Spring86-31
  P.S. Yaeger, 400(MLN):Dec85-1139
  639(VQR):Summer85-90
Sedlar, J., with N. Kolpas.  Modern South-
  west Cuisine.
  F. Fabricant, 441:7Dec86-18
Sedulius Scottus.  On Christian Rulers
  [and] The Poems.  (E.G. Doyle, ed and
  trans)
  F. Kelly, 112:Vol 17-186
See, C.  Golden Days.
  C. Sternhell, 441:30Nov86-9
  442(NY):29Dec86-96
von See, K., ed.  Neues Handbuch der
  Literaturwissenschaft.
  K.H. Kiefer, 343:Heft11-112
von See, K.  Skaldendichtung.
  H-P. Naumann, 224(GRM):Band35Heft1-101
Seebass, G.  Das Problem von Sprache und
  Denken.
  E. Baer, 567:Vol56No1/2-147
Seebohm, C.  The Last Romantics.
  M. Rubin, 441:21Dec86-14
Seebohm, H.  The Birds of Siberia.
  D. Durrant, 364:Feb86-109
Seebold, E.  Etymologie.*
  K. Müller, 682(ZPSK):Band38Heft4-447
von Seefranz-Montag, A.  Syntaktische Funk-
  tionen und Wortstellungsveränderung.*
  O. Fischer and F. van der Leek,
  297(JL):Sep85-497
Seel, G.  Die Aristotelische Modaltheorie.*
  E. Karger, 192(EP):Jul-Sep85-423
Seeley, T.D.  Honeybee Ecology.
  D. Galton, 617(TLS):10Jan86-47
Seelig, S.C.  The Shadow of Eternity.*
  R.B. Shaw, 402(MLR):Jul85-692
Seelye, H.N.  Teaching Culture.*  (2nd ed)
  S.S. Magnan, 276:Summer85-147
Seferis, G.  Meres 20 Aprili 1951 —
  4 Avgoustous 1956.
  H. Gifford, 617(TLS):12Dec86-1391
Segal, C.  Dionysiac Poetics and Euripides'
  "Bacchae."*
  H.E. Barnes, 131(CL):Summer85-269
Segal, C.  Pindar's Mythmaking.
  P. Murray, 617(TLS):21Nov86-1316
Segal, C. - see Whitman, C.H.
Segal, E., ed.  Oxford Readings in Greek
  Tragedy.
  J.F. Davidson, 67:Nov85-248
  E.M. Jenkinson, 161(DUJ):Dec84-95
Segal, G., ed.  The Soviet Union in East
  Asia.
  A.S. Whiting, 293(JASt):Nov84-151
Segal, H.P.  Technological Utopianism in
  American Culture.
  B. Goodwin, 617(TLS):18Apr86-425
  K.M. Roemer, 26(ALR):Spring/Autumn85-
  282
Segalen, V. and H. Manceron.  Correspon-
  dance.  (G. Manceron, ed)
  J-L. Coatalem, 450(NRF):Sep85-77

Segev, T. 1949 — The First Israelis.*
  E. Jackson, 441:2Feb86-13
Segonds, A. - see Kepler, J.
Segre, C. - see Ariosto, L.
Segrè, E. From X-Rays to Quarks.
  B.W. Sargent, 529(QQ):Winter85-884
Segreff, K-W. Moses Mendelssohn und die
  Aufklärungsästhetik im 18. Jahrhundert.
  D. Dowdey, 221(GQ):Fall85-606
Segurado, J., ed. Francisco D'Ollanda,
  "De aetatibus mundi imagines."
  J. Bury, 90:Jan85-44
Sehrt, E.T. Humor und Historie in Kip-
  lings Puck-Geschichten.
  R. Fricker, 38:Band103Heft1/2-243
Seibold, J.R. Pueblo y saber en la Feno-
  menologia del Espíritu de Hegel.
  A. Reix, 542:Jul-Sep85-337
Seibt, G.F. Griechische Söldner im
  Achaimenidenreich.
  R.J. van der Spek, 394:Vol38fasc1/2-
  254
Seide, G. Geschichte der Russischen Ortho-
  doxen Kirche im Ausland von der Gründung
  bis in die Gegenwart.
  H. Röhling, 688(ZSP):Band45Heft1-199
Seidel, F. Men and Woman.*
  W. Scammell, 148:Winter85-65
  G. Szirtes, 148:Summer85-51
Seideman, D. The New Republic.
  R. Caplan, 441:21Dec86-15
Seidenspinner-Núñez, D. The Allegory of
  Good Love.
  V. Marmo, 379(MedR):Apr85-155
Seidensticker, B. Palintonos harmonia.*
  A.L. Brown, 303(JoHS):Vol 105-199
Seidensticker, T. Die Gedichte des Šamar-
  dal ibn Šarīk.
  J.E. Montgomery, 294:Vol 16-149
Seidl, H. Aristoteles. (R. Berlinger, ed)
  Beiträge zu Aristoteles' Erkenntnislehre
  und Metaphysik. (R. Berlinger and W.
  Schräder, eds)
  L.J. Elders, 543:Mar86-586
Seidler, H. Österreichischer Vormärz und
  Goethezeit.*
  P. Horwath, 406:Winter85-490
Seidman, B. Absent at the Creation.
  J.M. Heaton, 323:Jan85-104
Seifert, H-U. Sade: Leser und Autor.
  M. Delon, 535(RHL):Sep/Oct85-879
Seifert, J. Selected Poetry. (G. Gibian,
  ed)
  D.J. Enright, 617(TLS):31Oct86-1222
Seigel, J. Bohemian Paris.
  R. Shattuck, 453(NYRB):18Dec86-66
  A. Weinstein, 441:23Mar86-30
Seiler, B.W. Die leidigen Tatsachen.*
  K.L. Berghahn, 406:Fall85-351
Seiler, H. and C. Lehmann, eds. Apprehen-
  sion.* (Pt 1)
  B. Comrie, 603:Vol9No3-459
  T.L. Markey, 350:Sep86-676
Seiler, H. and J. Stachowiak, eds. Appre-
  hension.* (Pt 2)
  T.L. Markey, 350:Sep86-676
Seiler, T.B. and W. Wannenmacher, eds.
  Concept Development and the Development
  of Word Meaning.
  D. Warding, 353:Vol23No3-512
Seiler-Dietrich, A. Die Literaturen
  Schwarzafrikas.
  B. Ischinger, 538(RAL):Winter85-618

de Seingalt, J.C. - see under Casanova de
  Seingalt, J.
Seip, J.A. Problemer og metode i historie-
  forskningen.
  P. Vinten-Johansen, 563(SS):Autumn85-
  461
Seitter, W. Menschenfassungen.
  R. Schlesier, 384:Sep/Oct85-928
Seitz, W.C. Abstract Expressionist Paint-
  ing in America.*
  D. Craven, 59:Dec85-499
  M. Welish, 473(PR):Vol52No3-299
Sekler, E.F. Josef Hoffmann: The Architec-
  tural Work.
  C. Jencks, 617(TLS):17Jan86-54
Selbmann, R. Dichterberuf im bürgerlichen
  Zeitalter.
  G.K. Hart, 221(GQ):Winter85-130
Selby, H., Jr. Song of the Silent Snow.
  R. Atwan, 441:21Sep86-26
  B. Morton, 617(TLS):5Sep86-978
Selden, R. Criticism and Objectivity.
  A. Easthope, 366:Spring85-130
  K.M. Newton, 97(CQ):Vol 14No2-178
Selden, R. A Reader's Guide to Contempor-
  ary Literary Theory.
  C. Baldick, 617(TLS):17Jan86-52
  L. Olsen, 70:May/Jun86-159
Self, D. Television Drama.
  A. Rissik, 157:No155-52
Seliktar, O. New Zionism and the Foreign
  Policy System of Israel.
  B. Wasserstein, 617(TLS):10Oct86-1123
Selinger, S. Calvin Against Himself.
  D.J. Wilcox, 551(RenQ):Autumn85-525
Selinker, L. and S. Gass. Workbook in
  Second Language Acquisition.
  H.H. Kleinmann, 399(MLJ):Autumn85-296
Sell, R.D. The Reluctant Naturalist of
  "Amelia."
  H. Reinhold, 38:Band103Heft3/4-506
  L. Speirs, 179(ES):Oct85-404
Sellin, B. The Life and Works of David
  Lindsay.
  K. Hume, 677(YES):Vol 15-335
Sellin, P.R. John Donne and "Calvinist"
  Views of Grace.*
  P. Dane, 67:May85-75
Seltzer, M. Henry James and the Art of
  Power.*
  M. Dickie, 301(JEGP):Oct85-580
  E.D. Ermarth, 445(NCF):Dec85-355
  J. Freedman, 432(NEQ):Jun85-323
  E. Prioleau, 27(AL):May85-335
  295(JML):Nov85-503
Selz, T.D. and M. Simensky. Entertainment
  Law.
  B.J. Wry, 476:Winter84-77
Selzer, R. Taking the World in for
  Repairs.
  D. Ackerman, 441:5Oct86-42
Sembach, K-J. Style 1930.
  S.M. Halpern, 441:28Sep86-26
Semmel, B. John Stuart Mill and the Pur-
  suit of Virtue.*
  R.W. Hoag, 319:Jul86-421
  D.N. Lindley, 637(VS):Spring85-555
Semowich, C.J., comp. American Furniture
  Craftsmen Working prior to 1920.
  D.D. Waters, 658:Winter85-314
Semprun, J. La Montagne blanche.
  R. Buss, 617(TLS):5Sep86-979

Sen, A.  Resources, Values and Develop-
ment.*
   B.M.B., 185:Apr86-693
de Senancour, É.P.  Obermann.  (J-M. Mon-
noyer, ed)
   Y. le Hir, 450(NRF):Jun85-63
   P. Lecoq, 535(RHL):Nov/Dec85-1073
Senckel, B.  Individualität und Totalität.
   O.W. Johnston, 221(GQ):Fall85-609
Seneca.  Apocolocyntosis.  (P.T. Eden, ed)
   D.C. and S.H. Braund, 313:Vol75-314
   M.S. Smith, 123:Vol35No2-302
Seneca.  Seneca's "Thyestes."  (R.J.
Tarrant, ed)
   E. Fantham, 627(UTQ):Summer86-435
Seneca.  Thyestes.  (J. Heywood, trans; J.
Daalder, ed)
   D. Kay, 447(N&Q):Sep84-427
Sénécal, A. - see Aubert de Gaspé fils, P.
Senelick, L.  Serf Actor.*
   J.A. Barnstead, 550(RusR):Jan85-84
   E.K. Bristow, 615(TJ):May85-243
   S. Golub, 130:Spring85-92
   L. Hecht, 574(SEEJ):Fall85-347
   N. Worrall, 575(SEER):Apr85-288
   N. Worrall, 610:Spring85-78
Senger, M.W.  Leonhard Culmann.
   J.W. Van Cleve, 406:Summer85-219
Sen Gupta, S.C.  A Shakespeare Manual.
   K. Tetzeli von Rosador, 156(ShJW):
   Jahrbuch1985-259
Seniff, D.P. - see Alfonso XI
Senkewicz, R.M.  Vigilantes in Gold Rush
San Francisco.
   J. Seelye, 617(TLS):6Jun86-612
Senkuttuvan, A., ed.  MNCs and ASEAN
Development in the 1980s.
   L. Lim, 293(JASt):May85-689
Senn, F.  Joyce's Dislocations.  (J.P.
Riquelme, ed)
   B. Benstock, 395(MFS):Winter85-784
   R.M. Kain, 329(JJQ):Winter86-229
   J. Kidd, 617(TLS):5Sep86-980
Senn, H.A.  Werewolf and Vampire in
Romania.*
   A. Stone, 203:Vol196No2-266
Sennett, R.  The Fall of Public Man.
   362:4Sep86-30
"Le sens du parfait de l'indicatif actif
en Latin."
   W. Ax, 260(IF):Band90-322
"A Sense of History."
   N. Ramsey, 441:5Jan86-17
Sensibar, J.L.  The Origins of Faulkner's
Art.*
   S.S. Baskett, 115:Summer85-381
   P.R. Broughton, 534(RALS):Spring83-41
   P.J. Egan, 27(AL):May85-345
   E.J. Higgins, 95(CLAJ):Jun86-490
   D. Roberts, 651(WHR):Spring85-88
   S.M. Ross, 395(MFS):Winter85-737
   R. Storey, 149(CLS):Winter85-559
   M. Yonce, 392:Summer85-372
   295(JML):Nov85-477
Sensibar, J.L. - see Faulkner, W.
Seppänen, L.  Meister Eckeharts Konzeption
der Sprachbedeutung.
   B.J. Koekkoek, 350:Dec86-941
Septimus, B.  Hispano-Jewish Culture in
Transition.
   H. Tirosh-Rothschild, 589:Jan85-199

Serbat, G. and others, eds.  É. Benveniste
aujourd'hui.
   P. Swiggers, 350:Jun86-458
Serebriakoff, V.  Mensa.
   A. Wooldridge, 617(TLS):14Feb86-158
Sergent, M. and K. Wilkins.  A Translation
Textbook.
   B.L. Knapp, 207(FR):May86-1024
Seron, X.  Aphasie et neuropsychologie.
   L. Millet, 192(EP):Apr-Jun85-274
Serpell, J.  In the Company of Animals.
   H. Ritvo, 441:26Oct86-46
Serres, M.  The Parasite.  Hermes.  (J.V.
Harari and D.F. Bell, eds)
   V. Nemoianu, 704(SFR):Spring85-105
Serres, M.  Rome, le livre des fondations.*
   P. Saint-Armand, 704(SFR):Winter85-435
Sérullaz, M., with others.  Musée du Lou-
vre, Cabinet des Dessins; Inventaire
Général des Dessins, Ecole Française:
Dessins d'Eugène Delacroix, 1798-1863.
   L. Johnson, 90:Mar85-170
Servet, M.  Restitución del Cristianismo.
(Á. Alcalá, ed)
   N.G. Round, 86(BHS):Jul85-296
Sessions, W.K.  The First Printers at
Ipswich in 1547-1548 and Worcester in
1549-1553.
   B.S. Benedikz, 354:Dec85-370
Seth, V.  The Golden Gate.
   P-L. Adams, 61:May86-99
   W. Balliett, 442(NY):14Jul86-82
   A. Hollinghurst, 617(TLS):4Jul86-733
   C. Iannone, 129:Sep86-54
   R. Mungo, 441:11May86-11
   M. Perloff, 29(APR):Nov/Dec86-37
Seth, V.  The Humble Administrator's
Garden.*
   C. Rawson, 617(TLS):7Feb86-137
Settis, S., ed.  Camposanto monumentale di
Pisa: Le Antichità.  (Vol 2)
   M.A.R. Colledge, 123:Vol35No1-220
Settis, S.  Memoria dell'antico nell'arte
italiana.
   B. Boucher, 617(TLS):12Dec86-1399
Settle, M.L.  Celebration.
   W. Boyd, 441:26Oct86-14
   442(NY):24Nov86-149
"The Settlement Cookbook."
   W. and C. Cowen, 639(VQR):Spring85-64
Setton, K.M.  The Papacy and the Levant.*
(Vols 3 and 4)
   W.H. McNeill, 551(RenQ):Winter85-728
Seung, T.K.  Semiotics and Thematics in
Hermeneutics.*
   D.H. Hirsch, 569(SR):Summer85-465
   J.A. Varsava, 125:Fall84-99
Seung, T.K.  Structuralism and Hermeneu-
tics.*
   D.H. Hirsch, 569(SR):Summer85-465
Dr. Seuss.  You're Only Old Once!
   E. Sorel, 441:23Mar86-39
Severin, T.  Tracking Marco Polo.
   S. Ferrell, 441:13Apr86-23
de Sevilla, I. - see under San Isidoro de
Sevilla
Sevin, D., I. Sevin and K. Bean.  Wie
geht's?  (2nd ed)
   I. Henderson, 399(MLJ):Spring85-96
Seward, D.  Napoleon's Family.
   442(NY):25Aug86-95
Seward, J.  Japanese in Action.*  (2nd ed)
   L.A. Serafim, 399(MLJ):Summer85-192

Sewell, B. In the Dorian Mode.*
   I. Murray, 161(DUJ):Jun84-261
   D. Rutenberg, 637(VS):Winter85-336
Sexton, A. The Complete Poems.
   D. Middlebrook, 472:Spring/Summer/Fall/
   Winter85-293
Seyersted, P. Hjalmar Hjorth Boyesen.
   R. Asselineau, 189(EA):Oct-Dec86-483
Seymour, G. In Honor Bound.
   639(VQR):Spring85-63
Seymour, M.C. - see Hoccleve, T.
Seznec, J. - see Diderot, D.
Sgard, J. L'Abbé Prévost.
   P. France, 617(TLS):31Oct86-1226
Sgrilli, P., ed. Il "Libro di Sidrac"
   salentino.
   R. Coluccia, 228(GSLI):Vol 162fasc520-
   615
Sguaitamatti, M. L'offrante de porcelet
   dans la coroplathie géléenne.
   R. Higgins, 303(JoHS):Vol 105-234
Shackelford, G.T.M. Degas: The Dancers.*
   A.A. McLees, 207(FR):Apr86-831
   C. Stuckey, 90:Jul85-465
Shackleton Bailey, D.R., ed. Anthologia
   Latina. (Vol 1, fasc 1)
   W.D. Lebek, 123:Vol35No2-293
   M.D. Reeve, 487:Summer85-174
Shackleton Bailey, D.R. Profile of
   Horace.*
   W.S. Anderson, 122:Jul85-274
Shackleton Bailey, D.R. - see Cicero
Shacochis, B. Easy in the Islands.
   J. Crace, 617(TLS):7Mar86-257
Shah, I. Kara Kush.
   P-L. Adams, 61:Jul86-80
   C.L. Sulzberger, 441:15Jun86-22
Shah, N.M., ed. Pakistani Women.
   H. Papanek, 293(JASt):Nov84-127
Shahar, D. Nin-Gal.
   J. Blot, 450(NRF):May85-108
Shaikh, S. Handbook of English-Arabic for
   Professionals.
   T.B. Irving, 399(MLJ):Winter85-407
Shaked, G. and A. Lelchuk, eds. Eight
   Great Hebrew Short Novels.
   N. Stiller, 287:Mar85-24
Shakespeare, W. The Comedy of Errors/Die
   Komödie der Irrungen.* (K. Tetzeli von
   Rosador, ed)
   R. Freifrau von Ledebur, 72:Band222
   Heft2-401
Shakespeare, W. The Contemporary Shake-
   speare Series. (A.L. Rowse, ed)
   R. Gross, 615(TJ):May85-254
Shakespeare, W. Hamlet.* (H. Jenkins, ed)
   M. Coyle, 447(N&Q):Mar84-116
Shakespeare, W. Hamlet, Prince of Denmark.
   (P. Edwards, ed)
   P. Conrad, 617(TLS):14Mar86-279
Shakespeare, W. Henry V.* (G. Taylor, ed)
   J. Feather, 447(N&Q):Mar84-115
   A. Hammond, 570(SQ):Autumn85-371
   D. Mehl, 156(ShJW):Jahrbuch1985-219
   B. Vickers, 541(RES):Aug85-415
Shakespeare, W. Julius Caesar. (A.
   Humphreys, ed)
   D. Birch, 610:Summer85-166
   M. Grivelet, 189(EA):Apr-Jun86-206
   D. Mehl, 156(ShJW):Jahrbuch1985-219

Shakespeare, W. King Richard II. (A.
   Gurr, ed)
   M. Dodsworth, 175:Summer85-186
   G. Monsarrat, 189(EA):Apr-Jun86-208
Shakespeare, W. King Richard III.* (A.
   Hammond, ed)
   S. Colley and R.C. Hassel, Jr.,
   570(SQ):Winter85-496
Shakespeare, W. Macbeth. (illustrated by
   Von) Othello. (illustrated by O. Zar-
   ate)
   H. Hammerschmidt, 156(ShJW):Jahrbuch
   1985-245
Shakespeare, W. A Midsummer Night's Dream.
   (H.F. Brooks, ed)
   G.K. Paster, 702:Vol 17-255
Shakespeare, W. A Midsummer Night's Dream.
   (R.A. Foakes, ed)
   G. Monsarrat, 189(EA):Apr-Jun86-208
Shakespeare, W. Romeo and Juliet. (G.B.
   Evans, ed) The Taming of the Shrew. (A.
   Thompson, ed) Othello. (N. Sanders, ed)
   M. Grivelet, 189(EA):Apr-Jun86-207
   K.P. Wentersdorf, 610:Summer85-164
Shakespeare, W. William Shakespeare: The
   Complete Works. (S. Wells and G. Taylor,
   eds)
   M. Bradbrook, 362:6Nov86-24
   D.J.R. Bruckner, 441:7Dec86-69
Shakespeare, W. Mr. William Shakespeares
   Comedies, Histories and Tragedies Pub-
   lished According to the True Original
   Copies. (M. Spevack, ed)
   H.N. Davies, 617(TLS):15Aug86-895
Shakespeare, W. Shakespeare's Plays in
   Quarto.* (M.J.B. Allen and K. Muir, eds)
   R. Fraser, 403(MLS):Spring85-90
   B. Gaines, 702:Vol 17-237
Shakespeare, W. The Taming of the Shrew.*
   (B. Morris, ed)
   D.F. Bratchell, 447(N&Q):Mar84-113
Shakespeare, W. The Taming of the Shrew.*
   (H.J. Oliver, ed)
   D.F. Bratchell, 447(N&Q):Mar84-113
   D. Mehl, 156(ShJW):Jahrbuch1985-219
   B. Vickers, 541(RES):Aug85-415
Shakespeare, W. Titus Andronicus. (E.M.
   Waith, ed)
   D. Birch, 610:Summer85-167
   M. Grivelet, 189(EA):Apr-Jun86-206
   D. Mehl, 156(ShJW):Jahrbuch1985-219
   J.L. Sanderson, 570(SQ):Winter85-498
Shakespeare, W. Troilus and Cressida.*
   (K. Muir, ed)
   R. Kimbrough, 570(SQ):Summer85-239
   D. Mehl, 156(ShJW):Jahrbuch1985-219
   B. Vickers, 541(RES):Aug85-415
Shakespeare, W. Troilus and Cressida.*
   (K. Palmer, ed)
   R. Kimbrough, 570(SQ):Summer85-239
   B. Vickers, 541(RES):Aug85-415
"Shakespeare inmitten der Revolutionen."
   J.L. Gunther, 570(SQ):Summer85-240
"Shakespeare Survey." (Vol 35) (S. Wells,
   ed)
   R. Freifrau von Ledebur, 72:Band222
   Heft2-405
   D.J. Palmer, 541(RES):Aug85-464
"Shakespeare Survey."* (Vol 36) (S. Wells,
   ed)
   V. Emeljanow, 611(TN):Vol39No1-44

"Shakespeare Survey."* (Vol 37) (S. Wells, ed)
   M. Grivelet, 189(EA):Apr-Jun86-205
"Shakespeare Survey." (Vol 38) (S. Wells, ed)
   K. Brown, 617(TLS):22Aug86-917
Shames, L. The Big Time.
   L. Uchitelle, 441:4May86-20
Shand, G.B. and R.C. Shady, eds. Play-Texts in Old Spelling.
   L.A. Beaurline, 551(RenQ):Autumn85-573
Shang Ming-hsuan. Liao Chung-k'ai chuan.
   F.G. Chan, 293(JASt):Nov84-174
Shange, N. A Daughter's Geography.*
   B. Brown, 95(CLAJ):Mar86-378
Shanin, T., ed. Late Marx and the Russian Road.
   D.A.J. Macey, 550(RusR):Oct85-418
Shankman, S. Impersonal Attractions.
   N. Callendar, 441:9Feb86-27
Shankman, S. Pope's "Iliad."*
   S.W. Brown, 529(QQ):Summer85-406
   J.V. Guerinot, 568(SCN):Fall85-45
   A. Manousos, 405(MP):Aug85-73
Shann, P. Untersuchungen zur strukturellen Semantik.
   G. Kleiber, 553(RLiR):Jul-Dec85-494
Lord Shannon. Lord Shannon's Letters to his Son. (E. Hewitt, ed)
   272(IUR):Autumn85-256
Shannon, A.C. The Medieval Inquisition.
   J.H. Mundy, 589:Apr85-490
Shannon, R. Gladstone.* (Vol 1)
   L.F. Barmann, 377:Jul84-115
Shapard, R. and J. Thomas, eds. Sudden Fiction.
   D. Kirk, 441:23Nov86-24
Shapcott, T. Hotel Bellevue.
   A. Sattin, 617(TLS):7Nov86-1255
Shapere, D. Reason and the Search for Knowledge.
   K. Harrison, 63:Dec85-558
   T. Nickles, 486:Jun85-310
   R. Torretti, 160:Apr85-166
Shapiro, A. The Courtesy.*
   A. Hudgins, 434:Summer86-526
Shapiro, B. and R.G. Frank, Jr. English Scientific Virtuosi in the 16th and 17th Centuries.
   M. Phillips, 192(EP):Apr-Jun85-275
Shapiro, B.J. Probability and Certainty in Seventeenth-Century England.*
   F.J. Levy, 401(MLQ):Dec84-407
   R.H. Popkin, 319:Jul86-416
   G.A.J. Rogers, 518:Apr85-84
   W.A. Wallace, 543:Dec85-375
Shapiro, D. Jasper Johns Drawings, 1954-1984.*
   K.D. Russell, 90:Aug85-542
   R. Walsh, 55:Apr85-28
Shapiro, H. The Light Holds.
   639(VQR):Summer85-98
Shapiro, J. and Liang Heng. Cold Winds, Warm Winds.
   J.K. Fairbank, 453(NYRB):17Jul86-33
   C. Wakeman, 441:22Jun86-7
Shapiro, K. Love and War, Art and God.*
   D. Wojahn, 491:Jun85-167
Shapiro, L. Perfection Salad.
   B. Ehrenreich, 441:23Mar86-36
Shapiro, M. The Sense of Grammar.*
   T.F. Shannon, 350:Mar86-233
          [continued]

[continuing]
   C.E. Townsend, 279:Vol29-143
   G. Urban, 355(LSoc):Jun85-239
Shapiro, M.C. and H.F. Schiffmann. Language and Society in South Asia.*
   L.A. Schwarzschild and R.K. Barz, 259(IIJ):Oct85-295
Shapiro, M.J. Language and Political Understanding.*
   F. Fischer, 488:Sep85-371
Shapiro, N.R. - see "Fables from Old French"
Shapiro, R. Origins.
   L.A. Marschall, 441:12Jan86-9
   442(NY):17Feb86-105
Shaplen, R. Bitter Victory.
   R.W. Apple, 441:5Oct86-14
Shapson, S. and V. D'Oyley, eds. Bilingual and Multicultural Education.
   E. Bialystok, 399(MLJ):Autumn85-301
   M. Heller, 350:Jun86-483
Sharma, B.N.K. History of the Dvaita School of Vedānta and its Literature.
   J.P. Olivelle, 318(JAOS):Apr-Jun84-337
Sharma, U. Women, Work, and Property in North-West India.
   H. Papanek, 293(JASt):Nov84-127
Sharnik, J. Remembrance of Games Past.
   M. Wexler, 441:16Nov86-25
Sharp, G. Making Europe Unconquerable.
   G.F. Kennan, 453(NYRB):13Feb86-3
   K.E. Meyer, 441:20Apr86-17
Sharp, M. False Face.
   639(VQR):Winter85-25
Sharp, R.A. Friendship and Literature.
   A.S. Byatt, 176:Nov86-48
Sharpe, L. Schiller and the Historical Character.*
   S.D. Martinson, 406:Fall85-357
   J.F. Reynolds, 400(MLN):Apr85-693
Sharpe, T. Wilt on High.*
   P. Lewis, 565:Summer85-50
   639(VQR):Autumn85-128
Sharpe, W. and L. Wallock, eds. Visions of the Modern City.
   N. Berry, 155:Autumn85-183
Sharples, R.W. - see Alexander of Aphrodisias
Sharratt, B. The Literary Labyrinth.*
   295(JML):Nov85-420
Sharratt, P. and F. Ecosse Romane.
   N.M. Cameron, 90:Oct85-719
Sharratt, P. and P.G. Walsh - see Buchanan, G.
Sharrock, R. Saints, Sinners and Comedians.*
   A.A. Devitis, 395(MFS):Winter85-812
   R. Kelly, 594:Fall85-329
   C. Linck, 70:Sep/Oct85-29
Shatto, S. - see Tennyson, A.
Shattuck, R. The Innocent Eye.*
   S. Bann, 617(TLS):23May86-573
   W. Fowlie, 569(SR):Fall85-lxxvi
   A. Sonnenfeld, 207(FR):Dec85-325
   639(VQR):Summer85-88
Shatyn, B. A Private War.
   G.A. Craig, 453(NYRB):10Apr86-7
Shavit, Z. Poetics of Children's Literature.
   D. Grylls, 617(TLS):29Aug86-948
Shaw, A. Black Popular Music in America.
   L. Birnbaum, 441:20Apr86-23

Shaw, A. Dictionary of American Pop/Rock.
E. Southern, 91:Spring85-124
Shaw, B.C. The Wool-Hat Boys.
639(VQR):Winter85-7
Shaw, G. and M. Lloyd, eds. Publications
Proscribed by the Government of India.
J. Katz, 617(TLS):29Aug86-951
Shaw, G.B. Agitations. (D.H. Laurence
and J. Rambeau, eds)
R. Scruton, 617(TLS):21Feb86-180
Shaw, G.B. Collected Letters.* (Vol 3)
(D.H. Laurence, ed)
W.H. Pritchard, 249(HudR):Winter86-673
Shaw, G.B. Shaw on Dickens. (D.H.
Laurence and M. Quinn, eds)
R. Maxwell, 637(VS):Summer86-646
G.B. Tennyson, 445(NCF):Dec85-366
Shaw, H.E. The Forms of Historical Fic-
tion.*
A.M. Duckworth, 637(VS):Winter85-308
Shaw, I. Paris/Magnum.
M. Nesbit, 59:Mar85-132
Shaw, J.B. Some of the Things I Did Not
Do.
B. Hooper, 573(SSF):Spring85-242
Shaw, V. The Short Story.*
G. Bas, 189(EA):Jan-Mar86-85
H. Bonheim, 402(MLR):Apr85-404
D. Hewitt, 541(RES):Nov85-624
G. Monteiro, 573(SSF):Fall85-491
"Shaw: The Annual of Bernard Shaw Studies."
(Vol 3) (D. Leary, ed)
H.F. Brooks, 611(TN):Vol39No1-41
B. Richardson, 637(VS):Winter85-344
"Shaw, The Annual of Bernard Shaw Studies."
(Vol 4) (S. Weintraub, ed)
B. Richardson, 637(VS):Spring86-470
Shawcross, J.T. Milton: A Bibliography
for the Years 1624-1700.*
R. Flannagan, 391:Mar85-20
Shawcross, J.T. With Mortal Voice.*
M. Evans, 541(RES):May85-270
Al-Shaykh, H. The Story of Zahra.
R. Irwin, 617(TLS):16May86-535
She, L. - see under Lao She
Shea, W., ed. Otto Hahn and the Rise of
Nuclear Physics.
J.R. Brown, 486:Jun85-317
Shea, W.L. The Virginia Militia in the
Seventeenth Century.*
J.F. Fausz, 656(WMQ):Apr85-279
Sheard, W.S. Antiquity in the Renaissance.
M.V., 90:Mar85-172
Shearman, J. The Early Italian Pictures
in the Collection of Her Majesty the
Queen.*
C. Lloyd, 278(IS):Vol40-120
Shears, R. and I. Gidley. The Rainbow
Warrior Affair.
J. Waldron, 617(TLS):4Jul86-728
Sheed, W. Frank and Maisie.*
J.M. Cameron, 453(NYRB):8May86-36
V. Glendinning, 362:15May86-25
P. Hebblethwaite, 617(TLS):30May86-589
Sheehan, J.B. The Boston School Integra-
tion Dispute.
J.D. Feaster, Jr., 432(NEQ):Dec85-628
Sheehan, S. A Missing Plane.
E. Lax, 441:19Oct86-9
Sheehan, T. The First Coming.
J.M. Cameron, 453(NYRB):4Dec86-23
A.A. Rhodes, 441:28Dec86-24

Sheehy, G. Spirit of Survival.
E.R. Lipson, 441:25May86-17
Sheerin, J. A Crack in the Ice.
M. Harmon, 272(IUR):Autumn85-234
B. O'Donoghue, 493:Aug85-67
Sheets-Johnstone, M., ed. Illuminating
Dance.
S.B. Fowler, 290(JAAC):Summer86-417
Shefter, M. Political Crisis/Fiscal
Crisis.*
J. Cohn, 129:May86-74
Sheidley, W.E. Barnabe Googe.*
J.M. Kennedy, 677(YES):Vol 15-273
Shelah, S. Proper Forcing.
S. Todorcevic, 316:Mar85-237
Shelby, G. The Edge of the Blade.
S. Altinel, 617(TLS):18Jul86-793
Sheldon, D. Dreams of an Average Man.*
E. Currie, 441:22Jun86-14
Shelford, R.W. A Naturalist in Borneo.
617(TLS):21Nov86-1327
Shell, M. Money, Language, and Thought.*
M.S. Roth, 478:Oct85-242
Shelley, L.I. Lawyers in Soviet Work Life.
G.G. Weickhardt, 550(RusR):Apr85-202
Shelley, M. Frankenstein. (B. Mosher,
illustrator)
D. Ketterer, 561(SFS):Nov85-337
A. Morvan, 189(EA):Jan-Mar86-97
Shelley, M.W. The Letters of Mary Woll-
stonecraft Shelley.* (Vol 2) (B.T.
Bennett, ed)
P.M.S. Dawson, 148:Spring85-85
Shelley, P.B. Shelley's "Adonais." (A.D.
Knerr, ed)
E.B. Murray, 340(KSJ):Vol34-187
M.A. Quinn, 661(WC):Fall85-196
Shelp, E.E. Born To Die?
C. Levine, 441:23Mar86-42
Shelp, E.E., ed. The Clinical Encounter.
R.M., 185:Oct85-222
Shelston, A., ed. Dickens: "Dombey and
Son" and "Little Dorrit."
W.H., 148:Winter85-92
Shelton, R. No Direction Home.
L. Mackinnon, 617(TLS):31Oct86-1228
D. McLeese, 441:12Oct86-18
B. Woffinden, 362:4Dec86-24
Shem, S. Fine.*
639(VQR):Summer85-91
Shennan, J.H. France before the Revolu-
tion.
D.J.F., 83:Spring85-126
Shepard, J. Paper Doll.
J. Lasdun, 441:9Nov86-9
R. Towers, 453(NYRB):18Dec86-29
Shepard, L. Green Eyes.
J. Clute, 617(TLS):20Jun86-683
Shepard, P. and B. Sanders. The Sacred
Paw.
W.P. Root, 469:Vol 11No2-118
Shepherd, D. and R. Slatzer, with D. Gray-
son. Duke.
P. Oakes, 617(TLS):9May86-507
Shepherd, J.C. and G.A. Jellicoe. Italian
Gardens of the Renaissance.
J. Summerson, 617(TLS):28Nov86-1353
Sheppard, A.D.R. Studies on the 5th and
6th Essays of Proclus' Commentary on the
Republic.
W. Beierwaltes, 53(AGP):Band67Heft2-
185

Sheppard, S. The Faerie King. (P.J.
Klemp, ed)
 W.B. Hunter, 568(SCN):Fall85-44
Sher, A. Year of the King.
 M. Wolf, 157:No158-47
Sher, R.B. Church and University in the
Scottish Enlightenment.
 J. Cater, 617(TLS):2May86-467
 J. Smitten, 173(ECS):Summer86-580
Sheridan, A. Michel Foucault.*
 H.M. Cavallari, 567:Vol56No3/4-315
Sheridan, D. - see Mitchison, N.
Sheridan, J. Leave the Fighting to
McGuigan.
 362:3Jul86-34
Sheridan, P. Penny Theatres of Victorian
London.
 M.R. Booth, 611(TN):Vol39No1-42
Sheringham, M. Beckett: "Molloy."
 A. Jenkins, 617(TLS):14Nov86-1281
Sherlock, J. The Golden Mile.
 R. Smith, 441:13Jul86-18
Sherman, C. Reading Voltaire's Contes.
 W.F. Edmiston, 207(FR):May86-977
Sherman, K. Words for Elephant Man.*
 J. Orange, 102(CanL):Winter84-103
Sherman, R. and A. Nadia Reisenberg.
 B. Gowen, 510:Spring86-51
Sherry, F. Raiders and Rebels.
 J.M. Elukin, 441:16Mar86-21
Sherry, H.J. Splashes.
 R. Spiess, 404:Autumn85-62
Sherry, R. - see O'Connor, F. and H. Hunt
Sherwin-White, A.N. Roman Foreign Policy
in the East, 168 B.C. to A.D. 1.
 K.R. Bradley, 121(CJ):Dec85/Jan86-167
 J. Briscoe, 123:Vol35No2-323
 F.W. Walbank, 313:Vol75-235
 R.D. Weigel, 124:Sep-Oct85-64
Sherwood, T.G. Fulfilling the Circle.
 J. Egan, 568(SCN):Spring-Summer85-5
 H. MacCallum, 627(UTQ):Summer85-409
 W. Schleiner, 551(RenQ):Summer85-370
 J. Shami, 539:Nov85-199
Sherzer, J. Kuna Ways of Speaking.*
 E.B. Basso, 355(LSoc):Mar85-85
Sherzer, W.M. Juan Marsé entre la ironía
y la dialéctica.
 L. Hickey, 86(BHS):Apr85-212
Shesgreen, S. Hogarth and the Times-of-
Day Tradition.*
 P. Brückmann, 627(UTQ):Spring85-293
 F.H. Dowley, 405(MP):Aug85-77
 G. Levitine, 173(ECS):Spring86-406
Shi, D.E. The Simple Life.*
 T.P. Thornton, 432(NEQ):Jun85-318
Shibusawa Masahide. Japan and the Pacific
Region.
 Hayashi Risuke, 285(JapQ):Jan-Mar85-85
Shideler, J.C. A Medieval Catalan Noble
Family.*
 A.R. Lewis, 589:Apr85-491
Shields, C. Various Miracles.
 C. Rooke, 376:Sep85-142
Shier, L.A. Terracotta Lamps from Karanis,
Egypt.
 C. Grande, 313:Vol75-284
Shiff, R. Cézanne and the End of Impres-
sionism.*
 T. Dolan, 446(NCFS):Spring-Summer86-
 389
 S. Scobie, 376:Jan86-129

Shikatani, G. A Sparrow's Food.
 C. Wiseman, 102(CanL):Summer85-188
Shikes, R.E. and S. Heller. The Art of
Satire.*
 T. Reese, 507:Jul/Aug85-314
Shipler, D.K. Arab and Jew.
 R. Sanders, 441:28Sep86-1
Shipps, J. Mormonism.*
 D. Martin, 617(TLS):7Mar86-251
Shirai, T., ed. Contemporary Industrial
Relations in Japan.
 K. Taira, 293(JASt):Nov84-203
Shirazi, M. Javady Alley.
 P. Lewis, 565:Winter84/85-42
Shirer, W.L. The Nightmare Years, 1930-
1940.
 R. Hopwood, 529(QQ):Autumn85-608
 V. Young, 31(ASch):Summer85-414
Shirley, G. Belle Starr.
 L. Horne, 106:Summer85-221
Shirley, J.W. and F.D. Hoeniger, eds.
Science and the Arts in the Renaissance.
 M. Kemp, 617(TLS):28Mar86-320
Shivers, A.S. The Life of Maxwell Ander-
son.*
 L.G. Avery, 534(RALS):Autumn83-250
"Shixue qingbao."
 M.C. Wiens, 293(JASt):Feb85-362
Shklovsky, V. A Sentimental Journey.*
 A.M., 125:Winter85-231
Shnayerson, R. The Illustrated History of
the Supreme Court of the United States.
 J.P. MacKenzie, 441:7Dec86-68
Shneidman, N.N. Dostoevsky and Suicide.
 R.L. Busch, 104(CASS):Summer85-220
 J.L. Rice, 550(RusR):Oct85-408
Shoaf, R.A. Dante, Chaucer, and the
Currency of the Word.
 J.M. Ferrante, 545(RPh):Feb86-393
 L. Patterson, 301(JEGP):Oct85-545
Shoaf, R.A. Milton, Poet of Duality.
 L. Newlyn, 617(TLS):8Aug86-871
Shoemaker, S. Identity, Cause and Mind.*
 J. Heal, 518:Jul85-156
 F.J., 185:Jan86-445
Shoemaker, S. and R. Swinburne. Personal
Identity.*
 M. Adam, 542:Oct-Dec85-567
 D.P. Behan, 518:Apr85-112
 D. Locke, 393(Mind):Apr85-302
 G. Madell, 479(PhQ):Apr85-214
 R.B. Schultz, 185:Apr86-641
Shoesmith, D.J. and T.J. Smiley. Multiple-
Conclusion Logic.
 D.N. Walton, 154:Spring85-179
"Shogun: The Shogun Age Exhibition."
 C.G. Kanda, 407(MN):Summer85-248
Sholton, M. - see Leskov, N.
Shomer, E. The Startle Effect.
 F. Allen, 496:Fall85-179
Shomu, N. and Akamatsu Katsumaro - see
under Nobori Shomu and Akamatsu Katsu-
maro
Shook, L.K. Étienne Gilson.
 V.J. Bourke, 377:Nov84-178
 D.J. Fitz Gerald, 319:Oct86-571
 J. Pelikan, 589:Oct85-1019
Shope, R.K. The Analysis of Knowing.*
 B. Aune, 543:Jun85-905
 S. Cohen, 484(PPR):Mar86-523
 Q. Gibson, 63:Mar85-105
 J. Harrison, 479(PhQ):Jan85-95

Siegel, P.N.  Shakespeare's English and Roman History Plays.
R.M. Adams, 453(NYRB):6Nov86-50
Siegelbaum, L.H.  The Politics of Industrial Mobilization in Russia, 1914-1917.
W.L. Duggan, Jr., 550(RusR):Oct85-425
A. Wood, 575(SEER):Jul85-461
Siegman, A. and S. Feldstein, eds.  Nonverbal Behavior and Communication.
G.W. Beattie, 567:Vol57No3/4-375
Siemek, A.  La Recherche morale et esthétique dans le roman de Crébillon fils.*
S. Davies, 208(FS):Jul85-344
Siemens, W.L.  Worlds Reborn.
L. Guerra-Cunningham, 238:Dec85-784
Siemon, J.R.  Shakespearean Iconoclasm.
C. Davidson, 130:Summer85-189
Sievers, S.L.  Flowers in Salt.*
C. Gluck, 293(JASt):Aug85-846
Siewierska, A.  The Passive.
S. Romaine, 353:Vol23No3-505
Sigel, J.  Wasan Bahaushe Gaskiyarsa.
A.H.M. Kirk-Greene, 538(RAL):Fall85-461
Siger de Brabant.  "Quaestiones in Metaphysicam:" Edition revue de la reportation de Munich; Texte inédit de la reportation de Vienne.  (W. Dunphy, ed)  "Quaestiones in Metaphysicam:"  Texte inédit de la reportation de Cambridge; Edition revue de la reportation de Paris.  (A. Maurer, ed)
B.C. Bazán, 154:Summer85-339
Signoret, S.  Adieu, Volodya.
D. Bair, 441:14Sep86-20
J. Mellors, 362:20Nov86-28
Sigurjónsson, Á.  Den politiske Laxness.
P. Carleton, 563(SS):Summer85-360
Silber, E.  The Sculpture of Epstein.
S. Gardiner, 362:11Dec86-24
Silberman, C.E.  A Certain People.*
E.S. Shapiro, 390:Dec85-52
Siler, D. - see Pradier, J.
Silk, L.  Economics in the Real World.
639(VQR):Spring85-59
Silk, M.S. and J.P. Stern.  Nietzsche on Tragedy.*
N. Davey, 323:Jan85-88
Sill, G.M.  Defoe and the Idea of Fiction, 1713-1719.*
D. Blewett, 401(MLQ):Jun84-199
A.M. Duckworth, 566:Spring86-194
J. Richetti, 141:Fall85-413
S. Sim, 83:Autumn85-242
Silliman, R.  Paradise.
M. Perloff, 29(APR):Jan/Feb86-37
Silva, A.I.S. - see under Souto Silva, A.I.
de Silva y Verástegui, S.  Iconografía del siglo X en el Reino de Pamplona-Nájera.
I. Mateo Gómez, 48:Oct-Dec85-433
Silver, B.R., ed.  Virginia Woolf's Reading Notebooks.*
M. Goldstein, 569(SR):Fall85-624
E. Warner, 541(RES):Nov85-596
Silver, C.G.  The Romance of William Morris.*
P. Faulkner, 326:Winter85/86-22
Silver, E.  Begin.*
D. Polish, 287:Nov-Dec85-28
Silver-Lillywhite, E.  All That Autumn.*
M. Kumin, 219(GaR):Spring85-169
C. Wright, 448:Vol23No1-118

Silverberg, R.  Star of Gypsies.
G. Jonas, 441:23Nov86-30
Silverman, K.  The Life and Times of Cotton Mather.*
H. Cohen, 617(TLS):21Nov86-1302
C.E. Hambrick-Stowe, 656(WMQ):Apr85-263
J.H. Kettner, 250(HLQ):Winter85-81
J. Walker, 568(SCN):Fall85-46
Silverman, K.  The Subject of Semiotics.*
R.E. Chumbley, 678(YCGL):No34-132
Sim, K.  David Roberts, R.A., 1796-1864.*
R.L. Ormond, 324:Jul86-540
Simak, C.D.  Highway of Eternity.
G. Jonas, 441:8Jun86-23
Simard, R.  Postmodern Drama.
B. Veracek, 610:Autumn85-266
Simenon, G.  The Couple from Poitiers.
442(NY):21Apr86-125
Simenon, G.  Intimate Memoirs, Including Marie-Jo's Book.*
V.A. Conley, 395(MFS):Winter85-832
Simenon, G.  Maigret's War of Nerves.
442(NY):14Apr86-111
Simeti, M.T.  On Persephone's Island.
P-L. Adams, 61:May86-99
A. Cornelisen, 441:20Apr86-14
Simic, C.  Selected Poems 1963-1983.
A. Libby, 441:12Jan86-17
Simkin, T. and others.  Volcanoes of the World.
C.H.V. Ebert, 293(JASt):Aug85-901
Simkin, T. and R.S. Fiske.  Krakatau 1883.
C.H.V. Ebert, 293(JASt):Aug85-901
Simmel, G.  On Women, Sexuality, and Love.
M.B., 185:Jan86-443
Simmerman, J.  Home.*
F. Skloot, 448:Vol23No3-132
Simmler, F.  Graphematisch-phonematische Studien zum althochdeutschen Konsonantismus insbesondere zur zweiten Lautverschiebung.*
R. Hinderling, 684(ZDA):Band114Heft1-3
H. Penzl, 685(ZDL):1/1985-95
Simmonds, N.E.  The Decline of Juridical Reason.
A.S., 185:Jan86-440
Simmonds, R.S.  The Two Worlds of William March.
J. Braham, 395(MFS):Winter85-740
B. Hitchcock, 9(AlaR):Apr85-138
M. Routh, 392:Fall85-481
295(JML):Nov85-526
Simmons, D.D.  Personal Valuing.
L. Kelly, 480(P&R):Vol 18No4-267
Simmons, J.  From the Irish.
T. Eagleton, 493:Aug85-64
Simmons, R.C. and P.D.G. Thomas, eds.  Proceedings and Debates of the British Parliaments Respecting North America, 1754-1783.  (Vol 2)
B.S. Schlenther, 83:Spring85-101
Simmons, S.  Body Blows.
W.J. Harding, 441:13Apr86-22
Simmons, S.  Wilderness Images.
P.M. St. Pierre, 102(CanL):Summer85-183
R. Stevenson, 628(UWR):Fall-Winter85-83
Simms, E.  The New Naturalist British Warblers.
J. Buxton, 617(TLS):11Apr86-400

Smith, G. Morality, Reason, and Power.
D.P. Calleo, 441:6Jul86-18
M. Ledeen, 129:Aug86-62
R. Steel, 61:Jun86-78
Smith, G. The Novel and Society.*
G.L. Stonum, 594:Winter85-441
Smith, G. "The Waste Land."
295(JML):Nov85-473
Smith, G.B. The Devil in the Dooryard.
J.A. West, 441:19Oct86-22
Smith, G.S. Songs to Seven Strings.
V. Aksyonov, 617(TLS):28Mar86-338
Smith, G.S. - see Galich, A.
Smith, H. Forgotten Truth.
H.A. Durfee, 543:Dec84-405
Smith, H. The Tension of the Lyre.*
K. Muir, 677(YES):Vol 15-275
W. Weiss, 156(ShJW):Jahrbuch1985-213
Smith, I.C. The Exiles.*
D. McDuff, 565:Summer85-72
Smith, I.C. The Last Summer.
P. Craig, 617(TLS):19Dec86-1428
Smith, I.C. A Life.
M. O'Neill, 617(TLS):19Dec86-1423
Smith, I.C. Selected Poems 1955-1980.*
(R. Fulton, ed)
A. Bold, 493:Oct85-58
K. McCarra, 571(ScLJ):Winter85-64
Smith, I.C. The Tenement.*
442(NY):13Jan86-84
Smith, J. The Complete Works of Captain
John Smith. (P.L. Barbour, ed)
J. Axtell, 617(TLS):21Nov86-1302
T.H. Breen, 453(NYRB):20Nov86-48
P.F. Gura, 165(EAL):Winter86/87-260
A. Vaughan, 441:29Jun86-27
Smith, J. The Frugal Gourmet.
W. and C. Cowen, 639(VQR):Autumn85-139
Smith, J.C. Nuremberg.*
90:Mar85-173
Smith, J.C.S. Nightcap.
R. Hill, 617(TLS):25Apr86-454
Smith, J.F. Language and Language Atti-
tudes in a Bilingual Community.
S.M. Embleton, 355(LSoc):Jun85-279
Smith, J.H. and W. Kerrigan, eds. Taking
Chances.*
D. Morton, 651(WHR):Summer85-178
J.M. Todd, 478:Oct85-249
Smith, J.P. The Man from Marseille.*
D. Fitzpatrick, 441:31Aug86-12
Smith, K.N. Elegy for a Soprano.
N. Callendar, 441:26Jan86-40
Smith, L. Family Linen.*
J.E. Jacobi, 580(SCR):Spring86-126
Smith, L. Lawrence Ferlinghetti.*
S. Wilson, 649(WAL):Feb86-364
Smith, L. The Japanese Print Since 1900.
Susamu Takiguchi, 463:Summer85-196
Smith, L.A. A Catalogue of Pre-Revival
Appalachian Dulcimers.
M. Collins, 187:Winter86-185
Smith, L.B. Treason in Tudor England.
G.R. Elton, 176:Jul/Aug86-41
Smith, L.P. - see under Pearsall Smith, L.
Smith, L.R. Kenneth Patchen.
C.F. Terrell, 659(ConL):Spring86-115
Smith, M. Doctor Blues.
G. Davenport, 569(SR):Spring85-321
Smith, M. - see de La Boëtie, É.
Smith, M.C. Stallion Gate.
T.R. Edwards, 453(NYRB):8May86-12
H.F. Mosher, 441:4May86-14

Smith, M.G. Pastoral Discipline and the
Church Courts.
R.A. Beddard, 161(DUJ):Dec84-137
Smith, M.V. and D. Maclennan, eds. Olive
Schreiner and After.
R. Ayling, 49:Apr85-77
Smith, N., ed. A Collection of Ranter
Writings from the 17th Century.
B. Nelson, 568(SCN):Spring-Summer85-10
Smith, N.B. and T.G. Bergin. An Old
Provençal Primer.
S. Belasco, 207(FR):Dec85-328
Smith, O. The Politics of Language 1791-
1819.*
A. Bony, 189(EA):Apr-Jun86-223
P.M.S. Dawson, 148:Summer85-67
Smith, P. Pound Revised.*
S. Moore, 70:Sep/Oct84-30
A. Ross, 468:Spring85-137
D. Seed, 447(N&Q):Jun84-286
Smith, P. Public and Private Value.*
R.A. Hartzell, 207(FR):May86-979
S. Monod, 549(RLC):Jan-Mar85-109
V. Nemoianu, 446(NCFS):Fall-
Winter85/86-184
S. Pinsker, 136:Vol 18No1-70
Smith, P. Redeeming the Time.
D. Murray, 441:16Nov86-25
Smith, P.H., ed. Letters of Delegates to
Congress, 1774-1789. (Vols 3-10)
C. Royster, 656(WMQ):Apr85-286
Smith, P.L. The Problem of Values in
Educational Thought.
N. Hellman, 321:Vol 19No2-163
Smith, R. Seasonal.
S. Scobie, 376:Jun85-132
Smith, R. The Red Smith Reader. (D.
Anderson, ed)
E.L. Galligan, 569(SR):Spring85-283
Smith, R. Toward an Authentic Interpreta-
tion of the Organ Works of César Franck.*
W.J. Gatens, 410(M&L):Apr85-144
Smith, R.B. An International History of
the Vietnam War. (Vol 1)
E.E. Moise, 293(JASt):Feb85-343
Smith, R.E.F. and D. Christian. Bread
and Salt.
G.L. Freeze, 104(CASS):Spring85-64
K.L. Nalibow, 574(SEEJ):Winter85-497
Smith, R.J. China's Cultural Heritage:
The Ch'ing Dynasty, 1644-1922.
R. Entenmann, 293(JASt):Feb85-381
H.G. Skaja, 485(PE&W):Jul85-323
Smith, R.J. Japanese Society.*
T.R.H. Havens, 293(JASt):Nov84-209
Smith, R.M. Liberalism and American Con-
stitutional Law.
W.M.S., 185:Jul86-893
Smith, R.N. The Harvard Century.
R.A. McCaughey, 441:7Sep86-16
Smith, R.R.R. - see Richter, G.M.A.
Smith, R.T. From the High Dive.
N.A. Brittin, 577(SHR):Summer85-293
Smith, S. W.H. Auden.
N. Jenkins, 617(TLS):13Jun86-643
Smith, S. Inviolable Voice.*
R.D. Sell, 541(RES):Feb85-129
Smith, S. Ritual Murders.
P.M. St. Pierre, 102(CanL):Summer85-
183
Smith, S. Stevie Smith: A Selection. (H.
Lee, ed)
J. Saunders, 565:Spring85-72

Smith, S.A. Red Petrograd.*
    M. McAuley, 575(SEER):Jul85-462
    D.J. Raleigh, 550(RusR):Jul85-309
Smith, S.B. New and Selected Poems.
    M. Harmon, 272(IUR):Autumn85-234
Smith, S.B. Reading Althusser.
    T.M., 185:Jul86-901
Smith, S.G. The Wallace.
    D. Devlin, 157:No158-45
Smith, S.J. Crime, Space and Society.
    L. Taylor, 362:11Dec86-23
Smith, T. Literary and Linguistic Works
    [1542, 1549, 1568]. (Pt 2) (B. Daniels-
    son, ed)
    K. Reichl, 72:Band222Heft2-378
Smith, T.D. R.A. Caton and the Fortune
    Press.
    D. Chambers, 503:Spring84-44
    J.H. Woolmer, 517(PBSA):Vol79No1-136
Smith, V. Selected Poems.
    G. Bitcon, 581:Sep85-352
Smith, W. Cosmos and Transcendence.
    J.C. Caiazza, 396(ModA):Summer85-274
Smith, W.D. The Ideological Origins of
    Nazi Imperialism.
    G.A. Craig, 453(NYRB):30Jan86-20
    I. Kershaw, 617(TLS):19Dec86-1416
    A.A. Rhodes, 441:30Mar86-19
Smith, W.J. and D. Gioia, eds. Poems from
    Italy.
    442(NY):3Mar86-107
Smith, W.S. Bishop of Everywhere.*
    B.B. Brown, 397(MD):Sep85-508
    B. Richardson, 637(VS):Winter85-344
Smolenaars, J.J.L. P. Papinius Statius,
    "Thebaid," A Commentary on Book 7. 1-451.
    D.E. Hill, 123:Vol35No1-187
Smoljan, A. and N. Jurgeneva, eds. Mich-
    ail Zoščenko v vospominanijach sovremen-
    nikov.
    W. Busch, 688(ZSP):Band45Heft1-190
Smolla, R.A. Suing the Press.
    D. Casse, 129:Nov86-81
    A. Lewis, 441:8Jun86-27
Smoodin, R. Inventing Ivanov.*
    I. Malin, 532(RCF):Fall85-190
    639(VQR):Autumn85-124
Smout, T.C. A Century of the Scottish
    People.
    H. Fraser, 617(TLS):24Oct86-1200
Smyth, A.P. Warlords and Holy Men.
    R.T. Farrell, 589:Oct85-1021
Smyth, D. Diplomacy and Strategy of
    Survival.
    R. Carr, 617(TLS):30May86-582
Smythe, D. Pershing.
    B. Atkinson, 441:28Sep86-27
    K. Jeffery, 617(TLS):31Oct86-1209
Šneerson, M. Aleksandr Solženicyn.
    V. Krasnov, 574(SEEJ):Summer85-220
Snelgrove, M. Sleep Tight Tonight.
    D. Devlin, 157:No158-45
Snell, K.D.M. Annals of the Labouring
    Poor.*
    J. Fisher, 637(VS):Summer86-644
Snellgrove, D. and H. Richardson. A Cul-
    tural History of Tibet.
    D.S. Lopez, Jr., 469:Vol 11No3-118
Snellgrove, D.L. and T. Skorupski, with P.
    Denwood. The Cultural Heritage of
    Ladakh. (Vol 2)
    J.C. Huntington, 293(JASt):Nov84-195

Snipes, K. Robert Penn Warren.*
    J.H. Justus, 578:Spring86-123
Snitow, A.B. Ford Madox Ford and the
    Voice of Uncertainty.*
    T.C. Moser, 301(JEGP):Oct85-569
    K.C. Rentz, 177(ELT):Vol28No1-98
    D. Schenker, 569(SR):Summer85-1viii
    J. Wiesenfarth, 594:Winter85-437
Snoeyenbos, M. and others, eds. Business
    Ethics.
    D. Muschamp, 63:Dec85-581
Snoeyenbos, M., R. Almeder and J. Humber,
    eds. Business Ethics, Corporate Values
    and Society.
    V. Di Norcia, 154:Summer85-368
Snorri Sturluson. Edda.* (A. Faulkes, ed)
    H. O'Donoghue, 541(RES):May85-250
Snow, K.M. and others. Subject Index for
    Children and Young People to Canadian
    Poetry in English.
    W.N., 102(CanL):Winter84-186
Snowden, C.T., C.H. Brown and M.R. Peter-
    sen, eds. Primate Communication.
    M. Dobrovolsky, 320(CJL):Summer85-200
Snowman, D. The World of Plácido Domingo.*
    E. Forbes, 415:Oct85-603
Snyder, C. Massachusetts Eye and Ear
    Infirmary.
    P. Cash, 432(NEQ):Sep85-482
Snyder, G. Passage Through India.
    E. Folsom, 649(WAL):Aug85-172
Snyder, G. and A. Peckolick. Herb Luba-
    lin.*
    507:Sep/Oct85-125
Snyder, J. Northern Renaissance Art.
    J. Russell, 441:1Jun86-11
Sobel, R. IBM vs. Japan.
    A. Pollack, 441:27Apr86-11
Sobel, R. and D.B. Sicilia. The Entrepren-
    eurs.
    C.R. Herron, 441:26Oct86-39
Sober, E. The Nature of Selection.*
    D.C. Culver, 486:Dec85-645
    D.H., 185:Jan86-443
Soboleva, N.A. Rossiyskaya gorodskaya i
    oblastnaya geral'dika XVIII-XIX vv.
    W.F. Ryan, 575(SEER):Jan85-123
Sobolevskij, A.I. Istorija russkogo lit-
    eraturnogo jazyka. (A.A. Alekseev, ed)
    D.S. Worth, 279:Vol29-177
Sobrino, J. and others. Repaso de español.
    (3rd ed)
    F. Nuessel, 399(MLJ):Spring85-114
Sodaro, M.J. and S.L. Wolchik, eds. For-
    eign and Domestic Policy in Eastern
    Europe in the 1980s.
    H. Hanak, 575(SEER):Oct85-632
Södergran, E. Complete Poems.
    J. Bankier, 563(SS):Spring85-226
    W.G. Jones, 562(Scan):Nov85-236
    J. Saunders, 565:Autumn85-74
Sōetsu, Y. - see under Yanagi Sōetsu
Sogliuzzo, A.R. Luigi Pirandello, Direc-
    tor.*
    S.V. Longman, 615(TJ):Oct85-392
Sohn, D.A. and E. Enger. Writing by Doing.
    S. Irujo, 399(MLJ):Summer85-216
Sohn Pow-Key. Early Korean Typography.
    (new ed)
    E.B. McCune, 293(JASt):Aug85-852
Sohnle, W.P. Stefan George und der
    Symbolismus.
    C. Gabriel, 52:Band20Heft1-103

Sorensen, T.C.   A Different Kind of Presidency.
639(VQR):Winter85-22
Sørensen, V.   Seneca.
G.W. Bowersock, 31(ASch):Autumn85-567
A.L. Motto and J.R. Clark, 121(CJ):
Oct/Nov85-76
E. Nelson, 124:Sep-Oct85-68
G.S., 185:Jul86-911
Sorestad, G.   Hold the Rain in Your Hands.
S. Scobie, 376:Jan86-126
Soria, J.M.N. - see under Nieto Soria, J.M.
Soriano, O.   A Funny Dirty Little War.
J. Coleman, 441:8Jun86-32
J. Updike, 442(NY):22Sep86-108
Sorin, G.   The Prophetic Minority.
J.V. Mallow, 287:Oct85-25
Sorley, C.H.   The Collected Poems of
Charles Hamilton Sorley.   (J.M. Wilson,
ed)
N. Corcoran, 617(TLS):28Feb86-214
P. Parker, 364:Feb86-105
V. Scannell, 493:Feb86-56
Sornberger, J., ed.   All My Grandmothers
Could Sing.
F.W. Kaye, 502(PrS):Winter85-116
Sorokin, J.S., ed.   Slovar' russkogo jaz-
yka XVIII veka: Vypusk 1.   Slovar' russ-
kogo jazyka XVIII veka: Pravila pol'zov-
anija slovarem.
G. Hüttl-Folter, 559:Vol9No1-97
Sorrentino, G.   Blue Pastoral.*
J. Byrne, 532(RCF):Spring85-135
Sosa, E., ed.   Essays on the Philosophy of
Roderick M. Chisholm.
J.E. Tomberlin, 449:Mar85-136
Soshuk, L. and A. Eisenberg, eds.   Momentous Century.
N. Yood, 287:May85-24
Soto, G.   Black Hair.
M. Jarman, 249(HudR):Summer85-338
D. Wojahn, 491:Jun85-171
Soucy, R.   French Fascism: The First Wave,
1924-1933.
D. Johnson, 617(TLS):26Sep86-1052
J.W. Scott, 441:20Apr86-20
Soulez, A., ed and trans.   Manifeste de
Cercle de Vienne et autres écrits.
T. Cordellier, 450(NRF):Nov85-104
"Sources and Analogues of Old English
Poetry."   (Vol 2) (D.G. Calder and
others, trans)
H. Kratz, 221(GQ):Fall85-599
T.A. Shippey, 179(ES):Jun85-272
Souster, R.   Going the Distance.*
M. Turner, 102(CanL):Spring85-151
Souster, R.   Queen City.
M. Braun, 99:Apr85-33
L. York, 102(CanL):Spring85-145
Soutet, O.   La littérature française de
la Renaissance.
H. Sonneville, 356(LR):Aug85-228
Southall, G.H.   The Continuing Enslavement
of Blind Tom, the Black Pianist-Composer
(1865-1887).   (Bk 2)
E. Southern, 91:Spring85-119
Souto, C.   Allgemeinste wissenschaftliche
Grundlagen des Sozialen.
J.C.E., 185:Apr86-691
Souto Silva, A.I.   El retablo de San
Miguel de los Navarros.
M. Estella, 48:Apr-Jun85-166

Souza, M.   Mad Maria.
J. Franco, 441:19Jan86-10
Souza, R.D.   The Poetic Fiction of José
Lezama Lima.*
R. Magráns, 345(KRQ):Vol32No4-436
C. Ruiz Barrionuevo, 240(HR):Autumn85-
517
Sowa, C.A.   Traditional Themes and the
Homeric Hymns.
E.S. de Angeli, 124:Mar-Apr86-278
R. Janko, 123:Vol35No2-378
Sox, D.   Relics and Shrines.
J. McManners, 617(TLS):3Jan86-8
Soyinka, W.   Soyinka: Six Plays.   A Play
of Giants.
D. Devlin, 157:No155-49
Soymié, M., ed.   Nouvelles contributions
aux études de Touen-houang.
P.W. Kroll, 116:Jul84-203
Sozzi, L. and V-L. Saulnier, eds.   La
Nouvelle française à la Renaissance.
K.M. Hall, 208(FS):Jan85-68
Spacks, P.M.   Gossip.*
S. Pickering, 569(SR):Fall85-lxxxiii
Spada, M.   Érotiques du merveilleux.
D. Coste, 535(RHL):Nov/Dec85-1083
Spaemann, R. and R. Löw.   Die Frage Wozu?*
J. Habermas, 384:Sep/Oct85-900
Spaeth, D.   Mies van der Rohe.*
M. Filler, 453(NYRB):12Jun86-26
H. Muschamp, 62:Dec85-14
J. Winter, 46:May85-80
Spagnoletti, G.   La letteratura italiana
del nostro secolo.
F. Donini, 617(TLS):7Mar86-255
Spalding, F.   Vanessa Bell.*
M. Goldstein, 569(SR):Fall85-624
M. Jones, 31(ASch):Winter84/85-129
W. Kendrick, 473(PR):Vol52No4-466
Spalding, F.   British Art Since 1900.
S. Gardiner, 362:24Apr86-32
Spalding, K.   Huarochirf.
G. Escobar M., 263(RIB):Vol35No1-73
Spang, K.   Ritmo y versificación/Teoría y
práctica del análisis métrico y rítmico.
W. Ferguson, 238:Sep85-522
Spanidou, I.   God's Snake.
N. Bromell, 441:14Sep86-13
Spanier, S.W.   Kay Boyle.
J. Koslow, 441:23Nov86-25
"The Spanish Civil War: A History in Pictures."
W. Herrick, 441:31Aug86-13
442(NY):14Jul86-85
Spanos, W.V., ed.   Martin Heidegger and
the Question of Literature.
D.H. Hirsch, 569(SR):Summer85-465
Sparagna, A.   La tradizione musicale a
Maranola.
M.S. Keller, 187:Fall86-563
Spariosu, M.   Literature, Mimesis, and
Play.*
V. Farenga, 478:Oct85-239
Spark, D., ed.   20 Under 30.
P. Lopate, 441:23Mar86-12
Spark, M. and D. Stanford.   Emily Bronte.
617(TLS):31Jan86-127
Sparshott, F.   The Cave of Trophonius and
Other Poems.
B. Pirie, 102(CanL):Winter84-91
Spasowski, R.   The Liberation of One.
P-L. Adams, 61:Apr86-131
J. Darnton, 441:30Mar86-6

Städele, A., ed and trans. Die Briefe des Pythagoras und der Pythagoreer.
  J. Mansfeld, 394:Vol38fasc1/2-215
Stadler, E. Dichtungen, Schriften, Briefe.* (K. Hurlebusch and K.L. Schneider, eds)
  H. Rollmann, 564:Nov85-286
Staehelin, M. - see "Beethoven-Jahrbuch"
Stafford, B.M. Voyage into Substance.*
  P. Adams, 173(ECS):Fall85-88
  W. Franklin, 658:Summer/Autumn85-193
  M.S. Kinsey, 446(NCFS):Fall-Winter85/86-183
  C. Rosen, 453(NYRB):6Nov86-55
  639(VQR):Winter85-16
Stafford, K.R. Having Everything Right.
  J. Tallmadge, 441:3Aug86-19
Stafford, W. A Glass Face in the Rain.
  M. Pearson, 577(SHR):Winter85-82
Stafford, W. Writing the Australian Crawl.
  R. McDowell, 249(HudR):Autumn85-514
Stafford, W.T. Books Speaking to Books.
  E. Safer, 402(MLR):Oct85-910
Stahl, A.M. The Merovingian Coinage of the Region of Metz.
  D.M. Metcalf, 589:Jan85-202
Stahl, H-P. Propertius, "Love" and "War."
  F. Cairns, 617(TLS):18Jul86-794
Stahnke, A. Aspazija.
  J. Silenieks, 104(CASS):Summer85-204
  A. Ziedonis, Jr., 574(SEEJ):Fall85-365
Staib, B. Semantik und Sprachgeographie.*
  N.C.W. Spence, 208(FS):Jul85-375
Staicar, T., ed. The Feminine Eye.
  D.M. Hassler, 395(MFS):Summer85-465
Staines, D. Tennyson's Camelot.*
  D.F. Goslee, 637(VS):Winter85-358
Stainton, L. Turner's Venice.
  J. Gage, 617(TLS):7Feb86-144
Stalberg, R. China's Puppets.
  M. Knight, 610:Autumn85-254
Staley, T.F., ed. British Novelists, 1890-1929: Traditionalists.
  R.M. Davis, 136:Vol 18No2-155
Staley, T.F., ed. Twentieth-Century Women Novelists.
  K. Watson, 447(N&Q):Dec84-550
Stalley, R.F. An Introduction to Plato's "Laws."*
  R. Kraut, 482(PhR):Jan85-123
Stallworthy, J. The Anzac Sonata.
  A. Haverty, 617(TLS):3Oct86-1118
Stallworthy, J., ed. The Oxford Book of War Poetry.*
  S. Hynes, 569(SR):Fall85-618
  H. Lomas, 249(HudR):Autumn85-388
Stallworthy, J. - see Owen, W.
Stalnaker, R.C. Inquiry.*
  T. Baldwin, 393(Mind):Oct85-627
  C.C., 185:Jan86-444
Stamaty, M.A. More Washingtoons.
  A. Gore, Jr., 441:14Dec86-9
Stamm, T.D. Gavarni and the Critics.*
  R. Snell, 54:Mar85-165
Stammerjohann, H. Französisch für Lehrer.*
  W. Schweickard, 72:Band222Heft1-213
Stamp, G. and A. Goulancourt. The English House 1860-1914.
  P. Davey, 617(TLS):8Aug86-872
Stancliffe, C. St. Martin and his Hagiographer.
  P. Brown, 589:Jul85-727
  I.N. Wood, 313:Vol75-267

Standing, S. Deception Pass.
  M. Kumin, 219(GaR):Spring85-169
Stanford, D.E. Revolution and Convention in Modern Poetry.*
  G.E. Murray, 219(GaR):Fall85-667
Stanford, D.E. - see Bridges, R.
Stanford, W.B. Greek Tragedy and the Emotions.*
  L. Spatz, 615(TJ):Mar85-126
Stang, S.J. - see Ford, F.M.
Stanguennec, A. and others. L'homme et ses normes. (Pt 1)
  P. Somville, 542:Jul-Sep85-351
Staniland, M. What Is Political Economy?*
  K-K.T., 185:Jul86-898
Stanislavsky, K. On the Art of the Stage.
  617(TLS):28Feb86-231
Stanislawski, M. Tsar Nicholas I and the Jews.*
  J. Boyarin, 287:Mar85-26
Stankiewicz, E. Grammars and Dictionaries of the Slavic Languages from the Middle Ages up to 1850.
  L. Djurović, 559:Vol9No1-103
Stankiewicz, E. Studies in Slavic Morphophonemics and Accentology.
  L.R. Micklesen, 279:Vol29-151
Stanley, E.G. and D. Gray, eds. Five Hundred Years of Words and Sounds.
  B. Cottle, 541(RES):Nov85-545
Stanley, G. Opening Day.
  L. Boone, 102(CanL):Winter84-136
Stanley-Baker, J. Japanese Art.
  R. Grant, 324:Jan86-128
Stannard, M. Evelyn Waugh: The Early Years, 1903-39.
  P.N. Furbank, 617(TLS):7Nov86-1237
Stansell, C. City of Women.
  M. Saxton, 441:30Nov86-19
Stansky, P. Redesigning the World.*
  F. Kirchhoff, 637(VS):Spring86-482
  E. Norwich, 139:Aug/Sep85-46
  D. Sutton, 39:Sep85-170
  H.W., 636(VP):Summer85-223
Stanton, M. Cries of Swimmers.*
  P. Stitt, 219(GaR):Winter85-849
Stanyukovich, K. Running to the Shrouds.
  P. Reading, 617(TLS):26Dec86-1456
Staples, S. Male-Female Comedy Teams in American Vaudeville, 1865-1932.
  J.M. Callahan, 615(TJ):Dec85-519
Stapleton, M. The Cambridge Guide to English Literature.*
  J.W. Blench, 161(DUJ):Dec84-133
  B. Cottle, 541(RES):Nov85-617
Stapleton, T.J. Husserl and Heidegger.
  W. Mays, 518:Apr85-91
Starck, T. and J.C. Wells, eds. Althochdeutsches Glossenwörterbuch.
  D.H. Green, 402(MLR):Jan85-203
Stark, D. The Old English Weak Verbs.*
  R. Hamer, 382(MAE):1985/2-345
Stark, M. Für und wider den Expressionismus.*
  W. Paulsen, 564:Sep85-238
Stark, S.S. The Dealers' Yard and Other Stories.*
  J. Saari, 42(AR):Summer85-366
Starkey, C.M. and N.W. Penn. What You Need To Know About ....
  R.E. Meyer, 399(MLJ):Winter85-445
Starkey, D. The Reign of Henry VIII.
  R. Mayne, 176:Jul/Aug86-49

Starn, R. Contrary Commonwealth.
  H. Butters, 551(RenQ):Winter85-701
Starobinski, J. Montaigne en mouvement.*
  P. Henry, 207(FR):Dec85-291
  S.F.R., 131(CL):Fall85-366
Stassen, L. Comparison and Universal Grammar.
  S. Romaine, 353:Vol23No3-507
Staten, H. Wittgenstein and Derrida.
  B. Harrison, 651(WHR):Winter85-359
States, B.O. Great Reckonings in Little Rooms.
  K. Elam, 617(TLS):7Mar86-250
  G. Weales, 219(GaR):Winter85-885
Stati, S. Il dialogo.
  R.J. Di Pietro, 205(ForL):Aug84-168
Statius. P. Papini Stati "Thebaidos" Libri XII. (D.E. Hill, ed)
  R. Mayer, 123:Vol35No2-289
"The Status of Women in Nepal."
  H. Papanek, 293(JASt):Nov84-127
"Status of Women in Sri Lanka."
  H. Papanek, 293(JASt):Nov84-127
Staud, G. A magyarországi jezsuita iskolai színjátékok forráisa I, 1561-1773.
  G.F. Cushing, 575(SEER):Oct85-584
Stauffer, H.W. Mari Sandoz.
  L. Horne, 106:Summer85-221
  A. Ronald, 649(WAL):May85-55
Stavrou, T.G., ed. Art and Culture in Nineteenth-Century Russia.*
  L. Dienes, 550(RusR):Oct85-412
Stead, C. Ocean of Story. (R.G. Geering, ed)
  P. Craig, 617(TLS):16May86-535
  E. White, 441:25May86-7
Stead, C.K. The Death of the Body.
  G. Strawson, 617(TLS):29Aug86-933
Stead, C.K. Poems of a Decade.*
  W. Scammell, 364:Jul85-80
Stead, C.K. Pound, Yeats, Eliot and the Modernist Movement.
  A.W. Litz, 617(TLS):10Oct86-1142
Stead, I.M., J.B. Bourke and D. Brothwell. Lindow Man.
  R. Bradley, 617(TLS):12Sep86-1010
Stead, M. Egyptian Life.
  P. Levi, 176:Jul/Aug86-45
Stead, R. Dry Water. (P. Varma, ed)
  W.J. Keith, 627(UTQ):Summer85-435
  H. Prest, 102(CanL):Winter84-151
Steadman, J.M. The Hill and the Labyrinth.*
  G.M. Ridden, 506(PSt):Dec85-93
  L. Roux, 189(EA):Apr-Jun86-213
Steadman, J.M. Milton's Biblical and Classical Imagery.*
  J.H. Sims, 568(SCN):Spring-Summer85-1
Steblin, R. A History of Key Characteristics in the Eighteenth and Early Nineteenth Centuries.
  K. Berger, 410(M&L):Oct85-388
Steblin-Kamenskij, M.I. Mir sagi.
  A. Liberman, 562(Scan):Nov85-211
Steblin-Kamenskij, M.I. Myth.*
  M. Ciklamini, 589:Apr85-492
  H. Pálsson, 562(Scan):Nov85-225
Stedman, P. The Symphony.
  J.H., 412:May83-141
Steegmuller, F. Apollinaire.
  617(TLS):19Dec86-1434
Steegmuller, F. - see Flaubert, G.
Steel, C. - see Proclus

Steel, D. Wanderlust.
  J. Gerston, 441:3Aug86-18
Steele, B. - see Lawrence, D.H.
Steele, H. Chasing the Gilded Shadow.
  M. Quilligan, 441:25May86-16
Steele, H.T. Bowl-o-Rama.
  C. Colman, 441:21Sep86-26
Steele, R. - see under "The Guardian"
Steele, R. and J. Gaillard. L'Express.
  T. Scanlan, 207(FR):Dec85-317
Steele, T. The Prudent Heart.*
  A. Hudgins, 434:Summer86-526
Steene, B. August Strindberg.*
  C. Waal, 563(SS):Spring85-225
Steever, S.B. Selected Papers on Tamil and Dravidian Linguistics.
  D.W. McAlpin, 318(JAOS):Oct-Dec84-784
Stéfan, J. Gnomiques.
  T. Cordellier, 450(NRF):Oct85-89
Stefanson, B. - see Bernanos, G.
Steffen, C.G. The Mechanics of Baltimore.
  W.H. Ridgway, 656(WMQ):Oct85-546
Steffler, J. The Grey Islands.
  S. Scobie, 376:Jan86-126
Stegagno Picchio, L. La Méthode philologique.
  T.R.H., 131(CL):Spring85-189
Steger, H., ed. Soziolinguistik. Anwendungsbereiche der Soziolinguistik.
  A. Mihm, 685(ZDL):1/1985-101
Steiger, K.P., ed. Das englische Drama nach 1945.
  G. Bas, 189(EA):Jan-Mar86-111
Stein, A. - see Kunert, G.
Stein, A.F. After the Vows Were Spoken.*
  T.A. Gullason, 395(MFS):Winter85-745
Stein, D. Ada.*
  L. Burnard, 617(TLS):7Mar86-242
Stein, D.L. The Golden Age Hotel.
  L.K. Mackendrick, 102(CanL):Fall85-146
  C. Matthews, 376:Jun85-128
Stein, G. and C. Van Vechten. The Letters of Gertrude Stein and Carl Van Vechten. (E. Burns, ed)
  H. Ford, 441:6Jul86-14
  W.H. Gass, 617(TLS):7Nov86-1235
Stein, H. Washington Bedtime Stories.
  G. Daugherty, 441:2Nov86-27
Stein, H.F. The Psycho-Dynamics of Medical Practice.
  R. Frankenberg, 617(TLS):16May86-542
Stein, J. The World of Marcus Garvey.
  M. Crowder, 617(TLS):13Jun86-662
  C.E. Walker, 441:13Apr86-19
Stein, J.B. The Soviet Bloc, Energy and Western Security.
  D. Wilson, 550(RusR):Apr85-211
Stein, L. - see Schoenberg, A.
Stein, P. Connaissance et emploi des langues à l'Île Maurice.*
  549(RLC):Jan-Mar85-110
Stein, P. Kreolisch und Französisch.
  A. Bollée, 547(RF):Band97Heft4-441
Stein, S.J. - see Byrd, W.S.
Stein-Karnbach, A. G.W. Leibniz und der Buchhandel.
  W. Grossmann, 517(PBSA):Vol79No2-246
Steinbach, H-R. Englishes im deutschen Werbefernsehen.
  K. Herr, 399(MLJ):Winter85-418
Steinbaugh, E. Winston Churchill.
  R.W. Schneider, 26(ALR):Spring/Autumn85-293

Stirling, N. Pearl Buck.
D.W. Petrie, 395(MFS):Winter85-727
K.J. Williams, 27(AL):Mar85-167
Stitt, P. The World's Hieroglyphic Beauty.
A. Brumer, 441:17Aug86-23
Stiver, H.E., Jr. and S. Kahan. Play and
Scene Preparation.
B. Bernhard, 615(TJ):Dec85-521
Stock, B. The Implications of Literacy.
D.P. Henry, 161(DUJ):Dec84-111
G.H. Martin, 366:Autumn85-298
W.J. Ong, 377:Jul84-108
E. Vance, 153:Fall85-55
Stock, J. Il Valore dei Disegni Antichi.
G. Naughton, 39:May85-358
Stockert, W. T. Maccius Plautus, "Aulula-
ria."
H.D. Jocelyn, 123:Vol35No2-268
Stocking, G.W., ed. Objects and Others.
S. Piggott, 617(TLS):25Jul86-808
Stockinger, L. Ficta Respublica.*
W. Barner, 221(GQ):Winter85-111
P.U. Hohendahl, 133:Band17Heft3/4-329
Stockman, D.A. The Triumph of Politics.
J.K. Galbraith, 453(NYRB):26Jun86-3
C. Johnson, 617(TLS):16May86-523
M. Kinsley, 441:11May86-3
442(NY):14Jul86-83
Stockman, N. Antipositivist Theories of
the Sciences.
D. Howard, 543:Dec85-377
Stockton, R.R. and F.W. Wayman. A Time of
Turmoil.
K. Ver Burg, 115:Spring84-153
Stodelle, E. Deep Song.
R. Bailey, 151:Jan85-44
S.A. Manning, 612(ThS):Nov85-205
Stoetzel, J. Les Valeurs du temps présent.
E. Morot-Sir, 207(FR):Oct85-162
Stokes, E. The Peasant Armed. (C.A.
Bayly, ed)
P.J. Marshall, 617(TLS):10Oct86-1144
Stokes, G., ed. Nationalism in the Bal-
kans.
R. Pearson, 575(SEER):Jul85-474
Stokes, R. The Function of Bibliography.*
(2nd ed)
P.S. Koda, 87(BB):Dec85-219
Stol, M. Letters from Yale.
W.L. Moran, 318(JAOS):Jul-Sep84-573
Stoler, A.L. Capitalism and Confrontation
in Sumatra's Plantation Belt, 1870-1979.
P. Carey, 617(TLS):28Feb86-223
Stoljar, S. An Analysis of Rights.*
T.M. Benditt, 185:Jan86-420
Stoltzfus, B. Alain Robbe-Grillet.
A. Jefferson, 617(TLS):7Mar86-254
E. Kafalenos, 268(IFR):Winter86-52
S. Lawall, 659(ConL):Fall86-423
Stolze, P. Untersuchungen zur Sprache der
Anzeigenwerbung in der zweiten Hälfte
des 18. Jahrhunderts.
R. Römer, 680(ZDP):Band104Heft3-475
Stolze, R. Grundlagen der Textübersetzung.
H.G. Vermeer, 257(IRAL):Aug85-261
Stone, A.E. Autobiographical Occasions
and Original Acts.*
R.A. Banes, 577(SHR):Winter85-70
P.M. Spacks, 131(CL):Summer85-286
Stone, D., Jr. Mellin de Saint-Gelais and
Literary History.*
Y. Bellenger, 535(RHL):Sep/Oct85-853
[continued]

[continuing]
A. Moss, 208(FS):Apr85-193
T. Thomson, 402(MLR):Apr85-459
Stone, J. Israel and Palestine.
R.A. Gerber, 390:Feb85-59
Stone, L. and J.C.F. An Open Elite?*
C. Hill, 551(RenQ):Summer85-337
F. McCormick, 566:Autumn85-91
Stone, M.E., ed. Jewish Writings of the
Second Temple Period.
G. Vermes, 617(TLS):27Jun86-718
Stone, R. Children of Light.
A. Alvarez, 453(NYRB):10Apr86-23
W. Balliett, 442(NY):2Jun86-105
J. Mellors, 362:10Apr86-28
J. Strouse, 441:16Mar86-1
M. Wood, 617(TLS):21Mar86-307
Stoneman, R. Daphne into Laurel.*
J. Griffin, 123:Vol35No2-368
Stonyk, M. Nineteenth-Century English
Literature.*
B.V. Qualls, 637(VS):Spring86-498
Stopp, K. Die Handwerkskundschaften mit
Ortsansichten.* (Vol 1)
70:May/Jun85-156
Storey, E. A Right to Song.
R.L. Brett, 541(RES):May85-283
J. Lucas, 637(VS):Spring85-538
M.K. Sutton, 661(WC):Fall85-207
L.J. Swingle, 340(KSJ):Vol34-194
Storey, G. and K.J. Fielding - see Dickens,
C.
Storey, M. - see Clare, J.
Storey, R. Pierrots on the Stage of
Desire.
B.L. Knapp, 446(NCFS):Spring-Summer86-
395
Story, G. It Never Pays to Laugh Too Much.
J. Ditsky, 649(WAL):Nov85-256
M. Jenoff, 99:Aug/Sep85-31
Story, G.L. Babine and Carrier Phonology.
S. Hargus, 350:Jun86-473
Story, G.M., W.J. Kirwin and J.D.A.
Widdowson, eds. Dictionary of Newfound-
land English.*
E.G. Stanley, 447(N&Q):Mar84-103
J. Tucker, 178:Dec85-484
"The Story of Muhammad Hanafiyyah." (L.F.
Brakel, trans)
A. Schimmel, 318(JAOS):Oct-Dec84-779
Stössel, A., ed. Afrikanische Keramik.
F.T. Smith, 2(AfrA):Aug85-91
Stott, W. Documentary Expression and
Thirties America.
617(TLS):19Dec86-1434
Stotz, C.M. Outposts of the War for
Empire.
70:May/Jun85-173
Stötzer, U. and others, eds. Grosses
Wörterbuch der deutschen Aussprache.
W. Braun, 682(ZPSK):Band38Heft4-420
Stouck, D. Major Canadian Authors.
A.E. Davidson, 627(UTQ):Winter84/85-
217
W.J. Keith, 301(JEGP):Jul85-460
M. Peterman, 649(WAL):May85-75
C. Thomas, 395(MFS):Summer85-431
G. Woodcock, 102(CanL):Spring85-143
Stout, H.S. The New England Soul.
A. Delbanco, 441:14Sep86-24
Stouten, J. Verlichting in de letteren.
P.F. Schmitz, 204(FdL):Mar85-78

Stovall, F. The Foreground of "Leaves of Grass."
J. Gatta, 183(ESQ):Vol31No4-272
Stove, D.C. Popper and After.*
J. Agassi, 488:Sep85-368
J.R. Brown, 154:Spring85-177
Stove, D.C. The Rationality of Induction.
D. Papineau, 617(TLS):19Dec86-1429
Stöver-Leidig, H., ed. Die Gedichte Thomas Tickells.
P. Rogers, 402(MLR):Apr85-426
Stowe, W.W. Balzac, James and the Realistic Novel.*
I.F.A. Bell, 447(N&Q):Dec84-567
A.W. Bellringer, 677(YES):Vol 15-325
R.P. Hoople, 106:Spring85-57
P. Nykrog, 131(CL):Fall85-375
R.B. Yeazell, 536(Rev):Vol7-43
"Strabon, 'Géographie.'" (Vol 9) (F. Lasserre, ed and trans)
Y. Janvier, 555:Vol59fasc1-118
Strachan, H. From Waterloo to Balaclava.
M. Carver, 617(TLS):25Apr86-440
Strachan, H. Wellington's Legacy.
B. Bond, 637(VS):Winter86-318
Strachan, W.J. Open Air Sculpture in Britain.
M. Yorke, 324:May86-416
Strachey, B. The Strachey Line.*
M. Fitz Herbert, 617(TLS):7Feb86-135
Strachey, B. and J. Samuels - see Berenson, M.
Strachey, J. and F. Partridge. Julia.
W. Kendrick, 473(PR):Vol52No4-466
Strachey, J. and A. Bloomsbury/Freud.*
(P. Meisel and W. Kendrick, eds)
P-L. Adams, 61:Feb86-88
R. Dinnage, 453(NYRB):8May86-15
J. Drummond, 362:20Mar86-29
R. Fuller, 364:Feb86-87
V. Glendinning, 617(TLS):28Mar86-334
P. Grosskurth, 627(UTQ):Spring86-306
Strack, F. Im Schatten der Neugier.*
R. Leroy, 133:Band18Heft1-87
Strahan, L. Just City and the Mirrors.*
D. Green, 381:Jun85-193
Strainchamps, E. and M.R. Maniates, with C. Hatch, eds. Music and Civilization.
A. Walker, 414:Vol71No3-375
Strand, M. Mr. and Mrs. Baby and Other Stories.*
A. Mars-Jones, 617(TLS):30May86-587
639(VQR):Autumn85-128
Strandberg, V. Religious Psychology in American Literature.
A.W. Bellringer, 402(MLR):Oct85-916
Strange, S. Casino Capitalism.
B.M. Rowland, 441:14Dec86-35
Straram, P. Blues clair/Quatre Quatuors en trains qu'amour advienne.
J. Moss, 102(CanL):Fall85-145
Strassberg, R.E. The World of K'ung Shang-jen.
P.S. Ropp, 293(JASt):Feb85-383
Strassi, S., ed. A Selective Publication and Description of the Greek Papyri (P. Leeds Museum) in the Leeds City Museum.
R. Coles, 123:Vol35No1-173
"Strategic Defenses."
M. MccGwire, 617(TLS):31Oct86-1214
Strauss, L. Studies in Platonic Political Philosophy.*
T. Molnar, 396(ModA):Winter85-82

Strauss, W.L. and M. van der Meulen, with others. The Rembrandt Documents.
C. Brown, 90:Jan85-46
Stravinsky, I. Selected Correspondence.* (Vol 2) (R. Craft, ed)
R. Holloway, 607:Mar85-37
A. Whittall, 410(M&L):Jul85-259
Stravinsky, I. Selected Correspondence.* (Vol 3) (R. Craft, ed)
P. Griffiths, 617(TLS):14Mar86-273
Stravinsky, V. and I. Dearest Bubushkin. (R. Craft, ed)
P. Griffiths, 617(TLS):14Mar86-273
Strawson, J. Daring to Excel.
M.R.D. Foot, 176:Jun85-61
Strayer, J.R., ed-in-chief. Dictionary of the Middle Ages. (Vols 1-5)
C.T. Wood, 589:Oct85-967
Streeck, J. Social Order in Child Communication.
S. Karimi, 350:Jun86-479
Street, J. Rebel Rock.
H. Kureishi, 617(TLS):8Aug86-874
Street, J.S. French Sacred Drama from Bèze to Corneille.*
G. Forestier, 535(RHL):Sep/Oct85-859
R. Griffiths, 402(MLR):Apr85-460
Streeter, T.W. Bibliography of Texas, 1795-1845. (2nd ed) (A. Hanna, ed)
C.C. Colley, 517(PBSA):Vol79No3-453
Strehler, G. and U. Ronfani. Io, Strehler.
H. Sachs, 617(TLS):10Oct86-1132
Streier, E-M. Bedrohung des Menschen durch Naturwissenschaft und Technologie?
F. Rottensteiner, 561(SFS):Jul85-223
Strelka, J. Stefan Zweig.*
D. Sevin, 133:Band17Heft3/4-372
Strelka, J.P. Exilliteratur.*
E. Glass, 400(MLN):Apr85-695
Strelka, J.P., ed. Literary Theory and Criticism.
T.R.H. and S.F.R., 131(CL):Fall85-380
P. Salm, 678(YCGL):No34-122
Strelka, J.P. - see Petzold, B.
Strelka, J.P. - see "Yearbook of Comparative Criticism"
Stricker, R. Robert Schumann.* (French title: Schumann, le musicien et la folie.)
A. Suied, 450(NRF):Feb85-115
Strier, R. Love Known.
I. Bell, 141:Fall85-404
D.W. Doerksen, 539:Nov85-305
J.R. Mulder, 551(RenQ):Autumn85-583
Strobel, K. Untersuchungen zu den Dakerkriegen Trajans.
F.A. Lepper, 123:Vol35No2-333
Strohm, R. Essays on Handel and Italian Opera.*
J. Keates, 617(TLS):31Jan86-118
C. Price, 415:Dec85-731
Strohm, R. Music in Late Medieval Bruges.
D. Leech-Wilkinson, 617(TLS):9May86-496
Strohmaier, I. - see Husserl, E.
Strohmeyer, J. Crisis in Bethlehem.
S. Greenhouse, 441:26Oct86-38
Ströker, E. Theorienwandel in der Wissenschaftsgeschichte.
L. Schäfer, 679:Band16Heft1-182
Stromberg-Stein, S. Louis Dudek.
C. McLay, 102(CanL):Summer85-144

Strong, E. My Darling Neighbour.
M. Harmon, 272(IUR):Autumn85-234
Strong, J.S. The Legend of King Aśoka.
R. Thapar, 293(JASt):Feb85-447
Strong, R. Art and Power.*
M. Dodsworth, 175:Spring85-92
Strong, R. Henry Prince of Wales and
England's Lost Renaissance.
C. Hill, 453(NYRB):23Oct86-19
R. Savage, 362:19Jun86-26
B. Worden, 617(TLS):13Jun86-635
Stroop, J. Molenaarsterm en molenge-
schiedenis.
D. Stellmacher, 685(ZDL):1/1985-131
Strosetzki, C. Rhétorique de la conversa-
tion.
G. Le Coat, 475:Vol 12No23-749
J.L. Pallister, 568(SCN):Winter85-69
Stroud, B. The Significance of Philosophi-
cal Scepticism.*
E. Craig, 483:Oct85-548
J. Dancy, 518:Oct85-235
S. Nathanson, 258:Dec85-431
M.T., 185:Jan86-445
Stroud, D. Sir John Soane, Architect.*
E. McParland, 90:Feb85-100
Struminger, L.S. What Were Little Girls
and Boys Made Of?
L. Czyba, 535(RHL):Sep/Oct85-892
Struthers, B. Censored Letters.
R. Potter, 526:Summer85-84
S. Scobie, 376:Sep85-144
Struthers, J.R., ed. The Montreal Story
Tellers.
J. Fitzgerald, 99:Jan86-36
Strutz, J., ed. Robert Musil und die kul-
turellen Tendenzen seiner Zeit.
G.C. Howes, 221(GQ):Winter85-136
Struve, G. Russkaia literatura v izgnanii.
(2nd ed)
A. McMillin, 402(MLR):Oct85-1004
V. Setchkarev, 550(RusR):Oct85-411
Struve, G.P. and others - see Akhmatova, A.
Struve, L.A. The Southern Ming, 1644-1662.
J.P. Dennerline, 293(JASt):Aug85-824
Stryk, L. Encounter with Zen. Collected
Poems 1953-1983.
G.S. Corseri, 219(GaR):Winter85-864
Stuart, E.R. The History of Prairie
Theatre.
D. Bessai, 627(UTQ):Summer85-433
R. Plant, 529(QQ):Winter85-740
D. Rubin, 99:May85-34
B. Somers, 108:Summer85-188
Stuart, F. Faillandia.
J. Melmoth, 617(TLS):17Jan86-57
Stuart, J. Clearing in the Sky and Other
Stories.
G. Hendrick, 573(SSF):Spring85-244
Stuart, R.C., ed. The Soviet Rural
Economy.
I. Stebelsky, 104(CASS):Spring85-90
K-E. Wadekin, 550(RusR):Oct85-430
Stuart-Fox, M., ed. Contemporary Laos.
J. Halpern, 293(JASt):May85-681
Stubbing, R.A., with R.A. Mendel. The
Defense Game.
J.S. Nye, Jr., 441:28Sep86-9
Stubbs, J.C. - see Fellini, F.
Stubbs, M. Discourse Analysis.*
Cheng Yumin, 596(SL):Vol39No2-175
M. Owen, 297(JL):Mar85-241

Studebaker, W. The Cleaving.
K. Riedell, 649(WAL):Feb86-376
"Studi goldoniani." (No 6)
K. Ringger, 547(RF):Band97Heft1-110
"Studien zur Nationalsprachlichen Entwick-
lung in Afrika."
M. Dietrich-Friedländer and C. El-
Solami-Mewis, 682(ZPSK):Band38Heft2-
196
"Studies in Eighteenth-Century Culture."
(Vol 10) (H.C. Payne, ed)
B.S. Hammond, 83:Autumn85-217
"Studies in Eighteenth-Century Culture."
(Vol 11) (H.C. Payne, ed)
J. Gray, 107(CRCL):Sep85-529
B.S. Hammond, 83:Autumn85-217
"Studies in Eighteenth-Century Culture."
(Vol 12) (H.C. Payne, ed)
B.S. Hammond, 83:Autumn85-217
J.W. Van Cleve, 221(GQ):Summer85-487
"Studies in Scottish Literature.* (Vol 17)
(G.R. Roy, ed)
A.H. MacLaine, 541(RES):Aug85-467
"Studies on Voltaire and the Eighteenth
Century." (Vol 199)
M.H. Waddicor, 208(FS):Apr85-209
"Studies on Voltaire and the Eighteenth
Century." (Vol 201)
M-E. Diéval, 535(RHL):Jan/Feb85-100
"Studies on Voltaire and the Eighteenth
Century." (Vol 228)
S. Soupel, 189(EA):Apr-Jun86-242
Stueck, W. The Wedemeyer Mission.
639(VQR):Spring85-53
Stump, D.V. and others, eds. Hamartia.
P. Properzio, 124:May-Jun86-353
Sturgeon, T. Godbody.
G. Jonas, 441:20Apr86-27
Sturlese, L. Dokumente und Forschungen zu
Leben und Werk Dietrichs von Freiberg.
K. Ruh, 684(ZDA):Band114Heft2-66
Sturluson, S. - see under Snorri Sturluson
Sturm, A. and F. Weerman. Generatieve syn-
taxis.
A. Hulk, 204(FdL):Mar85-61
Sturm, J. Morpho-syntaktische Untersuch-
ungen zur "phrase négative" im gespro-
chenen Französisch.*
F. Lebsanft, 209(FM):Apr85-109
Sturm, T. - see "Christopher Brennan"
Sturrock, J. Structuralism.
D. Attridge, 617(TLS):21Nov86-1306
Stussi, A. Avviamento agli studi di filol-
ogia italiana.
Y. Malkiel, 276:Summer85-154
Stussi, A. Studi e documenti di storia
della lingua e dei dialetti italiani.*
B. Richardson, 545(RPh):Feb85-375
P. Trifone, 708:Vol 11fasc1-132
Stutman, S. - see Wolfe, T. and A. Bern-
stein
Styan, J.L. Modern Drama in Theory and
Practice.* (Vols 1-3)
P. Thomson, 402(MLR):Jan85-140
de la Suarée, O. Sociedad y política en
la ensayística de Ramón Pérez de Ayala.
A.M. Aguirre, 140(CH):Vol7No1-91
Suarez, F. De juramento fidelitatis.
(L. Pereña and others, eds)
J-F. Courtine, 192(EP):Apr-Jun85-269
Suárez, J.A. La lengua tlapaneca de Malin-
altepec.
B. Comrie, 350:Mar86-223

Sweeney, J.G. 3d. Jonson and the Psychology of Public Theater.
  G. Parfitt, 551(RenQ):Winter85-772
Sweeney, M. The Lame Waltzer.
  M. Imlah, 617(TLS):16May86-540
  H. Lomas, 364:Mar86-87
Sweeney, V.G. The Emancipist.
  H. Benedict, 441:16Feb86-16
Sweet, F. The Film Narratives of Alain Resnais.
  F.A. Worth, 207(FR):Apr86-824
Sweezy, N. Raised in Clay.
  C. Counts, 139:Jun/Jul85-52
Swenson, M. New and Selected Things Taking Place.
  S. Birkerts, 472:Spring/Summer/Fall/Winter85-317
Swift, G. Waterland.* (French title: Le Pays des eaux.)
  A. Bony, 98:Jun-Jul85-639
  C. Jordis, 450(NRF):Apr85-105
Swift, J. The Complete Poems.* (P. Rogers, ed)
  C. Fabricant, 301(JEGP):Jul85-442
  N. Wood, 83:Spring85-108
Swift, J. The Dark Path of Our Names.
  W. Pavlich, 448:Vol23No3-135
"Jonathan Swift." (A. Ross and D. Woolley, eds)
  P. Danchin, 189(EA):Apr-Jun86-216
  566:Autumn85-77
Swiggers, P. Les conceptions linguistiques des Encyclopédistes.
  G. Kleiber, 553(RLiR):Jul-Dec85-455
  J. Leopold, 350:Mar86-205
Swinburne, R. Faith and Reason.*
  R.M. Adams, 449:Dec85-626
  D.J. Casey, 258:Jun86-215
Swinburne, R., ed. Space, Time and Causality.*
  D.H. Mellor, 518:Oct85-243
  G. Schlesinger, 393(Mind):Jan85-144
Swinden, P. The English Novel of History and Society, 1940-1980.
  M. Casserley, 617(TLS):7Mar86-258
  J. Hynes, 659(ConL):Spring86-90
  R.C. Schweik, 395(MFS):Summer85-365
  295(JML):Nov85-429
Swinfen, A. In Defense of Fantasy.
  L. Basney, 395(MFS):Winter85-848
Swing, E.S. Bilingualism and Linguistic Segregation in the Schools of Brussels.
  A. Langenakens, 355(LSoc):Jun85-282
Swir, A. Happy as a Dog's Tail.
  E. Hoffman, 441:16Feb86-14
Switten, M.L. The Cansos of Raimon de Miraval.
  N. Wilkins, 617(TLS):29Aug86-950
Swope, M. and W.H. Kerr, eds. American Classic.
  P-L. Adams, 61:Aug86-92
Sykes, C. Four Studies in Loyalty.
  617(TLS):25Apr86-459
Sylvan, M. Anne Charlotte Leffler.
  M.G. Lokrantz, 172(Edda):1985/5-322
Sylvester, E.J. Target: Cancer.
  H. Schmeck, 441:23Feb86-23
Sylvestre, P-F. Bougrerie en Nouvelle France.
  A. van den Hoven, 628(UWR):Fall-Winter85-94
"Symbolism in Polish Painting 1890-1914."
  A.S. Ciechanowiecki, 39:Feb85-137

Symcox, G. Victor Amadeus II.*
  J. Black, 161(DUJ):Jun84-284
  D. Thompson, 278(IS):Vol40-143
Symington, N. The Analytic Experience.
  P. Lomas, 617(TLS):31Oct86-1212
Symington, R. - see Fairley, B.
Symonds, J.A. The Memoirs of John Addington Symonds.* (P. Grosskurth, ed)
  42(AR):Summer85-369
Symonds, R. Oxford and Empire.
  A. Sykes, 617(TLS):28Nov86-1336
Symons, J. Bloody Murder.
  617(TLS):28Mar86-343
Symons, J. A Criminal Comedy.
  442(NY):3Feb86-106
Symons, J. The Criminal Comedy of the Contented Couple.
  T.J. Binyon, 617(TLS):25Apr86-454
Symons, J. Dashiell Hammett.*
  639(VQR):Summer85-80
Symons, J. A.J.A. Symons.
  617(TLS):15Aug86-899
Symons, T.H.B. and J.E. Page. Some Questions of Balance.*
  B. Neatby, 298:Spring85-153
Symons, V.J. Ch'ing Ginseng Management.
  A.Y-C. Lui, 302:Vol21No1-106
Synge, J.M. The Collected Letters of John Millington Synge.* (Vol 1) (A. Saddlemyer, ed)
  A.M. Gibbs, 402(MLR):Jan85-135
  H. Hunt, 610:Summer85-186
  H.F. Salerno, 177(ELT):Vol28No4-442
Synge, J.M. The Collected Letters of John Millington Synge.* (Vol 2) (A. Saddlemyer, ed)
  B. Dolan, 305(JIL):Jan85-51
  H. Hunt, 610:Summer85-186
  H.F. Salerno, 177(ELT):Vol28No4-442
  295(JML):Nov85-561
Sytova, A. and others, eds. The Lubok.
  D.E. Farrell, 550(RusR):Oct85-407
Syv, P. Danske Ordsproge. (Vol 1) (I. Kjaer and J.K. Sørensen, eds)
  C.S. Hale, 563(SS):Spring85-225
  U. Palmenfelt, 64(Arv):Vol39-220
Szambien, W. Jean-Nicholas-Louis Durand, 1760-1834.
  B. Bergdoll, 90:Jul85-464
Szanto, G. The Marriage of Heaven and Earth.
  A. Doueihi, 469:Vol 11No2-122
Szarkowski, J. and M.M. Hambourg. The Work of Atget.* (Vol 3)
  M. Nesbit, 59:Mar85-132
Szarkowsky, J. Looking at Photographs.
  Y. Michaud, 98:Aug-Sep85-761
Szarmach, P.E., ed. Studies in Earlier Old English Prose.
  70:Mar/Apr86-123
Szarota, E.M., ed. Das Jesuitendrama im deutschen Sprachgebiet.* (Vols 1-3)
  N. Griffin and P. Skrine, 402(MLR):Oct85-981
Szechi, D. Jacobitism and Tory Politics 1710-14.*
  G.M. Townend, 566:Autumn85-92
Szemerényi, O. Einführung in die vergleichende Sprachwissenschaft. (2nd ed)
  J. Schildt, 682(ZPSK):Band38Heft4-436
  K.H. Schmidt, 685(ZDL):3/1985-357
Sziborsky, L. - see Schelling, F.W.J.

367

"The Talmud of the Land of Israel." (J. Neusner, trans)
S. Lieberman, 318(JAOS):Apr-Jun84-315
Tamargo, M.L. La narrativa de Bioy Casares.
R.S. Minc, 238:Dec85-786
Tamaro, B.F. - see Forlati Tamaro, B.
Tambiah, S.J. Culture, Thought and Social Action.
R. Stirrat, 617(TLS):24Jan86-92
Taminiaux, J. Dialectic and Difference. (J. Decker and R. Crease, eds and trans)
R. Cobb-Stevens, 543:Jun86-787
Taminiaux, J. Recoupements.
J. Colette, 192(EP):Jul-Sep85-427
T.J. Harrison, 543:Sep85-172
T'an Ssu-t'ung. An Exposition of Benevolence. (Chan Sin-wai, trans)
C-T. Hung, 293(JASt):Aug85-804
Tancke, G. Die italienischen Wörterbücher von den Anfängen bis zum Erscheinen des "Vocabolario degli Accademici della Crusca" (1612).
C. Marello, 547(RF):Band97Heft4-445
Tang, T.N. Journal of a Vietcong.
L.H. Tan, 617(TLS):28Feb86-223
Tang, T.N., with D. Chanoff and D.V. Toai. A Vietcong Memoir.*
639(VQR):Autumn85-118
Tani, S. The Doomed Detective.*
B. Benstock, 301(JEGP):Apr85-293
Tanizaki, J. Éloge de l'ombre.
J. Aeply, 450(NRF):Nov85-110
Tanizaki, J. Naomi.*
J. Burnham, 617(TLS):4Apr86-357
J. Mellors, 362:10Apr86-28
Tanizaki, J. Some Prefer Nettles.
J. Haylock, 364:Nov85-109
Tannen, D. Conversational Style.*
D. Good, 353:Vol23No1-161
Tannen, D. and M. Saville-Troike, eds. Perspectives on Silence.
P.K. Bock, 350:Sep86-731
Tannenbaum, L. Biblical Tradition in Blake's Early Prophecies.*
F. Mouret, 549(RLC):Jul-Sep85-351
M.J. Tolley, 591(SIR):Summer85-300
Tanner, N.P. The Church in Late Medieval Norwich: 1370-1532.
E. Colledge, 589:Oct85-1026
Tanner, T. Thomas Pynchon.*
B. McHale, 107(CRCL):Mar85-138
Tanner, T.A. Frank Waters.
W.D. Laird, 517(PBSA):Vol79No1-144
Tanner, W.E. and J.D. Bishop, eds. Rhetoric and Change.
W.F. Woods, 126(CCC):Feb85-106
Tanselle, T. - see Melville, H.
"Tao Te Ching." (D.C. Lau, trans)
R.G. Henricks, 293(JASt):Nov84-177
H.D. Roth, 485(PE&W):Apr85-213
Taper, B. Balanchine.* (3rd ed)
J.R. Acocella, 151:Mar85-96
M. Mudrick, 249(HudR):Autumn85-520
Taplin, O. - see Macleod, C.
Tapply, W.G. The Marine Corpse.
N. Callendar, 441:5Oct86-28
Tapscott, S. American Beauty.*
C. Clausen, 27(AL):Mar85-140
295(JML):Nov85-570

Tarán, L. Speusippus of Athens.*
M. Isnardi Parente, 53(AGP):Band67 Heft1-102
H.A.S. Tarrant, 122:Jan85-78
de Taranco, F.M.G.O. and others - see under Garín Ortiz de Taranco, F.M. and others
Taranovski, K. Knjiga o Mandeljštamu.
M.J. Lotman, 279:Vol29-133
Tarasti, E. Myth and Music.
J.H., 412:Aug/Nov83-310
Tarcov, N. Locke's Education for Liberty.
J.T., 185:Jan86-455
Tarczylo, T. Sexe et Liberté au Siècle des Lumières.
G.S. Rousseau, 173(ECS):Fall85-116
Tarkenton, F., with H. Resnicow. Murder at the Super Bowl.
N. Callendar, 441:16Nov86-38
Tarn, N. At the Western Gates. The Desert Mothers.
G. Economou, 703:No14-167
Tarnowski-Seidel, H. Arthur Schnitzler, "Flucht in die Finsternis."
W. Riemer, 221(GQ):Spring85-291
M. Swales, 402(MLR):Jan85-236
Tarot, R. - see Ulrich, A.
Tarrant, H. Scepticism or Platonism?
J. Barnes, 520:Vol30No2-216
Tarrant, R.J. - see Seneca
Tarraube, J. Montesquieu auteur dramatique.
J.G. Rosso, 535(RHL):Jan/Feb85-98
Tarrow, S. Exile from the Kingdom.
B. Stoltzfus, 395(MFS):Winter85-829
295(JML):Nov85-455
Tarshis, L. World Economy in Crisis.
E. Kierans, 529(QQ):Winter85-850
Taruskin, R. Opera and Drama in Russia as Preached and Practiced in the 1860s.*
H.Z., 412:Feb83-61
Tasso, T. Creation of the World. (G. Cipolla, ed)
D.A. Trafton, 276:Winter85-330
Tasso, T. Tasso's Dialogues.* (C. Lord and D.A. Trafton, eds and trans)
J.R. Woodhouse, 447(N&Q):Sep84-429
Tatchell, P. AIDS.
D. Widgery, 362:4Sep86-21
Tate, C. Black Women Writers at Work.*
B. Brown, 95(CLAJ);Mar86-378
Tate, D. Bravo Burning.
S. Laschever, 441:27Apr86-22
Tate, R.B., ed. Essays on Narrative Fiction in the Iberian Peninsula in Honour of Frank Pierce.*
G.A. Davies, 86(BHS):Apr85-191
Tatian. "Oratio ad Graecos" and Fragments.* (M. Whittaker, ed and trans)
J.J. Thierry, 394:Vol38fasc1/2-220
Tatlow, A. and Tat Wai Wong, eds. Brecht and East Asian Theatre.*
A. Hsia, 678(YCGL):No34-151
Sun Fengcheng and Zhang Yushu, 52:Band20Heft3-297
Tatum, S. Inventing Billy the Kid.
R. Thacker, 298:Spring85-161
Tauber, W. Der Wortschatz des Hans Sachs.* (Vols 1 and 2)
F.G. Banta, 301(JEGP):Jul85-401
Tauber, W. - see Konrad von Haslau
Taubman, M. Gwen John.*
D. Thomas, 324:Jun86-468

369

Teichman, J. Illegitimacy.
  B. Baumrin, 449:Sep85-453
Teigen, P.M. Books, Manuscripts, and the
  History of Medicine.
  M.L. Russell, 470:Vol23-102
Teitelbaum, M.S. The British Fertility
  Decline.
  S.R. Johansson, 637(VS):Spring86-465
Teitelboim, V. Neruda.
  F. Alegria, 263(RIB):Vol35No4-470
Teitler, H.C. Notarii en Exceptores.
  T. Honoré, 123:Vol35No2-405
Teiwes, F.C. Leadership, Legitimacy, and
  Conflict in China.
  E. Friedman, 293(JASt):Aug85-825
Tejera, V. History as a Human Science.
  T.R. Spivey, 651(WHR):Summer85-189
Teleky, R., ed. The Oxford Book of French-
  Canadian Short Stories.*
  E. Dansereau, 102(CanL):Winter84-131
  K. Mezei, 677(YES):Vol 15-253
Teller, W.M. Consider Poor I.
  W. Howarth, 432(NEQ):Sep85-484
Telles, L.F. - see under Fagundes Telles,
  L.
Teloh, H. The Development of Plato's Meta-
  physics.*
  J.N. Moline, 53(AGP):Band67Heft3-296
Telotte, J.P. Dreams of Darkness.
  R.E. Wood, 500:Spring/Summer86-84
Temperli, S. Siegfried Lang (1887-1970).
  P. Skrine, 402(MLR):Jul85-764
  M. Winkler, 133:Band17Heft3/4-367
Temple, G. 100 Years of Mathematics.
  G.H. Moore, 556:Summer85-89
Temple, W. William Temple's Analysis of
  Sir Philip Sidney's "Apology for Poetry."
  (J. Webster, ed and trans)
  James Fitzmaurice, 568(SCN):Spring-
    Summer85-28
  J.R. Henderson, 604:Spring-Summer85-36
Tengström, S. Die Toledotformel und die
  Literarische Struktur der priesterlichen
  Erweiterungschichte im Pentateuch.
  B.O. Long, 318(JAOS):Oct-Dec84-770
Tennant, E., ed. The Adventures of Robina.
  D. Nokes, 617(TLS):24Jan86-81
  K.C. O'Brien, 362:27Feb86-27
Tennant, E. Black Marina.*
  J. Mellors, 364:Jul85-97
Tennant, E. Woman Beware Woman.* Queen
  of Stones.
  P. Lewis, 565:Winter84/85-42
Tennant, R. Joseph Conrad.
  T.C. Moser, 637(VS):Winter85-329
Tennenhouse, L., ed. Two Tudor Interludes.
  J. Wasson, 130:Summer85-183
Tennyson, A. Idylls of the King.* (J.M.
  Gray, ed)
  S. Shatto, 541(RES):Aug85-444
Tennyson, A. Tennyson's "Maud." (S.
  Shatto, ed)
  A.S. Byatt, 617(TLS):14Nov86-1274
Tennyson, G.B. Victorian Devotional
  Poetry.
  T. Winnifrith, 677(YES):Vol 15-329
Tennyson, G.B. - see Carlyle, T.
Teramoto, M. Die Psalmmotettendrucke des
  Johannes Petrejus (gedruckt 1538-1542).
  C. Meyer, 537:Vol71No1/2-200
de Terán, L.S. The Bay of Silence.
  L. Chamberlain, 617(TLS):23May86-554
    [continued]

[continuing]
  E. Fishel, 441:24Aug86-18
  J. Mellors, 362:29May86-25
de Terán, L.S. The High Place.
  D. Davis, 362:10Apr86-27
Terkel, S. Chicago.
  442(NY):8Dec86-155
Terkel, S. Talking to Myself.
  T. Parker, 617(TLS):7Mar86-243
Terlecki, T. Stanisław Wyspiański.
  J.T. Baer, 497(PolR):Vol30No4-454
Terrall, R. Wrap It in Flags.
  J. House, 441:12Jan86-16
  442(NY):17Feb86-102
Terras, V. F.M. Dostoevsky.*
  W.J. Leatherbarrow, 402(MLR):Jan85-249
  T. Pachmuss, 574(SEEJ):Spring85-104
Terras, V., ed. Handbook of Russian Liter-
  ature.
  42(AR):Summer85-369
  295(JML):Nov85-369
Terras, V. Vladimir Mayakovsky.
  J. Graffy, 575(SEER):Jul85-443
Terrell, C.F. A Companion to "The Cantos"
  of Ezra Pound.* (Vol 2)
  295(JML):Nov85-543
Terry, B. The Watermelon Kid.
  G.C., 569(SR):Spring85-xxxix
Terry, R.C. Victorian Popular Fiction,
  1860-80.*
  W. Hughes, 637(VS):Summer85-707
Terry, S.M. Poland's Place in Europe.
  R.A. Walawender, 497(PolR):Vol30No2-
    215
Terry, S.M., ed. Soviet Policy in Eastern
  Europe.*
  639(VQR):Winter85-21
Tertz, A. - see under Siniavski, A.
Tervooren, H. and H. Moser - see von Kraus,
  C.
Terwiel, B.J. A History of Modern Thai-
  land, 1767-1942.
  J.J. Wright, 293(JASt):May85-682
Terzani, T. Behind the Forbidden Door.
  F. Butterfield, 441:17Aug86-23
  D. Murphy, 617(TLS):20Jun86-674
Terzian, P. OPEC.
  P. McDonald, 617(TLS):25Jul86-820
Tesauro, P., ed. Libro de miseria de omne.
  J.C. Temprano, 240(HR):Autumn85-477
Tesch, G. Linguale Interferenz.
  H.H. Munske, 685(ZDL):2/1985-266
Tessin, C.G. Tableaux de Paris et de la
  cour de France 1739-1742. (G. von
  Proschwitz, ed)
  Y. Coirault, 535(RHL):Nov/Dec85-1066
  P. Larthomas, 209(FM):Oct85-249
  D. Williams, 402(MLR):Oct85-941
Tessonneau, R. - see Joubert, J.
Tetel, M. Lectures Scéviennes.*
  J.C. Nash, 188(ECr):Summer85-97
Tétreault, M.A. Revolution in the World
  Petroleum Market.
  P. McDonald, 617(TLS):25Jul86-820
Tetzeli von Rosador, K. - see Shakespeare,
  W.
Teubner, C. and S.G. Schonfeldt. The
  Great Dessert Book.
  W. and C. Cowen, 639(VQR):Autumn85-141
Teutonicus, J. - see under Johannes Teu-
  tonicus

Teveth, S.  Ben-Gurion and the Palestinian Arabs.*
  C. Townshend, 617(TLS):23May86-549
Teyssèdre, B.  Naissance du Diable (de Babylone aux grottes de la Mer Morte) [et] Le Diable et l'Enfer au temps de Jésus.
  G. Lascault, 450(NRF):Jun85-76
Tgahrt, R. and others.  Weltliteratur: Die Lust am Übersetzen im Jahrhundert Goethes.*
  H. Eichner, 406:Winter85-469
Thackara, J. and S. Jane.  New British Design.
  362:4Dec86-32
Thacker, C.  The Wildness Pleases.*
  L.W.B. Brockliss, 366:Spring85-145
Thaden, E.C.  Russia's Western Borderlands, 1710-1870.
  S.R. Burant, 497(PolR):Vol30No4-456
Thalberg, I.  Misconceptions of Mind and Freedom.
  R. Kirk, 518:Jul85-164
Thalmann, W.G.  Conventions of Form and Thought in Early Greek Epic Poetry.*
  W. Donlan, 124:May-Jun86-340
  W.C. Scott, 121(CJ):Feb/Mar86-258
Thaning, K.  Grundtvig.
  P.M. Mitchell, 563(SS):Summer85-352
Tharpe, J.  Walker Percy.
  V.A. Makowsky, 536(Rev):Vol7-305
Tharpe, J., ed.  Walker Percy.
  V.A. Makowsky, 536(Rev):Vol7-305
Thavenius, C.  Referential Pronouns in English Conversation.*
  X. Dekeyser, 38:Band103Heft1/2-131
Thayer, C.G.  Shakespearean Politics.*
  M.B. Rose, 536(Rev):Vol7-19
  R.H. West, 219(GaR):Summer85-453
"Le Théâtre."
  J. Moss, 102(CanL):Fall85-145
Theil, U.  Lockes Theorie der personalen Identität.
  G. Gawlick, 706:Band17Heft1-124
Theiler, W. - see Posidonius
Thelander, M., ed.  Talspråksforskning i Norden.
  S.R. Smith, 563(SS):Winter85-76
Thélot, J.  Poétique d'Yves Bonnefoy.*
  A.O. Sullivan, 207(FR):Mar86-625
Themerson, S.  Logic, Labels and Flesh.
  G. Turcotte, 616:Fall/Winter85-59
Themerson, S.  The Mystery of the Sardine.
  W. Blythe, 441:28Dec86-18
  N. Shack, 617(TLS):21Feb86-199
Theocritus.  Idylls and Epigrams.  (D. Hine, trans)
  D.M. Halperin, 676(YR):Summer85-587
Theodoridis, C., ed.  Photii Patriarchae Lexicon.  (Vol 1)
  J.J. Keaney, 24:Fall85-388
  C.J. Ruijgh, 394:Vol38fasc3/4-426
"Théories du cinéma."
  C.P. James, 207(FR):Dec85-309
Thériault, M.J.  Les Demoiselles de Numidie.
  N.B. Bishop, 102(CanL):Fall85-166
Thério, A.  Marie-Eve, Marie-Eve.
  E-M. Kroller, 102(CanL):Winter84-129
Theroux, P.  Half Moon Street.*
  W.H. Pritchard, 249(HudR):Spring85-125
Theroux, P.  The Imperial Way.
  442(NY):6Jan86-86

Theroux, P.  O-Zone.
  E. Korn, 617(TLS):31Oct86-1224
  A.R. Lee, 362:23Oct86-24
  S.F. Schaeffer, 441:14Sep86-12
Thesen, S.  Confabulations.
  S. Scobie, 376:Sep85-145
Thesen, S.  Holding the Pose.*
  L. Weir, 102(CanL):Winter84-105
Thesing, W.B.  The London Muse.*
  C. Miles, 366:Spring85-149
  W.S. Peterson, 396(ModA):Summer85-261
Theuerkauff, C.  Elfenbein Sammlung Reiner Winkler.
  M. Estella, 48:Apr-Jun85-168
Theunissen, M.  Selbstverwirklichung und Allgemeinheit.
  J. Habermas, 384:Sep/Oct85-905
Thevet, A.  Cosmographie de Levant.  (F. Lestringant, ed)
  M.J. Heath, 208(FS):Oct85-457
Thévoz, M.  Le Corps peint.
  F. de Mèredieu, 450(NRF):Feb85-109
Thiebaux, M.  Ellen Glasgow.
  M.R. Winchell, 106:Spring85-73
von Thiel, H.  Iliaden und Ilias.*
  W.J. Verdenius, 394:Vol38fasc3/4-397
Thiel, U.  Lockes Theorie der personalen Identität.*
  B. Doniela, 63:Dec85-573
Thiele, S.  Die Verwicklungen im Denken Wittgensteins.
  R. Sokolowski, 543:Dec84-408
  R. Wimmer, 489(PJGG):Band92Heft2-415
van Thienen, G. and others, comps.  Incunabula in Dutch Libraries.
  N. Barker, 78(BC):Spring85-113
Thierry, A. - see d'Aubigné, A.
Thiesse, A-M.  Le Roman du quotidien.
  A.T. Harrison, 207(FR):May86-1012
Thiher, A.  Words in Reflection.*
  C. Touloudis, 207(FR):Mar86-222
  R.R. Wilson, 107(CRCL):Jun85-292
  295(JML):Nov85-429
Thikian, A. and M. Armand.  Le Mouvement ouvrier bulgare.
  R.J. Crampton, 575(SEER):Oct85-638
wa Thiong'o, N.  Barrel of a Pen.
  P. Nazareth, 538(RAL):Summer85-276
Thiry, C.  Le "Jeu de l'Etoile" du manuscrit de Cornillon (Liège).
  K. Schoell, 547(RF):Band97Heft2/3-297
Thistlewood, D.  Herbert Read.
  P. Meeson, 89(BJA):Winter85-71
Tholfsen, T.R.  Ideology and Revolution in Modern Europe.
  639(VQR):Summer85-82
Thom, M. - see Contejean, C.
Thomas, A.  Intertidal Life.
  L. Hutcheon, 102(CanL):Fall85-94
  C. Rooke, 376:Jun85-129
Thomas, C. and J. Lennox.  William Arthur Deacon.*
  S. Neuman, 102(CanL):Summer85-176
Thomas, C., with G. Tremlett.  Caitlin.
  J. Kelly, 617(TLS):21Nov86-1299
Thomas, D.  Belladonna.
  W.J. Smith, 283:Winter84/85-13
Thomas, D.  The Collected Letters of Dylan Thomas.*  (P. Ferris, ed)
  R. Craft, 453(NYRB):24Apr86-15
  J. Haffenden, 493:Feb86-52
  C. Rawson, 617(TLS):2May86-475

Thompson, G.A., Jr.  Key Sources in Compar-
ative and World Literature.*
  G.R. Kaiser, 52:Band20Heft1-76
  J. Voisine, 549(RLC):Jul-Sep85-319
  J.K. Wikeley, 107(CRCL):Sep85-471
Thompson, G.R. - see Poe, E.A.
Thompson, J.  Hardcore.
  N. Callendar, 441:30Nov86-20
Thompson, J.  Language in Wycherley's
Plays.
  C. Kallendorf, 568(SCN):Fall85-35
  J.A. Vance, 173(ECS):Winter85/86-293
Thompson, J.  White Biting Dog.
  R.P. Knowles, 198:Spring85-84
  P. Walsh, 108:Winter85-143
Thompson, J.B.  Critical Hermeneutics.
  P.L. Bourgeois, 543:Jun85-912
Thompson, J.B.  Studies in the Theory of
Ideology.
  S.S., 185:Jan86-442
Thompson, J.C. and R.F. Vidmer.  Adminis-
trative Science and Politics in the USSR
and the United States.
  M.R. Beissinger, 550(RusR):Jan85-76
Thompson, K.  Eisenstein's "Ivan the
Terrible."
  G. Pirog, 574(SEEJ):Summer85-213
Thompson, K.  Exporting Entertainment.
  L. Braudy, 18:May86-59
Thompson, K.W., ed.  Moral Dimensions of
American Foreign Policy.
  T.W.P., 185:Apr86-671
Thompson, L.  Stig Dagerman.
  G.C. Schoolfield, 563(SS):Winter85-98
Thompson, L.  The Political Mythology of
Apartheid.*
  J. Levine, 676(YR):Summer86-610
Thompson, M.  All My Lives.
  L. Jones, 49:Oct85-127
Thompson, M.  Rubbish Theory.
  J. Culler, 153:Fall85-2
Thompson, R.H.  The Return from Avalon.
  L. Basney, 395(MFS):Winter85-848
  R. Dwyer, 561(SFS):Nov85-335
Thompson, S.  Wild Bananas.
  S. Vogan, 441:26Jan86-20
  442(NY):24Feb86-104
Thomsen, C.W.  Das englische Theater der
Gegenwart.
  B. Schulte-Middelich, 38:Band103
  Heft1/2-246
Thomson, A.  Materialism and Society in
the Mid-Eighteenth Century.
  D. Beeson, 208(FS):Apr85-213
Thomson, B.  The Post Impressionists.
  90:Aug85-545
Thomson, D.  Renaissance Paris.*
  W. Prinz, 683:Band48Heft4-573
Thomson, D.  Suspects.*
  G. Brown, 707:Summer85-226
Thomson, D.S., ed.  The Companion to
Gaelic Scotland.
  D.E. Meek, 588(SSL):Vol20-298
  B. Ó Cuív, 112:Vol 16-215
Thomson, J.  The Dark Stream.
  M. Laski, 362:3Jul86-32
Thomson, J.  The Seasons.*  (J. Sambrook,
ed)
  C.J. Rawson, 402(MLR):Apr85-428
Thomson, J.A.F.  The Transformation of
Medieval England, 1370-1529.
  M.J. Tucker, 589:Jul85-755

Thomson, J.M., ed.  Musical Delights.
  K. Spence, 415:Apr85-226
Thomson, P.  Shakespeare's Theatre.*
  A. Brissenden, 541(RES):Aug85-414
  R. Kift, 157:No157-51
Thomson, P. and G. Salgãdo.  The Everyman
Companion to the Theatre.
  S. Wall, 617(TLS):10Oct86-1132
Thomson, R.  Seurat.*
  E. Cowling, 617(TLS):28Mar86-323
Thomson, V.  A Virgil Thomson Reader.*
  T. Hathaway, 529(QQ):Summer85-328
Thomson, W.R.  The Latin Writings of John
Wyclyf.
  S. Wenzel, 589:Apr85-492
Thon, N., ed.  Quellenbuch zur Geschichte
der orthodoxen Kirche.
  H. Röhling, 688(ZSP):Band45Heft1-199
Thong, H.S. - see Du, N.
Thoreau, H.D.  Thoreau in the Mountains.
(W. Howarth, ed)
  R.H. Du Pree, 577(SHR):Winter85-67
Thoreau, H.D.  A Week on the Concord and
Merrimack Rivers; Walden, or Life in the
Woods; The Maine Woods; Cape Cod.  (R.F.
Sayre, ed)
  D. Donoghue, 617(TLS):25Apr86-435
Thoreau, H.D.  The Writings of Henry D.
Thoreau.*  (Vol 1: Journal, 1837-1844.)
(E.H. Witherell and others, eds)
  L. Ziff, 402(MLR):Jul85-705
Thorn, F. and C. - see "Domesday Book"
Thorndike, J.  Anna Delaney's Child.
  S. Posesorski, 441:7Sep86-22
Thorne, C.  The Issue of War.*
  I. Buruma, 453(NYRB):13Mar86-3
Thorne, R.G., ed.  The House of Commons
1790-1820.
  N. Gash, 617(TLS):24Oct86-1181
Thornton, L.  Unbodied Hope.
  L.L. Doan, 395(MFS):Winter85-866
Thornton, P.  Authentic Decor.*
  D. Sutton, 39:Jul85-2
Thornton, R.  The Hewed Out Light.
  B. Whiteman, 529(QQ):Winter85-842
Thornton, R.K.R.  The Decadent Dilemma.*
  D.M.R. Bentley, 637(VS):Winter85-352
  R. Crawford, 447(N&Q):Dec84-539
Thornton, R.K.R. - see Clare, J.
Thornton, R.K.R. - see Gurney, I.
Thorp, R.  Rainbow Drive.
  D. Fitzpatrick, 441:30Nov86-22
Thorpe, J.D.  John Milton.*
  R. Lejosne, 189(EA):Apr-Jun86-212
  A.K. Nardo, 551(RenQ):Summer85-378
  D.M. Rosenberg, 115:Spring84-156
  A-L. Scoufos, 179(ES):Aug85-366
  P. Stevens, 627(UTQ):Spring85-285
Thorpe, M., ed.  Peter Pears.
  R. Smith, 607:Dec85-51
Thorslev, P.L., Jr.  Romantic Contraries.*
  S.C. Behrendt, 141:Fall85-418
  P.M.S. Dawson, 148:Summer85-67
  R.F. Gleckner, 340(KSJ):Vol34-172
  N. Hilton, 478:Oct85-232
Thoss, D. and U. Jenni - see Pächt, O.
"Three Lives of the Last Englishmen."  (M.
Swainton, trans)
  J.D.A. Ogilvy, 191(ELN):Mar86-64
Thrower, N.J.W., ed.  Sir Francis Drake
and the Famous Voyage, 1577-1580.*
  E.S. Donno, 551(RenQ):Autumn85-548

Thuillier, J. Peut-on parler d'un pein-
ture "pompier"?
    J-C. Lebensztejn, 98:Mar85-225
Thurin, E.I. Emerson as Priest of Pan.*
    J.S. Martin, 106:Summer85-205
Thurley, G. The Romantic Predicament.
    639(VQR):Winter85-14
Thurman, J. Karen Blixen.
    E. Cederborg, 172(Edda):1985/5-319
Thurman, J. Isak Dinesen.*
    R. Baker, 469:Vol 11No2-86
    W. Harmon, 577(SHR):Winter85-73
    J. Kramer, 453(NYRB):17Jul86-21
Thurow, L.C. The Zero-Sum Solution.*
    A. Hacker, 453(NYRB):13Feb86-35
Thurston, A.F. and B. Pasternak, eds. The
Social Sciences and Fieldwork in China.
    R. Stross, 293(JASt):Feb85-385
Thwaite, A. Edmund Gosse.*
    M.M. Harper, 177(ELT):Vol28No2-209
    M. Lago, 31(ASch):Spring85-272
    P. Lewis, 565:Spring85-43
    M. Stocker, 637(VS):Winter86-330
    295(JML):Nov85-487
    639(VQR):Winter85-12
Thwaite, A. Poetry Today.
    C. Rawson, 617(TLS):7Feb86-137
Tiberg, E. Zur Vorgeschichte des Livländ-
ischen Krieges.
    D. Kirby, 575(SEER):Oct85-598
Tichane, R. Ching-te-Chen.*
    "Skipjack," 463:Winter85/86-439
Tichy, E. Onomatopoetische Verbalbil-
dungen des Griechischen.
    F. Skoda, 555:Vol59fasc1-97
    E. Tucker, 123:Vol35No2-314
Tien, H-M., ed. Mainland China, Taiwan,
and U.S. Policy.
    W. Kirby, 293(JASt):Feb85-387
Tierney, F.M. - see Sangster, C.
Tierney, N. William Walton.*
    T. Bray, 410(M&L):Jul85-279
Tietz, M. and V. Kapp, eds. La Pensée
religieuse dans la littérature et la
civilisation du XVIIe siècle en France.
    C.M. Probes, 475:Vol 12No22-379
Tigay, J.H. The Evolution of the
Gilgamesh Epic.
    J.G. Westenholz, 318(JAOS):Apr-Jun84-
    370
Tihanyi, E. Prophecies Near the Speed of
Light.
    J. Ditsky, 628(UWR):Fall-Winter85-77
    G. Russell, 526:Summer85-89
    C. Wiseman, 102(CanL):Summer85-188
Tilghman, B.R. But is it Art?*
    P. Fuller, 90:Aug85-542
    R. Shusterman, 89(BJA):Summer85-285
Tilley, N.M. The R.J. Reynolds Tobacco
Company.
    639(VQR):Autumn85-117
Tillinghast, R. Our Flag Was Still There.
    J. Holden, 651(WHR):Summer85-155
    M. Jarman, 249(HudR):Summer85-334
    D.E. Stanford, 385(MQR):Summer86-607
    T. Swiss, 569(SR):Fall85-lxxix
    639(VQR):Summer85-97
Tilly, C. Big Structures, Large Processes,
Huge Comparisons.
    B.M.D., 185:Apr86-680
Tilly, C. The Contentious French.
    G. Rudé, 617(TLS):4Jul86-729
    A.B. Spitzer, 441:6Apr86-11

"Timarion." (B. Baldwin, trans)
    D.J. Constantelos, 124:May-Jun86-346
Timko, M., F. Kaplan and E. Guiliano - see
"Dickens Studies Annual"
Timms, E. Karl Kraus, Apocalyptic Sati-
rist.
    D.J. Enright, 453(NYRB):6Nov86-46
    J.P. Stern, 362:23Oct86-28
Timms, E. and D. Kelley, eds. Unreal City.
    J. Melmoth, 617(TLS):1Aug86-845
Timpanaro, S. Il socialismo di Edmondo De
Amicis.
    E. Saccone, 400(MLN):Jan85-184
Tinker, H., ed. Burma. (Vol 1)
    F.N. Trager, 293(JASt):Nov84-251
Tintner, A.R. The Museum World of Henry
James.
    N. Bradbury, 617(TLS):26Sep86-1078
Tippett, M. Art at the Service of War.
    D. Farr, 529(QQ):Autumn85-604
    J. O'Brian, 627(UTQ):Summer85-509
Tiptree, J., Jr. The Starry Rift.
    G. Jonas, 441:10Aug86-29
Tirro, F. - see "Medieval and Renaissance
Studies"
Tirso de Molina. La celosa de sí misma.
(S. Maurel, ed)
    P. Heugas, 92(BH):Jan-Jun84-250
Tiryakian, E.A. and R. Rogowski, eds. New
Nationalisms of the Developed West.
    B. Anderson, 617(TLS):28Mar86-333
Tisano, V. Concordanze lemmatizzate delle
poesie in dialetto tursitano di Albino
Pierro.
    C. Muller, 552(RLiR):Jul-Dec85-465
Tischler, B.L. An American Music.
    K. Gann, 441:7Sep86-23
Tismar, J. Das deutsche Kunstmärchen des
zwanzigsten Jahrhunderts.*
    W. Anthony, 400(MLN):Apr85-696
Tison-Braun, M. L'Introuvable Origine.*
    P. Jourdan, 535(RHL):Mar/Apr85-328
Tisserant, J-M. - see Swedenborg, E.
Tissoni Benvenuti, A. and M.P. Mussini
Sacchi, eds. Teatro del Quattrocento.*
    A. Stäuble, 228(GSLI):Vol 162fasc518-
    276
Titley, N.M. Miniatures from Turkish Manu-
scripts.
    R. Hillenbrand, 59:Jun85-265
Titon, J.T., ed. Worlds of Music.
    L.V. Shumway, 187:Spring/Summer86-355
Titone, R. and M. Danesi. Applied Psycho-
linguistics.
    E. Bialystok, 399(MLJ):Winter85-425
Tittler, J. Narrative Irony in the Contem-
porary Spanish-American Novel.
    F. Burgos, 552(REH):Jan85-140
    D.W. Foster, 238:May85-318
    J.J. Hassett, 240(HR):Autumn85-515
Tjäder, J-O. Die nichtliterarischen lat-
einischen Papyri Italiens aus der Zeit
445-700. (Vol 2)
    J.D. Thomas, 123:Vol35No1-222
Tjulpanow, S.I. Erinnerungen an deutsche
Freunde und Genossen.
    I. Henker, 654(WB):5/1985-877
Toai, D.V. and D. Chanoff. The Vietnamese
Gulag.
    J.G. Dunne, 453(NYRB):25Sep86-25
    R. Shaplen, 441:13Jul86-17
Tobin, D.N. The Presence of the Past.*
    R.Z. Temple, 536(Rev):Vol7-329

Toby, R.P.   State and Diplomacy in Early
   Modern Japan.*
   R. Innes, 293(JASt):Feb85-408
Tocanne, B.   L'Idée de Nature en France
   dans la seconde moitié du XVIIe siècle.
   R. Behrens, 224(GRM):Band35Heft2-238
de Tocqueville, A.   Écrits sur le système
   pénitentiaire en France et à l'étranger.
   (M. Perrot, ed)
   J. Duvignaud, 450(NRF):May85-99
de Tocqueville, A.   Alexis de Tocqueville:
   Selected Letters on Politics and
   Society.*   (R. Boesche, ed)
   B.J.S., 185:Jul86-906
Toda, H., ed.   Saddharmapuṇḍarīkasūtra.
   O. von Hinüber, 259(IIJ):Apr85-137
Todd, J.   Jane Austen.*
   B. Roth, 594:Summer85-218
Todd, J., ed.   A Dictionary of British and
   American Women Writers 1660-1800.*
   F. Rosslyn, 97(CQ):Vol 14No3-274
Todd, L.   Modern Englishes.*
   P. Poussa, 439(NM):1985/1-140
Todd, O.   Jacques Brel.
   J. Abrate, 207(FR):Mar86-633
   E. Cameron, 364:Jun85-83
Todd, R.L.   Mendelssohn's Musical Educa-
   tion.*
   J-A. Ménétrier, 537:Vol71No1/2-206
   D. Seaton, 143:Issue37/38-224
Todorov, T.   Mikhail Bakhtin.*
   D. Donoghue, 533:Fall85-107
   J. Frank, 453(NYRB):23Oct86-56
   W.G. Regier, 223:Spring85-74
   P.S. Yaeger, 659(ConL):Summer86-246
Todorov, T.   The Conquest of America.*
   (French title: La Conquête de
   l'Amérique.)
   N. Le Coat, 188(ECr):Fall85-96
Todorov, T.   French Literary Theory Today.
   J. Beck, 545(RPh):Nov84-247
   M. Grimaud, 567:Vol58No1/2-151
Todorov, T.   Introduction to Poetics.*
   T.E. Morgan, 567:Vol57No1/2-125
Todorov, T.   Symbolism and Interpretation.
   S. Briosi, 603:Vol9No3-449
   G. Prince, 478:Oct85-241
Todorov, T.   Theories of the Symbol.*
   (French title: Théories du symbole.)
   E. Cobley, 376:Sep85-149
Todorović-Strähl, P. and O. Lurati, eds.
   Märchen aus dem Tessin.
   R. Schenda, 196:Band26Heft1/2-198
Togeby, K.   Grammaire française, I.
   T.J. Cox, 207(FR):May86-1017
du Toit, A. and H. Giliomee, eds.   Afri-
   kaner Political Thought.   (Vol 1)
   G.M. McSheffrey, 529(QQ):Spring85-228
Toivainen, J.   Inflectional Affixes Used
   by Finnish-Speaking Children Aged 1-3
   Years.
   T. Randoja, 350:Mar86-228
Tokaji, A.   Mozgalom és Hivatal.
   L. Kürti, 187:Spring/Summer86-367
Tokarczyk, R.   Prawa wierne naturze.
   W.J. Wagner, 497(PolR):Vol30No3-301
Tolkien, J.R.R.   The Monsters and the
   Critics and Other Essays.   (C. Tolkien,
   ed)
   R.L. Thomson, 447(N&Q):Sep84-412

Tolkien, J.R.R.   The Old English "Exodus."*
   (J. Turville-Petre, ed)
   W.G. Busse, 38:Band103Heft1/2-168
   A.M. Lucas, 382(MAE):1985/2-288
   A.H. Olsen, 179(ES):Apr85-169
Tolle, G.J.   Human Nature Under Fire.
   P.W. Zagorski, 389(MQ):Winter86-260
Tolley, A.T.   The Poetry of the Forties.
   W. Scammell, 617(TLS):2May86-476
Tolochko, P.P.   Drevnii Kiev.
   T.S. Noonan, 550(RusR):Jan85-101
Tolstoi, A.   Aelita.
   G. Benford, 441:2Feb86-9
Tolstoy, I.   James Clerk Maxwell.
   D.B. Wilson, 637(VS):Spring85-539
Tolstoy, L.   Childhood, Adolescence, Youth.
   (F. Solasko, trans)   Tales of Sevastopol;
   The Cossacks.   (R. Daglish and J. Fein-
   berg, trans)
   G.R. Jahn, 399(MLJ):Spring85-104
Tolstoy, L.N.   Tolstoy's Diaries.   (R.F.
   Christian, ed and trans)
   J. Bayley, 441:9Feb86-14
   H. Gifford, 617(TLS):14Feb86-155
   J. Updike, 442(NY):20Oct86-116
Tolstoy, N.   The Minister and the Massa-
   cres.
   R. Knight, 617(TLS):13Jun86-639
   P. Whitehead, 362:22May86-30
Tolstoya, S.   The Diaries of Sofia Tol-
   stoya.*   (O.A. Golinenko and others,
   eds and trans)
   P-L. Adams, 61:Apr86-131
   J. Bayley, 441:9Feb86-14
   A. Fitzlyon, 364:Feb86-94
   R. Görner, 176:Jun86-44
   V.L. Smith, 617(TLS):10Jan86-42
   442(NY):13Jan86-86
Toma, R.   Epistemă, ideologie, roman.
   F. Courriol, 549(RLC):Jul-Sep85-345
Tomalin, C. - see Mansfield, K.
Toman, J.   Wortsyntax.
   G.E. Booij, 361:Mar85-260
   S. Wolff, 660(Word):Apr85-83
Tombalani, M.   Bronzi figurati etruschi,
   italici, paleoveneti e romani del museo
   provinciale di Torcello.
   A. Hus, 555:Vol59fasc1-162
Tomberlin, J.E., ed.   Agent, Language, and
   the Structure of the World.*
   W. Barthelemy, 154:Autumn85-570
Tomes, N.   A Generous Confidence.
   C.L. Krasnick, 529(QQ):Autumn85-626
   M. Neve, 617(TLS):28Mar86-335
Tomin, Z.   Stalin's Shoe.
   C. Rumens, 617(TLS):31Jan86-113
Tomkies, M.   Out of the Wild.
   S. Mills, 617(TLS):21Mar86-314
Tomlin, E.W.F.   In Search of St. Piran.
   R.N. Bailey, 447(N&Q):Jun84-255
Tomlinson, C.   Collected Poems.
   M. Edwards, 617(TLS):21Mar86-308
   L. MacKinnon, 493:Oct85-55
   J. Mole, 176:Nov86-60
   R. Swigg, 364:Nov85-77
Tomlinson, C.   Eden.
   M. Edwards, 617(TLS):21Mar86-308
Tomlinson, C.   Notes from New York and
   Other Poems.*
   J. Saunders, 565:Autumn85-73
Tomlinson, C.   Poetry and Metamorphosis.
   M. Schiralli, 289:Fall85-123

[continued]

Trescases, P. Le Franglais: vingt ans
après.*
H. Ossipov, 207(FR):Apr86-838
Trethewey, E. Dreaming of Rivers.
K. Meadwell, 102(CanL):Summer85-140
D. Richards, 198:Summer85-104
Trevelyan, R. The Fortress.
617(TLS):31Jan86-127
Trevor, W. Fools of Fortune.*
G. Davenport, 569(SR):Spring85-321
Trevor, W. The News from Ireland.
P. Craig, 617(TLS):11Apr86-382
J. Fowles, 61:Aug86-89
M. Hulse, 176:Sep/Oct86-60
J. Mellors, 362:29May86-25
E. Spencer, 441:8Jun86-14
R. Towers, 453(NYRB):26Jun86-32
Trevor, W. A Writer's Ireland.
S. Connelly, 174(Éire):Summer85-144
639(VQR):Winter85-29
Trevor-Roper, H. Hermit of Peking.
617(TLS):10Oct86-1147
Trevor-Roper, H. Renaissance Essays.*
R.J.W. Evans, 453(NYRB):30Jan86-29
442(NY):13Jan86-86
Tribble, E. - see Pearsall Smith, L.
Tribe, I.M. Mountaineer Jamboree.
F.W. Childrey, Jr., 585(SoQ):Spring86-
89
Tribe, L.H. Constitutional Choices.*
G. Marshall, 617(TLS):18Apr86-410
Triem, E. New As a Wave.
M. Cary, 134(CP):Vol 18No1/2-141
J. Newman, 448:Vol23No3-116
Trifonov, Y. The Old Man.*
639(VQR):Spring85-61
Trigg, R. The Shaping of Man.
S.R.L. Clark, 483:Jul85-411
Trigg, R. Understanding Social Science.
R. Harré, 617(TLS):11Apr86-399
Trigger, B.G. and others. Ancient Egypt.
S.E. Sidebotham, 124:Jan-Feb86-193
Trimpi, W. Muses of One Mind.
V. Farenga, 124:Sep-Oct85-48
O.B. Hardison, Jr., 551(RenQ):Spring85-
157
M. Heath, 123:Vol35No1-195
D.G. Marshall, 481(PQ):Summer85-421
B.R. Rees, 303(JoHS):Vol 105-197
Trinkaus, C. The Scope of Renaissance
Humanism.
J. D'Amico, 539:Nov85-281
T.G.G., 278(IS):Vol40-124
D. Hay, 551(RenQ):Autumn85-511
Triphiodorus. Triphiodore, "La prise
d'Ilion."* (B. Gerlaud, ed and trans)
Triphiodorus, "Ilii Excidium."* (H.
Livrea, ed)
P. Chuvin, 555:Vol59fasc1-125
Tripp, J. Passing Through.
T. Curtis, 493:Feb86-62
S. O'Brien, 617(TLS):23May86-548
Tripp, R.P., Jr., ed and trans. More
about the Fight with the Dragon.
D.G. Calder, 589:Jul85-755
H. Schabram, 38:Band103Heft3/4-445
Tristan, F. Peregrinations of a Pariah.
(J. Hawkes, ed and trans)
617(TLS):10Oct86-1147
Tristan, F. The Workers' Union. (B.
Livingston, ed and trans)
S.P. Conner, 446(NCFS):Fall-
Winter85/86-191

Troinitskii, A. The Serf Population in
Russia, According to the 10th National
Census.
O. Crisp, 575(SEER):Apr85-317
Troitskii, S.M. Rossiia v XVIII veke.
C.S. Leonard, 550(RusR):Jul85-297
Troll, C.W. - see "Islam in India"
Trollope, A. The Complete Short Stories.*
(Vols 1-5) (B.J.S. Breyer, ed)
F.G. Navakas, 405(MP):Nov85-172
Trollope, A. The Letters of Anthony Trol-
lope.* (N.J. Hall, ed)
J. Carlisle, 639(VQR):Winter85-180
S. Gill, 541(RES):Aug85-446
D.D. Stone, 577(SHR):Summer85-288
Tromly, A. The Cover of the Mask.*
B.T. Gates, 637(VS):Autumn84-194
Trousdale, M. Shakespeare and the Rhetor-
icians.*
M. Coyle, 447(N&Q):Mar84-117
A. Drew-Bear, 702:Vol 17-298
H.F. Plett, 156(ShJW):Jahrbuch1985-253
J.W. Velz, 301(JEGP):Apr85-262
Trousson, R. Balzac disciple et juge de
Jean-Jacques Rousseau.*
D. Bellos, 208(FS):Jul85-349
J. Roussel, 535(RHL):Jul/Aug85-686
P. Stewart, 207(FR):Feb86-469
G. Woollen, 402(MLR):Jan85-171
Troxell, H.A. The Coinage of the Lycian
League.*
J. Zahle, 303(JoHS):Vol 105-242
Troy, N.J. The de Stijl Environment.*
R. Padovan, 46:Jan85-4
Troyat, H. Alexander of Russia.
A. McConnell, 550(RusR):Jan85-105
Troyat, H. Chekhov.*
J. Bayley, 453(NYRB):4Dec86-21
J. Koslow, 441:28Dec86-12
de Troyes, C. - see under Chrétien de
Troyes
Traux, C. Simply Delicious Cold Dishes.
W. and C. Cowen, 639(VQR):Autumn85-140
Trudgill, P. Accent, Dialect, and the
School.
A. Rowley, 685(ZDL):3/1985-396
Trudgill, P., ed. Applied Sociolinguis-
tics.
B. Spolsky, 350:Jun86-451
Trudgill, P. Coping with America.
S. Ferrell, 441:2Feb86-17
R. Hattersley, 617(TLS):7Feb86-147
Trudgill, P., ed. Language in the British
Isles.*
R.K.S. Macaulay, 350:Dec86-914
T.A. Watkins, 112:Vol 17-177
Trudgill, P. On Dialect.*
M. Görlach, 685(ZDL):3/1985-395
P. Mühlhäusler, 541(RES):Aug85-388
M. Yaeger-Dror, 350:Dec86-917
Trueblood, A.S. - see Machado, A.
Truett, J.C. and D.W. Lay. Land of Bears
and Honey.
L. Milazzo, 584(SWR):Winter85-130
Truffaut, L. Problèmes linguistiques de
traduction, allemand-français.
G. Thome, 72:Band222Heft2-434
Trujillo, A.L. - see under López Trujillo,
A.
Trujillo, R. - see Bello, A.
Truman, M. Murder in Georgetown.
N. Callendar, 441:10Aug86-23

Truman, M. Bess W. Truman.
K.S. Davis, 453(NYRB):4Dec86-28
H. Thomas, 441:13Apr86-9
Truscott, H., with H. Keller and F.
Schmidt. The Music of Franz Schmidt.
(Vol 1)
B. Northcott, 607:Mar85-38
D. Puffett, 415:Jul85-409
Trussler, S., ed. New Theatre Voices of
the Seventies.
A.E. Quigley, 397(MD):Sep85-500
Trusted, J. Free Will and Responsibility.
J.D., 185:Apr86-676
Trusted, J. An Introduction to the Philos-
ophy of Knowledge.
J. Harrison, 479(PhQ):Jan85-95
Trustram, M. Women of the Regiment.
G. Malmgreen, 637(VS):Summer86-624
Tryon, T. All That Glitters.
T. Nolan, 441:9Nov86-32
Trzebinski, E. The Kenya Pioneers.
R. Baldock, 617(TLS):31Jan86-107
Tsai, S-S.H. China and the Overseas
Chinese in the United States, 1868-1911.
E. Wickberg, 293(JASt):Aug85-829
Tsai, W-H. Patterns of Political Elite
Mobility in Modern China, 1912-1949.
R.K. Schoppa, 293(JASt):Aug85-830
Tsao, K-F. The Relationship Between
Scholars and Rulers in Imperial China.
L.D. Kessler, 293(JASt):Feb85-388
Tschudi, A. Chronicon Helveticum. (Pt 5)
(B. Stettler, comp)
R. Schenda, 196:Band26Heft1/2-200
Tschumi, R. La crise culturelle, ses cinq
siècles d'histoire et son dépassement.
J-M. Gabaude, 542:Jan-Mar85-66
Tsekourakis, D. Oi laikophilosophikes
pragmateies tou Ploutarchou.
A. Nikolaidis, 303(JoHS):Vol 105-193
Tshe-tan Zhabs-drung. Snyan-ngag me-long-
gi spyi-don sdeb-legs rig-pa'i 'char-sgo.
L.W.J. van der Kuijp, 259(IIJ):Jul85-
212
Tsopanakis, A.G. Homeric Researches.
P.V. Jones, 123:Vol35No2-377
Tsou, T. The Cultural Revolution and Post-
Mao Reform.
J.K. Fairbank, 453(NYRB):17Jul86-33
Tsoukalis, L., ed. Europe, America and
the World Economy.
S. Strange, 617(TLS):6Jun86-613
Tsu-yu, C. - see under Ch'en Tsu-yu
Tsuge, G., comp and trans. Anthology of
Sōkyoku and Jiuta Song Texts.
Y. Mitani, 187:Spring/Summer86-357
Tsuji, K. - see under Kiyoaki Tsuji
Tsukui, N. Ezra Pound and Japanese Noh
Plays.
Akiko Miyake, 468:Winter84-455
Ts'un-yan, L., with J. Minford - see under
Liu Ts'un-yan, with J. Minford
Tsung-i, J. and Tseng Hsien-t'ung - see
under Jao Tsung-i and Tseng Hsien-t'ung
Tsurumi, S. An Intellectual History of
Wartime Japan 1931-1945.
W.G. Beasley, 617(TLS):22Aug86-908
Tuan, Y-F. The Good Life.
D. Hall, 441:16Mar86-17
Tubb, J.N., ed. Palestine in the Bronze
and Iron Ages.
P.R.S. Moorey, 617(TLS):12Sep86-1010

Tucholsky, K. Castle Gripsholm.*
J. Mellors, 364:Dec85/Jan86-140
Tuck, A. Crown and Nobility 1272-1461.
N. Saul, 617(TLS):6Jun86-628
Tuck, R.C., ed. The Island Family Harris.
W. Baker, 102(CanL):Winter84-69
Tucker, B.M. Samuel Slater and the Ori-
gins of the American Textile Industry,
1790-1860.
T.W. Leavitt, 432(NEQ):Jun85-313
Tucker, E.F.J. Intruder into Eden.
L. Martines, 551(RenQ):Spring85-164
Tucker, G.H. Goodly Heritage.*
B. Roth, 594:Summer85-224
Tucker, L. Stephen and Bloom at Life's
Feast.*
A. Douglas, 305(JIL):May85-77
R.M. Kain, 395(MFS):Winter85-789
295(JML):Nov85-511
Tucker, N.B. Patterns in the Dust.
S.I. Levine, 293(JASt):May85-590
Tucker, P.H. Monet at Argenteuil.*
T. Shapiro, 207(FR):Apr86-825
Tucker, R.P. and J.F. Richards, eds.
Global Deforestation and the Nineteenth-
Century World Economy.
J.V. Thirgood, 293(JASt):Aug85-801
Tucker, R.W. and D.C. Hendrickson. The
Fall of the First British Empire.
L.D. Cress, 106:Fall85-307
P.D.G. Thomas, 83:Spring85-100
Tuetey, C.G. Classical Arabic Poetry.
A.F.L. Beeston, 617(TLS):29Aug86-950
Tugendhat, C. Making Sense of Europe.
J. Simpson, 362:23Jan86-33
Tugendhat, E. Traditional and Analytical
Philosophy.*
T.S. Champlin, 518:Jan85-29
R. Rorty, 311(JP):Dec85-720
Tullett, T. Clues to Murder.
P.D. James, 617(TLS):25Apr86-444
Tulpule, S.G. Classical Marāthī Litera-
ture.
E. Zelliot, 293(JASt):Nov84-241
Tumler, T. Der Tempusgebrauch der Ver-
gangenheit in der modernen italienischen
Prosa.
G. Lepschy, 545(RPh):Nov85-250
T'ung Shu-yeh. Ch'un-ch'iu Tso-chuan yen-
chiu.
J. Sailey, 318(JAOS):Jul-Sep84-529
Tunley, D. Harmony in Action. (2nd ed)
P. Standford, 415:Aug85-464
Tunnell, T. Crucible of Reconstruction.
639(VQR):Summer85-81
Tuohy, F. The Collected Stories.*
P. Lewis, 565:Spring85-43
Turbayne, C. - see Berkeley, G.
Turbet-Delof, G. - see Guilleragues, G.D.
Turcan, R. - see Firmicus
Turchetti, M. Concordia o tolleranza?
D.R. Kelley, 551(RenQ):Winter85-734
Turgenev, I.S. Stories and Poems in Prose.
(O. Shartse and others, trans)
G. Cox, 399(MLJ):Spring85-104
Turgenev, I.S. Turgenev's Letters.* (A.V.
Knowles, ed and trans) Turgenev Let-
ters.* (D. Lowe, ed and trans)
R.L. Jackson, 569(SR):Spring85-300
Turkle, S. The Second Self.*
M. Harney, 63:Dec85-520

Turnbull, G.  A Gathering of Poems 1950–
1980.
  J. Saunders, 565:Spring85–72
Turner, H.A. - see Wagener, O.
Turner, J.  Without God, Without Creed.*
  R.J. Neuhaus, 129:Apr86–76
Turner, J. and L. Emery, eds.  Perspec-
tives on Women in the 1980s.
  T. McCormack, 529(QQ):Summer85–429
Turner, J.A.  Kwang Tung or Five Years in
South China.
  R. Harris, 617(TLS):6Jun86–617
Turner, J.H. and D. Musick.  American
Dilemmas.
  J.L.H., 185:Jul86–916
Turner, L.  Voyage of a Different Kind.
  E. Jones, 298:Fall85–149
Turner, M.  Slaves and Missionaries.
  C.D. Rice, 637(VS):Winter86–338
Turner, R.V.  The English Judiciary in the
Age of Glanvill and Bracton, c. 1176–
1239.
  J. Sumption, 617(TLS):28Feb86–226
Turner, S.  Secrecy and Democracy.*
  Z. Steiner, 617(TLS):4Jul86–727
Turner, S. and R. Factor.  Max Weber and
the Dispute over Reason and Value.
  K.S., 185:Jul86–903
Turner, S. and B. Skiöld.  Handmade Paper
Today.*
  78(BC):Winter85–421
Turner, T.  The Diary of Thomas Turner
1754–1765.*  (D. Vasey, ed)
  S. Soupel, 189(EA):Apr–Jun86–220
Turner, V.  On the Edge of the Bush.
  G. Obeyesekere, 617(TLS):25Jul86–821
Turner, W.C. - see Mason, C.
"Turning the Tables."
  R. Grant, 324:May86–417
Turpin, C.  British Government and the
Constitution.
  G. Marshall, 617(TLS):7Mar86–241
Turpin, J.  John Hogan.
  P. Winkel, 174(Éire):Winter85–152
Tursi, J.A. and P.D. Cincinnato.  Italian —
Two and Three Years.
  J. Vizmuller-Zocco, 276:Spring85–84
Türstig, H-G.  Über Entstehungsprozesse in
der Philosophie des Nyāya-Vaiśeṣika-
Systems.
  W. Halbfass, 318(JAOS):Oct–Dec84–787
Turville-Petre, J. - see Tolkien, J.R.R.
Tushnet, M.  The American Law of Slavery,
1810–1860.
  G. Vandal, 106:Spring85–41
Tuska, J.  Billy the Kid.
  L. Horne, 106:Summer85–221
Tuska, J.  Dark Cinema.*
  J.P. Telotte, 500:Fall85–62
Tuska, J. and V. Piekarski, with P.J.
Blanding, eds.  The Frontier Experience.
  27(AL):May85–364
Tutin, C.  Bruckner.
  J.B., 412:Feb84–68
Tutuola, A.  La mia vita nel bosco degli
spiriti.
  J. Wilkinson, 538(RAL):Winter85–597
Twain, M.  Adventures of Huckleberry Finn.
(W. Blair and V. Fischer, eds)
  H. Kenner, 617(TLS):9May86–490
Twain, M.  The Adventures of Huckleberry
Finn (Tom Sawyer's Companion): A Fac-

simile of the Manuscript.*  (L.J. Budd,
ed)
  J. Nagel, 587(SAF):Autumn85–249
Twain, M.  Christian Science.
  J. Moynahan, 617(TLS):15Aug86–896
Twain, M.  Early Tales and Sketches.  (Vol
2) (E.M. Branch and R.H. Hirst, with H.E.
Smith, eds)
  P. Messent, 541(RES):Feb85–144
Twain, M.  The Science Fiction of Mark
Twain.*  (D. Ketterer, ed)
  H.B. Franklin, 561(SFS):Mar85–88
  J.L. Idol, Jr., 573(SSF):Fall85–495
  J.S. Tuckey, 27(AL):Dec85–672
Twain, M.  Selected Writings of an Amer-
ican Skeptic.  (V. Donyo, ed)
  E. Emerson, 587(SAF):Autumn85–253
Tweedie, J.  Internal Affairs.
  L. Heron, 362:24Jul86–26
Twitchell, J.B.  Dreadful Pleasures.*
  S. Schoenbaum, 453(NYRB):30Jan86–23
  R.E. Wood, 500:Spring/Summer86–84
Twitchell, J.B.  Forbidden Partners.
  R. Dinnage, 453(NYRB):4Dec86–39
Twitchell, J.B.  Romantic Horizons.*
  P.M.S. Dawson, 148:Summer85–67
  T.M. Kelley, 340(KSJ):Vol34–203
Twitchett, D.  Printing and Publishing in
Medieval China.*
  E.S. Rawski, 293(JASt):Nov84–187
"2PLUS2."  (4th issue)
  S. Romer, 617(TLS):10Jan86–36
Twombly, R.  Louis Sullivan.
  T.S. Hines, 441:6Apr86–3
  442(NY):12May86–127
Tyack, D., R. Lowe and E. Hansot.  Public
Schools in Hard Times.
  J. Rury, 42(AR):Fall85–496
Tydeman, W.  "Doctor Faustus."
  M. Willems, 189(EA):Apr–Jun86–210
Tydeman, W., ed.  Wilde: Comedies.
  N. Grene, 447(N&Q):Dec84–539
Tydeman, W. - see Robertson, T.
Tyler, A.  The Accidental Tourist.*
  A. Bloom, 434:Summer86–513
  P. Lewis, 364:Oct85–90
Tyler, F.  American Etchings of the Nine-
teenth Century.
  J.V. Turano, 16:Spring85–91
Tymieniecka, A-T., ed.  The Phenomenology
of Man and of the Human Condition.*
(Vol 1)
  J. Sivak, 542:Oct–Dec85–569
Tymn, M.B., ed.  The Year's Scholarship in
Science Fiction, Fantasy and Horror Lit-
erature: 1980.
  L. Hatfield, 128(CE):Mar85–276
Tymn, M.B. and R.C. Schoblin, eds.  The
Year's Scholarship in Science Fiction
and Fantasy: 1976–1979.
  L. Hatfield, 128(CE):Mar85–276
Tyng, A.  Beginnings.
  D.P. Doordan, 505:Apr85–125
Tyrrell, E., Jr.  The Liberal Crack-Up.
  639(VQR):Summer85–95
Tyrrell, J., comp.  Leoš Janáček: "Kat'a
Kabanová."*
  J.B., 412:May84–146
Tyrrell, W.B.  Amazons.*
  J. Fontenrose, 124:Sep–Oct85–61

[continued]

Vakar, G. Stixotvorenija. (E.N. Čvani
and S. Ljubenskaja, eds)
    N. Lee, 574(SEEJ):Fall85-352
Valdés, J. Lecturas básicas. (3rd ed)
    R.B. Klein, 399(MLJ):Winter85-434
Valdés, M.J. Shadows in the Cave.*
    R. Cardona, 240(HR):Summer85-384
Valdman, A. and others. Son et sens.
(3rd ed)
    B.B. Distelhorst, 399(MLJ):Summer85-
179
    P. Siegel, 207(FR):Oct85-176
Valdman, A., N.C. Mellerski and S.L. Heine.
Promenades et perspectives.
    B.B. Distelhorst, 399(MLJ):Summer85-
179
Valdman, A., N.C. Mellerski and M.
Lavergne. Scènes et séjours. (3rd ed)
    B.B. Distelhorst, 399(MLJ):Summer85-
179
    P. Siegel, 207(FR):Oct85-175
Vale, F. The Amorous Unicorn.
    B. Pirie, 102(CanL):Summer85-181
Vale, J. Edward III and Chivalry.*
    M. Keen, 382(MAE):1985/2-298
Valenstein, E.S. Great and Desperate
Cures.
    P-L. Adams, 61:May86-100
    M. Critchley, 453(NYRB):24Apr86-7
    S.W. Jackson, 441:6Apr86-30
Valent, I. La forma del linguaggio.
    J. Lambert, 542:Jul-Sep85-347
Valentin, J-M. Le Théâtre des Jésuites
dans les pays de langue allemande.
    N. Griffin and P. Skrine, 402(MLR):
Oct85-981
Valette, J-P. and R. Contacts. (3rd ed)
    M-N. Little, 207(FR):Feb86-500
Valin, J. Life's Work.
    N. Callendar, 441:16Nov86-38
Valin, R. Perspectives psychomécaniques
sur la syntaxe.*
    K-H. Körner, 72:Band222Heft1-217
Valin, R., W. Hirtle and A. Joly, eds.
Leçons de linguistique de Gustave Guil-
laume, 1956-1957.
    A. Lorian, 545(RPh):May85-492
Valkenier, E.K. The Soviet Union and the
Third World.
    R.O. Freedman, 104(CASS):Spring85-101
Valla, L. Dialogue sur le libre-arbitre.
(J. Chomarat, ed and trans)
    J. Jolivet, 542:Jul-Sep85-309
Valladares, A. Against All Hope.
    M. Falcoff, 129:Aug86-56
    R. Radosh, 441:8Jun86-11
del Valle-Inclán, R. Barbarische Komödien.
(F. Vogelsang, trans)
    H. Wentzlaff-Eggebert, 547(RF):Band97
Heft4-495
Vallee, L. and R. Findlay - see Osinski, Z.
de Valois, M. - see under Marguerite de
Valois
Van Antwerp, M.A. and S. Johns, eds. Dic-
tionary of Literary Biography Documen-
tary Series.* (Vol 4: Tennessee
Williams.)
    W.K. Holditch, 598(SoR):Autumn86-892
    L. Leverich, 534(RALS):Spring83-98
    R.B. Parker, 397(MD):Mar85-180

Vanbrugh, J. The Provoked Wife. (A.
Coleman, ed)
    B. Corman, 566:Autumn85-87
    H. Love, 402(MLR):Jan85-125
    F. McCormick, 447(N&Q):Mar84-126
Vance, J.A. Samuel Johnson and the Sense
of History.*
    P. Alkon, 173(ECS):Winter85/86-300
    J.J. Burke, Jr., 125:Spring85-346
    S. Soupel, 189(EA):Apr-Jun86-219
Vance, J.A. Joseph and Thomas Warton.
    D. Fairer, 173(ECS):Fall85-110
Vance, N. The Sinews of the Spirit.*
    D. Newsome, 617(TLS):8Aug86-856
Vancouver, G. A Voyage of Discovery to
the North Pacific Ocean and Round the
World 1791-1795.* (W.K. Lamb, ed)
    S. Soupel, 189(EA):Oct-Dec86-464
Van Deburg, W.L. Slavery and Race in
American Popular Culture.
    J. Rury, 42(AR):Spring85-247
Van Delft, L. Le moraliste classique.
    G. Mathieu-Castellani, 549(RLC):Jul-
Sep85-339
Vandenbroucke, R. Truths the Hand Can
Touch.
    A. Borreca, 609:Spring86-77
Van den Heuvel, J., ed. Album Voltaire.
    C. Mervaud, 535(RHL):May/Jun85-487
Vanderbilt, A.T. 2d. Treasure Wreck.
    A. Schmitz, 441:29Jun86-25
Vanderhaeghe, G. Man Descending.*
    A. Mars-Jones, 617(TLS):22Aug86-920
Vanderhaeghe, G. My Present Age.*
    D. Barbour, 102(CanL):Summer85-151
    A. Mars-Jones, 617(TLS):22Aug86-920
    C. Rooke, 376:Mar85-160
    D.O. Spettigue, 529(QQ):Winter85-836
Vanderhaeghe, G. The Trouble With Heroes
and Other Stories.
    L.K. MacKendrick, 198:Spring85-88
    E. McNamara, 102(CanL):Winter84-113
Van der Horst, P.W. - see Chaeremon
Van Diver, B.B. Roadside Geology of New
York.
    W. Sullivan, 441:12Jan86-21
Vandromme, P. Marcel, Roger et Ferdinand.
    C. Krance, 210(FrF):May85-246
Van Engen, J.H. Rupert of Deutz.
    J. Newell, 589:Oct85-1028
Van Esterik, P., ed. Women of Southeast
Asia.
    M.A. Muecke, 293(JASt):Nov84-252
Van Ghent, D. Keats.* (J.C. Robinson, ed)
    D. Birch, 541(RES):Aug85-440
    J.L. Hill, 115:Spring84-154
    H. Vendler, 591(SIR):Summer85-283
    L. Waldoff, 301(JEGP):Jan85-143
Van Greenaway, P. Mutants.
    J. Clute, 617(TLS):5Sep86-978
Vanhelleputte, M., ed. G.E. Lessing und
die Freiheit des Denkens.
    H.B. Nisbet, 402(MLR):Jan85-214
Van Herik, J. Freud on Femininity and
Faith.
    R. Hooks, 367(L&P):Vol32No2-53
Van Horne, J.C. and L.W. Formwalt - see
Latrobe, B.H.
Van Kley, D.K. The Damiens Affair and the
Unravelling of the Ancien Régime, 1750-
1770.
    D. Hudson, 173(ECS):Spring86-401

Vann, J.A.   The Making of a State.*
N.Z. Davis, 551(RenQ):Summer85-327
Vannebo, K.I.   En nasjon av skriveføre.
C. Creider, 350:Mar86-218
E. Haugen, 355(LSoc):Jun85-262
Vanneste, H.M.C.   Northern Review, 1945-
1956.*
J. Mulvihill, 102(CanL):Fall85-139
Van Nooten, B.A.   The Mahābhārata, Attrib-
uted to Kṛṣṇa Dvaipāyana.
F. Blackwell, 314:Winter-Spring85-247
Van Schendel, A.   L'Homme de l'eau.
L. Kovacs, 450(NRF):Mar85-114
Van Seters, J.   In Search of History.
E.D. Mallon, 125:Fall84-97
Vansittart, P.   Aspects of Feeling.
V. Bogdanor, 362:20Feb86-28
V. Cunningham, 617(TLS):24Jan86-81
J. Mellors, 364:Feb86-97
Vansittart, P.   Paths from a White Horse.*
A. Ross, 364:Nov85-108
Vaquero, Q.A., T. Marín Martínez and J.
Vives Gatell - see under Aldea Vaquero,
Q., T. Marín Martínez and J. Vives
Gatell
Varadpande, M.L.   Religion and Theatre.
N.A. Bert, 615(TJ):Mar85-127
Vardy, S.B. and A.H., eds.   Society in
Change.*
P. Longworth, 575(SEER):Oct85-599
Varela, J.L. - see de Larra, M.J.
Varey, S.   Henry St. John, Viscount Boling-
broke.
P. Lewis, 161(DUJ):Jun85-274
Varey, S. - see Lord Bolingbroke
Varga von Kibéd, A.   Die Philosophie der
Neuzeit.
W. Steinbeck, 342:Band76Heft3-348
Vargas Llosa, M.   The Perpetual Orgy.
J. Barnes, 441:21Dec86-10
Vargas Llosa, M.   The Real Life of Alejan-
dro Mayta.
P-L. Adams, 61:Mar86-112
J. Butt, 617(TLS):14Nov86-1290
R. Coover, 441:2Feb86-1
J. Updike, 442(NY):24Feb86-98
M. Wood, 453(NYRB):27Mar86-34
Vargas Llosa, M.   The War of the End of
the World.*   (Spanish title: La Guerra
del Fin del Mundo.)
A. Graham-Yooll, 364:Apr/May85-155
W.H. Pritchard, 249(HudR):Spring85-120
Varia, R.   Brancusi.
J. Russell, 441:7Dec86-11
Varloot, J. - see Diderot, D.
Varloot, J. and M. Delon - see Restif de
La Bretonne
Varma, D.P. - see Lewis, M.
Varma, P. - see Stead, R.
Varnedoe, K.   Vienna 1900: Art, Architec-
ture and Design.
C.E. Schorske, 453(NYRB):25Sep86-19
Varnhagen, R.L.   Rahel-Bibliothek.   (K.
Feilchenfeldt, ed)
T.H. Pickett, 221(GQ):Summer85-462
Varriano, J.   Italian Baroque and Rococo
Architecture.
A. Barnet, 441:8Jun86-37
E. Chaney, 617(TLS):240ct86-1198
Varvaro, A.   La parola nel tempo.
A. Castelvecchi, 708:Vol 11fasc1-135
Vasey, D. - see Turner, T.
Vasey, L. - see Lawrence, D.H.

Vasil'ev, L.M.   Semantika russkogo glagola.
H-J. Mattusch, 682(ZPSK):Band38Heft6-
777
Vassallo, P., ed.   The Magic of Words.
R. Gish, 649(WAL):Nov85-265
Vassberg, D.E.   Land in Society in Golden
Age Castile.
C.J. Jago, 551(RenQ):Summer85-342
Vasseur, A.M.   Passion puissance².
J.L. Pallister, 207(FR):May86-1004
Vassiltchikov, M.   The Berlin Diaries 1940-
1945 of Marie "Missie" Vassiltchikov.
(G. Vassiltchikov, ed)
A.J. Nicholls, 617(TLS):18Jul86-777
Vatai, F.L.   Intellectuals in Politics in
the Greek World, from Early Times to the
Hellenistic Age.*
D. Whitehead, 123:Vol35No2-408
Vatter, H.G.   The U.S. Economy in World
War II.
S. Strange, 617(TLS):6Jun86-613
Vattimo, G.   La Fine Della Modernità.
G. Borradori, 290(JAAC):Spring86-306
Vattuone, R.   Ricerche su Timeo.
R.J.A. Talbert, 303(JoHS):Vol 105-215
de Vaucher Gravili, A.   Loi et transgres-
sion.*
R.G. Pellegrini, 535(RHL):Jan/Feb85-89
de Vaugelas, C.F.   La Préface des "Remar-
ques sur la langue françoise."   (Z.
Marzys, ed)
W. Ayres-Bennett, 208(FS):Oct85-464
Vaughan, A.   Grub, Water and Relief.
A.J. Peacock, 637(VS):Spring86-495
Vaughan, F.   The Tradition of Political
Hedonism.
N. Jolley, 543:Mar86-589
Vaughan, R.   Herbert von Karajan.
G. Annan, 453(NYRB):29May86-22
J. Rockwell, 441:22Jun86-14
M. Tanner, 617(TLS):2May86-465
Vaughan, T.   The Works of Thomas Vaughan.*
(A. Rudrum, with J. Drake-Brockman, eds)
T.O. Calhoun, 191(ELN):Sep85-72
T. Willard, 627(UTQ):Summer85-411
Vázquez, J.A. and A.D. Kossoff - see Amor
y Vázquez, J. and A.D. Kossoff
Vecchio, F.   Textos de ayer y de hoy.
H.L. Ryan, 238:Dec85-801
van der Veen, B.K.   The Development of D.H.
Lawrence's Prose Themes, 1906-1915.
J.B. Foster, Jr., 395(MFS):Summer85-
354
de Vega Carpio, L.   Cartas.   (N. Marín,
ed)
M. Levisi, 304(JHP):Fall85-86
de Vega Carpio, L.   La Gatomaquia.   (C.
Sabor de Cortázar, ed)
V. Dixon, 402(MLR):Oct85-962
de Vega Carpio, L.   Las hazañas del segun-
do David.   (J.B. Avalle-Arce and G. Cer-
vantes Martín, eds)
D.W. Cruickshank, 304(JHP):Spring85-
261
Veiras, D.M. - see under Mariño Veiras, D.
Veith, G.E., Jr.   Reformation Spirituality.
J. Drury, 617(TLS):28Feb86-228
Veith, W.H. and W. Putschke, with L.
Hummel, eds.   Kleiner deutscher Sprach-
atlas.   (Vol 1, Pt 1)
H.F. Nielsen, 300:Oct85-189

Velasco Kindelan, M. La novela cortesana
y picaresca de Castillo Solórzano.
V. García Ruiz, 552(REH):May85-149
van de Velde, R.G. Prolegomena to Inferen-
tial Discourse Processing.
K. Allan, 350:Sep86-733
Vellacott, P. The Logic of Tragedy.
D. Sider, 124:Jan-Feb86-205
Vellay, M. Pierre Chareau.
R. Cardinal, 617(TLS):10Oct86-1133
Velleius Paterculus. The Caesarian and
Augustan Narrative (2.41-93). The
Tiberian Narrative (2.94-131). (A.J.
Woodman, ed)
G.W.M. Harrison, 124:Mar-Apr86-286
Veloudis, G. Deutsche Einflusse auf die
neugriechische Literatur 1750-1944.
R. Richer, 549(RLC):Oct-Dec85-470
Veltman, C. Language Shift in the United
States.*
M. Görlach, 260(IF):Band90-338
Vendler, H., ed. The Harvard Book of Con-
temporary American Poetry.*
C.K. Doreski, 30:Spring86-85
J. Gardner, 129:Jan86-50
V. Shetley, 676(YR):Spring86-429
Vendler, H. The Odes of John Keats.*
J. Bayley, 591(SIR):Winter85-551
W.H. Galperin, 340(KSJ):Vol34-177
J. Hill, 115:Fall84/Winter85-160
R.M. Ryan, 405(MP):Feb86-319
Vendler, H. Wallace Stevens.*
M. Beehler, 705:Spring85-57
J.S. Leonard, 27(AL):Oct85-522
639(VQR):Spring85-44
Vendrand-Voyer, J. Normes civiques et
métier militaire à Rome sous le Prin-
cipat.
B. Campbell, 313:Vol75-258
Venegas, A. Primera parte de las diferen-
cias de libros que hay en el universo.
F. Márquez Villanueva, 304(JHP):
Winter85-172
Venetus, P. - see under Paulus Venetus
Vennum, T., Jr. The Ojibwa Dance Drum.
C. Heth, 187:Spring/Summer86-343
Venturi, F. Settecento riformatore. (Vol
4, Pt 1)
M.S. Miller, 173(ECS):Summer86-561
J.M. Roberts, 617(TLS):21Mar86-309
Venturi, F. Settecento riformatore. (Vol
4, Pt 2)
M.S. Miller, 173(ECS):Summer86-561
Venturi, F. Studies in Free Russia.
A. Gleason, 550(RusR):Jul85-300
Venturini, F. Sulle strade del blues.
A. Prévos, 91:Fall85-232
Venturini, G. - see Ariosti, O.
Verani, H.J. Octavio Paz.
E.M. Santi, 263(RIB):Vol35No3-334
Verástegui, S.D. - see under de Silva y
Verástegui, S.
Verba, S. and G.R. Orren. Equality in
America.
G.T., 185:Jul86-915
Verbeke, G. Avicenna, Grundleger einer
neuen Metaphysik.
J. Jolivet, 542:Apr-Jun85-250
Verbeke, G. The Presence of Stoicism in
Medieval Thought.*
E.L. Fortin, 543:Sep84-146
A. Maurer, 319:Apr86-264
J.A. Weisheipl, 438:Summer85-365

Verchau, E. Theodor Fontane.
H-G. Richert, 133:Band17Heft3/4-358
Verdery, K. Transylvanian Villagers.
D. Deletant, 575(SEER):Jul85-470
M. Sozan, 104(CASS):Spring85-117
Verdi, G. Autobiographie à travers la
correspondance. (A. Oberdorfer, ed)
A. Suied, 450(NRF):Jan85-113
Verdi, R. Klee and Nature.*
D. Hall, 90:Dec85-911
Verdon, T.G., with J. Dally, eds. Monasti-
cism and the Arts.
P. Verdier, 377:Nov84-182
Verene, D.P. Hegel's Recollection.
S. Bungay, 290(JAAC):Summer86-415
Verey, C.D., T.J. Brown and E. Coatsworth,
eds. The Durham Gospels together with
Fragments of a Gospel Book in Uncial.
H. Gneuss, 38:Band103Heft3/4-455
Vergara, L. Rubens and the Poetics of
Landscape.*
L. Lerner, 131(CL):Spring85-169
Vergé, R. Entertaining in the French
Style.
F. Fabricant, 441:7Dec86-17
Vergez, R. Early Ukiyo-e Master.
B.W.R., 90:Oct85-729
Vergil. Vergil: "Aeneiden." (E. Kragge-
rud, ed and trans)
Ø. Andersen, 172(Edda):1985/6-373
Vergine, P.I. Studi su Charles Péguy.
S. Fraisse, 535(RHL):Jul/Aug85-695
Vergnaud, J-R. Dépendances et niveaux de
représentation en syntaxe.
D. Lightfoot, 350:Dec86-939
Vergote, A. Religion, foi, incroyance.
M. Adam, 542:Jan-Mar85-107
Vergote, H-B. Sens et répétition.
J. Brun, 192(EP):Jul-Sep85-428
Q. Lauer, 258:Dec85-427
Verhaeghe, J. Het mensbeeld in de Aristo-
telische Ethiek.
A.P. Bos, 394:Vol38fasc1/2-198
R. Brague, 192(EP):Jul-Sep85-430
Verhaeren, É. Les Campagnes hallucinées;
Les Villes tentaculaires.
I. Higgins, 208(FS):Jul85-357
Verhoeff, H. Les grandes tragédies de Cor-
neille.
J.H. Broome, 208(FS):Apr85-205
Verkruijsse, P.J. Mattheus Smallegange
(1624-1710).
70:May/Jun85-168
Verlaine, P. Les Poètes maudits. (M.
Décaudin, ed)
M. Bertrand, 535(RHL):Jan/Feb85-111
Verleun, J. and J. de Vries. Conrad's
"The Secret Agent" and the Critics: 1965-
1980."
E. Delgarno, 136:Vol 18No2-157
Vermazen, B. and M.B. Hintikka, eds.
Essays on Davidson.*
C. MacDonald, 393(Mind):Oct85-632
Vermeer, H.J. Aufsätze zur Translations-
theorie.
H. Witte, 257(IRAL):Aug85-263
Vermette, L. Domestic Life at Les Forges
du Saint-Maurice.
B.G. Carson, 658:Spring85-88
Vermorel, F. and J. Starlust.
G. Marcus, 62:Dec85-16

Vernant, J-P. and P. Vidal-Naquet. Mythe et tragédie en Grèce ancienne deux.
J. Gould, 617(TLS):26Sep86-1071
Vernay, H. Syntaxe et sémantique.*
N.L. Corbett, 545(RPh):May86-478
Vernon, B.D. Margaret Cole 1893-1980.
K.O. Morgan, 362:17Apr86-27
P. Willmott, 617(TLS):13Jun86-642
Vernon, J. La Salle.
P-L. Adams, 61:Jul86-78
D. Guy, 441:13Jul86-16
Vernon, J. Money and Fiction.*
J.S. Allen, 446(NCFS):Fall-Winter85/86-186
C. Gallagher, 637(VS):Spring86-463
P. Stevick, 395(MFS):Winter85-838
da Verona, R. - see under Raffaele da Verona
Verrier, A. The Road to Zimbabwe 1890-1980.
S. Uys, 617(TLS):14Mar86-270
Verschuren, H. Jean Pauls "Hesperus" und das zeitgenössische Lesepublikum.
W. Theiss, 224(GRM):Band35Heft3-356
Versteeg, M., S. Thomas and J. Huddleston, comps. Index to Fiction in "The Lady's Realm."*
S. Mitchell, 635(VPR):Spring85-40
Versteegh, K. Pidginization and Creolization.
B. Comrie, 353:Vol23No3-496
J. Heath, 350:Dec86-952
A.S. Kaye, 159:Fall85-201
Vertov, D. Kino-Eye.* (A. Michelson, ed)
D. Polan, 500:Fall85-60
Vertzberger, Y.Y.I. Misperceptions in Foreign Policymaking.
A.S. Whiting, 293(JASt):Aug85-803
de Verville, B. - see under Béroalde de Verville
"Verzeichnis der im deutschen Sprachbereich erschienen Drucke des XVI. Jahrhunderts." (Ser 1, Vol 1)
L.S. Thompson, 133:Band17Heft3/4-321
J.E. Walsh, 517(PBSA):Vol79No4-585
Vescovini, G.F. "Arti" e filosofia nel secolo XIV.
J. Jolivet, 542:Apr-Jun85-251
N.G. Siraisi, 589:Apr85-493
Vester, E. Instrument and Manner Expressions in Latin.*
W.J. Pepicello, 361:Jan85-185
Vestergaard, T. and K. Schroeder. The Language of Advertising.*
R. Draper, 453(NYRB):26Jun86-14
K.A. Hunold, 350:Dec86-959
J. Mellors, 364:Jun85-111
Veyne, P. Writing History.
D. Watson, 366:Autumn85-291
H. White, 617(TLS):31Jan86-109
Viallaneix, P. - see de Vigny, A.
Viard, J. Pierre Leroux et les socialistes européens.
J-J. Goblot, 535(RHL):Mar/Apr85-321
Vicente, G. Teatro. (T.R. Hart, ed)
C. Stern, 240(HR):Autumn85-484
Vickers, B., ed. Rhetoric Revalued.
P. France, 402(MLR):Oct85-892
Vickers, B., ed. Shakespeare: The Critical Heritage.* (Vol 6)
G. Bullough, 677(YES):Vol 15-282
Vickers, H. Cecil Beaton.*
T. Wolfe, 441:15Jun86-1

Vickery, J.B. Myths and Texts.*
S.C. Ausband, 577(SHR):Fall85-367
M. Bell, 402(MLR):Jul85-676
Vickery, W.N. and B.B. Sagatov, eds. Aleksandr Blok Centennial Conference.
B.F. Scherr, 574(SEEJ):Winter85-478
Vico, G. The New Science of Giambattista Vico. (T.G. Bergin and M.H. Fisch, trans)
D.P. Verene, 543:Dec85-378
Vico, G. Vico: Selected Writings. (L. Pompa, ed and trans)
D.P. Verene, 543:Mar85-678
Vidal, A.S. - see under Sánchez Vidal, A.
Vidal, F.C. - see under Canals Vidal, F.
Vidal, G. The Second American Revolution and Other Essays: 1976-1982.
P.F. Kress, 577(SHR):Winter85-93
Vidal, G. Vidal in Venice. (G. Armstrong, ed)
R. Craft, 453(NYRB):13Feb86-28
"The Vidas of the Troubadours."* (M. Egan, trans)
F.M. Chambers, 589:Jul85-673
Vidich, A.J. and S.M. Lyman. American Sociology.
D. Wrong, 617(TLS):24Jan86-91
Vieillard, F., ed. Le Roman de Troie en prose (version du Cod. Bodmer 147).
F. Bogdanow, 208(FS):Jul85-316
Viera, D.J. Bibliografia anotada de la vida i obra de Francesc Eiximenis (1340?-1409?).
C.B. Faulhaber, 545(RPh):Feb86-390
Viereck, W., ed. Studien zum Einfluss der englischen Sprache auf das Deutsche/ Studies on the Influence of the English Language on German.
K. Kehr, 685(ZDL):3/1985-406
Viereck, W., E.W. Schneider and M. Görlach, eds. A Bibliography of Writings on Varieties of English, 1965-1983.
R.R. Butters, 35(AS):Spring85-88
B. Carstensen, 685(ZDL):3/1985-404
G-J. Forgue, 189(EA):Apr-Jun86-195
J.T. Jensen, 350:Mar86-213
L. Todd, 260(IF):Band90-342
Vieregg, A. - see Huchel, P.
Vierne, S., ed. George Sand.
C. Campos, 402(MLR):Apr85-467
Vieth, D.M., ed. Essential Articles for the Study of Jonathan Swift's Poetry.
J.I. Fischer, 566:Spring86-195
Vieth, D.M. Rochester Studies, 1925-1982.*
L. Carver, 566:Autumn85-83
R. Ellrodt, 189(EA):Apr-Jun86-211
"The Vietnam Experience."
A. Barnett, 362:25Sep86-20
Vietta, S., ed. Die literarische Frühromantik.*
D.P. Haase, 221(GQ):Winter85-121
H.M.K. Riley, 133:Band17Heft3/4-343
Vietta, S. Neuzeitliche Rationalität und moderne literarische Sprachkritik.
H.A. Pausch, 107(CRCL):Sep85-551
Vigée, C. Le Parfum et la cendre, entretien sur trois continents.
A-M. Boyer, 188(ECr):Fall85-101
Vigezzi, B., ed. Federico Chabod e la "nuova storiografia" italiana (1919-1950).
C. Seton-Watson, 617(TLS):31Jan86-110

Vigil, E., ed. Woman of Her Word.
   B. Miller, 238:May85-326
Vigner, G. L'exercice dans la classe de
   français.
   P. Hagiwara, 399(MLJ):Spring85-90
Vignoles, K.H. Charles Blacker Vignoles.
   R.A. Buchanan, 637(VS):Autumn84-200
Vignuzzi, U. Il glossario latino-sabino
   di Ser Iacopo Ursello da Roccantica.
   A. Castelvecchi, 708:Vol 11fasc1-140
de Vigny, A. Les Destinées, poëmes philos-
   ophiques.* (P. Viallaneix, ed)
   J-P. Saint-Gérand, 535(RHL):Mar/Apr85-
   313
Vijn, J.P. Carlyle and Jean Paul.*
   G.B. Tennyson, 588(SSL):Vol20-271
Viksnins, G.J. Financial Deepening in
   ASEAN Countries.
   L. Stifel, 293(JASt):May85-692
Vilela, J.S. - see under Stichini Vilela,
   J.
Viljamaa, T. Infinitive of Narration in
   Livy.
   S. Oakley, 123:Vol35No1-190
Viljanen, K. Zum Wortschatz der wirt-
   schaftlichen Integration nach dem
   zweiten Weltkrieg in Europa.
   H.J. Hakkarainen, 439(NM):1985/3-418
Villalon-Galdames, A., comp. Bibliografía
   jurídica. (Vol 2)
   C. Garcia-Godoy, 263(RIB):Vol35No1-74
Villanueva, T. Shaking Off the Dark.
   R. Aguilar, 238:Dec85-793
Villar, L.M. Plasmador.
   R.A. Román Riefköhl, 238:Sep85-532
Villarreal, J.A. Clemente Chacón. The
   Fifth Horseman.
   E. Gonzales-Berry, 238:Dec85-791
Ville, G. La gladiature en occident des
   origines à la mort de Domitien.*
   J. Linderski, 122:Apr85-189
Villegas, R.N. Kayamanan.
   S. Markbreiter, 60:Sep-Oct85-132
Villey, M. Philosophie du droit. (Vol 2)
   (2nd ed)
   J-L. Gardies, 542:Jan-Mar85-65
Villiers, G. Buckingham. (C. Phipps, ed)
   D. Nokes, 617(TLS):25Apr86-452
Villon, F. Poésies. (J. Dufournet, ed)
   D.A. Fein, 207(FR):Mar86-605
   J. Fox, 208(FS):Oct85-453
Viñao Frago, A. Política y educación en
   los orígenes de la España contemporánea.
   P. Deacon, 86(BHS):Jul85-309
Vinaver, E. Entretiens sur Racine.
   R. Parish, 208(FS):Jul85-337
Vince, R.W. Ancient and Medieval Theatre.
   J.M. Walton, 610:Autumn85-227
Vincent, D. Bread, Knowledge and Freedom.
   H.G. Klaus, 72:Band222Heft1-189
Vincent, D., ed. Testaments of Radicalism.
   H.G. Klaus, 72:Band222Heft1-189
Vincent, J. - see Lindsay, D.
Vine, B. A Dark-Adapted Eye.
   T.J. Binyon, 617(TLS):28Nov86-1357
   K.C. O'Brien, 362:1May86-30
Vines, G. and L. Gamlin, eds. The Evolu-
   tion of Life.
   T. Bay, 441:5Oct86-54
Vining, R. On Appraising the Performance
   of an Economic System.
   639(VQR):Autumn85-136

Vinje, P.M. An Understanding of Love
   According to the Anchoress Julian of
   Norwich.
   S. Dickman, 589:Apr85-494
Vinson, J., ed. Restoration and 18th Cen-
   tury Prose and Poetry.
   P. Wagner, 72:Band222Heft2-475
Vinson, J., ed. 20th-Century Fiction.
   20th-Century Poetry. 20th-Century Drama.
   N. Bradbury, 541(RES):Aug85-453
Vinson, J. and D.L. Kirkpatrick, eds.
   Contemporary Poets. (4th ed)
   J. Barker, 617(TLS):15Aug86-900
Vinton, B. The Polish Prince.
   S.L. Cuba, 497(PolR):Vol30No1-105
Vinz, M. The Weird Kid.
   455:Mar85-64
"Bill Viola."
   L. Zippay, 127:Fall85-263
Viola, H.J. The National Archives of the
   United States.
   P.B. Hensley, 658:Winter85-321
Violato, G. La Principessa giansenista,
   saggi su Madame de La Fayette.
   E.B. Quallio, 475:Vol 12No22-393
Vion, M. Panique au Pellerin.
   J. Kolbert, 207(FR):Dec85-343
Viorst, J. Necessary Losses.
   F. Klagsbrun, 441:23Mar86-37
Viorst, M., ed. Making a Difference.
   J. Paradis, 441:19Oct86-49
Virgil - see under Vergil
Virgilio, N.A. Selected Haiku.
   R. Yarrow, 404:Autumn85-55
Virgillo, C., E.H. Friedman and L.T. Val-
   divieso. Aproximaciones al estudio de
   la literatura hispánica.
   C.S. Maier, 238:Dec85-803
Virgoe, N. and S. Yaxley, eds. The Ban-
   ville Diaries.
   R. Blythe, 617(TLS):26Dec86-1455
Virmaux, O. Les Héroïnes romanesques de
   Madame de Lafayette.
   J. Campbell, 208(FS):Jan85-72
"Visages de la féminité."
   M.M. Rowan, 475:Vol 12No23-752
Viscomi, J. Prints by William Blake and
   His Followers.
   R. Lister, 88:Fall85-80
Vishnevskaya, G. Galina.*
   E. Forbes, 415:Oct85-605
   639(VQR):Winter85-14
Visky, K. Spuren der Wirtschaftskrise
   der Kaiserzeit in den römischen Rechts-
   quellen.
   J.A. Crook, 123:Vol35No1-141
Visram, R. Ayahs, Lascars and Princes.
   D. Hiro, 617(TLS):13Jun86-654
Vitalis, O. - see under Orderic Vitalis
Viti, P., ed. Due commedie umanistiche
   pavesi.
   A. Stäuble, 228(GSLI):Vol 162fasc518-
   276
Vitz, P.C. and A.B. Glimcher. Modern Art
   and Modern Science.*
   J.A. Richardson, 289:Fall85-89
Vitzthum, R.C. Land and Sea.
   R. Morton, 106:Summer85-197
Vivante, P. The Epithets in Homer.*
   N. Austin, 122:Jan85-67
Vivante, P. Homer.
   S. Scully, 124:Jul-Aug86-417
   O. Taplin, 453(NYRB):13Mar86-39

Vlach, M. and Y. Buono. Catalogue collectif des impressions québécoises 1764-1820.
  S. Alston, 470:Vol23-106
Vladimov, G. Three Minutes' Silence.
  G. Hosking, 617(TLS):24Jan86-77
Vlasopolos, A. The Symbolist Method of Coleridge, Baudelaire, and Yeats.*
  R. Bienvenu, 549(RLC):Oct-Dec85-472
  S. Nalbantian, 678(YCGL):No34-142
Vliet, R.G. Scorpio Rising.*
  W. Lesser, 249(HudR):Autumn85-466
  639(VQR):Autumn85-126
Vogel, S. and F. N'Diaye. African Masterpieces from the Musée de l'Homme.
  J.M. Borgatti, 2(AfrA):May85-22
Vogel, S.M. African Aesthetics.
  R. Hobbs, 441:21Sep86-33
Vogel-Weidemann, U. Die Statthalter von Africa und Asia in den Jahren 14-68 n. Chr.
  B. Levick, 313:Vol75-301
von der Vogelweide, W. - see under Walther von der Vogelweide
Vogl, J. Das Frühwerk Valentin P. Kataevs.
  J.L. Laychuk, 104(CASS):Summer85-213
Vogler, C.M. The Nation State.
  B. Anderson, 617(TLS):28Mar86-333
Vogt, E., ed. Neues Handbuch der Literaturwissenschaft.* (Vol 2)
  A.M. Bowie, 123:Vol35No1-194
Vogt, J. Thomas Mann: "Buddenbrooks."
  J. Rieckmann, 221(GQ):Spring85-292
Voigt, E-M. - see "Lexikon des frühgriechischen Epos"
Voigt-Langenberger, P. Antifaschistische Lyrik in Frankreich, 1930-1945.
  I. Higgins, 208(FS):Oct85-500
Voigts, L.E. and M.R. McVaugh, eds. A Latin Technical Phlebotomy and Its Middle English Translation.
  F.M. Getz, 589:Oct85-1030
Voinovich, V. The Anti-Soviet Soviet Union.
  P-L. Adams, 61:Sep86-104
  S.F. Starr, 441:31Aug86-5
  442(NY):24Nov86-150
Voitle, R. The Third Earl of Shaftesbury, 1671-1713.*
  A.O. Aldridge, 173(ECS):Winter85/86-257
  S. Archer, 568(SCN):Spring-Summer85-9
  J.A. Bernstein, 566:Autumn85-78
  C. Cunliffe, 518:Jul85-143
Vojatzi, M. Frühe Argonautenbilder.
  S. Woodford, 303(JoHS):Vol 105-243
Volek, E. Cuatro claves para la modernidad.
  S. Merrim, 238:Sep85-531
Volk, O. Salzproduktion und Salzhandel mittelalterlicher Zisterzienserklöster.
  R.C. Hoffmann, 589:Oct85-1032
Volkan, V.D. and N. Itzkowitz. The Immortal Atatürk.*
  639(VQR):Spring85-46
Völker, K. Brecht-Kommentar.
  T. Reber, 193(ELit):Spring-Summer85-210
Völker, L., ed. "Komm, heilige Melancholie."
  R. Dove, 402(MLR):Apr85-494
Volkman, E. Warriors of the Night.
  639(VQR):Summer85-95

Volkman, E. and J. Cummings. The Heist.
  J. Quinlan, 441:28Dec86-19
Volkoff, V. Vladimir the Russian Viking.
  J. Greppin, 441:13Apr86-26
Volkov, S. Balanchine's Tchaikovsky.*
  J.R. Acocella, 151:Dec85-87
  H. Muschamp, 62:Jan86-13
Voll, J.O. Islam.
  J. Waterbury, 318(JAOS):Jul-Sep84-594
Vollen, G.E. The French Cantata.
  G. Sadler, 410(M&L):Oct85-370
van Vollenhoven, C. Van Vollenhoven on Indonesian Adat Law. (J.F. Holleman, ed)
  M.C. Hoadley, 293(JASt):May85-674
Vollenweider, M-L. Musée d'art et d'histoire de Genève: Catalogue raisonné des sceaux, cylindres, intailles et camées, III.
  M. Henig, 123:Vol35No1-212
Voloshinov, V.N. Marxism and the Philosophy of Language.
  S.M. Weber, 153:Winter85-94
de Voltaire, F.M.A. Corpus des notes marginales de Voltaire. (Vol 2)
  W.H. Barber, 208(FS):Oct85-473
de Voltaire, F.M.A. Correspondance. (Vol 8) (T. Besterman, ed)
  J.H. Brumfitt, 208(FS):Jan85-77
de Voltaire, F.M.A. Facéties. (J. Macary, ed)
  J-J. Didier, 356(LR):Aug85-230
de Voltaire, F.M.A. Voltaire: Russia under Peter the Great. (M. Jenkins, trans)
  J. Black, 83:Autumn85-248
Von Arx, J.P. Progress and Pessimism.
  R. Jann, 637(VS):Summer86-648
Vonnegut, K. Galápagos.*
  L. Rackstraw, 455:Dec85-78
"Voorgeschiedenis."
  R. Padovan, 46:Jan85-4
Vorce, M.H. Rebel Pen. (D. Garrison, ed)
  D.J. Leab, 441:12Jan86-28
van Voss, H. and others, eds. Studies in Egyptian Religion.
  E.S. Meltzer, 318(JAOS):Apr-Jun84-362
Voss, R. Die Artusepik Hartmanns von Aue.*
  D.H. Green, 402(MLR):Apr85-484
  W.C. McDonald, 400(MLN):Apr85-699
Vossenkuhl, W. Anatomie des Sprachgebrauchs.
  U. Steinvorth, 687:Jul-Sep85-470
Vosskamp, W., ed. Utopieforschung.*
  G.E. Grimm, 680(ZDP):Band104Heft2-271
  P. Kuon, 224(GRM):Band35Heft4-448
Vovelle, M. The Fall of the French Monarchy 1787-1792.
  W. Doyle, 83:Autumn85-229
  W. Scott, 384:Jan85-61
"Vox New College Spanish and English Dictionary." "Vox Compact College Spanish and English Dictionary." "Vox Super-Mini College Spanish and English Dictionary."
  L.J. Walker, 399(MLJ):Summer85-213
Voyenne, B. Les journalistes français.
  J-P. Déron, 98:Dec85-1207
Voyles, J.B. Gothic, Germanic, and Northwest Germanic.*
  H. Tiefenbach, 260(IF):Band90-331
Voznesenskaya, J. The Women's Decameron.
  L. Chamberlain, 617(TLS):14Mar86-266
  F. Weldon, 441:26Oct86-9

Vreuls, D. Let Us Know.
L. Graeber, 441:9Mar86-24
de Vries, J. Grundbegriffe der Scholastik.
R.A. Müller, 489(PJGG):Band92Heft1-217
Vroon, R. Velimir Xlebnikov's Shorter
Poems.*
J. Graffy, 575(SEER):Oct85-567
Vuarnet, J-N. Personnage anglais dans
une île.
S. Jaudeau, 450(NRF):Nov85-102
Vucinich, A. Empire of Knowledge.
G.A. Hosking, 575(SEER):Oct85-621
P.R. Josephson, 550(RusR):Apr85-214
Vuillemin, J. Nécessité ou contingence.
G. Stahl, 542:Apr-Jun85-237


Wachter, O. No More Secrets for Me.
M. Warnock, 617(TLS):31Oct86-1212
Wackernagel, J. Kleine Schriften. (Vol 3)
(B. Forssman, ed)
R. Sternemann, 682(ZPSK):Band38Heft4-
448
Waddell, G. and R.W. Liscombe. Robert
Mills's Courthouses and Jails.
P. Scott, 658:Winter85-299
Waddicor, M.H. - see Defontaines, P.F.G.
Waddington, C.H. Behind Appearance.
J.A. Richardson, 289:Fall85-89
Wade, A. Memories of the London Theatre
1900-1914.
B. Richardson, 637(VS):Spring86-470
Wade, E.L., ed. The Arts of the North
American Indian.
J. Russell, 441:1Jun86-11
Wade, R.A. Red Guards and Workers' Mili-
tias in the Russian Revolution.
L. Engelstein, 104(CASS):Spring85-77
M. McAuley, 575(SEER):Jul85-462
Wade, T. Prepositions in Modern Russian.
R. Sussex, 575(SEER):Apr85-284
Wade-Gayles, G. No Crystal Stair.*
C. Werner, 395(MFS):Summer85-420
Wadell, M-B. The Dream of the Salamander.
M. Ekelund, 341:Vol54No1-44
Wagatsuma, H. and G.A. De Vos. Heritage
of Endurance.
R. Dore, 407(MN):Summer85-235
L.H. Lynn, 293(JASt):Nov84-213
Wagenbach, K., ed. Franz Kafka.*
C. Koelb, 395(MFS):Winter85-822
Wagener, H. Carl Zuckmayer.
M. Goth, 221(GQ):Fall85-630
Wagener, O. Hitler.* (H.A. Turner, ed)
[shown in prev under ed]
N. Stone, 617(TLS):28Feb86-210
Wagenknecht, E. The Novels of Henry
James.*
A.W. Bellringer, 677(YES):Vol 15-325
R.P. Hoople, 106:Spring85-57
Wagenknecht, E. Henry David Thoreau.
R. Sattelmeyer, 183(ESQ):Vol31No3-190
Waggoner, H.H. American Visionary Poetry.*
A. Gelpi, 27(AL):Dec85-653
Wagner, A., ed. Contemporary Canadian
Theatre.
A. Filewod, 108:Fall85-143
D. Pavlovic, 193(ELit):Winter85-235
Wagner, A.M. Jean-Baptiste Carpeaux.
R. Dorment, 617(TLS):5Sep86-955

Wagner, D.L., ed. The Seven Liberal Arts
in the Middle Ages.
K.H. Jamieson, 377:Jul84-107
E. Lucki, 589:Jul85-730
Wagner, H. and N. MacCongáil. Oral Litera-
ture from Dunquin, Co. Kerry.
D. Ó Sé, 112:Vol 17-159
Wagner, H.R. Alfred Schutz.
D.J.G., 185:Apr86-660
Wagner, H.R. and C.L. Camp. The Plains
and the Rockies. (4th ed rev by R.H.
Becker)
M.D. Kaplanoff, 78(BC):Spring85-108
Wagner, J. Kommunikation und Spracherwerb
im Fremdsprachenunterricht.
P. Wagner, 257(IRAL):Feb85-73
Wagner, K. El Doctor Constantino Ponce de
la Fuente.
J-M. Laspéras, 92(BH):Jan-Jun84-231
Wagner, L.W. Ellen Glasgow.*
L. Pannill, 70:Sep/Oct84-29
M.R. Winchell, 106:Spring85-73
Wagner, M.L. Petr Chelčický
H. Kaminsky, 589:Apr85-463
Wagner, N. Geist und Geschlecht.
D.G. Daviau, 406:Fall85-365
Wagner, P. - see Cleland, J.
Wagner, R. Oper und Drama. (K. Krop-
finger, ed)
H.M.K. Riley, 133:Band18Heft2-174
Wagner, R-L. Essais de linguistique fran-
çaise.
G. Price, 208(FS):Jan85-122
Wagoner, M. Tobias Smollett.
P-G. Boucé, 189(EA):Oct-Dec86-460
Wagonner, N.M. Early Greek Coins from the
Collection of Jonathan P. Rosen.
B. Burrell, 124:Jan-Feb86-199
Wah, C.K. - see under Chin Kin Wah
Wahlgren, E. The Vikings and America.
J. Graham-Campbell, 617(TLS):5Dec86-
1382
Wain, J. Dear Shadows.
N. Berry, 617(TLS):25Apr86-445
M., 176:Jul/Aug86-30
G. Millar, 362:8May86-24
Wainwright, J. Selected Poems.
B. Morrison, 493:Aug85-62
Wainwright, L. The Great American Maga-
zine.
L.H. Lapham, 441:16Nov86-9
Wais, K. Europaïsche Literatur im Ver-
gleich.* (J. Hösle, D. Janik and W.
Theile, eds)
M. Delon, 535(RHL):May/Jun85-523
N. Segal, 208(FS):Jul85-371
Waite, P.B. The Man From Halifax.
M. Horn, 150(DR):Summer85-308
Waites, A. and R. Hunter, comps. The
Illustrated Victorian Songbook.
A. Lamb, 415:Aug85-466
Waith, E.M. - see Shakespeare, W.
Wakefield, D. French Eighteenth-Century
Painting.*
P. Conisbee, 59:Sep85-359
D. Irwin, 83:Spring85-122
Wakefield, T. The Discus Throwers.
D. Profumo, 617(TLS):31Jan86-112
Wakoski, D. Toward a New Poetry.
R. McDowell, 249(HudR):Autumn85-513
Walbank, F.W. Selected Papers.
S. Hornblower, 617(TLS):1Aug86-848

Walbank, F.W. and others, eds. Cambridge
  Ancient History.* (2nd ed) (Vol 7, Pt 1)
    R.J. Rowland, Jr., 124:May-Jun86-351
Walberg, G. Provincial Middle Minoan
  Pottery.
    P. Warren, 123:Vol35No2-415
Walcott, D. Collected Poems 1948-1984.
    J. Dickey, 441:2Feb86-8
    L. Mackinnon, 617(TLS):24Oct86-1185
Walcott, D. Midsummer.*
    B. Howard, 271:Fall85-156
Wald, A.M. The Revolutionary Imagination.*
    W.B. Rideout, 27(AL):Oct85-520
Waldbaum, J.C. and others. Metalwork from
  Sardis.*
    J.D. Muhly, 124:May-Jun86-339
Walden, K. Visions of Order.
    R. Thacker, 298:Spring85-161
Walden, S. The Ravished Image.*
    E. Langmuir, 90:May85-306
Waldenfels, B. In den Netzen der Lebens-
  welt.
    J. Habermas, 384:Sep/Oct85-905
Waldenfels, B. Phänomenologie in Frank-
  reich.
    K. Schuhmann, 687:Apr-Jun85-326
Waldheim, K. In the Eye of the Storm.
    G.A. Craig, 453(NYRB):9Oct86-3
    C.C. O'Brien, 617(TLS):17Jan86-63
Waldheim, K. Die Reichsidee bei Konstan-
  tin Frantz.
    G.A. Craig, 453(NYRB):9Oct86-3
"Kurt Waldheim's Hidden Past."
    G.A. Craig, 453(NYRB):9Oct86-3
Waldmann, B. Natur und Kultur im
  höfischen Roman um 1200.
    D.H. Green, 402(MLR):Jul85-747
Waldmann, R. Die Schweiz in ihren Märchen
  und Sennengeschichten.
    B. Bieri, 196:Band26Heft1/2-205
Waldrop, K. The Ruins of Providence.
    L. Goldstein, 385(MQR):Winter86-147
    J. McCann, 472:Spring/Summer86-241
Waldrop, K. The Space of Half an Hour.
  The Quest for Mount Misery. A Ceremony
  Somewhere Else.
    J. McCann, 472:Spring/Summer86-241
Wales, H.G.Q. Divination in Thailand.
    C.F. Keyes, 293(JASt):May85-685
Walker, A. Horses Make a Landscape Look
  More Beautiful.*
    639(VQR):Spring85-57
Walker, A. In Search of Our Mothers'
  Gardens.*
    P. Lewis, 565:Winter84/85-42
    V.A. Smith, 569(SR):Spring85-xxxi
Walker, A. National Heroes.
    D. Robinson, 617(TLS):17Jan86-69
Walker, A.G.H. Die nordfriesische Mundart
  der Bökingharde.
    T.L. Markey, 260(IF):Band90-354
Walker, B.G. The Crone.
    M. Rubin, 441:12Jan86-21
Walker, C. The Nightingale's Burden.
    M. Kumin, 219(GaR):Spring85-169
Walker, D. The Transparent Lyric.
    L. Bartlett, 27(AL):May85-355
    M.J. Bates, 141:Fall85-429
    J. Green, 134(CP):Vol 18No1/2-145
    W.S. Waddell, Jr., 705:Spring85-55
    295(JML):Nov85-404

Walker, D.C. Dictionnaire inverse de
  l'ancien français.*
    R. de Gorog, 545(RPh):May85-475
Walker, D.L. - see Henry, W.
Walker, D.P. Music, Spirit and Language
  in the Renaissance. (P. Gouk, ed)
    A. Grafton, 617(TLS):7Feb86-133
Walker, E. The Art of Bookbinding. (P.S.
  Koda, ed)
    F. Broomhead, 503:Winter84-190
Walker, G. The Politics of Frustration.
    J. Whyte, 617(TLS):21Mar86-297
Walker, G.F. Criminals in Love.
    P. Walsh, 108:Winter85-143
Walker, G.F. The Power Plays.
    B. Parker, 108:Summer85-190
Walker, G.L. The Chronicles of Doodah.
    C. Verderese, 441:2Feb86-16
Walker, I. - see Plato
Walker, J. Metaphysics and Aesthetics in
  the Works of Eduardo Barrias.*
    J. Hancock, 238:May85-316
    D. Stephens, 593:Spring85-77
Walker, J. The Once and Future Film.*
    D. Robinson, 617(TLS):17Jan86-69
Walker, J. Portraits: 5000 Years.*
    K. Garlick, 39:Mar85-210
Walker, J. - see Cunninghame Graham, R.B.
Walker, J.B. and J. The Light on Her
  Face.*
    N.P. Hurley, 435:Winter85-71
    F. Thompson, 500:Fall85-65
Walker, J.L. The Making of a Modernist.*
    M.J. Hoffman, 395(MFS):Summer85-408
    C.N. Pondrom, 659(ConL):Spring86-98
    R.L. White, 27(AL):Mar85-165
    295(JML):Nov85-556
Walker, J.M. Fugitive Angels.
    P. Stitt, 219(GaR):Summer85-414
Walker, K. A Piece of My Heart.
    M.F. Coburn, 441:25May86-15
Walker, K. - see Lord Rochester
Walker, L.A. A Loss for Words.
    H. Kenner, 441:5Oct86-47
Walker, P. Zola.
    D. Bellos, 617(TLS):11Apr86-396
Walker, P.D. "Germinal" and Zola's Philo-
  sophical and Religious Thought.
    R.B. Grant, 210(FrF):May85-244
    L. Kamm, 207(FR):May86-982
    S. Nalbantian, 188(ECr):Winter85-119
    B. Nelson, 593:Fall85-228
    D. Rounsaville, 446(NCFS):Spring-
      Summer86-381
Walker, R. Regency Portraits.
    G. Reynolds, 617(TLS):28Mar86-328
Walker, R.C.S., ed. Kant on Pure Reason.
    A.N. Perovich, Jr., 342:Band76Heft2-
      221
Walker, S.S., ed. The Court Rolls of the
  Manor of Wakefield from October 1331 to
  September 1333.
    A.R. De Windt, 589:Jan85-146
Wallace, A. The Prodigy.
    P-L. Adams, 61:Aug86-91
    S. Sutherland, 617(TLS):24Oct86-1183
    L. Thomas, 441:20Jul86-19
Wallace, B. Signs of the Former Tenant.*
    T. Whalen, 102(CanL):Winter84-75
Wallace, C.M. The Design of "Biographia
  Literaria."*
    D. Jasper, 161(DUJ):Dec84-123

Wallace, D. Chaucer and the Early Writings of Boccaccio.
 A. Wawn, 617(TLS):28Nov86-1356
Wallace, D.R. The Turquoise Dragon.*
 J.D. Houston, 649(WAL):Feb86-362
 M. Laski, 362:3Jul86-32
Wallace, E. The Council of Justice.
 M. Laski, 362:9Jan86-30
Wallace, I. The Seventh Secret.
 W. Lesser, 441:12Jan86-20
Wallace, J.D. Early Cooper and His Audience.
 B. Lee, 617(TLS):27Jun86-704
Wallace, K.Y., ed. La Estoire de seint Aedward le Rei.
 M.D. Legge, 208(FS):Apr85-180
 G.B. Speroni, 379(MedR):Apr85-131
Wallace, M. The Silent Twins.
 A. Clare, 617(TLS):28Feb86-212
 O. Sacks, 441:19Oct86-3
Wallace, R. God Be with the Clown.
 W.B. Clark, 27(AL):Mar85-146
 E. Folsom, 646:Winter86-36
 E.L. Galligan, 579(SAQ):Autumn85-439
 C. Wade, 616:Fall/Winter85-46
Wallace, R., ed. Light Year '85.
 639(VQR):Spring85-56
Wallace, R. and C. Zimmerman. The Work.*
 R.P. Knowles, 198:Spring85-84
Wallace, R.K. Jane Austen and Mozart.*
 B. Boyce, 579(SAQ):Spring85-231
 M.H. Frank, 301(JEGP):Jul85-445
 A. Leighton, 410(M&L):Apr85-162
 B. Roth, 594:Summer85-220
 K.E. Smith, 83:Spring85-121
Wallace, W.A. Galileo and His Sources.*
 M.A. Finocchiaro, 543:Dec85-335
Wallace, W.A. Prelude to Galileo.*
 J.A. Weisheipl, 488:Mar85-97
Wallace, W.L. Principles of Scientific Sociology.
 I.C. Jarvie, 486:Sep85-489
Wallace-Crabbe, C. The Amorous Cannibal.
 C. Boyle, 364:Nov85-79
 L. Mackinnon, 617(TLS):18Apr86-430
Wallace-Hadrill, A. Suetonius.*
 H.W. Bird, 487:Autumn85-290
 K.R. Bradley, 122:Jul85-254
 R.H. Martin, 123:Vol35No1-40
Wallace-Hadrill, J.M. The Frankish Church.
 U-R. Blumenthal, 377:Jul85-118
Wallach, A.T. Private Scores.
 E. Feldman, 441:16Nov86-14
Wallach-Faller, M. Ein alemannischer Psalter aus dem 14. Jahrhundert.
 A. Näf, 680(ZDP):Band104Heft1-146
Wallechinsky, D. Midterm Report.
 R. Plunket, 441:31Aug86-5
Waller, A.L. Reverend Beecher and Mrs. Tilton.
 B. Todd, 106:Fall85-329
Waller, B. Les Portes gigognes.
 R. Buss, 617(TLS):21Mar86-306
 F. de Martinoir, 450(NRF):Nov85-95
Waller, G.A. The Living and the Undead.
 S.S. Prawer, 617(TLS):8Aug86-870
 R.E. Wood, 500:Spring/Summer86-84
Waller, M.R. Petrarch's Poetics and Literary History.
 T. Barolini, 545(RPh):Aug85-135
Wallimann, I. Estrangement.
 D.G., 185:Jan86-452

Wallis, B., ed. Art After Modernism.
 M. Berger, 62:Dec85-17
Wallis, R. and K. Malm. Big Sounds from Small Peoples.
 L.W. Brunner, 414:Vol71No1-81
 C. Ehrlich, 415:Jan85-28
 J. Shepherd, 187:Winter86-171
Wallis, W. Biographer's Notes.
 L.T. Lemon, 502(PrS):Fall85-117
Wallner, F. Die Grenzen der Sprache und der Erkenntnis.
 R. Thurnher, 489(PJGG):Band92Heft2-425
Walpole, H. Contes hiéroglyphiques et autres bizarreries.
 A. Clerval, 450(NRF):Jun85-84
Walpole, H. Memoirs of King George II by Horace Walpole.* (J. Brooke, ed)
 D.G.C.A., 324:May86-420
Walpole, H. The Yale Edition of Horace Walpole's Correspondence.* (Vol 43) (E.M. Martz, with R.K. McClure and W.T. La Moy, eds)
 P. Rogers, 83:Spring85-103
Walpole, R.N., ed. Le Turpin français, dit le Turpin I.
 D.D.R. Owen, 617(TLS):21Mar86-311
Walser, M. Letter to Lord Liszt.*
 D.J. Enright, 453(NYRB):14Aug86-37
Walser, R. Les Enfants Tanner.
 R. Millet, 450(NRF):Oct85-106
Walser, R. Aus dem Bleistiftgebiet. (W. Morland and B. Echte, eds) Robert Walser Rediscovered. (M. Harman, ed)
 A. Cardinal, 617(TLS):10Jan86-33
Walsh, G.B. The Varieties of Enchantment.
 R.M. Harriott, 303(JoHS):Vol 105-198
 M. Lloyd, 123:Vol135No2-380
 W.G. Thalmann, 124:Sep-Oct85-56
Walsh, J. American War Literature: 1914 to Vietnam.*
 W.K. Buckley, 594:Fall85-331
 B. Gasser, 447(N&Q):Jun84-283
Walsh, J.E. Growing Up in British India.
 S. Hay, 293(JASt):May85-658
 P.J. Marshall, 637(VS):Autumn85-158
Walsh, J.K., ed. "El libro de los doze sabios, o Tractado de la nobleza y lealtad" [Ca. 1237].
 H. Goldberg, 545(RPh):Aug84-41
Walsh, M. and K. Williamson - see Smart, C.
Walsh, M.J. A History of Philosophy.
 M.A. Stewart, 518:Jul85-132
Walsh, W. R.K. Narayan.*
 C.R. Larson, 405(MP):Aug85-89
Walter, E. The Untidy Pilgrim. The Byzantine Riddle.
 F. Eberstadt, 617(TLS):17Jan86-56
Walter, H. and others. Enquête phonologique et variétés régionales du français.*
 N.L. Corbett, 545(RPh):Feb86-344
Walter, I. Secret Money.
 S. Aris, 617(TLS):28Feb86-222
Walters, A. Britain's Economic Renaissance.
 W. Eltis, 176:Sep/Oct86-70
 P. Jay, 617(TLS):30May86-579
Walters, W.A.W. and P. Singer, eds. Test-Tube Babies.
 C. Overall, 154:Winter85-728
Walthall, J.A. Prehistoric Indians of the Southeast.
 J.P. Pate, 9(AlaR):Apr85-137

394

Watson, J.R., ed. An Infinite Complexity.
  P. New, 161(DUJ):Dec84-125
  B. Ruddick, 148:Spring85-92
  P.D. Sheats, 340(KSJ):Vol34-175
Watson, J.R. Wordsworth's Vital Soul.*
  R. Sharrock, 447(N&Q):Mar84-143
  M. Wedd, 541(RES):Feb85-105
Watson, L. Heaven's Breath.*
  P. Zaleski, 469:Vol 11No1-104
Watson, O. Persian Lustre Ware.
  B. Gray, 39:Dec85-500
  B. Gray, 90:Nov85-819
Watson, P. The Nazi's Wife.
  D. Ryan, 441:5Jan86-16
Watson, R. The Literature of Scotland.*
  P. Morère, 189(EA):Jan-Mar86-113
  G.R.R., 588(SSL):Vol20-326
Watson, R. The Playfair Hours.*
  C.R., 90:Dec85-918
Watson, S. - see Mandel, M.
Watson, W. Gramsci x 3.*
  A. Filewod, 108:Spring85-145
  R.P. Knowles, 198:Spring85-84
Watson, W. Tang and Liao Ceramics.*
  "Skipjack," 463:Autumn85-311
Watson-Williams, H. The Novels of Natha-
lie Sarraute.*
  C. Britton, 208(FS):Jan85-109
Watt, D.C. Succeeding John Bull.
  M. Beloff, 176:Apr86-62
Watt, G. The Fallen Woman in the Nine-
teenth-Century English Novel.*
  R. Gagnier, 637(VS):Autumn85-159
  M. Moseley, 569(SR):Summer85-485
Watt, W.M. Islam and Christianity Today.
  P.J. Ryan, 258:Jun85-222
"Jean-Antoine Watteau: Einschiffung nach
Cythera."
  P. Conisbee, 59:Sep85-359
Wattel, H.L. The Policy Consequences of
John Maynard Keynes.
  P.C. Roberts, 617(TLS):4Jul86-744
Wattenberg, B. and K. Zinsmeister, eds.
Are World Population Trends A Problem?
  J. Lieberson, 453(NYRB):26Jun86-36
Wattenberg, B.J. The Good News is the Bad
News is Wrong.*
  639(VQR):Spring85-57
Watts, C. The Deceptive Text.
  R. Davis, 395(MFS):Winter85-798
  J.M. Szczypien, 136:Vol 18No3-224
  295(JML):Nov85-430
Watts, D.A. - see Rotrou, J.
Watts, P.M. Nicolaus Cusanus.*
  P.E. Sigmund, 551(RenQ):Winter85-716
Waugh, A. Another Voice.
  F. Raphael, 617(TLS):17Oct86-1157
Waugh, A. Brideshead Benighted.
  A. Goreau, 441:31Aug86-7
Waugh, E. The Essays, Articles and
Reviews of Evelyn Waugh.* (D. Gallagher,
ed)
  G. Weales, 219(GaR):Summer85-444
Waugh, E. Ninety-Two Days.
  617(TLS):28Feb86-231
Waugh, E. Remote People.* Waugh in Abys-
sinia.
  617(TLS):28Mar86-343
Waugh, L.R. and M. Halle - see Jakobson, R.
Waugh, L.R. and C.H. van Schooneveld, eds.
The Melody of Language.
  D. Brazil, 567:Vol56No3/4-371

Waugh, P. Metafiction.*
  A. Nadel, 395(MFS):Winter85-759
  U. Wicks, 343:Heft12-126
  R.R. Wilson, 107(CRCL):Jun85-292
  295(JML):Nov85-430
Waugh, T. Waterloo Waterloo.
  K.C. O'Brien, 362:1May86-30
  K. Milne, 617(TLS):7Mar86-257
Wawn, B. The Economies of the ASEAN Coun-
tries.
  L. Lim, 293(JASt):May85-689
Wayne, D.E. Penshurst.
  W.E. Cain, 551(RenQ):Winter85-770
Weale, A. Political Theory and Social
Policy.
  R. Dagger, 185:Oct85-203
Weales, G. Canned Goods as Caviar.*
  D. Powell, 617(TLS):24Oct86-1202
Wearing, J.P., comp. The London Stage
1920-1929.
  R. Berry, 130:Fall85-282
Weaver, G. A World Quite Round.
  S. Tanenhaus, 441:6Jul86-14
Weaver, M. Alvin Langdon Coburn.
  A. Grundberg, 441:7Dec86-21
Weaver, R., ed. The Anthology Anthology.
  G. Woodcock, 102(CanL):Summer85-152
Weaver, W. Red Earth, White Earth.
  T. Miller, 441:9Nov86-33
Weaver, W.W. Sauerkraut Yankees.
  J. Anderson, 650(WF):Jan85-57
Webb, B. The Diary of Beatrice Webb.*
  (Vol 4) (N. and J. MacKenzie, eds)
  A. Howard, 441:6Apr86-42
  442(NY):27Jan86-98
Webb, M., ed. Hollywood.
  C. James, 441:7Sep86-23
Webb, M.G. Even Cops' Daughters.
  N. Callendar, 441:22Jun86-25
Webb, P. Human Calorimeters.
  T.C. Holyoke, 42(AR):Fall85-497
Webb, P., with R. Short. Hans Bellmer.*
  S. Wilson, 90:Dec85-910
Webb, S.S. 1676.*
  J. Kukla, 658:Winter85-292
Webb, T., ed. English Romantic Hellenism,
1700-1824.*
  C. Rawson, 83:Autumn85-240
  C. Woodring, 340(KSJ):Vol34-199
Webber, C. and A. Wildavsky. A History of
Taxation and Expenditure in the Western
World.
  H. Stein, 441:3Aug86-11
Webber, J.M. Milton and his Epic Tradi-
tion.
  W. Weihermann, 38:Band103Heft3/4-484
Weber, A. and J.M. Bächtold. Zürich-
deutsches Wörterbuch. (3rd ed rev by
J.M. Bächtold, J.J. Sturzenegger and R.
Trüb)
  W.G. Moulton, 133:Band18Heft2-191
Weber, B. - see Crane, H.
Weber, D.J. Richard H. Kern.
  L. Milazzo, 584(SWR):Spring85-262
Weber, E. France, Fin de Siècle.
  P. Brooks, 441:14Sep86-15
  J.F. McMillan, 617(TLS):19Dec86-1417
  R. Shattuck, 453(NYRB):18Dec86-66
  442(NY):3Nov86-166
Weber, H. Geschichte der DDR.
  G.A. Craig, 453(NYRB):25Sep86-62

Weber, M. Gesammelte Aufsätze zur Wissen-
schaftslehre. (5th ed)
  C. Piché, 98:Oct85-954
Weber, M. Die mythologische Erzählungen
in Ovids Liebeskunst.
  E.J. Kenney, 123:Vol35No2-389
Weber, R. Company Spook.
  N. Callendar, 441:30Mar86-22
Weber, R. Seeing Earth.
  M. Boruch, 219(GaR):Winter85-904
  L. Goldstein, 385(MQR):Fall86-736
Weber, W.K. Training Translators and Con-
ference Interpreters.
  M.T. Krause, 399(MLJ):Winter85-448
Webster, B. - see David II
Webster, B.S. Blake's Prophetic Psychol-
ogy.*
  K. Everest, 83:Spring85-106
  C. Gallant, 661(WC):Fall85-165
Webster, C. From Paracelsus to Newton.*
  R.H. Popkin, 319:Jan86-125
Webster, D.B., with M.S. Cross and I.
Szylinger. Georgian Canada, Conflict
and Culture, 1745-1820.
  W.H. Siener, 656(WMQ):Jul85-417
Webster, E.M. The Moon Man.
  K. Burridge, 617(TLS):8Aug86-859
Webster, J. - see Temple, W.
Webster, J.C. Erastus D. Palmer.
  B.R., 90:Jun85-397
Weckmann, L. La herencia medieval de
México.
  C.J. Bishko, 589:Oct85-1034
Wedberg, A. A History of Philosophy.*
(Vol 2)
  R. Cormier, 568(SCN):Spring-Summer85-
  22
Wedde, I. Symmes Hole.
  P. Smelt, 617(TLS):26Dec86-1456
Wedgwood, A. A.W.N. Pugin and the Pugin
Family.
  R. O'Donnell, 90:Oct85-724
Weeks-Pearson, T. Dodo.
  J. Mellors, 362:24Apr86-34
  N. Shack, 617(TLS):23May86-553
Wees, W.C. and M. Dorland, eds. Words and
Moving Images.
  D. Clandfield, 627(UTQ):Summer85-519
Wehdeking, V., ed. Zu Alfred Andersch.
  R.W. Williams, 402(MLR):Apr85-503
Wehgartner, I. Attische weissgrundige
Keramik.
  D.C. Kurtz, 123:Vol35No2-341
Wehgartner, I. Corpus Vasorum Antiquorum.
(Deutschland, Band 51)
  T. Rasmussen, 303(JoHS):Vol 105-237
Wehle, W. Novellenerzählen.*
  W. Pabst, 224(GRM):Band35Heft1-114
Wehr, B. Diskurs-Strategien im Roman-
ischen.
  G. Kleiber, 553(RLiR):Jul-Dec85-457
Wehrli, B. Kommunikative Wahrheitsfindung.
  E. Glass, 221(GQ):Spring85-276
Wehrli, M. Literatur im deutschen Mittel-
alter.
  O. Sayce, 402(MLR):Oct85-969
Weideger, P. History's Mistress.
  A. Barnet, 441:4May86-41
Weidenhammer, D. Prometheus und Merlin.
  B. Guthmüller, 72:Band222Heft2-451
Weidman, J. Praying for Rain.
  W. Balliett, 442(NY):8Dec86-151
  H. Dudar, 441:21Sep86-11

Weigand, H.J. Critical Probings. (U.K.
Goldsmith and D. Goldschmidt, eds)
  H. Zohn, 221(GQ):Winter85-103
Weiger, J.G. The Substance of Cervantes.
  A.J. Close, 617(TLS):28Nov86-1352
Weigl, B. The Monkey Wars.
  639(VQR):Autumn85-130
Weigl, B. and T.R. Hummer, eds. The Imag-
ination as Glory.*
  639(VQR):Spring85-45
Weigley, R.F. Eisenhower's Lieutenants.
  P. Brown, 106:Spring85-107
Weikert, H-E. Tom Stoppards Dramen.
  P.H. Marsden, 38:Band103Heft3/4-512
  H.F. Plett, 72:Band222Heft2-424
Weil, S.E. Beauty and the Beasts.
  W.S. Ayres, 476:Winter84-74
  F.V. O'Connor, 127:Winter84-393
Weimann, R. Structure and Society in Lit-
erary History.
  S.V. Pradham, 150(DR):Spring85-131
Weimerskirch, P.J. Antonio Panizzi and
the British Museum Library.
  J.F. Fuggles, 354:Mar85-74
Weinberg, H.B. The American Pupils of
Jean-Louis Gérôme.
  A.S. Weller, 127:Spring85-73
Weinberg, K. The Figure of Faust in Val-
éry and Goethe.
  A. Dabezies, 549(RLC):Jul-Sep85-363
de Weinberg, M.B.F. - see under Fontanella
de Weinberg, M.B.
Weinbrot, H.D. Alexander Pope and the Tra-
ditions of Formal Verse Satire.*
  H. Erskine-Hill, 541(RES):Feb85-92
  W. Frost, 131(CL):Fall85-373
  G. Laprevotte, 549(RLC):Jul-Sep85-347
Weiner, A.R. and S. Means, eds. Literary
Criticism Index.
  27(AL):Mar85-189
Weiner, L.Y. From Working Girl to Working
Mother.
  639(VQR):Summer85-86
Weiner, M.A., with K. Goss. Maximum Immu-
nity.
  L. Lyon, 441:23Mar86-46
Weinig, M.A. Coventry Patmore.
  P.M. Ball, 402(MLR):Oct85-916
Weinman, I. Tailor's Dummy.
  N. Callendar, 441:20Apr86-32
  442(NY):18Aug86-75
Weinmayer, B. Studien zur Gebrauchssitua-
tion früher deutscher Druckprosa.*
  S. Calomino, 589:Jul85-732
  J.L. Flood, 402(MLR):Jan85-208
Weinreb, R.P. Visions et Révisions.*
  J.D. Brown and M.P. Leamon, 399(MLJ):
  Spring85-91
Weinrich, L., comp and trans. Quellen zur
deutschen Verfassungs-, Wirtschafts- und
Sozialgeschichte bis 1250.
  H. Kaminsky, 589:Jan85-232
Weinrich, P. Social Protest from the Left
in Canada 1870-1970.
  A.K. Richardson, 161(DUJ):Jun84-317
Weinsheimer, J. Imitation.
  H. Weber, 566:Spring86-216
Weinstein, B. The Civic Tongue.
  H.R. Dua, 355(LSoc):Dec85-527
Weinstein, M.A. Unity and Variety in the
Philosophy of Samuel Alexander.
  D. Emmet, 323:May85-204

West, R. Sunflower.
  L. Chamberlain, 617(TLS):25Jul86-818
  M. Wandor, 362:10Jul86-27
West, R. This Real Night.
  W. Lesser, 249(HudR):Autumn85-463
West, S. - see Homer
West, T. Ted Hughes.
  A. Haberer, 189(EA):Apr-Jun86-232
West, T. Horace Plunkett, Co-operation
  and Politics.
  T. Hoppen, 617(TLS):19Dec86-1432
West, T.W. and G.S., eds and trans. Plato
  and Aristophanes — Four Texts on Socra-
  tes.
  J. Barnes, 520:Vol30No3-326
West, W.J. - see Orwell, G.
Westall, O.M., ed. The Historian and the
  Business of Insurance.
  D. Meredith, 637(VS):Summer86-638
Westbrook, R. The Left-Handed Policeman.
  N. Callendar, 441:8Jun86-34
Westby, B.M. - see Rovira, C.
Westerfield, N.G. Welded Women.
  C.H. Taylor, 649(WAL):May85-94
Western, J.R. Monarchy and Revolution.
  R. Lejosne, 189(EA):Apr-Jun86-241
Westlake, D.E. Good Behavior.
  N. Callendar, 441:22Jun86-25
"Westland plc: The Government's Decision-
  making."
  J. Turner, 617(TLS):22Aug86-904
Westling, L. Sacred Groves and Ravaged
  Gardens.
  W.L. Andrews, 659(ConL):Summer86-257
  W.J. Stuckey, 395(MFS):Winter85-749
  295(JML):Nov85-404
Westlund, J. Shakespeare's Reparative
  Comedies.*
  P. Erickson, 301(JEGP):Oct85-551
  C. Kahn, 551(RenQ):Autumn85-581
Weston, S.B. Children of the Light.
  G. Jonas, 441:9Mar86-23
Westphal, P.B., ed. Strategies for
  Foreign Language Teaching, Communication,
  Technology, Culture.
  M-A. Reiss, 399(MLJ):Winter85-406
Weststeijn, W.G. Velimir Chlebnikov and
  the Development of Poetical Language in
  Russian Symbolism and Futurism.*
  J. Graffy, 575(SEER):Oct85-567
  M.M. Naydan, 574(SEEJ):Summer85-211
  R. Vroon, 550(RusR):Apr85-188
Westwater, M. The Wilson Sisters.
  W. Ruddick, 366:Autumn85-309
Westwood, J. Albion.
  T.A. Shippey, 617(TLS):30May86-583
van de Wetering, J. Murder by Remote
  Control.
  G. Wilson, 441:4May86-27
van der Wetering, J. The Rattle-Rat.
  M. Laski, 362:3Jul86-32
Wetherbee, W. Chaucer and the Poets.*
  R. Edwards, 219(GaR):Winter85-871
  P.G. Ruggiers, 107(CRCL):Sep85-511
Wetherell, W.D. The Man Who Loved Levit-
  town.
  R. Ward, 441:5Jan86-8
Wetherill, P.M., ed. Flaubert - la dimen-
  sion du texte.
  J. Bem, 535(RHL):Jul/Aug85-688
Wethey, H. Alonso Cano.
  D. Angulo Íñiguez, 48:Jan-Mar85-87

Wetzel, C-D. Die Worttrennung am Zeilen-
  ende in altenglischen Handschriften.
  C.T. Berkhout, 589:Apr85-465
  K. Dietz, 72:Band222Heft2-381
  A. Lutz, 260(IF):Band90-227
Wexler, A. Emma Goldman.
  639(VQR):Winter85-10
Wexler, J. The Bequest and Other Stories.
  J. Mills, 198:Autumn85-85
de Weydenthal, J., B.D. Porter and K. Dev-
  lin. The Polish Drama, 1980-82.
  J. Woodall, 575(SEER):Jan85-153
Weydt, G. and others - see "Simpliciana"
Weydt, H. Partikeln und Deutschunterricht.
  D. Nehls, 257(IRAL):Feb85-78
Weydt, H., ed. Partikeln und Interaktion.
  B.J. Koekkoek, 221(GQ):Spring85-270
  D. Nehls, 257(IRAL):Feb85-78
Weyergans, F. La Vie d'un bébé.
  R. Buss, 617(TLS):30May86-597
Whale, J.C. Thomas De Quincey's Reluctant
  Autobiography.
  P.F. Morgan, 635(VPR):Winter85-159
Whalen, R.W. Bitter Wounds.
  G. Best, 176:Jun85-48
Whalley, G. Studies in Literature and the
  Humanities. (B. Crick and J. Ferns, eds)
  P. Rae, 150(DR):Summer85-312
Whalley, G. - see Coleridge, S.T.
Whalley, J.I. Pliny the Elder "Historia
  Naturalis."
  K.S., 90:Jul185-471
Whalley, P. Robbers.
  T.J. Binyon, 617(TLS):27Jun86-711
Whallon, W. Inconsistencies.*
  J. Simpson, 447(N&Q):Sep84-413
Wharton, E. The House of Mirth; The Reef;
  The Custom of the Country; The Age of
  Innocence.
  J. Malcolm, 441:16Nov86-11
Wharton, T.F. "Henry the Fourth, Parts 1
  and 2."
  B.W. Kliman, 130:Winter85/86-383
Wharton, T.F. Samuel Johnson and the
  Theme of Hope.
  T. Jemielity, 481(PQ):Fall85-595
Wharton, W. Pride.*
  P. Duguid, 617(TLS):18Apr86-416
  M. Hulse, 176:Sep/Oct86-59
  J. Mellors, 362:24Apr86-34
Wheatcroft, G. The Randlords.*
  J.A. Livingston, 441:30Mar86-6
  L. Thompson, 453(NYRB):17Jul86-17
Wheatcroft, J. Slow Exposures.
  J. Neugeboren, 441:2Feb86-31
Wheeler, J.A. and W.H. Zurek, eds. Quan-
  tum Theory and Measurement.
  N. Cartwright, 486:Sep85-480
Wheeler, M. English Fiction of the Victor-
  ian Period, 1830-1890.*
  B.V. Qualls, 637(VS):Spring86-498
  G.B. Tennyson, 445(NCF):Dec85-363
Wheeler, M. - see "The Oxford Russian-
  English Dictionary"
Wheeler, R. Sword Over Richmond.
  H. Goodman, 441:27Apr86-23
Whelan, F.G. Order and Artifice in Hume's
  Political Philosophy.
  G.B. Herbert, 543:Jun86-788
Whelan, P. The Accrington Pals.
  D. Devlin, 157:No155-49

Williams, T. Moise und die Welt der Vernunft.
  D. Dziwas, 654(WB):4/1985-658
Williams, T. The Moon Pinnace.
  H.F. Mosher, 441:17Aug86-8
Williams, T. The Theater of Tennessee Williams. (Vols 1-7)
  W.K. Holditch, 598(SoR):Autumn86-892
Williams, W.C. The Doctor Stories.
  295(JML):Nov85-570
Williams, W.H. The Garden of American Methodism.
  J.B. Frantz, 656(WMQ):Apr85-292
Williams, W.L. Black Americans and the Evangelization of Africa, 1877-1900.
  G. Vandal, 106:Spring85-41
Williams, W.P. and C.S. Abbott. An Introduction to Bibliographical and Textual Studies.
  M.A. O'Donnell, 365:Summer85-37
Williamsen, V.G. The Minor Dramatists of Seventeenth-Century Spain.*
  A.L. Mackenzie, 86(BHS):Oct85-408
Williamson, A. Gilbert and Sullivan Opera. (rev)
  J.B., 412:Feb83-59
  A.F.L.T., 412:Aug/Nov84-304
Williamson, A. Introspection and Contemporary Poetry.*
  L. Coupe, 148:Winter85-88
  M. Dickie, 115:Fall84/Winter85-152
  C. Molesworth, 141:Summer85-324
Williamson, D. Fireside Tales of the Traveller Children.*
  N. Philip, 203:Vol96No1-135
Williamson, H. Methods of Book Design.* (3rd ed)
  A. Lerner, 354:Mar85-79
  W.S. Peterson, 517(PBSA):Vol79No2-258
Williamson, J. Consuming Passions.
  J.B. Ciulla, 441:15Jun86-17
  K. Milne, 362:10Apr86-26
Williamson, J. The Crucible of Race.*
  E.L. Ayers, 639(VQR):Spring85-337
Williamson, J. Wonder's Child.
  G.K. Wolfe, 395(MFS):Summer85-458
Williamson, J.G. Did British Capitalism Breed Inequality?
  J.H. Porter, 637(VS):Summer86-626
Williamson, R.A. Living the Sky.
  J.L. Davis, 649(WAL):Aug85-189
Willis, B. Lasting the Pace.
  A. Ross, 617(TLS):3Jan86-21
Willis, B. and P. Murphy. Starting with Grace.
  S. Fry, 362:18/25Dec86-55
Willis, D.K. Klass.
  639(VQR):Autumn85-135
Willis, P.C. - see Moore, M.
Willmot, R. The Ribs of Dragonfly.
  W.J. Higginson, 404:Autumn85-52
Willmott, H.P. The Barrier and the Javelin.
  T.W. Burkman, 293(JASt):Feb85-410
Willms, A. Die dialektale Differenzierung des Berberischen.
  K.H. Schmidt, 685(ZDL):2/1985-256
Wills, A. Organ.
  A. Bond, 415:Mar85-179
Wills, G. Cincinnatus: George Washington and the Enlightenment.*
  L.B. Miller, 656(WMQ):Oct85-527

Willson Cummer, W. and E. Schofield. Keos. (Vol 3)
  R.L.N. Barber, 303(JoHS):Vol 105-223
  S. Hood, 123:Vol35No2-417
Willumsen, D. Marie.
  S. Altinel, 617(TLS):18Jul86-793
Wilmot, J. - see under Lord Rochester
Wilner, E. Shekkinah.*
  639(VQR):Autumn85-130
Wilshere, A.D. - see Saint Edmund of Abingdon
Wilshire, B. Role Playing and Identity.*
  P.N. Campbell, 480(P&R):Vol 18No1-62
  M. Carlson, 449:Dec85-644
  D.M. Levin, 258:Jun85-211
Wilson, A. Diversity and Depth in Fiction.* (K. McSweeney, ed)
  P. Conradi, 148:Spring85-25
Wilson, A. Reflections in a Writer's Eye.
  F. King, 617(TLS):7Feb86-147
  M. Wexler, 441:7Sep86-23
  442(NY):20Oct86-131
Wilson, A. and J.L. A Medieval Mirror.
  C.R. Dowdell, 617(TLS):14Mar86-287
Wilson, A.J. The Life and Times of Sir Alfred Chester Beatty.
  J. White, 39:Nov85-403
Wilson, A.J. and D. Dalton, eds. The States of South Asia.
  A.T. Embree, 293(JASt):Feb85-450
  R.J. Young, 318(JAOS):Oct-Dec84-781
Wilson, A.N. Hilaire Belloc.*
  P. Lewis, 565:Spring85-43
  S. Rudikoff, 31(ASch):Autumn85-556
  S. Weintraub, 177(ELT):Vol28No2-202
  295(JML):Nov85-448
  639(VQR):Winter85-12
Wilson, A.N. Gentlemen in England.*
  A. Broyard, 441:9Mar86-7
  J. Mellors, 364:Oct85-86
Wilson, A.N. The Life of John Milton.*
  M. Fixler, 541(RES):May85-269
  R.S. Ide, 536(Rev):Vol7-89
Wilson, A.N. Love Unknown.
  W. Brandmark, 362:11Sep86-22
  J. Melmoth, 617(TLS):29Aug86-932
Wilson, A.N. Scandal.*
  W.H. Pritchard, 249(HudR):Spring85-126
  639(VQR):Summer85-91
Wilson, C. First with the News.
  A. Briggs, 362:2Jan86-23
  C. Carter, 324:Aug86-625
  J. Sutherland, 617(TLS):21Feb86-186
Wilson, C. Gallimaufy's Gospel.
  P. Reading, 617(TLS):30May86-588
Wilson, C.A. The Book of Marmalade.
  R. Fuller, 364:Jul85-107
Wilson, C.P. The Labor of Words.
  J. Buenker, 125:Spring85-353
  H. McNeil, 617(TLS):21Feb86-181
  R.W. Schneider, 26(ALR):Spring/Autumn85-293
Wilson, D. The Sun at Noon.
  A. Booth, 617(TLS):22Aug86-908
Wilson, D.M. Anglo-Saxon Art.*
  C.R. Dowdell, 39:May85-351
Wilson, D.M. The Bayeux Tapestry.*
  G. Zarnecki, 617(TLS):21Mar86-301
Wilson, D.M. The Forgotten Collector.
  T. Russell-Cobb, 324:Apr86-344
Wilson, E. The Fifties. (L. Edel, ed)
  J. Epstein, 441:31Aug86-3
    [continued]

Wolf, N.A.  Lautlehre der Mundart des Such-
ener Tals in der deutschen Sprachinsel
Gottschee.
  K. Rein, 685(ZDL):2/1985-239
Wolf, N.R.  Geschichte der deutschen
Sprache.*  (Vol 1)
  J. Schildt, 682(ZPSK):Band38Heft3-330
Wolf, T.  The Nonprofit Organization.
  S. Benedict, 476:Summer85-100
Wolf, U., ed.  Eigennamen.
  J. Habermas, 384:Sep/Oct85-899
Wolf, U.  Das Problem des moralischen
Sollens.
  J.C.E., 185:Apr86-692
Wolf, V.  Die Rezeption australischer Lit-
eratur im deutschen Sprachraum von 1845-
1979.*
  H. Ertl, 38:Band103Heft3/4-527
Wolf, W.  Ursprünge und Formen der Empfind-
samkeit im französischen Drama des 18.
Jahrhunderts (Marivaux und Beaumarchais).
  F. Baasner, 547(RF):Band97Heft2/3-321
Wolfart, H.C. and J.F. Carroll.  Meet
Cree.*  (rev)
  H.I. Aronson, 269(IJAL):Jul85-321
Wolfe, C.K.  Kentucky Country.*
  F.W. Childrey, Jr., 585(SoQ):Spring86-
  89
Wolfe, G.  The House of Appleton.
  R.W. Ryan, 87(BB):Mar85-47
Wolfe, L.  The Professor and the Prosti-
tute.
  J. Coleman, 441:1Jun86-21
Wolfe, M.  Invisible Weapons.
  H. Benedict, 441:24Aug86-18
Wolfe, P. - see Naudé, G.
Wolfe, P. - see de Peiresc, N.C.F.
Wolfe, T.  The Autobiography of an Amer-
ican Novelist.*  (L. Field, ed)  Welcome
to Our City.*  (R.S. Kennedy, ed)
  E. McNamara, 106:Spring85-115
Wolfe, T.  Sam et Charlie vont en bateau.
  P-Y. Petillon, 98:Dec85-1159
Wolfe, T. and A. Bernstein.  My Other Lone-
liness.*  (S. Stutman, ed)
  E. McNamara, 106:Spring85-115
Wolfe, T. and E. Nowell.  Beyond Love and
Loyalty.*  (R.S. Kennedy, ed)
  E. McNamara, 106:Spring85-115
Wölfel, K., ed.  Sammlung der zeitgenös-
sischen Rezensionen von Jean Pauls
Werken.
  W. Theiss, 224(GRM):Band35Heft3-356
Wolfenstine, M.R.  The Manual of Brands
and Marks.
  W.C. Watt, 567:Vol55No3/4-295
Wolff, C.  Magnus Hirschfeld.
  R. Dinnage, 617(TLS):5Sep86-964
Wolff, C.  Vernünfftige Gedancken von Gott,
der Welt und der Seele des Menschen,
auch allen Dingen überhaupt.  (C.A. Corr,
ed)
  R. Finster, 706:Band17Heft1-116
Wolff, C.G.  Emily Dickinson.
  E. Frank, 441:23Nov86-7
Wolff, G.  Providence.
  J. Beatty, 61:Feb86-85
  T.J. Binyon, 617(TLS):28Nov86-1357
  J. Carroll, 441:16Feb86-7
  442(NY):5May86-133
Wolff, G.  Theodore Roethke.
  R. Pooley, 402(MLR):Apr85-452

Wolff, J.  Rilkes Grabschrift.
  B.L. Bradley, 301(JEGP):Jan85-88
Wolff, R., ed.  Hans Fallada.
  M. Geisler, 221(GQ):Summer85-473
Wolff, R., ed.  Reiner Kunze.
  M. Eifler, 221(GQ):Fall185-636
  G.H. Weiss, 221(GQ):Fall185-637
Wolff, R., ed.  Thomas Manns "Dr. Faustus"
und die Wirkung.
  F.A. Lubich, 221(GQ):Summer85-471
Wolff, R.L.  Nineteenth-Century Fiction.*
(Vol 3)
  W.E. Smith, 517(PBSA):Vol79No1-153
Wolff, R.L.  Nineteenth-Century Fiction.
(Vol 4)
  J. Sutherland, 617(TLS):11Apr86-384
Wolff, R.P.  Understanding Marx.
  H. Denis, 542:Jul-Sep85-338
  J.E. Roemer, 185:Jan86-425
Wolff, T.  Back in the World.*
  P. Glasser, 455:Dec85-75
  D. Montrose, 617(TLS):24Jan86-82
Wolfson, N. and J. Manes, eds.  Language
of Inequality.
  J. Baugh, 350:Dec86-923
Wolfzettel, F.  Einführung in die franzö-
sische Literaturgeschichtsschreibung.
  J. von Stackelberg, 535(RHL):Nov/Dec85-
  1081
Wolfzettel, F., ed.  Der französische
Sozialroman des 19. Jahrhunderts.
  W. Engler, 224(GRM):Band35Heft3-362
Wolitzer, M.  Hidden Pictures.
  R. Kaveney, 617(TLS):28Nov86-1358
  G. Naylor, 441:8Jun86-12
  442(NY):18Aug86-73
Wolkski, W., ed.  Aspekte der sowjetrus-
sischen Lexikographie.
  D. Herberg, 682(ZPSK):Band38Heft4-441
Wolkstein, D. and S.N. Kramer.  Inanna:
Queen of Heaven and Earth.
  J. O'Brien, 124:Sep-Oct85-59
Woll, A.  Dictionary of the Black Theatre.
  E. Southern, 91:Spring85-124
Woll, J., with V.G. Treml.  Soviet Dissi-
dent Literature.*
  O. Matich, 550(RusR):Apr85-192
  D. Milivojević, 558(RLJ):Fall184-300
Wollasch, J., with others, eds.  Synopse
der cluniacensischen Necrologien.
  G. Constable, 589:Jan85-208
Wollheim, R.  The Thread of Life.*
  R. Eldridge, 543:Mar86-590
  R.M.M., 185:Jul86-890
  R. Puccetti, 529(QQ):Autumn85-632
  483:Apr85-278
Wollstonecraft, M.  A Critical Edition of
Mary Wollstonecraft's "A Vindication of
the Rights of Women: With Strictures on
Political and Moral Subjects."*  (U.H.
Hardt, ed)
  J.D.F., 447(N&Q):Mar84-137
Woloch, G.M. - see Grimal, P.
Wolosky, S.  Emily Dickinson.*
  W. Barker, 432(NEQ):Sep85-459
  N. Baym, 301(JEGP):Oct85-578
  J. Burbick, 357:Spring86-69
  R. Miller, 385(MQR):Fall186-760
  295(JML):Nov85-467
Wolsch, R.A. and L.A.C.  From Speaking to
Writing to Reading.
  S. Liggett, 126(CCC):Oct85-369
Wolter, A.B. - see Scotus, J.D.

Wright, A., D. Betteridge and M. Buckby.
Games for Language Learning. (new ed)
L.M. Crawford-Lange, 399(MLJ):Summer85-165
Wright, A.M. The Formal Principle in the
Novel.*
T. Braun, 447(N&Q):Dec84-561
A.M. Duckworth, 219(GaR):Fall85-655
J. Frank, 569(SR):Summer85-493
D.H. Richter, 599:Spring85-137
Wright, B. Baudelaire: "La Fanfarlo"
[together with] Scott, D.H.T. Baude-laire: "Le Spleen de Paris."
F.S. Heck, 207(FR):Apr86-791
N.H. Lewis, 446(NCFS):Spring-Summer86-365
R. Lloyd, 208(FS):Jan85-89
Wright, B. and T. Mellors - see Fromentin,
E. and P. Bataillard
Wright, C. Dutch Landscape Painting.
C.B., 90:Feb85-110
Wright, C. The Dutch Painters. (rev)
N. Powell, 39:Mar85-211
Wright, C. Frege's Conception of Numbers
as Objects.*
G. Currie, 84:Dec85-475
A. Hazen, 63:Jun85-251
M. Jubien, 316:Mar85-252
Wright, C. The French Painters of the
Seventeenth Century.
R. Spear, 617(TLS):28Mar86-321
Wright, C. The Other Side of the River.*
M. Jarman, 460(OhR):No37-129
Wright, C. Poussin Paintings.
R. Verdi, 90:Nov85-811
Wright, E. Franklin of Philadelphia.
B. De Mott, 61:Apr86-122
B. Granger, 165(EAL):Winter86/87-275
P. Maier, 441:18May86-39
D. Schaub, 129:Jun86-74
G.S. Wood, 617(TLS):29Aug86-945
Wright, E. The Man Who Changed His Name.
N. Callendar, 441:28Sep86-28
Wright, E. Psychoanalytic Criticism.*
C.B. Johnson, 343:Heft12-129
Wright, F. No Siege Is Absolute.
F. Allen, 496:Fall85-179
Wright, F.L. The Master Architect. (P.J.
Meehan, ed)
T. Brown, 45:May85-89
Wright, G. The Hound of Heaven.
N. Callendar, 441:1Jun86-46
Wright, G. Old South, New South.
M.P. Johnson, 453(NYRB):8May86-38
J.M. Wiener, 441:6Jul86-12
Wright, G. and D. Frith. Cricket's Golden
Summer.
G. Moorhouse, 364:Aug-Sep85-154
Wright, J. Collected Prose. (A. Wright,
ed)
W.S. Di Piero, 569(SR):Winter85-140
R. McDowell, 249(HudR):Autumn85-512
Wright, J.P. The Sceptical Realism of
David Hume.*
D. Garrett, 482(PhR):Jan85-131
J. King, 319:Apr86-275
R.J. Roth, 543:Jun86-792
Wright, J.R.B., ed. Ignatius Sancho (1729-1780).
E. Southern, 91:Spring85-119
Wright, M.R. - see Empedocles

Wright, R. Late Latin and Early Romance
in Spain and Carolingian France.*
R.J. Blake, 239:Vol2No1-161
F.W. Hodcroft, 382(MAE):1985/1-132
Wright, R. On Fiji Islands.
R. Fulford, 441:7Sep86-11
Wright, R. Sacred Rage.*
F. Halliday, 617(TLS):20Jun86-667
Wright, R. Veracruz.
D.J. Weber, 441:27Apr86-22
Wright, R. and R.L. Danish Emigrant
Ballads and Songs.
R.L. Baker, 292(JAF):Jul/Sep85-366
P.V. Bohlman, 187:Winter86-169
S.H. Rossel, 301(JEGP):Oct85-589
M. Schellinger, 563(SS):Spring85-203
Wright, T.R., ed. John Henry Newman.
J.L. Altholz, 637(VS):Winter86-320
Wright, T.R. The Religion of Humanity.
P. Clarke, 617(TLS):23May86-564
Wright, W. Lillian Hellman.
F. Rich, 441:23Nov86-1
Wrigley, C., ed. Warfare, Diplomacy and
Politics.
G. Best, 617(TLS):6Jun86-614
W. Thomas, 362:27Mar86-32
Wrigley, R. The Glow.
J. Carter, 219(GaR):Summer85-432
Wriston, W.B. Risk and Other Four-Letter
Words.
M. Mayer, 441:16Feb86-21
"The Writer and Human Rights."
M. Boruch, 219(GaR):Fall85-664
Wroth, M. The Poems of Lady Mary Wroth.*
(J.A. Roberts, ed)
K. Duncan-Jones, 541(RES):Nov85-565
Wu Hsiang-hsiang. Sun I-hsien hsien-sheng
chuan.
F.G. Chan, 293(JASt):Feb85-391
Wu, K-M. Chuang Tzu.*
S.A. Wawrytko, 485(PE&W):Oct85-453
Wu, Y-L. and C-H. Economic Development in
Southeast Asia.
L. Stifel, 293(JASt):May85-692
Wulstan, D. Tudor Music.
I. Fenlon, 617(TLS):31Jan86-118
Wunberg, G. Wiedererkennen.
W. Riemer, 221(GQ):Summer85-442
Wunberg, G. and J.J. Braakenburg, eds.
Die Wiener Moderne.*
L.J. King, 406:Summer85-239
W.E. Yates, 402(MLR):Jul85-762
Wunder, J.R., ed. At Home on the Range.
L. Milazzo, 584(SWR):Autumn85-547
Wunderli, P. Saussure-Studien.
T.M. Scheerer, 72:Band222Heft1-146
Wünsche, K. Der Volksschullehrer Ludwig
Wittgenstein.
K. Rutschky, 384:Jul85-618
Wurgaft, L.D. The Imperial Imagination.
W.H. New, 637(VS):Winter85-353
A. Roland, 293(JASt):Aug85-880
Wurlitzer, R. Slow Fade.*
I. Malin, 532(RCF):Spring85-155
Wurzel, W.U. Flexionsmorphologie und
Natürlichkeit.
A. Carstairs, 297(JL):Sep85-487
Wuthnow, R. and others. Cultural Analysis.
R.J. Anderson and W.W. Sharrock,
323:May85-215
Wüthrich, L. Wandgemälde von Müstair bis
Hodler.
P. Strieder, 90:Apr85-232

Yerkes, D. Syntax and Style in Old English.*
  C. Sisam, 541(RES):Aug85-393
  E.G. Stanley, 382(MAE):1985/1-133
Yevtushenko, Y. Ardabiola.*
  639(VQR):Autumn85-126
Yglesias, R. Hot Properties.
  J. Rascoe, 441:6Jul86-12
Yin, H.W. - see under Hua Wu Yin
Yndurāin, D. - see Calderón de la Barca, P.
Yoke, C.B. and D.M. Hassler, eds. Death and the Serpent.
  D.D. Elgin, 395(MFS):Winter85-852
  H. Kaminsky, 561(SFS):Nov85-330
Yolton, J.W. Perceptual Acquaintance from Descartes to Reid.*
  G. Brykman, 542:Jul-Sep85-325
  F. and E. Michael, 518:Oct85-214
  J.T. Stevenson, 173(ECS):Summer86-539
  R.S. Woolhouse, 393(Mind):Apr85-300
Yolton, J.W. Thinking Matter.*
  D. Berman, 518:Apr85-85
  D. Garber, 311(JP):Dec85-729
  R. McRae, 173(ECS):Winter85/86-265
  I. Tipton, 393(Mind):Jul85-478
Yomtoob, P. and T. Schwarz. The Gift of Life.
  D. Hellerstein, 441:2Nov86-36
Yoshida, K. Tanrokubon.
  K.B. Gardner, 407(MN):Spring85-110
Yoshinori, T. - see under Takeuchi Yoshinori
Yoshitsu, M.M. Caught in the Middle East.
  Itagaki Yūzō, 285(JapQ):Jul-Sep85-330
Young, A. Dada and After.*
  S. Scobie, 107(CRCL):Sep85-442
Young, A. The Poetical Works of Andrew Young. (E. Lowbury and A. Young, eds)
  J. Arlott, 493:Jan85-25
  D. Davis, 362:30Jan86-24
  G. Lindop, 617(TLS):13Jun86-643
  W. Scammell, 148:Winter85-65
Young, B. and B. Beck, eds. Robert Hunter Middleton, the Man and His Letters.
  J. Dreyfus, 617(TLS):7Mar86-259
Young, B.A. The Rattigan Version.
  M. Wandor, 362:20Nov86-30
Young, E. A Vindication of Providence.
  566:Autumn85-91
Young, G.V.C. and C.R. Clewer. Føroysk-Ensk Ordabók/Faroese-English Dictionary.
  J.F. West, 617(TLS):11Apr86-398
Young, G.V.C. and C. Foster. Captain François Thurot.
  C. Bewley, 617(TLS):12Dec86-1397
Young, H. and A. Sloman. The Thatcher Phenomenon.
  J. Turner, 617(TLS):12Sep86-993
Young, H.T. The Line in the Margin.*
  P.R. Olson, 131(CL):Fall85-378
Young, J. and K. Nakajima-Okano. Learn Japanese — New College Text. (Vol 1)
  F.K. Harada, 399(MLJ):Spring85-100
Young, J. and K. Nakajima-Okano. Learn Japanese — New College Text. (Vol 2)
  C.J. Quinn, Jr., 399(MLJ):Winter85-422
Young, J.D. Confucianism and Christianity.
  J. Spence, 293(JASt):Nov84-198
Young, J.S. The Weather Tomorrow.
  C.L. Crow, 649(WAL):May85-90
Young, K., C. Wolkowitz and R. McCullagh, eds. Of Marriage and the Market.
  C.C., 185:Apr86-679

Young, L.B. The Unfinished Universe.
  A. Lightman, 441:6Apr86-15
Young, P. Hawthorne's Secret.*
  R.K. Gollin, 445(NCF):Sep85-236
  L.J. Reynolds, 27(AL):Dec85-662
  D. Rifkind, 31(ASch):Autumn85-563
Young, P. Naseby 1645.
  K. Sharpe, 617(TLS):10Jan86-43
Young, R. Personal Autonomy.
  R. Lindley, 617(TLS):11Jul86-754
Young, R.M. Darwin's Metaphor.
  G. Beer, 617(TLS):1Aug86-836
Young, R.V. Richard Crashaw and the Spanish Golden Age.*
  R. Zim, 541(RES):May85-256
Young, T.D. The Past in the Present.*
  J.A.L. Lemay, 677(YES):Vol 15-352
Young, T.D. and G. Core - see Ransom, J.C.
Young, V.B. Waterfall.
  404:Summer85-52
Young, W. and D.E. Kaiser. Postmortem.*
  R.J. Margolis, 441:19Jan86-21
  F. Russell, 432(NEQ):Dec85-625
Yourcenar, M. Alexis.
  639(VQR):Winter85-25
Yourcenar, M. Mishima.* (French title: Mishima ou la vision du vide.)
  P-L. Adams, 61:Dec86-103
  M. Wood, 441:14Dec86-11
  442(NY):24Nov86-150
Yourcenar, M. Oriental Tales.*
  M. Gorra, 249(HudR):Winter86-669
Yourcenar, M. With Open Eyes.*
  R. Baker, 469:Vol 11No3-99
Yu, B. The Great Circle.*
  R.W. Dasenbrock, 468:Fall/Winter85-493
  S. Paul, 301(JEGP):Oct85-586
  J.A. Robinson, 27(AL):Mar85-179
Yu, L. - see under Lu Yu
Yudelman, D. The Emergence of Modern South Africa.
  D. Moodie, 529(QQ):Spring85-226
Yue Daiyun and C. Wakeman. To the Storm.*
  J.K. Fairbank, 453(NYRB):17Jul86-33
  J. Mirsky, 617(TLS):22Aug86-909
Yüeh, H. - see under Hsün Yüeh
Yule, H. and A.C. Burnell. Hobson-Jobson. (2nd ed, ed by W. Crooke)
  D.J. Enright, 617(TLS):11Apr86-397
Yule, P. Early Cretan Seals.
  M.H. Wiencke, 303(JoHS):Vol 105-237
Yuryenen, S. The Marksman.
  C. Emerson, 441:29Jun86-24
Yuyama, A. Kacchapa-jātaka.
  J.W. de Jong, 259(IIJ):Jul85-230
Yuyama, A. A Select Bibliography on the Sanskrit Language for the Use of Students in Sanskrit.
  B. Oguibenine, 259(IIJ):Jul85-207

de Zabaleta, J. El día de fiesta por la mañana y por la tarde. (C. Cuevas García, ed)
  R. ter Horst, 240(HR):Autumn85-497
Zac, S. La philosophie religieuse de Hermann Cohen.*
  J. Brun, 192(EP):Jul-Sep85-434
Zaccaria, V., ed. Il teatro umanistico veneto: La tragedia.
  A. Stäuble, 228(GSLI):Vol 162fasc518-276

Zacharasiewicz, T. Nachsommer des Bieder-
meier, Eine Freundin Adalbert Stifters.
    L.D. Wells, 400(MLN):Apr85-702
Zachary, H. The Venus Venture.
    N. Callendar, 441:11May86-32
    442(NY):23Jun86-100
Zacour, N.P. and H.W. Hazard, eds. A His-
tory of the Crusades. (Vol 5)
    R. Irwin, 617(TLS):7Mar86-237
Zadan, C. Sondheim and Co.
    B. Short, 441:7Dec86-12
Zaefferer, D. Frageausdrücke und Fragen
im Deutschen.
    G. von Schuch, 72:Band222Heft2-364
    G. Starke, 682(ZPSK):Band38Heft6-780
Zagajewski, A. Tremor.
    E. Hoffman, 441:16Feb86-14
Zagst, M. The Greening of Thurmond
Leaner.
    W. Ferguson, 441:3Aug86-18
Zak, W.F. Sovereign Shame.
    K. Muir, 570(SQ):Autumn85-370
Zaloga, S. and V. Madej. The Polish Cam-
paign 1939.
    M.A. Peszke, 497(PolR):Vol30No4-427
Zaluska, Y. and others. Dix siècles
d'enluminure italienne (VIe-XVIe
siècles).
    R. Gibbs, 90:Dec85-905
Zander, H. Shakespeare "bearbeitet."*
    W. Bies, 52:Band20Heft1-108
Zangrilli, F. L'arte novellistica di
Pirandello.*
    G.R. Bussino, 276:Spring85-83
Zapata, R. Luttes philosophiques en
U.R.S.S. 1922-1931.
    M.B. Adams, 550(RusR):Jul85-314
    D.J. Bakhurst, 575(SEER):Jul85-422
Zapperi, R. Der schwangere Mann.
    C. Lipp, 196:Band26Heft1/2-207
Zaret, D. The Heavenly Contract.
    W.M. Lamont, 617(TLS):10Jan86-43
Zarlino, G. On the Modes. (C.V. Palisca,
ed)
    B.V. Rivera, 308:Fall85-336
Zarnecki, G., J. Holt and T. Holland, eds.
English Romanesque Art 1066-1200.
    I. Wood, 59:Jun85-228
Zaroulis, N. Certain Kinds of Loving.
    S. Mernit, 441:16Nov86-24
Zarubina, N.D. and N.S. Ožegova. Putešest-
vie po Sovetskoj Strane.*
    G.F. Holliday, 558(RLJ):Fall84-290
Zarzyski, P. The Make-up of Ice.
    R. Wrigley, 649(WAL):Aug85-173
Zavala, I.M., ed. Historia y crítica de
la literatura española. (Vol 5)
    G. Gullón, 240(HR):Winter85-79
Zazoff, P. Die antiken Gemmen.
    M. Henig, 123:Vol35No1-163
Zeami. On the Art of Nō Drama.* (J.T.
Rimer and Yamazaki Masakazu, trans)
    S.L. Leiter, 615(TJ):May85-257
    L.C. Pronko, 130:Summer85-181
    A.H. Thornhill 3d, 293(JASt):Feb85-404
Zeffirelli, F. Zeffirelli.
    S.M.L. Aronson, 441:14Dec86-16
Zehnacker, H. - see Pliny
Zehnacker, H. and G. Hentz, eds. Hommages
à Robert Schilling.
    G. Capdeville, 555:Vol59fasc1-172

Zeitlin, F.I. Under the Sign of the
Shield.
    M. Heath, 123:Vol35No1-180
Zeitlin, I. Ancient Judaism.
    639(VQR):Autumn85-137
Zeitlin, M. The Civil Wars in Chile.
    N. Galleguillos Portales, 529(QQ):
    Summer85-394
Zeitlin, S.J., A.J. Kotkin and H.C. Baker.
A Celebration of American Family Folk-
lore.*
    H. Isaacson, 126(CCC):Dec85-503
Zelazny, R. Blood of Amber.
    G. Jonas, 441:23Nov86-31
Zelin, M. The Magistrate's Tael.
    J. Spence, 453(NYRB):16Jan86-41
Zelinsky-Wibbelt, C. Die semantische Be-
lastung von submorphematischen Einheiten
im Englischen.
    H. Käsmann, 38:Band103Heft1/2-141
Zell, H.M., C. Bundy and V. Coulon, eds.
A New Reader's Guide to African Litera-
ture.* (2nd ed)
    A. Dommergues, 189(EA):Oct-Dec86-478
Zeman, H., ed. Studien zur österreich-
ischen Erzählliteratur der Gegenwart.
    D.G. Daviau, 133:Band17Heft3/4-377
von Zemnszky, E. and R.J. Schulmann - see
von Steuben, F.W.L.A.
Zempel, S. - see Rølvaag, O.E.
Zemskaja, E.A., ed. Russkaja razgovornaja
reč'.
    J.L. Conrad, 574(SEEJ):Spring85-121
Zenkovsky, S.A., ed. The Nikonian Chron-
icle. (Vol 1)
    M.S. Flier, 574(SEEJ):Fall85-340
Zepeda, O. A Papago Grammar.*
    W.R. Miller, 399(MLJ):Spring85-101
Zeps, V.J. The Placenames of Latgola.
    W.R. Schmalstieg, 215(GL):Vol25No3-206
von Zesen, P. Sämtliche Werke. (Vols 2
and 13) (F. van Ingen, ed)
    E.A. Philippson, 301(JEGP):Apr85-304
Zetzel, J.E.G. Latin Textual Criticism in
Antiquity.
    J.N. Grant, 487:Spring85-86
    M.D. Reeve, 122:Jan85-85
Zevi, F., ed. Pompei 79.
    R. Ling, 313:Vol75-272
Zevit, Z. Matres Lectionis in Ancient
Hebrew Epigraphs.
    J. Barr, 318(JAOS):Apr-Jun84-374
Zeyi, P. - see under Peng Zeyi
Zhabs-drung, T-T. - see under Tshe-tan
Zhabs-drung
Zhadova, L.A. Malevitch.
    J. Beckett, 90:Feb85-106
Zhang Xianliang. Mimosa and Other Stories.
    P. Link, 441:6Jul86-16
Zheng Yi Li and others, eds. A New
English-Chinese Dictionary. (2nd ed)
    L. Yang, 399(MLJ):Winter85-407
Zhijuan, R. - see under Ru Zhijuan
Zholkovsky, A. Themes and Texts.*
    C. Gaudin, 478:Oct85-254
"Zhongguo lishi xue nianjian." (1979,
1981, 1982, 1983)
    M.C. Wiens, 293(JASt):Feb85-362
Zhongshu, W. - see under Wang Zhongshu
Zhu Jiajin, Ed. Treasures of the Forbid-
den City.
    M. Sullivan, 617(TLS):8Aug86-873

WITHDRAWAL